THE
C. S. LEW
INDEX

THE
C. S. LEWIS
INDEX

*A Comprehensive Guide
to Lewis's Writings and Ideas*

Compiled by
JANINE GOFFAR

Foreword by
WALTER HOOPER

CROSSWAY BOOKS • WHEATON, ILLINOIS
A DIVISION OF GOOD NEWS PUBLISHERS

The C. S. Lewis Index: A Comprehensive Guide to Lewis's Writings and Ideas

This edition published by Crossway Books, a division of Good News Publishers, 1300 Crescent Street Wheaton, Illinois 60187, 1998.

First published by La Sierra Press, Riverside, California, 1995.

Cover design: Cindy Kiple

Cover photo: Arthur P. Strong

Printed in the United States of America

Excerpts from *Surprised by Joy*, copyright © 1956 by C. S. Lewis and renewed 1984 by Arthur Owen Barfield, Executor of the Estate of C. S. Lewis. Reprinted by permission of Harcourt Brace Jovanovich, Inc.

Excerpts from *Reflections on the Psalms*, copyright © 1958 by C. S. Lewis and renewed 1986 by Arthur Owen Barfield, Executor of the Estate of C. S. Lewis. Reprinted by permission of Harcourt Brace & Company.

Excerpts from *Letters to Malcolm: Chiefly on Prayer*, copyright © 1964, 1963 by the Estate of C. S. Lewis and/or C. S. Lewis. Reprinted by permission of Harcourt Brace & Company.

Excerpts from *The Four Loves*, copyright © 1960 by Helen Joy Lewis and renewed 1988 by Arthur Owen Barfield. Reprinted by permission of Harcourt Brace & Company.

Excerpts from *Letters of C. S. Lewis*, copyright © 1966 by W. H. Lewis and the Executors of C. S. Lewis, reprinted by permission of Harcourt Brace & Company.

Excerpts from "Religion and Rocketry" and "On Obstinacy in Belief" in *The World's Last Night and Other Essays*, copyright © 1958, 1955 by C. S. Lewis and renewed 1986 by Arthur Owen Barfield. Reprinted by permission of Harcourt Brace & Company.

Excerpts from *Perelandra*, copyright © 1943 by the Estate of C. S. Lewis and/or C. S. Lewis. Reprinted by permission of The Bodley Head.

Permission is granted by Harper Collins Publishers for excerpts from *A Grief Observed*, copyright © 1961.

Permission is granted by Faber and Faber for excerpts from *A Grief Observed*, copyright © 1961.

Permission is granted by Macmillan Publishing Company for excerpts from *The Weight of Glory*, copyright © 1949.

Permission is granted by William B. Eerdmans Publishing Company for excerpts from *Christian Reflections*, copyright © 1967, and Letters to an American Lady, copyright © 1967.

Permission is granted by Curtis Brown and John Farquharson for excerpts from *God in the Dock, The Weight of Glory*, and *The World's Last Night and Other Essays*.

Permission is granted by Harper Collins Religious for excerpts from *Miracles*, copyright © 1960, *The Problem of Pain*, copyright © 1944, *The Screwtape Letters*, copyright © 1942, and *The Weight of Glory*.

Library of Congress Cataloging-in-Publication Data
Goffar, Janine.
    The C. S. Lewis index : a comprehensive guide to Lewis's writings
and ideas / compiled and edited by Janine Goffar ; foreword by
Walter Hooper. —1st Crossway Books ed.
    p.   cm.
    "First published by La Sierra Press, Riverside, California, 1995"—
T.p. verso.
    Includes bibliographical references.
    ISBN 0-89107-980-7
    1. Lewis, C. S. (Clive Staples), 1898-1963—Indexes. 2. Theology—
Indexes   I. Title.
BX5199.L53G64   1998
016.23'0092—dc21   98-9960

11	10	09	08	07	06	05	04	03	02	01	00	99	98
15	14	13	12	11	10	9	8	7	6	5	4	3	2	1

Dedication

Foreword

by *Walter Hooper*
Oxford, England

Nearly every week I get a letter beginning 'Can you tell me where this quotation from C. S. Lewis comes from . . .?' Before I discover what it is, my heart is in my mouth. I think 'What if I *can't* identify it! Don't they know how much Lewis wrote?' So far—and I really do mean 'so far'—I've been lucky and have been able to identify the things sent to me. But as more of Lewis's writings become available—and my memory fails—I've longed for, prayed for, such a work as this. As far as Lewis's own works are concerned, this *Index* is the most important book to be published since he died.

Many of those who ask me to identify quotations or ideas usually say 'The passage I'm thinking of runs something like this . . .' And in nearly every instance what the reader remembers is not as trenchant as what Lewis said. But who am I to point the finger? It happens to me too. I find that unless I go back again and again to Lewis's very clear meaning, I will unconsciously blur or dilute that meaning lest it 'offend' the very people who ought to be *shocked* by his words. If it is some great passage Lewis has writ-ten about God or His revelation in Christ, we have a responsibility to see that we don't rob it of all significance by making it weak enough or vague enough for some modern sensibilities. Lewis's ideas are like Aslan in the *Chronicles of Narnia*. They are neither 'tame' nor 'safe,' but they are *good*.

This *Index* of ideas is a very impor-tant publishing event because it will keep us in touch with what Lewis called 'Real Things.' He believed the Christian Faith to be a matter of objec-tive reality. Almost immediately after his conversion to the Faith in 1931 he wrote to his friend, Arthur Greeves, saying, 'Christianity is God expressing Himself through what we call "real things" . . . namely, the actual incarna-tion, crucifixion, and resurrection' (*They Stand Together,* October 18, 1931). God, he insisted in *Mere Christianity*, is 'the rock bottom, irreducible Fact on which all other facts depend' (MC IV, 6). In *Miracles*, God is described as a basic Fact whose existence it would be nonsensical to try to explain because this Fact is itself the ground or start-ing-point of all explanations' (II) and 'the basic, original, self-existent Fact which exists on its own right' (IV).

Lewis was by profession a teacher of English language and literature, and as this part of life belongs to God just as much as any other, he thought it ought to involve 'real learning.' In his essay, 'The Parthenon and the Optative,' Lewis distinguished between two types of education. One type, he said, 'begins with hard, dry things like grammar, and dates . . . and ends in Appreciation.' The other type, he says, 'begins in "appreciation" and ends in gush.'

Lewis himself had some slight tendency towards 'gush' before it was corrected. In his autobiography, *Surprised by Joy* (IX), he tells of his first meeting with the man who saw to it that his education was about Real Things. This was his father's old friend, Mr. W. T. Kirkpatrick, who was going to tutor Lewis for Oxford University. Lewis was fifteen when they met, and before he had spent five minutes in Mr. Kirkpatrick's part of England, he was spouting his 'opinion' of it. Mr. Kirkpatrick was not a man for vague, factless talk, and he cried, 'Stop!' After showing the boy that he knew nothing whatever about the subject, he said, 'Do you not see, then, that you had no right to have any opinion whatever on the subject?' Lewis came to love Mr. Kirkpatrick, and he never forgot this valuable lesson. Years later, in his novel *That Hideous Strength* Lewis tells us that the reason one of the weakest of his characters, Mark Studdock, is so weak is because 'He was a man of straw, a glib examinee in subjects that require no exact knowledge' (9:ii).

Most people in the West have no 'exact knowledge' of God and live as though He did not exist. For this reason, I imagine all who turn to this index will recognise how valuable Lewis's ideas are. More than that, those ideas are recognised by Christians of all denominations as a part of the Real Things that we must pass on to others.

The reader might at first be confused when he sees this *Index* in a book shop. There are already so many books about Lewis to chose from. Which should he or she choose? I don't believe the decision is as difficult as it looks. By the time Lewis had reached the end of his life, he had read a vast amount of criticism about many authors, including himself. In *An Experiment in Criticism* (XI) he asked himself which authors had helped *him* most. Whose books was it most vital that he have on his shelves? Was it the 'evaluative critics' who pretend to tell us what an author 'really means?' Was it the historians? Was it the emotive critics? Was it someone with a brand-new interpretation? No, he said. His greatest debt was to those often scorned as "Dry as dust," those who just plain point to where the Real Things are. "I have owed, and must continue to owe," he said

> far more to editors, textual critics, commentators, and lexicographers than to anyone else. Find out what the author actually wrote and what the hard words meant and what the allusions were to, and you have done far more for me than a hundred new interpretations or assessments could ever do.

Janine Goffar points directly to what the author C. S. Lewis 'actually wrote' and I am honoured that I have been given a chance to point to what I believe is the most valuable book we have on Lewis, and the one most likely to remain so.

Introduction

Within the theologically oriented books of C. S. Lewis lies an amazing array of topics, with unique wordings and ideas that reward the deeper reader at every turn of the page. Much has been done to bring these ideas into greater accessibility for both scholar and layperson. Still, the very thoroughness with which Lewis develops his points has usually meant some labor-intensive searching when one has wished to excavate and utilize these treasures in sermons, lectures, or personal study.

This index has been carefully constructed to aid in the location of C. S. Lewis's *theological ideas*. It is intended to work in two ways: first, as a guide to direct the user to passages relating to a desired topic of study; and second, to assist him or her in finding known C. S. Lewis passages, the source of which is unknown or has been forgotten. In this way the index may serve as something like a concordance, although it probably serves better the first purpose. For while every effort has been made to preserve Lewis's wordings when possible, space limitations have often required passages to be summarized or contracted. Thus the user is to be forewarned that the wording of the index frequently deviates from Lewis's wording. To flag this, a system of asterisks (*) is used (see below).

Scope: Fifteen books are included in this index; they were chosen for their theological orientation and suitability for idea indexing. Toward these

books the index could be considered comprehensive, in that it attempts to cover inclusively each of Lewis's primary ideas. It cannot be considered exhaustive because it does not include every instance of a word or phrase nor each small point.

It also does not attempt to index every proper noun; in fact, references to these are few and mostly given only when associated with an extractable idea.

Reference Abbreviations: Each reference is indexed in two ways: first, by page number for those who own editions paged exactly as those listed in the bibliography following this introduction; and second, by chapter and paragraph for the convenience of those with differing editions. The page citations are denoted by "•" and appear as follows: • WG 32 refers to *The Weight of Glory*, page 32. The paragraph citations are denoted by "❖" and appear as follows: ❖ SJ 4:3 refers to *Suprised by Joy*, chapter four, paragraph three. The latter citations will work with any edition the reader may have.

Two books, *Mere Christianity* and *God in the Dock*, are further divided into sections (in *Mere Christianity*, they are called "books.") These are given Roman numerals, so that GID III 2:4 refers to *God in the Dock*, section three, chapter two, paragraph four; MC I 3:6 refers to *Mere Christianity*, Book One, chapter three, paragraph six. A sample entry would look like the following:

Adoration and praise in prayer: "Begin where you are"—with the pleasures and blessings you are apprehending right now
  • LM 88-91 ❖ LM 17:1-13

The first citation refers to *Letters to Malcolm: Chiefly on Prayer*, p. 88-91, while the second citation refers to chapter 17, paragraphs 1-13.

The preface of a book is listed as "P"; paragraph references will then read like this: WG P:1 for *The Weight of Glory*, preface, paragraph one. In the indexed edition of *The Screwtape Letters*, there is the unique circumstance of having two prefaces. This is handled with "P" for the first preface, and "PP" for the second.

The first time a subject heading appears in this index it is set in bold faced type to highlight it.

Use of Asterisks: An *asterisk* (*) following an entry denotes either an entry which is placed under a subject heading chosen by the editor rather than Lewis's own word(s) or a close synonym, *or* an entry which is entirely an interpretation or summary of Lewis's idea in the editor's own words. Thus in either case the user is notified that he will not find the idea in just that wording.

An entry which is followed by a *double asterisk* (**) is an extrapolation from something Lewis has said to a subject which he did not there intend to address. An example of this would be all of the entries under the heading "Abortion," a subject Lewis never specifically addressed.

Entries without asterisks are not necessarily exact quotes, but the idea should be easy to find as worded.

An asterisk within a page or paragraph cross-reference denotes a reference which is only obscurely related to the primary reference.

Every effort has been made to place exact quotes within quote marks, however, due to the juggling of word order necessary to compose entries so that the subject word comes first, this has often not been possible.

Word Order: When reading an entry where the wording is transposed to facilitate indexing, the initial subject word or phrase of an entry (before the comma) is ordinarily to be placed at the first punctuation mark or at the end—whichever causes the entry to read sensibly. While this may be confusing at first, with greater use it should become intuitive.

Spelling: Spelling is according to American usage in the subject headings; otherwise it is British or American according to whichever spelling was used in the book being indexed.

Singular and Plural Noun Forms: For ease of use, plural noun subject headings have been located immediately following listings of the singular form, ignoring precise alphabetical order. Thus the user is instructed to look up subject nouns under the singular form. The exception to this rule is when the plural form involves more than just adding an "s" (e.g., Child/Children, Man/Men, and Activities/Activity). In these cases normal alphabetical order has been followed.

Dating of Letters: All of the index entries for letters found in the books *Letters of C. S. Lewis* and *Letters to an*

American Lady use the dating as Lewis did. For example, if he dated the letter "14/6/56" it appears in the index that way as well. The exception to this rule is that when the date is spelled out, such as "28 March 1961," the month name has been abbreviated to the first three letters, while the year has been shortened to the last two numbers, for example, "28 Mar 61."

Cross-References: A network of cross-references has been developed to guide the user to appropriate related headings. "*See also…*" would indicate a very closely related subject heading, whereas "*consider also…*" would suggest a less closely related heading.

In determining headings, a choice between synonyms has occasionally been made in order to bring material of a given subject together under a single heading.

Cross-references within page and paragraph references are handled differently. "*See also…*" would indicate a reference closely related to the primary reference, while a reference which is more obscurely related will contain an asterisk, for example, "*see also* MC 43*.*"

Search Method: When one is searching for a particular idea, the best method is to scan all the entries under related headings. Some comparable references may be listed separately because, though the idea is similar, the wording is unique.

Subheadings: Many attempts were made to divide the longer sections of the index, such as "Prayer," into subheadings, and in some cases such will be found. But Lewis makes

so many *different* points on these broad subjects that for the most part it proved to be impossible. Most headings are sufficiently self-limited. Where there are numerous entries to be gone through under a single heading, it is hoped that the reader may make some valuable discoveries among the other ideas encountered in his search.

Unusual Subject Headings: Attention should be drawn to a few important subject headings which have been used to tie related references together but which may be overlooked because they would not readily come to mind. These are: Destiny of lost Man; Destiny of redeemed Man; Evangelism, problems in; Obstacles to Christian faith; Obstacles to prayer; Paradoxes in Christianity; and Relations, interpersonal.

"Screwtape Proposes a Toast": The last portion of more recent editions of *The Screwtape Letters* contains a section entitled "Screwtape Proposes a Toast." This section is also included as a chapter in *The World's Last Night and Other Essays*. It is here indexed only as part of the latter book. Paragraph references to this chapter could be utilized with either source just by changing the chapter number. In *The World's last Night and Other Essays*, it is Chapter 4; in *The Screwtape Letters*, it would be "Chapter" 32.

Use of the Index Versus the Books: Although people have mentioned their enjoyment of just browsing through or reading the index by itself, the editor wishes to remind users of the importance of going back to the books themselves for the full idea and the exact wording. It could be said that in such an index, the editor necessarily acts somewhat editorially, as a commentator; and Lewis himself has pointed out the error of relying on commentators rather than referring back to the great writer: "...the great man, just because of his greatness, is much more intelligible than his modern commentator" (*God in the Dock*, 200).

World View of C. S. Lewis: C. S. Lewis held a world view which could be summarized in his own words as follows: "If you think of this world as a place intended for our happiness, you find it quite intolerable: think of it as a place of training and correction and it's not so bad... The people who try to hold an optimistic view of the world...become pessimists: the people who hold a pretty stern view of it become optimistic" (*God in the Dock*, 52).

Lewis loved life immensely, yet he retained a sober awareness of its dangers and sufferings, at times even flirting with a desire for death. This is not quite the paradox it seems. His hearty relish of life was precisely *because* he realized its potential for pain and horror, and therefore he more fully cherished all its loveliness, as one might treasure a rose garden on prison grounds.

This view has proven difficult to capture in one word for use as a subject heading. Many names have been tried, all of them inadequate. Noted Los Angeles radio commentator Dennis Prager, who shares this view, calls it "Prager's Tragic View of Life." But that wouldn't work as a subject heading. Perhaps we need a new word in the English language for this: *Tragicism.* But since that wouldn't work either as a heading, the passages which reflect this view of Lewis's have been placed—with some misgiving—under the topic "Pessimism, Lewis's."

Let us be thankful to God that, whatever else it is, Lewis's view—or that of any Christian's—is most definitely not in the end pessimistic.

Editor's Note

In his book *Perelandra*, C. S. Lewis has Ransom explaining to the "Lewis" of the book, "One never can see, or not till long afterwards, why [one] was selected for [a] job. And when one does, it is usually for some reason that leaves no room for vanity."

I cannot say for certain that God led me to prepare this index or, if so, why. But the task could not have been more joyful, and a further reason I will never need in this life.

My college English professor was Dr. Isaac Johnson, and though I am quite certain I left no lasting impression on him, he gave me a great and enduring gift: an assignment that included reading a portion of C. S. Lewis's book *Mere Christianity*. At the time, I was a nursing student with little interest in English class; but somehow the name C. S. Lewis stuck in my mind as an author who was worth going back to someday.

I am happy to say I had a great opportunity to do so while working as a nurse on cruise ships for two and a half years. We were busy in the medical department but still had plenty of off-duty time to sit on deck and read.

During that time, I read—among other things—the fifteen books included in this index, one after the other, and could recall passages easily in conversations with tolerant friends. But soon after leaving the ships, the ability to do so began to fade, and I missed being able to locate these loved passages easily. It was for this reason I began to create a "short" index for my personal use which soon grew to require a computer for alphabetizing.

Eight years later, with the encouragement of many friends, it has developed into a tool which I believe can help others access Lewis's ideas more easily. In addition to the more casual reader, I have especially envisioned its use by such people as ministers and teachers—busy people who may vaguely recall a "great passage" relevant to the topic of their next sermon or lesson plan, but who despair of finding it before week's end.

Some have inquired about my qualifications for producing such a work as this index. I think I know the answer: My father was a minister, my mother was an indexer of nursing literature, and my first teacher had an obsessive-compulsive personality disorder! Remember, C. S. Lewis did not have any degrees in Theology, either.

I have deliberately refrained from creating an exhaustive concordance-style index for two reasons: First, it would not have been possible for one person to undertake this, and a joint effort would likely have been economically unfeasible. Second, I have little doubt—and great hope—that such a tool will soon be made available in computerized form on CD-ROM. This seems the only reasonable way to go about such a project in our day.

But the need for an idea-oriented index of C. S. Lewis's works has existed for some time, and I sincerely hope *C. S. Lewis Index: Rumours from the Sculptor's Shop* will begin to fill this need.

Acknowledgments

I suppose no book is produced without assistance and encouragement from many sources. Mine is no exception. It is a real pleasure to be able to give grateful acknowledgment to the following people, without whom this book would never have seen the light of print:

First of all, to my beloved father, Pastor Wilford Goffar, who passed away in 1992. He always believed in me, and he shared with me his love for spiritual things. To my precious mother, Emma Goffar, who as senior indexer for a nursing index gave me my interest in organizing and indexing, as well as much-needed technical assistance. To my sister and brother-in-law, Colleen and Ernie Woodhouse, who kindly supplied me with computer time before I got my own. To Dr. Allen Shepherd, who has lent much support and encouragement with the project during our many years of friendship. To the C. S. Lewis Foundation of Redlands, California, and especially its founder and president, Dr. Stan Mattson, who has given great advice and real encouragement from the minute he saw the project. To my dear friend Pastor Emmett Watts, who encouraged me to "stay with it" near the end and helped me find a publisher. To Dale Haslem, my computer expert, who patiently programmed and reprogrammed as I changed my mind about format, which in the initial stages happened often. To my close friends and advisors, Hilda and Dan Smith, who first suggested that I think about publishing my work.

My editors, Dr. V. Bailey Gillespie and Stuart Tyner, deserve special thanks for their whole-hearted belief in this project, and for their great help in bringing it to publication. And to Dr. Lawrence Geraty, president of La Sierra University, I owe a debt of gratitude for his personal interest in the index and his determination to see it published.

I am also very grateful to Sharon Churches, who spent many late hours expertly proofreading the index and thinking of ways to improve it. Editorial assistant John Anthony and typist Elizabeth Cea earned my admiration and deep appreciation for their dedication to the project and careful attention to detail.

A heartfelt thank you goes to Marjorie Lamp Mead of the Marion E. Wade Center at Wheaton College, Wheaton, Illinois. Marjorie gave me a warm welcome when I was first there in 1989 and has provided unflagging support and wise counsel during my efforts to finish the project and secure a publisher. The Wade Center also awarded me a very much-appreciated research award—the Clyde S. Kilby Research Grant for 1991—just when my funds and courage were running low.

Walter Hooper was an answer to my prayers for guidance at a time when I was just beginning to think in terms of publication, and he has been most generous in his support of the project. While I have always greatly admired his own inestimable contribution to Lewis scholarship, I never dreamed I would someday meet him and have the honor of his writing a foreword for a book of mine. I will always be most grateful for his friendship, counsel, and support.

It was my pleasure and a real honor to meet Douglas Gresham, C. S. Lewis's stepson, at the West Coast opening of the movie *Shadowlands* recently. I thank him for his kind words for the index and for his dedication to the furthering of Lewis scholarship in many areas.

I would also like to thank the people at Curtis Brown Group Ltd. (representing the C. S. Lewis Estate), especially Elizabeth Stevens. Their kind permission, along with that of each of the other copyright holders, was crucial to the publication of this work, and is greatly appreciated.

Other people who have helped in innumerable and inestimable ways include: Dr. Jeremy Dyson; Dr. and Mrs. Paul Ford and the members of the Southern California C. S. Lewis Society which Dr. Ford founded, especially its current president, Carl Swift, Dr. George Musacchio, and Ginny Brown; Reverend Jerry Root; Dr. Wayne Martindale; Dr. Earle Hilgert; Attorneys Frederick J. Hickman and Harvey Hertz; dear friends Lilah Scalzo, Cynthia Vanderberg, Mildred Lee, Michelle Hesse, and Sharon Diaz; Jan and Garry Reynolds, who contributed more valuable computer expertise; Hans van de Lagemaat, a ship's officer and new Christian who first showed me the potential power of C. S. Lewis's writings, together with the Holy Spirit, to convince and convict an agnostic; Kathy O'Hanlon Carder, Dr. David Duffy, Professor Leonard Nelson, Jennifer Peterson, and the other members of my C. S. Lewis Discussion Group; and finally, Dr. Isaac Johnson, my college English professor who introduced me to C. S. Lewis, never guessing the impact that small reading assignment would have on my life.

To these and all others who have helped along the way, I offer my deepest gratitude and loving thanks.

Janine Goffar
Loma Linda, California
1994

The Editor of this index welcomes any corrections or comments. Please write to Janine Goffar, in care of La Sierra University Press, Riverside, CA 92515. Fax: 909-785-2199

Key to Abbreviations

Abbreviation Code	C. S. Lewis Book Title
GO	*A Grief Observed*
CR	*Christian Reflections*
FL	*The Four Loves*
GID	*God in the Dock*
L	*Letters of C. S. Lewis*
LAL	*Letters to an American Lady*
LM	*Letters to Malcolm: Chiefly on Prayer*
MC	*Mere Christianity*
M	*Miracles*
PP	*The Problem of Pain*
RP	*Reflections on the Psalms*
SL	*The Screwtape Letters*
SJ	*Surprised by Joy*
WG	*The Weight of Glory*
WLN	*The World's Last Night & Other Essays*

Bibliography

C. S. Lewis, *A Grief Observed,*
New York: Bantam Books, Inc., 1980 printing

C. S. Lewis, *Christian Reflections,*
Grand Rapids, MI: William B. Eerdmans Publishing Company, © 1967

C. S. Lewis, *The Four Loves,*
New York: Harcourt Brace Jovanovich, © 1960

C. S. Lewis, *God in the Dock,*
Grand Rapids, MI: William B. Eerdmans Publishing Company, © 1970

C. S. Lewis, *Letters of C. S. Lewis,*
New York: Harcourt Brace Jovanovich, © 1966

C. S. Lewis, *Letters to an American Lady,*
Grand Rapids, MI: William B. Eerdmans Publishing Company, © 1967

C. S. Lewis, *Letters to Malcolm: Chiefly on Prayer,*
New York: Harcourt Brace Jovanovich, © 1964

C. S. Lewis, *Mere Christianity,*
New York: Macmillan Publishing Company, Inc., © 1952

C. S. Lewis, *Miracles,*
New York: Macmillan Publishing Company, Inc., © 1960

C. S. Lewis, *The Problem of Pain,*
New York: Macmillan Publishing Company, Inc., 1978 printing

C. S. Lewis, *Reflections on the Psalms,*
New York: Harcourt Brace Jovanovich, © 1958

C. S. Lewis, *Screwtape Letters,*
New York: Macmillan Publishing Company, Inc., © 1959, 1961, 1982

C. S. Lewis, *Surprised by Joy,*
New York: Harcourt Brace Jovanovich, © 1955

C. S. Lewis, *The Weight of Glory,*
New York: Macmillan Publishing Company, Inc., © 1965

C. S. Lewis, *The World's Last Night & Other Essays,*
New York: Harcourt Brace Jovanovich, © 1960

Abandonment [by God]—*see also* Absence of God

Abandonment, Lewis describes his childhood fear of
• SJ 39 ❖ SJ 2:17

Abandonment, question of why we may sometimes feel a sense of, explained by Screwtape*
• SL 37-39 ❖ SL 8:3, 4

Abandonment: Screwtape rues the man who feels that every trace of God has vanished, and asks why he has been forsaken, and still obeys
• SL 39 ❖ SL 8:4

Abandonment, sense of, shared by Christ: "...God Himself, as man, submitted to man's sense of being abandoned"
• LAL 38 (*see also* GO 5; LAL 77)
❖ LAL 20/2/55 (*see also* GO 1:8; LAL Jul 21st 58)

Abandonment, sense of, shared by Christ: "The Father was not *really* absent from the Son when He said 'Why hast thou forsaken me?'"
• LAL 38 ❖ LAL 20/2/55

Abandonment, sense of, shared by Christ: "Is it that God Himself cannot be Man unless God seems to vanish at His greatest need?"
• LM 43-044 ❖ LM 8:10-12

Abolition of Man mentioned: "...it is almost my favorite among my books but in general has been almost totally ignored by the public"
• LAL 39 (*see also* L 204; MC 19)

❖ LAL 20/2/55 (*see also* L undated letter of May 1944; MC I 1:7)

Abortion: According to Screwtape, God's view is that human birth is important chiefly as the qualification for human death which is the gate to Heaven**
• SL 133-134 (*see also* SJ 117)
❖ SL 28:3 (*see also* SJ 7:21)

Abortion: Death an evil, but not the greatest evil (re: war and Pacifism)**
• WG 43 (*see also* GID 297, 311; M 125; SL 131-132) ❖ WG 3:18 (*see also* GID III 4:20; 8:1; M 14:28; SL 28:1)

Abortion: "I am not a woman...I did not think it my place to take a firm line about pains, dangers and expenses from which I am protected..." (re: birth control)**
• MC 9 ❖ MC P:10

Abortion: I am on neither side of the present controversy, but I think the abolitionists conduct their case very ill (re: capital punishment)**
• GID 340 ❖ GID IV Letter 12

Abortion: "...I have had a great dislike of people who, themselves in ease and safety, issue exhortations to men in the front line" (re: many things about which he chose to remain silent)**
• MC 9 ❖ MC P:10

Abortion: "...no *sin* simply as such, should be made a *crime*. Who the deuce are our rulers to enforce their opinions of sin on us?" (re: homosexuality)**
• L 281 ❖ L 1 Feb 58

Abortion: "Of course many acts which are sins against God are also injuries to our fellow-citizens, and must on that account...only...be made crimes"**
• L 281 ❖ L 1 Feb 58

Abraham as an example of someone who, for a high and terrible vocation, may have to turn his back on his own people and his father's house
• FL 183 ❖ FL 6:31

Abraham, test of, did not show God what he could endure (God already knew that)—it showed Abraham
• PP 101-102 (*see also* GO 61*)
❖ PP 6:13 (*see also* GO 3:36*)

---

* These items reflect some interpretation on the part of the editor; the idea will not be found in these exact words. *See Introduction, p. ix.*
** These items are ideas of Lewis's which the editor has placed under a topic Lewis did not there intend to address. *See Introduction, p. ix.*
Entries without asterisks *are not necessarily exact quotes,* but the idea should be easy to find as worded.

Absence of God—*see also* Abandonment

Absence of God, feeling of, in deep grief: "There is no answer. Only the locked door, the iron curtain, absolute zero. 'Them as asks don't get'"
- •GO 7 (*see also* GO 71, 80)
- ❖ GO 1:13 (*see also* GO 4:4, 24)

Absence of God, feeling of, in our greatest need: "But go to Him when your need is desperate...and what do you find? A door slammed in your face..."
- •GO 4-6 (*see also* GO 53-54; LAL 92)
- ❖ GO 1:7 (*see also* GO 3:25, 26; LAL 24 Sep 60)

Absence of God, feeling of: "The time when there is nothing at all in your soul except a cry for help may be just the time when God can't give it..."
- •GO 53-54 (*see also* LAL 92)
- ❖ GO 3:25 (*see also* LAL 24 Sep 60)

Absence of God: "Why is He so present a commander in our time of prosperity and so very absent a help in time of trouble?"
- •GO 5 ❖ GO 1:7

Absolute Being, God is the, in the sense that He alone exists in His own right; but God is not a generality
- •M 87 ❖ M 11:10

"Absolute," belief in the: "This was a religion that cost nothing...There was nothing to fear; better still, nothing to obey"
- •SJ 209-210 (*see also* GID 143; M 81, 93-94; MC 35, 136; Cost)
- ❖ SJ 13:18 (*see also* GID I 16:25; M 11:2, 19; MC I 4:6; IV 1:4; Cost)

"Absolute," belief in, yielded a life of "'desire without hope'"
- •SJ 210 ❖ SJ 13:19

Absolute Idealism, I thought that those who believed in "a God" came nearer to the truth of, than those who did not
- •SJ 215 ❖ SJ 14:5

"Absolute," Lewis's earlier belief about the
- •SJ 209-210, 215, 221, 222-223
- ❖ SJ 13:18; 14:5, 13, 14

Absolute, through the notion of the, God had taught me how a thing can be re-

vered not for what it can do to us but for what it is in itself
- •SJ 231 ❖ SJ 15:3

"**Absorption**" not accurate as a word to describe how human souls can be taken into the life of God and yet remain themselves
- •MC 141 (*see also* SL 38, 59, 81-82; WG 67) ❖ MC IV 2:3 (*see also* SL 8:3, 4; 18:3, 4; 13:4; WG 4:21, 22)

Absorption or "eating" as a principle of Hell: "Even in human life we have seen the passion to dominate, almost to digest, one's fellow"
- •SL xi (*see also* FL 160)
- ❖ SL P:19, 20 (*see also* FL 5:46)

Absorption or "eating" as a principle of Hell: "I feign that devils can, in a spiritual sense, eat one another; and us"
- •SL xi (*see also* SL xiii, 26, 37-38, 81, 141, 145; WLN 51-56, 69-70)
- ❖ SL P:19 (*see also* SL P:22; 5:2; 8:3; 18:3; 30:1; 31:1; WLN 4:1-13, 39)

Absorption or "eating" as a principle of Hell: "...the sucking of will and freedom out of a weaker self into a stronger" (—Screwtape)
- •SL 81 ❖ SL 18:3

Abstinence—*consider* Chastity; Temperance

Acceptance—*consider* Approval

Accommodation of clergymen who disbelieve what they preach: "I feel it is a form of prostitution"
- •GID 260, 265 (*see also* GID 89-90)
- ❖ GID II 16:12, 46 (*see also* GID I 10:2, 3)

Accommodation to unbelievers—*see* Conformity

Achievement, self-sufficiency the possible result of those vices that lead to worldly
- •PP 98 ❖ PP 6:9

Achievement: The only people who achieve much are those who want something so much that they seek it while the conditions are still unfavourable*
- •WG 30 ❖ WG 2:12

Achievements and triumphs, worldly, will all come to nothing in the end

• WLN 110 ❖ WLN 7:32

Acquaintance or general society has always meant little to me; I can't understand why a man should wish to know more people than he can make real friends of
• SJ 33 (*see also* L 245)
❖ SJ 2:12 (*see also* L 20 Oct 52)

Acquaintance with God—*see* Knowing God; Knowledge of God; Relationship with God

Acting—*consider* Pretending

Action, in the whole puzzle of grace and free will we profanely assume that divine and human, exclude one another
• LM 49-50 (*see also* GID 55; LM 68-69; MC 130; Moral effort) ❖ LM 9:11, 12 (*see also* GID I 4:30, 31—Ques. 8; LM 13:2-5; MC III 12:8; Moral effort)

Action, Kant thought that no, had moral value unless it were done out of pure reverence for the moral law (that is, without inclination)
• PP 99-101 ❖ PP 6:11-13

Action, regarding any proposed course of, God wants men to ask simply, "Is it righteous? Is it prudent? Is it possible?"
• SL 118 ❖ SL 25:6

Action, Screwtape advises preventing any repentance from being converted into: "The great thing is to prevent his doing anything"
• SL 60-61 ❖ SL 13:5

Action: "...to act on the light one has is almost the only way to more light"
• L 191-192 ❖ L 4 Jan 41

Action: We must sometimes act on our intellectual assent before we have real confidence (faith)
• L 199 (*see also* CR 42-43; MC 122-123; WLN 23-25) ❖ L 20 Jan 42 (*see also* CR 3:11; MC III 11:2-4; WLN 2:12, 13)

Actions—*see also* Behaviour; Works

Actions, a man who perseveres in doing just, gets in the end a certain quality of character (but right actions done for the wrong reason do not build "virtue")

• MC 77 (*see also* MC 127)
❖ MC III 2:8-10 (*see also* MC III 12:3)

Actions all go on having consequences, mostly unforeseeable, to the world's end
• L 294 ❖ L 17 Jun 60

Actions, ethical differences between Christianity and Materialism as they affect our social values and our
• GID 109-110 ❖ GID I 12:2-4

Actions: God and man cannot exclude one another, as man excludes man; "God did (or said) it" and "I did (or said) it" can both be true
• LM 68-69 (*see also* LAL 22, 23; LM 49-50, 81; MC 142-143*; PP 98-99*)
❖ LM 13:2-4 (*see also* LAL Nov 6/53; 27/xi/53; LM 9:11; 15:15; MC IV 2:9*; PP 6:10*)

Actions, human beings judge one another by their external; God judges them by their moral choices
• MC 85, 86 ❖ MC III 4:6, 7

Actions not any less free because God has foreknowledge
• MC 148-149 (*see also* SL 126-128; Free will) ❖ MC IV 3:11 (*see also* SL 27:3, 4; Free will)

Actions of love more important than having loving feelings
• MC 116, 117 (*see also* L 269; LM 115; MC 161) ❖ MC III 9:5, 9 (*see also* L undated letter just after 13 Mar 56; LM 21:12; MC IV 7:3)

Actions sometimes unite us; discussions usually separate us (re: reunion of churches)
• LM 16 ❖ LM 3:5

Actions, the more virtuous a man becomes the more he enjoys virtuous
• PP 100 (*see also* L 277; LM 114-116)
❖ PP 6:11 (*see also* L 18 Jul 57; LM 21:11-14)

Actions: We can perhaps train ourselves to ask how the thing which we are saying or doing at each moment will look when the irresistible light streams in on it
• WLN 113 ❖ WLN 7:38

Activist groups: Devil used to prevent

people from doing good works; now he just *organises* them**
•LAL 58 ❖ LAL 5/7/56

Activities, a man's most genuinely Christian, may fall entirely outside that part of his life which he calls "religious"
• LM 30-31❖ LM 6:6

Activities, cultural and religious, should be undertaken for their own sakes, not for the sake of prestige or merit
• WLN 31-39 (*see also* CR 10; L 216*; SL 59-60; Pride of pursuing "culture")
❖ WLN 3:1-11 (*see also* CR 1:15; L 3 Apr 49*; SL 13:4; Pride of pursuing "culture")

Activities, cultural: Work of a charwoman and the work of a poet can be done to the Lord; both become spiritual in the same way and on the same condition
• CR 24 (*see also* WG 26)
❖ CR 2:37 (*see also* WG 2:9)

Activities, even the noblest of our natural, will be sinful unless offered to God
• WG 25 ❖ WG 2:8

Activities for which we were created (e.g., prayer) appear as duties while we live on earth; will not be a delight until we are perfected
• LM 114-116 (*see also* L 277*; PP 100*; RP 97) ❖ LM 21:10-14 (*see also* L 18 Jul 57*; PP 6:12*; RP 9:7)

Activities: Hymn singing can undoubtedly be done to the glory of God—just as eating, or drinking beer, or playing darts
• CR 95-96 ❖ CR 8:6

Activities: Most men must glorify God by doing to His glory something which is not *per se* an act of glorifying, but which becomes so by being offered
• CR 24 ❖ CR 2:37

Activities, mundane, undertaken in humility better than cultural activities undertaken in pride
•L 182-183 ❖ L 16 Apr 40

Activities, no essential quarrel between human, and spiritual life
• WG 25-26 (*see also* CR 24; L 228)
❖WG 2:8 (*see also* CR 2:37; L 23 Apr 51)

Activities of culture and religion are seen by majority as marginal, amateurish, and rather effeminate next to the activities of the world of Business
• WLN 80-81 ❖ WLN 5:22

Activities of natural love and friendship: Nothing is too trivial to be transformed into works of Charity...a game, a joke, a drink together...
• FL 184 ❖ FL 6:34

Activities of religion as an end in themselves are infinitely dangerous
• LM 30 (*see also* RP 57-58; SL 35)
❖LM 6:4-6 (*see also* RP 6:6, 7; SL 7:4)

Activities, self-centredness slowly permeates every one of our, even when they are begun with the best of intentions
• PP 75-76 ❖ PP 5:5

Activities: The Christian "has no objection to comedies that merely amuse and tales that merely refresh...We can play, as we can eat, to the glory of God"
• CR 10 ❖ CR 1:15

Activities, we have no non-religious; only religious and irreligious
• LM 30 (*see also* CR 125, bottom*)
❖ LM 6:4 (*see also* CR 10:31*)

Activities we naturally like may be as much a part of our "service" to God as our hardest duties
• WG 130 ❖ WG 9:9

Activities which are for us, here and now, frivolous will be enjoyed in Heaven without frivolity (e.g., dance and games)
• LM 92-93 (*see also* LM 115-116*)
❖ LM 17:17 (*see also* LM 21:13*)

Activity a part of true mysticism: "...the ultimate Peace is silent through very density of life"*
• M 93 ❖ M 11:18

Activity, the bloom of innocence and the element of obedience is gradually rubbed off every
• PP 76 ❖ PP 5:5

Acts, Resurrection of Christ the central theme of every Christian sermon reported in the book of
• M 143 ❖ M 16:2

Adam—*see also* Unfallen man

Adam: If he could appear among us now, we would regard him as a savage; but the holiest among us would soon fall at his feet
•PP 79 (*see also Perelandra* 208*)
❖ PP 5:7 (*see also Perelandra* 17:11*)

Adam, regarding the belief that we were somehow involved in the sin of
•PP 70 (*see also* PP 86-87)
❖ PP 5:1 (*see also* PP 5:12)

Adam, sin of, was that of turning from God to self
•PP 75-76*, 80-83 ❖ PP 5:5*, 9, 10

Adam, speculation about the nature of
•L 237; PP 77-84
❖ L 10 Jan 52; PP 5:6-10

Addiction described as an Appreciative pleasure gone bad (turned into Need-pleasure)
•FL 26-27 ❖ FL 2:2, 3

Admiration—*see also* Appreciation; Appreciative love

Admiration, as of a father for his son, not the same thing as sinful Pride
•MC 113 ❖ MC III 8:11

Admiration as that element in love which wishes that its object should be what it is even if we were never to enjoy it
•FL 32-33 ❖ FL 2:12-14

Admiration, inequality furnishes opportunity for the immense pleasures of; the Incarnation sheds new light on this principle
•GID 84-85 (*see also* LAL 26, 27; SL 170; WG 115-116; WLN 68)
❖ GID I 9:7 (*see also* LAL 26/1/54; Feb 22/54; SL 32:39; WG 7:15; WLN 4:39)

Admiration: When we meet someone clever or beautiful, we ought to admire and love them; but is it not our choice to turn that kind of love into "being in love"?
•MC 101 (*see also* SL 88*)
❖ MC III 6:13 (*see also* SL 19:3*)

Adolescence—*see* Youth

Adonis, central idea in the myth of, is Death and Rebirth
•CR 83 (*see also* Death and Rebirth)
❖ CR 7:5 (*see also* Death and Rebirth)

Adonis, resemblance of, to Christ not at all accidental
•GID 29-30, 83; M 113-114; RP 106-108 (*see also* Mythology)
❖ GID I 2:8; 9:5; M 14:8, 9; RP 10:11, 12 (*see also* Mythology)

Adoration—*see also* Praise; Worship

Adoration and praise in prayer: "Begin where you are"—with the pleasures and blessings you are apprehending right now
•LM 88-91 ❖ LM 17:1-13

Adoration, every pleasure can be made a channel for; we can learn to recognise its divine source and give thanks for it in the same moment it is received
•LM 89-90 (*see also* GO 73)
❖ LM 17:6-9 (*see also* GO 4:7, 8)

Adoration, inequality furnishes opportunity for the immense pleasures of; the Incarnation sheds new light on this principle
•GID 84-85 (*see also* SL 170; WLN 115-116; WLN 68) ❖ GID I 9:7 (*see also* SL 32:39; WG 7:15; WLN 4:39)

Adoration, more than any other kind of prayer, should be a communal act
•LM 100 ❖ LM 19:1

Adoration of God through experience of pleasure: Any patch of sunlight will show you something about the sun which you couldn't get from books on astronomy
•LM 91 ❖ LM 17:13

Adoration vs. Gratitude: Gratitude says, "How good of God to give me this"; Adoration says, "What must be the quality of that Being..."
•LM 90 ❖ LM 17:8

Adoration: "We...shall not be able to adore God on the highest occasions if we have learned no habit of doing so on the lowest" (re: praise for small things)
•LM 91 ❖ LM 17:13

Adult life, I had (as a child) the gloomiest anticipation of
•SJ 22-23 (*see also* SJ 64-65)
❖ SJ 2:1 (*see also* SJ 4:11)

Adults and learned have (spiritually) no

advantage over the simple and the child
- PP 79 (*see also* LM 103; PP 75*)
- ❖ PP 5:7 (*see also* LM 19:7; PP 5:5*)

Adults (quote from E. Nesbitt): "'Grownups know that children can believe almost anything; that's why they tell you that the earth is round...'"
- L 113 ❖ L 30 Mar 27

Adulteries, Screwtape gives a recipe for luring humans into "noble," romantic, and tragic
- SL 88 ❖ SL 19:3

Adultery—*see also* Infidelity

Adultery not an offense against "sexual morality" but against honesty, gratitude, and common humanity
- GID 320 (*see also* FL 132-133)
- ❖ GID III 9:20 (*see also* FL 5:2)

Adultery, Screwtape speaks about
- SL 155; WLN 53 ❖ SL 32:5; WLN 4:5

Adultery, the sexual act carried out with fine feelings may still be plain
- FL 132-133 ❖ FL 5:2

"**Advantage**," Christ's, is the only reason He can help us (drowning swimmer analogy)
- L 234-235; MC 61
- ❖ L undated letter between 12 Sep 51 and 3 Dec 51; MC II 4:10

Advantage, on the important level the learned and the adult have no, over the simple and the child
- PP 79 (*see also* LM 103; PP 75*)
- ❖ PP 5:7 (*see also* LM 19:7; PP 5:5*)

Advantage, the Christian has a great, over other men—not by being less fallen but by knowing that he *is* a fallen man in a fallen world
- WLN 77 ❖ WLN 5:15

Adventures, first beginning of winter always excites me and makes me want
- L 264 ❖ L 16 Oct 55

Adversity—*see also* Difficulties

Adversity and prosperity both mentioned by Screwtape as possible means to separate men from God
- SL 132 ❖ SL 28:1

Advertisements—especially those with a sexy or a snobbish appeal—listed as a

means to distract us from God
- CR 168-169 ❖ CR 14:17, 18

Advertisements mentioned by Screwtape as one of many trivial things that can distract us from prayer if we already have a vague, overall sense of guilt
- SL 55 ❖ SL 12:4

Advertisements, our lives must be good, for Christianity in order to make it attractive
- L 247 ❖ L 8 Nov 52

Advertisers mentioned by Screwtape as influencing humans in determining what kind of person they ought to fall in love with
- SL 91 ❖ SL 20:3

Advertising creates desires for unnecessary things; this creates unnecessary work
- WLN 75-78 (*see also* MC 80)
- ❖ WLN 5:11-15 (*see also* MC III 3:4)

Advertising ("propaganda"), we grow up surrounded by, in favour of unchastity
- MC 92 ❖ MC III 5:8, 10

Advice, Christianity is not just good; it is the Truth
- GID 90-91, 101; MC 137; SL 108-109*
- ❖ GID I 10:5, 48; MC IV 1:6, 7; SL 23:4*

Advice, issuing: I dislike people who, themselves in ease and safety, issue exhortations to men in the front line
- MC 9 ❖ MC P:10

Advice, it is a curious fact that the, we can give to others we cannot give to ourselves; truth is more effective through any lips rather than our own
- L 195 ❖ L 19 Nov 41

Advice of others: "...the thing we know already...when said by *someone else* becomes suddenly operative"
- L 236 ❖ L 26 Dec 51

Aesthetic delight as described in quote from *Pepys's Diary*
- WG 57 ❖ WG 4:5

Aesthetic enjoyment of nature was certainly hallowed by our Lord's praise of the lilies
- CR 15 ❖ CR 2:7

"Aesthetic experience," I had labelled "Joy" as; but that answer too had bro-

ken down
- •SJ 221 (*see also* GID 175*; SJ 072)
- ❖ SJ 14:12 (*see also* GID I 21:7*; SJ 5:2)

Aesthetic experience, "Joy" labelled by Lewis as, in his early days at Oxford
- •SJ 205 (*see also* Joy)
- ❖ SJ 13:12 (*see also* Joy)

Aesthetic pleasure, "Joy" is distinct not only from pleasure in general but also from; it must have the stab, the pang, the longing
- •SJ 72 (*see also* SJ 221)
- ❖ SJ 5:2 (*see also* SJ 14:12)

Aesthetic rapture described most easily as a physical sensation
- •WG 57-58 (*see also* CR 139-140; SJ 168, 219) ❖ WG 4:5, 6 (*see also* CR 11:22; SJ 11:5; 14:10, 11)

Aesthetic satisfaction, belief in any supposed reality lends a certain sort of; "poetry" is the result, not the cause, of religious belief
- •WG 77-78 ❖ WG 5:9

Aesthetic satisfaction: The pleasure of Poetic language is the pleasure at finding anything vividly conveyed to the imagination*
- •CR 130-131 (*see also* GID 66*)
- ❖ CR 11:4 (*see also* GID I 5:9*)

Aesthetic satisfactions, if you reject, you will fall into sensual satisfactions (re: learning in wartime)
- •WG 23-4 (*consider also* Culture)
- ❖ WG 2:5 (*consider also* Culture)

Affection (chapter title)
- •FL 53-83 ❖ FL ch. 3

Affection, as in a parent, may degenerate into a continued and ruthless demand for sympathy, affection, and appreciation
- •GID 285 (*see also* FL 64-65, 73-76)
- ❖ GID III 3:7 (*see also* FL 3:18, 33-36)

Affection as the love in which our experience seems to differ least from that of the animals
- •FL 53 (*see also* FL 131)
- ❖ FL 3:1 (*see also* FL 5:1)

Affection "at its best practices a courtesy which is incomparably more subtle, sensitive, and deep than the public kind"
- •FL 68-70 ❖ FL 3:24

Affection between dogs and cats
- •FL 55, 56, 59 (*see also* LAL 72)
- ❖ FL 3:4, 7, 11 (*see also* LAL 22/2/58)

Affection broadens the mind; of all natural loves it is the most catholic, the least finical, the broadest
- •FL 59-60 ❖ FL 3:11

Affection by itself will "go bad on us"; we need a higher sort of love
- •FL 62, 76-77; 81-82 ❖ FL 3:13, 37, 44

Affection by itself—without charity— not a cause of lasting happiness; becomes greedy, jealous, naggingly solicitous, exacting
- •GID 285 ❖ GID III 3:7

Affection can unite people who, if they had not been put down in the same household or community, would have nothing to do with each other
- •FL 58-59 (*see also* CR 117)
- ❖ FL 3:10 (*see also* CR 10:6)

Affection, change is a threat to
- •FL 70-73 (*see also* L 274)
- ❖ FL 3:27-32 (*see also* L 10 Feb 57)

Affection, feelings of, cannot be manufactured
- •MC 105, 116-117 (*see also* SL 21)
- ❖ MC III 7:5; 9:5, 6 (*see also* SL 4:3)

Affection, homespun clothing of...the mere ease and ordinariness of the relationship (free as solitude, yet neither is alone)...no need to talk...
- •FL 57 ❖ FL 3:8

Affection, human, in its natural condition is tyrannically possessive; cannot stand seeing the beloved passing into a sphere where it cannot follow
- •L 274 (*see also* FL 70-73)
- ❖ L 10 Feb 57 (*see also* FL 3:27-32)

Affection, I can imagine nothing more disagreeable than to experience erotic love for more than a very short time without the homespun clothing of
- •FL 57 ❖ FL 3:8

Affection ignores the barriers of age, sex, class, and education—even of species
- •FL 54-55; 58-60 ❖ FL 3:4, 10, 11

Affection includes both Need-love and

Gift-love
•FL 62 (see also FL 54)
❖ FL 3:15 (see also FL 3:3)
Affection "is an affair of old clothes, and
ease, of the unguarded moment..."
•FL 67 ❖ FL 3:24
Affection is responsible for nine-tenths of
whatever solid and durable happiness
there is in our natural lives
•FL 80 ❖ FL 3:42
Affection is "sometimes as comfortable
and unemphatic as putting on your
soft slippers"*
•GO 6 ❖ GO 1:12
Affection is the humblest love; nothing to
be proud of; has a comfortable, quiet
nature; it lives with soft slippers, old
clothes [etc.]
•FL 56-57 ❖ FL 3:7
Affection is the most instinctive, in that
sense the most animal, of the loves;
can be fiercely jealous
•FL 71 ❖ FL 3:28
Affection: "Its objects have to be familiar...I
doubt if we ever catch Affection be-
ginning"
•FL 55 ❖ FL 3:6
Affection may at times conflict with char-
ity
•MC 115-116 ❖ MC III 9:4
Affection may be felt for an old friend, as
things about him which originally had
nothing to do with the friendship be-
come dear with familiarity
•FL 57 ❖ FL 3:8
Affection may become perverted, as in the
need to be needed (story of Mrs.
Fidget)
•FL 73-77, 82-83 (see also SL 121*, 123*)
❖ FL 3:33-37, 45 (see also SL 26:2, 5*)
Affection may exist apart from other kinds
of love, but often it blends and over-
laps with other loves
•FL 57-58 ❖ FL 3:8, 9
Affection may involve a certain taking for
granted which is right and proper up
to a point, but which would be an out-
rage in erotic love
•FL 56 ❖ FL 3:7
Affection may take liberties, as long as

they are not intended to (and will not)
hurt
•FL 68-69 ❖ FL 3:25
Affection: "Nearly all the characteristics
of this love are ambivalent. They may
work for ill as well as for good"
•FL 62 ❖ FL 3:13
Affection of a Mother is Gift-love but it is
also Need-love because it needs to be
needed
•FL 54 (see also FL 76)
❖ FL 3:3 (see also FL 3:37)
Affection, perversion of: Regarding the
devilish desire to dominate another,
to make his whole intellectual and
emotional life merely an extension of
one's own
•SL xi* (see also FL 160; Absorption)
❖ SL P:19, 20 (see also FL 5:46; Absorption)
Affection, perversion of, not a disease
which needs medical treatment but a
sin which needs spiritual direction
•FL 80-81 ❖ FL 3:43
Affection resembles charity only as the
moon resembles the sun*
•CR 23 ❖ CR 2:34
Affection, the familiar is in itself ground
for (e.g., love for one's country, family, or school)
•L 231
❖ L undated letter just after 19 Apr 51
Affection: There is a charm about those
moments when Appreciative love lies
curled up asleep and the ease and ordinariness of Affection wraps us
round
•FL 57 ❖ FL 3:8
Affection: "This warm comfortableness
...takes in all sorts of objects. It is in-
deed the least discriminating of loves"
•FL 54 ❖ FL 3:4
Affection: We feel we have a right to expect it, but in truth we have only "a
reasonable expectation of being loved
by our intimates..."
•FL 62-65 ❖ FL 3:16-19
Agape—see Charity
Age, "chronological snobbery" as the uncritical acceptance of the intellectual

climate common to our own, and the arbitrary discrediting of past thought
•SJ 207-208 (see also SJ 206, 212- 213, 216; SL 128-129; WLN 96)
❖ SJ 13:17 (see also SJ 13:14; 14:2, 7; SL 27:5; WLN 7:6)

Age, danger of taking our own, to be a final and permanent platform from which we can see all other ages objectively
•RP 121 (see also SJ 207-208; WLN 96)
❖ RP 12:3 (see also SJ 13:17; WLN 7:6)

Age, every, has its own outlook; we therefore need older books that will correct the characteristic mistakes of our own period
•GID 202 ❖ GID II 4:4

Age, historical perspective gained through education protects one against the errors of the current
•WG 28-29 ❖ WG 2:10

Age, Lewis mentions the injustice which every, does to its predecessor
•CR 82 ❖ CR 7:1

Age, modern theologians and Biblical critics have been obviously influenced by (and perhaps insufficiently critical of) the spirit of the, they grew up in
•CR 158 ❖ CR 13:11

Age, our own, is also a "period" with its own illusions; they are likeliest to lurk in those widespread assumptions which go unchallenged
•SJ 208 ❖ SJ 13:17

Age, probably every, gets (within certain limits) the science it desires (re: myth of popular Evolution)
•CR 84-85 ❖ CR 7:9

Age, rejection of a thing because it does not immediately appeal to our own, is to have "the self-complacent blindness of the stay-at-home"
•RP 130 ❖ RP 12:9

Age, the immensely formidable unity of Christianity can best be seen by going out of our own
•GID 204 ❖ GID II 4:6

Age, under the views of "subjectivism" it is useless to compare the moral ideas of one, with those of another; progress and decadence are meaningless words
•CR 73 (see also CR 075)
❖ CR 6:5 (see also CR 6:11)

Ages, between different, there is no impartial judge on earth, for no one stands outside the historical process
•RP 121 ❖ RP 12:3

Ages, Screwtape mentions that where learning makes a free commerce between the, there is possibility that errors of one age may be corrected by the truth of another
•SL 129 ❖ SL 27:5

Aging and youth listed by Screwtape as neutral situations which can work either for God's or the devil's purposes
•SL 89 ❖ SL 19:3

Aging: "As to the bug-bear of Old People's Homes, remember that...the things we have most dreaded sometimes turn out to be quite nice"
•LAL 94 ❖ LAL 24 Nov 60

Aging: "...as we grow older we remember the distant past better than what is nearer"
•SJ 232 ❖ SJ 15:5

Aging: Autumn is like old age; it's the best of the seasons, but it doesn't last
•L 308 ❖ L 27 Oct 63

Aging: Decay in one's desire for "the crowd" neither a bad sign nor a sign of increasing spirituality; is a natural development as one grows older
•L 245 ❖ L 20 Oct 52

Aging: Future defined by Screwtape as "something which everyone reaches at the rate of sixty minutes an hour, whatever he does, whoever he is"
•SL 119 ❖ SL 25:6

Aging: "Has this world been so kind to you that you should leave it with regret? There are better things ahead than any we leave behind"
•LAL 117 (see also LAL 114; Death)
❖ LAL 17 Jun 63 (see also LAL 19 Mar 63; Death)

Aging: I agree that it is just as well to be past the age when one expects or desires to attract the other sex...
•LAL 19 ❖ LAL Aug 1st [1953]

Aging: "I can well understand your fears about old age. And of course you are doing the very best thing in meditating on the sufferings of Our Lord"
•LAL 32 ❖ LAL Sep 19/54

Aging: "I do wonder why the doctors inflict such torture to delay what cannot in any case be very long delayed. Or why God does!"
•LAL 118 ❖ LAL 25 Jun 63

Aging: "I have seen men, for the most part, grow better not worse with advancing years..." (re: suffering as used by God in soul-making)
•PP 108 ❖ PP 6:18

Aging: "I too think there is lots to be said for being no longer young..."
•LAL 19 ❖ LAL Aug 1st [1953]

Aging: "I'll never be able to take real walks again...but it's wonderful how mercifully the desire goes when the power goes"
•LAL 70 ❖ LAL Nov 30th 57

Aging: "I'm afraid as we grow older life consists more and more in either giving up things or waiting for them to be taken from us..."
•LAL 95 ❖ LAL 9 Jan 61

Aging: "In your position I myself would prefer a 'Home'—or almost anything—to solitude"
•LAL 102 (see also LAL 109, 117, 120*) ❖ LAL 17 Jan 62 (see also LAL 8 Nov 62; 10 Jun 63; 6 Jul 63*)

Aging: "It is a pity that the old usually dislike one another"
•LAL 102 ❖ LAL 17 Jan 62

Aging: Lewis mentions the hardship of the elderly "living on investment income in a world of rising prices"
•L 235
❖ L undated letter just before 3 Dec 51

Aging like becoming an old car; we must look forward to the fine new machines awaiting us in the Divine garage
•LAL 78 (see also LAL 110) ❖ LAL Sep 30 58 (see also LAL 26 Nov 62)

Aging: Like you, I'm a tired traveller, near the journey's end
•LAL 118 ❖ LAL 17 Jun 63

Aging likened to a ship's journey into a black night...a deafening gale... breakers ahead*
•GO 39 ❖ GO 2:33

Aging: Memories (e.g., of holidays) improve with time
•L 71-72 ❖ L 31 Aug 21

Aging: No need to always think of death, but one should always take it into account (as with Christ's return, and the Judgment)
•WLN 110 ❖ WLN 7:31

Aging: No use maundering about lost youth; new horizons appearing
•MC 101 ❖ MC III 6:12

Aging: Only the other day a girl to whom death was mentioned replied "Oh, but by the time I'm that age, Science will have done something about it"
•GID 252, 266 ❖ GID II 14:9; 16:56

Aging: Screwtape advises how to aggravate the female's chronic horror of growing old
•SL 92 ❖ SL 20:3

Aging: Screwtape mentions the gradual decay of youthful loves and hopes as providing "admirable opportunities of wearing out a soul by attrition"
•SL 132 ❖ SL 28:1

Aging: "...some of the shrewdest minds I have met inhabited the bodies of old maids"
•PP 136 ❖ PP 9:9

Aging: "The increasing list of people to be prayed for is...one of the burdens of old age"
•LM 66 ❖ LM 12:13

Aging: The parable of the Unjust Judge teaches us that no evil habit is so ingrained that it cannot, even in old age, be whisked away
•LM 107 ❖ LM 20:1

Aging: "There is no way out of it: either one must die fairly young or else outlive many friends"
•LAL 82-83 ❖ LAL May 19th 59

Aging: "...though I get no more tired now than I did when I was younger, I take much longer to get un-tired afterwards"

•LAL 86 ❖ LAL Aug 3/59

Aging: Though now most of us live longer, other things have made old age harsher than it ever was before
•LAL 102 ❖ LAL 17 Jan 62

Aging: We are growing less kind to the elderly; any doctor will tell you that even prosperous people refuse to look after their parents
•GID 312 ❖ GID III 8:4

Aging: "We have *always* been forgetting things: but now, when we do so, we attribute it to our age"
•LAL 93-94 ❖ LAL 24 Nov 60

Aging: "We must 'sit light' not only to life itself but to all its phases. The useless word is 'encore'"*
•L 306 (*see also* L 161-162; LM 26-027; WLN 110; *Perelandra* 48*)
❖ L 21 Nov 62 (*see also* L 12 Sep 38; LM 5:10- 13; WLN 7:31; *Perelandra* 4:6*)

Aging: "Why shouldn't we have wrinkles? Honorable insignia of long service in this warfare"
•LAL 79 ❖ LAL Oct 30 58

Aging: Youth are generally less unwilling to die than the middle-aged and the old; "prosperity knits a man to the World"
•SL 132 ❖ SL 28:1

Aging: Youth is neither the wisest, happiest, or most innocent period in life; the attempt to prolong it loses all the value of the *other* parts of life
•LAL 19 ❖ LAL Aug 1st [1953]

Agnostic(s)—*see also* Sceptic(s); Unbeliever(s); *consider also* Atheist(s)

Agnostic argument from similarities between Christianity and Paganism works only if you know the answer
•GID 132 ❖ GID I 16:4

Agnostics and atheists, I would gladly believe that many, care for the things I care for (re: spontaneous, genuine enjoyment of "culture")
•WLN 49 ❖ WLN 3:28

Agnostics will talk about "man's search for God"—to me, as I was then, they might as well have talked about the mouse's search for the cat

•SJ 227 (*see also* CR 169)
❖ SJ 14:21 (*see also* CR 14:19)

Agnosticism—*consider also* Atheism; Obstacles to Christian faith; Scepticism

Agnosticism: Lewis's reply to a paper entitled "The Grounds of Modern Agnosticism," by H. H. Price
•GID 129-146 ❖ GID I ch. 16

Agnosticism of youth may be explained by ignorance; British school system no longer teaches Christianity
•GID 115 ❖ GID I 13:3

Aid—*see* Charity; Help; Helping

Akhenaten (Amenhetep IV): It is possible that Moses was influenced by his system of Monotheism, as expressed in the Egyptian poem *Hymn to the Sun*
•RP 85-89 ❖ RP 8:16-19

Alcohol—*consider also* Temperance

Alcohol and sex, without the attraction of, I fancy even adults would not find an evening party very endurable
•SJ 47 ❖ SJ 3:5

Alcohol: Hymn singing can undoubtedly be done to the glory of God—just as eating, or drinking beer, or playing darts*
•CR 95-96 ❖ CR 8:6

Alcohol: "...I know I should be very angry if the Mohammedans tried to prevent the rest of us from drinking wine"
•MC 101 ❖ MC III 6:14

Alcohol: "I...object to the tyrannic and unscriptural insolence of anything that calls itself a Church and makes teetotalism a condition of membership"
•L 262 ❖ L 16 Mar 55

Alcohol: Lewis mentions a woman who was "a rabid teetotaller"
•GID 319 ❖ GID III 9:15

Alcohol, mention of, with regard to our abuse of our bodies*
•GID 216 ❖ GID II 7:3

Alcohol: No doubt, if our minds are full of novels and our bodies full of alcohol, we shall turn any love we feel into "being in love"
•MC 101 ❖ MC III 6:14

Alcohol: Of course the wine of the Bible was real fermented wine and alcoholic
•L 262, 263 ❖ L 16 Mar 55; 14 May 55

Alcohol: Screwtape observes that temptation to overdrink is more successful during the "trough" periods of human experience—when men are dull and weary
•SL 41 ❖ SL 9:2

Alcohol: Sobriety mentioned by Lewis as one of the virtues attempted by his friends at Oxford, and a standard which he accepted in principle*
•SJ 201 ❖ SJ 13:6

Alcohol: Temperance fanatics who claim to have an unanswerable intuition that all strong drink is forbidden really can have nothing of the sort
•WG 37-38 (see also L 263)
❖ WG 3:8 (see also L 14 May 55)

Alcohol: Temperance not just a matter of drink; involves caution in the indulgence of bridge, clothes, golf, etc.
•MC 75-76 (see also LAL 53)
❖ MC III 2:5, 6 (see also LAL 19/3/56)

Alcohol: "To the alcoholic...no liquor gives any pleasure except that of relief from an unbearable craving" (re: Need-pleasures)
•FL 26 ❖ FL 2:2

Alcohol: "We are half-hearted creatures, fooling about with drink and sex and ambition when infinite joy is offered us..."*
•WG 3-4 ❖ WG 1:1

"All-I-want" state of mind, people in the, are being gluttonous and self-concerned even as they believe they are practicing temperance
•SL 76-78 ❖ SL 17:1-3

"All shall be well..." (quote from Lady Julian of Norwich)
•CR 123; GID 169; GO 75; L 186
❖ CR 10:22; GID I 20:Reply-11; GO 4:12; L 2 Jun 40

Allegorical (or hidden) meanings in things written or said
•RP 99-108 ❖ RP ch. 10

Allegorical (or hidden) meanings in Scripture
•RP 109-117 ❖ RP 11:1-13

Allegorical way of reading the Psalms is justified in principle, but this does not mean that all applications of it are fruitful, legitimate, or rational
•RP 120-121 ❖ RP 12:2, 3

Allegories, some of the, imposed on my books have been so ingenious and interesting that I often wish I had thought of them myself
•RP 99 ❖ RP 10:2

Allegory, definition of, ("...a composition...in which immaterial realities are represented by feigned physical objects...")
•L 283 ❖ L 29 Dec 58

"Allegory" is a word which can be used in wider or narrower senses; in one sense the whole material universe could be called an allegory
•L 273 ❖ L 10 Dec 56

Allegory, Lewis mentions medieval, as his own subject of study
•L 155-157 ❖ L 7 Jun 34

Allegory of Love, reference to the writing and content of
•L 127 (see also L 155-157*)
❖ L 10 Jul 28 (see also L 7 Jun 34*)

Allegory: Regarding the danger of applying allegorical interpretations to individual authors
•L 273 ❖ L 10 Dec 56

Allegory vs. Myth: "A myth is a story out of which ever varying meanings will grow..."; an allegory has one meaning
•L 271 ❖ L 22 Sep 56

Alms—see also Charity; Help; Helping

Alms: "Charity—giving to the poor—is an essential part of Christian morality"
•MC 81 ❖ MC III 3:7

Alms: If it were true that to receive money or gifts degraded the recipient, then every act of alms would be wicked
•LAL 58 ❖ LAL 5/7/56

Alms: It will not bother me at death to know I was "had for a sucker" by many impostors; but it would be a torment to know I had refused one person in need
•LAL 108 ❖ LAL 26 Oct 62

Alms: Parable of the Sheep and Goats makes our duty perfectly plain
•LAL 108 ❖ LAL 26 Oct 62

Aloneness—*see* Solitude

Alternative, The Shocking (chapter title)
•MC 51-56 ❖ MC II ch. 3

Alternatives—*see also* Choices

Alternatives, there are only three: 1) to be God, 2) to be like God and to share His goodness in creaturely response, and 3) to be miserable
•PP 53-54 ❖ PP 3:19

Altruistic vs. egoistic love as regards the love of God (God has no needs, thus His love is bottomlessly selfless)
•PP 49-54, esp. 50
❖ PP 3:17-19, esp. 3:17

Amateur (or "layman"), I write as one, to another
•RP 1-2 (*see also* CR 94, 152; GID 60, 62, 89, 332-333; L 219, 223; LM 101; MC 6; PP 10; WG 71; WLN 93-94)
❖ RP 1:1, 2 (*see also* CR 8:1; 13:1; GID I 4:56 (Ques. 14); 4:60 (Ques. 16); 10:1, 2; IV Letter 7; L 2 Sep 49; 28 Nov 50; LM 19:3; MC P:2; PP P:2; WG 4:28; WLN 7:1)

Ambition—*consider also* Competition; Money

Ambition: A man "should never give all his heart to anything which will end when his life ends"*
•WLN 110 ❖ WLN 7:31

Ambition, good and bad types of
•GID 55-56 ❖ GID I 4:34-36 (Ques. 9)

Ambition, we are half-hearted creatures fooling about with drink and sex and, when infinite joy is offered us
•WG 3-4 ❖ WG 1:1

Ambition: "When we want to be something other than the thing God wants us to be, we must be wanting what, in fact, will not make us happy"*
•PP 52 (*see also* PP 90; WG 118-119)
❖ PP 3:18 (*see also* PP 6:3; WG 7:18)

America and Russia, space race between: Great powers are seldom less dangerously employed than in fabricating costly objects and flinging them overboard
•CR 172; WLN 77
❖ CR 14:36; WLN 5:14

America, only yesterday I said to myself that I should like to see, if only one could see the quiet places and not the cities
•L 215 ❖ L undated letter of Jan 1949

American generosity, Lewis remarks on, which came his way during World War II
•L 213, 214 ❖ L 29 Jan 48; 29 May 48

Americans are far too medically minded; they read and think too much about health
•LAL 39 ❖ LAL 21/3/55

Americans mentioned
•L 81 (*see also* GID 3:18; L 53) ❖ L 16 Oct 22 (*see also* GID III 9:9; L 21 Jan 21)

Americans mentioned: "...every quarter a dull American don discovers for the first time what some Shakesperean play really meant"
•CR 157 ❖ CR 13:10

Americans mentioned: "This absurd notepaper is a present from an American"
•L 212 ❖ L 22 Dec 47

Analogy/ies—*see also* Metaphors; Language, imaginative; Language, metaphorical

Analogies, knowledge of God derived only by personal acquaintance and by
•FL 174-175 ❖ FL 6:20

Analogy is unavoidable and necessary for certain purposes—but there is some death in it (re: language of religion)
•CR 137 (*see also* CR 140)
❖ CR 11:18 (*see also* CR 11:23)

Analogy: "The footprints of the Divine are more visible in that rich soil than across rocks or slag-heaps" (i.e., abstract thinking)
•LM 52 ❖ LM 10:2

Analogy, we must not smuggle in the idea that we can throw away the, and get in behind it to a purely literal truth (re: God as "impassible")
•LM 51 ❖ LM 10:1

Angels, both good and bad kinds of, are "Supernatural" in relation to this spatio-temporal Nature; but good angels

are "Supernatural" in another sense as well
•M 170 ❖ M App. A:2

Angels, both good and bad kinds of, have likenesses to God which men lack: immortality and intuitive knowledge
•FL 15 ❖ FL 1:9

Angels, fallen—see also Devils

Angels, fallen ("beings in a different, and higher, 'Nature' which is partially interlocked with ours") have tampered with things inside our frontier—Nature*
•M 121 ❖ M 14:22

Angels, fallen, as "powerful, non-human beings, supernatural but created"*
•M 121 ❖ M 14:22

Angels, Friendship is the sort of love one can imagine between, (free of instinct, duties, jealousy, and the need to be needed)
•FL 111 (see also FL 124)
❖ FL 4:38 (see also FL 4:57)

Angels have no senses (their experience is purely intellectual and spiritual); that is why we know something about God which they don't
•GID 216 ❖ GID II 7:2

Angels: "I believe no angel ever appears in Scripture without exciting terror: they always have to begin by saying 'Fear not'"
•LAL 13; SL ix ❖ LAL 4/iii/53; SL P:14

Angels: I believe them to be real beings in the actual universe
•L 283 ❖ L 29 Dec 58

Angels: In art and literature, they are given wings in order to suggest the swiftness of unimpeded intellectual energy
•SL viii ❖ SL P:12

Angels, Lewis acknowledges a "heavy debt" to Ezekiel for his characterization of, in the Space Trilogy
•LAL 13 (see also LAL 72)
❖ LAL 4/iii/53 (see also LAL 22/2/58)

Angels, Lewis explains why many who believe in God cannot believe in
•M 154 ❖ M 16:20

Angels: Naked spirituality is in accordance with their nature; not, I think,

with ours
•LM 123-124 ❖ LM 22:20

Angels never knew the meaning of the word "ought"; there is no morality in Heaven
•LM 115 ❖ LM 21:13

Angels ("spirits"): When we see them we shall know that we have always known them*
•SL 147-148 ❖ SL 31:4

Angels: The Hebrew word Kherub is from the same root as Gryphon
•LAL 13-14 ❖ LAL 31/3/53

Angels, use of imagery to describe: Creatures higher in the natural order than ourselves must be represented symbolically if at all
•SL viii ❖ SL P:12

Angels, we are in one most blessed sense nearer to Jesus than to
•LAL 13 ❖ LAL 4/iii/53

Anger—see also Wrath

Anger, absence of, can be an alarming symptom; presence of indignation may be a good one (re: cursings in the Psalms)
•RP 29-30 ❖ RP 3:18, 19

Anger against "an apparently ruthless and idiotic cosmos" is really an unconscious homage to something in or behind that cosmos which is authoritative
•CR 65-67, 69-70 (see also MC 45-46*)
❖ CR 5:19, 24 (see also MC II 1:5, 6*)

Anger against God: When I was an atheist, I maintained that God did not exist; I was also very angry at God for not existing, and for creating a world
•SJ 115 (see also SJ 171)
❖ SJ 7:20 (see also SJ 11:8)

Anger against oneself "'worketh not the righteousness of God'. One must never be either content with, or impatient with, oneself"
•LAL 29 ❖ LAL Mar 31st 54

Anger, fear tames, —the fear that my own unforgivingness will exclude me from all the promises
•LAL 93 ❖ LAL 28 Oct 60

Anger: "...how madly one cherishes that

base part as if it were one's dearest possession..."
- LAL 93 ❖ LAL 28 Oct 60

Anger is love's renewal; reconciliation between two people is fullest when the anger has been fully expressed (re: "wrath" of God)
- LM 96-97 ❖ LM 18:8, 9

Anger ("just, generous, scalding indignation") is the fluid that love bleeds when you cut it
- LM 97 ❖ LM 18:9

Anger ("rudeness") in unbelievers shows fear that there "might be something in it after all"*
- LAL 90 ❖ LAL 26 Mar 60

Anger, speaking in: Slowing down the *speed* of the conversation is sometimes helpful; also sitting down
- LAL 94 ❖ LAL 24 Nov 60

Anger spreads; when one angry man bursts out, others become equally angry
- LAL 56 ❖ LAL 21/5/56

Anger toward God in times of difficulty: "I was getting from it the only pleasure a man in anguish can get; the pleasure of hitting back"
- GO 45-46 ❖ GO 3:9

Anglican Church—*see* Church of England

Anglican theology, letter regarding conflict in
- GID 327 ❖ GID IV Letter 2

Anglicans, it would be idle to pretend that we, are a striking example of the gusto expressed in the Psalms
- RP 52 ❖ RP 5:10

Anglo-Catholic, what unites the Evangelical and the, against the "Liberal" or "Modernist" Christian
- GID 336 ❖ GID IV Letter 9

Anglo-Catholicism, Lewis describes his childhood experience with, as a student at "Belsen"
- SJ 33-34 ❖ SJ 2:14

Animal behaviour: "There are instincts I had never dreamed of: big with the promise of real morality"
- L 242 ❖ L 28 May 52

Animal creation: How strange that God

brings us into such intimate relations with creatures of whose real purpose and destiny we remain forever ignorant
- LAL 109 ❖ LAL 26 Oct 62

Animal, everything man does to an, is either a lawful exercise or a sacrilege abuse of an authority by divine right
- PP 138 ❖ PP 9:11

Animal experimentation—*see* Vivisection

Animal furs: I like them *on* the beasts
- LAL 46 ❖ LAL 9/10/55

Animal, if you want to make sure of keeping your heart intact, you must give it to no one—not even an
- FL 169 ❖ FL 6:13

Animal, in so far as the tame, has a real self or personality, it owes this almost entirely to its master
- PP 139, 141 (*see also* MC 166, 170)
- ❖ PP 9:11, 13 (*see also* MC IV 7:13; 8:11)

Animal, man is an, called or raised to be something more than an animal; there may be more than analogy between this and the taking of man into God
- RP 115-116, 134 ❖ RP 11:11; 12:13

Animal, man's love for an, as an analogy useful to our conception of God's love for us
- PP 43-44, 47 ❖ PP 3:11, 14

Animal Pain (chapter title)
- PP 129-143 ❖ PP ch. 9

Animal pain: Animals are incapable of sin or of virtue, therefore they can neither deserve pain nor be improved by it
- PP 129 ❖ PP 9:1

Animal pain, I find that the problem of, is just as tough when I concentrate on creatures I dislike as on ones I could make pets of
- L 303 ❖ L 29 Dec 61

Animal pain: If God is good, then the appearance of divine cruelty in the animal world must be a false appearance
- GID 167-168, 170; PP 129-130
- ❖ GID I 20:Reply-6, 15; PP 9:1

Animal pain, problem of, is appalling because the Christian explanation of human pain cannot be extended to

Animals: Lewis makes the case for their having "sentience without consciousness" (re: animal pain)
•PP 131-133 ❖ PP 9:4, 5

Animals, Lewis pokes fun at the idea of putting clothing on
•LAL 115 ❖ LAL 19 Mar 63

Animals, love for: "I think God wants us to love Him *more*, not to love creatures (even animals) *less*"
•LAL 61 (*see also* FL 165*, 170-171, 190-191*) ❖ LAL 18/8/56 (*see also* FL 6:3, 4, 15, 44*)

Animals, Man meant to be the mediator through whom, apprehend so much of the Divine splendour as their irrational nature allows
•PP 78 ❖ PP 5:6

Animals, man's power over, has been abused; requires intervention
•WG 114 ❖ WG 7:12

Animals, of the small, I think Hamsters are the most amusing—and I am also fond of mice
•L 265 ❖ L 16 Oct 55

Animals, possible immortality of
•PP 136-143 (*see also* LAL 110)
❖ PP 9:9-14 (*see also* LAL 26 Nov 62)

Animals, Psalmist's appreciation for, is almost certainly reached through the idea of God as Creator and sustainer of all; they are our fellow-dependents
•RP 84-85 (*see also* RP 88-89)
❖ RP 8:14 (*see also* RP 8:18)

Animals, question of whether there are, anywhere except on earth and, if they exist, whether they have rational souls
•WLN 84-86 ❖ WLN 6:6-9

Animals, Reason enables men to inflict a great amount of pain on; this power they have exploited to the full
•PP 14 ❖ PP 1:1

Animals, regarding the question of immortality of wild
•PP 141-143 (*see also* GID 169) ❖ PP 9:13, 14 (*see also* GID I 20:Reply-11)

Animals, tame, are the only "natural" animals, since Man was appointed by God to have dominion over the beasts
•PP 138 ❖ PP 9:11

Animals, tame, at the zoo reminded Lewis of the world before the Fall
•L 154-155; SJ 237-238
❖ L 14 Jun 32; SJ 15:8, 9

Animals, tame: Their mere sentience is reborn to soulhood in us as our mere soulhood is reborn to spirituality in Christ
•PP 141 (*see also* GID 169; MC 170)
❖ PP 9:13 (*see also* GID I 20:Reply-11; MC IV 8:11)

Animals, The Pains of (chapter title)
•GID 161-171 ❖ GID I ch. 20

Animals, those who find in, a relief from the demands of human companionship will be well advised to examine their real reasons
•FL 79 ❖ FL 3:41

Animals, we can learn the lesson of *trust* from the; how well a sick dog trusts if one has to do things that hurt it
•LAL 56 (*see also* WLN 23-24)
❖ LAL 26/4/56 (*see also* WLN 2:12)

Animals: We know neither what they are nor why they are
•GID 167; PP 129
❖ GID I 20:Reply-6; PP 9:1

Animals: We now have good reason to believe that they existed long before men
•PP 133 ❖ PP 9:6

Animals: What strikes you is their cheerful fatuity, the pointlessness of nearly all they do
•L 217 ❖ L 4 Apr 49

Animals, when a hard-worked shepherd or carter remains kind to, his back may well be patted; not ours (who have met them solely as pets)
•RP 84 ❖ RP 8:14

Animals, whether, are sub-personal or not they are never loved as if they were; the fact or illusion of personality is always present
•FL 49 ❖ FL 2:44

Anna Karenina, story of, mentioned as an example of unredeemed, poisonous Eros
•FL 160 ❖ FL 5:46

Annunciation mentioned

Anthroposophist, it would not be pleasant to have to explain to an M.P.H. that one's father was an
•L 172 ❖ L 3 Dec 39

Anthroposophists, Harwood and then Barfield embraced the doctrines of Steiner and became; this was a really dreadful thing
•SJ 205-207 (see also L 89)
❖ SJ 13:14-17 (see also L 7 Jul 23)

Anthroposophy: "Here were gods, spirits, afterlife and pre-existence, initiates, occult knowledge, meditation"
•SJ 206 ❖ SJ 13:14

Antichrist, we have been warned that *all but* conclusive evidence against Christianity will appear with
•WLN 92 ❖ WLN 6:28

Anticipation: In time of war, it was usually the reserve who had to *watch* the carnage, not the troops who were in it, whose nerve broke first*
•L 250 ❖ L 17 Jul 53

Anticipation of pain and of death a cause of much acute mental suffering in Man; is the result of Reason
•PP 14 (see also GO 9)
❖ PP 1:1 (see also GO 1:18)

Anticipation: "The approach of any fate is usually also the preparation for it" (quote from George MacDonald)
•L 186 (see also L 219)
❖ L 2 Jun 40 (see also L 2 Sep 49)

Anxiety(ies)—see also Worry; consider also Difficulties; Faith

Anxieties, like all afflictions, can be taken as our share in the Passion of Christ
•LM 41 ❖ LM 8:5

Anxieties of everyday domestic life more of a hindrance to devotional life than any passion or appetite
•FL 137-138 ❖ FL 5:10

Anxieties should not be regarded as a defect of faith; they are afflictions, not sins
•LM 41-43 ❖ LM 8:5

Anxieties, worldly, often pour into our lives on the eve of conversion or at a time we might receive Grace; devil is very active at such junctures

•L 227-228 (see also SL 172; WLN 70)
❖ L 5 Mar 51 (see also SL 32:40; WLN 4:40)

Anxiety: Analogy of the Front Line to illustrate how we should live day to day, "not adding the past or future to the present"
•LAL 69 ❖ LAL Oct 20th 57

Anxiety and suffering: "It doesn't really matter whether you grip the arms of the dentist's chair or let your hands lie in your lap. The drill drills on"
•GO 38 ❖ GO 2:31

Anxiety and suspense, there is nothing like, for barricading a human's mind against God (—Screwtape)
•SL 28 ❖ SL 6:1

Anxiety described as "the circular movement of the mind"
•L 285; LM 41 ❖ L 29 Apr 59; LM 8:4

Anxiety: If God wanted me to live like the lilies of the field, why didn't He give me the same lack of nerves and imagination as they enjoy?
•LAL 21, 22, 79 (see also GO 84)
❖ LAL Aug 10th 53; Nov 6/53; Oct 30 58 (see also GO 4:32)

Anxiety is not only a pain which we must ask God to assuage but also a weakness we must ask Him to pardon—for He's told us to take no care for the morrow
•LAL 23 ❖ LAL 27/xi/53

Anxiety itself is a cross we must submit to God—not all the things we are afraid might happen*
•SL 29 (see also LAL 60)
❖ SL 6:2 (see also LAL 3/8/56)

Anxiety: "...Our Lord says to you "Peace, child, peace. Relax. Let go. Underneath are the everlasting arms. Let go, I will catch you"*
•LAL 117 ❖ LAL 17 Jun 63

Anxiety: "Remember one is given strength to bear what happens to one, but not the 100 and 1 different things that *might* happen"*
•LAL 60 (see also LAL 58, 69, 103; SL 29)
❖ LAL 3/8/56 (see also LAL 14/6/56; Oct 20th 57; 4 May 62; SL 6:2)

Anxiety: "Remember, tho' we struggle against things because we are afraid of them, it is often the other way round—we get afraid *because* we struggle"
•LAL 117 ❖ LAL 17 Jun 63

Anxiety that gnaws like fire: "If I knew any way of escape I would crawl through sewers to find it" (re: justification of suffering)
•PP 105 ❖ PP 6:16

Anxiety: "The dreadful thing, as you know, is the waking each morning—the moment at which it all flows back on one"*
•LAL 88 ❖ LAL 18 Oct 59

Anxiety: "The great thing with unhappy times is to take them bit by bit and hour by hour...it is seldom the *present* the exact present, that is unbearable"*
•LAL 58 (*see also* LAL 60, 69, 103; SL 29, 67-71*)
❖ LAL 14/6/56 (*see also* LAL 3/8/56; Oct 20th 57; 4 May 62; SL 6:2; ch. 15*)

Anxiety, Jesus' prayer in Gethsemane shows that, is part of our human destiny; the perfect Man experienced it
•LM 42-43 ❖ LM 8:9

Anxiety, your, about the future is a thing we can all understand, and *very* hard to bear; I pray you may be supported in it as you were before
•LAL 47 ❖ LAL 26/10/55

Apocalypse—*see* Second Coming

Apocalyptic, Christian, foretells a sudden, violent end imposed from without; "...a curtain rung down on the play — Halt!"
•WLN 101 ❖ WLN 7:12

Apocalyptic literature naturally produced by those trained to expect apocalypse (the Jews)
•WLN 97 ❖ WLN 7:7

Apocalyptic writings, to most modern tastes, appear tedious and unedifying; predictions of Jesus seen as "much the same sort of thing"
•WLN 95 ❖ WLN 7:5

Apocryphal gospels mentioned
•CR 156 ❖ CR 13:8

Apologetic(s)—*see also* Argument; *consider also* Evangelism

Apologetic of Christian beliefs cannot rely on Science for basis; Science is always switching positions
•GID 92 (*see also* GID 39, 44; WLN 83-84) ❖ GID I 10:8 (*see also* GID I 3:3, 12; WLN 6:1-3)

Apologetics: "A man can't always be defending the truth; there must be a time to feed on it"
•RP 7 ❖ RP 1:12

Apologetics: Analogy is unavoidable and necessary for certain purposes—but there is some death in it (re: language and religion)*
•CR 137 ❖ CR 11:18

Apologetics, Christian (chapter title)
•GID 89-103 ❖ GID I ch. 10

Apologetics, Christian: We must be able to meet our enemies on their own ground (by being educated)
•WG 28 (*see also* CR 17)
❖ WG 2:10 (*see also* CR 2:18)

Apologetics dangerous to one's own faith; no doctrine seems to me so unreal as one that I have just successfully defended in a public debate
•GID 103, 128; L 209
❖ GID I 10:50; 15:4; L 2 Aug 46

Apologetics, definition of: "Defence"
•GID 89 ❖ GID I 10:2

Apologetics, discussion of Christian
•GID 89-103 ❖ GID I ch. 10

Apologetics: If the "emotional" religious sayings contain real information, you will not get it without meeting them with a certain readiness to find it*
•CR 136-137, 141 ❖ CR 11:16, 25

Apologetics, Theological language—which is essential to,—is in a sense alien to religion, omitting nearly all that really matters by its very precision
•CR 135-136 ❖ CR 11:13-15

Apologist, Christian, must defend Christianity itself—not his own religion
•GID 90 ❖ GID I 10:4

Apologist must continually fall back from the web of his own arguments into Reality—from Christian apologetics into

Christ Himself
•GID 103 ❖ GID I 10:50
Apologist must face up to what he finds
disagreeable in the doctrines
•GID 91 ❖ GID I 10:6
Apologist must keep abreast of recent
movements in theology
•GID 91-92 ❖ GID I 10:7
Apologist, purpose of Christian, misun-
derstood by modern audiences (they
think you are preaching Christianity
because it is good for society, etc.)
•GID 90-91, 101 (see also MC 137; SL
108-109*) ❖ GID I 10:5, 48 (see also MC
IV 1:6, 7; SL 23:4*)
Apologist represents John Baptist; the
Preacher (the Evangelist, the man on
fire) represents the Lord
•GID 221-222 ❖ GID II 8:10
Apologists are opposed not by the irreligion of their hearers, but by their
vague, Pantheistic religion
•M 81 ❖ M 11:2
Apologizing: Regarding those who make
an elaborate show of always "unnec-
essarily asking, or insufferably offer-
ing, forgiveness"*
•FL 185 ❖ FL 6:36
Apostle's Creed, doctrine of the Second
Coming as part of ("He shall come
again to judge the quick and the
dead")
•WLN 93 ❖ WLN 7:1
Apostle's Creed, in the, we are reminded
to believe in the forgiveness of sins;
this is not nearly so easy as I once believed
•WG 121 ❖ WG 8:1
Appetite(s)—see also Desire(s)
"Appetite for God" as expressed in the
Psalms ("It has all the cheerful spon-
taneity of a natural, even a physical,
desire")
•RP 50-53 (see also GID 130)
❖ RP 5:8-10 (see also GID I 16:2)
Appetite for God, early belief in Heaven
and Hell may render impossible the
development of the
•RP 40-41 (see also GID 130-131*; SJ
231) ❖ RP 4:15 (see also GID I 16:2, 3*;

SJ 15:3)
Appetite, God makes no, in vain (re:
man's natural appetite for knowledge
and beauty)
•WG 27 ❖ WG 2:9
Appetite, God makes no, in vain ("...my
desire for Paradise...[is] a pretty good
indication that such a thing exists")*
•WG 8-9 (see also MC 120)
❖ WG 1:6 (see also MC III 10:5)
Appetites and passions not as big a hin-
drance to our prayers as the anxieties
and decisions of everyday domestic
life
•FL 137-138 ❖ FL 5:10
Appetites would give us very little trouble
if the imagination were obedient
•LM 17 (see also GID 217; L 126; LAL
111) ❖ LM 3:9 (see also GID II 7:3; L 1
Apr 28; LAL 26 Nov 62)
Apple in the Genesis story was a magic
apple of knowledge (full of sugges-
tion); in the developed doctrine, story
is simply one of disobedience
•PP 71-72 (see also Genesis)
❖ PP 5:2 (see also Genesis)
Apple [of Eden] may have been literal, but
the question is of no consequence
•PP 80 ❖ PP 5:8
Appreciation—see also Gratitude; Praise
Appreciation, a growing, of people sim-
ply because they happen to be there
as a by-product of Affection
•FL 58-60 ❖ FL 3:10, 11
Appreciation for things such as "un-
spoiled forests that we shall never
see..." a form of disinterested love
•FL 32-33 ❖ FL 2:12-14
Appreciative love differentiated from
Need-love and Gift-love
•FL 25-33, esp. 33 (see also Gift-love;
Need-love) ❖ FL 2:1-14, esp. 2:14 (see
also Gift-love; Need-love)
Appreciative love "gazes and holds its
breath and is silent, rejoices that such
a wonder should exist even if not for
him..."
•FL 33 ❖ FL 2:14
Appreciative love not a basic element in
Affection; but Affection can make ap-

preciations possible which, but for it, might never have existed
•FL 56, 58-59 ❖ FL 3:7, 10

Appreciative love, through Grace God can awaken in man an, towards Himself
•FL 191 ❖ FL 6:46

Appreciative pleasure, Eros transforms a Need-pleasure into
•FL 135-136 ❖ FL 5:6

Appreciative pleasure vs. Need-pleasure
•FL 25-30 ❖ FL 2:2-8

Approval by God comes not because we are good; God makes us good because He loves us
•MC 64 ❖ MC II 5:6

Approval by God is the promise—and the weight—of glory
•WG 11-13 ❖ WG 1:9, 10

Aquinas, Thomas, said of all his own theology, "It reminds me of straw"
•LM 82 ❖ LM 15:17

Archaeology: "The whole modern estimate of primitive man is based upon that idolatry of artefacts which is a great corporate sin of our own civilisation"*
•PP 74 ❖ PP 5:3

Architecture, Christianity for me was associated with ugly
•SJ 172 (consider also Cathedral/s)
❖ SJ 11:8 (consider also Cathedral/s)

Architecture compared to rhyming poetry: "...a need, and the answer of it following so quickly that they make a single sensation"
•L 66 ❖ L 7 Aug 21

Architecture: I would loathe a house that is nearly all glass; I like to feel indoors when I'm in*
•LAL 46 ❖ LAL 9/10/55

Architecture: "...the base utility for which alone we build now"
•L 100 ❖ L undated letter of "April or May" 1925

Architecture: Wyvern Priory was the first building that I ever perceived to be beautiful*
•SJ 58 ❖ SJ 4:4

Arguing—consider also Quarrelling

Arguing: "I hope one is rewarded for all

the stunning replies one thinks of one does not utter!" —but more than we suspect comes out in our manner, etc.*
•LAL 109-110 ❖ LAL 8 Nov 62

Arguing: Slowing down the speed of the conversation is sometimes helpful; also sitting down*
•LAL 94 ❖ LAL 24 Nov 60

Argument—see also Apologetics; Debate-(ing)

Argument against existence of God, regarding the, which demands concrete evidence*
•SL 38 (see also God, existence of)
❖ SL 8:4 (see also God, existence of)

Argument by correspondence, Lewis expresses distaste for
•L 223, 234
❖ L undated letter of Jan 1950; undated letter just before 3 Dec 51

Argument, denominational differences may be widened and sharpened by discussion or
•L 228-229, 230 (see also L 223)
❖ L 23 Apr 51; undated letter just before 27 Mar 51 (see also L undated letter of Jan 1950)

Argument depends upon rational intuition; is at an end when any one of the self-evident steps cannot be seen
•WG 35 (see also CR 75*)
❖ WG 3:4 (see also CR 6:12*)

Argument: "Discussions usually separate us; actions sometimes unite us" (re: re-union of churches)*
•LM 16 ❖ LM 3:5

Argument for the existence of God not unimportant; faith as intellectual assent a necessary pre-condition for faith as trust or confidence
•GID 173 ❖ GID I 21:2

Argument has a life of its own; is impartial
•GID 128 ❖ GID I 15:3

Argument, I can still remember my first metaphysical: whether the future is like a line you can't see or like a line that is not yet drawn
•SJ 32 ❖ SJ 2:11

Argument in the realm of philosophy and

religion no longer as effective as it used to be; people more influenced by jargon than by argument for truth*
•SL 7-8 (*see also* SL 43)
❖ SL 1:1, 2 (*see also* SL 9:4)

Argument, Lewis's early attempts at, after studying with Kirkpatrick: "Most of it, as I now see, was incredibly crude and silly"
•SJ 173 ❖ SJ 11:9

Argument, silence during an, can be of an emphatic, audible, and even dialectical character
•LM 77 (*see also* LAL 110)
❖ LM 15:1 (*see also* LAL 8 Nov 62)

Argument: The modern method is to assume that your opponent is wrong and then to explain how he became so silly—rather than first showing *that* he is wrong
•GID 273 ❖ GID III 1:6

Argument, those who lose their Christian faith not usually reasoned out of it by honest; just drift away
•MC 124 (*see also* CR 42)
❖ MC III 11:6 (*see also* CR 3:10)

Argument, use of emotive vs. descriptive words in: "Stagnant" rather than "permanent" to describe traditional morality is to infer an unfair metaphor*
•CR 76 (*see also* SL 119)
❖ CR 6:14 (*see also* SL 25:6)

Argument, use of intellectual, in evangelism: "Uneducated people are not irrational people..."
•GID 99 ❖ GID I 10:39, 40

Aristotelian ethics: two definitions
•CR 44-45 ❖ CR 4:2

Aristotle and the value of culture as limited by Christian belief: "Of the great pagans Aristotle is on our side"
•CR 15 ❖ CR 2:10

Aristotle mentioned as having been well reconciled with Christianity by Thomas Aquinas
•L 186 ❖ L 2 Jun 40

Aristotle mentioned by Screwtape
•SL 169; WLN 68
❖ SL 32:28; WLN 4:38

Aristotle noted that the more virtuous a

man becomes, the more he enjoys virtuous actions
•PP 100 ❖ PP 6:11

Aristotle: Nothing separates Pagan theology from Christianity so much as Aristotle's doctrine that God moves the universe to love Him, Himself unmoved
•PP 51-52 (*see also* GID 174*)
❖ PP 3:17 (*see also* GID I 21:5*)

Aristotle: When he writes in praise of a certain kind of self-love, we may feel that here we strike something essentially sub-Christian
•GID 193 ❖ GID II 2:1

Arius, religion of, mentioned
•GID 206 ❖ GID II 4:8

Army, I am surprised I did not dislike the, more
•SJ 188 ❖ SJ 12:10

Army: "I met there both the World and the great goddess Nonsense"
•SJ 194 ❖ SJ 12:16

Army, Lewis describes his service in the
•SJ 186-198 (*see also* L 33-46)
❖ SJ 12:6-13:1 (*see also* L 28 Jan 17 to undated letter just before 27 Jan 19)

Army: "Straight tribulation is easier to bear than tribulation which advertises itself as pleasure" [such as school]
•SJ 188 ❖ SJ 12:10

Arnold, Matthew, quote from: "Nor does the being hungry prove that we have bread"
•GID 260; WG 8
❖ GID II 16:18; WG 1:6

Arnold, Matthew: "The present inordinate esteem of culture by the cultured began, I think, with Matthew Arnold..."
•CR 12 ❖ CR 2:2

Arrogance—*see also* Pride

Arrogance a result of inner insecurity
•LAL 27-28 (*see also* SL 162-163; WLN 60-61) ❖ LAL Mar 10/54 (*see also* SL 32:22, 23; WLN 4:22, 23)

Arrogance may be produced by cruelty and oppression ("We reimburse ourselves for cuffs and toil by a double dose of self-esteem")*
•SJ 107 ❖ SJ 7:8

Arrogance ("self-importance") as one of the "deadly serious passions" lived out in Hell*
•SL ix ❖ SL P:16

Art(s)—*see also* Culture; Literature

Art, abstract: When no one can agree on the subject of a picture—whether it's a horse or a ship or an orange—I give it up*
•LAL 30 ❖ LAL Mar 31st 54

Art: "All of the great poets, painters, and musicians of old could produce great work 'to order'"
•RP 128 ❖ RP 12:8

Art, analogy that we are a Divine work of, useful to our conception of God's love for us
•PP 42-43, 47 (*see also* LM 34, 69; MC 44, 173) ❖ PP 3:10, 14 (*see also* LM 6:16; 13:4; MC II 1:4; IV 9:7)

Art and philosophy are but clumsy imitations of the soul's never-completed attempt to communicate its unique vision of God to all the others
•PP 150 (*see also* FL 92-93*)
❖ PP 10:7 (*see also* FL 4:9*)

Art as a form of culture in which "culture" is irrelevant when the enjoyment is genuine
•WLN 33-34 ❖ WLN 3:5, 6

Art as pattern and balance: "The principle of art has been defined as 'the same in the other'" (re: parallelism in the Psalms)
•RP 3-4 ❖ RP 1:6

Art can teach without at all ceasing to be art (and much great art sets out deliberately to do so)
•L 222
❖ L undated letter just before 9 Jan 50

Art: Cultural "sensitivity," like "experience," is a potentiality and therefore neutral; neither can be an end to Christians*
•CR 24 ❖ CR 2:38

Art, distinction between sacred, and iconography ("that which is meant merely as the starting point for devotion and meditation")
•CR 2 ❖ CR 1:2

Art: Editors of "Scrutiny" mentioned who believed in a relationship between the quality of a person's response to art and his fitness for humane living
•CR 13 ❖ CR 2:2

Art: Every real Friendship is a kind of rebellion; it may be a rebellion of real artists against popular ugliness or of charlatans against civilised taste [etc.]
•FL 114 ❖ FL 4:45

Art for art's sake ("serious irreligious art") is all balderdash; art is healthy only when aiming at innocent recreation or serving as a handmaid of moral truth
•L 182 (*see also* L 74)
❖ L 16 Apr 40 (*see also* L 3 May 22)

Art, in literature and, no man who bothers about originality will ever be original
•MC 190 (*see also* L 201; WG 119; Originality) ❖ MC IV 11:15 (*see also* L undated letter just after 29 Jul 42; WG 7:19; Originality)

Art: It is taken as basic among all the "culture" of our age that whenever artists and audience lose touch, the fault must be on the side of the audience
•WLN 45 (*see also* WLN 78-79)
❖ WLN 3:20 (*see also* WLN 5:18)

Art, like love, "ceases to be a devil only when it ceases to be a god"
•L 182 (For the same quote used regarding erotic love, see CR 35; FL 17)
❖ L 16 Apr 40 (For the same quote used regarding erotic love, see CR 2:55; FL 1:13)

Art: Many modern novels, poems, and pictures are not good work because they are not *work* at all; "they are mere puddles of spilled sensibility or reflection"
•WLN 80 ❖ WLN 5:21

Art of all kinds had better be done well or not at all; we have no duty to "appreciate" the ambitious
•WLN 80-81 (*see also* WLN 78-79)
❖ WLN 5:21, 22 (*see also* WLN 5:18)

Art or literature, "low-brows" who genuinely enjoy, vs. "snobs" who feign enjoyment of it ("I...prefer the live dog

to the dead lion")
- WLN 38-39 (*see also* CR 10)
❖ WLN 3:12 (*see also* CR 1:15)

Art, Screwtape speaks on the representation of the nude in
- SL 92 ❖ SL 20:3

Art: Surrealism and "pictures painted by chimpanzees" mentioned as being "part of the general 'Highbrow racket'"
- GID 251 ❖ GID II 14:5

Art, the Crucifixion did not become a frequent motive of Christian, until the generations which had seen real crucifixions were all dead
- LM 85 ❖ LM 16:10

Art: The value of icons depends very little on their perfection as artefacts
- CR 2 ❖ CR 1:2

Art: Use of images (in prayer), for me, is very limited; but focussing one's eyes on almost any object is a help towards concentration*
- LM 84 ❖ LM 16:3, 4

Art: Use of pictures and images of Jesus in worship: The artistic merits or demerits are a distraction
- LM 84 ❖ LM 16:4

Art: "We—even our poets and musicians and inventors—never, in the ultimate sense, *make*. We only build. We always have materials to build from"
- LM 73 (*see also* M 32-33; Creativity) ❖ LM 14:3 (*see also* M 4:14; Creativity)

Art, works of: The operation of comparing and preferring does little good*
- SJ 145-146 ❖ SJ 9:22

Arts, according to Screwtape, have been successfully infected with the horror of the Same Old Thing and demand for continual novelty
- SL 117 ❖ SL 25:4

Arts and literature: Until modern times nobody ever suggested that they were an end in themselves
- GID 279-280 ❖ GID III 2:4, 5

Arts and sciences, Christianity never intended to replace or supersede the ordinary; it is rather a director which will set them all to the right jobs

- MC 79 ❖ MC III 3:2

Arts ("culture"), on Christianity and the value of*
- CR 12-36 ❖ CR ch. 2

Arts, no one is really maintaining that a fine taste in the, is a condition of salvation
- CR 14 (*see also* L 224) ❖ CR 2:4 (*see also* L 7 Dec 50)

Arts, pleasure in the, possibly more varied, intense, and lasting than vulgar or "popular" pleasure (though this has not been proved)
- CR 21 ❖ CR 2:28

Arts, we should not regard pleasure in the, as meritorious
- CR 21 ❖ CR 2:28

Artist must take into account the tastes and capacity of his audience; haughty indifference to them is not genius nor integrity, but laziness and incompetence
- WLN 80 (*see also* WLN 78-79) ❖ WLN 5:21 (*see also* WLN 5:18)

Artist ["Painter"], God is the; we are only the picture
- MC 173 (*see also* LM 34, 69; MC 44; PP 42-43) ❖ MC IV 9:7 (*see also* LM 6:16; 13:4; MC II 1:4; PP 3:10)

Artists, I wonder if, don't lose something of the love of earth by seeing it in eye-sensations only
- L 63 ❖ L 1 Jul 21

Artists now seem to prefer "significant" or "contemporary" work to good work
- WLN 72 ❖ WLN 5:2

Arthur, Charles Williams' interest in [the medieval], mentioned
- L 244 ❖ L 2 Oct 52

Arthur, it is a remarkable fact that the post-medieval interest in, has been almost exclusively Protestant
- L 264 ❖ L 22 Sep 55

Arthur, Lewis's childhood friend, mentioned or referred to
- SJ 46, 130-131, 142, 143, 149-152, 155, 157-158, 160, 162, 164, 173, 199 ❖ SJ 3:5; 8:14-18; 9:18; 10:1-3, 6, 10, 11, 13, 16, 17, 18; 11:9; 13:3, 4

Arthur, we may without disgrace believe in a historical
• CR 162 ❖ CR 13:25

Ascension Day, Psalm 8 as an appropriate reading for
• RP 132-134 ❖ RP 12:11-13

Ascension, doctrine of, an essential part of the doctrine of the Resurrection
• M 145-149 ❖ M 16:4-11

Ascension, I think it very rash to assume that the story of the, is mere allegory
• GID 35 ❖ GID I 2:13

Ascension, imagery such as that of upward motion in the: Impossible to know how much of a representation is symbolical and how much is literal
• CR 164-166 ❖ CR 13:30-35

Ascension of Christ described specifically in only two places in the Bible —books of Acts and St. Mark— though implied throughout the New Testament
• M 148 ❖ M 16:10, 11

Ascension of Christ: Meaning of the text "I go to prepare a place for you"
• M 149, 157 ❖ M 16:12, 25

Ascension story can be dropped only if we regard the Resurrection appearances as those of a ghost or hallucination
• M 148-149 ❖ M 16:11

Ascetic practices necessary as a means; as an end they would be abominable
• PP 112 ❖ PP 7:3

Ascetic practices only useful so far as they strengthen the will against the passions as a preparation for offering the whole man to God
• PP 112 ❖ PP 7:3

Asceticism—see also Renunciation; Self-denial; consider also Fasting; Mysticism

Asceticism, Christian, involves respect for the thing rejected which is not found in pagan asceticism
• GID 149 ❖ GID I 17:5

Asceticism should be an exercise in controlling the body, not in renouncing it (for we shall have bodies in Heaven)
• M 163 (see also GID 148-149)
❖ M 16:32 (see also GID I 17:5)

Asceticism: The reward is self-mastery,

and the danger pride
• PP 112 ❖ PP 7:3

Asceticism vs. tribulation sent by God: They accomplish very different things
• PP 112 ❖ PP 7:3

Asceticism, wrong kind of, torments the self; the right kind kills the selfness
• GID 195 ❖ GID II 2:4

Asia, I have played with the idea that Christianity was never intended for
• L 152-153 (see also GID 265-266*; MC 65, 176-177) ❖ L 8 Apr 32 (see also GID II 16:50, 51*; MC II 5:8; IV 10:4)

Aslan answers the question, "What might Christ become like, if there really were a world like Narnia and He chose to be incarnate...in that world...?"
• L 283 ❖ L 29 Dec 58

Aslan, of course I'm not committed to a real belief in
• L 251 ❖ L 3 Aug 53

Asleep, to know that one is dreaming is to be no longer perfectly, (re: a realization of our incomplete awareness of God)
• FL 192 (see also LM 75; RP 92)
❖ FL 6:47 (see also LM 14:11; RP 9:3)

Ass, God used an, to convert the prophet —perhaps we shall be allowed a stall near it in the celestial stable
• L 193-194 ❖ L 15 May 41

Ass, the body as Brother (an expression of St. Francis'): "...a useful, sturdy, lazy, obstinate, patient, lovable and infuriating beast..."
• FL 143; LAL 89
❖ FL 5:19, 20; LAL 22 Dec 59

Assent—see Belief

Association ("connivance") with the ungodly, dangers and temptations of
• RP 66-75; SL 45-48
❖ RP ch. 7; SL ch. 10

Association: "People who bore one another should meet seldom; people who interest one another, often"*
• FL 116 ❖ FL 4:47

Association, we should avoid, with people who are cruel, etc.—not because we are too good for them, but because, in a sense, we are not good enough

•RP 71-74 (*see also* SL 45-48*)
❖ RP 7:9-16 (*see also* SL ch. 10*)
Association with people for the wrong reason—hoping to be on good terms with our bad neighbors to get "pickings"
•RP 69-75 ❖ RP 7:6-17
Association with the wrong people: Fear of being accused of priggery increases the temptation to consort with people whose behaviour we disapprove
•RP 71-72 (*see also* SL 48)
❖ RP 7:10 (*see also* SL 10:4)
Association with unbelievers: "All mortals tend to turn into the thing they are pretending to be" (—Screwtape)
•SL 46 ❖ SL 10:2
Association with unbelievers makes faith harder even when their opinions on any other subject are known to be worthless
•CR 42 ❖ CR 3:10
Association with unbelievers: There is a subtle play of looks and tones and laughs by which one can imply that he agrees with those to whom he is speaking
•SL 46 ❖ SL 10:1, 2
Association with unbelievers: "They know well enough what we are believing or trying to believe...and regard it as total illusion" (re: Psalmists' dark experience)*
•CR 127 ❖ CR 10:38
Assurance about prayer, as in our requests of people, is not from knowing things about the Giver but from knowing *him*
•WLN 6-8 (*see also* LM 49; WLN 26-27*) ❖ WLN 1:12-15 (*see also* LM 9:8; WLN 2:14*)
Assurance: "As organs in the Body of Christ...we are assured of our eternal self-identity..."
•WG 117 ❖ WG 7:16
Assurance or belief as a psychological state, like we have about the existence of furniture: This comes and goes; don't depend on it
•L 199 ❖ L 20 Jan 42
Assurance that we are chosen, quote from

Luther regarding
•L 252 ❖ L 3 Aug 53
Athanasian Creed discussed briefly ("...that work is not exactly a creed and was not by St. Athanasius")
•GID 205 ❖ GID II 4:8
Athanasius mentioned as one who "stood for the Trinitarian doctrine, 'whole and undefiled'" when world was slipping back into the religion of Arius
•GID 206 ❖ GID II 4:8
Atheism—*consider also* Materialism; Obstacles to Christian faith; Scepticism
Atheism and Pessimism, my own, were fully formed before I went to Bookham [to study with Kirkpatrick]
•SJ 139-140 (*see also* CR 164; SJ 190) ❖ SJ 9:16 (*see also* CR 13:28; SJ 12:12)
Atheism: Anger against "an apparently ruthless and idiotic cosmos" is really an unconscious homage to something in or behind the cosmos which is authoritative
•CR 65-67, 69-70 (*see also* MC 45-46*) ❖ CR 5:19, 24 (*see also* MC II 1:5, 6*)
Atheism: Both those who believe in God and those who disbelieve face many hours of doubt
•CR 41 ❖ CR 3:9
Atheism, consistent, involves philosophical and emotional abstinences, just as real Christianity does
•GID 250-251 ❖ GID II 14:3
Atheism, discussion of
•MC 45-46 ❖ MC II 1:5, 6
Atheism has come down in the world since those days [with Kirkpatrick], and mixed itself in politics and learned to dabble in dirt
•SJ 139 ❖ SJ 9:15
Atheism: Heroic anti-theism has a contradiction at centre: If a Brute made the world then he also made the standard by which we judge him to be a Brute
•CR 65-67 (*see also* CR 69-70; MC 45-46*) ❖ CR 5:19 (*see also* CR 5:24; MC II 1:5, 6*)
Atheism: "How right you are when you say, 'Christianity is a terrible thing for

a life-long atheist to have to face'"
•L 298 ❖ L 9 May 61

Atheism, I felt [in my youth] the force of Lucretius' argument for: "'Had God designed the world, it would not be A world so frail and faulty as we see'"
•SJ 65 ❖ SJ 4:11

Atheism of my tutor [William T. Kirkpatrick] was chiefly of the anthropological and pessimistic kind
•SJ 139 ❖ SJ 9:15

Atheism ("the anti-Christian position") no longer considered self-evident by scholars*
•GID 221 ❖ GID II 8:8

Atheism: "The number of clear and determined atheists is apparently not very large"
•GID 101 (see also GID 128)
❖ GID I 10:45 (see also GID I 15:4)

Atheism, there is something holier about the, of a Shelley than about the theism of a Paley (re: the good atheist's indignation against the cosmos)
•CR 69-70 ❖ CR 5:24, 25

Atheism too simple; if the whole universe has no meaning, we should never have found out that it has no meaning
•MC46 ❖ MC II 1:6

Atheist(s)—see also Agnostic(s); Sceptic(s); Unbeliever(s)

Atheist, a young, cannot guard his faith too carefully; dangers lie in wait for him on every side
•SJ 226 ❖ SJ 14:19

Atheist, a young man who wishes to be a sound, cannot be too careful of his reading; there are traps everywhere...
•SJ 191 ❖ SJ 12:13

Atheist, Lewis describes how he became an
•SJ 58-70 ❖ SJ 4:4-20

Atheist, liberal theology which denies the miraculous will make the unlearned man either a Roman Catholic (if he disagrees) or an, (if he agrees)
•CR 153 ❖ CR 13:2

Atheist might say that "your vaunted Jesus was really the same sort of crank or charlatan as all the other writers of apocalyptic"
•WLN 95 ❖ WLN 7:5

Atheist, Screwtape mentions a sound, whom he kept safe for Hell by keeping his mind on ordinary "real life" rather than on logic and reason
•SL 9-10 ❖ SL 1:3

Atheist, when I was an, I had moods in which Christianity looked terribly probable
•MC 123-124 (see also CR 41)
❖ MC III 11:5 (see also CR 3:9)

Atheist, when I was an, I maintained that God did not exist; I was also very angry with God for not existing and for creating a world
•SJ 115 (see also CR 65-67*, 70*; SJ 171)
❖ SJ 7:20 (see also CR 5:19-20*, 24-26*; SJ 11:8)

Atheist, why I was an, (the pessimist's case against God, and an answer to it)
•PP 13-25 ❖ PP ch. 1

Atheists and agnostics, I would gladly believe that many, care for the things I care for (re: spontaneous, genuine enjoyment of "culture")
•WLN 49 ❖ WLN 3:28

Atheists, don't you think that all you, are strangely unsuspicious people? (re: discussion about science and religion)
•GID 75
❖ GID I 7:41 (last line of chapter)

Atheists, even, express their rage against God although (or because) He does not, in their view, exist
•PP 95 ❖ PP 6:7

Atheists, how many professed, have been honestly argued out of their faith?
•CR 42-43; MC 124
❖ CR 3:10; MC III 11:6

Atheists, I expect justice and courtesy from many; it is the liberal "Christians" that are the most arrogant and intolerant
•L 229 (see also GID 327*)
❖ L 23 Apr 51 (see also GID IV Letter 2*)

Atheists, in 1926 the hardest boiled of all the, I knew remarked that the evidence for the historicity of the Gospels was really surprisingly good

•SJ 223-224 (*see also* SJ 235-236)
❖ SJ 14:15 (*see also* SJ 15:7)

Atheists, in my experience the bitterest opposition comes neither from thoroughgoing believers nor from, but from semibelievers of all complexions
•RP 7-8 ❖ RP 1:13

Atheists, many hard, come from pious homes; religious education often has exactly the opposite effect to that which was intended
•LAL 32 ❖ LAL Sep 19/54

Atheists, some, question the problem of existence in a world of suffering; this is almost infinitely superior to fatuous contentment with a profane life
•PP 95 ❖ PP 6:7

Athletic competition—*see* Games

Atlantis, the great continent had sunk like, (re: his mother's death)
•SJ 21 ❖ SJ 1:23

Atmosphere, I learned that we should attempt a total surrender to whatever, was offering itself at the moment; to find the most dismal and dripping wood...
•SJ 199 (*see also* SJ 145-146)
❖ SJ 13:3 (*see also* SJ 9:22)

Atonement, Anselmic theory of, mentioned
•L 197, 201 ❖ L 21 Dec 41; 13 Oct 42

"Atonement," meaning of the word, to modern minds ("compensation")
•GID 96-97 ❖ GID I 10:20

Atonement of Christ for us more like paying a debt than taking a punishment
•MC 58-59 ❖ MC II 4:6

Atonement: "...the resulting conflict is resolved by God's own assumption of the suffering nature which evil produces"*
•PP 84 ❖ PP 5:11

Atonement, theories of, need not be used if not found to be helpful
•L 197 ❖ L 21 Dec 41

Atonement, theories of ("...no explanation will ever be quite adequate to the reality")
•MC 57-61 ❖ MC II 4:3-11

Atonement: Understanding about how it works is not essential to our accepting it; in fact a man would not know how it works until he has accepted it
•MC 58-59 (*see also* L 197-198)
❖ MC II 4:4, 5 (*see also* L 21 Dec 41)

Attempting obedience—*see* Moral effort

Attend: "The only imperative that nature utters is, 'Look. Listen. Attend.'"
•FL 36 (*see also* LM 88-90*)
❖ FL 2:21 (*see also* LM 17:1-10*)

Attend, the real labour (in recognising the presence of God) is to remember and to
•LM 75 ❖ LM 14:11

Attention essential to the recognition of pleasures as blessings from God
•LM 90 ❖ LM 17:10

Attention (to a book or lecture), the moment I begin thinking about my, I have *ipso facto* ceased attending
•L 221 ❖ L 27 Sep 49

Augustine, quote from Saint: "God gives where He finds empty hands"
•LAL 73 ❖ LAL 31/3/58

Augustine, quote from Saint: "God wants to give us something, but cannot, because our hands are full—there's nowhere for Him to put it"
•PP 96 (*see also* GO 53-54*)
❖ PP 6:8 (*see also* GO 3:25, 26*)

Augustine, quote from Saint: "Thou hast made us for Thyself, and our heart has no rest till it comes to Thee"
•FL 189 (*see also* GID 252; *consider also* God–shaped hollow)
❖ FL 6:41 (*see also* GID II 14:7; *consider also* God–shaped hollow)

Augustine, Saint: Everyone talks as if he *wanted* unbaptised infants to go to Hell
•PP 96-97 ❖ PP 6:8

Augustine, Saint: His *Confessions* mentioned as worthwhile reading for a Christian
•L 299 ❖ L 9 May 61

Augustine, Saint: I reject his method of dissuading us from inordinate love of our fellow creatures
•FL 167-169 ❖ FL 6:7-13

Augustine, Saint, makes it plain that pride

does not only go before a fall but is a fall—a fall of our attention from God to ourselves
•CR 7 ❖ CR 1:10

Augustinianism mentioned (re: grace and free will)
•LM 49 ❖ LM 9:11

Author(s)—*see also* Writers

Author, Christian, sees his own temperament and experience as of no value except as a medium through which something universally profitable appeared to him
•CR 8 ❖ CR 1:13

Author, it is frustrating to have discovered a new, and not to be able to tell anyone how good he is (re: the naturalness of spontaneous praise)
•RP 95 ❖ RP 9:6

Author, liking an, may be as involuntary and improbably as falling in love
•SJ 190 ❖ SJ 12:12

Authors, according to secular literary criticism the great, are innovators, pioneers, explorers; they are always "breaking fetters"; they are themselves
•CR 3 ❖ CR 1:4

Authors, better to read original, than commentators
•GID 200 (*see also* L 122-123)
❖ GID II 4:1 (*see also* L 12 Dec 27)

Authors, Christian, do not have "self-expression" as their goal; of every idea and method they do not ask 'Is it mine?' but "Is it good?'
•CR 7-9 ❖ CR 1:11-14

Authors, Christian, must hold to same rules as those who write secular literature
•CR 1 ❖ CR 1:1

Authors, Christian, needed whose Christianity is latent
•GID 93 ❖ GID I 10:9

Authors, Christian, who were of help to Lewis, listed
•GID 260 ❖ GID II 16:16

Authors don't necessarily understand the meaning of their own stories better than anyone else

•L 273 (*see also* L 271*)
❖ L 10 Feb 57 (*see also* L 22 Sep 56*)

Authors, modern Christian, are anxious to allow to the enemy every advantage he can with any show of fairness claim*
•M 164-165 ❖ M 17:1

Authors, professional, mentioned as one group of "culture-sellers" whose ranks should probably include some Christians
•CR 20-21 ❖ CR 2:23-25

Authors should never conceive themselves as bringing into existence beauty or wisdom which did not exist before, but as reflecting eternal Beauty and Wisdom
•CR 7 (*see also* Originality)
❖ CR 1:11 (*see also* Originality)

Authors, the only non-Christian, who seemed to me really to know anything were the Romantics (and even they were tinged with something like religion)
•SJ 213-214 ❖ SJ 14:3, 4

Authors, what is the point of reading contemporary, because they happen to be alive?
•L 225-226
❖ L undated letter of Jan 1951

Authority and experience supply us with material for our Reason, which in turn tells us about truth and falsehood
•WG 34 ❖ WG 3:3

Authority and religious experience as the two grounds on which our poetic [religious] expressions are believed
•CR 137-138 ❖ CR 11:17-19

Authority exercised with humility and obedience accepted with delight are the very lines along which our spirits live
•WG 115 ❖ WG 7:15

Authority, historical evidence, and religious experience as three of the things on which a Christian may base his belief
•WLN 17 ❖ WLN 2:6

Authority, human and divine, as regarding the question of Pacifism

•WG 45-51 ❖ WG 3:21-30

Authority: Human nature wants to be left to itself, wants to keep well away from anything better or stronger or higher than itself*
•MC 154 (*see also* MC 111)
❖ MC IV 5:2 (*see also* MC III 8:5)

Authority, I base the Faith on, which has grown up in the Church and won the assent of great doctors
•GID 181 (*see also* PP 71-72)
❖ GID I 22:11 (*see also* PP 5:2)

Authority, misuse of, may provoke resentment; in this sin both parties share
•CR 119-120 (*see also* RP 24-26)
❖ CR 10:9-12 (*see also* RP 3:9-11)

Authority, most of our beliefs must be based on trusted, rather than on proof
•MC 63 (*see also* CR 26*, 41, 43; GID 276; SJ 174; WLN 17)
❖ MC II 5:4 (*see also* CR 2:40*; 3:9, 12; GID III 1:17; SJ 11:12; WLN 2:6)

Authority, most of us accept the truths we believe on expert; must be frequently used instead of reasoning as a method of getting conclusions
•WG 35-36 ❖ WG 3:5, 6

Authority, my youthful rationalism was based on what I believed to be the findings of the sciences—which I had to take on trusted
•SJ 174 (*see also* SJ 170)
❖ SJ 11:12 (*see also* SJ 11:7)

Authority of husbands over wives and parents over children was part of the original plan; but a kind of equality became necessary due to the Fall
•WG 114-115 ❖ WG 7:12-15

Authority of man over beast has been abused; requires intervention
•WG 114 ❖ WG 7:12

Authority: "One of the things my reason tells me is that I ought to check the results of my own thinking by the opinions of the wise"
•CR 26 ❖ CR 2:40

Authority, reason, and experience: "... on these three, mixed in varying proportions all our knowledge depends"
•CR 41 (*see also* CR 26*, 43)

❖ CR 3:9 (*see also* CR 2:40*; 3:12)

Authority, those who have little, over others may be thankful; it is hard to be just, and power corrupts
•CR 119-120; RP 25
❖ CR 10:10; RP 3:10

Authority, value of, in checking or superseding our own thinking is much greater in the sphere of Conscience than in that of Reason
•WG 36 ❖ WG 3:6

Authority vs. obedience: A child can be trained in the art of obedience before it has reason and age enough to learn to command
•L 179 (*see also* WG 36-37)
❖ L 26 Mar 40 (*see also* WG 3:6)

Authority, we no longer rely on tradition and, for truth; we must get it ourselves or go without it
•M 42 (*see also* GID 276)
❖ M 6:6 (*see also* GID III 1:17)

Automobiles—*see also* Cars

Automobiles, our bodies are like; they wear out ("We must just look forward to the fine new machines—latest Resurrection model...")
•LAL 78 (*see also* LAL 110) ❖ LAL Sep 30 58 (*see also* LAL 26 Nov 62)

Autumn: "It sounds fantastic to say that one can be enamored of a season, but that is something like what happened" (on reading *Squirrel Nutkin*)
•SJ 16-17 ❖ SJ 1:16

Autumn like old age: the best of the seasons, but it doesn't *last*
•L 308 ❖ L 27 Oct 63

Autumn mentioned as a season Lewis enjoyed
•L 30, 31; LAL 45
❖ L 27 Sep 16; 30 Oct 16; LAL 5/10/55

Autumn, our, goes slowly; the trees keep their leaves for weeks
•L 264-265 ❖ L 16 Oct 55

Avarice—*consider also* Money

Avarice, considerable mortification of our, may be necessary if we are to value and seek worthwhile jobs (it is usually the insane jobs that lead to big money)

•WLN 78 ❖ WLN 5:16

Avarice ("greed"), what looks like, may actually be the result of Pride
•MC 110 ❖ MC III 8:3, 4

Avarice, Screwtape mentions one cause of, as the perverted thirst for continual novelty
•SL 117 ❖ SL 25:4

Avarice, the great and permanent temptation of marriage is not to sensuality but to
•FL 138 ❖ FL 5:10

Avoidance of God/truth/etc.—*see* Evasion of...

Awake, God is that object to admire which is simply to be
•RP 92 (*see also* LM 75)
❖ RP 9:3 (*see also* LM 14:11)

Awake: "To know that one is dreaming is to be no longer fully asleep. But for news of the fully waking world you must go to my betters"
•FL 192 ❖ FL 6:47

Awe—*see also* Numinous; *consider also* Reverence

Awe as "an emotion very like fear, with the important difference that it need imply no estimate of danger"
•GID 174-175 ❖ GID I 21:6

Awe as the emotion aroused by the presence of divinity ("Numinous")
•GID 174-175 ❖ GID I 21:6

Awe, childhood listed as one of the avenues for experience of Numinous
•PP 24-25 ❖ PP 1:16

Awe: Either it is a mere twist in the human mind (serving no biological function) or else it is a direct experience of the supernatural
•PP 20-21 ❖ PP 1:11

Awe: "I think the lion, when he has ceased to be dangerous, will still be awful"
•PP 143 ❖ PP 9:14

Awe, I was brought into the region of, by the realization that the object of Joy was something other and outside; something sheerly objective
•SJ 220, 221 ❖ SJ 14:12

Awe in prayer: We ought to be simultaneously aware of closest proximity

and infinite distance
•LM 13 ❖ LM 2:13

Awe is preserved by the anthropomorphic image of God as a grave old king with a long beard
•GO 35-36 ❖ GO 2:27

Awe: The object which excites it is called the Numinous
•PP 17-21 ❖ PP 1:5-11

Axioms, either the maxims of traditional morality must be accepted as, of practical reason which cannot be argued; or else there are no values at all
•CR 75 ❖ CR 6:12

Axioms: Lewis points out that certain beliefs such as belief in God cannot be proven without self-evident inferences which just have to be "seen"*
•WG 36 ❖ WG 3:4

Baby, Christian renewal likened to the birth of a: Just as a baby might, if he had the choice, we may prefer to stay in the warmth and safety of the womb
•MC 187 (*see also* MC 154-155*, 173; SL 147*) ❖ MC IV 11:9 (*see also* MC IV 5:3, 4*; 9:7; SL 31:3*)

Baby pleasing his father with first steps as analogy to us: "God is easy to please, but hard to satisfy" (quote from George MacDonald)
•MC 172 (*see also* PP 46*; SL 39)
❖ MC IV 9:5 (*see also* PP 3:13*; SL 8:4)

"Baby talk" as it is used in both Affection and Eros not unique to humans; some birds use infantile sounds in the same way
•FL 58 ❖ FL 3:9

Backsliders not usually reasoned out of their faith by honest argument; just drift away*
•MC 124 (*see also* CR 42; Obstacles to Christian faith)
❖ MC III 11:6 (*see also* CR 3:10; Obstacles to Christian faith)

Bad man, picture of a, for whom we find ourselves moved by a truly ethical demand for justice (re: doctrine of Hell)
•PP 120-121 (*see also* PP 128)
❖ PP 8:5 (*see also* PP 8:13)

Bad people—*see also* Wicked

Bad people do not know about either good or evil; good people know about both
•MC 87 ❖ MC III 4:10

Bad people, how are we to behave in the presence of very
•RP 68-74 (*see also* SL 45-48*; Association...) ❖ RP 7:5-16 (*see also* SL ch. 10*; Association...)

Bad people: "If the Divine call does not make us better, it will make us very much worse. Of all bad men religious bad men are the worst"
•RP 31-32 (*see also* L 301; RP 28)
❖ RP 3:20 (*see also* L 20 Dec 61; RP 3:17)

Bad people, Lewis differentiates two kinds of, and our reaction to them: the powerful, prosperous and impenitent, and those whose wickedness has not paid
•RP 68 ❖ RP 7:5

Bad people: "One has to keep on saying 'But for the grace of God, there go I'"*
•LAL 107 ❖ LAL 2 Oct 62

Bad people: To them, "death represents the final defeat of the systematic self-regarding caution and egoism which has been the sole occupation of life"
•L 190
❖ L undated letter just after 11 Aug 40

Badness—*see also* Evil; Sinfulness; Wickedness

Badness: A bad man, happy, is a man without the least inkling that his actions are not in accord with the laws of the universe
•PP 93 ❖ PP 6:5

Badness: A moderately bad man knows he is not very good; a thoroughly bad man thinks he is all right
•MC 87 (*see also* GID 56-57; LAL 95; PP 55, top; 67; Self-knowledge)
❖ MC III 4:10 (*see also* GID I 4:38; LAL 9 Jan 61; 61; PP 4 prelim. quote; 4:15; Self-knowledge)

Badness, as soon as we perceive our, the "wrath" of God appears inevitable; otherwise it seems a barbarous doctrine
•PP 58 ❖ PP 4:6

Badness, belief that, is either an unavoidable legacy from animal ancestors or merely the result of our being finite encourages us to shift responsibility
•PP 65-66 ❖ PP 4:14

Badness: Each person is in reality far bet-

---

* These items reflect some interpretation on the part of the editor; the idea will not be found in these exact words. *See Introduction, p. ix.*
** These items are ideas of Lewis's which the editor has placed under a topic Lewis did not there intend to address. *See Introduction, p. ix.*
Entries without asterisks are not necessarily exact quotes, but the idea should be easy to find as worded.

ter *and* worse than is ever imagined*
•L 267 ❖ L 8 Feb 56

Badness: I find it easier to understand the great crimes, for the raw material for them exists in us all; mere disagreeableness is mysterious
•LAL 27-28 ❖ LAL Mar 10/54

Badness is not bad in the same way that goodness is good; badness is spoiled goodness (re: Dualism)
•MC 49 ❖ MC II 2:9, 10

Badness: We must guard against the feeling that if *all* men are as bad as the Christians say, then badness must be very excusable
•PP 62 ❖ PP 4:10

Balance—*consider also* Moderation

Balance or tension between the secular (or "Natural") and the spiritual ("Supernatural"): "I have no use for mere *either-or* people"
•L 228 (*see also* WG 25-26)
❖ L 23 Apr 51 (*see also* WG 2:7, 8)

Balder—*consider also* Myth; Mythology; Paganism

Balder, beauty of
•GID 279 ❖ GID III 2:2

Balder, Christ is more than, not less (as God is more than a god, not less); Incarnation transcends myth in conveying abstract reality to humans
•GID 67 (*see also* Myth of "dying god")
❖ GID I 5:13 (*see also* Myth of "dying god")

Balder, I knew nothing about; but instantly I was uplifted into huge regions of northern sky... (Lewis describes his first reading of *Tegner's Drapa*)
•SJ 17 (*see also* SJ 73)
❖ SJ 1:17 (*see also* SJ 5:4)

Balder, I loved, before Christ
•GID 132 ❖ GID 16:4

Balder, myth of, has similarities to the story of Christ; this resemblance can be interpreted in different ways
•RP 105-108; WG 82-85
❖ RP 10:11-13; WG 5:14,15

Band, analogy of a musical, to illustrate the importance and operation of mo-

rality
•MC 71-73 ❖ MC III 1:3-8

Band, God meant humility to be like players in one, or organs in one body; the Christian community is the best instrument for learning about God
•MC 144 ❖ MC IV 2:15, 16

Band-wagoning—*consider also* Inner Rings

"Band-wagoning," or consorting with people for the wrong motives—especially bad people
•RP 69-75 (*see also* SL 45-48*)
❖ RP 7:6-17 (*see also* SL ch. 10*)

Baptism as one of three things which spreads the Christ-life to us
•MC 62, 65 ❖ MC II 5:3, 7

Baptism calls a Christian not into a collective but into a Body (like a family)
•WG 112 ❖ WG 7:9

Baptism, don't bother at all about the question of a person being "made a Christian" by
•L 239 ❖ L 18 Mar 52

Baptism: "Our life as Christians begins by being baptised into a death"; our most joyous festivals centre upon the broken body and the shed blood
•RP 52 ❖ RP 5:10

Baptism: "That night [on reading *Phantastes* by George MacDonald] my imagination was, in a certain sense, baptized; the rest of me...took longer"
•SJ 181 ❖ SJ 11:19

Baptists mentioned as an "extreme Protestant sect"
•GID 241 ❖ GID II 12:2

Barber, story of the, who prayed for Lewis to come (re: efficacy of prayer)
•WLN 3 ❖ WLN 1:1, 2

Barfield and Harwood embraced the doctrines of Steiner and became Anthroposophists; this was a really dreadful thing
•SJ 205-207 (*see also* L 89)
❖ SJ 13:14-17 (*see also* L 7 Jul 23)

Barfield, Owen, Lewis describes a conversation with his good friend, in which they discussed "Christina dreams," *Dymer*, and immortality

•L 76-77 (*see also* L 78)

❖ L 24 May 22 (*see also* L 30 Jun 22)

Barfield, Owen: Lewis's "Second Friend" who disagreed with him about everything yet influenced him greatly
•SJ 199-200 (*see also* SJ 225)

❖ SJ 13:4 (*see also* SJ 14:17)

Barfield, Owen, mentioned briefly
•LAL 80 ❖ LAL Dec 25th 58

Barfield, the Great War with, began with his conversion to Anthroposophy
•SJ 207, 212 ❖ SJ 13:16; 14:1

Bargaining, as for the element of, in the Psalms (Do this and I will praise you), that silly dash of Paganism certainly existed
•RP 97 ❖ RP 9:8

Bargaining with God: I have often, on my knees, been shocked to find what absurd adjustments or compromises I was, half-consciously, proposing
•RP 97-98 ❖ RP 9:4

Barriers to faith—*see* Obstacles to Christian faith

Bawdy—*see also* Humor

Bawdy humour, Screwtape outlines the usefulness and limitations of, for his purposes
•SL 50-51 ❖ SL 11:4

Bawdy mentioned as the only living folk art left
•L 146 ❖ L 25 Dec 31

Bawdy ought to be outrageous and extravagant; must have nothing cruel about it; must not approach anywhere near the pornographic
•L 146 ❖ L 25 Dec 31

Baxter mentioned as the coiner of the term "mere Christians"
•GID 336 ❖ GID IV Letter 9

BBC talks, dates of
•L 198 ❖ L 21 Dec 41

BBC talks, mention of giving, (which later became the book *Mere Christianity*)
•L 193 ❖ L 15 May 41

Beach, Lewis's liking for, expressed
•SJ 182 (*see also* L 29, 41, 218)

❖ SJ 12:1 (*see also* L undated letter between Oct 1915 and 27 Sep 16; 16 Feb 18; 16 Aug 49)

Beatific Vision—*see also* Vision of God

Beatific Vision, the old parson was not seeking the, and did not even believe in God
•SJ 202 (*see also* CR x)

❖ SJ 13:8 (*see also* CR P:9)

Beatitudes: "It is safe to tell the pure in heart that they shall see God, for only the pure in heart want to"
•PP 145 ❖ PP 10:1

Beatitudes: More than one kind of poverty meant in the words, "Blessed are the poor"
•MC 180-181 ❖ MC IV 10:11, 12

Beauty and knowledge, pursuit of, need not exclude God; an appetite for these things exists in the human mind and God makes no appetite in vain
•WG 27 ❖ WG 2:9

Beauty, appreciation of, that we shall never ourselves see or enjoy as a form of disinterested love
•FL 32-33 ❖ FL 2:12-14

Beauty as discovered in Lewis's childhood: "Then came the Beatrix Potter books, and here at last beauty"
•SJ 15 ❖ SJ 1:13

Beauty, earth's, hints at the future healing of Spirit and Nature
•M 159 ❖ M 16:27

Beauty exalts, but beauty also lulls (as in King James—"Authorised"—version of the Bible)
•GID 231 ❖ GID II 10:4

Beauty has smiled, but not to welcome us; we long to meet with some response, yet "we have been mere spectators"
•WG 14-17 ❖ WG 1:11-13

Beauty in literature: "I was at last made free of the secret that others had, like me, found there 'enormous bliss' and been maddened by beauty"
•SJ 103 ❖ SJ 7:4

Beauty [in nature, etc.]: We do not want merely to *see* beauty, but also to be united with it
•WG 16 ❖ WG 1:13

Beauty is often transfigured in memory; "how often some momentary glimpse of beauty in boyhood is 'a whisper

Which memory will warehouse as a shout'"
•LM 122 ❖ LM 22:17

Beauty, Lewis mentions wondering [in his youth] whether, was objective
•SJ 192 (*see also* CR 71)
❖ SJ 12:14 (*see also* CR 5:27)

Beauty: Light and shadows make up so much of the beauty of the world
•LAL 80 ❖ LAL Dec 25th 58

Beauty mistakenly thought to be the object of our desire; but beauty and memories are only good images of what we really desire
•WG 6-7 ❖ WG 1:4, 5

Beauty, murder of, cannot be attributed to any particular set of evil men but to society in general
•L 211 ❖ L 15 Oct 47

Beauty, my experience is that women rather distrust and dislike, in men
•LAL 112 ❖ LAL 2 Jan 63

Beauty, natural: "...of every created thing I praise, I should say, 'In some way, in its unique way, like Him who made it'"*
•GO 73 (*see also* LM 90)
❖ GO 4:7 (*see also* LM 17:8)

Beauty: No reason why it, like logic and moral standards, should not also have an objective reality
•CR 71 ❖ CR 5:27

Beauty, nowhere in my childhood drawings is there a single line drawn in obedience to the idea of; this absence of beauty is characteristic of my childhood
•SJ 6 ❖ SJ 1:4

Beauty of God experienced partly through our bodies
•LAL 110-111 (*see also* LM 17-18)
❖ LAL 26 Nov 62 (*see also* LM 3:9)

Beauty of nature (and works of art): I was cured once and for all of the pernicious tendency to compare and prefer
•SJ 146 (*see also* FL 34-35)
❖ SJ 9:22 (*see also* FL 2:17, 18)

Beauty of the Lord, The Fair (chapter title)
•RP 44-53 ❖ RP ch. 5

Beauty, Psalmist's effort to keep the Law

springs not from servile fear but from love of moral
•RP 59-60 ❖ RP 6:9

Beauty, the externals of Christianity made no appeal to my sense of; Christianity for me was mainly associated with ugly architecture, music, and poetry
•SJ 171-172 ❖ SJ 11:8

Beauty, the whole world of, was opening before me... (re: Lewis's youthful experiences of "Joy")
•SJ 169 ❖ SJ 11:5

Beauty, there (in the dormitory at "Belsen") I came to know the ghastly, of the full moon
•SJ 25 (*see also* SJ 34, 60, 171)
❖ SJ 2:4 (*see also* SJ 2:14; 4:6; 11:8)

Beauty withers when we try to make it an absolute ("Put first things first...")
•L 228 (*see also* FL 39; First things)
❖ L 23 Apr 51 (*see also* FL 2:28; First things)

Beauty: Wyvern Priory was the first building that I ever perceived to be beautiful
•SJ 58 ❖ SJ 4:4

Before We Can Communicate (chapter title)
•GID 254-257 ❖ GID II ch. 15

Begetting: Could there have been many sons begotten by God, as Jesus was?
•MC 157-159 ❖ MC IV 6:2

Begetting, Making and (chapter title)
•MC 135-140 ❖ MC IV ch. 1

Begetting vs. creating: We are created, Jesus was begotten
•MC 137-140, 150 (*see also* Father and Son) ❖ MC IV 1:8-16; 4:2 (*see also* Father and Son)

Beginning, The (chapter title)
•SJ 230-238 ❖ SJ ch. 15

Behavior—*consider also* Action(s); Responsibility, personal; Works

Behavior, a genuine conversion will be known by an improvement in outward —just as a tree is known by its fruit
•MC 175-176 ❖ MC IV 10:2

Behavior, attempts to excite fear about

bases his, may include historical evidence, religious experience, authority, or all of these
•WLN 17 (see also GID 175)
❖ WLN 2:6 (see also GID 21:8, 9)

Belief: If we really believe that our real home is elsewhere, why should we not look forward to the arrival?
•LAL 83-84 (see also SL 132*)
❖ LAL Jun 7th 59 (see also SL 28:1*)

Belief in any supposed reality lends a certain sort of aesthetic satisfaction; "poetry" is the result and not the cause of religious belief
•WG 77-78 ❖ WG 5:9

Belief in God and understanding of what He is like is best acquired through experience of Him —e.g., in the moral and devotional life*
•M 90 (see also GID 170; MC 135-136; Experience) ❖ M 11:14 (see also GID I 20:Reply-15) MC IV 1:2, 3; Experience)

Belief in God may be described in Theological or Poetical language; Theological language is in a sense alien to religion, omitting all that's important
•CR 135-136 ❖ CR 11:13-15

Belief in God, scientific proof not the same kind of proof required for, since belief is different from knowledge
•WLN 14-16, 20-21 (see also WLN 92)
❖ WLN 2:3, 4, 9 (see also WLN 6:28)

Belief in God stated in Theological language: "I believe in incorporeal entity, personal in the sense that it can be the subject and object of love..."
•CR 135 ❖ CR 11:13

Belief in God: The evidence cannot be so weak as to warrant the view that all whom it convinces are indifferent to the evidence
•WLN 18 ❖ WLN 2:7

Belief in Heaven should be a corollary to belief in God, not the other way around
•FL 189-190; GO 79; LM 120; RP 39-42; SJ 231 (see also L 290*)
❖ FL 6:42; GO 4:21; LM 22:8; RP 4:13-17; SJ 15:3 (see also L 3 Dec 59*)

Belief in the forgiveness of sins easily slips away if we don't keep on polishing it up
•WG 121 ❖ WG 8:1

Belief is the result of causes ("I believe this is true because my parents do") or reasons ("I believe this is true because it can be proved")*
•GID 271-277 ❖ GID III ch. 1

Belief: Materialist may understand the kind and degree of conviction expressed in a Christian's "I believe" if he thinks about his own "I don't believe it"
•WLN 15 ❖ WLN 2:4

Belief may be hostile to perfect imaginative enjoyment
•WG 77 ❖ WG 5:8

Belief: "Momentous matter, if believed, will arouse emotion whatever the language" (re: Poetical religious language)
•CR 136 ❖ CR 11:16

Belief not the same thing as knowledge; scientific proof not required*
•WLN 14-16 (see also WLN 92; MC 32-33) ❖ WLN 2:3, 4 (see also WLN 6:28; MC I 4:2, 3)

Belief, obstinacy in: "There are times when we can do all that a fellow creature needs if he will only trust us"—may require trust in the teeth of senses
•WLN 23-24 (see also CR 42-43; L 199; MC 122-123) ❖ WLN 2:12 (see also CR 3:10-12; L 20 Jan 42; MC III 11:2-5)

Belief, On Obstinacy in (chapter title)
•WLN 13-30 ❖ WLN ch. 2

Belief: Only the practice of Faith resulting in the habit of Faith will ever cement our belief so that we are not continually assailed by doubts
•CR 41-42 ❖ CR 3:9

Belief or disbelief of most people results from their upbringing and from the prevailing tone of the circles they live in
•CR 170-171 ❖ CR 14:28

Belief, religious: Lewis attempts to show that religious language carries significance—if you are prepared to meet it half-way, with good will

•CR 129-141, esp. 135, 141
❖ CR ch. 11, esp. 11:12, 23
Belief, religious: theories about what it is (Freud: a complex; Frazer: a by-product of agriculture; Tylor: comes from dreams about the dead, etc.)
•WLN 18 ❖ WLN 2:7
Belief, religious, which is purely a result of conditioning mentioned with satisfaction by Screwtape
•SL 110-111 ❖ SL 24:1
Belief, struggle with: Bible gives us one short prayer—"Lord I believe, help Thou my unbelief"
•L 239 ❖ L 18 Mar 52
Belief: The Christian does not claim to have proof that God exists, but he does not necessarily have the least actual doubt
•WLN 15-16 ❖ WLN 2:4
Belief, the moment one asks oneself "Do I believe?" all, seems to go
•L 221 ❖ L 27 Sep 49
Belief, the sense in which scientists proportion their, to the evidence, and the sense in which Christians do not, defined and discussed
•WLN 13-30 ❖ WLN ch. 2
Belief: "...there is evidence both for and against the Christian propositions which fully rational minds, working honestly, can assess differently"
•WLN 20, 21 ❖ WLN 2:8, 9
Belief vs. imagination: "I can picture very few of the things I believe in ...thought, time, atoms...New York, nor even...my mother's face"
•L 288 ❖ L 8 Sep 59
Belief vs. imagination: It is a mistake to suppose that children believe the things they imagine
•SJ 59-60, 82 ❖ SJ 4:6; 5:15
Belief: "We too often mean by it 'having confidence or assurance as a psychological state'"; this comes and goes
•L 199 ❖ L 20 Jan 42
Belief, without a firm, and the assistance of Grace, our feelings will continually assault our conviction like a blast furnace against a snowflake

•CR 41-43, esp. 43
❖ CR 3:9-12, esp.3:12
Belief: "You never know how much you really believe anything until its truth or falsehood becomes a matter of life and death to you"
•GO 25, 41-43 ❖ GO 2:9; 3:3, 4
Beliefs—see also Doctrines
Beliefs and liturgy, proper relationship between
•GID 333 ❖ GID IV Letter 7
Beliefs cannot be dependent on our moods and feelings
•MC 123-124 (see also CR 42-43)
❖ MC III 11:4, 5 (see also CR 3:11, 12)
Beliefs, Christian, always remain intellectually possible but never intellectually compulsive; probably when this ceases to be so the world will be ending
•WLN 92 (see also WLN 28)
❖ WLN 6:28 (see also WLN 2:16)
Beliefs, Christian ("What Christians Believe" — Book II of Mere Christianity)
•MC 43-66 ❖ MC Book II
Beliefs do not automatically remain alive in the mind; must be fed
•MC 124 ❖ MC III 11:6
Beliefs, Lewis states he based his own, about religion on authority, reason, and experience, though he admits others' reason and experience may produce different results
•CR 41 ❖ CR 3:9
Beliefs may vary in strength from weak opinion to complete subjective certitude
•WLN 14-15, 20-21 ❖ WLN 2:4, 9
Beliefs, most of our, must be based on trustworthy authority rather than on proof
•MC 63; WG 35-36; WLN 17 (see also CR 26*, 41, 43; GID 276; SJ 174) ❖ MC II 5:4; WG 3:5, 6; WLN 2:6 (see also CR 2:40*; 3:9, 12; GID III 1:17; SJ 11:12)
Beliefs, new, must fight to maintain a foothold against our habitual ways of thinking (e.g., a rational belief in miracles)
•M 166-167 ❖ M 17:4

Beliefs, real, may differ from the professed and may lurk in the turn of a phrase or the choice of an epithet (re: beliefs implicit in literature)
•CR 28-29 ❖ CR 2:48

Beliefs, specific, ("dogma") essential for religion to be practical
•GID 129-146, esp. 139-140
❖ GID I ch. 16, esp. 16:21

Beliefs: Whether they are true or not must be discovered by reasoning before it is asked whether people's motives for believing them are proper or improper
•GID 271-274 ❖ GID III 1:1-7

Beloved, God as our true
•FL 190-191; PP 147; SL 148
❖ FL 6:44, 45; PP 10:3; SL 31:5

Beloveds—*see* Loved ones

"Belsen" (Lewis's first school) described
•SJ 24-37, 49 ❖ SJ 2:4-16; 3:8

Beneficence—*see also* Charity; Humanitarianism

Beneficence, law of, involves not doing some good to some men at some times—since if you do *this* good, you can't at the same time do *that* (re: Pacifism)
•WG 41-42 ❖ WG 3:16

Bereavement—*see also* Grief

Bereavement: A prolonged ritual of sorrow—visiting graves, keeping anniversaries, etc.—is like mummification; it makes the dead far more dead
•GO 65-66 ❖ GO 3:42-44

Bereavement: After a loved one's death, a slow process begins in which they become more and more imaginary—the reality is no longer there to check us*
•GO 19-24 (*see also* GO 59, 64-65, 75-77) ❖ GO 2:3-7 (*see also* GO 3:33, 34, 41; 4:13-17)

Bereavement: All lovers are eventually separated, even if both die at exactly the same moment
•GO 58-59, 63-64 ❖ GO 3:33, 40

Bereavement: "An odd by-product of my loss is that I'm aware of being an embarrassment to everyone I meet" (re: Lewis's wife's death)
•GO 10-11 ❖ GO 1:19, 20

Bereavement, effect of, on a long relationship vs. a shorter one ("I had not grown *accustomed* to happiness")
•L 301 ❖ L 20 Dec 61

Bereavement, effect of, on a long relationship vs. a shorter one ("...so much more intertwined with your whole life")
•L 289-290 ❖ L 3 Dec 59

Bereavement: Faces of our loved ones are difficult to remember after they're gone—all the expressions crowd together in our memory and cancel out into a blur*
•GO 16-17 ❖ GO 1:31

Bereavement: "Her absence is like the sky, spread over everything"
•GO 11 ❖ GO 1:21

Bereavement: "How often...will the vast emptiness astonish me like a complete novelty and make me say, 'I never realized my loss till this moment?'"
•GO 67 ❖ GO 3:47

Bereavement: "How wicked it would be, if we could, to call the dead back!"*
•GO 89 ❖ GO 4:40

Bereavement: I believe there is something beyond death; but the moment one tries to use that as a consolation the belief crumbles
•L 290; RP 41 (*see also* FL 189-190; GO 28-30, 79*) ❖ L 3 Dec 59; RP 4:16 (*see also* FL 6:41-43; GO 2:13-16; 4:21*)

Bereavement: I can't help suspecting that the dead also feel the pains of separation from their loved ones
•GO 58 (*see also* GO 31)
❖ GO 3:33 (*see also* GO 2:17)

Bereavement: "I have learned now that while those who speak about one's miseries usually hurt one, those who keep silence hurt more"
•L 289 ❖ L 3 Dec 59

Bereavement: "I will turn to her as often as possible in gladness. I will even salute her with a laugh. The less I mourn her the nearer I seem to her"
•GO 66 ❖ GO 3:44

Bereavement: In going to places where H. and I had been happy, I unexpectedly

found that her absence is no more emphatic in those places than anywhere else
- •GO 11 ❖ GO 1:21

Bereavement: In the loss of a child, a mother may find comfort in the idea of Heaven, but her specifically maternal happiness must be written off
- •GO 29-30 ❖ GO 2:16

Bereavement is a universal and integral part of our experience of love; it is not the interruption of the dance, but the next figure
- •GO 58-59 (see also GO 14-15, 63-64)
- ❖ GO 3:33 (see also GO 1:28; 3:40)

Bereavement is in some ways easier for the unbeliever; he may rage and shake his fist at the universe, but we must try to believe that God is our true Beloved
- •FL 191 ❖ FL 6:45

Bereavement, later stages of: Lewis gives reasons why, with the sense that one is "feeling better," there comes a sort of shame
- •GO 62-64 ❖ GO 3:38-40

Bereavement: Lewis describes the embarrassment his stepsons felt when he mentioned their mother, who had died: "It's the way boys are"
- •GO 8-9 ❖ GO 1:16, 17

Bereavement, Lewis's: "Up till this I always had too little time. Now there is nothing but time"*
- •GO 39 ❖ GO 2:32

Bereavement likened to having one leg cut off; the fierce pain stops, but you will never be a biped again
- •GO 61-62 (see also GO 64*, 67, 71)
- ❖ GO 3:37 (see also GO 3:40*; 3:47; 4:3)

Bereavement: Marriage as "one ship" which must chug along on only a single engine after the death of one's spouse*
- •GO 39 ❖ GO 2:33

Bereavement: No use applying to Heaven for earthly comfort; there is no earthly comfort in the long run—Heaven can give only heavenly comfort
- •FL 190 (see also GO 28-30; L 290; LAL 49) ❖ FL 6:43 (see also GO 2:13-16; L 3

Dec 59; LAL 16/12/55)

Bereavement (on the death of Charles Williams): "I find that all that talk about 'feeling that he is closer to us than before' isn't just talk"
- •L 206 ❖ L 18 May 45; 20 May 45

Bereavement, praise of God and of our loved one in: "Don't we in praise somehow enjoy what we praise, however far we are from it?"
- •GO 72 (see also RP 95)
- ❖ GO 4:5 (see also RP 9:6)

Bereavement, prayer in: "There is no answer. Only the locked door, the iron curtain, the vacuum, absolute zero. 'Them as asks don't get'"
- •GO 7 (see also GO 4-6, 53-54, 71, 80; LAL 92) ❖ GO 1:13 (see also GO 1:7-11; 3:25, 26; 4:4, 24; LAL 24 Sep 60)

Bereavement: Reunion with deceased loved ones not to be the goal of our Christian life*
- •FL 189-191 (see also GO 28-29, 79; L 290; RP 41) ❖ FL 6:41-43 (see also GO 2:13-16; 4:21; L 3 Dec 59; RP 4:16)

Bereavement: The happiness I had before H. [Joy] seems insipid now; I don't want to go back again and be happy in that way*
- •GO 70 ❖ GO 4:2

Bereavement: "...the moments I feel nearest to Joy are precisely those when I mourn her least"
- •LAL 92 (see also GO 51-53, 64-65)
- ❖ LAL 24 Sep 60 (see also GO 3:22-24, 41)

Bereavement: "...there is spread over everything a vague sense of wrongness, of something amiss"*
- •GO 40 ❖ GO 3:1

Bereavement: To reach the state in which my years of marriage should appear in retrospect a charming episode in my interminable life would be the worst fate*
- •GO 70 ❖ GO 4:2

Bereavement, "vast emptiness" of
- •GO 39, 67 ❖ GO 2:32; 3:47

Bereavement: "What's wrong with the world to make it so flat, shabby, worn-

out looking?"*
•GO 40-41 ❖ GO 3:1

Bergson, [Henri], the more modern form of nature religion would be the religion started, in a sense, by
•GID 86 ❖ GID I 9:9

Bergson, Lewis mentions reading, in a convalescent camp during the War: "He did not abolish my old loves, but he gave me a new one"
•SJ 198 ❖ SJ 13:1

Bergson, on reading, one Divine attribute—that of necessary existence—rose above my horizon
•SJ 204, 211 ❖ SJ 13:11, 20

Bergson, the most profound expositions of Creative Evolution (or "Life-Force" philosophy) come from
•MC 35 ❖ MC I 4:6

Beyond Personality: or First Steps in the Doctrine of the Trinity (Book IV of *Mere Christianity*)
•MC 135-190 ❖ MC Book IV

Bible—*see also* Scripture; *consider also* Epistles; Gospel(s); Jesus, teaching of

Bible addressed not to our intellectual curiosity but to our conscience and our will (re: the Dominical utterances)*
•PP 119 (*see also* L 169-170)
❖ PP 8:2 (*see also* L 5 Nov 39)

Bible: Apocalyptic writings, to most modern tastes, appear tedious and unedifying; predictions of Jesus seen as "much the same sort of thing"
•WLN 95 ❖ WLN 7:5

Bible: Apocryphal gospels mentioned
•CR 156 ❖ CR 13:8

Bible, archaic language in: I find that people react to archaism most diversely—it antagonizes some, and helps others
•LM 7 ❖ LM 1:18

Bible: Argument that all books before the invention of printing were copied and recopied till unrecognizable used by some to defend historical scepticism
•GID 242 ❖ GID II 12:3

Bible as literature: Bible can be read as merely human literature; nothing will ever prove either interpretation

•RP 116-117 (*see also* WG 35; *consider also* Proof) ❖ RP 11:12 (*see also* WG 3:4; *consider also* Proof)

Bible as literature: "I was by now too experienced in literary criticism to regard the Gospels as myths. They had not the mythical taste"
•SJ 236 (*see also* CR 154-155; GID 101, 158-159) ❖ SJ 15:7 (*see also* CR 13:4, 5; GID I 10:47; 19:4, 5)

Bible as literature: Its poetry depends largely upon parallelism which translates into any language
•L 188; RP 3-5 ❖ L 16 Jul 40; RP 1:5-7

Bible as literature: Lewis's view of the Old Testament as "the same sort of material as all other literature...but all taken into the service of God's word"
•RP 111 ❖ RP 11:4

Bible as literature: New Testament has nothing at all to tell us of literature, but we may notice what kinds of metaphor it uses
•CR 3-5 ❖ CR 1:5-7

Bible as literature: Passage in Mark 8 given as example of a sequence which is logically, emotionally, and imaginatively perfect
•CR 155-156 ❖ CR 13:6

Bible as literature: "Some of the parables do work like poetic similes; but then others work like philosophic illustrations"
•CR 3-4 ❖ CR 1:5

Bible as literature: Story of Christ addressed to the imaginative side of us no less than to the intellectual side (re: Christ as Perfect Myth and Perfect Fact)
•GID 67; M 133-134 (ftnt.)
❖ GID I 5:13; M 15:2 (ftnt.)

Bible as literature: Story of Jesus is no legend
•GID 158-159 (*see also* CR 154-155; GID 101; SJ 236) ❖ GID I 19:4, 5 (*see also* CR 13:4, 5; GID I 10:47; SJ 15:7)

Bible as literature taken up to be the vehicle of God's word (rather than the conversion of God's word into literature)

•RP 109-119, esp. 116
❖ RP ch. 11, esp. 11:11
Bible as literature: There is a sense in which the Bible cannot be read except as literature (e.g., Psalms must be read as poems)
•RP 3 ❖ RP 1:4
Bible as Word of God, proof of: "Proof rests on the unprovable, which just h̀as to be 'seen'" (re: Reason, and judging truth vs. falsehood)**
•WG 35 (see also RP 116-117; consider also Proof) ❖ WG 3:4 (see also RP 11:12; consider also Proof)
Bible: "Beware of the argument that 'the Church gave the Bible and therefore the Bible can never give us grounds for criticising the Church'"
•L 302 ❖ L 28 Dec 61
Bible: Book of Genesis achieves the idea of true Creation and of a transcendent Creator
•RP 110-111 ❖ RP 11:3
Bible: Deborah's song of triumph over Sisera in Judges V might be as old as the battle that gave rise to it back in the thirteenth century
•CR 115 ❖ CR 10:2
Bible: Either the Book of John is reportage pretty close to the facts, or some writer suddenly anticipated the whole technique of modern narrative
•CR 155 ❖ CR 13:5
Bible: Ezekiel 16 as "one of the most moving and graphic chapters of the whole Old Testament"
•RP 130 ❖ RP 12:9
Bible: Genesis account of Creation told in the form of a folk tale, but relays the idea of Creation in the rigorous sense of the word
•M 33 (see also GID 42; RP 109-111) ❖ M 4:15 (see also GID I 3:9; RP 11:2,3)
Bible—historicity: A theology which denies historicity of nearly everything in the Gospels, if offered to the uneducated man, can produce one of two effects
•CR 153 ❖ CR 13:2
Bible—historicity: At least some narratives

in the Bible are universally admitted to be unhistorical (e.g., parables); this may extend to Jonah and Job
•L 286-287 (see also PP 71-72; GID 42, 57-58; M 33, 133-134, ftnt.)
❖ L 7 May 59 (see also PP 5:2; GID I 3:9; 4:41, 42; M 4:15; 15:2—ftnt.)
Bible—historicity: Book of Jonah described as having few historical attachments, grotesque in incident, and not without a distinctly Jewish humour
•CR 154-155 (see also L 286)
❖ CR 13:5 (see also L 7 May 59)
Bible—historicity: Earliest stratum of the Old Testament contains many truths in a form which I take to be legendary or even mythical
•WG 84 (see also L 303)
❖ WG 5:15 (see also L 21 Mar 62)
Bible—historicity: Gospels do not qualify as legends
•GID 158-159 (see also CR 154-155; GID 101; SJ 236) ❖ GID I 19:4, 5 (see also CR 13:4, 5; GID I 10:47; SJ 15:7)
Bible—historicity: Historicity of the Gospel of John
•CR 154-155; GID 158-159, 179-180
❖ CR 13:5; GID I 19:5; 22:8, 9
Bible—historicity: I do not hold that every sentence of the Old Testament has historical or scientific truth
•RP 109 ❖ RP 11:2
Bible—historicity: "...I find no difficulty in accepting the [miracle of] Peter's walking on the water as historical"
•CR 145 ❖ CR 12:11
Bible—historicity: In 1926 the hardest boiled of all atheists I knew remarked that the evidence for the historicity of the Gospels was really surprisingly good
•SJ 223-224 (see also SJ 235-236)
❖ SJ 14:15 (see also SJ 15:7)
Bible—historicity: Miraculous elements in a Bible narrative do not for me preclude its historicity; for this reason I have been called a Fundamentalist
•RP 109-110 ❖ RP 11:2
Bible—historicity: New Testament is, in my opinion, historical

Bible, most embarrassing verse in the (Mark 13:30: "Verily I say unto you, that this generation shall not pass, till all these things be done")
•WLN 98 ❖ WLN 7:8, 9

Bible: Narrative of Christ's prayer in Gethsemane an example of how only portions of certain events were recalled and recorded by Bible writers
•LM 46-47 ❖ LM 9:3

Bible: Narrative of Tertullos' speech against St. Paul an example of how only portions of certain events were recalled and recorded by Bible writers
•LM 47 ❖ LM 9:4

Bible—New Testament, chronology of writing, misunderstood (Epistles written before the Gospels)
•GID 232 (see also M 143-144)
❖ GID II 10:7 (see also M 16:1-3)

Bible—New Testament demands that whatever is most highly valued on the natural level is to be abandoned the moment it conflicts with the service of God
•CR 14 ❖ CR 2:5

Bible—New Testament has nothing at all to tell us of literature; but we may notice what kind of metaphor it uses
•CR 3-5 ❖ CR 1:5-7

Bible—New Testament: I think we can still believe culture to be innocent after reading N.T.; I cannot see that we are encouraged to think it important
•CR 15 ❖ CR 2:8

Bible—New Testament, in the, history reigns supreme and Truth is incarnate (whereas in the Old Testament, truths may be in legendary or mythical form)
•WG 84 ❖ WG 5:15

Bible—New Testament is, in my opinion, historical
•GID 57-58 (see also Bible—historicity)
❖ GID I 4:42 (Ques. 10) (see also Bible—historicity)

Bible—New Testament is more prosaic, in some ways less splendid, than the Old Testament
•M 133-134 (ftnt.) ❖ M 15:2 (ftnt.)

Bible—New Testament passages which may speak to the issue of the value of "culture" in the life of the Christian
•CR 14-15 ❖ CR 2:5-8

Bible—New Testament: Story of Jesus is no legend
•GID 158-159 (see also CR 154-155; GID 101; SJ 236) ❖ GID I 19:4, 5 (see also CR 13:4, 5; GID I 10:47; SJ 15:7)

Bible—New Testament: The passage in Mark 13:30-32 together with Mark 15:34 make up the strongest evidence that the N.T. is historically reliable
•WLN 98-99 ❖ WLN 7:9

Bible—New Testament: The undermining of the old orthodoxy [belief in the miraculous] has been mainly the work of divines engaged in N.T. criticism
•CR 153 ❖ CR 13:3

Bible—New Testament: What a tissue of quotations from the Old Testament it is
•RP 26-27 ❖ RP 3:13

Bible—New Testament (without going into details) gives us a pretty clear hint of what a fully Christian society would be like
•MC 80-82 ❖ MC III 3:4-6

Bible: "Not one jot of Revelation will be proved false; but so many new truths might be added"
•L 267 ❖ L 8 Feb 56

Bible not to be used as an encyclopedia; we need to steep ourselves in its tone or temper and so learn its overall message
•RP 112 ❖ RP 11:5

Bible—Old Testament contains fabulous elements
•GID 57-58 (see also CR 154-155; GID 42; L 286; M 33, 133-134, ftnt.; PP 71)
❖ GID I 4:42 (Ques. 10) (see also CR 13:5; GID I 3:9; L 7 May 59; M 4:15; 15:2—ftnt.; PP 5:2)

Bible—Old Testament, earliest stratum of, contains many truths in a form which I take to be legendary or even mythical
•WG 84 (see also L 303)
❖ WG 5:15 (see also L 21 Mar 62)

Bible—Old Testament gives an account of

how God selected the Jews and spent several centuries hammering into their heads the sort of God He was
•MC 54 ❖ MC II 3:9

Bible—Old Testament: I do not hold that every sentence of the Old Testament has historical or scientific truth
•RP 109 ❖ RP 11:2

Bible—Old Testament is less rich in many kinds of imaginative beauty than the Pagan mythologies
•M 133-134 (ftnt.) ❖ M 15:2 (ftnt.)

Bible—Old Testament: Myth has been raised by God above itself, qualified and compelled by Him to serve purposes which of itself it would not have served
•RP 111 ❖ RP 11:4

Bible—Old Testament: One of the rewards of reading the Old Testament is that you discover what a tissue of quotations from it the New Testament is
•RP 26-27 ❖ RP 3:13

Bible—Old Testament: Our ancestors seem to think that those authors wrote with a pretty full understanding of Christian theology
•RP 34 (See entire chapter)
❖ RP 4:2 (See entire chapter 4)

Bible, one can respect and at moments envy the Fundamentalist's view of the, (as "ultimate truth in systematic form")
•RP 112 ❖ RP 11:6

Bible: Perhaps the writings of St. Paul let through what matters more than ideas —a whole Christian life in operation
•RP 114 ❖ RP 11:9

Bible: Poets of the "Song of Songs" probably never dreamed of any but a secular and natural purpose in what they composed
•RP 111 ❖ RP 11:4

Bible (Psalms): Through all the horrible distortions of the human medium, I have gained something I might not have gained from a flawless exposition
•RP 114 (see also Psalms)
❖ RP 11:10 (see also Psalms)

Bible, quoting from, to support a point ("text-hunting") may be Puritanical, but it is also scholastic, patristic, apostolic, and Dominical
•CR 27 ❖ CR 2:43

Bible, read in the right spirit, will bring us to Christ—the true Word of God
•L 247 (see also L 287)
❖ L 8 Nov 52 (see also L 7 May 57)

Bible reading also requires inspiration, and a right spirit
•L 287 ❖ L 7 May 59

Bible reading on your own—with prayer for guidance—as the best starting point for understanding doctrines*
•L 233 ❖ L 13 Jun 51

Bible: Regarding critics who take the Book of John to be a "spiritual romance"
•CR 154-155 ❖ CR 13:5

Bible, ritual, and miracle as avenues for knowing God
•GID 143-144 ❖ GID I 16:26

Bible: Second meanings (the "spiritual" ones) may not always have been intended by the author—but they also do not obliterate the first, plainer meaning
•RP 128-129 ❖ RP 12:9

Bible study—see also Devotional life; Devotions

Bible study: "...there is no question of learning a subject but of steeping ourselves in a Personality..."
•RP 113-114 ❖ RP 11:9

Bible, technique for dealing with inconsistent passages in the: "...it is better to hold two inconsistent views than to ignore one side of the evidence"*
•L 251-252 ❖ L 3 Aug 53

Bible: The "Gospels" were composed later (after the epistles) for the benefit of those who had already accepted the "gospel"
•GID 232; M 143-144; SL 108
❖ GID II 10:7; M 16:2; SL 23:3

Bible: The Gospels were written not to make Christians, but to edify Christians already made; few people are converted by studying Jesus' life as biography

•CR 163 ❖ CR 13:28

Biblical criticism: I distrust the modern theologians as critics; their literary experience lacks a wide and deep experience of literature in general
•CR 154 (see also CR 161)
❖ CR 13:22 (see also CR 13:22)

Biblical criticism: In using linked hypotheses to support genesis of texts, a critic unwittingly reduces the probability of his conclusion to almost nothing
•CR 163 ❖ CR 13:27

Biblical criticism made even more difficult for the modern reviewer by the differences in customs, language, race-characteristics, etc.
•CR 161-162 ❖ CR 13:22-23

Biblical Criticism, Modern Theology and (chapter title)
•CR 152-166 ❖ CR ch. 13

Biblical criticism: Regarding critics who take the Book of John to be a "spiritual romance"
•CR 154-155 ❖ CR 13:5

Biblical criticism: Regarding the statement that something in a Gospel cannot be historical because it shows a theology too developed for so early a date
•CR 164 ❖ CR 13:28

Biblical criticism: Scepticism need not be reserved for the New Testament and the Creeds; try doubting something else
•CR 164 (see also CR 162*)
❖ CR 13:29 (see also CR 13:25*)

Biblical criticism: The kind of textual criticism which finds that every old book was made by six anonymous authors with scissors and paste is dying out
•GID 134-135 ❖ GID I 16:8

Biblical criticism: The reconstruction of the history of an ancient text can sound very convincing, but the results cannot be checked by fact
•CR 160-161 ❖ CR 13:20

Biblical criticism: "The undermining of the old orthodoxy has been mainly the work of divines engaged in the work of New Testament criticism" (re: belief in the miraculous)
•CR 153 ❖ CR 13:3

Biblical criticism: You cannot know that everything in the representation of a thing is symbolical unless you have access to the thing and can compare it...
•CR 165-166 ❖ CR 13:31-35

Biblical revelation not intended for gratification of curiosity; is purely practical*
•GID 43 (see also PP 119)
❖ GID I 3:10 (see also PP 8:2)

Billboard making as an example of work whose sole value lies in the money it brings (vs. "necessary" work such as farming, teaching, etc.)
•WLN 75-76 ❖ WLN 5:11

Billiard ball analogy to show that laws of Nature do not in themselves produce events
•GID 77; M 58-59 ❖ GID I 8:4; M 8:7

Billiard ball analogy to show that the laws of Nature tell what will happen *provided that* there's no interference (re: Miracles)
•GID 73-74; M 56-57
❖ GID I 7:24-28; M 8:2, 5

Biographical items of interest on C. S. Lewis—see Lewis

Bios, or biological life (vs. *Zoë*, or spiritual life) mentioned
•MC 139-140, 153, 154
❖ MC IV 1:15; 2:9; 4:10; 5:1

Birth, according to Screwtape God's view is that human, is important chiefly as the qualification for human death which is the gate to Heaven
•SL 133-134 (see also SJ 117*)
❖ SL 28:3 (see also SJ 7:21*)

Birth, Christian renewal likened to a: Just as an ordinary baby might, if he had the choice, we may prefer to stay in the warmth and safety of the womb
•MC 187 (see also MC 154-155*, 173; SL 147*) ❖ MC IV 11:9 (see also MC IV 5:3*; 9:7; SL 31:3*)

Birth control, I have said nothing about; not my place

•MC 9 ❖ MC P:10

Birth control I won't give a view on; I'm certainly not prepared to say it is always wrong
•L 268 ❖ L 13 Mar 56

Birth: "I have even (I'm afraid) caught myself wishing that I had never been born, wh. is sinful. Also meaningless if you think it out"
•L 166 (see also SJ 115-116)
❖ L 8 May 39 (see also SJ 7:19-21)

Birth, New—see New Birth

Blame: I am rather sick of the modern assumption that, for all events, "WE" are never responsible: it is always our rulers, or parents, or education...
•LAL 15 (see also Responsibility, personal) ❖ LAL May 30th 53 (see also Responsibility, personal)

Blessing, when we lose one, another is often most unexpectedly given in its place
•LAL 86 ❖ LAL Aug 3/59

Blessings: "...all that is given to a creature with free will must be two-edged" (even pain)*
•PP 107, 118 ❖ PP 6:18; 8:1

Blessings, earthly, only suggest what we were really made for
•MC 120 ❖ MC III 10:5

Blessings: "God wants to give us something, but cannot, because our hands are full—there's nowhere for Him to put it" (quote from St. Augustine)
•PP 96 (see also GO 53-54*; LAL 73)
❖ PP 6:8 (see also GO 3:25, 26*; LAL 31/3/58)

Blessings: Imitation of Christ includes looking at everything as something that comes from God*
•GID 50 ❖ GID I 4:11 (Ques. 3)

Blessings: "It seems to me that we often, almost sulkily, reject the good that God offers us because, at that moment, we expected some other good"
•LM 26 ❖ LM 5:10

Blessings ("riches"), no kind of, is a passport to the Kingdom of Heaven (e.g., happiness, strength, etc.)
•FL 16 ❖ FL 1:11

Blessings, obstacles to our perception of ordinary, as being from God: inattention, greed, and conceit
•LM 90 ❖ LM 17:10

Blessings of God often turned to occasions for quarrelling, jealousy, excess, etc.
•GID 152 ❖ GID I 18:4

Blessings of God, we ought to be able to appreciate ordinary pleasures as*
•LM 89-90 ❖ LM 17:6-9

Blessings, temporal (e.g., friends, books or brains) not given us to keep; we must learn to care for something else more
•L 161-162 (see also L 306; LM 27, 90)
❖ L 12 Sep 38 (see also L 21 Nov 62; LM 5:12, 13; 17:10)

Blessings, temporal, look like broken toys in times of fear and pain; we are reminded that they were never intended to possess our heart*
•PP 106 (see also FL 192)
❖ PP 6:17 (see also FL 6:47)

Blessings: We can learn to recognise their divine source and give thanks for them in the same moment they are received
•LM 89-90 (see also GO 73*)
❖ LM 17:6-9 (see also GO 4:7, 8*)

Blood sacrifice, Homer's idea of, to restore a ghost to rationality may strikingly anticipate the truth
•RP 37-38 ❖ RP 4:8

Blood, too much emphasis on, in hymns dealing with the Crucifixion
•LM 85 ❖ LM 16:10

Bloodery (chapter title)
•SJ 83-100 ❖ SJ ch. 6

Blue Flower, before I was six years old I was a votary of the
•SJ 7 (see also The Pilgrim's Regress, p. xii) ❖ SJ 1:4 (see also The Pilgrim's Regress P:16)

Boarding school, life àt a vile, is a good preparation for the Christian life; it teaches one to live by hope and faith
•SJ 36-37 ❖ SJ 2:16

Bodleian Library, description of
•L 125-126 ❖ L 31 Mar 28

Bodies are like cars; they wear out (we

must just look forward to the fine new machines—latest Resurrection model)
•LAL 78 ❖ LAL Sep 30 58

Bodies are like machines; they wear out ...but through my body God showed me that whole side of His beauty which is embodied in color, sound, smell and size
•LAL 110-111 (*see also* LM 17-18)
❖ LAL 26 Nov 62 (*see also* LM 3:9)

Bodies, men's belief that their, are their own causes much of the modern resistance to chastity
•SL 97-98 ❖ SL 21:4

Bodies, we shall have, in Heaven
•M 126, 159-163 ❖ M 14:30; 16:27-32

Bodies which we will inherit at the Resurrection not made of the same atoms we ruled before
•M 151 (*see also* GID 33)
❖ M 16:15 (*see also* GID I 2:11)

Body as "Brother Ass" (an expression of Saint Francis'): "...a useful, sturdy, lazy, obstinate, patient, lovable and infuriating beast..."
•FL 143; LAL 89
❖ FL 5:19, 20; LAL 22 Dec 59

Body, as Christians we are organs in a
•MC 159 ❖ MC IV 6:3

Body, Christianity enjoins respect for the human, even while asceticism may be practiced
•GID 148-149 (*see also* M 163; consider also Matter) ❖ GID I 17:5 (*see also* M 16:32; *consider also* Matter)

Body, Christianity has no quarrel with the, as such; demands only that we set right a *misdirection* of our nature
•PP 104 ❖ PP 6:15

Body, Christianity is almost the only one of the great religions which thoroughly approves of the; some kind of body will be given us even in Heaven
•MC 91 (*see also* M 161-162; WG 18, 72-73*) ❖ MC III 5:7 (*see also* M 16:30; WG 1:14; 4:30*)

Body, heaven is a, because the blessed remain eternally different; and each has something unique to tell all the others about God

•PP 150 (*see also* FL 92-93; L 242-243*)
❖ PP 10:7 (*see also* FL 4:9; L 20 Jun 52*)

Body, human: Moral rules are like directions for running a machine
•MC 69 (*see also* MC 54; RP 60-61*)
❖ MC III 1:1 (*see also* MC II 3:7, 8; RP 6:10, 11*)

Body, human: We are the machine; God is the Inventor
•MC 173 ❖ MC IV 9:7

Body (i.e., physical desires) vs. Soul (i.e., "imagination") in temptation: "If the imagination were obedient, the appetites would give us very little trouble"
•GID 216-217; LM 17 *see also* LAL 111)
❖ GID II 7:3; LM 3:9 (*see also* LAL 26 Nov 62)

Body, if our human, cannot inherit the kingdom, that is not because it is too solid and distinct but because it is too flimsy and transitory
•WG 69 ❖ WG 4:25

Body important to our realization of God's glory; but for our body all that we receive through the senses would go unpraised
•LM 17-18 (*see also* LAL 110-111)
❖ LM 3:9 (*see also* LAL 26 Nov 62)

Body, in Christian life we are not homogeneous units but different and complimentary organs of a mystical (re: women in the clergy)
•GID 238 ❖ GID II 11:10

Body, Man has held three views of his: 1) filthy and shameful, 2) glorious, or 3) as St. Francis called it, "Brother Ass" —useful, lazy, infuriating, etc.
•FL 142-143 (*see also* LAL 89)
❖ FL 5:19, 20 (*see also* LAL 22 Dec 59)

Body, my, is now like an empty house; it had such a different importance while it was the body of H.'s [Joy's] lover
•GO 12 (*see also* GO 4)
❖ GO 1:22 (*see also* GO 1:6)

Body: "No doubt it has often led me astray: but not half so often, I suspect, as my soul has led it astray"
•LAL 111 ❖ LAL 26 Nov 62

Body of Christ—*see also* Church; Membership

Body of Christ: Christ rejoices in the differences of the members
•L 224 ❖ L 7 Dec 50

Body of Christ exemplified by the image of the family
•WG 110-112 ❖ WG 7:6-9

Body of Christ: God meant humanity to be like players in one band, or organs in one body; the Christian body is the best instrument for learning about God
•MC 144 ❖ MC IV 2:15, 16

Body of Christ, if we want to help others we must add ourselves to the
•MC 65 ❖ MC II 5:8

Body of Christ: Our concern about "outsiders" is more reason to get *inside* ourselves, where we can help; to add a new finger to the Body of Christ
•L 196 ❖ L 8 Dec 41

Body of Christ: "Those who are, or can become, His sons, are our real brothers ... It is spiritual, not biological, kinship that counts"*
•WLN 91 ❖ WLN 6:22

Body of Christ, we are all "special" as members in the
•L 242-243 ❖ L 20 Jun 52

Body of Christ, we become part of, in membership
•L 224; WG 110 ❖ L 7 Dec 50; WG ch. 7

Body of the risen Jesus was a solid body; He was not a ghost (what this reveals about life after death)
•M 145-163 ❖ M 16:5-32

Body, our resurrected: Some hints about this New Nature are given us in Jesus' miracles of anticipation (e.g., walking on water, raising of Lazarus)
•M 150-153 ❖ M 16:19

Body, our resurrected, will not be made of the same atoms; even in this life its actual ingredients change
•GID 33 (*see also* M 151)
❖ GID I 2:11 (*see also* M 16:15)

Body provides comic relief in sexual love; one of its functions in our lives is to play the part of buffoon
•FL 143-144 ❖ FL 5:19-21

Body regarded by ancient philosophers as

a mere encumbrance, but Christians believe it will be harmonised with the spirit and resurrected
•M 172 ❖ M App. A:11

Body, resurrection of—*see* Resurrection

Body sometimes seen as "the bad part" of one; this is a misunderstanding
•L 175 ❖ L 17 Jan 40

Body, St. Paul has told us that a, is a unity of different members (re: the unique vision that each soul has of God)
•PP 150 ❖ PP 10:7

Body, the rapture of the saved soul will "'flow over'" into the glorified body (reference to quote from St. Augustine)
•WG 18 ❖ WG 1:14

Body, "Transposition" throws a new light on the doctrine of the resurrection of the; all our earthly sensations are to be flooded with new meaning
•WG 72 (*see also* WG 67-68)
❖ WG 4:30 (*see also* WG 4:22)

Body, we are members of one, but differentiated members, each with his own vocation
•WG 26-27 (*see also* PP 150-151)
❖ WG 2:9 (*see also* PP 10:7, 8)

Body will not continue indefinitely supplying us with the physical media of emotion (re: flatness of emotions after a crisis passes)
•LM 46 ❖ LM 9:2

Bomb, [atomic], mentioned
•GID 312 ❖ GID III 8:2, 3, 6

Bomb, small statement regarding use of the atomic, in Japan
•L 225
❖ L undated letter just after 7 Dec 50

Book(s)—*see also* Literature; *consider also* Authors; Poetry; Reading; Writing

Book, almost anything can be read into any, if you are determined enough
•RP 99 ❖ RP 10:2

Book/author relationship as analogy to God's relationship to the world (re: miracles)
•M 98 (*consider also* Play/Play analogy) ❖ M 12:6 (*consider also* Play/Play analogy)

Book, let him write a, about it...let him do anything but act (—Screwtape, referring to the human's renewed state of grace)
•SL 60 ❖ SL 13:5

Book on prayer, I have never met a, which was much use...
•LM 62 ❖ LM 12:1

Book reviewing—*see* Literary criticism

Book, there is nothing nicer than to buy a doubtful looking, and then to discover that it is topping
•L 30
❖ L undated letter just before 27 Sep 16

Book, to read a, marked by you is almost the nearest thing to a conversation
•L 172 ❖ L 3 Dec 39

Books: "*War and Peace* is in my opinion *the* best novel..."
•L 201 (*see also* WG 23)
❖ L 13 Oct 42 (*see also* WG 2:5)

Books, all the, were beginning to turn against me; the most religious authors were clearly those on whom I could really feed—the others seemed "tinny"
•SJ 213-214 (*see also* SJ 225)
❖ SJ 14:3 (*see also* SJ 14:17)

Books: "...an anthology of love poems for public and perpetual use would probably be as sore a trial to literary taste as *Hymns Ancient and Modern*"
•RP 94 ❖ RP 9:5

Books: Better to read original authors than commentators
•GID 200 (*see also* L 122-123)
❖ GID II 4:1 (*see also* L 12 Dec 27)

Books: Biblical criticism attempts to reconstruct the genesis of the ancient texts; but I have watched reviewers do this to my own books with 100% failure
•CR 158-160 (*see also* Biblical criticism)
❖ CR 13:13-20 (*see also* Biblical criticism)

Books, devotional: Lewis mentions a "curious drabness which characterises so many 'little books on religion'"
•L 193 ❖ L 10 Apr 41

Books, devotional vs. doctrinal: Many find that "the heart sings unbidden while...working their way through a tough bit of theology..."
•GID 205 ❖ GID II 4:7

Books, effect of, on children: Certain bad elements may not have as profound an effect as we may fear
•CR 32-33 ❖ CR 2:53

Books: First editions of *The Screwtape Letters* and *The Great Divorce* both belong to the worst war-period and are scrubby little things on rotten paper...
•LAL 12 ❖ LAL Nov 10th 52

Books, how did we enjoy, so much when we did not know what was at the center of them?
•L 173 (*see also* L 143*, 181-182)
❖ L 18 Dec 39 (*see also* L 24 Oct 31*; 26 Mar 40)

Books: "How one's range of interest grows..."
•L 148 ❖ L 17 Jan 32

Books, I couldn't tell you which of the, I read are professional reading and which are for pleasure
•L 275 ❖ L 16 Mar 57

Books, I don't want my dog to bark approval of my (re: God needing or wanting our praise)
•RP 93 ❖ RP 9:4

Books, I make every effort to cling to the old life of, [while in the army]
•L 38 ❖ L undated letter postmarked 22 Jul 17

Books: "I went to the Coll far more disposed to excuse my literary tastes than to plume myself on them. But this innocence did not last..."
•SJ 103 ❖ SJ 7:3, 4

Books, if you wish to avoid God select your, very carefully; safer to stick to the papers
•CR 168-169 (*see also* SJ 191)
❖ CR 14:17, 18 (*see also* SJ 21:13)

Books, it is a very silly idea that in reading, you must never "skip"
•MC 145 ❖ MC IV 2:15, 16

Books: "It is important to acquire early in life the power of reading sense wherever you happen to be"
•SJ 56-57 ❖ SJ 4:1

Books, Lewis describes his childhood as being greatly influenced by endless
•SJ 10 (*see also* SJ 45-46)
❖ SJ 1:8 (*see also* SJ 3:4)

Books, Lewis lists the sources for his, in a letter to a critic
•L 205 ❖ L 29 Oct 44

Books: Lewis makes suggestions for Christian reading in several areas
•L 298-299 ❖ L 9 May 61

Books: Lewis mentions *The Abolition of Man* as "almost my favorite among my books but in general has been almost totally ignored by the public"
•LAL 39 (*see also* L 204; MC 19)
❖ LAL 20/2/55 (*see also* L undated letter of May 1944; MC I 1:7)

Books, Lewis mentions, "where the doctrine is as good...as the art"
•L 222 ❖ L 9 Jan 50

Books: "Liking an author may be as involuntary and improbable as falling in love"
•SJ 190 ❖ SJ 12:12

Books, mistaken preference for modern, rather than old nowhere more rampant than in theology
•GID 201 ❖ GID II 4:2

Books: More are needed by Christians on other subjects with Christianity latent
•GID 93; L 208
❖ GID I 10:9; L 10 Dec 45

Books, most of my, are evangelistic; they are addressed to those who did not know they were in need of forgiveness and a Saviour
•GID 181-182 ❖ GID I 22:13

Books, my brother and I learned that, can be taken on a journey and that hours of golden reading can so be added to its other delights
•SJ 56-57 (*see also* L 203, 265)
❖ SJ 4:1 (*see also* L 31 Jan 43; 5 Dec 55)

Books: "Never in my life had I read a work of fiction, poetry, or criticism in my own language except because...I liked the taste of it"
•SJ 102-103 ❖ SJ 7:3

Books, old vs. new: The Apologist should choose the old books over the new, because they contain those truths of which our own age is neglectful
•GID 92 ❖ GID I 10:7

Books, old: "...when a learned man is presented with any statement in an ancient author, the one question he never asks is whether it is true"
•SL 128-129 (*see also* L 145-146*)
❖ SL 27:5 (*see also* L 22 Nov 31*)

Books, On the Reading of Old (chapter title)
•GID 200-207 ❖ GID II ch. 4

Books one finds antipathetic, we all know how difficult it is to grasp or retain the substance of
•GID 179 ❖ GID I 22:4

Books, one thing Arthur taught me was to love the bodies of; the set up of the page, the feel and smell of the paper...
•SJ 164 (*see also* GID 278)
❖ SJ 10:18 (*see also* GID III 2:1)

Books or music in which we thought the beauty was located will betray us if we trust to them; these things are only good images of what we really desire
•WG 6-7 (*see also* Beauty)
❖ WG 1:4, 5 (*see also* Beauty)

Books, people in, can almost become members of one's own family
•L 173 ❖ L 18 Dec 39

Books read at an early age, going back to, illuminates the origins of things in one's mental outfit
•L 109-110 ❖ L 4 Jul 26

Books, ready-made collections of: "How I abominate such culture for the many"
•L 70 (*see also* SL 60)
❖ L 7 Aug 21 (*see also* SL 13:4*)

Books: Regarding the unbeliever who "commonly wishes to maintain his superiority to the great mass of mankind who turn to books for mere recreation"
•CR 10 (*see also* WLN 38-39, 41)
❖ CR 1:15 (*see also* WLN 3:11, 12, 14)

Books, Screwtape mentions that only the learned read old, and they are the least likely to be influenced by them (as they subscribe to Historical Point of View)

•SL 128-129 (*see also* SL 43, 133)
❖ SL 27:5 (*see also* SL 9:4; 28:2)

Books, Screwtape refers to the spiritual dangers to his side of humans reading, they greatly enjoy as opposed to reading the "right" books
•SL 58, 60 (*see also* L 216; LAL 54; SJ 102-103; WLN 33- 34)
❖ SL 13:3, 4 (*see also* L 3 Apr 49; LAL 20/3/56; SJ 7:3; WLN 3:5, 6)

Books, self-forgetfulness through the enjoyment of*
•WLN 39 ❖ WLN 3:12

Books, some of the allegories imposed on my, have been so ingenious and interesting that I often wish I had thought of them myself
•RP 99 ❖ RP 10:2

Books: "The best Dickens always seems to me to be the one I have read last"
•L 289 ❖ L 5 Nov 59

Books, the great blessing of my youth was that I grew up in a world of cheap and abundant
•SJ 147 ❖ SJ 9:23

Books, the key to my, is Donne's maxim, "The heresies that men leave are hated most"; the things I assert most vigorously are those that I resisted long...
•SJ 213 ❖ SJ 14:2

Books: "The more 'up to date' the book is, the sooner it will be dated" (re: Prayer Book)
•LM 12 ❖ LM 2:11

Books: "Those who have greatly cared for any book whatever may possibly come to care, some day, for good books"
•WLN 39 ❖ WLN 3:12

Books: What is the point in reading contemporary authors just because they happen to be alive?
•L 225-226
❖ L undated letter of Jan 1951

Books which became for Lewis a medium of "Joy": *Squirrel Nutkin*
•SJ 16-17 ❖ SJ 1:16

Books which became for Lewis a medium of "Joy": *Saga of King Olaf*
•SJ 17 ❖ SJ 1:17

Books which became for Lewis a medium of "Joy": *Siegfried and the Twilight of the Gods*
•SJ 72-78 ❖ SJ 5:3-10

Books which became for Lewis a medium of "Joy": other Norse mythology
•SJ 78 ❖ SJ 5:11

Books, why old, are better than modern books
•GID 200-207 ❖ GID II ch. 4

Books, you may have noticed that the, you really love are bound together by a secret thread
•PP 145 ❖ PP 10:2

Books, your friends do not see the common quality in all the, you really love, and often wonder why, liking this, you should also like that
•PP 145 ❖ PP 10:2

Books, your library in Heaven will contain only the, you gave away or lent on earth
•GID 216 (*see also* MC 190*)
❖ GID II 7:1 (*see also* MC IV 11:15*)

Books, your "Second Friend" has read all the right, but has got the wrong thing out of every one
•SJ 199 ❖ SJ 13:4

Bore, it's so much easier to pray for a, than to go and see him
•LM 66 ❖ LM 12:12

Bores mentioned "whose history you know well after a short acquaintance...because they had nothing to say and would not be silent"
•L 136 ❖ L 9 Sep 29

"Born again"—*see also* New Birth

Born again, ye must be, (Obedience as an imperative is not really obedience at all)
•LM 115 ❖ LM 21:12

Boxen: Animal-land and India were united into the single state of Boxen; they belonged to my outer world, not my inner world of "Joy"
•SJ 78-79 (*see also* SJ 82)
❖ SJ 5:12, 13 (*see also* SJ 5:14)

Boxen described in detail
•SJ 79-82 ❖ SJ 5:12-15

Branch, it is like cutting off the, you are

sitting on when you argue against God; you are arguing against the very power that enables you to argue at all
•MC 52-53 ❖ MC II 3:4

Branch, they have sawn off the, they were sitting on (re: Freudian and Marxist belief that all thoughts are tainted at the source)
•GID 272 (consider also Thought)
❖ GID III 1:4 (consider also Thought)

Bravery—see Courage

Breakfast: "He that but looketh on a plate of ham and eggs to lust after it, hath already committed breakfast with it in his heart" (re: having mumps)
•LAL 28 ❖ LAL Mar 10/54

Brevity of life—see Life, brevity of

Bribe, Heaven is not a; offers nothing that a mercenary soul can desire
•PP 145 ❖ PP 10:1

Bribe, my withers are quite unwrung by the fear that I was lured into Christianity by a; by the hope of everlasting life
•LM 120 (see also FL 189-190; RP 42; SJ 231) ❖ LM 22:8 (see also FL 6:42; RP 4:17; SJ 15:3)

Bribe, those who have attained everlasting life know very well that it is no mere, but the very consummation of their earthly discipleship
•WG 5 ❖ WG 1:3

Bribe, until a certain spiritual level has been reached the promise of immortality will always operate as a
•GID 131 (Compare with WG 3-5*; see also Immortality)
❖ GID I 16:3 (Compare with WG 1:1-3*; see also Immortality)

"**Bridegroom**" as a term used in Scripture to represent God (lending the image of Eros rather than of Friendship)
•FL 112-113, 124 (see also PP 45-46)
❖ FL 4:42, 58 (see also PP 3:13)

Bridegroom, Christ as, to the Church
•RP 128-132 ❖ RP 12:9, 10

Bridegroom, Christ as, turns out not to be a mere arbitrary interpretation of certain Bible passages but to have roots in the whole history of religion

•RP 128-130 ❖ RP 12:9

Britain—see also England; Ireland; Scotland

Britain, National Health System of, mentioned or referred to
•LAL 71, 84, 116
❖ LAL 14/1/58; Jul 7th 59; 10 Jun 63

Britain, school system of, discussed with regard to the transmission of Christianity
•GID 114-119 ❖ GID I ch. 13

British Empire, as a youth I hated whatever I knew or imagined of the
•SJ 173 ❖ SJ 11:10

Broken toys, all our little happinesses look like, in times of fear and pain; we are reminded that they were never intended to possess our heart
•PP 106 ❖ PP 6:17

"Broken toys and faded flowers," even the imagining of supernatural love towards God has at times made all other objects of desire look like
•FL 192 ❖ FL 6:47

"**Brother** Ass," the body as, (an expression of Saint Francis'): "...a useful, sturdy, lazy, obstinate, patient, lovable and infuriating beast..."
•FL 143; LAL 89
❖ FL 5:19, 20; LAL 22 Dec 59

Brother, Lewis's—see Lewis, Warren Hamilton

Brothers: "Those who are, or can become, His sons, are our real brothers... It is spiritual, not biological, kinship that counts"
•WLN 91 ❖ WLN 6:22

Brotherhood, I have long known that the talk about, wherever it occurs, is hypocrisy (re: racial prejudice)
•LAL 43 ❖ LAL 7/6/55

Buddha, miracles performed by, are hardly credible if we accept his teaching that Nature is an illusion from which we must escape
•M 133 ❖ M 15:2

Buddha never claimed to be God or the Son of God; there is no parallel to Jesus in other religions
•GID 157-158 ❖ GID I 19:3

Buddha's view of the value of culture: "Buddha was, I believe, anti-cultural, but here...I speak under correction"
•CR 15 ❖ CR 2:10

Buddhism an example of the fact that belief in immortality can exist without a belief in God at all
•RP 40 ❖ RP 4:14

Buddhism as an anti-nature religion which tells us that nature is evil and illusory
•M 119 (see also GID 86*)
❖ M 14:20 (see also GID I 9:9*)

Buddhism, doctrine of immortality is central in, yet immortality regarded as a nightmare, not a prize
•GID 130-131 ❖ GID I 16:2, 3

Buddhism is only a Hindu heresy, and a simplification inferior to the thing simplified
•CR 71 ❖ CR 5:26

Buddhism is the greatest of the Hindu heresies; not real Paganism
•GID 102 ❖ GID I 10:49

Buddhism mentioned as a system which exposes our total nature to death (while Christianity demands only that we set right a *misdirection* of our nature)
•PP 104 ❖ PP 6:15

Buddhism mentioned as the only civilised religion which is genuinely Pacifist
•WG 47 ❖ WG 3:26

Buddhism, miraculous elements of, not essential to that religion (vs. Christianity, where one Grand Miracle is the whole point)
•GID 80 (see also M 68*)
❖ GID I 9:1 (see also M 10:1*)

Buddhist who concentrates on the Buddhist teaching about mercy as an example of those who belong to Christ without knowing it
•MC 176-177 ❖ MC IV 10:4

Bultitude the bear (at Whipsnade Zoo) mentioned
•L 154 ❖ L 14 Jun 32

Bultmann, [Rudolph]: Regarding his strange claim that no personality of Our Lord is presented in the New Testament
•CR 156-157 ❖ CR 13:7, 8

"Bulverism" (in debate) tries to show that the other man has causes and not reasons and that we have reasons and not causes
•GID 275 ❖ GID III 1:12

"Bulverism" Or, The Foundation of Twentieth Century Thought (chapter title)
•GID 271-277 ❖ GID III ch. 1

Bunyan, [Paul], an uneducated believer, was able to write a book that has astonished the whole world—because Christianity is an education in itself
•MC 75 ❖ MC III 2:4

Bunyan, [Paul], mentioned as an author of books "where the doctrine is as good...as the art"
•L 222
❖ L undated letter just before 9 Jan 50

Bureaucracy—see also Organization(s)

Bureaucracy: In every institution there is something which sooner or later works against the very purpose for which it came into existence*
•LM 43 ❖ LM 8:10

Bureaucracy, my symbol for Hell is something like the, of a police state or the offices of a thoroughly nasty business concern
•SL x (see also That Hideous Strength)
❖ SL P:17 (see also That Hideous Strength)

Bureaucratic evils described (principle of "Dog eat dog," etc.)*
•SL x-xi ❖ SL P:18

Bureaucrats, I like bats better than
•SL x ❖ SL P:17

Bus, in Limbo there is a faint melancholy because everyone knows they have missed the
•L 164 ❖ L 5 Apr 39

Bus, Lewis writes of his free-choice conversion to Theism while riding on the top of a
•SJ 224-225, 228 (see also GID 261)
❖ SJ 14:16, 22 (see also GID II 16:19-22)

Business—consider also Commercialism

Business matters, Lewis describes his own lack of competence in
•LAL 61 ❖ LAL Sep 8/56

Business of Heaven, Joy is the serious
•LM 93 ❖ LM 17:17
Business of Hell: to undermine faith and prevent the formation of virtues*
•SL 25 ❖ SL 5:1
Business of life—*see also* Goal of [Christian] life
Business of life is to learn to like contact with God, since that contact cannot be avoided for long
•GID 47 (*see also* MC 183; WG 13)
❖ GID I 3:17 (*see also* MC IV 10:17; WG 1:10)
Business of life is to purge away hatred
•CR 118 ❖ CR 10:7
Business of life: the glory of God and, as our only means to glorifying Him, the salvation of human souls
•CR 14 (*see also* CR 12, 26)
❖ CR 2:4 (*see also* CR 2:1, 42)
Business, world of, "does with such efficiency so much that never really needed doing"
•WLN 81 (see entire chapter 5)
❖ WLN 5:22 (see entire chapter 5)
Busy-body, one must be careful lest the desire to be a, should disguise itself as a vocation to help the "fallen"
•RP 69 ❖ RP 7:5

Cake: God's idea is to eat the cake and have it; the creatures are to be one with Him and yet themselves (—Screwtape)
•SL 38 (*see also* Personality)
❖ SL 8:4 (*see also* Personality)
Cake: Screwtape mentions satisfaction over seeing men paying for the cake and not eating it (re: debunking emotion as "mere sentiment" when it is pleasurable)
•SL 144 (*see also* SL 42*, 56*)
❖ SL 30:4 (*see also* SL 9:2*; 12:4*)
Calling—*see* Vocation
Calvary—*see also* Crucifixion; Death of Christ
Calvary as an instance of self-giving which touches a rhythm not only of all creation but of all being
•PP 152 ❖ PP 10:10
Calvary as the ultimate answer to all those who object to the doctrine of hell
•PP 128 ❖ PP 8:12
Calvary: "God Himself, as man, submitted to man's sense of being abandoned"
•LAL 38 (*see also* GO 5; LAL 77; Abandonment) ❖ LAL 20/2/55 (*see also* GO 1:8; LAL Jul 21st 58; Abandonment)
Calvary: "Is it that God Himself cannot be Man unless God seems to vanish at His greatest need?"
•LM 43-44 ❖ LM 8:10-12
Calvary: "The Father was not *really* absent from the Son when He said 'Why hast thou forsaken me?'"

•LAL 38 ❖ LAL 20/2/55

Calvin, John: Modernist Christians maintain, as stoutly as Calvin, that there's no reason why God's dealings should appear just or merciful to us
•L 177 ❖ L 18 Feb 40

Calvinism—*consider also* Predestination

Calvinism, could one introduce the idea of a bad God through a sort of extreme: We are so depraved that our ideas of goodness count for nothing?
•GO 36-38 (*see also* CR 68-69, 79; PP 37-39) ❖ GO 2:28-30 (*see also* CR 5:22, 23; 6:19; PP 3:1-5)

Calvinist, if I were a, this symptom would fill me with despair (re: the experience of prayer as a burden rather than a delight)
•LM 113 ❖ LM 21:7

Camaraderie among fellow sufferers (such as soldiers) makes tribulation easier to bear
•SJ 188 ❖ SJ 12:10

Cambridge, description of
•L 052
❖ L undated letter postmarked 8 Dec 20

Cambridge, Lewis mentions being made a Professor at
•LAL 32 (*see also* LAL 35) ❖ LAL Sep 19/54 (*see also* LAL Nov 1st 54)

Cambridge, Lewis writes after resigning his fellowship at, "...I shall haunt the place whence the most valued of my honours came"
•L 308 ❖ L 25 Oct 63

Cambridge: Magdalene College, Cambridge, compared to Magdalen College of Oxford
•LAL 35 (*see also* LAL 32) ❖ LAL Nov 1st 54 (*see also* LAL Sep 19/54)

Cancer—*consider also* Illness, terminal

Cancer, and cancer, and cancer...my mother, my father, my wife; I wonder who is next in the queue
•GO 12 (*see also* L 275)
❖ GO 1:23 (*see also* L 6 Mar 57)

Cancer: "I think this disease now ranks as a *plague*..."*
•L 285 ❖ L 29 Apr 59

Candles, controversy over: Screwtape

mentions "what that pestilent fellow Paul used to teach about food and other unessentials"
•SL 75 ❖ SL 16:5

Candles on altars, Screwtape mentions
•SL 87 ❖ SL 19:3

Cannibalism, spiritual, as a principle of Hell: "I feign that devils can, in a spiritual sense, eat one another; and us"
•SL xi, xiii (*see also* SL 26, 37-38, 81, 141, 145; WLN 51-56, 69-70)
❖ SL P:19, 22 (*see also* SL 5:2; 8:3; 18:3; 30:1; 31:3; WLN 4:1-13, 39)

Cannibalism, spiritual, as a principle of Hell: "Even in human life we have seen the passion to dominate, almost to digest, one's fellow"
•SL xi (*see also* FL 160)
❖ SL P:19, 20 (*see also* FL 5:46)

Canoe, no one can paddle his own, but everyone can paddle someone else's
•L 236 (*see also* L 195*)
❖ L 26 Dec 51 (*see also* L 19 Nov 41*)

Canonization of saints, comment on
•GID 337 ❖ GID IV Letter 10

Canonization of saints: I only hope there'll be no scheme for this in the Church of England
•LM 15 ❖ LM 3:3

Capital punishment—*see* Punishment, capital

Car, aging like becoming an old; we must just look forward to the fine new machines awaiting us in the Divine garage ("latest Resurrection model")
•LAL 78 (*see also* LAL 110)
❖ LAL Sep 30 58 (*see also* LAL 26 Nov 62)

Car, I number it among my blessings that my father had no; the deadly power of rushing about wherever I pleased had not been given me
•SJ 156-157 ❖ SJ 10:9

Cars: "...a modern boy travels a hundred miles with less sense of liberation and pilgrimage and adventure than his grandfather got from traveling ten"
•SJ 157 ❖ SJ 10:9

Cars: "The truest and most horrible claim made for modern transport is that it

'annihilates space'. It does"
•SJ 157 ❖ SJ 10:9

Cardinal Difficulty of Naturalism, The (chapter title)
•M 12-24 ❖ M ch. 3

Cardinal Virtues," The (chapter title)
•MC 74-78 ❖ MC III ch. 2

Career(s)—*see also* Job(s); Occupation(s); Work

Career choice: We must try to earn our living by doing well what would be worth doing even if we had not our living to earn
•WLN 78 (*see also* MC 80)
❖ WLN 5:16 (*see also* MC III 3:4)

Cares—*see also* Anxiety; Difficulties; Worry; *consider also* Faith

Cares of everyday domestic life more of a hindrance to devotion to God in marriage than sex
•FL 137-138 ❖ FL 5:10

Carnal sins—*see* Sins of the flesh

Carolers look like angels, may be juvenile delinquents!*
•GID 306 ❖ GID III 7:1, 2

Case for Christianity (original title for the first book included in *Mere Christianity*)
•MC 17-66 ❖ MC I ch. 1-10

Categorical Imperative mentioned as being the substance of Kantian ethics
•CR 44-45 ❖ CR 4:2

Cathedral at Salisbury compared with the cathedral at Wells
•L 99-100 ❖ L undated letter of "April or May" 1925

Cathedral at St. Albans, Lewis mentions, as "the poorest English cathedral I have yet seen"
•L 95-96 ❖ L 4 Jul 24

Cathedral at Wells, mention of ("...wonderfully satisfying to look at")
•L 66 ❖ L 7 Aug 21

Cathedral of Truro "the poorest almost that I have ever seen"
•L 121 ❖ L 3 Sep 27

Cathedrals, so many generations have contributed to building our old, that they must be regarded as midway between a work of art and a work of

nature
•L 264 ❖ L 22 Sep 55

Catholic, I would rather not discuss why I am not a*
•L 223, 228-229, 230 (*see also* LAL 11)
❖ L undated letter of Jan 1950; 23 Apr 51; undated letter just before 27 Mar 51 (*see also* LAL Nov 10 52)

Catholic: Lewis describes what unites the Evangelical and the Anglo-Catholic against the "Liberal" or "Modernist" Christian
•GID 336 ❖ GID IV Letter 9

Catholic, liberal theology which denies the miraculous will make the unlearned man either a Roman, (if he disagrees), or an atheist (if he agrees)
•CR 153 ❖ CR 13:2

"Catholic," meaning of the word, to modern minds ("Papistical")
•GID 97 ❖ GID I 10:22

Catholic, Roman: "One can respect, and at moments envy, both the Fundamentalist's view of the Bible and the Roman Catholic's view of the Church"
•RP 112 ❖ RP 11:6

Catholic, Tolkien was a, and I had been (implicitly) warned never to trust a Papist*
•SJ 216 ❖ SJ 14:6

Catholic University Encyclopedia mentioned
•LAL 108 ❖ LAL 26 Oct 62

Catholics: Lewis mentions that, among his audiences, strict and well-informed Christian statements usually came from Anglo-and Roman Catholics
•GID 241 ❖ GID II 12:2

Catholics or Catholicism mentioned or referred to
•L 50, 268 ❖ L 4 Feb 20; 13 Mar 56

Catholics: "Romans" listed among those who have retained more of the gusto of the Psalmists than the Anglicans
•RP 52 ❖ RP 5:10

Catholicism: Lewis describes his childhood experiences with high "Anglo-Catholicism" while a student at "Belsen"

•SJ 33-34 ❖ SJ 2:14

Catholicism: Nothing would give such strong support to the Papal claims as the Pope functioning as the head of Christendom
  •L 165 (consider also Reunion)
  ❖ L 8 May 39 (consider also Reunion)

Catholicism: "What do they mean by 'Error has no rights'?" (re: an article Lewis had read, on Tolerance)*
  •L 254 ❖ L 16 Jan 54

Cats—consider also Pets

Cats and dogs, affection between: "I bet no dog would ever confess it to the other dogs"
  •FL 56 (see also FL 54-55)
  ❖ FL 3:7 (see also FL 3:4)

Cats and dogs, affection between: I notice that the common age is a bond stronger than common species
  •LAL 72 ❖ LAL 22/2/58

Cats and dogs should always be brought up together; it broadens their minds so
  •FL 59 ❖ FL 3:11

Cats as Pharisees: When he sits and stares you out of countenance he is thanking God that he is not as these dogs, or these humans, or as other cats
  •LAL 40 ❖ LAL 21/3/55

Cats: "Give my love to Fanda: I am very 'cat-minded'"
  •LAL 39 ❖ LAL 20/2/55

Cats, I can't understand the people who say, are not affectionate; our Siamese is almost suffocatingly so
  •LAL 107 ❖ LAL 2 Oct 62

Cats, I have a great respect for; they are very shrewd people and would probably see through the analyst a good deal better than he'd see through them
  •LAL 97 ❖ LAL 24 Feb 61

Cats, it is strange that anyone should dislike; but cats themselves are the worst offenders—they seldom seem to like one another
  •LAL 105 ❖ LAL 31/7/62

Cats, Lewis mentions Hugo Dyson as sharing his love of
  •L 145 ❖ L 22 Nov 31

Cats: No creature can give such a crushing "snub" as a cat; our Tom thinks I'm not quite socially up to his standards, and he makes this very clear
  •LAL 108 ❖ LAL 2 Oct 62

Cats: The cat is a Pharisee and always has a good conscience; the dog, being an honest and humble person, always has a bad one
  •LAL 40 ❖ LAL 21/3/55

Cats: "...the Siamese are delicate and fascinating creatures. Ours adores me..."
  •LAL 82 ❖ LAL Jan 26th 59

Cats, we are both ruled by; Joy's Siamese—my "stepcat"—is the most terribly conversational animal I ever knew...
  •LAL 105 ❖ LAL 3/7/62

Cats: "We are now told by the learned that Siamese are not royal cats at all..."
  •LAL 83 ❖ LAL May 19th 59

Cause, those who are readiest to die for a, may easily become those who are readiest to kill for it
  •RP 28 ❖ RP 3:17

Causes, crusades, meetings, movements, etc. as ends in themselves mentioned by Screwtape as serving his purposes
  •SL 35 (see also Means and ends)
  ❖ SL 7:4 (see also Means and ends)

Causes, Lewis explains his "culpably defective" interest in large impersonal movements and
  •SJ 32-33 ❖ SJ 2:12

Causes, salvation (according to Screwtape) may also go to people who gave their lives for wrong, thinking them to be right*
  •SL 26 ❖ SL 5:2

Celebrities: Film stars and crooners mentioned by Screwtape as useful in drawing thousands of souls away from God
  •SL 158-159; WLN 56-57
  ❖ SL 32:13; WLN 4:13

Celebrity, people will go out of their way to meet a, or a politician even when it is known that the person leads a vile and mischievous life
  •RP 67, 71 (see also LAL 27*; RP 90)
  ❖ RP 7:3, 9 (see also LAL Feb 22/54*)

RP 9:2)

Celtic mythology soon became, if not a rival, yet a humble companion, to Norse
•SJ 114 (*see also* L 48; SJ 165)
❖ SJ 7:18 (*see also* L 25 May 19; SJ 11:1)

Cemetery, sentimental tending of a plot in a: "...all this churchyard stuff was and is simply hateful, even inconceiv-able, to me"
•GO 22-24 ❖ GO 2:7

Centaur as an illustration of how "Na-ture" might one day be fully harmonised with "Spirit"
•M 126, 161 (*see also* M 163*; PP 98*)
❖ M 14:30; 16:29 (*see also* M 16:32*; PP 6:10*)

Centipede, Screwtape mentions assuming the form of a large
•SL 103 ❖ SL 22:6

Ceremonial, English people have not the talent for graceful; they go through it lumpishly..."
•L 103 ❖ L 14 Aug 25

Certainty—*see* Assurance

Cesspool, according to Alexander Whyte the true Christian's nostril is to be con-tinually attentive to the inner
•LM 97-98 ❖ LM 18:13

Change—*see also* Transformation; *consider also* Growth, Christian; Improvement; Perfection

Change, any given, in society is at least as likely to destroy the liberties and amenities we already have as to add new ones (re: "progress")
•CR 92 ❖ CR 7:22

Change as a threat to Affection: "We don't want the old, familiar faces to become brighter or more beautiful" etc.
•FL 70-73 (*see also* L 274)
❖ FL 3:27-32 (*see also* L 10 Feb 57)

Change, essential, in our souls cannot be brought about by moral effort
•MC 165 (*see also* LAL 48; Moral ef-fort) ❖ MC IV 7:12 (*see also* LAL 9/11/65; Moral effort)

Change essential in the Christian life; we are like eggs—must be hatched or go bad
•MC 169 ❖ MC IV 8:9

Change, I dread any; the old wine is to me always better...We must sit light to life and all its phases
•L 306 (*see also* L 161-162*; LM 26-27; WLN 110) ❖ L 21 Nov 62 (*see also* L 12 Sep 38*; LM 5:10- 13; WLN 7:31)

Change in a beloved may elicit a sense of outrage (as in a conversion to Chris-tianity)
•L 274 (*see also* FL 70-73; SL 18*) ❖ L 10 Feb 57 (*see also* FL 3:27-32; SL 3:6*)

Change in us will not be completed in this life
•MC 173-174, 175 ❖ MC IV 9:8; 10:1

Change, Screwtape describes how he has perverted the enjoyment of, into a de-mand for continual novelty and hor-ror of the Same Old Thing
•SL 116-117 ❖ SL 25:3, 4

Change, Screwtape mentions human en-joyment of, balanced by a desire for permanence—which combine to en-able people to appreciate Rhythm (such as seasons)
•SL 116 ❖ SL 25:2

Change, Screwtape mentions the human tendency to resist making, in them-selves ("...a hard, tight, settled core of resolution to go on being what it is...")
•SL 157; WLN 55
❖ SL 32:10; WLN 4:10

Changes, on the making of, in the liturgy: "Take care. It is so easy to break eggs without making omelettes"
•LM 6 ❖ LM 1:13

Channeling—*consider* Spiritualism

Character and temperament cannot be changed by moral effort; we must al-low it to be done for us by God*
•MC 165 (*see also* Moral effort)
❖ MC IV 7:12, 13 (*see also* Moral effort)

Character changes a little each time we make a choice for right or wrong
•MC 86-87, 107, 117 (*see also* RP 136; SL 53-54; WG 102-103; WLN 54-55)
❖MC III 4:8, 9; 7:9; 9:8 (*see also* RP 12:16; SL 12:1; WG 6:12; WLN 4:10)

Character, decline of, consists of small wrong choices*
•SL 156-157; WLN 54-55 (*see also* MC

86-87, 117; RP 136; SL 53-54; WG 101-103)

❖ SL 32:10; WLN 4:10 (*see also* MC III 4:8, 9; 9:8; RP 12:16; SL 12:1; WG 6:12)

Character judgment—*see* Judging

Character: "...surely what a man does when he is taken off his guard is the best evidence for what sort of man he is?"*

•MC 164 ❖ MC IV 7:12

Character, there is in ourselves just as in others a fatal flaw in our, on which the hopes and plans of other people have again and again shipwrecked

•GID 151-155 (*see also* GID 121-123)

❖ GID I ch. 18 (*see also* GID I 14:4-8)

Character transformation—*see* Transformation

Character virtues more important than outward obedience

•MC 77, 127, 164-165

❖ MC III 2:8; 12:3; IV 7:12

Character virtues such as charity, submissiveness to God's will, etc. are *graces*—gifts from the Holy Spirit—not our own merits*

•L 219 (*consider also* Righteousness by faith/grace) ❖ L 2 Sep 49 (*consider also* Righteousness by faith/grace)

Character will not be altered by God through force

•GID 152-153 ❖ GID I 18:5

Character-building: Difficult personality traits in our loved ones give us an opportunity to practice forgiveness*

•FL 186-187 ❖ FL 6:37

"Charientocracy" defined as when entry into the ruling class becomes the reward of culture, instead of culture being a privilege of the ruling class

•WLN 44-45 ❖ WLN 3:19

"Charientocracy": I don't think we are in danger of a Theocracy, but of something only one degree less intolerable: a "Charientocracy"

•WLN 40-41 (see entire chapter 3)

❖ WLN 3:13 (see entire chapter 3)

Charity—*see also* Alms; Help; Helping; Humanitarianism; Love

Charity, acts of, are jobs that had better be done well or not at all

•WLN 80-81 ❖ WLN 5:22

Charity, all of us need, since there is something in each of us that cannot be naturally loved

•FL 181, 183 ❖ FL 6:29, 30

Charity begins at home (and so does uncharity)

•GID 285 ❖ GID III 3:6

Charity (chapter title)

•FL 163-192; MC 115-118

❖ FL ch. 6; MC III ch. 9

Charity (Christian love) is an affair of the will

•MC 115, 117-118 (*see also* L 269; LM 115)

❖ MC III 9:2, 9, 10 (*see also* L undated letter just after 13 Mar 56; LM 21:12)

"Charity," devil substitutes for the positive word, the negative word "Unselfishness"

•SL 121 (*see also* WG 3*)

❖ SL 26:2 (*see also* WG 1:1*)

Charity, discussion of Christian

•MC 115-118 ❖ MC III ch. 9

Charity: "...every stranger whom we feed or clothe is Christ. And this is apparently Gift-love to God whether we know it or not"

•FL 178 ❖ FL 6:24

Charity, folly of trying to manufacture feelings of, even as we pray for charity

•SL 21 (*see also* MC 105, 116-118)

❖ SL 4:3 (*see also* MC III 7:4; 9:5, 6, 9, 10)

Charity, for many of us the great obstacle to, is fear of [financial] insecurity

•MC 82 ❖ MC III 3:7

Charity, forced, vs. "a deeper, less conscious Charity" which enables us to want to do the right thing

•FL 185 (*see also* PP 100*)

❖ FL 6:36 (*see also* PP 6:11*)

Charity, giving money is only *one* way of showing; giving time and toil is better—and harder

•L 255-256 ❖ L 18 Feb 54

Charity (giving to the poor) an essential part of Christian morality

•MC 81 ❖ MC III 3:7

Charity, having to accept, makes palpable the total dependence in which we always live anyway*
•LAL 57 ❖ LAL 14/6/56

Charity: I sometimes think that shame does as much towards preventing good acts and straightforward happiness as any of our vices can do (re: Lewis's awkwardness at discussing his wife's death with her sons)*
•GO 9 ❖ GO 1:17

Charity: If it were true that to receive money or gifts degraded the recipient, then every act of alms would be wicked
•LAL 58 ❖ LAL 5/7/56

Charity may at times conflict with affection
•MC 115-116 ❖ MC III 9:4

Charity may lead to affection toward those you now dislike
•MC 116-117 (see also MC 161)
❖ MC III 9:5, 6 (see also MC IV 7:3)

"Charity," meaning of the word, to modern minds ("Alms" or "a charitable organization", etc.)
•GID 97 ❖ GID I 10:23

Charity must come to the help of any natural love if it is to remain sweet; feelings of love are not enough
•FL 163 (see also FL 81-83, 124, 159-160; GID 285; L 198-199; SL 124)
❖ FL 6:1 (see also FL 3:44, 45; 4:59; 5:45, 46; GID III 3:7; L undated letter just before 20 Jan 42; SL 26:5)

Charity: Only safe rule is to give more than we can spare
•MC 81-82 ❖ MC III 3:7

Charity, opportunities for practicing, are never lacking; in everyone, including ourselves, there is that which requires forbearance and forgiveness
•FL 186 ❖ FL 6:37

Charity, pride hinders our; we are tempted to spend more on tipping, hospitality, etc. than on those who really need our help
•MC 82 ❖ MC III 3:7

Charity, the fact that you are giving money to a, does not mean that you need not try to find out whether that charity is a fraud or not
•MC 75 ❖ MC III 2:4

Charity, the Gift-love of, comes by Grace
•FL 178 ❖ FL 6:24, 25

Charity: "...the proper aim of giving is to put the recipient in a state where he no longer needs our gift"*
•FL 76 ❖ FL 3:37

Charity, the total commitment of Eros is an example of how we are to exercise
•FL 153-154, 158 ❖ FL 5:35, 43

Charity, through the Grace of, God can awaken in man a supernatural Appreciative love towards Himself
•FL 191 ❖ FL 6:46

Charity toward differences in others: "A real desire to believe all the good you can of others and to make others as comfortable as you can..." (re: cultural and generational differences in propriety)
•MC 88-89 ❖ MC III 5:1

Charity: We cannot give God anything that is not His already*
•MC 125 (see also SL 96-99)
❖ MC III 11:9 (see also SL 21:2-6)

Charity, works of, do not excuse poor workmanship; much charitable work is not good work*
•WLN 71 ❖ WLN 5:1

"Charming," in English, has come to be a tepid and even patronising word
•RP 54 ❖ RP 6:1

Chastity—see also Sexual morality

Chastity as a difficult Christian principle: It must at least be attempted
•MC 92, 93-94 ❖ MC III 5:8, 11, 12

Chastity as one of the things which has decreased in value by abuse of the word "Puritanism"
•SL 47 ❖ SL 10:3

Chastity, men's belief that their bodies are their own causes much of the modern resistance to
•SL 97-98 ❖ SL 21:4

Chastity, mention of Charles Williams' lecture on
•L 177 (see also L 178, 196-197) ❖ L 11 Feb 40 (see also L 3 Mar 40; 21 Dec 41)

Chastity mentioned as one of "the severer virtues" which Lewis came to realize might have relevance in his own life*
•SJ 192 (see also SJ 201)
❖ SJ 12:14 (see also SJ 13:6)
Chastity, rule of, remains the same for all Christians at all times whereas the rule of propriety changes with time and place
•MC 88-89 ❖ MC III 5:1
Chastity: Screwtape advises promoting the lie that an excess of physical exercise and consequent fatigue is helpful toward this virtue
•SL 79 ❖ SL 17:4
Chastity, Screwtape advises Wormwood on the value of excess in food to attacks on human
•SL 79 ❖ SL 17:4
Chastity: When the devil fails to tempt us in this area (his attacks don't last forever), he tries to persuade us that chastity is unhealthy*
•SL 90-91 ❖ SL 20:1
Cheating—see Dishonesty
Check (chapter title)
•SJ 165-181 ❖ SJ ch. 11
Checkmate (chapter title)
•SJ 212-229 ❖ SJ ch. 14
Cheerfulness: A Christian society is to be a cheerful society, full of singing and rejoicing, and regarding worry or anxiety as wrong
•MC 80 ❖ MC III 3:4
Cheerfulness: "...I think we all sin by needlessly disobeying the apostolic injunction to 'rejoice' as much as by anything else" (re: guilt and humility)
•PP 67 ❖ PP 4:15
Chess game analogy to show that traditional morality does not provide answers to every particular moral problem with which we may be confronted
•CR 56 ❖ CR 4:27
Chess game as analogy to how God uses certain of Satan's weapons, such as Death, to defeat Satan himself
•M 128-129 ❖ M 14:34
Chess game used to illustrate how fixed laws are essential to freedom of choice

•PP 34, 71 ❖ PP 2:15; 5:1
Chesterton, G. K.: "His humor was of the kind which I like best"—no general tone of flippancy or jocularity; not separable from the argument itself
•SJ 190-191 ❖ SJ 12:12
Chesterton, G. K.: "I did not know what I was letting myself in for"—for an Atheist cannot be too careful of his reading
•SJ 190-192 ❖ SJ 12:12
Chesterton, G. K.: "...I liked him for his goodness"
•SJ 191 ❖ SJ 12:12
Chesterton "had more sense than all the other moderns put together; bating, of course, his Christianity"
•SJ 213 ❖ SJ 14:3
Chesterton mentioned as an author of books "where the doctrine is as good... as the art"
•L 222
❖ L undated letter just before 9 Jan 50
Chesterton's Everlasting Man, I read, and for the first time I saw the whole Christian outline of history set out in a form that seemed to me to make sense
•SJ 223 (see also L 298; SJ 235)
❖ SJ 14:15 (see also L 9 May 61; SJ 15:7)
Child, in the loss of a, the mother may find comfort in the idea of Heaven, but her specifically maternal happiness must be written off
•GO 29-30 ❖ GO 2:16
Child pleasing his father with first steps as analogy to us: "God is easy to please, but hard to satisfy" (quote from George MacDonald)
•MC 172 (see also PP 46*; SL 39)
❖ MC IV 9:5 (see also PP 3:13*; SL 8:4)
Child, the learned and the adult have (spiritually) no advantage over the simple and the
•PP 79 (see also LM 103; PP 75*)
❖ PP 5:7 (see also LM 19:7; PP 5:5*)
Childhood—see also Youth
Childhood, dreams of, and the dreams of adolescence have much in common— but boyhood stretches between them

like an alien territory
•SJ 71-72 ❖ SJ 5:1, 2

Childhood listed as one of the avenues for experience of the Numinous
•PP 24-25 ❖ PP 1:16

Childhood: "I fancy that most of those who think at all have done a great deal of their thinking in the first fourteen years"
•SJ 63 ❖ SJ 4:10

Childhood, in our, we already had spiritual experiences as pure and momentous as any we have undergone since
•PP 79 (see also PP 24-25; SJ chapters 1-5) ❖ PP 5:7 (see also PP 1:16; SJ chapters 1-5)

Childhood, Lewis's: "I am a product of long corridors, empty sunlit rooms, upstairs indoor silences, attics explored in solitude...Also, of endless books"
•SJ 10 ❖ SJ 1:8

Childhood, the short but seemingly immemorial "always" of
•FL 56 (see also L 266)
❖ FL 3:6 (see also L 8 Feb 56)

Childhood, you and I who still enjoy fairy tales have less reason to wish, back; we have kept its pleasures and added some grown-up ones as well
•LAL 17 ❖ LAL Jun 22d 53

Child-rearing—consider also Child(ren); Father(s); Family; Mother(s); Motherhood; Youth

Child-rearing: Affection of a parent may degenerate into a continued and ruthless demand for sympathy, affection, and appreciation
•GID 285 (see also FL 64-65, 73-76)
❖ GID III 3:7 (see also FL 3:18, 33-36)

Child-rearing: Human beings must be trained in obedience almost before they have moral intuitions*
•WG 36-37 (see also L 179)
❖ (see also L 26 Mar 40)

Child-rearing: Importance of courtesy of parents toward children (especially young adults)
•FL 66 (see also GID 282-286)
❖ (see also GID III ch. 3)

Child-rearing involves a Gift-love which must work toward its own abdication; we must aim at making ourselves superfluous
•FL 76 ❖ FL 3:37

Child-rearing: Parents are not Providence; their bad intentions may be frustrated as their good ones (re: not giving a child religious education)
•LAL 32 ❖ LAL Sep 19/54

Child-rearing: Parents who "live for their family" may not be doing their family a favor (re: Gift-love based on a need to be needed)
•FL 73-77, 82-83 (see also L 198-199*; MC 167*; SL 121*, 123*)
❖ FL 3:33-37, 45 (see also L undated letter just before 20 Jan 42*; MC IV 7:3*; SL 26:2, 5*)

Child-rearing: The process of being brought up, however well it is done, cannot fail to offend
•CR 92 ❖ CR 7:20

Children—see also Family members; Loved ones

Children calling parents by their first names a perverse practice
•WG 111 ❖ WG 7:7

Children, effect of books on: Certain bad elements may not have as profound an effect as we may fear
•CR 32-33 ❖ CR 2:53

Children: "Every child is sometimes infuriating; most children are not infrequently odious" (re: opportunities for practising tolerance and forgiveness)
•FL 186 ❖ FL 6:37

Children, happiness of our: We would rather see them suffer much than be happy in contemptible and estranging modes (like God, with us)
•PP 41 ❖ PP 3:8

Children: "Hardly any amount of oppression from above takes the heart out of a boy like oppression from his fellows"
•SJ 31 ❖ SJ 2:11

Children, modern, are poor creatures; they keep asking Maureen, "What shall we do now?"

•L 169 ❖ L 18 Sep 39

Children, parents' anxiety about, "being a credit to them" is nothing compared to the anxiety of children that their parents should not be an absolute disgrace
•L 172 ❖ L 3 Dec 39

Children (quote from E. Nesbitt): "Grownups know that children can believe almost anything; that's why they tell you that the earth is round..."
•L 113 ❖ L 30 Mar 27

Children, religious education for, often has exactly the opposite effect to that which was intended; how many hard atheists come from pious homes
•LAL 32 ❖ LAL Sep 19/54

Children suffer not (I think) less than their elders, but differently (re: Lewis's grief on the loss of his mother)
•SJ 18-19 ❖ SJ 1:20

Children, when Christ said we were to be like, He did not mean we were to be fools; He wants a child's heart, but a grown-up's head
•MC 74-75 ❖ MC III 2:4

Children who lose parents in a divorce, letter regarding
•L 221 ❖ L 22 Sep 49

Children's literature: My knowledge of it is really very limited...
•L 304 ❖ L 31 Jul 62

Chocolate, analogy of boy asking whether sex involves eating, to our wondering whether heaven will be like things we know on earth
•M 160 (see also WG 67-69*)
❖ M 16:28 (see also WG 4:22-24*)

Choice—see also Freedom of choice; Free will

Choice, before God closed in on me I was offered what now appears a moment of wholly free
•SJ 224 (see also GID 261)
❖ SJ 14:16 (see also GID II 16:19-22)

Choice: Choosing self as the center rather than God is the basic sin behind all particular sins
•PP 75 ❖ PP 5:5

Choice, every moral, involves two things:

1) the act of choosing, and 2) the feelings and impulses which are the raw material of one's choice
•MC 84 ❖ MC III 4:4

Choice, God created us with the power of
•MC 52-53 ❖ MC II 3:2-5

Choice itself would soon cease if God removed by miracle the results of each wrong choice
•PP 71 (see also PP 34)
❖ PP 5:1 (see also PP 2:15)

Choice: Our power to choose marks the difference between the Laws of Nature (e.g., gravity) and the Law of Human Nature
•MC 18 ❖ MC I 1:3-4

Choice (quote from Law): "If you have not chosen the Kingdom of God, it will make in the end no difference what you have chosen instead"
•WG 131 ❖ WG 9:11

Choice: The efficacy of prayer cannot be either asserted or denied without an exercise of the will—choosing or rejecting faith
•M 180-181 ❖ M App. B:20, 21

Choice, today is our chance to make the right; it will not last forever
•MC 66 ❖ MC II 5:9

Choice, we have a, whether to respond to Christ
•GID 87-88 (see also M 93-94*)
❖ GID I 9:11 (see also M 11:19, 20*)

Choice, we have the power of; God won't alter people's character against their will
•GID 152-153 ❖ GID I 18:5

Choice which could lead to scoundrelism will come, when it does come, in no very dramatic colours
•WG 101-102 ❖ WG 6:12

Choices—see also Decisions; Moral decisions; Moral judgements

Choices, little, are of infinite importance since good and evil increase at compound interest
•MC 117 (see also RP 136)
❖ MC III 9:8 (see also RP 12:16)

Choices of life, Lewis describes, as choices between crosses: "The more one can

accept that fact...the less, I believe, one suffers"*
- LAL 96 ❖ LAL 9 Jan 61

Choices, Screwtape advocates leading humans to believe that their wrong, are trivial and revocable
- SL 53-54 ❖ SL 12:1

Choices, small, for right or wrong slowly turn our central self into a heavenly or a hellish creature
- MC 86-87, 107 (see also WG 102-103) ❖ MC III 4:8, 9; 7:9 (see also WG 6:12)

Choices, tempters try to elicit small wrong, which later harden into habit and then into evil principles
- SL 156-157; WLN 54-55 ❖ SL 32:10; WLN 4:10

Choices, there are only three: 1) to be God, 2) to be like God and to share His goodness in creaturely response, and 3) to be miserable
- PP 53-54 ❖ PP 3:19

Choir boys singing without personal emotion as an image that comes to mind while reading the Psalms, side by side with images of creatures full of emotion
- CR 114 (see also CR 121) ❖ CR 10:1 (see also CR 10:14)

Choir music—consider Hymns; Music, church

Choirs: Let them sing well or not at all ("Good works" had better also be good work)
- WLN 80 ❖ WLN 5:22

Chopin, music of, mentioned ("Preludes")
- L 28 ❖ L undated letter just after letter of Oct 1915

"Chosen people," Hebrews' claim to be, is strong
- CR 116-117 ❖ CR 10:4-6

"Chosen people" not chosen for their own sake but for the sake of the unchosen
- M 118 (see also GID 85) ❖ M 14:18 (see also GID I 9:7)

Chosen people obtain burden as well as blessing
- GID 84-85; M 116, 118 ❖ GID I 9:7, 8; M 14:15, 18

"Chosen people," we do not like the idea of a; we prefer to think that all nations and individuals start level in the search for God
- GID 84; M 116 ❖ GID I 9:7; M 14:15

Christ—see also Jesus

Christ addresses Himself to the savage, the child, and the poet in each of us no less than to the philosopher, etc. (re: Christ as Perfect Myth and Perfect Fact)
- GID 67; M 133-134 (ftnt.) ❖ GID I 5:13; M 15:2 (ftnt.)

Christ also experienced the absence of God the Father in a time of difficulty— "Why hast thou forsaken me?"
- GO 5 (see also LAL 38, 77; LM 43-44) ❖ GO 1:8 (see also LAL 20/2/55; Jul 21st 58; LM 8:10-12)

Christ as Bridegroom to the Church
- RP 128-132 ❖ RP 12:9, 10

Christ as Priest-King prefigured by the mysterious Melchizedek
- RP 122-124 ❖ RP 12:4, 5

Christ as the archetypal Man in whose suffering, resurrection, and victories all men (unless they refuse) can share
- RP 133-134 ❖ RP 12:12

Christ as the center of all doctrines and truth*
- GID 103 (see also GID 37) ❖ GID I 10:50 (see also GID I 2:15)

Christ as the perfect Penitent
- MC 56-61 ❖ MC II ch. 4

Christ as well as man received divine virtue by imitation
- CR 5-6 ❖ CR 1:6-10

Christ, birth of: For those who first read the Psalms about the birth of Christ, that birth primarily meant something very militant—the hero, champion
- RP 124-125 ❖ RP 12:5

Christ, death and resurrection of, echoed in the Natural world
- GID 82-84, 86 (see also GID 37; M 98, 111-116, 125, 130*, 161; PP 149*; RP 106-107) ❖ GID I 9:4-6, 8 (see also GID I 2:15; M 12:7; 14:5-14, 29, 35*; 16:29; PP 10:7*; RP 10:11)

Christ, death of—see Death of Christ

Christ did not die for men because of their merit, but because He is love and He loves infinitely
•M 52 (*see also* M 122; WLN 86)
❖ M 7:14 (*see also* M 14:24; WLN 6:10)

Christ did not preach any brand-new morality; the Golden Rule sums up what everyone had always known to be right
•MC 78 (*see also* CR 47, 51, 53, 77; MC 19; PP 63; RP 27; Law of Nature; book *The Abolition of Man*)
❖ MC III 3:1 (*see also* CR 4:7, 17, 22; 6:16; MC I 1:7; PP 4;10; RP 3:13; Law of Nature; book *The Abolition of Man*)

Christ died for men, not for societies or states
•WG 117 (*see also* GID 109-110; MC 73; WG 19; WLN 68)
❖ WG 7:16 (*see also* GID I 12:3; MC III 1:9; WG 1:15; WLN 4:39)

Christ died for men precisely because men are *not* worth dying for; to make them worth it
•WLN 86 (*see also* M 52, 122)
❖ WLN 6:10 (*see also* M 7:14; 14:24)

Christ died, not for valuable men, but for sinners—human souls whose value, out of relation to God, is zero
•WG 115 (*see also* WLN 53)
❖ WG 7:14 (*see also* WLN 4:8)

Christ, earthly life of, involved the killing of His human desires at every turn
•MC 155 ❖ MC IV 5:5

Christ: either God or a complete lunatic
•GID 101, 157-158, 261- 262; L 181; M 109; MC 55-56; PP 23-24; RP 135-136; WG 91 ❖ GID I 10:46; 19:3; II 16:23, 24; L 26 Mar 40; M 14:2; MC II 3:12, 13; PP 1:14; RP 12:15; WG 5:23

Christ: "...every mode of human excellence is implicit in his historical human character" although not all were fully developed
•CR 3 ❖ CR 1:5

Christ gave us an example of how to treat the wicked whose wickedness has not "paid"—e.g., the poor and miserable outcasts of society
•RP 68-69 ❖ RP 7:5

Christ, goodness of, led to His death because of the nature of goodness and the nature of this world
•RP 105 ❖ RP 10:10

Christ has ascended into Heaven, and in due time will become the Conqueror and Ruler of all things, including death and the devil (re: Psalm 8)
•RP 133 ❖ RP 12:11

Christ Himself is the true Word of God; Bible will bring us to Him
•L 247 ❖ L 8 Nov 52

Christ: How if He were mistaken, and the Being He called Father was horribly different from what He had supposed?
•GO 34 ❖ GO 2:24

Christ, humanity of, as a permanent thing seems understressed, as if He once became a man and then reverted to being simply God
•RP 134 (*see also* M 123)
❖ RP 12:13 (*see also* M 14:26)

Christ: I certainly think He was not omniscient, if only because a human brain would not be capable of omniscient consciousness
•PP 134 (*see also* MC 147-148; WLN 99)
❖ PP 9:6 (*see also* MC IV 3:10; WLN 7:10)

Christ, imitation of—*see* Imitation of Christ

Christ, in transcending and thus abrogating, also fulfills, both Paganism and Judaism
•RP 129 ❖ RP 12:9

Christ, incarnation of—*see* Incarnation

Christ is dimly present in the good side of even inferior teachers
•L 247 ❖ L 8 Nov 52

Christ is more than Balder, not less (as God is more than a god, not less); Incarnation transcends myth in conveying abstract reality to humans
•GID 67 (*see also* Myth of "dying god")
❖ GID I 5:13 (*see also* Myth of "dying god")

Christ is the Resurrection and the Life, because He was able to perform dying perfectly and thus defeat death

•M 130 ❖ M 14:35

Christ: "...it is difficult in reading the Gospels not to believe...that He smiled"
•CR 4 ❖ CR 1:5

Christ, it seems to me impossible to retain our belief in the Divinity of, while abandoning or neglecting the doctrine of the Second Coming
•WLN 93 ❖ WLN 7:1

Christ: Jewish convert tended to stress Christ as king and conqueror; Gentile more likely to start from the priestly sacrificial and intercessory role
•RP 124 ❖ RP 12:5

Christ, look for, and you will find Him—and with Him everything else thrown in
•MC 190 (see also GO 79*; MC 118-119)
❖ MC IV 11:15 (see also GO 4:21*; MC III 10:1)

Christ, mission of, like a diver recovering a precious object from deep slime
•GID 82; M 111-112 (see also M 135)
❖ GID I 9:4; M 14:5 (see also M 15:5)

Christ, our conception of what it will be like to be with, as symbolical as our conception of other aspects of Heaven
•WG 10 ❖ WG 1:8

Christ, pain or the threat of pain reminds me that my true good is in another world and my only real treasure is
•PP 106 ❖ PP 6:17

Christ, Passion of, as "the human situation writ large" (anxiety, suspense, hope, loneliness—even feeling forsaken by God)
•LM 42-44 (see also GO 5; LAL 38, 77)
❖ LM 8:6-12 (see also GO 5:8; LAL 20/2/55; Jul 21st 58)

Christ, Passion of: "The 'hiddenness' of God perhaps presses most painfully on those who are in another way nearest to Him..."
•LM 44 ❖ LM 8:12

Christ, perfection of, must be interpreted in a sense which admits of His feeling the full range of temptations
•L 189
❖ L undated letter just after 11 Aug 40

Christ, play as analogy to the union of two

natures—human and divine—in the Person of, (as when an author puts himself in a play as one of the characters)
•CR 171-172 ❖ CR 14:30-32

Christ, return of—see Second Coming of Christ

Christ, story of, demands from us not only a religious and historical response but also an imaginative response; it is a Myth which became Fact
•GID 67; M 133-134 (ftnt.)
❖ GID I 5:13; M 15:2 (ftnt.)

Christ: The fact that He denied all sin of Himself is no small argument of His Deity
•RP 135-136 (see also GID 157)
❖ RP 12:15 (see also GID I 19:2)

Christ: The fact that He forgave sins is an argument for His Deity
•GID 157; MC 55
❖ GID I 19:2; MC II 3:11

Christ: The idea of His priesthood involves the recognition of a priesthood independent of and superior to Aaron's
•RP 123-124 ❖ RP 12:4, 5

Christ, the union between God and Nature in the Person of, admits no divorce; He will not go out of Nature again...
•M 123 (see also RP 134)
❖ M 14:26 (see also RP 12:13)

Christ, those who have heard the claims of, must come to terms with them—or else be guilty of inattention or evasion
•GID 265-266 ❖ GID II 16:50

Christ, thoughts regarding the temptations felt by
•L 189-191
❖ L undated letter just after 11 Aug 40

Christ was not a kind of composite being but "perfect God and perfect man"
•L 191 (see also L 210)
❖ L undated letter just after 11 Aug 40 (see also L undated letter of 1947)

Christ: What He may have meant when He said that the Son does only what He sees the Father doing

•CR 6 ❖ CR 1:9

Christ, what the risen body of, reveals about life after death
•M 145-163 ❖ M 16:5-32

Christ, why the death of, was necessary ("...no explanation will ever be quite adequate to the reality")
•MC 56-61 (see also Atonement)
❖ MC II ch. 4 (see also Atonement)

Christ: You cannot fit His earthly life into any time-relations with His life as God
•MC 147-148 ❖ MC IV 3:10

Christendom must fully confess its specific contribution to the sum of human cruelty and treachery
•FL 49 ❖ FL 2:43

Christendom, reunion of—see Reunion

Christendom still an immensely formidable unity despite many divisions
•GID 204 ❖ GID II 4:6

Christian, a more complete enjoyment of literature as one of the materialistic gains of being a
•L 173 (see also L 143*, 181-182)
❖ L 18 Dec 39 (see also L 24 Oct 31*; 26 Mar 40)

Christian, advice to a new: "You've only just enlisted. Don't go off challenging enemy champions"
•L 241 ❖ L 15 May 52

Christian Apologetics (chapter title)
•GID 89-103 ❖ GID I ch. 10

"Christian" as a term of description will become a useless word if we spiritualize its meaning
•MC 11 ❖ MC P:13-14

"Christian" as a term of description has come to include almost no idea of belief; usually a vague term of approval
•GID 97 ❖ GID I 10:24

"Christian" as a word which has a deep, ambiguous, disputable and (for many purposes) useless sense; also a shallower, clear, useful sense
•L 288-289 ❖ L 8 Sep 59

Christian Behaviour (Book III of Mere Christianity)
•MC 69-131 ❖ MC Book III

Christian belief which is purely a result of conditioning mentioned by Screwtape

•SL 110-111 ❖ SL 24:1

Christian belief—see also Beliefs

Christian beliefs ("What Christians Believe"—Book II of Mere Christianity)
•MC 43-66 ❖ MC Book II

Christian Church—see Church

Christian, every, is to become a little Christ
•MC 153 (see also Imitation of Christ)
❖ MC IV 4:10 (see also Imitation of Christ)

Christian faith, Lewis describes how he lost his, in his youth
•SJ 58-70 (see also PP 13-15)
❖ SJ 4:4-20 (see also PP 1:1)

Christian growth—see Growth, Christian

Christian has a great advantage over other men, not by being less fallen but by knowing that he is a fallen man in a fallen world
•WLN 77 ❖ WLN 5:15

Christian history: Christendom must fully confess its specific contribution to the sum of human cruelty and treachery
•FL 49 ❖ FL 2:43

Christian, I ceased to be a, at "Chartres" (Lewis's boarding school in Wyvern, England)
•SJ 58 ❖ SJ 4:4

"Christian," I have used the word, to mean one who accepts the common doctrines of Christianity
•MC 9, 11 ❖ MC P:11, 14

Christian idea of God is the only one on the market if you are looking for something superpersonal—something more than a person
•MC 141 ❖ MC IV 2:2

Christian, if you are a, you do not have to believe that all the other religions are simply wrong all through
•MC 43 (see also GID 54, 132; SJ 235)
❖ MC II 1:1 (see also GID I 4:27; 16:4; SJ 15:7)

Christian is not a man who never goes wrong, but a man who is enabled to repent
•MC 64 ❖ MC II 5:6

Christian is to Christ as a mirror to an object; divine virtue received by imitation and reflection

•CR 5-6 (*see also* Mirror/s)
❖ CR 1:8-10 (*see also* Mirror/s)
Christian, Jewish, and Moslem view of the universe is that there is something beyond Nature which refutes the scientists' picture of futility
•CR 59 ❖ CR 5:5
Christian, Lewis mentions some of the factors which caused him to become a, (or at least a supernaturalist)*
•CR 41 ❖ CR 3:9
Christian, Lewis observes that even as an atheist the authors he most enjoyed were
•SJ 213-214 ❖ SJ 14:3
Christian life—*consider also* Activities; Christianity, practice of; Life
Christian life: "...a Christian is not a man who never goes wrong, but a man who is enabled to repent..."
•MC 64 ❖ MC II 5:5
Christian life: Activities of religion as an end in themselves are infinitely dangerous*
•LM 30 (*see also* RP 57-58; SL 35)
❖ LM 6:4-6 (*see also* RP 6:6, 7; SL 7:4)
Christian life ("Christ-life") is spread by three things: baptism, belief, and Holy Communion
•MC 62-65 ❖ MC II 5:1-7
Christian life consists of doing most of the same things as before, but in a new spirit
•WG 23 ❖ WG 2:5
Christian life defends us from the collective, not by isolating us, but by making us organs in the mystical Body
•WG 116 (*see also* Collective)
❖ WG 7:16 (*see also* Collective)
Christian life, goal of—*see* Goal of Christian life
Christian life: If we share in the life of Christ, we shall catch the kind of life He has (and spread it to other men) by what I call "good infection"
•MC 153 (*see also* MC 157, 162, 163, 186) ❖ MC IV 4:8-10 (*see also* MC IV 5:8; 7:5, 8; 11:7)
Christian life: In all of us God still holds

only a part; there is, we have to admit, a line of demarcation between God's part in us and the enemy's region*
•LM 31 ❖ LM 6:8
Christian life is a school where they can always use your previous work whatever subject it was on
•SJ 146 ❖ SJ 9:22
Christian life, life at a vile boarding school is in a way a good preparation for the, in that it teaches one to live by hope and faith
•SJ 36-37 ❖ SJ 2:16
Christian life, necessity of daily devotions in
•GID 266 (*see also* L 220; MC 124, 168-169*; SJ 226*; WG 132*) ❖ GID II 16:52, 53 (*see also* L undated letter between 6 Sep 49 and 22 Sep 49; MC III 11:6; IV 8:8*; SJ 14:20*; WG 9:13*)
Christian life, practical aspects of
•MC 160-166 ❖ MC IV ch. 7
Christian life, Screwtape lists obstacles to perseverance in: ("The routine of adversity, the gradual decay of youthful loves and youthful hopes...")*
•SL 132 ❖ SL 28:1
Christian life, Screwtape mentions the law of Undulation which refers to the human tendency to experience peaks and troughs, especially in the
•SL 36-39 (*see also* SL 40-44)
❖ SL ch. 8 (*see also* SL ch. 9)
Christian life, Screwtape speaks about the periods of "dryness" humans may experience in their, which he calls the "Troughs"
•SL 13-14, 36-44 ❖ SL 2:3; ch. 8, 9
Christian life: "The Christian thinks any good he does comes from the Christ-life inside him"
•MC 64 ❖ MC II 5:6
Christian life, things that can help us in our: rational thinking, advice of good friends and good books, etc.*
•WG 129-130 ❖ WG 9:8
Christian life, whole basis of, is to "put on Christ"; Christianity offers nothing else at all
•MC 166, 169-170 ❖ MC IV 8:1, 10

Christian literature—*see* Literature, Christian

Christian Marriage (chapter title)
•MC 95-103 ❖ MC III ch. 6

Christian may come to feel he is part of an "inner ring" (vis-a-vis "the unbelievers") and thus develop a form of Spiritual Pride
•SL 110-113 (*see also* RP 65; SL 34)
❖ SL 24:1-5 (*see also* RP 6:14; SL 7:2)

Christian movements always excite opposition eventually; claims of real Christianity are offensive to the World (re: Christian revival at Oxford)
•GID 222-223 ❖ GID II 8:12

Christian outlook described: "...men who see this world as the vestibule of eternity, who regard pride as the greatest of the sins [etc.]"*
•GID 219 ❖ GID II 8:3

Christian political parties, problems inherent in the creation of
•GID 196-199 (*see also* WG 114)
❖ GID II ch. 3 (*see also* WG 7:12)

Christian regeneration—*see* New Birth

Christian revival, current, may be a fad ("Fashion")
•GID 222 ❖ GID II 8:11

Christian "revival": Ease of getting an audience for discussion of "religion" does not prove that more people are becoming religious
•GID 250 ❖ GID II 14:2

Christian revival: If real, it works slowly and obscurely in small groups
•GID 222 ❖ GID II 8:11

Christian Scientists mentioned
•L 257 ❖ L 1 Nov 54 (first letter)

Christian story has neither the monolithic grandeur of Unitarian conceptions nor the richness of Polytheism (re: Christian theology as "poetry")
•WG 75 ❖ WG 5:5

Christian theology—*see* Theology

Christian universe, the horror of, was that it had no door marked "Exit"; the materialist's universe was attractive because it offered limited liabilities
•SJ 171 (*see also* GO 33; Limited liabilities) ❖ SJ 11:8 (*see also* GO 2:22; Limited liabilities)

Christian vs. Jewish picture of Judgement: One cries to God for mercy instead of justice; the other cries to God for justice instead of injustice
•RP 9-19, esp. 10-12
❖ RP ch. 2, esp. 2:3-6

Christian vs. Jewish attitude in the face of Judgement: Psalmists exhibit Jewish confidence; the Christian trembles because he knows he is a sinner
•CR 122-125, esp. 125
❖ CR 10:22- 30, esp. 10:29, 30

Christian vs. pantheistic view of God
•M 81-94; MC 43-45 (*see also* Pantheism) ❖ M ch. 11; MC II 1:3, 4 (*see also* Pantheism)

"Christian," whether to classify certain denominations (e.g., Quakers) as, is a linguistic, not a religious question
•L 288-289 ❖ L 8 Sep 59

Christians and soldiers are still men; neither conversion nor enlistment in the army is really going to obliterate our human life (re: learning in war-time)
•WG 23-24 ❖ WG 2:5, 6

Christians cannot be judged simply by comparing the *product*; you need to know what kind of raw material Christ is working on (tooth paste analogy)
•GID 59; MC 177-178 (*see also* L 242*)
❖ GID I 4:46-52 (Ques. 12); MC IV 10:5 (*see also* L 28 May 52*)

Christians, common grounds which unite "mere": their belief in Creation, Fall, Incarnation, Second Coming, and Four Last Things
•GID 336 (*see also* Christianity, "mere") ❖ GID IV Letter 9 (*see also* Christianity, "mere")

Christians do not even agree on the importance of their disagreements
•MC 8 ❖ MC P:6

Christians in modern England often feel, as the Psalmists did, the ineffectiveness of their cause
•CR 127 ❖ CR 10:37

Christians increasingly live on a spiritual island; we shall perhaps find increas-

ing reasons to value God's Law over the current ways of thinking
●RP 64-65 (*see also* SL 110-113)
❖ RP 6:14 (*see also* SL 24:1-5)
Christians' ineffectiveness in this world a result of ceasing to think of the next
●MC 118 (*see also* GID 150*)
❖ MC III 10:1 (*see also* GID I 17:7*)
Christians, liberal—*see* Liberal Christians
Christians, "Modernist"—*see* Modernist
Christians, our life as, begins by being baptised into a death; our most joyous festivals centre upon the broken body and the shed blood
●RP 52 ❖ RP 5:10
Christians vs. non-Christians: If Christianity is true, why aren't the Christians all nicer?
●MC 175-183 ❖ MC IV ch. 10
Christianity, a description of the origin of, (and of all developed religion)
●PP 16-25 ❖ PP 1:4-17
Christianity always remains intellectually possible but never intellectually compulsive; probably when this ceases to be so, the world will be ending
●WLN 92 (*see also* WLN 28)
❖ WLN 6:28 (*see also* WLN 2:16)
Christianity and Culture (chapter title)
●CR 12-36 ❖ CR ch. 2
Christianity and Hinduism as the only two religions which could possibly be the maturity of Paganism
●SJ 235-236 (*see also* CR 71; GID 102, 132) ❖ SJ 15:7 (*see also* CR 5:26; GID I 10:49; 16:4)
Christianity and Hinduism as "the two serious options for an adult mind"
●CR 71 ❖ CR 5:26
Christianity and Hinduism the only two things worth considering; most other religions are heresies of these
●GID 102 ❖ GID I 10:49
Christianity and Literature (chapter title)
●CR 1-11 ❖ CR ch. 1
"Christianity And..." mentioned by Screwtape as the desired alternative to "mere Christianity" which is troublesome to his cause

●SL 115-116 (*see also* GID 60*)
❖ SL 25:1 (*see also* GID I 4:56 Ques. 14*)
Christianity and other religions can hardly avoid coincidental ideas
●WG 82-83 (*consider also* Islam; Judaism; Mythology) ❖ WG 5:15 (*consider also* Islam; Judaism; Mythology)
Christianity and politics, Screwtape discusses a profitable relationship between, from his point of view
●SL 108-109 ❖ SL 23:4
Christianity and "Religion" (chapter title)
●M 81-94 ❖ M ch. 11
Christianity and the doctrine of the Incarnation works into our minds differently from the way other belief systems do
●M 131 ❖ M 14:36
Christianity-and-water: "Do not attempt to water Christianity down. There must be no pretence that you can have it with the Supernatural left out"*
●GID 99 (*see also* GID 260; L 170)
❖ GID I 10:41 (*see also* GID II 16:12; L 8 Nov 39)
Christianity-and-water, the view which says there is a God in Heaven and everything is all right, is too simple
●MC 46-48 (*see also* LM 75-76; SL 73-74) ❖ MC II 2:1-5 (*see also* LM 14:13; SL 16:3)
Christianity, Answers to Questions on (chapter title)
●GID 48-62 (*see also* GID 258-267)
❖ GID I ch. 4 (*see also* GID II ch. 16)
Christianity anticipated by Paganism
●RP 37-38 (*see also* GID 132; SJ 235-236; Death and Rebirth; Paganism)
❖ RP 4:8 (*see also* GID I 16:4; SJ 15:7; Death and Rebirth; Paganism)
Christianity, argument against, based on size is a primitive error
●GID 39-41, 74-75; M 48-54 (*see also* PP 13) ❖ GID I 3:4-6; 7:29-41; M 7:7-17 (*see also* PP 1:1)
Christianity, arguments for and against other life in the universe both used as arguments against
●CR 174; M 50; WLN 83-84
❖ CR 14:46; M 7:10; WLN 6:1-3

Christianity as a "myth" which has outlived all of its defenders and all of its adversaries
•GID 63-67 (see also Myth)
❖ GID I ch. 5 (see also Myth)

Christianity as it relates to politics and economics discussed briefly
•MC 78-83 ❖ MC III 3:2-8

Christianity as one of the only two religions which could possibly be the maturity of Paganism (the other is Hinduism)
•SJ 235 (see also CR 71; GID 102)
❖ SJ 15:7 (see also CR 5:26; GID I 10:49)

Christianity as the completion of other religions such as paganism
•GID 132 (see also SJ 235-236; Death and Rebirth pattern; Paganism)
❖ GID I 16:4 (see also SJ 15:7; Death and Rebirth pattern; Paganism)

Christianity as the tradition in which we may most reasonably believe we have the consummation of all religion
•GID 144 ❖ GID I 16:26

Christianity as Truth: always complex, as is reality (re: the knotty and ambiguous doctrine of Hell)*
•PP 119 (see also M 165; Reality)
❖ PP 8:3 (see also M 17:2; Reality)

Christianity as Truth: an account of facts, not just a patent medicine
•GID 108-109 (see also GID 101)
❖ GID I 12:1 (see also GID I 10:48)

Christianity as Truth: "If it were true, what it tells us would be bound to be difficult"
•MC 137 (see also M 85-86)
❖ MC IV 1:9 (see also M 11:7)

Christianity as Truth: It is not merely good advice, good for society, etc.; it is the Truth
•GID 90-91, 101-102; MC 137; SL 108-109*
❖ GID I 10:5, 48; MC IV 1:6; SL 23:4*

Christianity as Truth not transparent to reason; we could not have invented it ourselves; it has the rough, male taste of reality
•PP 25 ❖ PP 1:16

Christianity as Truth: We could make it easier if we were making it up
•MC 145 (see also MC 46-48) ❖ MC IV 2:17 (see also MC II 2:2, 4, 5; IV 1:9)

Christianity as Truth will never be fully comprehensible; much will remain puzzling to the end
•L 181 ❖ L 26 Mar 40

Christianity asserts that God is good; that He made all things good, but that one of those things, free will, included the possibility of evil
•PP 69 ❖ PP 5:1

Christianity both world-affirming and world-denying
•GID 147-150 ❖ GID I ch. 17

Christianity cannot operate as a bribe (in its offer of eternal life)
•GID 131 (see also FL 189-190; LM 120; PP 145*; RP 42; SJ 231; WG 3-5)
❖ GID I 16:3 (see also FL 6:42; LM 22:8; PP 10:2*; RP 4:17; SJ 15:3; WG 1:1-3)

Christianity, case against: If Christianity is true, why aren't the Christians all nicer?
•MC 175-183 ❖ MC IV ch. 10

Christianity, case against, quite strong due to the problem of pain
•GID 265 ❖ GID II 16:47

Christianity, Case for, (original title for the first book included in Mere Christianity)
•MC 17-66 ❖ MC I ch. 1-10

Christianity ("Christendom") must fully confess its specific contribution to the sum of human cruelty and treachery
•FL 49 ❖ FL 2:43

Christianity ("Christendom") still an immensely formidable unity despite many divisions
•GID 204 ❖ GID II 4:6

Christianity, common reproach against: Its dogmas are unchanging, while human knowledge is in continual growth
•GID 38 ❖ GID I 3:1

Christianity, defenders of, opposed not by irreligion but by vague, Pantheistic religion
•M 81 (see also Religion, minimal; Pantheism) ❖ M 11:2 (see also Religion,

minimal; Pantheism)

Christianity defined: "...the faith preached by the Apostles, attested by the Martyrs, embodied in the Creeds, expounded by the Fathers"*
•GID 90 ❖ GID I 10:4

Christianity defines the world as enemy-occupied territory; tells how the rightful king has landed
•MC 51 ❖ MC II 2:11, 12

Christianity, demands of, offensive to the World
•GID 222-223 ❖ GID II 8:12

Christianity demands only that we set right a *misdirection* of our nature, unlike other systems (Buddhism) which require mortification of the total nature
•PP 104 ❖ PP 6:15

Christianity directly opposed to the World
•GID 265 ❖ GID II 16:46

Christianity dismissed by some as being a substitute for the real well-being we have failed to achieve on earth; this theory has a great deal of plausibility
•CR 37-38 (see entire chapter)
❖ CR 3:2 (see entire chapter)

Christianity dismissed on the grounds that it is "wish-fulfillment" illogical; "...our wishes may favour either side or both"
•WLN 18-20 (*see also* GID 272-274; GO 45; SJ 171, 172, 203*)
❖ WLN 2:8 (*see also* GID III 1:5-7; GO 3:9; SJ 11:7, 9; 13:10*)

Christianity dismissed on the grounds that for some it is tainted with desire for personal gain does not help us decide whether it is true or not
•GID 273-274 ❖ GID III 1:7

Christianity, divisions within—*see also* Divisions

Christianity, divisions within and without: Those who are at the heart of each division are all closer to one another than those who are at the fringes*
•LAL 11-12 (*see also* GID 60; MC 9)
❖ LAL Nov 10th 52 (*see also* GID I 4:56—Ques. 14; MC P:9)

Christianity does not avoid being poetical; all world views yield poetry to those who believe them by the mere fact of being believed
•WG 81-82 (*see also* CR 136)
❖ WG 5:13 (*see also* CR 11:16)

Christianity does not begin by offering comfort, but dismay (the diagnosis of sin)
•MC 39 (*see also* GID 58, 243-244; L 193; PP 55*; WLN 19) ❖ MC I 5:4 (*see also* GID I 4:45—Ques. 11; II 12:6; L 15 May 41; PP 4:1*) WLN 2:8)

Christianity does not help us if it brings no healing to the impotent will; a mere statement of the highest ethical principles is not enough
•GID 328-329 ❖ GID IV Letter 4

Christianity does not involve the belief that all things were made for man; man technically insignificant
•M 51 ❖ M 7:11, 12

Christianity does not offer earthly comfort; there is no earthly comfort in the long run*
•FL 190 (*see also* GO 28-30; L 290; LAL 49) ❖ FL 6:43 (*see also* GO 2:13-16; L 3 Dec 59; LAL 16/12/55)

Christianity does not replace technical knowledge; when it tells you to feed the hungry, it doesn't give you lessons in cookery
•GID 48 ❖ GID I 4:1

Christianity does not simply replace our natural life and substitute a new one; it exploits our natural activities to its own ends
•WG 25 (*consider also* Personality)
❖ WG 2:8 (*consider also* Personality)

Christianity does not tell of a human search for God, but of something done by God for, to, and about Man
•M 116 (*see also* GID 144, top; M 83; PP 51; SJ 227) ❖ M 14:15 (*see also* GID I 16:26; M 11:4; PP 3:17; SJ 14:21)

Christianity does not want us to reduce by one atom the hatred we feel for cruelty and treachery (re: forgiveness)
•MC 106 ❖ MC III 7:6

Christianity enables us to love the world better

•GID 150 (*see also* World)

❖ GID I 17:7 (*see also* World)

Christianity: Error of thinking it is a private affair often reacted to by the opposite error of making it a collective affair

•WG 108 ❖ WG 7:3

Christianity, evidence or "proof" of—*see* Proof; *consider* Doubt

Christianity, externals of, made no appeal to my sense of beauty; Christianity for me was mainly associated with ugly architecture, music, and poetry

•SJ 171-172 ❖ SJ 11:8

Christianity: greatest truth or greatest fraud

•GID 111-112 ❖ GID I 12:9

Christianity, Is, Hard or Easy? (chapter title)

•MC 166-170 ❖ MC IV ch. 8

Christianity has nothing to say to those who feel no need of forgiveness

•MC 38-39 (*see also* CR 46-47; GID 95, 181, 243-244; PP 55-58)

❖ MC I 5:4 (*see also* CR 4:7; GID I 10:15, 22:13, II 12:6, 7; PP 4:1-4)

Christianity: Here the learned and the adult have no advantage over the simple and the child

•PP 79 (*see also* LM 103; PP 75*)

❖ PP 5:7 (*see also* LM 19:7; PP 5:5*)

Christianity, I believe in, as I believe that the Sun has risen—not only because I see it, but because by it I see everything else

•WG 92 (*see also* WG 69; M 110; SJ 180*; Sun) ❖ WG 5:24 (*see also* WG 4:24; M 14:3; SJ 11:19*; Sun)

Christianity: I can't believe that a belief against which so many and various defensive weapons have been found necessary is wholly lacking in plausibility

•WLN 18 ❖ WLN 2:7

Christianity: I *do* get that sudden feeling that the whole thing is hocus-pocus, but it hardly worries me now

•L 227 ❖ L 5 Mar 51

Christianity: If it is false, it is of no importance; if true, it is of infinite importance

•GID 101-102 (*see also* GID 108-109)

❖ GID I 10:48 (*see also* GID I 12:1)

Christianity: If it is only a mythology, it is not the one I like best; I like Greek, Irish, and Norse mythology much better

•WG 76 ❖ WG 5:6

Christianity: If it is true, why aren't all the Christians nicer than all the non-Christians?

•MC 175-183 (*see also* GID 59)

❖ MC IV ch. 10 (*see also* GID I 4:46-52)

Christianity, in a sense, creates rather than solves the problem of pain, for in the midst of a painful world it assures us that ultimate reality is loving

•PP 24 ❖ PP 1:15

Christianity, in modern English audiences one often encounters a, tainted with Pantheistic elements and theological vagueness

•GID 240-241 ❖ GID II 12:2

Christianity, in spite of its revolutionary and apocalyptic elements, can be delightfully humdrum about earning one's living (re: "cultural" occupations)

•CR 20 ❖ CR 2:23

Christianity, intellectual honesty regarding—*see* Intellectual dishonesty; Intellectual honesty

Christianity is addressed only to penitents, only to those who admit their disobedience to the known moral law

•CR 46-47 (*see also* GID 243-244; MC 38-39)

❖ CR 4:7 (*see also* GID II 12:6; MC I 5:4)

Christianity is always either doing, or repenting for not having done, all the things which secular humanitarianism enjoins

•GID 147 ❖ GID I 17:2

Christianity is as hard as nails and tender at the same time

•L 250 (*see also* MC 167-175; SJ 229)

❖ L 17 Jul 53 (*see also* MC IV 8:4-11; SJ 14:23)

Christianity: Is its attraction merely that of arousing and satisfying our imaginations?

•WG 74-75 ❖ WG 5:3

Christianity is like toothpaste—how much better it makes a person's teeth depends upon what they were like when he started brushing
•GID 59; MC 177-178 (see also L 242*)
❖ GID I 4:46-52 (Ques. 12); MC IV 10:5 (see also L 28 May 52*)

Christianity is the real text; Nature is only the commentary
•M 130 (see also GID 84*)
❖ M 14:35 (see also GID I 9:6*)

Christianity: It seems to me impossible to retain our belief in the Divinity of Christ while abandoning or neglecting the doctrine of the Second Coming
•WLN 93 ❖ WLN 7:1

Christianity, Lewis's philosophical steps toward conversion to, described
•WG 91-92 ❖ WG 5:23, 24

Christianity, Lewis's view of, as a youth—and the causes of his doubt
•SJ 62-66 ❖ SJ 4:9-12

Christianity, liberal—see Liberal Christianity

Christianity, magical element of, can never be reduced to zero; if it is, what remains is only morality, or culture, or philosophy (re: Holy Communion)
•LM 104 ❖ LM 19:11

Christianity makes demands on one, as does consistent atheism
•GID 250-251 (see also SJ 226)
❖ GID II 14:3 (see also SJ 14:19)

Christianity makes duty a self-transcending concept and endeavors to escape from the region of mere morality in its ethics
•CR 45 (see also GID 112, 144; LM 114-115; MC 130-131; PP 65*)
❖ CR 4:2 (see also GID I 12:10; 16:26; LM 21:11-13; MC III 12:9; PP 4:13*)

Christianity makes people either very much better or very much worse (e.g., record of persecution by "Christians")
•L 301 (see also L 164*; RP 28-32)
❖ L 20 Dec 61 (see also L 5 Apr 39*; RP 3:17-20)

Christianity may be the only safeguard against the dangers of increasing worldly collectivism
•WG 109 (see also Collective)
❖ WG 7:5 (see also Collective)

Christianity, "mere"—consider also Denominational differences; Doctrinal differences

Christianity, "mere," as the essence of the experience of Joy**
•GID 203-204 ❖ GID II 4:5

Christianity, "mere": Baxter mentioned as the coiner of the term "mere Christians"
•GID 336 ❖ GID IV Letter 9

Christianity, "mere," I have always in my books been concerned simply to put forward
•L 262 (see also PP 10)
❖ L 16 Mar 55 (see also PP P:2)

Christianity, "mere": "I have written as a member of the Church of England, but I have avoided controversial questions as much as possible"
•RP 7 ❖ RP 1:13

Christianity, "mere": Lewis lists the common grounds which unite "mere" Christians
•GID 336 ❖ GID IV Letter 9

Christianity, "mere," Lewis relates why he explains and defends only
•MC 6-9 ❖ MC P:2-9

Christianity, "mere," like a hall out of which doors open into several rooms
•MC 11-12 ❖ MC P:15-16

Christianity, "mere," mentioned by Screwtape as troublesome to his cause: "What we want...is to keep them in the state of mind I call 'Christianity And'"
•SL 115-116 ❖ SL 25:1

Christianity, "mere," not an alternative to the creeds of existing communions
•MC 11-12 ❖ MC P:15

Christianity, "mere": Standards for this are best acquired from old books
•GID 201 ❖ GID II 4:3

Christianity, "mere": Theological controversies must be put in their proper perspective by having a standard of plain, central ("mere") Christianity

•GID 201 ❖ GID II 4:3

Christianity, "mere," turns out to be no insipid interdenominational transparency, but something positive, self-consistent, and inexhaustible
•GID 203 ❖ GID II 4:5

Christianity, "mere": "When all is said (and truly said) about the divisions of Christendom, there remains, by God's mercy, an enormous common ground"
•CR vii—quote from unpublished letter ❖ CR P:1—quote from unpublished letter

Christianity, "Modernist"—see Modernist Christianity

Christianity must preach the diagnosis (of sin) before it can win a hearing for the cure
•GID 243-244; PP 55 (see also GID 95, 181-182; MC 38-39)
❖ GID II 12:6; PP 4:1 (see also GID I 10:15; 22:13; MC I 5:4)

Christianity never intended to dissipate the sense of our own nothingness; it comes to intensify it
•M 51 ❖ M 7:11

Christianity no longer needs to be feigned for social reasons; "that fact covers a good deal of what is called the decay of religion"
•GID 219-220, 253 ❖ GID II 8:5; 14:11

Christianity not a solitary religion; we must go to church
•L 224 (see also Church attendance)
❖ L 7 Dec 50 (see also Church attendance)

Christianity not a solitary religion; is already institutional in the earliest of its documents
•WG 106 ❖ WG 7:1

Christianity not believed because of its poetic attraction; "poetry," or aesthetic enjoyment, is the result and not the cause of belief
•WG 77-78 ❖ WG 5:9

Christianity not merely good advice for society; it is the truth
•GID 90-91, 101; MC 137; SL 108-109
❖ GID I 10:5; I 10:48; MC IV 1:6, 7; SL 23:4

Christianity not necessarily declining; social church-going declining
•GID 219-220 ❖ GID II 8:5

Christianity not the conclusion of a philosophical debate on the origins of the universe but a catastrophic historical event
•PP 24 ❖ PP 1:15

Christianity not the sort of religion anyone would have made up; has that "queer twist" of real things
•MC 46-48 (see also MC 137*, 145; M 165*; PP 25)
❖ MC II 2:2-5 (see also MC IV 1:9*; 2:16; M 17:2*; PP 1:16)

Christianity not transparent to reason; we could not have invented it ourselves
•PP 25 ❖ PP 1:16

Christianity offers the attractions neither of optimism nor of pessimism
•WG 75-76 (see also GID 52; SJ 204)
❖ WG 5:5 (see also GID I 4:18, 19 - Ques. 5; SJ 13:11)

Christianity offers us a refreshing return to inequality and opportunity for reverence
•WG 113, 116 (see also GID 84-85*)
❖ WG 7:10, 15 (see also GID I 9:7*)

Christianity, On the Transmission of (chapter title)
•GID 114-119 ❖ GID I ch. 13

Christianity, one Grand Miracle is the whole point of; in other religions the miraculous elements are not so essential
•GID 80 (see also M 68)
❖ GID I 9:1 (see also M 10:1)

Christianity, opposition to, may sometimes call itself "Christianity"*
•GID 223 ❖ GID II 8:13

Christianity, practical effect of, in this world: 1) Tries to make things better; 2) Fortifies us against what cannot be changed
•GID 49 ❖ GID I 4:6-8 (Ques. 2)

Christianity, practical effect of, in this world: It is in favour of all knowledge and all that will help the human race

•GID 57 (*see also* CR 58-59*; GID 55, 147-150; PP 113-114; WLN 111-112)
❖ GID I 4:40 (*see also* CR 5:4*; GID I 4:32, 33 [Ques. 9]; ch. 17; PP 7:4; WLN 7:33, 34)

Christianity, practice of—*see also* Christian life

Christianity, practice of, consists of the imitation of Christ—referring every experience, pleasant or unpleasant, to God and asking His will
•GID 50 (*see also* Imitation of Christ)
❖ GID I 4:11 (Ques. 3) (*see also* Imitation of Christ)

Christianity, practice of: "It is more like painting a portrait than like obeying a set of rules"
•MC 162 ❖ MC IV 7:5

Christianity, practice of, more important than what we preach
•L 261 (*see also* LAL 29*, 96*)
❖ L 2 Feb 55 (*see also* LAL March 31st 54; 24 Feb 61)

Christianity, practice of, much harder than preaching (re: humility)
•LAL 29 ❖ LAL Mar 31st 54

Christianity, practice of: Practice may be imperfect, yet the precept still profitable
•GID 283-284 ❖ GID III 3:4

Christianity, practice of: We must try in our own lives to be such good advertisements for Christianity as will make it attractive
•L 247 ❖ L 8 Nov 52

Christianity prefigured in mythology and Paganism
•GID 57-58, 66-67, 83-84, 132, 175; L 258; M 113-115, 133-134 (ftnt.); PP 25; RP 105-108; SJ 62, 223-224, 235-236; WG 82-84 ❖ GID I 4:42 (Ques. 10); 5:11-13; 9:5, 6; 16:4; 21:7; L 1 Nov 54; M 14:9-14; 15:2 (ftnt.); PP 1:16; RP 10:11, 12; SJ 4:9; 14:15; 15:7; WG 5:14, 15

Christianity prefigured in poetry and the romances
•L 143 ❖ L 24 Oct 31

Christianity primarily the fulfillment of the Jewish religion, but also the fulfillment of what was vaguely hinted

at in all religions at their best
•GID 54 (*see also* Death and Rebirth pattern; Paganism)
❖ GID I 4:27 (Ques. 8) (*see also* Death and Rebirth pattern; Paganism)

Christianity referred to as "the Christian mythology" by Lewis while a scholar at Oxford (prior to his becoming a Christian)
•SJ 214, 215 ❖ SJ 14:4, 5

Christianity, reunion of—*see* Reunion

Christianity, Screwtape discusses how, used merely as a means to social justice can work to the devil's advantage
•SL 108-109 (*see also* MC 137)
❖ SL 23:4 (*see also* MC IV 1:6, 7)

Christianity seems at first to be all about morality—duties and rules, guilt and virtue—yet it leads you out of all that, into something beyond
•MC 130-131 (*see also* CR 45; GID 144*; LM 114-115; PP 65)
❖ MC III 12:9 (*see also* CR 4:2; GID I 16:26*; LM 21:11-14; PP 4:13)

Christianity takes the whole of you, brains and all; is an education in itself
•MC 75 ❖ MC III 2:4

Christianity tells how the demands of the law have been met on our behalf, how God Himself became a man to save man from the disapproval of God
•MC 39 ❖ MC I 5:4

Christianity, the central miracle asserted by, is the Incarnation
•GID 81-88; M 68, 108-131
❖ GID I ch. 6; M 10:1; ch. 4

Christianity, the enemy attempts to make, a private affair
•WG 107-108 ❖ WG 7:3

Christianity, the God of, is alive and pulling at the other end of the cord; may demand something of you
•M 81, 93-94 (*see also* GID 142-143; MC 35, 136; SJ 209-210*; *consider also* Cost)
❖ M 11:2, 19 (*see also* GID I 16:25; MC I 4:6; IV 1:4; SJ 13:18*; *consider also* Cost)

Christianity: The idea that it brought a new ethical code into the world is an error; Jesus' commands are paralleled in classical, Egyptian and Chinese

texts
•CR 46-47, 51, 52-53, 55, 77 (see also Law of Nature; book *The Abolition of Man*) ❖ CR 4:5-7, 17, 20-22, 26; 6:16 (see also Law of Nature; book *The Abolition of Man*)

Christianity the only religion which teaches that Nature is not irrelevant to spiritual beatitude; Heaven will involve a natural environment
•M 161-162 (see also MC 91; Matter; Nature) ❖ M 16:30 (see also MC III 5:7; Matter; Nature)

Christianity, road into and out of, usually the same; therefore "semi-Christianity" may be useful at times
•L 297 (see also CR 22, 23)
❖ L undated letter of Feb 61 (see also CR 2:29, 34)

Christianity, the sort of arguments against, which our reason can be persuaded to accept at the moment of yielding to temptation are often preposterous
•CR 43 (see also Obstacles to Christian faith) ❖ CR 3:12 (see also Obstacles to Christian faith)

Christianity, the "watered" versions of, which leave out the darker elements and include only pure consolation: No real belief in them can last
•LM 75-76 (see also MC 46-47; Christianity-and-water)
❖ LM 14:13 (see also MC II 2:1-5; Christianity-and-water)

Christianity, the whole cosmic story according to, though full of tragic elements, yet fails of being a tragedy
•WG 75 ❖ WG 5:5

Christianity the worst enemy of totalitarian government; gives the individual a standing ground against the State
•GID 118 (see also MC 73)
❖ GID I 13:9 (see also MC III 1:9)

Christianity: "...there is evidence both for and against the Christian propositions which fully rational minds, working honestly, can assess differently"

•WLN 20, 21 ❖ WLN 2:8, 9

Christianity, there is no doctrine I would more willingly remove from, than the doctrine of Hell
•PP 118 ❖ PP 8:1

Christianity: "This is not 'a religion,' nor 'a philosophy.' It is the summing up and actuality of them all"
•SJ 236 ❖ SJ 15:7

Christianity: To accept the Incarnation brings God nearer, or near in a new way—and this, I found, was something I had not wanted
•SJ 237 ❖ SJ 15:8

Christianity, to preach, in Paul's day meant primarily to preach the Resurrection
•M 143-144 ❖ M 16:1, 2

Christianity, transmission of: adults to children
•GID 119 ❖ GID I 13:11

Christianity, transmission of, only possible by Christians
•GID 116 ❖ GID I 13:5, 6

Christianity, unbelievers who speak of, with reverence vs. those who are rude: the rudeness shows fear that there "might be something in it after all"
•LAL 90 ❖ LAL 26 Mar 60

Christianity vs. Materialism: Ethical differences as they affect social values
•GID 109-110 ❖ GID I 12:2, 3

Christianity vs. other religions: How much more one has in common with a *real* Jew or Muslim than with a wretched, liberalising specimen of the same classes*
•LAL 11-12 (see also GID 60*; MC 9*)
❖ LAL Nov 10th 52 (see also GID I 4:56—Ques. 14*; MC P:9*)

Christianity vs. Science: Christian theology can fit in science, art, and morality; Science cannot fit in any of these things, not even itself

Christianity vs. Science: Lewis examines the view that miracles were accepted in earlier days because people had a false conception of the universe and Man's place in it

•M 48-54 ❖ M 7:7-17

Christianity vs. Science: Lewis examines the view that miracles were accepted in earlier days because people didn't know the laws of Nature
•M 45-48 ❖ M 7:2-6

Christianity, we believe, as we believe that the sun is in the sky at midday—not because we clearly see the sun but because we can see everything else
•M 110; WG 92 (see also WG 69*)
❖ M 14:3; WG 5:24 (see also WG 4:24*)

Christianity: We fear lest it may prove too inconvenient
•WG 127 (see also Self-reservation)
❖ WG 9:4 (see also Self-reservation)

Christianity, we have been warned that all but conclusive evidence against, will appear with Antichrist; after that, all evidence will be on the other side
•WLN 92 ❖ WLN 6:28-30

Christianity, what is the value of the magical element in, for me
•LM 104 ❖ LM 19:10

Christianity: What it tells us about equality, vicariousness, nature, interdependence, and death
•GID 84-87 ❖ GID I 9:7-10

Christianity, what they now call the "demythologizing" of, can easily be the "remythologizing" of it—and substituting a poorer mythology for a richer
•LM 52 (see also M 74-75)
❖ LM 10:2 (see also M 10:13)

Christianity: Whether it is true or not must be discovered by reasoning before it is asked whether people's motives for believing it are improper
•GID 273-274 (see also WLN 18-20; Wish-fulfilment) ❖ GID III 1:7 (see also WLN 2:8; Wish-fulfilment)

Christianity which has died out in England is nominal Christianity, so that only those who really believe now profess
•LAL 15 ❖ LAL 9th May 53

Christianity, whole basis of, is to "put on Christ"; Christianity offers nothing else at all
•MC 166, 169-170 ❖ MC IV 8:1, 10

Christianity works for improvement in this world
•GID 49, 57, 147-150; PP 113-114; WLN 111 (see also CR 58-59*; Heaven on earth) ❖ GID I 4:6-8 (Ques. 2), 39-40 (Ques. 9); ch. 17; PP 7:4; WLN 7:33, 34 (see also CR 5:4*; Heaven on earth)

Christianity, you cannot subtract the miraculous in; it is precisely the story of a great Miracle
•GID 80; M 68 (see also M 108, 133)
❖ GID I 9:1; M 10:1 (see also M 14:1; 15:2)

"Christina dreams" mentioned: The love dream makes a man incapable of real love
•L 76 (see also L 78)
❖ L 24 May 22 (see also L 30 Jun 22)

Christ-life is spread by three things: baptism, belief, and Holy Communion
•MC 62-65 ❖ MC II 5:1-7

Christ-likeness—see Imitation of Christ

Christmas: After Boxing Day, perhaps we shall have a little quiet in which to remember the birth of Christ
•GID 310 ❖ GID III 7:15

Christmas as an example of a religious festival or act of worship which can be separated from the vision of God, thereby becoming a rival to God
•RP 48-49 ❖ RP 5:7

Christmas, commercialism of, in Britain
•GID 301-303 ❖ GID III ch. 5

Christmas, commercialism of, in general
•GID 304-305 ❖ GID III ch. 6

Christmas, commercialism of, is one of my pet abominations
•L 265-266 ❖ L 17 Dec 55

Christmas: "Every year the merciless spate of correspondence makes this season more pestilential and less festal for me"
•L 300 ❖ L 3 Dec 61

Christmas, I'm afraid I hate the weeks just before; so much of the fuss has nothing to do with the Nativity at all
•LAL 50 ❖ LAL 19/12/55

Christmas: Long before Dec. 25th everyone is worn out
•GID 305 ❖ GID III 6:3

Christmas Psalm, Psalm 45, shows us so

many aspects of the Nativity we could never get from carols or even from the gospels (e.g., Christ as Bridegroom)
•RP 127-132 ❖ RP 12:8-10

Christmas Psalms: For those who first read them as Psalms about the birth of Christ, that birth primarily meant something militant—the hero, the champion
•RP 124-125 ❖ RP 12:5

Christmas, story illustrating contrast between the Nativity and the racket of, (Lady on bus: "Oh Lor'! They bring religion into everything...")
•LAL 80 (see also LAL 89) ❖ LAL Dec 29/58 (see also LAL 22 Dec 59)

Christmas, the horrid commercial racket of: "I send no cards and give no presents except to children"
•LAL 23 ❖ LAL 27/xi/53

Christmas to me is mainly hard work—write, write, write, till I wickedly say that if there were less good will (in the mail) there would be more peace
•LAL 23-24 (see also LAL 37, 88, 112) ❖ LAL Jan 1st 54 (see also LAL 29/1/55; 22 Dec 59; 2 Jan 63)

Christmas, What, Means to Me (chapter title)
•GID 304-305 ❖ GID III ch. 6

Christmas, Xmas and (chapter title)
•GID 301-303 ❖ GID III ch. 5

"Chronicles of Narnia": Aslan answers the question, "What might Christ be like if there really were a world like Narnia and He became incarnate in it?"
•L 283 ❖ L 29 Dec 58

"Chronicles of Narnia," Lewis mentions what led him to write, ("...the fairy tale was the genre best fitted for what I wanted to say")
•L 260, 307 ❖ L undated letter just before 2 Feb 55; 2 Dec 62

"Chronicles of Narnia": Lewis mentions that when he wrote The Lion, the Witch, and the Wardrobe he had no notion of writing the other six books
•L 307 ❖ L 2 Dec 62

"Chronicles of Narnia": Lewis mentions

that writing for children modified his habits of composition
•L 307 ❖ L 2 Dec 62

"Chronicles of Narnia": "No, no, I'm not committed to a real belief in Aslan..."
•L 251 ❖ L 17 Jul 53

"**Chronological snobbery**": the uncritical acceptance of the intellectual climate common to our own age, and the arbitrary discrediting of past thought
•SJ 207-208 (see also RP 121, 130; SJ 206, 212-213, 216, SL 128-129; WLN 96)
❖ SJ 13:17 (see also RP 12:3, 9; SJ 13:14; 14:2, 7; SL 27:5; WLN 7:6)

Church—see also Body of Christ

Church activities, as an end in themselves, are infinitely dangerous—can become an idol that hides both God and my neighbors
•LM 30 (see also RP 57-58; SL 35)
❖ LM 6:4-6 (see also RP 6:6, 7; SL 7:4)

Church, affection for a particular, must be treated as a natural affection (like Patriotism) and subjected to the same limitations
•FL 48-49 ❖ FL 2:43

Church and State, separation of—see Separation of Church and State

Church architecture, Uncle H. taught me appreciation of
•L 66 (see also Cathedral/s)
❖ L 7 Aug 21 (see also Cathedral/s)

Church as a medium of the Holy Spirit
•L 243 ❖ L 20 Jun 52

Church as the Bride of Christ
•RP 128-132 ❖ RP 12:9, 10

Church attendance and membership, importance of
•WG 106-120 (see also Membership)
❖ WG ch. 7 (see also Membership)

Church attendance: As soon as I became a Theist I started attending church as a way of "flying my flag"—though the idea of churchmanship was to me wholly unattractive
•SJ 233 ❖ SJ 15:6

Church attendance: David's dancing as a valuable contrast to the merely dutiful "church-going" and "saying our prayers" to which religion is often re-

duced
- RP 45-46 ❖ RP 5:4

Church attendance from social pressure declining; thus the "decline of religion" may be a misperception
- GID 219-220 (see also GID 253)
- ❖ GID II 8:5 (see also GID II 14:11)

Church attendance: God "may be trusted to know when we need bed even more than Mass"
- LAL 24 (see also LAL 38)
- ❖ LAL Jan 1st 54 (see also LAL 20/2/55)

Church attendance, I saw, as a kind of collective; a wearisome "get-together" affair
- SJ 234 ❖ SJ 15:6

Church attendance, importance of: Adoration, more than any other act, should be a communal act*
- LM 100 ❖ LM 19:1

Church attendance, importance of: "...I found it was the only way of flying your flag"
- GID 61-62 ❖ GID I 4:59, 60 (Ques. 16)

Church attendance, importance of: It will teach us humility and charity; "Regular but cool...is no bad symptom"
- L 224-225 ❖ L 7 Dec 50

Church attendance, importance of: "We have to be continually reminded of what we believe"
- MC 124 (see also MC 78)
- ❖ MC III 11:6 (see also MC III 3:1*)

Church attendance: Lewis maintains that his distaste for "the collective" may be partly traced to his mother's funeral**
- SJ 20 ❖ SJ 1:21

Church attendance only on great annual festivals likens one to a Pagan (in the best sense) who makes his bow to the Unknown—and at other times Forgotten
- RP 46-47 ❖ RP 5:5

Church attendance: Some of us find it more natural to approach God in solitude; but Christianity is not a solitary religion—we must go to church
- L 224 ❖ L 7 Dec 50

Church, Christian, offers us a refreshing return to inequality and opportunity

for reverence
- WG 113, 116 (see also GID 84-85*)
- ❖ WG 7:10, 15 (see also GID I 9:7*)

Church claims to be the bearer of a revelation; if that is true, we should expect to find in it things opaque to our reason though not contrary to it
- GID 238 ❖ GID II 11:11

Church, divisions within—see Division(s)

Church exists for nothing else but to draw men into Christ
- MC 169-170 ❖ MC IV 8:10

Church-going—see Church attendance

Church: "I think the 'low' church milieu that I grew up in did tend to be too cosily at ease in Sion" (re: intimacy without awe in prayer)*
- LM 13 ❖ LM 2:14

Church: "...if a man can't be cured of churchgoing, the next best thing is to send him all over the neighborhood looking for the church that 'suits' him..." (—Screwtape)
- SL 72 ❖ SL 16:1

Church, in every, there is something which sooner or later works against the very purpose for which it came into existence
- LM 43 ❖ LM 8:10

Church is the Bride, and Christ is the Bridegroom; therefore priests, as representatives of Christ, must be male
- GID 236-237 ❖ GID II 11:6, 7

Church, it is extraordinary how inconvenient it is for your family if you get up early to go to
- GID 61 ❖ GID I 4:60 (Ques. 16)

Church, it takes all sorts to make a; Heaven will display far more variety than Hell (re: differences of worship style)
- LM 10 ❖ LM 2:3

Church itself mentioned by Screwtape as his ally in keeping humans out of God's camp (incomprehensible liturgy, bad lyrics, errant church-goers, etc.)
- SL 12-14 ❖ SL 2:2-4

"Church," meaning of the word, to modern minds ("a sacred building" or "the clergy"—does not suggest "the com-

pany of the faithful")
•GID 97 ❖ GID I 10:25

Church members: Screwtape advises
tempting them to criticize their
church, whereas "the Enemy" [God]
wants pupils, not critics
•SL 72-73 ❖ SL 16:2

Church membership—*see* Membership

Church music—*see* Music; Hymns

Church of England—*see also* Anglican(s);
Anglo-Catholicism

Church of England, history of, is likely to
be very short if the current trend of
theological thought continues
•CR 166 ❖ CR 13:36

Church of England, I am a very ordinary
layman of the, not especially "high"
nor especially "low"
•MC 6 ❖ MC P:2

Church of England, I only hope there'll be
no scheme for the canonization of
saints in the
•LM 15 ❖ LM 3:3

Church of England, I think St. Paul has
told us what to do about the divisions
in the
•L 170 ❖ L 8 Nov 39

Church of England: It would be idle to
pretend that we Anglicans are a striking example of the gusto expressed in
the Psalms
•RP 52 ❖ RP 5:10

Church of England: Its clergymen need to
define doctrinal boundary lines and
defend them
•GID 89-90 ❖ GID I 10:2, 3

Church of England mentioned ("There is
more real poverty, even actual want,
in English vicarages than there is in
the homes of casual labourers")
•LAL 15-16 ❖ LAL May 30th 53

Church of England, Screwtape mentions
High and Low parties of, as example
of the value to his cause of small, self-
righteous factions within the Church
•SL 34 ❖ SL 7:2

Church of England: Screwtape mentions
the conflicts between "high" and
"low" churchmen which are kept active as long as Paul's advice is not

brought to mind
•SL 75 ❖ SL 16:5

Church of England: "The Tableland [in *The
Pilgrim's Regress*] represents *all* high
and dry states of mind, of which High
Anglicanism then seemed to me to be
one"
•L 170 ❖ L 8 Nov 39

Church organization vs. the congregational principle discussed by
Screwtape: The congregational principle makes each church into a kind
of club or faction
•SL 73 ❖ SL 16:2

Church: "Our real journey to God involves constantly turning our backs
on [Nature]; passing from the dawn-
lit fields into some poky little
church..."
•FL 39 ❖ FL 2:27

Church, saying one's private prayers in a:
usually too many distractions
•LM 17 ❖ LM 3:8

Church, Screwtape mentions criticism of
one's, —its organization, services, etc.
—as serving his purposes
•SL 72-73 ❖ SL 16:2

Church, Screwtape rejoices to see the, dividing itself up into small, self-righteous factions
•SL 34 (*see also* SL 72-73, 75)
❖ SL 7:2 (*see also* SL 16:2, 5)

Church, Screwtape ruefully describes, as
"...spread out through all time and
space and rooted in eternity, terrible
as an army with banners"
•SL 12 ❖ SL 2:2

Church service(s)—*see also* Liturgy; Worship, corporate; *consider also* Praise

Church service, the perfect, would be one
we were almost unaware of; our attention would have been on God
•LM 4 ❖ LM 1:5

Church services
•LM 3-8 ❖ LM ch. 1

Church services: An uncritical attitude, a
laying open of the mind in humble receptivity to any nourishment available, described by Screwtape as dangerous to his cause

•SL 73 ❖ SL 16:2

Church services: "...any form will do me if only I'm given time to get used to it"
•LM 101 ❖ LM 19:2

Church services: Anything the congregation *can do* may be properly offered to God in public worship; but in modern England we can't sing
•GID 331 (*see also* Hymns)
❖ GID IV Letter 6 (*see also* Hymns)

Church services are merely an attempt at worship and praise, never fully successful; only a dim reflection of how it will be in Heaven
•RP 96 ❖ RP 9:6

Church services: "I think our business as laymen is to take what we are given and make the best of it"
•LM 4, 5 ❖ LM 1:3, 10

Church services, incense as part of, merely a question of ritual—not of doctrine; some find it helpful and others don't
•L 243
❖ L undated letter just after 20 Jun 52

Church services: Judging of others who may worship in a different fashion than we do ("It takes all sorts to make a world; or a church")
•LM 10 ❖ LM 2:3

Church services may have cultural value, but that is not what they exist for
•CR 94 ❖ CR 8:2

Church services: My whole position really boils down to an entreaty for permanence and uniformity
•LM 4-5 ❖ LM 1:3-8

Church services: "never anything can be amiss When simpleness and duty tender it"
•LM 101 ❖ LM 19:2

Church services: "...nothing should be done or sung or said in church which does not aim...either at glorifying God or edifying the people or both"
•CR 94 ❖ CR 8:2

Church services: Sacred dance as part of the worship service may be proper in a place like, say, Africa
•GID 331 ❖ GID IV Letter 6

Church services: Screwtape mentions candles on altars
•SL 87 (*see also* SL 75)
❖ SL 19:3 (*see also* SL 16:5)

Church services should not go overtime
•GID 332 ❖ GID IV Letter 7

Church services, tastes in: If we cannot lay down our tastes at the church door, surely we should at least bring them in to be humbled*
•GID 336 ❖ GID IV Letter 8

Church services: What pleased me most about a Greek Orthodox mass I once attended was that there seemed to be no prescribed behaviour for the congregation
•LM 10 ❖ LM 2:3

Church: The Christian community is the one really adequate instrument for learning about God
•MC 144 ❖ MC IV 2:15, 16

Church: "...the fussy, time-wasting botheration of it all! the bells, the crowds, the umbrellas, the notices, the bustle, the perpetual arranging..."
•SJ 234 ❖ SJ 15:6

Church, the parish, is a descendent of both the Temple of Jerusalem and the synagogues, which represented two separate functions (sacrifice/teaching)
•RP 45 ❖ RP 5:3

Church, though I liked clergymen as I liked bears, I had as little wish to be in the, as in the zoo (re: Lewis's conversion to Theism)
•SJ 234 ❖ SJ 15:6

Church unity—*see* Unity; *consider* Reunion

Church, when no man goes to, except because he seeks Christ the number of actual believers can at last be determined
•GID 220 ❖ GID II 8:5

Church, when you go to, you are really listening in to the secret wireless from the friendly side of the civil war in the universe
•MC 51 ❖ MC II 2:12

Church will outlive the universe, along with its members
•WG 116 ❖ WG 7:16

Churches—*see also* Denominations; Religions

Churches in modern cities "huddle between the sky-scraping offices..."
•L 100 ❖ L undated letter of "April or May" 1925

Cigars: "I once knew two bad boys who smoked secretly..."
•CR 38-39 ❖ CR 3:4

Cigars, we should all like to believe that there are, in Heaven...that Heaven will mean the happy past restored
•GO 29 ❖ GO 2:14

Circle analogy for our earthly lives which touch each other in relationships (while our eternal lives will be spheres or globes)
•GO 27 ❖ GO 2:12

Circumstances, so often one's inner state seems to have so little connection with the
•LAL 83 (*see also* SJ 78, 118-119)
❖ LAL Jun 7th 59 (*see also* SJ 5:12; 8:1)

Cities in any country interest me only if I want to hear an opera or buy a book
•L 215 ❖ L undated letter of Jan 1949

Cities: Man's attempt to win safety and ease from Nature seems to lead on to universal suburbia*
•L 211 ❖ L 15 Oct 47

Cities, modern, "where the churches huddle between the sky-scraping offices..."
•L 100 ❖ L undated letter of "April or May" 1925

"**City**" contrasted by "country" is part of our appreciation of Nature; this was not the case with the Psalmists—towns were few and very small
•RP 76-77 ❖ RP 8:2

City, no man loves his, because it is great, but because it is his (quote from "one of the Greeks")
•FL 46 ❖ FL 2:40

Civil authority—*see* Government

Civil claims (e.g., of nation or party or class) must not supersede God's claims on us
•WG 24-25 ❖ WG 2:6

Civil law, morality of obeying, when it tells me to serve in the wars
•WG 33-53 ❖ WG ch. 3

Civil obedience not related to the kind and degree of obedience which a creature owes to its Creator; on the former I have nothing to say
•PP 115 ❖ PP 7:6

Civil Service mentioned as among the instruments of an increasingly tyrannical State
•L 259-260
❖ L 22 Dec 54 (second letter)

Civilizations—*see* Cultures

Claims—*see also* Cost; Demands

Claims of God must not be superseded by claims of country or party or class
•WG 24-25 ❖ WG 2:6

Claims of God on us: There is no area in our lives on which God has no claim
•WG 130 (*see also* MC 167*; SJ 172; SL 95-99) ❖ WG 9:9 (*see also* MC IV 8:4*; SJ 11:8; SL ch. 21)

Claims of God on us: We are like taxpayers, dreading a rise in the tax
•WG 129 ❖ WG 9:7

Claims of real Christianity offensive to the World
•GID 222-223 ❖ GID II 8:12

Class distinctions: "...I don't mean to ignore (in fact I find it nice) the distinction between a peasant's grandson like myself and those of noble blood"
•LAL 26 (*see also* LAL 27) ❖ LAL 26/1/54 (*see also* LAL Feb 22/54)

Class distinctions: People "do not get their qualities from a class: they belong to a class because they have those qualities"
•GID 309 ❖ GID III 7:12

Class, middle, as the social group which gave society the majority of its scientists, physicians, philosophers, artists, etc.
•SL 168; WLN 66
❖ SL 32:33; WLN 4:33

Clergy, argument against women in the (Priests serve as representatives of God, who is masculine; therefore women not suited for this role)
•GID 234-239 ❖ GID II ch. 11

Clergy of Church of England: "There is more real poverty, even actual want, in English vicarages than there is in the homes of casual labourers"
•LAL 15-16 ❖ LAL May 30th 53

Clergy: "One is sometimes (not often) glad not to be a great theologian; one might so easily mistake it for being a good Christian"*
•RP 57 ❖ RP 6:6

Clergy, regarding the modern tendency to blame, for apostasy from the Church (I think it more wholesome to concentrate on the faults of the laity)
•LAL 15 ❖ LAL May 30th 53

Clergy, we must not expect the, to put out a political programme for us; that is not what they are trained to do
•MC 79 ❖ MC III 3:3

Clergyman, description of an Irish, whose only interest was the search for evidence of "human survival"; this man influenced Lewis's view of immortality
•SJ 202 ❖ SJ 13:8

Clergyman, Screwtape mentions, who waters down the faith so much that he shocks his parishioners with his unbelief
•SL 73-74 (see also Christianity-and-water) ❖ SL 16:3 (see also Christianity-and-water)

Clergyman, Screwtape mentions, who preaches a broad range of opinions—all calculated to shock and grieve his parents and their friends
•SL 74 ❖ SL 16:4

Clergyman, Screwtape mentions, who "revolves endlessly round the little treadmill of his fifteen favourite Psalms and twenty favourite lessons"
•SL 74 ❖ SL 16:3

Clergyman who comes to hold unorthodox opinions cannot honestly continue his ministry; clergy have duty to support church doctrines
•GID 89-90 (see also GID 260, 265) ❖ GID I 10:2, 3 (see also GID II 16:12, 46)

Clergymen, even from the pens of, you

will meet Naturalistic assumptions
•M 164-165 (see also CR 152-166) ❖ M 17:1 (see also CR ch. 13)

Clergymen, intellectual dishonesty of, who disbelieve what they preach: "I feel it is a form of prostitution"
•GID 260 (see also GID 89-90, 265*) ❖ GID II 16:12 (see also GID I 10:2, 3; II 16:46*)

Clergymen, missionary to the, of one's own church is an embarrassing role—though perhaps very urgently necessary (re: modern theology)
•CR 166 ❖ CR 13:36

Clergymen, modern, are anxious to allow to the enemy every advantage he can with any show of fairness claim
•M 164-165 ❖ M 17:1

Clergymen must face up to what they find disagreeable in the doctrines*
•GID 91 ❖ GID I 10:6

Clergymen must keep abreast of recent movements in theology*
•GID 91-92 ❖ GID I 10:7

Clergymen, purpose of the preaching of, misunderstood by modern audiences (they think you are preaching Christianity because it is good for society, etc.)
•GID 90-91 ❖ GID I 10:5

Clergymen: Some of them are among those people who are slowly ceasing to be Christians but still call themselves by that name
•MC 176 ❖ MC IV 10:4

Clergymen, teaching of, must aim at presenting that which is timeless in the language of our own age
•GID 93, 94, 96-98 (see also GID 242-243, 254-257, 338) ❖ GID I 10:10, 12, 18-38 (see also GID II 12:4, 5; ch. 15; IV Letter 11)

Clergymen, though I liked, as I liked bears, I had as little wish to be in the Church as in the zoo (re: Lewis's conversion to Theism)
•SJ 234 ❖ SJ 15:6

Cliches—see Expressions

"Climates of opinion," I take a very low view of; all discoveries are made and

all errors are corrected by those who ignore the "climate of opinion"
•PP 134 (*consider also* Spirit of the Age)
❖ PP 9:6 (*consider also* Spirit of the Age)

Clique(s)—*see also* Coteries; *consider also* Inner Rings

Clique, Screwtape wants the Church to be small so that its members may acquire the self-righteousness of a
•SL 33-34 (*see also* SL 72-73)
❖ SL 7:2 (*see also* SL 16:2)

Clock analogy to show that entropy hasn't always been the rule: "A clock can't run down unless it has first been wound up"
•M 152 (*see also* GID 33-34)
❖ M 16:17 (*see also* GID I 2:12)

Clothes: "...I am one of those on whom Nature has laid the doom that...whatever they wear they will always look as if they had come out of an old clothes shop"
•SJ 67 ❖ SJ 4:14

Clothes: Lewis describes a phase in which he aspired to be a flashy dresser
•SJ 67 ❖ SJ 4:14

Clothes, Lewis's dislike for fancy
•SJ 22 (*see also* LAL 17; SJ 67) ❖ SJ 2:1 (*see also* LAL Jun 22d 53; SJ 4:14)

Clothes: Lewis's dislike for new suits
•LAL 116 ❖ LAL 22 Apr 63

Clouds, Lewis's enjoyment of all types of
•SJ 152 (*see also* L 110)
❖ SJ 10:4 (*see also* L 10 Jan 27)

Co-dependence—*consider also* Dependence; Interdependence; Need to be needed

Co-dependence: What Christianity tells us about interdependence and vicariousness ("It will not in any way allow me to be an exploiter...")**
•GID 87 ❖ GID I 9:10

Co-dependence, which is evil in the world of selfishness and necessity, is good in the world of love and understanding (re: hierarchical inequality, interdependency, etc.)**
•M 120 ❖ M 14:20

Coghill, Neville: He was a man after my own heart; I soon had the shock of dis-

covering that he was a Christian
•SJ 212 ❖ SJ 14:2

Collective—*see also* Crowd(s); *consider also* Society

Collective activities, like health and politics, must be considered only as a means to something more important ("to be happy at home")
•WG 108-109 ❖ WG 7:4

Collective, Christian life defends us from, not by isolating us, but by making us organs in the mystical Body
•WG 116 (*see also* PP 150-151*)
❖ WG (*see also* PP 10:8*)

Collective, decay in one's desire for, neither a bad sign nor a sign of increasing spirituality; is a natural development as one grows older*
•L 245 ❖ L 20 Oct 52

Collective, dominance of, as seen in the insect world named as one of two things "that some of us most dread for our own species"
•SJ 8-9 ❖ SJ 1:6

Collective, Friendship withdraws men from the, as surely as solitude itself could do
•FL 90 (*see also* FL 88, 97)
❖ FL 4:5 (*see also* FL 4:2, 17)

Collective, I hated the, as much as any man can hate anything
•SJ 173 ❖ SJ 11:10

Collective, I saw church-going as a kind of; a wearisome "get-together" affair
•SJ 234 ❖ SJ 15:6

Collective idea in the extreme seen in prisoner numbering system
•WG 112 ❖ WG 7:8

Collective, Lewis maintains that his distaste for the, may be partly traced to his mother's funeral
•SJ 20 ❖ SJ 1:21

Collective, modern outlook values, above the individual; this disparages Friendship
•FL 90 ❖ FL 4:5

Collectivism as opposite error to isolation
•WG 108 ❖ WG 7:3

Collectivism of our life necessary but has deathly properties; our only safeguard

is in the Christian life
- •WG 109 ❖ WG 7:5

Collectivism, secular, vs. Christian membership
- •WG 110-113 ❖ WG 7:5-13

Comfort, Christian religion does not begin by offering; it begins in dismay (the diagnosis of sin)
- •MC 39 (see also GID 58, 243-244; L 193; PP 55*; WLN 19*)
- ❖ MC I 5:4 (see also GID I 4:45 Ques. 11; II 12:6; L 15 May 41; PP 4:1*; WLN 2:8*)

Comfort is the one thing you cannot get by looking for it; but if you look for truth, you may find comfort in the end
- •MC 39 ❖ MC I 5:4

Comfort, there is no good applying to Heaven for earthly; there is no earthly comfort in the long run
- •FL 190 (see also GO 28-30; L 290; LAL 49) ❖ FL 6:43 (see also GO 2:13-16; L 3 Dec 59; LAL 16/12/55)

Comforts, one fights for one's remaining, ("I didn't call Him 'God' either; I called Him 'Spirit'")—re: Lewis's road to conversion
- •SJ 223 ❖ SJ 14:14

Coming to God—see Search for God; Surrender

Commandment(s)—see also Law(s); Moral law(s)

Commandment, Meditation on the Third (chapter title)—regarding the formation of "Christian" political parties
- •GID 196-199 ❖ GID II ch. 3

Commandment, sixth: In the commandment "Thou shalt not kill" the word "kill" means "murder" (re: pacifism and capital punishment)
- •L 247; MC 106-107
- ❖ L 8 Nov 52; MC III 7:7

Commandment, third: We cannot assume that all who use God's name without reverential prefixes are making careless use of it
- •GID 335-336 ❖ GID IV Letter 8

Commandments, the two great, must be translated "Behave as if you loved God and man"—for no man can love because he is told to

- •LM 115 (see also MC 115, 117-118; L 269)
- ❖ LM 21:12 (see also MC III 9:2, 9, 10; L undated letter just after 13 Mar 56)

Commercialism—consider also Economics; Materialism

Commercialism: Advertising creates desires for unnecessary things; this creates unnecessary work*
- •WLN 75-78 (see also CR 168-169; MC 80) ❖ WLN 5:11-15 (see also CR 14:18; MC III 3:4)

Commercialism: "...buying and selling things...seems to have become almost more important than either producing or using them"
- •LAL 50 ❖ LAL 19/12/55

Commercialism of Christmas in Britain
- •GID 301-303 ❖ GID III ch. 5

Commercialism of Christmas in general
- •LAL 23, 50
- ❖ LAL 27/xi/53; 19/12/55

Commercialism: "...'sales-resistance' is the sin against the Holy Ghost"*
- •CR 92 ❖ CR 7:21

Commercialism, the degraded, of our minds is as much the result of the new requirement for "built-in obsolescence" as it is its cause
- •WLN 72 (see also CR 92)
- ❖ WLN 5:3-5 (see also CR 7:21)

Commercialism: The Myth of Evolutionism pleases those who want to sell things to us; nothing ought to last
- •CR 92 ❖ CR 7:21

Commercialism: Youth have the least sales-resistance; maybe that is why there is a tendency in the modern world to prolong that period
- •LAL 19-20 ❖ LAL Aug 1st [1953]

Commitment: A man "should never give all his heart to anything which will end when his life ends"*
- •WLN 110 ❖ WLN 7:31

Common ground, when all is said about the divisions of Christendom there remains (by God's mercy) an enormous
- •CR vii—quote from unpublished letter (see also Christianity, "mere")
- ❖ CR P:1—quote from unpublished

letter (*see also* Christianity, "mere")
Common people—*see* Low-brow(s); Vulgar
Communication: Lewis describes the inadequacy of language in communicating the essence of our lives to others
•CR 140 ❖ CR 11:23
Communication: Thinking as other than the succession of linked concepts which we use when we successfully convey our "thought" to one another (re: Poetic language in religion)
•CR 139-140 ❖ CR 11:22, 23
Communication with deceased loved ones: Is God a clown who whips away one bowl of soup only to replace it with another of the same soup?
•GO 15-16 (*see also* GO 28-29)
❖ GO 1:29 (*see also* GO 2:14)
Communication with deceased loved ones: Lewis describes an experience of what seemed like the presence of his wife after her death*
•GO 85-87 ❖ GO 4:33-35
Communication with audiences: Lewis lists terms which are used differently by the layman than by the clergyman or theologian
•GID 96-98 ❖ GID I 10:20-37
Communication with "outsiders": Plain language is necessary in Christian apologetics and preaching
•GID 96-98, 183, 243- 244, 254-257, 338
❖ GID I 10:18-38; 22:16, 17; II 12:4, 5; ch. 15; IV ch. 11
Communication with "outsiders," problems in
•GID 254-257 ❖ GID II ch. 15
Communication with "outsiders": We need to be on guard against the use of slang or jargon peculiar to our own circle
•GID 256-257 ❖ GID II 15:11-13
Communion, Holy: As Christians, our most joyous festivals centre upon the broken body and the shed blood
•RP 52 ❖ RP 5:10
Communion, Holy, as one of three things which spread the Christ-life to us
•MC 62, 65 ❖ MC II 5:3, 7
Communion, Holy, as the one church function in which we are commanded by the New Testament to partake
•GID 61 ❖ GID I 4:57, 58 (Ques. 15)
Communion, Holy, as the only rite which we know to have been instituted by Our Lord Himself (and therefore cannot be altered)
•L 224 ❖ L 7 Dec 50
Communion, Holy: Discussion of the controversy over what happens to the bread and wine
•LM 101-105 ❖ LM 19:4-13
Communion, Holy, gives the act of eating a new meaning (a refutation of Development as explaining the continuity between all spiritual and natural things)
•WG 70 ❖ WG 4:27
Communion, Holy: I haven't written about it because I am not good enough at Theology; I have nothing to offer
•LM 101 ❖ LM 19:3
Communion, Holy: I need not be tormented by the question "What is this?" The command, after all, was Take, eat: not Take, understand
•LM 104-105 ❖ LM 19:13
Communion, Holy: I should define this magic as "'objective efficacy which cannot be further analysed'"
•LM 103 ❖ LM 19:8
Communion, Holy: Is it not in some ways an advantage that the little thin, cold wafer can't pretend the least resemblance to that with which it unites me?
•GO 75-76 ❖ GO 4:13, 14
Communion on, Holy: Private communions are extraordinarily moving; I am in danger of preferring them to those in church
•LAL 115 ❖ LAL 19 Mar 63
Communion, Holy: The Sacrament as a supernatural event
•LM 9 ❖ LM 2:1
Communion, Holy: The Sacraments show the value of matter and the senses in God's scheme*
•M 163 ❖ M 16:32
Communion, Holy, vs. "Mass": Screwtape relishes the quarrel over which of

these labels to use
•SL 75 ❖ SL 16:5

Communion, in Holy, God gives Himself to men; thus in this act of worship, among others, God communicates His presence to men
•RP 93 ❖ RP 9:4

Communion, Lewis relates making his first, in his youth—which he did only to please his father
•SJ 161-162 ❖ SJ 10:15

Communions—*see* Denominations

Communism and Fascism potent because of the good they contain or imitate
•L 176 ❖ L 17 Jan 40

Communism fixes men's affections on the Future, according to Screwtape, and is therefore to be encouraged in men's thinking
•SL 68-69 ❖ SL 15:3

Communism, like other monomaniacal systems, has arbitrarily selected some one maxim of traditional morality and isolated it from the rest as all-important
•CR 75 ❖ CR 6:10, 11

Communism mentioned by Screwtape
•SL 161; WLN 59
❖ SL 32:17; WLN 4:17

Communism mentioned with reference to the universal acceptance of traditional morality
•CR 52-53 ❖ CR 4:21

Communism: Screwtape mentions a form of Pacifism which is adopted not on moral grounds but from "a dash of purely fashionable and literary communism"
•SL 45-46 ❖ SL 10:1

Communism: The Myth of Evolutionism has been built into the state religion of Russia; is essential to Leftist politics (as well as to the political Right)*
•CR 93 ❖ CR 7:22

Communist committed to a sinking ship
•GID 44 ❖ GID I 3:11

Community, Christian—*see* Body of Christ; Church

Companionship (such as among people who work together) is only the ma-trix of Friendship; real Friendship is something more
•FL 94-98 ❖ FL 4:11-19

Compass analogy: Free will is a needle that can choose to point North or not
•MC 179 ❖ MC IV 10:7

Compassion—*see* Pity; Sympathy; *consider* Help; Helping; Humanitarianism

Competition—*consider also* Ambition; Pride

Competition as the main principle of Hell; what one gains, another loses (—Screwtape)
•SL 81 (*see also* SL 37, 85)
❖ SL 18:3 (*see also* SL 8:3; 19:1)

Competition, dangers of: To want to dance well or look nice is all right; when you want to look nicer than all the others you are going wrong
•GID 55-56 ❖ GID I 4:34-36 (Ques. 9)

Competition: "Games...seem to me to lead to ambition, jealousy, and embittered partisan feeling, quite as often as to anything else"
•SJ 129 ❖ SJ 8:13

Competition, Lewis's dislike for athletic
•SJ 90, 96-98, 107, 113-114, 129-130 (*see also* L 61*, 75*; LAL 46)
❖ SJ 6:11, 20-23; 7:9, 18; 8:13 (*see also* L 29 May 21*; 18 May 22*; LAL 9/10/55)

Competition: Pride is competitive by its very nature; it gets no pleasure out of having something, only out of having more of it than the next man
•MC 109-110 ❖ MC III 8:3

Competitive egoisms (as in the pursuit of "culture" for the sake of prestige or merit) can only impoverish social life
•WLN 35, bottom (*consider also* Pride of pursuing "culture")
❖ WLN 3:8 (*consider also* Pride of pursuing "culture")

Complacency, the difficulty of converting an uneducated man nowadays lies in his
•CR 23 ❖ CR 2:35

Compliment, God has paid us the intolerable, of loving us, in the deepest, most tragic, most inexorable sense
•PP 41, 42, 53 ❖ PP 3:8, 10, 18

Compromise harder than going in for the full treatment; we are like eggs—must be hatched or go bad
•MC 169 (see also Self-surrender; Surrender) ❖ MC IV 8:9 (see also Self-surrender; Surrender)

Compromise not acceptable to God though He will be merciful to our failures
•WG 130 ❖ WG 9:9

Compromise, there is no question of a, between the claims of God and the claims of anything else; in a sense, "religion" must occupy the whole of life
•WG 25 ❖ WG 2:7

"Compulsion" (by God) in conversion process
•SJ 224-225, 229, 237 (see also GID 261) ❖ SJ 14:16, 23; 15:8 (see also GID II 16:19-22)

Compulsion, I detest every kind of religious
•GID 61 (see also Separation of Church and State)
❖ GID I 4:58 (Ques. 15) (see also Separation of Church and State)

Compulsion: "The hardness of God is kinder than the softness of men, and His compulsion is our liberation"
•SJ 229 (see also GID 261*)
❖ SJ 14:23 (see also GID II 16:19-22*)

Compulsion: The most deeply compelled action is also the freest
•GID 261 (see also LM 49-50*; SJ 224-225) ❖ GID II 16:19-22 (see also LM 9:11*; SJ 14:16)

Conceit—see also Pride

Conceit as an obstacle to a proper appreciation of all ordinary pleasures as means for adoring God
•LM 90 ❖ LM 17:10

Conceit: "If you think you are not conceited, it means you are very conceited indeed"
•MC 114 ❖ MC III 8:14

Concentration Camp (chapter title)
•SJ 22-41 ❖ SJ ch. 2

Conception—see Miracle of Conception

Conclusion, The Practical (chapter title)
•MC 62-66 ❖ MC II ch. 5

Conditioning, religious belief which is purely a result of, mentioned by Screwtape*
•SL 110-111 ❖ SL 24:1

Confessing our sins, by, we do more than give God information; we put ourselves on a personal footing with Him
•LM 20-21 ❖ LM 4:6, 7

Confession, advantages of, include an increased feeling of forgiveness and a gain in self-knowledge
•L 249-250 ❖ L 6-7 Apr 53

Confession and Absolution, our church enjoins, on no one but leaves it free to all
•L 192 ❖ L 4 Jan 41

Confession (as to a friend) never tells the whole truth; we must not mistake our inevitably limited utterances for a full account of the worst that is inside
•PP 59-60 ❖ PP 4:7

Confession: Confiding to a confessor no more inappropriate than confiding to one's doctor
•L 219 ❖ L 6 Sep 49

Confession: I have found that my feelings of shame and disgust at my own sins do not correspond to what my reason tells me about their comparative gravity
•LM 99 ❖ LM 18:16

Confession: I take it that the view of our Church is that everyone may use it but none is obliged to
•L 243, 249-250
❖ L 20 Jun 52; 6-7 Apr 53

Confession: "If there is a particular sin on your conscience, repent and confess it. If there isn't, tell the despondent devil not to be silly"
•LAL 77 (see also LM 32-34; SL 54-55*) ❖ LAL Jul 21st 58 (see also LM 6:11-17; SL 12:2-4*)

Confession: It is not for me to decide for you, but if you do not [go to confession], you should at least make a list of your sins on a piece of paper...
•GID 123-124 ❖ GID I 14:9

Confession: Remember it's not the psychoanalyst over again; his advice or "un-

derstanding" is of secondary importance
- L 192 ❖ L 4 Jan 41

Confirmation, Lewis relates his, in his youth —which was done to please his father
- SJ 161-162 ❖ SJ 10:15

Conformity—*see also* Peer pressure

Conformity ("accommodation") of clergymen who disbelieve what they preach: "I feel it is a form of prostitution"
- GID 260, 265 (*see also* GID 89-90) ❖ GID II 16:12, 46 (*see also* GID I 10:2, 3)

Conformity: Dangers of associating with people whose behaviour we disapprove*
- RP 66-75, esp. 72-73; SL 45-48 (*see also* Association) ❖ RP ch. 7, esp. 7:11-14; SL ch. 10 (*see also* Association)

Conformity, desire for social, can lead to a gradual rejection of God's law and His Grace (—Screwtape)
- SL 156-157; WLN 55 ❖ SL 32:10; WLN 4:10

Conformity, Pride can be the result of overcoming the temptation to, and determining to be different*
- SL 164; WLN 62-63 ❖ SL 32:27; WLN 4:27

Conformity, tempters make use of the desire for, especially in young people
- SL 163-164; WLN 62 (*see also* SL 45-48) ❖ SL 32:25, 26; WLN 4:25, 26 (*see also* SL ch. 10)

Conformity to the World must be limited; "...there comes a time when we must show that we disagree"*
- GID 262 (*see also* RP 71-74; SL 45-48*) ❖ GID II 16:29 (*see also* RP 7:9-16; SL ch. 10*)

Confucianism and Stoicism, the purely moral systems like, are philosophies for aristocrats
- CR 71 ❖ CR 5:26

Confucianism mentioned as one of the world-affirming religions
- GID 147 ❖ GID I 17:2

Connaitre (knowledge-by-acquaintance) vs. *savoir* (direct knowledge about)— specifically regarding the love of God
- FL 174-175 (*see also* GID 170; WLN 25, 29, 30) ❖ FL 6:20 (*see also* GID I 20:Reply-15; WLN 2:13, 18)

Connivance—*see also* Association with unbelievers; Conformity

Connivance (chapter title)
- RP 66-75 ❖ RP ch. 7

Conscience—*see also* Guilt

Conscience: A bad man, happy, is a man without the least inkling that his actions are not in accord with the laws of the universe*
- PP 93 ❖ PP 6:5

Conscience aided by having the imitation of Christ as our goal
- MC 162 ❖ MC IV 7:5

Conscience analogous to Reason (both mean the whole man judging, either between good and evil or between truth and falsehood)
- WG 34 ❖ WG 3:3

Conscience as one of the things God gave us to defend ourselves against Satan
- MC 54 ❖ MC II 3:9

Conscience has two meanings: pressure we feel to do what we think is right, and judgment as to what is right and wrong
- WG 33-38 ❖ WG 3:2-9

Conscience, how to awaken, in modern audiences
- GID 244 ❖ GID II 12:8

Conscience, human, seen in modern religious thought as of no value at all
- L 177 ❖ L 18 Feb 40

Conscience: I've met people who felt guilty but did not seem to be, and others who were guilty and didn't seem to feel guilt
- LM 33 ❖ LM 6:12

Conscience, Lewis describes a false, which tormented him as a child regarding his nightly prayers
- SJ 61-62 ❖ SJ 4:7, 8

Conscience, my long-evaded encounter with God happened at a time when I was making a serious effort to obey my
- CR 169 ❖ CR 14:20

Conscience, my, tells me that if there is an absolutely wise and good Person I owe Him obedience
•CR 27 ❖ CR 2:42

Conscience, need for awakening, in modern men (including Christians)
•PP 55-59 (see also GID 95-96, 181-182, 243-244; MC 38-39)
❖ PP 4:1-6 (see also GID I 10:15-17; 22:13; II 12:6-8; MC I 5:4)

Conscience not a product of Nature as shown by the fact that we all make moral judgments
•M 38 ❖ M 5:10

Conscience not a separate faculty, like a sense; can be altered by argument
•WG 33 ❖ WG 3:1

Conscience, nothing gives one a more spuriously good, than keeping rules—even if there has been a total absence of all real charity and faith
•LAL 38 ❖ LAL 20/2/55

Conscience, operation of, involves three elements (as does Reason): reception of facts, perception of self-evident truth, and skill in arranging facts...
•WG 34-36; 39 ❖ WG 3:3-6, 11

Conscience, Screwtape advocates the use of Noise to silence the, ("Music and silence—how I detest them both!")*
•SL 102-103 (see also CR 168*, 170*)
❖ SL 22:5 (see also CR 14:18*, 27*)

Conscience, sin breeds more sin by strengthening sinful habit and weakening the
•PP 116 ❖ PP 7:9

Conscience, social, as currently being re-awakened can be used as a mere excuse for evading our own personal faults
•PP 60-61 ❖ PP 4:8

Conscience, that voice which speaks in your, and in some of your intensest joys may be in fact the closest contact you have with the mystery...(re: attempting contact with ultimate Reality)
•CR 170 ❖ CR 14:27

Conscience, the more you try to obey your, the more your conscience will demand of you; the Christian way is different: harder, and easier
•MC 167 ❖ MC IV 8:3, 4

Conscience, the pleasures of a good, may be what Psalmists are referring to when they speak of the Law being sweeter than honey (according to one great scholar)
•RP 55-56 ❖ RP 6:4

Conscience, when our, won't come down to brass tacks and will only vaguely accuse, we must ignore it
•LM 34 ❖ LM 6:14, 17

Consciences, dogs and cats both have; the dog, being honest and humble, always has a bad one but the cat is a Pharisee and always has a good one
•LAL 40 ❖ LAL 21/3/55

Consorting/contact with the ungodly—see Association...

Contact with God—consider also Devotional life; Evasion of God; Presence of God; Relationship with God; Seeking God

Contact with God: "...how could the initiative lie on my side? ...if Shakespeare and Hamlet could ever meet, it must be Shakespeare's doing"
•SJ 227 (see also SJ 216, 223; Initiative)
❖ SJ 14:20 (see also SJ 14:7, 14; Initiative)

Contact with God in prayer: Having our prayers considered means more than having them granted; we can bear to be refused but not to be ignored*
•LM 52-53 ❖ LM 10:3

Contact with God in prayer: Screwtape points out that the humans do not desire it as much as they suppose
•SL 22-23 (see also LM 75, 114; M 94; MC 66) ❖ SL 4:4 (see also LM 14:12; 21:8; M 11:19; MC II 5:9)

Contact with God in prayer: We ought to be simultaneously aware of closest proximity and infinite distance
•LM 13 ❖ LM 2:13

Contact with God: Initiative lies wholly on His side
•GID 143-144 (see also CR 169; MC 144; PP 51-52; SJ 216, 227)
❖ GID I 16:26 (see also CR 14:19; MC

IV 2:13; PP 3:17; SJ 14:7, 20, 21)

Contact with God: It is important in prayer to have an awareness of God and myself as real entities facing each other, in actual contact with each other
• LM 77-82 ❖ LM ch. 15

Contact with God means either bliss or horror; cannot be avoided for long; business of life is to learn to like it
• GID 47 (see also MC 183; SJ 232; WG 13) ❖ GID I 3:17 (see also MC IV 10:17; SJ 15:4; WG 1:10)

Contact with God: Prayer is an effort toward unity with God; here, at least, the distortion of God's voice through man is not total
• LM 69-70 ❖ LM 13:6

Contact with God, prayer is either sheer illusion or personal
• WLN 8 ❖ WLN 1:16

Contact with God: Screwtape mentions that anything, even a sin, which has the total effect of moving a man closer to God works against the devil's purpose*
• SL 125-126 (see also SL 56, 87-89) ❖ SL 27:1 (see also SL 12:5; 19:3)

Contact with God: "There comes a moment when people who have been dabbling in religion...suddenly draw back. Supposing we really found Him?"
• M 94 ❖ M 11:19

Contact with God, we receive the new life through; Lewis calls this "good infection"
• MC 153, 157, 162, 163, 186 ❖ MC IV 4:8, 10; 5:8; 7:5, 8; 11:7

Contact with God, we shrink from too naked a, [in prayer] because we are afraid of the divine demands upon us which it might make too audible
• LM 114 (see also CR 43; LM 75; SL 22-23, 54-55; WG 127-128) ❖ LM 21:8 (see also CR 3:12; LM 14:12; SL 4:4; 12:3; WG 9:5)

"Contemplation" of our inner activities is incompatible with our "enjoyment" of them; e.g., you cannot hope and think about hoping at the same time

• SJ 217-219 (see also GID 65-66; L 221) ❖ SJ 14:9, 10 (see also GID I 5:8, 9; L 27 Sep 49)

Contemptus mundi has sometimes been reckoned a Christian virtue; but Christianity is both world-affirming and world-denying
• GID 147-150, esp. 148 (see also World) ❖ GID I ch. 17, esp. 17:3 (see also World)

Contemptus mundi is dangerous and may lead to Manicheeism, while love of the creature is also dangerous
• L 183 ❖ L 16 Apr 40

"Contrite hearts," how to understand expressions such as, which are used in the Prayer Book
• GID 120-124 ❖ GID I 14:2-10

Controversial doctrines—see Doctrines, difficult

Controversy/ies—see also Debate(ing)

Controversies in theology—see Theological controversy(ies); consider Doctrinal differences

Controversies, two ways in which, can cease: by being settled, or by gradual and imperceptible change of custom
• GID 335 ❖ GID IV Letter 7

Controversy, I am on neither side of the capital punishment, but I think the abolitionists conduct their case very ill
• GID 340 ❖ GID IV Letter 12

Convalescent homes: "In your position I myself would prefer a 'Home'—or almost anything—to solitude"
• LAL 102 ❖ LAL 17 Jan 62

Convalescent homes ("Old People's Homes"): Sometimes the things we have most dreaded turn out to be quite nice
• LAL 94 ❖ LAL 24 Nov 60

Convalescent homes ("Old People's Homes"): "If you ever do have to go to a Home, Christ will be there just as much as in any other place"
• LAL 94 ❖ LAL 24 Nov 60

Convalescent ("nursing") homes, Screwtape mentions humans who die in costly, amid doctors, nurses, and friends who all lie to them about their

condition
- •SL 26-27 (see also L 275*; SL 146)
- ❖ SL 5:2 (see also L 6 Mar 57*; SL 31:3)

Conversation(s)—see also Talk(ing); Speech

Conversation among friends as "the golden sessions," when each feels himself to be among his betters
- •FL 104-105 ❖ FL 4:30

Conversation, angry: Slowing down the speed of the conversation is sometimes helpful; also sitting down
- •LAL 94 ❖ LAL 24 Nov 60

Conversation: As a youth Lewis made it his rule that at "social functions" he must never speak of any subject in which he felt the slightest interest
- •SJ 48 ❖ SJ 3:6

Conversation between men may be invaded and spoiled by "silly women" who are not really interested in the same things
- •FL 107-110 ❖ FL 4:33-37

Conversation, Christian must guard against unprotesting participation in evil
- •RP 72-74 (see also GID 262; SL 45-48)
- ❖ RP 7:11-13 (see also GID II 16:29; SL ch. 10)

Conversation, I remember nothing about the "grown-up," in that house but Uncle Gussie talked to me about Things
- •SJ 43 (see also FL 109*)
- ❖ SJ 3:1 (see also FL 4:35*)

Conversation, in my experience "grown-up," meant conversation about politics, money, deaths, and digestion
- •SJ 136 ❖ SJ 9:11

Conversation "in the charmed circle of one's own set and caste" vs. that with a stranger "whose aitches are uncertain"
- •L 106 (see also GID 127*)
- ❖ L 5 Jan 26 (see also GID I 15:2, 3*)

Conversation: "Kirk excited and satisfied one side of me. Here was talk that was really about something"
- •SJ 137 ❖ SJ 9:11

Conversation, Lewis describes the dull, of his fellow officers in the army: Subjects were shop, sport, and theatrical news
- •L 39 ❖ L undated letter just after one postmarked 10 Oct 17

Conversation, Lewis's distaste for "grown-up"
- •L 173; SJ 43, 48, 134, 136
- ❖ L 1 Jan 40; SJ 3:1, 6; 9:6, 11

Conversation, Lewis's distaste for information and fact-oriented, reflected in a description of a dull walk
- •L 150-151 (see also L 173)
- ❖ L 20 Mar 32 (see also L 1 Jan 40)

Conversation: "One used to be told as a child, 'Think what you're saying.' Apparently we also need to be told, 'Think what you're thinking'"*
- •LM 45 ❖ LM 8:14

Conversation: Protests against sins of the tongue are all over the Psalms
- •RP 75 ❖ RP 7:16

Conversation: Screwtape points out ways in which human laughter and humour can be used to serve diabolical purposes
- •SL 49-52 ❖ SL ch. 11

Conversation should be polite at home as in public
- •GID 285-286 (see also FL 66-70)
- ❖ GID III 3:8, 9 (see also FL 3:22-26)

Conversation, silence a good refuge when during evil, one does not wish to offend or appear to agree (although there is a limit)
- •RP 72-73 (see also GID 262*; SL 45-48*) ❖ RP 7:11-13 (see also GID II 16:29*; SL ch. 10*)

Conversation: "The only two kinds of talk I wanted were the almost purely imaginative and the almost purely rational..."
- •SJ 136-137 ❖ SJ 9:11

Conversation: When things are of high value and easily destroyed, we must talk with great care, and perhaps the less we talk the better (re: "culture")*
- •WLN 34 (see also WLN 37)
- ❖ WLN 3:6 (see also WLN 3:11)

Conversations, regarding women trying to

enter men's, ("We all appear as dunces when feigning an interest in things we know nothing about")
- FL 106-110 ❖ FL 4:32-37

Conversations with those one cares nothing about, on subjects that bore one, mentioned by Screwtape as a method to distract humans from God
- SL 55 ❖ SL 12:4

Conversion—*see also* New Birth; *consider also* Evangelism; Surrender

Conversion, a genuine, will be known by an improvement in outward behaviour, just as a tree is known by its fruit
- MC 175-176 ❖ MC IV 10:2

Conversion: "'Any road out of Jerusalem must also be a road into Jerusalem'"* (re: the possible value of "sub-Christian" literature)*
- CR 22, 23 (*see also* L 297) ❖ CR 2:29, 34 (*see also* L undated letter of Feb 61)

Conversion, culture as a route to: not for all people; there is a shorter and safer way...
- CR 24 ❖ CR 2:36

Conversion, devil very active on the eve of; anxieties and doubts pour in
- L 227-228 (*see also* SL 172; WLN 70) ❖ L 5 Mar 51 (*see also* SL 32:40; WLN 4:40)

Conversion different from intellectual assent
- GID 221 ❖ GID II 8:10

Conversion: Does it depend on our choice or God's choice?
- L 251-252 (*see also* Predestination) ❖ L 8 Aug 53 (*see also* Predestination)

Conversion, feelings of excitement that may sometimes accompany, never last; don't depend on them
- L 241 ❖ L 15 May 52

Conversion: Few people are converted from scepticism to liberal Christianity; most unbelievers, when they come in at all, come in a good deal further
- LM 119 ❖ LM 22:5

Conversion: Few people are converted by studying Jesus' life simply as biography—the Gospels were written, not to make Christians, but to edify Christians
- SL 108 (*see also* M 143-144) ❖ SL 23:3 (*see also* M 16:2)

Conversion, freedom of choice involved in: The most deeply compelled action is also the freest*
- GID 261 (*see also* LM 49-50*; SJ 224-225) ❖ GID II 16:19-22 (*see also* LM 9:11*; SJ 14:16)

Conversion: "If we are to convert our heathen neighbors, we must understand their culture. We must 'beat them at their own game'"
- CR 17 (*see also* WG 28) ❖ CR 2:18 (*see also* WG 2:10)

Conversion, in religious, as in romantic love, the old self turns out to be not so dead as he pretended
- FL 159 ❖ FL 5:44

Conversion, Lewis describes his: "...the steady, unrelenting approach of Him whom I so earnestly desired not to meet"
- SJ 228 ❖ SJ 14:23

Conversion, Lewis describes the freedom of choice involved in his, to Theism
- SJ 224-225 (*see also* GID 261) ❖ SJ 14:16 (*see also* GID II 16:19-22)

Conversion, Lewis mentions Dyson and Tolkien as the "immediate human causes" of his
- L 197 (*see also* SJ 216, 225) ❖ L 21 Dec 41 (*see also* SJ 14:6, 17)

Conversion, Lewis mentions some of the factors relevant in his, e.g., authority, reason, and experience*
- CR 41 ❖ CR 3:9

Conversion, Lewis mentions that on the eve of his, he realized his need for total surrender
- SJ 228 ❖ SJ 14:22

Conversion, Lewis writes of his, to Theism while riding on a bus: It was strangely unemotional; I was moved by no desires or fears
- SJ 224-225, 228 (*see also* GID 261) ❖ SJ 14:16, 22 (*see also* GID II 16:19-22)

Conversion, Lewis's: Agnostics will talk about "man's search for God." To me,

they might as well have talked about the mouse's search for the cat
- •SJ 227 (*see also* CR 169)
- ❖ SJ 14:21 (*see also* CR 14:19)

Conversion, Lewis's: "But who can duly adore that Love which will open the high gates to a prodigal who is brought in kicking, struggling, resentful..."
- •SJ 229 (*see also* GID 261)
- ❖ SJ 14:23 (*see also* GID II 16:19-22)

Conversion, Lewis's: He mentions that without his early experiences of romantic *Sehnsucht*, his conversion would have been more difficult
- •CR 23 (*see also* SJ 3-21, 71-82, 165-181; Joy)
- ❖ CR 2:33 (*see also* SJ ch. 1, 5, 11; Joy)

Conversion, Lewis's: [I was] the most dejected and reluctant convert in all England...brought in kicking, struggling, resentful...
- •SJ 228-229 ❖ SJ 14:23

Conversion, Lewis's: "I was the object rather than the subject in this affair. I was decided upon"
- •GID 261 (*see also* SJ 226-229; Initiative) ❖ GID II 16:20 (*see also* SJ 14:20-23; Initiative)

Conversion, Lewis's imminent, indicated in a letter to Owen Barfield: "Terrible things are happening to me"
- •L 141
- ❖ L undated letter just after 10 Jun 30

Conversion, Lewis's: My long-evaded encounter with God happened at a time when I was making a serious effort to obey my conscience
- •CR 169 ❖ CR 14:20

Conversion, Lewis's philosophical steps toward, described
- •WG 91-92 ❖ WG 5:23, 24

Conversion, Lewis's: The final step was taken on the way to Whipsnade Zoo one morning
- •SJ 237-238 ❖ SJ 15:8, 9

Conversion, Lewis's: "There was no strain of music from within, no smell of eternal orchards at the threshold, when I was dragged through the doorway..."
- •SJ 230-231 ❖ SJ 15:2

Conversion likened to the experience of a man who, after long sleep, still lying motionless in bed, becomes aware that he is now awake
- •SJ 237 ❖ SJ 15:8

Conversion, methods of—*see* Evangelism

Conversion, obstacles to—*see* Obstacles to Christian faith

Conversion of rebellious wills cost God crucifixion
- •MC 179 ❖ MC IV 10:9

Conversion: One can't be thinking it over forever; can begin to try to be a disciple before one is a professed theologian
- •L 191 ❖ L 4 Jan 41

Conversion process, "compulsion" by God in
- •SJ 224-225, 229, 237 (*see also* GID 261)
- ❖ SJ 14:16, 23; 15:8 (*see also* GID II 16:19-22)

Conversion process not the same for everyone; we must be careful not to demand that the salvation of our loved ones conform to some pattern of our own
- •L 261 ❖ L 2 Feb 55

Conversion process not without its distresses; I send you my condolences and congratulations
- •L 238 ❖ L 29 Feb 52

Conversion, regarding the disappointment or anticlimax which comes in the first few weeks after
- •SL 13-14 (*see also* LM 26-27; MC 100; SL 36-37, 42-44*)
- ❖ SL 2:3 (*see also* LM 5:10-13; MC III 6:11, 12; SL 8:1, 2; 9:3, 4*)

Conversion requires an alteration of the will and the intervention of the supernatural
- •GID 221 ❖ GID II 8:10

Conversion, Screwtape advises preventing any, from being acted upon; "The great thing is to prevent his doing anything"
- •SL 60-61 ❖ SL 13:5

Conversion, Screwtape describes how to exploit the inevitable falling off of

emotion which humans experience after
•SL 36-44 ❖ SL ch. 8, 9

Conversion, Screwtape reassures Wormwood that even after, many converts can still be reclaimed for Hell ("...*habits*...are still in our favour")
•SL 11 ❖ SL 2:1

Conversion, steps in and after, outlined*
•L 191-192 ❖ L 4 Jan 41

Conversion: "The difficulty of converting an uneducated man nowadays lies in his complacency"
•CR 23 ❖ CR 2:35

Conversion, the fervour we experienced in the first days of our, will likely die away; do not miserably try to conjure it back
•LM 26-27 (*see also* SL 13-14)
❖ LM 5:10-13 (*see also* SL 2:3)

Conversion to Christianity may elicit a sense of outrage in family members
•FL 71-72; L 274
❖ FL 3:29, 30; L 10 Feb 57

Conversion, we must prefer the, rather than the punishment of very evil men, and prefer it infinitely—but the demand for justice may be ethical
•PP 121-122 ❖ PP 8:5

Conviction—*see* Self-knowledge; Sinfulness

Convictions—*see* Beliefs

Cooking, the whole time-wasting business of, is hardly worth it when one is on one's own
•LAL 86 ❖ LAL 21 Aug 59

Cooperation of churches—*see* Reunion

Cord, God as alive and pulling at the other end of the, makes people more uncomfortable than an impersonal God
•M 94 (*see also* GID 142-143*; LM 114; M 81, MC 35*; SL 22-23*)
❖ M 11:19 (*see also* GID I 16:25*; LM 21:8; M 11:2; MC I 4:6*; SL 4:4*)

Corn-king ("dying god"), is not Christ simply another
•M 113-115, 136-137 (*see also* GID 29-30, 37, 83-84; Myth of "dying God")
❖ M 14:8-14; 15:8 (*see also* GID I 2:8, 15; 9:5, 6; Myth of "dying God")

Coronation of the Queen of England seen as a symbol of the situation of humanity itself—called by God, yet inadequate to the responsibility
•LAL 18-19 ❖ LAL Jul 10 53

Corporate self-complacency, the real traitor to our order is not the man who speaks, within that order, of its faults but the man who flatters our
•WLN 36 ❖ WLN 3:9

Corporate superiority, sense of, which may develop in a circle of Friends
•FL 116-124 (*see also* Inner Rings)
❖ FL 4:48-57 (*see also* Inner Rings)

Correspondence—*see also* Letter(s); Letter-writing

Correspondence, a heavy responsibility rests on those who forage through a dead man's, and publish it indiscriminately
•L 108 ❖ L 5 Jun 26

Correspondence, Lewis expresses distaste for argument by
•L 223, 224
❖ L undated letter of Jan 1950; undated letter just before 3 Dec 51

Correspondence, my, is mostly with women; the female is by nature a much more "epistolatory" animal than the male
•L 242 ❖ L 28 May 52

Correspondents, you are one of the minority of my female, who didn't gradually fade away as soon as they heard I was married
•LAL 74 ❖ LAL 15/4/58

Corruption—*see also* Sinfulness

Corruption, Screwtape speaks on small-scale political
•SL 154, 156; WLN 52, 54
❖ SL 32:5, 10; WLN 4:5, 10

Corruption: The greatest evil is not now done in Dickensian "dens of crime" but rather in clean, carpeted offices by quiet men with white collars...*
•SL x ❖ SL P:17

Cost, both the tempter and Our Lord tell us to count the, of becoming a Christian
•WG 131 ❖ WG 9:12

Cost, Counting the (chapter title)
•MC 171-175 ❖ MC IV ch. 9

Cost, counting the, takes on a new meaning when one realizes that if the Divine call does not make us better, it will make us very much worse
•RP 32 ❖ RP 3:20

Cost: In the religion of "the Absolute," there was nothing to fear; better still, nothing to obey—this was a religion that cost nothing
•SJ 209-210 ❖ SJ 13:18

Cost: It costs God nothing to create nice things, but to convert rebellious wills cost Him crucifixion
•MC 179 ❖ MC IV 10:9

Cost: Lewis mentions that in the religion of "Higher Thought" which he adopted at Wyvern there was nothing to be obeyed
•SJ 60 ❖ SJ 4:6

Cost: "Life-force" is a sort of tame God—all thrills, no cost
•MC 35 (see also SL 33)
❖ MC I 4:6 (see also SL 7:1)

Cost: Minimal religion (without dogma) cannot convince, convert, or console; is not costly enough
•GID 143 ❖ GID I 16:25

Cost of being a Christian—see also Demands of God; consider also Self-reservation

Cost of being a Christian: It is not so much of our time and attention that God demands; it is ourselves
•WG 130 (see also MC 167; SJ 172*)
❖ WG 9:9 (see also MC IV 8:4; SJ 11:8*)

Cost of being a Christian: We are afraid of getting in over our heads, of running up "too big a bill to pay"
•WG 126-132 (see also CR 43*; LM 114*)
❖ WG ch. 9 (see also CR 3:12*; LM 21:8*)

Cost of being a Christian: Whatever is most highly valued on the natural level is to be abandoned without mercy the moment it conflicts with the service of God*
•CR 14 ❖ CR 2:5

Cost of calling in the heavenly Dentist: He

will give you the full treatment
•MC 171-175 ❖ MC IV ch. 9

Cost of leaving home and family as part of the allegory of Bride and Bridegroom: a vocation is at first a costly honour
•RP 130-132 ❖ RP 12:10

Cost: Pantheism attractive because its God does nothing, demands nothing; He will not pursue you*
•M 81, 93-94 ❖ M 11:2, 19

Cost: The God of Christianity is alive and pulling at the other end of the cord; may demand something of you*
•M 81, 93-94 ❖ M 11:2, 19

Cost: The vague religion of feeling God in nature, etc. is attractive because it is all thrills and no work*
•MC 136 ❖ MC IV 1:4

"Coterie" as one of the derogatory names often given to sets of friends by the envious people outside
•FL 112 ❖ FL 4:41

Coterie ("clique"), Screwtape wants the Church to be small so that its members may acquire the self-righteousness of a
•SL 33-34 ❖ SL 7:2

Coterie is a self-appointed aristocracy; to become a coterie is one of the temptations of every set of Friends
•FL 118, 122 ❖ FL 4:49, 55

Coterie, the congregational principle [of church organization] makes each church into a kind of club or
•SL 73 ❖ SL 16:2

Coteries, I have a holy terror of
•L 48 ❖ L 25 May 19

Coteries, people who think alike tend to gravitate together into, where they do not encounter much opposition; complacent dogmatism thrives
•GID 127 (see also L 106*; consider also Inner Rings) ❖ GID I 15:2 (see also L 5 Jan 26*; consider also Inner Rings)

Counting the Cost (chapter title)
•MC 171-175 ❖ MC IV ch. 9

"Country" contrasted by "town" is part of our appreciation of Nature; this was not the case with the Psalmists—

towns were few and very small
- •RP 76-77 ❖ RP 8:2

Country of the Blind (by Wells) mentioned as an illustration of how thought and the use of language to convey thought may be changing
- •CR 140-141 ❖ CR 11:23, 24

Country ("quiet places"), Lewis mentions his fondness for, as opposed to cities which interested him only for cultural reasons
- •L 215 ❖ L undated letter of Jan 1949

Courage, according to Screwtape pride may be a consequence of human
- •SL 135 (*see also* SL 140)
- ❖ SL 29:1 (*see also* SL 30:1)

Courage: "As Johnson points out, where courage is not, no other virtue can survive except by accident"
- •SJ 161 ❖ SJ 10:15

Courage, folly of trying to manufacture feelings of, even as we pray for courage
- •SL 21 ❖ SL 4:3

Courage, ideal of, (as found in literature) may provide temptation, but for some it may prove a schoolmaster to the ideal of martyrdom
- •CR 22 ❖ CR 2:30

Courage is not simply *one* of the virtues, but the form of every virtue at the testing point (—Screwtape)
- •SL 137 ❖ SL 29:6

Courage, Jesus not a man of immense natural, as seen by Gethsemane
- •L 210-211 (*see also* Gethsemane)
- ❖ L undated letter of 1947 (*see also* Gethsemane)

Courage of the perfected Christian, having been learned in Gethsemane, may have no "honour" about it (re: value of "honour" in literature)
- •CR 22 ❖ CR 2:30

Courage of two kinds mentioned: the kind that faces danger, and the kind that "sticks it" under pain
- •MC 76 ❖ MC III 2:7

Courage: When pain is to be borne, courage helps more than knowledge, human sympathy more than courage,

and the love of God more than all
- •PP 10 ❖ PP P:1

Courage: You needn't worry about not feeling brave; Our Lord didn't, in Gethsemane
- •L 250 (*see also* L 166, 189, 285; LAL 41; LM 41-43; Gethsemane) ❖ L 17 Jul 53 (*see also* L 8 May 39; undated letter just after 11 Aug 40; 29 Apr 59; LAL 2 Apr 55; LM 8:5-11; Gethsemane)

Courtesy as one of the Christian virtues
- •MC 80 ❖ MC III 3:4

Courtesy at home: "...Affection at its best practices a courtesy which is incomparably more subtle, sensitive, and deep than the public kind"
- •FL 67-68 (*see also* GID 285-286)
- ❖ FL 3:24 (*see also* GID III 3:8, 9)

Courtesy at home, discussion of the importance of
- •FL 66-70; GID 282-286
- ❖ FL 3:22-26; GID III ch. 3

Courtesy of parents toward children (especially young adults), importance of
- •FL 66 ❖ FL 3:22

Courtesy, there is a distinction between public and domestic, but the root principle of both is the same
- •FL 67 ❖ FL 3:24

Courtship: A real disagreement on the issue of putting God first should make itself felt early enough to prevent a marriage from occurring*
- •FL 173-174 ❖ FL 6:19

Courtship mentioned by Screwtape as the time for sowing the seeds of domestic hatred
- •SL 120 ❖ SL 26:1

Courtship, Screwtape advises causing humans during, to think they have solved their problems through "love" when in fact they have only postponed them
- •SL 120 ❖ SL 26:1

Coverdale as the Bible translation Lewis mainly used in working on the Psalms
- •RP 7 ❖ RP 1:11

Cowardice—*see also* Fear

Cowardice, alone among the vices, is purely painful—horrible to anticipate,

horrible to feel, horrible to remember
•SL 136 ❖ SL 29:4

Cowardice: An honesty or mercy which yields to danger will be honest or merciful only on conditions; Pilate was merciful till it became risky
•SL 137-138 ❖ SL 29:6

Cowardice: "As Johnson points out, where courage is not, no other virtue can survive except by accident"
•SJ 161 ❖ SJ 10:15

Cowardice as one of the things that protected Lewis as he became interested in the the Occult (in his youth)
•SJ 175-176, 177 ❖ SJ 11:13, 14, 16

Cowardice is almost the only vice at which men still feel shame (—Screwtape)
•SL 137 ❖ SL 29:5

"Cowardice," Lewis describes his own pessimism as
•SJ 117 (see also SJ 171*)
❖ SJ 7:21 (see also SJ 11:8*)

Cowardice mentioned by Screwtape as one of those things which can be passed off as funny, if boasted of with humorous exaggerations and grotesque gestures
•SL 51 ❖ SL 11:5

Cowardice, the act of, is all that matters; the emotion of fear is, in itself, not sin (—Screwtape)
•SL 139 ❖ SL 29:8

Cowper, William: He had literally nothing to tell anyone about, yet one reads a whole volume of his letters with unfailing interest
•L 124 (see also L 146)
❖ L 25 Feb 28 (see also L 22 Nov 31)

"Create" means to make; "beget" is to become the father of (re: Jesus as the "begotten" Son of God)
•MC 138, 150 (see also Father and Son)
❖ MC IV 1:11-13; 4:2 (see also Father and Son)

Creation—consider also Evolution

Creation an exclusively Christian doctrine; in polytheism the gods are usually the product of a universe already in existence
•GID 149 (see also M 8; RP 78, 82)

❖ GID I 17:6 (see also M 2:9; RP 8:4, 11)

Creation an explicit doctrine in ancient Judaism (unlike many other religions); this had consequences for their entire way of thinking
•RP 77-85 ❖ RP 8:3-15

"Creation" as applied to human authorship a misleading term; we rearrange elements He has provided
•L 203 (see also CR 6-7; GID 276; LM 73; M 32-33; Originality)
❖ L 20 Feb 43 (see also CR 1:10, 11; GID III 1:19; LM 14:3; M 4:14; Originality)

Creation as expressed in the various mythologies—Egyptian, Babylonian, Norse and Greek
•RP 78 ❖ RP 8:4

Creation as one of the beliefs which unite all Christians everywhere
•GID 336 ❖ GID IV Letter 9

Creation as part of Christian beliefs
•MC 45 ❖ MC II 1:4

Creation as separation: "Can it be that the more perfect the creature is, the further this separation must at some point be pushed?" (re: Jesus as Man)
•LM 44 ❖ LM 8:12

Creation: "Because God created the Natural—invented it out of His love and artistry—it demands our reverence..."
•GID 148 ❖ GID I 17:5

Creation: Because God created the natural level, we cannot cease to fight against the death which mars it
•GID 150 ❖ GID I 17:7

Creation: Burden of proof now rests on those who deny that nature has some cause beyond herself
•GID 39 ❖ GID I 3:3

Creation defined: "...the whole universe ...(is) produced by the will of a perfect, timeless, unconditioned God who is above and outside all that He makes"
•RP 79-80 ❖ RP 8:6

Creation, doctrine of, leaves Nature full of manifestations which show the presence of God (even as it separates God and Nature)
•RP 80-81 ❖ RP 8:8-10

Creation: "Either the stream of events had a beginning or it had not. If it had, then we are faced with something like creation"
•GID 78-79 ❖ GID I 8:8, 9

Creation: Entropy is the rule in nature; but a clock can't run down unless it has first been wound up*
•M 152 (see also GID 33-34; Entropy)
❖ M 16:17 (see also GID I 2:12; Entropy)

Creation: "Everything God has made has some likeness to Himself"—space, matter, insects, mammals, and man
•MC 139 ❖ MC IV 1:14

Creation: First beginning must have been outside the ordinary processes of nature
•GID 210-211 ❖ GID II 5:10

Creation: Genesis account achieves the idea of true Creation and of a transcendent Creator
•RP 110-111 ❖ RP 11:3

Creation, Genesis account of, told in the form of a folk-tale, but relays the idea of "creation" in the rigorous sense of the word
•M 33 (see also GID 42; RP 109-111)
❖ M 4:15 (see also GID I 3:9; RP 11:2, 3)

Creation: God "caused things to be other than Himself that, being distinct, they might learn to love Him, and achieve union instead of mere sameness"
•PP 151 (see also L 242-243)
❖ PP 10:8 (see also L 20 Jun 52)

Creation: God's creative act is timeless; in this sense God did not create the universe long ago but creates it at this minute—at every minute
•M 177, 178 ❖ M App. B:10, 15

Creation: Humans not capable of weighing the question of whether creating the world, with its possibility of suffering, was better than not creating it
•PP 35-36, 70 ❖ PP 2:17; 5:1

Creation, I have no difficulty accepting the view that the Genesis account of, is derived from earlier Semitic stories which were Pagan and mythical
•RP 110 ❖ RP 11:3

Creation: If a Brute made the world, then he also made the standard by which we judge him to be a Brute (re: Heroic Pessimism or anti-theism)
•CR 65-67 (see also CR 69-70; MC 45-46*) ❖ CR 5:19 (see also CR 5:24; MC II 1:5, 6*)

Creation, in any unambiguous sense, seems in reality to be a surprisingly rare doctrine among the religions of the world
•RP 78 ❖ RP 8:4

Creation: Mentally limited beings studying a painting used to illustrate the impossibility of discovering by science how God works on Nature** (illustration borrowed from Bergson; used regarding all miracles)
•M 97 ❖ M 12:5

Creation: No theory I have yet come across is a big improvement on the words "In the beginning God made Heaven and Earth"
•M 33 ❖ M 4:15

Creation of a world seems to require certain intrinsic necessities—matter, environment, fixed laws, etc. (re: Divine omnipotence)
•PP 29-35 (see also PP 71)
❖ PP 2:6-16 (see also PP 5:1)

Creation of individuals, purpose of God in the, includes the never-completed attempt by each soul to communicate its unique vision of God to all the others
•PP 150 (see also FL 92-93*)
❖ PP 10:7 (see also FL 4:9*)

Creation of man, conjectures about the Genesis account of
•RP 115-116 ❖ RP 11:11

Creation of man described as the calling or raising of an animal to be something more than an animal
•RP 115 ❖ RP 11:11

Creation of Man: "I fancy the 'beauties of nature' are a secret God has shared with us alone. That may be one of the reasons why we were made..."
•LM 18 ❖ LM 3:9

Creation of Man: Speculation about the nature of Adam
•L 237; PP 77-84

❖ L 10 Jan 52; PP 5:6-10

Creation of Man: When it is said that God made man in His image, different images are brought to different minds—but the substance is the same
•GID 45-46 ❖ GID I 3:15, 16

Creation of the universe was purely from Gift-love, not from any kind of Divine Need-love
•FL 175-176 ❖ FL 6:21

Creation, one result of believing in, is to see Nature not as a mere datum but as an achievement
•RP 83 ❖ RP 8:12

Creation, purpose of our: To be a part of the gift Jesus presents to the Father is the only thing we were made for
•MC 170 ❖ MC IV 8:12

Creation, purpose of our: We were made not primarily that we may love God but that God may love us
•PP 48 ❖ PP 3:15

Creation: Reality is a very *long* story, with a complicated plot; what we know of reality through Nature is only a very small part (re: miracles)**
•M 98-99 ❖ M 12:7

Creation: regarding the impossibility of "tinkering with the creation as though this or that element of it could have been removed"
•PP 35 ❖ PP 2:16

Creation, something tragic may be inherent in the very act of; the anguish that lies across our lives may not *solely* be due to some pre-historic catastrophe
•LM 91 ❖ LM 17:15

Creation, St. Jerome said that Moses described, "after the manner of a popular poet" (which is to say, mythically)
•RP 109 ❖ RP 11:2

Creation: "The great work of art was made for the sake of all it does and is, down to the curve of every wave and the flight of every insect" (re: prayer as an end as well as a means)
•LM 56 ❖ LM 10:11

Creation: "The relation between Nature and Supernature...becomes intelligible if the Supernatural made the Natural"
•GID 276 ❖ GID III 1:18, 19

Creation: "This act, as it is for God, must always remain totally inconceivable to man"
•LM 72-73 ❖ LM 14:1-3

Creation: "To say that God created Nature, while it brings God and Nature into relation, also separates them"; the created and the Creator cannot be one
•RP 80 ❖ RP 8:8

Creation: Universe was made for Christ and everything is to be gathered together in Him
•MC 170 ❖ MC IV 8:10

Creation vs. Evolution: We should not base our apologetic on some recent development in Science (re: scientific attitude towards Christianity)**
•GID 92 (*see also* GID 39, 44; WLN 83-84) ❖ GID I 10:8 (*see also* GID I 3:3, 12; WLN 6:1-3)

Creation: "Was it better for God to create than not to create?"—I am sure that, if the question has a meaning, the answer must be Yes
•PP 70 (*see also* PP 35-36)
❖ PP 5:1 (*see also* PP 2:17)

Creation: "Was Nature—space and time and matter—created precisely in order to make many-ness possible?"
•MC 159 ❖ MC IV 6:2

Creation, we find in Plato a clear Theology of, in the Judaic and Christian sense
•RP 79-80, 82 ❖ RP 8:6, 11

Creation: When God made space and worlds and air, he knew what the sky would mean to us; it is of all things sensuously perceived the most like infinity (re: our images of Heaven)
•M 158 ❖ M 16:26

Creation, whole point of, is that God was not content to be all; He intends to be all *in all* (vs. Pantheism, in which God is all)
•LM 70 ❖ LM 13:9

Creation: Whole world of nature invented and formed by "that great Imagination...for Its own delight and

for the delight of men and angels and...beasts"*
•RP 5 ❖ RP 1:8

Creationist's ("religious") view vs. materialist's view of the universe: Neither can be proved by science*
•MC 32 ❖ MC I 4:2

Creative Evolution—*see also* Emergent Evolution; Life-force

Creative Evolution and Progress, philosophies of, bear reluctant witness to the truth that our real goal is elsewhere
•WG 8 ❖ WG 1:5

Creative Evolution, discussion of
•MC 35 ❖ MC I 4:6

Creative Evolution fixes men's affections on the future, according to Screwtape, and is therefore encouraged in men's thinking by the devils
•SL 68-69 ❖ SL 15:3

Creative Evolution gives the comfort of belief in God without the cost
•MC 35 (*consider also* Cost)
❖ MC I 4:6 (*consider also* Cost)

Creative Evolutionist committed to a sinking ship
•GID 44 ❖ GID I 3:11

"Creative," meaning of the word, to modern minds ("The idea of creation in the theological sense is absent...")
•GID 97 ❖ GID I 10:26

Creativity—*see also* Originality

Creativity: Author should never conceive himself as bringing into existence beauty or wisdom which did not exist before; he reflects eternal Beauty and Wisdom
•CR 6-7 ❖ CR 1:10, 11

Creativity: "Human will becomes truly creative and truly our own when it is wholly God's..."
•PP 102 (*consider also* Personality)
❖ PP 6:14 (*consider also* Personality)

Creativity: "...we can create nothing new, but can only rearrange our material provided through sense data"
•GID 276 ❖ GID III 1:19

Creativity: We can never actually create but can only re-combine elements borrowed from the real universe
•M 32-33 ❖ M 4:14

Creativity: "We—even our poets and musicians and inventors—never, in the ultimate sense, *make*. We only build. We always have materials to build from"
•LM 73 (*see also* L 203-204; M 32-33)
❖ LM 14:3 (*see also* L 20 Feb 43; M 4:14)

Creator and creature, relationship between, is unique but analogies from the various types of love between creatures can be useful (examples listed)
•PP 41-47 ❖ PP 3:9-14

Creator and creature, relationship between: Human action and Divine action need not exclude one another
•LM 68-71, 72-75 (*see also* LM 49-50, 81; MC 142-143) ❖ LM 13:2-10; 14:1-11 (*see also* LM 9:10-12; 15:15; MC IV 2:9)

Creator and Creature, there is a union between, which is "given" by the relationship; this is different from the union of wills reached through grace
•LM 69 (*see also* Creature)
❖ LM 13:5 (*see also* Creature)

Creator, God as: "[God] is the opaque centre of all existences...He is so brim-full of existence that He can give existence away..."
•M 88 ❖ M 11:11

Creator, God as: If a Brute made the world, then he also made the standard by which we judge him to be a brute (re: Heroic Pessimism or anti-theism)
•CR 65-67 (*see also* CR 69-70; MC 45-46*) ❖ CR 5:19 (*see also* CR 5:24; MC II 1:5, 6*)

Creator, God as: one of the Christian beliefs
•MC 45 ❖ MC II 1:4

Creator, God is the glad; He values matter and the senses and all that can be called Nature
•M 163 ❖ M 16:32

Creator, one seldom meets people who have grasped the evidence of a supernatural God and yet deny that He is the
•M 33 ❖ M 4:15

Creator, praise of: "...of every created thing I praise, I should say, 'In some way, in its unique way, like Him who made it'"*
•GO 73 (see also LM 90)
❖ GO 4:7 (see also LM 17:8)

Creature, civil obedience not related to the kind and degree of obedience which a, owes to its Creator
•PP 115 ❖ PP 7:6

"Creature" defined as "an essentially dependent being whose principle of existence lies not in itself but in another" (re: Fall of Man)
•PP 75 ❖ PP 5:5

Creature, every, is nearer to its creator than it can be to superior *creatures* (e.g., angels)
•LAL 13 ❖ LAL 4/iii/53

Creature, God can no more be in competition with a, than Shakespeare can be in competition with Viola (re: God as "selfish" or "unselfish")
•PP 49 ❖ PP 3:17

Creature, love of the, is dangerous ("Not bad you see, just very very small") while *contemptus mundi* is also dangerous
•L 183 (consider also Body; Matter)
❖ L 16 Apr 40 (consider also Body; Matter)

"Creature," meaning of the word, to modern minds ("beast", or "irrational animal"—does not suggest "a created being")
•GID 97 ❖ GID I 10:27

Creature, the better stuff a, is made of, the better—and worse—it can become
•MC 53 (see also MC 181)
❖ MC II 3:5 (see also MC IV 10:13)

Creature, the highest good of a, must be creaturely—that is, derivative or reflective—good
•CR 7 ❖ CR 1:10

Creature, the proper good of a, is to surrender itself to its Creator—and when it does so, it is good and happy
•PP 90 (see also PP 52; WG 118-119)
❖ PP 6:3 (see also PP 3:18; WG 7:18)

Creatures, all, are other than God—yet God is in them as they can never be in one another (re: the creature's relationship to the Creator)
•LM 73-74 (see also LM 68)
❖ LM 14:5 (see also LM 13:3)

Creatures, as, God is the ground of our being; He is always both within us and over against us
•LM 68 ❖ LM 13:3

Creatures, as, we have a Need-love for God which is incalculably increased by our being fallen creatures; Grace enables us to accept this need gladly
•FL 179-181 ❖ FL 6:26-28

Creatures, as, we have nothing we have not received; but we have received the power to be something more than receptacles (re: causative power of prayer)
•LM 50 ❖ LM 9:12

Creatures, by being created, are in some sense separated from the Creator; Jesus, in becoming Man, experienced this aspect of humanity as well
•LM 44 ❖ LM 8:12

Creatures can never "call their souls their own," or set up independently of God
•PP 80 (see also L 251; SJ 172, 228, 237; SL 95-99; WG 130-131)
❖ PP 5:8 (see also L 17 Jul 53; SJ 11:8; 14:22; 15:8; SL ch. 21; WG 9:9, 10)

Creatures, God gives the higher, power to will His will; the lower ones simply execute it automatically
•LM 74-75 ❖ LM 14:9

Creatures, God is the only good of all; He has not arbitrarily made us such that He is our only good
•PP 53 ❖ PP 3:19

Creatures higher in the natural order than ourselves must be represented symbolically if at all (re: use of imagery to describe angels)
•SL viii ❖ SL P:12

Creatures, I think it dangerous to suppose that Satan created all disagreeable or dangerous
•L 257 ❖ L 1 Nov 54 (first letter)

Creatures, it passes reason to explain why any, not to say creatures such as we,

should have a value so prodigious in their Creator's eyes
•PP 47 ❖ PP 3:14

Creatures, we are only; our highest activity must be response, not initiative (re: love of God)
•PP 51 ❖ PP 3:17

Creatures, we tend to feel that surely we can't be *quite*, —that surely we must have a little native luminosity?
•FL 180 ❖ FL 6:27

Creatureliness, our, creates responsibility to the One who made us*
•MC 73 ❖ MC III 1:8

Creatureliness, our: We are the machine; God is the inventor*
•MC 173 (*see also* Machine)
❖ MC IV 9:7 (*see also* Machine)

Creaturely role, in obedience we consciously act our, and reverse the act by which man fell
•PP 100-101 ❖ PP 6:12

Crime, "Humanitarian" view of: All crime is pathological; demands not retributive punishment but cure—a dangerous view
•GID 287-294 (*see also* GID 313; L 304)
❖ GID III 4:1-14 (*see also* GID III 8:7-9; L 25 May 62)

Crime: Only the concept of desert connects punishment with morality and justice; if crime is merely a disease, it cannot be pardoned—must be cured
•GID 288, 294, 313, 339 (*see also* PP 93-94, 120-122; L 304)
❖ GID III 4:4, 13; 8:7; IV Letter 12 (*see also* PP 6:6; 8:5, 6; L 25 May 62)

Crime, under the humanitarian view of, (where it is viewed as a "disease" which must be "cured"), rulers become owners
•GID 313 ❖ GID III 8:8

Crime, white collar: The greatest evil is not now done in Dickensian "dens of crime" but rather in clean, carpeted offices by quiet men with white collars
•SL x ❖ SL P:17

Crimes, I find it easier to understand the great, for the raw material of them

exists in us all; mere disagreeableness is mysterious
•LAL 27-28 ❖ LAL Mar 10/54

Criminal justice—*see* Justice

Criminal law—*see also* Punishment

Criminal law protects the criminal more than the victim
•GID 306-310, esp. 307
❖ GID III ch. 6, esp. 6:7

Crisis, emotions may be flat after a, passes; that isn't ingratitude, only exhaustion
•LM 46 ❖ LM 9:2

Crisis, relief after: Like at sea, "once you have doubled the point and got into smooth water, the point doesn't take long to hide below the horizon"
•LM 46 ❖ LM 9:1

Crisis, worry and suspense in a: "...if only one could go underground, hibernate, sleep it out"*
•LM 41 ❖ LM 8:4

Criticism, Biblical—*see* Biblical criticism

Criticism, literary—*see* Literary criticism

Criticism, Modern Theology and Biblical (chapter title)
•CR 152-166 ❖ CR ch. 13

Criticism of one's church, its organization, services, etc. mentioned by Screwtape as serving his purposes
•SL 72-73 ❖ SL 16:2

Criticism of others—*see also* Judging

Criticism of others: It is important to realize that there is some really fatal flaw in *you* which causes others the same despair
•GID 123, 151-155 (*see also* FL 186)
❖ GID I 14:7, 8; ch. 18 (*see also* FL 6:37)

Criticism of others: "Those who do not think about their own sins make up for it by thinking incessantly about the sins of others"*
•GID 124 (*see also* GID 154; LAL 95)
❖ GID I 14:10 (*see also* GID I 18:10; LAL 9 Jan 61)

Criticism, textual, which finds that every old book was made by six anonymous authors with scissors and paste is beginning to die out
•GID 134-135 ❖ GID I 16:8

Criticism: "The human mind is generally

far more eager to praise and dispraise than to describe and define"
•FL 27 ❖ FL 2:3

Critics, "fatal," who make every distinction a distinction of value
•FL 27 ❖ FL 2:3

Critics, Lewis wrote concerning his: "To call them liars would be as undeserved a compliment as to say that a dog was bad at arithmetic"
•LAL 51 ❖ LAL 8/2/56

Critics, Lewis's: Letter written to a critic he felt was "thorough and perceptive" in his review of Lewis's sources
•L 205 ❖ L 29 Oct 44

Critics mentioned as one group of "culture-sellers" whose ranks should probably include some Christians
•CR 20-21 ❖ CR 2:23-25

Cross: Avoidance of suffering and self-preservation is not what life is about; all Jesus' followers must take up the cross
•CR 155 (see also FL 168, 170)
❖ CR 13:6 (see also FL 6:10, 14)

Cross, bear your, for if you try to get rid of it you will probably find another and worse one (quote from *Imitation of Christ*)
•LAL 86 ❖ LAL Aug 3/59

Cross comes before the crown and tomorrow is a Monday morning
•WG 18 ❖ WG 1:15

Cross, crown not promised without the
•L 166 ❖ L 8 May 39

Cross did not become a frequent motive of Christian art until the generations which had seen real crucifixions were all dead
•LM 85 ❖ LM 16:10

"Cross," meaning of the word, to modern minds (It now very faintly, if at all, conveys the idea of execution by torture)
•GID 97 ❖ GID I 10:28

Cross, the command to take up your, is followed by Christ telling us, "My yoke is easy and my burden light"
•MC 168 ❖ MC IV 8:5-7

Cross, with the, before our eyes we have little excuse to forget our insolvency (re: our real condition of total dependence upon God and one another)
•LAL 58 ❖ LAL 14/6/56

Cross-Examination (chapter title)
•GID 258-267 ❖ GID II ch. 15

Crowd—see also Collective

Crowd, if you wish to avoid God live in a; avoid silence and solitude...
•CR 168 (see also SL 102-103*)
❖ CR 14:17, 18 (see also SL 22:5*)

Crowd, the modern undergraduate lives in a; caucus has replaced friendship
•WG 107 ❖ WG 7:2

Crowd, the weariness we feel in a, is because we see so many faces but can do no more than see them—like reading the first page of a hundred books
•L 253-254 ❖ L 9 Jan 54

Crown not promised without the cross
•L 166 (see also WG 18)
❖ L 8 May 39 (see also WG 1:15)

Crown, the sternest feminist need not grudge my sex the, offered to it in the Pagan or the Christian mystery; the one is of paper and the other is of thorns
•FL 149 (see also FL 147)
❖ FL 5:28 (see also FL 5:25)

Crowns, tinsel, of lineage, beauty, talent, fame, etc.: All such things may be enjoyed provided one takes them lightly enough
•LAL 111 ❖ LAL 10 Dec 62

Crucifixes—see Icons

Crucifixion—see also Calvary; Death of Christ

Crucifixion as an example of an evil exploited by God to produce a complex good (while the role of Judas remains simply evil)
•PP 111 ❖ PP 7:2

Crucifixion: Christ also experienced the absence of the Father in a time of difficulty—"Why hast thou forsaken me?"*
•GO 5 ❖ GO 1:8

Crucifixion did not become a frequent motive of Christian art until the gen-

erations which had seen real crucifixions were all dead
•LM 85 ❖ LM 16:10

Crucifixion, God created the universe already foreseeing the
•FL 176 ❖ FL 6:21

Crucifixion, God saw the, in the act of creating the first nebula (re: the fall of Man)
•PP 84 ❖ PP 5:11

Crucifixion, hymns dealing with: too much emphasis on blood
•LM 85 ❖ LM 16:10

Crucifixion, image of, evokes sheer physical horror; leaves no room for the fruitful emotions (compassion, gratitude)
•LM 85 ❖ LM 16:10

Crucifixion, in actual fact, was a sight very unlike most of our religious pictures and images
•LM 42 ❖ LM 8:6

"Crucifixion," meaning of the word, to modern minds (It now very faintly, if at all, suggests the idea of execution by torture)
•GID 97 ❖ GID I 10:28

Crucifixion of Christ, why the, was necessary ("...no explanation will ever be quite adequate to the reality")
•MC 56-61 (see also Atonement)
❖ MC II ch. 4 (see also Atonement)

Crucifixion, the conversion of rebellious wills cost God
•MC 179 ❖ MC IV 10:9

Crucifixion: The Father was not really absent from the Son when He said, "Why hast thou forsaken Me?"
•LAL 38 ❖ LAL 20/2/55

Crucifixion: "The sense of dereliction cannot be a bad symptom for Our Lord Himself experience it in its depth— 'Why hast thou forsaken me?'"
•LAL 77 ❖ LAL Jul 21st 58

Crucifixion: "There will come a day for all of us when 'it is finished.' God help us all"*
•LAL 64-65 ❖ LAL 4/1/57

Crucifixion: "To God, God's last words are 'Why hast thou forsaken me?'"
•LM 43-44 ❖ LM 8:10-12

Cruelty, a recollection of all one's own, will help to make prayer for one's enemies real
•L 183 ❖ L 16 Apr 40

Cruelty, Christianity does not want us to reduce by one atom the hatred we feel for treachery and
•MC 106 ❖ MC III 7:6

Cruelty: Even if all suffering were man-made, we should like to know the reason for the enormous permission to torture their fellows which God gives to men
•PP 89 ❖ PP 6:1

Cruelty, every vice leads to; even good emotions such as pity can lead through anger to cruelty
•PP 65 ❖ PP 4:12

Cruelty, in justifying, to animals (as in vivisection) we put ourselves also on the animal level; we choose the jungle and must abide by our choice
•GID 228 (see also Vivisection)
❖ GID II 9:10 (see also Vivisection)

Cruelty "is surely more evil than lust and the World at least as dangerous as the Flesh"
•SJ 109 ❖ SJ 7:11

Cruelty mentioned by Screwtape as one of those things which can be passed off as funny—a "practical joke"— without disapproval from one's fellows
•SL 51 ❖ SL 11:5

Cruelty, self-contempt as a source of
•GID 194-195 ❖ GID II 21:2, 3

Cruelty: The more cruel you are, the more you will hate
•MC 117 ❖ MC III 9:7, 8

Cruelty to one another accounts for perhaps four-fifths of the suffering of men
•PP 89 ❖ PP 6:1

Cruelty: "Where oppression does not completely and permanently break the spirit, has it not a natural tendency to produce retaliatory pride and contempt?"
•SJ 107 ❖ SJ 7:8

Crying: "If you must weep, weep: a good honest howl! I suspect we—and espe-

cially my sex—don't cry enough now-
adays"
•LAL 26 ❖ LAL Feb 22/54
Crying: The bath of self-pity disgusts me...
(re: Lewis's grief at the loss of his wife)
•GO 2 ❖ GO 1:4
Cube analogy to explain God as Trinity
•MC 141-142; CR 79-80; M 85 (*see also*
GID 182)
❖ MC IV 2:5-7; CR 6:21; M 11:6 (*see also*
GID I 22:14)
Cultural activities and spiritual life, no es-
sential quarrel between
•CR 24; WG 25-27 (*see also* CR 10)
❖ CR 2:37; WG 2:8, 9 (*see also* CR 1:15)
"Cultural activities," I have no: I like the
Bacchae because it's exciting, not be-
cause it is—loathsome word!— "cul-
tured"
•LAL 54 (*see also* SL 60*)
❖ LAL 20/3/56 (*see also* SL 13:4*)
Cultural activities not intrinsically spiri-
tual and meritorious; the work of a
Beethoven must be offered to God just
as the work of a charwoman
•CR 24; WG 26 ❖ CR 2:37; WG 2:9
Cultural activities, plausible reasons have
never been lacking for putting off,
until a suitable moment (re: education
in time of war)
•WG 22; 29-30 ❖ WG 2:4, 12
Cultural activities undertaken in pride
worse than mundane activities undertaken in humility
•L 182-183 ❖ L 16 Apr 40
Cultural activities: "We can play, as we can
eat, to the glory of God" (re: the reading of comedies and tales)
•CR 10 ❖ CR 1:15
Cultural activities: Work of a charwoman
and the work of a poet can be done to
the Lord; both become spiritual in the
same way and on the same condition
•CR 24; WG 26 ❖ CR 2:37; WG 2:9
Cultural and religious activities should be
undertaken for their own sakes, not
for the sake of prestige or merit
•WLN 31-39 (*see also* CR 10; L 216; SL
59-60; Pride of pursuing "culture")
❖ WLN 3:1-11 (*see also* CR 1:15; L 3 Apr

49; SL 13:4; Pride of pursuing "culture")
Cultural differences may cause the rule of
propriety to change, but the rule of
chastity remains the same for all
Christians at all times
•MC 88-89 ❖ MC III 5:1
Cultural education has the indirect value
of helping us to meet our enemies on
their own ground
•WG 28 (*see also* CR 17)
❖ WG 2:10 (*see also* CR 2:18)
Cultural occupations such as teaching,
writing, etc. may be justified provided
there is a demand for "culture" and
that culture is in fact harmless
•CR 20 ❖ CR 2:23
Cultural "refinement": Where it is most
named it is most absent
•WLN 32 ❖ WLN 3:2
Cultural "sensitivity," like "experience,"
is a potentiality and therefore neutral;
neither can be an end to Christians
•CR 24 ❖ CR 2:38
Culture—*consider also* Art; Education;
Intellectual(ism); Knowledge; Music;
Poetry; Taste
Culture: "The desirable habit of mind, if
it is to come at all, must come as a by-
product, unsought"
•WLN 35 (*see also* CR 10)
❖ WLN 3:7 (*see also* CR 1:15)
"Culture" a name given from outside to
activities which are not themselves
interested in "culture" at all, and
would be ruined the moment they
were
•WLN 33-34 ❖ WLN 3:5
Culture, according to Newman, looks like
virtue "only at a distance"; does not
make men better
•CR 18 ❖ CR 2:20
Culture and knowledge, pride a danger
in the love of
•WG 27-28 (*see also* CR 10*, 014*, 17*;
L 182-183; PP 76; SL 60*; WLN 34-36)
❖ WG 2:9 (*see also* CR 1:15*; 2:6, 16*; L 16
Apr 40; PP 5:5; SL 13:4*; WLN 3:6-8)
Culture and sanctity: Both are hard to di-
agnose and easy to feign
•WLN 47 ❖ WLN 3:24

Culture, appetite for: The existence of the impulse and the faculty prove that they must have a proper function in God's scheme
•WG 27 ❖ WG 2:9

"Culture" as a collective name for certain valuable activities is a permissible word, but culture as a cause or a banner is unendurable
•WLN 38 ❖ WLN 3:11

Culture as a route to conversion: not for all people; there is a shorter and safer way...
•CR 24 ❖ CR 2:36

Culture as a weapon, Gregorian view of: "If we are to convert our heathen neighbors, we must understand their culture"
•CR 17 (see also CR 21; WG 28)
❖ CR 2:18 (see also CR 2:26; WG 2:10)

Culture, Christianity and (chapter title)
•CR 12-36 ❖ CR ch. 2

"Culture" defined indirectly as "...liberal knowledge..."*
•CR 18 ❖ CR 2:20

"Culture" defined indirectly as "...a fine taste in the arts..."*
•CR 14 ❖ CR 2:4

"Culture" defined indirectly as literature, art, and knowledge*
•CR 23 ❖ CR 2:34

"Culture" defined indirectly as "the cultivation of the intellect..."*
•CR 18 ❖ CR 2:20

"Culture" defined: "...intellectual and aesthetic activity"*
•CR 12 ❖ CR 2:1

Culture: Editors of "Scrutiny" mentioned who believed in a relationship between the quality of a person's response to art and his fitness for humane living
•CR 13 ❖ CR 2:2

Culture: Good taste in poetry or music not necessary to salvation, as evidenced by the humble charwoman who revels in hymns
•L 224 (see also CR 13-14)
❖ L 7 Dec 50 (see also CR 2:3, 4)

Culture, I conclude that, has a distinct part to play in bringing certain souls to Christ
•CR 24 ❖ CR 2:36

Culture, I think we can still believe, to be innocent after we have read the New Testament; I cannot see that we are encouraged to think it important
•CR 15 ❖ CR 2:8

Culture: If it is of little relative value, how is one justified in spending so much time and energy on it?*
•CR 12-25 ❖ CR 2:1-38

"Culture" irrelevant to those actually in pursuit of cultural activities such as deep and genuine enjoyment of literature and the other arts
•WLN 33-35 (see also L 70, 216*; SL 58-60*)
❖ WLN 3:5-7 (see also L 7 Aug 21; 3 Apr 49*; SL 13:3, 4*)

Culture is a storehouse of the best (sub-Christian) values—values which are of the soul, not the spirit, and which will save no man
•CR 23, 26 ❖ CR 2:34, 41

Culture: It is taken as basic by all the "culture" of our age that whenever artists and audience lose touch, the fault must be on the side of the audience
•WLN 45 (see also WLN 78-79)
❖ WLN 3:20 (see also WLN 5:18)

Culture, Lewis expresses distaste for standardized, (specifically, a series called The Hundred Best Books which he found at a hotel)
•L 70 (see also SL 60*)
❖ L 7 Aug 21 (see also SL 13:4*)

Culture: Lewis reacts against the notion that good taste somehow defines the true Church, or that course, unimaginative people are less likely to be saved
•CR 13 (see also L 224)
❖ CR 2:3 (see also L 7 Dec 50)

Culture, Lewis's own case for the value of, stated
•CR 20-25 ❖ CR 2:23-38

Culture, Lewis's own case for the value of, restated simply
•CR 27-28 ❖ CR 2:45

"Culture," majority are convinced that the activities of, are essentially marginal, amateurish, and rather effeminate activities (compared with Business)
•WLN 80-81 ❖ WLN 5:22

"Culture," many modern exponents of, speak of the most precious and fragile things with the roughness of an auctioneer, as if selling us a Hoover
•WLN 37 ❖ WLN 3:11

Culture may be a road into Jerusalem; for others it is a road out
•CR 22, 23 (see also L 297)
❖ CR 2:29, 34 (see also L undated letter of Feb 61)

Culture: New Testament demands that whatever is most valued on natural level is to be abandoned without mercy the moment it conflicts with service of God
•CR 14 ❖ CR 2:5

Culture, New Testament passages which may speak to the issue of the value of, in the life of the Christian
•CR 14-15 ❖ CR 2:5-8

Culture: Newman felt it may provide innocent distraction at those moments of spiritual relaxation which would otherwise lead to sin
•CR 18 (see also CR 21)
❖ CR 2:20 (see also CR 2:27)

Culture: Lewis discusses Newman's view of the cultivation of the intellect as a justifiable end in itself, while remaining wholly distinct from virtue
•CR 18-19 ❖ CR 2:20, 21

Culture: "No one, presumably, is really maintaining that a fine taste in the arts is a condition of salvation"
•CR 14 (see also L 224)
❖ CR 2:4 (see also L 7 Dec 50)

Culture ordinarily a privilege of the ruling class; when entry into the ruling class becomes the reward of culture, we have a "Charientocracy"
•WLN 44-45 ❖ WLN 3:19

Culture: Pleasure in the arts possibly more varied, intense, and lasting than vulgar or "popular" pleasure (though this has not been proved)

•CR 21 ❖ CR 2:28

Culture, pleasure of, is good in itself; a "sinful" pleasure means a good offered and accepted under conditions which involve a breach of the moral law
•CR 21 (consider also Pleasure)
❖ CR 2:27 (consider also Pleasure)

Culture: Pride of activities such as reading a certain book in order to make clever comments about it to one's friends mentioned by Screwtape*
•SL 58, 60 (see also L 216)
❖ SL 13:3, 4 (see also L 3 Apr 49)

Culture: Pursuit of knowledge and beauty need not exclude God
•WG 27 ❖ WG 2:9

Culture: Question of whether its value can be reconciled with the Christian belief that the end of human life is salvation in Christ and glorifying of God
•CR 12-25 ❖ CR 2:1-38

Culture records man's striving for those ends which, though not the true end of man (the fruition of God), have nevertheless some degree of similarity to it
•CR 26 ❖ CR 2:41

Culture: Regarding the evil tendency to love knowledge and discernment more than the object known and discerned
•CR 17; WG 28 ❖ CR 2:16; WG 2:9

"Culture": "The moment good taste knows itself, some of its goodness is lost"*
•SJ 104 ❖ SJ 7:4

Culture, the present inordinate esteem of, by the cultured began, I think, with Matthew Arnold
•CR 12 ❖ CR 2:2

"Culture," the whole modern world ludicrously over-values books and learning and what they call
•L 269 ❖ L 2 Apr 56

Culture: There was no question of restoring to it the kind of status which I had given it before my conversion
•CR 19 ❖ CR 2:22

"Culture," to be engaged with, for the sake

of prestige or merit endangers the very enjoyment of the activities and impoverishes social life
•WLN 34-36 ❖ WLN 3:6-8

Culture: To my childhood nurse I owe my lifelong immunity from the false identification which some people make of refinement with virtue*
•SJ 5 ❖ SJ 1:3

Culture, undesirable states of, include the modern student's belief that poetry is something assigned and tested on—no other purpose for it is realised*
•WLN 47 ❖ WLN 3:25

Culture, value of: A cultured person is usually aware that reality is very odd and that the ultimate truth *must* have the characteristics of strangeness...
•CR 23 ❖ CR 2:35

Culture, value of, in the life of the already-converted: "...since we must rest and play, where can we do so better than here—in the suburbs of Jerusalem?"
•CR 24 ❖ CR 2:37

Culture, values reflected in, resemble the regenerate life only as the moon resembles the sun
•CR 23 (*see also* CR 24)
❖ CR 2:34 (*see also* CR 2:37)

Culture: We should not regard pleasure in the arts as meritorious
•CR 21 ❖ CR 2:28

Culture, what the intellectual and religious authorities have had to say about the value of, (Aristotle, Plato, Buddha, Augustine, Milton, Newman, etc.)
•CR 15-19 ❖ CR 2:8-22

Culture: While it may not always be harmless, the ranks of the culture-sellers (teachers, writers, etc.) should probably include some Christians
•CR 20-21 ❖ CR 2:23-25

"Culture": Why it is a poor qualification for entry into a ruling class
•WLN 31-49 ❖ WLN ch. 3

Culture: Young people "now sometimes suppress an incipient taste for classi-cal music or good literature because it might prevent their Being Like Folks" (re: Conformity)
•SL 164; WLN 62
❖ SL 32:25; WLN 4:25

Cultures, ethics of different: "...may we not recognize in modern thought a very serious exaggeration of the ethical differences between different cultures?"
•CR 54-55 (*see also* MC 24)
❖ CR 4:24 (*see also* MC I 2:7)

Cultures, people of modern , no better in God's eyes than people in other ages who excelled in different virtues (courage, chastity) but were cruel*
•PP 64 ❖ PP 4:11

Cultures, two arguments used to obscure the substantial moral agreement within different
•CR 78 ❖ CR 6:17

Cultures, within different, we find substantial agreement as to moral values with considerable local differences of emphasis...
•CR 77-78 (*see also* CR 47, 52; MC 19, 24; PP 63; book *The Abolition of Man*)
❖ CR 6:16 (*see also* CR 4:7, 21; MC I 1:6, 7; 2:7; PP 4:10; book *The Abolition of Man*)

"**Cultured**" increasingly means little unofficial, self-appointed aristocracies in which people can feel superior to the mass
•WLN 41 ❖ WLN 3:14

"Cultured," why some people go to such lengths to prove that they are not
•WLN 31-38, 41 ❖ WLN 3:1-11, 14

Curiosity, Jesus' sayings addressed not to our intellectual, but to our conscience and our will
•L 169-170; PP 119
❖ L 5 Nov 39; PP 8:2

Cursing Psalms can show us the proper object of utter hostility—wickedness, especially our own
•RP 136 ❖ RP 12:16

Cursings, The (chapter title)
•RP 20-33 ❖ RP ch. 3

Cynicism, self-contempt as a source of
　•GID 194-195 ❖ GID II 2:2,3

Daily—*see also* Day
Daily dose: I pray for just so much self-
　knowledge as I can bear and use at the
　moment; the little daily dose
　　•LM 34 ❖ LM 6:14
Daily, necessity of dying, ("...however of-
　ten we think we have broken the re-
　bellious self we shall still find it alive")
　　•PP 92 ❖ PP 6:3
Damocles, sword of, really hangs over all
　mortals
　　•L 280 ❖ L 6 Nov 57
Damocles, we live always under the
　sword of
　　•LAL 65, 69
　　❖ LAL 17/1/57; Oct 20th 57
Dance and game are frivolous and unim-
　portant down here, for "down here"
　is not their natural place; will be en-
　joyed in Heaven without frivolity
　　•LM 92-93 (*see also* LM 115-116*)
　　❖ LM 17:17 (*see also* LM 21:13*)
Dance: David danced before the ark; this
　helps to remind us that Judaism is an
　ancient religion
　　•RP 44 ❖ RP 5:2
Dance, eternal, of self-sacrifice "makes
　heaven drowsy with the harmony"
　　•PP 153 ❖ PP 10:11
Dance, God as a kind of, —a dynamic,
　pulsing activity
　　•MC 152, 153 ❖ MC IV 4:6, 8
Dance: I can dance no better than a centi-
　pede with wooden legs (re: use of im-
　ages like play and dance for the high-

  * These items reflect some interpretation on the part of the editor; the idea will not be found in these exact words. *See Introduction, p. ix.*
 ** These items are ideas of Lewis's which the editor has placed under a topic Lewis did not there intend to address. *See Introduction, p. ix.*
  Entries without asterisks are not necessarily exact quotes, but the idea should be easy to find as worded.

est things)
•LM 92 ❖ LM 17:16

Dance, sacred, as part of the worship service may be proper in a place like, say, Africa
•GID 331 ❖ GID IV Letter 6

Dance, world is a, in which good, descending from God, is disturbed by evil arising from the creatures
•PP 84 ❖ PP 5:11

Dances, neighborhood, which young Lewis hated: "Even adults, I fancy, would not find an evening party very endurable without the attraction of sex and...alcohol"
•SJ 46-48 (see also SJ 160)
❖ SJ 3:5, 6 (see also SJ 10:13)

Dancing of David a valuable contrast to merely dutiful "church-going" and "saying our prayers"; we may regard it with envy and hope to be infected by it
•RP 45-46 ❖ RP 5:4

Danger, a chastity or honesty or mercy which yields to, will be chaste or honest or merciful only on conditions; Pilate was merciful till it became risky
•SL 137-138 ❖ SL 29:6

Danger, Screwtape observes that, (such as in a war) brings moral issues to the point
•SL 137 ❖ SL 29:5, 6

Dangers of National Repentance (chapter title)
•GID 189-192 ❖ GID II ch. 1

Daniel, Book of, mentioned
•LAL 108 ❖ LAL 2 Oct 62

Dante: His angels are the best in literature; before them we sink in awe
•SL ix ❖ SL P:15

Dante, in, the lost souls are entirely concerned with their past; not so the saved
•LAL 99 ❖ LAL 5 Jun 61

Dante Society mentioned
•LAL 41, 62
❖ LAL 24/3/55; Sep 8/56

Dante: When he saw the great apostles in heaven they affected him like mountains (re: the necessity for awe in prayer)
•LM 13 ❖ LM 2:14

"Dark Night of the Flesh" as a term given by Lewis to the experience of the Psalmists in their fear of certain evils
•CR 125-128 ❖ CR 10:31-40

Darwinian theorem—see also Evolution

Darwinian theorem in biology not the same as the modern myth of evolutionism or developmentalism or progress in general
•WLN 101 (see also CR 83-86; WG 89-90) ❖ WLN 7:14 (see also CR 7:5-12; WG 5:22)

Darwinism gives no support to the belief that natural selection, working upon chance variations, has a general tendency to produce improvement
•WLN 103 ❖ WLN 7:18

Darwinism, Watson's defence of, leaves one with the question "Was [evolution] devised not to get in facts but to keep out God?"
•WG 89 ❖ WG 5:22

Date-setting for Second Coming impossible; we must be ready at all moments
•WLN 106-109 (see also GID 266)
❖ WLN 7:24-29 (see also GID II 16:54-56)

Dating—see Courtship

David danced before the ark; didn't care whether he was making a fool of himself or not
•RP 44 ❖ RP 5:2

David, dancing of, a valuable contrast to merely dutiful "church-going" and "saying our prayers"; we may regard it with envy and hope to be infected by it
•RP 45-46 ❖ RP 5:4

Davidman, Joy—see Joy (Lewis's wife)

Day—see also Daily

Day, Lewis describes an ordinary, for him while at Oxford
•L 144 (see also L 214)
❖ L 22 Nov 31 (see also L 29 May 48)

Day, Lewis describes what he considers a "normal" or ideal
•SJ 141-143 ❖ SJ 9:18

Day, what is our first job each
•MC 169 ❖ MC IV 8:8

10:7*; RP 10:11)

Death and Rebirth pattern in Christianity transcends our conscience and our reason; is the consummation of all religion
•GID 144 ❖ GID I 16:26

Death and Rebirth pattern in Nature seen in the buried seed and the re-arising corn
•GID 37, 84; M 113-115; PP 103
❖ GID I 2:15; 9:6; M 14:9-14; PP 6:15

Death and Rebirth pattern in Paganism prefigured Christianity
•GID 57-58, 66-67, 83-84, 132, 175; L 258; M 112-116; MC 54; PP 25; RP 105-108; SJ 62, 223-224, 235-236; WG 82-84
❖ GID I 4:42 (Ques. 10); 5:11-13; 9:5, 6; 16:4; 21:7; L 1 Nov 54; M 14:8-14; MC II 3:9; PP 1:16; RP 10:11, 12; SJ 4:9; 14:15; 15:7; WG 5:14, 15

Death and Rebirth pattern in Nature because it was first in her Creator
•M 112-115 ❖ M 14:7-14

Death and Rebirth pattern never restores the previous individual organism
•GID 33; M 151
❖ GID I 2:11; M 16:15, 16

Death and Rebirth, pattern of, also seen in the history of human thought (re: rich, imaginative thought vs. logical analysis)
•M 161 ❖ M 16:29

Death and Rebirth, pattern of, never restores the previous individual organism; universal movement is from more order to less
•M 151-152 ❖ M 16:16, 17

Death and Rebirth, pattern of, not accidental in mythology or nature; teaches truth that man himself must undergo some sort of death if he would truly live
•RP 106-107 ❖ RP 10:11

Death and Resurrection are what the great story is about, and this is hinted at on every level in Nature
•M 98 ❖ M 12:7

Death and resurrection of Christ echoed in the natural world
•GID 82-84, 86 (see also GID 37; M 98,

111-116, 125, 130*, 161; PP 149*; RP 106-107)
❖ GID I 9:4-6, 8 (see also GID I 2:15; M 12:7; 14:5-14, 29, 35*; 16:29; PP 10:7*; RP 10:11)

Death, anticipation of: "It remains true that I have, almost all my life, been quite unable to feel that horror of nonentity, of annihilation..."
•SJ 117 ❖ SJ 7:21

Death, anticipation of: To think, in sunny and confident times, that we shall die and rot is easier if we have seen that sort of thing happening before (re: inevitability of the new school term)*
•SJ 36-37 ❖ SJ 2:16

Death as an important part of the process of perfection
•MC 175 ❖ MC IV 10:1

Death as means of redemption: Christianity is unique in that it teaches that the terrible task has already in some sense been done for us
•PP 104 ❖ PP 6:15

Death as means of redemption, doctrine of, not peculiar to Christianity and cannot be escaped by ceasing to be a Christian
•PP 103 ❖ PP 6:15

Death as separation: "What am I to do with that daily portion of my thoughts which has for so many years been hers?"
•L 289-290 ❖ L 3 Dec 59

Death as the inevitable result of choosing to remain in the womb rather than going through the birth process (re: New Birth)
•MC 187 (see also MC 173, 190*; SL 147*)
❖ MC IV 11:9 (see also MC IV 9:7; 11:15*; SL 31:3*)

Death both a punitive sentence and a safety device; once fallen, natural immortality would be the one utterly hopeless destiny for man
•M 129-130 (see also LAL 47*)
❖ M 14:35 (see also LAL 26/10/55*)

Death: By willing and humble surrender to it Man undoes his act of rebellion

•M 129-130 ❖ M 14:35

Death, can you not see, as the friend and deliverer? It means stripping off that body which is tormenting you...
•LAL 117 ❖ LAL 17 Jun 63

Death, Christ as conqueror of, and (death's patron) the devil (re: Psalm 8)
•RP 133 ❖ RP 12:11

Death, Christian view of: It is the result of sin and the triumph of Satan; but it is also the means of redemption from sin, God's medicine for Man
•M 128 ❖ M 14:34

Death, Christian view of: It is the triumph of Satan, the punishment of sin, and the last enemy; yet only he who loses his life will save it
•M 125 ❖ M 14:28

Death, Christianity integrates positive and negative attitudes toward: "Of all men, we hope most of death; yet...we cannot cease to fight against [it]"
•GID 149-150 ❖ GID I 17:7

Death defeated by Christ in the Resurrection
•GID 159 ❖ GID I 19:6

Death *does* matter, and very solemnly
•L 230 (*see also* GO 16)
❖ L 27 Mar 51 (*see also* GO 1:30)

Death *does* matter; more horrible to Jesus than to us
•GID 149-150 (*see also* L 190-191)
❖ GID I 17:7 (*see also* L undated letter between 11 Aug 40 and 4 Jan 41)

Death, effect of, on a long relationship vs. a shorter one ("...so much more intertwined with your whole life")
•L 289-290 ❖ L 3 Dec 59

Death, effect of, on a short relationship vs. a longer one ("I had not grown *accustomed* to happiness")
•L 301 ❖ L 20 Dec 61

Death: Eternal life will probably also be eternal dying in the sense of self-conquest
•PP 151-152 ❖ PP 10:9, 10

Death, experiences of visions or hearing voices at the moment of, are all very well attested and in quite a different category from ordinary ghost stories

•LAL 24 ❖ LAL Jan 1st 54

Death, fear of, not unique to a wartime situation; war does not make death more frequent or more painful
•WG 30-31 (*see also* PP 115-116)
❖ WG 2:14 (*see also* PP 7:8)

Death, Greek religious belief about, is shown at the beginning of the *Iliad*...
•RP 37 ❖ RP 4:8

Death: "Has this world been so kind to you that you should leave it with regret? There are better things ahead than any we leave behind"
•LAL 117 ❖ LAL 17 Jun 63

Death: "He that loseth his life shall find it"; surely this is the main purpose of our life—to "die," to relinquish one's freedom and independence
•LAL 97-98 ❖ LAL 28 Mar 61

Death, how Satan might have produced human
•M 129 ❖ M 14:35

Death: "I do wonder why the doctors inflict such torture to delay what cannot in any case be very long delayed. Or why God does!"
•LAL 118 ❖ LAL 25 Jun 63

Death: I have never been able to find it anything but extraordinary and rather incredible; one cannot believe something has turned into nothing
•L 59 ❖ L 23 Apr 21

Death: "I was unexpectedly revived from a long coma...to be brought back and have all one's dying to do again was rather hard"
•L 307 ❖ L 17 Sep 63

Death, in a recent discussion of, a girl replied "Oh, but by the time I'm *that* age Science will have done something about it"
•GID 252, 266 ❖ GID II 14:9; 16:56

Death in the Psalms (chapter title)
•RP 34-43 ❖ RP ch. 4

Death, inevitability of: "There will come a day for all of us when 'it is finished.' God help us all"
•LAL 64-65 ❖ LAL 4/1/57

Death is Satan's great weapon and also God's great weapon; our supreme dis-

grace and our only hope
•M 125 (*see also* M 128-130; SL 131)
❖ M 14:28 (*see also* M 14:34, 35; SL 28:1)

Death: It is hard to have patience with people who say, "Death doesn't matter"; you might as well say that birth doesn't matter
•GO 16 ❖ GO 1:30

Death: It is useless to worry about future destruction; didn't people know that they were going to die anyway?
•GID 266 ❖ GID II 16:56

Death, it seems clear that in most parts of the Old Testament, there is little or no belief in life after
•RP 36, 38-39 ❖ RP 4:6, 9-12

Death, jokes about, point to the fact that we find our own animality either objectionable or funny ("spirit" and "organism" not at home together)
•M 127 ❖ M 14:32

Death, Lewis mentions twice sensing the presence of a person after their
•L 290 ❖ L 3 Dec 59

Death, life after—*see* Life after death; Immortality; *consider* Dead, state of the; Eternal life; Future life; Purgatory

Death likened to having a painful tooth out
•LAL 84; SL 147 (*see also* Dentist analogy) ❖ LAL Jul 7th 59; SL 31:3 (*see also* Dentist analogy)

Death, living with the knowledge of Joy's impending: "You would be surprised ...to know how much of a strange sort of happiness and even gaiety there is..."
•L 275 ❖ L 6 Mar 57

Death, no need to always think of one's approaching, but we should always take it into account (as with Christ's return, and the Judgement)
•WLN 110 ❖ WLN 7:31

Death of a person changes one's view of that person ("...one finds out that it is a natural process")
•L 138 ❖ L 27 Oct 29

Death of Charles Williams "has made my faith stronger than it was a week ago"
•L 206 ❖ L 18 May 45; 20 May 45

Death of Christ—*see also* Calvary; Crucifixion; *consider also* Atonement; Redemption

Death of Christ: Christ did not die for men because of their merit, but because He is love and He loves infinitely
•M 52 (*see also* M 122*; WLN 86)
❖ M 7:14 (*see also* M 14:24*; WLN 6:10)

Death of Christ: Christ died for men, not for societies or states
•WG 117 (*see also* GID 109-110*; MC 73*; WG 19*; WLN 68*)
❖ WG 7:16 (*see also* GID I 12:3*; MC III 1:9*; WG 1:15*; WLN 4:39*)

Death of Christ: Christ died not for valuable men, but for sinners—human souls whose value, out of relation to God, is zero
•WG 115 (*see also* WLN 53)
❖ WG 7:14 (*see also* WLN 4:8)

Death of Christ has somehow put us right with God and given us a fresh start
•MC 57 ❖ MC II 4:3

Death of Christ is the remedy for the Fall; it was the means by which He conquered Death
•M 125 ❖ M 14:28

Death of Christ necessary precisely because men are *not* worth dying for; to make them worth it
•WLN 86 (*see also* M 52, 122*)
❖ WLN 6:10 (*see also* M 7:14; 14:24*)

Death of Christ, redemption through: Is this the only mode of Redemption that is possible? Here we ask what is wholly unknowable
•WLN 87 ❖ WLN 6:12

Death of Christ: The goodness of Christ led to His death, because of the nature of goodness and the nature of this world
•RP 105 ❖ RP 10:10

Death of Christ: "There the degree of accepted Death reaches the utmost bounds of the imagination and perhaps goes beyond them"
•PP 103 ❖ PP 6:14

Death of Christ was a martyrdom (done on our behalf), which remains the supreme enacting and perfection of

Christianity
•PP 102 ❖ PP 6:14

Death of Christ was for you as if you had
been the only man in the world
•MC 147 ❖ MC IV 3:7

Death of Christ, why the, was necessary
("...no explanation will ever be quite
adequate to the reality")
•MC 56-61 (see also Atonement)
❖ MC II ch. 4 (see also Atonement)

Death of Lewis's father mentioned: "...all
the fortitude (even playfulness) which
he displayed in his last illness..."
•SJ 215 ❖ SJ 14:6

Death of self-will involves the necessity
of dying daily; "...however often we
think we have broken the rebellious
self we shall still find it alive"
•PP 92 ❖ PP 6:3

Death of the body is due to the conflict
between "spirit" and "nature" which
began as a result of the Fall; Christ's
death is the remedy
•M 125-126 ❖ M 14:28-30

Death: Only a perfect Man could perform
dying perfectly; Christ is the repre-
sentative "Die-er" of the universe
•M 130 ❖ M 14:35

Death, only three things we can do about:
to desire it, to fear it, or to ignore it—
the third alternative is surely the most
uneasy and precarious
•LAL 84 ❖ LAL Jun 7th 59

Death penalty—see Capital punishment

Death (quote from Thomas Browne): "I am
not so much afraid of death, as
ashamed of it"
•GID 87, 150; M 129
❖ GID I 9:10; 17:7; M 14:35

Death, Reason enables Man to foresee his
own, which causes acute mental suffering since he keenly desires permanence
•PP 14 (see also GO 9)
❖ PP 1:1 (see also GO 1:18)

Death, regarding the objection that, ought
not to be final—that we ought to be
given a second chance: "Finality must
come sometime..."
•PP 124 ❖ PP 8:8

Death, Resurrection tends to confirm only
one idea about: that the righteous
dead will return to earth one day as
solid men (quote from Isaiah 26:19)
•M 145-146 ❖ M 16:6

Death, Sadducees were holding to the
older Jewish view of, which had apparently changed greatly by Our
Lord's time
•RP 39 ❖ RP 4:12

Death: Saying "I'll be happy when God
calls me" not morbid; if we really believe that our real home is elsewhere,
why should we not look forward to
the arrival?
•LAL 83-84 (see also SL 132*)
❖ LAL Jun 7th 59 (see also SL 28:1*)

Death, scientific hope of defeating, a real
rival to Christianity
•L 167 ❖ L 9 Jul 39

Death, Screwtape describes a human's,
and subsequent passage into Heaven
•SL 146-148 ❖ SL 31:2-5

Death, Screwtape observes that humans
tend to regard, as the prime evil and
survival as the greatest good
•SL 131 ❖ SL 28:1

Death, self-surrender is in our fallen state
a kind of
•PP 91 ❖ PP 6:3

Death, spiritual essence of, is the opposite
of freedom—hence the mortal images
of rigidity, suffocation, etc.
•L 190
❖ L undated letter just after 11 Aug 40

Death, temptation to fear of, attacks most
fiercely the best and the worst of men;
Lewis explains why (re: Christ's fear
in Gethsemane)
•L 189-190
❖ L undated letter just after 11 Aug 40

Death, the Jewish conception of life after,
("Sheol"), was common to many an-
cient religions
•RP 37 ❖ RP 4:8

Death, the process of transformation of
our natural loves into Charity will always involve a kind of
•FL 187-188 ❖ FL 6:38

Death, the times when I can desire, come

not when the world seems harshest but when there seems to be most of Heaven already here
•L 289 ❖ L 5 Nov 59

Death: The world is like a picture with a golden background; you must step off the background [into death] before you can see the gold
•PP 148 ❖ PP 10:5

Death: The young are generally less unwilling to die than the middle-aged and the old; "prosperity knits a man to the World"
•SL 132 ❖ SL 28:1

Death: "There is no way out of it: either one must die fairly young or else outlive many friends"
•LAL 82-83 ❖ LAL May 19th 59

Death: "There's nothing discreditable in dying: I've known the most respectable people do it!"
•LAL 64-65 ❖ LAL Jul 3/57

Death, threat of, ("Sword of Damocles") really hangs over all mortals
•L 280 (see also LAL 65, 69) ❖ L 6 Nov 57 (see also LAL 17/1/57; Oct 20th 57)

Death, time itself is one more name for; the past is the past and that is what time means
•GO 28 ❖ GO 2:12

Death: To me the materialist's universe had the enormous attraction that it offered limited liabilities; death ended all
•SJ 171 (see also GO 33; consider also Limited liabilities)
❖ SJ 11:8 (see also GO 2:22; consider also Limited liabilities)

Death, to very bad people, "represents the final defeat of the systematic self-regarding caution and egoism which has been the sole occupation of life"
•L 190
❖ L undated letter just after 11 Aug 40

Death, total disfigurement of: "The ugliest man alive is an angel of beauty compared with the loveliest of the dead" (re: seeing his mother after her death)
•SJ 20 (see also SJ 195-196)

❖ SJ 1:21 (see also SJ 12:17)

Death, two views on: that it doesn't matter, or that it is the greatest of all evils; Christianity countenances neither
•M 125 ❖ M 14:28

Death, war forces us to think about; Screwtape finds this "disastrous" to his cause ("One of our best weapons, contented worldliness, is rendered useless")
•SL 27 ❖ SL 5:2

Death, war makes, real to us; it is good to be always aware of our own mortality
•WG 31-32 ❖ WG 2:14

Death, we are more than half in love with easeful, —if only we could be sure it wouldn't hurt
•L 190-191
❖ L undated letter just after 11 Aug 40

Death: "We hate the division which makes possible the conception of either corpse or ghost"
•M 128 ❖ M 14:32

Death: "We shall get out of it all sooner or later, for 'even the weariest river Winds somewhere safe to sea'"
•LAL 120-121 ❖ LAL 6 Jul 63

Death, what Christianity tells us about: that it is an appalling horror, a stinking indignity—and yet somehow good
•GID 86-87 (see also M 128-130)
❖ GID I 9:10 (see also M 14:34, 35)

Death: "What have you and I got to do but to make our exit? When they told me I was in danger...I don't remember feeling distressed"
•LAL 114 (see also LAL 115-116, 118)
❖ LAL 19 Mar 63 (see also LAL 22 Apr 63; 25 Jun 63)

Death, what the risen body of Christ reveals about life after
•M 145-163 ❖ M 16:5-32

Death: "When you die, and if prison visiting is allowed, come down and look me up in Purgatory...It is all rather fun—solemn fun—isn't it?"
•L 307 (see also LAL 119)
❖ L 17 Sep 63 (see also LAL 25 Jun 63)

Death, where other systems (like Buddhism) expose our total nature to, Christianity demands only that we set right a *misdirection* of our nature
•PP 104 ❖ PP 6:15

Death would be better than to live through another war
•L 166 ❖ L 8 May 39

Debate—*see also* Argument

Debate: "A man can't always be defending the truth; there must be a time to feed on it"*
•RP 7 ❖ RP 1:12

Debate between Christian and unbeliever: There is evidence both for and against the Christian propositions which fully rational minds can assess differently
•WLN 20 ❖ WLN 2:8

Debate between Christian and unbeliever: "There is no need to suppose stark unreason on either side. We need only suppose error"
•WLN 21 ❖ WLN 2:9

Debate: "Bulverism tries to show that the other man has causes and not reasons and that we have reasons and not causes"
•GID 275 ❖ GID III 1:12

Debate, Lewis's early attempts at, after studying with Kirkpatrick: "Most of it, as I now see, was incredibly crude and silly"*
•SJ 173 ❖ SJ 11:9

Debate, Lewis's liking for: "I am fond of a tumble in the surf"*
•WLN 87 ❖ WLN 6:11

Debate, silence during a, can be of an emphatic, audible, and even dialectical character
•LM 77 (*see also* LAL 110)
❖ LM 15:1 (*see also* LAL 8 Nov 62)

Debate, success in, dangerous to one's own faith; no doctrine seems to me so unreal as one that I have just successfully defended in a public debate
•GID 103, 128; L 209
❖ GID I 10:50; 15:4; L 2 Aug 46

Debate with "enemy champions" no task for a new Christian
•L 241 ❖ L 15 May 52

Debating: Alone among unsympathetic companions, I hold certain views timidly; back among Friends these same views become once more indisputable*
•FL 114 ❖ FL 4:44

Debating: "Discussions usually separate us; actions sometimes unite us" (re: re-union of churches)*
•LM 16 ❖ LM 3:5

Debating, emotion vs. "coolness" in: The ancient Persians debated everything twice: once when they were sober, and once when they were drunk
•LM 45 ❖ LM 8:14

Debating: I can still remember my first metaphysical argument: whether the future was like a line you can't see or like a line that is not yet drawn
•SJ 32 ❖ SJ 2:11

Debating: "One used to be told as a child: 'Think what you're saying.' Apparently we also need to be told, 'Think what you're thinking'"*
•LM 45 ❖ LM 8:14

Debating with those who feel "corporate superiority" toward you
•FL 120-121 ❖ FL 4:53

Deceit/Deception—*see* Dishonesty

Decision for Christ: One can't be thinking it over forever; can begin to try to be a disciple before one is a professed theologian
•L 191 ❖ L 4 Jan 41

Decision, today is our chance to make the right; it will not last forever
•MC 66 ❖ MC II 5:9

Decisions—*see also* Choices

Decisions about right and wrong aided by having the imitation of Christ as our goal
•MC 162 ❖ MC IV 7:5

Decisions, either way, always cost something; indecision is comfortable
•GID 250 ❖ GID II 14:3

Decisions, little, are of infinite importance since good and evil increase at compound interest
•MC 117 (*see also* MC 86-87; RP 136; SL 53-54; WG 102-103*; WLN 54-55)

❖ MC III 9:7, 8 (*see also* MC III 4:8, 9; RP 12:16; SL 12:1; WG 6:12*; WLN 4:10)

Decisions, moral—*see* Ethics; Moral decisions; Values

Decline of Religion, The (chapter title)
•GID 218-223 ❖ GID II ch. 8

Defense—*see* Apologetic(s)

Degree: "A certain degree of a thing might be good and a further degree of the same thing bad"
•L 158 (*see also* Balance; Moderation; Temperance) ❖ L 8 Mar 37 (*see also* Balance; Moderation; Temperance)

Deism as a system of thought which moved out with its time (vs. Christianity, which has survived)
•GID 65 ❖ GID I 5:7

Deists and Pantheists: Among the latter, we must emphasize the relative independence of the creatures; among the former, the divine presence in all things
•LM 74 ❖ LM 14:8

Deity of Christ—*see* Jesus (especially entries beginning with "Jesus: either ...")

Delight, as expressed in the Psalms, is very much centred on the Temple and its services
•RP 45-48, 50 ❖ RP 5:3-6, 8

Delight, the most valuable thing the Psalms do for me is to express that same, in God which made David dance
•RP 45 ❖ RP 5:4

Delinquents in the Snow (chapter title)
•GID 306-310 (*see also* RP 33)
❖ GID III ch. 6 (*see also* RP 3:21)

Demand of the New Testament: Whatever is most highly valued on the natural level is to be abandoned without mercy the moment it conflicts with the service of God
•CR 14 ❖ CR 2:5

Demands of God—*see also* Claims...; Cost of being a Christian

Demands of God: It is not so much of our time and attention that God demands; it is ourselves
•WG 130 (*see also* MC 167; SJ 172*)

❖ WG 9:9 (*see also* MC IV 8:4; SJ 11:8*)

Demands of God on our lives, we fear, may prove too inconvenient
•WG 127 (*see also* Self-reservation)
❖ WG 9:4 (*see also* Self-reservation)

Demands of God on us, our fear of, contributes to our reluctance to pray
•LM 114 (*see also* CR 43; LM 75; M 94; SL 22-23*, 54-55; WG 127-128)
❖ LM 21:8 (*see also* CR 3:12; LM 14:12; M 11:19; SL 4:4*; 12:3; WG 9:5)

Demands of God on us, our fear of, may be one of the causes of our weak faith*
•CR 43 (*see also* Obstacles to Christian faith) ❖ CR 3:12 (*see also* Obstacles to Christian faith)

Demands of God which we least like in fact marshall us where we should want to go if we knew what we wanted
•PP 52 (*see also* PP 90; WG 118-119)
❖ PP 3:18 (*see also* PP 6:3; WG 7:18)

Demands of real Christianity offensive to the World
•GID 222-223 ❖ GID II 8:12

Democracy—*consider also* Equality

"Democracy" as a principle of education results in the absurd philosophy that dunces and idlers must not be made to feel inferior to industrious students
•SL 166-168; WLN 64-66 (*see also* FL 73) ❖ SL 32:31-33; WLN 4:31-33 (*see also* FL 3:32)

"Democracy," corruption of the word, has given the devil an advantage (as meaning we must all be "equal," it is used to sanction Envy and discredit excellence)
•SL 161-170; WLN 59-68
❖ SL 32:19-39; WLN 4:19-39

"Democracy" in the diabolical sense (in which equality/conformity is prized) "leads to a nation without great men, a nation mainly of subliterates"
•SL 168-169; WLN 66-67
❖ SL 32:33-36; WLN 4:33-36

Democracy increasing in the outer world; Christianity offers us refreshing returns to inequality and opportunities for reverence

•WG 116 (*see also* GID 84-85; WG 113)

❖ WG 7:15 (*see also* GID I 9:7; WG 7:10)

Democracy is all very well as a political device, but it must not intrude into the spiritual, or even the aesthetic, world (re: choosing of church music)

•CR 98 ❖ CR 8:11

Democracy, the belief that values are subjective is eternally incompatible with freedom and

•CR 81 (*see also* CR 56; Subjectivism; Value/s) ❖ CR 6:22 (*see also* CR 4:27; Subjectivism; Value/s)

Democracy, true ground of, lies in the fact that fallen men are so wicked they can't be trusted with much power over their fellows

•WG 113-114 (*see also* GID 197)

❖ WG 7:10-12 (*see also* GID II 3:3)

Democracy vs. totalitarianism: If Christianity is true, then the individual is incomparably more important than a civilisation, for he is everlasting

•MC 73 (*see also* GID 118*; MC 159-160*; Individuals)

❖ MC III 1:9 (*see also* GID I 13:9*; MC IV 6:3*; Individuals)

Demon, if Eros is honoured without reservation and obeyed unconditionally it becomes a

•FL 154 ❖ FL 5:36

Demons—*see* Angels, fallen; Devils

Demonology, regarding the pseudo-science of

•M 121 ❖ M 14:22

Denomination, affection for a particular, must be treated as a natural affection (like Patriotism) and subjected to the same limitations*

•FL 48-49 ❖ FL 2:43

Denomination, deciding which, to join: We must ask, "Are these doctrines true?" —not a matter of preference

•MC 11-12 ❖ MC P:15

Denominations—*see also* Religions

Denominations and religions: At the center of each there is something or a Someone who speaks with the same voice

•MC 9 (*see also* LAL 11)

❖ MC P:9 (*see also* LAL Nov 10 52)

Denominations: "Divisions between Christians are a sin and a scandal, and Christians ought at all times to be making contributions towards reunion..."

•GID 60 ❖ GID I 4:56 (Ques. 14)

Denominations: "Extremist" elements in every church are nearest one another; the liberal and "broad-minded" people could never be united

•GID 60 (*see also* LAL 11-12)

❖ GID I 4:56 (Ques. 14) (*see also* LAL Nov 10 52)

Denominations, I offer no help to anyone who is hesitating between two Christian

•MC 6 ❖ MC P:2

Denominations: Screwtape rejoices to see the Church dividing itself up into small, self-righteous factions

•SL 34 ❖ SL 7:2

Denominations: "...those who are at the heart of each division are all closer to one another than those who are at the fringes"*

•LAL 11-12 (*see also* GID 60; MC 9)

❖ LAL Nov 10th 52 (*see also* GID I 4:56—Ques. 14; MC P:9)

Denominations: "When all is said (and truly said) about the divisions of Christendom, there remains, by God's mercy, an enormous common ground"

•CR vii—quote from unpublished letter (*see also* Christianity, "mere")

❖ CR P:1—quote from unpublished letter (*see also* Christianity, "mere")

Denominations, whether to classify certain, (e.g., Quakers) as "Christian" is a linguistic, not a religious question

•L 288-289 ❖ L 8 Sep 59

Denominations which hate each other on earth may end up in hell together— and will be astonished and resentful at the situation*

•SL 171; WLN 69

❖ SL 32:40; WLN 4:40

Denominations within Christianity, Christianity still an immensely formidable

unity despite many
•GID 204 ❖ GID II 4:6

Denominational differences—*consider also*
Christianity, "mere"; Differences; Doctrinal differences

Denominational differences: Christians do not even agree on the importance of their disagreements
•MC 8 ❖ MC P:6

Denominational differences, I am no guide on questions of; I have always in my books been concerned simply to put forward "mere" Christianity
•L 262 ❖ L 16 Mar 55

Denominational differences: I think St. Paul has told us what to do about them (re: division of "high" vs. "low" in the Church of England)*
•L 170 ❖ L 8 Nov 39

Denominational differences: Lewis lists the beliefs which unite "mere" Christians everywhere*
•GID 336 ❖ GID IV Letter 9

Denominational differences may be widened and sharpened by discussion or argument
•L 228-229, 230 (*see also* L 223)
❖ L 23 Apr 51; undated letter just before 27 Mar 51 (*see also* L undated letter of Jan 1950)

Denominational differences: "Our divisions should never be discussed except in the presence of those who have already come to believe..."
•MC 6 ❖ MC P:2

Denominational differences: "When all is said (and truly said) about the divisions of Christendom, there remains, by God's mercy, an enormous common ground"
•CR vii—quote from unpublished letter
❖ CR P:1—quote from unpublished letter

Denominational groups: The real traitor to our order is not the man who speaks, within that order, of our faults but the man who flatters our self-complacency (re: "the cultured")**
•WLN 36 ❖ WLN 3:9

Dentist analogy: "Christ says...I don't want to drill the tooth, or crown it, or stop it, but to have it out"
•MC 167 ❖ MC IV 8:4

Dentist analogy: Death likened to having a painful tooth out
•LAL 84 ❖ LAL Jul 7th 59

Dentist analogy for Purgatory: "I hope that when the tooth of life is drawn and I am 'coming round,' a voice will say, 'Rinse your mouth out with this'"
•LAL 84; LM 109 (*see also* SL 146*, 147)
❖ LAL Jul 7th 59; LM 20:12 (*see also* SL 31:2*, 3)

Dentist analogy: Once you call Him in, He will give you the full treatment
•MC 171 ❖ MC IV 9:2, 3

Dentist analogy: Repentance of sins like having a painful tooth out
•GID 124 (*see also* RP 32)
❖ GID I 14:10 (*see also* RP 3:21)

Dentist analogy: "Surely it [the Law of God] could be more aptly compared to the dentist's forceps or the front line than to anything enjoyable and sweet"
•RP 55 ❖ RP 6:3

Dentist analogy to suffering:" It doesn't really matter whether you grip the arms of the dentist's chair or let your hands lie in your lap. The drill drills on"
•GO 38 ❖ GO 2:31

Dentist analogy: "What do people mean when they say, 'I am not afraid of God because I know He is good?' Have they never been to a dentist?"
•GO 50-51 ❖ GO 3:19

Dependence—*see also* Interdependence

Dependence, actual and total, of those who call themselves "independent" since they live on inherited wealth
•LAL 21, 57-58, 112
❖ LAL Aug 10th 53; 14/6/56; 10 Dec 62

Dependence, having to accept money makes palpable the total, in which we always live anyway
•LAL 57-58 ❖ LAL 14/6/56

Dependence is our real condition; suffering helps to cure us of the illusion of "independence"
•LAL 20-21 ❖ LAL Aug 10th 53

Dependence is our real condition; poverty

merely reveals it to us
•LAL 111-112 ❖ LAL 10 Dec 62
Dependence of all people upon each other:
We are born helpless; we need others
physically, emotionally, intellectually
•FL 11-12 (see also GID 85-86, 87; LAL
57, 111-112) ❖ FL 1:3 (see also GID I 9:8,
10; LAL 14/6/56; 10 Dec 62)
Dependence upon God—consider also
Moral effort; Righteousness by faith/
grace; Works
Dependence upon God, fear teaches us
our
•PP 106 ❖ PP 6:17
Dependence upon God, Grace can help us
to accept our total, and even to find
joy in it
•FL 179-181 ❖ FL 6:26-28
Dependence upon God has to begin all
over again every day
•L 220 (see also GID 266; LM 27; MC
124; WG 132) ❖ L undated letter just
before 22 Sep 49 (see also GID II 16:52,
53; LM 5:14; MC III 11:6; WG 9:13)
Dependence upon God: "It is when we no-
tice the dirt that God is most present
in us..."
•L 199 ❖ L 20 Jan 42
Dependence upon God, moral effort use-
ful to show us our complete
•MC 94; 124-125; 127-131 (see also CR
169*; PP 65*) ❖ MC III 5:12; 11:7; 12:3-
9 (see also CR 169*; PP 4:13*)
Dependence upon God, our daily and
hourly, for our virtue*
•SJ 226; SL 62 (see also L 220; WG 132;
Daily...) ❖ SJ 14:20; SL 14:1 (see also L
undated letter just before 22 Sep 49;
WG 9:13; Daily...)
Dependence upon God, pain teaches us
our
•PP 95-98 (see also LAL 49*)
❖ PP 6:8, 9 (see also LAL 16/12/55*)
Dependence upon God: Perhaps in heaven
they will feel happiest who have been
forced to begin practising it here on
earth
•LAL 49 ❖ LAL 16/12/55
Dependence upon God, Screwtape la-
ments the fact that the "patient" is

daily increasing his conscious
•SL 131 ❖ SL 28:1
Dependence upon God: The only thing
one can usually change in one's situ-
ation is oneself—and yet one can't
change that either; we must ask Our
Lord to so do*
•LAL 48 ❖ LAL 9/11/55
Dependence upon God: The state of having to depend solely upon God is what
we all dread most; we will not turn to
Him as long as He leaves us anything
else...
•LAL 49 ❖ LAL 16/12/55
Dependence upon God, troubles and misery eventually may be seen as having
brought us to
•L 220
❖ L undated letter just before 22 Sep 49
Depravity, doctrine of Total: Could one introduce the idea of a bad God through
thinking we are so depraved that our
ideas of goodness count for nothing?*
•GO 36-38 (see also CR 68-69*, 79; PP
37-39) ❖ GO 2:28-30 (see also CR 5:22,
23*; 6:19; PP 3:1-5)
Depravity, doctrine of Total, may turn
Christianity into a form of devil-wor-
ship (since, if we are totally depraved,
our idea of good is worth nothing)
•PP 37-38 ❖ PP 3:3
Depravity, doctrine of Total, mentioned
with regard to self-contempt as a
source of cruelty
•GID 194 ❖ GID II 2:2
Depravity, I disbelieve the doctrine of To-
tal, partly because if our depravity
were total we should not know our-
selves to be depraved
•PP 66-67 (see also CR 25)
❖ PP 4:15 (see also CR 2:40)
Depravity [of Man]—see also Original sin;
Sinfulness
Depression—consider also Bereavement;
Grief; Unhappiness
Depression: An unhappy man wants dis-
tractions? —Only as a dog-tired man
wants a blanket on a cold night; he'd
rather lie there shivering...*
•GO 4 ❖ GO 1:6

it comes to Thee" (quote from St. Augustine)
- FL 189 (*see also* GID 252)
❖ FL 6:41 (*see also* GID II 14:7)

Desire for God will also awaken the fear of losing Him
- LM 76 ❖ LM 14:16

Desire for God: Your soul is a hollow made to fit a particular swelling in the infinite contours of the divine substance
- PP 147, 151 ❖ PP 10:3, 9

Desire for Heaven already in us but not yet attached to the true object
- WG 6 ❖ WG 1:4

Desire for Heaven: "...even if there were pains in heaven, all who understand would desire them"
- PP 126 (*see also* PP 152; SL 148)
❖ PP 8:9 (*see also* PP 10:9; SL 31:5)

Desire for Heaven not simply a desire for longevity or jewellery or social splendours; also we claim to know that our desire is not simply erotic
- WG 65 ❖ WG 4:17

Desire for Heaven not usually recognized as such; often mistaken as desire for wealth, women, travel, etc.
- MC 119 (*see also The Pilgrim's Regress, p. ix-xiii*) ❖ MC III 10:2, 3 (*see also The Pilgrim's Regress P:13-17*)

Desire for Heaven: Screwtape points out that youth have an inveterate appetite for Heaven; "Real worldliness is a work of time..."
- SL 133 ❖ SL 28:2

Desire for Heaven: Sometimes I do not think we desire heaven but more often I wonder whether, in our heart of hearts, we have ever desired anything else
- PP 145 ❖ PP 10:2

Desire for Heaven: "This secret fire goes out when you use the bellows; turn your back on it and attend to your duties, and then it will blaze"
- PP 148 ❖ PP 10:5

Desire for knowledge: The only people who achieve much are those who want knowledge so badly that they seek it while conditions are still unfavourable
- WG 30 ❖ WG 2:12

Desire for our heavenly country may be mistaken as desire for Beauty
- WG 6-7 ❖ WG 1:5

Desire for our own far-off country an inconsolable secret about which we are shy to speak
- WG 6-7 ❖ WG 1:5

Desire for Paradise may not prove that I shall enjoy it, but it indicates that such a thing exists (God makes no appetite in vain)
- WG 8-9 (*see also* WG 27)
❖ WG 1:6 (*see also* WG 2:9)

Desire for a "vague something" as suggested all one's life in experiences of nature, music, poetry, etc. seems to me possibly *not* a product of one's own mind
- L 144 ❖ L 24 Oct 31

Desire for the transtemporal: Can we suppose that reality offers any satisfaction to it?
- WG 8-9 ❖ WG 1:6

Desire for the ultimate reward increased by obedience
- WG 5 ❖ WG 1:3

Desire (for things like walking): "...it's wonderful how mercifully the desire goes when the power goes" (e.g., in sickness or old age)
- LAL 70 ❖ LAL Nov 30th 57

Desire: "...God intends to give us what we need, not what we now think we want"
- PP 53 ❖ PP 3:18

Desire: God's love for us is "a burden of glory not only beyond our deserts but also, except in rare moments of grace, beyond our desiring"
- PP 47 ❖ PP 3:14

Desire, I must keep alive in myself the, for my true country—which I shall not find till after death
- MC 120 ❖ MC III 10:5

Desire, I was sick with; that sickness better than health (re: a period in Lewis's adolescence)
- SJ 118-119 ❖ SJ 8:1

Desire, if you sit down to brood on the, and attempt to cherish it, the desire itself will evade you
•PP 148, 149 ❖ PP 10:5, 7

Desire, inherent dialectic of: If I mistook the images and sensations of Joy for Joy itself they soon confessed themselves inadequate
•SJ 219-220 (*see also The Pilgrim's Regress*, p. ix-xiii) ❖ SJ 14:11 (*see also The Pilgrim's Regress* P:13-17)

Desire: "It is the object that makes the desire itself desirable or hateful" (re: "Joy")
•SJ 220 ❖ SJ 14:12

Desire, Joy as a, which owes all its character to its object; the form of the desired is in the desire
•SJ 220 ❖ SJ 14:12

Desire, "Joy" defined as an unsatisfied, which is itself more desirable than any other satisfaction
•SJ 18 ❖ SJ 1:18

Desire ("Joy"): "Our best havings are wantings"
•L 289 ❖ L 5 Nov 59

Desire, Lewis states that no kind of, was present at all when he was converted to Theism
•SJ 230-231 ❖ SJ 15:2

Desire, "Northernness" was essentially a, and implied the absence of its object
•SJ 82 ❖ SJ 5:15

Desire, Object of: I ought to have seen that it was further away and less subjective than a system of mythology— had, in fact, only shown through that system
•SJ 168-169 ❖ SJ 11:5

Desire, object of our: "...he who has God and everything else has no more than he who has God only"
•WG 10 (*see also* PP 96*)
❖ WG 1:8 (*see also* PP 6:8*)

Desire, object of our: To lose it is to lose everything
•PP 146-147 ❖ PP 10:2

Desire, object of: "that something" which we are always looking for, watching for, listening for, from childhood to old age
•PP 146 ❖ PP 10:2

Desire, object of: "The thing I am speaking of is not an experience. You have experienced only the want of it"
•PP 148 ❖ PP 10:5

Desire, object of: "Whatever you try to identify with it turns out to be not it but something else"
•PP 149 ❖ PP 10:6

Desire, object of your: If it ever became manifest, you would know it; you would say, "Here at last is the thing I was made for"
•PP 146 (*see also* MC 170*)
❖ PP 10:2 (*see also* MC IV 8:12*)

Desire, object of your: "You have never *had* it. All the things that have ever deeply possessed your soul have been but hints of it..."
•PP 146 ❖ PP 10:2

Desire of each person is unique: "We cannot tell each other about it. It is the secret signature of each soul"
•PP 146 ❖ PP 10:2

Desire, speculation about the nature and object of our: "If this opinion is not true, something better is"
•PP 149 ❖ PP 10:6

Desire that no earthly experience can satisfy probably means I was made for another world
•MC 120 ❖ MC III 10:5

Desire, the, —much more the satisfaction—has always refused to be fully present in any experience
•PP 149 ❖ PP 10:6

Desire, the man of good will who is saddled with an abnormal, vs. "the equable virtue of some who are psychologically sound"
•L 242 (*consider also* Raw material)
❖ L 28 May 52 (*consider also* Raw material)

Desire: The settled happiness and security which we all desire God withholds from us; but joy, pleasure, and merriment He has scattered broadcast
•PP 115 ❖ PP 7:7

Desire: There can be a merely impulsive,

headstrong, greedy desire even for spiritual things—a desire which is "flesh" and not "spirit"
•LM 65 ❖ LM 12:11

Desire, this, always summons you away from yourself—even the desire itself lives only if you abandon it (re: desire for heaven)
•PP 148, 149 ❖ PP 10:5, 7

Desire to be accepted and welcomed by Nature as one part of our spiritual longings
•WG 14-17 (see also FL 78-79*; L 154-155*) ❖ WG 1:11-13 (see also FL 3:40*; L 14 Jun 32)

Desire to be "in" (as in an Inner Ring) almost excludes the possibility; "Until you conquer the fear of being an outsider, an outsider you will remain"
•WG 103 (see also Inner Rings)
❖ WG 6:14 (see also Inner Rings)

Desire to be needed—see Need to be needed

Desire: "We can hope only for what we can desire" (re: the negative notions we form of Heaven)
•WG 66 ❖ WG 4:19

Desire, we remain conscious of a, which no natural happiness will satisfy
•WG 8 ❖ WG 1:6

Desire: "When we want to be something other than the thing God wants us to be, we must be wanting what, in fact, will not make us happy"
•PP 52 (see also PP 90; WG 118-119)
❖ PP 3:18 (see also PP 6:3; WG 7:18)

"'Desire without hope,'" belief in "the Absolute" yielded a life of
•SJ 210 ❖ SJ 13:19

Desires: "All that you are, sins apart, is destined, if you will let God have His good way, to utter satisfaction"
•PP 147 ❖ PP 10:3

Desires, earthly life of Christ involved the killing of his human, at every turn
•MC 155 ❖ MC IV 5:5

Desires for unnecessary things are created by advertising for purely economic motives; this creates unnecessary work

•WLN 75-76, 78 ❖ WLN 5:11, 12, 15

Desires, in following the will of God Paradisal man was but carrying out his own
•PP 98 ❖ PP 6:10

Desires, our impossible, as one of the things Screwtape advocates silencing by the use of Noise
•SL 102-103 (see also CR 168*)
❖ SL 22:5 (see also CR 14:18*)

Desires, the nature religions simply affirm my natural, and the anti-religions simply contradict them; Christianity does neither
•GID 86 ❖ GID I 9:9

Desires, we inherit a whole system of, which do not necessarily contradict God's will but steadfastly ignore it
•PP 98-99 ❖ PP 6:10

Despair, Screwtape lists means of creating human, (routine of adversity, gradual decay of youthful loves and hopes, etc.)*
•SL 132 ❖ SL 28:1

Despair over one's own sinfulness mentioned by Screwtape as "a greater sin than any of the sins which provoke it"
•SL 138 ❖ SL 29:7

Despair, Screwtape mentions the quiet, which humans feel of ever overcoming chronic temptation
•SL 132 ❖ SL 28:1

Desperateness for love: "The greed to be loved is a fearful thing..."*
•GID 285 (see also FL 64-65, 73-76)
❖ GID III 3:7 (see also FL 3:18, 33-36)

Desperateness may prevent our perception of God's presence; "Perhaps your own reiterated cries deafen you to the voice you hoped to hear"
•GO 53-54 (see also GO 4-6; LAL 92)
❖ GO 3:24, 25 (see also GO 1:7-11; LAL 24 Sep 60)

Destinations, all day long we are helping each other to one or the other of these eternal
•WG 18-19 ❖ WG 1:15

Destiny—consider also Choice(s); Fate; Will of God

Destiny, if a transtemporal good is our

real, then any other object on which our desire fixes must be in some degree fallacious
•WG 6 ❖ WG 1:4

Destiny, is it possible for men to be too much concerned with their own eternal?—in one sense, yes
•RP 39-40 (see also WG 3, 18- 19)
❖ RP 4:13-15 (see also WG 1:1, 15)

Destiny of all creation: to eventually be rescued from decay, restored to shape, and then to subserve the splendour of remade humanity*
•GID 33 (see also M 149)
❖ GID I 2:11 (see also M 16:12)

Destiny of each person: Contact with God will mean either bliss or horror*
•GID 47 ❖ GID I 3:17

Destiny of each person: Dullest person you meet today may one day be a creature you would be tempted to worship, or else a creature of horror and corruption*
•WG 18-19 ❖ WG 1:15

Destiny of each person: Each of us is developing a character which will have to be endured—or enjoyed—forever*
•MC 87 ❖ MC III 4:9

Destiny of each person: For the first time, to see every one as he really is; "there will be surprises"*
•MC 86 ❖ MC III 4:7

Destiny of each person: How will you feel when "the real world" fades away and the Presence of God becomes palpable, immediate, and unavoidable?*
•MC 183 ❖ MC IV 10:17

Destiny of each person: "In each of us there is something growing up which will of itself be hell unless it is nipped in the bud"*
•GID 155 (see also MC 77-78; PP 122-123, 127) ❖ GID I 18:11 (see also MC III 2:12; PP 8:7, 11)

Destiny of each person: "In the end that Face which is the delight or the terror of the universe must be turned upon each of us..."*
•WG 13 ❖ WG 1:10

Destiny of each person: Infallible judg-

ment will be passed on what each of us is; "We shall know and all creation will know too"*
•WLN 113 ❖ WLN 7:37

Destiny of each person (Play analogy): "We are led to expect that the Author will have something to say to each of us on the part that each of us has played"*
•WLN 106 ❖ WLN 7:22

Destiny of each person: "Shall we, perhaps, in Purgatory, see our own faces and hear our own voices as they really were?"*
•RP 8 ❖ RP 1:13

Destiny of each person: Someday we shall hear God's infallible judgment on us, and realise that in some dim fashion we could have known it all along*
•WLN 112-113 ❖ WLN 7:36, 37

Destiny of each person: The day is coming when you will wake to find that you have attained it, or else that it was within your reach but you have lost it forever*
•PP 148 ❖ PP 10:4

Destiny of each person: to see God without disguise, which will strike either irresistible love or irresistible horror into every creature*
•MC 66 (see also GID 47)
❖ MC II 5:9 (see also GID I 3:17)

Destiny of each person: We walk every day on the razor edge of two incredible possibilities*
•WG 15-16 ❖ WG 1:12

Destiny of each person: "...when the term ends we might find ourselves facing the public opinion of that larger world"*
•PP 63 (see also PP 61, bottom)
❖ PP 4:10 (see also PP 4:9)

Destiny of lost Man—see also Hell

Destiny of lost Man: Even if their experience contained no pain and much pleasure, that black pleasure would send any soul flying to its prayers in terror
•PP 126 (see also PP 152)
❖ PP 8:9 (see also PP 10:9)

Destiny of lost Man: God is that Object "not to appreciate which is to have lost the greatest experience, and in the end to have lost all"*
•RP 92 ❖ RP 9:3

Destiny of lost Man, I have sometimes wondered whether the, is as the Greeks believed—to disintegrate in soul as in body ("witless psychic sediment")
•RP 37 ❖ RP 4:8

Destiny of lost Man: "I now see that I spent most of my life doing *neither* what I ought *nor* what I liked" (said by a patient of Screwtape's, already in Hell)*
•SL 56 ❖ SL 12:4

Destiny of lost Man: If we will not learn to eat the only food that the universe grows, then we must starve eternally*
•PP 54 ❖ PP 3:19

Destiny of lost Man: "It is, of course, impossible to imagine what the consciousness of such a creature...would be like"*
•PP 126 ❖ PP 8:9

Destiny of lost Man: Screwtape points out that what really gladdens the Devil's heart is to get a man's soul and give him *nothing* in return*
•SL 42 (*see also* SL 56, 144*)
❖ SL 9:2 (*see also* SL 12:4; 30:4*)

Destiny of lost Man: "...there is on each of us a load which, if nothing is done about it, will in fact break us..."*
•GID 121, 123 ❖ GID I 14:3, 4, 7

Destiny of lost Man: "They enjoy forever the horrible freedom they have demanded, and are therefore self-enslaved..."*
•PP 127-128 ❖ PP 8:11

Destiny of lost Man: They have asked to be left alone; alas, I am afraid that is what He does*
•PP 128 ❖ PP 8:12

Destiny of lost Man: To be a creature in a state of war and hatred with God means madness, horror, idiocy, rage, impotence, and eternal loneliness*
•MC 86-87 ❖ MC III 4:8

Destiny of lost Man: To enter hell is to be banished from humanity, while to enter heaven is to become more human than you ever succeeded in being on earth*
•PP 125 ❖ PP 8:9

Destiny of lost Man: "...to live wholly in the self and to make the best of what he finds there. And what he finds there is Hell"*
•PP 123 (*see also* GID 155; MC 77-78*)
❖ PP 8:7 (*see also* GID I 18:11; MC III 2:12*)

Destiny of lost Man: to lose the object of our secret, life-long desire ("If we lose this, we lose all")*
•PP 147-148 ❖ PP 10:3, 4

Destiny of lost Man: to miss the end for which we were formed, and the only thing that satisfies*
•WG 131 ❖ WG 9:11

Destiny of lost Man: We can be both banished from the presence of Him and erased from the knowledge of Him who knows all*
•WG 15-16 ❖ WG 1:12

Destiny of Man—*consider also* Goal of Christian life

Destiny of Man, as well as his humble origins, analogized by the life of Christ— His humiliations and victories
•RP 134 ❖ RP 12:13

Destiny of Man clearly involves a "remaking" of Nature
•M 120 (*see also* GID 87; M 149)
❖ M 14:21 (*see also* GID I 9:11; M 16:12)

Destiny of Man: To wish God had designed for us a less glorious and less arduous destiny is to wish not for more love but for less
•PP 43, 44 ❖ PP 3:10, 11

Destiny of Nature: Nature is to be fully harmonised with Spirit*
•M 159-161 ❖ M 16:27-29

Destiny of Nature: not to be unmade but remade*
•M 149 (*see also* GID 87)
❖ M 16:12 (*see also* GID I 9:11)

Destiny of Nature: "...our species, rising after its long descent, will drag all Nature up with it..."

•M 122 ❖ M 14:24

Destiny of Nature: "Something is being pulled down and something going up in its place"—like a house being rebuilt*
•M 155 ❖ M 16:21

Destiny of Nature: The destiny which Christianity promises to man clearly involves a "re-making" of Nature
•M 120 ❖ M 14:21

Destiny of Nature: to be redeemed and cured, but not tamed or sterilised; we shall still be able to recognise her*
•M 66-67 ❖ M 9:7

Destiny of Nature: "...to come right. The bad dream will be over: it will be morning"
•MC 170 ❖ MC IV 8:12

Destiny of redeemed humanity is to be something more glorious than unfallen humanity would have been
•M 122-123 (see also GID 87*)
❖ M 14:24 (see also GID I 9:11*)

Destiny of redeemed Man—see also Heaven

Destiny of redeemed Man: a complete cleansing, as if we have shuffled off for good a defiled, wet, clinging garment*
•SL 146 ❖ SL 31:2

Destiny of redeemed Man: a New Nature; some hints about this New Nature are given us in Jesus' miracles of anticipation
•M 150-153 ❖ M 16:13-19

Destiny of redeemed Man: a return to inequality, and the "the immense pleasures of admiration"*
•GID 85 (see also WG 115-116)
❖ GID I 9:7 (see also WG 7:15)

Destiny of redeemed Man: All earthly delights, even the delights of virtue itself, will seem half-nauseous in comparison with meeting our true Beloved*
•SL 148 ❖ SL 31:5

Destiny of redeemed Man: All our earthly sensations will be flooded with new meaning*
•WG 68-73, esp. 73 (see also WG 18)

❖ WG 4:23-30, esp. 4:30 (see also WG 1:14)

Destiny of redeemed Man: "All that you are, sins apart, is destined, if you will let God have His good way, to utter satisfaction"*
•PP 147 ❖ PP 10:3

Destiny of redeemed Man as promised in the New Testament: "Some day, God willing, we shall get in"*
•WG 17 ❖ WG 1:13

Destiny of redeemed Man: Beyond all possibility of doubt you will say, "Here at last is the thing I was made for"*
•PP 146 ❖ PP 10:2

Destiny of redeemed Man: complete reconciliation to boundless freedom with a delicate and beautiful order (re: dance and play in Heaven, without frivolity)*
•LM 92 ❖ LM 17:17

Destiny of redeemed Man: "...each of the redeemed shall forever know and praise some one aspect of the divine beauty better than any other creature can"*
•PP 150 (see also FL 92-93)
❖ PP 10:7 (see also FL 4:9)

Destiny of redeemed Man: Each one will receive a new name, which will always remain a secret between God and him*
•PP 149-150 ❖ PP 10:7

Destiny of redeemed Man: effortless power over all matter*
•GID 33 ❖ GID I 2:11

Destiny of redeemed Man: Forever submitting to obedience, he becomes through all eternity more and more free*
•PP 127-128 ❖ PP 8:11

Destiny of redeemed Man: Glory*
•WG 3-19 ❖ WG ch. 1

Destiny of redeemed Man: "God will look to every soul like its first love because He is its first love"*
•PP 147 ❖ PP 10:3

Destiny of redeemed Man: Grace will expand all our natures into the full richness of the diversity which God in-

tended when He made them*
•LM 10 ❖ LM 2:3
Destiny of redeemed Man: "Human will becomes truly creative and truly our own when it is wholly God's..."*
•PP 102 (consider also Personality)
❖ PP 6:14 (consider also Personality)
Destiny of redeemed Man: Humble souls will have the surprise of discovering that on certain occasions they sinned much less than they had thought*
•WG 123 ❖ WG 8:4
Destiny of redeemed Man: I can now only tell you about the fields of my boyhood; perhaps the day is coming when I can take you for a walk through them*
•LM 122 ❖ LM 22:15
Destiny of redeemed Man: "If we were perfected, prayer would not be a duty, it would be delight. Some day, please God, it will be"*
•LM 114 (see also L 277*)
❖ LM 21:11 (see also L 18 Jul 57*)
Destiny of redeemed Man is not less but more unimaginable than mysticism would lead us to suppose
•M 159 ❖ M 16:27
Destiny of redeemed Man: It appears that his powers will be almost unlimited (Bible texts given in footnote)*
•M 135 ❖ M 15:5
Destiny of redeemed Man: It may be possible to think too much of our own potential glory; it is never possible to think too much of our neighbor's*
•WG 18 ❖ WG 1:15
Destiny of redeemed Man: Light of Heaven will transform our natural experiences from "pencilled lines on flat paper" to three-dimensional reality*
•WG 68-69, 72 ❖ WG 4:23, 24, 30
Destiny of redeemed Man: Memory as we now know it is a dim foretaste of a power which the soul will exercise hereafter*
•LM 121-122 ❖ LM 22:15
Destiny of redeemed Man: "Nature" and "Spirit" are to be fully harmonised—

rather like a Centaur than a mounted knight*
•M 126, 160-161 (see also M 163; PP 98*) ❖ M 14:30; 16:29 (see also M 16:32; PP 6:10*)
Destiny of redeemed Man: new bodies ("latest Resurrection model")*
•LAL 78 (see also LAL 110) ❖ LAL Sep 30 58 (see also LAL 26 Nov 62)
Destiny of redeemed Man: "No doubt there are already...faint hints of what mould each is designed for, or what sort of pillar he will be"*
•WG 118 ❖ WG 7:17
Destiny of redeemed Man: "The door on which we have been knocking all our lives will open at last"*
•WG 14-15 ❖ WG 1:11
Destiny of redeemed Man: The faces of our friends shall laugh upon us with amazed recognition*
•LM 124 ❖ LM 22:21
Destiny of redeemed Man: "The Scotch catechism says that man's chief end is 'to glorify God and enjoy Him forever'" (and these are the same thing)
•RP 96-97 ❖ RP 9:6
Destiny of redeemed Man: the vision and enjoyment of God*
•WG 66-67 (see also FL 15)
❖ WG 4:20, 21 (see also FL 1:9)
Destiny of redeemed Man: "The whole man is to drink joy from the fountain of joy"*
•WG 17-18 (see also RP 97*; Joy)
❖ WG 1:14 (see also RP 9:7*; Joy)
Destiny of redeemed Man: The wounds of the martyrs will turn into beauties in Heaven*
•GID 216 ❖ GID II 7:1
Destiny of redeemed Man: "There is no question of finding for him a place... The place was there first. The man was created for it"*
•WG 119 ❖ WG 7:18
Destiny of redeemed Man: He will put on that greater glory of which Nature is only the first sketch*
•WG 17 ❖ WG 1:13
Destiny of redeemed Man: Think of your-

self as a seed, waiting to come up in the Gardener's good time, up into the *real* world, the real waking*
•LAL 119 (*consider also* Life as a "bad dream") ❖ LAL 28 Jun 63 (*consider also* Life as a "bad dream")

Destiny of redeemed Man: To be a creature that is in harmony with God and with other creatures is heaven: joy and peace and knowledge and power*
•MC 86-87 ❖ MC III 4:8

Destiny of redeemed Man: To be a part of the gift Jesus presents to the Father is the only thing we were made for*
•MC 170 ❖ MC IV 8:12

Destiny of redeemed Man: to become a real Man, strong, radiant, wise, beautiful, and drenched in joy
•GID 112 ❖ GID I 12:10

Destiny of redeemed Man: to be recalled to a new life, which will be in some sense a bodily life*
•M 126 ❖ M 14:30

Destiny of redeemed Man: "...to be united with that Life...is, strictly speaking, the only thing worth a moment's consideration"*
•M 155 ❖ M 16:22

Destiny of redeemed Man: to be very much more himself than he was before*
•MC 141 (*see also* MC 189-190; PP 125; SL 38, 59; WG 117-118)
❖ MC IV 2:3 (*see also* MC IV 11:13-15; PP 125; SL 8:3; 13:4; WG 7:17)

Destiny of redeemed Man: to become [as] gods*
•GID 87, 112; GO 85; L 257, 284; MC 174-175, 187 (*see also* GID 178*; MC 137-140*; RP 82*)
❖ GID I 9:11; 12:10; GO 4:32; L 1 Nov 54; 20 Jan 59; MC IV 9:11; 11:9 (*see also* GID I 22:3*; MC IV 1:1-16*; RP 8:11*)

Destiny of redeemed Man: To enter heaven is to become more human than you ever succeeded in being on earth; to enter hell is to be banished from humanity*
•PP 125 (*see also* WG 117-119)

❖ PP 8:9 (*see also* WG 7:17, 18)

Destiny of redeemed Man: to gain an utter knowledge of our sinfulness and to embrace the pain of it*
•SL 148 ❖ SL 31:5

Destiny of redeemed Man: to have that central music in every pure experience which had always just evaded memory at last recovered*
•SL 148 ❖ SL 31:4

Destiny of redeemed Man to include a fulfilling of our humanity
•WG 67 (*see also* MC 141, 189-190; GID 131; PP 125, 144-154; SL 59; WG 117-118) ❖ WG 4:21, 22 (*see also* MC IV 2:3; 11:13-15; GID I 16:3; PP 8:9; ch. 10; SL 13:4; WG 7:17)

Destiny of redeemed Man: to meet Jesus, our true Beloved, whom we have loved all our life*
•SL 148 (*see also* FL 190-191; PP 147)
❖ SL 31:5 (*see also* FL 6:44, 45; PP 10:3)

Destiny of redeemed Man: to meet our angels ("spirits"), whom we shall realize we have always known*
•SL 147-148 ❖ SL 31:4

Destiny of redeemed Man: to meet people one has met on earth only in books (Lewis is here referring to Samuel Johnson)*
•L 173 ❖ L 18 Dec 39

Destiny of redeemed Man: to understand, as God does, our own individuality*
•PP 147 ❖ PP 10:3

Destiny of redeemed Man: true personality*
•WG 117-118 (*see also* Personality)
❖ WG 7:17 (*see also* Personality)

Destiny of redeemed Man: We may be at last reunited with God in a love offered from the height of the utter individualities He has liberated us to be*
•SL xii ❖ SL P:20

Destiny of redeemed Man: We may hope "finally to emerge, if not altogether from time, at any rate from the tyranny, the unilinear poverty, of time"*
•RP 137-138 ❖ RP 12:17

Destiny of redeemed Man: We shall find that God is our true Beloved ("When

we see the face of God, we shall know that we have always known it")*
- FL 190-191; PP 147; SL 148
- ❖ FL 6:44, 45; PP 10:3; SL 31:5

Destiny of redeemed Man, what the risen body of Christ reveals about*
- M 145-163 (see also GID 32-33)
- ❖ M 16:5-32 (see also GID I 2:11)

Destiny of redeemed Man: When he reaches the place he was made for, his nature is fulfilled and his happiness attained*
- PP 52 (see also PP 90; WG 118-119)
- ❖ PP 3:18 (see also PP 6:3; WG 7:18)

Destiny of Redeemed who have "learned their driving in a hard school"*
- MC 181-182 ❖ MC IV 10:14

Destiny, our whole, seems to lie not in being "ourselves" but in becoming clean mirrors filled with the image of a face that is not ours
- CR 6-7 ❖ CR 1:10

Destiny, we must carry the weight of our neighbors'
- WG 18-19 ❖ WG 1:15

Destruction (as in Hell) means the unmaking, or cessation, of the destroyed
- PP 125 ❖ PP 8:9

Determinism defined: "It rejects as an illusion our spontaneous conviction that our behaviour has its ultimate origin in ourselves"
- LM 36 ❖ LM 7:5

Determinism seems to be implicit in a scientific view of the world, but may not preclude belief in God
- LM 36-37 ❖ LM 7:5, 6

Developmentalism, myth of—see Evolution(ism)

Devil—see also Satan

Devil always sends errors into the world in pairs of opposites; we must go straight through between both errors
- MC 160 (see also WLN 94-95; WG 108)
- ❖ MC IV 6:4 (see also WLN 7:4; WG 7:3)

Devil as the Prince of this World: "Is this state of affairs in accordance with God's will or not?"
- MC 51-54 ❖ MC II 3:1-6

Devil attempts "to make Christianity a private affair while banishing all privacy"
- WG 118 ❖ WG 7:3

Devil became the devil through Pride
- MC 109 ❖ MC III 8:2

Devil: Both the tempter and Our Lord tell us to count the cost of becoming a Christian
- WG 131 ❖ WG 9:12

Devil cannot bear scorn—can be driven out by jeering and flouting him (quote from Luther)
- SL 5 ❖ SL prelim. quote

Devil cannot endure to be mocked (quote from Thomas More)
- SL 5 ❖ SL prelim. quote

Devil, Christ as conqueror of death and the, (re: Psalm 8)
- RP 133 ❖ RP 12:11

Devil: Christianity says that he was created by God, was good when he was created, and went wrong; now he occupies the world
- MC 50-51 ❖ MC II 2:11, 12

Devil could make nothing but has infected everything; is the usurping lord of this age
- L 301 (see also L 257)
- ❖ L 20 Dec 61 (see also L 1 Nov 54)

Devil is a liar; not everything Screwtape says should be assumed to be true even from his own angle
- SL 4 ❖ SL PP:3

Devil is very active near the altar or on the eve of conversion; anxieties, doubts pour in
- L 227-228 (see also SL 172; WLN 70)
- ❖ L 5 Mar 51 (see also SL 32:40; WLN 4:40)

Devil laughs to see us overcoming cowardice or lust or ill-temper by learning to think that they are beneath our dignity
- MC 112 ❖ MC III 8:8

Devil: "Like a good chess player, he is always trying to manoeuvre you into a position where you can save your castle only by losing your bishop"
- WG 118 ❖ WG 7:3

Devil loves curing a small fault by giving

you a great one
•MC 113 ❖ MC III 8:10

Devil, Paganism seen by some as nothing but the direct work of the; "he 'makes his lies as like the truth as he can'"
•RP 106 ❖ RP 10:11

Devil, not essential to believe in the
•L 261 ❖ L 2 Feb 55

Devil seldom tries to deceive with a direct lie (re: temptation to protect our things temporal, which contains the truth that we can be too fanatical)
•WG 129-130 ❖ WG 9:8

Devil, temptation probably not the only mode in which the, can corrupt and impair
•GID 169 ❖ GID I 20:Reply-12

Devil: "The association between him and me in the public mind has already gone quite as deep as I wish..."
•WG 94 ❖ WG 6:3

Devil: The humorous and civilised image of Mephistopheles has helped to strengthen the illusion that evil is liberating
•SL ix (see also SL 33)
❖ SL P:15 (see also SL 7:1)

Devil, the various artistic and literary symbols used to represent the, discussed
•SL viii-ix ❖ SL P:12-15

Devil used to prevent people from doing good works; now he just organises them
•LAL 58 ❖ LAL 5/7/56

Devil was an archangel once; natural gifts like niceness will only make your fall more terrible
•MC 181 ❖ MC IV 10:13

Devil, whenever we find that our religious life is making us feel better than others we may be sure we are being acted on by the
•MC 111 ❖ MC III 8:7

Devils—see also Angels, fallen

Devils and angels both "Supernatural" in relation to this spatio-temporal Nature; but good angels lead a life which is "Supernatural" in another sense as well
•M 170 (see also FL 15)

❖ M App. A:2 (see also FL 1:9)

Devil(s), existence of
•GID 56-57 ❖ GID I 4:38 (Ques. 9)

Devils have "faith" in the sense of intellectual assent, but not "faith" in the sense of trust or confidence
•GID 173 ❖ GID I 21:2

Devils, "hunger" of the, in Hell is the passion to dominate, almost to digest, one's fellow; even in human life ("love") we see this
•SL xi (see also FL 160; SL 26, 37-38, 81, 141, 145; WLN 51-56, 69-70)
❖ SL P:19, 20 (see also FL 5:46; SL 5:2; 8:3; 18:3; 30:1; 31:1; WLN 4:1-13, 39)

Devils, Lewis describes his belief about, ("They do not differ in nature from good angels, but their nature is depraved")
•SL vii-xii ❖ SL P:8-21

Devils mentioned as "'fallen' angels"
•M 170 ❖ M App. A:2

Devil(s), our awareness of, may vary according to how much we are in Satan's power
•GID 56-57 ❖ GID I 4:38 (Ques. 9)

Devils, Screwtape laments that disbelief in, takes away their ability to terrorize, while belief in their existence precludes materialism and scepticism
•SL 32-33 ❖ SL 7:1

Devils: Screwtape mentions that the fact that they are mostly comic figures in the modern imagination helps his cause
•SL 33 (see also SL ix)
❖ SL 7:1 (see also SL P:15)

Devils ("Tempters") try to elicit small wrong choices which later harden into evil principles
•SL 156-157; WLN 54-55 (see also MC 86-87, 117; RP 136; SL 53-54; WG 101-103)
❖ SL 32:10; WLN 4:10 (see also MC III 4:8, 9; 9:8; RP 12:16; SL 12:1; WG 6:12)

Devils, there are two equal and opposite errors into which our race may fall about the: disbelief, and excessive interest
•SL 3 ❖ SL PP:2

Devils, use of imagery to describe: Creatures higher in the natural order than ourselves must be represented symbolically if at all
•SL viii ❖ SL P:12

Devotion to God: We cannot give God anything that is not His already
•MC 125 (*see also* SL 96-99)
❖ MC III 11:9 (*see also* SL 21:2-6)

Devotion to God: What St. Paul had to say on the hindrance of marriage related not to sex but to the multiple distractions of domesticity
•FL 137-138 ❖ FL 5:10

Devotions—*see also* Prayer(s); *consider also* Obstacles to prayer

Devotions, carrying out one's private, in a church: Usually there are too many distractions
•LM 17 ❖ LM 3:8

Devotions, human distaste for religious, when one is feeling vague guilt mentioned by Screwtape*
•SL 54-55 ❖ SL 12:3

Devotions: "I don't think we ought to try to keep up our normal prayers when we are ill and over-tired. I would not say this to a beginner..."*
•LAL 38 (*see also* LAL 24)
❖ LAL 20/2/55 (*see also* LAL Jan 1st 54)

Devotions: "If the few, the very few, minutes we now spend on intercourse with God are a burden to us rather than a delight, what then?"*
•LM 113-114 ❖ LM 21:7

Devotions, importance of daily, to train the habit of faith
•MC 124 (*see also* L 220; GID 266; MC 168-169; SJ 226*; SL 062*; WG 132)
❖ MC III 11:5, 6 (*see also* L undated letter just after 6 Sep 49; GID II 16:52, 53; MC IV 8:8; SJ 14:20*; SL 14:1*; WG 9:13)

Devotions: "Perhaps prayers as a secret indulgence which Father disapproves may have a charm they lacked in houses where they were commanded"*
•LAL 32 ❖ LAL Sep 19/54

Devotions, personal, should be undertaken in the morning*
•MC 169 (*consider also* Morning)
❖ MC IV 8:8 (*consider also* Morning)

Devotions, personal, should not be reserved for bed-time—obviously the worst hour for any action which needs concentration*
•LM 16-17 (*see also* L 256)
❖ LM 3:7 (*see also* L 31 Jul 54)

Devotions, regarding the "irksomeness" of private*
•LM 112-117 ❖ LM ch. 21

Devotions to saints
•L 243
❖ L undated letter just after 20 Jun 52

Devotions to saints, propriety of, may infer propriety of devotions to stars and whales
•GID 334 (*see also* L 243)
❖ GID IV Letter 7 (*see also* L undated letter between 20 Jun 52 and 2 Oct 52)

Devotions to saints: There is clearly a theological defense to it, and also a great danger
•LM 15 ❖ LM 3:3

Devotions to saints, there's a lot to be said against, but at least they remind us that we are very small people compared to them
•LM 13 ❖ LM 2:14

Devotions to saints: While Christendom is divided about prayer *to* saints, we are all agreed about praying *with* them
•LM 15 ❖ LM 3:4

Devotional books: Lewis mentions a "curious drabness which characterises so many 'little books on religion'"
•L 193 ❖ L 10 Apr 41

Devotional books vs. doctrinal books: Many find that "the heart sings unbidden while...working their way through a tough bit of theology..."
•GID 205 ❖ GID II 4:7

Devotional life—*see also* Prayer(s); *consider also* Obstacles to prayer

Devotional life, anxieties of everyday domestic life more of a hindrance to, than any passion or appetite
•FL 137-138 ❖ FL 5:10

Devotional life as a means to correct the

growing emptiness of our idea of God
•M 90 ❖ M 11:14

Devotional life destroyed by construc-
tions of a "historical Jesus" which cannot in fact be worshipped
•SL 106-108 ❖ SL 23:3, 4

Devotional life: Lewis describes his realization of the need for "continual, conscious recourse" to God (whom He
then called "Spirit") for his virtue*
•SJ 226 (see also SL 62; consider also Dependence upon God; Works)
❖ SJ 14:20 (see also SL 14:1; consider also
Dependence upon God; Works)

Devotional life, my own rules about, are
as follows...
•L 256 (see also LM 16-18)
❖ L 31 Jul 54 (see also LM 3:6-11)

Devotional life: Turning to God became a
painful effort after the Fall, since
man's inclination had become self-
ward*
•PP 76, 83 (see also PP 91)
❖ PP 5:5, 10 (see also PP 6:3)

Devotional life: We feel our time is "our
own," and God's share in it is a tribute we must pay out of "our own"
pocket*
•PP 75 ❖ PP 5:5

Devotional life, we must be open to new
blessings in our, and not lament that
the first fervours of our conversion
have died away
•LM 26-27 (see also SL 13-14*)
❖ LM 5:10-13 (see also SL 2:3*)

Devotional reading: "Don't worry if your
heart won't respond; do the best you
can"
•L 192 ❖ L 4 Jan 41

Devotional reading, Lewis suggests
sources for
•L 192, 299 (see also LM 62*)
❖ L 4 Jan 41; 9 May 61 (see also LM 12:1*)

Diagnosis (of sin) must be preached before the remedy (the Gospel)
•GID 243-244; PP 55 (see also GID 95-
96, 181-182; MC 38-39)
❖ GID II 12:6; PP 4:1 (see also GID I
10:15-17; 22:13; MC I 5:4)

Dialectic of desire, the inherent: If I mis-

took the images and sensations of Joy
for Joy itself, they soon confessed
themselves inadequate
•SJ 219-220 (see also The Pilgrim's Regress, p. ix-xiii, esp. p. xiii)
❖ SJ 14:11 (see also The Pilgrim's Regress
P:13-17, esp. P:17)

Dialogue—see Argument; Discussion;
Debate(ing)

Diary, I am thankful that Theism cured me
of the time-wasting and foolish practice of keeping a
•SJ 233 ❖ SJ 15:5

Diary-keeping after Joy's death: "Are
these jottings morbid? ...By writing it
all down...I believe I get a little outside it"*
•GO 9-10 ❖ GO 1:18

Diary: "You put down each day what you
think important; but of course you
cannot each day see what will prove
to have been important in the long
run"
•SJ 233 ❖ SJ 15:5

Dickens' Christmas Carol: Absence of any
interest in the Incarnation is significant
•GID 219 ❖ GID II 8:3

Dickens mentioned as the great author on
mere affection (storge)
•L 254 ❖ L 23 Jan 54

Dickens, the best, always seems to me to
be the one I have read last
•L 289 ❖ L 5 Nov 59

Diet: Christianity-and-Vegetarianism
mentioned by Screwtape as a useful
alternative to "mere Christianity"
•SL 115 ❖ SL 25:1

Diet, medical: "...perhaps having to fast for
medical reasons is a just punishment
for not having fasted enough on
higher grounds!"
•LAL 35 (see also LAL 104-105)
❖ LAL Nov 1st 54 (see also LAL 3/7/62)

Diet: Screwtape mentions "what that pestilent fellow Paul used to teach about
food and other unessentials..."
•SL 75 ❖ SL 16:5

Differences—see also Denominational differences; Doctrinal differences

Differences between people like differences between organs of a body
- MC 159 (*see also* GID 238)
- ❖ MC IV 6:3 (*see also* GID II 11:10)

Differences, even in heaven we shall have, and remain a "body" of unique members; we shall not all be the same, or appreciate God in the same way
- PP 150-151 ❖ PP 10:7, 8

Differences in kind make for real unity (re: Christian membership)
- WG 110-111 (*see also* PP 150-151)
- ❖ WG 7:6, 7 (*see also* PP 10:7, 8)

Differences in others, charity toward: Lewis suggests believing all the good you can of others, and making them as comfortable as you can
- MC 88-89 ❖ MC III 5:1

Differences in others seen as a claim to superiority; Screwtape observes that humans tend to resent them
- SL 163; WLN 61
- ❖ SL 32:23; WLN 4:23

Differences, in the Body of Christ we all have; no one is like anyone else— "All different and all necessary to the whole and to one another"
- L 242-243 ❖ L 20 Jun 52

Differences: "It takes all sorts to make a world; or a church... Heaven will display far more variety than Hell" (re: differences of worship style)
- LM 10 ❖ LM 2:3

Differences of opinion: "...there is evidence both for and against the Christian propositions which fully rational minds...can assess differently"*
- WLN 20, 21 ❖ WLN 2:8, 9

Differences [of people], if God has no use for all these, I do not see why He should have created more souls than one
- PP 147 ❖ PP 10:3

Difficult doctrines—*see* Doctrines, difficult; *consider* Difficulties in Scripture

Difficult passages in the Psalms: "... it was the sound principle of nursery gastronomy to polish off the nasty things first..."
- RP 6-7, 34 ❖ RP 1:10; 4:1

Difficult times, the great thing with, is to take them bit by bit and hour by hour; it is seldom the exact present that is unbearable
- LAL 58 (*see also* LAL 60, 69, 103; SL 29, 67-71*)
- ❖ LAL 14/5/45 (*see also* LAL 3/8/56; Oct 20th 57; 4 May 62; SL 6:2; ch. 15*)

Difficulties—*see also* Crisis; Grief; Pain; Problems; Sorrow; Suffering; Trouble(s); Tribulation(s)

Difficulties: Adversity and prosperity both mentioned by Screwtape as possible means of separating humans from God
- SL 132 ❖ SL 28:1

Difficulties as a threat to faith: "The conclusion I dread is not, 'So there's no God after all,' but, 'So this is what God's really like...'"*
- GO 5 ❖ GO 1:9

Difficulties: "Bear your cross, for if you try to get rid of it you will probably find another and worse one" (quote from *Imitation of Christ*)
- LAL 86 ❖ LAL Aug 3/59

Difficulties, Christian attitude toward: The crown is not promised without the Cross*
- L 166 ❖ L 8 May 39

Difficulties: "...Divine punishments are also mercies and particular good is worked out of particular evil..."*
- SJ 77 ❖ SJ 5:9

Difficulties, empathy for another's: Lewis demonstrates that it is more effective if we can admit our own handicap in being able to truly empathize*
- LM 40-41 ❖ LM 8:2

Difficulties, fellow-pupils can often help each other solve, better than their teachers can; I write as one amateur to another
- RP 1-2 ❖ RP 1:1, 2

Difficulties, how to think about, (may bring us closer to God; do not last forever)*
- LAL 47 ❖ LAL 26/10/55

Difficulties, human, which provide the devil "admirable opportunities of

wearing out a soul by attrition" listed by Screwtape
•SL 132 ❖ SL 28:1

Difficulties: "I have learned now that while those who speak about one's miseries usually hurt one, those who keep silence hurt more"
•L 289 ❖ L 3 Dec 59

Difficulties: "I must try not to let my own present unhappiness harden my heart against the woes of others!"*
•LAL 64 ❖ LAL 4/1/57

Difficulties: If we could steadfastly remember God, I suppose we should need no misfortunes
•L 227 (see also L 161-162)
❖ L 5 Mar 51 (see also L 12 Sep 38)

Difficulties in Scripture—see also Questions

Difficulties in Scripture: "Behind the shocking passage be sure there lurks some great truth which you don't understand"
•L 253 ❖ L 8 Aug 53

Difficulties in Scripture, doctrine, etc: "There is always hope if we keep an unsolved problem fairly in view; there's none if we pretend it's not there"*
•LM 59 ❖ LM 11:8

Difficulties in Scripture: If we are free to delete all inconvenient data we shall have no theological difficulties; but also no solutions and no progress
•LM 59 ❖ LM 11:8

Difficulties in Scripture: "The troublesome fact, the apparent absurdity...is precisely the one we must not ignore"
•LM 59 ❖ LM 11:8

Difficulties in Scripture: "Where we find a difficulty we may always expect that a discovery awaits us" (e.g., in the Psalms)
•RP 28 ❖ RP 3:16

Difficulties, Lewis proposes a healthy attitude toward*
•GID 52 ❖ GID I 4:18, 19 (Ques. 5)

Difficulties may have names—Cancer, War, Unhappiness—but the reality is each hour or moment that comes; one

never gets the full impact of the thing itself
•GO 12-13 (see also GO 42-43)
❖ GO 1:24 (see also GO 3:3)

Difficulties ("misfortune"), men are not angered by, but by difficulties conceived as injury; the more claims on life we make, the more often we feel injured
•SL 95-96 (see also SL 141)
❖ SL 21:2 (see also SL 30:2)

Difficulties of everyday domestic life more of a hindrance to devotion to God in marriage than sex
•FL 137-138 ❖ FL 5:10

Difficulties, our human: "We are not on an untrodden path. Rather, on the main road"—shared also with our Master
•LM 44 ❖ LM 8:13

Difficulties: "Part of every misery is...the fact that you don't merely suffer but have to keep on thinking about the fact that you suffer"
•GO 9 (see also PP 14)
❖ GO 1:18 (see also PP 1:1)

Difficulties remind me that my only real treasure is Christ
•PP 106 ❖ PP 6:17

Difficulties remind us that our real home is elsewhere—and why should we not look forward to the arrival?*
•LAL 83-84 (see also CR 37; L 227; PP 106, 115; SL 132)
❖ LAL Jun 7th 59 (see also CR 3:2; L 5 Mar 51; PP 6:17; 7:7; SL 28:1)

Difficulties such as poverty and overwork brought on by human stupidity and avarice rather than by "the churlishness of nature"
•PP 89 ❖ PP 6:1

Difficulties, talking to others about our: "Often...the person we speak to is at that moment full of troubles we know nothing about"
•LAL 40-41 ❖ LAL 24/3/55

Difficulties ("tests") do not tell God what we can endure, they tell us
•PP 101-102 (see also GO 61)
❖ PP 6:13 (see also GO 3:36)

Difficulties: The apparent stone will be bread to us if we believe that a Father's hand put it into ours, in mercy or in justice or even in rebuke*
•LM 53 ❖ LM 10:3

Difficulties: "The great thing...is to live from day to day and hour to hour not adding the past or future to the present"
•LAL 69 (see also LAL 58, 60, 97, 103; SL 29, 67- 71*)
❖ LAL Oct 20th 57 (see also LAL 14/6/56; 3/8/56; Oct 30 58; 4 May 62; SL 6:2; ch. 15*)

Difficulties: The only thing one can usually change in one's situation is oneself—and yet one can't change that either; we must ask Our Lord to do so*
•LAL 48 ❖ LAL 9/11/55

Difficulties: The practice of Christianity includes referring every experience, pleasant or unpleasant, to God and asking His will
•GID 50 ❖ GID I 4:11 (Ques. 3)

Difficulties, the temptation as we try to sympathize with another's, is to attempt reassurances
•LM 41 ❖ LM 8:3

Difficulties ("troughs"), Screwtape explains why Christians seem to experience more, ("He wants them to learn to walk and must therefore take away His hand")*
•SL 37-39 ❖ SL 8:3, 4

Difficulties: "We are under the harrow and can't escape. Reality, looked at steadily, is unbearable"*
•GO 32 ❖ GO 2:20

Difficulties: "...we do not usually think about the next world till our hopes in this have been pretty well flattened out..."*
•CR 37 ❖ CR 3:2

Difficulties: What we regard as a mere hideous interruption and curtailment of life is really the concrete situation
•L 221 (see also L 161-162; SL 95-97*)
❖ L 22 Sep 49 (see also L 12 Sep 38; SL 21:2, 3*)

Difficulties which the Psalmists experienced (out of which their self-righteous utterances grew) included ostracism, ineffectiveness, and humiliation
•CR 125-128 ❖ CR 10:30-40

Difficulty, anger toward God in time of: "I was getting from it the only pleasure a man in anguish can get; the pleasure of hitting back"
•GO 45-46 ❖ GO 3:9

Difficulty, the approach of any, is usually also the preparation for it (quote from George MacDonald)
•L 186 (see also L 219)
❖ L 2 Jun 40 (see also L 2 Sep 49)

Difficulty, why is God so present a commander in our time of prosperity and so very absent a help in time of
•GO 4-5 (see also Absence of God)
❖ GO 1:7 (see also Absence of God)

Digestion, our feelings and moods (the "look" of the world) tell us more about the state of our passions and even our, than about reality
•CR 43; MC 123-124
❖ CR 3:11; MC III 11:5

Dimension, concept of, to help explain concept of a super-personal and trinitarian God
•MC 141-142 ❖ MC IV 2:5-7

Diminishing returns: When we take pleasures at times or in ways or in degrees which God has forbidden, we get increasing craving for diminishing pleasure*
•SL 41-42 (see also SL 55, 116-117)
❖ SL 9:2 (see also SL 12:4; 25:3, 4)

Directions for living, in the law of God one finds the real and well-grounded
•RP 60-61 ❖ RP 6:10, 11

Directions, moral laws are like, for running a machine
•MC 69-70 (see also Machine)
❖ MC III 1:1, 2 (see also Machine)

Disadvantages, we must learn to live with our own set of, (no excuse for throwing up the sponge)
•L 180 ❖ L 26 Mar 40

Disagreeableness in people: Probable cause is inner insecurity

•LAL 27-28 (*see also* SL 162-163*; WLN 60-61*) ❖ LAL Mar 10/54 (*see also* SL 32:22, 23*; WLN 4:22, 23*)

Disagreeableness, mere, is harder to understand than the great crimes, for the raw material of them exists in us all
•LAL 27-28 ❖ LAL Mar 10/54

Disagreement with unbelievers may sometimes be necessary; "...there comes a time when we must show that we disagree"
•GID 262 (*see also* L 249; RP 71- 74; SL 45-48*) ❖ GID II 16:29 (*see also* L 6-7 Apr 53; RP 7:9-16; SL ch. 10*)

Disagreement between denominations— *see* Denominational differences

Disappointment: "'Blessed are they that expect little, for they shall not be disappointed'"
•LAL 96 (*see also* SL 95-96)
❖ LAL 24 Feb 61 (*see also* SL 21:2)

Disappointment: In every department of life it marks the transition from dreaming aspiration to laborious doing (re: anti-climax after conversion)
•SL 13 (*see also* LM 26; MC 100)
❖ SL 2:3 (*see also* LM 5:10; MC III 6:11, 12)

Disappointment, Screwtape mentions that the sense of, in humans can easily be turned into a sense of injury
•SL 141 (*see also* SL 95-96)
❖ SL 30:2 (*see also* SL 21:2)

Disappointment: "When we lose one blessing, another is often most unexpectedly given in its place"*
•LAL 86 ❖ LAL Aug 3/59

Disappointment with oneself often mistaken for true repentance
•L 195 ❖ L 19 Nov 41

Discipleship—*consider* Example, Christian

Discouragement ("Despair") over one's own sinfulness mentioned by Screwtape as "a greater sin than any of the sins which provoke it"
•SL 138 ❖ SL 29:7

Discouragement ("despair"), Screwtape mentions the quiet, which humans feel of ever overcoming chronic temptation

•SL 132 ❖ SL 28:1

Discouragement, Screwtape lists means of creating human, ("The routine of adversity, the gradual decay of youthful loves and youthful hopes...")*
•SL 132 ❖ SL 28:1

Discussion(s)—*see also* Conversation; Debate(ing); Argument

Discussion, silence during a, can be of an emphatic, audible, and even dialectical character*
•LM 77 (*see also* LAL 110)
❖ LM 15:1 (*see also* LAL 8 Nov 62)

Discussions, intellectual, about God: We must continually fall back from the web of our own arguments into Reality—from Christian apologetics to Christ Himself*
•GID 103 ❖ GID I 10:50

Discussions, regarding women trying to enter men's, ("We all appear as dunces when feigning an interest in things we know nothing about")
•FL 106-110 ❖ FL 4:32-37

Discussions usually separate us; actions sometimes unite us (re: the re-union of churches)
•LM 16 ❖ LM 3:5

Disease(s)—*see also* Illness(es)

Disease and deformity: Temptation probably not the only mode in which the Devil can corrupt and impair, as seen in the deformed woman of Luke 13:16
•GID 169 ❖ GID I 20:Reply-12

Disease has its own pleasures of which health knows nothing
•L 137 (*see also* L 106-107, 159, 202, 302, 304; LAL 37; SJ 189)
❖ L 9 Sep 29 (*see also* L undated letter postmarked 25 Jan 26; undated letter just after 2 Sep 37; 31 Jan 43; Dec 61; 25 May 62; LAL 29/1/55; SJ 12:11)

Disease, perversions of Affection are not a, which needs medical treatment but a sin which needs spiritual direction
•FL 80-81 ❖ FL 3:43

Disease: Regarding the view that all crime is more or less pathological (in which "punishment" becomes "healing" or "curing")*

•GID 287-294, 313, 339-340; L 304
❖ GID III 4:1-14; 8:7-9; IV Letter 12; L 25 May 62

Disease, Satan is associated with, in Scripture; I by no means reject the view that disease may be caused by a created being other than man
•PP 89 (ftnt.), 136 ❖ PP 6:1 (ftnt.); 9:7

Diseases, one easily gets to dread the doctors more than the
•LAL 107 ❖ LAL 2 Oct 62

Diseases, we have Scriptural authority for Satan originating
•L 257 ❖ L 1 Nov 54 (first letter)

Disguise—*consider also* Pretending

Disguise, what pops out before a man has time to put on a, is the truth
•MC 164-165 ❖ MC IV 7:12

Dishonesty—*consider also* Intellectual dishonesty; Intellectual honesty

Dishonesty ("falsehood") is habit-forming (a warning to dishonest tax-collectors)*
•RP 15-16 ❖ RP 2:10

Dishonesty in our work: "Few of us have always, in fair measure, given our pupils or patients or clients...what we were being paid for"
•RP 13 ❖ RP 2:8

Dishonesty in schoolwork: How can any man prefer the galley-slave labour of transcription to the freeman's work of attempting an essay on his own?
•L 291 ❖ L 10 Dec 59

Dishonesty: Lying and deceit as "sins of the tongue" which are protested against in the Psalms
•RP 75 ❖ RP 7:16

Dishonesty: "*One* trouble about habitual liars is that, since you can't believe anything they say, you can't feel the slightest interest in it"
•LAL 107 ❖ LAL 2 Oct 62

Dislike—*see* Hatred

Dismay—*see* Fear

Disney, Walt: "...it is not the ugliness of the ugly figures but the simpering dolls, intended for our sympathy..."
•SJ 151 ❖ SJ 10:3

Disney, Walt, mentioned with regard to

Dwarfs
•SJ 54-55 ❖ SJ 3:13

Disney, Walt, mentioned as one of those whose minds were dominated by the myth of popular Evolutionism
•CR 82 ❖ CR 7:3

Distance: Having no car, I measured distances by the standard of man walking on his two feet
•SJ 156-157 ❖ SJ 10:9

Distractions listed which can help us avoid God (money, sex, status, health, the radio, etc.)
•CR 168-169 ❖ CR 14:17, 18

Distractions listed which have greater power over us when we are feeling vague guilt (useless conversation, staring at a dead fire, staying up late at night)
•SL 54-56 ❖ SL 12:3, 4

Distractions which can help us avoid God: Noise*
•SL 102-103 ❖ SL 22:5

"**Dither**," regarding the word
•LAL 16, 17-18
❖ LAL May 30th 53; Jun 22d 53

Diver analogy of Christ's life, death, and resurrection
•GID 82; M 111-112, 135 (*see also* GID 159-160*) ❖ GID I 9:4; M 14:5; 15:5 (*see also* GID I 19:7*)

Diversity—*see also* Differences

Diversity, grace will expand all our natures into the rich fullness of the, which God intended when He made them
•LM 10 ❖ LM 2:3

Diversity: "It takes all sorts to make a world; or a church...Heaven will display far more variety than Hell" (re: differences in worship style)
•LM 10 ❖ LM 2:3

Divine concepts illustrated by mundane, earthly acts and language
•WG 56 (*see also* Imagery)
❖ WG 4:4 (*see also* Imagery)

Divine Goodness (chapter title)
•PP 37-54 (*see also* God, goodness of)
❖ PP ch. 3 (*see also* God, goodness of)

Divine humility: God is not proud, He

stoops to conquer; He will have us even though we have shown that we prefer everything else to Him
•PP 97 (*see also* LAL 49; SJ 229) ❖ PP 6:8 (*see also* LAL 16/12/55; SJ 14:23)

Divine Omnipotence (chapter title)
•PP 26-36 (*see also* Omnipotence of God) ❖ PP ch. 2 (*see also* Omnipotence of God)

Divine punishments are also mercies and particular good is worked out of particular evil
•SJ 77 ❖ SJ 5:9

Divine reality is like a fugue; all His acts are different but they all rhyme or echo to one another
•GID 37 ❖ GID I 2:15

Divinity of Christ, it seems to me impossible to believe in the, while abandoning or neglecting the doctrine of the Second Coming
•WLN 93 (*see also* Jesus as ...) ❖ WLN 7:1 (*see also* Jesus as ...)

Division(s)—*consider also* Denomination(s); Reunion

Division, those who are at the heart of each, are all closer to one another than those who are at the fringes (both within Christianity and without)
•LAL 11-12 (*see also* GID 60; MC 9) ❖ LAL Nov 10th 52 (*see also* GID I 4:56—Ques. 14; MC P:9)

Divisions of Christendom, when all is said about the, there remains by God's mercy an enormous common ground
•CR vii—quote from unpublished letter (*see also* Christianity, "mere") ❖ CR P:1—quote from unpublished letter (*see also* Christianity, "mere")

Divisions within Christianity a sin and a scandal; we must pray for re-union
•GID 60 ❖ GID I 4:56 (Ques. 14)

Divisions within Christianity: Christians do not even agree on the importance of their disagreements*
•MC 8 ❖ MC P:6

Divisions within Christianity not so dispiriting when seen from without; Christianity still an immensely formidable unity

•GID 204 ❖ GID II 4:6

Divisions within Christianity: Screwtape rejoices to see the Church dividing itself up into small, self-righteous factions
•SL 34 (*see also* SL 72-73, 75) ❖ SL 7:2 (*see also* SL 16:2, 5)

Divisions within Christianity should never be discussed except in the presence of those who are already Christians
•MC 6 ❖ MC P:2

Divisions within the Church of England ("High" vs. "Low"): I think St. Paul has told us what to do about them
•L 170 ❖ L 8 Nov 39

Divorce, discussion of
•MC 96-102 ❖ MC III 6:3-14

Divorce, letter regarding children who lose parents in a
•L 221 ❖ L 22 Sep 49

Divorce, letter to a lady contemplating
•L 240 (For related letters, see L 218-221, 227, and 236) ❖ L 13 May 52 (For related letters, see L 2 Sep 49 through 27 Sep 49; 5 Mar 51; 8 Jan 52)

Docetism mentioned with regard to whether Christ, in the flesh, was omniscient
•PP 134 (*consider also* Omniscience) ❖ PP 9:6 (*consider also* Omniscience)

Dock, in testing our faith God makes us occupy the, and the bench all at once—to show *us* the quality of our faith
•GO 61 ❖ GO 3:36

Dock, Man is on the Bench and God in the
•GID 240-244, esp. 244 (*see also* GID 95; L 181*) ❖ GID II ch. 12, esp. 12:7 (*see also* GID I 10:15; L 26 Mar 40*)

Doctor, let the, tell me I shall die unless I do so-and-so, but whether life is worth having on those terms is not a question for him or any other man
•GID 315 ❖ GID III 8:15

Doctors: Aren't they hideously overworked?
•LAL 121 ❖ LAL 6 Jul 63

Doctors: "Few of us have always, in full measure, given our pupils or patients

or clients...what we were being paid for"*
•RP 13 ❖ RP 2:8

Doctors, I do wonder why the, inflict such torture to delay what cannot in any case be very long delayed—or why God does
•LAL 118 ❖ LAL 25 Jun 63

Doctors: "I was only too glad to let [my doctor] off with the merest skeleton account of my own state—I found it such a boring subject"
•LAL 121 ❖ LAL 9 Jul 63

Doctors mentioned as "unpromising subjects" for Christianity
•L 249 ❖ L 6-7 Apr 53

Doctors merely stimulate Nature's functions or remove what hinders them to cause healing
•GID 30; M 139-140
❖ GID I 2:8; M 15:14

Doctors, one easily gets to dread the, more than the diseases
•LAL 107 ❖ LAL 2 Oct 62

Doctors who lie to their patients about their terminal condition mentioned with satisfaction by Screwtape
•SL 26-27 (see also L 275)
❖ SL 5:2 (see also L 6 Mar 57)

Doctrinal belief and liturgy, proper relationship between
•GID 333 ❖ GID IV Letter 7

Doctrinal differences—see also Christianity, "mere"; Denominational differences; Division(s); Theological controversies; Theology

Doctrinal differences: Example of Pope Gregory, on arriving in Heaven and finding he'd been wrong about something: It was the funniest thing he'd ever heard (story from *Paradiso*)*
•CR 11 ❖ CR 1:16

Doctrinal differences: "I assume that the Holy Spirit would not have allowed [them] to grow up in the church...unless [that] also was true and useful..."**
•PP 72 ❖ PP 5:1

Doctrinal differences: "There is our freedom, our chance for a little gener-

osity, a little sportsmanship"*
•LM 120-121 ❖ LM 22:10

Doctrinal issues must not be tacitly or implicitly settled by mere changes in liturgy (e.g., regarding propriety of devotions to Mary)
•GID 332-333 ❖ GID IV Letter 7

Doctrinal positions are not "adjustable to contemporary thought," etc., as some theologians seem to believe—as if we were trying to make rather than to learn
•LM 104 ❖ LM 19:12

Doctrine, changes in, must be accompanied by thorough reasoning based on Scripture along with a solemn act of penitence
•GID 333 ❖ GID IV Letter 7

Doctrine, exaggeration of a, may result in a reaction—making the opposite error
•WLN 94-95 ❖ WLN 7:4

Doctrine, how Christian, can be unchanging in the face of growing scientific knowledge
•GID 38-47 ❖ GID I ch. 3

Doctrine, no, seems to me so unreal as one that I have just successfully defended in a public debate
•GID 103, 128; L 209
❖ GID I 10:50; 15:4; L 2 Aug 46

Doctrine of Total Depravity—see Depravity

Doctrines—see also Beliefs

Doctrines, additional: "Christianity And..." mentioned by Screwtape as the desired alternative to "mere Christianity," which is troublesome to his cause*
•SL 115-116 ❖ SL 25:1

Doctrines all connected: "Divine reality is like a fugue. All His acts are different, but they all rhyme or echo to one another"
•GID 37 ❖ GID I 2:15

Doctrines are not God; they are only a kind of map—but maps are essential if you want to go anywhere
•MC 136 ❖ MC IV 1:4

Doctrines, best starting point for an understanding of, is Bible reading on

your own—with prayer for guidance*
•L 233 ❖ L 13 Jun 51

Doctrines, church, must be supported by its clergy
•GID 89-90 (see also GID 260, 265)
❖ GID I 10:2, 3 (see also GID II 16:12, 46)

Doctrines, differing—see Doctrinal differences

Doctrines, difficult—see also Difficulties in Scripture; Questions

Doctrines, difficult: "Do all theoretical problems conceal shirkings by the will?"*
•L 202 ❖ L 22 Dec 42

Doctrines, difficult: If we are free to delete all inconvenient data, we shall have no theological difficulties; but also no solutions and no progress*
•LM 59 ❖ LM 11:8

Doctrines, difficult: "...it was the sound principle of nursery gastronomy to polish off the nasty things first..." (re: the repellent Psalms)*
•RP 6-7 ❖ RP 1:10

Doctrines, difficult, must not be avoided (puzzling or repellent elements conceal precisely what we do not yet know and need to know)
•WG 9-10 ❖ WG 1:7

Doctrines, difficult: "There is always hope if we keep an unsolved problem fairly in view; there's none if we pretend it's not there"*
•LM 59 ❖ LM 11:8

Doctrines, difficult, we must accept the challenge of
•GID 91 ❖ GID I 10:6

Doctrines, difficult: "Whenever you find any statement in Christian writings which you can make nothing of, do not worry. Leave it alone"
•MC 126 ❖ MC III 12:1

Doctrines, difficult: "Where we find a difficulty we may always expect that a discovery awaits us"*
•RP 28 ❖ RP 3:16

Doctrines, few of us have followed the reasoning on which the, we believe are based*

•WG 35 ❖ WG 3:5

Doctrines, fundamental Christian, unchanging in the face of increasing knowledge
•GID 44-45 (see also GID 92)
❖ GID I 3:13, 14 (see also GID I 10:7)

Doctrines, it is almost impossible to state the negative effect which certain, have on me without seeming to mount an attack against them (re: Holy Communion)
•LM 101 ❖ LM 19:4

Doctrines, Lewis's attack on author Vidler's premise that certain, may have to be "outgrown"
•LM 31-32 (see also LM 59)
❖ LM 6:9, 10 (see also LM 11:8)

Doctrines: Most of our beliefs must be based on trusted authority rather than on proof*
•MC 63; WG 35-36; WLN 17 (see also CR 26*, 41, 43; GID 276; SJ 174) ❖ MC II 5:4; WG 3:5, 6; WLN 2:6 (see also CR 2:40*; 3:9, 12; GID III 1:17; SJ 11:12)

Doctrines, only a minority of world religions have a systematic series of, (a "theology")
•WG 74 ❖ WG 5:2

Doctrines relevant to a particular age not necessarily irrelevant to other times*
•WLN 97 (see also RP 121, 130; Age)
❖ WLN 7:6 (see also RP 12:3, 9; Age)

Doctrines: Screwtape mentions the clergyman who waters down the faith so much that he shocks his parishioners with his unbelief*
•SL 73-74 (see also Christianity-and-water) ❖ SL 16:3 (see also Christianity-and-water)

Doctrines, specific, essential for religion to be practical
•GID 129-146 ❖ GID I ch. 16

Doctrines, standing firm amidst winds of ("...we must at all costs not move with the times")
•GID 91-92 ❖ GID I 10:7

Doctrines, struggle with believing: Bible gives us one short prayer—"Lord I believe, help Thou my unbelief"
•L 239 ❖ L 18 Mar 52

Doctrines, we must not rely on Science to prove; it is always switching positions
•GID 92 (*see also* GID 39, 44; WLN 83-84) ❖ GID I 10:8 (*see also* GID I 3:3, 12; WLN 6:1-3)

Dog(s)—*consider also* Pets

Dog, analogy of, trying to form a conception of human life: All the details in its pictures would be derived from canine experience
•CR 165 (*see also* M 89—limpet analogy) ❖ CR 13:33, 34 (*see also* M 11:13, 14—limpet analogy)

Dog: "...conjectures as to why God does what He does are probably of no more value than my dog's ideas of what I am up to when I sit and read"
•RP 115 ❖ RP 11:11

Dog, how well a sick, trusts one if one has to do things that hurt it; we can take a lesson from this
•LAL 56 (*see also* WLN 23-24) ❖ LAL 26/4/56 (*see also* WLN 2:12)

Dog, I don't want my, to bark approval of my books (re: God needing or wanting our praise)
•RP 93 ❖ RP 9:4

Dog, I prefer the live, to the dead lion (re: low-brows who genuinely enjoy art or literature vs. snobs who feign enjoyment of same)
•WLN 38-39 (*see also* CR 10) ❖ WLN 3:12 (*see also* CR 1:15)

Dog, Lewis describes his family, named "Tim"
•SJ 162-163 ❖ SJ 10:16

Dog, man's love for a, as an analogy useful to our conception of God's love for us
•PP 43-44, 47 ❖ PP 3:11, 14

Dog/master relationship as analogy to relationship between the Christian and God
•GID 50 ❖ GID I 4:12 (Ques. 3)

Dog, reference to the Lewis's family, who presented them with ten puppies
•LAL 71, 72 ❖ LAL 14/1/58; 22/2/58

Dog, the woman who makes a, the centre of her life loses not only her human usefulness but also the proper pleasure of dog-keeping
•GID 280 ❖ GID III 2:6

Dog which cannot understand pointing as analogy to people who cannot understand the meaning of things because they insist on only looking at facts
•WG 71-72 ❖ WG 4:29

Dog who would rather be dirty than have a bath as analogy to ourselves (re: purpose of trials and pain)
•PP 107 ❖ PP 6:17

Dogs and cats, affection between: "I bet no dog would ever confess it to the other dogs"
•FL 56 (*see also* FL 54-55) ❖ FL 3:7 (*see also* FL 3:4)

Dogs and cats, affection between: I notice that the common *age* is a bond stronger than common species
•LAL 72 ❖ LAL 22/2/58

Dogs and cats both have consciences; the dog, being honest and humble, always has a bad one but the cat is a Pharisee and always has a good one
•LAL 40 ❖ LAL 21/3/55

Dogs and cats should always be brought up together; it broadens their minds so
•FL 59 ❖ FL 3:11

Dogs, we treat our, as though they were "almost human"; they become almost human in the end
•MC 166, 170 (*see also* PP 139, 141) ❖ MC IV 7:13; 8:11 (*see also* PP 9:11, 13)

Dogma and the Universe (chapter title)
•GID 38-47 ❖ GID I ch. 3

Dogma essential in practical religion
•GID 129-146, esp. 139-140 ❖ GID I ch. 16, esp. 16:21

Dogma, how Christian, can be unchanging in the face of growing scientific knowledge
•GID 38-47 ❖ GID I ch. 3

"Dogma," meaning of the word, to modern minds ("Used by people only in a bad sense to mean 'unproved assertion delivered in an arrogant manner'")
•GID 97 ❖ GID I 10:29

Dogma, Religion Without (chapter title)

•GID 129-146 ❖ GID I ch. 16

Dogma, religion without, not a practical religion
•GID 138-141 ❖ GID I 16:19-22

Dogmatic definition, example of a, which even a minimalist might find himself subscribing to if forced to make his religion practical*
•GID 140 ❖ GID I 16:22

"Doing things": I bet the things which "had to be done" in your room didn't really *have* to be done at all; very few things really do
•LAL 113 (*see also* LAL 105-106, 107)
❖ LAL 8 Jan 63 (*see also* LAL 31/7/62; 3 Sep 62)

Dolphins: If they are proved to be rational we have no more right to enslave them than to enslave our fellowmen
•CR 174 ❖ CR 14:44

Domestic ...—*see also* Home; Family ...

Domestic animals—*see* Cats; Dogs; Pets

Domestic distractions more of a hindrance to devotion to God in marriage than sex
•FL 137-138 ❖ FL 5:10

Domestic drudgery is excellent as an alternative to idleness or hateful thoughts; otherwise it is maddening
•L 92 ❖ L 17-25 Mar 24

Domestic happiness more essential to women than to men
•GID 321 ❖ GID III 9:27

Domestic hatred, courtship mentioned by Screwtape as the time for sowing the seeds of
•SL 120 ❖ SL 26:1

Domestic hatred usually expresses itself more in the manner of speech than in the words themselves
•SL 17-18 ❖ SL 3:5

Domestic manners—*see also* Courtesy

Domestic manners, discussion of
•FL 66-70; GID 282-286
❖ FL 3:22-26; GID III ch. 3

Domestic nastiness, you have no idea how many instances of, come before me in my mail; the only "ordinary" homes seem to be the ones we don't know

much about
•LAL 45-46 ❖ LAL 5/10/55

Domestic relations—*see* Family relations; Relations, interpersonal

Domestic work the most important work in the world
•L 262 ❖ L 16 Mar 55

Domesticity—*consider also* Homeliness

Domesticity, fundamental principles of
•GID 284-286 ❖ GID III 3:6-11

Domesticity is no passport to heaven on earth but a sea full of hidden rocks and perilous ice shores; is an arduous vocation
•GID 284 ❖ GID III 3:6

Domesticity, the suburban villas of Surrey suggested Happiness and filled me with desire for a, which I had never known
•SJ 132-133 ❖ SJ 9:1

Domination: The passion to dominate one's fellow almost totally is a principle of Hell; there, it is called "eating" one another
•SL xi (*see also* FL 160; SL 26, 37-38, 81, 141, 145; WLN 51-56, 69-70)
❖ SL P:19, 20 (*see also* FL 5:46; SL 5:2; 8:3; 18:3; 30:1; 31:1; WLN 4:1-13, 39)

Don(s)—*see also* Teacher(s)

Don, I knew that there was hardly any position in the world save that of a, in which I was fitted to earn a living
•SJ 183 (*see also* CR 20)
❖ SJ 12:2 (*see also* CR 2:23)

Don (professor), Lewis describes his work as a, at Oxford
•L 214 ❖ L 29 May 48

Dons mentioned as one group of "culture-sellers" whose ranks should probably include some Christians
•CR 20-21 ❖ CR 2:23-25

Donkey, St. Francis thought of the body as like a: useful, lazy, loveable, infuriating, pathetic, and absurdly beautiful
•FL 143 (*see also* LAL 89)
❖ FL 5:19, 20 (*see also* LAL 22 Dec 59)

Donne's analogy of the symphony: We are now merely tuning our instruments [in anticipation of the "symphony" of

Heaven]
•RP 97 (see also LM 116)
❖ RP 9:7 (see also LM 21:15)
Door, for me the horror of the Christian universe was that it had no, marked "Exit"; materialist's universe offered limited liabilities—death ended all
•SJ 171 (see also GO 33; SJ 228; consider also Limited liabilities)
❖ SJ 11:8 (see also GO 2:22; SJ 14:22; consider also Limited liabilities)
Door, I have gradually been coming to feel that the, is no longer shut and bolted; was it my own frantic need that slammed it in my face?
•GO 53-54 (see also GO 71, 80)
❖ GO 3:25, 26 (see also GO 4:4, 24)
Door on which we have been knocking all our lives will open at last—when we are at last accepted by God, and welcomed "into the heart of things"
•WG 14-16 ❖ WG 1:11, 12
Door slammed in your face, go to God when your need is desperate and you may find the
•GO 4-6, 7 (see also LAL 92)
❖ GO 1:7-11, 13 (see also LAL 24 Sep 60)
Doubt—see also Scepticism; consider also God, existence of
Doubt, a drop of disturbing, fell into my Materialism on reading [Maurice] Maeterlinck
SJ 175 ❖ SJ 11:12
Doubt, both those who believe in God and those who disbelieve face many hours of
•CR 41 (see also Atheism)
❖ CR 3:9 (see also Atheism)
Doubt, complete trust could have no room to grow except where there is also room for, (re: trust in God)
• WLN 25-26 ❖ WLN 2:13
Doubt, Lewis describes his, about God after the death of his wife
•GO 4-6 (see entire book)
❖ GO 1:7-11 (see entire book)
Doubt often pours into our lives on the eve of conversion or at a time we might receive Grace; devil is very active at such junctures

•L 227-228 (see also SL 172; WLN 70)
❖ L 5 Mar 51 (see also SL 32:40; WLN 4:40)
Doubt: Only the practice of Faith resulting in the habit of Faith will ever cement our belief so that we are not continually assailed by doubts
•CR 41-42 ❖ CR 3:9
Doubt, struggle with: Bible gives us one short prayer—"Lord I believe, help Thou my unbelief"
•L 239 ❖ L 18 Mar 52
Doubt that your prayer will be answered not necessarily a sin; Our Lord had no such assurance when He prayed in Gethsemane
•LM 60 (see also Gethsemane)
❖ LM 11:12 (see also Gethsemane)
Doubt: "We are not necessarily doubting that God will do the best for us; we are wondering how painful the best will turn out to be"
•L 285 ❖ L 29 Apr 59
Doubt: We may imagine God has let us down at the very moment help was on its way
•L 219 ❖ L 2 Sep 49
Doubts—see Questions
Drama—consider Art; Culture; Literature; Play
Drawing as an example of the difficulty inherent in representing a spiritual reality by earthly concepts and images
•WG 60-62; 68-69 (see also M 85)
❖ WG 4:10-12, 23, 24 (see also M 11:6)
Drawing, our natural experiences are like a; our risen life will be the reality
•WG 68-69 ❖ WG 4:22-24
Dream, life as a bad
•MC 170 (see also LAL 47, 57, 69, 119-120; SL 147)
❖ MC IV 8:12 (see also LAL 26/10/55; 21/5/56; Oct 20 57; 28 Jun 63; SL 31:3)
Dreams, I have dreamed, but not seen visions; but don't think all that matters a hoot
•L 251 (see also L 269*)
❖ L 17 Jul 53 (see also L undated letter just before 2 Apr 56*)
Dreams, Screwtape mentions the gradual

decay of youthful, as providing "admirable opportunities of wearing out a soul by attrition"
•SL 132 ❖ SL 28:1

Dreams, we are here in the land of; but cock-crow is coming
•LAL 119-120 ❖ LAL 28 Jun 63

Dreaming and waking as analogy to Christianity vs. Science ("Which is more real?")
•WG 92 ❖ WG 5:24

"Dreaming spires" of Oxford
•SJ 184 ❖ SJ 12:3

Dreaming, to know that one is, is to be no longer perfectly asleep (regarding a realization of our incomplete awareness of God)
•FL 192 (see also LM 75; RP 92)
❖ FL 6:47 (see also LM 14:11; RP 9:3)

"**Dressing** up as Christ"—see Imitation of Christ

Drink(ing)—see Alcohol

Drowning man analogy to show that philosophical definiteness about details can never be the *first* necessity once a belief in God has been accepted
•M 75-76 ❖ M 10:15

Drowning man analogy to show that Christ's "advantage" is the only reason He can help us
•L 234-235; MC 61
❖ L undated letter between 12 Sep 51 and 3 Dec 51; MC II 4:10

Drowning man analogy to show that when you are most desperate for help may be just the time when God can't give it (drowning man clutches and grabs)
•GO 53-54 (see also LAL 92*)
❖ GO 3:25 (see also LAL 24 Sep 60*)

"**Dryness**," Screwtape speaks about the periods of, which humans may experience in the Christian life ("the Troughs")
•SL 13-14, 36-44 ❖ SL 2:3; ch. 8, 9

Dualism as the theory that God produces good, while some equal and independent Power produces evil
•PP 69 (see also SL vii)
❖ PP 5:1 (see also SL P:9)

Dualism at first seems gratifying and plausible, but has two fatal difficulties—one metaphysical, and the other moral
•GID 22-23 ❖ GID I 1:3-6

Dualism discussed
•GID 21-24; MC 48-51
❖ GID I ch. 1; MC II 2:6-11

Dualism gives evil a positive nature, like that of good—but if cruelty and kindness were equally ultimate, by what standard could one reprove the other?
•GID 22-23 ❖ GID I 1:5-7

Dualism, New Testament allows one to go very near; Devil is the usurping lord of this age
•L 301 ❖ L 20 Dec 61

Dualism, Norse form of, a manly creed, nobler by many degrees than most philosophies of the moment; yet still only a half-way house
•GID 24 ❖ GID I 1:8

Dualism, philosophical difficulty with the concept of
•M 31-32 ❖ M 4:12-14

Dualism, you wouldn't be surprised at the space I give to, if you knew how attractive it is to some simple minds
•L 201-202 ❖ L 13 Oct 42

Dualist, if you think that God and Nature are self-existent and independent of each other you are a
•M 31 ❖ M 4:12

Dust and ashes, the wild hopes which tempt man to seek a heaven on earth by breaking the moral law prove to be
•PP 114 ❖ PP 7:5

Duties, attend to your, and then it [your secret desire for heaven] will blaze
•PP 148 ❖ PP 10:5

Duties, human distaste for religious, (such as prayer) when one is feeling vague guilt mentioned by Screwtape
•SL 54-55 ❖ SL 12:3

Duties, if we were perfected many of our behaviours which now appear as, would be a delight—e.g., prayer ("Someday, please God, it will be")
•LM 114-116 (see also L 277; PP 100; RP 97) ❖ LM 21:11-14 (see also L 18 Jul 57; PP 6:11; RP 9:7)

Duties may become pleasurable to us, but then they can no longer be a means of learning self-surrender
•PP 99, 101 ❖ PP 6:10, 13

Duties, Screwtape advises keeping the human's mind off the most elementary, and directing it instead to the most advanced and spiritual ones
•SL 16 ❖ SL 3:2

Duties, when we carry out our religious, we are like people digging channels in a waterless land, so that when water [delight] comes we are ready for it
•RP 97 ❖ RP 9:7

Duty—*consider also* Vocation

Duty: Activities we naturally like may be as much a part of our "service" to God as our hardest duties
•WG 130 ❖ WG 9:9

Duty, by doing what one's, does not demand one can make oneself less fit for the duties it *does* demand
•LAL 53 ❖ LAL 19/3/56

Duty, Christianity makes, a self-transcending concept and endeavors to escape from the region of mere morality in its ethics
•CR 45 (*see also* GID 112*, 144; LM 114-115; MC 130-131; PP 65)
❖ CR 4:2 (*see also* GID I 12:10*; 16:26; LM 21:11-13; MC III 12:9; PP 4:13)

Duty, devotion to, mentioned as one of "the severer virtues" which Lewis came to realize might have relevance in his own life
•SJ 192 ❖ SJ 12:14

Duty, doing our: "To play well the scenes in which we are 'on' concerns us much more than guessing about future scenes"
•WLN 104 ❖ WLN 7:19

Duty, each must do his, in that state of life to which God has called him; don't be too easily convinced God wants you to do all sorts of work you needn't do
•LAL 53 (*see also* LAL 72)
❖ LAL 19/3/56 (*see also* LAL 22/2/58)

Duty, every, is a religious duty
•WG 24 ❖ WG 2:6

Duty, fear of, as a reason for avoiding truth

•GID 110-111 (*see also* Obstacles to Christian faith; Self-reservation)
❖ GID I 12:6-8 (*see also* Obstacles to Christian faith; Self-reservation)

Duty is always conditioned by evil—by lack of love in myself, or by the general diffused evil of the world
•LM 116 ❖ LM 21:14

Duty is only a substitute for love (of God and of other people); a perfect man would never act from a sense of duty—he'd always want to do the right thing
•L 277; LM 114-116
❖ L 18 Jul 57; LM 21:11-14

Duty is what you call obedience before it becomes Love*
•LM 114-115 ❖ LM 21:11, 12

Duty, meanwhile we are to go on doing our, ("The world might stop in ten minutes...")
•GID 266 ❖ GID II 16:55

Duty, morality, and the Law essential until a man really loves God and his fellow man
•LM 114-116 (*see also* PP 100*; SL 39*)
❖ LM 21:11-14 (*see also* PP 6:11*; SL 8:4*)

Duty, most of the behaviour which is now, would be spontaneous and delightful if we were, so to speak, good rose-trees
•LM 116 (*see also* L 277; PP 100*)
❖ LM 21:14 (*see also* L 18 Jul 57; PP 6:11*)

Duty of planning for future acts of justice and charity is a present duty (as are all duties), though its material is in the future
•SL 69 (*see also* SL 70)
❖ SL 15:4 (*see also* SL 15:5)

Duty, prayer as a, which often feels like a burden: "The fact that prayers are often set as penances tells its own tale"
•LM 113-114 ❖ LM 21:5-7

Duty: There is no area in our lives on which God has no claim
•WG 130 (*see also* SJ 172*; SL 95-99)
❖ WG 9:9 (*see also* SJ 11:8*; SL ch. 21)

Duty to posterity not the only duty we have as Christians; we must remem-

ber that what may be upon us at any moment is not merely an End but a Judgment
•WLN 111 ❖ WLN 7:33

Duty, we have a, as Christians to leave the world (even in a temporal sense) "better" than we found it
•PP 113-114 (see also GID 49, 57, 147-150; MC 118; WLN 111)
❖ PP 7:4 (see also GID I 4:6, 7, 40; ch. 17; MC III 10:1; WLN 7:33, 34)

Dying—see also Death; consider also Illness, terminal

Dying daily, necessity of, ("...however often we think we have broken the rebellious self we shall still find it alive")
•PP 92 (see also GID 195; Daily...; Self-surrender; Surrender)
❖ PP 6:3 (see also GID II 2:4; Daily...; Self-surrender; Surrender)

"Dying god" myth—consider also Death and Rebirth pattern

"Dying god" myth came true once
•GID 57-58, 66-67, 83-84; M 113-115; SJ 235-236 (see also GID 132*)
❖ GID I 4:42 (Ques. 10); 5:11-13; 9:5, 6; M 14:9-14; SJ 15:7 (see also GID I 16:4*)

"Dying god" myth: In 1926 the hardest boiled of all the atheists I knew remarked, "Rum thing. It almost looks as if it had really happened once"
•SJ 223-224, 235-236 ❖ SJ 14:15; 15:7

Dying, Lewis's attitude toward
•LAL 47, 114, 115-116, 117, 118, 119; L 73, 166; MC 170* (see also Death)
❖ LAL 26/10/55; 19 Mar 63; 22 Apr 63; 17 Jun 63; 25 Jun 63; 28 Jun 63; L 7 Apr 22; 8 May 39; MC IV 8:12* (see also Death)

Dying, Lewis's attitude toward, vs. being killed (the latter wakes the instinct for self-preservation into fierce activity)
•LAL 114 ❖ LAL 19 Mar 63

Dying: Screwtape mentions with satisfaction humans who die in costly nursing homes amid doctors, nurses, and friends who lie to them about their condition
•SL 26-27 (see also L 275; SL 146)
❖ SL 5:2 (see also L 6 Mar 57; SL 31:3)

Dymer, mention of writing the long poem
•L 73, 76-77, 80, 92, 110
❖ L 2 Apr 22; 15 Apr 22; 24 May 22; 20 Sep 22; 17-25 Mar 24; 6 Jul 26

"Dynamic" is one of the words invented by this age which sums up what it likes and I abominate
•L 179 (see also L 204*)
❖ L 22 Mar 40 (see also L undated letter of May 1944*)

Dyson, Hugo, mentioned ("...he is a Christian and a lover of cats")
•L 145 ❖ L 22 Nov 31

Dyson, H.V.V. (Hugo), mentioned by Lewis as one who gave him "much help in getting over the last stile" on the road to Christianity
•SJ 216 (see also L 197; SJ 225)
❖ SJ 14:6 (see also L 21 Dec 41; SJ 14:17)

Earth—*see also* World

Earth, a Christian cannot believe any of those who promise a heaven on
•PP 114 ❖ PP 7:5

Earth, almost all our modern philosophies have been devised to convince us that the good of man is to be found on this
•WG 7-8 ❖ WG 1:5

Earth may be the one lost sheep that the Shepherd went in search of; Christianity not wedded to an anthropocentric view of the universe
•GID 42-43, 100; M 122; WLN 86-87 (*see also* M 51-52*)
❖ GID I 3:9; 10:42; M 14:24; WLN 6:11 (*see also* M 7:13, 14*)

Earth: Our only real security is in Heaven and thus earth affords only imitations
•LAL 49 (*see also* FL 190)
❖ LAL 16/12/55 (*see also* FL 6:43)

Earth, the dream of making a Heaven on, mentioned by Screwtape as a temptation especially successful with youth
•SL 133 ❖ SL 28:2

Earth, the less one can think about happiness on, the less, I believe, one suffers
•LAL 96 (*see also* SL 95-96*)
❖ LAL 9 Jan 61 (*see also* SL 21:2*)

Earthly attachments, achievements, etc. — *see* Worldly attachments, achievements, etc.

Earthly comfort, there is no good applying to Heaven for; there is no earthly comfort in the long run

•FL 190 (*see also* GO 28-30; L 290; LAL 49) ❖ FL 6:43 (*see also* GO 2:13-16; L 3 Dec 59; LAL 16/12/55)

Easter as an example of a religious festival or act of worship which can be separated from the vision of God, thereby becoming a rival to God
•RP 48-49 ❖ RP 5:7

Easter, everyone writes to me at, so that what ought to be a bright spot in the year threatens to become for me a very dark one
•LAL 30 ❖ LAL 17th Apr 54

Eating alone: The whole time-wasting business of cooking is hardly worth it when one is on one's own
•LAL 86 ❖ LAL 21 Aug 59

Eating and reading are two pleasures that combine admirably, although not all books are suitable for mealtime reading
•SJ 142 ❖ SJ 9:18

"Eating" or absorption as a principle of Hell: "I feign that devils can, in a spiritual sense, eat one another; and us"
•SL xi (*see also* SL xiii, 26, 37-38, 81, 141, 145; WLN 51-56, 69-70)
❖ SL P:19 (*see also* SL P:22; 5:2; 8:3; 18:3; 30:1; 31:1; WLN 4:1-13, 39)

"Eating" or absorption as a principle of Hell: "Even in human life we have seen the passion to dominate, almost to digest, one's fellow"
•SL xi (*see also* FL 160)
❖ SL P:19, 20 (*see also* FL 5:46)

"Eating" or absorption as a principle of Hell: "...the sucking of will and freedom out of a weaker self into a stronger" (—Screwtape)
•SL 81 ❖ SL 18:3

Ecclesiastes, I would not now willingly spare from my Bible something in itself so anti-religious as the nihilism of
•RP 115 ❖ RP 11:10

Ecclesiastes: "We get there a clear, cold picture of man's life without God"
•RP 115 ❖ RP 11:10

Economic system, our, is based on lending money at interest; condemned by Moses, Aristotle, and the Christians
•MC 81 ❖ MC III 3:6

---

* These items reflect some interpretation on the part of the editor; the idea will not be found in these exact words. *See Introduction, p. ix.*

** These items are ideas of Lewis's which the editor has placed under a topic Lewis did not there intend to address. *See Introduction, p. ix.*

Entries without asterisks are not necessarily exact quotes, but the idea should be easy to find as worded.

Economics—*see also* Commercialism

Economics and politics discussed briefly with regard to Christianity
- MC 78-83 ❖ MC III 3:2-8

Economics, the class system at Wyvern College was an answer to those who derive all the ills of society from
- SJ 110 ❖ SJ 7:13

Economy, in our, "wants have to be created in order that people may receive money for making things"; work worth doing has become the privilege of a few
- WLN 76 (*see also* MC 80)
❖ WLN 5:12 (*see also* MC III 3:4)

Economy, our fatal and insane: The practical task for us is to consider how we can live within it as little hurt and degraded as possible
- WLN 77 (*consider also*, Commercialism) ❖ WLN 5:14 (*consider also*, Commercialism)

Ecumenism—*see* Reunion

Eden—*consider* Adam; Fall of Man; Unfallen Man

Edinburgh is a wonderful city, with a castle on a crag and mountains beyond it...
- LAL 52 ❖ LAL 4/3/56

Educated and uneducated people, widest cleavage between, is their degree of scepticism about, and perspective gained from, History
- GID 241 (*see also* GID 94-95)
❖ GID II 12:3 (*see also* GID I 10:13)

Education—*see also* School(s); Teacher(s); *consider also* Culture; Knowledge; Learning

Education a necessary tool in Christian evangelism; we must be able to meet our enemies on their own ground
- WG 28 (*see also* CR 17)
❖ WG 2:10 (*see also* CR 2:18)

Education: "A society which is predominantly Christian will propagate Christianity through its schools: one which is not, will not"
- GID 116 ❖ GID I 13:6

Education, almost our whole, has been directed to silencing this shy, inner voice of longing
- WG 7 (*see also* MC 119)
❖ WG 1:5 (*see also* MC III 9:2)

Education cannot be postponed until we are secure (re: education in time of war)
- WG 21-22 ❖ WG 2:4

Education, Christianity is an, in itself
- MC 75 ❖ MC III 2:4

Education creates strong sense of history; lack of historical perspective in uneducated men is a problem when one is trying to present the Christian faith
- GID 94-95, 241-242
❖ GID I 10:13; II 12:3

Education, cultural: Question of whether its value can be reconciled with the belief that the end of human life is salvation in Christ and glorifying of God
- CR 12-25 (*see also* Culture)
❖ CR 2:1-38 (*see also* Culture)

Education, "democracy" as a principle of, results in the absurd philosophy that dunces and idlers must not be made to feel inferior to industrious students
- SL 166-168; WLN 64-66 (*see also* FL 73) ❖ SL 32:31-33; WLN 4:31-33 (*see also* FL 3:32)

"Education" held by many to be the thing that will eventually put right whatever is wrong with man
- GID 252 ❖ GID II 14:9

Education, historical perspective gained through, protects one against the errors of the current age
- WG 28-29 ❖ WG 2:10

Education, in modern cultural, poetry is something assigned and tested on; the modern student does not know that poetry ever had any other purpose
- WLN 47 ❖ WLN 3:25

Education in secular subjects: Is it justifiable for Christians?
- WG 20-32 ❖ WG ch. 2

Education in wartime, three enemies of, are excitement, frustration, and fear
- WG 29-32 (*see also* SL 67-71*)
❖ WG 2:12-14 (*see also* SL ch. 15*)

Education is only the most fully conscious of the channels whereby each

generation influences the next
•GID 116 ❖ GID I 13:5

Education: Means may hamper ends, such as when examinations prevent people from becoming learned*
•WG 109 ❖ WG 7:5

Education, modern, not content to teach a subject; aims at creating Plasticine characters who can simulate orthodox responses and have no tastes of their own
•WLN 42-44, 46 ❖ WLN 3:16-18, 20

Education, nationally suicidal type of, which keeps the promising child back because the idlers and dunces might be "hurt" if it were advanced
•FL 73; WLN 64-66
❖ FL 3:32; WLN 4:31-33

Education: Newman's view of the cultivation of the intellect as a justifiable end in itself, while remaining wholly distinct from virtue
•CR 18-19 ❖ CR 2:20, 21

Education now organizes a boy's whole life, to the exclusion of all solitude; if a Wordsworth were born today he would be "cured" before he was twelve
•WLN 41-42 ❖ WLN 3:15, 16

Education of youth about Christianity is remedy for agnosticism or indifference
•GID 115 ❖ GID I 13:3

Education as one way of transmitting Christianity from one generation to the next
•GID 116 ❖ GID I 13:5, 6

Education, our whole, tends to fix our minds on this world
•MC 119 ❖ MC III 10:2

Education: Question of how much time and energy God wants us to spend on nonmoral perfection, such as the cultivation of the intellect
•CR 19 (see entire chapter)
❖ CR 2:21 (see entire chapter)

Education: Regarding the evil tendency to love knowledge and discernment more than the object known and discerned*
• CR 17; WG 28 (see also Pride of pursuing "culture") ❖ CR 2:16; WG 2:9 (see also Pride of pursuing "culture")

Education, religious, for children often has exactly the opposite effect to that which was intended; how many hard atheists come from pious homes
•LAL 32 ❖ LAL Sep 19/54

Education, Screwtape forecasts much success for his side if all, becomes state education
•SL 168; WLN 66
❖ SL 32:33; WLN 4:33

Education, state system of, not likely to tolerate radically Christian elements
•GID 118 ❖ GID I 13:9

Education: "...the greatest service we can do to education today is to teach fewer subjects"
•SJ 112-113 ❖ SJ 7:17

Education: "The only people who achieve much are those who want knowledge so badly that they seek it while conditions are still unfavourable"
•WG 30 ❖ WG 2:12

Education: Training for anything whatever that is good will always help us in the true training for the Christian life
•SJ 146 ❖ SJ 9:22

Education, value of: Secular learning might be embodied in the Magi; [and] the Talents in the parable might include "talents" in the modern sense
•CR 14-15 ❖ CR 2:7

Efficacy of Prayer (chapter title)
•WLN 3-11 ❖ WLN ch. 1

Effort, moral—see Moral effort

Egalitarianism—consider Democracy; Equality

Eggs hatching to birds as an analogy for the necessity of change in our nature
•MC 169 ❖ MC IV 8:9

Eggs, it is so easy to break, without making omelettes (Lewis advises caution in making changes in the liturgy)
•LM 6 ❖ LM 1:13

Ego, Christian must wage endless war against the clamour of the, (though he loves and approves selves as such)
•GID 194-195 (see also SL 63-66*)

❖ GID II 2:3 (*see also* SL 14:3-5*)

Egoism—*see also* Self-centredness

Egoism, as in the pursuit of "culture" for the sake of prestige or merit, can only impoverish social life*
•WLN 34-35 (*see also* Pride of pursuing "culture") ❖ WLN 3:6-8 (*see also* Pride of pursuing "culture")

Egoism, even in human life [as in Hell] we see the desire to indulge one's, through another as well as through oneself
•SL xi (*see also* Domination)
❖ SL P:19 (*see also* Domination)

Egotism—*see* Arrogance; Pride

Egotist, the choice which could lead to becoming a treacherous, will come in no very dramatic colours
•WG 101-102

Egyptian poem *Hymn to the Sun* was written by Pharaoh Amenhetep IV; it shows an astonishing lead into Monotheism
•RP 85-89 ❖ RP 8:16-19

Elderly—*see also* Aging

Elderly, we are growing less kind to the; any doctor will tell you that even prosperous people refuse to look after their parents
•GID 312 ❖ GID III 8:4

Eldils mentioned (beings in Lewis's books *Out of the Silent Planet, Perelandra,* and *That Hideous Strength*)
•LAL 12, 13 ❖ LAL 4/iii/53

Elitism—*consider* Inner Rings

Elixir of life, I remind the reader that a particular medicine is not to be mistaken for the
•PP 114 ❖ PP 7:5

Embarrassment—*see also* Shame

Embarrassment or awkwardness, Lewis describes, which is felt by people who are grieving as well as by those around them
•GO 8-11 ❖ GO 1:16-20

Embroidery, Psalm 119 is a pattern like, done stitch by stitch, through long, quiet hours—for the pleasure of getting a thing "just so"
•RP 58-59 ❖ RP 6:8, 9

Emergent Evolution—*see also* Creative Evolution; Evolutionism; *consider also* Entropy; Life-force

Emergent Evolution, discussion of
•MC 35 ❖ MC I 4:6

Emergent Evolution equated with "Mellontolatry, the worship of the future"; described as "a fuddled religion"
•GID 21 ❖ GID I 1:1

Emergent Evolution involves the belief that what is coming next will be an improvement; this belief is unwarranted
•GID 21 (*see also* CR 85; WLN 101)
❖ GID I 1:1 (*see also* CR 7:11; WLN 7:13)

Emergent Evolution, the obviousness which most people seem to find in the idea of, seems to be a pure hallucination
•WG 90-91 ❖ WG 5:23

"Emergent God" (the God of the Naturalist) vs. "transcendent God" (the God of the Supernaturalist)
•M 30 ❖ M 4:10

Emotion(s)—*see also* Aesthetic rapture; Affection; Anxiety; Courage; Desire; Fear; Feelings; Grief; Guilt; Happiness; Hatred; Hope; Jealousy; Joy; Longing; Love; Pain; Pleasure

Emotion, a fabricated, is a miserable affair (re: trying to pray without words)
•LM 11 ❖ LM 2:5

Emotion, even genuinely religious, is only a servant
•L 269
❖ L undated letter just before 2 Apr 56

Emotion ("fervour") we experienced in the first days of our conversion will likely die away; do not miserably try to conjure it back
•LM 26-27 (*see also* SL 13-14)
❖ LM 5:10-13 (*see also* SL 2:3)

Emotion generated by poetic language is the emotion of pleasure at finding anything vividly conveyed to the imagination
•CR 130-131 (*see also* GID 66*)
❖ CR 11:4 (*see also* GID I 5:9*)

Emotion: I feel fairly sure the superiority

of Poetic language over Ordinary language does not consist in discharging or arousing more emotion
- •CR 130-131, 132-134
- ❖ CR 11:4, 5, 7-11

Emotion, I had bred in me very early a certain distrust of, as something uncomfortable and embarrassing and even dangerous
- •SJ 4 (see also SJ 33, 66*, 133, 158-159*)
- ❖ SJ 1:1 (see also SJ 2:13; 4:13*; 9:2, 3; 10:11*)

Emotion in evangelistic appeals: "There are many different ways of bringing people into His Kingdom, even some ways that I specially dislike!"**
- •GID 262 ❖ GID II 16:28

Emotion in evangelistic appeals often still successful
- •GID 99, 244 ❖ GID I 10:39; II 12:9

Emotion in poetical religious language: "Momentous matter, if believed, will arouse emotion whatever the language"
- •CR 136 ❖ CR 11:16

Emotion in poetical religious language a by-product of the conveying of real information
- •CR 129-141, esp. 134, 140
- ❖ CR ch. 11, esp. 11:11, 23

Emotion in religion ("religious experience") comes and goes, especially goes; the operation of Faith is to retain what is obvious during the moments of grace*
- •GID 175-176 ❖ GID I 21:9

Emotion in religious experience is a by-product of our attention to a particular Object
- •CR 140 ❖ CR 11:22

Emotion: Lewis's fear and dislike of "sentimentalism"*
- •SJ 66, 133, 173, 190
- ❖ SJ 4:13; 9:2, 3; 11:10; 12:12

Emotion mentioned by Screwtape as useful to his ends when a patient thinks, in a negative situation (such as war), that it reveals "reality"
- •SL 142-144 ❖ SL 30:4

Emotion: "My lifelong fear of sentimen-

talism ought to have qualified me to become a vigorous 'debunker'"*
- •SJ 173 ❖ SJ 11:10

Emotion, never try to generate, by will power (e.g., emotion in prayer, or a prayerful frame of mind)
- •L 256 (see also L 202; LM 23; SJ 61-62*; SL 20-21, 125)
- ❖ L 31 Jul 54 (see also L 22 Dec 42; LM 4:19; SJ 4:8*; SL 4:3; 27:1)

Emotion of Awe in religious experience
- •GID 174-175 (see also PP 17-21)
- ❖ GID I 21:6 (see also PP 1:5-11)

Emotion: Perhaps real love—like that in a society of pure intelligences—is not an emotion, and does not need an attendant emotion
- •GO 85-88, esp. 87
- ❖ GO 4:33-35, esp. 4:35

Emotion, Poetic language often expresses, not for its own sake but in order to inform us about the object which aroused the emotion
- •CR 132, 134 ❖ CR 11:7, 11

Emotion: Religious and most other experiences cannot be conveyed to one another except by Poetic language—by hints, similes, metaphors, and emotions
- •CR 137-138, 140 ❖ CR 11:19, 23

Emotion, religious, cannot be our regular spiritual diet; feelings come and go (re: attempts to excite fear about the Second Coming)
- •WLN 109 ❖ WLN 7:30

Emotion, religious, is only a servant which we can rejoice in when it comes; don't be worried about flat feelings
- •L 192 ❖ L 4 Jan 41; 29 Jan 41

Emotion, religious: Many find that "the heart sings unbidden while...working their way through a tough bit of theology with a pipe in their teeth..."
- •GID 205 ❖ GID II 4:7

Emotion: Screwtape advises how to use the law of Undulation (the "Peaks" and "Troughs" of human experience) to further the devil's purposes
- •SL 40-44 ❖ SL ch. 9

Emotion: Screwtape mentions the law of

things men need or like
•WLN 77, 79 ❖ WLN 5:14, 19

Enchantment, it is our painful duty to wake the world from an, (re: Myth of Evolutionism)
•CR 93 ❖ CR 7:23

Enchantment, you and I have need of the strongest spell to wake us from the evil, of worldliness which has been laid on us for nearly a hundred years
•WG 7 ❖ WG 1:5

Encore: Is God a clown who whips away one bowl of soup only to replace it with another of the same soup? (re: communication with dead loved ones)*
•GO 15-16 (*see also* GO 28-29)
❖ GO 1:29 (*see also* GO 2:14)

"Encore" is the one prayer God may never grant; do not miserably try to conjure back the past ("Leave those bulbs alone and the new flowers will come up")
•LM 27 (*see also* LM 90; *Perelandra* 48, 50*) ❖ LM 5:12 (*see also* LM 17:10; *Perelandra* 4:6, 8*)

Encore, the useless word is; we must "sit light" to life and all its phases
•L 306 (*see also* L 161-162*; LM 26-27; WLN 110) ❖ L 21 Nov 62 (*see also* L 12 Sep 38*; LM 5:10- 13; WLN 7:31)

End of the world—*see also* Second Coming; *consider also* Destiny of lost Man; Destiny of redeemed Man; Heaven; Hell

End of the world: "Christian apocalyptic ...foretells a sudden, violent end imposed from without...a curtain rung down on the play —Halt!"
•WLN 101 ❖ WLN 7:12

End of the world, God without disguise will invade at the; too late then to choose sides
•MC 66 ❖ MC II 5:9

End of the world: Great thing is to be found at one's post when the Inspection comes
•GID 266; WLN 111-112
❖ GID II 16:55; WLN 7:34

End of the world: "I do not find that pic-

tures of physical catastrophe...help one so much as the naked idea of Judgment"
•WLN 113 ❖ WLN 7:38

End of the world: If it's going to occur, and the Jews were trained to expect it, it is very natural that they should produce apocalyptic literature
•WLN 97 ❖ WLN 7:7

End of the world means contact with God; how will we feel then?
•MC 183 (*see also* GID 47; MC 66)
❖ MC IV 10:17 (*see also* GID I 3:17; MC II 5:9)

End of the world seen by some as Christ's central message; Dr. Albert Schweitzer is associated with this school of thought
•WLN 94-95 ❖ WLN 7:3, 4

End of the world: "That it will come when it ought, we may be sure; but we waste our time in guessing when that will be"
•WLN 106 ❖ WLN 7:22

End of the world: "What is important is not that we should always fear (or hope) about the End but that we should always remember, always take it into account"
•WLN 110 ❖ WLN 7:31

End of the world: "...when the term ends we might find ourselves facing the public opinion of that larger world"
•PP 63 (*see also* PP 61, bottom)
❖ PP 4:10 (*see also* PP 4:9)

Ends—*see* Means and ends

Endings and changes, Lewis's dislike of
•L 306 (*see also* L 161-162)
❖ L 21 Nov 62 (*see also* L 12 Sep 38)

Endings: Lewis mentions stowing memories away "with the faintly melancholy feeling of things going past"
•L 117 (*see also* GD 28)
❖ L 26 Apr 27 (*see also* GD 2:12)

Endurance—*see* Steadfastness

Enemies, loving our, does not mean thinking them nice
•MC 105, 108 (*see also* MC 115-117)
❖ MC III 7:5, 10 (*see also* MC III 9:2-6)

Enemies, prayer for: How to make it real
•L 183 ❖ L 16 Apr 40

Enemies, prayer for: I find it helpful to remember that one is joining in *Christ's* prayer for them
•L 226
❖ L undated letter just before 7 Feb 51

Enemies, prayer for: "I'd sooner pray for God's mercy than for His justice on my friends, my enemies, and myself"
•LAL 14 ❖ LAL 17/4/53

Enemies, prayer for our, —then away to other subjects—better than allowing them to become an obsession, to haunt our minds
•LAL 28 (*see also* LAL 44)
❖ LAL Mar 10/54 (*see also* LAL 21/6/55)

Enemies, the filth that our, fling at the Holy One either does not stick, or, sticking, turns into glory (re: charge that God committed adultery with Mary)
•GID 32 ❖ GID I 2:9

Enemies, we are under orders to pray for our
•MC 11-12 ❖ MC P:16

Enemies, we must be able to meet our, on their own ground (by being educated)
•WG 28 (*see also* CR 17; Unbelievers)
❖ WG 2:10 (*see also* CR 2:18; Unbelievers)

Enemy, loving your, means wishing his good rather than feeling fond of him
•MC 108 ❖ MC III 7:10

Enemy, your: If you do him a good turn you will find yourself disliking him less
•MC 116 (*see also* MC 161)
❖ MC III 9:5 (*see also* MC IV 7:3)

Engine, God invented us as a man invents an
•MC 54 ❖ MC II 3:7

Engine, I travel with my back to the
•GID 266 (*see also* CR 106)
❖ GID II 16:55 (*see also* CR 9:14)

England, Christianity which has died out in, is *nominal* Christianity; so that only those who really believe now profess
•LAL 15 ❖ LAL 9th May 53

England, Christians in modern, often feel—as the Psalmists did—the ineffectiveness of their cause
•CR 127 ❖ CR 10:37

England, "decline" of religion in, may be a misperception
•GID 218-220 (*see also* GID 253*)
❖ GID II 8:1-7 (*see also* GID II 14:11*)

England, fogginess of: "One pines for lights and, scarcely less, *shadows*, which make up so much of the beauty of the world"
•LAL 80 ❖ LAL Dec 25th 58

England, Lewis's first impressions of, (at age nine)
•SJ 24-25 ❖ SJ 2:3, 4

England: Scenery of Surrey described
•SJ 132, 134, 146-147 ❖ SJ 9:1, 6-8, 22

England, the town of Wyvern healed my quarrel with; the great blue plain below us and, behind, those green, peaked hills...
•SJ 58 ❖ SJ 4:4

England, to believe in the popular religion of modern, is retrogression—like believing the earth is flat
•MC 136-137 ❖ MC IV 1:5, 6

English people "have not the talent for graceful ceremonial. They go through it lumpishly..."
L 103 ❖ L 14 Aug 25

English take their "sense of humour" so seriously that a deficiency in this area is almost the only deficiency at which they feel shame (—Screwtape)
•SL 51 ❖ SL 11:5

English, when you want to be typically, you pretend to be very hospitable, honest, and hearty
•L 133
❖ L undated letter postmarked 13 Apr 29

Enjoyment, all, spontaneously overflows into praise unless something checks it
•RP 93-94 ❖ RP 9:5

Enjoyment: "I think we delight to praise what we enjoy because the praise not merely expresses but completes the enjoyment..."
•RP 95 (*see also* GO 72)
❖ RP 9:6 (*see also* GO 4:5)

"Enjoyment" of an experience is incom-

patible with the contemplation of it; e.g., we cannot feel grief and think about feeling grief at the same time
- •SJ 217-219 (see also GID 65-66; L 221)
- ❖ SJ 14:9, 10 (see also GID I 5:8, 9; L 27 Sep 49)

Enjoyment of anything for its own sake better than abandoning what you really like in favour of the "best" people, the "important" books, etc.*
- •SL 58-60 (see also CR 10; L 216; LAL 54; WLN 31-35)
- ❖ SL 13:3, 4 (see also CR 1:15; L 3 Apr 49; LAL 20/3/56; WLN 3:2-7)

Enjoyment of God is no more separable from praise than the brightness a mirror receives is separable from the brightness it sheds
- •RP 96 ❖ RP 9:6

Enjoyments, the true, must be spontaneous...those who read poetry to improve their mind will never improve their mind by reading poetry
- •WLN 35 (see also CR 10; SL 58-60)
- ❖ WLN 3:7 (see also CR 1:15; SL 13:3, 4)

Enlightenment—see also Understanding
Enlightenment: "...to act on the light one has is almost the only way to more light"
- •L 191-192 ❖ L 4 Jan 41

Entertainment—see also Play; Pleasure(s); Games
Entertainment, the miracle at Cana sanctified an innocent sensual pleasure and could be taken to sanctify at least a recreational use of "culture" as
- •CR 15 ❖ CR 2:7

Entropy—consider also Emergent Evolution
Entropy, degradation, and disorganization the rule in the universe
- •CR 58 (see also CR 85; GID 33)
- ❖ CR 5:3 (see also CR 7:11; GID I 2:12)

Entropy: "Everything suggests that organic life is going to be a very short and unimportant episode in the history of the universe"
- •CR 58 ❖ CR 5:3

Entropy: Resurrection of Jesus as "the first movement of a great wheel beginning to turn in the direction opposite to that..."*
- •M 146 ❖ M 16:6

Entropy, science cannot be expected to anticipate the reversal of, since it is based on observation
- •M 151-152; GID 33-34
- ❖ M 16:16, 17; GID I 2:12

Entropy: the actual cosmic reality
- •GID 208-211 (see also PP 14-15)
- ❖ GID II ch. 5 (see also PP 1:1)

Entropy: "The movement from more order to less almost serves to determine the direction in which Time is flowing"
- •M 151-152 (see also PP 25)
- ❖ M 16:16 (see also PP 1:16)

Entropy: the real cosmic wave
- •GID 44 (see also GID 33*)
- ❖ GID I 3:11 (see also GID I 2:12*)

Entropy the universal rule in nature, but not universal absolutely; a clock can't run down unless it has first been wound up
- •M 152 (see also GID 33-34)
- ❖ M 16:17 (see also GID I 2:12)

Environment and heredity are used by God to create "the secret signature of each soul," the incommunicable and unappeasable Desire we each have in a unique way
- •PP 147 ❖ PP 10:3

Environment, Christianity does not teach us to desire a total release from
- •M 162 (see also Matter; Nature)
- ❖ M 16:30 (see also Matter; Nature)

Environment: Man's attempt to win safety and ease from Nature seems to lead on to universal suburbia*
- •L 211 ❖ L 15 Oct 47

Environment (preferably a social environment) essential to freedom of choice; a creature with no environment would have no choices to make
- •PP 29-30 ❖ PP 2:6-11

Environment ("space") listed as part of "the old field" of Nature which is not be to be unmade, but remade
- •M 149 (see also M 162-163)
- ❖ M 16:12 (see also M 16:30-32)

Envy—*see also* Jealousy

Envy always brings the charge nearest to the truth that she can think up; it hurts more (re: those envious of real Friendships)
•FL 112 ❖ FL 4:41

Envy as one of the "deadly serious passions" lived out in Hell
•SL ix ❖ SL P:16

Envy of those who do not understand Friendship toward circles of Friends
•FL 112 ❖ FL 4:41

Envy of those whom we feel to be superior to ourselves now sanctioned by our current usage of the word "democratic"
•SL 162-163; WLN 60-61
❖ SL 32:20-24; WLN 4:20-24

Epicureanism as a system of thought which moved out with its time (vs. Christianity, which has survived)
•GID 65 ❖ GID I 5:7

Episcopal—*see* Anglican(s); Church of England

Epistles, even St. Peter admits being stumped by the Pauline
•L 251 ❖ L 3 Aug 53

Epistles of New Testament written before the Gospels
•GID 232 (*see also* M 143-144)
❖ GID II 10:7 (*see also* M 16:1-3)

Epistles of St. Paul: I cannot be the only reader to wonder why God withheld from St. Paul the gift of lucidity and orderly exposition
•RP 113 ❖ RP 11:8

Epistles of St. Paul: Perhaps his writings let through what matters more than ideas—a whole Christian life in operation
•RP 114 ❖ RP 11:9

Equality—*consider also* Democracy

Equality a quantitative term; love often knows nothing of it
•WG 115 ❖ WG 7:15

Equality (as in marriage) not the Divine plan but a necessity due to the Fall
•WG 113-116 (*see also* FL 148-149*; M 119-120, 124*; MC 102-103)
❖ WG 7:10-15 (*see also* FL 5:26-28*; M

14:20, 26*; MC III 6:17)

"Equality" as the attitude that "I'm as good as you" turns a person away from almost every road which might finally lead him to Heaven
•SL 170; WLN 68
❖ SL 32:39; WLN 4:39

Equality: "I cannot conceive how one would get through the boredom of a world in which you never met anyone more clever, or more beautiful...than yourself"
•GID 85 ❖ GID I 9:7

Equality: "...I don't mean to ignore (in fact I find it nice) the distinction between a peasant's grandson like myself and those of noble blood"*
•LAL 26 (*see also* LAL 27)
❖ LAL 26/1/54 (*see also* Feb 22/54)

Equality: In the Church we recover our real inequalities, and are offered refreshing opportunities for reverence and worship
•WG 113-116 ❖ WG 7:10-15

Equality in the sense of not allowing differences is a principle of the governments of tyrants and dictators; "Democracy" now a misused word
•SL 161-170, esp. 164-165; WLN 59-68, esp. 63 ❖ SL 32:19-39, esp. 32:28; WLN 32:19-39, esp. 32:28

Equality is for me in the same position as clothes; it is a result of the Fall and the remedy for it
•WG 114 ❖ WG 7:13

Equality is our only defense against one another's cruelty
•WG 115 ❖ WG 7:14

Equality: Most men, as Aristotle observed, do not like to be merely equal with other men; tend to build themselves into groups where they can feel superior
•WLN 41 ❖ WLN 3:14

Equality of man ("Brotherhood"): I have long known that the talk about Brotherhood, wherever it occurs, is hypocrisy*
•LAL 43 ❖ LAL 7/6/55

Equality of men and women does not

mean that they are interchangeable (regarding women in the clergy)
•GID 238 ❖ GID II 11:10

Equality of the sexes as citizens or intellectual beings not absolutely repugnant to Pauline thought
•CR 4 ❖ CR 1:6

Equality: Opportunity for reverence, which the church offers us, is a refreshing change from the necessary democracy of the world*
•WG 116 (see also GID 84-85; WG 113) ❖ WG 7:15 (see also GID I 9:7; WG 7:10)

Equality, the claim to, is made only by those who feel themselves to be in some way inferior
•SL 162-163; WLN 60-61 (see also LAL 27-28) ❖ SL 32:22; WLN 4:22 (see also LAL Mar 10/54)

Era(s)—see Age(s)

Eros—see also Love; Sexual love; consider also Lust; Marriage

Eros (at his height) regards pleasure as a by-product
•FL 136 ❖ FL 5:8

Eros, between the best possible lovers, is intermittent; the old self soon turns out to be not so dead as he pretended
•FL 159 ❖ FL 5:44

Eros "ceases to be a devil only when it ceases to be a god" (quote from M. de Rougemont)
•CR 35; FL 17-18, 39; L 182 (see also FL 83, 151*, 156-157*, 160, 166*) ❖ CR 2:55; FL 1:13, 14, 29; L 16 Apr 40 (see also FL 3:45; 5:31*; 5:39-41*; 5:46; 6:5*)

Eros (chapter title)
•FL 131-160 ❖ FL ch. 5

Eros, dangers of, unless ruled by Charity
•FL 151-160 ❖ FL 5:31-46

Eros, definition of: "...that state which we call 'being in love'"; sexuality only one ingredient
•FL 131 ❖ FL 5:1

Eros ("erotic love") may lead to real Friendship and real Friendship may easily lead to erotic love
•FL 98-99 (see also FL 106) ❖ FL 4:21 (see also FL 4:31)

Eros ("erotic love"), nothing so enriches,

as the discovery that the Beloved can deeply and truly enter into Friendship with the Friends you already had
•FL 99 ❖ FL 4:21

Eros: "...half the love songs and poems in the world will tell you that the Beloved is your fate or destiny, no more your choice than a thunderbolt..."
•FL 125-126 ❖ FL 4:61

Eros, "honoured without reservation and obeyed unconditionally, becomes a demon"
•FL 154, 160 ❖ FL 5:36, 46

Eros, I can imagine nothing more disagreeable than to experience, for more than a very short time without the homespun clothing of Affection
•FL 57 ❖ FL 3:8

Eros involves good-natured mockery; until they have a baby to laugh at, lovers are always laughing at each other
•FL 151 ❖ FL 5:30

Eros, it is one of God's jokes that a passion so soaring as, should be linked with an appetite connected like all appetites with mundane factors like...
•FL 142 ❖ FL 5:18

Eros itself may be idolised; this is a greater danger than that lovers will idolise each other
•FL 155-157, 159 (see also FL 20-21) ❖ FL 5:37-41 (see also FL 1:18)

Eros makes a man really want, not a woman, but one particular woman, thus transforming Need-pleasure into Appreciative pleasure
•FL 135-136 ❖ FL 5:6

Eros notoriously the most mortal of our loves; "What is baffling is the combination of this fickleness with his protestations of permanency"
•FL 157-158 ❖ FL 5:42

Eros obliterates the distinction between giving and receiving
•FL 137 ❖ FL 5:8

Eros: Of some people a total renunciation of this love is required; of others, a transformation
•FL 154 (see also FL 183) ❖ FL 5:35 (see also FL 6:31)

Eros, perverted: "Plato was right after all. Eros, turned upside down, blackened, distorted, and filthy, still bore the traces of his divinity" (re· pederasty at Wyvern College)
•SJ 109-110 ❖ SJ 7:12

Eros, schools of thought regarding the voice of, (Platonic, Shavian, Christian)
•FL 151-154 ❖ FL 5:33-35

Eros, sexual element within, labelled "Venus"
•FL 131-132 ❖ FL 5:1

Eros, speaking with grandeur and transcendence of self-regard, may sound like a message from God—but may urge to evil as well as to good
•FL 151, 156-157 (see also FL 18, 166) ❖ FL 5:31, 32, 38-41 (see also FL 1:14; 6:5)

Eros, temptations of, when we are "in love" speak with the voice of "quasi-religious duties, acts of pious zeal to love"
•FL 156-157 ❖ FL 5:40

Eros tends to turn "being in love" into a sort of religion; opposition makes lovers feel like martyrs
•FL 154 ❖ FL 5:36

Eros, the work of carrying out the promises of, is indeed the whole Christian life seen from one particular angle
•FL 160 ❖ FL 5:45

Eros: There is a charm about those moments when Appreciative love lies curled up asleep and the ease and ordinariness of Affection wraps us round
•FL 57 ❖ FL 3:8

Eros: Though we can have erotic love and friendship for the same person, in some ways nothing is less like a Friendship than a love-affair
•FL 91 ❖ FL 4:8

Eros, total commitment of, is an example of the love we ought to exercise towards God and Man
•FL 153-154, 158 ❖ FL 5:35, 43

Eros vs. Friendship: If only one were possible, which should we choose?
•FL 99-100 ❖ FL 4:22

Eros wants the Beloved, while mere sexual desire wants it, the thing in itself
•FL 134 ❖ FL 5:4

Eros, we must do the works of, even when Eros is not present
•FL 159 ❖ FL 5:45

Eros: What comes first is rarely mere sexual appetite, but a delighted preoccupation with the Beloved in her totality
•FL 133-134 ❖ FL 5:3

Eros, what is offered as Friendship may be mistaken for, on the other side with painful and embarrassing results
•FL 106 ❖ FL 4:31

Eros: When he is in us we would rather share unhappiness with the Beloved than be happy on any other terms
•FL 149-150 (see also FL 168) ❖ FL 5:29 (see also FL 6:10)

Eros, without diminishing desire, reduces the nagging, addictive character of mere appetite and makes abstinence easier
•FL 138 ❖ FL 5:10

Erotic love—see Eros

"Error of Stoicism," Pascal referred to: thinking we can do always what we can do sometimes (e.g., prayers without words)
•LM 11 ❖ LM 2:5

Error usually contains or imitates some truth; that is what makes it potent (re: Fascism and Communism)*
•L 176 ❖ L 17 Jan 40

Error: "What do they mean by 'Error has no rights'? (re: an article Lewis read, on Tolerance)
•L 254 ❖ L 16 Jan 54

Errors, devil always sends, into the world in pairs of opposites; we must go straight through between both errors
•MC 160 (see also WG 108) ❖ MC IV 6:4 (see also WG 7:3)

Errors in our thinking: Example of Pope Gregory, on arriving in Heaven and finding he'd been wrong about something: It was the funniest thing he'd ever heard (story from "Paradiso")*
•CR 11 ❖ CR 1:16

Errors in thinking may remove ordinary checks to evil and deprive good intentions of their natural support (re: "subjectivism")
•CR 72 ❖ CR 6:1

Errors, reactive: Martin Luther compared humanity to a drunkard who, after falling off his horse on the right, falls off it next time on the left
•WLN 94-95 ❖ WLN 7:4

Esoteric, lust for the, may take many forms including a desire for "the delicious sense of secret intimacy" (re: "Inner Rings")
•WG 100 ❖ WG 6:10

Essentials—*consider also* Priorities

Essentials vs. non-essentials: Good taste in poetry or music not necessary to salvation*
•CR 13-14; L 224 ❖ CR 2:3, 4; L 7 Dec 50

Essentials vs. non-essentials: "I'm sure a man can get to Heaven without being accurate about Methuselah's age"
•L 261 ❖ L 2 Feb 55

Essentials vs. non-essentials: Screwtape lauds the devils' labour toward causing humans to forget what Paul had to say "about food and other unessentials"*
•SL 75 ❖ SL 16:5

Eternal, all that is not, is eternally out of date (re: the irrelevance of meeting people in Heaven for whom you had only natural love on earth)
•FL 188 ❖ FL 6:39

Eternal aspect of sin: "It may be that salvation consists not in the cancelling of [sins] but in the perfected humility that bears the shame forever..."*
•PP 61 (*see also* L 236; SL 148) ❖ PP 4:9 (*see also* L 8 Jan 52; SL 31:5)

Eternal life—*see also* Immortality; *consider also* Destiny of redeemed Man; Heaven; Salvation

Eternal life, a crucifixion of the natural self is the passport to
•WG 117 (*consider also* Personality) ❖ WG 7:16 (*consider also* Personality)

Eternal life: According to Screwtape, God's view is that human birth is important chiefly as the qualification for human death, which is the gate to Heaven
•SL 133-134 (*see also* SJ 117*) ❖ SL 28:3 (*see also* SJ 7:21*)

Eternal life, at my conversion I did not yet believe in; I now number that among my greatest mercies (God was to be obeyed simply because He was God)
•SJ 231 (*see also* FL 189-190; LM 120; RP 39-42, esp. 42) ❖ SJ 15:3 (*see also* FL 6:42; LM 22:8; RP 4:12-17, esp. 4:17)

Eternal life, belief in, coming too soon, may render impossible the development of the appetite for God; personal hopes and fears have got in first
•RP 39-40 (*see also* FL 189-190; GID 130-131; LM 120; SJ 231) ❖ RP 4:13-15 (*see also* FL 6:41-44; GID I 16:2, 3; LM 22:8; SJ 15:3)

Eternal life: "Christianity asserts that every individual human being is going to live for ever..."
•MC 73 ❖ MC III 1:9

Eternal life, hope for, is a Christian virtue rather than a form of escapism or wishful thinking
•MC 118 ❖ MC III 10:1

Eternal life: How can it loom less than large if it is believed in at all?
•LM 120 (*see also* WG 3-5*) ❖ LM 22:7, 9 (*see also* WG 1:1-3*)

Eternal life: I believed in God for a whole year before any belief in the future life was given me
•RP 42 (*see also* FL 189-190; LM 120; SJ 231) ❖ RP 4:17 (*see also* FL 6:41, 42; LM 22:8; SJ 15:3)

Eternal life, I cannot sufficiently admire the divine tact of training the chosen race for centuries before even hinting at
•GID 131 (*see also* M 145-146; RP 39-42; SJ 231) ❖ GID I 16:3 (*see also* M 16:6; RP 4:12-16; SJ 15:3)

Eternal life, if it turned out there was no such thing as, would that be a moment for changing sides?
•LM 120 ❖ LM 22:8

Eternal life, in the end it will make no difference what we chose instead of; we shall have missed the thing we were made for, the only thing that satisfies
•WG 131 ❖ WG 9:11

Eternal life, is it possible for men to be too much concerned with their own? — In one sense, yes
•RP 39-40 (see also WG 3, 18-19)
❖ RP 4:13-15 (see also WG 1:1, 15)

Eternal life, most of us find that our belief in, is strong only when God is at the centre of our thoughts
•RP 41 (see also FL 189-190; GID 130-131; GO 79; LM 120; SJ 231)
❖ RP 4:16 (see also FL 6:41-44; GID I 16:2, 3; GO 4:21; LM 22:8; SJ 15:3)

Eternal life no mere bribe, but the consummation of our earthly discipleship
•WG 5 ❖ WG 1:3

Eternal life, Psalmists (and other Old Testament writers) probably had little or no belief in*
•RP 36, 38-39 ❖ RP 4:6, 9-12

Eternal life, why God did not teach the Jewish people early about
•RP 39-42 (see also GID 130-131; SJ 231)
❖ RP 4:12-16 (see also GID I 16:2, 3; SJ 15:3)

Eternal life will probably also be eternal dying in the sense of self-conquest
•PP 151-152 ❖ PP 10:9, 10

Eternal life, you will not get, by simply feeling the presence of God in flowers or music (re: importance of theology)
•MC 136 ❖ MC IV 1:4

Eternity, for God, is the endless present; not simply an older time
•LM 110 ❖ LM 20:16

Eternity, humans live in time but God destines them to; He therefore wants them to attend to eternity and to the Present (—Screwtape)
•SL 67-68 ❖ SL 15:2

Eternity, if we think of time as a line we probably ought to think of, as a plane or solid (of which earthly life is the base-line)
•PP 123-124 ❖ PP 8:8

Eternity, in the perspective of, the categories of pain and pleasure recede as vaster good and evil looms in sight
•PP 126 (see also SL 148)
❖ PP 8:9 (see also SL 31:5)

Eternity, natural loves can hope for, only in so far as they have allowed themselves to be taken into the eternity of Charity
•FL 187 ❖ FL 6:38

Eternity, perspective of: "I suppose that our whole present life, looked back on from there, will seem only a drowsy half-waking...but cockcrow is coming..."
•LAL 119-120 ❖ LAL 28 Jun 63

Eternity, perspective of: One sometimes wonders why God thinks the game worth the candle; but we have not yet seen the game*
•LM 91-92 ❖ LM 17:15

Eternity, perspective of: "...how different the content of our faith will look when we see it in the total context" *
•L 267 ❖ L 8 Feb 56

Eternity, the Present is the point at which time touches; in the present moment alone freedom and actuality are offered us
•SL 68 ❖ SL 15:2

Ethical and social values of the Christian vs. the Materialist
•GID 109-110 ❖ GID I 12:2-4

Ethical code, idea that Christianity brought a new, into the world is a grave error; Jesus' commands are paralleled in classical, Egyptian, and Chinese texts
•CR 46-47, 51, 52-53, 55, 77 (see also Law of Nature; book *The Abolition of Man*) ❖ CR 4:5-7, 17, 20-22, 26; 6:16 (see also Law of Nature; book *The Abolition of Man*)

Ethical codes, those who say they are choosing between, are already assuming a code (since one must appeal to moral principles in order to choose)
•CR 51 ❖ CR 4:16

Ethical decisions, factors in making: facts, intuition, reasoning, and regard for

authority
•WG 33-39 ❖ WG 3:1-11

Ethical element [of Judeo-Christianity] cannot be abstracted and set up as a religion on its own
•GID 144 ❖ GID I 16:26

Ethical injunctions, ultimate, have always been premisses, never conclusions; unless the ethical is assumed from the outset, no argument will bring you to it
•CR 55-56 ❖ CR 4:26

Ethical principles, a mere statement of even the highest, is not enough; Christianity does not help us if it brings no healing to the impotent will
•GID 328-329 ❖ GID IV Letter 4

Ethical standards: Within different cultures we find substantial agreement with considerable local differences of emphasis
•CR 77-78 (see also CR 54-55; MC 19, 24; PP 63; book The Abolition of Man)
❖ CR 6:16, 17 (see also CR 4:24; MC I 1:6, 7; 2:7; PP 4:10; book The Abolition of Man)

Ethical system, in order to "choose" an, we must first be in an ethical vacuum where we can view all Ethical Systems from the outside
•CR 47-48 (see also CR 50-51)
❖ CR 4:9 (see also CR 4:16)

Ethical systems, I deny that we have any choice to make between clearly differentiated, or that we have any power to make a new ethical system
•CR 55 ❖ CR 4:25

Ethical systems, two ways of differentiating: as bodies of ethical injunctions, or as systematic analyses and explanations of our moral experience
•CR 44-45 ❖ CR 4:2

Ethical teaching strikingly similar in Zarathustra, Jeremiah, Socrates, Gautama, and Christ—teachers widely separated in space and time
•PP 63 (see also CR 44-56, 77; MC 19, 78; RP 27; Law of Nature; book The Abolition of Man)
❖ PP 4:10 (see also CR ch. 4; 6:16; MC I

1:7; III 3:1; RP 3:13; Law of Nature; book The Abolition of Man)

Ethical theories, the very act of studying, as theories exaggerates the practical differences between them
•CR 45 ❖ CR 4:3

Ethics—see also Moral decisions; Moral judgements; Moral law; Moral thought; Morality; Values

Ethics, a person's theory of, arises out of the practical ethics he already attempts to obey—and again, the theory reacts on his judgement of what to do
•CR 45 ❖ CR 4:3

Ethics, all men alike stand condemned by their own codes of, and are thereby conscious of guilt
•PP 21-22 ❖ PP 1:12

Ethics: All the modern attempts at developing a new value consist of selecting and isolating one maxim of traditional morality as all-important
•CR 75 ❖ CR 6:10

Ethics: All the modern attempts at developing new moral codes are contractions of something already given
•CR 53, 56 ❖ CR 4:22, 27

Ethics, Aristotelian: two definitions
•CR 44-45 ❖ CR 4:2

Ethics: Attempting to imitate Christ will help us decide issues of right and wrong*
•MC 162 ❖ MC IV 7:5

Ethics, Christian: two definitions
•CR 44-45 ❖ CR 4:2

Ethics, Christianity makes duty a self-transcending concept and endeavors to escape from the region of mere morality in its
•CR 45 (see also LM 114-115; GID 112, 144; MC 130-131; PP 65*)
❖ CR 4:2 (see also LM 21:11-13; GID I 12:10; 16:26; MC III 12:9; 4:13*)

Ethics defined indirectly as "...what ought to be done..."*
•CR 45 ❖ CR 4:3

Ethics, in a certain sense it is no more possible to invent a new, than to place a new sun in the sky
•CR 53, 56, 75 (see also Law of Nature)

❖ CR 4:22, 27; 6:9 (*see also* Law of Nature)

Ethics, Kantian, mentioned as referring primarily to the Categorical Imperative ("Kant did not differ remarkably from other men on the content of ethics...")
•CR 44-45 (*see also* CR 55-56)
❖ CR 4:2 (*see also* CR 4:26)

Ethics: "...may we not recognize in modern thought a very serious exaggeration of the ethical differences between different cultures?"
•CR 54-55 (*see also* CR 77-78; MC 19, 24) ❖ CR 4:24 (*see also* CR 6:16; MC I 1:6, 7; 2:7)

Ethics, medical: Doctors who lie to their patients about their terminal condition mentioned with satisfaction by Screwtape
•SL 26-27 (*see also* L 275)
❖ SL 5:2 (*see also* L 6 Mar 57)

Ethics, medical: "I do wonder why the doctors inflict such torture to delay what cannot in any case be very long delayed. Or why God does"
•LAL 118-119 ❖ LAL 25 Jun 63

Ethics, medical: Let the doctor tell me I shall die unless I do so-and-so, but whether life is worth having on those terms is not a question for him...
•GID 315 ❖ GID III 8:15

Ethics, On (chapter title)
•CR 44-56 ❖ CR ch. 4

Ethics: Our emotional reactions to our own behaviour are of limited ethical significance; the shame I feel toward my sins doesn't correspond to their gravity
•LM 99 ❖ LM 18:16

Ethics, preservation of the human race as a basis for a code of: Is it a duty, and if so, on what grounds do we assume it is a duty?
•CR 48 ❖ CR 4:10, 11

Ethics: Question of whether the preservation of the human race is an imperative imposed by instinct
•CR 48-52 ❖ CR 4:12-19

Ethics, regarding the Communist, Futurist, Aristocratic, and Racialist systems of (all have selected some one maxim of traditional morality as all-important)
•CR 75 ❖ CR 6:11

Ethics, *Screwtape Letters* is, served with an imaginative seasoning
•L 234
❖ L undated letter just before 3 Dec 51

Ethics, situation: "I do not want a sensitivity which will show me how different each temptation to lust or cowardice is from the last...how unamenable to general rules"**
•CR 24-25 ❖ CR 2:38

Ethics, situation: "...if war is ever lawful, then peace is sometimes sinful"**
• GID 326 ❖ GID IV Letter 1

Ethics, social, of Christianity: We have a duty to leave the world (even in a temporal sense) better than we found it
•PP 113-114 (*see also* GID 49, 57, 147-150; MC 118; WLN 111)
❖ PP 7:4 (*see also* GID I 4:6, 7, 40; ch. 17; MC III 10:1; WLN 7:33, 34)

Ethics, Stoical: two definitions
•CR 44-45 ❖ CR 4:2

Ethics: Survival can have no value apart from the prior value of what survives
•L 158 (*see also* GID 297, 311; SL 131; WG 43*) ❖ L 13 Jan 37 (*see also* GID III 4:20; 8:1; SL 28:1; WG 3:18*)

Ethics: The activity of those who urge us to adopt new moralities is in the long run always directed against our freedom
•CR 56 (*see also* CR 81)
❖ CR 4:27 (*see also* CR 6:22)

Ethics: "...there can be no moral motive for entering a new morality unless that motive is borrowed from the traditional morality..."
•CR 52-53 ❖ CR 4:21

Ethics: Those who expect us to adopt a moral code to "preserve the species" have themselves already a moral code and tacitly assume that we do too
•CR 51 (*see also* CR 55)
❖ CR 4:16 (*see also* CR 4:25)

Ethics: Traditional morality does not pro-

vide answers to every particular moral problem with which we may be confronted (chess game analogy)
•CR 56 ❖ CR 4:27

Ethics, under views of "subjectivism" it is useless to compare the, of one age or society with those of another; progress and decadence are meaningless words
•CR 73 (see also CR 75)
❖ CR 6:5 (see also CR 6:11)

Ethics, we shall perhaps find increasing reasons to value Christian, over the current ways of thinking
•RP 64-65 (see also SL 110-113)
❖ RP 6:14 (see also SL 24:1-5)

Eucharist—see Communion, Holy

Eugenics as part of the false hope the devil wishes us to have for turning this Earth into Heaven
•SL 133 ❖ SL 28:2

Europe, would you agree that the un-Christening of much of, is an even bigger change than its Christening?
•L 258 ❖ L 1 Nov 54 (second letter)

Euthanasia for pets: "...rejoice that God's law allows you to extend to Fanda that last mercy which...we are forbidden to extend to suffering humans"
•LAL 61 ❖ LAL 18/8/56

Evangelicals and Anglo-Catholics, common ground between, more important than their differences
•GID 336 (see also Christianity, "mere") ❖ GID IV Letter 9 (see also Christianity, "mere")

Evangelism—see also Apologetic(s); Witnessing; consider also Preaching

Evangelism and witness: Though conversion requires the intervention of the supernatural, we still have work to do in preparing the intellectual climate*
•GID 221 ❖ GID II 8:10

Evangelism: Attempts to excite fear about Hell cannot succeed as a permanent influence on conduct*
•RP 41-42 (see also LM 76)
❖ RP 4:16 (see also LM 14:15)

Evangelism: Christians' ineffectiveness in this world a result of ceasing to think

of the next*
•MC 118 (see also GID 150*)
❖ MC III 10:1 (see also GID I 17:7*)

Evangelism, education a necessary tool in Christian; we must be able to meet our enemies on their own ground*
•WG 28 (see also CR 17)
❖ WG 2:10 (see also CR 2:18)

Evangelism: Great Britain is as much part of the mission field as China
•GID 94 ❖ GID I 10:12

Evangelism: If the "emotional" religious sayings contain real information, you will not get it without meeting them with a certain readiness to find it*
•CR 141 (see also CR 135)
❖ CR 11:25 (see also CR 11:12)

Evangelism: "If we are to convert our heathen neighbors, we must understand their culture. We must 'beat them at their own game'"*
•CR 17 (see also WG 28)
❖ CR 2:18 (see also WG 2:10)

Evangelism: Lewis mentions the "intolerable pride" of going around asking people if they are saved*
•L 64 ❖ L 1 Jul 21

Evangelism, the practical method of: to convert our adult and adolescent neighbors
•GID 119 ❖ GID I 13:11

Evangelism, methods of: intellectual vs. emotional approach
•GID 99, 244 ❖ GID I 10:39, 40; II 12:9

Evangelism, methods of: which sins should be emphasized
•GID 244 ❖ GID II 12:8

Evangelism: "One must take comfort in remembering that God used an ass to convert the prophet..."*
•L 193-194 ❖ L 15 May 41

Evangelism: "Our business is to present that which is timeless...in the particular language of our own age"*
•GID 93-94 ❖ GID I 10:10

Evangelism: Pagans more responsive to Christianity than the modern, post-Christian man*
•GID 172 ❖ GID I 21:1

Evangelism, problems in—consider also

Obstacles to Christian faith

Evangelism, problems in: a firm disbelief in the principle of salvation by faith in Jesus*
•GID 101-102 ❖ GID I 10:48

Evangelism, problems in: "A sense of sin is almost totally lacking"*
•GID 95-96 (see also GID 181-182, 243-244; MC 38-39*; PP 55-57)
❖ GID I 10:15-17 (see also GID I 22:13; II 12: 6-8; MC I 5:4*; PP 4:1-4

Evangelism, problems in: combatting the idea of God as merely a "great spiritual force"*
•M 81 (see also GID 71; M 93-94; MC 35; SL 33; Religion, minimal)
❖ M 11:2 (see also GID I 6:9; M 11:19; MC I 4:6; SL 7:1; Religion, minimal)

Evangelism, problems in, do not usually include much determined atheism*
•GID 100-101 ❖ GID I 10:45

Evangelism, problems in: "For the modern man the roles are reversed. He is the judge: God is in the dock"
•GID 244 (see also GID 95; L 181*)
❖ GID II 12:17 (see also GID I 10:15; L 26 Mar 40*)

Evangelism, problems in: History is regarded with scepticism by the uneducated man, while "Science" is considered reliable*
•GID 241-242 (see also GID 94-95, 252)
❖ GID II 12:3 (see also GID I 10:13, 14; II 14:8, 9)

Evangelism, problems in: "It is very difficult to produce arguments on the popular level for the existence of God"*
•GID 100 ❖ GID I 10:44

Evangelism, problems in: Modern audiences think you are preaching Christianity because you like it or think it good for society, etc.*
•GID 90-91, 101 (see also MC 137; SL 108-109) ❖ GID I 10:5, 48 (see also MC IV 1:6, 7; SL 23:4)

Evangelism, problems in: Opponents of Christianity may be ignorant of the Faith they suppose themselves to be rejecting (re: Socratic Club)*

•GID 127 ❖ GID I 15:3

Evangelism, problems in: "...our present task is chiefly to convert and instruct infidels"*
•GID 94 ❖ GID I 10:12

Evangelism, problems in: terms which are commonly misunderstood by the modern, uneducated man (e.g., "Atonement," "Creature," "Dogma," etc.)*
•GID 96-98 ❖ GID I 10:18-38

Evangelism, problems in: "...the almost total absence from the minds of my audience of any sense of sin"
•GID 243-244 (see also GID 95-96, 181-182; MC 38-39; PP 55)
❖ GID II 12:6 (see also GID I 10:15-17; 22:13; MC I 5:4; PP 4:1)

Evangelism, problems in: the belief that since the earth is so small it must be insignificant*
•GID 99-100 (see also GID 39-42, 74-75; M 48-54) ❖ GID I 10:42 (see also GID I 3:4-9; I 7:29- 41; M 7:7-17)

Evangelism, problems in: the belief that a certain amount of "religion" is desirable but one mustn't carry it too far*
•GID 101 (see also Self-reservation)
❖ GID I 10:48 (see also Self-reservation)

Evangelism, problems in: the belief that the story of Jesus is a legend*
•GID 101 (see also CR 154-155; GID 158-159; SJ 236) ❖ GID I 10:47 (see also CR 13:4, 5; GID I 19:4, 5; SJ 15:7)

Evangelism, problems in: the danger to one's own faith ("No doctrine...seems to to me so spectral, so unreal as one that I have just successfully defended...")
•GID 103, 128; L 209
❖ GID I 10:50; 15:4; L 2 Aug 46

Evangelism, problems in: the difference between what the ordinary man believes Christianity to be and the picture of the universe he has gotten from science*
•GID 68 (see also M 68-69)
❖ GID I 6:2 (see also M 10:2)

Evangelism, problems in: "The difficulty of converting an uneducated man

nowadays lies in his complacency"*
•CR 23 ❖ CR 2:35

Evangelism, problems in: the embarrassing supporter who tries to help, but whose arguments are invalid*
•GID 100 ❖ GID I 10:44

Evangelism, problems in: The moment people have gone away from our lecture, they go back to a world where the opposite position is taken for granted*
•GID 93 ❖ GID I 10:9

Evangelism, problems in: The opposition we meet is not usually based on malice or suspicion, but on genuine doubt
•GID 242 ❖ GID II 12:3

Evangelism, problems in: "...to keep before the audience's mind the question of Truth (they think you recommend Christianity because it is good)
•GID 101 (see also GID 90-91, 108-109)
❖ GID I 10:48 (see also GID I 10:5; 12:1)

Evangelism, problems in: Uneducated people are sceptical about history and the authenticity of ancient texts; they lack historical perspective*
•GID 94-95, 241-242
❖ GID I 10:13, 14; II 12:3

Evangelism, problems in: We are mistaken to think Materialism our only considerable adversary (others include Theosophy, Spiritualism, etc.)
•GID 240-241 ❖ GID II 12:2

Evangelism, problems in: We must be aware of our audience's race, age, and intelligence
•GID 240 ❖ GID II 12:1

Evangelism, problems in: We must learn and use the language of our audience, including the vernacular
•GID 93, 94, 96-98, 254-257, 338 ❖ GID I 10:10, 12, 18-38; II ch. 15; IV Letter 11

Evangelism, problems in: Within the English proletariat is found a Christianity tainted with Pantheistic elements and theological vagueness*
•GID 240-241 ❖ GID II 12:2

Evangelism: The "real business of life" is the glory of God, and, as our only means of glorifying Him, the salvation of souls*
•CR 14 ❖ CR 2:4

Evangelism: "There are many different ways of bringing people into His kingdom, even some ways that I specially dislike!"
•GID 262 (see also GID 258-259)
❖ GID II 16:28 (see also GID II 16:3, 4)

Evangelism: There are two kinds of outsiders whom the theologian needs to study: the uneducated, and those who are educated in some way but not in his way*
•CR 152-153 ❖ CR 13:1, 2

Evangelism, translation into vernacular necessary in
•GID 183 (see also Translation)
❖ GID I 22:16, 17 (see also Translation)

Evangelism: "What a wonderful power is in the direct appeal which disregards the temporary climate..."
•L 177 ❖ L 11 Feb 40

Evangelism: What doesn't suit us may suit possible converts of a different type
•L 268 ❖ L 13 Mar 56

Evangelism: What we want is not more books about Christianity, but more books by Christians on other subjects—with their Christianity latent*
•GID 93 ❖ GID I 10:9

Evangelist or preacher represents the Lord; the apologist represents John Baptist
•GID 221-222 ❖ GID II 8:10

Evangelistic, most of my books are; they are addressed to those who did not know they were in need of forgiveness and a Saviour
•GID 181-182 ❖ GID I 22:13

Evasion, corporate guilt or a social conscience can be used as an, of our own personal faults
•PP 60-61 ❖ PP 4:8

Evasion of Christ not manly: "...you do know that you ought to be a Man, not an ostrich, hiding its head in the sand"
•GID 111 ❖ GID I 12:8

Evasion of God—consider also Contact with God; Self-reservation

Evasion of God because of the desire "to

call one's soul one's own" is both shameful and futile*
•SJ 237 (*see also* PP 80; SJ 172, 228; WG 130-131; Limited liabilities)
❖ SJ 15:8 (*see also* PP 5:8; SJ 11:8; 14:22; WG 9:9, 10; Limited liabilities)

Evasion of God: Business of life is to learn to like contact with God, since that contact cannot be avoided for long
•GID 47 (*see also* MC 183; WG 13)
❖ GID I 3:17 (*see also* MC IV 10:17; WG 1:10)

Evasion of God: Distractions listed which have greater power to cause us to evade God when we are feeling vague guilt (useless conversations, etc.)*
•SL 54-56 ❖ SL 12:3, 4

Evasion of God: "Do not let us deceive ourselves. No possible complexity which we can give to our picture of the universe can hide us from God..."
•GID 47 ❖ GID I 3:17

Evasion of God: Lewis lists many things which will help you to avoid God, if that is what you desire ("Avoid silence...Live in a crowd..." etc.)
•CR 168-169 (*see also* SL 102-103*)
❖ CR 14:17, 18 (*see also* SL 22:5*)

Evasion of God: My long-evaded encounter with God happened at a time when I was making a serious effort to obey my conscience
•CR 169 ❖ CR 14:20

Evasion of God: "The presence which we voluntarily evade is often, and we know it, His presence in wrath"
•LM 75 ❖ LM 14:12

Evasion of God: The secret wish that our faith should *not* be very strong may be one of the causes of our weak faith*
•CR 43 ❖ CR 3:12

Evasion of God: Was Evolution devised not to get in facts but to keep out God?*
•WG 89 ❖ WG 5:22

Evasion of God: "We may ignore, but we can nowhere evade, the presence of God. The world is crowded with Him"
•LM 75 ❖ LM 14:11

Evasion of God: "We shrink from too naked a contact [in prayer], because we are afraid of the divine demands upon us which it might make too audible"*
•LM 114 (*see also* CR 43; M 94; SL 22-23*, 54-55; WG 127-128)
❖ LM 21:8 (*see also* CR 3:12; M 11:19; SL 4:4; 12:3; WG 9:5)

Evasion of Grace likened to venipuncture: Do the approaches of Grace often hurt because the spiritual vein in us hides itself from the celestial surgeon?
•LAL 118-119 ❖ LAL 25 Jun 63

Evasion of truth: Those who have heard the claims of Christ must come to terms with them, or else be guilty of inattention or evading the question
•GID 265-266 ❖ GID II 16:50

Evasion of truth out of fear of duty: "...a blunting of his whole mental edge will result. He has lost his intellectual virginity"
•GID 110-111 (*see also* Self-reservation) ❖ GID I 12:6-8 (*see also* Self-reservation)

Evasion of truth usually deliberate*
•GID 110-111; WG 35
❖ GID I 12:6-8; WG 3:4

Evasion, the idealistic doctrine that sin is merely a result of our being finite can be used as an
•PP 65-66 ❖ PP 4:14

Evasion, to recognize the ground for my, was of course to recognize both its shame and its futility ("to call one's soul one's own")
•SJ 237 ❖ SJ 15:8

Evening, would it were, and all was well (quote from unspecified source)
•L 166 ❖ L 8 May 39

Everlasting arms, underneath are the; let go, [Jesus] will catch you
•LAL 117 ❖ LAL 17 Jun 63

Everlasting Man, I read Chesterton's, and for the first time saw the whole Christian outline of history set out in a form that seemed to me to make sense
•SJ 223 (*see also* L 298; SJ 235)
❖ SJ 14:15 (*see also* L 9 May 61; SJ 15:7)

"**Everythingism**" (Lewis's word for Monism) discussed
- M 165 ❖ M 17:2

Evil—*see also* Badness; Sin; Sinfulness; Wickedness; *consider also* Pain, problem of

Evil a perversion of good
- GID 22-23 (*see also* CR 21; LM 69, 89; MC 49; SL 41-42)
- ❖ GID I 1:5 (*see also* CR 2:27; LM 13:4; 17:5; MC II 2:9; SL 9:2)

Evil a perversion of good: "...the ugliest things in human nature are perversions of good or innocent things"
- PP 94 ❖ PP 6:6

Evil and God (chapter title)
- GID 21-24 ❖ GID I ch. 1

Evil and good—*see* Good and evil

Evil comes from the abuse of free will
- PP 135 (*see also* M 121-122; MC 52-53; PP 69) ❖ PP 9:7 (*see also* M 14:23; MC II 3:3, 4; PP 5:1)

Evil did not frustrate the good that God intended when He created the world; rather evil provides the fuel for a second, more complex kind of good
- PP 84 (*see also* PP 110-111)
- ❖ PP 5:11 (*see also* PP 7:2)

Evil: "...Divine punishments are also mercies and particular good is worked out of particular evil..."
- SJ 77 ❖ SJ 5:9

Evil, duty is always conditioned by, (by lack of love in myself, or by the general diffused evil of the world)
- LM 116 ❖ LM 21:14

Evil habits: The parable of the Unjust Judge teaches us that none are so ingrained that they cannot, even in old age, be whisked away
- LM 107 ❖ LM 20:1

Evil, how terrible that there should be even a kind of *pleasure* in thinking
- L 222-223 (*see also* FL 82, 113; GID 154; LAL 92-93; LM 94-95; MC 108; RP 22-24) ❖ L 12 Jan 50 (*see also* FL 3:45; 4:43; GID I 18:9; LAL 28 Oct 60; LM 18:1, 2; MC III 7:11; RP 3:6-8)

Evil, human race may be a local pocket of, in which the standard of decency is vastly inferior to that of the larger universe
- PP 62-63 ❖ PP 4:10

Evil, if an illusion, would still be real; therefore the Christian Science theory is too simple and gains nothing
- L 257 ❖ L 1 Nov 54 (first letter)

Evil, in contemplating, we find ourselves moved by a truly ethical demand for justice (re: the "intolerable" doctrine of Hell)
- PP 120-122 ❖ PP 8:5

Evil is a parasite, not an original thing
- MC 50 ❖ MC II 2:10

Evil is the pursuit of some good in the wrong way*
- MC 49-50 (*see also* CR 21; LM 89)
- ❖ MC II 2:9, 10 (*see also* CR 2:26; LM 17:5)

Evil: Jesus Himself "plumbed the depths of that worst suffering which comes to evil men who at last know their own evil"
- RP 127 (*consider also* Self-knowledge)
- ❖ RP 12:7 (*consider also* Self-knowledge)

Evil may be exploited by God for His redemptive purpose (as in the case of suffering), thereby producing a complex good
- PP 110-111 ❖ PP 7:2

Evil, pain rouses men to the presence of, in their existence; they may either rebel (with the possibility of deeper repentance later) or make a change
- PP 95 ❖ PP 6:7

Evil people—*see* Bad people; Wicked

Evil, problem of, no more urgent for us than for the great majority of monotheists down through the ages
- GID 22 (*consider also* Pain, problem of) ❖ GID I 1:2 (*consider also* Pain, problem of)

Evil, some pain may be necessary to awaken us to the existence of, ("Pain is unmasked, unmistakable evil")
- PP 92-98, 106-107 ❖ PP 6:5-9, 17

Evil, the art of life consists in tackling each immediate, as well as we can
- WG 44-45 ❖ WG 3:20

Evil, the attempt to explain, lies in the realm of theology
•CR 69-71, esp. 71
❖ CR 5:24-26, esp. 5:26

Evil, the greatest, is not now done in Dickensian "dens of crime" but rather in clean, carpeted offices by quiet men with white collars...
•SL x ❖ SL P:17

Evil, the humourous and civilised image of Mephistopheles has helped to strengthen the illusion that, is liberating
•SL ix (see also SL 33)
❖ SL P:15 (see also SL 7:1)

Evil, two sub-Christian theories on the origin of, (Monism and Dualism) vs. the doctrine of the Fall of Man
•PP 69 ❖ PP 5:1

Evil usually contains or imitates some good, which accounts for its potency (re: Fascism and Communism)
•L 176 ❖ L 17 Jan 40

Evil vs. good: "There is no neutral ground in the universe: every square inch, every split second, is claimed by God and counterclaimed by Satan"*
•CR 33 ❖ CR 2:54

Evil which God chiefly uses to produce "complex good" is pain; pain lacks the tendency to proliferate which sin has
•PP 116-117 ❖ PP 7:9

Evil within ourselves never fully known to us
•GID 121-123, 153; PP 59-60 (see also L 183; MC 87; SL 16)
❖ GID I 14:4-8; 18:6, 7; PP 4:7 (see also L 16 Apr 40; MC III 4:10; SL 3:2)

Evils: "Cruelty is surely more evil than lust and the World at least as dangerous as the Flesh"
•SJ 109 ❖ SJ 7:11

Evils, greatest, are not death and pain (re: Pacifism)
•WG 43 (see also GID 297, 311, 322*; L 158*, 166; M 125; SL 131-132)
❖ WG 3:18 (see also GID III 4:20; 8:1; 9:28*; L 13 Jan 37*; 8 May 39; M 14:28; SL 28:1)

Evils, necessary: "Government is at its best a necessary evil. Let's keep it in its place"
•L 281 (see also WLN 40)
❖ L 1 Feb 58 (see also WLN 3:13)

Evils, necessary: Let us not mistake them for good (re: collective activities—politics, armies, laws, and institutions)
•WG 108-109 ❖ WG 7:4

Evils, necessary: There are such things as necessary evils; but the infliction of pain must always be justified (re: vivisection)
•GID 224-225 ❖ GID II 9:3

Evils, spiritual, which we share with the devils (pride, spite) far worse than the sensual evils which we share with the beasts
•LAL 111 (see also FL 111-112; GID 98; MC 94-95, 108-112; SJ 109)
❖ LAL 26 Nov 62 (see also FL 4:39; GID I 10:36; MC III 5:14; 8:1-8; SJ 7:11)

Evolution—consider also Creation

Evolution and the fall of Man, a version offered by Lewis of*
•PP 77-85 ❖ PP 5:6-11

Evolution as a biological theorem vs. Evolutionism or Developmentalism "which is certainly a Myth"
•CR 82-93, esp. 83-86
❖ CR ch. 7, esp. 7:5-12

Evolution as a purely biological theorem does not in itself explain the origin of organic life, nor does it discuss the origin and validity of reason
•CR 86 ❖ CR 7:12

Evolution as a purely biological theorem does not attempt to tell you how the universe as a whole arose, or what it is, or whither it is tending
•CR 86 ❖ CR 7:12

Evolution: "As to Man being 'in Evolution' I agree, tho' I shd. rather say 'in process of being created'"
•L 228 ❖ L 23 Apr 51

Evolution, Biological, is a theory about how organisms change; progress is the exception and degeneration the rule
•CR 58 (see also CR 85; GID 33)
❖ CR 5:3 (see also CR 7:11; GID I 2:12)

Evolution, Creative—see Creative Evolution; Emergent Evolution

Evolution: Darwinism gives no support to the belief that natural selection, working upon chance variations, has a general tendency to produce improvement
- WLN 103 ❖ WLN 7:18

Evolution, Emergent—see Creative Evolution; Emergent Evolution

Evolution: "If by saying that man rose from brutality you mean simply that man is physically descended from animals, I have no objection"*
- PP 72 ❖ PP 5:2

Evolution, in my opinion the modern conception of, is simply a myth, supported by no evidence whatever
- WLN 100-104, esp. 101
❖ WLN 7:12-19, esp. 7:13

Evolution: In subjectivism, where reason is thought to be the by-product of blind evolutionary process, there is no reason to suppose that logic yields truth
- CR 72 (see also Reason; Subjectivism)
❖ CR 6:2 (see also Reason; Subjectivism)

Evolution: In the normal act of generation there passes "the form of those pre-human organisms which the embryo will recapitulate in the womb"*
- M 13 ❖ M 15:12

Evolution in the strict biological sense differentiated from "Evolutionism"—the belief that the very formula of universal process is from imperfect to perfect
- WG 89-90 ❖ WG 5:22

Evolution, many of the changes produced by, are not improvements by any conceivable standard
- WLN 103 (see also CR 85; GID 21)
❖ WLN 7:18 (see also CR 7:11; GID I 1:1)

Evolution not a doctrine of moral, or even of biological, improvement, but of biological changes
- L 218 (see also CR 85)
❖ L 1 Aug 49 (see also CR 7:11)

Evolution: On the Christian view, the "Next Step" has already appeared—and it is really new

- MC 184-188 ❖ MC IV 11:2-10

Evolution only a momentary ripple in the real cosmic wave of entropy; the trend of the universe is downward
- GID 44 (see also GID 33*)
❖ GID I 3:11 (see also GID I 2:12*)

Evolution or "naturalism": "Was it devised not to get in facts but to keep out God?"
- WG 89 ❖ WG 5:22

Evolution, people are being taught the most absurd versions of Darwin's theory of
- L 113 ❖ L 30 Mar 27

Evolution: "To those—and they are now the majority—who see human life merely as a development and complication of animal life..."*
- FL 90 ❖ FL 4:5

Evolution, transformation found in, as a parallel to Christian transformation
- MC 183-187 ❖ MC IV 11:1-9

Evolution vs. entropy: "The march of all things is from higher to lower"; "Developmentalism" is made plausible by a kind of trick
- GID 208-211 ❖ GID II ch. 5

Evolution: We now have good reason to believe that animals existed long before men*
- PP 133 ❖ PP 9:6

Evolution, what difficulties I have about, are not religious
- RP 115 ❖ RP 11:11

Evolution: "'...you need much more faith in science than in theology'" (quote from unknown source)
- L 113 ❖ L 30 Mar 27

Evolutionary doctrine that badness is an unavoidable legacy from our animal ancestors encourages us to shift responsibility for our behaviour from ourselves
- PP 65-66 ❖ PP 4:14

Evolutionary picture of reality developed in the nineteenth and early twentieth centuries sometimes referred to as "Wellsianity"—but this is misleading
- CR 82 (see also WG 79—ftnt.)
❖ CR 7:3 (see also WG 5:11—ftnt.)

Evolutionary world picture of such people as H. G. Wells described and refuted
•CR 82-93; WG 79-81
❖ CR ch. 7; WG 5:11, 12

Evolutionism—*see also* Creative Evolution; Emergent Evolution

Evolutionism, a certain degree of, is inherent in Christianity (as in Nature developing from the formless to the finished)
•M 121 ❖ M 14:22

Evolutionism, definition of: "...the belief that the very formula of universal process is from imperfect to perfect"
•WG 90 ❖ WG 5:22

Evolutionism, evidence proving, to be a Myth: chronology and internal evidence
•CR 83-88 ❖ CR 7:6-16

Evolutionism: If my own mind is a product of the irrational, how shall I trust my mind when it tells me about Evolution?
•CR 89 (*see also* Reason)
❖ CR 7:16 (*see also* Reason)

Evolutionism, in the best versions of the Myth of, all ends in nothingness
•CR 88 ❖ CR 7:14

Evolutionism is perhaps the deepest habit of mind in the contemporary world
•WG 90 ❖ WG 5:22

Evolutionism, modern politics would be impossible without the Myth of, which obscures truisms that would be fatal to the political Left and Right
•CR 92-93 ❖ CR 7:22

Evolutionism, Myth of, as expressed in literature (Wells, Keats, Wagner, Shaw, etc.)
•CR82-88 ❖ CR 7:3-15

Evolutionism, Myth of, defined as the idea "that small or chaotic or feeble things perpetually turn themselves into large, strong, ordered things"
•CR 90 ❖ CR 7:18

Evolutionism, Myth of, has been built into the state religion of Russia; is essential to the political Left and the political Right of modern times
•CR 93 ❖ CR 7:22

Evolutionism, Myth of: "I grew up believing in this Myth and I have felt—I still feel—its almost perfect grandeur"
•CR 89 ❖ CR 7:17

Evolutionism, Myth of: I speak of this Myth as a thing to be buried because I believe that its dominance is already over
•CR 89 ❖ CR 7:17

Evolutionism, Myth of: "It appeals to every part of me except my reason"
•CR 93 ❖ CR 7:23

Evolutionism, Myth of: "It gives us almost everything the imagination craves—irony, heroism, vastness, unity in multiplicity, and a tragic close"
•CR 93 ❖ CR 7:23

Evolutionism, Myth of: "It is one of the most moving and satisfying world dramas which have ever been imagined"
•CR 86 ❖ CR 7:12

Evolutionism, Myth of, must be treated with respect; it has a vast appeal
•CR 93 ❖ CR 7:23

Evolutionism, Myth of: Reasons for its popularity listed
•CR 90-93 ❖ CR 7:18-22

Evolutionism, Myth of: "That it has embedded in it many true particulars I do not doubt: but in its entirety, it simply will not do"
•CR 89 ❖ CR 7:16

Evolutionism (or Developmentalism or Progress) not the same as the Darwinian theorem in biology; is an illegitimate transition from it
•WLN 101 (*see also* CR 83-86; WG 89-90) ❖ WLN 7:14 (*see also* CR 7:5-12; WG 5:22)

Evolutionism, popular, called a Myth by Lewis because it is "the imaginative and not the logical result of what is vaguely called 'modern science'"
•CR 82-83 ❖ CR 7:4

Evolutionism, story of the universe as told by the Myth of, ("The proper drama is preceded...")
•CR 86-88 ❖ CR 7:13, 14

Evolutionism, the masses are shielded

from fear of cosmic futility by popular, in which "Evolution" simply means "improvement"
•CR 58 ❖ CR 5:3

Evolutionism, the Romantic poetry and music in which popular, found their natural counterpart are going out of fashion
•CR 90 ❖ CR 7:17

Exaggeration, doesn't the mere fact of putting something into words of itself involve an
•LM 112-113, 116 ❖ LM 21:2, 15

Exaggeration: It is almost impossible to state the negative effect certain doctrines have on me without seeming to mount an attack against them*
•LM 101 ❖ LM 19:4

Exaggeration of a doctrine results in danger of a reaction—making the opposite error (re: extreme views of the doctrine of the Second Coming)
•WLN 94-95 (see also MC 160; WG 108*) ❖ WLN 7:4 (see also MC IV 6:4; WG 7:3*)

Exaggeration seems to be inherent in the mere act of writing
•L 137 ❖ L 9 Sep 29

Exam, compulsory questions on, as an analogy to attempting difficult virtues such as chastity
•MC 93 ❖ MC III 5:11

Example, Christian: Practice may be imperfect, yet the precept still profitable*
•GID 283-284 ❖ GID III 3:4

Example, Christian: Practice much harder than preaching (re: humility)*
•LAL 29 ❖ LAL Mar 31st 54

Example, Christian: What we practice is more important than what we preach, when it comes to the conversion of others*
•L 261 (see also L 247; LAL 96)
❖ L 2 Feb 55 (see also L 8 Nov 52; LAL 24 Feb 61)

Example, Christian: "...when I err, my error infects everyone who believes me"*
•PP 117 ❖ PP 7:9

Example setting: We must try in our own lives to be such good advertisements for Christianity as will make it attractive
•L 247 ❖ L 8 Nov 52

Excellence, devil is working toward discrediting and then eliminating every kind of human, by misuse of the word "democracy" to mean we must all be "equal"
•SL 164-165, 168-169; WLN 63, 66-67 (see also FL 73) ❖ SL 32:28, 33-37; WLN 4:28, 33-37 (see also FL 3:32)

Excellence, not the business of the Church to encourage the natural man's instinctive hatred of, (re: the choosing of church music)
•CR 97-98 ❖ CR 8:11

Excitement—see Emotion(s); Feeling(s)

Exclusive circles—see also Inner Rings

Exclusive circles among Friends ("Friendship may be 'about' almost nothing except the fact that it excludes")
•FL 114-127, esp. 121-122
❖ FL 4:46-62, esp. 4:54, 55

Exclusive circles: Being "in" is a pleasure that cannot last
•WG 103 ❖ WG 6:15

Exclusive focus on object of love is dangerous to that love; this illustrates a universal law
•GID 280 ❖ GID III 2:6

Exclusivity, secret pleasure of, in belonging to an "Inner Ring"
•WG 93-105 (see also FL 115-127; Inner Rings) ❖ WG ch. 6 (see also FL 4:46-62; Inner Rings)

Excuses, the fact that we make, for our bad behaviour shows that we are aware of the Law of Nature (Law of Right and Wrong)
•MC 20-21 ❖ MC I 1:10

Excuses, true repentance vs. asking God to accept our
•GID 124 ❖ GID I 14:9

Excuses, two remedies for the danger of making
•WG 123-124 ❖ WG 8:4, 5

Excusing: Belief that badness is either an unavoidable legacy from animal an-

cestors or merely a result of being finite encourages us to shift responsibility
- •PP 65-66 ❖ PP 4:14

Excusing vs. forgiveness
- •WG 122-125 ❖ WG 8:3-6

Excusing: We must guard against the feeling that if *all* men are as bad as the Christians say, then badness must be very excusable
- •PP 62 ❖ PP 4:10

Exegesis, I cannot apply to divine matters a method of, which I have rejected in my secular ("profane") studies (re: interpretation of Jesus' words)
- •WG 51 ❖ WG 3:29

Exegetics, I suggest two rules for: 1) never take the images literally; 2) when the purport of the image seems to conflict with the abstract, trust the image
- •LM 52 ❖ LM 10:2

Exercise, Screwtape advises promoting the lie that an excess of physical, and consequent fatigue are helpful in combatting sexual temptation
- •SL 79 ❖ SL 17:4

Existence: Humans not capable of weighing the question of whether creating the world, with its possibility of suffering, was better than not creating
- •PP 35-36, 70 ❖ PP 2:17; 5:1

Existence: I felt it something of an outrage that I had been created without my permission
- •SJ 171 (*see also* GO 32*; SJ 115)
- ❖ SJ 11:8 (*see also* GO 2:20*; SJ 7:19, 20)

Existence: I found in Bergson a refutation of the old idea that the universe might not have existed
- •SJ 204, 211 ❖ SJ 13:11, 20

Existence: "I have even (I'm afraid) caught myself wishing that I had never been born, wh. is sinful. Also meaningless if you think it out"
- •L 166 (*see also* SJ 115-116)
- ❖ L 8 May 39 (*see also* SJ 7: 19-21)

Existence: Lewis describes his early pessimism which would have preferred non-existence itself to even the mildest unhappiness

- •SJ 117 (*see also* SJ 171; Pessimism, Lewis's)
- ❖ SJ 7:21 (*see also* SJ 11:8; Pessimism, Lewis's)

Existence of God—*see* God, existence of

Existence: "When once one has dropped the absurd notion that reality is an arbitrary alternative to 'nothing,' one gives up being a pessimist..."
- •SJ 204 ❖ SJ 13:11

Existentialism, two schools of, mentioned with references to Sartre and Kierkegaard
- •L 297-298
- ❖ L undated letter of Feb 61

"Exit," for me the horror of the Christian universe was that there was no door marked; the materialist's universe offered limited liabilities
- •SJ 171 (*see also* GO 33; *consider also* Limited liabilities)
- ❖ SJ 11:8 (*see also* GO 2:22; *consider also* Limited liabilities)

Expectations—*consider also* Disappointment

Expectations, lowering our: "'Blessed are they that expect little for they shall not be disappointed'"
- •LAL 96 ❖ LAL 24 Feb 61

Expectations, lowering our: People who try to hold an optimistic view of this world become pessimists; people who hold a stern view of it become optimistic*
- •GID 52 ❖ GID I 4:18, 19 (Ques. 5)

Expectations, lowering our: "...the less one can think about happiness on earth, the less, I believe, one suffers"*
- •LAL 96 ❖ LAL 9 Jan 61

Expectations: The more claims we make on life, the more often we will feel injured*
- •SL 95-96 ❖ SL 21:2

Experience—*consider also* Religious experience

Experience: A great philosopher once said that where Virtue is concerned "Experience is the mother of illusion"
- •SL 133 ❖ SL 28:2

Experience, all our, is only an "appear-

ance"; the reality lies "behind the scenes," as illustrated by stage sets in a theatre
- GID 245-249 (see also CR 169-172; LM 78-81) ❖ GID II ch. 13 (see also CR 14:21-32; LM 15:5-15)

Experience and adoration of God through pleasure
- LM 88-91 ❖ LM 17:1-13

Experience and authority supply us with material for our Reason, which in turn tells us about truth and falsehood
- WG 34 ❖ WG 3:3

Experience and learning, variety of, protects one against the errors of the current age
- WG 28-29 ❖ WG 2:10

Experience and taste do not always confirm what is real and what is a substitute (re: religion as reality or substitute)
- CR 38-41 ❖ CR 3:3-9

Experience as an avenue for revelation of God: "...those who seek will find comment sufficient whereby to understand it in such degree as they need..."
- CR 113 ❖ CR 9:26

Experience by itself proves nothing; is colored by the preconceptions we bring to it
- GID 25-26; M 3 ❖ GID I 2:1; M 1:1, 2

Experience essential to full understanding of anything ("One must look both along and at everything")
- GID 212-215 ❖ GID II ch. 6

Experience essential to understanding truths about life (no real teaching possible; every generation starts from scratch)
- L 166 ❖ L 8 May 39

Experience is such an honest thing; you may take any number of wrong turnings, but keep your eyes open and you will not be allowed to go far without warnings
- SJ 177 ❖ SJ 11:14

"Experience," like "sensitivity," is a potentiality, therefore neutral; neither can be an end to Christians
- CR 24 ❖ CR 2:38

Experience, many people draw from Keats the strange doctrine that, in itself is good (re: sub-Christian or anti-Christian values derived from literature)
- CR 16-17 ❖ CR 2:13

Experience of God the best material for correcting our abstract conception of God
- M 90 (see also GID 170*; MC 135-136) ❖ M 11:14 (see also GID I 20:Reply-15*; MC IV 1:2, 3)

Experience of God's blessings ("pleasures") essential to our adoration of Him; without it we will not have "tasted and seen"
- LM 91 ❖ LM 17:13

Experience of something, such as pain, vs. scientific-like knowledge about it (looking "along" vs. looking at)
- GID 212-215 ❖ GID II ch. 6

Experience of something, such as pain, seems somehow unconnected and irrelevant to our reading or writing about it (re: writing of The Problem of Pain)
- L 172 ❖ L 3 Dec 39

Experience of spiritual things essential to our understanding of them ("'Spiritual things are spiritually discerned'" —WG 65)
- WG 54-73 ❖ WG ch. 4

Experience, reason, and authority: "...on these three, mixed in varying proportions all our knowledge depends"
- CR 41 (see also CR 43; WLN 17) ❖ CR 3:9 (see also CR 3:12; WLN 2:6)

Experience, religious—see Religious experience

Experience vs. intellectual apprehension: While we are loving or bearing pain we are not intellectually apprehending personality or pain
- GID 65-66 (see also L 172*, 221; SJ 217-219) ❖ GID I 5:8 (see also L 3 Dec 39*; 27 Sep 49; SJ 14:9, 10)

Experience, what we learn from, depends on the kind of philosophy we bring to it
- M 3 (see also GID 25-26) ❖ M 1:2 (see also GID I 2:1)

Experiences, anti-Christian, as a possible means of God working on us
•MC 162-163 ❖ MC IV 7:7

Experiences, most human, cannot be communicated by Scientific language; require the use of Poetic language
•CR 138, 140 ❖ CR 11:20, 23

Experiences, our natural, are only like pencilled lines on flat paper; in the risen life we shall experience "the real world" for the first time
•WG 68-69 ❖ WG 4:22-24

Experiences, Poetic language can convey to us the quality of, which we have not had, or perhaps can never have...
•CR 133 ❖ CR 11:8, 9

Experiences, religious, did not occur at all in my childhood, although I was taught the usual things and made to say my prayers and taken to church
•SJ 7 ❖ SJ 1:5

Experiences which arise from natural causes become religious in religious people (re: fear in the Psalmists)*
•CR 125 (see also LM 30)
❖ CR 10:31 (see also LM 6:4-6)

Experiment, cosmic: My real fear is not of materialism; I am more afraid that we are really rats in a trap—or worse still, rats in a laboratory*
•GO 33 ❖ GO 2:22

Exploitation, Man's, of other men and nature an indication of how we would treat other-worldly creatures*
•WLN 89-90 ❖ WLN 6:18-22

Expressions—see also Jargon

Expressions of our own circle, we must be on guard against using; they may delude ourselves as well as mystify outsiders
•GID 256-257 ❖ GID II 15:11-13

Expressions, religious, like "God is love" not merely expressions of emotion; they convey real information if you will meet them half-way—with good will
•CR 129-141, esp. 135-137, 141
❖ CR ch. 11, esp. 11:12-18, 25

Expressions used in Christianity: Retain what is helpful to you; leave alone what is not*
•MC 157 ❖ MC IV 5:9

Expressions used in Christianity, some common, related to the idea of "being born again"
•MC 163-164 ❖ MC IV 7:10, 11

External actions, human beings judge one another by their; God judges them by their moral choices
•MC 85, 86 ❖ MC III 4:6, 7

External obedience may be deceiving: "...a cold, self-righteous prig who goes regularly to church may be nearer to hell than a prostitute"*
•MC 94-95 ❖ MC III 5:14

External obedience, we can deceive ourselves by our*
•SL 54 ❖ SL 12:2

Externals, God is not deceived by
•MC 76 ❖ MC III 2:6

Externals of Christianity made no appeal to my sense of beauty; Christianity was associated for me with ugly architecture, ugly music, and bad poetry
•SJ 171-172 ❖ SJ 11:8

Extramarital relationships—see Infidelity

Extraterrestrial life, arguments for and against the presence of, both used as arguments against Christianity
•CR 174; GID 40; M 50; WLN 83-84
❖ CR 14:46; GID I 3:5; M 7:10; WLN 6:1-4

Extraterrestrial life, contact with: At the very least we shall corrupt any alien rational species with our vices and infect it with our diseases
•CR 173 ❖ CR 14:40

Extraterrestrial life, contact with: Only if we had a redemptive function would contact between us and unknown races be other than a calamity
•WLN 88 ❖ WLN 6:14-16

Extraterrestrial life, contact with: "I have wondered...whether the vast astronomical distances may not be God's quarantine precautions"
•WLN 91 ❖ WLN 6:24

Extraterrestrial life, contact with: I fear the practical problems which will arise if we ever meet rational creatures which

are not human
•WLN 89 ❖ WLN 6:18-20
Extraterrestrial life, contact with: "I look forward with horror to contact with the other inhabited planets, if there are such"
•GID 267 (*see also* Space travel)
❖ GID II 16:57, 58 (*see also* Space travel)
Extraterrestrial life, contact with: The starry heavens would become an object to which good men could look up only with feelings of shame, pity, and guilt
•WLN 90 ❖ WLN 6:20
Extraterrestrial life, contact with: "We know what our race does to strangers. Man destroys or enslaves every species he can"
•WLN 89 ❖ WLN 6:18
Extraterrestrial life, contact with: We would probably send missionaries, who would probably try to "civilize" the "natives"
•WLN 90 ❖ WLN 6:21
Extraterrestrial life: If other rational species exist, it is not necessary to suppose that they also have fallen; this shows the real freedom of man*
•PP 85 (*see also* WLN 86-87)
❖ PP 5:11 (*see also* WLN 6:10, 11)
Extraterrestrial life: If there is life on other planets, we shall hardly find it nearer than the stars
•CR 173 ❖ CR 14:39
Extraterrestrial life: In the drama of earth's history, only the Author knows the outcome; and the audience (angels, "company of heaven") may have an inkling*
•WLN 105 ❖ WLN 7:22
Extraterrestrial life: It is wise to face the possibility that the whole human race is a local pocket of evil within the larger universe*
•PP 62-64 ❖ PP 4:10, 11
Extraterrestrial life: Lewis speculates what it would be like to visit other worlds and meet beings wholly different from us (*if* we were not fallen)
•WLN 88-89 ❖ WLN 6:17

Extraterrestrial life: Other rational species may not exist; there is not at present a shred of empirical evidence that they do
•WLN 91 ❖ WLN 6:24
Extraterrestrial life, possible kinds of, which might be discovered: rational but innocent; both good and bad; needing Redemption but not given it; diabolical
•CR 174-176 ❖ CR 14:48-52
Extraterrestrial life, question of*
•M 51-52, 122-123 (*see also* GID 100)
❖ M 7:13; 14:24 (*see also* GID I 10:42)
Extraterrestrial life: Question of whether other rational species in the universe (if they exist) are fallen and, if so, whether they have been redeemed
•WLN 86-88 ❖ WLN 6:10-14
Extraterrestrial life: Question of whether there are animals anywhere except on earth and, if they exist, whether they have rational souls
•WLN 84-86 ❖ WLN 6:6-9
Extraterrestrial life, question of, explored and rejected as relevant to the claims of Christianity*
•WLN 83-92 ❖ WLN ch. 6
Extraterrestrial life: "We are not fit yet to visit other worlds. We have filled our own with massacre, torture, syphilis, famine..."
•CR 173 ❖ CR 14:41
Extraterrestrial life: We do not know about such things, and it is to be expected that we would not know*
•GID 43-44 ❖ GID I 3:9, 10
Extraterrestrial life: We have been shown the plan only in so far as it concerns ourselves; we do not know about other life in the universe
•MC 170 ❖ MC IV 8:10
Extraterrestrial life: We need to know more about these other species before we can say what theological corollaries or difficulties their discovery would raise
•CR 174 ❖ CR 14:47
Extremes, all, except extreme devotion to God serve the devil's purpose (—

Screwtape, re: extreme patriotism and extreme pacifism)
- •SL 33-35 (*see also* SL 25)
- ❖ SL 7:2, 3 (*see also* SL 5:1)

Extremes: Devil always sends errors into the world in pairs of opposites; we must go straight through between both errors
- •MC 160 (*see also* WLN 94-95; WG 108)
- ❖ MC IV 6:4 (*see also* WLN 7:4; WG 7:3)

Extremes: Screwtape advises Wormwood that if a patient can't be kept out of the Church, he ought to be attached to some faction ("party") within it*
- •SL 72-73, 75 ❖ SL 16:2, 5

Extremism—*see* Fanaticism

Eye, if thy right, offend thee...
- •L 228 (*see also* WG 118)
- ❖ L 23 Apr 51 (*see also* WG 7:17)

Eye, The Seeing (chapter title)
- •CR 167-176 ❖ CR ch. 14

Eyes: When reason itself becomes the object of study, it is as if we take out our own eyes to look at them; this yields "subjectivism"
- •CR 72 (*see also* L 221)
- ❖ CR 6:2 (*see also* L 27 Sep 49)

Ezekiel 16 mentioned as "one of the most moving and graphic chapters of the whole Old Testament"
- •RP 130 ❖ RP 12:9

Ezekiel, Lewis acknowledges a "heavy debt" to, in his characterization of angels in the Space Trilogy
- •LAL 13 ❖ LAL 4/iii/53

Facade, all our experience is only a; reality lies "behind the scenes"
- •GID 245-249 (*see also* CR 169-172; LM 78-81) ❖ GID II ch. 13 (*see also* CR 14:21-32; LM 15: 5-15)

Facade, what appears to us as reality is really only a, —both ourselves and the things around us (re: attempting contact with ultimate Reality)
- •CR 169-170 (*see also* LM 78-81)
- ❖ CR 14:21-24 (*see also* LM 15:5-15)

Face, Lewis describes his, as an adolescent: "I am the kind of person who gets told, 'And take that look off your face too'"
- •SJ 94 (*see also* SJ 188, 200- 201*, 217)
- ❖ SJ 6:18 (*see also* SJ 12:10; 13:5*; 14:8)

Face of God turns on each of us in the end, conferring either glory or shame
- •WG 13 (*see also* GID 47; WG 18-19)
- ❖ WG 1:10 (*see also* GID I 3:17; WG 1:15)

Face of God, when we see the, we shall know that we have always known it
- •FL 190 (*see also* SL 147*)
- ❖ FL 6:44 (*see also* SL 31:4*)

Faces of those we love are difficult to remember after they're gone; all the expressions crowd together in our memory and cancel out into a blur
- •GO 16-17❖ GO 1:31

Faces, what we see when we think we are looking into the depths of Scripture may sometimes be only the reflection of our own silly

---

* These items reflect some interpretation on the part of the editor; the idea will not be found in these exact words. *See Introduction, p. ix.*

** These items are ideas of Lewis's which the editor has placed under a topic Lewis did not there intend to address. *See Introduction, p. ix.*
Entries without asterisks are not necessarily exact quotes, but the idea should be easy to find as worded.

•RP 121 ❖ RP 12:3

Facing God—*see* Contact with God

Fact, God as the ultimate; the fountain of all other facthood
•M 6-7, 87, 88, 91, 95, 110, 155; MC 158
❖ M 2:5, 6; 11:9-11, 15; 12:1; 14:4; 16:22; MC IV 6:2

Faction(s)—*consider also* Coterie(s)

Faction ("party"), Screwtape advises Wormwood that if a patient can't be kept out of Church he ought to be attached to some, within it
•SL 72-73, 75 ❖ SL 16:2, 5

Factory analogy to character judgement: "To judge the management of a factory, you must consider not only the output but the plant"
•MC 178 (*see also* GID 59) ❖ MC IV 10:5, 6 (*see also* GID I 4:52 (Ques. 12)

Factory work prevents people from giving full play to their faculties; this is an insoluble problem
•GID 48 ❖ GID I 4:1

Failure in overcoming chronic temptation, encouragement regarding ("...the only fatal thing is to lose one's temper and give it up")
•L 199 (*see also* MC 93-94; WG 132*; Moral effort) ❖ L 20 Jan 42 (*see also* MC III 5:12; WG 9:13*; Moral effort)

Failures, God will be merciful to our, but He cannot accept compromise
•WG 130 ❖ WG 9:9

Failures will be forgiven; it is acquiescence that is fatal
•L 199; MC 94; WG 132
❖ L 20 Jan 40; MC III 5:12; WG 9:13

Fair Beauty of the Lord, The (chapter title)
•RP 44-53 ❖ RP ch. 5

Fair play, rule of, seems to be known by all people everywhere
•MC 17-26 (*see also* CR 44-45, 72-81; M 34-38; RP 13; book *The Abolition of Man*) ❖ MC I 1:1 to 2:8 (*see also* CR 4:1-27, 6:1-23; M 5:1-11; RP 2:8; book *The Abolition of Man*)

Fairness and honesty in our work: "Few of us have always, in full measure, given our pupils or patients or clients

...what we were being paid for"
•RP 13 ❖ RP 2:8

Fairness in our work: We have not always done quite our fair share of tiresome work if we found a colleague who would do it
•RP 13-14 ❖ RP 2:8

Fairies are still believed in many parts of Ireland and greatly feared
•LAL 33 ❖ LAL Oct 9th 54

Fairy tales, I turned to writing, because that seemed the form best fitted for what I wanted to say
•L 260, 307 ❖ L undated letter just before 2 Feb 55; 2 Dec 62

Fairy tales, Lewis describes his youthful enjoyment of
•SJ 54-55 ❖ SJ 3:13

Fairy tales, you and I who still enjoy, have less reason to wish childhood back; we have kept its pleasures and added some grown-up ones as well
•LAL 17 ❖ LAL Jun 22d 53

Faith (chapter title)
•MC 121-126, 126-131
❖ MC III ch. 11, 12

Faith—*see also* Belief; Trust; *consider also* Grace; Obstacles to Christian faith; Righteousness by faith/grace

Faith, a mere change of scene can decrease my, at first; God is less credible when I pray in a hotel bedroom than when I am in College
•CR 42 ❖ CR 3:10

Faith, absence of, that your prayer will be answered not necessarily a sin; Our Lord had no such assurance when He prayed in Gethsemane
•LM 60 ❖ LM 11:12

Faith as a choice: The efficacy of prayer cannot be either asserted or denied without an exercise of the will— choosing or rejecting faith
•M 180-181 ❖ M App. B:20, 21

Faith as a gift we must pray for
•CR 43; GID 174 ❖ CR 3:12; GID I 21:5

Faith as a virtue: A firm and settled belief is required because "though Reason is divine, human reasoners are not"
•CR 43 ❖ CR 3:12

Faith as confidence vs. intellectual assent (swimming analogy)
•L 199 (*see also* CR 42-43; GID 172-173; MC 122-123; WLN 23-25)
❖ L 20 Jan 42 (*see also* CR 3:11; GID I 21:2; MC III 11:2-4; WLN 2:12, 13)

Faith as intellectual assent usually involves a degree of excess subjective certitude, even in matters of science and history
•GID 173-174 ❖ GID I 21:4

Faith as the art of holding on to things your reason has once accepted in spite of your changing moods
•MC 123-124 ❖ MC III 11:5

Faith as the art of holding on to things your reason has once accepted in spite of apparent evidence against them*
•WLN 13-30 (*see also* CR 42-43)
❖ WLN ch. 2 (*see also* CR 3:10-12)

Faith as the power of continuing to believe what we once thought to be true until cogent reasons for honestly changing our minds are brought before us
•CR 42 ❖ CR 3:10

Faith as the power to go on believing not in the teeth of reason but in the teeth of our feelings and emotions
•CR 43 ❖ CR 3:11, 12

Faith: Assent or confidence in God moves us from the logic of speculative thought into what might be called the "logic" of personal relations
•WLN 29-30 ❖ WLN 2:18

Faith, being around unbelievers makes, harder even when their opinions on other subjects are known to be worthless
•CR 42 ❖ CR 3:10

Faith, difficulties as threat to: "The conclusion I dread is not, 'So there's no God after all,' but, 'So this is what God's really like...'"*
•GO 5 ❖ GO 1:9

Faith, discussion of
•CR 41-43; MC 121-131; GID 172-176; WLN 13-30 ❖ CR 3:9-12; GID I ch. 21; MC III ch. 11; WLN ch. 2

Faith does not exclude us from dismay, as evidenced by Gethsemane
•L 285 (*see also* L 166, 189-191, 210-211, 250; Gethsemane) ❖ L 29 Apr 59 (*see also* L 8 May 39; undated letter just after 11 Aug 40; undated letter of 1947; 17 Jul 53; Gethsemane)

Faith, elements of, involve philosophical argument, our own moral and spiritual experience, and history
•GID 175 (*see also* WLN 17)
❖ GID I 21:8, 9 (*see also* WLN 2:6)

Faith: Existence of God is a speculative question as long as it is a question at all; once answered, you are faced with a Person who demands your confidence
•WLN 26-27 (*see also* MC 123)
❖ WLN 2:14 (*see also* MC III 11:4, 5)

Faith healing mentioned by Screwtape as a useful addition to "mere Christianity" ("If they must be Christians, let them...be Christians with a difference")
•SL 115-116 ❖ SL 25:1

Faith healing, question of
•L 224-225, 226 (*see also* CR 149-150; L 251) ❖ L 7 Dec 50; undated letter just before 7 Feb 51 (*see also* CR 12:23; L 17 Jul 53)

Faith, how many who lose their, have been honestly *argued* out of it?
•CR 42-43; MC 124
❖ CR 3:10; MC III 11:6

Faith, I base, on authority which has grown up in the Church and won the assent of great doctors
•GID 181 (*see also* PP 71-72)
❖ GID I 22:11 (*see also* PP 5:2)

Faith, I think the life of, is easier to me because of these memories (of school terms and the hope of the holiday)
•SJ 36-37 ❖ SJ 2:16

Faith, if our, were stronger we might be less tenderly treated (re: not drawing conclusions about God's favor toward us when our prayers are granted)*
•WLN 10-11 ❖ WLN 1:21

Faith in Christ, out of, good actions will inevitably come
•MC 129 ❖ MC III 12:7

Faith in God, a Christian's, is often more

than may be merited by philosophical premises, but less than He deserves
•GID 173, 176 ❖ GID I 21:4, 9

Faith in God and understanding of what He is like is best acquired through experience of Him—e.g., in the moral and devotional life*
•M 90 (*see also* GID 170; MC 135-136; Experience) ❖ M 11:14 (*see also* GID I 20:Reply-15; MC IV 1:2, 3; Experience)

Faith in God not parallel to faith of a scientist trying to prove a hypothesis when evidence is against it; love involves trusting beyond the evidence
•WLN 13-30, esp. 26
❖ WLN ch. 2, esp. 2:13, 14

Faith in God (or in a person), difficulty of sustaining, while we are waiting to hear from Him
•L 219 ❖ L 2 Sep 49

Faith in God: "Our relation to those who trusted us only after we were proved innocent in court cannot be the same as…to those who trusted us all through"
•WLN 29 ❖ WLN 2:17

Faith in God: "That demand for our confidence which a true friend makes of us is exactly the same that a confidence trickster would make"
•WLN 28 ❖ WLN 2:16

Faith in God: "The saying 'Blessed are those that have not seen and have believed'…says in effect, 'You should have known Me better'"
•WLN 28-29 ❖ WLN 2:17

Faith in Heaven weakens when used for the purpose of promoting hope of reunion with loved ones
•FL 189-190 (*see also* GO 28-29, 79; L 290; RP 41; SJ 231*)
❖ FL 6:41-43 (*see also* GO 2:13-16; 4:21; L 3 Dec 59; RP 4:16; SJ 15:3*)

Faith in prayer based upon having a certain idea of God's character
•LM 49 (*see also* WLN 7-8, 25-27*)
❖ LM 9:8 (*see also* WLN 1:14, 15; 2:13, 14*)

Faith in prayer: "Even the kind that says

'Help thou my unbelief' may make way for a miracle"
•LM 60 ❖ LM 11:12

Faith in prayer: "For most of us the prayer in Gethsemane is the only model. Removing mountains can wait"
•LM 57-61, esp. 60
❖ LM ch. 11, esp. 11:10

Faith in prayer: In Mark 11, there is no doubt at all that what we are to believe is precisely that we shall get all the things we ask for
•CR 147 ❖ CR 12:14

Faith in prayer: The efficacy of prayer cannot be either asserted or denied without an exercise of the will—choosing or rejecting faith
•M 180-181 ❖ M App. B:20, 21

Faith in prayer: "The faith that moves mountains is a gift from Him who created mountains"
•CR 150 ❖ CR: 12:25

Faith in prayer, two seemingly contradictory kinds of, recommended by Scripture: Praying "Thy will be done" and praying with a sure belief
•CR 142-151, esp. 142-144
❖ CR ch. 12, esp. 12:1-9

Faith in prayer: "…we ought perhaps to regard the worker of miracles, however rare, as the true Christian norm and ourselves as spiritual cripples"
•CR 150 ❖ CR 12:25

Faith in prayer: Whatever else faith may mean, I feel quite sure it does not mean psychological certitude manufactured from within
•CR 150 ❖ CR 12:25

Faith (intellectual assent) a necessary precondition for faith as trust or confidence
•GID 173 ❖ GID I 21:2

Faith, justification by: Lewis mentions that a Methodist complained that he said nothing about this in his BBC talks (which later became *Mere Christianity*)
•L 198 (*see also* Righteousness by faith/grace) ❖ L 21 Dec 41 (*see also* Righteousness by faith/grace)

Faith, Lewis describes his, as a "house of

cards": "If my house has collapsed at one blow, that is because it was a house of cards"
•GO 42 (*see also* GO 44-45, 48, 61)
❖ GO 3:3 (*see also* GO 3:5-7, 13, 36)

Faith, Lewis discusses the kinds of, which we see exercised in the miracles of Jesus
•CR 144-146 ❖ CR 12:10, 11

Faith moving mountains: The point is that the condition of doing such a mighty work is unwavering, unhesitating faith
•CR 146-147 ❖ CR 12:13

Faith moving mountains, whether Jesus was using hyperbole when He talked about
•CR 146 ❖ CR 12:13

Faith not a state of mind which can be "worked up"
•LM 60 ❖ LM 11:11

Faith not the same thing as knowledge; does not require the same kind of proof as Science does*
•WLN 14-16 (*see also* WLN 92; MC 32-33) ❖ WLN 2:3, 4 (*see also* WLN 6:28; MC I 4:2, 3)

Faith, obstinacy in: "There are times when we can do all that a fellow creature needs if he will only trust us"—may require trust in the teeth of senses
•WLN 23-24 (*see also* CR 42-43; MC 122-123) ❖ WLN 2:12 (*see also* CR 3:10-12; MC III 11:2-5)

Faith of a child which accepts imagery such as harps and golden streets may be deceived, yet in the deepest sense not deceived
•WG 66 ❖ WG 4:19

"Faith" of a kind often generated in children, which regards God as a magician: Its disappointment may be of no religious importance
•SJ 20-21 ❖ SJ 1:22

Faith, one must train the habit of
•MC 123-124 (*see also* CR 41-42)
❖ MC III 11:5, 6 (*see also* CR 3:9)

Faith, one of the causes of our weak, may be the secret wish that our faith should *not* be very strong

•CR 43 (*see also* LM 114; Obstacles to Christian faith) ❖ CR 3:12 (*see also* LM 21:7; Obstacles to Christian faith)

Faith, only the practice of, resulting in the habit of Faith will ever cement our belief so that we are not continually assailed by doubts
•CR 41-42 ❖ CR 3:9

Faith, only, vouches for the connection between prayer and event
•LM 48-49 ❖ LM 9:6-8

Faith, operation of, is to retain for the will and the intellect what is irresistible and obvious during the moments of special grace
•GID 176 ❖ GID I 21:9

Faith, our struggle is to achieve and retain, on a much lower level—to believe that there *is* a Listener, and that He will listen to our prayers
•LM 61 (*see also* LM 67-68)
❖ LM 11:15 (*see also* LM 13:1)

Faith: "Reason may win truths; without Faith she will retain them just so long as Satan pleases"
•CR 43 ❖ CR 3:12

Faith, religious, which is purely a result of conditioning mentioned by Screwtape
•SL 110-111 ❖ SL 24:1

Faith, Screwtape laments that suffering is largely ineffective as an attack on, since humans have been told it is an essential part of Redemption
•SL 27 ❖ SL 5:3

Faith: "Some people feel guilty about their anxieties and regard them as a defect of faith. I don't agree at all"
•LM 41 ❖ LM 8:5

Faith, steps in training the habit of
•MC 124 ❖ MC III 11:6

Faith: Surely the faith Peter lacked was faith in the particular event (walking on water), not a faith in God's goodness
•CR 145-146 ❖ CR 12:11

Faith, tests of our, not sent in order that God might find out its quality; God already knows that—they show *us* its quality

•GO 61 (*see also* PP 101-102)
❖ GO 3:36 (*see also* PP 6:13)
Faith, the American in the old story defined, as "the power of believing what we know to be untrue" (Lewis follows with his own definition)
•CR 42 ❖ CR 3:10
Faith, the eye of: "To some, God is discoverable everywhere; to others, nowhere. Much depends on the seeing eye"*
•CR 171 (*see also* CR 172)
❖ CR 14:29 (*see also* CR 14:34)
Faith: "The moment one asks oneself, 'Do I believe?' all belief seems to go"
•L 221 ❖ L 27 Sep 49
Faith, two kinds of: a settled intellectual assent, and trust or confidence
•GID 172-173 (*see also* L 199; WLN 23-24) ❖ GID I 21:2 (*see also* L 20 Jan 42; WLN 2:12)
Faith, undermining of, and prevention of the formation of virtues listed by Screwtape as "the real business" of Hell
•SL 25 ❖ SL 5:1
Faith vs. Works—*see also* Moral effort; Works
Faith vs. Works: Faith arises after a man has tried his level best and found that he fails*
•MC 94, 124-125, 127-131 (*see also* CR 169*; PP 065) ❖ MC III 5:12; 11:7; 12:3-9 (*see also* CR 14:20, 21*; PP 4:13)
Faith vs. Works: "I personally rely on the paradoxical text; 'Work out your own salvation...for it is God that worketh in you'"*
•GID 55 (*see also* LM 49; MC 130)
❖ GID I 4:30, 31 (Ques. 8) (*see also* LM 9:11; MC III 12:8)
Faith vs. Works: In the parable of the Sheep and the Goats, you see nothing about Predestination or even faith—all depends on works
•L 251 ❖ L 3 Aug 53
Faith vs. Works, question of, is like asking which blade in a pair of scissors is most necessary
•MC 129 ❖ MC III 12:7

Faith: We must expect that God's operations will often appear to us far from beneficent and far from wise, since His knowledge of our needs exceeds our own
•WLN 24-25 ❖ WLN 2:13
Faith, we shall proceed to, only by acting as if we had it
•L 199 ❖ L 20 Jan 42
Faith: Without a firm belief and the assistance of Grace, our feelings will continually assault our conviction like a blast furnace against a snowflake
•CR 41-43 ❖ CR 3:9-12
Faith, you need much more, in science than in theology (quote from unknown source)
•L 113 ❖ L 30 Mar 27
Faith: "You never know how much you really believe anything until its truth or falsehood becomes a matter of life and death to you"
•GO 25, 41-43 ❖ GO 2:9; 3:3, 4
Faithfulness or perseverance in the Christian life, Screwtape lists obstacles to: "The routine of adversity, the gradual decay of youthful loves..."*
•SL 132 ❖ SL 28:1
Faithfulness or perseverance, obstacles to Christian: old habits*
•SL 11 (*consider also* Obstacles to Christian faith) ❖ SL 2:1 (*consider also* Obstacles to Christian faith)
Faithfulness or perseverance, obstacles to Christian: vague guilt*
•SL 54-56 ❖ SL 12:3, 4
Faithfulness, Screwtape laments that suffering is probably not an obstacle to, since humans have been told that it is an essential part of Redemption*
•SL 27 ❖ SL 5:3
Faithfulness: Screwtape rues the man who feels that every trace of God has vanished, and asks why he has been forsaken, and still obeys*
•SL 39 ❖ SL 8:4
Fall—*consider also* Unfallen man
Fall as one of the beliefs which unite all Christians everywhere
•GID 336 ❖ GID IV Letter 9

Fall, at the, the will of man had no resource but to force back by main strength the new thoughts and desires arising from the tidal wave of mere nature
•PP 82 ❖ PP 5:10

Fall did not deprave our knowledge of the Law in the same degree as it depraved our power to fulfil it
•CR 79 (see also Depravity, doctrine of Total) ❖ CR 6:19 (see also Depravity, doctrine of Total)

Fall, doctrine of the, and the doctrine of Evolution not related in any important way
•L 218 ❖ L 1 Aug 49

Fall, doctrine of the, states that man is now a horror to himself and to God and ill-adapted to the universe because of his abuse of free will
•PP 69, 72 ❖ PP 5:1, 3

Fall enabled God to express His goodness through the total drama of a world of free agents and their rebellion against Him
•PP 84 (see also PP 110-111)
❖ PP 5:11 (see also PP 7:2)

Fall, equality (as in marriage) became a necessity due to the
•WG 113-116 (see also MC 102-103)
❖ WG 7:10-15 (see also MC III 6:17)

Fall: First sin described by St. Augustine as the result of Pride, of the movement whereby a creature tries to set up on its own
•PP 75 ❖ PP 5:5

Fall, Genesis story of the, as a scriptural myth: Apple was a magic apple of knowledge; in the developed doctrine, story is simply one of disobedience
•PP 71-72 (see also Genesis)
❖ PP 5:2 (see also Genesis)

Fall of Man, a version offered by Lewis of the
•PP 77-85 ❖ PP 5:6-11

Fall of Man as part of Christian beliefs*
•MC 45 ❖ MC II 1:4

Fall of Man created conflict between "spirit" and "nature" which causes disintegration and death of the body; Christ's death is the remedy
•M 125-126 ❖ M 14:28-30

Fall of Man happened because he tried to set up on his own
•MC 52-53 ❖ MC II 3:2-6

Fall of Man may be unique in the universe, yet its redemption spreads outward and exalts all creatures
•M 122-123 (see also WLN 87-88)
❖ M 14:24-26 (see also WLN 6:13, 14)

Fall of Man, Science has nothing to say either for or against the doctrine of the
•PP 72-74, esp. 74 ❖ PP 5:3

Fall of Man, The (chapter title)
•PP 69-88 ❖ PP ch. 5

Fall of Man: Was it in accordance with the will of God?
•MC 51-54 ❖ MC II 3:1-6

Fall of Man was not the result of sexual corruption, but the book of Genesis suggests sexual corruption was caused by the Fall
•MC 53 ❖ MC II 3:6

Fall, our habitual gravitation away from God and toward self is a product of the
•PP 76 (see also PP 83, 91)
❖ PP 5:5 (see also PP 5:10; 6:3)

Fall, Paganism includes a hazy doctrine of, but no real doctrine of Creation
•GID 149 (consider also Paganism)
❖ GID I 17:6 (consider also Paganism)

Fall: Question of whether other rational species in the universe (if they exist) are fallen and, if so, whether they have been redeemed
•WLN 86-88 ❖ WLN 6:10-14

Fall: Question of whether the eating of the fruit [in Genesis] was literal or not is of no consequence
•PP 80 ❖ PP 5:8

Fall, since the, no organization or way of life has a natural tendency to go right (regarding family life)
• GID 284 ❖ GID III 3:6

Fall, story of, as an example of a myth built into a systematic and fully believed theology (vis-a-vis myths told by primitive man)
•L 303 ❖ L 21 Mar 62

Fall, turning to God became a painful ef-

fort after the, since man's inclination had become self-ward
•PP 83 (see also PP 91)
❖ PP 5:10 (see also PP 6:3)

Fall, work became punitive because of the
•L 187-188 ❖ L 16 Jul 40

Fallen creatures, we are all, and all very hard to live with
•LAL 110 ❖ LAL 8 Nov 62

Fallen Man, faults of newly, included pride, ambition, self-admiration, competition, envy, and insecurity
•PP 83 ❖ PP 5:10

Fallen Man, natural immortality would be the one utterly hopeless destiny for
• M 129-130 (see also LAL 47*)
❖ M 14:35 (see also LAL 26/10/55*)

Fallen Man not simply an imperfect creature but also a rebel who must lay down his arms
•MC 59 ❖ MC II 4:7

Falsehood—see also Dishonesty

Falsehood is habit-forming (a warning to dishonest tax-collectors)
•RP 15-16 ❖ RP 2:10

Familiarity and intimacy discussed: "I am not sure that the distinction between intimacy and familiarity is really very profound"
•L 136-138 ❖ L 9 Sep 29

Families: The very same conditions of intimacy which make Affection possible also make possible a peculiarly incurable hatred

Family; Family members—see also Domestic; Home; Loved ones

Family courtesy, importance of
•FL 66-70; GID 282-286
❖ FL 3:22-26; GID III ch. 3

Family, does not our, seem at first rather improbable? One's relatives are not necessarily like oneself—still less, like one's idea of that self (re: Hebrews as the "Chosen" people)
•CR 117 ❖ CR 10:6

Family intended to be the image on the natural level of the Christian Body
•WG 112 ❖ WG 7:9

Family, it is extraordinary how inconvenient it is for your, if you get up

early to go to Church
•GID 61 ❖ GID I 4:60 (Ques. 16)

Family life, fundamental principles of
•GID 284-286 ❖ GID III 3:6-11

Family life not a panacea; it is difficult and has its own temptations and corruptions
•GID 284-286 ❖ GID III 3:4-11

Family may become indignant when a member rises *above* the homely *ethos* as well as when one should fall from it into something worse
•FL 70-73, esp. 73
❖ FL 3:27-32, esp. 3:32

Family members, how to forgive
•LAL 92-93 ❖ LAL 28 Oct 60

Family members may develop an appreciation for one another which might otherwise never develop
•FL 58-60 ❖ FL 3:10, 11

Family members, Screwtape discusses prayers for, ("Make sure they are always very 'spiritual'..."; keep attention on grievances, etc.)
•SL 16-17 ❖ SL 3:3

Family members who are difficult: "It's the mixture, or alternation, of resentment and affection that is so very uneasy, isn't it?"
• LAL 92-93 ❖ LAL 28 Oct 60

Family members who change may be ridiculed; "Change is a threat to Affection"
•FL 70-73 (see also L 274)
❖ FL 3:27-32 (see also L 10 Feb 57)

Family needs redemption; must be offered to God
•GID 285 ❖ GID III 3:6

Family of God—see also Body of Christ

Family of God: "Those who are, or can become, His sons, are our real brothers... It is spiritual, not biological, kinship that counts"*
•WLN 91 ❖ WLN 6:22

Family offers us the first step beyond self-love; patriotism offers us the first step beyond family selfishness
•FL 41❖ FL 2:33

Family ("our nearest and dearest") must be turned down when they come be-

tween us and our obedience to God
- FL 172 ❖ FL 6:17

Family relations—*see also* Domestic...; Domesticity; Relations, interpersonal

Family relations: Domestic hatred usually expresses itself more in the manner of speech than in the words themselves*
- SL 17-18 ❖ SL 3:5

Family relations: Screwtape mentions the diabolical value of "a good settled habit of mutual annoyance: daily pinpricks"
- SL 15, 17-18 ❖ SL 3:1, 5

Family relations: Screwtape mentions the irritating mannerisms which each person assumes the other is doing just to annoy
- SL 17 ❖ SL 3:4

Family relations: Screwtape mentions the diabolical value of a person's oversensitive interpretations of everything said and done
- SL 17-18 ❖ SL 3:5

Family relations: Story of "Mrs. Fidget" who gave unreasonable and unwanted service to her family in the name of "love"
- FL 73-76; 82-83 (*see also* L 198-199*; MC 167*; SL 121*, 123*)
❖ FL 3:33-36, 45 (*see also* L undated letter just before 20 Jan 42*; MC IV 7:3*; SL 26:2, 5*)

Family relations: "What is commonly called 'sensitiveness' is the most powerful engine of domestic tyranny, sometimes a life-long tyranny"*
- RP 14 ❖ RP 2:9

Family, Screwtape decries the: "...[it] is like the organism, only worse; for the members are more distinct, yet also united..."
- SL 82 ❖ SL 18:5

Family, Screwtape describes with contempt a loving Christian
- SL 102 ❖ SL 22:4

Family structure as a model for Christian membership (each person is almost a species in himself; they are not interchangeable)

- WG 110-112 ❖ WG 7:6-9

Fanaticism: Devil always sends errors into the world in pairs of opposites; we must go straight through between both errors*
- MC 160 (*see also* WLN 94-95; WG 108)
❖ MC IV 6:4 (*see also* WLN 7:4; WG 7:3)

Fanaticism: Exaggeration of a doctrine results in danger of reaction—making the opposite error (re: extreme views of the doctrine of the Second Coming)*
- WLN 95 ❖ WLN 7:4

Fanaticism: We may embrace tasks never intended for us
- WG 129-130 ❖ WG 9:8

Fanatics: "It is great men, potential saints, not little men, who become merciless fanatics"—may become ready to kill for their cause
- RP 28 ❖ RP 3:17

Fanatics who claim to have an unanswerable intuition that all strong drink is forbidden really can have nothing of the sort
- WG 37-38 (*see also* L 263)
❖ WG 3:8 (*see also* L 14 May 55)

Fascism and Communism potent because of the good they contain or imitate
- L 176 ❖ L 17 Jan 40

Fashion(s)—*see also* Modern...

Fashions and Vogues, Screwtape points out that the desire for novelty is indispensable if Hell is to produce
- SL 117 ❖ SL 25:4

Fashions: "...I am conscious of a partly pathological hostility to what is fashionable"
- L 179 ❖ L 26 Mar 40

Fashions in thought, according to Screwtape, are useful to distract the attention of men from their real dangers
- SL 117-118 ❖ SL 25:5

Fasting—*consider also* Asceticism; Self-denial

Fasting as practise for "meeting the real enemy"
- GID 54 ❖ GID I 4:25 (Ques. 8)

Fasting asserts the will against the appetite—the reward being self-mastery

and the danger pride
- PP 112 ❖ PP 7:3

Fasting: "...every missed meal can be converted into a fast if taken in the right way"
- LAL 20 ❖ LAL Aug 10th 53

Fasting: In a perfect Christian his feasts would be as Christian as his fasts
- WG 130 ❖ WG 9:9

Fasting: "...perhaps having to fast for medical reasons is a just punishment for not having fasted enough on higher grounds!"
- LAL 35 (see also LAL 104-105)
❖ LAL Nov 1st 54 (see also LAL 3/7/62)

Fatal flaw, some, always brings the selfish and cruel people to the top, and it all slides back into misery and ruin (re: world's futility without God)
- MC 54 ❖ MC II 3:7, 8

Fatal flaw, you have a, in your character which prevents God from making you happy
- GID 151-155 (see also GID 121-123)
❖ GID I ch. 18 (see also GID I 14:4-9)

Fatal flaw, you have a, on which the hopes and plans of others have again and again shipwrecked, just as your plans have on theirs
- GID 123, 153 (see also FL 186*)
❖ GID I 14:7, 8; 18:6, 7 (see also FL 6:37*)

Fatal thing, the only, is to lose one's temper and give up (re: chronic temptations)
- L 199 (see also MC 94; WG 132)
❖ L 20 Jan 42 (see also MC III 5:12; WG 9:13)

Fate—see also Destiny; consider also Will of God

Fate, Lewis mentions the error of mistaking the dictates of passion for the decree of, (as in a marriage between unbelievers)
- L 160-161 (see also MC 100, 101)
❖ L 10 Jun 38 (see also MC III 6:11, 13)

Fate, the approach of any, is usually also the preparation for it (quote from George MacDonald)
- L 186 (see also L 219)

❖ L 2 Jun 40 (see also L 2 Sep 49)

Father(s)—see also Parent(s); consider also Loved ones

Father and Son as names for God and Christ suggest the erroneous idea that one was there first
- MC 150-151 ❖ MC IV 4:2-4

Father and Son: Could there have been many sons begotten by God, as Jesus was?
- MC 157-159 ❖ MC IV 6:2

"Father" as a term used in Scripture to represent God (a term denoting Affection rather than Friendship)
- FL 112-113, 124 (see also PP 44-45)
❖ FL 4:42, 58 (see also PP 3:12)

Father, dear Sergeant Ayres became to me almost like a
- SJ 196 ❖ SJ 12:17

Father, every man has a grudge against his, and his first teacher; the process of being brought up, however well it is done, cannot fail to offend
- CR 92 ❖ CR 7:20

Father, letter to a lady who had just lost her, through death: Death does matter, and very solemnly
- L 230 ❖ L 27 Mar 51

Father, Lewis compares his, to his father's two brothers
- L 139-140 ❖ L 21 Dec 29

Father, Lewis makes reference to caring for his, during his last illness
- L 136-138 ❖ L 9 Sep 29

Father, Lewis mentions the death of his, and his feelings regarding it
- L 138-139 ❖ L 27 Oct 29

Father, Lewis mentions the death of his: "...all the fortitude (even playfulness) which he displayed in his last illness ..."
- SJ 215 (see also L 138; SJ 123)
❖ SJ 14:6 (see also L 27 Oct 29; SJ 8:6)

Father, Lewis mentions the guilt he felt regarding his relationship with his*
- SJ 125 (see also L 162)
❖ SJ 8:7 (see also L 12 Sep 38)

Father, Lewis relates his confirmation and first Communion which he made only to please his
- SJ 161-162 ❖ SJ 10:15

Father, Lewis's
- •SJ 3-5, 9-10, 18-19, 23, 29-31, 37-41, 49, 54, 57, 64-65, 80-81, 119-129, 133, 134, 135, 143, 156, 160-162, 164, 183-184, 186
- ❖ SJ 1:1, 2, 8, 19, 20; 2:1, 2, 10, 17-19; 3:7, 8, 13; 4:2, 11; 5:13, 14; 8:2-12; 9:2, 6, 9, 18; 10:9, 14-16, 19-21; 12:2, 5

Father, Lewis's: "Be thankful you have nothing to reproach yourself in your relations with your father (I had lots)"
- •L 162 ❖ L 12 Sep 38

Father, Lewis's: "He could never empty, or silence, his own mind to make room for an alien thought"
- •SJ 184 ❖ SJ 12:2

Father, Lewis's: "His intense desire for my total confidence co-existed with an inability to listen (in any strict sense) to what I said"
- •SJ 184 (see also SJ 120-121)
- ❖ SJ 12:2 (see also SJ 8:4)

Father, Lewis's: Kirk told my father, "You may make a writer or a scholar out of him, but you'll not make anything else"
- •SJ 183 (see also CR 20*)
- ❖ SJ 12:2 (see also CR 2:23*)

Father, Lewis's letter to his, from a hospital during the war: "Come and see me, I am homesick, that is the long and the short of it"
- •L 20 Jun 18 ❖ L 042-043

Father, Lewis's: "[My father had] more power of confusing an issue or taking up a fact wrongly than any man I have ever known"
- •SJ 120-121 ❖ SJ 8:4

Father, Lewis's: "...my long-suffering father offered me a fourth year at Oxford during which I read English..."
- •SJ 212 ❖ SJ 14:1

Father, Lewis's: The attempt made "to break through the artificiality of our intercourse and admit him to my real life...was a total failure"
- •SJ 183-184 ❖ SJ 12:2

Father, Lewis's: "With the cruelty of youth I allowed myself to be irritated by traits in my father which, in other elderly men, I have since regarded as lovable foibles"
- •SJ 160 (see also FL 64*; GID 285)
- ❖ SJ 10:14 (see also FL 3:17*; GID III 3:7)

"Father of Lights," God as the
- •RP 80, 110 (see also CR 136)
- ❖ RP 8:7; 11:3 (see also CR 11:16)

Father pleased with baby's first steps as analogy to God with us: "God is easy to please, but hard to satisfy" (quote from George MacDonald)
- •MC 172 (see also PP 46*; SL 39)
- ❖ MC IV 9:5 (see also PP 3:13*; SL 8:4)

Father's love for a son as an analogy useful to our conception of God's love for us
- •PP 44-45, 47 (see also FL 112-113, 124)
- ❖ PP 3:12, 14 (see also FL 4:42, 58)

Fathers: "That son would have borne patiently and humorously from any other old man the silliness which enraged him in his father"
- •GID 285 (see also SJ 160)
- ❖ GID III 3:7 (see also SJ 10:14)

Fatherhood, Divine, not at all comparable to earthly fathers who are afraid to restrain or instruct their children
- •PP 44 ❖ PP 3:12

Fatigue—see also Tiredness

Fatigue makes women talk more and men talk less; this can cause much secret resentment, even between lovers
- •SL 142 ❖ SL 30:3

Fatigue, Screwtape advises promoting the lie that an excess of physical exercise and consequent, is helpful toward combatting sexual temptation
- •SL 79 ❖ SL 17:4

Fatigue, Screwtape mentions the diabolical uses that can be made of, ("It is not fatigue simply as such that produces anger, but unexpected demands on a man already tired") .
- •SL 141-142 ❖ SL 30:2

Fault(s)—see also Flaw(s); Sin(s)

Fault, devil loves curing a small, by giving you a great one
- •MC 113 ❖ MC III 8:10

Faults, God loves us in spite of our, as we should love each other

•GID 154 (*see also* GID 122-123*)
❖ GID I 18:8, 9 (*see also* GID I 14:7, 8*)
Faults, God may love us in spite of our, but He cannot cease to will their removal
    •PP 46 (*see also* MC 172)
    ❖ PP 3:13 (*see also* MC IV 9:4)
Faults in ourselves hard to see
    •GID 121-124, 153; PP 59- 60 (*see also* MC 087*; SL 016) ❖ GID I 14:4-10; 18:6, 7; PP 4:7 (*see also* MC III 4:10*; SL 3:2)
Faults in ourselves: "...if, on consideration, one can find no faults on one's own side, then cry for mercy: for this *must* be a most dangerous delusion"
    •LAL 95 ❖ LAL 9 Jan 61
Faults in ourselves, two opposite errors in admitting: making melodramatic sins out of small matters, or slurring things over
    •GID 124, 153 ❖ GID I 14:9; 18:7
Faults in ourselves: When a man is getting better, he understands more clearly the evil left in him
    •MC 87 (*see also* GID 56-57; MC 164; PP 55, top; 67; Self-knowledge)
    ❖ MC III 4:10 (*see also* GID I 4:38; MC IV 7:12; PP 4:prelim. quote; 4:15; Self-knowledge)
Faults of newly fallen man included pride, ambition, self-admiration, competition, envy, and insecurity
    •PP 83 ❖ PP 5:10
Faults of others, abstain from thinking about; "It is healthier to think of one's own"
    •GID 124, 154; LAL 95
    ❖ GID I 14:10; 18:10; LAL 9 Jan 61
Faults, regarding the dead now having knowledge of all our: "So be it. Look your hardest, dear...I wouldn't hide if I could..."
    •GO 83-84 ❖ GO 4:30
Fear—*see also* Awe; *consider also* Cowardice; Worry
Fear and grief, sensations of, are the same—the same fluttering in the stomach, the same restlessness
    •GO 1 (*see also* GO 38-39)

❖ GO 1:1 (*see also* GO 2:32)
Fear as a form of pain which helps us in our return to obedience and charity (reminds us that our true good is in another world)
    •PP 105-106 ❖ PP 6:17
Fear as one of the things that protected Lewis as he became interested in the Occult (in his youth)
    •SJ 175-176, 177 ❖ SJ 11:13, 14, 16
Fear, attempt to excite, about Hell cannot succeed as a permanent influence on conduct
    •RP 41-42 (*see also* LM 76)
    ❖ RP 4:16 (*see also* LM 14:15)
Fear, attempt to excite, about the Second Coming will not succeed since fear is an emotion and it is impossible to maintain any emotion for very long
    •WLN 109 ❖ WLN 7:30
Fear becomes easier to master when the mind is diverted from the thing feared to the fear itself
    •SL 29 ❖ SL 6:3
Fear: "Cowardice, alone among the vices, is purely painful—horrible to anticipate, horrible to feel, horrible to remember"
    •SL 136 ❖ SL 29:4
Fear ("dismay") not excluded by greater faith, as evidenced by Gethsemane*
    •L 285 (*see also* L 166, 189- 191, 210-211, 250; Gethsemane) ❖ L 8 May 39 (*see also* L 8 May 39; undated letter just after 11 Aug 40; undated letter of 1947; 17 Jul 53; Gethsemane)
Fear during wartime as an enemy to educational pursuits
    •WG 30-31 (*see also* SJ 183*; SL 67-71)
    ❖ WG 2:14 (*see also* SJ 12:2*; SL ch. 15)
Fear: God never teaches us to fear anything but Himself; as the hymn says, "Fear Him ye saints and you will then have nothing else to fear"
    •LAL 60 ❖ LAL 3/8/56
Fear, human, contains two elements: a) physical sensations, and b) mental images of what will happen *if*; (a) without (b) often felt as pleasurable
    •GID 170 ❖ GID I 20:Reply-14

Fear: In time of war, it was usually the reserve who had to *watch* the carnage, not the troops who were in it, whose nerve broke first
•L 250 ❖ L 17 Jul 53

Fear is horrid, but there's no reason to be ashamed of it; Our Lord was afraid (dreadfully so) in Gethsemane
•LAL 41 ❖ LAL 2nd Apr 55

Fear is the lowest form of religion; but a safe, or tame, God is a fantasy
•LM 76 ❖ LM 14:14

Fear isn't repentance, but it's alright as a beginning
•L 196 ❖ L 8 Dec 41

Fear itself is a cross we must submit to God, rather than all the things we are afraid might happen*
•SL 29 (*see also* LAL 60)
❖ SL 6:2 (*see also* LAL 3/8/56)

Fear, Lewis describes his early religious experience (while a student at "Belsen") as involving a great deal of
•SJ 33-34 ❖ SJ 2:14

Fear, Lewis's, of insects: "'...they are like French locomotives—they have all the works on the outside'" (quote from Owen Barfield)
•SJ 8-9 (*see also* L 257; LAL 21)
❖ SJ 1:6, 7 (*see also* L 1 Nov 54; LAL Aug 10th 53)

Fear, Lewis's, of poverty, large spiders, and heights
•LAL 21 ❖ LAL Aug 10th 53

Fear: Not all the things you fear can happen to you; the one (if any) that does will perhaps turn out very different from what you think
•LAL 60 (*see also* SL 29)
❖ LAL 3/8/56 (*see also* SL 6:2)

Fear of allowing our natural self to be killed
•MC 154 (*see also* MC 164, 167, 174*; Self-reservation) ❖ MC IV 5:2 (*see also* MC IV 7:11; 8:4; 9:10*; Self-reservation)

Fear of death: "Pain is terrible, but surely you need not have fear as well? Can you not see death as the friend and deliverer?"
•LAL 117 ❖ LAL 17 Jun 63

Fear of death, temptation to, attacks most fiercely the best and the worst of men; Lewis explains why (re: Christ's fear in Gethsemane)
•L 189-190
❖ L undated letter just after 11 Aug 40

Fear of duty as reason for avoiding truth
•GID 110-111 (*see also* Obstacles to Christian faith; Self-reservation)
❖ GID I 12:6-8 (*see also* Obstacles to Christian faith; Self-reservation)

Fear of [financial] insecurity must be recognised as a temptation; it hinders our charity
•MC 82 ❖ MC III 3:7

Fear of Hell, God accepts us even when we choose Him out of
•PP 97 ❖ PP 6:8

Fear of losing our things temporal as a reason for avoiding God
•WG 126-132 (*see also* Self-reservation)
❖ WG ch. 9 (*see also* Self-reservation)

Fear of poverty, Lewis describes the development of his, as a child
•SJ 64-65❖ SJ 4:11

Fear: "Remember, tho' we struggle against things because we are afraid of them, it is often the other way round—we get afraid *because* we struggle"
•LAL 117 ❖ LAL 17 Jun 63

Fear: Screwtape observes that danger brings moral issues to the point
•SL 137 ❖ SL 29:5, 6

Fear tames wrath—the fear that my own unforgivingness will exclude me from all the promises
•LAL 93 ❖ LAL 28 Oct 60

Fear: That day I noticed how a greater terror overcomes a less; in the midst of the shelling, a poor shivering mouse made no attempt to run from me
•SJ 195 ❖ SJ 12:17

Fear: "...the *act* of cowardice is all that matters; the emotion of fear is, in itself, no sin..." (—Screwtape)
• SL 139 ❖ SL 29:8

Fear ("timidity") and pessimism may prevent me from gambling, but they also tempt me to avoid those risks and adventures which every man ought to

take*
- RP 29 ❖ RP 3:18

Fear, you can't really share someone else's weakness or pain or ; there's a limit to the "one flesh" [of marriage]
- GO 13 ❖ GO 1:26

Fears, irrational: I am inclined to think a real objective curiosity will usually have a cleansing effect (re: his own fear of spiders)
- SJ 9 ❖ SJ 1:6

Feast, Friendship compared to a, in which God spreads the board, chooses the guests, and, we may dare to hope, presides as Host
- FL 126-127 ❖ FL 4:61

Feeling(s)—*see also* Emotion(s); Passion; Sensation(s)

Feeling, do I hope that if, disguises itself as thought I shall feel less? (re: intellectualizing God and the problem of pain when one is grieving)
- GO 38 (*see also* GO 41, 43*)
- ❖ GO 2:31 (*see also* GO 3:3, 4*)

Feeling "hurt": Most times people who "hurt" us did not intend to, and are quite unconscious of the whole thing
- LAL 59 (*see also* LAL 96-97)
- ❖ LAL 3/8/56 (*see also* LAL 24 Feb 61)

"Feeling hurt" so seldom means merely sorrow—usually mixed with wounded pride, self-justification, fright, even desire for retaliation
- LAL 56-57 ❖ LAL 21/5/56

Feeling, mere, continues to assault whatever view we embrace—Theism or atheism
- CR 41 ❖ CR 3:9

Feeling of being or not being forgiven is not what matters
- LAL 77 (*see also* LM 32-34; SL 21)
- ❖ LAL Jul 21st 58 (*see also* LM 6:11-17; SL 4:3)

Feeling of spiritual awe—*see* Awe; Numinous

Feeling, the couple whose marriage will be endangered by lapses of mere, are those who have idolised Eros (romantic love)
- FL 159 ❖ FL 5:45

Feeling the presence of God not the same as the presence of God; the former may be due to imagination, and the latter may not bring consolation
- LAL 38-39 ❖ LAL 20/2/55

Feeling, we cannot rely on, to support our prayers; in it there is so much that is not ours—weather, health, etc.
- LM 116 (*see also* SL 21)
- ❖ LM 21:16 (*see also* SL 4:3)

Feelings accompanying my emotions, by themselves, are of very mediocre interest to me; their value is in what they are about
- CR 139-140 (*see also* SJ 168, 218- 220, 238; WG 57-59) ❖ CR 11:22 (*see also* SJ 11:5; 14:10-12; 15:10; WG 4:5-7)

Feelings and moods change; that is why Faith is such a necessary virtue
- MC 123-124 ❖ MC III 11:5

Feelings and moods tell us more about the state of our passions and even our digestion than about reality (re: constancy in faith)
- CR 43 ❖ CR 3:11

Feelings are not what God principally cares about; Christian love is an affair of the will
- MC 115, 117-118 (*see also* L 269; LM 115)
- ❖ MC III 9:2, 9, 10 (*see also* L undated letter just before 2 Apr 56; LM 21:12)

Feelings as unreliable witnesses: "When a witness has once been proved unreliable, turn him out of the court" (re: religion as reality or substitute)
- CR 40 ❖ CR 3:8

Feelings come and go, and when they come a good use can be made of them; they cannot be our regular spiritual diet
- WLN 109 ❖ WLN 7:30

Feelings come and go as God pleases; obedience is the key to all doors
- L 225 ❖ L 7 Dec 50

Feelings, don't be worried about flat; religious emotion is only a servant which we can rejoice in when it comes
- L 192 ❖ L 4 Jan 41; 29 Jan 41

Feelings: Holy Spirit may be most opera-

tive when you can feel it least
•L 241 ❖ L 15 May 52

Feelings in prayer: "...we must never in prayer strive to extort 'by maistry' what God does not give"*
•SJ 61-62 (see also L 202, 256; LM 23; SL 20-21, 125; SJ 168)
❖ SJ 4:8 (see also L 22 Dec 42; 31 Jul 54; LM 4:19; SL 4:3; 27:1; SJ 11:5)

Feelings: Love, hate, fear, hope, anger, desire, and lust all mentioned as "inner activities" which can be aborted or "spoiled" by introspection*
•SJ 218-219 ❖ SJ 14:10

Feelings not important in themselves; it is by his will alone that man is good or bad
•L 210 ❖ L undated letter of 1947

Feelings of affection cannot be manufactured
•MC 105, 116-117 (see also SL 21)
❖ MC III 7:5; 9:5, 6 (see also SL 4:3)

Feelings of belief ("belief-feelings") do not follow reason except by long training; they follow the grooves and ruts which already exist in the mind
•M 166-167 ❖ M 17:4

Feelings of bravery and love, folly of trying to manufacture, even as we pray for courage and charity
•SL 21 ❖ SL 4:3

Feelings of disappointment or anticlimax which may come in the first few weeks after one's conversion
•SL 13-14 (see also LM 26-27; SL 36-37, 42-44; MC 100*) ❖ SL 2:3 (see also LM 5:10-13; SL 8:1, 2; 9:3, 4; MC 100*)

Feelings of excitement never last; don't depend on them (e.g., when newly converted)
•L 241 (see also SL 42-43)
❖ L 15 May 52 (see also FL 9:3)

Feelings of excitement never last (e.g., in marriage, learning to fly, etc.); don't depend on them
•MC 99-101 (see also FL 28*; GID 320-321; LM 26-27*; SL 13)
❖ MC III 6:9-12 (see also FL 2:6*; GID III 9:23, 24; LM 5:11, 12; SL 2:3)

Feelings of gratitude, like other feelings,

must not be bothered about; must simply be acted
•L 202 ❖ L 22 Dec 42

Feelings of love not enough; something else must come to help if it is to remain sweet
•FL 163 (see also FL 81-83, 124, 159-160; GID 285; L 198-199; SL 124)
❖ FL 6:1 (see also FL 3:44, 45; 4:59; 5:45, 46; GID III 3:7; L undated letter just before 20 Jan 42; SL 26:5)

Feelings of love not reliable in marriage; hence the need for a promise
•MC 96-99 (see also L 184; SL 82-84*)
❖ MC III 6:4-9 (see also L 18 Apr 40; SL 18:6)

Feelings, Our Lord will give us right, if He wishes; important thing is to keep on doing what you are told
•L 216 (see also LM 115)
❖ L 3 Apr 49 (see also LM 21:12)

Feelings ("passive" actions) are weakened by repetition while active habits are strengthened; the more one feels without acting the less he will be able to act
•SL 60-61 ❖ SL 13:5

Feelings: Screwtape advises tempting the human to go to work on "the desperate design of recovering his old feelings by sheer will power" (after conversion)
•SL 42 ❖ SL 9:3

Feelings: "So often, whether for good or ill, one's inner state seems to have so little connection with the circumstances"*
•LAL 83 (see also SJ 78, 118-119)
❖ LAL Jun 7th 59 (see also SJ 5:12; 8:1)

Feelings: The enjoyment and the contemplation of our inner activities are incompatible; the surest way of spoiling a pleasure (etc.) is to start examining it*
•SJ 217-219 (see also GID 65-66; L 221)
❖ SJ 14:9, 10 (see also GID I 5:8; L 27 Sep 49)

Feelings: The sense of the Holy Spirit's presence is a super-added gift for which we give thanks when it comes*

•LAL 38-39 ❖ LAL 20/2/55

Feelings: They are not *you*, but only a thing that happens to you
•L 233 ❖ L 13 Jun 51

Feelings: Without a firm belief and the assistance of Grace, our feelings will continually assault our conviction like a blast furnace against a snowflake
•CR 41-43 ❖ CR 3:9-12

Feigning—*see* Imitation; Pretending

Fellowship, Christian, primarily means fellowship with Christ
•WG 112 ❖ WG 7:9

Female aspects in men: "...there ought spiritually to be a...woman in every man" (and vice versa)
•L 237 ❖ L 10 Jan 52

Females—*see* Women

Feminism—*consider also* Equality; Marriage; Men; Women

Feminism and "women's rights" mentioned
•L 117-118 ❖ L 9 Jul 27

Feminist, the sternest, need not grudge my sex the crown offered to it in the Pagan or the Christian mystery; the one is of paper and the other is of thorns
•FL 149 (*see also* FL 147)
❖ FL 5:28 (*see also* FL 5:25)

Fidelity in marriage—*see* Adultery; Infidelity; Marriage

Fidget, story of Mrs., as an example of a perversion of Gift-love
•FL 73-76, 82-83 (*see also* L 198-199*; MC 167*; SL 121, 123*) ❖ FL 3:33-36, 45 (*see also* L undated letter just before 20 Jan 42; MC IV 7:3*; SL 26:2, 5*)

Fighting—*see* Quarrelling

Film star or other celebrity, people will go out of their way to meet, even when it is known that they live a vile and mischievous life
•RP 67, 71 (*see also* LAL 27*)
❖ RP 7:3, 9 (*see also* LAL Feb 22/54)

Film stars and popular singers mentioned by Screwtape as useful in drawing thousands of souls away from God
•SL 158-159; WLN 56-57
❖ SL 32:13; WLN 4:13

Films, as you know I'm rather allergic to
•LAL 59 ❖ LAL 3/8/56

Financial insecurity, fear of, must be recognised as a temptation; it hinders our charity
•MC 82 ❖ MC III 3:7

First and Second Things (chapter title) (re: a universal law of values)
•GID 278-281 ❖ GID III ch. 2

First and second things: "Second things are always corrupted when they are put first..." (re: the over-valuing of "culture")
•L 269 ❖ L 2 Apr 56

First job each day, what is our
•MC 169 ❖ MC IV 8:8

First things, our deepest concern should be for, and our next deepest for second things, and so on...this is what St. Augustine called "ordinate loves"
•LM 22 ❖ LM 4:14

First things, when put first, increase the value of second things
•L 248 (*see also* GID 150*)
❖ L 8 Nov 52 (*see also* GID I 17:7*)

First things: When we put them first we get second things thrown in; when we put second things first we lose both
•L 228 (*see also* FL 166; GID 280; L 269; MC 118-119; RP 49; WG 109) ❖ L 23 Apr 51 (*see also* FL 6:5; GID III 2:7; L 2 Apr 56; MC III 9:1; RP 5:7; WG 7:4)

First Years, The (chapter title)
•SJ 3-21 ❖ SJ ch. 1

Fish tank used to illustrate how Nature is a relatively closed system, but vulnerable to a larger reality which includes it and created it
•M 60-61 ❖ M 8:9

Flatlander(s)—*consider also* Pictures

Flatlander (a creature who perceives only two dimensions) could never comprehend that a picture stood for a three-dimensional world
•WG 61-62, 64 ❖ WG 4:12, 15

Flatlanders, we cannot comprehend the Trinity any more than the, could comprehend a cube
•CR 79-80; M 85; MC 142 (*see also* GID 182; Trinity)

❖ CR 6:21; M 11:6; MC IV 2:7 (*see also* GID I 22:14; Trinity)

Flattery as one of the "sins of the tongue" which are protested against in the Psalms
•RP 75 ❖ RP 7:16

Flaw(s)—*see also* Fault(s)

Flaw, some fatal, always brings the selfish and cruel people to the top and it all slides back into misery and ruin (re: world's futility without God)
•MC 54 ❖ MC II 3:7, 8

Flaw, you have a fatal, in your character which prevents God from making you happy
•GID 151-155 (*see also* GID 121-123) ❖ GID I ch. 18 (*see also* GID I 14:4-9)

Flaw, you have a fatal, on which the hopes and plans of others have again and again shipwrecked, just as your plans have on theirs
•GID 123, 153 (*see also* FL 186*) ❖ GID I 14:7, 8; 18:6, 7 (*see also* FL 6:37*)

Flaws in our own characters hard to see
•GID 121-123, 153; PP 59-60 (*see also* MC 87*; SL 16) ❖ GID I 14:4-8; 18:6, 7; PP 4:7 (*see also* MC III 4:10*: SL 3:2)

Flaws, we are helped in learning charity by other people's
•FL 186 ❖ FL 6:37

Flesh, sins of the, are bad but they are the least bad of all sins
•MC 94-95 (*see also* FL 111-112*; L 175; LAL 111) ❖ MC III 5:14 (*see also* FL 4:39*; L 17 Jan 40; LAL 26 Nov 62)

Flesh, sins of the: "Cruelty is surely more evil than lust and the World at least as dangerous as the Flesh"
•SJ 109 ❖ SJ 7:11

Flesh, temptations of the, are more successful during the "trough" periods of human experience—when one is dull and weary (—Screwtape)
•SL 41 ❖ SL 9:2

Flippancy defined by Screwtape: "...every serious subject is discussed in a manner which implies that they have already found a ridiculous side to it"
•SL 52 ❖ SL 11:6

Flippancy mentioned by Screwtape as deadening the intellect and effectively armouring humans against God
•SL 52 ❖ SL 11:6

Flippancy parodies merriment as indulgence parodies love
•WG 19 ❖ WG 1:15

Flying: Original thrill dies away and is replaced by a quieter, more lasting interest (as with love)
•MC 100-101 ❖ MC III 6:11, 12

Fog in England: "One pines for lights and, scarcely less, *shadows*, which make up so much of the beauty of the world"
•LAL 80 ❖ LAL Dec 25th 58

Fog, indulgence [in sin] brings; virtue—even attempted virtue—brings light
•MC 94 ❖ MC III 5:13

Fog, what will all our speculations and evasions count when the anesthetic, of "nature" fades away and we are faced with the Presence of God?
•MC 183 (*consider also* Contact with God; Destiny of each person) ❖ MC IV 10:17 (*consider also* Contact with God; Destiny of each person)

Food—*consider also* Eating; Gluttony

Food, Screwtape advises Wormwood on the value of excess in, to attacks on human chastity
•SL 79 ❖ SL 17:4

Food: Screwtape mentions "what that pestilent fellow Paul used to teach about food and other unessentials..."
•SL 75 ❖ SL 16:5

Footstep in the hall, was that a real
•M 94 (*consider also* Contact with God) ❖ M 11:19 (*consider also* Contact with God)

Foreknowledge, Divine—*see also* Omniscience

Foreknowledge, Divine, does not preclude our free will
•MC 148-149 (*see also* SL 126-128; Free will) ❖ MC IV 3:11 (*see also* SL 27:3, 4; Free will)

Foreknowledge, Divine: God created the universe already foreseeing the Crucifixion
•FL 176 ❖ FL 6:21

Forgetfulness: "We have *always* been for-
getting things: but now, when we do
so, we attribute it to our age"
  •LAL 93-94 (*consider also* Aging)
  ❖ LAL 24 Nov 60 (*consider also* Aging)
Forgiveness (chapter title)
  •MC 104-108 ❖ MC III ch. 7
Forgiveness a lovely idea until we have
something to forgive
  •MC 104 ❖ MC III 7:2
Forgiveness, a man who admits no guilt
can accept no
  •PP 122 ❖ PP 8:6
Forgiveness: After each failure, ask for-
giveness, pick yourself up, and try
again
  •MC 93-94 ❖ MC III 5:12
Forgiveness: After we have repented we
should remember the price of our for-
giveness and be humble
  •PP 61 (*see also* L 236)
  ❖ PP 4:9 (*see also* L 8 Jan 52)
Forgiveness and Christian love of one's
enemy does not preclude the concept
of punishment
  •MC 106-108 ❖ MC III 7:8-10
Forgiveness, asking for, must not consist
in asking God to accept our excuses
  •WG 122 ❖ WG 8:3
Forgiveness, asking for, reflects accep-
tance of blame; excusing reflects de-
nial of blame
  •WG 122 ❖ WG 8:3
Forgiveness, at the highest level of repen-
tance, is valued chiefly as a symptom
or seal of the restoration of an infi-
nitely valued relationship
  •LM 95 ❖ LM 18:3
Forgiveness by its nature is for the unwor-
thy
  •LAL 85 ❖ LAL Jul 7th 59
Forgiveness, Christianity has nothing to
say to those who feel no need of
  •MC 38-39 (*see also* CR 46-47; GID 95,
181; 243-244; PP 55-58)
  ❖ MC I 5:4 (*see also* CR 4:7; GID I 10:15,
22:13, II 12:6, 7; PP 4:1-4)
Forgiveness, discussion of
  •MC 104-108 ❖ MC III ch. 7
Forgiveness does not necessarily include

an immediate restoration of trust; it
means the killing of resentment and
the desire for revenge
  •WG 124 ❖ WG 8:6
Forgiveness: "Failures will be forgiven; it
is acquiescence that is fatal"
  •WG 132 (*see also* L 199; WG 130)
  ❖ WG 9:13 (*see also* L 20 Jan 40; WG
9:9)
Forgiveness: "I find *fear* a great help—the
fear that my own unforgivingness will
exclude me from all the promises"
  •LAL 93 ❖ LAL 28 Oct 60
Forgiveness: "I hope, now that you know
you are forgiven, you will spend most
of your remaining strength in *forgiving*. Lay all the old resentments
down..."
  •LAL 118 ❖ LAL 25 Jun 63
Forgiveness, I realize that until about a
month ago I never really believed in
God's
  •L 232 (*see also* L 236)
  ❖ L 5 Jun 51 (*see also* L 8 Jan 52)
Forgiveness: "I think if God forgives us
we must forgive ourselves. Otherwise
it is almost like setting ourselves up
as a higher tribunal than Him"
  •L 230 ❖ L 19 Apr 51
Forgiveness: In Christianity it is made
perfectly clear that if we do not forgive we shall not be forgiven
  •MC 104 ❖ MC III 7:3
Forgiveness, in offering, for having bro-
ken the moral Law, Christianity reaffirms the Law
  •CR 46-47 ❖ CR 4:7
Forgiveness: It is at first sight so easy to
forgive, but then one wakes up five
minutes later and finds one hasn't really forgiven at all
  •LAL 56 (*see also* LAL 120)
  ❖ LAL 21/5/56 (*see also* LAL 6 Jul 63)
Forgiveness: Like learning to swim, the
moment it happens it seems so easy
you wonder why you didn't do it
years ago
  •LAL 120 ❖ LAL 6 Jul 63
Forgiveness: "Love may forgive all infirmities and love still in spite of them:

but Love cannot cease to will their removal" (re: love of God)
•PP 46 ❖ PP 3:13
Forgiveness, many people lack a feeling of, without the act of Confession
•L 250 (*see also* Confession)
❖ L 6-7 Apr 53 (*see also* Confession)
Forgiveness means looking steadily at the sin, seeing it in all its dirt and horror, and yet still being reconciled to the man who has done it
•WG 123-124 ❖ WG 8:5
Forgiveness must include that of the incessant provocations of daily life (bossy mother-in-law, bullying husband, nagging wife, etc.)
•WG 125❖ WG 8:7
Forgiveness: "My resource is to look for some action of my own which is open to the same charge as the one I'm resenting"
•LM 27-28 ❖ LM 5:15
Forgiveness not easy; has to be done over and over again
•RP 24-25 (*see also* LAL 120)
❖ RP 3:10 (*see also* LAL 6 Jul 63)
Forgiveness of enemies: "...we must forgive all our enemies or be damned"
•GID 190-191 ❖ GID II 1:3
Forgiveness of others: What it involves
•WG 124 ❖ WG 8:6
Forgiveness of ourselves vs. forgiveness of others (in our own case we accept excuses too easily; in other people's cases not easily enough)
•WG 124-125 ❖ WG 8:6
Forgiveness of sins: A divine action is elicited by our petition (re: prayer as cause)
•LM 50 ❖ LM 9:12
Forgiveness of sins, I had been a Christian for many years before I *really* believed in the
•LAL 74, 85
❖ LAL 15/4/58; Jul 7th 59
Forgiveness of sins, no mere man could claim the power of, as Jesus did
•MC 55 ❖ MC II 3:11
Forgiveness of sins not easy to believe in
•WG 121❖ WG 8:1

Forgiveness, On (chapter title)
•WG 121-125 ❖ WG ch. 8
Forgiveness: "...only a few weeks ago I realised suddenly that I at last *had* forgiven the cruel schoolmaster who had so darkened my childhood"
•LAL 120 (*see also* LM 106)
❖ LAL 6 Jul 63 (*see also* LM 20:1)
Forgiveness: Only a Person can forgive (re: God as a personal God—"more like a mind than it is like anything else")
•MC 37-38 ❖ MC I 5:3
Forgiveness ought not to rest on the quality of the other person's penitence; it may no doubt be very imperfect, as is our own
•LAL 95 ❖ LAL 9 Jan 61
Forgiveness, our own, conditional on our forgiveness of others
•WG 121-122; 125 ❖ WG 8:2, 7
Forgiveness: Regarding "If you forgive you will be forgiven": "...one is safe as long as one keeps on trying"
•LAL 120 ❖ LAL 6 Jul 63
Forgiveness: Regarding those who make an elaborate show of always "unnecessarily asking, or insufferably offering, forgiveness"
•FL 185 ❖ FL 6:36
Forgiveness: Remember that God has promised to forgive you *as*, and only *as*, you forgive them
•LAL 93, 95 (*see also* LAL 120)
❖ LAL 28 Oct 60; 9 Jan 61 (*see also* LAL 6 Jul 63)
Forgiveness: Sin, once repented and forgiven, is gone, annihilated, white as snow—though we may continue to feel sorrow for being that kind of person
•L 236 (*see also* PP 61; SL 148*)
❖ L 8 Jan 52 (*see also* PP 4:9; SL 31:5*)
Forgiveness: The *feeling* of being or not being forgiven is not what matters
•LAL 77 (*see also* LM 32-34; SL 21)
❖ LAL Jul 21st 58 (*see also* LM 6:11-17; SL 4:3)
Forgiveness: "To be a Christian means to forgive the inexcusable, because God

has forgiven the inexcusable in you"
•WG 125❖ WG 8:6

Forgiveness vs. condoning: To condone an evil is simply to ignore it, to treat it as if it were good; but forgiveness needs to be accepted as well as offered
•PP 122 ❖ PP 8:6

Forgiveness vs. excusing
•WG 122-125 ❖ WG 8:3-6

Forgiving and being forgiven may be two words for the very same thing
•LAL 120; LM 106-107
❖ LAL 6 Jul 63; LM 20:1

Forgiving not the same as excusing; almost exact opposites
•WG 122 ❖ WG 8:3

Formality: "English people have not the talent for graceful ceremonial. They go through it lumpishly..."
•L 103 ❖ L 14 Aug 25

Formality, Lewis maintains that his "boorish inaptitude" for, may be partly traced to his mother's funeral
•SJ 20 ❖ SJ 1:21

Fornication, the reason prostitution is worse than ordinary, is that it has no end in view except money
•WLN 75 ❖ WLN 5:11

Fornication: Why it is no longer felt to be a sin
•GID 244 ❖ GID II 12:8

Fortitude includes two kinds of courage: the kind that faces danger, and the kind that "sticks it" under pain
•MC 76 ❖ MC III 2:7

Fortune, it is a curious truth that good, is nearly always followed by more good fortune and bad, by more bad
•SJ 130 ❖ SJ 8:14

Fortune's Smile (chapter title)
•SJ 149-164 ❖ SJ ch. 10

Founding of the Oxford Socratic Club, The (chapter title)
•GID 126-128 ❖ GID I ch. 15

Fountain, God as a, (Our loved ones are as portraits to the Original, and as rivulets to the Fountain)
•FL 191 ❖ FL 6:44

Fountain of energy and beauty which is God: "If you are close to it, the spray

will wet you..."
•MC 153 ❖ MC IV 4:8

Fountain of facthood, God as the
•M 88, 155 (see also M 6-7, 87; 91, 110; MC 158) ❖ M 11:11; 16:22 (see also M 2:5, 6; 11:9, 10, 15; 14:4; MC IV 6:2)

Fountain of joy, the whole man is to drink joy from the
•WG 17-18 (see also RP 97*)
❖ WG 1:14 (see also RP 9:7*)

Fountain of life, we know which road we must take to the, and none who has seriously followed the directions complains that he has been deceived
•GID 43 ❖ GID I 3:10

Four Last Things as one of the beliefs which unite all Christians everywhere
•GID 336 ❖ GID IV Letter 9

Fox had been dislodged from the Hegelian Wood and was now running in the open... (re: Lewis's path to conversion)
•SJ 225 ❖ SJ 14:17

Francis de Sales, Saint, recommended for reading
•LAL 44, 48 ❖ LAL 21/6/55; 9:11/55

Frazer, Sir James George, as a source for the "dying God" myth (The Golden Bough)
•GID 83 (see also M 69; SJ 223-224)
❖ GID I 9:5 (see also M 10:3; SJ 14:15)

Free will—see also Choice; Freedom of choice; Will

Free will and grace, the whole puzzle about: "We profanely assume that divine and human action exclude one another..."
•LM 49-50 (see also GID 55; LM 68-69*; MC 130; Moral effort) ❖ LM 9:11, 12 (see also GID I 4:30, 31 — Ques. 8; LM 13:2-5*; MC III 12:8; Moral effort)

Free will and Predestination, question of, is to my mind indiscussible, insoluble; I suspect it is meaningless
•L 245-246 (consider also Predestination) ❖ L 20 Oct 52 (consider also Predestination)

Free will did not frustrate the good that God intended when He created the world; rather evil provides the fuel for a second, more complex kind of good

sonal, —that is, to "die"
- LAL 97-98 ❖ LAL 28 Mar 61

Freedom, obedience is the road to
- WG 113 (see also SL 37-38)
- ❖ WG 7:9 (see also SL 8:3)

Freedom of choice—see also Choice; Free will

Freedom of choice, chess game used to illustrate how fixed laws are essential to
- PP 34, 71 ❖ PP 2:15; 5:1

Freedom of choice implies the existence of things to choose between
- PP 29 ❖ PP 2:8

Freedom of choice involved in Lewis's conversion to Theism: I believe that this came nearer to being a perfectly free act than most that I have ever done
- SJ 224 (see also GID 261)
- ❖ SJ 14:16 (see also GID II 16:19-22)

Freedom of choice: The most deeply compelled action is also the freest
- GID 261 (see also LM 49-50*; SJ 224-225) ❖ GID II 16:19-22 (see also LM 9:11*; SJ 14:16)

Freedom of man best stated by saying that if there are other rational species in the universe, then it is not necessary to suppose that they have fallen
- PP 85 (see also WLN 86-87)
- ❖ PP 5:11 (see also WLN 6:10, 11)

Freedom of obedience, Screwtape discusses the paradoxical, which humans can experience
- SL 37-38 ❖ SL 8:3

Freedom, the activity of those who urge us to adopt new moralities is in the long run always directed against our
- CR 56 ❖ CR 4:27

Freedom, the belief that values are subjective is eternally incompatible with democracy and; the very idea of freedom presupposes some objective moral law
- CR 81 (see also Subjectivism; Value/s) ❖ CR 6:22 (see also Subjectivism; Value/s)

Freedom: "The hardness of God is kinder than the softness of men, and His com-

pulsion is our liberation"
- SJ 229 (see also GID 261*)
- ❖ SJ 14:23 (see also GID II 16:19-22*)

Freedom, the real inter-relation between God's omnipotence and Man's, is something we can't find out
- L 252 ❖ L 3 Aug 53

Freedom, the spiritual essence of death is the opposite of, hence the mortal images of rigidity, suffocation, etc.
- L 190
- ❖ L undated letter just after 11 Aug 40

Freud: If he is right, the universal pressure of the wish that God should not exist must be enormous...
- WLN 19 (see also Wish-fulfilment)
- ❖ WLN 2:8 (see also Wish-fulfilment)

Freud, philosophy of, mentioned as being in direct contradiction to Christianity
- MC 84 ❖ MC III 4:3

Freudians have discovered that we exist as bundles of complexes
- GID 271 ❖ GID III 1:2

Freudians, we are greatly indebted to, for exposing the cowardly evasions of really useful self-knowledge which we had all been practising...
- LM 34 ❖ LM 6:16

Friend, Arthur and Barfield were the types of every man's First and Second, (the First is our alter ego; the Second is the antiself)
- SJ 199 ❖ SJ 13:4

Friend, finding a true, is as great a wonder as first love—or even a greater
- SJ 131 ❖ SJ 8:18

Friend, God as our, whom we trust even when much evidence seems to disprove His existence or His good intentions
- WLN 26-30 ❖ WLN 2:13-18

Friend, I have no duty to be anyone's, and no man has a duty to be mine
- FL 103 ❖ FL 4:28

Friend, Lewis's childhood: "I had been so far from thinking such a friend possible that I had never even longed for one..."
- SJ 131 ❖ SJ 8:18

Friend, the First, is our alter ego—the man

who first reveals to you that you are not alone in the world (shares all your secret delights)
•SJ 199 ❖ SJ 13:4

Friend, the only, to walk with is one who so exactly shares your taste for each mood of the countryside that you needn't talk
•SJ 142 (*see also* PP 145-146; RP 95; SJ 200*) ❖ SJ 9:18 (*see also* PP 10:2; RP 9:6; SJ 13:4*)

Friend, the Second: "He has read all the right books but has got the wrong thing out of every one"
•SJ 199 ❖ SJ 13:4

Friend, the Second, is the antiself—the man who disagrees with you about everything (although he shares your interests)
•SJ 199-200 ❖ SJ 13:4

Friend, the Second: "When you set out to correct his heresies, you find that he forsooth has decided to correct yours!"
•SJ 199-200 ❖ SJ 13:4

Friends agree that some question, little regarded by others, is of great importance; they need not agree about the answer
•FL 97 ❖ FL 4:18

Friends, Christian, as a way in which the Holy Spirit speaks to us
•L 243 ❖ L 20 Jun 52

Friends, dangers of associating with ungodly
•RP 66-75, esp. 72-73; SL 45-48 (*see also* Association)
❖ RP ch. 7, esp. 7:11-14; SL ch. 10 (*see also* Association)

Friends, either one must die fairly young or outlive many
•LAL 82-83 ❖ LAL May 19th 59

Friends end up knowing and loving each other better than if their initial interest had been in each other as such
•FL 104 ❖ FL 4:29

Friends find solitude about them whether they want it or not; they would be glad to reduce it, and be joined by a third
•FL 97 (*see also* FL 91-92)

❖ FL 4:16, 17 (*see also* FL 4:8, 9)

Friends hardly ever talk about their friendship; they are side by side, absorbed in some common interest
•FL 91, 98 (*see also* FL 104)
❖ FL 4:18, 19 (*see also* FL 4:29)

Friends, I see few of the old warnings about Choice of, (—Screwtape)
•SL 47 ❖ SL 10:3

Friends, in each of my, there is something that only some other friend can fully bring out
•FL 92, 104-105 ❖ FL 4:9, 30

Friends, in Heaven the faces of our, shall laugh upon us in amazed recognition
•LM 124 ❖ LM 22:21

Friends indirectly defined as "joint seekers of the same God, the same beauty, the same truth"*
•FL 99 ❖ FL 4:22

Friends: "Is any pleasure on earth as great as a circle of Christian friends by a good fire?"
•L 197 ❖ L 21 Dec 41

Friends, Lewis describes a period he went through in which nearly all his, seemed "to be selfish or even false"
•L 222-223 ❖ L 12 Jan 50

Friends, like companions, will be doing something together, but something more inward, less widely shared and less easily defined
•FL 98 ❖ FL 4:19

Friends may come to feel humbled before all the others in their group; "Sometimes he wonders what he is doing there among his betters"
•FL 104-105 (*see also* FL 124-125)
❖ FL 4:30 (*see also* FL 4:59)

Friends ("peers"), we all wish to be judged by our; theirs is the praise we really covet and the blame we really dread
•FL 114 (*see also* WLN 112)
❖ FL 4:44 (*see also* WLN 7:36)

Friends, sets of, often suspected of being "stuck-up prigs who think themselves too good for us" by those who know nothing of Friendship
•FL 112 (*see also* FL 123-124)
❖ FL 4:41 (*see also* FL 4:57)

Friends, talk among: "...when the whole world, and something beyond the world, opens itself to our minds...an Affection mellowed by the years enfolds us"
•FL 104-105 ❖ FL 4:30

Friends, the very condition of having, is that we should want something else besides; those who are going nowhere can have no fellow travellers
•FL 98 ❖ FL 4:20

Friends, walking tours with: "Those are the golden sessions; when four or five of us after a hard day's walking have come to our inn..."
•FL 105 (see also L 117)
❖ FL 4:30 (see also L 26 Apr 27)

Friends who are pursuing "alien visions" and do not understand what you see in a particular book or landscape (re: desire for heaven)
•PP 145-146 (see also RP 95; SJ 142, 199-200)
❖ PP 10:2 (see also RP 9:6; SJ 9:18; 13:4)

Friends who disagree: You modify one another's thought; and "out of this perpetual dogfight a community of mind and a deep affection emerge"
•SJ 199-200 ❖ SJ 13:4

Friendship, a common point of view was the cause rather than the result of our, (re: C. Williams, J.R.R. Tolkien, D. Sayers, C. S. Lewis)
•L 287-288 ❖ L 15 May 59

Friendship a luminous, tranquil, rational world of relationships freely chosen; seems to raise us to the level of angels
•FL 89 ❖ FL 4:3

Friendship: Acquaintance or general society means little to me; I can't understand why a man should wish to know more people than he can make real friends of
•SJ 33 (see also L 245)
❖ SJ 2:12 (see also L 20 Oct 52)

Friendship always involves at least a partial indifference to outside opinion; this may lead to a wholesale indifference which is arrogant and inhuman
•FL 114-118 ❖ FL 4:47, 48

Friendship among workers who make good work their common goal: the only "Inner Ring" worth reaching
•WG 104-105 ❖ WG 6:17

Friendship and Affection: Things about an old friend which originally had nothing to do with the friendship become dear with familiarity
•FL 57 ❖ FL 3:8

Friendship and other love best when between those who acknowledge the same law, where each are "related in the right way to Love Himself"
•FL 173-174 ❖ FL 6:19

Friendship as an Appreciative love: "Sometimes he wonders what he is doing there among his betters. He is lucky beyond desert to be in such company"
•FL 104-105 ❖ FL 4:29, 30

Friendship arises when two or more companions discover some interest or insight in common which each believed to be unique to himself
•FL 96-97 ❖ FL 4:16-18

Friendship, Authorities tend to distrust, among their subjects; every real Friendship is a pocket of potential resistance
•FL 88, 112, 113-116 ❖ FL 4:2, 40, 43-47

Friendship between those who share a negative vision or point of view: "...we all know the perilous charm of a shared hatred or grievance"
•FL 113 ❖ FL 4:43

Friendship can be a school of virtue or of vice; makes good men better and bad men worse
•FL 115 ❖ FL 4:46

Friendship (chapter title)
•FL 87-127 ❖ FL ch. 4

Friendship: Christ says, "You have not chosen one another but I have chosen you for one another"
•FL 125-127 ❖ FL 4:61

Friendship compared to a feast in which God spreads the board, chooses the guests, and, we may dare to hope, presides as Host
•FL 126-127 ❖ FL 4:61

Friendship does not always need to be treated solemnly; "'God who made good laughter' forbid"
•FL 127 ❖ FL 4:62

Friendship, erotic love greatly enriched by the discovery that the Beloved can deeply and truly enter into, with the Friends you already had
•FL 99 ❖ FL 4:21

Friendship, every real, is a sort of secession, even a rebellion; may be unwelcome to those in authority
•FL 114-115 ❖ FL 4:45

Friendship: "Few value it because few experience it"
•FL 88 ❖ FL 4:2

Friendship, great thing in, is to turn from the demand to *be* loved to the wish to love
•L 245 ❖ L 20 Oct 52

Friendship has been by far the chief source of my happiness
•SJ 33 ❖ SJ 2:12

Friendship, in our society the matrix of common interests which makes up, exists between the sexes in some groups but not in others
•FL 105-107 ❖ FL 4:31, 32

Friendship: In this love, the important question is, "Do you see the same truth?"—or at least, "Do you care about the same truth?"
•FL 97, 102-103 ❖ FL 4:18, 27

Friendship indirectly defined as "travellers on the same quest" with a common vision*
•FL 99 ❖ FL 4:21

Friendship is born when two people share their vision; "And instantly they stand together in an immense solitude"
•FL 97 (*see also* SJ 32: "...we two or we few stand together...")
❖ FL 4:16 (*see also* SJ 2:12—"...we two or we few stand together...")

Friendship is unnecessary, has no survival value; rather it is one of those things which give value to survival
•FL 100-103, esp. 103 (*see also* FL 88, 94) ❖ FL 4:23-28, esp. 4:28 (*see also* FL 4:2, 11)

Friendship "is utterly free from Affection's need to be needed"
•FL 102 ❖ FL 4:26

Friendship, it has actually become necessary in our time to rebut the theory that every firm and serious, is really homosexual
•FL 90-94 ❖ FL 4:6-10

Friendship: "It would almost seem that Providence...quite overrules our previous tastes when it decides to bring two minds together" (re: improbability of one's taste in books)*
•SJ 190 ❖ SJ 12:12

Friendship largely free from instinct, duties, jealousy, and the need to be needed; is the sort of love one can imagine between angels
•FL 111 (*see also* FL 124)
❖ FL 4:38 (*see also* FL 4:57)

Friendship, lending or giving aid when we are in need not the stuff of; the occasions for it are almost interruptions
•FL 101-102 ❖ FL 4:26

Friendship, life has no better gift to give than real
•FL 105 ❖ FL 4:30

Friendship like Heaven in that each person can communicate a different aspect of God to all the rest
•FL 92-93 (*see also* PP 150)
❖ FL 4:9 (*see also* PP 10:7)

Friendship, love between God and Man rarely represented in Scripture as; more often as Affection ("Father") and Eros ("Bridegroom")
•FL 112-113, 124 (*see also* PP 44-46)
❖ FL 4:42, 58 (*see also* PP 3:12, 13)

Friendship may be "about" almost nothing except the fact that it excludes others ("...the degrading pleasure of exclusiveness")
•FL 121-122 ❖ FL 4:54, 55

Friendship may be called a "spiritual" love, but this does not mean it is in itself holy or inerrant
•FL 111-112 (*see also* FL 124)
❖ FL 4:39 (*see also* FL 4:57-59)

Friendship may develop slowly or with "amazing and elliptical speed"

•FL 97 ❖ FL 4:16

Friendship mostly between men and men or between women and women, as the sexes seldom share the companionship of common activities
•FL 105-106 ❖ FL 4:31

Friendship must be *about* something; that is why those pathetic people who simply "want friends" can never make any
•FL 98 ❖ FL 4:20

Friendship must exclude, but it must not come to take pleasure in its exclusivity
•FL 122 ❖ FL 4:55

Friendship must not become a "mutual admiration society," yet must be full of mutual admiration
•FL 124 (*see also* FL 112)
❖ FL 4:59 (*see also* FL 4:41)

Friendship: "No one can mark the exact moment at which friendship becomes love" (re: his relationship with Joy Davidman)
•LAL 65 ❖ LAL 17/2/57

Friendship not a reward for our discrimination and good taste; it is the instrument by which God reveals to each the beauties of all the others
•FL 126 ❖ FL 4:61

Friendship not merely a disguise or elaboration of Eros; those who cannot conceive this betray the fact that they have never had a Friend
•FL 91 ❖ FL 4:8

Friendship: "Nothing, I suspect, is more astonishing in any man's life than the discovery that there do exist people very, very like himself"
•SJ 131 ❖ SJ 8:18

Friendship: "Nothing makes an absent friend so present as a disagreement" (re: discussion about prayer by letter with his "friend" Malcolm)
•LM 3 ❖ LM 1:1

Friendship often confused with the Companionship which grows up among those who work and socialize together; but real Friendship is something more

•FL 95-98 ❖ FL 4:11-19

Friendship, passage from *Pilgrim's Progress* indicates how we can taste the illustrious experience of, with safety
•FL 124-125 ❖ FL 4:59, 60

Friendship: "People who bore one another should meet seldom; people who interest one another, often"
•FL 116 ❖ FL 4:47

Friendship, Pride is the danger to which, is naturally liable; may come to take pleasure in the exclusion of "Outsiders"
•FL 114-127 (*see also* Inner Rings)
❖ FL 4:46-62 (*see also* Inner Rings)

Friendship, question of maintaining an old, where there is no longer spiritual communion
•L 245 ❖ L 20 Oct 52

Friendship, real, may easily lead to erotic love and erotic love to real Friendship
•FL 98-99 (*see also* FL 106)
❖ FL 4:21 (*see also* FL 4:31)

Friendship the least natural of loves, the least instinctive and necessary—we can live and breed without it
•FL 88 (*see also* FL 94, 100-103)
❖ FL 4:2 (*see also* FL 4:11, 23-28)

Friendship: The modern undergraduate lives in a crowd; caucus has replaced friendship
•WG 107 ❖ WG 7:2

Friendship the most spiritual of loves, so the danger which besets it is spiritual too (Pride); it must invoke the divine protection if it is to remain sweet
•FL 111-112, 123-124 (*see also* FL 163)
❖ FL 4:38, 39, 57-59 (*see also* FL 6:1)

Friendship, the typical expression of opening, is something like, "What? You too? I thought I was the only one"
•FL 96, 113 (*see also* SJ vii)
❖ FL 4:16, 43 (*see also* SJ P:1)

Friendship: There is a charm about those moments when Appreciative love lies curled up asleep, and the ease and ordinariness of Affection wraps us round
•FL 57 ❖ FL 3:8

Friendship: To this day my vision of the

world is one in which "we two" or "we few" stand together against something stronger and larger
•SJ 32 (*see also* FL 97: "...they stand together..."; SJ 176: "...we few...")
❖ SJ 2:12 (*see also* FL 4:16: "...they stand together..."; SJ 11:13: "...we few...")
Friendship, true, is the least jealous of loves
•FL 92 ❖ FL 4:9
Friendship, two not the necessary number for; it is not even the best
•FL 91-92 (*see also* FL 97)
❖ FL 4:8 (*see also* FL 4:17)
Friendship (unlike Eros) is uninquisitive about such things as marital status and occupation; what matters is, "Do you see the same truth?"
•FL 102-103 ❖ FL 4:27
Friendship, very few modern people think of, as a love at all; it is thought to be a diversion, not a main course in life's banquet
•FL 87-88 ❖ FL 4:1
Friendship vs. erotic love: If only one were possible, which should we choose?
•FL 99-100 ❖ FL 4:22
Friendship vs. "Inner Rings": The exclusivity of friendship (or any wholesome group) is accidental
•WG 104-105 (*see also* FL 115-122)
❖ WG 6:16, 17 (*see also* FL 4:47-55)
Friendship: "We live in a world starved for solitude, silence, and privacy, and therefore starved for meditation and true friendship"
•WG 107❖WG 7:2
Friendship, what is offered as, may be mistaken for Eros on the other side—with painful and embarrassing results
•FL 106 ❖ FL 4:31
Friendship which dwindles into a coven of wanglers and manipulators meets a just doom—it sinks back into the mere practical Companionship which was its matrix
•FL 123 ❖ FL 4:56
Friendship, why, was valued more in ancient and medieval times than in modern times

•FL 89-90 ❖ FL 4:3-5
Friendship (with his brother): "Here came that moment...which you would have so appreciated and which cannot be fully enjoyed alone..."
•L 174 ❖ L 9 Jan 40
Friendship "withdraws men from the collective 'togetherness' as surely as solitude itself could do"
•FL 90 (*see also* FL 88, 97)
❖ FL 4:5 (*see also* FL 4:2, 17)
Friendships, are not all life-long, born when at last you meet a person who has some inkling of that something which you were born desiring?
•PP 146 (*see also* RP 95*)
❖ PP 10:2 (*see also* RP 9:6*)
Friendships which grow apart as interests change illustrate the irrelevance of meeting people in Heaven for whom you had only natural love on earth
•FL 188 ❖ FL 6:39
Front Line, analogy of, to illustrate how we should live day to day, "not adding the past or future to the present"
•LAL 69 ❖ LAL Oct 20th 57
Fruit—*consider also* Works
Fruit, a tree is known by its; a genuine conversion will be known by an improvement in outward behaviour
•MC 175-176 ❖ MC IV 10:2
Fruit, if the Bride does not bear, it may be supposed that the marriage was an illusion
•RP 132 ❖ RP 12:10
Fruition, "Joy" as desire but also
•SJ 166 ❖ SJ 11:3
Fruition of God: My idea of it is a huge, risky extrapolation from a very few and short experiences here on earth
•GO 82 (*consider also* Joy)
❖ GO 4:27 (*consider also* Joy)
Fulfillment—*see also* Satisfaction
Fulfillment: "When we want to be something other than the thing God wants us to be, we must be wanting what, in fact, will not make us happy"*
•PP 52 (*see also* PP 90; WG 118-119)
❖ PP 3:18 (*see also* PP 6:3; WG 7:18)

Fun—*see also* Pleasure(s)

Fun defined by Screwtape as "a sort of emotional froth arising from the play instinct"; he points out that it can be used to divert humans from duties
- SL 50 ❖ SL 11:3

Fun mentioned by Screwtape as having "wholly undesirable tendencies; it promotes charity, courage, contentment, and many other evils"
- SL 50 ❖ SL 11:3

Fun, the world is sillier and better, than they make out
- L 217 ❖ L 4 Apr 49

Fun, to become holy must be great
- MC 188 ❖ MC IV 11:10

Fun: "We are never safe, but we have plenty of fun and some ecstasy"; the settled happiness and security we all desire God withholds from us
- PP 115 ❖ PP 7:7

Fundamentalism: One can respect and at moments envy the Fundamentalist's view of the Bible (as "ultimate truth in systematic form")
- RP 112 ❖ RP 11:6

Fundamentalist, I have been suspected of being what is called a, since miraculous elements in a Bible narrative do not for me preclude its historicity
- RP 109 (*see also* CR 163)
❖ RP 11:2 (*see also* CR 13:28)

Funeral of a Great Myth, The (chapter title—re: popular Evolutionism)
- CR 82-93 ❖ CR ch. 7

Furs: I like them *on* the beasts
- LAL 46 ❖ LAL 9/10/55

Futilitate, De ["On Futility"] (chapter title)
- CR 57-71 ❖ CR ch. 5

Futility—*see also* Pessimism

Futility, difficulty inherent in accusing the universe of: "An accusation always implies a standard"
- CR 65-66 (*see also* PP 15*)
❖ CR 5:19 (*see also* PP 1:2*)

Futility: How any man can take it for granted that existence is not futile beats me...
- CR 57 ❖ CR 5:2

Futility of the world without God: "Some fatal flaw always brings the selfish and cruel people to the top and it all slides back into misery and ruin"
- MC 54 ❖ MC II 3:7, 8

Futility: Our sense that the universe is futile really implies a belief that it is not futile at all—that values are objective, rooted in moral reality
- CR 67 ❖ CR 5:20

Futility: Our very condemnation of reality as being futile carries an unconscious allegiance to that same reality as the source of our moral standards
- CR 69-70 ❖ CR 5:24

Futility, question of whether our feeling of, (along with all human thought) can be set aside as merely subjective and irrelevant to the real universe
- CR 60-71 (*see also* Thought)
❖ CR 5:9-27 (*see also* Thought)

Futility, the masses are shielded from fear of cosmic, by popular Evolutionism in which "Evolution" simply means "improvement"
- CR 58 ❖ CR 5:3

Futility, three possible attitudes toward the scientists' idea of long-term: to accept it; to deny that view of the universe; or to work against it
- CR 59 ❖ CR 5:5

Future—*consider also* Planning

Future, a mind so little sanguine as mine about the, ...
- SJ 173 (*see also* SJ 183)
❖ SJ 11:10 (*see also* SJ 12:2)

Future, a schoolboy learns to keep the, in its place; if he allowed infiltrations from the coming term into the present holidays he would despair
- SJ 158 ❖ SJ 10:11

Future defined by Screwtape as "something which everyone reaches at the rate of sixty minutes an hour, whatever he does, whoever he is"; we can't know it
- SL 118-119 ❖ SL 25:6

Future destruction, useless to worry about: Didn't people know they were going to die anyway?

•GID 266 ❖ GID II 16:56

Future, doing our daily duty more important than predictions about the, (play analogy)
•WLN 104-106 ❖ WLN 7:19-23

Future, don't worry about feeling brave over possible evils in the, —Our Lord didn't, in Gethsemane
•L 250 (see also Courage)
❖ L 17 Jul 53 (see also Courage)

Future, fear of—see also Fear; Worry

Future, fear of: In time of war, it was usually the reserve who had to watch the carnage, not the troops who were in it, whose nerve broke first
•L 250 ❖ L 17 Jul 53

Future, fear of: "The great thing...is to live from day to day and hour to hour not adding the past or future to the present"
•LAL 69 (see also LAL 58, 60, 97, 103; SL 29, 67-71*) ❖ LAL Oct 20th 57 (see also LAL 14/6/56; 3/8/56; Oct 30 58; 4 May 62; SL 6:2; ch. 15*)

Future, fear of: "We are not necessarily doubting that God will do the best for us; we are wondering how painful the best will turn out to be"*
•L 285 ❖ L 29 Apr 59

Future, I look upon the immediate, with great apprehension; moral collapse follows upon spiritual collapse
•GID 265 ❖ GID II 16:44

Future life—see also Eternal life; Immortality

Future life, at my conversion I did not yet believe in a; I now number that among my greatest mercies (God was to be obeyed simply because He was God)
•SJ 231 (see also FL 189-190; LM 120; RP 39-42, esp. 42) ❖ SJ 15:3 (see also FL 6:42; LM 22:8; RP 4:12-17, esp. 4:17)

Future life, belief in, should be a corollary to belief in God, not the other way around
•FL 189-190; GO 79 (see also L 290*; LM 120; RP 39-42)
❖ FL 6:42; GO 4:21 (see also L 3 Dec 59*; LM 22:8; RP 4:13-17)

Future life: How can it loom less than large if it is believed in at all?

•LM 120 (see also WG 3-5*)
❖ LM 22:7, 9 (see also WG 1:1-3*)

Future must be left in God's hands ("We may as well, for God will certainly retain it whether we leave it to Him or not")
•WG 30 (see also GO 38*)
❖ WG 2:13 (see also GO 2:31*)

Future, never commit your virtue or your happiness to the
•WG 30 (see also SL 67-71)
❖ WG 2:13 (see also SL ch. 15)

Future of our society, two determinants of: advance of science, and the changed relationship between Government and subjects
•GID 312-313 ❖ GID III 8:5-7

Future, predictions of, not useful: "The world might stop in ten minutes; meanwhile, we are to go on doing our duty"
•GID 266 (see also WLN 111-112)
❖ GID II 16:54-56 (see also WLN 7:34)

Future, Screwtape observes that God wants men to think about the, just so much as is necessary for planning acts of justice and charity
•SL 69 ❖ SL 15:4

Future (Screwtape): "We want a whole race perpetually in pursuit of the rainbow's end, never honest, nor kind, nor happy now..."
•SL 70 ❖ SL 15:4

Future, sober work for the, within the limits of ordinary morality and prudence, is not discouraged by Christianity and its belief about the End
•WLN 111-112 (see also GID 49, 57, 147-150, 266; PP 113-114)
❖ WLN 7:33, 34 (see also GID I 4:6, 7, 40; ch. 17; II 16:55; PP 7:4)

Future, thinking about, inflames hope and fear; Screwtape advises tempting humans to dwell on it (as well as on the Past) rather than the Present
•SL 67-71 ❖ SL 15:3-5

Future, those whose hopes are all based on the terrestrial, do not entrust much to it (re: "Life-Force" religion)
•GID 119 ❖ GID I 13:11

Future, uncertainty about, as a barricade to the human mind against God (—Screwtape)
•SL 28-29 ❖ SL 6:1, 2
Future, your anxiety about the, is a thing we can all understand, and *very* hard to bear; I pray you may be supported in it as you were before
•LAL 47 ❖ LAL 26/10/55

Gambling as one of the two sins Lewis mentioned that he was never tempted to commit (the other was "pederasty")
•SJ 101 (*see also* GID 59-60)
❖ SJ 7:1 (*see also* GID I 4:53, 54)
Gambling, I do not feel myself qualified to give advice about permissible and impermissible
•MC 9 ❖ MC P:10
Gambling, if I have no temptation for, this does not mean I am better than those who do; my timidity and pessimism are themselves temptations to avoid risk
•RP 29 ❖ RP 3:18
Gambling on a small scale, such as raffles, discussed
•GID 59-60 ❖ GID I 4:53, 54 (Ques. 13)
Games and dance are frivolous and unimportant down here, for "down here" is not their natural place; will be enjoyed in Heaven without frivolity
•LM 92-93 (*see also* LM 115-116*)
❖ LM 17:17 (*see also* LM 21:13*)
Games, I was useless at
•SJ 94 (*see also* L 75)
❖ SJ 6:18 (*see also* L 18 May 22)
Games: "It is a serious matter to choose wholesome recreations: but they would no longer be recreations if we pursued them seriously"
•CR 33-34 ❖ CR 2:54
Games, Lewis's dislike for
•SJ 90, 96-98, 107, 113-114, 129-130 (*see also* L 61*, LAL 46)

---

* These items reflect some interpretation on the part of the editor; the idea will not be found in these exact words. *See Introduction, p. ix.*
** These items are ideas of Lewis's which the editor has placed under a topic Lewis did not there intend to address. *See Introduction, p. ix.*
Entries without asterisks are not necessarily exact quotes, but the idea should be easy to find as worded.

❖ SJ 6:11, 20-23, 7:9, 18; 8:13 (*see also* L 29 May 21*; LAL 9/10/55)

Games: Making them organized and compulsory in school banished the element of play
•SJ 98 (*see also* SJ 107)
❖ SJ 6:22, 23 (*see also* SJ 7:9)

Games: "Not to like them is a misfortune, because it cuts you off from companionship with many excellent people who can be approached in no other way"
•SJ 129-130 ❖ SJ 8:13

Games seem to me to lead to ambition, jealousy, and embittered partisan feeling, quite as often as to anything else
•SJ 129 ❖ SJ 8:13

Garden as analogy to love: Both must be tended, and our tending must be combined with God's grace
•FL 163-165 ❖ FL 6:2

Garden, as long as I live my imagination of Paradise will retain something of my brother's toy
•SJ 7 (*see also* SJ 8, 16)
❖ SJ 1:4 (*see also* SJ 1:5, 15)

Garden, Joy (Lewis's wife) described as being like a, "...more secret, more full of fragrant and fertile life, the further you entered"
•GO 73 ❖ GO 4:6

Garden of the Hesperides, I had been wrong in supposing that I really desired; I was also wrong in supposing that I desired Joy itself
•SJ 220 ❖ SJ 14:12

Gardener, God as: "Think of yourself as a seed patiently waiting in the earth; waiting to come up a flower in the Gardener's good time..."
•LAL 119 (*see also* FL 163-165)
❖ LAL 28 Jun 63 (*see also* FL 6:2)

Generalities are the lenses with which our intellects have to make do (but God does not require such makeshifts)
•LM 55 ❖ LM 10:8

Generation(s)—*consider* Age(s)

Genesis account of Creation, I have no difficulty accepting the view that the, is derived from earlier Semitic stories

which were Pagan and mythical
•RP 110 ❖ RP 11:3

Genesis account of creation of man, conjectures about the
•RP 115-116 ❖ RP 11:11

Genesis account of Creation told in the form of a folk tale, but relays the idea of "creation" in the rigorous sense of the word
•M 33 (*see also* GID 42; RP 109-111)
❖ M 4:15 (*see also* GID I 3:9; RP 11:2, 3)

Genesis, book of, achieves the idea of true Creation and of a transcendent Creator
•RP 110-111 ❖ RP 11:3

Genesis story of the Fall as a scriptural myth: Apple was a magic apple of knowledge; in the developed doctrine story is simply one of disobedience
•PP 71-72 ❖ PP 5:2

"Genius," God as
•GID 31, 36; M 137, 138-139
❖ GID I 2:9, 15; M 15:9, 12

Genius, I don't like; it is the results I like (re: literature)
•L 154 ❖ L 14 Jun 32

Genuflection mentioned by Screwtape as a good source of conflict between "high" and "low" churchmen as long as Paul's advice is not brought to their minds
•SL 75 ❖ SL 16:5

Germans, reference to, in a letter written during World War II
•L 217 ❖ L 4 Apr 49

Gethsemane: a glaring instance contrary to the idea that the New Testament promises an invariable granting of our prayers
•WLN 5 ❖ WLN 1:7

Gethsemane, answer to criticism regarding Lewis's assumption that Christ felt fearful in
•L 189
❖ L undated letter just after 11 Aug 40

Gethsemane, Christ's faith did not save Him from dismay in
•L 285 (*see also* L 189, 210-211, 250)
❖ L 29 Apr 59 (*see also* L undated letter just after 11 Aug 40; undated letter

of 1947; 17 Jul 53)

Gethsemane, for most of us the prayer in, is the only model; removing mountains can wait
•LM 60 ❖ LM 11:10

Gethsemane: I am thankful that that scene of all others in our Lord's life did not go unrecorded
•L 166 (see also L 189, 250)
❖ L 8 May 39 (see also L undated letter just after 11 Aug 40; 17 Jul 53)

Gethsemane: It is clear that the knowledge of His death must somehow have been withdrawn from Jesus before He prayed
•LM 42 ❖ LM 8:6

Gethsemane: Jesus "chose on that night to plumb the depths of Christian experience, to resemble not the heroes of His army but the very weakest..."
•CR 150 ❖ CR 12:25

Gethsemane, Jesus' prayer in, shows that anxiety is part of our human destiny; the perfect Man experienced it
•LM 42-43 ❖ LM 8:9

Gethsemane: "Lest any trial incident to humanity should be lacking, the torments of hope—of suspense, anxiety—were at the last moment loosed upon Him"
•LM 42 ❖ LM 8:6

Gethsemane: Our Lord descends into the humiliation of praying on His own behalf (but when He does, certitude about His Father's will apparently is withdrawn)
•LM 61 ❖ LM 11:14

Gethsemane, Our Lord didn't feel brave in
•L 250 ❖ L 17 Jul 53

Gethsemane, our Lord made a petitionary prayer in, (and did not get what He asked for)
•LM 35-36 ❖ LM 7:1, 2

Gethsemane, Our Lord was afraid in; fear is horrid, but there's no reason to be ashamed of it
•LAL 41 ❖ LAL 2nd Apr 55

Gethsemane, prayer in: Disciples only heard the opening words—then fell asleep; they record those words as if they were the whole
•LM 47 ❖ LM 9:3

Gethsemane, prayer in: The reservation "Nevertheless, not my will but thine" seems inconsistent with the New Testament demand for a sure belief
•CR 143-144 ❖ CR 12:4-9

Gethsemane, prayer in: We may be sure Jesus prayed aloud; people did everything aloud in those days
•LM 47 ❖ LM 9:3

Gethsemane refutes the idea that the people whose prayers are answered are "a sort of court favorites, people who have influence with the throne"
•WLN 10 ❖ WLN 1:20

Gethsemane shows us that the absence of such faith as ensures the granting of a prayer is not necessarily a sin
•LM 60 ❖ LM 11:12

Gethsemane, the courage of the perfected Christian has been learned in, and may have no "honour" about it (re: value of "honour" in literature)
•CR 22 ❖ CR 2:30

Gethsemane: The fact that Jesus made His request with a reservation—"not my will, but thine"—does not remove the prayer's petitionary character
•LM 36 ❖ LM 7:2

Gethsemane, the Perfect Man brought to, a strong will to escape suffering and death combined with a perfect readiness for obedience
•PP 113 ❖ PP 7:3

Ghost, confusion between Spirit and, has done much harm
•M 92 ❖ M 11:16

Ghost, Jesus had to assure the disciples that He was not a; He had a body
•M 145-148 ❖ M 16:6-10

Ghosts and insects, Lewis describes a childhood fear of: "...to this day I would rather meet a ghost than a tarantula"
•SJ 8-9 (see also SJ 177)
❖ SJ 1:6, 7 (see also SJ 11:16)

Gift, faith as a, which we must ask for
•GID 174 ❖ GID I 21:5

Gifts: It is much harder to receive than to

give but, I think, much more blessed (—Joy Lewis, in letter to an American lady)
•LAL 76 ❖ LAL Jun 6th [1958]

Gifts, natural—*see also* Talents

Gifts, natural, can cause us to forget our need of God as surely as wealth
•MC 180-181 (*see also* L 221)
❖ MC IV 10:11-13 (*see also* L 22 Sep 49)

Gifts of God—*see* Blessings

Gifts of help: We must all learn to receive as well as to give
•LAL 57, 58 (*see also* LAL 75-76; 111-112) ❖ LAL 14/6/56; 5/7/56 (*see also* LAL Jun 6th [1958]; 10 Dec 62)

Gifts of the Spirit—*consider also* Glossolalia

Gifts of the Spirit, giving of, may not have been possible until the Ascension of Christ; there is a mystery here that I will not even attempt to sound
•RP 126 ❖ RP 12:6

Gifts to God, all our, are like the intrinsically worthless present of a child, which a father values indeed, but only for the intention (re: church music)*
•CR 99 ❖ CR 8:12

Gifts: Unless we learn to receive, how could others have the pleasure, and the spiritual growth, of giving things? (—Joy Lewis, in letter to American lady)
•LAL 75-76 (*see also* LAL 61-62)
❖ LAL Jun 6th [1958] (*see also* LAL Sep 8/56)

Gift-love—*see also* Love

Gift-love (as in parenting) must work toward its own abdication; we must aim at making ourselves superfluous
•FL 76 ❖ FL 3:37

Gift-love for God vs. Need-love and Appreciative love for Him: "Gift-love longs to serve..."
•FL 33 ❖ FL 2:13, 14

Gift-love, God implants in us a natural, but in addition He can bestow a far greater gift—Divine Gift-love, which is wholly disinterested
•FL 176-177 ❖ FL 6:22-24

Gift-love may become perverted, as in the need to be needed (story of Mrs. Fidget)
•FL 73-77, 82-83 (*see also* L 198-199*; MC 167*; SL 121*, 123*) ❖ FL 3:33-37, 45 (*see also* L undated letter just before 10 Jan 42; MC IV 7:3*; SL 26:2, 5*)

Gift-love, Need-love, and Appreciative love differentiated
•FL 11-21, 33 (*see also* FL 175-184)
❖ FL ch. 1; 2:14 (*see also* FL 6:21-34)

Gift-love of Charity comes by Grace
•FL 178 ❖ FL 6:24, 25

Gift-love the most God-like love
•FL 19 ❖ FL 1:16

Gift-love to God includes our charity to those in need; "every stranger whom we feed or clothe is Christ"
•FL 178 ❖ FL 6:24

Giving, the proper aim of, is to put the recipient in a state where he no longer needs our gift
•FL 76 ❖ FL 3:37

Giving to the poor—*see* Alms; Charity

Giving up things: "I'm afraid as we grow older life consists more and more in either giving up things or waiting for them to be taken from us..."
•LAL 95 ❖ LAL 9 Jan 61

Glorifying God—*see also* Praise

Glorifying God: Most men must glorify God by doing to His glory something which is not *per se* an act of glorifying but which becomes so by being offered
•CR 24 ❖ CR 2:37

Glorifying God: "The Scotch catechism says that man's chief end is 'to glorify God and enjoy Him forever'" (and these are the same thing)
•RP 96-97 ❖ RP 9:6

Glorifying God: "There is...a sense in which all natural agents, even inanimate ones, glorify God continually by revealing the powers He has given them" —re: church musicians
•CR 98 (*see also* CR 95)
❖ CR 8:11(*see also* CR 8:5)

Glorifying God, two levels of: one in which intention is irrelevant, and another in which all depends on intention (re: church music)

•CR 98 ❖ CR 8:12

Glorifying God: "We can play, as we can eat, to the glory of God" (re: the reading of comedies and tales)
•CR 10 ❖ CR 1:15

Glorifying of God and the salvation of souls as "the business of life"
•CR 14 (*see also* CR 12, 26; GO 30)
❖ CR 2:4 (*see also* CR 2:1, 42; GO 2:16)

Glory as brightness, splendour, luminosity
•WG 11, 16-17 ❖ WG 1:9, 13

Glory: Filth that our enemies fling at the Holy One either does not stick, or, sticking, turns into glory (re: charge that God committed adultery with Mary)
•GID 32 ❖ GID I 2:9

Glory: From Idealism I had come one step nearer to understanding the words, "We give thanks to thee for thy great glory"
•SJ 210-211 ❖ SJ 13:19

Glory, God's love for us is a burden of, not only beyond our deserts but also mostly beyond our desiring
•PP 47 ❖ PP 3:14

"Glory," I was lamenting that a, had passed away (re: the passing of the "thrill," for Lewis, out of Norse literature)
•SJ 166 ❖ SJ 11:2

Glory, in the sense of obtaining approval by God, is scriptural; perfect humility dispenses with modesty
•WG 11-13 ❖ WG 1:9, 10

Glory, it may be possible to think too much of our own potential, but not of our neighbor's
•WG 18 ❖ WG 1:15

Glory means acceptance by God, and welcome into the heart of things
•WG 14-15 ❖ WG 1:11

"Glory," nature gave the word, a meaning for me
•FL 37 (*see also* FL 153-154)
❖ FL 2:23 (*see also* FL 5:35)

Glory of God—*see also* God, greatness of

Glory of God cannot be diminished by our refusal to worship Him, any more than a lunatic can put out the sun by scribbling the word "darkness" on the walls of his cell
•PP 53 ❖ PP 3:18

Glory of God described as the "beauty so old and new" and "the light behind the sun" (re: Lord's Prayer)
•LM 28 (*see also* SJ 236)
❖ LM 5:17 (*see also* SJ 15:7)

Glory of God, pleasures are shafts of the, as it strikes our sensibility
•LM 89 ❖ LM 17:4

Glory of God to be worshipped for its own sake
•GID 130 (*see also* FL 189-190*; RP 4:15, 16; SJ 77, 211*, 231)
❖ GID I 16:2 (*see also* FL 6:42*; RP 40-41; SJ 5:9; 13:19*; 15:3)

Glory of redeemed humanity will exalt all creatures, including those who have never fallen
•M 122-123 ❖ M 14:24

Glory, promise of, is highly relevant to our deep desire
•WG 14-15 ❖ WG 1:11

Glory, promise of, only possible by the work of Christ
•WG 13 ❖ WG 1:10

Glory, promise of: What it involves
•WG 3-19 ❖ WG ch. 1

Glory, The Weight of (chapter title)

Glory: We are taught to "give thanks to God for His great glory," as if we owed Him thanks just for being what He necessarily is; and so indeed we do
•SJ 77 (*see also* GID 130; SJ 211, 231)
❖ SJ 5:9 (*see also* GID I 16:2; SJ 13:20; 15:3)

Glory, we give thanks to thee for thy great: God as both a noun (a "substance") and an adjective or quality ("glory")
•LM 86 ❖ LM 16:12

Glossolalia as an example of how glorifying God may not always edify our neighbor
•CR 94 ❖ CR 8:3

Glossolalia "glorified God firstly by being miraculous and involuntary, and secondly by the ecstatic state of mind in which the speaker was"
•CR 95 ❖ CR 8:5

Glossolalia, it is very hard to believe that

in all instances of, the Holy Ghost is operating
- •WG 55 ❖ WG 4:2

Glossolalia mentioned as an example of how "Transposition" works
- •WG 54-55, 64-65 ❖ WG 4:1-2, 15-17

Glossolalia, whether all instances of, are manifestations of hysteria
- •WG 54-66 ❖ WG 4:1-18

Gluttony of those people in the "All-I-want" state of mind who believe they are practicing temperance ("gluttony of Delicacy")
- •SL 76-78 ❖ SL 17:1-3

Gluttony: Screwtape advises Wormwood on the value of excess in food for attacks on human chastity
- •SL 79 ❖ SL 17:4

Gluttony: Women, according to Screwtape, are more often tempted to gluttony of Delicacy ("All-I-want...") while men are more often tempted to gluttony of Vanity
- •SL 78 ❖ SL 17:3

Gnosticism as a system of thought which moved out with its time (vs. Christianity, which has survived)
- •GID 65 ❖ GID I 5:7

Goal—see also Purpose

Goal ("end") of all human endeavor is to be happy at home (quote from Johnson)
- •L 262; WG 108-109
- ❖ L 16 Mar 55; WG 7:4

Goal ("job") of life is to determine truth or untruth of Christianity and then to devote all energy either to serving it or to exposing the humbug
- •GID 112 ❖ GID I 12:9

Goal of Christian life: "Business of life" is to learn to like contact with God, since that contact cannot be avoided for long*
- •GID 47 (see also MC 183; WG 13)
- ❖ GID I 3:17 (see also MC IV 10:17; WG 1:10)

Goal of Christian life: "Business of life" is to purge away hatred*
- •CR 118 ❖ CR 10:7

Goal of Christian life is to "die," to relinquish one's freedom and independence
- •LAL 97-98 ❖ LAL 28 Mar 61

Goal of Christian life is to press on toward Heaven (our "true country") and to help others do the same
- •MC 120 ❖ MC III 10:5

Goal of Christian life: "The great thing is to be found at one's post as a child of God, living each day as though it were our last..."*
- •GID 266; WLN 111-112
- ❖ GID II 16:55; WLN 7:34

Goal of Christian life: The proper good of a creature is to surrender itself to its Creator—and when it does so, it is good and happy*
- •PP 90 (see also PP 52; WG 118-119)
- ❖ PP 6:3 (see also PP 3:18; WG 7:18)

Goal of Christian life: to be as little as possible "ourselves," but rather to become clean mirrors filled with the image of a face that is not ours*
- •CR 6-7 ❖ CR 1:10

Goal of Christian life: to be such good advertisements for Christianity as will make it attractive*
- •L 247 ❖ L 8 Nov 52

Goal of Christian life: to become a little Christ, united with God
- •MC 153 ❖ MC IV 4:8-10

Goal of Christian life: to "glorify God and enjoy Him forever"*
- •GO 30 ❖ GO 2:16

Goal of Christian life: to imitate Christ; this goal will help us decide issues of right and wrong
- •MC 162 (see also MC 166)
- ❖ MC IV 7:5 (see also MC IV 8:1)

Goal of Christian life: "To play well the scenes in which we are 'on'..."*
- •WLN 104 ❖ WLN 7:19

Goal of Christian life: "We are bidden to 'put on Christ,' to become like God"*
- •PP 53-54 (see also SL 158*; WLN 56*)
- ❖ PP 3:18, 19 (see also SL 32:13*; WLN 4:13*)

Goal of Christians in thinking about the Judgment: "...to dress our souls not for the electric lights of the present world

but for the daylight of the next"*
•WLN 113 ❖ WLN 7:38

Goal of human life [from the Christian perspective]: Salvation in Christ and the glorifying of God (re: how to reconcile this with the value of "culture")
•CR 12, 14 (see also CR 26)
❖ CR 2:1, 4 (see also CR 2:42)

Goal of human life not to be the avoidance of suffering or of self-preservation; all Christ's followers must take up the cross*
•CR 155 (see also FL168, 170; Safety)
❖ CR 13:6 (see also FL 6:10, 14; Safety)

Goal of life (or "civilization"), what should be the main?
•GID 280-281 ❖ GID III 2:7-10

Goal of man, true: the fruition of God
•CR 26 ❖ CR 2:41

Goals: "When we want to be something other than the thing God wants us to be, we must be wanting what, in fact, will not make us happy"*
•PP 52 (see also PP 90; WG 118-119)
❖ PP 3:18 (see also PP 6:3; WG 7:18)

God—consider also Supernatural

God, a man is "nearest" to, when he is most surely approaching his final union with God, and the vision and enjoyment of God
•FL 15 (see also WG 66-67)
❖ FL 1:9 (see also WG 4:20)

God, a safe or tame, is a fantasy
•LM 76 ❖ LM 14:14

God, absence of—see Absence of God; consider Abandonment

God, acts of worship and observances of religious festivals can become substitutes for
•RP 48-49 ❖ RP 5:7

God, adoration of, through experience of pleasure: Any patch of sunlight will show you something about the sun which you couldn't get from books on astronomy
•LM 91 ❖ LM 17:13

God and Christ: Using the names Father and Son suggest the erroneous idea that one was there first
•MC 150-151 ❖ MC IV 4:2-4

God and His creation not fully conceivable to Man
•GID 43 (see also L 252; M 110; RP 115)
❖ GID I 3:9 (see also L 3 Aug 53; M 14:4; RP 11:11)

God and Joy, no slightest hint was vouchsafed me that there ever had been or ever would be any connection between
•SJ 230 (see also Joy)
❖ SJ 15:2 (see also Joy)

God and man cannot exclude one another, as man excludes man; "God did (or said) it" and "I did (or said) it" can both be true
•LM 68-69 (see also LAL 22, 23; LM 49-50, 81; MC 142-143)
❖ LM 13:2-4 (see also LAL Nov 6/53; 27/xi/53; LM 9:11; 15:15; MC IV 2:9)

God and Man, love between, rarely represented in Scripture as Friendship; more often described as Affection ("Father") and Eros ("Bridegroom")
•FL 112-113, 124 (see also PP 44-46)
❖ FL 4:42, 58 (see also PP 3:12, 13)

God and nothing else is the true goal of men and the satisfaction of their needs
•RP 40-41 (see also GO 79*; WG 14-15)
❖ RP 4:15 (see also GO 4:21*; WG 1:11, 12)

God and the Incarnation, example of attempt to describe, without the use of metaphorical language
•GID 71; M 79 ❖ GID I 6:9; M 10:19

God and the moral law, Lewis's attempt to describe the relationship between, (Possibly God neither obeys nor creates the moral law; Good is uncreated)
•CR 79-80 ❖ CR 6:21

God, anger toward, in time of difficulty: "I was getting from it the only pleasure a man in anguish can get; the pleasure of hitting back"
•GO 45-46 ❖ GO 3:9

God, "appetite" for, as expressed in the Psalms ("It has all the cheerful spontaneity of a natural, even a physical, desire")
•RP 50-53 (see also GID 130)
❖ RP 5:8-10 (see also GID I 16:2)

God, approval by, comes not because we are good; God makes us good because He loves us
•MC 64 ❖ MC II 5:6

God, approval by, is the promise—and the weight—of glory
•WG 11-13 ❖ WG 1:9, 10

God as a "bright blur," our imagining of, may be an obstacle to prayer; this idol needs to be broken before we begin
•LM 78, 82, 83 (see also LM 91)
❖ LM 15:5, 17; 16:1 (see also LM 17:12)

God as a Fountain: "If you are close to it, the spray will wet you..."
•MC 153 ❖ MC IV 4:8

God as a Fountain: Our loved ones are as portraits to the Original, and as rivulets to the Fountain
•FL 191 ❖ FL 6:44

God as a Fountain: "The whole man is to drink joy from the fountain of joy"
•WG 17-18 (see also RP 97*)
❖ WG 1:14 (see also RP 9:7*)

God as "a god" and more—not less (as Christ is more than Balder, not less)
•GID 67 ❖ GID I 5:13

God as a grave old king with a long beard: This anthropomorphic image at least gets in the idea of oldness and mystery
•GO 35-36 ❖ GO 2:27

God as a "great spiritual force" commands a friendly interest; temperature drops when you speak of a personal, definitive God
•M 81 (see also GID 71; M 93-94; MC 35; SL 33; Religion, minimal)
❖ M 11:2 (see also GID I 6:9; M 11:19; MC I 4:6; SL 7:1; Religion, minimal)

God as a kind of Dance—a dynamic, pulsing activity (re: Trinity)
•MC 152, 153 ❖ MC IV 4:6, 8

God as a kind of "magician" to children: I imagine that disappointment of this kind of faith is of no religious importance
•SJ 20-21 ❖ SJ 1:22

God as a Person—see God, personal

God as a Sea: We are tempted to be careful not to get out of our depth and lose our things temporal
•WG 128 (see also FL 181)
❖ WG 9:6 (see also FL 6:28)

God as "a smooth inclined plane on which there is no resting...indeed we are now of such a nature that we must slip off" (re: sin of self-centredness)
•PP 76 (see also PP 83, 91)
❖ PP 5:5 (see also PP 5:10; 6:3)

God as an impersonal "life-force" is well and good; but God Himself, alive, pulling at the other end of the cord, is another matter
•M 93-94 (see also GID 142-143; LM 114; M 81; MC 35; SL 22-23)
❖ M 11:19 (see also GID I 16:25; LM 21:8; M 11:2; MC I 4:6; SL 4:4)

God as an utterly concrete Being whom Man can fear, love, address, and "taste"
•RP 87 ❖ RP 8:17

God as Angler: He "played his fish and I never dreamed that the hook was in my tongue"
•SJ 211 ❖ SJ 13:20

God as Artist [or "Painter"]: We are only the picture
•MC 173 (see also LM 34, 69; MC 44)
❖ MC IV 9:7 (see also LM 6:16; 13:4; MC II 1:4)

God as Artist: We are a Divine work of art; an artist, over the most loved picture of his life, will spend much time and effort perfecting it
•PP 42-43, 47 ❖ PP 3:10, 14

God as Author, Producer, and Audience (in the stage-play of prayer)
•LM 81 (see also Prayer as soliloquy)
❖ LM 15:15 (see also Prayer as soliloquy)

God as both a noun (a "substance") and an adjective or quality ("glory")
•LM 86 ❖ LM 16:12

God as Cosmic Sadist vs. a kind surgeon whose intentions are wholly good
•GO 49-50 (see also GO 35, 43- 44, 45-46; L 162; LAL 118-119)
❖ GO 3:17 (see also GO 2:26; 3:4, 5, 9˘; L 12 Sep 38; LAL 25 Jun 63)

God as Creator—see also Creator

God as Creator: "[God] is the opaque centre of all existences...He is so brim-full of existence that He can give existence away..."
•M 88 ❖ M 11:11

God as Creator: He values matter and the senses and all that can be called Nature
•M 163 ❖ M 16:32

God as Creator: If a Brute made the world, then he also made the standard by which we judge him to be a Brute (re: Heroic Pessimism or anti-theism)
•CR 65-67 (see also CR 69-70; MC 45-46*) ❖ CR 5:19 (see also CR 5:24; MC II 1:5, 6*)

God as Creator: one of the Christian beliefs
•MC 45 ❖ MC II 1:4

God as Dentist: "Christ says...I don't want to drill the tooth, or crown it, or stop it, but to have it out"
•MC 167 ❖ MC IV 8:4

God as Dentist: "I hope that when the tooth of life is drawn and I am 'coming round,' a voice will say, 'Rinse your mouth out with this'" (re: Purgatory)
•LAL 84; LM 109 (see also SL 146*, 147) ❖ LAL Jul 7th 59; LM 20:12 (see also SL 31:2*, 3)

God as Dentist: "It doesn't really matter whether you grip the arms of the dentist's chair or let your hands lie in your lap. The drill drills on"
•GO 38 ❖ GO 2:31

God as Dentist: Once you call Him in, He will give you the full treatment
•MC 171 ❖ MC IV 9:2, 3

God as Dentist: Repentance of sins like having a painful tooth out
•GID 124 (see also RP 32) ❖ GID I 14:10 (see also RP 3:21)

God as Dentist: "Surely it [the Law of God] could be more aptly compared to the dentist's forceps or the front line than to anything enjoyable and sweet"
•RP 55 ❖ RP 6:3

God as Dentist: "What do people mean when they say, 'I am not afraid of God because I know He is good?' Have they never been to a dentist?"
•GO 50-51 ❖ GO 3:19

God as Eternal Vet whose operations may hurt, but only for our own good
•GO 75 (see also GO 46-47) ❖ GO 4:12 (see also GO 3:10, 11)

God as First Cause, "Ens Realissimum," or "Unmoved Mover": Such a God fails to invite a personal approach
•GID 174 (see also PP 51-52*) ❖ GID I 21:5 (see also PP 3:17*)

God as "Force," belief in, gives the thrills of religion without the cost
•MC 35 (see also GID 143; M 81*, 93-94*; SL 33*; Cost) ❖ MC I 4:6 (see also GID I 16:25; M 11:2*, 19*; GI 19*; SL 7:1*; Cost)

God as "Force" just as metaphorical as "Father"
•GID 71; M 74-75 ❖ GID I 6:9; M 10:13

God as Gardener: "Think of yourself as a seed patiently waiting in the earth; waiting to come up a flower in the Gardener's good time..."
•LAL 119 (see also FL 163-165) ❖ LAL 28 Jun 63 (see also FL 6:2)

God as "Genius"
•GID 31, 36; M 137, 138-139 ❖ GID I 2:9, 15; M 15:9, 12

God as Helper: The help He intends to give us is help to become perfect—nothing less
•MC 171-175 ❖ MC IV ch. 9

God as Hunter: "He was the hunter (or so it seemed to me) and I was the deer. He stalked me like a redskin, took unerring aim, and fired"
•CR 169 (see also SJ 227; Initiative) ❖ CR 14:19 (see also SJ 14:20, 21; Initiative)

God as "I AM": In declaring this, God proclaims the mystery of self-existence
•M 87 ❖ M 11:10

God as immeasurably superior to ourself: We must recognize our nothingness before we can know Him at all
•MC 111 ❖ MC III 8:6

God as Inventor: We are only the machine
•MC 173 (see also Machine)

❖ MC IV 9:7 (*see also* Machine)

God as Man—*see also* Incarnation

God as Man, difficulty of imagining, ("But the physical sciences, no less than theology, propose for our belief much that cannot be imagined")
•WLN 99 ❖ WLN 7:10

God as "my Adversary" (before Lewis's conversion)
•SJ 216, 227 ❖ SJ 14:7, 20

God as One "without whom Nothing is strong" —and Nothing is very strong
•SL 56 ❖ SL 12:4

God as our Friend whom we trust even when much evidence seems to disprove His existence or His good intentions
•WLN 26-30 ❖ WLN 2:13-18

God as our true Beloved (earthly loved ones are as portraits to the Original, and as rivulets to the Fountain)
•FL 190-191 (*see also* PP 147; SL 148)
❖ FL 6:44, 45 (*see also* PP 10:3; SL 31:5)

God as Painter: We are a Divine work of art; an artist, over the most loved picture of his life, will spend much time and effort perfecting it
•PP 42-43, 47 ❖ PP 3:10, 14

God as Painter: We are only the picture
•MC 173 (*see also* LM 34, 69; MC 44)
❖ MC IV 9:7 (*see also* LM 6:16; 13:4; MC II 1:4)

God as perceived in Christian imagery
•M 73-80 (*see also* GID 68, 70-71)
❖ M 10:12-20 (*see also* GID I 6:2, 8, 9)

God as Perfect Myth and Perfect Fact (in Christ)
•GID 67 (*see also* M 133-134, ftnt.; SJ 236; Myth of "dying god")
❖ GID I 5:13 (*see also* M 15:2—ftnt.; SJ 15:7; Myth of "dying god")

God as Surgeon: Do the approaches of Grace often hurt because the spiritual vein in us hides itself from the celestial surgeon?
•LAL 118-119 ❖ LAL 25 Jun 63

God as Surgeon: "The more we believe that God hurts only to heal, the less we can believe that there is any use in begging for tenderness"
•GO 49-50 ❖ GO 3:17

God as Surgeon: "We *force* God to surgical treatment: we won't (mentally) diet..."
•L 162 (*see also* L 227*)
❖ L 12 Sep 38 (*see also* L 5 Mar 51*)

God as "the Absolute Being" in the sense that He alone exists in His own right (but God is not a generality)
•M 87 (*see also* M 169)
❖ M 11:10 (*see also* M App. A:1)

God as "the Absolute" taught me how a thing can be revered not for what it can do to us but for what it is in itself
•SJ 231 ❖ SJ 15:3

God as "the Absolute": "This was a religion that cost nothing...There was nothing to fear; better still, nothing to obey"
•SJ 209-210 (*see also* GID 143; M 81, 93-94; MC 35, 136; Cost)
❖ SJ 13:18 (*see also* GID I 16:25; M 11:2, 19; MC I 4:6; IV 1:4; Cost)

God as "the completely real, external, invisible Presence" there with us in the room who, according to Screwtape, is never fully knowable by humans
•SL 22 ❖ SL 4:4

God as "the Desirable" or "the real Desirable"
•SJ 166, 168, 177, 204
❖ SJ 11:3, 5, 14; 13:10

God as "the Father of Lights" who gives us all our understanding*
•RP 80, 110 (*see also* CR 136)
❖ RP 8:7; 11:3 (*see also* CR 11:16)

God as the great Rival, the ultimate object of human jealousy: "The bitterness of some unbelief...is really due to this"
•FL 61 (*see also* FL 70-73; L 274; SL 18)
❖ FL 3:13 (*see also* FL 3:27-32; L 10 Feb 57; SL 3:6)

God as the ground of our existence (with a kind of paternal claim on us) and a benefactor (with a claim on our gratitude); we owe Him obedience
•CR 27 ❖ CR 2:42

God as "the increasingly knowable Lord"
•WLN 30 ❖ WLN 2:18

God as the "light from behind the sun"*

•LM 28 (*see also* SJ 236)
❖ LM 5:17 (*see also* SJ 15:7)
God as the "light from beyond Nature"
•M 120 (*see also* GID 84*)
❖ M 14:20 (*see also* GID I 9:6*)
God as "the naked Other, image-less...unknown, undefined, desired"*
•SJ 221 ❖ SJ 14:12
God as the Presence which will someday become palpable, immediate, and unavoidable
•MC 183 (*see also* GID 47; MC 66)
❖ MC IV 10:17 (*see also* GID I 3:17; MC II 5:9)
God as "the pure light" who walked the earth when incarnated
•LM 71 (*see also* MC 151; SJ 236; Light)
❖ LM 13:10 (*see also* SJ 15:7; MC IV 4:4; Light)
God as the Sovereign of Nature
•GID 32; M 32, 132
❖ GID I 2:10; M 4:14; 15:1
God as the ultimate Fact, the fountain of all other facthood
•M 6-7, 87, 88, 91, 95, 110, 155; MC 158
❖ M 2:5, 6; 11:9-11, 15; 12:1; 14:4; 16:22; MC IV 6:2
God as the ultimate reality does not mean "not a person" but "a person and more"; this is shown in the doctrine of the Trinity
•GID 185 (*see also* MC 140-141)
❖ GID I 23:2 (*see also* MC IV 2:2)
God as transcendental Interferer
•SJ 172 (*see also* SJ 228, 237*)
❖ SJ 11:8 (*see also* SJ 14:22; 15:8*)
God as Trinity (three Beings)—*see* Trinity
God as vet vs. vivisector
•GO 46 (*see also* GO 33, 44, 75)
❖ GO 3:10, 11 (*see also* GO 2:22; 3:5; 4:12)
God, avenues for seeking knowledge about, (miracles, inspired teachers, and enjoined ritual)
•GID 143-144 ❖ GID I 16:26
God, avoidance of—*see* Evasion of God
God, awareness of the presence of, has often been unwelcome—for He comes not only to raise up but to cast down; to deny, to rebuke, to interrupt

•LM 75 (*see also* Evasion)
❖ LM 14:12 (*see also* Evasion)
God, belief in, may be described in Theological or Poetical language; Theological language is in a sense alien to religion, omitting all that's important
•CR 135-136 ❖ CR 11:13-15
God, belief in, ought to come before belief in a future life—not the other way around
•FL 189-190; GO 79; LM 120; RP 39-42; SJ 231 (*see also* L 290*)
❖ FL 6:42; GO 4:21; LM 22:8; RP 4:13-17; SJ 15:3 (*see also* L 3 Dec 59*)
God, belief in, stated in Theological language: "I believe in incorporeal entity, personal in the sense that it can be the subject and object of love..."
•CR 135 ❖ CR 11:13
God, both those who believe in, and those who disbelieve face many hours of doubt
•CR 41 (*see also* Atheism)
❖ CR 3:9 (*see also* Atheism)
God, business of life is to learn to like contact with, since that contact cannot be avoided for long
•GID 47 (*see also* MC 183; WG 13)
❖ GID I 3:17 (*see also* MC IV 10:17; WG 1:10)
God cannot be affected with love because He *is* love, in the same way that water is exempt from getting wet
•M 92-93 ❖ M 11:17
God can't be used as a road to another end, such as reunion with deceased loved ones
•GO 79 (*see also* FL 189-190; GO 28-29; L 290; RP 41)
❖ GO 4:21 (*see also* FL 6:41-43; GO 2:14; L 3 Dec 59; RP 4:16)
God, Christian idea of, is the only one on the market if you are looking for something superpersonal—something more than a person
•MC 141 ❖ MC IV 2:2
God, Christian vs. Pantheistic view of
•M 81-94; MC 43-45
❖ M ch. 11; MC II 1:3, 4
God: Christianity asserts that He is good,

that He made all things good, but that one of those things, free will, included the possibility of evil
•PP 69 ❖ PP 5:1

God, claims of—*see* Claims of God; Demands of God

God closed in on me...
•SJ 224 (*see also* CR 169; GID 261)
❖ SJ 14:16 (*see also* CR 14:19; GID II 16:19-22)

God communicates His presence to men in the process of being worshipped
•RP 93 ❖ RP 9:4

God, contact with—*see* Contact with God

God created the world because He was not content to be all; He intends to be all *in all* (vs. Pantheism, in which God is all)
•LM 70 ❖ LM 13:9

God demands not so much of our time and attention, but ourselves
•WG 130 (*see also* MC 167; SJ 172*)
❖ WG 9:9 (*see also* MC IV 8:4; SJ 11:8*)

God, demands of— *see* Claims of God; Demands of God

God, desire for—*see* Desire for God; *consider* Joy; Seeking God

God, difference between believing in, and in many gods is not one of arithmetic
•RP 82 (*consider also* Gods)
❖ RP 8:11 (*consider also* Gods)

God, difficulties as threat to faith in: "The conclusion I dread is not, 'So there's no God after all,' but, 'So this is what God's really like...'"*
•GO 5 ❖ GO 1:9

God, discovery of: "Much depends on the seeing eye"; "What is required is a certain faculty of recognition"
•CR 171, 172 ❖ CR 14:29, 34

God: "Divine reality is like a fugue. All His acts are different, but they all rhyme or echo to one another"
•GID 37 ❖ GID I 2:15

God: Does He seem real to me? It varies, just as with lots of other things I firmly believe in
•L 251 (*see also* L 288)
❖ L 17 Jul 53 (*see also* L 8 Sep 59)

God does nothing simply of Himself

which can be done by His creatures; Creation seems to be delegation through and through
•LM 70 ❖ LM 13:8

God, "Emergent," (the God of the Naturalist) vs. "transcendent God" (the God of the Supernaturalist)
•M 30 ❖ M 4:10

God, enjoyment of, (in Heaven), is a concept which is difficult for most of us to imagine, while our idea of Heaven's negations is vivid
•WG 66-67 ❖ WG 4:20

God, enjoyment of, no more separable from praise than the brightness a mirror receives is separable from the brightness it sheds
•RP 96 ❖ RP 9:6

God, even the mere desire for, is itself more desirable than any other satisfaction**
•SJ 17-18 (*see also* Joy)
❖ SJ 1:18 (*see also* Joy)

God: "Every idea of Him we form, He must in mercy shatter"; prayer may facilitate this
•LM 82 (*see also* GO 76-78, 82-83; SL 22*)
❖ LM 15:17 (*see also* GO 4:15-18, 27-28; SL 4:4*)

God: Every soul in Heaven, seeing Him in her own way, will communicate that unique vision to all the rest
•FL 92-93 (*see also* PP 150)
❖ FL 4:9 (*see also* PP 10:7)

God: Everything He has made has some likeness to Himself—space, matter, insects, mammals, and man
•MC 139 ❖ MC IV 1:14

God, example of a definition of, as expressed by Christian dogma: "...he is a righteous creator...who demands of you justice and mercy"
•GID 140 ❖ GID I 16:22

God, existence of—*see also* Doubt; Scepticism; *consider also* Agnosticism; Atheism; Theism

God, existence of: Argument for Theism not unimportant; faith as intellectual assent a necessary pre-condition for

faith as trust or confidence
•GID 173 ❖ GID I 21:2

God, existence of, cannot be proven ("Proof rests on the unprovable which has to be just 'seen'")**
•WG 35 (consider also Proof)
❖ WG 3:4 (consider also Proof)

God, existence of: Descartes' Ontological Proof mentioned
•GID 173 (see also L 143)
❖ GID I 21:3 (see also L 24 Oct 31)

God, existence of: "...if we fully understood what God is we should see that there is no question whether He is"
•M 88 ❖ M 11:11

God, existence of, is a question of no serious importance if nothing much is staked on it; suffering makes it relevant and personal
•GO 43 ❖ GO 3:4

God, existence of, is a speculative question as long as it is a question at all; once answered, you are faced with a Person who demands your confidence
•WLN 26-27 (see also MC 123)
❖ WLN 2:14 (see also MC III 11:4, 5)

God, existence of: "...It is a remarkable fact that no canonical writer has ever used Nature to prove God" (quote from Pascal)
•PP 13 ❖ PP 1 prelim. quote

God, existence of: "It is very difficult to produce arguments on the popular level for the existence of God"
•GID 100 ❖ GID I 10:44

God, existence of: "...oddly...people are usually disposed to hear the divinity of Our Lord discussed before going into the existence of God"
•GID 100 ❖ GID I 10:45

God, existence of: On reading Bergson one Divine attribute, that of necessary existence, rose above my horizon
•SJ 204, 211 ❖ SJ 13:11, 20

God, existence of: The Christian does not claim to have proof, but he does not necessarily have the least actual doubt
•WLN 15-16 ❖ WLN 2:4

God, existence of: "The conclusion I dread is not, 'So there's no God after all,' but,

'So this is what God's really like'..." (re: problem of suffering)
•GO 5 ❖ GO 1:9

God: Existence of the Supernatural may be deduced from the experience of Awe if it is not a mere twist in the human mind
•PP 20-21 (see also Supernatural)
❖ PP 1:11 (see also Supernatural)

God, existence of: Various arguments for Theism mentioned
•GID 173 ❖ GID I 21:3

God, existence of: When I was an Atheist I was angry at God for not existing and also for creating a world
•SJ 115 (see also CR 65-67*, 70*)
❖ SJ 7:20 (see also CR 5:19-20*, 24-26*)

God, existence of: Screwtape explains why God doesn't use His power to be more explicitly present to human souls
•SL 38 ❖ SL 8:4

God, experience and adoration of, through pleasure
•LM 88-91 ❖ LM 17:1-13

God, experience of, not totally unimaginable ("...the Transposition can be in its own way adequate")
•WG 72-73 ❖ WG 4:30

God, face of, is delight or terror of the universe; will one day be turned upon each of us, conferring either glory or shame
•WG 13 (see also GID 47)
❖ WG 1:10 (see also GID I 3:17)

God, fruition of, as "the true end of man"
•CR 26 (see also Goal of ...)
❖ CR 2:41 (see also Goal of ...)

God gives back with His right hand what He takes away with His left (re: restoration of our self-love in its proper form)
•SL 65 (see also GID 194*; L 155)
❖ SL 14:4 (see also GID II 2:3*; L undated letter of 1933)

God gives what He has, not what He has not; He gives the happiness that there is, not the happiness that is not
•PP 54 ❖ PP 3:19

God, glorifying—see Glorifying God

God, glory of—see Glory of God

God, goodness and love of, defined and discussed
•PP 37-54 ❖ PP ch. 3

God, goodness of—*see also* Goodness

God, goodness of: A bad God would never have thought of baits like love, or laughter, or daffodils, or a frosty sunset
•GO 36 ❖ GO 2:27

God, goodness of, differs from ours not as white from black but as a perfect circle from a child's first attempt to draw a wheel
•PP 39 ❖ PP 3:4

God, goodness of, expressed through the total drama of a world of free agents and their rebellion against Him
•PP 84 (*see also* PP 110-111)
❖ PP 5:11 (*see also* PP 7:2)

God, goodness of: "God is goodness. He can give good, but cannot need or get it"; thus His love is bottomlessly selfless
•PP 50 ❖ PP 3:17

God, goodness of: "God is not merely good, but goodness; goodness is not merely divine, but God" (re: relationship between God and the moral law)
•CR 80 ❖ CR 6:21

God, goodness of: "If God's goodness is inconsistent with hurting us, then either God is not good or there is no God"
•GO 31 ❖ GO 2:18

God, goodness of: Lewis and his friends discuss whether one can really believe in a universe where the majority are damned, and also in the goodness of God
•L 169-170 (*see also* PP 118-119)
❖ L 5 Nov 39 (*see also* PP 8:1)

God, goodness of, may differ from our ideas of goodness but it cannot be sheerly different
•PP 37-39 (*see also* CR 67-69, 79; GO 36-38; PP 48-49) ❖ PP 3:2-4 (*see also* CR 5:21-23; 6:19; GO 2:28-30; PP 3:16)

God, goodness of: "The more we believe that God hurts only to heal, the less we can believe there is any use begging for tenderness"
•GO 49-51 ❖ GO 3:17-19

God, goodness of: What reason have we to believe that God is "good"? Doesn't all the *prima facie* evidence suggest exactly the opposite?
•GO 33-34 ❖ GO 2:23

God, goodness of: "Wrath" of God is a mere corollary from His goodness
•PP 58 ❖ PP 4:5, 6

God, greatness of, hinted at by the greatness of the material universe
•GID 42 (*see also* M 53*)
❖ GID I 3:8 (*see also* M 7:16*)

God, hardness of, is kinder than the softness of men, and His compulsion is our liberation
•SJ 229 (*see also* GID 261)
❖ SJ 14:23 (*see also* GID II 16:19-22)

God has individual attention to spare for each one of us ("You are as much alone with Him as if you were the only being He had ever created")
•MC 147 ❖ MC IV 3:7

God has no need of our praise; that miserable idea is answered by the words "If I be hungry I will not tell *thee*"
•CR 98-99; RP 93 (*see also* MC 113-114*)
❖ CR 8:12; RP 9:4 (*see also* MC III 8:12*)

God has no needs; if He chooses to need us, it is because we need to be needed
•PP 49-52 ❖ PP 3:17, 18

God has no needs ("Need-love"); His love is pure Gift-love
•FL 11-12, 175-176 ❖ FL 1:1-3; 6:21, 22

God has nothing to give us but Himself; we must make room for Him in our souls
•WG 130 (*see also* PP 53-54)
❖ WG 9:9 (*see also* PP 3:18, 19)

God: "He has paid us the intolerable compliment of loving us, in the deepest, most tragic, most inexorable sense"
•PP 41, 42, 53 ❖ PP 3:8, 10, 18

God: "...he who has God and everything else has no more than He who has God only"
•WG 10 (*see also* PP 96*)
❖ WG 1:8 (*see also* PP 6:8*)

God, "hiddenness" of, perhaps presses most painfully on those who are in another way nearest to Him (re: Passion of Christ)
• LM 44 ❖ LM 8:12

God Himself is the fuel for the human machine, which He invented
• MC 54 (see also Machine)
❖ MC II 3:7 (see also Machine)

God: His love for us and His knowledge of us are not distinct from one another; He sees because He loves, and therefore loves although He sees
• GO 84 ❖ GO 4:31

God: How to approach the idea that He "demands" praise (as in the Psalms)
• RP 90-98 ❖ RP ch. 9

God, how to avoid: Avoid silence or solitude; concentrate on money, sex, status, health, your own grievances; keep the radio on; live in a crowd...
• CR 168-169 (see also SL 102-103*)
❖ CR 14:17, 18 (see also SL 22:5*)

God, I believed in, before I believed in Heaven
• LM 120; SJ 231 (see also FL 189-190; RP 42) ❖ LM 22:8; SJ 15:3 (see also FL 6:42; RP 4:17)

God, I distinguished my philosophical, from "the God of popular religion"; I didn't call Him "God" either; I called Him "Spirit" [while a student at Oxford]
• SJ 222 ❖ SJ 14:14

God, I will not believe in the Managerial, and his general laws; God's grand design has no unconsidered by-products or consequences
• LM 53-56 ❖ LM 10:4-11

God, idea of, demanding praise reminded me of the dictator or celebrity who demands continued assurance of his own virtue
• RP 90-91 ❖ RP 9:2

God, if a good, made the world why has it gone wrong? —This question raises the other question, "Where do we get our idea of 'just' and 'unjust'?"
• MC 45-46 (see also Moral law, objectivity of) ❖ MC II 1:5, 6 (see also Moral law, objectivity of)

God: "If He can be known it will be by self-revelation on His part, not by speculation on ours"
• GID 144 ❖ GID I 16:26

God: If He is Love, He is, by definition, something more than mere kindness
• PP 40-41, 46 ❖ PP 3:7, 8, 13

God: If His power could vanish and His other attributes remain, we should still owe Him the same kind and degree of allegiance as we do now
• SJ 232 ❖ SJ 15:4

God: If image of a fatherly-looking man is dropped, a more absurd image replaces it (like gas or fluid); not possible to get rid of imagery
• M 74-75 (see also GID 71; LM 74; M 87, 91-92) ❖ M 10:13, 14 (see also GID I 6:9; LM 14:9; M 11:10, 15, 16)

God: If, in our own experience of Him, we recognize Him to be good, then despite appearances to the contrary, He cannot be a power of darkness (re: animal pain)
• GID 167-168, 170 (see also PP 130)
❖ GID I 20:Reply-11, 15 (see also PP 9:1)

God: If we come to believe He is evil, we usually find ourselves asking the "Great God" to curse him and bring him to nought
• GID 171 ❖ GID I 20:Reply-17

God, if we do not love, it may be that what we are trying to love is not yet God; to love Him we must know Him
• PP 53 ❖ PP 3:18

God: "If you do not at all know God, of course you will not recognize Him, either in Jesus or in outer space"
• CR 172 ❖ CR 14:35

God, imagery of—see Anthropomorphic images; Imagery

God, imitation of—see Imitation of Christ; Imitation of God

God, implications of believing in an impersonal
• GID 139-143 ❖ GID I 16:21-25

God, in order to find, it is perhaps not always necessary to leave His creatures behind; the world is crowded with

Him
•LM 75 ❖ LM 14:11

God in the Dock (chapter title)
•GID 240-244 (*see also* GID 95)
❖ GID II ch. 12 (*see also* GID I 10:15)

God in the dock—*see also* God on trial

God in us: We believe that the Holy Spirit can be really present and operative in us, but not that we are "parts" of God (as the Pantheists believe)
•PP 87 (*see also* LM 68-70)
❖ PP 5:13 (*see also* LM 13:2-9)

God is at the heart of all our deepest desires*
•WG 14-16 (*see also* RP 40-41)
❖ WG 1:11, 12 (*see also* RP 4:15)

God is both further from us, and nearer to us, than any other being
•PP 41 ❖ PP 3:9

God is concrete and individual in the highest degree, as evidenced by His very concrete creation
•M 87 (see entire chapter)
❖ M 11:9 (see entire chapter)

God is easy to please but hard to satisfy (quote from George MacDonald)
•MC 172 (*see also* PP 46; SL 39)
❖ MC IV 9:5 (*see also* PP 3:13; SL 8:4)

God is, if I may say it, very unscrupulous; there are traps everywhere for Atheists
•SJ 191 (*see also* SJ 226)
❖ SJ 12:13 (*see also* SJ 14:19)

"God is love" does not mean that "love is God"; if we ignore this distinction we may come to believe the human loves' claim to divinity
•FL 17-18 ❖ FL 1:13

"God is love," Lewis begins an explanation of the statement that
•FL 174-176 ❖ FL 6:20, 21

"God is Love" means also that in the Trinity something analogous to "society" exists, making possible the reciprocity of love within the Divine Being
•PP 29 (*see also* PP 151)
❖ PP 2:7 (*see also* PP 10:8)

God is met as a Person in prayer, just as we, by confessing our sins and making known our requests, assume the high rank of persons before Him
•LM 20-21 ❖ LM 4:6-8

God is more, not less, than what we know of Him
•GID 43 (*see also* GID 185)
❖ GID I 3:9 (*see also* GID I 23:2)

God is more than a Person; we must not imagine the joy of His presence too exclusively in terms of our present poor experience of personal love
•WG 11 (*see also* God, personal)
❖ WG 1:8 (*see also* God, personal)

God is not always delightful in men's imaginations (re: whether Christian theology is "poetry"—aesthetic satisfaction)
•WG 76 ❖ WG 5:7

God is not an amoral force but a righteous Creator, with demands on us (an example of a dogmatic definition which is excluded by truly minimal religion)
•GID 140 ❖ GID I 16:22

God is "not far from any one of us"; an utterly concrete Being whom Man can fear, love, address, and "taste"
•RP 87 ❖ RP 8:17

God is not in space, but space is in God
•LM 122 ❖ LM 22:16

God is not in Time; has no history
•M 176-177; MC 146-149; RP 137 (*see also* L 217; LM 48, 109-110; SL 127)
❖ M App. B:10; MC IV 3:5-12; RP 12:17 (*see also* L 1 Aug 49; LM 9:5; 10:14-17; SL 27:4)

God is not proud; according to Screwtape, "He is cynically indifferent to the dignity of His position..." (re: prayer)
•SL 21 ❖ SL 4:4

God is not proud; He stoops to conquer; He will have us even when we come to Him because there is "nothing better" now to be had
•PP 97 (*see also* LAL 49; SJ 229) ❖ PP 6:8 (*see also* LAL 16/12/55; SJ 14:23)

God "is related to the universe more as an author is related to a play than as one object in the universe is related to another"
•CR 168 ❖ CR 14:14

God is revealed to us as *super-personal,* which is very different from being *impersonal* (re: God as three Persons instead of *a* Person)
•L 305 ❖ L undated letter of Aug 1962

God is that Object to admire which is simply to be awake, to have entered the real world; not to appreciate which is to have lost the greatest experience
•RP 92 (*see also* LM 75)
❖ RP 9:3 (*see also* LM 14:11)

God is the ground of our being; He is always both within us and over against us
•LM 68 ❖ LM 13:3

God is "the thing we most need and the thing we most want to hide from"
•MC 38 ❖ MC I 5:3

God is to be obeyed simply because He is God—and revered not for what He can do for us but for what He is in Himself
•SJ 231 (*see also* FL 189-190; LM 120; RP 39-42) ❖ SJ 15:3 (*see also* FL 6:42; LM 22:8; RP 4:12-17)

God is unspeakable not by being indefinite but by being too definite for the unavoidable vagueness of language
•M 91 (*see also Perelandra* 33*)
❖ M 11:15 (*see also Perelandra* 3:2*)

God: It is much wiser to think of the Divine presence being in particular objects than just of "omnipresence," which gives the idea of something like a gas
•LM 74 (*see also* M 74-75, 87, 91-92)
❖ LM 14:9 (*see also* M 10:13; 11:10, 16)

God: "It is not simply that God has arbitrarily made us such that He is our only good. Rather God is the only good of all creatures"
•PP 53 ❖ PP 3:19

God: It is useful at least to "practice the absence of God, to become increasingly aware of our unawareness"
•FL 192 ❖ FL 6:47

God, it seems to me appropriate that the speech of, should sometimes be poetry (e.g., Psalms)
•RP 5 ❖ RP 1:8

God, knowing/knowledge of—*see* Knowing God; Knowledge of God; Relationship with God

God, language to describe—*see* Language, imaginative; Language, metaphorical; *consider* Anthropomorphic imagery; Imagery

God, Lewis's idea of, as a child ("...neither as Savior or as Judge, but merely as a magician...")
•SJ 21 ❖ SJ 1:22

God limits His own power to alter people's character
•GID 152-153 ❖ GID I 18:5

God, looking for, by exploring space is like reading all Shakespeare's plays in the hope that you will find Shakespeare as one of the characters
•CR 167-168 ❖ CR 14:10-14

God, love of—*see* Love of God

God loveth not Himself as Himself but as Goodness; and if there were aught better than God, He would love that and not Himself (quote from *Theol. Germ.,* XXXII)
•PP 152 ❖ PP 10:10

God, Man has the completest resemblance to, which we know of
•MC 139 ❖ MC IV 1:15

God, Man's attempt to describe, as seen in analogy of limpets trying to describe Man to one another
•M 89-90 ❖ M 11:13, 14

God, Man's attempt to understand, as seen in analogy of a dog trying to form a conception of human life—all the details would be derived from canine experience*
•CR 165 ❖ CR 13:33, 34

God, masculine imagery regarding, implies a truth we must not ignore (re: women in the clergy)
•GID 236-239 ❖ GID II 11:6-12

God may be more than moral goodness: He is not less...The moral realm may exist to be transcended, but first we must admit its claims upon us and try our best
•PP 65 (*see also* LM 114-115; Morality)
❖ PP 4:13 (*see also* LM 21:11-13; Moral-

ity)

God mentioned by Screwtape as being "a hedonist at heart" who offers "pleasures for evermore"
•SL 101, 116 ❖ SL 22:3; 25:2

God: "...mere movement in space will never bring you any nearer to Him or any farther from Him than you are at this very moment"
•CR 168 ❖ CR 14:16

God, Must Our Image of, Go? (chapter title)
•GID 184-185 ❖ GID I ch. 23

God, my idea of, has to be shattered time after time; He shatters it Himself—He is the great iconoclast
•GO 76-78; LM 82 (see also GO 82-83; SL 022*) ❖ GO 4:15-18; LM 15:17 (see also GO 4:27, 28; SL 4:4*)

God, my idea of the fruition of, is a huge, risky extrapolation from a very few and short experiences here on earth
•GO 82 (consider also Joy)
❖ GO 4:27 (consider also Joy)

God, my long-evaded encounter with, happened at a time when I was making a serious effort to obey my conscience
•CR 169 ❖ CR 14:20

God, name of: We cannot assume that all who use it without reverential prefixes are making careless use of it
•GID 335-336 ❖ GID IV Letter 8

God, nature of—see also Trinity

God, nature of: Trinity as described in early Christian writings was never philosophically definite; those writers were not writing to satisfy curiosity
•M 75-76 ❖ M 10:15

God: Nearness by likeness vs. nearness of approach
•FL 14-19 ❖ FL 1:8-16

God: No man nor angel can say nor conceive what He is or what He does
•PP 154 ❖ PP 10:11

God: Nothing in His work is accidental, or merely a by-product; all results are intended from the first
•LM 53-56; M 124, 158 (see also GID 36-37) ❖ LM 10:4-11; M 14:26; 16:26 (see

also GID I 2:15)

God of popular "religion" not a concrete Being but "being in general" about which nothing can be truly asserted
•M 85-88 ❖ M 11:7-10

God of whom no dogmas are believed (as in mere "Theism") is only a shadow, powerless to excite either fear or love
•GID 142-143 (see also Religion, minimal) ❖ GID I 16:24-25 (see also Religion, minimal)

God, omnipotence of
•PP 26-36 ❖ PP ch. 2

God, omnipotence of, means power to do all that is intrinsically possible, not to do the intrinsically impossible
•PP 26-28 ❖ PP 2:2-4

God, omnipotence of: Regarding the impossibility of "tinkering with the creation as though this or that element of it could have been removed"
•PP 35 ❖ PP 2:16

God, omnipresence of: "The higher the creature, the more, and also the less, God is in it; the more present by grace, and the less present...as mere power"
•LM 74 ❖ LM 14:9

God, omnipresence of: "We may ignore, but we can nowhere evade, the presence of God...The real labour is to remember, to attend"
•LM 75 (see also Evasion)
❖ LM 14:11 (see also Evasion)

God, omnipresence of: Wiser to think of the Divine presence being in particular objects than just of "omnipresence," which gives the idea of something like a gas
•LM 74 (see also M 74-75, 87, 91-92)
❖ LM 14:9 (see also M 10:13; 11:10, 16)

God, omniscience of: God created the universe already foreseeing the Crucifixion
•FL 176 ❖ FL 6:21

God, omniscience of: How can God foresee our acts, and yet leave us free not to do them?
•MC 148-149 (see also SL 126-128; Free will) ❖ MC IV 3:11 (see also SL 27:3, 4; Free will)

God, omniscience of: How it was affected

by His becoming a man
- •MC 147-148 (*see also* PP 134; WLN 99)
- ❖ MC IV 3:10 (*see also* PP 9:6; WLN 7:10)

God, omniscience of: Our Lord has reminded us not to pray as if we have forgotten it
- •LM 19 ❖ LM 4:2

God, omniscience of, with regard to prayer: If God is omniscient, why do we need to confess our sins and "make known" our requests?
- •LM 19-22 (*see also* CR 142*; GID 104-105; L 149, 217)
- ❖ LM 4:1-9 (*see also* CR 12:2*; GID I 11:1-5; L 21 Feb 32; 1 Aug 49)

God on trial—can't win ("We treat God as the police treat a man when he is arrested; whatever He does will be used against Him")*
- •GID 40; M 50 ❖ GID I 3:5; M 7:10

God on trial: In the Gospels we see that we are simply *not* invited to speak, to pass judgement on Him—He will do the judging*
- •L 181 ❖ L 26 Mar 40

God on trial: Men want to know whether God can be acquitted for creating such a world; Man is on the Bench and God is in the Dock
- •GID 95, 244 ❖ GID I 10:15; II 12:17

God or "something beyond" hinted at by Man's rationality
- •M 27-29 ❖ M 4:5-8

God, our glimpse of, will be blurred if we do not keep ourselves clean and bright (as a lens)
- •MC 144 ❖ MC IV 2:13, 14

God, our habitual gravitation away from, and toward self is a product of the Fall
- •PP 76 (*see also* PP 83, 91)
- ❖ PP 5:5 (*see also* PP 5:10; 6:3)

God, our need for, can never end—but our awareness of it can
- •FL 31 ❖ FL 2:9

God, our need for: Our whole being is one vast need, crying out for Him...
- •FL 13-14 ❖ FL 1:7

God, our picture of, is too often like the schoolboy's: as the sort of person who stops you having a good time*
- •MC 69 ❖ MC III 1:1

God: Our understanding of what He is like is best acquired through experience of Him—e.g., in the moral life and in the devotional life
- •M 90 (*see also* GID 170*; MC 135-136)
- ❖ M 11:14 (*see also* GID I 20:Reply-15*; MC IV 1:2, 3)

God, our whole life belongs to
- •MC 125 (*see also* SL 96-99)
- ❖ MC III 11:9 (*see also* SL 21:2-6)

God, Pantheist vs. Christian idea of
- •M 84-85 (*see also* Pantheism)
- ❖ M 11:6 (*see also* Pantheism)

God, personal: Christianity is the only religion which says God is more than a person, not less
- •MC 140-141 (*see also* GID 185; WG 11)
- ❖ MC IV 2:2 (*see also* GID I 23:2; WG 1:8)

God, personal (Christian) vs. impersonal (pantheistic)
- •GID 139-140*; M 81-94; MC 43-45 (*see also* Pantheism)
- ❖ GID I 16:21, 22*; M ch. 11; MC 6:3, 4 (*see also* Pantheism)

God, personal: For many people, the word "personal" means "corporeal"; thus a "personal God" would only mean an anthropomorphic God
- •GID 98, 255 ❖ GID I 10:32; II 15:5

God, personal: "...God Himself, alive, pulling at the other end of the cord...that is quite another matter"
- •M 93-94 (*see also* GID 142-143; LM 114; M 81; MC 35; SL 22-23)
- ❖ M 11:19 (*see also* GID I 16:25; LM 21:8; M 11:2; MC I 4:6; SL 4:4)

God, personal: Only a Person can forgive*
- •MC 37-38 ❖ MC I 5:3

God, personal: "...the Christians are the only people who offer any idea of what a being that is beyond personality could be like"
- •MC 140-141 (*see also* GID 185)
- ❖ MC IV 2:2 (*see also* GID I 23:2)

God, pessimist's case against the existence of, and an answer to it

•PP 13-25 ❖ PP ch. 1

God, presence of—*see* Presence of God

God, Psalmists expressed longing for the mere presence of, while they did not know that He would die to offer them eternal joy
•RP 50 ❖ RP 5:8

God, Psalms express the same delight in, that made David dance
•RP 45 ❖ RP 5:4

God reflected in nature: "The created glory may be expected to give us hints of the uncreated; for the one is derived from the other..."
•FL 38 ❖ FL 2:25

God, relationship with—*see* Contact with God; Relationship with God

God, religion (prayer, sacrament, repentance, adoration) as the sole avenue to knowledge about the reality of
•GID 46 ❖ GID I 3:16

God represented in Scripture by words such as "Father" and "Bridegroom," lending the images of Affection and Eros rather than of Friendship
•FL 112-113, 124 (*see also* PP 44-46)
❖ FL 4:42, 58 (*see also* PP 3:12, 13)

God, revelation of—*see* Revelation of God

God: Saying He is "infinite" must not encourage us to think of Him as a formless "everything"
•M 87 (*see also* Pantheism)
❖ M 11:10 (*see also* Pantheism)

God says to man, "You must be strong with *my* strength and blessed with *my* blessedness, *for I have no other to give you*" (taken from G. MacDonald)
•PP 53 ❖ PP 3:19

God, scientific logic not the same logic required for trust in, because once you accept that He is, you move from speculative thought to a *relationship*
•WLN 21-30, esp. 26-27, 30 (*see also* LM 49) ❖ WLN 2:10-18, esp. 2:14, 18 (*see also* LM 9:8)

God, separation from—*see* Separation from God

God, space travel has nothing to do with discovering, —to some, God is discoverable everywhere; to others, nowhere

•CR 171 ❖ CR 14:29

God: That voice which speaks in your conscience and in some of your intensest joys may be in fact the closest contact you have with the mystery...*
•CR 170 ❖ CR 14:27

God ("the Creator") has sovereignty *de facto* as well as *de jure*; He has the power as well as the kingdom and the glory
•SJ 232 (*see also* LM 28)
❖ SJ 15:3, 4 (*see also* LM 5:17)

God, The Rival Conceptions of (chapter title)
•MC 43-46 ❖ MC II ch. 1

God ("the Supernatural"): If so stupendous a thing exists, ought it not to be as obvious as the sun in the sky? — Not more than a window is obvious
•M 40-41 ❖ M 6:3-5

God, The Three-Personal (chapter title)
•MC 140-145 ❖ MC IV ch. 2

God: "Though we can only guess the reasons, we can at least observe the consistency, of His ways" (re: the format of the Bible)
•RP 115 ❖ RP 11:11

God: Through my body He showed me that whole side of His beauty which is embodied in colour, sound, smell and size
•LAL 110-111 (*see also* LM 17-18)
❖ LAL 26 Nov 62 (*see also* LM 3:9)

God, timelessness of—*see* Time; *consider* Omniscience of God

God, to be with, as the only thing we were made for*
•MC 170 (*see also* FL 189-191)
❖ MC IV 8:12 (*see also* FL 6:42-45)

God: To make things which are not Itself, and thus become in a sense capable of being resisted by its own handiwork, is the most astonishing feat of Deity
•PP 127 ❖ PP 8:11

God, "troublesome" complexity of: The real musician is troublesome to the man who wishes to indulge in untaught "musical appreciation" (etc.)
•M 85-86 ❖ M 11:7

God: Turn His "wrath" into mere disapproval, and you also turn His love into mere humanitarianism
•LM 96-97 (see also PP 58)
❖ LM 18:6-9 (see also PP 4: 5, 6)

God, undefined by dogma, has no practical value; the minimal religion cannot be acted upon
•GID 140-141 ❖ GID I 16:22-24

God, undefined, difficult to believe in at all—unconscious assumptions usually operate*
•GID 141 ❖ GID I 16:23

God, use of imaginative language to describe
•GID 184-185 (see also Language, imaginative) ❖ GID I ch. 23 (see also Language, imaginative)

God, vision of—see Vision

"God" vs. "gods," Lewis differentiates the nature of
•RP 82 (see also Gods)
❖ RP 8:11 (see also Gods)

God "wants a world full of beings united to Him but still distinct"
•SL 38 (see also GID 131; MC 141; SL 59, 81; WG 67, 117-118; Personality)
❖ SL 8:3 (see also GID I 16:3; MC IV 2:3; SL 13:4; 18:3, 4; WG 4:21, 22; 7:16, 17; Personality)

God wants to give us something, but cannot, because our hands are full—there's nowhere for Him to put it" (quote from St. Augustine)
•PP 96 (see also GO 53-54*; LAL 73)
❖ PP 6:8 (see also GO 3:25, 26*; LAL 31/3/58)

God: We can be both banished from His presence and erased from His knowledge—or we can be at last summoned inside
•WG 15-16 ❖ WG 1:12

God, we do not usually turn to, till our hopes in this world have been pretty well flattened out—and when they are revived we not infrequently abandon Him
•CR 37 ❖ CR 3:2

God: "We may ignore, but we can nowhere evade, the presence of God. The world is crowded with Him...The real labour is to remember, to attend"
•LM 75 ❖ LM 14:11

God: We must expect that His operations will often appear to us far from beneficent and far from wise, since His knowledge of our needs exceeds our own
•WLN 24-25 ❖ WLN 2:13

God, we picture, as a kind of employment committee whose job it is to find suitable careers for souls; but the place was there first—the man was made for it
•WG 118-119 (see also PP 52, 147- 148*)
❖ WG 7:18 (see also PP 3:18; 10:3*)

God, we regard, as an airman regards his parachute; it's there for emergencies but he hopes he'll never have to use it
•PP 96 ❖ PP 6:8

God, we treat, as the police treat a man when he is arrested: Whatever he does will be used in evidence against Him
•GID 40; M 50 ❖ GID I 3:5; M 7:10

God: What He is will be known only through a personal experience of Him in our lives*
•GID 170 (see also M 89-90; MC 135-136) ❖ GID I 20:Reply-15 (see also M 11:14; MC IV 1:2, 3)

God: What to do with passages of Scripture which seem to show that He is evil
•L 252-253 ❖ L 8 Aug 53

God: "What would really satisfy us would be a God who said of anything we happened to like doing, 'What does it matter so long as they are contented?'"
•PP 40 ❖ PP 3:7

God: When He arrives (and only then) the half-gods can remain (re: natural loves)
•FL 166 ❖ FL 6:5

God, when I was an Atheist I was angry at, for not existing and also for creating a world
•SJ 115 (see also CR 65-67*, 70*; SJ 171)
❖ SJ 7:20 (see also CR 5:19-20*, 24-26*; SJ 11:8)

God, when we see the face of, we shall know that we have always known it

•FL 190 (*see also* SL 147*)
❖ FL 6:44 (*see also* SL 31:4*)

God, where the real, is present the shadows of that God do not appear; elements of Nature-religion are strikingly absent from the teachings of Jesus
•M 115-116 (*see also* GID 84)
❖ M 14:14 (*see also* GID I 9:6)

God, why I did not believe in
•PP 13-15 ❖ PP 1:1

God will look to every soul like its first love because He is its first love
•PP 147 ❖ PP 10:3

God: "You asked for a loving God; you have one. The great spirit you so lightly invoked...is present: not a senile benevolence...but the consuming fire..."
•PP 46-47 ❖ PP 3:14

God's love—*see* Love of God

God's presence—*see* Presence of God

God's reasons, our conjectures about, are probably of no more value than my dog's ideas of what I am up to when I sit and read
•RP 115 ❖ RP 11:11

God's will—*see* Will of God

Gods: According to Screwtape, God had hoped to make humans into Saints or gods, things like Himself—but "His whole experiment is petering out"
•SL 158; WLN 56
❖ SL 32:13; WLN 4:13

Gods are strange to mortal eyes, and yet not strange; when a human finally meets them he will not say, "Who *are* you?" but "So it was *you* all the time"
•SL 147 (*see also* FL 190)
❖ SL 31:4 (*see also* FL 6:44)

Gods, in the Bible we are told we are, and if we allow it we will truly be made into gods or goddesses
•MC 174-175, 187 (For Lewis's differentiation between "God" and "gods," see RP 82) ❖ MC IV 9:11; 11:9 (For Lewis's differentiation between "God" and "gods," see RP 8:11)

"Gods" is not really the plural of God—God has no plural; even in Paganism

they are, like us, creatures or products
•RP 82 (*see also* GID 67)
❖ RP 8:11 (*see also* GID I 5:13)

Gods, multiple—*see also* Paganism; Polytheism

Gods, re: our becoming: "For I think that Jesus Christ is...the only original Son of God, through whom others are enabled to 'become sons of God'"*
•GID 178 (*see also* MC 137-140)
❖ GID I 22:3 (*see also* MC IV 1:10-16)

Gods, regarding the tendency of the natural loves to become
•FL 17-21 (*see also* FL 39, 83, 151, 156-157, 160, 166; CR 35*; L 182) ❖ FL 1:13-18 (*see also* FL 1:28, 29; 3:45; 5:31, 32, 39-41, 46; 6:5; CR 2:56*; L 16 Apr 40)

Gods, some thoughts regarding the idea that men might become
•L 284 ❖ L 20 Jan 59

Gods, something or someone whispered to the unfallen creatures that they could become; could cease directing their lives to their Creator
•PP 79-80 ❖ PP 5:8

Gods, suffering may be necessary to turn finite creatures (with free wills) into
•L 257 ❖ L 1 Nov 54 (first letter)

Gods, the day will come when we shall be those, described in Scripture
•GID 87 ❖ GID I 9:11

Gods, those who believed in many, very seldom regarded those gods as creators of the universe and self-existent
•M 8 (*see also* GID 149; RP 78, 82)
❖ M 2:9 (*see also* GID I 17:6; RP 8:4, 11)

Gods, we are to become*
•GO 85 (*see also* WLN 9)
❖ GO 4:32 (*see also* WLN 1:18)

Gods, we are to become ageless
•GID 112 ❖ GID I 12:10

Gods: "When God arrives (and only then) the half-gods can remain" (re: natural loves)
•FL 166 ❖ FL 6:5

God-shaped hollow: "It is not simply that God has arbitrarily made us such that He is our only good. Rather God is the only good of all creatures"*
•PP 53 (*see also* FL 189)

❖ PP 3:19 (*see also* FL 6:41)

God-shaped hollow: "...the soul is but a hollow which God fills"*
• PP 151 ❖ PP 10:9

God-shaped hollow: "Your soul has a curious shape because it is a hollow made to fit a particular swelling in the...contours of the divine substance"*
• PP 147 ❖ PP 10:3

Golden Bough, by Sir James George Frazer, mentioned (as a source for the "dying God" myth)
• GID 83 (*see also* L 106; M 69; SJ 223-224) ❖ GID I 9:5 (*see also* L 5 Jan 26; M 10:3; SJ 14:15)

Golden Bough, my tutor [William T. Kirkpatrick] was great on the; his atheism was chiefly of the anthropological and pessimistic kind
• SJ 139 ❖ SJ 9:15

Golden Rule a summing up of what everyone had always known to be right
• MC 78 (*see also* Morality) ❖ MC III 3:1 (*see also* Morality)

Golden Rule cannot really be carried out until we learn to love God, and we cannot learn to love God except by learning to obey Him
• MC 82 (*see also* LM 114-115) ❖ MC III 3:8 (*see also* LM 21:11, 12)

Golden Rule, Christianity does not profess to have a detailed political programme for applying the, to a particular society at a particular moment
• MC 78-79 ❖ MC III 3:2, 3

Golden Rule mentioned in a letter to a child
• L 277 ❖ L 18 Jul 57

Good and bad: First kind (virtue, vice), besides being good or bad in itself, also makes the possessor good or bad; the second (pleasure, pain) does not
• CR 34-36 ❖ CR 2:55-58

Good and evil—*see also* Evil

Good and evil, argument for a supernatural source for our ideas of
• M 34-38 (*see also* CR 67-71, 72-81; GID 275-276; MC 17-39; 45-46) ❖ M ch. 5 (*see also* CR 5:20-27; ch. 6; GID III 1:15; MC Book I; II 1:6)

Good and evil both increase at compound interest; hence little decisions are of infinite importance
• MC 117 (*see also* MC 86-87; RP 136; SL 53-54; WG 102-103*; WLN 54-55) ❖ MC III 9:8 (*see also* MC III 4:8, 9; RP 12:16; SL 12:1; WG 6:12*; WLN 4:10)

Good and evil, good people know about both; bad people do not know about either
• MC 87 ❖ MC III 4:10

Good and evil: "If the Divine call does not make us better, it will make us very much worse. Of all bad men religious bad men are the worst"
• RP 31-32 (*see also* L 310; RP 28) ❖ RP 3:20 (*see also* L 20 Dec 61; RP 3:17)

Good and evil, many preferences which seem to some to be simply "matters of taste" are visible to the trained critic as choices between
• CR 29 (*see also* Moral choices) ❖ CR 2:48 (*see also* Moral choices)

Good and evil not equal; badness is not even bad in the same way in which goodness is good
• GID 23 (*see also* Dualism) ❖ GID I 1:7 (*see also* Dualism)

Good and evil: "There is a kind of gravitation in the mind whereby good rushes to good and evil to evil" (re: Lewis's early interest in the Occult)
• SJ 176 ❖ SJ 11:13

Good and evil: "When natural things look most divine, the demoniac is just round the corner" (re: Venus, or sexual love)
• FL 144-145 ❖ FL 5:21

Good, God can make complex, out of simple evil such as suffering—though this does not excuse those who do the simple evil
• PP 110-111 ❖ PP 7:2

Good Infection (chapter title)
• MC 149-153 ❖ MC IV ch. 4

"Good infection" analogy: Good things as well as bad are caught by a kind of infection; if you are close to the fountain [of God], the spray will wet you
• MC 153 (*see also* MC 157, 162, 163,

186) ❖ MC IV 4:8, 10 (see also MC IV 5:8; 7:5, 8; 11:7)

Good or evil, how we decide what is
•WG 33-39 (see also Ethics; Moral decisions; Moral judgements)
❖ WG 3:1-11 (see also Ethics; Moral decisions; Moral judgements)

Good people, a world of contentedly, would be just as much in need of salvation as a miserable world, and may be more difficult to save
•MC 182 ❖ MC IV 10:15

Good people, description of truly*
•GID 252; MC 114, 130-131, 187-188; SL 64-65 ❖ GID II 14:9; MC III 8:13; 12:9; IV 11:10; SL 14:4

Good people, description of truly: A perfect man would never act from a sense of duty; he'd always *want* the right thing more than the wrong one*
•L 277 (see also LM 114-116; PP 100)
❖ L 18 Jul 57 (see also LM 21:11-14; PP 6:11)

Good people: "I now want to begin considering what the Christian idea of a good man is..."
•MC 83 ❖ MC III 4:1

Good people: In a perfect Christian, his feasts would be as Christian as his fasts*
•WG 130 ❖ WG 9:9

Good people know about both good and evil; bad people do not know about either
•MC 87 ❖ MC III 4:10

"Good" people, Lewis describes his friends at Oxford as, ("by decent Pagan standards")
•SJ 201 ❖ SJ 13:6

Good people: "...some old people whose state of grace we can hardly doubt seem to have got through their seventy years with surprising ease"*
•PP 104 ❖ PP 6:15

Good people, warning to contentedly: "...if virtue comes easily to you—beware! Much is expected from those to whom much is given"
•MC 180-181 ❖ MC IV 10:11-13

Good, simple, (descending from God) vs.

complex good (where evil is exploited by God for His redemptive purpose—e.g., suffering)
•PP 110-111 (see also PP 117)
❖ PP 7:2 (see also PP 7:9)

Good, the proper, of a creature is to surrender itself to its Creator—and when it does so, it is good and happy
•PP 90 (see also PP 52; WG 118-119)
❖ PP 6:3 (see also PP 3:18; WG 7:18)

Good, to us in our present state, means primarily remedial or corrective good (since Man, as a species, spoiled himself)
•PP 88 ❖ PP 5:14

Good vs. evil: "There is no neutral ground in the universe: every square inch, every split second, is claimed by God and counterclaimed by Satan"*
•CR 33 ❖ CR 2:54

Good, whatever misery God permits will be for our ultimate, (unless by our rebellion we convert it to evil)
•L 166 (see also GID 52*; LAL 114; Will of God)
❖ L 8 May 39 (see also GID I 4:18, 19 Ques. 5*; LAL 8 Feb 63; Will of God)

Good Work and Good Works (chapter title)
•WLN 71-81 ❖ WLN ch. 5

Good works—see Works; consider Charity; Humanitarianism; Moral effort

Goodness—see also Morality; Virtue; consider also Moral effort; Works

Goodness: A man may console himself for his other vices by a conviction that "his heart's in the right place" and "he wouldn't hurt a fly"*
•PP 56 ❖ PP 4:2

Goodness approved and loved and desired (but not acted) will not keep a man from Hell; indeed they may make him more amusing when he gets there
•SL 31 ❖ SL 6:5

Goodness, [as a youth] I felt the "charm" of, as a man feels the charm of a woman he has no intention of marrying
•SJ 191 ❖ SJ 12:12

Goodness, could it be that we are so de-

praved that our ideas of, count for nothing?
- GO 36-38 ❖ GO 2:28-30

Goodness, Divine (chapter title)
- PP 37-54 ❖ PP ch. 3

Goodness: Each person is in reality far better *and* worse than is ever imagined*
- L 267 ❖ L 8 Feb 56

Goodness may be enhanced by suffering: "I have seen men, for the most part, grow better not worse with advancing years..."*
- PP 108 ❖ PP 6:18

Goodness: For many modern people, even the wish is difficult—like the man who prayed, "Oh Lord, make me chaste" and added, "But please don't do it just yet"
- MC 92 ❖ MC III 5:9

Goodness, forced, vs. "a deeper, less conscious Charity" which enables us to want to do the right thing
- FL 185 ❖ FL 6:36

Goodness: God does not love us because we are good; He makes us good because He loves us
- MC 64 ❖ MC II 5:6

Goodness, God loveth not Himself as Himself but as; if there were aught better than God, He would love that and not Himself (quote from *Theol. Germ.*, XXXII)
- PP 152 ❖ PP 10:10

Goodness, God may be more than moral; He is not less...the moral realm may exist to be transcended, but first we must admit its claims upon us and try our best
- PP 65 (*see also* LM 114-115; Morality) ❖ PP 4:13 (*see also* LM 21:10-12; Morality)

Goodness, God's idea of, may differ from ours but is surely not opposite ours
- PP 37-39 (*see also* GO 36-38; PP 48-49) ❖ PP 3:2-4 (*see also* GO 2:28-30; PP 3:16)

Goodness, God's idea of, may differ from ours in some ways but it cannot be radically different

- CR 79 (*see also* CR 67-69) ❖ CR 6:19 (*see also* CR 5:21-23)

Goodness ("holiness") is irresistible; if even 10% of the world's population had it, would not the whole world be converted and happy before year's end?
- LAL 19 ❖ LAL Aug 1st [1953]

Goodness, I have never felt the dislike of, which seems to be quite common in better men than me; I lacked the bloodhound sensitivity for hypocrisy
- SJ 191 ❖ SJ 12:12

Goodness: I was brought up to believe that goodness must be disinterested, and that any hope of reward or fear of punishment contaminated the will
- SJ 231 (*see also* LM 120; RP 39-42; compare with WG 3-5*) ❖ SJ 15:3 (*see also* LM 22:8; RP 4:12-17; compare with WG 1:1-3*)

Goodness: Improvement can be initiated by at first pretending you are better than you are; if this is hypocrisy, then I maintain hypocrisy can do a man good*
- SJ 192-193 ❖ SJ 12:14

"Goodness" in modern times is thought to be merely "kindness"; thus many convince themselves that they are "good" when they are merely happy (unannoyed)
- PP 56 ❖ PP 4:2

Goodness is itself; badness is only spoiled goodness (re: Dualism)
- MC 49-50 ❖ MC II 2:9, 10

Goodness is not simply a law but also a begetting love; not merely divine, but God (re: relationship between God and the moral law)
- CR 80 ❖ CR 6:21

Goodness: It is by his will alone that a man is good or bad; feelings by themselves are not of any importance
- L 210 ❖ L undated letter of 1947

Goodness *may* be enhanced by suffering; but suffering, like all that is given to creatures with free will, is two-edged*
- PP 107, 118 (*see also* L 257*; PP 95) ❖ PP 6:18; 8:1 (*see also* L 1 Nov 54—

first letter*; PP 6:7)

Goodness: Modern Western cultures no better in God's eyes than people in other ages who excelled in different virtues (courage, chastity) but were cruel*
•PP 64 ❖ PP 4:11

Goodness ("morality") a mountain we cannot climb by our own efforts; if we could we should only perish in the ice and unbreathable air of the summit
•GID 112-113 (see also Moral effort)
❖ GID I 12:10, 11 (see also Moral effort)

Goodness: Most people never thoroughly intend it (quote from William Law)
•PP 66 ❖ PP 4:14

Goodness of Christ led to His death because of the nature of goodness and the nature of this world
•RP 105 ❖ RP 10:10

Goodness of God—see God, goodness of

Goodness of people a manifestation of the goodness of God; "Only by being in some respect like Him...has any earthly Beloved excited our love"
•FL 190 (see also L 10 Feb 57)
❖ FL 6:44 (see also L 274)

Goodness, people in Heaven are filled with, as a mirror is filled with light
•MC 130-131 (see also MC 144)
❖ MC III 12:9 (see also MC IV 2:13, 14)

Goodness, progress means increasing, and happiness—not mere longevity
•GID 311 (see also GID 296-297; L 158*; SL 131*; WG 43*)
❖ GID III 8:1 (see also GID III 4:20; L 13 Jan 37*; SL 28:1*; WG 3:18*)

Goodness: Right actions done for the wrong reason do not help to build "virtue"
•MC 77 (see also MC 127, 164- 165)
❖ MC III 2:8 (see also MC III 12:3; IV 7:12)

Goodness ("sanctity") and culture: Both are hard to diagnose and easy to feign
•WLN 47 ❖ WLN 3:24

Goodness: Screwtape observes that in order to be greatly and effectively wicked a man needs some virtue
•SL 135-136 (see also SL 105-106*;

WLN 56*)
❖ SL 29:2 (see also SL 23:1*; WLN 4:13*)

Goodness: Someday even the delights of virtue itself will seem half-nauseous in comparison to meeting our true Beloved*
•SL 148 ❖ SL 31:5

Goodness: "The Christian thinks any good he does comes from the Christ-life inside him"
•MC 64 ❖ MC II 5:5, 6

Goodness: The more one likes the right thing and the less one has to try to be good, the better
•L 277 ❖ L 18 Jul 57

Goodness: "The more virtuous a man becomes the more he enjoys virtuous actions"
•PP 100 (see also LM 114-116) 116)
❖ PP 6:11 (see also LM 21:11-14) 21:11-14)

Goodness: When a man is getting better, he understands more clearly the evil left in him
•MC 87 (see also GID 57; LAL 95; MC 164; PP 55, top; PP 67; Self-knowledge)
❖ MC III 4:10 (see also GID I 4:38; LAL 9 Jan 61; 61; MV IV 7:12; PP 4:prelim. quote; 4:15; Self-knowledge)

Goodness: "You cannot make men good by law: and without good men you cannot have a good society"
•MC 72 ❖ MC III 1:7

"Goody-goody," description of a: "...the docile youth who has neither revolted against nor risen above the routine pietisms and respectabilities of his home"
•WLN 47 ❖ WLN 3:25

Gospel as "good news" not meaningful to modern men; sense of guilt lacking
•GID 95, 181-182, 243-244; MC 38-39; PP 55-57 ❖ GID I 10;15; 22:13; II 12:6-8; MC I 5:4; PP 4:1-4

Gospel, as "good news" to the people in Paul's day, consisted of the Resurrection and its consequences
•M 143-144 ❖ M 16:2

Gospel directly opposed to the World
•GID 265 ❖ GID II 16:46

Gospel of John, historicity of
- •CR 154-155; GID 158-159, 179-180
- ❖ CR 13:5; GID I 19:5; 22:8, 9

Gospel of St. Luke mentioned regarding the Annunciation
- •L 146-146 ❖ L 25 Dec 31

Gospels, Apocryphal, mentioned
- •CR 156 ❖ CR 13:8

Gospels do not qualify as legends
- •GID 158-159 (*see also* CR 154-155; GID 101; SJ 236)
- ❖ GID I 19:4, 5 (*see also* CR 13:4, 5; GID I 10:47; SJ 15:7)

Gospels: Either the Book of John is reportage pretty close to the facts, or some writer suddenly anticipated the whole technique of modern narrative
- •CR 155 ❖ CR 13:5

Gospels, first real work of, is to raise the question, "Who or What is this?"
- •L 181 (*see also* GID 156-158; WG 91; MC 54-56) ❖ L 26 Mar 40 (*see also* GID I 19:1-3; WG 5:23; MC II 3:10-13)

Gospels, I was by now too experienced in literary criticism to regard the, as myths; they had not the mythical taste
- •SJ 236 (*see also* CR 154-155; GID 101, 158-159) ❖ SJ 15:7 (*see also* CR 13:4, 5; GID I 10:47; 19:4, 5)

Gospels: I was told I'd find a figure whom I couldn't help loving; well, I could
- •L 181 ❖ L 26 Mar 40

Gospels, in 1926 the hardest boiled of all the atheists I knew remarked that the evidence for the historicity of the, was really surprisingly good
- •SJ 223-224 (*see also* SJ 235-236)
- ❖ SJ 14:15 (*see also* SJ 15:7)

Gospels, Lewis relates his early impression of the, ("...very little definite teaching...")
- •L 82 ❖ L 28 Oct 22

Gospels: Materials for a full biography of Jesus have been withheld from men; few people are converted by studying Jesus' life simply as biography
- •SL 108 ❖ SL 23:3

Gospels probably based on acts and sayings which the disciples deliberately learned by heart—a much surer

method of transmission than writing
- •L 211 ❖ L undated letter of 1947

Gospels, the Epistles of the New Testament were written before the
- •GID 232 (*see also* M 143-144)
- ❖ GID II 10:7 (*see also* M 16:2)

Gospels were written, not to make Christians, but to edify Christians already made
- •SL 108 (*see also* M 143-144)
- ❖ SL 23:3 (*see also* M 16:2)

Gossip: The rule is, "When in doubt, don't tell"; I have nearly always regretted doing the opposite and never once regretted holding my tongue*
- •LAL 54-55 ❖ LAL 15/4/56

Gossiping ("circulation of rumours") as one of the "sins of the tongue" which are protested against in the Psalms
- •RP 75 ❖ RP 7:16

Government—*see also* Politics; *consider also* Democracy

Government, actual, "is and always must be oligarchical. Our effective masters must be more than one and fewer than all"
- •GID 314 ❖ GID III 8:12

Government, all forms of, can work to the devil's advantage; Democracy only less so
- •SL 168-169; WLN 67
- ❖ SL 32:35; WLN 4:35

Government, Christianity the worst enemy of totalitarian; gives the individual a standing ground against the State
- •GID 118 (*see also* MC 73)
- ❖ GID I 13:9 (*see also* MC III 1:9)

Government: Civil obedience not related to the kind and degree of obedience which a creature owes to its Creator; on the former I have nothing to say
- •PP 115 ❖ PP 7:6

Government: Civil Service mentioned as among the instruments of an increasingly tyrannical State
- •L 259-260
- ❖ L 22 Dec 54 (second letter)

Government ("criminal law") increasingly protects the criminal and ceases to

protect his victim
•GID 306-310, esp. 307
❖ GID III ch. 6, esp. 6:7

Government: Dangers of the use of political power to achieve religious goals
•GID 196-199; 315
❖ GID II ch. 3; III 8:15

Government, grounds on which the, demands my obedience must not include religious grounds; I detest theocracy
•GID 315 (Compare with GID 318*)
❖ GID III 8:16 (Compare with GID III 9:7, 8*)

Government: "I do think the State is becoming increasingly tyrannical..."
•L 259 ❖ L 22 Dec 54

Government, I dread, in the name of science ("technocracy"); that is how tyrannies come in
•GID 314-315 ❖ GID III 8:15-18

Government: In Britain we have been spared the almost world-wide difficulty of the "small man" in getting his case heard in court*
•RP 11 ❖ RP 2:4

Government is at its best a necessary evil; let's keep it in its place
•L 281 (see also WLN 40; Separation of Church and State)
❖ L 1 Feb 58 (see also WLN 3:13; Separation of Church and State)

Government: Lewis mentions his anti-Government nature as a student at Oxford
•SJ 209 ❖ SJ 13:17

Government: Of all tyrannies a tyranny sincerely exercised for the good of its victims may be the most oppressive
•GID 292 ❖ GID III 4:10

Government, our dilemma is between our need for, and our need for independence
•GID 314-316 ❖ GID III 8:13-20

Government: Politico-social programmes good only so far as they don't trample on people's rights for the sake of their good
•L 226-227 (see also WLN 111)
❖ L 7 Feb 51 (see also WLN 7:33)

Government: Revolutions seldom cure the evil against which they are directed; they always beget a hundred others
•GID 309 ❖ GID III 7:12

Government-sponsored education: Screwtape forecasts much success for his side if all education becomes state education
•SL 168; WLN 66
❖ SL 32:33; WLN 4:33

Government: "The State exists simply to promote and to protect the ordinary happiness of human beings in this life"
•MC 169 ❖ MC IV 8:10

Government: The very idea of freedom presupposes an objective moral law which overarches rulers and ruled alike; subjectivism incompatible with democracy*
•CR 81 (see also CR 56*)
❖ CR 6:22 (see also CR 4:27*)

Government: Theocracy has been abolished because priests are wicked men like ourselves
•WG 114 (see also GID 197)
❖ WG 7:12 (see also GID II 3:3)

Government: "There is nothing left of which we can say to them, 'Mind your own business.' Our whole lives are their business"
•GID 313-314 ❖ GID III 8:10, 11

Government: "You cannot make men good by law: and without good men you cannot have a good society"*
•MC 72 ❖ MC III 1:7

Governments, Theocracy the worst of all possible; the loftier the pretensions of power, the more meddlesome, inhuman, and oppressive it will be
•WLN 40, 48 ❖ WLN 3:13, 27

Governmental claims must not supersede God's claims on us
•WG 24-25 ❖ WG 2:6

Grace—see also Help; consider also Blessings; Faith

Grace and becoming sons of God: "...the approach, however initiated and supported by Grace, is something we do"
•FL 16-17 (see also FL 19)

❖ FL 1:12 (*see also* FL 1:16)

Grace and free will, the whole puzzle about: "We profanely assume that divine and human action exclude one another..."
•LM 49-50 (*see also* GID 55; LM 68-69*; MC 130; Moral effort) ❖ LM 9:11, 12 (*see also* GID I 4:30, 31—Ques. 8; LM 13:2-5*; MC III 12:8; Moral effort)

Grace assists our reason and our belief so that our feelings do not continually assault our conviction like a blast furnace against a snowflake*
•CR 43 ❖ CR 3:12

Grace, by, God gives the higher creatures power "to will His will ('and wield their little tridents')"
•LM 74-75 ❖ LM 14:9

Grace can help us to accept our total dependence upon God, and even to find joy in it
•FL 179-181 ❖ FL 6:26-28

Grace, do the approaches of, often hurt because the spiritual vein in us hides itself from the celestial surgeon?
•LAL 118-119 ❖ LAL 25 Jun 63

"Grace," I avoided the word, because I didn't think it carried much clear meaning to the uninstructed readers...
•L 223 ❖ L 28 Nov 50

Grace: More given by pressing steadily on through interruptions such as doubt or anxiety
•L 227-228 ❖ L 5 Mar 51

Grace, none of us have any right to; it is God's free bounty
•L 241 ❖ L 15 May 52

Grace not usually given us in advance; only *daily* support for the *daily* trial
•L 250 (*see also* SL 62; WG 30; Daily...)
❖ L 17 Jul 53 (*see also* SL 14:1; WG 2:13; Daily...)

Grace, salvation by—*see* Salvation by faith/grace; *consider* Moral effort; Righteousness by faith/grace; Works

Grace: Screwtape mentions this special form of the presence of God which comes to humans upon repentance, and protects them from the devil's assaults

•SL 57-58 ❖ SL 13:1, 2

Grace, Screwtape points out that the human desire for social conformity can lead to a gradual rejection of God's
•SL 156-157; WLN 55 ❖ SL 32:10; WLN 4:10

Grace, steps leading to the rejection of, (e.g., the hardening of wrong choices into habit by steady repetition)
•SL 156-157; WLN 54-55 (*see also* Choices)
❖ SL 32:10; WLN 4:10 (*see also* Choices)

Grace, the "garden" of human love must be tended and our tending must be combined with God's
•FL 163-165 ❖ FL 6:2

Grace, the Gift-love of Charity comes by
•FL 178 ❖ FL 6:24, 25

Grace, operation of, in the life of a man of good will, saddled with—and defeated by—an abnormal desire
•L 242 ❖ L 28 May 52

Grace: Virtues such as charity, submissiveness to God's will, etc. are *graces*—gifts from the Holy Spirit—not our own merits
•L 219 ❖ L 2 Sep 49

Grace, we are sure that all the good in us comes from, yet we can also know that every kind act we do will be accepted by Christ
•L 251-252 ❖ L 3 Aug 53

Grace, we should not expect an endowment of, for life; only a hope for enough to meet the daily and hourly temptations*
•SL 62 (*see also* Daily...)
❖ SL 14:1 (*see also* Daily...)

Graft—*see* Corruption

Graham, Billy: Lewis mentions meeting him in 1955
•GID 265 ❖ GID II 16:49

Grail legend: I do not doubt that it represents an imaginative and literary response to the doctrine of Transubstantiation...
•L 295-296 (*see also* L 264, 266, 269-270)
❖ L 26 Sep 60 (*see also* L 22 Sep 55; 17 Dec 55; 9 May 56)

Grand Miracle, The (chapter title)

•GID 80-88; M 108-131
❖ GID I ch. 9; M ch. 14
Gratitude—*see also* Appreciation; Praise
Gratitude, *act* your, and let feelings look after themselves
•L 202 ❖ L 22 Dec 42
Gratitude for small things: "We...shall not be able to adore God on the highest occasions if we have learned no habit of doing so on the lowest"
•LM 91 ❖ LM 17:13
Gratitude to God, one moment of, will help to head us off from the abyss of abstraction about God
•M 90 ❖ M 11:14
Gratitude vs. Adoration: Gratitude says, "How good of God to give me this"; Adoration says, "What must be the quality of that Being..."
•LM 90 ❖ LM 17:8
Gratitude: We can learn to recognise the divine source of a pleasure or blessing and give thanks for it in the same moment it is received
•LM 89-90 (*see also* GO 73*)
❖ LM 17:6-9 (*see also* GO 4:7, 8*)
Graveyard, sentimental tending of a plot in a: "...all this churchyard stuff was and is simply hateful, even inconceivable, to me"
•GO 22-24 ❖ GO 2:7
Gravitation away from God, "the journey homeward to habitual self," must, we think, be a product of the Fall
•PP 76 (*see also* PP 83, 91)
❖ PP 5:5 (*see also* PP 5:10; 6:3)
Gravitation, there is a kind of, in the mind whereby good rushes to good and evil to evil
•SJ 176 ❖ SJ 11:13
Great Britain—*see also* England; Ireland; Scotland
Great Britain is as much part of the mission field as China
•GID 94 ❖ GID I 10:12
Great Divorce mentioned
•L 259 ❖ L 22 Dec 54 (first letter)
Great Knock, The (chapter title)
•SJ 132-148 ❖ SJ ch. 9
Great Sin, The (chapter title) [re: Pride]

•MC 108-114 ❖ MC III ch. 8
Greatness: "It is great men, potential saints, not little men, who become merciless fanatics"—may become ready to kill for their cause*
•RP 28 (*see also* L 301; RP 31-32)
❖ RP 3:17 (*see also* L 20 Dec 61; RP 3:20)
Greece, trip to, mentioned
•LAL 89, 90-91
❖ LAL 13 Feb 60; 19/4/60
Greed—*see also* Avarice; *consider also* Money
Greed, what looks like, may actually be the result of Pride
•MC 110 ❖ MC III 8:3, 4
Greek Orthodox mass, what pleased me about a, I once attended was that there seemed to be no prescribed behaviour for the congregation
•LM 10 ❖ LM 2:3
Greek religious belief about death is shown at the beginning of the Iliad...
•RP 37 ❖ RP 4:8
Greeks did not believe that the gods were really like the beautiful human shapes their sculptors gave them (re: use of imagery to describe angels)
•SL viii ❖ SL P:13
Greeks: "The Jews were not, like the Greeks, an analytical and logical people; indeed, except the Greeks, no ancient peoples were"
•RP 46 ❖ RP 5:5
"Green Hills" [the Castlereagh Hills, County Down, Ireland] mentioned or described
•SJ 7-8, 152-154 ❖ SJ 1:4, 5; 10:4, 6
Green, Roger Lancelyn: Only the other week a reviewer said that a fairy tale of his was influenced by fairy tales of mine (re: Biblical criticism)
•CR 160 ❖ CR 13:19
Greeves, Arthur, and his love of "the homely"
•L 146; SJ 152, 157-158, 199
❖ L 22 Nov 31; SJ 10:3; 10:10; 13:3
Greeves, Arthur, mentioned ("When Arthur and I talk late...there is...a magical feeling of successful conspiracy")

•L 137 ❖ L 9 Sep 29

Gresham, David and Douglas: "I cannot talk to them about her [Joy, who had died]. The moment I try, there appears on their faces...embarrassment"
•GO 8-9 ❖ GO 1:16, 17

Gresham, David and Douglas, mentioned or referred to (Lewis's stepsons)
•L 275, 276; LAL 65, 68, 92
❖ L 16 Mar 57; 8 May 57; LAL 17/1/57; Aug 12th 57; 24 Sep 60

Gresham, Douglas: "My younger stepson is the greatest comfort to me"
•LAL 92 ❖ LAL 24 Sep 60

Gresham, Joy—*see* Joy (Lewis's wife)

Grief—*see also* Bereavement; Sorrow; *consider also* Death; Difficulties; Pain; Suffering

Grief, absence of God in: "But go to Him when your need is desperate, when all other help is vain, and what do you find? A door slammed in your face..."
•GO 4-6 (*see also* GO 53-54; LAL 92)
❖ GO 1:7-11 (*see also* GO 3:25, 26; LAL 24 Sep 60)

Grief, anticipatory, (quote from G. Mac-Donald): "The approach of any fate is usually also the preparation for it"*
•L 186 (*see also* L 219)
❖ L 2 Jun 40 (*see also* L 2 Sep 49)

Grief: As my health improves, I feel the loss of Joy more; I suppose the capacity for happiness must reawake before one becomes fully aware of its absence
•LAL 106 ❖ LAL 31/7/62

Grief as "the continually renewed shock of setting out...on familiar roads and being brought up short by the grim frontier post that now blocks them"
•L 289-290 ❖ L 3 Dec 59

Grief: At the very moment when I mourned H. [Joy] least, I remembered her best... It was as if the lifting of the sorrow removed a barrier
•GO 52-53 (*see also* GO 64-65; LAL 92)
❖ GO 3:22-24 (*see also* GO 3:41; LAL 24 Sep 60)

Grief: "Children suffer not (I think) less than their elders, but differently" (re: Lewis's loss of his mother)

•SJ 18-19 ❖ SJ 1:20

Grief feels like fear, or suspense, or waiting; just hanging about waiting for something to happen
•GO 38-39 ❖ GO 2:32

Grief feels like fear—the same fluttering in the stomach, the same restlessness
•GO 1 ❖ GO 1:1

Grief feels like suspense because of the frustration of so many impulses that had become habitual
•GO 55 ❖ GO 3:28

Grief: "I dread the moments when the house is empty. If only they would talk to one another and not to me"
•GO 1 (*consider also* Solitude)
❖ GO 1:2 (*consider also* Solitude)

Grief: "I find it hard to take in what anyone says...yet I want the others to be about me"
•GO 1 ❖ GO 1:2

Grief: "I have learned that while those who speak about one's miseries usually hurt one, those who keep silence hurt more"
•L 289 ❖ L 3 Dec 59

Grief: "I suppose I am recovering physically from a good deal of mere exhaustion"
•GO 51-52 ❖ GO 3:22

Grief: If we try to use the hope of "Heaven" as a compensation for earthly bereavement, belief in it crumbles away
•L 290; RP 41 (*see also* FL 189-190; GO 79*) ❖ L 3 Dec 59; RP 4:16 (*see also* FL 6:41-43; GO 4:21*)

Grief is like a bomber circling round and dropping its bombs each time the circle brings it overhead, whereas physical pain may be continuous
•GO 46-47 ❖ GO 3:11

Grief is like a long, winding valley...sometimes you are presented with exactly the same sort of country you thought you had left behind miles ago
•GO 69 ❖ GO 4:1

Grief isn't a state but a process; it keeps on changing—like a winding road with quite a new landscape at each

bend
- •LAL 92 (*see also* GO 68-69)
- ❖ LAL 24 Sep 60 (*see also* GO 4:1)

Grief: Lewis demonstrates that empathy for another's difficulty is more effective if we can admit our own handicap in being able to truly empathize*
- •LM 40-41 ❖ LM 8:2, 3

Grief: Lewis describes the embarrassment or awkwardness which is felt by people who are grieving as well as by those around them
- •GO 8-11 ❖ GO 1:16-20

Grief Lewis felt on the death of his friend Charles Williams: "Lots, lots of pain, but not a particle of depression or resentment"
- •L 206 ❖ L 18 May 45; 20 May 45

Grief like being concussed; and "Why should the desperate imaginings of a man dazed...be especially reliable?"
- •GO 1, 45 ❖ GO 1:2; 3:8

Grief, night-time anguish of: "...mad, midnight endearments and entreaties spoken into the empty air"
- •GO 29 ❖ GO 2:15

Grief, night-time anguish of: "...the mad, midnight moments..."
- •GO 41 ❖ GO 3:2

Grief, night-time anguish of: "Tonight all the hells of young grief have opened again..."
- •GO 66-67 ❖ GO 3:45

Grief, no one ever told me about the laziness of; I loathe the slightest effort
- •GO 3-4 ❖ GO 1:6

Grief not a state but a process; like a walk in a winding valley which gives you a new landscape every few miles
- •L 300 ❖ L 3 Dec 61

Grief Observed, A: "Are these jottings morbid?"
- •GO 9 ❖ GO 1:18

Grief Observed, A: Aren't all these notes the senseless writhings of a man who won't accept his suffering?
- •GO 38 ❖ GO 2:31

Grief Observed, A: "By writing it all down...I believe I get a little outside it"
- •GO 10 ❖ GO 1:18

Grief Observed, A: "Do I hope that if feeling disguises itself as thought I shall feel less?"
- •GO 38 (*see also* GO 41)
- ❖ GO 2:31 (*see also* GO 3:3)

Grief Observed, A: "I thought I could describe a *state*; make a map of sorrow. Sorrow, however, turns out to be not a state but a process"
- •GO 68 ❖ GO 4:1

Grief Observed, A: "In so far as this record was a defense against total collapse, a safety valve, it has done some good"
- •GO 68 ❖ GO 4:1

Grief Observed, A: "The notes have been about myself, and about H., and about God. In that order. The order and the proportions exactly [wrong]"
- •GO 71-72 ❖ GO 4:5

Grief Observed, A: "Why should the desperate imaginings of a man dazed...be especially reliable?"
- •GO 45 ❖ GO 3:8

Grief over a loved pet: I will never laugh at anyone for this
- •LAL 61 ❖ LAL 18/8/56

Grief: "Part of every misery...is the fact that you don't merely suffer but have to keep on thinking about the fact that you suffer"
- •GO 9 (*see also* PP 14)
- ❖ GO 1:18 (*see also* PP 1:1)

Grief, passionate, does not link us with the dead but cuts us off from them
- •GO 64 ❖ GO 3:41

Grief: "Perhaps being maddeningly busy is the best thing for me. Anyway I am"
- •L 295 ❖ L 5 Aug 60

Grief, recovery from: "And this time [while walking] the face of nature was not emptied of its beauty and the world didn't look...like a mean street"
- •GO 69 (*see also* GO 41)
- ❖ GO 4:2 (*see also* GO 3:2)

Grief, recovery from: Lewis gives reasons why, with the sense that one is "feeling better," there comes a sort of shame
- •GO 62-64 ❖ GO 3:38-40

Grief, recovery from: "There was no sud-

den, striking, and emotional transition. Like the warming of a room or the coming of daylight"
•GO 71 ❖ GO 4:4

Grief, stages of, recur over and over; nothing "stays put"
•GO 67, 68-69 ❖ GO 3:45; 4:1

Grief: The agonies must die away; but what will follow? Just this apathy, this dead flatness? Does grief finally subside into boredom...?
•GO 41 ❖ GO 3:2

Grief: The desperateness of our need may prevent our perception of God's presence
•GO 53-54 (see also GO 4-6; LAL 92)
❖ GO 3:24, 25 (see also GO 1:7-11; LAL 24 Sep 60)

Grief: "The dreadful thing, as you know, is the waking each morning—the moment at which it all flows back on one"*
•LAL 88 ❖ LAL 18 Oct 59

Grief: "...the moments at which I feel nearest to Joy are precisely those when I mourn her least"
•LAL 92 (see also GO 51-53, 64-65)
❖ LAL 24 Sep 60 (see also GO 3:22-24, 41)

Grief: "The moments at which you call most desperately and clamorously to God for help are precisely those when you seem to get none"
•LAL 92 (see also GO 4-6, 53-54)
❖ LAL 24 Sep 60 (see also GO 1:7-11; 3:24-26)

Grief: "The remembered voice—that can turn me at any moment to a whimpering child"
• GO 17 ❖ GO 1:31

Grief: "Up till this I always had too little time. Now there is nothing but time"
•GO 39 ❖ GO 2:32

Grief, vanity as one cause of the shame we feel as the intense pain of, begins to lessen ("We want to prove...that we are lovers on the grand scale...")
•GO 62-63 ❖ GO 3:38, 39

Grief wants distractions? —only as a dog-tired man wants an extra blanket on a cold night; he'd rather lie there shivering than get up and find one
•GO 4 ❖ GO 1:6

Grief, when people keep silent about your, the sense of general isolation makes a sort of fringe to the sorrow itself
•L 289 ❖ L 3 Dec 59

Grief: "When we lose one blessing, another is often most unexpectedly given in its place"*
•LAL 86 ❖ LAL Aug 3/59

Grief, work in time of: "Except at my job—where the machine seems to run on much as usual—I loathe the slightest effort"
•GO 3 ❖ GO 1:6

Grief: "You are probably very exhausted physically. Hug that and all the little indulgences to which it entitles you"
•L 290 ❖ L 3 Dec 59

Grieving, intellectualizing God and the problem of pain when one is: "Do I hope that if feeling disguises itself as thought I shall feel less?"*
•GO 38 (see also GO 41, 43)
❖ GO 2:31 (see also GO 3:3, 4)

Group activities—see Collective activities

Groups—see also Collective; Collectivism; Coteries; Inner Rings

Groups or societies: If you join just to be "in," your pleasure will be short-lived
•WG 103 (see also Inner Rings)
❖ WG 6:15 (see also Inner Rings)

Groups, since men do not like to be merely equal we find them building themselves into, within which they can feel superior to the mass
•WLN 41 ❖ WLN 3:14

Groups: "The real traitor to our order is not the man who speaks, within that order, of its faults, but the man who flatters our corporate self-complacency"
•WLN 36 (re: "the cultured")
❖ WLN 3:9 (re: "the cultured")

Growing up: Lewis mentions that, as a child, he had "the gloomiest anticipation of adult life"
•SJ 22-23 (see also SJ 64-65)
❖ SJ 2:1 (see also SJ 4:11)

Growth, Christian—*see also* Change; Improvement; Perfection; Transformation

Growth, Christian: "A *perfect* man would never act from a sense of duty; he'd always *want* the right thing more than the wrong one"*
- L 277 (*see also* LM 114-116; PP 100)
- ❖ L 18 Jul 57 (*see also* LM 21:11-14; PP 6:11)

Growth, Christian: Baby pleasing his father with first steps as analogy to us: "God is easy to please, but hard to satisfy" (quote from G. MacDonald)*
- MC 172 (*see also* PP 46*; SL 39)
- ❖ MC IV 9:5 (*see also* PP 3:13*; SL 8:4)

Growth, Christian: Christianity is like toothpaste—how much better it makes a person's teeth depends on what they were like when he started brushing*
- GID 59; MC 177-178 (*see also* L 242*)
- ❖ GID I 4:46-52 (Ques. 12); MC IV 10:5 (*see also* L 28 May 52*)

Growth, Christian: "Do not sit down and start watching your own mind to see if it is coming along. That puts a man quite on the wrong track"
- MC 128 (*see also* Introspection)
- ❖ MC III 12:5 (*see also* Introspection)

Growth, Christian: "...every advance...in the spiritual life opens to one the possibility of blacker sins as well as brighter virtues"
- L 301 (*see also* RP 28-32)
- ❖ L 20 Dec 61 (*see also* RP 3:17-20)

Growth, Christian: God intends to make us perfect—nothing less*
- MC 171-175 ❖ MC IV ch. 9

Growth, Christian: "It is more like painting a portrait than like obeying a set of rules"*
- MC 162 ❖ MC IV 7:5

Growth, Christian: Just as an ordinary baby might, if he had the choice, we may prefer to stay in the warmth and safety of the womb rather than be born and grow*
- MC 187 (*see also* MC 173; SL 147)
- ❖ MC IV 11:9 (*see also* MC IV 9:7; SL 31:3)

Growth, Christian, leads not only to peace but to knowledge*
- MC 87 ❖ MC III 4:10

Growth, Christian, likened to a mountain walk toward a village at the top which is our home*
- FL 15-16 ❖ FL 1:10-12

Growth, Christian, likened to a tin soldier being turned into a real man: He thinks he is being killed, and will not be made into a man if he can help it*
- MC 154-155 ❖ MC IV 5:3

Growth, Christian, likened to the stages of development of a fetus to a baby: If we had been conscious, we might not have wanted to be changed into babies*
- MC 173 (*see also* MC 187)
- ❖ MC IV 9:7 (*see also* MC IV 11:9)

Growth, Christian, ("nearness of approach") a slow and painful—though by no means unaided—task*
- FL 19 ❖ FL 1:16

Growth, Christian: Nearness [to God] by likeness vs. nearness of approach*
- FL 14-19 ❖ FL 1:8-16

Growth, Christian: Our failures will be forgiven; the only fatal thing is to lose one's temper and give it up*
- L 199; MC 94; WG 132
- ❖ L 20 Jan 40; MC III 5:12; WG 9:13

Growth, Christian: Screwtape observes that God ("the Enemy") works on us from the centre outwards, gradually bringing our behaviour under the new standard
- SL 15 (*see also* SL 31; Works)
- ❖ SL 3:1 (*see also* SL 6:5; Works)

Growth, Christian: Screwtape observes that it is during the "trough" periods, much more than during the "peak" periods, that Christian growth occurs
- SL 39 (see entire chapter)
- ❖ SL 8:3 (see entire chapter)

Growth, Christian: "...the approach, however initiated and supported by Grace, is something we must do" (re: becoming sons of God)*
- FL 16-17 (*see also* FL 19)
- ❖ FL 1:12 (*see also* FL 1:16)

Growth, Christian: "The unfinished pic-

ture would so like to jump off the easel and have a look at itself"*
•LM 34 (*see also* MC 128; God as Painter) ❖ LM 6:16 (*see also* MC III 12:5; God as Painter)

Growth, Christian, through studying the teachings of Our Lord: "...there is no question of learning a subject but of steeping ourselves in a Personality..."*
•RP 113-114 ❖ RP 11:9

Growth, Christian: "...what is meat for a grown person might be unsuited to the palate of a child" (re: Song of Solomon)*
•GID 264 ❖ GID II 16:40

Guilt—*see also* Conscience

Guilt, a man who admits no, can accept no forgiveness
•PP 122 ❖ PP 8:6

Guilt: "A recovery of the old sense of sin is essential to Christianity"
•PP 57 ❖ PP 4:4

Guilt, all men are conscious of; they stand condemned, not by alien codes of ethics, but by their own
•PP 21-22 ❖ PP 1:12

Guilt: "All the rabbit in us is to disappear—the worried, conscientious, ethical rabbit as well as the cowardly and sensual rabbit"*
•GID 112 ❖ GID I 12:10

Guilt: Any fixing of the mind on old evils beyond what is necessary for repentance and forgiveness is certainly useless and usually bad for us
•LAL 98-99 ❖ LAL 5 Jun 61

Guilt: Christianity has nothing to say to people who do not feel that they need any forgiveness*
•MC 38-39 (*see also* CR 46-47; GID 95, 181, 243-244, PP 55)
❖ MC I 5:4 (*see also* CR 4:7; GID I 10:15; 22:13; II 12:6; PP 4:1)

Guilt, corporate, or a social conscience can be used as a mere excuse for evading our own personal faults
•PP 60-61 ❖ PP 4:8

Guilt: Emotion of shame valuable not as an emotion but because of the insight to which it leads

•PP 67 ❖ PP 4:15

Guilt enables us to perceive the "wrath" of God as inevitable, a mere corollary from God's goodness
•PP 58 ❖ PP 4:5, 6

Guilt, feeling of, was a thing I hardly knew in my youth; "It took me as long to acquire inhibitions as others (they say) have taken to get rid of them"
•SJ 69 ❖ SJ 4:18

Guilt, humiliation is different from; perhaps we all dislike it so much that we tend to disguise it from ourselves by treating blunders as sins
•LAL 106-107 ❖ LAL 3 Sep 62

Guilt: "I come back to St. John: 'if our heart condemn us, God is greater than our heart'"
•LAL 77; LM 34
❖ LAL Jul 21st, 58; LM 6:14

Guilt: "If there is particular sin on your conscience, repent and confess it. If there isn't, tell the despondent devil not to be silly"
•LAL 77 ❖ LAL Jul 21st 58

Guilt is washed out not by time but by repentance and the blood of Christ; after repentance we should remember the price of our forgiveness and be humble
•PP 61 (*see also* L 236*)
❖ PP 4:9 (*see also* L 8 Jan 52*)

Guilt: I've met people who felt guilty but did not seem to be, and others who were guilty and didn't seem to feel guilt
•LM 33 ❖ LM 6:12

Guilt: Jesus Himself "plumbed the depths of that worst suffering which comes to evil men who at last know their own evil"
•RP 127 (*consider also* Self-knowledge)
❖ RP 12:7 (*consider also* Self-knowledge)

Guilt, Lewis mentions, which he felt regarding his relationship with his father*
•SJ 125 (*see also* L 162)
❖ SJ 8:7 (*see also* L 12 Sep 38)

Guilt, mere emotion of: I believe that all

sadness not arising from either repentance (hastening to amendment)
or pity (hastening to assistance) is bad*
•PP 67 ❖ PP 4:15

Guilt (or "shame"), lowering one's moral
standards in order to prevent: "It is
mad work to remove hypocrisy by
removing the temptation to hypocrisy"
•PP 57 ❖ PP 4:3

Guilt produced in us by those unlovable
people who demand to be loved
•FL 65 (see also GID 285)
❖ FL 3:18 (see also GID III 3:7)

Guilt, Psycho-analysis is partly to blame
for the decline of our sense of, by intimating that shame is a dangerous and
mischievous thing
•PP 56-57 ❖ PP 4:3

Guilt: Psychologists are talking nonsense
when they tell us that all guilt-feelings
are untrustworthy and pathological
•LM 32-33 ❖ LM 6:12

Guilt: Regret for the consequences of our
innocent blunders different from guilt
for sins; we must try not to confuse
the two*
•LAL 106-107 ❖ LAL 3 Sep 62

Guilt: Screwtape points out that God does
not want a person to think too much
of his sins; the sooner the man turns
his attention outward, the better
•SL 66 (see also LM 33)
❖ SL 14:5 (see also LM 6:13)

Guilt, sense of, lacking in modern audi-
ences
•GID 95, 181-182, 243-244; PP 55-57
❖ GID I 10:15; 22:13; II 12:6-8; PP 4:1-4

Guilt, sense of: method for awakening it
in modern audiences
•GID 96 ❖ GID I 10:16, 17

Guilt shared by those who observe sin and
do not condemn it
•PP 117 ❖ PP 7:9

Guilt: "Some people feel guilty about their
anxieties, and regard them as a defect
of faith. I don't agree at all"
•LM 41 ❖ LM 8:5

Guilt, the biggest sinners are conscious of,
and thereby capable of real repentance
•SL 165-166; WLN 64

❖ SL 32:29; WLN 4:29

Guilt: The holier a man is, the more aware
he is of his sinfulness
•PP 67 (see also LAL 95; MC 87, 164;
PP 55, top)
❖ PP 4:15 (see also LAL 9 Jan 61; MC
III 4:10; IV 7:12; PP 4:prelim. quote)

Guilt, two principal causes for the decline
of the sense of
•PP 56-57 ❖ PP 4:2, 3

Guilt: "Unless Christianity is wholly false,
the perception of ourselves which we
have in moments of shame must be
the only true one..."
•PP 56-57 ❖ PP 4:3

Guilt, vague, which never flowers into real
repentance increases one's reluctance
to think about God (almost anything
can distract us)
•SL 54-56 ❖ SL 12:3, 4

Guilt, vague, which we are reluctant to
face mentioned by Screwtape as having the capacity to shut humans off
"more and more from all real happiness"
•SL 55 ❖ SL 12:4

Guilt: We must be aware of our own sinfulness, but a continual poring over
the "sink" can breed its own perverse
pride*
•LM 98-99 ❖ LM 18:13-15

Guilt: "What the devil loves is that vague
cloud of unspecified guilt feeling or
unspecified virtue by which he lures
us into despair or presumption"
•LAL 77 ❖ LAL Jul 21st 58

Guilt, what to do about vague feelings of,
which do not seem to be connected
with particular wrong-doing
•LM 32-34 (see also LAL 77)
❖ LM 6:11-17 (see also LAL Jul 21st 58)

Guilt: When our conscience won't come
down to brass tacks and will only
vaguely accuse, we must ignore it
•LM 34 ❖ LM 6:17

Guns and Good Company (chapter title)
•SJ 182-196 ❖ SJ ch. 12

Habit, no evil, is so ingrained that it cannot, even in old age, be whisked away
•LM 107 ❖ LM 20:1

Habit, obedience mentioned by Screwtape as a
•SL 126 (*see also* CR 24-25*)
❖ SL 27:3 (*see also* CR 2:38*)

Habit renders any pleasure at once less pleasant and harder to forgo
•SL 55 ❖ SL 12:4

Habit, tempters try to elicit small wrong choices which later harden into, and then into evil principles
•SL 156-157; WLN 54-55 (*see also* SL 53-54; Choices) ❖ SL 32:10; WLN 4:10 (*see also* SL 12:1; Choices)

Habits, active, are strengthened by repetition but passive ones (feelings) are weakened; the more one feels without acting the less he will be able to act
•SL 60-61 ❖ SL 13:5

Habits: "It is only in so far as they reach the will and are there embodied in habits that the virtues are really fatal to us" (—Screwtape)
•SL 31 ❖ SL 6:5

Habits: When pleasures such as vanity, excitement, and flippancy are made into habits they are rendered at once less pleasant and harder to forego
•SL 55 ❖ SL 12:4

Habits, old, (both mental and bodily) mentioned by Screwtape as obstacles to human steadfastness in faith
•SL 11 ❖ SL 2:1

Hades, Lewis describes a haunting impression he experienced at Great Bookham over which hung an atmosphere like the Pagan
•SJ 150 ❖ SJ 10:2

"**Hades**" of Greek religious belief is neither Heaven nor Hell; it is almost nothing
•RP 37 (*see also* M 145)
❖ RP 4:8 (*see also* M 16:6)

Hades, regarding the doctrine of Christ descending into, and preaching to the dead
•L 238 ❖ L 31 Jan 52

Hades, the land of the dead, differentiated from Gehenna, the land of the lost
•L 238 ❖ L 31 Jan 52

Hail Marys: Salutes to the Virgin Mary better avoided lest she begin to be treated as a divinity
•L 243 (*see also* Devotions to saints; Mary)
❖ L undated letter just after 20 Jun 52 (*see also* Devotions to saints; Mary)

"**Half-way**," Lewis attempts to show that religious language carries significance if you are prepared to meet it, —with a certain good will
•CR 129-141, esp. 135, 141
❖ CR ch. 11, esp. 11:12, 23

Hamilton family mentioned (Lewis's mother's family)
•SJ 3, 42-44, 158-159
❖ SJ 1:1; 3:1, 2; 10:11

Hamlet—*see* Play illustration

Handicaps: "...a life, by natural standards, crippled and thwarted [is] not only no bar to salvation, but might easily be one of its conditions"*
•CR 14 ❖ CR 2:5

Happiness—*consider also* Life; Satisfaction; Unhappiness

Happiness, a right to, doesn't for me make much more sense than a right to be six feet tall or to have good weather
•GID 318 ❖ GID III 9:5

Happiness achieved in love not by good lovers but by good people
•GID 321 (*see also* FL 159-160)

---

* These items reflect some interpretation on the part of the editor; the idea will not be found in these exact words. *See Introduction, p. ix.*

** These items are ideas of Lewis's which the editor has placed under a topic Lewis did not there intend to address. *See Introduction, p. ix.*

Entries without asterisks are not necessarily exact quotes, but the idea should be easy to find as worded.

❖ GID III 9:24 (*see also* FL 5:45)

Happiness, Affection is responsible for nine-tenths of whatever solid and durable, there is in our natural lives
•FL 80 ❖ FL 3:42

Happiness, all our worldly schemes of, were always doomed to final frustration
•WG 31-32 ❖ WG 2:14

Happiness and peace, God cannot give us, apart from Himself; there is no such thing
•MC 54 ❖ MC II 3:7

Happiness and preservation of the human race of secondary importance to having people of a certain sort, behaving in a certain way
•GID 297 (*see also* GID 311)
❖ GID III 4:20 (*see also* GID III 8:1)

Happiness and security, the settled, which we all desire God withholds from us, for it would teach us to rest our hearts in this world
•PP 115 ❖ PP 7:7

Happiness, [as a youth] I was far more eager to escape pain than to achieve
•SJ 171, 228 (*see also* SJ 117*)
❖ SJ 11:8; 14:22 (*see also* SJ 7:21*)

Happiness, capacity for, must reawake before one becomes fully aware of its absence (re: illness while grieving)
•LAL 106 ❖ LAL 31/7/62

Happiness, Christ did not teach and suffer that we might become...more careful of our own
•FL 170 (*see also* CR 155; FL 168)
❖ FL 6:14 (*see also* CR 13:6; FL 6:10)

Happiness ("comfort") is the one thing you cannot get by looking for it; but if you look for truth, you may find happiness ("comfort") in the end**
•MC 39 ❖ MC I 5:4

Happiness did not come to Joy early in life; a thousand years of it would not have made her *blasée*
•GO 18 ❖ GO 2:1

Happiness, domestic, more essential to women than to men
•GID 321 ❖ GID III 9:27

Happiness, earthly, is perhaps addictive; the withdrawal more like lacking

bread than cake
•L 301 ❖ L 20 Dec 61

Happiness, even in, we must remember that the crown is not promised without the Cross
•L 166 (*see also* WG 18)
❖ L 8 May 39 (*see also* WG 1:15)

Happiness, fatal principle that we have a "right" to, will eventually cause our civilization to be swept away
•GID 322 ❖ GID III 9:28

Happiness found in which religion? — "While it lasts, the religion of worshipping oneself is the best"
•GID 58 ❖ GID I 4:43, 44 (Ques. 11)

Happiness, God gives the, that there is, not the happiness that is not
•PP 54 ❖ PP 3:19

Happiness, God intends for us a deep, strong, unshakable kind of
•MC 78 ❖ MC III 2:12

Happiness: "...God intends to give us what we need, not what we now think we want"
•PP 53 ❖ PP 3:18

Happiness, great thing is to stop thinking about
•L 227 ❖ L 5 Mar 51

Happiness, having, not necessarily the same thing as having what's good for you (if it was, the problem of pain would be unanswerable)
•PP 26, 37-54 ❖ PP 2:1, ch. 3

Happiness, I had been warned—I had warned myself—not to reckon on worldly; we were even promised sufferings—they were part of the program
•GO 41-42 ❖ GO 3:3

Happiness I had before H. [Joy] seems insipid now; I don't want to go back again and be happy in *that* way
•GO 70 ❖ GO 4:2

Happiness, I sometimes think that awkward and senseless shame does as much towards preventing straightforward, as any of our vices can do
•GO 9 ❖ GO 1:17

Happiness, if you think of this world as a place intended simply for our, you

will find it quite intolerable
•GID 51-52 ❖ GID I 4:17-19 (Ques. 5)

Happiness, it is incredible how much, —
even gaiety—we sometimes had together after all hope was gone (re: wife
Joy's terminal illness)
•GO 13 ❖ GO 1:25

Happiness, it is not settled, but momentary joy that glorifies the past
•SJ 8 ❖ SJ 1:5

Happiness: Lewis describes what is meant
by our having the right to "the pursuit of happiness"
•GID 318-319 ❖ GID III 9:9-14

Happiness, Lewis mentions friendship as
having been the chief source of his
•SJ 33 ❖ SJ 2:12

Happiness, life offers just sufficient, to
give us the fear of losing it and, when
it is lost, the poignant misery of remembering
•PP 14 (see also GO 9*)
❖ PP 1:1 (see also GO 1:18*)

Happiness: "Marriage is not otherwise
unhappy than as life is unhappy"
(quote from Johnson)
•L 128 ❖ L 2 Aug 28

Happiness, my father's people were true
Welshmen who had not much of the
talent for
•SJ 3 ❖ SJ 1:1

Happiness, never commit your, to the fu-
ture
•WG 30 (see also SL 67-71)
❖ WG 2:13 (see also SL ch. 15)

Happiness of a creature lies in self-surrender; no one can make that surrender
but himself, and he may refuse (re:
doctrine of hell)
•PP 118 ❖ PP 8:1

Happiness of Man: When he reaches the
place he was made for, his nature is
fulfilled and his happiness attained
•PP 52 (see also WG 118-119)
❖ PP 3:18 (see also WG 7:18)

Happiness of our loved ones: We would
rather see them suffer much than be
happy in contemptible and estranging
modes (like God, with us)
•PP 41 ❖ PP 3:8

Happiness of the kind brought by money
and natural gifts such as intelligence
and popularity may cause us to forget our need for God
•MC 180 ❖ MC IV 10:11

Happiness or unhappiness ("one's inner
state") so often seems to have little to
do with the circumstances*
•LAL 83 (see also SJ 78, 118-119)
❖ LAL Jun 7th 59 (see also SJ 5:12; 8:1)

Happiness: Our attempt to hang on to a
belief in our intrinsic goodness and
lovableness has kept us from being
happy
•FL 180-181 ❖ FL 6:27, 28

Happiness: Our modest prosperity and
the happiness of our children is not
enough to make us blessed; if we have
not learned to know God, we will be
wretched
•PP 97 ❖ PP 6:8

Happiness, perfect, which "being in love"
seems to promise turns out again and
again to be illusory
•GID 320-321 ❖ GID III 9:23-25

Happiness, progress means increasing
goodness and, —not mere longevity
•GID 311 (see also GID 296-297; L 158*;
SL 131*; WG 43*)
❖ GID III 8:1 (see also GID III 4:20; L 13
Jan 37*; SL 28:1*; WG 3:18*)

Happiness: The Hamiltons were a cooler
race; they went straight for happiness
as experienced travelers go for the best
seat in a train
•SJ 3 ❖ SJ 1:1

Happiness: "...the less one can think about
happiness on earth, the less, I believe,
one suffers"
•LAL 96 (see also SL 95-96*)
❖ LAL 9 Jan 61 (see also SL 21:2*)

Happiness: The proper good of a creature
is to surrender itself to its Creator—
and when it does so, it is good and
happy
•PP 90 ❖ PP 6:3

Happiness, the suburban villas of Surrey
suggested, and filled me with desire
for a domesticity which I had never
known

•SJ 132-133 ❖ SJ 9:1

Happiness, there is no other way to the, for which we were made than to become united to God
•MC 153 ❖ MC IV 4:8

Happiness: [This period of my life] consisted chiefly of moments when I was too happy to speak...*
•SJ 118 ❖ SJ 8:1

Happiness, to how few of us He *dare* send, because He knows we will forget Him
•L 227 (*see also* L 161-162*)
❖ L 5 Mar 51 (*see also* L 12 Sep 38*)

Happiness, vague guilt mentioned by Screwtape as having the capacity to shut humans off more and more from all real
•SL 55 ❖ SL 12:4

Happiness: Walking in Surrey, with the whole weekend's reading ahead, I suppose I reached as much happiness as is ever to be reached on earth
•SJ 147 ❖ SJ 9:22

Happiness, we depend for a very great deal of our, on circumstances outside all human control
•GID 318 ❖ GID III 9:5

Happiness, We Have No Right To, (chapter title)
•GID 317-322 (*see also* L 221)
❖ GID III ch. 9 (*see also* L 22 Sep 49)

Happiness, we have no right to ("An awful symptom is that part of oneself still regards troubles as interruptions")*
•L 161-162 ❖ L 12 Sep 38

Happiness: "...what a grim business even a happy human life is when you read it rapidly through to the inevitable end..."
•L 187 ❖ L 12 Jul 40

Happiness, what we would call our, is not the end God chiefly has in view; He desires our perfection, and knows this will make us happy
•PP 48 ❖ PP 3:15

Happiness: "When we want to be something other than the thing God wants us to be, we must be wanting what, in fact, will not make us happy"
•PP 52 (*see also* WG 118-119)

❖ PP 3:18 (*see also* WG 7:18)

Happiness, world divided into those who like, and those who don't
•WG xvi ❖ WG Introduction, para. 21

Happinesses of life, all our little, look like broken toys in times of fear and pain; we are reminded that they were never intended to possess our heart
•PP 106 (*see also* FL 192)
❖ PP 6:17 (*see also* FL 6:47)

Harwood, A. C.: Lewis's friend at Oxford ("He is the sole Horatio known to me in this age of Hamlets")
•SJ 200-201 (*see also* L 78)
❖ SJ 13:5 (*see also* L 30 Jun 22)

Harwood and then Barfield embraced the doctrines of Steiner and became Anthroposophists; this was a really dreadful thing
•SJ 205-207 (*see also* L 89)
❖ SJ 13:14-17 (*see also* L 7 Jul 23)

"**Hate**," how we are to understand the word, as used in the text "If any man come to me and hate not his father and mother..."
•FL 171-173 (*see also* FL 165-166; GID 191-192; RP 131-132) ❖ FL 6:16-19 (*see also* FL 6:4; GID II 1:4; RP 12:10)

Hating your father and your mother, Christ's exhortation about, profitable only to those who read it with horror
•RP 131-132 ❖ RP 12:10

Hatred, all kinds of love carry in them the seeds of
•FL 82-83 ❖ FL 3:45

Hatred and malice in humans are disappointing to Screwtape when they are directed against imaginary scapegoats ("the Germans") rather than real persons
•SL 30-31 ❖ SL 6:4, 5

Hatred and vindictiveness forbidden in Judaism just as in Christianity; the reaction of the Psalmists to injury, though natural, is profoundly wrong
•RP 26 ❖ CR 3:12, 13

Hatred as an element in some forms of "love"
•FL 64, 82-83, 160 ❖ FL 3:17, 45; 5:46

Hatred, courtship mentioned by Screwtape

as the time for sowing the seeds of domestic
•SL 120 ❖ SL 26:1

Hatred, domestic, usually expresses itself more in the manner of speech than in the words themselves
•SL 17-18 ❖ SL 3:5

Hatred for sin but not the sinner: We have no trouble doing this with ourselves
•MC 105-106 ❖ MC III 7:4-6

Hatred, if we cause, in another by injuring him we are guilty not only of the original injury but of provoking sin
•RP 24, 25-26 (see also CR 118-120)
❖ RP 3:9, 11 (see also CR 10:9-10)

Hatred in the Jewish culture did not need to be disguised for sake of social decorum; we therefore see it in the Psalms in its "wild" or natural state
•RP 23 (see also CR 118)
❖ RP 3:7 (see also CR 10:7)

Hatred in the Psalms: "Psalm 109 is as unabashed a hymn of hate as was ever written"
•CR 118 ❖ CR 10:7

Hatred in the Psalms: We should be wicked if we approved it, or (worse still) used it to justify similar passions in ourselves
•RP 22 ❖ RP 3:6

Hatred is a great anodyne for shame
•SL 136 ❖ SL 29:4

Hatred is often the compensation by which a frightened man reimburses himself for the miseries of fear; the more he fears, the more he will hate (re: war)
•SL 136 ❖ SL 29:4

Hatred is the natural result of oppression and injustice; an uninhibited expression of this is found in the Psalms
•CR 118-119 (see also RP 24-26)
❖ CR 10:9 (see also RP 3:9-11)

Hatred leads to cruelty, which leads to more hatred; a vicious circle
•MC 117 ❖ MC III 9:7, 8

Hatred made possible by the very same conditions of intimacy which make Affection possible
•FL 64 (see also GID 285*)

❖ FL 3:17 (see also GID III 3:7*)

"Hatred" of Esau [in Malachi 1:2-3] meant his rejection by God
•FL 172 ❖ FL 6:17

Hatred or grievance, we all know the perilous charm of a shared, (re: friendship between those who share a negative point of view)
•FL 113 ❖ FL 4:43

Hatred, the natural loves that are allowed to become gods do not remain loves but can become complicated forms of
•FL 19-20 (see also FL 47*, 154*)
❖ FL 1:16 (see also FL 2:40*; 5:36*)

Hatred, we are creatures who actually find pleasure in
•MC 108 (see also L 222-223)
❖ MC III 7:11 (see also L 12 Jan 50)

Hatred: We are far more subtle than the Psalmists in disguising our ill will from others and from ourselves
•RP 23 ❖ RP 3:8

Havard, Dr. Humphrey, noted as reading to the "Inklings" his paper on the clinical experience of pain (which later became appendix to *The Problem of Pain*)
•L 176 (see also L 197)
❖ L 3 Feb 40 (see also L 21 Dec 41)

Headship (as Christ is to man and man is to woman) is divine virtue received by imitation
•CR 4-6 ❖ CR 1:6-10

Headship in marriage—see Marriage

Healing always a function of Nature; doctors merely stimulate Nature's functions or remove what hinders them
•GID 30; M 139-140
❖ GID I 2:8; M 15:14

Healing, faith, question of
•L 224-225, 226 (see also CR 149-150; L 251) ❖ L 7 Dec 50; undated letter just before 7 Feb 51 (see also CR 12:23; L 17 Jul 53)

Healing, faith, Screwtape mentions, as a useful addition to "mere Christianity" ("If they must be Christians, let them ...be Christians with a difference")
•SL 115-116 ❖ SL 25:1

Healing, Jesus' miracles of: Lewis discusses the kinds of faith we see exercised in the miracles of Jesus
•CR 144-145 ❖ CR 12:10, 11

Healing, Jesus' miracles of: The Power that always was behind all healings puts on a face and hands
•M 139-140 (see also GID 30)
❖ M 15:13, 14 (see also GID I 2:8)

Healing, Jesus' miracles of: Why it is idle to complain that He healed only those whom He happened to meet
•M 140 ❖ M 15:14

Health a great blessing, but must not become the main object; you are only likely to get health if you want other things more—food, fresh air, etc.
•MC 118-119 ❖ MC III 10:1

Health and politics, we think about such things as, only in order to be able to think about something else
•WG 109 (see also GID 280-281)
❖ WG 7:4 (see also GID III 2:6-10)

Health and sickness listed by Screwtape as neutral situations which can work either for God's or the devil's purposes
•SL 89 ❖ SL 19:3

Health as a gift which could cause us to forget our need of God
•MC 180-181 (see also L 221)
❖ MC IV 10:11 (see also L 22 Sep 49)

Health, concentrating on one's, listed as a means of avoiding God
•CR 168 ❖ CR 14:17, 18

Health, over-emphasis on, in America: I get the impression that in your country people are far too medically minded; they read and think too much about health
•LAL 39 ❖ LAL 21/3/55

Health system of Britain mentioned or referred to
•LAL 71, 84, 116
❖ LAL 14/1/58; Jul 7th 59; 10 Jun 63

Heart, a man should never give all his, to anything which will end when his life ends
•WLN 110 ❖ WLN 7:31

Heart, the precious alabaster box (like Mary Magdalene's) which one must break over the Holy Feet is one's
•LAL 35-36 ❖ LAL Nov 1st 54

Heart: "Thou has made us for Thyself, and our heart has no rest till it comes to Thee" (quote from St. Augustine)
•FL 189 (see also GID 252)
❖ FL 6:41 (see also GID II 14:7)

Heathen—see Pagans; Unbelievers

Heathen religions—see Mythology; Pagan myth; Paganism

Heaven (chapter title)
•PP 144-154 ❖ PP ch. 10

Heaven—see also Destiny of redeemed Man; Eternal life

Heaven, according to Screwtape God's view is that human birth is important chiefly as the qualification for human death which is the gate to
•SL 133-134 (see also SJ 117*)
❖ SL 28:3 (see also SJ 7:21*)

Heaven, aim at, and you will get earth "thrown in"
•MC 118 ❖ MC III 10:1

Heaven, analogy of boy asking whether sex involves eating chocolates to our wondering whether, will be like things we know on earth
•M 160 ❖ M 16:28

Heaven, analogy of boy in dungeon being shown a drawing of the outside world to our attempt to understand, by our natural experiences
•WG 67-69 ❖ WG 4:22-24

Heaven and Hell, belief in, coming too soon, may render impossible the development of the appetite for God; personal hopes and fears have got in first
•RP 39-40 (see also FL 189-190; GID 130-131; LM 120; SJ 231)
❖ RP 4:13-15 (see also FL 6:41-44; GID I 16:2, 3; LM 22:8; SJ 15:3)

Heaven and hell, source of nearly all Biblical references to, is Our Lord Himself; we must not be afraid to mention them
•WG 20-21 ❖ WG 2:2

Heaven, any adult notion of, is forced to deny of that state most of the things

our nature desires
•WG 66 ❖ WG 4:19

Heaven as a life in Christ and a vision of God vs. Heaven as a bodily life: Christians have difficulty reconciling the two
•M 159 ❖ M 16:27

Heaven as an object of purely carnal, self-centred hope: "Such belief is fortunately very brittle"
•LM 76 ❖ LM 14:15

Heaven as described by metaphorical language not to be misunderstood; it is a merely symbolical attempt to express the inexpressible
•MC 121 ❖ MC III 10:6

Heaven as described by Scriptural imagery may have little natural appeal at first
•WG 9, 11 ❖ WG 1:7, 9

Heaven as glimpsed in a zoo with tame animals*
•L 154-155 (see also SJ 237-238)
❖ L 14 Jun 32 (see also SJ 15:8, 9)

Heaven: "As long as I live my imagination of Paradise will retain something of my brother's toy garden"
•SJ 7 ❖ SJ 1:4

Heaven as perceived by the image of the blue sky: an image intended by God
•M 157-158 ❖ M 16:25, 26

Heaven as "the fully waking world"
•FL 192 (see also LM 75; RP 92; Life as a "bad dream")
❖ FL 6:47 (see also LM 14:11; RP 93; Life as a "bad dream")

Heaven as the place we were made for: We were made for it, rather than it being made for us; and we will not be ourselves until we are there
•WG 118-119 (see also PP 52, 147- 148; consider also Personality)
❖ WG 7:18 (see also PP 3:18; 10:3; consider also Personality)

Heaven: At my conversion I did not yet believe in a future life; I now number that among my greatest mercies (God was to be obeyed simply because He was God)*
•SJ 231 (see also FL 189-190; LM 120; RP 39-42, esp. 42) ❖ SJ 15:3 (see also FL 6:42; LM 22:8; RP 4:12-17, esp. 4:17)

Heaven, belief in, should be a corollary to belief in God, not the other way around
•FL 189-190; GO 79; LM 120; RP 39-42; SJ 231 (see also L 290*)
❖ FL 6:42; GO 4:21; LM 22:8; RP 4:13-17; SJ 15:3 (see also L 3 Dec 59*)

Heaven, Biblical descriptions of, nearly always contain an appeal to desire; to hope for our own good is not a bad thing
•WG 3 (compare with GID 131; WG 66) ❖ WG 1:1 (compare with GID I 16:3; WG 4:19)

Heaven constantly associated with palms, crowns, white robes, thrones, etc.; this makes no immediate appeal to me at all
•WG 11 (see also WG 9, 66)
❖ WG 1:9 (see also WG 1:7; 4:19)

Heaven, desirable aspects of, include promise of Glory; Lewis describes what this involves
•WG 3-19 ❖ WG ch. 1

Heaven, desirable aspects of—see also Destiny of redeemed Man

Heaven, desirable aspects of: the vision and enjoyment of God*
•WG 66-67 (see also FL 15)
❖ WG 4:20, 21 (see also FL 1:9)

Heaven, desire for, already in us but not yet attached to the true object
•WG 6 ❖ WG 1:4

Heaven, desire for, may not prove that I shall enjoy it, but it indicates that such a thing exists (God makes no appetite in vain)
•WG 8-9 (see also WG 27)
❖ WG 1:6 (see also WG 2:9)

Heaven, desire for, not simply a desire for longevity or jewellery or social splendours; also we claim to know that our desire is not simply erotic
•WG 65 ❖ WG 4:17

Heaven desired most when there seems to be most of Heaven already here; "It is the bright frontispiece which whets one to read the story itself"

•L 289 ❖ L 5 Nov 59

Heaven, enjoyment of, not possible for those who have not allowed process of character improvement to begin on earth
•MC 78 (see also FL 187)
❖ MC III 2:12 (see also FL 6:38)

Heaven, even if there were pains in, all who understand would desire them
•PP 126 (see also PP 152; SL 148)
❖ PP 8:9 (see also PP 10:9; SL 31:5)

Heaven, everyone in, is filled with good-ness as a mirror is filled with light
•MC 130-131 (see also MC 144)
❖ MC III 12:9 (see also MC IV 2:13, 14)

Heaven, experience of, not totally un-imaginable ("...the Transposition can be in its own way adequate")
•WG 72-73 ❖ WG 4:30

Heaven, faith in, weakens when used for the purpose of promoting hope of re-union with loved ones
•FL 189-190 (see also GO 28-30, 79; L 290; RP 41; SJ 231*)
❖ FL 6:41-43 (see also GO 2:13-16; 4:21; L 3 Dec 59; RP 4:16; SJ 15:3*)

Heaven: "For it is one thing to see the land of peace from a wooded ridge...and another to tread the road that leads to it" (quote from St. Augustine)*
•SJ 230 ❖ SJ 15 prelim. quote

Heaven, four senses of the word, listed
•M 157 ❖ M 16:25

Heaven: God's nature is such that "union with that Nature is bliss and separa-tion from it horror. Thus Heaven and Hell come in"
•SJ 232 (see also GID 47)
❖ SJ 15:4 (see also GID I 3:17)

Heaven (God's presence) as the only thing we were made for
•MC 170 ❖ MC IV 8:12

Heaven, having new bodies in, compared to horse-riding bareback
•M 163 (see also M 126, 161)
❖ M 16:32 (see also M 14:30; 16:29)

Heaven, He came down from: This phrase can almost be transposed into "Heaven drew earth up into it"
•LM 70-71 ❖ LM 13:10

Heaven, hills and valleys of, will be to earthly ones not as a copy is to the original but as the flower to the root, or the diamond to the coal
•LM 123 ❖ LM 22:19

Heaven, hope of: Life at a vile boarding school is in a way a good preparation for the Christian life, in that it teaches one to live by hope and by faith*
•SJ 36-37 ❖ SJ 2:16

Heaven: How can it loom less than large if it is believed in at all?
•LM 120 (see also WG 3-5*)
❖ LM 22:7, 9 (see also WG 1:1-3*)

Heaven, I believed in God before I be-lieved in
•LM 120; FL 189-190; RP 42; SJ 213
❖ LM 22:8; FL 6:42; RP 4:17; SJ 15:3

Heaven: "I feel...that to make the life of the blessed dead strictly timeless is inconsistent with the resurrection of the body"*
•LM 109-110 ❖ LM 20:13-15

Heaven, I have met no people who dis-believed in Hell and also had a living and life-giving belief in
•LM 76 ❖ LM 14:14

Heaven: "I remind myself that...my true good is in another world and my only real treasure is Christ" (re: purpose of trials and pain)*
•PP 106 ❖ PP 6:17

Heaven, idea that, comes not to fulfill but to destroy our nature must be pre-vented whenever possible
•WG 67 (see also MC 141; SL 59; Per-sonality) ❖ WG 4:21, 22 (see also MC IV 2:3; SL 13:3, 4; Personality)

Heaven: "If I find in myself a desire which no experience in this world can sat-isfy, the most probable explanation is that I was made for another world"
•MC 120 (see also Desire)
❖ MC III 10:5 (see also Desire)

Heaven: If it is our real destiny, then any other object on which our desire fixes must be in some degree fallacious
•WG 6 ❖ WG 1:4

Heaven, if it turned out there was no such thing as, would that be a moment for changing sides?

•LM 120 ❖ LM 22:8

Heaven: If praise perfects enjoyment I can more easily understand how Heaven can be a state in which men and angels perpetually praise God

•RP 96 (see also GO 72*)

❖ RP 9:6 (see also GO 4:5*)

Heaven, if some earthly things are missing in, it will be because something better will leave no room for them (e.g., the sexual life)

•M 160 ❖ M 16:28

Heaven: If we really believe that our real home is elsewhere, why should we not look forward to the arrival?

•LAL 83-84 (see also PP 115; SL 132)

❖ LAL Jun 7th 59 (see also PP 7:7; SL 28:1)

Heaven, if we try to use the hope of, as a compensation for earthly misery (e.g., bereavement) belief in it crumbles away

•L 290; RP 41 (see also FL 189-190; GO 79*) ❖ L 3 Dec 59; RP 4:16 (see also FL 6:41-43; GO 4:21*)

Heaven, imagery such as that used by hymn-writers to describe, not altogether inappropriate to the reality

•WG 66 ❖ WG 4:19

Heaven: "In the perfect and eternal world the Law will vanish. But the results of having lived faithfully under it will not"

•LM 116 ❖ LM 21:14

Heaven, in the perfected humility of, it may be that we will bear the shame of our sins forever—glad that it should be common knowledge to the universe

•PP 61 (see also L 236; SL 148)

❖ PP 4:9 (see also L 8 Jan 52; SL 31:5)

Heaven in the sense of being united with God: Christ's divine Nature never left it

•M 155 ❖ M 16:22

Heaven, in, there will be no anguish and no duty of turning from our earthly beloveds, for we shall find them all in Him

•FL 190-191 ❖ FL 6:44

Heaven is a city, and a Body, because the blessed remain eternally different; and each has something unique to tell all the others about God

•PP 150 (see also FL 92-93; L 242-243*)

❖ PP 10:7 (see also FL 4:9; L 20 Jun 52*)

"Heaven is a state of mind," remark that, bears witness to the wintry and death-like phase in which we are now living

•M 161-163 ❖ M 16:30, 31

Heaven is an acquired taste (whereas Limbo, I am told, is a place of perfect natural happiness)

•L 164 ❖ L 5 Apr 39

Heaven is like friendship in that each person can communicate a different aspect of God to all the rest

•FL 92-93 (see also PP 150)

❖ FL 4:9 (see also PP 10:7)

Heaven is more than we think, not less; we shall be more, not less, than we were on earth

•WG 69 ❖ WG 4:23-25

Heaven is the home of humanity, but hell was not made for men; therefore we know much more about heaven than hell

•PP 125, 127 ❖ PP 8:9, 10

Heaven is wherever the will is perfectly offered back to the Creator in delighted obedience

•PP 91 ❖ PP 6:3

Heaven, it is more important that, should exist than that any of us should reach it

•SJ 211, 222 ❖ SJ 13:19; 14:13

Heaven, in the end it will make no difference what we chose instead of; we shall have missed the thing we were made for, the only thing that satisfies

•WG 131 ❖ WG 9:11

Heaven, Joy is the serious business of, (e.g., pleasure, such as dance and games)

•LM 93 ❖ LM 17:17

Heaven, joys of, are an "acquired taste" and certain ways of life may render the taste impossible of acquisition

•PP 61 ❖ PP 4:9

Heaven: Lewis speculates what it would

be like to visit other worlds and meet beings wholly different from us** •WLN 88-89 ❖ WLN 6:17

Heaven likely to be a development of what we know here; our natural experiences are like a drawing of which the risen life will be the reality •WG 67-69 ❖ WG 4:21-25

Heaven, looking for, by exploring space is like seeing all Shakespeare's plays in the hope that you will find Stratford as one of the places •CR 167-168 ❖ CR 14:10

Heaven: Love, by definition, seeks to enjoy its object; that is why love for God makes heaven its goal •PP 145 ❖ PP 10:1

Heaven: Meaning of the text "I go to prepare a place for you" •M 149, 157 ❖ M 16:12, 25

Heaven means union with God and Hell means separation from Him; any other belief is probably mischievous superstition •RP 41 ❖ RP 4:15

Heaven, missing, is to miss the end for which we were formed and the only thing that satisfies •WG 131 ❖ WG 9:11

Heaven: Most of us find that our belief in the future life is strong only when God is at the centre of our thoughts •RP 41 (see also FL 189-190; GID 130-131; GO 79; LM 120; SJ 231) ❖ RP 4:16 (see also FL 6:41-44; GID I 16:2, 3; GO 4:21; LM 22:8; SJ 15:3)

Heaven: Nature as "the instrument for that music which will...arise between Christ and us" •M 162 ❖ M 16:30

Heaven: Nature is to be redeemed and cured, but not tamed or sterilised; we shall still be able to recognise her •M 66-67 ❖ M 9:7

Heaven: Nature not to be unmade, but remade; the old field of space, time, matter, and the senses is to be weeded and sown for a new crop* •M 149 (see also GID 87) ❖ M 16:12 (see also GID I 9:11)

Heaven, no need to suppose that the distinction between the sexes will disappear in •M 160 ❖ M 16:28

Heaven: "No one, I presume, can imagine life in the glorified body...I can picture very few of the things I believe in" •L 288 ❖ L 8 Sep 59

Heaven not a bribe; offers nothing that a mercenary soul can desire •PP 145 ❖ PP 10:1

Heaven: Nothing can enter there that cannot become heavenly; must have at least allowed the process to begin here on earth (re: natural loves) •FL 187 (see also MC 78) ❖ FL 6:38 (see also MC III 2:12)

Heaven on earth, a Christian cannot believe any of those who promise a •PP 114 ❖ PP 7:5

Heaven on earth, dream of making, mentioned by Screwtape as a temptation which is especially successful with youth •SL 133 ❖ SL 28:2

Heaven on earth, modern philosophies try to persuade you that it is possible to build a •WG 8 ❖ WG 1:5

Heaven on earth, Screwtape mentions wanting men to be "hagridden by the Future"—absorbed by visions of an imminent hell or a •SL 69 ❖ SL 15:4

Heaven on earth, war tends to shatter our hope of building, and not a moment too soon •WG 32 ❖ WG 2:14

Heaven, one element of belief in the "Absolute" had much of the quality of; yet it yielded a life of "desire without hope" •SJ 210 ❖ SJ 13:19

Heaven, our difficulty in desiring, a result of lack of education about it and an inability to recognize it as the object of our most acute desire •MC 119 ❖ MC III 10:2

Heaven, our fear of the unknown about,

may prevent us from having the courage to go through the birth process (i.e., New Birth or death itself)**
•MC 187 (*see also* MC 154-155, 173; SL 147) ❖ MC IV 11:9 (*see also* MC IV 5:3; 9:7; SL 31:3)

Heaven, our only real security is in; thus earth affords only imitations
•LAL 49 (*see also* FL 190)
❖ LAL 16/12/55 (*see also* FL 6:43)

Heaven, our presuppositions regarding, are only as a picture is to three-dimensional reality
•WG 66-69 ❖ WG 4:19-24

Heaven, our total dependence upon God in: Perhaps they will feel happiest who have been forced to begin practising it here on earth
•LAL 49 ❖ LAL 16/12/55

Heaven (our "true country") as the thing we were made for, which we shall not find till after death
•MC 120 ❖ MC III 10:5

Heaven, ownership forbidden in; each soul will be eternally engaged in giving away to all the rest that which it receives
•PP 149, 151 ❖ PP 10:7, 9

Heaven: Present self a shadow of our future self*
•WG 117-118 ❖ WG 7:17

Heaven, promises in Scripture regarding, listed
•WG 10 ❖ WG 1:8

Heaven, reality as seen from: "...how different the content of our faith will look when we see it in the total context"*
•L 267 ❖ L 8 Feb 56

Heaven, regarding the use of imagery to describe
•M 157-163; MC 121
❖ M 16:25-32; MC III 10:6

Heaven, regarding the use of imaginative language to describe
•WG 56; 66-69 ❖ WG 4:4, 19-25

Heaven, Screwtape compares a love-filled Christian home with the description one human writer made of: "the regions where...all that is not music is silence"

•SL 102 ❖ SL 22:4

Heaven, Screwtape describes a human's death and subsequent passage into
•SL 146-148 ❖ SL 31:2-5

Heaven, Screwtape mentions the "acceleration in the rhythm of celestial experience" which is Laughter and Music and Joy in
•SL 50 ❖ SL 11:2

Heaven, Screwtape points out that youth have an inveterate appetite for; "Real worldliness is a work of time..."
•SL 133 ❖ SL 28:2

Heaven, Scripture itself uses imagery to describe; all intelligible descriptions must be of things within our experience
•WG 9-11 ❖ WG 1:7-9

Heaven, some kind of body will be given us even in
•MC 91 (*see also* M 159-163; WG 18, 72-73*) ❖ MC III 5:7 (*see also* M 16:27-32; WG 1:14; 4:30*)

Heaven: "The created glory may be expected to give us hints of the uncreated; for the one is derived from the other and in some fashion reflects it"
•FL 38 ❖ FL 2:25

Heaven, the letter and spirit of Scripture forbid us to suppose a sexual life in; something better will leave no room for it
•M 159-160 ❖ M 16:28

Heaven: "The point is not that God will refuse you admission..."; no external conditions can make a "Heaven" for us if we have not begun a transformation here
•MC 77-78 (*see also* GID 155; PP 122-123, 127*) ❖ MC III 2:12 (*see also* GID I 18:11; PP 8:7, 11*)

Heaven, the things in, originated with matter; let us therefore bless matter
•LM 123 ❖ LM 22:19

Heaven, the vision and enjoyment of God will outweigh all the negations we now perceive about
•WG 66-67 (*see also* FL 15)
❖ WG 4:20 (*see also* FL 1:9)

Heaven, the wounds of the martyrs will

turn into beauties in
•GID 216 ❖ GID II 7:1

Heaven: "There have been times when I
think we do not desire heaven but
more often I find myself wondering
whether...we have ever desired anything else"
•PP 145 ❖ PP 10:2

Heaven, there is no good applying to, for
earthly comfort; there is no earthly
comfort in the long run
•FL 190 (see also GO 28-30; L 290; LAL
49) ❖ FL 6:43 (see also GO 2:13-16; L 3
Dec 59; LAL 16/12/55)

Heaven, there is no morality in; angels
never knew the meaning of the word
"ought"
•LM 115 ❖ LM 21:13

Heaven: Think of yourself as a seed, waiting to come up in the Gardener's good
time, up into the *real* world
•LAL 119 ❖ LAL 28 Jun 63

Heaven: Thinking about what it will be
like is not unimportant to the practice
of the Christian life
•M 162-163 ❖ M 16:31

Heaven, to enter, is to become more human than you ever succeeded in being on earth; to enter hell is to be banished from humanity
•PP 125 (see also WG 117-119)
❖ PP 8:9 (see also WG 7:17, 18)

Heaven, to hope for, is a Christian virtue
rather than a form of escapism or
wishful thinking
•MC 118 ❖ MC III 10:1

Heaven: To lose this is to lose all*
•PP 146-147 ❖ PP 10:2

Heaven: To shrink back from Nature into
negative spirituality ("Heaven is a
state of mind") is as if we ran away
from horses instead of learning to ride
•M 162-163 ❖ M 16:31, 32

Heaven too often desired chiefly as an escape from Hell
•RP 42 ❖ RP 4:18

Heaven, various conjectures about,
("Guesses, only guesses. If they are
not true, something better will be")
•LM 121-124 ❖ LM 22:12-22

Heaven, we are afraid that, is a bribe and
that if we make it our goal we shall
no longer be disinterested; it is not so
•PP 145 ❖ PP 10:1

Heaven, we are shy of mentioning, nowadays; we are afraid of being told that
we are trying to escape the duty of
improving the world ("pie in the sky")
•PP 144 ❖ PP 10:1

Heaven: "We can hope only for what we
can desire"
•WG 66 ❖ WG 4:19

Heaven: We may hope it includes the general fabric of our earthly life with its
affections and relationships
•FL 187 (see also PP 139)
❖ FL 6:38 (see also PP 9:11)

Heaven: "We must believe...that every
negation will be only the reverse side
of a fulfilling"
•WG 67 ❖ WG 4:22

Heaven: "We need not suppose that the
necessity for something analogous to
self-conquest will ever be ended"
•PP 151-152 ❖ PP 10:9, 10

Heaven, we shall be true persons only in
•WG 117-119; PP 125 (see also Person-
ality) ❖ WG 7:16-18; PP 8:9 (see also
Personality)

Heaven: We should all like to believe that
Heaven will mean the happy past
restored...family reunions...cigars...
•GO 28-29 ❖ GO 2:14

Heaven, whether we shall know and love
one another in
•L 248 (see also LM 124)
❖ L 8 Nov 52 (see also LM 22:21)

Heaven, whether we shall know our loved
ones in, and whether those relationships will have any continued significance
•FL 187-188 ❖ FL 6:38, 39

Heaven will answer our questions, but not
by showing us subtle reconciliations
between our contradictory notions;
the notions will be knocked from under us...
•GO 83 ❖ GO 4:28, 29

Heaven will be a place of dance and play
without frivolity

•LM 92-93 (*see also* LM 115-116)
❖ LM 17:17 (*see also* LM 21:13)

Heaven will display far more variety than Hell, since grace will expand all our natures into that richness of diversity God intended when He made them
•LM 10 ❖ LM 2:3

Heaven will involve a natural environment as well as being a spiritual state
•M 161-162 (*consider also* Matter; Nature) ❖ M 16:30 (*consider also* Matter; Nature)

Heaven, your library in, will contain only those books you gave away or lent on earth
•GID 216 ❖ GID II 7:1

Heaven, your place in, will seem to be made for you and you alone, because you were made for it—stitch by stitch, as a glove is made for a hand
•PP 147-148 ❖ PP 10:3

Hebrew poets are our predecessors in a way that the Pagan writers could not be; they have Something the Pagans have not (re: Psalms)
•CR 116 ❖ CR 10:4

Hebrews—*see also* Jews; Judaism

Hebrews' claim to be the "Chosen" people is strong
•CR 116-117 ❖ CR 10:4-6

Hebrews, like other people, had mythology; as they were the chosen people so their mythology was the chosen mythology
•M 133-134 (ftnt.) ❖ M 15:2 (ftnt.)

Hebrews mentioned
•L 58 (*see also* L 193)
❖ L undated letter just before 23 Apr 21 (*see also* L 10 Apr 41)

Hebrews, we Gentile Christians need reminding that the, are spiritually *senior* to us
•L 263 (*see also* CR 116*)
❖ L 14 May 55 (*see also* CR 10:3*)

Hegel mentioned by Screwtape as a "propagandist" indispensable to his side
•SL 161; WLN 59 (*see also* SJ 222-223)
❖ SL 32:17; WLN 4:17 (*see also* SJ 14:14)

Hegel, the great Prussian philosopher, mentioned as holding a pantheistic view of God
•MC 44 ❖ MC II 1:3

Hegel: "When Hegel saw in history the progressive self-manifestation of absolute spirit he was a Historicist"
•CR 101 (*see also* CR 103)
❖ CR 9:3 (*see also* CR 9:7)

Hegelian Wood, the fox had been dislodged from the, and was now running in the open... (re: Lewis's path to conversion)
•SJ 225 ❖ SJ 14:17

Hegelianism mentioned
•CR 157, 163; SJ 209
❖ CR 13:10, 26; SJ 13:18

Heights, Lewis's fear of: "...poverty frightens me more than anything else except large spiders and the tops of cliffs"
•LAL 21 ❖ LAL Aug 10th 53

Hell (chapter title)
•PP 118-128 ❖ PP ch. 8

Hell—*see also* Destiny of lost Man; Hades; Sheol; *consider also* Dead, state of

Hell, according to Screwtape, produces a "peculiar kind of clarity"
•SL 13 ❖ SL 2:2

Hell, all of God's mercy cannot remove the fact of, ("So much mercy, yet still there is Hell")
•PP 119-120 ❖ PP 8:3

Hell and Heaven, source of nearly all Biblical references to, is Our Lord Himself; we must not be afraid to mention them
•WG 20-21 ❖ WG 2:2

Hell as a state where everyone is perpetually concerned with his own dignity and advancement, where everyone has a grievance (etc.)
•SL ix ❖ SL P:16

Hell as an object of purely carnal, self-centred fear which the old divines attempted to arouse: The effect did not last long
•LM 76 ❖ LM 14:15

Hell as Lewis pictured it (like a nasty business concern) is a society held together entirely by fear and greed
•SL x ❖ SL P:18

Hell as privation: The day is coming when you will wake to find that you have attained *it*, or else that it was within your reach but you have lost it forever
•PP 148 (*see also* WG 15-16)
❖ PP 10:4 (*see also* WG 1:12)

Hell as "that fierce imprisonment in the self..."
•PP 152 ❖ PP 10:10

Hell as the correct technical term for what my bad temper will be in a million years if I am immortal
•MC 73 ❖ MC III 1:9

Hell as "the darkness outside" where being fades away into nonentity
•PP 127 ❖ PP 8:10

Hell, attempt to excite fear about, cannot succeed as a permanent influence on conduct
•RP 41-42 (*see also* LM 76)
❖ RP 4:16 (*see also* LM 14:15)

Hell, belief in, has caused human tragedy; of the other tragedies which come from not believing in it we are told less
•PP 119 ❖ PP 8:2

Hell, common objections regarding the doctrine of
•PP 118-128 ❖ PP ch. 8

Hell, definition of, as something growing in ourselves which will of itself *be hell* unless it is nipped in the bud
•GID 155 (*see also* GID 121; MC 77-78, PP 122-123) ❖ GID I 18:11 (*see also* GID I 14:3; MC III 2:12; PP 8:7)

Hell described by Screwtape as "the cold and dark of utmost space"*
•SL 54 ❖ SL 12:1

Hell: Destruction, we should assume, means the unmaking or cessation of the destroyed
•PP 125 ❖ PP 8:9

Hell: Divine punishments are also mercies*
•SJ 77 ❖ SJ 5:9

Hell, doctrine of, is complex—knotty and ambiguous—as is all of Christianity, indeed all of reality
•PP 119 (*see also* Reality)
❖ PP 8:3 (*see also* Reality)

Hell, doors of, are locked on the *inside*

•PP 127 ❖ PP 8:11

Hell, "eating" or absorption as a principle of (...the sucking of will and freedom out of a weaker self into a stronger")
•SL 81 (*see also* SL xi, xiii, 26, 37-38, 141, 145; WLN 51-56, 69-70)
❖ SL 18:3 (*see also* SL P:19, 20, 22; 5:2; 8:3; 30:1; 31:1; WLN 4:1-13, 40)

Hell: Even if it contained only pleasure, that black pleasure would be such as to send any soul, not already damned, flying to its prayers in nightmare terror
•PP 126 (*see also* PP 152)
❖ PP 8:9 (*see also* PP 10:9)

Hell: God's nature is such that "union with that Nature is bliss and separation from it horror. Thus Heaven and Hell come in"
•SJ 232 (*see also* GID 47)
❖ SJ 15:4 (*see also* GID I 3:17)

Hell, good intentions and admired virtues will not keep a man from; indeed they may make him more amusing when he gets there
•SL 31 ❖ SL 6:5

Hell (Hades), regarding the doctrine of Christ's descending into, and preaching to the dead
•L 238 ❖ L 31 Jan 52

Hell: Hades, the land of the dead, differentiated from Gehenna, the land of the lost
•L 238 ❖ L 31 Jan 52

Hell, Heaven too often desired chiefly as an escape from
•RP 42 ❖ RP 4:18

Hell, "hunger" of the devils in, is the passion to dominate, almost to digest, one's fellow; even in human life ("love") we see this
•SL xi (*see also* FL 160; SL 26, 37-38, 81, 141, 145; WLN 51-56, 69-70)
❖ SL P:19, 20 (*see also* FL 5:46; SL 5:2; 8:3; 18:3; 30:1; 31:1; WLN 4:1-13, 39)

Hell, I have met no people who fully disbelieved in, and also had a living and life-giving belief in Heaven
•LM 76 ❖ LM 14:14

Hell: I notice that our Lord usually

emphasises the idea, not of duration, but of *finality*
•PP 126-127 ❖ PP 8:10

Hell, in all discussions of, we should keep steadily before our eyes the possible damnation, not of our enemies nor our friends, but of ourselves
•PP 128 ❖ PP 8:13

Hell, it is hardly complimentary to God that we should choose Him as an alternative to; yet even this He accepts
•PP 97 ❖ PP 6:8

Hell, Lewis offers an explanation for his interest in writing about
•SJ 33-34 ❖ SJ 2:14

Hell means separation from God and Heaven means union with God; any other belief is probably mischievous superstition
•RP 41 ❖ RP 4:15

Hell, my symbol for, is something like the bureaucracy of a police state or the offices of a thoroughly nasty business concern
•SL x (*see also* book, *That Hideous Strength*) ❖ SL P:17 (*see also* book, *That Hideous Strength*)

Hell was never made for men as heaven was; therefore we know much more about heaven than hell
•PP 125, 127 ❖ PP 8:9, 10

Hell, our Lord speaks of, under three symbols: 1) Punishment, 2) Destruction, and 3) Privation, exclusion, or banishment
•PP 124 ❖ PP 8:9

Hell: Punishment of lost souls is based on retribution (ill-desert), but is less a sentence imposed on one than the mere fact of being what one is
•PP 122-123 (*see also* GID 155; MC 77-78*; PP 127*) ❖ PP 8:7 (*see also* GID I 18:11; MC III 2:12*; PP 8:11*)

Hell, real business of, listed by Screwtape as the undermining of faith and the prevention of the formation of virtues
•SL 25 ❖ SL 5:1

Hell referred to by Screwtape as "the Kingdom of Noise"
•SL 146 ❖ SL 31:2

Hell, regarding the imagery which conveys the impression of frightful pain in
•PP 124-126 ❖ PP 8:9

Hell: Regarding the objection that the ultimate loss of a single soul means the defeat of Omnipotence
•PP 127-128 ❖ PP 8:11

Hell: Regarding the objection that we ought to be given a "second chance": "Finality must come sometime..."
•PP 124 ❖ PP 8:8

Hell, safest road to, is the gradual one—the gentle slope, soft underfoot...
•SL 56 (*see also* SL 53-54*)
❖ SL 12:5 (*see also* SL 12:1*)

Hell, Screwtape refers to "the realism, dignity, and austerity" of; Music and joyful laughter are unknown there
•SL 50 ❖ SL 11:2

Hell, the "intolerable" doctrine of: In contemplating evil we find ourselves moved by a truly ethical demand for justice
•PP 120-122 ❖ PP 8:5

Hell: The lost man "has his wish—to live wholly in the self and to make the best of what he finds there. And what he finds there is Hell"
•PP 123 (*see also* GID 155)
❖ PP 8:7 (*see also* GID I 18:11)

Hell, the one principle of, is—"I am my own" (quote from G. MacDonald)
•SJ 212 ❖ SJ 14 prelim. quote

Hell, the only place outside Heaven where you can be perfectly safe from all the dangers and perturbations of love is
•FL 169 ❖ FL 6:13

Hell, the ultimate answer to all those who object to the doctrine of
•PP 128 ❖ PP 8:12

"Hell," the word translated, in the Psalms simply means "the land of the dead"—the state of all the dead, good and bad alike, *Sheol*
•RP 36 ❖ RP 4:6

Hell, there is no doctrine that I would more willingly remove from Christianity than the doctrine of
•PP 118 ❖ PP 8:1

Hell: "...this doctrine is one of the chief

grounds on which Christianity is attacked as barbarous and the goodness of God impugned"
•PP 119 ❖ PP 8:2

Hell, to enter, is to be banished from humanity; to enter heaven is to become more human than you ever succeeded in being on earth
•PP 125 (see also WG 117-119*)
❖ PP 8:9 (see also WG 7:17, 18*)

Hell, whole philosophy of, rests on the recognition that one self is not another self—what one gains, another loses; competition is synonymous with existence
•SL 081 ❖ SL 18:3

Help—see also Alms; Charity; Grace

Help comes from God in all sorts of ways: through nature, other people, books, even anti-Christian experiences
•MC 162-163 ❖ MC IV 7:7

Help ("Grace") not usually given us in advance; only daily support for the daily trial
•L 250 (see also SL 62; Daily...)
❖ L 17 Jul 53 (see also SL 14:1; Daily...)

Help, having to accept, makes palpable the total dependence in which we always live anyway
•LAL 57 ❖ LAL 14/6/56

Help, in offering supernatural, toward keeping the moral Law, Christianity reaffirms the Law
•CR 46-47 ❖ CR 4:7

Help, lending or giving, when friends are in need is not the stuff of Friendship; the occasions for it are almost interruptions
•FL 101-102 ❖ FL 4:26

Help, one must get over any false shame about accepting necessary; one never has been "independent"
•LAL 111-112 (see also LAL 20-21)
❖ LAL 10 Dec 62 (see also LAL Aug 10th 53)

Help the "fallen," one must be careful lest the desire to patronise and be a busybody should disguise itself as a vocation to
•RP 69 ❖ RP 7:5

Help, the moments at which you call most desperately to God for, are precisely those when you seem to get none
•LAL 92 (see also GO 4-6, 53-54)
❖ LAL 24 Sep 60 (see also GO 1:7-11; 3:24-26)

Help, we must all learn to receive, as well as to give
•LAL 57, 58 (see also LAL 75-76)
❖ LAL 14/6/56; 5/7/56 (see also LAL Jun 6th 58)

Help, when you are most desperate for, may be just when God can't give it; like the drowning man who can't be helped because he clutches and grabs
•GO 53-54 (see also Drowning Man analogy)
❖ GO 3:24, 25 (see also Drowning Man analogy)

Help which God wants to give us is help to become perfect—nothing less
•MC 171-175 ❖ MC IV ch. 9

Helping others, I liked the superior feeling of, and for me it is much harder to receive than to give, but, I think, much more blessed (—Jóy Lewis)
•LAL 76 ❖ LAL Jun 6th [1958]

Helping people—see also Alms; Charity; Humanitarianism

Helping people: Lewis demonstrates that empathy for another's difficulty is more effective if we can admit our own handicap in being able to truly empathize*
•LM 40-41 ❖ LM 8:2

Helping people: "It's so much easier to pray for a bore than to go and see him"
•LM 66 ❖ LM 12:12

Helping people: The temptation as we try to sympathize with another's difficulty is to attempt reassurances*
•LM 41 ❖ LM 8:3

Helping the beggar—a fellow creature— at your door: In what sense is this also helping Jesus—the Creator? (re: the creature's relationship to the Creator)
•LM 73 ❖ LM 14:4

Heredity and environment are used by God to create "the secret signature of each soul," the incommunicable and

unappeasable Desire we each have in a unique way
•PP 147 ❖ PP 10:3

Heredity, we may have made so little use of a good, that we are no better than those we regard as fiends
•MC 86 (*see also* L 183; MC 180-182) ❖ MC III 4:7 (*see also* L 16 Apr 40; MC IV 10:11-14)

Heroic Pessimism has a contradiction at its centre: If a Brute made the world, then he also made the standard by which we judge him to be a Brute
•CR 65-67 (*see also* CR 69-70; MC 45-46*) ❖ CR 5:19 (*see also* CR 5:24; MC II 1:5, 6*)

Hero-worship: Film stars and crooners mentioned by Screwtape as useful in drawing thousands of souls away from God*
•SL 158-159; WLN 56-57 ❖ SL 32:13; WLN 4:13

Hero-worship: People will go out of their way to meet a celebrity or politician even when it is known that the person leads a vile and mischievous life*
•RP 67, 71 (*see also* LAL 27*; RP 90) ❖ RP 7:3, 9 (*see also* LAL Feb 22/54*; RP 9:2)

Hierarchy: Hierarchical inequality holds sway in the realm beyond Nature, where loves makes the difference
•M 119-120 (*see also* WG 113-116; Equality; Inequality) ❖ M 14:20 (*see also* WG 7:10-15; Equality; Inequality)

Hierarchy in marriage discussed*
•FL 148-149; MC 102-103 ❖ FL 5:26-28; MC III 6:15-17

Hierarchy: "To be high or central means to abdicate continually...all good masters are servants..."*
•M 124 ❖ M 14:26

"High" church activities such as genuflecting and crossing oneself mentioned by Screwtape as a good source of conflict between "high" and "low" churchmen
•SL 75 ❖ SL 16:5

"High" church vs. "low" church: "I think the 'low' church milieu that I grew up in did tend to be too cosily at ease in Sion" (re: necessity for awe in prayer)
•LM 13 ❖ LM 2:14

Highbrow(s)—*see also* Intellectual(ism); Prigs; Snobs

"Highbrow" converts: First lesson they must learn is that of humility through acquiescence to such things as hymn-singing
•GID 331 (*see also* CR 96-97) ❖ GID IV Letter 6 (*see also* CR 8:7-10)

Highbrow, I did not notice that Wyvern [College] was making me into a, in the bad sense
•SJ 100, 104 ❖ SJ 6:27; 7:4

Highbrow: Surrealism and "pictures painted by chimpanzees" mentioned as being "part of the general 'Highbrow racket'"
•GID 251 ❖ GID II 14:5

Highbrow vs. Lowbrow music in church
•CR 94-99 ❖ CR ch. 8

"Highbrows," conversions from among the, not likely to be widely influential; many highly literate people simply ignore what the "Highbrows" are doing
•GID 251 ❖ GID II 14:5

Higher can descend into the lower; because of this, Christ can descend into the death of the body for us
•M 130 ❖ M 14:35

Higher you rise the lower you can descend; fully regenerate man will recover his body
•M 172-173 ❖ M App. A:11

Highest does not stand without the lowest (quote from *Imitation of Christ*)
•FL 14, 20, 25, 32, 124, 144; LM 87; RP 88 ❖ FL 1:7, 18; 2:1, 13; 4:58; 5:20; LM 16:13; RP 8:17

High-minded, we must not be too, (re: petitionary prayer)
•LM 23, 35, 36 (*see also* LM 97) ❖ LM 4:20; 7:1, 3 (*see also* LM 18:9)

"**Hiking**" as an example of words which make "specialised and self-conscious stunts" out of activities which have before been ordinary
•L 259 ❖ L 22 Dec 54

Hindu-Christian debate, Lewis mentions:

"I always thought the real difference was the rival conceptions of God"
•L 305 ❖ L undated letter of Aug 1962

Hindus as "Pagan"—but not in the popular modern sense, which means pretty nearly "irreligious"
•LAL 60, 62 ❖ LAL 3/8/56; Sep 8/56

Hindus, I have known nice (and nasty)
•LAL 60 ❖ LAL 3/8/56

Hindus mentioned as holding a pantheistic view of God
•MC 44 ❖ MC II 1:3

Hindus: Regarding their spirituality, which takes the form of despising matter
•LAL 60 ❖ LAL 3/8/56

Hindus: What do they *deny*? Truth must surely involve exclusions?
•L 267 (*see also* L 285*)
❖ L 8 Feb 56 (*see also* L 30 Apr 59*)

Hinduism and Christianity as the only two religions which could possibly be the maturity of Paganism
•SJ 235-236 (*see also* CR 71; GID 102, 132*) ❖ SJ 15:7 (*see also* CR 5:26; GID I 10:49; 16:4*)

Hinduism and Christianity as "the two serious options for an adult mind"
•CR 71 ❖ CR 5:26

Hinduism and Christianity the only two religions worth considering; most other religions are heresies of these
•GID 102 ❖ GID I 10:49

Hinduism, higher, as an anti-nature religion which simply contradicts our natural desires (vs. Christianity, which neither contradicts nor affirms them)
•GID 86; M 119 ❖ GID I 9:9; M 14:20

Hinduism, miraculous elements of, not essential to that religion (vs. Christianity, which is precisely the story of a great Miracle)
•M 68 (*see also* GID 80*)
❖ M 10:1 (*see also* GID I 9:1*)

Historian misreading a document as analogy to the Christian pictured by the ordinary man as explaining away "mistaken" anthropomorphic thinking about God
•GID 69 ❖ GID I 6:3

Historian, whenever one turns from the, to the writings of the people he deals with there is always such a difference
•L 123 ❖ L 12 Dec 27

Historical evidence, religious experience, and authority as three of the things on which a Christian may base his belief
•WLN 17 ❖ WLN 2:6

"Historical Jesus," belief in, promoted by Screwtape since such a construct cannot in fact be worshipped ("...first we make Him solely a teacher...")
•SL 106-108 ❖ SL 23:3, 4

"Historical Point of View" defined by Screwtape, and mentioned as that which prevents learned men from being influenced by their reading of old books
•SL 128-129 (*see also* SL 43, 118*, 133)
❖ SL 27:5 (*see also* SL 9:4; 25:6*; 28:2)

"Historical Point of View," Screwtape advises encouraging, among humans
•SL 43 ❖ SL 9:4

Historicism (chapter title)
•CR 100-113 ❖ CR ch. 9

"Historicism" defined indirectly as "...a reading of history..."*
•CR 104 (*see also* CR 108)
❖ CR 9:7 (*see also* CR 9:16)

"Historicism" defined: "...the belief that men can, by the use of their natural powers, discover an inner meaning in the historical process"
•CR 100 ❖ CR 9:1

Historicism evident in the various Pagan mythologies
•CR 102-104 ❖ CR 9:5-7

Historicism: History is, in one sense, a story written by the finger of God; but have we the text? (re: "Historicism")
•CR 104-105 ❖ CR 9:9

Historicism: How can we say what the "point" of the story is if we have not yet read the end?
•CR 106 ❖ CR 9:14

Historicism, Keats' *Hyperion* is the epic of
•CR 101 ❖ CR 9:3

Historicism, Lewis's contention that, is an illusion and that Historicists are, at best, wasting their time

•CR 101 ❖ CR 9:4

Historicism, lowest form of, is the doctrine that our calamities (or more often our neighbours' calamities) are divine condemnations or punishments
•CR 101 ❖ CR 9:5

Historicism: Our own present experience as the part of history in which we may find divine comment or revelation
•CR 113 ❖ CR 9:26

Historicism: Play analogy (the defective manuscript) to show how the fragments we have of history can tell us nothing about the meaning of history as a whole
•CR 111-112 ❖ CR 9:23, 24

Historicism: Revelation of God in history may be seen in the great events of the creeds, and in "primary history"—our own experience
•CR 112-113 ❖ CR 9:26

Historicism seems to me a waste of time, or worse; the philosophy of history is a discipline for which we mortal men lack the necessary data
•CR 110 ❖ CR 9:21

"Historicism" [the derivation of metahistorical meaning from history] vs. "scientism" [the derivation of conclusions about God from science]
•CR 112 ❖ CR 9:25

Historicism: The important parts of the past, for the Christian Historicist, must be those which reveal the purposes of God
•CR 108 ❖ CR 9:17

Historicism which sees calamities as "judgements" not countenanced by Christianity
•CR 101-102 ❖ CR 9:5

Historicist may say that events fell out as they did because of some ultimate, transcendent necessity in the ground of things
•CR 101 ❖ CR 9:2

Historicist takes history to be the self-manifestation of Spirit, the story written by the finger of God
•CR 109 (see also CR 105, 106)
❖ CR 9:18 (see also CR 9:12, 14)

Historicist tries to get from historical premises conclusions which are metaphysical or theological (vs. historians, who try to get historical conclusions)
•CR 100-101 ❖ CR 9:2

Historicists, it is usually theologians, philosophers, and politicians who become
•CR 101 ❖ CR 9:4

Historicity of the Bible—see Bible—historicity

History, a pernicious type of patriotism occurs when the young are indoctrinated in knowably false or biased
•FL 44 ❖ FL 2:37

History as seen by various Pagan mythologies, and the "Historicism" evident in them
•CR 102-104 ❖ CR 9:5-7

History cannot prove the miraculous; if we believe miracles to be impossible, no amount of historical evidence will convince us
•M 3-4 (see also GID 27-28)
❖ M 1:3 (see also GID I 2:4)

History, Christian—see Christian history

History, contrast drawn between Judaic/Christian thought and Pagan/Pantheistic thought regarding the significance of, is in some measure illusory (re: "Historicism")
•CR 102-103 ❖ CR 9:6, 7

History, documented vs. traditional
•L 133
❖ L undated letter postmarked 13 Apr 29

"History," does not what we call, in fact leave out nearly the whole of real life?
•LAL 81 ❖ LAL Jan 26th 59

History, God has no; is not in Time
•MC 148 (see also Time)
❖ MC IV 3:10 (see also Time)

History, human, largely depends on unpredictables (such as the birth of great men) —re: one objection to petitionary prayer
•LM 39 ❖ LM 7:11

History: I am often struck how unimportant the things the historians make so much of seem to have been to ordinary people at the time

•LAL 81 ❖ LAL Jan 26th 59
History: "I do not much believe in the
Renaissance as generally described by
historians"
•SJ 71 ❖ SJ 5:1
History, if the Incarnation really happened
it is the central chapter of earth's
•GID 81 ❖ GID I 9:2
History, Incarnation illuminates the rest of,
including the patterns of nature and
the whole character of the nature reli-
gions
•GID 81-86; M 108-131
❖ GID I 9:3-8; M ch. 14
History is, in one sense, a story written by
the finger of God; but have we the
text? (re: "Historicism")
•CR 104-105 ❖ CR 9:9
History, no real beginnings to literary; one
must start with the first chapter of
Genesis
•L 125 ❖ L 31 Mar 28
History of Man like a play in which we
see only one small scene, the one in
which we are "on"; useless to try and
guess the plot*
•WLN 104-106 ❖ WLN 7:19-23
History, perspective of, gained through
education protects one against the er-
rors of the current age
•WG 28-29 ❖ WG 2:10
History, perspective of, lacking in the uneducated man; this is one difficulty in
presenting the Christian faith to mod-
ern unbelievers
•GID 94-95, 241-242
❖ GID I 10:13; II 12:3
History regarded with scepticism by the
uneducated man, while "Science" is
considered reliable; this has implications for evangelism
•GID 241-242 (see also GID 94-95, 252)
❖ GID II 12:3 (see also GID I 10:13, 14;
II 14:8, 9)
History, revelation of God in, may be seen
in the great events of the creeds and
in "primary history"—our own experience (re: "Historicism")
•CR 112-113 ❖ CR 9:26
History, sense of personal, seems to be

lacking in most people
•L 123 ❖ L 12 Dec 27
History, the key to, is that God designed
the human machine to run on Himself, and apart from Him there is no
happiness or peace
•MC 54 (see also Human machine)
❖ MC II 3:8 (see also Human machine)
History: The real historian is troublesome
when we want to romance about "the
old days" (analogy to the "troublesome" complexity of God)
•M 86 ❖ M 11:7
"History," the word, has several senses—
the past only, the total content of time,
etc.
•CR 105 ❖ CR 9:10, 11
History: Those we regard as historically
important may turn out to be minor
characters, having importance only by
giving occasion to states of soul in others
•CR 110 ❖ CR 9:20
History vs. science: "The scientist studies
those elements in reality which repeat
themselves. The historian studies the
unique" (re: "Historicism")
•CR 112 ❖ CR 9:25
History, we know next to nothing about;
a single second of lived time contains
more than can be recorded (re: "Historicism")
•CR 107 ❖ CR 9:15
History: What historians retain of the past
is more like the contents of an old
drawer than like an intelligent
epitome of some longer work
•CR 109 ❖ CR 9:19
Hitler and Stalin, when I pray for, two
things help me to make the prayer
real...You and I are not at bottom so
different from these ghastly creatures
•L 183 (see also MC 87*)
❖ L 16 Apr 40 (see also MC III 4:9*)
Hitler mentioned by Screwtape
•SL 154; WLN 52 ❖ SL 32:4; WLN 4:4
Hobbes, [Thomas]: Regarding his defini-
tion of Revengefulness as "Desire by
doing hurt to another to make him
condemn some fact of his own"
•PP 94 ❖ PP 6:6

Hobbies and little luxuries as possible means of avoiding love in order to not be hurt
•FL 169 ❖ FL 6:13

Hobbies, even in your, has there not always been some secret attraction which the others are curiously ignorant of? (re: desire for heaven)
•PP 146 ❖ PP 10:2

Holidays, memories of, improve with time
•L 71-72 ❖ L 31 Aug 21

Holiness—*consider also* Righteousness; Sanctity

Holiness as encountered by Lewis in the book *Phantastes*, by George MacDonald
•L 167; SJ 179 (*consider also* Books)
❖ L 9 Jul 39; SJ 11:18, 19 (*consider also* Books)

Holiness is not dull; when one meets the real thing it is irresistible
•LAL 19 ❖ LAL Aug 1st [1953]

Holiness: "The fine flower of unholiness can grow only in the close neighborhood of the holy" (—Screwtape)
•SL 172; WLN 70
❖ SL 32:40; WLN 4:40

Holiness: The holier a man is, the more he is aware of his sinfulness
•PP 67 (*see also* LAL 95; MC 87, 164; PP 55, top)
❖ PP 4:15 (*see also* LAL 9 Jan 61; MC III 4:10; IV 7:12; PP 4:prelim. quote)

Holiness: To become holy must be great *fun*
•MC 188 ❖ MC IV 11:10

Hollow, the soul is but a, which God fills
•PP 151 (*see also* FL 189*; PP 53*)
❖ PP 10:9 (*see also* FL 6:41*; PP 3:19*)

Hollow, your soul is a, made to fit a particular swelling in the infinite contours of the divine substance
•PP 147 ❖ PP 10:3

Holy Ghost—*see* Holy Spirit

Holy people, a description of truly
•MC 187-188 (*see also* Good people)
❖ MC IV 11:10 (*see also* Good people)

Holy places, things, and days: If they cease to remind us that all ground is holy and every bush a Burning Bush,

then the hallows begin to do harm
•LM 75 ❖ LM 14:10

Holy Spirit—*see also* Trinity

Holy Spirit as the third Person of the Trinity described
•MC 152 ❖ MC IV 4:6, 7

Holy Spirit, gift of: Ascension (withdrawal of the incarnate God) may have been the necessary condition of God's presence in another mode
•RP 126 ❖ RP 12:6

Holy Spirit guides us not only from within but also through Scripture, the Church, Christian friends, books, etc.
•L 243 ❖ L 20 Jun 52

Holy Spirit ("Holy Ghost"), it is very hard to believe that in all instances of Glossolalia the, is operating
•WG 55 ❖ WG 4:2

Holy Spirit, I prefer to make no judgment concerning the inspiration of writers by the
•GID 264 ❖ GID II 16:37, 38

Holy Spirit, if the, speaks in the man, then in prayer God speaks to God
•LM 68 (*see also* LAL 22, 23; LM 49-50*, 81; MC 142-143)
❖ LM 13:2 (*see also* LAL 6 Nov/53; 27/xi/53; LM 9:11*; 15:15; MC IV 2:9)

Holy Spirit may be most operative when you can feel it least
•L 241 ❖ L 15 May 52

Holy Spirit, we believe that the, can be really present and operative in the human spirit, but not that we are "parts" of God (as the Pantheists believe)
•PP 87 (*see also* LM 68-70)
❖ PP 5:13 (*see also* LM 13:2-9)

Holy Spirit, we may not always *sense* the presence of the, in the same way that the sexual act may or may not be attended with pleasure
•LAL 38-39 ❖ LAL 20/2/55

Home—*consider also* Domestic ...; Family

Home, charity begins at, (and so does uncharity)
•GID 285 ❖ GID III 3:6

Home, discussion of courtesy at
•FL 66-70 ❖ FL 3:22-26

Home, courtesy at: "You must really give

no kind of preference to yourself; at a party it is enough to conceal the preference"
•FL 67-68 ❖ FL 3:24

Home: "It is a hard thing—nay, a wicked thing—when a man is felt to be a stranger in his own house" (re: Lewis's family home in Belfast)
•SJ 123 ❖ SJ 8:7

Home, Lewis mentions enjoying freedom from the restrictive customs of his childhood
•L 137-138 ❖ L 9 Sep 29

Home, Lewis's ambivalent feelings toward his, in Belfast
•L 137, 139 (see also SJ 37-41, 119-128)
❖ L 9 Sep 29; 27 Oct 29 (see also SJ 2:17-19; 8:2-12)

Home, Lewis's: "I have never been able to resist the retrogressive influence of this house..."
•L 137-138 (see also L 84)
❖ L 9 Sep 29 (see also L 25 Dec 22)

Home, Lewis's: The suburban villas of Surrey suggested Happiness, and filled me with desire for a domesticity which I had never known
•SJ 132-133 ❖ SJ 9:1

"Home" not a panacea; home life is difficult and has its own temptations and corruptions
•GID 284-286 ❖ GID III 3:4-11

Home not a place where you can dispense with civility; there is nowhere this side of heaven where we can simply "be ourselves"
•GID 285-286 (see also FL 66-70)
❖ GID III 3:8, 9 (see also FL 3:22-26)

Home: "Our Father refreshes us on the journey with some pleasant inns, but will not encourage us to mistake them for home"
•PP 115 ❖ PP 7:7

Home, our real, is elsewhere; if we really believe this, why should we not look forward to the arrival?
•LAL 83-84 (see also MC 118; PP 115; SL 132; WG 3-5)
❖ LAL Jun 7th 59 (see also MC III 10:1; PP 7:7; SL 28:1; WG 1:1-3)

Home, Screwtape describes with loathing a love-filled Christian, and compares it to Heaven
•SL 102 ❖ SL 22:4

Home, the last thing we want is to make everywhere else just like our own
•FL 42 ❖ FL 2:34

Home, thoughts regarding behaviour at
•GID 282-286 ❖ GID III ch. 3

Home, to be happy at, is the end of all human endeavour (quote from Johnson)
•L 262; WG 108-109
❖ L 16 Mar 55; WG 7:4

Homes for old people: "If you ever do have to go to a Home, Christ will be there just as much as in any other place"
•LAL 94 ❖ LAL 24 Nov 60

Homes for old people: "In your position I myself would prefer a 'Home'—or almost anything—to solitude"
•LAL 102 ❖ LAL 17 Jan 62

Homes for old people: Remember that the things we have most dreaded sometimes turn out to be quite nice
•LAL 94 ❖ LAL 24 Nov 60

"Homeliness" was a key word in Arthur's imagination; he looked for it not only in literature but also in out-of-door scenes and taught me to do the same
•SJ 152, 157-158, 199 (see also L 146)
❖ SJ 10:3, 10; 13:3 (see also L 22 Nov 31)

Home-making—see also Domesticity

Home-making the most important work in the world
•L 262 ❖ L 16 Mar 55

Homer, Lewis's reading of, as a pupil at Great Bookham
•SJ 140-141, 144-145 ❖ SJ 9:17, 20, 21

Homer's idea that only a drink of sacrificial blood can restore a ghost to rationality may show Pagan anticipation of the truth
•RP 37-38 ❖ RP 4:8

Hometown, love for one's: "'No man loves his city because it is great, but because it is his'" (quote from "one of the Greeks")
•FL 46 ❖ FL 2:40

Homosexual activity: "We attack this vice not because it is the worst but because it is, by adult standards, the most disreputable and unmentionable..."*
•SJ 108-109 ❖ SJ 7:11, 12

Homosexual behaviour among schoolboys at Wyvern College ("...the vice in question is one to which I had never been tempted...")*
•SJ 87-89, 92, 101, 108-110
❖ SJ 6:8, 9, 15; 7:1, 11, 12

Homosexual, it has actually become necessary in our time to rebut the theory that every firm and serious friendship is really
•FL 90-94 ❖ FL 4:6-10

Homosexuals, Lewis mentions highbrow, "who dominate so much of the world of criticism and won't be very nice to you unless you are in their set"
•L 292 ❖ L 17 May 60

Homosexuals, Lewis mentions the persecution of, by "snoopers and busy-bodies"
•L 292 ❖ L 17 May 60

Homosexuality mentioned as a sin which should not also be a "crime" ("Who the deuce are our rulers to enforce their opinions about sin on us?")
•L 281, 292 ❖ L 1 Feb 58; 17 May 60

Honesty, according to Screwtape no human ever comes *very* near to
•SL 34 ❖ SL 7:3

Honesty and fairness in our work: "Few of us have always, in full measure, given our pupils or patients or clients ...what we were being paid for"
•RP 13 ❖ RP 2:8

Honesty, importance of strict: Falsehood is habit-forming
•RP 15-16 ❖ RP 2:10

Honesty in seeking Truth—*see also* Evasion; Truth

Honesty in seeking Truth even when it may turn out to be inconvenient
•GID 110-112 (*see also* WG 35*)
❖ GID I 12:6-9 (*see also* WG 3:4*)

Honesty in seeking Truth: "If Christianity is untrue, then no honest man will want to believe it...if it is true, every honest man will want to believe it"
•GID 108-109 ❖ GID I 12:1

Honesty in seeking Truth in a civilization like ours: "...I feel that everyone has to come to terms with the claims of Jesus Christ upon his life..."
•GID 265-266 ❖ GID II 16:50, 51

Honesty, intellectual, of the historian who has based his work on the misreading of a document
•GID 69 ❖ GID I 6:3

Honesty, issue of intellectual, for clergymen who disbelieve what they preach: "I feel it is a form of prostitution"
•GID 260 (*see also* GID 89-90, 265*)
❖ GID II 16:12 (*see also* GID I 10:2, 3; II 16:46*)

Honesty, issue of intellectual, for the clergyman who denies the miraculous in the Gospels*
•CR 153; M 164 ❖ CR 13:1, 2; M 17:1

Honesty: "Strict veracity" mentioned as one of "the severer virtues" which Lewis came to realize might have relevance in his own life*
•SJ 192 (*see also* SJ 201)
❖ SJ 12:14 (*see also* SJ 13:6)

Honesty: "What I like about experience is that it is such an honest thing...the universe rings true wherever you fairly test it"
•SJ 177 ❖ SJ 11:15

Honesty which yields to danger will be honest only on conditions
•SL 137-138 ❖ SL 29:6

Honor as one of the values implicit in medieval romance
•CR 16, 21-22 ❖ CR 2:13, 29, 30

Honor resembles virtue only as the moon resembles the sun*
•CR 23 ❖ CR 2:34

Honor, to the perfected Christian the ideal of, is simply a temptation; his courage has a better root, and may have no honor about it (re: value of "honour" in literature)
•CR 22 ❖ CR 2:30

Hooker, [Richard], has answered the contention that Scripture must contain everything important or even everything necessary

CR 15 ❖ CR 2:9

Hooper, Walter, letters written by, to the American Lady
●LAL 122-124
❖ LAL 27 Jul 63; 10 Aug 63

Hope (chapter title)
●MC 118-121 ❖ MC III ch. 10

Hope, Christian virtue of, may be growing languid due to the popular conception of Heaven merely as a state of mind
●M 162-163 ❖ M 16:31

Hope for an eternal world a Christian virtue; it is one of the things we are meant to do
●MC 118 (see also LAL 83-84; PP 115; SL132; WG 3-5)
❖ MC III 10:1 (see also LAL Jun 7th 59; PP 7:7; SL 28:1*; WG 1:1-3)

Hope, Heaven as an object of purely carnal and self-centred: "Such belief is fortunately very brittle"
●LM 76 ❖ LM 14:15

Hope during Joy's illness: "A dungeon is never harder to bear than when the door is open and the sunshine and bird song float in..."
●L 276 ❖ L 12 May 57

Hope, life at a vile boarding school is in a way a good preparation for the Christian life in that it teaches one to live by
●SJ 36-37 ❖ SJ 2:16

Hope, on the theological virtue of
●WG 66-69 ❖ WG 4:19-25

Hope (quote from Johnson): "The natural process of the mind is not from enjoyment to enjoyment but from hope to hope"
●L 128 (see also L 161*)
❖ 2 Aug 28 (see also L 10 Jun 38*)

Hope: "We can hope only for what we can desire" (re: the negative notions we form of Heaven)
●WG 66 ❖ WG 4:19

Hopes, Screwtape mentions the gradual decay of youthful, as providing "admirable opportunities of wearing out a soul by attrition"
●SL 132 ❖ SL 28:1

"**Horrid** Red Things" (chapter title)

●GID 68-71; M 68-80
❖ GID I ch. 6; M ch. 10

Horse, Christ's work of making New Men not like teaching a, to jump better and better but like turning a horse into a winged creature
●MC 182, 183 ❖ MC IV 10:16; 11:1

Horse: Martin Luther compared humanity to a drunkard who, after falling off his horse on the right, falls off it next time on the left
●WLN 94-95 ❖ WLN 7:4

Horse, the God-ward will of unfallen ("Paradisal") man rode his happiness like a well-managed
●PP 98 ❖ PP 6:10

Horse-riding bareback as analogy to having new bodies in Heaven
●M 163 (see also M 126, 161)
❖ M 16:32 (see also M 14:30; 16:29)

Hospital(s)—see also Nursing homes

Hospital, no Christian building except perhaps a church is more self-explanatory than a Christian
●GID 147 ❖ GID I 17:1

Hospitals and nurses, Joy's description of, in a letter to an American Lady
●LAL 75 ❖ LAL Jun 6th [1958]

Hospitality as a showy form of generosity (vs. real charity)
●MC 82 ❖ MC III 3:7

Hostility ("rudeness") in unbelievers shows fear that there "might be something in it after all"*
●LAL 90 ❖ LAL 26 Mar 60

Hotel/prison analogy to illustrate how thinking of this world as a place intended for our happiness may bring disillusionment
●GID 52 ❖ GID I 4:18, 19 (Ques. 5)

Hours, I love the empty, silent, dewy, cobwebby
●LAL 78 (see also Morning)
❖ LAL Sep 30 58 (see also Morning)

House, a new, is a tiring nuisance until the new ways which it demands have become habits
●LAL 70 ❖ LAL Nov 30th 57

House, Christianity is like a, with many rooms

•MC 11-12 ❖ MC P:15

House, I would loathe a, which is nearly all glass; I like to feel indoors when I'm in
•LAL 46 ❖ LAL 9/10/55

House, imagine yourself as a living; God comes in to rebuild it (He intends to live in it Himself)
•MC 174 (see also M 155)
❖ MC IV 9:10 (see also M 16:21)

House of cards, if my house was a, the sooner it was knocked down the better (re: Lewis's test of faith when his wife died)
•GO 44-45 ❖ GO 3:5-7

House of cards, Lewis describes his faith as a: "If my house has collapsed at one blow, that is because it was a house of cards"
•GO 42 (see also GO 48, 61)
❖ GO 3:3 (see also GO 3:13, 36)

House of cards, Lewis describes his idea of God as a possible
•GO 78-79 ❖ GO 4:20

House: We live amid all the anomalies, inconveniences, hopes and excitements of a house that is being rebuilt (New Nature)
•M 155 ❖ M 16:21

Housework: Domestic drudgery is excellent as an alternative to idleness or hateful thoughts; otherwise it is maddening
•L 92 ❖ L 17-25 Mar 24

Huck Finn tried the experiment [of prayer] and then, not unnaturally, never gave Christianity a second thought
•LM 60 ❖ LM 11:10

Human action and Divine action need not exclude each other; "God did (or said) it" and "I did (or said) it" can both be true
•LM 68-69 (see also LAL 22, 23; LM 49-50, 81; MC 142- 143)
❖ LM 13:2-4 (see also LAL Nov 6/53; 27/xi/53; LM 9:11; 15:15; MC IV 2:9)

Human beings—see also Humanity; Man; People

Human beings are composite creatures akin on one side to the angels, and on the other to tom-cats (re: seeing the humour in sexual love)
•FL 142 ❖ FL 5:18

Human beings, we cannot rely on; they will let us down
•MC 163 ❖ MC IV 7:9

Human body—see Body, human

Human condition: "...nothing about us except our neediness is, in this life, permanent"*
•FL 33 ❖ FL 2:15

Human condition: "We are born helpless. As soon as we are fully conscious we discover loneliness. We need others..."
•FL 11-12 (see also Interdependence)
❖ FL 1:3 (see also Interdependence)

Human condition: "When you have realised that our position is nearly desperate you will begin to understand what the Christians are talking about"*
•MC 39 ❖ MC I 5:4

Human destiny—see Destiny of lost Man; Destiny of Man; Destiny of redeemed Man

Human existence—see Existence

Human history largely depends on unpredictables (such as the birth of great men) —re: one objection to petitionary prayer
•LM 39 ❖ LM 7:11

Human history like a play in which we see only one small scene, the one in which we are "on"; useless to try and guess the plot
•WLN 104-106 ❖ WLN 7:19-23

Human life has always been lived on the edge of a precipice; war creates no absolutely new situation (re: education in time of war)
•WG 21 ❖ WG 2:4

Human life, many modern philosophies view, merely as an animal life of unusual complexity (in the same way Scripture can be read as merely human literature)
•RP 116-117 (see also WG 64*)
❖ RP 11:12 (see also WG 4:15*)

Human machine, Christian morality

claims to be a technique for putting the human, right (as does psycho-analysis)
•MC 83 ❖ MC III 4:2

Human machine, God Himself is the fuel for the
•MC 54 ❖ MC II 3:7

Human machine, moral rules are directions for running the
•MC 69 (see also RP 60-61*)
❖ MC III 1:1 (see also RP 6:10, 11*)

Human machine, we are the; God is the Inventor
•MC 173 ❖ MC IV 9:7

Human machines, our bodies are like; they wear out
•LAL 110-111 (see also LAL 78)
❖ LAL 26 Nov 62 (see also Sep 30 58)

Human mind, in every, God and Nature have a common frontier
•M 31 ❖ M 4:12

Human mind, Pantheism is the permanent natural bent of the
•M 81-84, esp. 82 (see also L 227*; M 164-167*) ❖ M 11:1-5, esp. 11:4 (see also L 5 Mar 51*; M 17:1-4*)

Human nature—see also Man

Human nature is fallen and needs correction; this Christian view differs from both Manichaean repudiation and Stoic superiority
•GID 148-149 (see also M 161-163*; Original sin) ❖ GID I 17:5 (see also M 16:30-32*; Original sin)

Human Nature, The Law of (chapter title)
•MC 17-21 ❖ MC I ch. 1

Human Pain (chapter title)
•PP 89-109, 110-117 ❖ PP ch. 6, 7

Human race may be a "local pocket of evil" in which the standard of decency is vastly inferior to that of the larger universe
•PP 62-63 ❖ PP 4:10

Human race, preservation of—see Preservation of the human race

Human reason and morality listed as "proofs of the Supernatural"
•M 43 (see also GID 275-276; MC 17-39; WG 88-89, 91; Reason)
❖ M 6:7 (see also GID III 1:13-16; MC Book I; WG 5:21, 24; Reason)

Human situation—consider also Life; Pain; Pessimism

Human situation, coronation of the Queen of England seen as a symbol of the,
—called by God, yet inadequate to the responsibility
•LAL 18-19 ❖ LAL Jul 10 53

Human situation: "Does not every movement in the Passion write large some common element in the sufferings of our race?"
•LM 43 ❖ LM 8:10, 11

Human situation: "...even a boy can recognize that there is desert all round him though he, for the nonce, sits in an oasis"*
•SJ 65 ❖ SJ 4:11

Human spirit—see Spirit

Human value, apart from God, is zero
•WG 115 (see also WLN 53)
❖ WG 7:14 (see also WLN 4:8)

Human weakness—see Weakness, human

Human wickedness—see also Sinfulness; Wickedness

Human Wickedness (chapter title)
•PP 55-68 ❖ PP ch. 4

Humans—see Human beings; People

"Humanism" coming to be used simply as a term of disapprobation
•CR 78 (see also WLN 49)
❖ CR 6:18 (see also WLN 3:28)

Humanism, Scientific, fixes men's affections on the Future and therefore, says Screwtape, it is to be encouraged in men's thinking
•SL 68-69 ❖ SL 15:3

Humanism, scientific: Many of its votaries know very little science
•L 160
❖ L undated letter just before 10 Jun 38

Humanist, a scientific, may urge us to get rid of traditional morality and make our sole end the exploitation of nature for the comfort and security of posterity
•CR 52-53 ❖ CR 4:21

"Humanist" mentioned as a word whose meaning is changing
•WLN 49 (see also CR 78)

❖ WLN 3:28 (*see also* CR 6:18)

Humanists mentioned with reference to the injustice which every age does to its predecessor
•CR 82 ❖ CR 7:1

Humanists, the whole philosophy of Becoming has been vigorously challenged by the American; this points to the decline of Evolutionism
•CR 89-90 ❖ CR 7:17

Humanitarian Theory of Punishment, The (chapter title)
•GID 287-300 (*see also* GID 313; Punishment) ❖ GID III ch. 4 (*see also* GID III 8:7-9; Punishment)

Humanitarianism—*see also* Charity; World, improvement of

Humanitarianism: A strong sense of our common miseries an excellent spur to the removal of all the miseries we can; no need to believe in "heaven on earth"*
•PP 114 ❖ PP 7:5

Humanitarianism: As Christians we cannot cease to fight against all kinds of suffering; Christianity is both world-affirming and world-denying*
•GID 147-150 ❖ GID I ch. 17

"Humanitarianism," Christians must reject the covert attempt to drive mercy out of the world by calling it such names as "Sentimentality" and
•PP 56 ❖ PP 4:2

Humanitarianism: In Christianity, provision for the poor is less important than the salvation of souls—and yet very important
•GID 147-150, esp. 148 ❖ GID I ch. 17, esp. 17:5

Humanitarianism: Law of beneficence involves not doing some good to some men at some times—since if you do *this* good you can't at the same time do *that* (re: Pacifism)*
•WG 41-42 ❖ WG 3:16

Humanity—*see also* Man

Humanity: In heaven we will be more human than we ever succeeded in being on earth
•PP 125; WG 117-119 (*see also* Personality) ❖ PP 8:9; WG 7:17, 18 (*see also*

Personality)

Humanity, interdependence of all: We are born helpless; we need others physically, emotionally, and intellectually*
•FL 11-12 ❖ FL 1:3

Humanity, interdependence of: "Always, in some mode or other, one has lived on others...we are members of one another..."
•LAL 111-112 (*see also* LAL 20-21) ❖ LAL 10 Dec 62 (*see also* LAL Aug 10th 53)

Humanity, interdependence of: "It is a law of the natural universe that no being can exist on its own resources"*
•GID 85 (*see also* M 118) ❖ GID I 9:8 (*see also* M 14:19)

Humanity, interdependence of: The Christian doctrine of vicariousness will not allow me any dream of living on my own*
•GID 87; M 118 ❖ GID I 9:10; M 14:19

Humanity, interdependence of: "We are all members of one another and must all learn to receive as well as to give"*
•LAL 57 ❖ LAL 14/6/56

Humanity of Christ—*see also* Incarnation

Humanity of Christ as a permanent thing seems under-stressed, as if He once became a man and then reverted to being simply God
•RP 134 (*see also* M 123) ❖ RP 12:13 (*see also* M 14:26)

Humanity's "place in the universe (its greatness and littleness, its humble origins, and—even on the natural level—amazing destiny)"
•RP 134 ❖ RP 12:13

Humiliation—*see also* Shame

Humiliation as part of "the Dark Night of the Flesh" which the Psalmists experienced—out of which their self-righteous utterances grew
•CR 125-128, esp. 127-128 ❖ CR 10:30-40, esp. 10:38-40

Humiliation different from guilt; perhaps we all dislike it so much that we tend to disguise it from ourselves by treating blunders as sins
•LAL 106-107 ❖ LAL 3 Sep 62

Humiliation ("oppression"): Where it does not completely and permanently break the spirit, has it not a tendency to produce retaliatory pride and contempt?*
•SJ 107 ❖ SJ 7:8

Humiliation: We should mind it less if we were humbler
•LAL 29 ❖ LAL Mar 31st 54

Humility—*consider also* Self-contempt

Humility, 1st step toward acquiring, is to realize that one is proud
•MC 114 ❖ MC III 8:14

Humility, 2nd step toward acquiring, is a serious attempt to practice the Christian virtues
•MC 124 ❖ MC III 11:7

Humility, a man is never so proud as when striking an attitude of, (said in reference to himself)
•CR 14 ❖ CR 2:4

Humility: After repentance and being forgiven, we may continue to feel sorrow for being that kind of person—and be humbled by it
•L 236 (*see also* PP 61; SL 148*)
❖ L 8 Jan 52 (*see also* PP 4:9; SL 31:5*)

Humility, after the first shock, is a cheerful virtue; it is the high-minded unbeliever, with his "faith in human nature," who is really sad
•PP 67 ❖ PP 4:15

Humility as seen in the child-like pleasure of being praised
•WG 12 ❖ WG 1:10

Humility, Divine: God is not proud, He stoops to conquer; He will have us even though we have shown that we prefer everything else to Him
•PP 97 (*see also* LAL 49; SJ 229) ❖ PP 6:8 (*see also* LAL 16/12/55; SJ 14:23)

Humility: I prefer to combat the "I'm special" feeling not by the thought "I'm no more special than anyone else," but by feeling "Everyone is as special as me"
•L 242-243 (*see also* SL 64)
❖ L 20 Jun 52 (*see also* SL 14:4)

Humility, false, ("false modesty") never works with me; if a man tells me he

can't do something I always believe him*
•LAL 34 ❖ LAL Nov 1st 54

Humility, false: "There can be no surer proof of a confirmed pride than a belief that one is sufficiently humble" (quote from Law)*
•LAL 96; PP 55, top (*see also* CR 14; MC 114; SL 62-63)
❖ LAL 24 Feb 61; PP 4 prelim. quote (*see also* CR 2:4; MC III 8:14; SL 14:2)

Humility, false, which Screwtape detects in a newly converted man who thinks he is showing great condescension in going to church with his commonplace neighbors
•SL 14 ❖ SL 2:4

Humility, I wish I had gotten a bit further with, myself; if I had, I could probably tell you a bit more about the relief...of taking the fancy-dress off
•MC 114 ❖ MC III 8:12

Humility: If we cannot lay down our tastes at the church door, surely we should at least bring them in to be humbled
•GID 336 ❖ GID IV Letter 8

Humility in saints not a false humility; when they say that they are vile, they are recording truth with scientific accuracy
•PP 67-68 ❖ PP 4:15

Humility is the road to pleasure
•WG 113 ❖ WG 7:9

Humility: "It is the humble and the meek who have all the blessings in the *Magnificat*"
•LAL 29 ❖ LAL Mar 31st 54

Humility, knowledge of God leads to
•MC 114 ❖ MC III 8:12

Humility learned through acquiescence to such things as hymn singing: "The door is *low* and one must stoop to enter"
•GID 331 (*see also* CR 96-97; *consider also* Hymns) ❖ GID IV Letter 6 (*see also* CR 8:9, 10; *consider also* Hymns)

Humility: Lewis describes what it would be like to meet a truly humble person
•MC 114 ❖ MC III 8:13

Humility means self-forgetfulness rather

than a low opinion of one's talents and character
- •SL 63-66 ❖ SL 14:3-5

Humility mentioned by Screwtape as a virtue which is less of a problem to the devil as long as men are aware that they have it
- •SL 62-63 ❖ SL 14:2

Humility: One's own sins are a much more profitable theme than the sins of others
- •LAL 95 ❖ LAL 9 Jan 61

Humility, perfect, dispenses with modesty
- •WG 13 ❖ WG 1:10

Humility: "The hard sayings of our Lord are wholesome to those only who find them hard"*
- •GID 191-192 (see also GID 182*; RP 131-132) ❖ GID II 1:4 (see also GID I 22:13*; RP 12:10)

Humility, true end of, is to turn our attention away from ourselves to God
- •SL 63-66 ❖ SL 14:3-5

Humility, truly humble people do not think about; do not think about themselves at all
- •MC 114 (see also SL 62-66)
- ❖ MC III 8:13 (see also SL ch. 14)

Humility: We must recognize our nothingness before we can know God at all*
- •MC 111 ❖ MC III 8:6

Humility: "...We should mind humiliation less if we were humbler"
- •LAL 29 ❖ LAL Mar 31st 54

Humor—see also Bawdy; Jokes

Humor a dangerous thing to try when learning to write
- •L 28 ❖ L undated letter between Oct 1915 and 27 Sep 16

Humor: "...a little comic relief in a discussion does no harm, however serious the topic may be"
- •RP 90 ❖ RP 9:1

Humor a necessary ingredient in "Venus," or sexual love
- •FL 138-144 ❖ FL 5:11-21

Humor and laughter, Screwtape points out ways in which, can be used to serve diabolical purposes
- •SL 49-52 ❖ SL ch. 11

Humor and playfulness, Eros involves;

until they have a baby to laugh at, lovers are always laughing at each other
- •FL 151 ❖ FL 5:30

Humor between the sexes: "...it is healthy that each should have a lively sense of the other's absurdity"
- •FL 110-111 ❖ FL 4:37

Humor, Book of Jonah is not without a distinctly Jewish vein of
- •CR 155 (see also L 286)
- ❖ CR 13:5 (see also L 30 Apr 59)

Humor, comment on the use of, in writing on Christian themes
- •GID 259 ❖ GID II 15:7-10

Humor: Flippancy defined by Screwtape: "...every serious subject is discussed in a manner which implies that they have already found a ridiculous side to it"
- •SL 52 ❖ SL 11:6

Humor: Flippancy mentioned by Screwtape as deadening the intellect and effectively armouring humans against God
- •SL 52 ❖ SL 11:6

Humor in [G.K.] Chesterton's books: "His humor was of the kind which I like best"—no general tone of flippancy or jocularity; not separable from the argument itself
- •SJ 190-191 ❖ SJ 12:12

Humor: "In my own experience the funniest things have occurred in the gravest and most sincere conversations"
- •RP 90 ❖ RP 9:1

Humor in the New Testament, I think there may be some; if there were more, we modern Occidentals may not see it
- •L 272 ❖ L 6 Dec 56

Humor in the Old Testament, we Gentiles probably miss; humor varies so much from culture to culture
- •L 272, 286 ❖ L 6 Dec 56; 30 Apr 59

Humor, merriment, and play as found among those who have taken each other seriously with regard for their eternal destiny
- •WG 19 ❖ WG 1:15

Humor not attributable to Satan, for hu-

mor involves a sense of proportion and a power of seeing yourself from the outside
•SL ix (*see also* SL xii-xiii)
❖ SL P:16 (*see also* SL P:22)
Humor: Screwtape mentions certain shameful things which can be passed off as funny and thus escape disapproval from one's fellows (cruelty, cowardice)
•SL 51 ❖ SL 11:5
Humor: Screwtape rues a female who "Looks as if butter wouldn't melt in her mouth, and yet has a satirical wit" (which "the Enemy" also grins at!)
•SL 101 (*see also* SL 124*)
❖ SL 22:2 (*see also* SL 26:5*)
Humor, the English take their sense of, so seriously that a deficiency in this area is almost the only deficiency at which they feel shame (—Screwtape)
•SL 51 ❖ SL 11:5
Humor, use of, [by people with barbaric taste] as a kind of shield to "protect themselves from anything which might disturb the muddy puddle inside"
•L 112 ❖ L 1 Apr 27
Humor: We do not need to always partake of friendship solemnly; "'God who made good laughter' forbid"
•FL 127 ❖ FL 4:62
Humor: We must acknowledge certain things in life to be serious and yet treat them often lightly as a game (re: Friendship)
•FL 127 ❖ FL 4:62
Humpty Dumpty analogy to show that entropy has not always been the rule
•M 152 ❖ M 16:17
Humpty Dumpty analogy to show the disorganizational character of the universe (entropy)
•GID 33-34; M 152
❖ GID I 2:12; M 16:17
Hunger—*see also* Appetite
"Hunger" of the devils in Hell is the passion to dominate, almost to digest, one's fellow; even in human life ("love") we see this

•SL xi (*see also* FL 160; SL 26, 37-38, 81, 141, 145; WLN 51-56, 69-70)
❖ SL P:19, 20 (*see also* FL 5:46; SL 5:2; 8:3; 18:3; 30:1; 31:1; WLN 4:1-13, 39)
Hunger, quote from Matthew Arnold regarding: "Nor does the being hungry prove that we have bread"
•GID 260; WG 8
❖ GID II 16:18; WG 1:6
Hunter, God was the, and I was the deer; He stalked me like a redskin, took unerring aim, and fired
•CR 169 (*see also* SJ 227; Initiative)
❖ CR 14:19 (*see also* SJ 14:20, 21; Initiative)
"**Hurt**," feeling, so seldom means merely sorrow; usually mixed with wounded pride, self-justification, fright, even desire for retaliation
•LAL 56-57 ❖ LAL 21/5/56
"Hurt" feelings: Most times people who "hurt" us did not intend to, and are quite unconscious of the whole thing
•LAL 59 (*see also* LAL 96-97)
❖ LAL 3/8/56 (*see also* LAL 24 Feb 61)
Husband—*see also* Marriage; Men
Husband, in Christian marriage, is the head of the wife just in so far as he is to her what Christ is to the Church
•FL 148-149 (*see also* GID 238; L 184-185) ❖ FL 5:26-28 (*see also* GID II 11:10; L 18 Apr 40)
Hymn, I question whether the badness of a really bad, can be so irrelevant to devotion as the badness of a bad devotional picture
•CR 2 ❖ CR 1:2
Hymn to the Sun, the Egyptian poem written by Amenhetep IV, shows an astonishing leap into Monotheism; Moses was possibly influenced by this
•RP 85-89 ❖ RP 8:16-19
Hymns—*see also* Music, church
Hymns about the Crucifixion: They must be the work of people so far above me that they can't reach me, or of people with no imagination at all (or both)
•LM 85-86 ❖ LM 16:10
Hymns: "...an anthology of love poems for public and perpetual use would prob-

ably be as sore a trial to literary taste as *Hymns Ancient and Modern*"
•RP 94 ❖ RP 9:5

Hymns, bad, are partly responsible for the unscriptural belief about family reunions "on the further shore"—the happy past restored
•GO 28-29 ❖ GO 2:14

Hymns: Christianity for me was associated with ugly music*
•SJ 172 ❖ SJ 11:8

Hymns: Good taste in poetry or music not necessary to salvation, as evidenced by the humble charwoman who revels in hymns
•L 224 (*see also* CR 13-14)
❖ L 7 Dec 50 (*see also* CR 2:3, 4)

Hymns: I considered them to be fifth-rate poems set to sixth-rate music
•GID 61-62 (*see also* SL 12*)
❖ GID I 4:10 (Ques. 16) (*see also* SL 2:2*)

Hymns, I naturally loathe nearly all, (but tolerating them teaches humility and charity)
•L 224 ❖ L 7 Dec 50

Hymns, letter expressing Lewis's distaste for
•GID 330-331 (*see also* LAL 60) ❖ GID IV Letter 6 (*see also* LAL 3/8/56)

Hymns, low-brow people who like, may be better Christians than ourselves
•L 224 ❖ L 7 Dec 50

Hymns: Neither the best choir singing, nor the heartiest bellowing from the pews, must be taken to signify that any religious activity is going on
•CR 96 ❖ CR 8:8

Hymns: "The 'sentimentality and cheapness' of much Christian hymnody had been a strong point in my own resistance to conversion..."
•CR 13 ❖ CR 2:3

Hymns: "We should be cautious of assuming that we know what their most banal expressions actually stand for in the minds of uneducated, holy persons"
•CR 13 (ftnt.) ❖ CR 2:3 (ftnt.)

Hymns were (and are) extremely disagreeable to me

•SJ 234 ❖ SJ 15:6

Hymns: "What I, like many other laymen, chiefly desire in church are fewer, better, and shorter hymns; especially fewer"
•CR 96 ❖ CR 8:6

Hyperbole, whether Jesus was using, when He talked about faith moving mountains
•CR 146 ❖ CR 12:13

Hypochondria in America: I get the impression that in your country people are far too medically minded; they read and think too much about health*
•LAL 39 ❖ LAL 21/3/55

Hypochondria ("self-pity for imaginary distresses"), according to Screwtape, vanishes upon five minutes of genuine toothache*
•SL 58 ❖ SL 13:3

Hypochondriac temperaments will always tend to think true what they most wish to be false (re: the wish that God should not exist)
•WLN 19 ❖ WLN 2:8

Hypocrisy—*see also* Self-righteousness

Hypocrisy: "A man is never so proud as when striking an attitude of humility"*
•CR 14 ❖ CR 2:4

Hypocrisy: How can people obviously full of Pride appear to themselves very religious?—I am afraid it is because they are worshipping an imaginary God*
•MC 111 ❖ MC III 8:7

Hypocrisy: "Humans are very seldom either totally sincere or totally hypocritical. Their moods change, their motives are mixed..."
•LAL 97 (*see also* LAL 95*) ❖ LAL 28 Mar 61 (*see also* LAL 9 Jan 61*)

Hypocrisy, I lacked the bloodhound sensitivity for, and have never felt the dislike of goodness quite common in better men than me
•SJ 191 ❖ SJ 12:12

Hypocrisy, if pretending to be better than you are is, then I must conclude that hypocrisy can do a man good

•SJ 192-193 (*see also* MC 161-162; Imitation) ❖ SJ 12:14 (*see also* MC IV 7:2-4; Imitation)

Hypocrisy in someone is no excuse for not heeding their good advice*
•GID 283-284 ❖ GID III 3:4

Hypocrisy, it is mad work to remove, by removing the temptation to hypocrisy (re: the attempt to overcome shame by the theories of Psychoanalysis)
•PP 56-57 ❖ PP 4:3

Hypocrisy: Real beliefs may differ from the professed and may lurk in the turn of a phrase or the choice of an epithet (re: beliefs implicit in literature)*
•CR 28-29 ❖ CR 2:48

Hypocrites in church, Screwtape mentions using, to create disappointment in the newly converted human
•SL 14 ❖ SL 2:4

Hypocrites in church: Why should their vices prove hypocrisy if I, being what I am, consider myself to be in some sense a Christian?
•SL 14 ❖ SL 2:4

Hypocrites, it is much clearer to say, are bad Christians than that they are not Christians*
•MC 11 ❖ MC P:14

Hypocrites more curable than "goody-goodies" who are content in their routine piety and respectability and are attempting no deception
•WLN 47-48 ❖ WLN 3:25, 26

I Broaden My Mind (chapter title)
•SJ 56-70 ❖ SJ ch. 4

Iconoclast, God is the great; my idea of Him has to be shattered time after time, and He shatters it Himself
•GO 76-78; LM 82 (*see also* GO 82-83; SL 22*) ❖ GO 4:15; LM 15:17 (*see also* GO 4:27, 28; SL 4:4*)

Iconoclastic, all reality is
•GO 77 ❖ GO 4:16

Iconography, distinction between sacred art and, (iconography being "that which is meant merely as the starting point for devotion and meditation")
•CR 2 ❖ CR 1:2

Icons—*consider also* Art

Icons: Their value depends very little on their perfection as artifacts; two sticks tied crosswise may kindle as much devotion as the work of Leonardo
•CR 2 ❖ CR 1:2

Icons: To me their danger is obvious; images of the Holy can easily become holy images—sacrosanct*
•GO 76 ❖ GO 4:15

"Idealism" as a term used with reference to morality may cause us to forget that morality is an absolute necessity for the human race
•MC 69-70 ❖ MC III 1:2

Idealism can be talked and even felt; it cannot be lived
•SJ 226 ❖ SJ 14:20

Idealism, I thought that those who believed in "a God" came nearer to the

---

truth of Absolute, than those who did not
•SJ 215 ❖ SJ 14:5

Idealism in marriage: One of the miracles of love is that it gives a power of seeing through its own enchantments and yet not being disenchanted*
•GO 83-84 ❖ GO 4:30, 31

Idealism, of course there had long been an ethic (theoretically) attached to my
•SJ 225 ❖ SJ 14:18

Idealism, philosophical, turns out to be disguised Theism
•WG 91 ❖ WG 5:23

Idealism was then the dominant philosophy at Oxford
•SJ 209 ❖ SJ 13:17

Idealist's and Pantheist's idea of the material universe is that it is not quite real; is a kind of mirage
•CR 59 ❖ CR 5:5

Idealists, what I learned from the, is that it is more important that Heaven should exist than that any of us should reach it
•SJ 210-211 (see also SJ 222)
❖ SJ 13:19 (see also SJ 14:13)

Idolatry: Mental images, pictures, and statues present an obvious danger; images of the Holy can easily become holy images–sacrosanct*
•GO 76 ❖ GO 4:15

Idolatry of an earthly Beloved: Loving God too little a greater danger than loving any human too much*
•FL 170 ❖ FL 6:15

Idolatry of love: "Where a true Eros is present resistance to his commands feels like an apostasy"; temptations feel like duties
•FL 155-157 (see also FL 20-21, 151)
❖ FL 5:37-41 (see also FL 1:18; 5:31, 32)

Idolatry: "We love everything in one way too much (i.e., at the expense of our love for Him) but in another way we love everything too little" (re: our pets)*
•LAL 61 (see also FL 165, 170-171, 190-191) ❖ LAL 18/8/56 (see also FL 6:3, 4, 15, 44)

Iliad, Greek religious belief is shown at the beginning of the
•RP 37 ❖ RP 4:8

Illness(es)—see also Disease(s)

Illness and health listed by Screwtape as neutral situations which can work either for God's or the devil's purposes
•SL 89 ❖ SL 19:3

Illness, I have seen the last, produce treasures of fortitude and meekness from most unpromising subjects (re: this world as a "'vale of soul-making'")
•PP 108 ❖ PP 6:18

Illness, I number a small, among the minor pleasures of life
•L 106-107; SJ 189 (see also L 137, 159,202, 302, 304; LAL 37)
❖ L undated letter postmarked 25 Jan 26; SJ 12:11 (see also L 9 Sep 29; undated letter just after 2 Sep 39; L 31 Jan 43; 20 Dec 61; 25 May 62; LAL 29/1/55)

Illness, Lewis describes his own (eventually fatal)
•L 278, 280, 300, 301-302, 305; LAL 119, 121, 122 ❖ L 24 Aug 57; 6 Nov 57; 28 Oct 61; 20 Dec 61; 10 Aug 62; undated letter of Aug 62; LAL 28 Jun 63; 9 Jul 63; 16th Jul 63

Illness: Lewis makes reference to his own declining health
•LAL 67, 68, 70, 86, 89-90, 98, 102, 103-104, 106, 113, 119, 121 ❖ LAL Jun 18th 57; Aug 12th 57; Nov 3d 57; Nov 30th 57; Aug 3/59; 13 Feb 60; 21 Apr 61; 6 Apr 62; Ascension Day 62; 3 Sep 62; 8 Jan 63; 26/1/63; 28 Jun 63; 9 Jul 63

Illness, Lewis's: "I was only too glad to let [my doctor] off with the merest skeleton account of my own state—I found it such a boring subject"
•LAL 121 ❖ LAL 9 Jul 63

Illness, men and women are quite diversely affected by; women worry that they can't do things, and men are grateful for the excuse not to do things
•LAL 105 ❖ LAL 31/7/62

Illness: Prayer for the sick is unquestionably right and can do real good
•L 226 (see also CR 148; SL 126)
❖ L undated letter just before 7 Feb 51

tianity
- GID 68-71; M 68-80 (*see also* GID 45-46; M 91-94) ❖ GID I ch. 6; M ch. 10 (*see also* GID I 3:15, 16; M 11:15-20)

Imagery, in trying to take the, out of Christianity a poorer mythology is being substituted for a richer
- LM 52 (*see also* M 74-75)
❖ LM 10:2 (*see also* M 10:13)

Imagery, it is probable that most of the early Christians never thought of their faith without anthropomorphic
- WG 85-86 ❖ WG 5:16-18

Imagery preserves the recognition of God's positive and concrete reality which evaporates in abstract thought
- M 91-92 (*see also* LM 51-52, 74)
❖ M 11:16 (*see also* LM 10:1; 14:9)

Imagery, Scriptural, used to describe Heaven not to be misunderstood; it is merely an attempt to express the inexpressible
- MC 121 ❖ MC III 10:6

Imagery, Scripture itself uses, to describe heaven; all intelligible descriptions must be of things within our experience
- WG 9-11 ❖ WG 1:7-9

Imagery such as that of upward motion in the Ascension: Impossible to know how much of a representation is symbolical and how much is literal
- CR 164-166 ❖ CR 13:30-35

Imagery such as that used by hymn writers to describe Heaven not altogether inappropriate to the reality
- WG 66 ❖ WG 4:19

Imagery, the philosophical problem of religious, stated ("...is it not very strange that an Apocalypse can furnish heaven with nothing more than...crowns, thrones, and music...?")
- WG 56 ❖ WG 4:4

Imagery, the unbeliever's difficulties with the miraculous usually begin with his contempt or disgust for Christian
- M 68-70 ❖ M 10:2-4

Imagery, there is no good substitute for religious; any language we attempt to substitute would be open to all the same objections

- GID 71 (*see also* LM 51-52*; M 74-75, 79) ❖ GID I 6:9 (*see also* LM 10:1, 2*; M 10:13, 19)

Imagery, two rules for: 1) Never take the images literally; 2) When the purport of the image seems to conflict with the abstraction, trust the image
- LM 52 ❖ LM 10:2

Imagery, use of, goes back beyond Christianity into Judaism
- M 76-77 ❖ M 10:16

Imagery, use of, to describe devils and angels: Creatures higher in the natural order than ourselves must be represented symbolically if at all
- SL viii ❖ SL P:12

Imagery, use of, to describe God
- GID 184-185 ❖ GID I ch. 23

Imagery, use of, to describe Heaven
- M 157-163; MC 121
❖ M 16:25-32; MC III 10:6

Imagery, use of "vulgar" [common]: If it gets across to the unbeliever what he desperately needs to know, the vulgarity must be endured
- GID 182 ❖ GID I 22:14, 15

Imagery used by Christians does not affect the miraculousness of what is asserted; e.g., Christ coming "down" from a local heaven
- GID 45-46 ❖ GID I 3:15, 16

Imagery used by Christians not to be identified with the thing believed; e.g., God pictured as a human form but believed to have no body
- M 73 (*see also* GID 69-70)
❖ M 10:12 (*see also* GID I 6:5-8)

Imagination—*consider also* Pretending

Imagination and thought processes may be changing, along with the way language is used to convey thought
- CR 140-141 ❖ CR 11:23, 24

Imagination as it may have related to Creation
- GID 276 ❖ GID III 1:18, 19

Imagination: "I think that all things reflect heavenly truth, the imagination not least"
- SJ 167 ❖ SJ 11:4

Imagination, if the, were obedient the appetites would give us very little

trouble
•LM 17 (*see also* GID 217; L 126; LAL 111) ❖ LM 3:9 (*see also* GID II 7:3; L 1 Apr 28; LAL 26 Nov 62)

Imagination: Invention is essentially different from reverie; in my [childhood] daydreams I was training myself to be a fool; in Animal-land, a novelist
•SJ 15 ❖ SJ 1:14

Imagination is distinct from thought; thought may be sound while accompanying images are false
•GID 69-71; M 70-71; 73 (*see also* WG 85-87) ❖ GID I 6:5-9; M 10:6-9, 11 (*see also* WG 5:18)

"Imagination," it became important [at Oxford] to distinguish, not only from "Fancy" but also from "Fantasy"
•SJ 203 ❖ SJ 13:10

Imagination: It is a mistake to suppose that children believe the things they imagine; [in chronicling Animal-land] I never mistook imagination for reality
•SJ 59-60, 82 ❖ SJ 4:6; 5:15

Imagination, it seems to me that, is something other than having mental images (re: Poetic language in religion)
•CR 138-140 ❖ CR 11:22, 23

Imagination, limitations of human: The act of creation, as it is for God, must always remain totally inconceivable to man*
•LM 72-73 ❖ LM 14:1-3

Imagination, Myth of Evolutionism gives the, almost everything it craves—irony, heroism, vastness, unity in multiplicity, and a tragic close
•CR 93 ❖ CR 7:23

Imagination, that night my, was baptized; the rest of me, not unnaturally, took longer (on reading the book *Phantastes*, by George MacDonald)
•SJ 181 ❖ SJ 11:19

Imagination, the emotion generated by poetic language is the emotion of pleasure at finding anything vividly conveyed to the
•CR 130-131 (*see also* GID 66*)
❖ CR 11:4 (*see also* GID I 5:9*)

Imagination, the power to visualize can sometimes serve true; very often it merely gets in the way (re: mental images in prayer)
•LM 85 (*see also* SL 21-22)
❖ LM 16:5-13 (*see also* SL 4:4)

"Imagination," three senses of the word, outlined
•SJ 15-16 ❖ SJ 1:14

Imagination, use of, in Lewis's writings described by himself as an attempt to embody his religious belief in symbolical or mythopeic forms
•L 260 (*see also* L 283 and specific book names) ❖ L undated letter just before 2 Feb 55 (*see also* L 29 Dec 58 and specific book names)

Imagination: "We are inveterate poets. When a quantity is very great we cease to regard it as a mere quantity. Our imaginations awake" (re: universe)
•M 52-53 ❖ M 7:16

Imagination would never have made me either wiser or better; but it still had, at however many removes, the shape of the reality it reflected (re: "Joy")
•SJ 167 ❖ SJ 11:4

Imaginative enjoyment, belief may be hostile to perfect
•WG 77 ❖ WG 5:8

Imaginative, except for the toy garden and the Green Hills my childhood was not
•SJ 8 ❖ SJ 1:5

Imaginative experience vs. Christian experience: Comparison is like that of the Sun's reflection in a dewdrop and the Sun itself
•SJ 167 ❖ SJ 11:4

Imaginative language—*see* Language, imaginative

Imagining, even the, of a supernatural love towards God has at times made all other objects of desire look like "broken toys and faded flowers"
•FL 192 (*see also* PP 106*)
❖ FL 6:47 (See PP 6:17*)

Imagining heaven: "No one, I presume, can imagine life in the glorified body ...I can picture very few of the things I believe in"
•L 288 ❖ L 8 Sep 59

Imitation—*see also* Pretending

Imitation as the mode in which each rung of a hierarchical ladder receives original divine virtue (Christ from God, man from Christ, etc.)
•CR 4-6 ❖ CR 1:6-10

Imitation can help toward becoming better; when a boor first enters the society of courteous people what can he do, for a while, except imitate the motions?
•SJ 192-193 ❖ SJ 12:14

Imitation may pass into initiation; for some it is a good beginning (re: values of culture as a reflection of spiritual values)
•CR 23 ❖ CR 2:34

Imitation of Christ as our goal will help us decide issues of right and wrong
•MC 162 ❖ MC IV 7:5

Imitation of Christ is sometimes, to an almost comic degree, not addressed to my condition
•LM 62 ❖ LM 12:1

Imitation of Christ mentioned as a book for meditative and devotional reading ("a little bit at a time, more like sucking a lozenge...")
•L 299 ❖ L 9 May 61

Imitation of Christ ("putting on Christ") not one among many jobs a Christian has to do; it is the whole of Christianity
•MC 166 ❖ MC IV 8:1

Imitation of Christ says "Bear your cross, for if you try to get rid of it you will probably find another and worse one"
•LAL 86 ❖ LAL Aug 3/59

Imitation of Christ: The Order of the Divine mind, embodied in the Divine Law, is beautiful; what should a man do but try to reproduce it in his daily life?*
•RP 59 ❖ RP 6:9

Imitation of Christ, the practice of Christianity consists of; Lewis describes what this means
•GID 50 ❖ GID I 4:11 (Ques. 3)

Imitation of Christ the whole purpose of becoming a Christian
•MC 153 ❖ MC IV 4:10

Imitation of Christ: "We are bidden to 'put on Christ,' to become like God"
•PP 53-54 (*see also* SL 158*; WLN 56*)
❖ PP 3:18, 19 (*see also* SL 32:13*; WLN 4:13*)

Imitation of God is what we must attempt in loving other people
•GID 152-154 (*see also* GID 123)
❖ GID I 18:4-9 (*see also* GID I 14:7, 8)

Imitation of God ("nearness of approach") a slow and painful—though by no means unaided—task
•FL 19 ❖ FL 1:16

Imitation of God, our, must be an imitation of Jesus, for this is the Divine life operating under human conditions
•FL 17 ❖ FL 1:12

Immaculate Conception defined (vs. Virgin Birth): It is a Roman Catholic doctrine which asserts that the mother of Jesus was born free of original sin
•L 232 ❖ L 13 Jun 51

"Immaculate Conception," meaning of the term, to modern minds ("Virgin Birth")
•GID 98 ❖ GID I 10:30

Immortality—*see also* Eternal life; Life after death; Salvation

Immortality, at my conversion I did not yet believe in; I now number that among my greatest mercies (God was to be obeyed simply because He was God)
•SJ 231 (*see also* FL 189-190; LM 120; RP 39-42, esp. 42) ❖ SJ 15:3 (*see also* FL 6:42; LM 22:8; RP 4:12-17, esp. 4:17)

Immortality, belief about, in Buddhism: "Salvation from immortality, deliverance from reincarnation, is the very core of its message"
•GID 130-131 ❖ GID I 16:2, 3

Immortality, belief in, can exist without a belief in God at all (e.g., in Buddhism)
•RP 40 ❖ RP 4:14

Immortality, belief in, coming too soon, may render impossible the development of the appetite for God; personal hopes and fears have got in first
•RP 39-40 (*see also* FL 189-190; GID 130-131; LM 120; SJ 231)

also Perfection

Improvement can be initiated by at first pretending you are better than you are; if this is hypocrisy, then I must conclude that hypocrisy can do a man good*
- •SJ 192-193 (*see also* Pretending)
- ❖ SJ 12:14 (*see also* Pretending)

Improvement, emergent evolution involves the belief that what is coming next will be an; this belief is unwarranted
- •GID 21 (*see also* CR 85; WLN 101)
- ❖ GID I 1:1 (*see also* CR 7:11; WLN 7:13)

Improvement, looking for, in yourself puts you on the wrong track
- •MC 128 (*see also* LM 34; Introspection) ❖ MC III 12:5 (*see also* LM 6:16; Introspection)

Improvement, mere, is not redemption (though redemption improves people); the change must go deeper than that
- •MC 182, 183 ❖ MC IV 10:16; 11:1

Improvement of this world—*see* World, improvement of

Incarnation—*consider also* Virgin Birth

Incarnation and God, example of attempt to describe, without the use of metaphorical language
- •GID 71; M 79 ❖ GID I 6:9; M 10:19

Incarnation as one of the beliefs which unite all Christians everywhere
- •GID 336 ❖ GID IV Letter 9

Incarnation as "the central event in the history of the Earth"
- •M 108 ❖ M 14:2

Incarnation as the "Dying God myth" come true; "By becoming fact it does not cease to be a myth"
- •GID 66-67 (*see also* M 133-134, ftnt.; Myth of "dying god")
- ❖ GID I 5:11 (*see also* M 15:2—ftnt.; Myth of "dying god")

Incarnation as "the missing chapter" in the novel of history
- •GID 80-88; M 109-110
- ❖ GID I ch. 9; M 14:3

Incarnation as the supreme example of God's iconoclasm; it leaves all previous ideas of the Messiah in ruins
- •GO 76-77 ❖ GO 4:15

Incarnation, belief in, brings God nearer, or near in a new way—and this, I found, was something I had not wanted
- •SJ 237 ❖ SJ 15:8

Incarnation: "Do we suppose that the scene of God's earthly life was selected at random?—that some other scene would have served better?"
- •WLN 97 ❖ WLN 7:7

Incarnation: "'He came down from Heaven' can almost be transposed into 'Heaven drew earth up into it'"
- •LM 70-71 ❖ LM 13:10

Incarnation: I have thought that the human and divine natures together made one Person; that there was a human *soul* involved
- •L 200-201 (*see also* L 210) ❖ L 29 Jul 42 (*see also* L undated letter of 1947)

Incarnation, I knew nothing yet about the; the God to whom I [first] surrendered was sheerly nonhuman
- •SJ 230 ❖ SJ 15:1

Incarnation: "...in it human life becomes the vehicle of Divine life." (as literature becomes the vehicle of God's word in Scripture)
- •RP 116 ❖ RP 11:11

Incarnation is strangely like many myths which have haunted religion from the first, yet it is not like them
- •PP 25; SJ 236 (*see also* GID 58, 63- 67, 83-84, 132, 175; M 113-115; WG 82-85)
- ❖ PP 1:16; SJ 15:7 (*see also* GID I 4:42; ch. 5; 9:5, 6; 16:4; 21:7; M 14:8-14; WG 5:15)

Incarnation is the central point of Christianity; for this reason, you cannot strip Christianity of its miraculous elements
- •GID 80; M 68, 108
- ❖ GID I 9:1; M 10:1; 14:1

Incarnation: It is difficult to imagine God as Man—but the physical sciences also propose for our belief much that cannot be imagined
- •WLN 99 ❖ WLN 7:10

Incarnation: Jesus as God *and* Man not fully conceivable to us; but neither can we conceive how the spirit of any man dwells within his natural organism
•M 110-111 ❖ M 14:4

Incarnation: "Men can read the life of Our Lord (because it is a human life) as nothing but a human life"
•RP 116 ❖ RP 11:12

Incarnation, miracle of, discussed ("The Grand Miracle")
•GID 80-88; M 108-131
❖ GID I ch. 9; M ch. 14

Incarnation not an episode in the life of God: the Lamb is slain—and therefore presumably born, grown to maturity, and risen—from all eternity
•WLN 99-100 ❖ WLN 7:11

Incarnation of Christ as a man likened to a man becoming a slug or crab
•MC 155 ❖ MC IV 5:4

Incarnation of Christ as a man likened to a diver bringing up a precious object from deep slime
•M 111-112 (*see also* GID 82; M 135)
❖ M 14:5, 6 (*see also* GID I 9:4, 5; M 15:5)

Incarnation of Christ, how "Transposition" may contribute to our understanding of the mechanism of
•WG 70-71 ❖ WG 4:28

Incarnation of Christ is the central point of Christianity—and if it happened at all, it is the central chapter of earth's history
•GID 80-82; M 108-109 (*see also* M 68)
❖ GID I 9:1-4; M 14:1, 2 (*see also* M 10:1)

Incarnation of Jesus as God *and* man, discussion of
•L 210 ❖ L undated letter of 1947

Incarnation of Jesus as history vs. myth: "If ever a myth had become fact, had been incarnated, it would be just like this"
•SJ 236 (*see also* Bible as literature)
❖ SJ 15:7 (*see also* Bible as literature)

Incarnation, play as analogy to the: "One might imagine a play in which the dramatist introduced himself as a character into his own play"
•CR 171-172 ❖ CR 14:30-32

Incarnation, Psalm 45 most valuable for the light it throws on the
•RP 127-130 ❖ RP 12:8

Incarnation, purpose of, explained
•MC 56-61 (*see also* MC 154-157)
❖ MC II ch. 4 (*see also* MC IV ch. 5)

Incarnation, purpose of: to enable men to become sons of God
•MC 154 ❖ MC IV 5:1

Incarnation, purpose of: to turn creatures into sons
•MC 182 ❖ MC IV 10:16

Incarnation, question of extraterrestrial life as it relates to the
•WLN 84-87 ❖ WLN 6:3-12

Incarnation sheds new light on the principle of inequality; I begin to see how it can survive as a supreme beauty in a redeemed universe
•GID 84-85 (*see also* WG 115-116)
❖ GID I 9:7 (*see also* WG 7:15)

Incarnation, story of the, not transparent to reason; we could not have invented it ourselves
•PP 25 (*see also* MC 46-47, 137*, 145)
❖ PP 1:16 (*see also* MC II 2:2-5; IV 1:9*; 2:17)

Incarnation is the central miracle asserted by Christians; is the chapter on which the whole novel turns, and it illuminates all of history and nature
•GID 81-88; M 108-131
❖ GID I ch. 6; M ch. 14

Incarnation: "The union between God and Nature in the Person of Christ admits no divorce. He will not *go out of* Nature again..."
•M 123 (*see also* RP 134)
❖ M 14:26 (*see also* RP 12:13)

Incarnation to some seems to imply particular merit in humanity, but in fact it implies just the reverse: a particular demerit and depravity
•WLN 86, 88 (*see also* M 52, 122)
❖ WLN 6:10, 15 (*see also* M 7:14; 14:24)

Incarnation transcends myth in conveying abstract reality to humans (as myth transcends thought); Christ is more than Balder, not less
•GID 66-67 (*see also* M 133-134, ftnt.*)

❖ GID I 5:10-13 (*see also* M 15:2—ftnt.*)

Incarnation, two views of: It was occasioned only by the Fall, or it would have occurred for Glorification and Perfection without the Fall
•M 123 ❖ M 14:25

Incarnation: Weariness, frustration, pain, doubt, and death "are, from before all worlds, known by God from within"
•LM 70-71 ❖ LM 13:10

Incense as part of church worship merely a question of ritual, not of doctrine; some find it helpful and others don't
•L 243
❖ L undated letter just after 20 Jun 52

Inclination(s)—*see* Desire(s)

Indecision ("floating") is a very agreeable operation; a decision either way costs something
•GID 250 ❖ GID II 14:3

Independence—*consider also* Self-centeredness; Self-reservation

Independence: At each step (in Lewis's conversion process) one had less chance 'to call one's soul one's own'"*
•SJ 237 ❖ SJ 15:8

Independence from God, to "call their souls their own," was what men desired from the beginning—but that is to live a lie, for our souls are not our own
•PP 80 (*see also* L 251; SJ 172, 228, 237; SL 95-99; WG 130-131)
❖ PP 5:8 (*see also* L 17 Jul 53; SJ 11:8; 14:22; 15:8; SL ch. 21; WG 9:9, 10)

Independence: "I became my own only when I gave myself to Another"
•L 251 (*see also* MC 141, 188-190; PP 152; SL 59; WG 117-118)
❖ L 17 Jul 53 (*see also* MC IV 2:3; 11:11-15; PP 10:10; SL 13:4; WG 7:16, 17)

Independence, main purpose of life is to reach the point at which we have relinquished personal freedom and, — that is, to "die"
•LAL 97-98 ❖ LAL 28 Mar 61

Independence ("selfish privacy"), sacrifice of, which is demanded in Christianity is repaid by growth of personality
•WG 113 ❖ WG 7:9

"Independence," suffering helps to cure us of the illusion of
•LAL 20-21 ❖ LAL Aug 10th 53

Independence, the state of being indebted to no one, is eternally impossible
•LAL 20-21 (*see also* LAL 112) ❖ LAL Aug 10th 53 (*see also* LAL 10 Dec 62)

Independence: Who is more totally dependent than what we call the man "of independent means"—every shirt he wears is made by other people
•LAL 21 (*see also* LAL 57-58, 112)
❖ LAL Aug 10th 53 (*see also* LAL 14/6/56; 10 Dec 62)

"**Independent**," living on inherited wealth makes one not, but more dependent than most
•LAL 57-58 ❖ LAL 14/6/56

"Independent," one never *has* been; poverty merely *reveals* the helpless dependence which has all the time been our real condition
•LAL 111-112 ❖ LAL 10 Dec 62

Indignation may be a good symptom, though it may lead to bitter personal vindictiveness (as in the Psalms)
•RP 30-31 ❖ RP 3:19

Individual, in Old Testament times, seems to have been less separated from others; blessings on one's remote posterity were blessings on oneself
•RP 42-43 ❖ RP 4:18

Individual, the Old Testament seems to ignore our conception of the
•PP 87-88 ❖ PP 5:13

Individuals are immortal only as new creatures
•WG 120 ❖ WG 7:19

Individuals are incomparably more important than states or civilizations; they are everlasting
•GID 109-110; MC 73; SL 170; WG 19, 116-117; WLN 68
❖ GID I 12:2, 3; MC III 1:9; SL 32:39; WG 1:15; 7:16; WLN 4:39

Individuals, purpose of God in creating, includes the never-completed "attempt by each soul to communicate its unique vision [of God] to all the others"

•PP 150 (*see also* FL 92-93)

❖ PP 10:7 (*see also* FL 4:9)

Individualism, if abandoned, will be given back to us when we become organs in the Body of Christ

•WG 117 (*see also* MC 141, 188- 190; SL 59; Personality)

❖ WG 7:16 (*see also* MC IV 2:3; 11:11-15; SL 13:4; Personality)

Individualist or Totalitarian, a Christian must not be either

•MC 159-160 ❖ MC IV 6:3

Individuality—*see also* Personality

Individuality being lost in humans today —through a corruption of the word "democracy"

•SL 158-170; WLN 56-68

❖ SL 32:13-39; WLN 4:13-39

Individuality: I wonder what prevents the growth of rich, strongly marked personal peculiarities now-a-days

•L 124 ❖ L 25 Feb 28

Individuality, the ins and outs of your, are no mystery to God; and one day they will no longer be a mystery to you

•PP 147 ❖ PP 10:3

Industry, modern, a radically hopeless system; the dullness of the work prevents its workers from giving full play to their faculties

•GID 48 ❖ GID I 4:1

Inequality—*consider also* Equality

Inequality, Christianity offers us a refreshing return to, and opportunities for reverence

•WG 113-116 ❖ WG 7:10-15

Inequality, hierarchical, holds sway in the the realm beyond Nature, where love makes the difference

•M 119-120 ❖ M 14:20

Inequality: "...I don't mean to ignore (in fact I find it nice) the distinction between a peasant's grandson like myself and those of noble blood"*

•LAL 26 (*see also* LAL 27)

❖ LAL 26/1/54 (*see also* Feb 22/54)

Inequality, Incarnation sheds new light on the principle of, ("...the immense pleasures of admiration")

•GID 84-85 (*see also* SL 170; WLN 68)

❖ GID I 9:7 (*see also* SL 32:39; WLN 4:39)

Infection, analogy of: Good things as well as bad are caught by a kind of infection; if you are close to the fountain [of God], the spray will wet you

•MC 153 (*see also* MC 157, 162, 163, 186) ❖ MC IV 4:8, 10 (*see also* MC IV 5:8; 7:5, 8; 11:7)

Infection, Good (chapter title)

•MC 149-153 ❖ MC IV ch. 4

Inference—*see also* Logic; Reason

Inference: It is clear that everything we know is inferred from our sensations

•M 14 ❖ M 3:4

Inference, validity of, is what the whole popular scientific picture depends upon; yet at the same time science asks me to believe that Reason is accidental

•WG 88-89 (*see also* M 12-24; Reasoning) ❖ WG 5:21 (*see also* M ch. 3; Reasoning)

Inferiority complex: Unmusical laymen may "look with the restless and resentful hostility of an inferiority complex" on all who try to improve their taste*

•CR 97 ❖ CR 8:9

Inferiority, feelings of, are what prompt people to make claims to equality

•SL 162-163; WLN 60-61

❖ SL 32:22; WLN 4:22

Inferiority, feelings of, ("inner insecurity") as the probable cause of mere disagreeableness in people

•LAL 27-28 ❖ LAL Mar 10/54

Infidelity—*see also* Adultery

Infidelity, a society which tolerates, is a society adverse to women, who are more often the victims than the culprits

•GID 321-322 ❖ GID III 9:27

Infidelity in marriage, discussion of

•GID 317-322; MC 95-101

❖ GID III ch. 9; MC III 6:1-13

Infidelity in marriage, letters to a lady with the problem of

•L 218-221 (*see also* L 227-228, 236, 240)

❖ L 2 Sep 49 through 27 Sep 49 (*see also* L 5 Mar 51; 8 Jan 52; 13 May 52)

Influence on others: "...what will really influence them, for good or ill, is not anything I do or say but what *I am*"
•LAL 96 (*see also* L 261; Witnessing) ❖ LAL 24 Feb 61 (*see also* L 2 Feb 55; Witnessing)

Ingratiation ("band-wagoning"), or consorting with people for the wrong motives—especially bad people*
•RP 69-75 (*see also* SL 45-48*) ❖ RP 7:6-17 (*see also* SL ch. 10*)

Inhibitions, it took me as long to acquire, as others (they say) have taken to get rid of them
•SJ 69 ❖ SJ 4:18

Initiative for knowing God lies wholly on God's side
•GID 143-144; MC 144 (*see also* PP 51-52; SJ 216) ❖ GID I 16:26; MC IV 2:13 (*see also* PP 3:17; SJ 14:7)

Initiative, how could the, lie on my side? If Shakespeare and Hamlet could ever meet, it must be Shakespeare's doing (re: human contact with God)
•SJ 227 (*see also* CR 169; SJ 223) ❖ SJ 14:20 (*see also* CR 14:19; SJ 14:14)

Initiative, our highest activity must be response and not
•PP 51 ❖ PP 3:17

"Inklings" mentioned or referred to
•L 170, 171, 176, 178, 197 (*see also* L 169, 287-288) ❖ L 11 Nov 39; 24 Nov 39; 3 Feb 40; 3 Mar 40; 21 Dec 41 (*see also* L 5 Nov 39; 15 May 39)

Inner activities, "enjoyment" of, is incompatible with the "contemplation" of them; e.g., you cannot hope and think about hoping at the same time
•SJ 217-219 (*see also* GID 65-66; L 221) ❖ SJ 14:9, 10 (*see also* GID I 5:8, 9; L 27 Sep 49)

Inner cesspool, according to Alexander Whyte the true Christian's nostril is to be continually attentive to the
•LM 97-98 ❖ LM 18:13

Inner life vs. outer life: "Where there are hungry wastes, starving for Joy, in the one, the other may be full of cheerful bustle and success..."
•SJ 78, 118-119 (*see also* LAL 83)

❖ SJ 5:12; 8:1 (*see also* LAL Jun 7th 59)

Inner Ring(s)—*consider also* "Band-wagoning"; Coteries; Snobbery

Inner Ring of Oxford professors described*
•L 59-60 ❖ L 10 May 21

Inner Ring of Wyvern College—the "Bloods"—described*
•SJ 83-100 (*see also* SJ 108) ❖ SJ ch. 6 (*see also* SJ 7:10)

Inner Ring of Wyvern College: "And from it, at school as in the world, all sorts of meanness flow..."*
•SJ 108 ❖ SJ 7:10

Inner Ring of Wyvern College: To get to the top and to remain there was the absorbing preoccupation of school life (as it is of adult life)*
•SJ 108 ❖ SJ 7:10

Inner Ring, The (chapter title)
•WG 93-105 ❖ WG ch. 6

Inner Ring which one may imagine he is part of as a Christian (vis-a-vis "the unbelievers")
•SL 110-113 (*see also* RP 65*; SL 34) ❖ SL 24:1-5 (*see also* RP 6:14*; SL 7:2)

Inner Rings as exclusive circles of Friends ("Friendship may be 'about' almost nothing except the fact that it excludes")*
•FL 114-127, esp. 121-122 ❖ FL 4:46-62, esp. 4:54, 55

Inner Rings: Being "in" is a pleasure that cannot last; if you join any group just to be "in," your pleasure will be short-lived
•WG 103 ❖ WG 6:15

Inner Rings cannot have from within the charm they had from the outside; by the very act of admiring you it has lost its magic
•WG 103 ❖ WG 6:15

Inner Rings, dangers of belonging to, may include deriving pleasure from the loneliness and humiliation of the outsiders
•WG 99 ❖ WG 6:9

Inner Rings: Desire to be "in" almost excludes the possibility; "Until you conquer the fear of being an outsider, an

outsider you will remain"
•WG 103 ❖ WG 6:14

Inner Rings, desire to belong to, is one of the great mainsprings of human action
•WG 100-101 ❖ WG 6:11

Inner Rings, desire to belong to, is one of the most dominant elements of our lives
•WG 96-97 (see also SJ 108*)
❖ WG 6:6 (see also SJ 7:10*)

Inner Rings, desire to belong to, likely to become one of the chief motives of your professional life
•WG 100-101 ❖ WG 6:11

Inner Rings, desire to belong to, may be a true index of our real situation: We may ultimately be left utterly outside, or at last be summoned inside**
•WG 15-16 ❖ WG 1:12

Inner Rings, identifying marks of
•WG 95-96 (see also SJ 108*)
❖ WG 6:4, 5 (see also SJ 7:10*)

Inner Rings: If one holds together for a good purpose (such as friendship), the exclusions are in a sense accidental
•WG 104 (see also FL 115-122)
❖ WG 6:16 (see also FL 4:47-55)

Inner Rings in Church: Screwtape advises that if the human can't be kept out of Church, he ought to be attached to some faction or party within it*
•SL 72-73, 75 ❖ SL 16:2, 5

Inner Rings in Church: Screwtape relishes watching the Church divide itself up into small, self-righteous factions*
•SL 34 (see also SL 72-73, 75)
❖ SL 7:2 (see also SL 16:2, 5)

Inner Rings, in the genuine, negative sense, exist for the pleasure of exclusion
•WG 104 ❖ WG 6:16

Inner Rings (meaning exclusive inner circles or groups of people such as may form among those who work together)
•WG 93-105 (see also FL 115-127; L 135)
❖ WG ch. 6 (see also FL 4:46-62; L undated letter postmarked 17 Jul 29)

Inner Rings not necessarily an evil in

themselves, but the desire to belong to one may be dangerous
•WG 98-99 ❖ WG 6:8

Inner Rings, passion for, can make men who are not yet very bad do very bad things
•WG 103 ❖ WG 6:13

Inner Rings, quest of belonging to, must be broken; and then a surprising result will follow: that of true professional enjoyment
•WG 104-105 ❖ WG 6:17

Inner Rings: Since men do not like to be merely equal with other men, we find them building themselves into groups where they can feel superior to others*
•WLN 41 ❖ WLN 3:14

Inner Rings, tangible profits of belonging to, include sense of secret intimacy
•WG 100 ❖ WG 6:10

Inner Rings, young people should not follow desire to enter
•WG 104-105 ❖ WG 6:17, 18

Innocence, bloom of, is gradually rubbed off every activity we undertake
•PP 76 ❖ PP 5:5

Innovation—see also Change(s)

Innovation in the liturgy: "Take care. It is so easy to break eggs without making omelettes"
•LM 6 ❖ LM 1:13

Insect world, there are moments when the, appears to be Hell itself visibly in operation around us
•GID 170-171 ❖ GID I 20:Reply-13, 16

Insects: "...in the hive and the anthill we see fully realized the two things that some of us most dread for our own species..."
•SJ 8-9 ❖ SJ 1:6

Insects, intense activity and fertility of, bear a dim resemblance to the unceasing activity and creativeness of God
•MC 139 ❖ MC IV 1:14

Insects, Lewis's dislike of: "'...they are like French locomotives—they have all the works on the outside'" (quote from

Owen Barfield)
- SJ 8-9 (*see also* L 257; LAL 21)
- ❖ SJ 1:6, 7 (*see also* L 1 Nov 54; LAL Aug 10th 53)

Insecurity ("inferiority"), feelings of, are what prompt people to make claims to equality
- SL 162-163; WLN 60-61
- ❖ SL 32:22; WLN 4:22

Insecurity, inner, as the probable cause of mere disagreeableness in people
- LAL 27-28 ❖ LAL Mar 10/54

Insight—*see* Introspection; Self-knowledge

Insignificance, Christianity never intended to dissipate the sense of our own; it comes to intensify it
- M 51 ❖ M 7:11

Insignificance of Man in the universe: We may be the one lost sheep whom the Shepherd came in search of
- GID 42-43, 100; M 122; WLN 86-87 (*see also* M 51-52*)
- ❖ GID I 3:9; 10:42; M 14:24; WLN 6:11 (*see also* M 7:13, 14)

Insignificance of Man: "...my very early reading...had lodged very firmly in my imagination the vastness and cold of space, the littleness of Man"
- SJ 65 ❖ SJ 4:11

Insignificance of Man to space and time, and of space and time to God: "Without such sensations there is no religion"
- M 51 ❖ M 7:11

Insignificance of Man: When one considers the sky and stars, it seems strange that God should be concerned with man— yet He has given us extraordinary honour (re: Psalm 8)
- RP 132 ❖ RP 12:11

Insomnia: Except for anxiety, nothing is more hostile to sleep than anger toward a loved one ("...the alternation of resentment and affection...")
- LAL 92-93 ❖ LAL 28 Oct 60

Insomnia, Lewis mentions having difficulty with
- LAL 89, 98, 113, 120 ❖ LAL 13 Feb 60; 21 Apr 61; 26/1/63; 6 Jul 63

Insomnia: Sleep is a jade who scorns her suitors but woos her scorners; the great secret (if one can do it) is not to *care* whether you sleep
- LAL 23 ❖ LAL 27/xi/53

Inspection, great thing is to be found at one's post when the, comes
- GID 266; WLN 111-112
- ❖ GID II 16:55; WLN 7:34

Inspiration, Bible *reading* also requires
- L 287 ❖ L 7 May 59

Inspiration: Lewis's view of the Old Testament as "the same sort of material as any other literature...but all taken into the service of God's word"
- RP 111 ❖ RP 11:4

Inspiration may operate in a wicked man without his knowing it
- L 287 ❖ L 7 May 59

Inspiration of all true and edifying writings other than the Bible
- L 287 ❖ L 7 May 59

Inspiration of Scripture, what Lewis believed about the
- RP 19, 109-119 (*see also* L 242, 286-287) ❖ RP 2:14; ch. 11 (*see also* L 28 May 52; 7 May 59)

Inspiration of the Bible: I suppose there was a Divine pressure over all phases—writing, preserving and canonizing, etc.
- RP 111 (*see also* RP 123)
- ❖ RP 11:4 (*see also* RP 12:4)

Inspiration of the Bible: "The total result is not 'the Word of God' in the sense that every passage, in itself, gives impeccable science or history"
- RP 112 (*see also* Bible—historicity)
- ❖ RP 11:5 (*see also* Bible—historicity)

Inspiration of writers by the Holy Spirit, I prefer to make no judgment concerning
- GID 264 ❖ GID II 16:37, 38

Inspiration, some thoughts regarding the divine authority and, of Scripture
- L 286-287 (*see also* Scripture/s)
- ❖ L 7 May 59 (*see also* Scripture/s)

Instinct: "If you do not arrange our instincts in a hierarchy of comparative dignity, it is idle to tell us to obey instinct, for the instincts are at war" (re:

"instinct" to preserve the human race)
•CR 51 ❖ CR 4:16

Instinct, it is dangerous to take any, and set it up as the thing we ought to follow at all costs; will make us into devils if we use it as an absolute guide
•MC 23-24 ❖ MC I 2:5

Instinct, question of whether the preservation of the human race is an imperative imposed by
•CR 48-52 (see also Preservation of the human race) ❖ CR 4:12-19 (see also Preservation of the human race)

Instinct to preserve the human race: "Why should this instinct [if it is an instinct] be preferred to all my others? It is certainly not my strongest"
•CR 50, 55 ❖ CR 4:15, 25

Instincts are in conflict; the satisfaction of one demands the denial of another
•CR 50 ❖ CR 4:15

Instincts themselves cannot furnish us with grounds for grading the instincts in a hierarchy; must be judged by some other standard (re: "instinct" to preserve the human race)
•CR 50-51, 74 ❖ CR 4:15, 16; 6:7

Institution(s)—see also Bureaucracy; Organization(s)

Institution, in every, there is something which sooner or later works against the very purpose for which it came into existence
•LM 43 ❖ LM 8:10

Institution, my symbol for Hell is something like the bureaucracy of a police state or the offices of a thoroughly nasty business
•SL x (see also book, That Hideous Strength) ❖ SL P:17 (see also book, That Hideous Strength)

Institutional evils described (principle of "Dog eat dog," etc.)
•SL x-xi ❖ SL P:18

Instruments, we are now merely tuning our, as Donne says—learning to praise God, in anticipation of the "symphony" of Heaven
•RP 97 (see also LM 116)
❖ RP 9:7 (see also LM 21:15)

Intellect, Newman's view of the cultivation of the, as a justifiable end in itself, while remaining wholly distinct from virtue
•CR 18-19 ❖ CR 2:20, 21

Intellect, Screwtape observes that the way to prepare for an assault of moral temptation upon a human is to darken his
•SL 95 ❖ SL 21:2

Intellect, the teaching of Jesus cannot be grasped by, alone; it demands a response from the whole man
•RP 112-114 ❖ RP 11:7-9

Intellectual and aesthetic activity, attempts to suspend, would only result in substituting a worse cultural life for a better (re: learning in war-time)
•WG 23 ❖ WG 2:5

Intellectual approach vs. emotional approach in evangelism
•GID 99, 244 ❖ GID I 10:39; II 12:9

Intellectual assent a necessary pre-condition for faith as trust or confidence
•GID 173 ❖ GID I 21:2

Intellectual assent not the same thing as conversion
•GID 221 ❖ GID II 8:10

Intellectual attacks of the heathen must be met by intellectual answers (re: value of education for the Christian)
•WG 28 ❖ WG 2:10

Intellectual development: Are you often struck with how late people's lives begin, so to speak?*
•L 123 ❖ L 12 Dec 27

Intellectual discussions about religion: We must continually fall back from the web of our arguments into Reality— from Christian apologetics to Christ Himself*
•GID 103 ❖ GID I 10:50

Intellectual dishonesty of clergymen who disbelieve what they preach: "I feel it is a form of prostitution"
•GID 260 (see also GID 89-90, 265*)
❖ GID II 16:12 (see also GID I 10:2, 3; II 16:46*)

Intellecual dishonesty of the historian who has based his work on the misread-

ing of a document
•GID 69 ❖ GID I 6:3

Intellectual dishonesty of the man who evades Christianity from fear of duty: "He has lost his intellectual virginity"
•GID 110-111 (see also WG 35*)
❖ GID I 12:6-8 (see also WG 3:4*)

Intellectual honesty/dishonesty—consider also Evasion; Truth

Intellectual honesty in considering Christianity and seeking Truth (even when it may turn out to be inconvenient)
•GID 108-113, 265-266 (consider also Truth) ❖ GID I ch. 12; II 16:50, 51 (consider also Truth)

Intellectual honesty in seeking Truth in civilizations like ours: "...I feel that everyone has to come to terms with the claims of Jesus Christ upon his life..."
•GID 265-266 ❖ GID II 16:50, 51

Intellectual honesty, issue of, for the modern theologian or clergyman who denies the miraculous in the Gospels*
•CR 153; M 164 ❖ CR 13:1, 2; M 17:1

Intellectual laziness: "God is no fonder of intellectual slackers than of any other slackers"; He wants us to use every bit of intelligence we have
•MC 74-75 ❖ MC III 2:4

Intellectual ("learned") life is, for some, a duty
•WG 29 ❖ WG 2:11

Intellectual life not the only road to God, nor the safest, but may be the road for some
•WG 27-28 ❖ WG 2:9

Intellectual life one of the appointed approaches to the Divine reality
•WG 32 ❖ WG 2:14

Intellectual, looking back on my life I am astonished that I did not become a satiric, of the type we all know so well
•SJ 173 ❖ SJ 11:10

Intellectual processes, emotion vs. "coolness" in our, (e.g., discussions of prayer): "I suppose one must try the problem in both states"
•LM 45 ❖ LM 8:14

Intellectual satisfaction vs. "Joy": "I did

not yet reflect on the difference..."
•SJ 78 ❖ SJ 5:11

Intellectuals, I suppose my Romanticism was destined to divide me from the orthodox, as soon as I met them
•SJ 173 ❖ SJ 11:10

"Intellectuals," the word, increasingly means little unofficial, self-appointed aristocracies in which people can feel superior to the mass
•WLN 41 ❖ WLN 3:14

"Intellectuals," why some people go to such lengths to prove that they are not
•WLN 31-38, 41 ❖ WLN 3:1-11, 14

Intellectualism—see also Culture; consider also Education; Highbrow(s); Knowledge

Intellectualism: A high natural gift of reason identified with a greater tendency to refuse the life of Christ (quote from Theologia Germanica)*
•CR 17 ❖ CR 2:16

Intellectualism: Regarding the evil tendency to love knowledge and discernment more than the object known and discerned*
•CR 17; WG 28 (see also Pride of pursuing "culture") ❖ CR 2:16; WG 2:9 (see also Pride of pursuing "culture")

Intellectualizing God and the problem of pain when one is grieving: "Do I hope that if feeling disguises itself as thought I shall feel less?"*
•GO 38 (see also GO 41, 43)
❖ GO 2:31 (see also GO 3:3, 4)

Intelligence, anyone who is honestly trying to be a Christian will soon find his, being sharpened; Christianity is an education in itself
•MC 75 (see also L 255*)
❖ MC III 2:4 (see also L 30 Jan 54*)

Intelligence as a gift which could cause us to forget our need of God
•MC 180-181 ❖ MC IV 10:11

Intelligence, Christ never meant that we were to remain children in; He wants us to use every bit of intelligence we have
•MC 74-75 ❖ MC III 2:4

Intelligence: Knowledge may be increas-

ing, but there is no evidence for advancement in intelligence (re: whether Bible is still applicable today)
•GID 57 ❖ GID I 4:41, 42 (Ques. 10)

Intemperance, there can be, in work just as in drink; what feels like zeal may be only fidgets or even the flattering of one's self-importance
•LAL 53 ❖ LAL 19/3/56

Intentions, good, will not keep a man from Hell; indeed they may make him more amusing when he gets there (— Screwtape)*
•SL 31 ❖ SL 6:5

Interdependence—*see also* Dependence; *consider also* Need to be needed

Interdependence of all humanity: We are born helpless; we need others physically, emotionally, intellectually*
•FL 11-12 ❖ FL 1:3

Interdependence of all humanity: "We are all members of one another and must all learn to receive as well as to give"*
•LAL 57 ❖ LAL 14/6/56

Interdependence of everything and everyone: "It is a law of the natural universe that no being can exist on its own resources"*
•GID 85 (*see also* M 118)
❖ GID I 9:8 (*see also* M 14:19)

Interdependence of humanity: "Always, in some mode or other, one has lived on others...we are members of one another..."*
•LAL 111-112 (*see also* LAL 20-21)
❖ LAL 10 Dec 62 (*see also* LAL Aug 10th 53)

Interdependence of humanity: The Christian doctrine of vicariousness will not allow me any dream of living on my own*
•GID 87; M 118(*see also* Independence)
❖ GID I 9:10; M 14:19 (*see also* Independence)

Interdependence of people: All the same principles which are evil in the world of selfishness and necessity are good in the world of love and understanding*
•M 120 ❖ M 14:20

Interdependence ("vicariousness"), what

Christianity tells us about: "It will not in any way allow me to be an exploiter..."*
•GID 87 ❖ GID I 9:10

Interests, even in your, has there not always been some secret attraction which the others are curiously ignorant of? (re: desire for heaven)
•PP 145-146 (*see also* RP 95)
❖ PP 10:2 (*see also* RP 9:6)

Interests, temptation to guard our worldly
•WG 126-132 (*see also* Self-reservation; Worldly...) ❖ WG ch. 9 (*see also* Self-reservation; Worldly...)

Interference by God in the world to correct the results of our abuse of free will would result in the exclusion of free will
•PP 33-34, 71 (*see also* PP 84; Miracles)
❖ PP 2:15; 5:1 (*see also* PP 5:11; Miracles)

Interference: Human nature wants to be left to itself, wants to keep well away from anything better or stronger or higher than itself*
•MC 154 (*see also* Independence; Self-reservation) ❖ MC IV 5:2 (*see also* Independence; Self-reservation)

"Interference," I hated no other word so much as; but Christianity seemed to place at the center a transcendental Interferer
•SJ 172 (*see also* SJ 228, 237*)
❖ SJ 11:8 (*see also* SJ 14:22; 15:8*)

Interference, in personal relations I could forgive much neglect more easily than the least degree of what I regarded as
•SJ 116-117 ❖ SJ 7:21

Interpersonal relations—*see* Relations, interpersonal; People

Interruption, one treats as an, of one's self-chosen vocation, the vocation actually imposed on one
•L 212 ❖ L 22 Dec 47

Interruption, what we regard as a mere hideous, and curtailment of life is really the concrete situation
•L 221 (*see also* L 161-162; SL 95-97*)
❖ L 22 Sep 49 (*see also* L 12 Sep 38; SL 21:2, 3*)

Interruptions, part of oneself still regards troubles as
•L 162 ❖ L 12 Sep 38

Intimacy and familiarity discussed: "I am not sure that the distinction between intimacy and familiarity is really very profound"
•L 136-138 ❖ L 9 Sep 29

Intolerance: In our day it is the "undogmatic" and "liberal" so-called Christians that are the most arrogant and intolerant
•L 229 ❖ L 23 Apr 51

Introspection—*see also* Self- examination; Self-knowledge

Introspection about one's own sins healthier than thinking about the sins of others
•GID 124 (*see also* LAL 95)
❖ GID I 14:10 (*see also* LAL 9 Jan 61)

Introspection as it relates to "Joy": "The surest way of spoiling a pleasure [is] to start examining your satisfaction"
•SJ 218-219 (*see also* GID 65-66*)
❖ SJ 14:10, 11 (*see also* GID I 5:8*)

Introspection, avoid, in prayer (as to whether one's mind is in the right frame)
•L 256 (*see also* LM 23; SJ 61-62*; SL 20-21*) ❖ L 31 Jul 54 (*see also* LM 4:19; SJ 4:7, 8*; SL 4:3*)

Introspection: Comment about discerning one's own feeling of depression
•L 215 ❖ L 10 Nov 48

Introspection: Contemplation and enjoyment of our inner activities are incompatible; you cannot hope and think about hoping at the same moment
•SJ 217-219 (*see also* GID 65-66; L 221)
❖ SJ 14:9, 10 (*see also* GID I 5:8; L 27 Sep 49)

Introspection: God wants to turn man's attention away from self to Him, and to one's neighbors; even of his sins God does not want a man to think too much*
•SL 63-66 ❖ SL 14:3-5

Introspection: "I had proved that there was a fully conscious 'I' whose connections with the 'me' of introspection were loose and transitory"
•SJ 197-198 ❖ SJ 13:1

Introspection: "I suspect that, save by God's direct miracle, spiritual experience can never abide introspection"
•WG 65-66 ❖ WG 4:18

Introspection is of no use at all in deciding which of two experiences is a substitute and which is the real thing (re: religion as reality or substitute)
•CR 40 ❖ CR 3:8

Introspection is productive in recognizing spiritually negative states like fear as states of your own mind, but destructive in positive states (like devotion or charity)*
•SL 29-30 ❖ SL 6:3

Introspection: Looking for improvement in yourself puts you on the wrong track
•MC 128 ❖ MC III 12:5

Introspection: One of the results of my Theistic conversion was a marked decrease in the fussy attentiveness which I had so long paid to my own mind
•SJ 232-233 ❖ SJ 15:5

Introspection: Screwtape advises trying to turn humans' attention inward, on themselves, and away from God
•SL 20-21 (*see also* SL 16, 29-30, 65-66)
❖ SL 4:3 (*see also* SL 3:2; 6:3; 14:5)

Introspection: Screwtape points out that God does not want a person to think too much of his sins; the sooner the man turns his attention outward, the better*
•SL 66 (*see also* LM 33)
❖ SL 14:5 (*see also* LM 6:13)

Introspection seldom reveals our most obvious defects; humans tend toward a horror and neglect of the obvious
•SL 16 (*see also* GID 121-124, 153)
❖ SL 3:2 (*see also* GID I 14:4-10; 18:6, 7)

Introspection, such as the reflection "My feelings are now growing more devout," fixes one's attention on self and away from God
•SL 30 ❖ SL 6:3

Introspection: "The attempt to discover by introspective analysis our own spiri-

tual condition...may be the quickest road to presumption or despair"
•WG 66 ❖ WG 4:18

Introspection: "The unfinished picture would so like to jump off the easel and have a look at itself"
•LM 34 (consider also God as Painter) ❖ LM 6:16 (consider also God as Painter)

Introspection: "There is also a merely morbid and fidgety curiosity about one's self—the slop-over from modern psychology—which surely does no good?"*
•LM 34 ❖ LM 6:16

Introspection: We must be aware of our own sinfulness, but a continual poring over the "sink" might breed its own perverse pride*
•LM 98-99 ❖ LM 18:13-15

Intuition (self-evident truth) defined as that which "no good man has ever dreamed of doubting"
•WG 38 (see also WG 37, 39, 41) ❖ WG 3:9 (see also WG 3:7, 11, 15)

Intuition, you cannot produce rational, by argument because argument depends upon rational intuition
•WG 35 (see also CR 75*) ❖ WG 3:4 (see also CR 75*)

Intuitions, basic, which cannot be argued about: ultimate preference of the will for love rather than hatred, and happiness rather than misery
•WG 37 ❖ WG 3:7

Invasion, The (chapter title)
•MC 46-51 ❖ MC II ch. 2

Inventor, God is our
•MC 173 (see also Body, human) ❖ MC IV 9:7 (see also Body, human)

Inventors: "We—even our poets and musicians and inventors—never, in the ultimate sense, make. We only build. We always have materials to build from"
•LM 73 (see also Creativity) ❖ LM 14:3 (see also Creativity)

Invocation of Saints—consider also Devotions to Saints

Invocation of saints: "I accept the author-

ity of the Benedicite for the propriety of invoking...saints" [as opposed to devotions to saints]
•GID 334 ❖ GID IV Letter 7

Ireland (Belfast), scenery of, described
•SJ 7, 11, 152-156 ❖ SJ 1:4, 9; 10:4-8

Ireland (Donegal): "All the mountains look like mountains in a story, and there are wooded valleys, and golden sands, and the smell of peat..."
•LAL 32 (see also LAL 45) ❖ LAL Sep 19/54 (see also LAL 5/10/55)

Ireland, fairies are still believed in many parts of, and greatly feared
•LAL 33 (see also L 234) ❖ LAL Oct 9th 54 (see also L undated letter between 12 Sep 51 and 3 Dec 51)

Ireland, I have [recently] been in really quiet and unearthly spots in my native
•L 234 ❖ L undated letter between 12 Sep 51 and 3 Dec 51

Irish, when you want to be typically, you try to be very witty and dashing and fanciful
•L 133 ❖ L undated letter postmarked 13 Apr 29

Islam as the greatest of the attempts to minimalize religion; is a simplification of Jewish and Christian traditions
•GID 139 ❖ GID I 16:20

Islam is only a Christian heresy, and a simplification inferior to the thing simplified
•CR 71 ❖ CR 5:26

Islam is the greatest of the Christian heresies; not real Paganism
•GID 102 ❖ GID I 10:49

Islam: "Mahometans" mentioned with regard to the doctrine of Hell
•PP 119 ❖ PP 8:3

Islam: Mohammed never claimed to be God or the Son of God; there is no parallel to Jesus in other religions
•GID 157-158 ❖ GID I 19:3

Islam ("Mohammedanism") mentioned with reference to teetotalism
•MC 75 ❖ MC III 2:5

Islam ("Mohammedanism"), miraculous elements of, not essential to that reli-

gion (vs. Christianity, where one Grand Miracle is the whole point)
•GID 80; M 68 ❖ GID I 9:1; M 10:1

Islamic writings, passage from, quoted: "The heaven and earth and all between, thinkest thou I made them in jest?"
•GID 182 ❖ GID I 22:13

Isolation, Christian view regarding
•WG 106-120 (*consider also* Independence) ❖ WG ch. 7 (*consider also* Independence)

Isolation, opposite error of, is collectivism
•WG 108 ❖ WG 7:3

Israel—*see also* Jew(s); Judaism; Hebrews

Israel, People of, obtain burden as well as blessing
•GID 84-85; M 116, 118
❖ GID I 9:7, 8; M 14:15, 18

Jargon—*see also* Expressions

Jargon mentioned by Screwtape as more effective than argument in keeping people from the Church
•SL 7-8 (*see also* SL 43)
❖ SL 1:1 (*see also* SL 9:4)

Jargon of our own circle, we must be on guard against using; it may delude ourselves as well as mystify outsiders
•GID 256-257 ❖ GID II 15:11-13

Jargon used in Christianity: Retain what is helpful to you and leave alone what is not*
•MC 157 ❖ MC IV 5:9

Jargon used in Christianity which is related to the idea of "being born again"
•MC 163-164 ❖ MC IV 7:10, 11

Jealous people, how to deal with
•LAL 44 ❖ LAL 21/6/55

Jealousy—*see also* Envy

Jealousy a characteristic of affection without charity
•GID 285 ❖ GID III 3:7

Jealousy as a factor in women who try to break up their husbands' Friendships
•FL 110 ❖ FL 4:36

Jealousy, God as the ultimate object of human, (that beauty which may at any moment steal from me a loved one's heart)
•FL 61 (*see also* FL 70-73; L 274; SL 18)
❖ FL 3:13 (*see also* FL 3:27-32; L 10 Feb 57; SL 3:6)

Jealousy: Human affection cannot stand seeing the beloved passing into a

sphere where it cannot follow
•L 274 ❖ L 10 Feb 57

Jealousy of Affection is closely connected with its reliance on what is old and familiar; change is a threat to Affection
•FL 70-73 (see also L 274)
❖ FL 3:27-32 (see also L 10 Feb 57)

Jealousy of Affection will probably be expressed by ridicule
•FL 71 ❖ FL 3:28

Jealousy, poisonous nature of indulged, no matter how just the cause
•L 219 ❖ L 2 Sep 49

Jealousy, Screwtape mentions the maternal, which may be felt when a son develops a new interest (such as religion)
•SL 18 (see also FL 61, 70-73)
❖ SL 3:6 (see also FL 3:13, 27-32)

Jerome (St. Jerome) on "culture"
•CR 16 ❖ CR 2:13

Jerome (St. Jerome) said that Moses described Creation "after the manner of a popular poet" (which is to say, mythically)
•RP 109 ❖ RP 11:2

Jerusalem, any road out of, must also be a road into Jerusalem (re: possible value of "sub-Christian" literature)
•CR 22 (see also L 297) ❖ CR 2:29 (see also L undated letter of Feb 61)

Jerusalem, since we must rest and play where can we do so better than here—in the suburbs of, (re: value of culture)
•CR 24 ❖ CR 2:37

Jerusalem, we would be at
•SJ 238 ❖ SJ 15:10

Jesus—see also Christ

Jesus: Although He is the "begotten Son of God" there was never a time before the Father produced the Son
•MC 138, 150 ❖ MC IV 1:11-13; 4:1-5

Jesus and modern scholarship: "No net less wide than a man's whole heart, nor less fine of mesh than love, will hold the sacred Fish"
•RP 119 ❖ RP 11:15

Jesus: appalling nature of His theological

remarks
•GID 156-157; MC 54-55
❖ GID I 19:2; MC II 3:10-12

Jesus appropriated to Himself many prophecies in the Old Testament; this helps to show that Bible passages can and do have multiple meanings
•RP 117-119, 120 ❖ RP 11:14, 15; 12:1

Jesus as God and man, discussion of
•L 210 ❖ L undated letter of 1947

Jesus as God and man not fully conceivable to us, but then neither can we conceive how the spirit of any man dwells within his natural organism
•M 110-111 ❖ M 14:4

Jesus as "lit by a light from beyond the world"
•SJ 236 ❖ SJ 15:7

Jesus as Man: "Can it be that the more perfect the creature is, the further this separation [from the Father] must at some point be pushed?"
•LM 44 ❖ LM 8:12

Jesus as Man, in Gethsemane, experienced the very human torments of hope—suspense and anxiety
•LM 42 ❖ LM 8:6

Jesus as Man: "Is it that God Himself cannot be Man unless God seems to vanish at His greatest need?"
•LM 43-44 ❖ LM 8:10-12

Jesus as our model—the Jesus "not only of Calvary, but of the workshop, the roads, the crowds..."
•FL 17 ❖ FL 1:12

Jesus as the "begotten" Son of God: "What God begets is God; just as what man begets is man"
•MC 138, 150 ❖ MC IV 1:11-13; 4:2

Jesus as the begotten Son of God
•MC 137-140, 150 ❖ MC IV 1:8-16; 4:2

Jesus as the begotten Son of God: Could there have been many sons begotten by God, as Jesus was?
•MC 157-159 ❖ MC IV 6:2

Jesus as the Lord who, despite His transcendence, is "not far from any one of us"—an utterly concrete Being whom Man can fear, love, address, and "taste"*

•RP 87 ❖ RP 8:17

Jesus as "a man born among the Jews who claimed to be...the Something which is at once the awful haunter of nature and the giver of the moral law"
•PP 23 ❖ PP 1:14

Jesus as "the pure light" who walked the earth
•LM 71 (see also MC 151; SJ 236; Light)
❖ LM 13:10 (see also SJ 15:7; MC IV 4:4; Light)

Jesus as the self-expression of the Father—what the Father has to say: There was never a time when He was not saying it
•MC 151 ❖ MC IV 4:4

Jesus becoming a man likened to a man becoming a slug or crab
•MC 155 ❖ MC IV 5:4

Jesus, belief in a "historical," promoted by Screwtape since such a construct cannot in fact be worshipped ("...first we make Him solely a teacher...")
•SL 106-108 ❖ SL 23:3, 4

Jesus can be known only through a personal experience of Him in our lives*
•GID 170 (see also M 89-90; MC 135-136) ❖ GID I 20:Reply-15 (see also M 11:14; MC IV 1:2, 3)

Jesus' childhood, we may suspect, contained both gentleness and a certain astringency
•RP 6 ❖ RP 1:9

Jesus Christ as the "Son" of God
•MC 135-140, 150-151
❖ MC IV ch. 1; 4:2, 3

Jesus Christ as the Son of God: "Christians believe that Jesus Christ is the Son of God because He said so"
•CR 137 ❖ CR 11:18

Jesus Christ is "the only original Son of God, through whom others are enabled 'to become sons of God'"
•GID 178 ❖ GID I 22:3

"Jesus Christ is the Son of God" is a poetical statement, conveying information which is much more than analogical (re: language of religion)
•CR 137 ❖ CR 11:18

Jesus Christ, those who have heard the claims of, must come to terms with them—or else be guilty of inattention or evading the question
•GID 265 ❖ GID II 16:50

Jesus Christ, What Are We to Make of? (chapter title)
•GID 156-160 ❖ GID I ch. 19

Jesus: Christians think the main thing He came to earth to do was to suffer and be killed
•MC 56-57 ❖ MC II 4:2

Jesus claimed to have power to forgive sins; this claim would be preposterous unless He was God
•MC 55 (see also GID 157, 180)
❖ MC II 3:11 (see also GID I 19:2; 22:9)

Jesus, contrasts within the personality of: peasant shrewdness, intolerable severity, and irresistible tenderness
•CR 156-157 ❖ CR 13:8

Jesus: Death is even more horrible in His eyes than in ours
•GID 149-150 ❖ GID I 17:7

Jesus, early Christians' beliefs about: He is eternally "with God," yet also was God; all things, including Life, arose within Him...
•M 76 ❖ M 10:15

Jesus: Either He was a raving lunatic of an unusually abominable type, or else He was, and is, precisely what He said; there is no middle way
•PP 23-24 ❖ PP 1:14

Jesus: "Either God or a bad man" argument useful in Christian apologetics
•GID 101 ❖ GID I 10:46

Jesus: either God or a lunatic
•WG 91 ❖ WG 5:23

Jesus: either God or a megalomaniac
•GID 157-158 (see also M 109)
❖ GID I 19:3 (see also M 14:2)

Jesus: either God or an arrogant paranoic
•RP 135-136 ❖ RP 12:15

Jesus: either the Son of God or a lunatic or the devil; we cannot say He was merely a great moral teacher
•MC 55-56 (see also CR 137; GID 261-262; L 181)
❖ MC II 3:11-13; 4:1 (see also CR 11:18; GID II 16:23, 24; L 26 Mar 40)

Jesus elicited no mild approval from

people who met Him; He produced mainly three effects—Hatred, Terror, and Adoration
- GID 158 ❖ GID I 19:3

Jesus: "Every good teacher, within Judaism as without, has anticipated Him"; He was not "original" in His teaching
- RP 27 (see also CR 47, 51, 53, 77; MC 78; PP 63; Law of Nature; book *The Abolition of Man*)
  ❖ RP 3:13 (see also CR 4:7, 17, 22; 6:16; MC III 3:1; PP 4:10; Law of Nature; book *The Abolition of Man*)

Jesus ("God") as our true Beloved, whom we have loved all our life
- FL 190-191; PP 147; SL 148
  ❖ FL 6:44, 45; PP 10:3; SL 31:5

Jesus: "God Himself, as man, submitted to man's sense of being abandoned"
- LAL 38 (see also LAL 77; Abandonment) ❖ LAL 20/2/55 (see also LAL Jul 21st 58; Abandonment)

Jesus: "'He came down from Heaven' can almost be transposed into 'Heaven drew earth up into it'"
- LM 70-71 ❖ LM 13:10

Jesus: His "advantage" of being God as well as Man is the only reason He can help us (drowning swimmer analogy)
- L 234-235; MC 61
  ❖ L undated letter between 12 Sep 51 and 3 Dec 51; MC II 4:10

Jesus' humanity included the possibility of ignorance (as in not knowing the day and hour of His return; also, His question, "Who touched Me?" was real)
- WLN 99-100 ❖ WLN 7:10, 11

Jesus: I was told that in the Gospels I would find a figure whom I couldn't help loving; well, I could
- L 181 ❖ L 26 Mar 40

Jesus identified Himself with both the sufferer and the king, the two figures that meet us in the Psalms
- RP 120-121 ❖ RP 12:2

Jesus: "If anything is common to all believers, and even to many unbelievers, it is the sense that in the Gospel they have met a personality"

- CR 156 ❖ CR 13:8

Jesus: "If you do not at all know God, of course you will not recognize Him, either in Jesus or in outer space"
- CR 172 ❖ CR 14:35

Jesus: "...in becoming Man, He bowed His neck beneath the sweet yoke of heredity and environment"
- RP 5-6 ❖ RP 1:9

Jesus in Gethsemane "chose on that night to plumb the depths of Christian experience, to resemble not the heroes of His army but the very weakest..."
- CR 150 (see also Gethsemane)
  ❖ CR 12:25 (see also Gethsemane)

Jesus, in Gethsemane, descends into the humiliation of praying on His own behalf (but when He does, certitude about His Father's will is apparently withdrawn)
- LM 61 ❖ LM 11:14

Jesus incarnate: I have thought that the human and divine natures together made one Person—that there was a human *soul* involved
- L 200-201 (see also L 210) ❖ L 29 Jul 42 (see also L undated letter of 1947)

Jesus, incarnation of—see Incarnation

Jesus: It is clear that the knowledge of His death must somehow have been withdrawn from Him before He prayed in Gethsemane
- LM 42 ❖ LM 8:6

Jesus: Lewis mentions his belief that the Son (as God) is subject to the Father
- L 198 ❖ L 21 Dec 41

Jesus, life of: Materials for a full biography have been withheld from men; few people are converted by studying Jesus' life simply as biography
- SL 108 ❖ SL 23:3

Jesus, life of, not an episode in the life of God; He was born, He died, and was raised from all eternity
- WLN 99-100 ❖ WLN 7:11

Jesus, men can read the life of, as nothing but a human life (because it is a human life)
- RP 116 ❖ RP 11:12

Jesus' mind and language were clearly

steeped in the Psalter and the Old Testament; He very seldom introduced a novelty
- •RP 22, 26-27 (*see also* CR 121)
- ❖ RP 3:4, 13 (*see also* CR 10:15)

Jesus' mode of consciousness not fully comprehensible to us, but then neither is the actual mechanism of *man's* consciousness
- •M 110-111 ❖ M 14:4

Jesus: Much about His earthly life cannot be imagined (e.g., His unconsciousness in sleep, the twilight of reason in His infancy, etc.)
- •WLN 99 ❖ WLN 7:10

Jesus not a man of iron nerves; did not feel very brave in Gethsemane
- •L 250 (*see also* L 166, 189, 210-211, 285; Gethsemane) ❖ L 17 Jul 53 (*see also* L 8 May 39; undated letter just after 11 Aug 40; undated letter of 1947; 29 Apr 59; Gethsemane)

Jesus not just a great moral teacher
- •MC 137 (*see also* SL 106-108)
- ❖ MC IV 1:6-8 (*see also* SL 23:3)

Jesus, omniscience of: How the omniscience of God was affected by His becoming a man
- •MC 147-148 (*see also* PP 134)
- ❖ MC IV 3:10 (*see also* PP 9:6)

Jesus, omniscience of: "The answer of the theologians is that the God-Man was omniscient as God, and ignorant as Man"
- •WLN 99 ❖ WLN 7:10

Jesus: One sees so very little of Him in ordinary situations; difficult to see His "moral perfection"
- •L 181 ❖ L 26 Mar 40

Jesus, predictions of, seen as being in a class with other apocalyptic writings, which to most modern tastes appear tedious and unedifying
- •WLN 95 ❖ WLN 7:5

Jesus: Regarding Bultmann's strange claim that no personality of Our Lord is presented in the New Testament
- •CR 156-157 ❖ CR 13:7, 8

Jesus, regarding the claim that the real teaching of, was misunderstood by

His early followers and has been recovered only by modern scholars
- •CR 157-158 ❖ CR 13:10

Jesus' sayings addressed not to our intellectual curiosity but to our conscience and our will (e.g., Dominical utterances regarding Hell)
- •PP 119 (*see also* L 169-170)
- ❖ PP 8:2 (*see also* L 5 Nov 39)

Jesus, sayings of, as they relate to Pacifism
- •WG 48-51 ❖ WG 3:26-29

Jesus, sayings of: Do even pious people, in their reverence for the more radiantly divine element, sometimes attend too little to their sheer common sense?
- •LAL 103 ❖ LAL 4 May 62

Jesus, sayings of, must be taken in the sense they would naturally have borne in the time and place of utterance
- •WG 50-51 ❖ WG 3:29

Jesus, sayings of: "The hard sayings of Our Lord are wholesome to those only who find them hard"
- •GID 191-192 (*see also* GID 182*; RP 131-132) ❖ GID II 1:4 (*see also* GID I 22:13*; RP 12:10)

Jesus, sayings of: Three ways to take the command to turn the other cheek
- •WG 49-51 ❖ WG 3:28, 29

Jesus, sayings of, which are hard: If we take one literally, we must take them all literally (re: Pacifism)
- •WG 48-49 ❖ WG 3:27

Jesus, sayings of, which are very different from what any other teacher has said, listed
- •GID 157, 160 ❖ GID I 19:2, 9

Jesus shared the suffering not only of the righteous but of the guilty—that which comes to evil men who at last know their own evil
- •RP 127 (*consider also* Self-knowledge)
- ❖ RP 12:7 (*consider also* Self-knowledge)

Jesus' sonship to God the solid reality; biological sonship merely a diagrammatic representation of that
- •M 91 ❖ M 11:15

Jesus, teaching of: Depth and sanity of His moral teaching almost generally admitted
- GID 156; M 109 (*see also* MC 55-56*)
- ❖ GID I 19:1; M 14:2 (*see also* MC II 3:12, 13*)

Jesus, teaching of, not given us in that cut-and-dried, fool-proof, systematic fashion we might have expected or desired
- RP 112-113 ❖ RP 11:7

Jesus, teaching of: "Our Lord's replies are never straight answers and never gratify curiosity"
- L 169-170 (*see also* PP 119)
- ❖ L 5 Nov 39 (*see also* PP 8:2)

Jesus, teaching of: "Taken by a literalist, He will always prove the most elusive of teachers"
- RP 119 ❖ RP 11:15

Jesus, teaching of: "...there is no question of learning a subject but of steeping ourselves in a Personality..."
- RP 113-114 ❖ RP 11:9

Jesus, teaching of: We must be cautious to assume that any circumstance in the culture of first-century Palestine was a hampering or distorting influence
- WLN 97 ❖ WLN 7:7

Jesus: The first real work of the Gospels is to raise the question, "Who or What is this?"
- L 181 (*see also* GID 156-158; WG 91; MC 54-56) ❖ L 26 Mar 40 (*see also* GID I 19:1-3; WG 5:23; MC II 3:10-13)

Jesus: "There have been too many historical Jesuses—a liberal Jesus, a pneumatic Jesus, a Barthian Jesus..." (re: exegesis of dominical utterances)
- WG 51 ❖ WG 3:29

Jesus, there is no parallel to, in other religions; Buddha and Mohammed never claimed to be God or the Son of God
- GID 157-158 ❖ GID I 19:3

Jesus: "To God, God's last words are 'Why hast thou forsaken me?'"
- LM 43 ❖ LM 8:10

Jesus: Trying to grasp His teaching by intellect alone like trying to bottle a sunbeam; it demands a response from the whole man

- RP 113-114 ❖ RP 11:7, 9

Jesus: Unless He really is what He says He is, He is not lovable or even tolerable
- L 181 (*see also* GID 156-158; WG 91; MC 54-56) ❖ L 26 Mar 40 (*see also* GID I 19: 2, 3; WG 5:23; MC II 3:10-13)

Jesus uttered few commands which cannot be paralleled in classical, ancient Egyptian, Ninevite, Babylonian, or Chinese texts
- CR 47, 51, 52-53, 77 (*see also* MC 19, 78; PP 63; RP 27; book *The Abolition of Man*) ❖ CR 4:7, 17, 20-22; 6:16 (*see also* MC I 1:7; III 3:1; PP 4:10; RP 3:13; book *The Abolition of Man*)

Jesus was different from other teachers; said "I am the Truth, and the Way, and the Life"...
- GID 160 ❖ GID I 19:9

Jesus "was not at all like the psychologist's picture of the integrated, balanced, adjusted, happily married, employed popular citizen"
- FL 81 ❖ FL 3:43

Jesus: We are not invited to pass any moral judgement on Him, however favorable
- L 181 (*consider also* God on trial)
- ❖ L 26 Mar 40 (*consider also* God on trial)

Jesus: Weariness, frustration, pain, doubt, and death "are, from before all worlds, known by God from within"
- LM 70-71 ❖ LM 13:10

Jesus: "When God becomes man, that Man, of all others, is least comforted by God, at His greatest need. There is a mystery here..."
- WLN 10-11 ❖ WLN 1:21

Jesus: Who He said He was
- GID 157; MC 54-55 (*see also* GID 180) ❖ GID I 19:2; MC II 3:10 (*see also* GID I 22:9)

Jesus' words to His Mother better understood if we realize that the iron element in His nature likely came from her
- CR 121 (*see also* RP 6) ❖ CR 10:14 (*see also* RP 1:9)

Jesus, you can't regard the earthly life of,

as an episode in the eternal life of the Son
•L 191
❖ L undated letter just after 11 Aug 40

Jew(s)—*see also;* Hebrew(s); Judaism; *consider also* Psalmist(s)

Jew, for the ancient, the enjoyment of the Temple festivals combined many elements into his "love of God"—social pleasure, anticipation of rest, etc.
•RP 46-47 ❖ RP 5:5

Jew, for us the very name, is associated with finance, shopkeeping, moneylending, etc.; but the ancient Jews were peasants or farmers
•RP 76, 83 ❖ RP 8:2, 13

Jews, a special illumination was vouchsafed to the, and then to the Christians; but there is also some divine light given to all men
•WG 83 ❖ WG 5:15

Jews, century after century it was hammered into the, that earthly prosperity is not the reward of seeing God
•RP 43 ❖ RP 4:19

Jews: "Chosen people" not chosen for their own sake but for the sake of the unchosen
•M 118 (*see also* GID 84-85)
❖ M 14:18 (*see also* GID I 9:7, 8)

Jews: God "selected one particular people and spent several centuries hammering into their heads the sort of God He was..."
•MC 54 ❖ MC II 3:9

Jews' ("Hebrews'") claim to be the "Chosen" people is strong
•CR 116-117 ❖ CR 10:4-6

Jews: It is an admirable thing that the sacred literature should have been entrusted to a people whose poetry should remain poetry in any language
•L 188 ❖ L 16 Jul 40

Jews, it was the, who fully identified the awful Presence haunting mountaintops with the Lord who "loveth righteousness" (identified Law with Lawgiver)
•PP 23 ❖ PP 1:13

Jews: I've been much struck in conversation with a Jewess by the extent to which Jews see humour in the O.T. where we don't
•L 272 ❖ L 6 Dec 56

Jews, Jesus' followers were all; if the story of Jesus were a legend, it would be very odd for it to grow up among the most monotheistic people in the world
•GID 158 ❖ GID I 19:4

Jews mentioned with reference to "the Gestapo" and forgiveness
•MC 104 ❖ MC III 7:2

Jews: "...my wife, who is a Jewess by blood, holds two views which will interest you..."
•L 285-286 ❖ L 30 Apr 59

Jews, our own religion begins among the, a people familiar with pain and suffering
•PP 16 ❖ PP 1:3

Jews under the Germans mentioned as example of what happens when rulers become owners and certain differences are considered "diseases" which must be "cured"
•GID 313 ❖ GID III 8:7-9

Jews: We as Christians believe that God chose that race for the vehicle of His own Incarnation, and are indebted to Israel beyond all possibility of repayment
•RP 28 ❖ RP 3:15

Jews: We Gentile Christians need to be reminded that the Hebrews are spiritually *senior* to us
•L 263 (*see also* CR 116*)
❖ L 14 May 55 (*see also* CR 10:3*)

Jews were no sailors—therefore all islands were remote (re: Psalm 97:1)
•RP 52 (*see also* RP 84)
❖ RP 5:9 (*see also* RP 8:13)

Jews were not, like the Greeks, an analytical and logical people; indeed, except the Greeks, no ancient peoples were
•RP 46 ❖ RP 5:5

Jews, while the temple was still standing, must have felt that their sacrificial service was the reality and the Christian one a mere substitute
•CR 37 ❖ CR 3:1

Jewish convert tends to stress Christ as king and conqueror; Gentile more likely to start from the priestly sacrificial and intercessory role
•RP 124 ❖ RP 12:5

Jewish, Moslem, and Christian view of the universe is that there is something beyond Nature which refutes the scientists' picture of futility
•CR 59 ❖ CR 5:5

Jewish nation and Mary the mother of Jesus as example of God's undemocratic way of working—His selectiveness
•GID 84-85; M 116 ❖ GID I 9:7; M 14:15

Jewish people obtained burden as well as blessing by being "chosen"
•GID 84-85; M 116, 118
❖ GID I 9:7, 8; M 14:15, 18

Jewish people themselves seem to shrink from the ancient rituals; they have not rebuilt the Temple nor revived the sacrifices
•RP 45 ❖ RP 5:2

Jewish people, why God did not teach the, early about immortality
•RP 39-42 (see also GID 130-131; SJ 231)
❖ RP 4:12-16 (see also GID I 16:2, 3; SJ 15:3)

Jewish religion, Christianity primarily the fulfillment of, but also the fulfillment of what was vaguely hinted at in all religions at their best
•GID 54 (see also Death and Rebirth pattern; Paganism)
❖ GID I 4:27 (Ques. 8) (see also Death and Rebirth pattern; Paganism)

Jewish rituals, we would not have enjoyed the ancient; every temple in the world (Parthenon and Temple at Jerusalem) was a sacred slaughterhouse
•RP 44-45 ❖ RP 5:2

Jewish vs. Christian attitude in the face of judgement: Psalmists exhibit Jewish confidence; the Christian trembles because he knows he is a sinner
•CR 122-125, esp. 125
❖ CR 10:22-30, esp. 10:29, 30

Jewish vs. Christian picture of Judge-

ment: One cries to God for justice instead of injustice; the other cries to God for mercy instead of justice
•RP 9-19, esp. 10-12
❖ RP ch. 2, esp. 2:3-6

Joad, C.E.M.
•GID 21, 22, 23 ❖ GID I 1:1, 2, 7

Joad, C.E.M., inquiry by, regarding Lewis's chapter on animal pain—and Lewis's answer
•GID 161-171 ❖ GID I ch. 20

Job and Jonah, Books of, described as having few even pretended historical attachments (re: Biblical criticism)
•CR 154 ❖ CR 13:5

Job, Book of: Calvin doubted whether the story of Job were history or fiction
•RP 109 ❖ RP 11:2

Job, Book of, clearly establishes that suffering is not *always* sent as punishment (that it sometimes is, is suggested by parts of Old Testament and Revelation)
•L 237 ❖ L 31 Jan 52

Job, Book of: Lesson taught in this book (that earthly prosperity is not the probable reward of seeing God) was grimly illustrated to the Jews
•RP 43 ❖ RP 4:19

Job, Book of: "No explanation of the problem of unjust suffering is there given: that is not the point of the poem"
•CR 70 ❖ CR 5:25

Job, Book of: Story of Job may be unhistorical, as are the parables
•L 286 (see also Bible—historicity)
❖ L 7 May 59 (see also Bible—historicity)

Job, Book of: Temptation to worship Nature seen in Job 31:26-28
•RP 80-81 ❖ RP 8:8

Job, Book of: Whole point of it is that the man who criticizes divine justice by the ordinary standard of good receives the divine approval
•CR 70 ❖ CR 5:25

Job, Book of: Why it appears to me unhistorical (unconnected with all history, no genealogy, etc.)
•RP 109-110 (see also RP 122)

❖ RP 11:2 (*see also* RP 12:4)

Job(s)—*see also* Vocation; Work

Job choice: We must try to earn our living by doing well what would be worth doing even if we had not our living to earn
 •WLN 78 (*see also* MC 80)
 ❖ WLN 5:16 (*see also* MC III 3:4)

Job satisfaction: "What a difference it makes to work with nice people and to do work that you can believe in"
 •LAL 51 ❖ LAL 8/2/56

Job, when we begin a new, we have the discharge of the vocation as our end; by the third week we have our own personal goals in mind
 •PP 75-76 ❖ PP 5:5

Job, witnessing on one's: A Christian should not take money for supplying one thing and use the opportunity to supply a quite different thing*
 •CR 21 ❖ CR 2:25

Job, witnessing on one's: The mere presence of Christians in the ranks will inevitably provide an antidote*
 •CR 21 ❖ CR 2:25

Job-hunting, even in youth, is a heartbreaking affair...
 •LAL 20 ❖ LAL Aug 10th 53

Jobs, it is usually the insane, that lead to big money; they are often also the least laborious
 •WLN 78 ❖ WLN 5:16

Jobs, the neglect of doing good work in our, not according to Biblical precept
 •WLN 71 ❖ WLN 5:1

John, Book of: Either this is reportage pretty close to the facts, or some writers suddenly anticipated the whole technique of modern narrative
 •CR 155 ❖ CR 13:5

John, Book of: I have been reading poems, romances, legends, and myths all my life; I know that not one of them is like this
 •CR 154-155 ❖ CR 13:5

John, historicity of the Gospel of
 •CR 154-155; GID 158-159, 179-180
 ❖ CR 13:5; GID I 19:5; 22:8, 9

John the Baptist, circumstances regarding the birth of, discussed
 •GID 328 ❖ GID IV Letter 3

Johnson, I quite agree about; if one had not experienced it, it wd. be hard to understand how a dead man out of a book can almost be a member of one's family
 •L 173 ❖ L 18 Dec 39

Johnson, personality of Boswell's: That union "of profound gravity and melancholy with that love of fun and nonsense which Boswell never understood..."
 •CR 156 ❖ CR 13:8

Johnson, quote from [Samuel]: "Marriage is not otherwise unhappy than as life is unhappy"
 •L 128 ❖ L 2 Aug 28

Johnson, quote from [Samuel]: "People need to be reminded more often than they need to be instructed" (re: Morality)
 •L 128; MC 78
 ❖ L 2 Aug 28; MC III 3:1

Johnson, quote from [Samuel]: "The natural process of the mind is not from enjoyment to enjoyment but from hope to hope"
 •L 128 ❖ L 2 Aug 28

Johnson, quote from [Samuel]: "To be happy at home is the end of all human endeavour"
 •L 262; WG 108-109
 ❖ L 16 Mar 55; WG 7:4

Joke, it is frustrating to hear a good, and find no one to share it with (the perfect hearer died a year ago)
 •RP 95 (*see also* LAL 82)
 ❖ RP 9:6 (*see also* LAL May 19th 59)

Joke, the fact that we have bodies is the oldest, there is (re: Eros and sexual love)
 •FL 143 ❖ FL 5:20

Jokes—*see also* Bawdy; Humor

Jokes about death point to the fact that we find our own animality either objectionable or funny ("spirit" and "organism" not at home together)
 •M 127 ❖ M 14:32

Jokes about sex a symptom of our es-

trangement, as spirits, from Nature and as animals, from Spirit*
•M 160 ❖ M 16:29

Jokes about sex embody an attitude which endangers the Christian life far less than reverential gravity
•FL 140 ❖ FL 5:15

Jokes, according to Screwtape, "turn on sudden perception of incongruity" and are a promising field for temptation
•SL 50 ❖ SL 11:4

Jokes: Bawdy ought to be outrageous and extravagant; must have nothing cruel about it, and must not approach anywhere near the pornographic
•L 146 ❖ L 25 Dec 31

Jokes, it is one of God's, that a passion so soaring as Eros should be linked with an appetite connected like all appetites with mundane factors like...
•FL 142 ❖ FL 5:18

Jokes, one classifies, according to the person one wants to tell them to
•L 132
❖ L undated letter postmarked 13 Apr 29

Jokes: Screwtape outlines the usefulness and limitations of bawdy humour to his purposes
•SL 50-51 ❖ SL 11:4

Jonah, Book of, described as having few historical attachments, grotesque in incident, and not without a distinct, though edifying, vein of Jewish humour
•CR 154-155 ❖ CR 13:5

Jonah, story of, may be unhistorical, as are the parables
•L 286 (see also M 133-134, ftnt.)
❖ L 7 May 59 (see also M 15:2—ftnt.)

Joseph in Potiphar's house, thoughts regarding the story of, (e.g., "Why was Joseph imprisoned and not killed?")
•L 178 ❖ L 25 Feb 40

Joseph's reaction to the Virgin Birth shows that early Christians perceived miracles as being contrary to Nature
•GID 26, 72-73, 100; M 46-47
❖ GID I 2:2; 7:1-10; 10:43; M 7:5

Journalists mentioned who neither know

nor care what words mean
•GID 309 ❖ GID III 7:11

Journalists: That they can be saved "is a doctrine, if not contrary to, yet certainly above, reason" (re: their misuse of the word "Pagan")
•LAL 62 ❖ LAL Sep 8/56

"Journey homeward to habitual self," what we feel then has been well described by Keats as the, (re: our spiritual longings)
•WG 14 ❖ WG 1:11

"Journey homeward to habitual self," or the gravitation away from God, must be a product of the Fall
•PP 76 (see also PP 83, 91)
❖ PP 5:5 (see also PP 5:10; 6:3)

Journey (of life), our Father refreshes us on the, with some pleasant inns, but will not encourage us to mistake them for home (re: doctrine of suffering)
•PP 115 ❖ PP 7:7

Joy (Lewis's wife), death of
•L 293; LAL 91
❖ L 15 Jun 60; LAL 15 Jul 60

Joy (Lewis's wife) described as being like a sword
•GO 72-73 (see also GO 49)
❖ GO 4:6-9 (see also GO 3:15)

Joy (Lewis's wife) described as being like a garden "...more secret, more full of fragrant and fertile life, the further you entered"
•GO 73 ❖ GO 4:6

Joy (Lewis's wife): "For those few years H. [Joy] and I feasted on love; every mode of it—solemn and merry, romantic and realistic..."
•GO 6 ❖ GO 1:12

Joy (Lewis's wife): "Happiness had not come to her early in life. A thousand years of it would not have made her blasée"
•GO 18 ❖ GO 2:1

Joy (Lewis's wife); "Her mind was lithe and quick and muscular as a leopard... How many bubbles of mine she pricked!"
•GO 3 ❖ GO 1:5

Joy (Lewis's wife): Her remission of can-

cer after prayer mentioned
- •LAL 81, 82, 88 (see also LAL 67; WLN 3-4*)
- ❖ LAL Jan 26th 59; 6/5/59; 18 Oct 59 (see also LAL Jun 18th 57; WLN 1:3*)

Joy (Lewis's wife): "...I once praised her for her 'masculine virtues'...there was something of the Amazon..."
- •GO 56 ❖ GO 3:29

Joy (Lewis's wife): "If we had never fallen in love we should have none the less always been together, and created a scandal"
- •GO 56 ❖ GO 3:29

Joy (Lewis's wife), letter from, to an American lady
- •LAL 75-76 ❖ LAL Jun 6th [1958]

Joy (Lewis's wife): Lewis describes an experience of what seemed like her presence after her death
- •GO 85-87 ❖ GO 4:33-35

Joy (Lewis's wife) mentioned
- •LAL 67-71, 73, 74, 77-83, 85, 87-93, 103, 105, 106, 115
- ❖ LAL Jun 18th 57-22/2/58; 31/3/58; 15/4/58; Jul 21st 58-Jun 7th 59; Jul 7th 59; 21 Aug 59-28 Oct 60; 4 May 62; 3/7/62; 31/7/62; 19 Mar 63

Joy (Lewis's wife), possible reference to, whose prayer for recovery from cancer was seemingly answered
- •WLN 3-4 (see also GO 34-35; LAL 67, 81) ❖ WLN 1:3 (see also GO 2:25; LAL Jun 18th 57; Jan 26th 59)

Joy (Lewis's wife), probable reference to the illness of
- •LAL 63 ❖ LAL 20 Oct 56

Joy (Lewis's wife), reference to
- •L 272, 275-280, 285, 293, 298, 300, 301
- ❖ L 14 Nov 56; 6 Mar 57 through 6 Nov 57; 30 Apr 59; 15 Jun 60; 9 May 61; 3 Dec 61; 20 Dec 61

Joy (Lewis's wife), reference to: "...I may soon be, in rapid succession, a bridegroom and a widower"
- •LAL 63, 64
- ❖ LAL Nov 16/56; Dec 12th 56

Joy (Lewis's wife), reference to: "I have married a lady suffering from cancer"
- •LAL 65 ❖ LAL 17/1/57

Joy (Lewis's wife), reference to: "My wife is now home, bed-ridden, and dying"
- •LAL 66 ❖ LAL 13th Apr 57

Joy (Lewis's wife), reference to: "There is no great mystery about my marriage. I have known the lady a long time..."
- •LAL 65 ❖ LAL 17/2/57

Joy (Lewis's wife): "She liked more things and liked them more than anyone I have known"
- •GO 18 ❖ GO 2:1

Joy (Lewis's wife): "She was my daughter and my mother, my pupil and my teacher, my subject and my sovereign...my friend, shipmate, fellow-soldier..."
- •GO 55-56 ❖ GO 3:29

Joy (Lewis's wife): She was "My mistress; but at the same time all that any man friend (and I have good ones) has ever been to me. Perhaps more"
- •GO 56 ❖ GO 3:29

Joy (Lewis's wife): "The moments at which I feel nearest to Joy are precisely those when I mourn her least"
- •LAL 92 (see also GO 51-53, 64-65)
- ❖ LAL 24 Sep 60 (see also GO 3:22-24, 41)

Joy—see also Desire; Longing(s); consider also Aesthetic delight; Sehnsucht

Joy, 1st instance of Lewis's experience of, came through the memory of a memory (recalling his brother's toy garden)
- •SJ 7, 16 ❖ SJ 1:4, 15

Joy, 2nd instance of Lewis's experience of, came through the book Squirrel Nutkin by Beatrix Potter
- •SJ 16-17 ❖ SJ 1:16

Joy, 3rd instance of Lewis's experience of, came through Longfellow's Saga of King Olaf
- •SJ 17 ❖ SJ 1:17

Joy: "...a single, unendurable sense of desire and loss, which suddenly became one with the loss of the whole experience..."
- •SJ 73 ❖ SJ 5:4

Joy, a technical term which must be sharply distinguished both from Hap-

piness and from Pleasure
•SJ 18 ❖ SJ 1:18

Joy: "...all images and sensations, if idola-
trously mistaken for Joy itself, soon
honestly confessed themselves inadequate"; they are only reminders
•SJ 220 ❖ SJ 14:11

Joy, all, reminds; it is never a possession,
always a desire for something longer
ago or further away or still "about to be"
•SJ 78 ❖ SJ 5:10

Joy and anguish, physical sensations of,
are exactly the same
•WG 57-59, 63 ❖ WG 4:5-7, 13

Joy: "And at once I knew (with fatal
knowledge) that to 'have it again' was
the supreme and only important object of desire"
•SJ 73 ❖ SJ 5:4

Joy and laughter mentioned by Screwtape
as "a meaningless acceleration in the
rhythm of celestial experience" in
Heaven
•SL 50 ❖ SL 11:2

Joy, Arthur and I both knew the stab of,
and that—for both—the arrow was
shot from the North
•SJ 130 ❖ SJ 8:18

Joy as a desire which owes all its character to its object; the form of the desired is in the desire
•SJ 220 ❖ SJ 14:12

Joy as a state of my own mind never had
the kind of importance I once gave it;
it was valuable only as a pointer or
signpost to something other and outer
•SJ 238 (see also GO 82*)
❖ SJ 15:10 (see also GO 4:27*)

Joy as a thing we look to find described in
books all our life*
•L 270 ❖ L 26 Jun 56

Joy as desire for God and His glory*
•WG 3-19 (see also The Pilgrim's Re-
gress, pp. ix-xiii) ❖ WG ch. 1 (see also
The Pilgrim's Regress, P:13-17)

Joy as desire for Heaven*
•PP 144-150 (see also MC 118-121)
❖ PP 10:1-7 (see also MC III ch. 10)

Joy as desire, yet also fruition
•SJ 166 (see also SJ 17-18*)

❖ SJ 11:3 (see also SJ 1:18*)

Joy (as distinct from mere pleasure, still
more amusement) emphasises our pilgrim status; always reminds, beckons,
awakens desire
•L 289 ❖ L 5 Nov 59

Joy as experienced by Lewis through Wag-
nerian music and Norse and Celtic
mythology
•SJ 71-78, 114 (see also SJ 165-167)
❖ SJ 5:1-11; 7:18 (see also SJ 11:1-5)

Joy as it related (or did not relate) to
Lewis's interest in the Occult during
his youth
•SJ 175-177 (see also SJ 204)
❖ SJ 11:13-15 (see also SJ 13:10)

Joy as met through music*
•WG 7 (see also SL 50)
❖ WG 1:5 (see also SL 11:2)

Joy as met through Nature*
•SJ 77; WG 16-17 (see also The Pilgrim's
Regress, p. ix) ❖ SJ 5:10; WG 1:13, 14
(see also The Pilgrim's Regress, P:13)

Joy as met through various works of lit-
erature*
•GID 203-204 (see also WG 7; The Pil-
grim's Regress, p. ix)
❖ GID II 4:5 (see also WG 1:5; The
Pilgrim's Regress, P:13)

Joy as "the odour which is death to us until
we allow it to become life"*
•GID 203-204 ❖ GID II 4:5

Joy can return as we remember our past
experiences of Joy*
•SJ 73, 166 ❖ SJ 5:4; 11:3

Joy: Considered only in its quality, the sensation might almost equally well be
called a particular kind of unhappiness or grief (but it is a kind we want)
•SJ 18 (see also SL 148*)
❖ SJ 1:18 (see also SL 31:5*)

Joy defined: "...an unsatisfied desire which
is itself more desirable than any other
satisfaction"
•SJ 17-18 ❖ SJ 1:18

Joy described or referred to as a "longing"
•SJ 16, 72, 166, 175, 177, 217; WG 7*,
8*, 14-16*; The Pilgrim's Regress, pp. ix,
xii, xiii ❖ SJ 1:15; 5:2; 11:3, 13, 14; 14:8;
WG 1:5*, 11*, 12*; The Pilgrim's Regress

P:13, 17, 18

Joy, essence of, is expressed by "mere" Christianity*
•GID 203-204 ❖ GID II 4:5

Joy (experience of the "Numinous") originally appears to be a special form of aesthetic experience, until religion comes and retrospectively transforms it*
•GID 174-175 (see also SJ 205, 221; The Pilgrim's Regress xi-xiii)
❖ GID I 21:6, 7 (see also SJ 13:12; 14:12; The Pilgrim's Regress P:12-17)

Joy: First and deadly error is to make a state of mind your aim, and the second error is to attempt to produce it
•SJ 168 ❖ SJ 11:5

Joy, flippancy is a thousand miles away from
•SL 52 ❖ SL 11:6

Joy: "For it is one thing to see the land of peace from a wooded ridge...and another to tread the road that leads to it" (quote from St. Augustine)*
•SJ 230 ❖ SJ 15 prelim. quote

Joy, for many years [at "Belsen"], was not only absent but forgotten
•SJ 34 ❖ SJ 2:15

Joy: God and nothing else is the true goal of men and the satisfaction of their needs*
•RP 40-41 (see also GO 79; WG 14-15)
❖ RP 4:15 (see also GO 4:21; WG 1:11, 12)

Joy: "I believe...that the old stab...has come to me as often and as sharply since my conversion as at any time of my life whatever"
•SJ 238 ❖ SJ 15:10

Joy: "I concluded that it was a mood or a state within myself which might turn up in any context. To 'get it again' became my constant endeavor..."
•SJ 169 ❖ SJ 11:5

Joy: "I did not yet ask, Who is the desired? only What is it?"
•SJ 221 ❖ SJ 14:12

Joy: "I did not yet reflect on the difference between it and the merely intellectual satisfaction of getting to know the Eddaic universe"

•SJ 78 ❖ SJ 5:11

Joy, I gradually realized that my scholarly delight in literature was something quite different from the original
•SJ 165 ❖ SJ 11:2

Joy: "I had hoped that the heart of reality might be of such a kind that we can best symbolize it as a place; instead, I found it to be a Person"
•SJ 230 ❖ SJ 15:2

Joy: I had labelled it "aesthetic experience"; but that answer too had broken down
•SJ 221 (see also GID 175*; SJ 72)
❖ SJ 14:12 (see also GID I 21:7*; SJ 5:2)

Joy, I saw that all my waitings and watchings for, had been a futile attempt to contemplate the enjoyed
•SJ 219 ❖ SJ 14:11

Joy, I sometimes wonder whether all pleasures are not substitutes for
•SJ 170 ❖ SJ 11:6

Joy: "If I find in myself a desire which no experience in this world can satisfy, the most probable explanation is that I was made for another world"*
•MC 120 ❖ MC III 10:5

Joy, images or sensations of: "I knew now that they were merely the mental track left by the passage of Joy...the wave's imprint on the sand"
•SJ 219 ❖ SJ 14:11

Joy ("imagination") would never have made me wiser or better; but it still had, at however many removes, the shape of the reality it reflected*
•SJ 167 ❖ SJ 11:4

Joy: "...in a sense the central story of my life is about nothing else..."
•SJ 17 ❖ SJ 1:18

Joy: In childhood we have spiritual experiences as pure and momentous as any since*
•PP 79 (see also PP 24-25; SJ chapters 1-5 ❖ PP 5:7 (see also PP 1:16; SJ chapters 1-5)

Joy: In Heaven we shall recover at last that central music in every pure experience which had always just evaded memory*

•SL 148 ❖ SL 31:4

Joy, infinite, offered us but we are like an ignorant child content to make mudpies in a slum
•WG 3-4 ❖ WG 1:1

Joy, introspection as it relates to: "The surest way of spoiling a pleasure [is] to start examining your satisfaction"
•SJ 218-219 (see also GID 65-66*)
❖ SJ 14:10, 11 (see also GID I 5:8*)

Joy is distinct not only from pleasure in general but even from aesthetic pleasure; it must have the stab, the pang, the longing
•SJ 72 (see also SJ 221)
❖ SJ 5:2 (see also SJ 14:12)

Joy is the serious business of Heaven
•LM 93 ❖ LM 17:17

Joy, it is not settled happiness but momentary, that glorifies the past
•SJ 8 ❖ SJ 1:5

Joy: Its Object is imageless, though our imagination salutes it with a hundred images
•SJ 221 ❖ SJ 14:12

Joy: Its visitations were the moments of clearest consciousness we had, when we ached for that impossible reunion...
•SJ 222 ❖ SJ 14:13

Joy itself, considered simply as an event in my own mind, turned out to be of no value at all; all the value lay in that of which Joy was the desiring
•SJ 220 ❖ SJ 14:12

Joy labelled by Lewis as "aesthetic experience" in his early days at Oxford
•SJ 205, 221 ❖ SJ 13:1Joy2; 14:12

Joy labelled by Lewis as "romantic delusion" as he resolved to put it away [during his early years at Oxford]*
•SJ 201, 203 ❖ SJ 13:7, 9

Joy, Lewis describes three episodes of imaginative experience which he later labelled
•SJ 16-18 ❖ SJ 1:15-18

Joy, Lewis's description of a memory of a certain instance of: "...the remembering...was itself a new experience of just the same kind"

•SJ 73, 166 (see also SJ 16)
❖ SJ 5:4; 11:3 (see also SJ 1:15)

Joy, Lewis's experience of, on reading the words Siegfried and the Twilight of the Gods
•SJ 72-73 ❖ SJ 5:3, 4

Joy, Lewis's interest in planetary science fiction described as something courser and stronger than
•SJ 35-36 ❖ SJ 2:15

Joy makes nonsense of our common distinction between having and wanting; there, to have is to want and to want is to have
•SJ 166 (see also SJ 17-18*)
❖ SJ 11:3 (see also SJ 1:18*)

Joy mentioned by Screwtape as a cause of human laughter and music: He admits it has no meaning for devils
•SL 50 ❖ SL 11:2

Joy most easily described as a physical sensation*
•WG 58 (see also SJ 168, 219)
❖ WG 4:6 (see also SJ 11:5; 14:10, 11)

Joy: My idea of the fruition of God is a huge, risky extrapolation from a very few and short experiences here on earth*
•GO 82 ❖ GO 4:27

Joy, nature soon ceased to be (for me) a reminder of the books and became herself a medium of the real
•SJ 77 ❖ SJ 5:10

Joy: "No slightest hint was vouchsafed me that there ever had been or ever would be any connection between God and Joy. If anything, it was the reverse"
•SJ 230 ❖ SJ 15:2

Joy not a desire for our own past (though that may come into it)*
•SJ 16 ❖ SJ 1:15

Joy not a disguise of sexual desire; "I repeatedly followed that path—to the end"
•SJ 169-170 (see also GO 6-7*; SJ 203-204*)
❖ SJ 11:6 (see also GO 1:12*; SJ 13:10*)

Joy not usually recognized as desire for Heaven*
•MC 119 ❖ MC III 10:2

Joy, Object of: I ought to have seen that it was further away and less subjective than a system of mythology—had, in fact, only shown through that system
•SJ 168-169 ❖ SJ 11:5

Joy, object of: If it ever became manifest, you would know it; you would say, "Here at last is the thing I was made for"*
•PP 146 (see also MC 170)
❖ PP 10:2 (see also MC IV 8:12)

Joy, object of: "...that something which you were born desiring," which you are always looking for, watching for, listening for, from childhood to old age*
•PP 146 ❖ PP 10:2

Joy, object of: "You have never had it. All the things that have ever deeply possessed your soul have been but hints of it..."*
•PP 146 ❖ PP 10:2

Joy of loving God no more separable from praise than the brightness a mirror receives is separable from the brightness it sheds
•RP 96 ❖ RP 9:6

Joy: "Our best havings are wantings"
•L 289 ❖ L 5 Nov 59

Joy, praise is the mode of love which always has some element of, in it
•GO 72 ❖ GO 4:5

Joy, Psalmists did not know that God would die to offer them eternal, yet they express a longing for Him—for His mere presence
•RP 50 ❖ RP 5:8

Joy, pursuit of: You may take any number of wrong turnings, but keep your eyes open and you will not be allowed to go very far without warnings
•SJ 177 ❖ SJ 11:14

Joy, return of, while at Oxford: "I was off once more into the land of longing, my heart at once broken and exalted ..."*
•SJ 217 ❖ SJ 14:8

Joy, satisfaction of: "...to be united with that Life in the eternal Sonship of Christ is...the only thing worth a moment's consideration"*
•M 155 ❖ M 16:22

Joy: "Slowly, and with many relapses, I came to see that the magical conclusion was just as irrelevant to Joy as the erotic conclusion had been"
•SJ 177 (see also SJ 203-204)
❖ SJ 11:14 (see also SJ 13:10)

Joy: Take away the object, and what is left? —a whirl of images, a fluttering sensation in the diaphragm, a momentary abstraction
•SJ 168 (see also WG 57-59)
❖ SJ 11:5 (see also WG 4:5-7)

Joy: The feelings accompanying my emotions, by themselves, are of very mediocre interest to me—their value is in what they are about*
•CR 139-140 (see also SJ 168, 218- 220, 238; WG 57-59)
❖ CR 11:22 (see also SJ 11:5; 14:10-12; 15:10; WG 4:5-7)

Joy: The Flesh and the Devil could not offer me the supreme bribe—it was not in their gift; and the World never even pretended to have it
•SJ 178 (see also SJ 176)
❖ SJ 11:17 (see also SJ 11:13)

Joy, the "stab" of
•SJ 21, 78, 130, 166
❖ SJ 1:23; 5:11; 8:18; 11:3

Joy: "The whole man is to drink joy from the fountain of joy"
•WG 17-18 (see also RP 97*)
❖ WG 1:14 (see also RP 9:7*)

Joy: "...there arose at once, almost like heartbreak, the memory of Joy itself..."
•SJ 73 (see also SJ 16, 166)
❖ SJ 5:4 (see also SJ 1:15; 11:3)

Joy: There arose the fatal determination to recover the old thrill, and at last the moment when I was compelled to realize that all such efforts were failures
•SJ 166 ❖ SJ 11:3

Joy ("thirst for the Uncreated") cannot be satisfied by any earthly Beloved*
•FL 155, 189-191 ❖ FL 5:37; 6:41-45

Joy: "This secret fire goes out when you use the bellows; turn your back on it and attend to your duties, and then it will blaze"*
•PP 148 ❖ PP 10:5

Joy, to be drenched in, as part of our destiny
•GID 112 ❖ GID I 12:10

Joy: "To tell you the truth, the subject has lost nearly all interest for me since I became a Christian..."
•SJ 238 ❖ SJ 15:10

Joy, to try and produce the "thrill" of, as a state of mind turns religion into a self-caressing luxury
•SJ 168 ❖ SJ 11:5

Joy vs. Pleasure: I doubt whether anyone who has tasted "Joy" would exchange it for all the pleasures in the world
•SJ 18 (see also SL 148*)
❖ SJ 1:18 (see also SL 31:5*)

Joy vs. Pleasure: "Joy" has only one characteristic in common with Pleasure: Anyone who has experienced it will want it again
•SJ 18 ❖ SJ 1:18

Joy vs. Pleasure: "Joy is never in our power and pleasure often is"
•SJ 18 ❖ SJ 1:18

Joy vs. sexual pleasure: "You might as well offer a mutton chop to a man who is dying of thirst as offer sexual pleasure to the desire I am speaking of"
•SJ 170 (see also SJ 203-204)
❖ SJ 11:6 (see also SJ 13:10)

Joy vs. the Occult: Raising a spirit might have been extremely interesting, "but the real Desirable would have evaded one..."
•SJ 177 ❖ SJ 11:14

Joy vs. "wishful thinking": "Now what, I asked myself, were all my delectable mountains and western gardens but sheer Fantasies?"*
•SJ 203-204 ❖ SJ 13:10

Joy was frightened away by greedy impatience to snare it, destroyed by introspection, and vulgarized by false assumptions about its nature
•SJ 169 ❖ SJ 11:5

Joy: What is wanted is not a "thrill" or a state of mind; real Joy is a by-product
•SJ 168 ❖ SJ 11:5

Joy: "Whatever you try to identify with it turns out to be not it but something else"*
•PP 149 ❖ PP 10:6

Joy, where the inner life may be starving for, the outer life may be full of cheerful bustle and success (and vice versa)
•SJ 78, 118-119 (see also LAL 83)
❖ SJ 5:12; 8:1 (see also LAL Jun 7th 59)

Joy which Lewis felt on reading the book Phantastes, by George MacDonald: "If it had once eluded me by its distance, it now eluded me by its proximity"*
•SJ 179-181 ❖ SJ 11:18, 19

Joy which Lewis felt on reading the book Phantastes: "...never had the wind of Joy blowing through any story been less separable from the story itself"
•SJ 180 ❖ SJ 11:19

Joy which Lewis felt on reading the book Phantastes: "Up till now each visitation of Joy had left the common world momentarily a desert..."
•SJ 181 ❖ SJ 11:19

Joy which Lewis's wife experienced as she went about her work one day: "... and instantly she entered into joy"
•GO 54-55 ❖ GO 3:27

Joys and sorrows, all of our, are not merely emotions; they are about something—a by-product of attending to something
•CR 139 (see also SJ 168, 218-220, 238; WG 57-59) ❖ CR 11:22 (see also SJ 11:5; 14:10-12; 15:10; WG 4:5-7)

Joys, that voice which speaks in your conscience and in some of your intensest, may be in fact the closest contact you have with the mystery... (re: attempting contact with ultimate Reality)
•CR 170 ❖ CR 14:27

Judaic ethics, Our Lord constantly repeated and reinforced the; He very seldom introduced a novelty
•RP 26-27 (see also CR 47; MC 78; PP 63; Law of Nature)
❖ RP 3:13 (see also CR 4:7; MC III 3:1; PP 4:10; Law of Nature)

Judaism—see also Jew(s)

Judaism, all that was best in, survives in Christianity
•GID 102 ❖ GID I 10:49

Judaism an ancient religion, more like Paganism in its externals and attitudes than like all the stuffiness which the word "religion" now suggests
•RP 44 ❖ RP 5:2

Judaism: As Christians there is a tragic depth to our worship, which Judaism lacked; our most joyous festivals centre upon the broken body and the shed blood
•RP 52 ❖ RP 5:10

Judaism: "...Christ, in transcending and thus abrogating, also fulfills, both Paganism and Judaism..."
•RP 129 ❖ RP 12:9

Judaism, Creation an explicit doctrine in ancient, (unlike many other religions); this had consequences for their entire way of thinking
•RP 77-85 ❖ RP 8:3-15

Judaism in its earlier stages had no belief in immortality; the glory or splendour of God is worshipped for its own sake
•GID 130-131; M 145-146 (see also RP 38-40; SJ 231) ❖ GID I 16:2, 3; M 16:6 (see also RP 4:11-15; SJ 15:3)

Judaism, in, the Bride of God is the whole nation of Israel
•RP 129 ❖ RP 12:9

Judaism, one will find imagery in, just as in Christianity (e.g., God pictured as living above "'in the high and holy place'")
•M 76-77, 78 ❖ M 10:16, 19

Judaism, the essence of sacrifice in, was not that men gave animals to God but that by their doing so God gave Himself to men
•RP 93 ❖ RP 9:4

Judaism, the only living, is Christianity; the modern Jewish religion is archaic, pedantic, and sectarian (Joy's view)
•L 285-286 ❖ L 30 Apr 59

Judaism, the sacrificial rites in, became separated from unity with God; their punctual performance came to be seen as the only thing God wanted
•RP 49 ❖ RP 5:7

Judas: Although God can make complex good out of simple evil, that fact does not excuse the simple evil; the role of Judas remains simply evil
• PP 110-111 ❖ PP 7:2

Judas' reaction to the hard sayings of Jesus (brother and child against parent, etc.): He took to them as a duck takes to water
•GID 191-192 (see also FL 165-166) ❖ GID II 1:4 (see also FL 6:4)

Judas: You will carry out God's purpose, however you act, but it makes a difference to you whether you serve like Judas or like John
•PP 111 ❖ PP 7:2

Judgement by our peers: "Theirs is the praise we really covet and the blame we really dread"
•FL 114 (see also WLN 112) ❖ FL 4:44 (see also WLN 7:36)

Judgement, Christian picture of: We must pin all our hopes on the mercy of God and the work of Christ, not on our own goodness
•RP 13 ❖ RP 2:8

Judgement, Christian vs. Jewish attitude in the face of: Psalmists exhibit Jewish confidence; the Christian trembles because he knows he is a sinner
•CR 122-125, esp. 125 ❖ CR 10:22-30, esp. 10:29 30

Judgement, Christian vs. Jewish picture of: One cries to God for mercy instead of judgement; the other cries to God for justice instead of injustice
•RP 9-19, esp. 10-12 ❖ RP ch. 2, esp. 2:3-6

Judgement, Day of: "If there is any concept which cannot...be removed from the teaching of Our Lord, it is that of the great separation"
•CR 122-123 ❖ CR 10:22

Judgement, Day of: It is from Jesus' own words that the picture of "Doomsday" has come into Christianity
•CR 123 ❖ CR 10:22

Judgement, for the Psalmists, is apparently an occasion of universal rejoicing; they ask for it
•RP 9-10 (see also CR 123) ❖ RP 2:2 (see also CR 10:24)

Judgement: "Happy are those whom it finds labouring in their vocations, whether they were merely going out to feed the pigs or laying good plans..."
•WLN 111 (see also GID 266)
❖ WLN 7:34 (see also GID II 16:55)

Judgement, I can find the Jewish conception of a civil, useful by picturing myself as the defendant instead of the plaintiff
•RP 16-17 ❖ RP 2:11

Judgement: "I do not find that pictures of physical catastrophe...help one so much as the naked idea of Judgment"
•WLN 113 ❖ WLN 7:38

Judgement, if there is any thought at which a Christian trembles it is the thought of God's
•RP 9 (see also CR 122-125)
❖ RP 2:1 (see also CR 10:22-29)

Judgement, in Psalms, not something that the conscience-stricken believer fears but something the downtrodden believer hopes for
•CR 123-124 ❖ CR 10:24-28

"Judgement" in the Psalms (chapter title)
•RP 9-19 (see also CR 122-128)
❖ RP ch. 2 (see also CR 10:22-40)

Judgement, in the, we may find that the heaviest charge against each of us turns not upon the things he has done but upon those he never did
•RP 9 ❖ RP 2:1

Judgement of others—see Judging others

Judgement, our goal in thinking about: "...to dress our souls not for the electric lights of the present world but for the daylight of the next"
•WLN 113 ❖ WLN 7:38

"Judgement" should be taken not as a sentence or reward, but as the Verdict; someday an absolutely correct verdict will be passed on what each of us is
•WLN 112-113 ❖ WLN 7:35-37

Judgement, someday we shall hear God's infallible, on us and perhaps we shall realise that in some dim fashion we could have known it all along
•WLN 113 (consider also Self-knowl-

edge) ❖ WLN 7:37 (consider also Self-knowledge)

Judgement: Sooner or later the wicked need to realize their own sinfulness; right must be asserted (re: the "intolerable" doctrine of Hell)*
•PP 120-122 ❖ PP 8:5

Judgement, the spark of desire for, which is seen first in the Psalms burns clear in the Magnificat
•CR 122 ❖ CR 10:20

Judgement: The unanswerable and (by then) self-evident truth about each of us will be known to all
•WLN 113 ❖ WLN 7:37

"Judgement," the word, evokes a criminal trial: the Judge on the bench, the accused in the dock...but what our Lord had in view was a civil trial (re: Parable of Unjust Judge)
•CR 123-124 ❖ CR 10:23-25)

Judgement: We can perhaps train ourselves to ask how the thing we are saying or doing at each moment will look when the irresistible light streams in
•WLN 113 ❖ WLN 7:38

Judgement, what alarms us in the Christian picture of, is the infinite purity of the standard against which our actions will be judged
•RP 13 (see also CR 125)
❖ RP 2:8 (see also CR 10:29)

Judgement, what may be upon us at any moment is not merely an End but a, (re: necessity of working for the good of posterity)
•WLN 111 ❖ WLN 7:33

"Judgements," Historicism which sees calamities as, not countenanced by Christianity
•CR 101-102 ❖ CR 9:5

Judgements, we have all encountered, on ourselves in this life; every now and then we discover what our fellow creatures really think of us
•WLN 112 (see also FL 114)
❖ WLN 7:36 (see also FL 4:44)

Judges, Book of: The word we translate as "Judges" might almost be rendered "Champions"; they perform more as

rescuers of the Israelites
•RP 12; CR 124 ❖ RP 2:6; CR 10:27

Judging a person's Christianity simply by behaviour is not possible; you need to know what kind of raw material Christ is working on (tooth paste analogy)
•GID 59; MC 177-178 (*see also* L 242*)
❖ GID I 4:46-52 (Ques. 12); MC IV 10:5 (*see also* L 28 May 52*)

Judging: A recollection of all one's own cruelty will help to make prayer for one's enemies real*
•L 183 ❖ L 16 Apr 40

Judging: In a sense, the world is quite right to judge Christianity by its results; Christ told us to judge by results
•MC 176 ❖ MC IV 10:2

Judging others: Condemnation of sin can be dangerous to charity and humility (though the alternative is to condone it, thus sharing guilt)*
•PP 117 ❖ PP 7:9

Judging others: "Human beings judge one another by their external actions. God judges them by their moral choices"
•MC 85, 86 ❖ MC III 4:6, 7

Judging others: "I'd better keep my breath to cool my own porridge"*
•GO 66 ❖ GO 3:44

Judging others: If Christianity is true, why aren't all the Christians nicer than all the non-Christians?
•MC 175-183 ❖ MC IV ch. 10

Judging others: It is important to realize that there is some really fatal flaw in *you* which causes others the same despair*
•GID 123, 151-155 (*see also* FL 186)
❖ GID I 14:7, 8; ch. 18 (*see also* FL 6:37)

Judging others: "It is not for us to say who, in the deepest sense, is or is not close to the spirit of Christ"
•MC 11 ❖ MC P:13

Judging others: "...let's go on disagreeing but don't let us *judge*"
•L 268 ❖ L 13 Mar 56

Judging: Others *may* be sinners; ask yourself, "Why should their vices prove hypocrisy if I can consider that I am in some sense a Christian?"*
•SL 14 ❖ SL 2:4

Judging others: "'Mind one's own business' is a good rule in religion as in other things..." (re: varying tastes in worship styles)
•L 268 ❖ L 13 Mar 56

Judging others: "Those who do not think about their own sins make up for it by thinking incessantly about the sins of others"*
•GID 124 (*see also* GID 154; LAL 95)
❖ GID I 14:10 (*see also* GID I 18:10; LAL 9 Jan 61)

Judging others who may worship in a different fashion than we do
•LM 10 ❖ LM 2:3

Judging: "The human mind is generally far more eager to praise and dispraise than to describe and define"*
•FL 27 ❖ FL 2:3

Judging: "What can you ever really know of other people's souls—of their temptations, their opportunities, their struggles?"—We can only know ourselves
•MC 183 ❖ MC IV 10:17

Julian of Norwich, Lady, would have us "loving and peaceable," not only to our "even-Christians," but to "ourself"
•GID 193 (*see also* L 183)
❖ GID II 2:1 (*see also* L 16 Apr 40)

Julian of Norwich, quote from: "All shall be well..."
•CR 123; GID 169; GO 75; L 186
❖ CR 10:22; GID I 20:Reply-11; GO 4:12; L 2 Jun 40

Julian of Norwich, vision of Lady
•GID 37 ❖ GID I 2:15

Jung, philosophy of, mentioned as being in direct contradiction to the philosophy of Freud
•MC 84 ❖ MC III 4:3

Justice—*consider also* Punishment

Justice an old name for what we now call "fairness"; it includes honesty, give and take, truthfulness, and keeping promises
•MC 76 ❖ MC III 2:7

Justice: "Criminal law increasingly protects the criminal and ceases to protect his victim"

•GID 307 ❖ GID III 7:7

Justice, in contemplating evil we find ourselves moved by a truly ethical demand for, (re: the "intolerable" doctrine of Hell)
•PP 120-122 ❖ PP 8:5

Justice, mercy detached from, grows unmerciful (re: "Humanitarian" concept of punishment)
•GID 294 ❖ GID III 4:13

Justice requires that punishment be based on retribution or desert
•GID 287-300, 313, 339-340; L 304; PP 93-94, 120-122 ❖ GID III ch. 4; 8:7-9; IV Letter 12; L 25 May 62; P:P 6:6; 8:5, 6

Justice: Sooner or later the wicked need to realize their own sinfulness; right must be asserted (re: the "intolerable" doctrine of Hell)
•PP 120-122 ❖ PP 8:5

Justice system in Britain: We have been spared the almost world-wide difficulty of the "small man" in getting his case heard in court*
•RP 11 (see also CR 124)
❖ RP 2:4 (see also CR 10:26)

Justice, the ferocity of the Psalms (which we are to make no concession to) is mixed with a passionate craving for
•CR 121-122 ❖ CR 10:17

Justice, there is a current lack of thirst for; having discovered oppression, the new man immediately asks how he can join the ranks of the oppressors (re: craving for justice in the Psalms)
•CR 122; RP 69-70
❖ CR 10:18, 19; RP 7:7, 8)

Justice, there is in many of the Psalms a fatal confusion between the desire for, and the desire for revenge
•RP 18 ❖ RP 2:14

Justification by faith—*see also* Salvation by faith/grace; *consider also* Righteousness by faith/grace

Justification by faith, Lewis mentions a Methodist who complained that he said nothing about, in his BBC talks (which later became *Mere Christianity*)
•L 198 ❖ L 21 Dec 41

Kant: "If God were a Kantian, who would not have us till we came to Him from the purest and best motives, who could be saved?"
•PP 98 ❖ PP 6:8

Kant, [Immanuel], and the Stoics responsible for the notion that to desire our own good and earnestly hope for the enjoyment of it is a bad thing; not part of the Christian faith
•WG 3 ❖ WG 1:1

Kant mentioned as being at the root of a certain philosophical preconception we all suffer from which makes the idea of a New Nature shocking
•M 154 ❖ M 16:20

Kant mentioned as having nearly been reconciled with Christianity by Lady Julian of Norwich
•L 186 ❖ L 2 Jun 40

Kant thought that no action had moral value unless it were done out of pure reverence for the moral law (that is, without inclination)
•PP 99-101 ❖ PP 6:11-13

Kant was right; the imperative is categorical
•CR 55-56 (see also CR 44-45)
❖ CR 4:26 (see also CR 4:2)

Kant's distinction between the Noumenal and the Phenomenal self mentioned
•SJ 197 ❖ SJ 13:1

"Kantian Ethics" mentioned as primarily referring to the Categorical Imperative ("Kant did not differ remarkably from

---

* These items reflect some interpretation on the part of the editor; the idea will not be found in these exact words. *See Introduction, p. ix.*
** These items are ideas of Lewis's which the editor has placed under a topic Lewis did not there intend to address. *See Introduction, p. ix.* Entries without asterisks are not necessarily exact quotes, but the idea should be easy to find as worded.

other men on the content of ethics...")
- •CR 44-45 ❖ CR 4:2

Key, your soul is a, made to unlock one of the doors in the house with many mansions
- •PP 147 ❖ PP 10:3

Kierkegaard, I can't read, myself, but some people find him helpful
- •L 299 ❖ L 9 May 61

Kierkegaard is regarded as the pioneer of religious Existentialism
- •L 297-298
- ❖ L undated letter of Feb 61

"Kill" in the sixth Commandment means "Murder"
- •L 247; MC 106-107
- ❖ L 8 Nov 52; MC III 7:7

Killing—*see also* Capital punishment; Death; *consider also* Pacifism; War

Killing may sometimes be justified, in my opinion
- •PP 111-112 ❖ PP 7:2

Killing, regarding the man who "just feels" that all, of human beings is in all circumstances an absolute evil
- •WG 39-41 ❖ WG 3:12-14

"Kindness" is a quality fatally easy to attribute to ourselves on inadequate grounds; we think we are kind when we are only happy (unannoyed)
- •PP 56 ❖ PP 4:2

"Kindred souls," mention of
- •FL 92, 96-97 ❖ FL 4:9, 16

King James Version—*see* Bible, King James Version

Kirk [William T. Kirkpatrick]: From him, I learned something about the honor of the intellect and the shame of voluntary inconsistency
- •SJ 173 ❖ SJ 11:9

Kirk [William T. Kirkpatrick] had been a Presbyterian and was now an Atheist
- •SJ 139 ❖ SJ 9:14

Kirk [William T. Kirkpatrick] was a "Rationalist" of the old, high and dry, nineteenth-century type
- •SJ 139 (*see also* SJ 171)
- ❖ SJ 9:15 (*see also* SJ 11:8)

Kirk [William T. Kirkpatrick] told my father, "You may make a writer or a scholar out of him, but you'll not make anything else"
- •SJ 183 (*see also* CR 20*)
- ❖ SJ 12:2 (*see also* CR 2:23*)

Kirkpatrick, William T., a tribute by Lewis to his teacher
- •L 53-54 (*see also* L 59)
- ❖ L 28 Mar 21 (*see also* L 23 Apr 21)

Kirkpatrick, William T.: "He never attacked religion in my presence"
- •SJ 140 ❖ SJ 9:16

Kirkpatrick, William T.: "Here was a man who thought not about you but about what you said"
- •SJ 137 ❖ SJ 9:11

Kirkpatrick, William T., (Lewis's tutor) mentioned or referred to
- •CR 164; L 42, 49, 64; SJ 126, 128-148, 160, 160, 164, 171, 180, 183 ❖ CR 13:28; L 20 Jun 18; 22 Jun 29; 1 Jul 21; SJ 8:8, 12-19; ch. 9; 10:14, 18-21; 11:8, 19; 12:2

Kirkpatrick, William T.: "My debt to him is very great, my reverence to this day undiminished"
- •SJ 148 ❖ SJ 9:24

Kirkpatrick, William T., referred to as "a hard, satirical atheist" and "the...man who taught me to think"*
- •M 69 ❖ M 10:3

Kneeling in prayer: "I won't say this doesn't matter. The body ought to pray as well as the soul"
- •LM 17 (*see also* SL 20)
- ❖ LM 3:9 (*see also* SL 4:2)

Kneeling in prayer: "The relevant point is that kneeling does matter, but other things matter even more"
- •LM 18 ❖ LM 3:10

Knocking: "Don't knock and it shall be opened to you"—this is how it seems [in grief]; a clamorous need seems to shut one off from the thing needed
- •LAL 92 (*see also* GO 4-6, 53-54)
- ❖ LAL 24 Sep 60 (*see also* GO 1:7-11; 3:24-26)

Knowing God—*see also* Knowledge of God; Relationship with God

Knowing God: "As long as you are proud you cannot know God"
- •MC 111 ❖ MC III 8:6

Knowing God: Assurance about prayer, as in our requests of people, is not from knowing things about the Giver but from knowing *Him*
•WLN 6-8 (*see also* LM 49; WLN 26-27*) ❖ WLN 1:12-15 (*see also* LM 9:8; WLN 2:14*)

Knowing God essential if we are to love Him ("...and if we know Him, we shall in fact fall on our faces")
•PP 53 ❖ PP 3:18

Knowing God: "Every idea of Him we form, He must in mercy shatter"; prayer may facilitate this
•LM 82 (*see also* GO 76-78, 82-83; SL 22*) ❖ LM 15:17 (*see also* GO 4:15-18, 27-28; SL 4:4*)

Knowing God: Experience of God the best material for correcting our abstract conception of God
•M 90 (*see also* MC 135-136)
❖ M 11:14 (*see also* MC IV 1:2, 3)

Knowing God: Experience of His blessings ("pleasures") essential to our adoration of Him; without it we will not have "tasted and seen"
•LM 91 ❖ LM 17:13

Knowing God: If we have not learned to know God we will be wretched, in spite of earthly prosperity
•PP 97 ❖ PP 6:8

Knowing God: "If you do not at all know God, of course you will not recognize Him, either in Jesus or in outer space"
•CR 172 ❖ CR 14:35

Knowing God: Initiative lies wholly on God's side; He shows more of Himself to some than to others
•MC 143-144 (*see also* CR 169; GID 143-144; PP 51-52; SJ 216, 226-227)
❖ MC IV 2:11-13 (*see also* CR 14:19; GID I 16:26; PP 3:17; SJ 14:7; 14:20, 21)

Knowing God leads to humility; "...He wants you to know Him; wants to give you Himself"
•MC 114 ❖ MC III 8:12

Knowing God: "The instrument through which you see God is your whole self"
•MC 144 ❖ MC IV 2:14, 15

Knowing God: "...the one really adequate instrument for learning about God is the whole Christian community, waiting for Him together"
•MC 144 ❖ MC IV 2:16

Knowing God: "The saying 'Blessed are those that have not seen and have believed'...says in effect, 'You should have known Me better'"
•WLN 28-29 ❖ WLN 2:17

Knowing God through nature: We can get hints, but must not try to find a direct path through it and beyond it to an increasing knowledge of God
•FL 38 ❖ FL 2:26

Knowing God through prayer: In it, God shows Himself to us
•WLN 8 ❖ WLN 1:16

Knowing God: "To know God is to know that our obedience is due to Him..."
•SJ 231-232 ❖ SJ 15:3

Knowing God: We have a knowledge-by-acquaintance of the Person we believe in; we trust not because "a God" exists, but because "this God" exists
•WLN 25, 29-30 ❖ WLN 2:13, 17, 18

Knowledge—*see also* Education; Learning; *consider also* Culture; Intellectual(ism); Self-knowledge; Truth

Knowledge: A belief in the objectivity and validity of reason must be maintained *or* all thoughts are accidents and we can know no truths and have no knowledge*
•CR 60-63, 71, 72-81, 89; GID 21, 52-53, 136-138, 272, 274-276; M 12-24, 34, 105; MC 45-46; SJ 208; WG 88-92 (*see also* Reason) ❖ CR 5:9-13, 27; ch. 6; 7:16; GID I 1:1; 4:21; 16:13-17; III 1:4, 9, 13-16; M ch. 3; 5:1; 13:16; MC II 1:6; SJ 13:17; WG 5:21-24 (*see also* Reason)

Knowledge about ourselves—*see* Self-knowledge

Knowledge about such things as how the Atonement works not essential to our acceptance of them; we might not know how they work until we've accepted them*
•MC 58-59 (*see also* L 197-198)
❖ MC II 4:4, 5 (*see also* L 21 Dec 41)

Knowledge, all, depends on the validity

of inference (re: subjectivity vs. objectivity of human thought)
- •CR 62-63 ❖ CR 5:12, 13

Knowledge, all our, depends on authority, reason, and experience, mixed in varying proportions
- •CR 41 (see also CR 26*, 43)
- ❖ CR 3:9 (see also CR 2:40*; 3:12)

Knowledge, all possible, depends on the validity of reasoning; Naturalism discredits our processes of reasoning, thereby discrediting Naturalism itself
- •M 12-24, 34, 105 (see also CR 60-61, 71, 72-81, 89; GID 21, 52-53, 136-138; 272*, 274-276; MC 45-46; SJ 209-209; WG 88-91)
- ❖ M ch. 5; 5:1; 13:16 (see also CR 5:9, 10, 27; ch. 6; 7:16; GID I 1:1; 4:21; 16:13-17; GID III 1:4*; 1:9, 13-16; MC II 1:6; SJ 13:17; WG 5:21-24)

Knowledge and beauty, pursuit of, need not exclude God; an appetite for these things exists in the human mind and God makes no appetite in vain
- •WG 27 ❖ WG 2:9

Knowledge and beauty, search for, cannot be postponed until men are secure (re: education in time of war)
- •WG 21-22 ❖ WG 2:4

Knowledge and learning as a catalyst for religious emotion: Many find that the heart sings unbidden while working through a tough bit of theology*
- •GID 205 ❖ GID II 4:7

"Knowledge-by-acquaintance," the humblest of us can have some, of Love Himself; but no man has direct "knowledge about" God—only analogies
- •FL 174-175 (see also GID 170)
- ❖ FL 6:20 (see also GID I 20:15)

Knowledge-by-acquaintance, we have a, of the Person we believe in; we (as Christians) trust not because "a God" exists, but because this God exists
- •WLN 25, 29-30 ❖ WLN 2:13, 17, 18

Knowledge by experience: Through religious experience Christians believe that they get a sort of verification (or perhaps falsification) of their tenets*

- •CR 137-138 ❖ CR 11:19

Knowledge, desire for, is one of the things that distinguishes Man from the other animals
- •GID 108 ❖ GID I 12:1

Knowledge, entire mass of our, is illuminated by the doctrine of the Incarnation
- •M 109-110 ❖ M 14:3

Knowledge, first-hand, easier and more delightful to acquire than second-hand knowledge (re: reading original authors rather than commentators)
- •GID 200 ❖ GID II 4:1

Knowledge: "[For the Theist] the human mind in the act of knowing is illuminated by the Divine reason"
- •M 22 ❖ M 3:29

Knowledge gained by obedience: "When a man is getting better, he understands more and more clearly the evil that is still left in him"*
- •MC 87 (see also GID 56-57; MC 94, 164; PP 55, top; PP 67; Self-knowledge)
- ❖ MC III 4:10 (see also GID I 4:38; MC III 5:13; IV 7:12; PP 4:prelim. quote; PP 4:15; Self-knowledge)

Knowledge, how Christian doctrine can be unchanging in the face of growing scientific
- •GID 38-47 ❖ GID I ch. 3

Knowledge: If our inferences do not give a genuine insight into reality, then we can know nothing (re: reason)
- •GID 274-275, 277 ❖ GID III 1:11, 22-27

Knowledge may be increasing, but there is no evidence for advancement in intelligence (re: whether Bible is still applicable today)
- •GID 57 ❖ GID I 4:41, 42 (Ques. 10)

Knowledge: Newman's view of the cultivation of the intellect as a justifiable end in itself, while remaining wholly distinct from virtue
- •CR 18-19 ❖ CR 2:20, 21

Knowledge not superseded by more knowledge; possibility of progress demands that there be an unchanging element

•GID 44-45, 47 ❖ GID I 3:13, 14, 16

Knowledge of God—*see also* Knowing God; Relationship with God

Knowledge of God, avenues for seeking: miracles, inspired teachers, and enjoined ritual
•GID 143-144 ❖ GID I 16:26

Knowledge of God "by acquaintance" ("connaitre") vs. direct "knowledge about" God ("savoir")—specifically regarding the love of God
•FL 174-175 (*see also* GID 170; WLN 25, 29, 30) ❖ FL 6:20 (*see also* GID I 20:Reply-15; WLN 2:13, 18)

Knowledge of God derived only by personal acquaintance and by analogies
•FL 174-175 ❖ FL 6:20

Knowledge of God, gaining, through the intellectual life: It is not the only road to God, nor the safest, but it may be the appointed road for us
•WG 27-28 ❖ WG 2:9

Knowledge of God: "...if we fully understood *what* God is we should see that there is no question whether He is"
•M 88 ❖ M 11:11

Knowledge of God: "Much depends on the seeing eye"; "What is required is a certain faculty of recognition"*
•CR 171, 172 ❖ CR 14:29, 34

Knowledge of God, our own experience as an avenue for
•CR 113 (*see also* Experience)
❖ CR 9:26 (*see also* Experience)

Knowledge of God: Through prayer, God pours out a knowledge of Himself
•SL 21 ❖ SL 4:4

Knowledge of God, two sources for, discussed: the universe and the moral law; the better source is the moral law
•MC 37 ❖ MC I 5:3

Knowledge of God: What He is will be known only through a personal experience of Him in our lives*
•GID 170 (*see also* M 89-90)
❖ GID I 20:Reply-15 (*see also* M 11:14)

Knowledge, our, about spiritual things may be weak but at the least we know enough to know that we have fallen short

•WG 65-66 ❖ WG 4:18

Knowledge, pride a danger in the love of
•WG 27-28 (*see also* CR 10*, 14*, 17*; L 182-183; PP 76; SL 60*; WLN 34-36)
❖ WG 2:9 (*see also* CR 1:15*; 2:6, 16*; L 16 Apr 40; PP 5:5; SL 13:4*; WLN 3:6-8)

Knowledge: Regarding the evil tendency to love knowledge and discernment more than the object known and discerned
•CR 17; WG 28 (*see also* Pride of pursuing "culture") ❖ CR 2:16; WG 2:9 (*see also* Pride of pursuing "culture")

Knowledge ("scholarship"), transitory nature of all, including that of theology
•CR 162 ❖ CR 13:25

Knowledge: Screwtape advises that generations are to be kept from learning from past ages by inculcating the Historical Point of View
•SL 128-129 (*see also* SL 43, 118*, 133)
❖ SL 27:5 (*see also* SL 9:4; 25:6*; 28:2)

Knowledge, technical, not replaced by Christianity; when Christianity tells you to feed the hungry, it doesn't give you lessons in cookery
•GID 48 ❖ GID I 4:1

Knowledge: "The only people who achieve much are those who want knowledge so badly that they seek it while the conditions are still unfavourable"
•WG 30 ❖ WG 2:12

Knowledge, validity of, cannot be explained by perpetual happy coincidence
•CR 64-65 ❖ CR 5:17

Knox's translation of the Bible mentioned as being particularly good
•GID 231 ❖ GID II 10:5

Lamb, wrath of: If even the lamb is not the symbol of the harmless, where shall we turn? (re: phrases in the Bible which "should make our blood run cold")
•CR 120 ❖ CR 10:13

Landscape—*see also* Scenery

Landscape, the sky is to me one of the principal elements of any
•SJ 152 (*see also* L 110)
❖ SJ 10:4 (*see also* L 10 Jan 27)

Landscape, you have stood before some, which seems to embody what you have been looking for all your life—but your friend sees something different
•PP 145-146 (*see also* RP 95; SJ 142)
❖ PP 10:2 (*see also* RP 9:6; SJ 9:18)

Landscapes are religiously ambivalent; i.e., may be a preparation or medium for meeting God, *or* may be a distraction and impediment
•L 268
❖ L undated letter just before 2 Apr 56

Landscapes, one becomes more tolerant of various, after one's twentieth year
•L 63 ❖ L 1 Jul 21

Language—*see also* Words; *consider also* Expressions; Jargon

Language is a changing thing; "If you have a vernacular liturgy you must have a changing liturgy"
•LM 6-7 (*see also* GID 230-231)
❖ LM 1:11-17 (*see also* GID II 10:3)

Language a changing thing; sometimes the change of definition spoils the word for practical use (as in "Christian" and "gentleman")
•MC 10-11 (*see also* GID 333)
❖ MC P:12-14 (*see also* GID IV Letter 7)

Language, advice to a child regarding the use of, in writing
•L 270-271 ❖ L 26 Jun 56

Language, An Interpretation of Prayer Book, ("Miserable Offenders"—chapter title)
•GID 120-128 ❖ GID I ch. 14

Language, archaic, as is found in the Prayer Book: I find that people react to archaism most diversely—it antagonises some, and helps others
•LM 7 ❖ LM 1:18

Language, corruption of human, mentioned by Screwtape as giving the devil an advantage (re: the word "Democracy")*
•SL 161; WLN 59-60
❖ SL 32:19; WLN 4:19

Language, emotion in poetical religious: "Momentous matter, if believed, will arouse emotion whatever the language"
•CR 136 ❖ CR 11:16

Language, imaginative—*see also* Anthropomorphic images; Imagery; Language, metaphorical; Symbolism

Language, imaginative, as used in the thought of the ordinary man when picturing Christianity
•GID 68 (*see also* M 68-69)
❖ GID I 6:2 (*see also* M 10:2)

Language, imaginative, defense of the use of, in Christian literature and thinking
•GID 68-71; M 68-80 (*see also* GID 45-46; M 91-94) ❖ GID I ch. 6; M ch. 10 (*see also* GID I 3:15, 16; M 11:15-20)

Language, imaginative, defense of the use of, in describing God
•GID 184-185 ❖ GID I ch. 23

Language, imaginative, such as that used by hymn writers in describing Heaven not altogether inappropriate to the reality
•WG 66 ❖ WG 4:19

Language, imaginative, to describe

* These items reflect some interpretation on the part of the editor; the idea will not be found in these exact words. *See Introduction, p. ix.*
** These items are ideas of Lewis's which the editor has placed under a topic Lewis did not there intend to address. *See Introduction, p. ix.*
Entries without asterisks are not necessarily exact quotes, but the idea should be easy to find as worded.

Heaven
•M 157-163; MC 121
❖ M 16:25-32; MC III 10:6

Language, imaginative, used by Christians not to be identified with the thing believed; e.g., God pictured as a human form although He has no body
•GID 69-71; M 73
❖ GID I 6:5-8; M 10:12

Language, in my opinion there is no specifically religious
•CR 129 ❖ CR 11:1

Language in which we express our religious beliefs and experiences not a special language, but something that ranges between the Ordinary and the Poetical
•CR 135 ❖ CR 11:13

Language, inadequacy of, in communicating the essence of our lives
•CR 140 ❖ CR 11:23

Language is a living thing and words are bound to throw out new senses as a tree throws out new branches
•M 171-172 ❖ M App. A:11

Language, learned, has its value in making brevity possible
•GID 256 (see also GID 98)
❖ GID II 15:10 (see also GID I 10:38)

Language, learning a new: The great thing is to learn to think in it
•SJ 141 ❖ SJ 9:17

Language, metaphorical—see also Analogy(ies); Language, imaginative

Language, metaphorical, Christian theology shares with poetry the use of
•WG 85 ❖ WG 5:16

Language, metaphorical: Example of attempt to describe God and the Incarnation without the use of metaphor
•GID 71; M 79 ❖ GID I 6:9; M 10:19

Language, metaphorical, necessary in describing things other than physical objects
•GID 71; M 72; WG 88
❖ GID I 6:9; M 10:10; WG 5:20

Language, metaphorical: Seemingly trivial metaphors more adequate to illustrate high matters than those which

sneak into our minds when we relax our vigilance
•M 129 ❖ M 14:34

Language, metaphorical, to describe Heaven not to be misunderstood; it is merely a symbolical attempt to express the inexpressible
•MC 121 ❖ MC III 10:6

Language, metaphorical, to describe God: "...we can make our language more polysyllabic and duller; we cannot make it more literal"
•GID 71; M 79; WG 87 (see also L 147*)
❖ GID I 6:9; M 10:19; WG 5:20 (see also L 17 Jan 32*)

Language, modern, necessary in presenting timeless truths
•GID 93, 94 ❖ GID I 10:10, 12

Language, most human experiences cannot be communicated by Scientific; require the use of Poetic language
•CR 138, 140 ❖ CR 11:20, 23

Language, no living, can be timeless; you might as well ask for a motionless river
•LM 6 ❖ LM 1:11

Language not an infallible guide but it contains, with all its defects, a good deal of stored insight and experience (re: calling Need-love "love")
•FL 12 ❖ FL 1:5

Language of religion—see also Expressions

Language of religion: Analogy is unavoidable and necessary for certain purposes—but there is some death in it
•CR 137 ❖ CR 11:18

Language of Religion, The (chapter title)
•CR 129-141 ❖ CR ch. 11

Language: One obvious difference between poetry and straight prose is that poetry contains a great many more adjectives
•CR 131 ❖ CR 11:5

Language, plain, necessary in Christian apologetics and preaching
•GID 96-98, 183, 242-243, 254-257, 338
❖ GID I 10:18-38; 22:16, 17; II 12:4, 5; ch. 15; IV Letter 11

Language, Poetic, can convey to us the

quality of experiences which we have not had, or perhaps can never have...
•CR 133 ❖ CR 11:8, 9

Language, Poetic, is by no means merely an expression, nor a stimulant, of emotion but a real medium of information
•CR 130-134, esp. 134
❖ CR 11:4-11, esp. 11:11

Language, Poetic: Its pleasure is the pleasure at finding anything vividly conveyed to the imagination
•CR 130-131 (see also GID 66*)
❖ CR 11:4 (see also GID I 5:9*)

Language, Poetic, often expresses emotion not for its own sake but in order to inform us about the object which aroused the emotion
•CR 132, 134 ❖ CR 11:7, 11

Language, Poetic: Such information about religion as it has to give can be received only if you are prepared to meet it half-way—with good will
•CR 135, 137, 141
❖ CR 11:12, 16, 18, 25

Language, Poetic, uses factors within our experience so that they become pointers to something outside our experience
•CR 133 ❖ CR 11:9

Language, Poetic, vs. Ordinary or Scientific language: Poetic language vividly conveys factual information to the imagination
•CR 130-131 (see also GID 66*)
❖ CR 11:3, 4 (see also GID I 5:9*)

Language, Poetic, works with "subtle and sensitive exploitations of imagination and emotion" to convey information (re: language and religion)
•CR 137 ❖ CR 11:18

Language, private, (of our own circle) is to be guarded against; it may delude ourselves as well as mystify outsiders
•GID 256-257 ❖ GID II 15:11-13

Language, religious experiences cannot be conveyed to one another except by Poetic, —by hints, similes, metaphors, and emotions
•CR 137-138, 140 ❖ CR 11:19, 23

Language, the same process of attrition which empties good, of its virtue also empties bad language of much of its vice (re: ignorance in readers)
•CR 32-33 ❖ CR 2:53

Language: "...the unconscious linguistic process is continually degrading good words and blunting useful distinctions"
•GID 333 ❖ GID IV Letter 7

Language, Theological: "In it we are attempting...to state religious matter in a form more like that we use for scientific matter"
•CR 135 ❖ CR 11:13

Language, Theological, is in a sense alien to religion, omitting nearly all that really matters by its very precision
•CR 135-136 ❖ CR 11:13-15

Language, Theological, often necessary but it is not the language religion naturally speaks
•CR 135 ❖ CR 11:13

Language too vague to describe God; He is unspeakable not by being indefinite but by being too definite
•M 91 (see also Perelandra 33*)
❖ M 11:15 (see also Perelandra 3:2*)

Laodiceanism appreciated by Screwtape: "A moderated religion is as good for us as no religion at all—and more amusing"*
•SL 43 (see also SL 75)
❖ SL 9:3 (see also SL 16:5)

Laodiceanism ("lukewarm and complacent") and extremism ("Unbalanced and prone to faction") both mentioned by Screwtape as serving his purposes*
•SL 33 ❖ SL 7:2

Last night, what if this present were the world's, (quote from Donne)
•WLN 109 (see also WLN 111-113)
❖ WLN 7:29 (see also WLN 7:34-38)

Last-day events will be in a sense normal (there are always wars and rumours of wars, etc.)*
•WLN 108 (see also WG 22*)
❖ WLN 7:27 (see also WG 2:4*)

Laughter and humour, Screwtape points out ways in which, can be used to serve diabolical purposes

•SL 49-52 (*see also* Humour)

❖ SL ch. 11 (*see also* Humour)

Laughter mentioned by Screwtape as "a meaningless acceleration in the rhythm of celestial experience"; he admits it has no meaning for devils
•SL 50 ❖ SL 11:2

Laughter, Screwtape divides the causes of human, into Joy, Fun, the Joke Proper, and Flippancy
•SL 50 ❖ SL 11:2

Law(s)—*see also* Commandment(s); Moral law(s); Principles; Rules; *consider also* Legalism

Law, a development of Hooker's conception of, (re: "proper" laws, such as the law of Prudence, and "lower" laws, such as the law of gravity)
•PP 82 and ftnt. ❖ PP 5:10 and ftnt.

Law and punishment: "Mercy, detached from Justice, grows unmerciful" (re: "Humanitarian" concept of punishment)
•GID 294 (*see also* Punishment)
❖ GID III 4:13 (*see also* Punishment)

Law: Christianity brought no new ethical code into the world; Jesus' commands are paralleled in classical, ancient Egyptian, Babylonian, and Chinese texts
•CR 46-47, 51, 52-53, 55, 77 (*see also* Law of Nature; book *The Abolition of Man*) ❖ CR 4:5-7, 17, 20-22, 26; 6:16 (*see also* Law of Nature; book *The Abolition of Man*)

Law, Christianity offers forgiveness for having broken the moral, and supernatural help towards keeping it, and by doing so re-affirms it
•CR 46-47 ❖ CR 4:7

Law ("morality") connected with a Lawgiver ("Numinous") in the third stage or element of religion; this is the most surprising jump
•PP 22-23 ❖ PP 1:13

Law, criminal, protects the criminal more than the victim
•GID 306-310, esp. 307
❖ GID III ch. 6, esp. 6:7

Law, duty, and morality are essential until a man really loves God and his fellow man
•LM 114-116 (*see also* L 277; PP 100*)
❖ LM 21:11-14 (*see also* L 18 Jul 57; PP 6:11*)

Law, effort of the Psalmist to keep the, springs not from servile fear but from love of moral beauty
•RP 59-60 ❖ RP 6:9

Law: God enjoins what is good because it is good; not a mere arbitrary toss-up
•RP 60-61 (*see also* CR 79-81; PP 100)
❖ RP 6:10, 11 (*see also* CR 6:20-22; PP 6:12)

Law, I submit that the Fall did not deprave our knowledge of the, in the same degree as it depraved our power to fulfil it
•CR 79 (*see also* Depravity, doctrine of Total) ❖ CR 6:19 (*see also* Depravity, doctrine of Total)

Law, in order to transcend the moral, we must first admit its claims upon us, try to meet those claims, and admit our failure
•PP 65 (*see also* LM 114-115; MC 94, 124-125, 127-131) ❖ PP 4:13 (*see also* LM 21:11-13; MC III 5:12; 11:7; 12:3-9)

Law, in the perfect and eternal world, will vanish; but the results of having lived faithfully under it will not
•LM 116 ❖ LM 21:14

Law: Judges are trained in a science which originally accepted guidance from the Law of Nature, and from Scripture
•GID 288 ❖ GID III 4:5

Law, moral, cannot be separated; it is all one ("Every vice leads to cruelty")*
•PP 65 ❖ PP 4:12

Law, moral, exists to be transcended; yet while God may be more than moral goodness, He is not less; "The road to the promised land runs past Sinai"
•PP 65 (*see also* CR 45; LM 114-116; MC 130-131) ❖ PP 4:13 (*see also* CR 4:2; LM 21:11-14; MC 12:9)

Law: Moral realm exists to be transcended, but until we are perfected we have the category of duty*
•LM 114-116 (*see also* CR 45; GID 144;

L 277; MC 130-131; PP 65, 100*) ❖ LM 21:11-14 (see also CR 4:2; GID I 16:26*; L 18 Jul 57; MC III 12:9; PP 4:13; 6:11*)

Law of decent behaviour seems to be known by all people everywhere
•MC 17-26 (see also CR 44-56, 72-81; M 34-38; RP 13; book The Abolition of Man) ❖ MC I 1:1 to 2:8 (see also CR 4:1-27, 6:1-23; M 5:1-11; RP 2:8; book The Abolition of Man)

Law of diminishing returns as regards pleasure
•SL 116-117 (see also SL 41-42, 55) ❖ SL 25:3, 4 (see also SL 9:2; 12:4)

Law of God a better indication of God's character than the universe itself; universe is beautiful but also terrifying and dangerous
•MC 37 ❖ MC I 5:3

Law of God associated with "the all piercing, all detecting sunshine...luminous, severe, disinfectant, exultant" in Psalm 19
•RP 63-64 (see also RP 81) ❖ RP 6:13 (see also RP 8:9)

Law of God "can take on a cancerous life of its own and work against the thing for whose sake it existed" —through legalism
•RP 57-58 ❖ RP 6:6, 7

Law of God: I believe that God commands certain things because they are right, not that they are right because He commands them
•PP 100 (see also CR 79-80; RP 61) ❖ PP 6:12 (see also CR 6:20, 21; RP 6:11)

Law of God in the Psalms
•RP 54-65 (see also GID 130) ❖ RP ch. 6 (see also GID I 16:2)

Law of God, keeping of, not a kind of bargain for a reward, but it affects our character
•MC 86-87 ❖ MC III 4:8

Law of God must have shown with an extraordinary radiance when the Jews compared it with the laws of Pagan deities (requiring baby sacrifices, etc.)
•RP 62, 64 ❖ RP 6:12, 14

Law of God seen by the Psalmists as enjoyable and sweet; this was to me at first very mysterious
•RP 54-55 (see also GID 130) ❖ RP 6:1-3 (see also GID I 16:2)

Law of God: "Surely it could be more aptly compared to the dentist's forceps or the front line than to anything enjoyable and sweet"
•RP 55 ❖ RP 6:3

Law of God, the assertion by the Psalmist that the, is "true" means that in it you find the real, well-grounded directions for living
•RP 60-61 ❖ RP 6:10, 11

Law of God, to the Psalmist, was a subject for study; thus he might develop a delight as in one's favorite subject—and is then open to the danger of spiritual pride
•RP 56-57 ❖ RP 6:5

Laws of God always based upon what is intrinsically good—something we ought to do even if God had not commanded it
•PP 100-101 (see also CR 79-80; RP 61) ❖ PP 6:12 (see also CR 6:20, 21; RP 6:11)

Laws of God are like directions for running a machine
•MC 69 (see also Machine) ❖ MC III 1:1 (see also Machine)

Laws of God, attempting obedience to, teaches us our dependence upon Him
•MC 94, 124-125, 127-131 (see also CR 169*) ❖ MC III 5:12; 11:7; 12:3-9 (see also CR 14:20, 21*)

Law of Human Nature, The (chapter title)
•MC 17-21 ❖ MC I ch. 1

Law of Nature—see also Moral law

Law of Nature: Behind all laws of the state there is a Natural Law; otherwise, the actual laws of the state become an absolute which cannot be judged
•GID 318 (Compare with GID 315*) ❖ GID III 9:7, 8 (Compare with GID III 8:16*)

Law of Nature, if a man will read the Encyclopedia of Religion and Ethics he will no longer doubt that there is a universally accepted
•CR 77 ❖ CR 6:16

Law of Nature, if there is no, there is no

•SL 40-44 ❖ SL ch. 9

Law of Undulation, Screwtape mentions, which refers to the human tendency to experience peaks and troughs in every department of life
•SL 36-39 ❖ SL ch. 8

Law, one mustn't make the Christian life into a punctilious system of, like the Jewish; it raises scruples when we don't keep it, and presumption when we do
•LAL 38 ❖ LAL 20/2/55

Law: Pleasures of a good conscience suggested by one scholar as what the Psalmists are referring to when they speak of the Law being sweeter than honey
•RP 55-56 ❖ RP 6:4

Law: Possibly what lies beyond existence ...is not simply a law but also a begetting love...God is not merely good, but goodness...
•CR 80 ❖ CR 6:21

Law, Psalm 119 as the Psalm specially devoted to the
•RP 58-60 ❖ RP 6:8, 9

Law, Psalmist probably felt about the, as he felt about his poetry; both involved exact and loving conformity to an intricate pattern
•RP 59 ❖ RP 6:9

Law, Psalmists' delight in, is a delight in having touched firmness—like a pedestrian weary of muddy short-cuts
•RP 62 ❖ RP 6:11

"Law" referred to in Psalms does not mean simply the Ten Commandments; it is the whole complex legislation contained in Leviticus, Numbers and Deuteronomy
•RP 56 ❖ RP 6:5

Law ("rules") in common life: Alternative is not freedom but tyranny*
•GID 286 ❖ GID III 3:10

Law, Screwtape points out that humans tend to develop vague theories about the, in order to escape its demands
•SL 157; WLN 55
❖ SL 32:10; WLN 4:10

Law, St. Paul recognized our inability to

keep the, but at the same time he asserted our power to perceive the Law's goodness and rejoice in it
•CR 79 ❖ CR 6:19

Law, The Reality of the (chapter title)
•MC 26-30 ❖ MC I ch. 3

Law, we as Christians may find increasing reasons to value God's, over the current ways of thinking
•RP 64-65 (see also SL 47-48*, 110-113*)
❖ RP 6:14 (see also SL 10:4*; 24:1-5*)

Law, we cannot discover our failure to keep God's, except by trying our hardest—but all this trying leads to our saying to God, "You must do this; I can't"
•MC 127-128 ❖ MC III 12:5

Law: We may treat the regimental rules as a dead letter or counsel of perfection, but neglect of them is going to cost every man his life
•PP 64 ❖ PP 4:10

Law, What Lies Behind the (chapter title)
•MC 31-35 ❖ MC I ch. 4

Law, William: Serious Call to a Devout and Holy Life mentioned as the best book on "prides, superiorities, and affronts"
•LAL 44-45 ❖ LAL 30/6/55

Law, William, quote from: "I earnestly beseech all who conceive they have suffered an affront to believe that it is very much less than they suppose"
•LAL 96-97 (see also LAL 59)
❖ LAL 24 Feb 61 (see also LAL 3/8/56)

Law, William, quote from:"If the heavenly life is not grown up in you, it signifies nothing what you have chosen in the stead of, or why you have chosen it"
•CR 12 ❖ CR 2 prelim. quote

Law, William, quote from: "There can be no surer proof of a confirmed pride than a belief that one is sufficiently humble"
•LAL 96; PP 55, top (see also CR 14; MC 114; SL 62-63)
❖ LAL 24 Feb 61; PP 4 prelim. quote (see also CR 2:4; MC III 8:14; SL 14:2)

Law, William: Serious Call to a Devout and

Holy Life mentioned
•L 143, 299 ❖ L 24 Oct 31; 9 May 61
Law: "You cannot make men good by law: and without good men you cannot have a good society"
•MC 72 ❖ MC III 1:7
Laws of God—*see* Law of God
Laws of Nature—*see* Law of Nature
Laws of the state, behind all, there is a Natural Law; otherwise, the actual laws of the state become an absolute which cannot be judged
•GID 318 (Compare with GID 315*)
❖ GID III 9:7, 8 (Compare with GID III 8:16*)
Lawgiver, belief in the existence of a, imports despair rather than comfort
•L 193 (*see also* MC 039; PP 055*) ❖ L 15 May 41 (*see also* MC I 5:4; PP 4:1*)
Layman (or "amateur"), I am not a real theologian but only a
•CR 94, 152; GID 60, 62, 89, 332-333; L 219, 223; LM 101; MC 6; PP 10; RP 1-2; WG 71; WLN 93-94
❖ CR 8:1; 13:1; GID I 4:56 (Ques. 14); 4:60 (Ques. 16); 10:1, 2; IV Letter 7; L 2 Sep 49; 28 Nov 50; LM 19:3; MC P:2; PP P:2; RP 1:1, 2; WG 4:28; WLN 7:1
Laymen, it is more wholesome for us to dwell on the faults of the, rather than on those of the clergy
•LAL 15 ❖ LAL May 30th 53
Laymen, job of finding the Christian solution to our social problems is really on us
MC 79 ❖ MC III 3:3
Lazarus: I think he, not St. Stephen, ought to be celebrated as the first martyr; "to be brought back and have all one's dying to do again was rather hard"
•GO 48; L 307 (*see also* LAL 119)
❖ GO 3:12; L 17 Sep 63 (*see also* LAL 25 Jun 63)
Lazarus, miracle of raising, a simple reversal yet it anticipates the general resurrection of all men
•M 150-151 ❖ M 16:15
Lazarus, we follow One who stood and wept at the grave of; as Christians we hope most of death, yet cannot cease

to fight against it
•GID 149-150 ❖ GID I 17:7
Laziness, a besetting sin all my life has been one which I never suspected—that of
•L 187-188 ❖ L 16 Jul 40
Laziness means more work in the long run (analogy of lazy boys to our desire to keep our personal happiness)
•MC 168 ❖ MC IV 8:6
Laziness of grief, no one ever told me about the; I loathe the slightest effort
•GO 3-4 ❖ GO 1:6
Learned—*see also* Intellectual
Learned and the adult have no advantage over the simple and the child, on the only level of any importance
•PP 79 (*see also* LM 103; PP 75*)
❖ PP 5:7 (*see also* LM 19:7; PP 5:5*)
Learned ("intellectual") life not the only road to God, nor the safest, but may be the road for some
•WG 27-28 ❖ WG 2:9
Learned life is, for some, a duty
•WG 29 ❖ WG 2:11
Learned life one of the appointed approaches to the Divine reality
•WG 32 ❖ WG 2:14
Learning—*see also* Education; Knowledge
Learning a new language: The great thing is to learn to think in it
•SJ 141 ❖ SJ 9:17
Learning as a catalyst for religious emotion: Many find that "the heart sings unbidden...while working their way through a tough bit of theology..."*
•GID 205 ❖ GID II 4:7
Learning in secular subjects: Is it justifiable for Christians?
•WG 20-32 ❖ WG ch. 2
Learning in War-Time (chapter title)
•WG 20-32 ❖ WG ch. 2
Learning may be hampered by such things as examinations (an example of how means may hamper ends)*
•WG 109 ❖ WG 7:5
Learning, no one has time to finish; the longest human life leaves a man, in any branch of learning, a beginner
•WG 30 ❖ WG 2:13

Learning, plausible reasons have never been lacking for putting off our, (re: education in time of war)
•WG 22, 29-30 ❖ WG 2:4, 12

Learning, Screwtape mentions that where, makes a free commerce between the ages there is possibility that the errors of one age may be corrected by the truth of another
•SL 129 ❖ SL 27:5

Learning: What we learn from experience depends on the kind of philosophy we bring to it
•M 3 (see also GID 25-26)
❖ M 1:2 (see also GID I 2:1)

Leaving (a place, job, etc.): "There will never be a time when you can't leave Cambridge; there could easily be one when you couldn't return"*
•L 288 ❖ L 19 Jun 59

Leaving home and family as part of the allegory of Bride and Bridegroom; a vocation is at first a costly honour
•RP 130-132 ❖ RP 12:10

Leaving things behind: "There is a 'rumness,' a ghostliness, about even a Windsor chair when it says, 'You will not see me again'"
•SJ 131 ❖ SJ 8:19

Legal system in Britain: We have been spared the almost world-wide difficulty of the "small-man" in getting his case heard in court*
•RP 11 (see also CR 124)
❖ RP 2:4 (see also CR 10:26)

Legalism—see also Law(s); Moral law(s); Obedience; Righteousness by faith/grace

Legalism: "All the rabbit in us is to disappear—the worried, conscientious, ethical rabbit as well as the cowardly and sensual rabbit"*
•GID 112 ❖ GID I 12:10

Legalism as "the sin, and simultaneously the punishment, of the Scribes and Pharisees"
•RP 57-58 ❖ RP 6:7

Legalism: Faced with the great issues of Christianity, can you really remain wholly absorbed in your own blessed

"moral development"?*
•GID 112 ❖ GID I 12:9

Legalism: For most of us, "...gospel replaces law and longing transforms obedience as gradually as the tide lifts a grounded ship"*
•WG 5 ❖ WG 1:3

Legalism: "Nothing gives one a more spuriously good conscience than keeping rules, even if there has been a total absence of all real charity and faith"*
•LAL 38 ❖ LAL 20/2/55

Legalism: One mustn't make the Christian life into a punctilious system of *law*, like Jews; it raises scruples when we don't keep it and presumption when we do
•LAL 38 ❖ LAL 20/2/55

Legalism: Sacrificial rites in Judaism became separated from unity with God; their punctual performance came to be seen as the only thing God wanted*
•RP 49 ❖ RP 5:7

Legalism: Screwtape lauds the devils' labour toward causing humans to forget what Paul had to say "about food and other unessentials"*
•SL 75 ❖ SL 16:5

Legalism: "Scruples are always a bad thing—if only because they usually distract us from real duties"*
•LM 33 (see also SL 66)
❖ LM 6:13 (see also SL 14:5)

Legalism, self-righteousness and anxiety as the results of
•RP 57-58 ❖ RP 6:6, 7

Legalism: "You cannot make men good by law: and without good men you cannot have a good society"*
•MC 72 ❖ MC III 1:7

Legalists described by Screwtape: "Some were all rules and relics and rosaries; others were all drab clothes, long faces and petty traditional abstinences"*
•SL 171; WLN 69
❖ SL 32:40; WLN 4:40

Legend(s)—see also Myth(s); Mythology

Legends, the Gospels do not qualify as
•GID 158-159 (see also CR 154-155; GID 101; SJ 236) ❖ GID I 19:4, 5 (see

also CR 13:4, 5; GID I 10:47; SJ 15:7)

Leisure, a good deal of the high-sounding doctrine of, is only a defense of laziness
•L 187-188 ❖ L 16 Jul 40

Leisure, our, is a matter of serious concern; there is no neutral ground in the universe (re: reading)
•CR 33-34 ❖ CR 2:54

Lending money at interest is what our whole economic system is based on, yet Moses, Aristotle, and the Christians agreed in condemning it
•MC 81 ❖ MC III 3:6

Lenten lands: It may be that our physical, sense-perceiving body sleeps in death, and the intellectual soul is sent to Lenten lands...
•LM 123 ❖ LM 22:20

Leprechauns, I doubt if you will find any, in Eire now; the Radio has driven them away
•LAL 62 ❖ LAL Sep 8/56

Leprechauns mentioned ("smaller than men")
•LAL 33 ❖ LAL Oct 9th 54

Let's Pretend (chapter title)
•MC 160-166 ❖ MC IV ch. 7

Letter, what a pleasant change to get a, which does *not* say all the conventional things
•L 307 ❖ L 27 Sep 63

Letters: "It is an essential of the happy life that a man would have almost no mail and never dread the postman's knock"
•SJ 143 ❖ SJ 9:18

Letters to Malcolm: Chiefly on Prayer, mention of writing
•LAL 116 ❖ LAL 22 Apr 63

Letters: When one is grieving, not only writing but even reading a letter is too much
•GO 3 ❖ GO 1:6

Letters: Why they are so hard to write and so much harder to read is that people confine themselves to news
•L 54
❖ L undated letter just after 28 Mar 21

Letter-writing—*see also* Correspondence

Letter-writing, Lewis's distaste for
•LAL 23-24, 30, 32, 37, 50, 71, 82, 88, 104, 112; 113-114; L 300; SJ 143
❖ LAL Jan 1st 54; 17th Apr 54; Sep 19/54; 29/1/55; 19/12/55; 14/1/58; 6/5/59; 22 Dec 59; Ascension Day 1962; 2 Jan 63;26/1/63; L 3 Dec 61; SJ 9:18

Letter-writing, Lewis's: "...you could hardly conceive what hundreds of hours a year I spend coaxing a rheumatic wrist to drive this pen across paper"
•LAL 66 (*see also* LAL 71)
❖ LAL 17/2/57 (*see also* LAL 14/1/58)

Letter-writing on Sunday as "Sabbath-breach"
•LAL 53 ❖ LAL 4/3/56

Letter-writing: Women love it and men loathe it
•LAL 104 ❖ LAL Ascension Day 1962

Lewis, C. S.—*consider also* Pessimism, Lewis's

Lewis acknowledges the limits of his own scope and knowledge*
•CR 94, 152; GID 60, 62, 89; L 219, 223; LM 101; MC 6; PP 10; RP 1-2; WG 71; WLN 93-94 ❖ CR 8:1; 13:1; GID I 4:56 (Ques. 14); I 4:60 (Ques. 16); 10:1, 2; L 2 Sep 49; 28 Nov 50; LM 19:3; MC P:2; PP P:2; RP 1:1, 2; WG 4:28; WLN 7:1

Lewis, Albert—*see* Father, Lewis's

Lewis describes a phase in which he aspired to be a flashy dresser
•SJ 67 ❖ SJ 4:14

Lewis describes himself as "a dogmatic Christian untinged with Modernist reservations and committed to supernaturalism in its full rigour"
•CR 44 ❖ CR 4:1

Lewis describes himself as a "middle-aged moralist"
•WG 93-94 ❖ WG 6:2, 3

Lewis describes himself as a person "of the old square-rigged type" for whom "the world as it is becoming is simply *too much*..."
•L 177 ❖ L 18 Feb 40

Lewis describes himself as a "quiet ruminant" who loathes "the stir" and "the sense of 'great issues'"

•L 179 ❖ L 22 Mar 40

Lewis describes himself as a romantic
- •SJ 5, 7, 173 (see also SJ 152, 201, 203)
- ❖ SJ 1:2, 4; 11:10 (see also SJ 10:4; 13:7, 9)

Lewis describes himself as a youth: "I was, in my ineffective way, a tender-hearted creature..."
- •SJ 65 ❖ SJ 4:11

Lewis describes himself at his conversion as "the most dejected and reluctant convert in all England"
- •SJ 228-229 ❖ SJ 14:23

Lewis describes himself in adolescence: "I was sick with desire; that sickness better than health"
- •SJ 118-119 ❖ SJ 8:1

Lewis describes his ancestors and relatives
- •SJ 3-4, 42-46 ❖ SJ 1:1; 3:1-4

Lewis describes his childhood fear of abandonment
- •SJ 39 ❖ SJ 2:17

Lewis describes his conversion: "...the steady, unrelenting approach of Him whom I so earnestly desired not to meet"
- •SJ 228 ❖ SJ 14:23

Lewis describes his early religious experience (while a student at "Belsen") as involving a great deal of fear
- •SJ 33-34 ❖ SJ 2:14

Lewis describes his face as an adolescent: "I am the kind of person who gets told, 'And take that look off your face too'"
- •SJ 94 (see also SJ 188, 200-201*, 217)
- ❖ SJ 6:18 (see also SJ 12:10; 13:5*; 14:8)

Lewis describes his futile efforts as a schoolboy to produce by sheer will-power prayers which were vivid in the imagination and the affections
- •SJ 61-62 (see also L 256*)
- ❖ SJ 4:8 (see also L 31 Jul 54*)

Lewis describes his military service
- •SJ 186-198 (see also L 33-46)
- ❖ SJ 12:6-13:1 (see also L 28 Jan 17 to undated letter just before 27 Jan 19)

Lewis describes his own (eventually fatal) disease
- •L 278, 280, 300, 301-302, 305; LAL 119, 121, 122 ❖ L 24 Aug 57; 6 Nov 57;

28 Oct 61; 20 Dec 61; 10 Aug 62; undated letter of Aug 62; LAL 28 Jun 63; 9 Jul 63; 16th Jul 63

Lewis describes his own lack of competence in business matters
- •LAL 61 ❖ LAL Sep 8/56

Lewis describes his work as a professor ("Don") at Oxford
- •L 214 ❖ L 29 May 48

Lewis describes some of the opposition which he encountered after becoming a Christian
- •GID 252 ❖ GID II 14:9

Lewis describes taking the final step in his conversion to Christianity while on a trip to Whipsnade Zoo
- •SJ 237-238 ❖ SJ 15:8, 9

Lewis describes the duality of his inner and outer lives during adolescence: "The two lives do not seem to influence each other at all"
- •SJ 78, 118-119 (see also LAL 83)
- ❖ SJ 5:12; 8:1 (see also LAL Jun 7th 59)

Lewis explains his "culpably defective" interest in large impersonal movements and causes
- •SJ 32-33 ❖ SJ 2:12

Lewis, Florence Hamilton—see Mother, Lewis's

Lewis: "In the course of life I could put up with any amount of monotony far more patiently than even the smallest disturbance, bother, bustle..."
- •SJ 116-117 ❖ SJ 7:21

Lewis indicates his imminent conversion to Christianity in a letter to Owen Barfield: "Terrible things are happening to me"
- •L 141
- ❖ L undated letter just after 10 Jun 30

Lewis, Joy Davidman Gresham—see Joy (Lewis's wife)

Lewis: Kirk told my father, "You may make a writer or a scholar of him, but you'll not make anything else"
- •SJ 183 (see also CR 20*)
- ❖ SJ 12:2 (see also CR 2:23*)

Lewis makes reference to his own declining health
- •LAL 67, 68, 70, 86, 89-90, 98, 102, 103-

104, 106, 113, 119, 121 ❖ LAL Jun 18th 57; Aug 12th 57; Nov 3d 57; Nov 30th 57; Aug 3/59; 13 Feb 60; 21 Apr 61; 6 Apr 62; Ascension Day 62; 3 Sep 62; 8 Jan 63; 26/1/63; 28 Jun 63; 9 Jul 63

Lewis mentions being "a barbarously early riser...I love the empty, silent, dewy, cobwebby hours"
•LAL 78 (see also Morning)
❖LAL Sep 30 58 (see also Morning)

Lewis mentions friendship as having been the chief source of his happiness
•SJ 33 ❖ SJ 2:12

Lewis mentions his anti-Government nature as a student at Oxford
•SJ 209 ❖ SJ 13:17

Lewis mentions his dislike of solitude
•LAL 117 (see also LAL 120)
❖ LAL 10 Jun 63 (see also LAL 6 Jul 63)

Lewis mentions his fear of poverty
•LAL 21 (see also LAL 79) ❖ LAL Aug 10th 53 (see also LAL Oct 30 58)

Lewis mentions his fear of spiders
•L 257; LAL 21 (see also SJ 8-9)
❖ L 1 Nov 54; LAL Aug 10th 53 (see also SJ 1:6, 7)

Lewis mentions medieval allegory as his own subject of study
•L 155-157 ❖ L 7 Jun 34

Lewis mentions that his long-evaded encounter with God happened at a time when he was making a serious attempt to obey his conscience
•CR 169 ❖ CR 14:20

Lewis mentions The Abolition of Man as almost his favorite among his own books
•LAL 39 (see also L 204; MC 19)
❖ LAL 20/2/55 (see also L undated letter of May 1944; MC I 1:7)

Lewis observes that even as an atheist the authors he most enjoyed were Christian
•SJ 213-214 ❖ SJ 14:3

Lewis, on himself: "I was big for my age, a great lout of a boy..."
•SJ 94, 96 ❖ SJ 6:18, 20

Lewis, on himself: "...I'm not a man for crowds and Best Clothes"
•LAL 17 (see also SJ 22, 67)

❖ LAL Jun 22d 53 (see also SJ 2:1; 4:14)

Lewis, on himself: My task was simply that of a translator, turning Christian doctrine into language that unscholarly people could understand
•GID 183 ❖ GID I 22:16

Lewis, on himself: "Talking too much is one of my vices..."
•LAL 55 ❖ LAL 15/4/56

Lewis, on himself: "The things I assert most vigorously are those that I resisted long and accepted late"
•SJ 213 ❖ SJ 14:2

Lewis, on his childhood: "I am a product of long corridors, empty sunlit rooms, upstairs indoor silences, attics explored in solitude...Also, of endless books"
•SJ 10 ❖ SJ 1:8

Lewis, on his own religion: "I am a very ordinary layman of the Church of England, not especially 'high' nor especially 'low'..."
•MC 6 ❖ MC P:2

Lewis, on his own works: "I am glad you like my stories. They are the part of my work I like best"*
•LAL 62 ❖ LAL Sep 8/56

Lewis, on his own writing as a child: He mentions trying not to make his stories interesting from the start, or (he believed) they wouldn't be like grown-up stories
•CR 33 ❖ CR 2:53

Lewis, the imaginative, is older and more basic than either the religious writer or the critic
•L 260
❖ L undated letter just before 2 Feb 55

Lewis views himself as having the label of "professional controversialist and itinerant prize-fighter"
•L 159
❖ L undated letter just after 2 Sep 37

Lewis, Warren Hamilton, letters written by, to the American Lady
•LAL 99, 100, 101 ❖ LAL 12th Jul 61; 20th Aug 61; 7th Oct 61

Lewis, Warren Hamilton, mentioned or referred to (C. S. Lewis's brother)

•LAL 45, 65-66, 92, 116, 117; SJ 6-7, 11-14, 18-19, 32, 38-41, 54, 56-57, 76, 91, 119, 126-128, 131, 149-150, 215
❖ LAL 5/10/55; 17/2/57; 24 Sep 60; 19 May 63; 10 Jun 63; SJ 1:4, 9-12, 20; 2:12, 17, 18; 3:13; 4:1; 5:7; 6:14; 8:2, 8-12; 8:19; 10:1, 2; 14:6

Lewis's conversion—see Conversion, Lewis's

Lewis's disclaimers of himself as an "expert" or a "real theologian"
•CR 94, 152; GID 60, 62, 89, 332-333; L 219, 223; LM 101; MC 6; PP 10; RP 1-2; WG 71; WLN 93-94
❖ CR 8:1; 13:1; GID I 4:56 (Ques. 14); 4:60 (Ques. 16); 10:1, 2; IV Letter 7; L 2 Sep 49; 28 Nov 50; LM 19:3; MC P:2; PP P:2; RP 1:1, 2; WG 4:28; WLN 7:1

Lewis's dislike for fancy clothes
•SJ 22 (see also LAL 17; SJ 67) ❖ SJ 2:1 (see also LAL Jun 22d 53; SJ 4:14)

Lewis's dislike for new suits
•LAL 116 ❖ LAL 22 Apr 63

Lewis's father's family mentioned
•SJ 3 ❖ SJ 1:1

Lewis's mother's family—see Hamilton family

Lewis's own moral development: "When I first came to the University I was as nearly without a moral conscience as a boy could be"*
•PP 38 ❖ PP 3:4

Liabilities, limited—see Limited liabilities
Liars—consider also Dishonesty
Liars, one trouble about habitual, is that since you can't believe anything they say, you can't feel the slightest interest in it
•LAL 107 ❖ LAL 2 Oct 62

Liars, to call them, would be as undeserved a compliment as to say that a dog was bad at arithmetic (re: his critics)
•LAL 51 ❖ LAL 8/2/56

Liberal ...—consider also Modern ...
Liberal Christianity "can only supply an ineffectual echo to the massive chorus of agreed and admitted unbelief"
•LM 119 ❖ LM 22:4

Liberal Christianity: Few people are con-verted from scepticism to this; most unbelievers, when they come in at all, come in a good deal further
•LM 119 ❖ LM 22:5

Liberal Christianity is stagnant
•GID 91 ❖ GID I 10:6

Liberal Christianity: The liberal writers who are continually whittling down the truth of the Gospel are turning people away from the church
•GID 260 (see also GID 99*; L 170; LM 75-76; MC 46-48; SL 73-74) ❖ GID II 16:12 (see also GID I 10:41*; L 5 Nov 39; LM 14:13; MC II 2:1-5; SL 16:3)

Liberal Christians are honest men and preach their version of Christianity, as we preach ours, because they believe it to be true
•LM 120 ❖ LM 22:6

"Liberal" Christians are the most arrogant and intolerant
•L 229 (see also GID 327*) ❖ L 23 Apr 51 (see also GID IV Letter 2*)

Liberal Christians want the security of a religion so contrived that no possible fact could ever refute it
•LM 121 ❖ LM 22:11

"Liberal" Christians who disbelieve in the supernatural genuinely believe that writers of my sort are doing a great deal of harm
•LM 118-119 ❖ LM 22:1-3

"Liberal" (or "modern") Christianity defined as excluding any real Supernaturalism*
•GID 89 ❖ GID I 10:2

Liberal theology—see Theology, liberal
"Liberalism" coming to be used simply as a term of disapprobation
•CR 78 ❖ CR 6:18

Liberalism mentioned by Screwtape as a subject for human criticism and warnings just at the times when men are becoming slaves and tyrants
•SL 118 ❖ SL 25:5

Liberation of instinct as one of the values implicit in modern literature
•CR 16, 21-22 ❖ CR 2:13, 29

Liberty—see Freedom
Library, Lewis's enjoyment of the: "...the

books, silence, the distant
sound of bat and ball...bees buzzing
at the open windows, and freedom"
•SJ 113-114 ❖ SJ 7:18

Lie(s); Lying—*see* Dishonesty

Life—*consider also* Pessimism, Lewis's;
World

Life: A man "should never give all his
heart to anything which will end
when his life ends"
•WLN 110 ❖ WLN 7:31

Life, a man should "sit loose" to his own
individual, remembering how short,
precarious, and temporary it is
•WLN 110 (*see also* L 161-162, 306; LM
26-27) ❖ WLN 7:31 (*see also* L 12 Sep
38; 21 Nov 62; LM 5:10-13)

Life, a man's, may be stolen away not by
sweet sins but in a dreary flickering
of the mind over it knows not what
and knows not why...
•SL 56 (*see also* SL 42*, 144*)
❖ SL 12:4 (*see also* SL 9:2*; 30:4*)

Life, a person who leads an incomplete
and crippled, having never been in
love, etc. as illustration of the loss incurred by those who never learn to appreciate God
•RP 92 ❖ RP 9:3

Life: A single second of lived time contains
more than can be recorded; therefore
we know next to nothing about history (re: "Historicism")*
•CR 107 ❖ CR 9:15

Life: According to Screwtape, God's view
is that human birth is important
chiefly as the qualification for human
death which is the gate to Heaven
•SL 133-134 (*see also* SJ 117*)
❖ SL 28:3 (*see also* SJ 7:21*)

Life, according to the Christian picture of
the universe, is "a mingled yarn, good
and ill together"
•WG 75-76 ❖ WG 5:5

Life after death—*see also* Dead, state of the;
Eternal life; Immortality

Life after death: "Can I honestly say that I
believe she [Joy] is now anything?
...What do I really think?"
•GO 24-27 ❖ GO 2:8-12

Life after death: "I find that this question,
however important it may be in itself,
is not after all very important in relation to grief"
•GO 27 ❖ GO 2:12

Life after death, I have been given no assurance about H.'s [Joy's]
•GO 7-8 ❖ GO 1:13, 14

Life after death: "I think I was much
helped by my own father after his
death; as if Our Lord welcomed the
newly dead with the gift of some
power..."
•L 230 ❖ L 27 Mar 51

Life after death, it seems clear that in most
parts of the Old Testament there is
little or no belief in
•RP 36, 38-39 ❖ RP 4:6, 9-12

Life after death: Lewis mentions twice
sensing the presence of a person after
their death
•L 290 ❖ L 3 Dec 59

Life after death, the Jewish conception of,
("Sheol") was common to many an-
cient religions
•RP 37 ❖ RP 4:8

Life after death, what the risen body of
Christ reveals about
•M 145-163 ❖ M 16:5-32

Life: "Ah well, it will not last forever.
There will come a day for all of us
when 'it is finished'"
•LAL 64-65 (*see also* LAL 66, 120- 121)
❖ LAL 4/1/57 (*see also* LAL 17/2/57;
6 Jul 63)

Life, all your, you are slowly turning into
a heavenly or a hellish creature
•MC 86-87, 107 (*see also* MC 117; RP
136*; SL 53-54; WLN 54-55*)
❖ MC III 4:8, 9; 7:9 (*see also* MC III 9:6-
8; RP 12:16*; SL 12:1; WLN 4:10)

Life and death, I wish, were not the only
alternatives; one could imagine a "via
media"
•L 73 ❖ L 7 Apr 22

Life: "And how or why did such a reality
blossom (or fester) here and there into
the terrible phenomenon called consciousness?"
•GO 32 ❖ GO 2:20

Life: Are you often struck with how *late* most people's lives begin, so to speak?
•L 123 ❖ L 12 Dec 27

Life as a "bad dream"
•MC 170 (*see also* LAL 47, 57, 69, 119-120; SL 147)
❖ MC IV 8:12 (*see also* LAL 26/10/55; 21/5/56; Oct 20 57; 28 Jun 63; SL 31:3)

Life as a school in which we must practice the "duty" of prayer, just as we must learn grammar if we are ever to read the poets
•LM 115-116 (*see also* L 277*)
❖ LM 21:12-15 (*see also* L 18 Jul 57*)

Life as a "valley of tears" cursed with labour, hemmed round with necessities, tripped up with frustrations, etc.
•LM 92 ❖ LM 17:17

Life at a vile boarding school is in a way a good preparation for the Christian life in that it teaches one to live by hope and by faith
•SJ 36-37 ❖ SJ 2:16

Life (at its best) as "the bright frontispiece which whets one to read the story itself"*
•L 289 ❖ L 5 Nov 59

Life, brevity of, may be a Divine mercy; how much greater a mess we would make if more were entrusted to us
•PP 124 (*see also* M 129-130*)
❖ PP 8:8 (*see also* M 14:35*)

Life, business of—*see* Business of life

Life, Christian—*see* Christian life

Life: Circle analogy for our earthly lives which touch each other in relationships (while our eternal lives will be spheres or globes)
•GO 27 ❖ GO 2:12

Life, each human, is part of only one small scene in a vast play; it is useless to try and guess when the end will come*
•WLN 104-106 ❖ WLN 7:19-23

Life, earthly, can be thought of as the baseline to the plane or solid of eternity; must be drawn straight
•PP 123-124 ❖ PP 8:8

Life, ease of, may be one of the "riches" which make salvation difficult*
•PP 104 (*see also* CR 14; Riches)

❖ PP 6:15 (*see also* CR 2:5; Riches)

Life, everything suggests that organic, is going to be a very short and unimportant episode in the history of the universe
•CR 58 ❖ CR 5:3

Life, extraterrestrial—*see* Extraterrestrial life

Life, futility of—*see* Futility

Life, goal ("end") of human: Salvation in Christ and the glorifying of God (re: how to reconcile this with the value of "culture")
•CR 12, 14 (*see also* CR 26)
❖ CR 2:1, 4 (*see also* CR 2:42)

Life, goal of Christian—*see* Goal of Christian life

Life has never been "normal"; always full of crises, alarms, difficulties, emergencies (re: education in time of war)
•WG 22 (*see also* WLN 108)
❖ WG 2:4 (*see also* WLN 7:27)

Life has no better gift to give than real Friendship
•FL 105 ❖ FL 4:30

Life has to be taken day by day and hour by hour; help not usually given us in advance
•L 250 (*see also* SL 62; Daily ...)
❖ L 17 Jul 53 (*see also* SL 14:1; Daily ...)

Life, he that loseth his, shall find it; surely this is the main purpose of our life—to "die," to relinquish one's freedom and independence
•LAL 97-98 ❖ LAL 28 Mar 61

Life, human, has always been lived on the edge of a precipice; war creates no absolutely new situation (re: education in time of war)
•WG 21 ❖ WG 2:4

Life, human: Many modern philosophies view it merely as an animal life of unusual complexity (the same way Scripture can be read as merely human literature)
•RP 116-117 (*see also* WG 64*)
❖ RP 11:12 (*see also* WG 4:15*)

Life: "I am not sure that the great canyon of anguish which lies across our lives is *solely* due to some pre-historic ca-

tastrophe"
•LM 91 ❖ LM 17:15

Life: I felt it something of an outrage that I had been created without my own permission
•SJ 171 (see also GO 32*; SJ 115)
❖ SJ 11:8 (see also GO 2:20*; SJ 7:19, 20)

Life, I now see that I spent most of my, doing *neither* what I ought *nor* what I liked (said by a "patient" of Screwtape's, already in Hell)
•SL 56 (see also SL 42*, 144*)
❖ SL 12:4 (see also SL 9:2*; 30:4*)

Life, I suppose that our whole present, will someday seem only a drowsy half-waking; we are here in the land of dreams—but cockcrow is coming...
•LAL 119-120 ❖ LAL 28 Jun 63

Life, if we really believe that this, is a "wandering to find home," and that home is elsewhere, why should we not look forward to the arrival?
•LAL 83-84 (see also SL 132)
❖ LAL Jun 7th 59 (see also SL 28:1)

Life, in a sense "religion" must occupy the whole of; there is no question of compromise between the claims of God and the claims of anything else
•WG 25 ❖ WG 2:7

Life, in every department of, disappointment marks the transition from dreaming aspiration to laborious doing (re: anti-climax after conversion)
•SL 13 (see also LM 26; MC 100)
❖ SL 2:3 (see also LM 5:11, 13; MC III 6:11, 12)

Life, in the course of, I could put up with any amount of monotony far more patiently than even the smallest disturbance, bother, bustle..."
•SJ 116-117 ❖ SJ 7:21

Life: In the law of God one finds the real, well-grounded directions for living
•RP 60-61 ❖ RP 6:10, 11

Life, in the New Testament the art of, itself is an art of imitation (re: "originality" in literature)
•CR 6 ❖ CR 1:10

Life, inherent difficulty of—see also Difficulty/ies; consider also Pessimism; Pes-

simism, Lewis's

Life, inherent difficulty of: "An awful symptom is that part of oneself still regards troubles as 'interruptions'"
•L 161-162 ❖ L 12 Sep 38

Life, inherent difficulty of: "...even a boy can recognize that there is desert all round him though he, for the nonce, sits in an oasis"*
•SJ 65 ❖ SJ 4:11

Life, inherent difficulty of: "I had been warned...not to reckon on worldly happiness. We were even promised sufferings. They were part of the program"
•GO 41-42 ❖ GO 3:3

Life, inherent difficulty of: "...no doubt what we regard as a mere hideous interruption and curtailment of life is really...the concrete situation..."
•L 221 ❖ L 22 Sep 49

Life, inherent difficulty of, (quote from Johnson): "Marriage is not otherwise unhappy than as life is unhappy"
•L 128 ❖ L 2 Aug 28

Life, inherent difficulty of: "The more one can accept that fact, the less one can think about happiness on earth, the less, I believe, one suffers"
•LAL 96 (see also SL 95-96)
❖ LAL 9 Jan 61 (see also SL 21:2)

Life, inherent difficulty of: "...there is no good applying to Heaven for earthly comfort; there is no earthly comfort in the long run"
•FL 190 (see also GO 28-30; L 290; LAL 49; MC 39)
❖ FL 6:43 (see also GO 2:13-16; L 3 Dec 59; LAL 16/12/55; MC I 5:4)

Life, inherent difficulty of: "We are not on an untrodden path. Rather, on the main road"—shared also with our Master
•LM 44 ❖ LM 8:13

Life, inner vs. outer: "So often, whether for good or ill, one's inner state seems to have so little connection with the circumstances"*
•LAL 83 ❖ LAL Jun 7th 59

Life, inner vs. outer: "Where there are hun-

gry wastes, starving for Joy, in the one, the other may be full of cheerful bustle and success..."
•SJ 78, 118-119 ❖ SJ 5:12; 8:1

Life is habit-forming; having once tasted it, even pessimists are subject to the impulse of self-preservation
•SJ 116 (see also LAL 114)
❖ SJ 7:21 (see also LAL 19 Mar 63)

Life is like a picture with a golden background; you must step off the picture [into death] before you can see the gold*
•PP 148 ❖ PP 10:5

Life, it is an essential of the happy, that a man would have almost no mail and never dread the postman's knock
•SJ 143 ❖ SJ 9:18

Life, it seems to me one can hardly say anything either bad enough or good enough about
•L 266-267 ❖ L 8 Feb 56

Life, it'll be nice when we all wake up from this, which has indeed something like nightmare about it
•LAL 69 (see also LAL 47, 57; MC 170; SL 147)
❖ LAL Oct 20th 57 (see also LAL 26/10/55; 21/5/56; MC IV 8:12; SL 31:3)

Life, job of every man's, is to determine truth or untruth of Christianity and then to devote all energy either to serving it or to exposing the humbug*
•GID 112 ❖ GID I 12:9

Life, Lewis's view of, in his youth: "...I had very definitely formed the opinion that the universe was, in the main, a rather regrettable institution"*
•SJ 63 ❖ SJ 4:10

Life, long-term futility is no ground for diminishing our efforts to make human, while it lasts, less painful and less unfair than it has been...
•CR 58-59 (see also World, improvement of) ❖ CR 5:4 (see also World, improvement of)

Life, main object of: To press on toward Heaven (our "true country") and to help others do the same
•MC 120 ❖ MC III 10:5

Life, main purpose of, is to "die," to relinquish one's freedom and independence
•LAL 97-98 ❖ LAL 28 Mar 61

Life, meaning of, being questioned since the eschatological hopes of our Christian ancestors have rather faded out
•CR 57 ❖ CR 5:1

Life, meaning of: If it has no meaning, we should have never have found out that it has none—just as "dark" has no meaning to creatures without eyes*
•MC 46 ❖ MC II 1:6

Life, meaning of: "We believe that those who seek will find comment sufficient whereby to understand it in such a degree as they need"*
•CR 113 ❖ CR 9:26

Life, moral judgement that, is better than death is necessary before preservation of the human race can be deemed valuable
•M 37-38 (see also MC 29-30*; WG 43)
❖ M 5:9 (see also MC I 3:5*; WG 3:18)

Life, [most] choices of, are choices between Crosses; "the more one can accept that fact...the less, I believe, one suffers"**
•LAL 96 ❖ LAL 9 Jan 61

Life: My real fear is not of materialism; I am more afraid that we are really rats in a trap—or worse still, rats in a laboratory
•GO 33 ❖ GO 2:22

Life, no part of our, is our own
•MC 125 (see also SL 96-99)
❖ MC III 11:9 (see also SL 21:2-6)

Life of humanity itself in this world is precarious, temporary, provisional; all worldly achievements and triumphs will come to nothing in the end
•WLN 110 ❖ WLN 7:31, 32

Life offers just sufficient happiness to give us the fear of losing it and, when it is lost, the poignant misery of remembering
•PP 14 (see also GO 9*)
❖ PP 1:1 (see also GO 1:18*)

Life: "...oh, what a business life is. Well, both you and I have most of it behind,

not ahead...Nightmares don't last"
•LAL 57 (see also LAL 47)
❖ LAL 21/5/56 (see also LAL 26/10/55)
Life on earth not forever; wouldn't it be ghastly to be *immortal* on earth? It will all one day go away like a dream
•LAL 47 ❖ LAL 26/10/55
Life on other planets—see Extraterrestrial life
Life, one discovers new snags and catches in, every day
•L 185 ❖ L 21 Apr 40
Life, ordinary men not so much in love with, as is usually supposed; we love drugs, sleep, irresponsibility, even easeful death...
•L 190-191
❖ L undated letter just after 11 Aug 40
Life, origin of — see also Creation; Evolution
Life, origin of: First beginning must have been outside the ordinary processes of nature
•GID 210-211 ❖ GID II 5:10
Life: Our experience is coloured through and through by books and plays and the cinema; it takes skill to disentangle the things we have learned for ourselves
•MC 100, 101 ❖ MC III 6:10, 13
Life: "Our Father refreshes us on the journey with some pleasant inns, but will not encourage us to mistake them for home"
•PP 115 ❖ PP 7:7
Life: Progress, for me, means increasing goodness and happiness of individual lives, not mere longevity
•GID 311 (see also GID 296-297; L 158*; SL 131*; WG 43*)
❖ GID III 8:1 (see also GID III 4:20; L 13 Jan 37*; SL 28:1*; WG 3:18*)
Life: "Say what you like, Barfield, the world is sillier and better fun than they make out"*
•L 217 ❖ L 4 Apr 49
Life, Screwtape mentions the law of Undulation which refers to the human tendency to experience peaks and troughs in every department of

•SL 36-39 (see also SL 40-44)
❖ SL ch. 8 (see also SL ch. 9)
Life, Screwtape observes that what humans call a "normal," is the exception
•SL 134 (see also WG 21-22)
❖ SL 28:3 (see also WG 2:4)
Life, self-sacrifice and discomfort in this, not limited to Christians
•GID 53 ❖ GID I 4:24, 25 (Ques. 8)
Life, shortness of: Screwtape observes that real worldliness is a work of time, and maintains that is why God allows humans so little of it
•SL 133 ❖ SL 28:2, 3
Life, suffering in: "It doesn't really matter whether you grip the arms of the dentist's chair or let your hands lie in your lap. The drill drills on"
•GO 38 ❖ GO 2:31
Life, supernatural, as given to both good and bad angels vs. the kind of supernatural life given only to a creature who voluntarily surrenders himself to it
•M 170 (see also FL 15)
❖ M App. A:2, 3 (see also FL 1:9)
Life, the art of, consists in tackling each immediate evil as well as we can
•WG 44-45 ❖ WG 3:20
Life, the gradual reading of one's own, seeing a pattern emerge, is a great illumination
•L 266 ❖ L 8 Feb 56
Life: "The great thing...is to live from day to day and hour to hour not adding the past or future to the present"
•LAL 69 (see also LAL 79; SL 029, 67-71) ❖ LAL Oct 20th 57 (see also LAL 14/6/56; 3/8/56; Oct 30 58; 4 May 62; SL 6:2; ch. 15)
Life, the more claims on, that we make the more often we will feel injured; men are not angered by misfortune as such but by misfortune conceived as injury
•SL 95-96 (see also LAL 96; SL 141)
❖ SL 21:2 (see also LAL 9 Jan 61; SL 30:2)
Life: The proud and the self-righteous are more in danger of finding it satisfactory than the feckless and dissipated
•PP 98 ❖ PP 6:9

Life: "The reality is a queer mixture of idyll, tragedy, farce, melodrama..."
•L 266-267 ❖ L 8 Feb 56

Life, the ultimate Peace is silent through very density of
•M 93 ❖ M 11:18

Life, the word "religion" carries the suggestion that this is one more department of; but either it is an illusion or else our whole life falls under it
•LM 29-31 ❖ LM 6:3-8

Life: "...there is nothing here that will do us good: the sooner we are safely out of this world the better"
•L 166 ❖ L 8 May 39

Life: Think of yourself as a seed, waiting to come up in the Gardener's good time, up into the *real* world
•LAL 119 ❖ LAL 28 Jun 63

Life, ultimate questions such as the meaning of, not part of most people's thinking
•GID 252-253 (*see also* SL 8-9*)
❖ GID II 14:10 (*see also* SL 1:2, 3*)

Life: "We are never safe, but we have plenty of fun, and some ecstasy"; the settled happiness and security we all desire God withholds from us
•PP 115 ❖ PP 7:7

Life: We must learn to live with our own set of disadvantages; they are no excuse for throwing up the sponge
•L 180 ❖ L 26 Mar 40

Life: We must live each day as though it were our last, but plan as though our world might last a hundred years
•GID 266 (*see also* WLN 110-112)
❖ GID II 16:55 (*see also* WLN 7:31-34)

Life, we must "sit light" to, and all its phases
•L 306 (*see also* L 161-162*; LM 26-27; WLN 110; *Perelandra* 48*)
❖ L 21 Nov 62 (*see also* L 21 Sep 38*; LM 5:10-13; WLN 7:31; *Perelandra* 4:6*)

Life: "We shall get out of it all sooner or later, for 'even the weariest river Winds somewhere safe to sea'"
•LAL 120-121 ❖ LAL 6 Jul 63

Life, what a grim business even a happy human, is when you read it rapidly through to the inevitable end
•L 187 ❖ L 12 Jul 40

Life, what seems to us the easiest conditions in, may really be the hardest
•L 221 ❖ L 22 Sep 49

Life, what we regard as an interruption and curtailment of, is really the concrete situation
•L 221 (*see also* L 161-162; SL 95-97*)
❖ L 22 Sep 49 (*see also* L 12 Sep 38; SL 21:2, 3*)

Life, when the most important things happen in your, you may not recognize it at once
•MC 128 ❖ MC III 12:5

Life Force, according to Shavian Romanticism the voice of Eros is the voice of the, seeking parents or ancestors for the superman
•FL 152-153 ❖ FL 5:34

"Life-force," God as an impersonal, is well and good; but God Himself, alive, pulling at the other end of the cord, is another matter
•M 93-94 (*see also* GID 142-143*; LM 114; M 81; MC 35; SL 22-23*)
❖ M 11:19 (*see also* GID I 16:25*; LM 21:8; M 11:2; MC I 4:6; SL 4:4*)

"Life-force" God commands a friendly interest; temperature drops when you speak of a personal, definitive God
•M 81 (*see also* GID 142-143*; *consider also* Cost) ❖ M 11:2 (*see also* GID I 16:25*; *consider also* Cost)

"Life-force" God just as metaphorical as Father
•GID 71; M 74-75 ❖ GID I 6:9; M 10:13

Life-Force philosophy, discussion of
•MC 35 ❖ MC I 4:6

"Life-force" religion—*see also* Religion, minimal

"Life-Force" religion not necessarily transmitted to next generation; those who base all their hopes on the terrestrial future do not entrust much to it
•GID 119 ❖ GID I 13:11

"Life-Force" religion: The "Life-Force" is a sort of tame God—all thrills, no cost
•MC 35 (*see also* GID 142-143; M 81*; 93-94*; SL 33*; Cost)

❖ MC I 4:6 (*see also* GID I 16:25; M 11:2*, 19*; SL 7:1*; Cost)

Life Force, Screwtape mentions, which the Devil himself would worship if he worshipped anything but himself
•SL 103-104 ❖ SL 22:6

Life-force worship as a form of Pantheism
•M 83 ❖ M 11:4

Light—*see also* Truth

Light analogy to show how, when we reflect Christ, we shall still remain ourselves and different from one another
•MC 188 ❖ MC IV 11:12

Light and Shade (chapter title)
•SJ 101-117 ❖ SJ ch. 7

Light and shadows make up so much of the beauty of the world
•LAL 80 ❖ LAL Dec 25th 58

Light, danger that a high natural gift of reason may come to think of itself as the true Eternal (quote from *Theologia Germanica*)
•CR 17 ❖ CR 2:16

Light, even attempted virtue brings; indulgence brings fog
•MC 94 ❖ MC III 5:13

"Light from behind the sun," the glory of God described as
•LM 28 ❖ LM 5:17

Light, in Heaven everyone is filled with goodness as a mirror is filled with
•MC 130-131 (*see also* MC 144)
❖ MC III 12:9 (*see also* MC IV 2:13, 14)

Light: In the Incarnation, the pure light walks the earth; the darkness, received into the heart of Deity, is there swallowed up
•LM 71 ❖ LM 13:10

Light, looking at, vs. looking "along" light as analogy to understanding truth
•GID 212-215 ❖ GID II ch. 6

Light: "Nature is being lit up by a light from beyond Nature"
•M 120 (*see also* GID 84*)
❖ M 14:20 (*see also* GID I 9:6*)

Light of Heaven will illuminate our natural experiences and change them from "pencilled lines on flat paper" to three-dimensional reality*
•WG 68-69, 72 ❖ WG 4:23, 24, 30

Light: The Person of the Gospels described as "...numinous, lit by a light from beyond the world"
•SJ 236 ❖ SJ 15:7

Light: The problem we all face is how to dress our souls not for the electric lights of the present world but for the daylight of the next
•WLN 113 ❖ WLN 7:38

Light: "...to act on the light one has is almost the only way to more light"
•L 191-192 ❖ L 4 Jan 41

Light: We can perhaps train ourselves to ask how the thing which we are saying or doing at each moment will look when the irresistible light streams in upon it
•WLN 113 ❖ WLN 7:38

Light, we cannot see, though by light we can see things—as we must use analogies to know about God
•FL 174-175 (*see also* M 109-110; WG 69, 92)
❖ FL 6:20 (*see also* M 14:3; WG 4:24; 5:24)

Light which has lightened every man from the beginning may shine more clearly but cannot change; every good teacher has anticipated Christ
•RP 26-27 (*consider also* Law of Nature)
❖ RP 3:13 (*consider also* Law of Nature)

Lights, God as the Father of, who gives us all our understanding*
•RP 80, 110 (*see also* CR 136)
❖ RP 8:7; 11:3 (*see also* CR 11:16)

Likings—*see also* Taste(s)

Likings and Loves for the Sub-human (chapter title)
•FL 25-49 ❖ FL ch. 2

Lilies, aesthetic enjoyment of nature was certainly hallowed by our Lord's praise of the
•CR 15 ❖ CR 2:7

Lilies of the field, if God wanted me to live like the, why didn't He give me the same lack of nerves and imagination as they enjoy?
•LAL 21, 22, 79 (*see also* GO 84-85)
❖ LAL Aug 10th 53; Nov 6/53; Oct 30 58 (*see also* GO 4:32)

Lilies That Fester (chapter title)
•WLN 31-49 ❖ WLN ch. 3

Limbo described as a place "for souls already lost"
•PP 124 (ftnt.) ❖ PP 8:8 (ftnt.)

Limbo, I am told, is a place of perfect *natural* happiness—although there is a faint melancholy because everyone will know they have missed the bus
•L 164 ❖ L 5 Apr 39

Limbo mentioned by Screwtape
•SL 156, 158; WLN 54, 56
❖ SL 32:9, 13; WLN 4:9, 13

Limited liabilities—*see also* Self-reservation; *consider also* Cost of being a Christian; Independence

Limited liabilities, Christ's teaching was never meant to confirm my preference for safe investments and
•FL 168 (*see also* CR 155; SJ 203; SL 133)
❖ FL 6:10 (*see also* CR 13:6; SJ 13:9; SL 28:2)

Limited liabilities, I had always aimed at SJ 228 ❖ SJ 14:22

Limited liabilities, only God can help us with our desire for
•WG 132 (*see also* CR 43*)
❖ WG 9:13 (*see also* CR 3:12*)

Limited liabilities, our craving for
•WG 126-132 (*see also* LM 114*)
❖ WG ch. 9 (*see also* LM 21:8*)

Limited liabilities, to me the materialist's universe had the enormous attraction that it offered you; death ended all
•SJ 171 (*see also* GO 33)
❖ SJ 11:8 (*see also* GO 2:22)

Limpets trying to describe Man to one another as analogy to Man's attempt to describe God
•M 89-90 (*see also* CR 165—dog analogy) ❖ M 11:13, 14 (*see also* CR 13:33, 34—dog analogy)

Lindsay, David: Lewis acknowledges a debt to his book *Voyage to Arcturus* in the writing of *The Screwtape Letters*
•SL xiii ❖ SL P:22

Lindsay, David: *Voyage to Arcturus* mentioned by Lewis as the "real father" of his own planet books

•L 205 ❖ L 29 Oct 44

Lion, I think the, when he has ceased to be dangerous, will still be awful
•PP 143 ❖ PP 9:14

Lion, the Witch and the Wardrobe: "I think it frightens some adults, but very few children"
•L 228 ❖ L 5 Mar 51

Lion, the Witch and the Wardrobe mentioned
•LAL 14, 34, 35 (*consider also* Aslan)
❖ LAL 17/4/53; Oct 9th 54; Nov 1st 54 (*consider also* Aslan)

Literal vs. symbolical interpretation of Biblical conceptions such as Resurrection and Ascension: Impossible to know how much should be taken symbolically
•CR 164-166 ❖ CR 13:30-35

Literalism—*see also* Bible; Fundamentalism; Scripture(s)

Literalism: If we take one of the hard sayings of Jesus literally, we must take them all literally (re: Pacifism)*
•WG 48-49 ❖ WG 3:27

Literalism: In reality a certain amount of "reading between the lines" is necessary; if we took every remark at face value we should soon be in difficulty*
•CR 31-32 ❖ CR 2:52

Literalism: People who take the symbols of harps and crowns literally might as well think that when Christ told us to be like doves, He meant us to lay eggs*
•MC 121 ❖ MC III 10:6

Literalism: Taken by a literalist [or taken only intellectually], Jesus will always prove the most elusive of teachers*
•RP 112-113 ❖ RP 11:7

Literary criticism attempts to reconstruct the genesis of texts; but in the case of the Bible, the results cannot be checked by fact
•CR 158-161 (*see also* Biblical criticism)
❖ CR 13:13-20 (*see also* Biblical criticism)

Literary criticism: Better to read original authors than commentators
•GID 200 (*see also* L 122-123)
❖ GID II 4:1 (*see also* L 12 Dec 27)

Literary criticism: Danger of invoking

"thus saith the Lord" at the end of every expression of our pet aversions
•CR 30-31 (see also CR 34-35; RP 31)
❖ CR 2:51 (see also CR 2:55; RP 3:20)

Literary criticism: I admit bad taste to be, in some sense, "a bad thing," but I do not think it per se "evil"
•CR 36 ❖ CR 2:57

Literary criticism, key words of modern (creative/derivative; spontaneity/ convention; freedom/rules)
•CR 3 ❖ CR 1:4

Literary criticism, language of modern, conflicts with the mind of the New Testament, in which "originality" is clearly the prerogative of God alone
•CR 3, 6-7 ❖ CR 1:3, 4, 10

Literary criticism, much bad, results from efforts of critics to get a worktime result out of something that never aimed at producing more than pleasure
•CR 34 ❖ CR 2:54

Literary criticism, on Christian
•CR 28-36 ❖ CR 2:46-58

Literary criticism: Regarding the danger of applying allegorical interpretations to individual authors*
•L 273 ❖ L 10 Dec 56

Literary criticism, the basis of all, should be the maxim that an author never brings into existence beauty or wisdom which did not exist before...
•CR 7 (consider also Originality)
❖ CR 1:11 (consider also Originality)

Literary criticism: "...the most rankling hatred of all other critics and of nearly all authors may come from the most honest and disinterested critic..."
•RP 28-29 ❖ RP 3:17

Literary enjoyment should be spontaneous and disinterested—not for the sake of prestige or merit
•WLN 34-35, 39 (see also L 70, 216; LAL 54; SL 60)
❖ WLN 3:6, 7, 12 (see also L 7 Aug 21; 3 Apr 49; LAL 20/3/56; SL 13:4)

Literary history, only satisfactory opening for any study of, is the first chapter of Genesis

•L 125 ❖ L 31 Mar 28

Literary (textual) criticism which finds that every old book was made by six anonymous authors with scissors and paste is beginning to die out
•GID 134-135 ❖ GID I 16:8

Literature—see also Bible as literature; Books; Poetry; Reading; consider also Culture

Literature, a great deal of, was meant to be read for entertainment; critics must not try to judge it as something it was not intended to be
•CR 33-34 ❖ CR 2:54

Literature, a more complete enjoyment of, as one of the materialistic gains of being a Christian
•L 173 (see also L 181-182*)
❖ L 18 Dec 39 (see also L 26 Mar 40*)

Literature, according to Newman you cannot have a Christian; it is a contradiction in terms to attempt a sinless Literature of sinful man
•CR 16 ❖ CR 2:13

Literature: All the books were beginning to turn against me; the most religious authors were clearly the ones on whom I could really feed—others seemed "tinny"
•SJ 213-214 (see also SJ 225)
❖ SJ 14:3 (see also SJ 14:17)

Literature: "...all the greatest poems have been made by men who valued something else much more than poetry"
•CR 10 ❖ CR 1:15

Literature: An author may be "original" and yet completely dependent on a supernatural teacher
•CR 7-9 ❖ CR 1:12-14

Literature and art are healthy only when aiming at innocent recreation or serving as handmaids to religious or moral truth —Art for its own sake is balderdash
•L 182 ❖ L 16 Apr 40

Literature and the arts, until modern times nobody even suggested that, were an end in themselves
•GID 279-280 ❖ GID III 2:4, 5

Literature as a form of culture in which

"culture" is irrelevant when the enjoyment is genuine
- WLN 33-35 (*see also* L 70, 216; SL 58-60) ❖ WLN 3:5-7 (*see also* L 7 Aug 21; 3 Apr 49; SL 13:3, 4)

Literature as a medium of spiritual longing
- WG 6-7 (*see also* SJ 78, 165, 211; *The Pilgrim's Regress*, p. ix)
- ❖ WG 1:5 (*see also* SJ 5:11; 11:2; 13:20; *The Pilgrim's Regress*, P:12)

Literature as a medium of spiritual truth: The book *Phantastes* by George MacDonald was "full of what I felt to be holyness before I really knew what it was..."*
- L 167 (*see also* GID 203-204; SJ 179)
- ❖ L 9 Jul 39 (*see also* GID II 4:6; SJ 11:18, 19)

Literature: [As a student at "Belsen"] I developed a great taste for all the fiction I could get about the ancient world
- SJ 35 ❖ SJ 2:15

Literature as self-expression, Christian theory of literary criticism opposes the idea of
- CR 7-8 ❖ CR 1:11-13

Literature: Attitudes of expressionist vs. Christian authors toward the self
- CR 7-9 ❖ CR 1:12-14

Literature becomes the vehicle of God's word in Scripture (rather than God's word being converted into literature)
- RP 109-119, esp. 116
- ❖ RP ch. 11, esp. 11:11

Literature, Bible as—*see* Bible as literature

Literature carries good and evil of two kinds: The first, besides being good and bad in itself, also makes the reader good or bad; the second does not
- CR 34-36 ❖ CR 2:55-58

Literature, children's: My knowledge of it is really very limited...
- L 304 ❖ L 31 Jul 62

Literature, Christian, defined as "work aiming at literary value and written by Christians for Christians"
- CR 3 ❖ CR 1:3

Literature, Christian: On the principles of Christian literary theory and criticism

- CR 3-11 ❖ CR 1:3-16

Literature, Christian: "The rules for writing a good passion play or a good devotional lyric are simply the rules for writing tragedy or lyric in general"
- CR 1 ❖ CR 1:1

Literature, Christianity and (chapter title)
- CR 1-11 ❖ CR ch. 1

Literature: Christianity prefigured in poetry and the romances
- L 143 ❖ L 24 Oct 31

Literature: Christianity prefigured in mythology and Paganism
- GID 57-58, 66-67, 83-84, 132, 175; L 258; M 113-115, 133-134, ftnt; PP 25; RP 105-108; SJ 62, 223-224, 235-236; WG 82-84 ❖ GID I 4:42 (Ques. 10); 5:11-13; 9:5, 6; 16:4; 21:7; L 1 Nov 54; M 14:9-14; 15:2—ftnt.; PP 1:16; RP 10:11, 12; SJ 4:9; 14:15; 15:7; WG 5:14, 15

Literature, differences between Christian and unbeliever in their approach to, (The Christian author does not ask, "Is it mine?", but "Is it good?")
- CR 9-10 ❖ CR 1:14, 15

Literature, enjoyment of, before and after conversion (can finally see the real point)
- L 192 (*see also* L 143, 173, 181-182*)
- ❖ L 29 Jan 41 (*see also* L 24 Oct 31; 18 Dec 39; 26 Mar 40*)

Literature: Fiction may be perfectly serious in that people often express their deepest thoughts, speculations, desires, etc. in a story
- L 261 ❖ L 2 Feb 55

Literature: "Finally I awoke from building the temple to find that the God had flown"—I no longer got the old thrill [from literature]
- SJ 165-166 ❖ SJ 11:2

Literature: "From these books [Norse mythology] again and again I received the stab of Joy"
- SJ 78 (*see also* Norse . . .)
- ❖ SJ 5:11 (*see also* Norse . . .)

Literature, genuine appreciation of, most likely to develop where teachers do not force pupils to feign it
- WLN 42-43 ❖ WLN 3:16, 17

Literature, great, seems to vulgar taste at first a pale reflection of the "thrillers" or "triangle dramas" which it prefers
•CR 40 ❖ CR 3:7

Literature: Heroic Pessimism has a contradiction at its centre: If a Brute made the world, then he also made the standard by which we judge him to be a Brute
•CR 65-67 (see also CR 69-70; MC 45-46*) ❖ CR 5:19 (see also CR 5:24; MC II 1:5, 6*)

Literature: How did we enjoy all these books so much when we did not know what was at the centre of them?
•L 173 (see also L 143*, 181-182, 192) ❖ L 18 Dec 39 (see also L 24 Oct 31*; 26 Mar 40; 29 Jan 41)

Literature, humor in: The kind Lewis says he likes best is humor not separable from the argument, but rather the "bloom" on the dialectic itself
•SJ 190-191 ❖ SJ 12:12

Literature, I could not doubt that the sub-Christian or anti-Christian values implicit in most, did actually infect many readers
•CR 16 ❖ CR 2:13

Literature: I don't like genius; it is the results I like, such as *Paradise Lost* and *The Divine Comedy*
•L 154 ❖ L 14 Jun 32

Literature, I gradually realized that my scholarly delight in, was something quite different from the original Joy
•SJ 165 ❖ SJ 11:2

Literature: I turned to writing fairy tales because that seemed the form best fitted for what I wanted to say
•L 260, 307 ❖ L undated letter just before 2 Feb 55; 2 Dec 62

Literature: "I was at last made free of the secret that others had, like me, found there 'enormous bliss' and been maddened by beauty"
•SJ 103 ❖ SJ 7:4

Literature: "I went to the Coll far more disposed to excuse my literary tastes than to plume myself on them. But this innocence did not last..."
•SJ 103 ❖ SJ 7:3, 4

Literature, idolatry of both erotic love and domestic affections was the great error of nineteenth-century
•FL 20 ❖ FL 1:18

Literature: "In all Shakespeare's works the conception of good...seems to be purely worldly"
•CR 16 ❖ CR 2:13

Literature, in art and, no man who bothers about originality will ever be original
•MC 190 (see also L 201; WG 119) ❖ MC IV 11:15 (see also L undated letter just after 29 Jul 42; WG 7:19)

Literature is always in some sense derivative rather than original
•CR 6-7 (see also Originality) ❖ CR 1:10, 11 (see also Originality)

Literature: It is taken as basic by all the "culture" of our age that whenever artists and audience lose touch, the fault must be on side of the audience
•WLN 45 (see also WLN 78-79) ❖ WLN 3:20 (see also WLN 5:18)

Literature: Lewis calls himself unqualified to evaluate "modern literary trends"
•GID 264 ❖ GID II 16:41, 42

Literature: Lewis mentions medieval allegory as his own subject of study
•L 155-157 ❖ L 7 Jun 34

Literature: Many modern novels and poems "are not good work because they are not *work* at all. They are mere puddles of spilled sensibility and reflection"
•WLN 80 ❖ WLN 5:21

Literature, Middle Ages, faults of: garrulity and coarseness
•L 29 ❖ L undated letter between Oct 1915 and 27 Sep 16

Literature, modern education in: Every pupil is presented with the choice, "Read the poets whom we approve, and say what we say about them, or be a prole"
•WLN 46 (see also WLN 42-44) ❖ WLN 3:20 (see also WLN 3:16-18)

Literature, modern: "Mere animalism,

however disguised as "honesty," "frankness," or the like, is not dangerous, but fatal"*
•CR 22 ❖ CR 2:31

Literature: Modern science fiction assumes moral thought to be merely a subjective thing like one's taste in food, which can vary from species to species
•CR 61 ❖ CR 5:11

Literature: My first delight in Valhalla and Valkyries began to turn itself imperceptibly into a scholar's interest in them
•SJ 165 ❖ SJ 11:2

Literature: "...my whole bent had been toward things pale, remote, and evanescent; the water-color world of Morris...Malory...the twilight of Yeats"
•SJ 198 (see also SJ 17)
❖ SJ 13:1 (see also SJ 1:17)

Literature, myth of Evolutionism as expressed in
•CR 82-88 ❖ CR 7:3-15

Literature, neither of my parents had the least taste for the kind of, to which my allegiance was given the moment I could choose books for myself
•SJ 4-5 (see also SJ 7-8)
❖ SJ 1:2 (see also SJ 1:5)

Literature, Norse, Lewis's taste for
•GID 278; L 110-111, 205; SJ 17, 72-78, 114-115, 130, 163-164, 165-169, 211; WG 76 ❖ GID III 2:1; L 8 Feb 27; 29 Oct 44; SJ 1:17; 5:3-11; 7:19, 20; 8:15-18; 10:17; 11:1-6; 13:20; WG 5:6

Literature: One of the conscious causes Lewis listed for his rising doubt in the Christian faith (as a youth) was his reading of the classics
•SJ 62 ❖ SJ 4:9

Literature or art, "low-brows" who genuinely enjoy, vs. "snobs" who feign enjoyment of it ("I...prefer the live dog to the dead lion")
•WLN 38-39 (see also CR 10)
❖ WLN 3:12 (see also CR 1:15)

Literature: "Plainly, it does not matter at what point you first break into the system of European poetry. Only

keep your ears open and your mouth shut..."
•SJ 53 ❖ SJ 3:12

Literature: Poetic language can convey to us the quality of experiences which we have not had, or perhaps can never have...
•CR 133 (see also Poetic language)
❖ CR 11:8, 9 (see also Poetic language)

Literature ("poetry"), for the modern student, is something assigned and tested on; he does not know that it ever had any other purpose
•WLN 47 ❖ WLN 3:25

Literature: Regarding the cultured unbeliever who "commonly wishes to maintain his superiority to the great mass of mankind who turn to books for mere recreation"
•CR 10 (see also WLN 38-39, 41; SL 58-60) ❖ CR 1:15 (see also WLN 3:11, 12, 14; SL 13:3-5)

Literature: Romantic poetry and music as natural counterparts to the Myth of Evolutionism
•CR 90 ❖ CR 7:17

Literature, salvation of a single soul more important than all the world's
•CR 10 ❖ CR 1:15

Literature: Satire tends to bore me
•L 135 ❖ L 29 Aug 29

Literature, scheme of values presupposed in most imaginative, has not become very much more Christian since the time of St. Jerome
•CR 16 ❖ CR 2:13

Literature: St. Augustine felt Tragedy to be a kind of sore; the spectator suffers, yet loves his suffering, and this is a miserabilis insania...
•CR 15 ❖ CR 2:11

Literature: "The books I liked best under [Smewgy's] teaching were Horace's Odes, Aeneid IV, and Euripides' Bacchae"
•SJ 113 ❖ SJ 7:17

Literature, the canon of "functionalism" has disabled, for half its functions
•SL xiv ❖ SL P:26

Literature: The Christian has no objection

to comedies and tales, for he thinks that we can play, as we can eat, to the glory of God
•CR 10 ❖ CR 1:15

Literature: The ideal of courage may provide a temptation, but for some it may prove a schoolmaster to the ideal of martyrdom
•CR 22 ❖ CR 2:30

Literature: The ideal of romantic love may be a danger, but for some it has proved a schoolmaster to better things
•CR 22 ❖ CR 2:31

Literature, the New Testament has nothing at all to tell us of, but we may notice what kinds of metaphor it uses
•CR 3-5 ❖ CR 1:5-7

Literature, "...the odour which is death to us until it becomes life" as that Christian element which Lewis met in various works of
•GID 203-204 ❖ GID II 4:5

Literature: The only non-Christian authors who seemed to me really to know anything were the Romantics; even they were tinged with something like religion
•SJ 214 ❖ SJ 14:4

Literature, the real vacuity is all with those who make, a self-existent thing to be valued for its own sake
•CR 10 ❖ CR 1:15

Literature: The same process of attrition which empties good language of its virtue also empties bad language of its vice (re: ignorance in readers)
•CR 32-33 ❖ CR 2:53

Literature, those who like reading for its own sake are those who truly enjoy the great
•L 152 ❖ L 8 Apr 32

Literature: "Those who read poetry to improve their minds will never improve their minds by reading poetry. For the true enjoyments must be spontaneous..."
•WLN 35 ❖ WLN 3:7

Literature, use of filth and obscenity in, a sign of a culture that has lost its faith
•GID 264-265 ❖ GID II 16:43, 44

Literature: Value presupposed in modern literature: the life of liberated instinct
•CR 16, 21-22 ❖ CR 2:13, 29

Literature: Values presupposed in medieval romance: honour and sexual love
•CR 16, 21-23 ❖ CR 2:13, 29-34

Literature: Values presupposed in nineteenth-century fiction: sexual love and material prosperity
•CR 16, 21-23 ❖ CR 2:13, 29-34

Literature: Values presupposed in romantic poetry: enjoyment of nature; Sehnsucht [longing] awakened by the past, the remote, or the imagined supernatural
•CR 16, 21-23 ❖ CR 2:13, 29-34

Literature: What the intellectual and religious authorities had to say about the value of "culture" (Aristotle, Plato, Buddha, Augustine, Milton, Newman, etc.)
•CR 15-19 ❖ CR 2:8-22

Literature: "When a boy passes from nursery literature to school stories he is going down, not up"
•SJ 35 ❖ SJ 2:15

Literature: "You and I who still enjoy fairy tales have less reason to wish actual childhood back. We have kept its pleasures and added some grown-up ones"
•LAL 17 ❖ LAL Jun 22d 53

Liturgical style, tastes in: If we cannot lay down our tastes at the church door, surely we should at least bring them in to be humbled*
•GID 336 ❖ GID IV Letter 8

Liturgiology, I cannot take an interest in; indeed for the laity I sometimes wonder if an interest in it is not rather a snare
•L 305 ❖ L undated letter of Aug 1962

Liturgiology: There is almost no subject in the world on which I have less to say
•LM 3-4 ❖ LM 1:2

Liturgy—see also Church services; Prayer, corporate; Worship, corporate

Liturgy and [doctrinal] belief, proper relationship between

•GID 333 ❖ GID IV Letter 7

Liturgy, doctrinal issues must not be tacitly or implicitly settled by mere changes in, (e.g., regarding devotions to Mary)
•GID 332-333 ❖ GID IV Letter 7

Liturgy, if you have a vernacular, you must have a changing liturgy
•LM 6-7 (see also GID 230-231)
❖ LM 1:11-17 (see also GID II 10:3)

Liturgy, Lewis advises caution in making changes in the, ("Take care. It is so easy to break eggs without making omelettes")
•LM 6 ❖ LM 1:13

Liturgy: My whole position really boils down to an entreaty for permanence and uniformity
•LM 4-5 ❖ LM 1:3-8

Liturgy should not go overtime
•GID 332 ❖ GID IV Letter 7

Living alone: All the rubs and frustrations of a joint life—even at its worst—seem to me better than solitude*
•LAL 109 (see also LAL 102, 117, 120*)
❖ LAL 8 Nov 62 (see also LAL 17 Jan 62; 10 Jun 63; 6 Jul 63*)

Living alone: The whole time-wasting business of cooking is hardly worth it when one is on one's own
•LAL 86 ❖ LAL 21 Aug 59

"Living for others" may end up making the "others" miserable
•FL 73-77, 82-83; MC 167 (see also L 198-199; SL 121, 123) ❖ FL 3:33-37, 45; MC IV 7:3 (see also L undated letter just before 20 Jan 42; SL 26:2, 5)

Living in a beauty spot: Original thrill dies away and is replaced by a quieter, more lasting interest (as with love)
•MC 100-101 ❖ MC III 6:11, 12

Living, process of, seems to consist in coming to realize truths so ancient and simple that, if stated, they sound like barren platitudes
•L 166 ❖ L 8 May 39

Living together perhaps better than making vows you do not intend to keep
•MC 97 ❖ MC III 6:5

Lock and key as analogy to how each soul has a curious shape (its individuality), made to fit a particular part of God
•PP 147 (see also FL 189*; PP 53*, 151)
❖ PP 10:3 (see also FL 6:41*; PP 6:41*; 10:9)

Logic—see also Reason(ing)

Logic: A belief in the objectivity and validity of reason must be maintained or all thoughts are accidents and we can know no truths and have no knowledge*
•CR 60-63, 71, 72-81, 89; GID 21, 52-53, 136-138, 272, 274-276; M 12-24, 34, 105; MC 45-46; SJ 208; WG 88-92 ❖ CR 5:9-13, 27; ch. 6; 7:16; GID I 1:1; 4:21; 16:13-17; III 1:4, 9, 13-16; M ch. 3; 5:1; 13:16; MC II 1:6; SJ 13:17; WG 5:21-24

Logic and reason, Screwtape advises keeping human minds on ordinary "real life" rather than on
•SL 8-10 ❖ SL 1:2-4

Logic, assent or confidence in God moves us from the, of speculative thought into the "logic" of personal relations
•WLN 29-30 ❖ WLN 2:18

Logic, I conclude that, is a real insight into the way in which real things have to exist [and is not merely subjective]
•CR 63 (consider also Subjectivism)
❖ CR 5:14 (consider also Subjectivism)

Logic, I had to admit that our, was participation in a cosmic Logos
•SJ 209 ❖ SJ 13:17

Logic, scientific, not the same kind of logic required for trust in God because, once you accept that He is, you move from speculative thought to relationship
•WLN 21-30, esp. 26-27, 30 (see also LM 49; MC 32) ❖ WLN 2:10-18, esp. 2:14, 18 (see also LM 9:8; MC I 4:2)

Logic, the physical sciences depend on the validity of, just as much as metaphysics; if logic is discredited science must go down with it
•CR 61-64 (see also CR 72, 89)
❖ CR 5:11-13 (see also CR 6:3; 7:16)

Logic, use of, with uneducated people in evangelism*
•GID 99 ❖ GID I 10:39, 40

Logic: We must combine a steadfast faith in inference as such with scepticism about each particular instance of inference (as people make mistakes)
•CR 67-68 ❖ CR 5:22

Logic: "When logic says a thing must be so, Nature always agrees"; this validity of knowledge cannot be explained by perpetual happy coincidence
•CR 64-65 ❖ CR 5:17

Logical Positivist, born a little later Kirk [William T. Kirkpatrick, Lewis's tutor] would have been a
•SJ 135 ❖ SJ 9:10

Loisy, Alfred, and the Modernist Movement mentioned
•GID 67 (ftnt.) ❖ GID I 5:12 (ftnt.)

Loki Bound: "...the only work I completed at this time was a tragedy, Norse in subject and Greek in form"
•SJ 114-115 ❖ SJ 7:19, 20

Loneliness—*consider also* Solitude

Loneliness: All the rubs and frustrations of a joint life—even at its worst—seem to me better than solitude*
•LAL 109 (*see also* LAL 117, 120)
❖ LAL 8 Nov 62 (*see also* LAL 10 Jun 63; 6 Jul 63)

Loneliness, as soon as we are fully conscious we discover; we need others
•FL 11-12 ❖ FL 1:3

Loneliness: Having free time because you don't matter to anyone is much worse than losing your Saturday afternoons to serve on a committee*
•WG 98 ❖ WG 6:6

Loneliness in old age: "In your position I myself would prefer a 'Home'—or almost anything—to solitude"
•LAL 102 (*see also* Aging)
❖ LAL 17 Jan 62 (*see also* Aging)

Loneliness that spreads out like a desert: "If I knew any way of escape I would crawl through sewers to find it" (re: all kinds of suffering)
•PP 105 ❖ PP 6:16

Longevity, mere, of species or of men a contemptible ideal
•GID 311 (*see also* GID 297; L 158*; SL 131*; WG 43*)

❖ GID III 8:1 (*see also* GID III 4:20; L 13 Jan 37*; SL 28:1*; WG 3:18*)

Longfellow's *Saga of King Olaf*, the third instance of Lewis's experience of "Joy" or longing came through
•SJ 17 ❖ SJ 1:17

Longing—*see also* Desire; Joy; *Sehnsucht*

Longing, almost our whole education has been directed to silencing this shy inner voice of
•WG 7 (*see also* MC 119)
❖ WG 1:5 (*see also* MC III 9:2)

Longing comes through beauty but its object is often misinterpreted
•WG 6-7 ❖ WG 1:5

Longing, I was off once more into the land of, my heart at once broken and exalted... (re: the return of "Joy" while Lewis was a student at Oxford)
•SJ 217 (*see also* SJ 155)
❖ SJ 14:8 (*see also* SJ 10:7)

"Longing," Joy described or referred to as a
•SJ 16, 72, 166, 175, 177, 217; *The Pilgrim's Regress*, pp. ix, xii, xiii
❖ SJ 1:15; 5:2; 11:3, 13, 14; 14:8; *The Pilgrim's Regress* P: 13, 17, 18

Longing, our life-long, is no mere neurotic fancy but the truest index of our real situation
•WG 15-16 ❖ WG 1:12

Longing, Psalmists expressed, for the mere presence of God—while they did not know that He would die to offer them eternal joy
•RP 50 ❖ RP 5:8

Longing (*Sehnsucht*), the low line of the Castlereagh Hills which we saw from the nursery windows taught me
•SJ 7 ❖ SJ 1:4

Longing, the supposed satisfaction to our deepest, just fades away...something has evaded us
•MC 119 ❖ MC III 10:2

Longings awakened by nature gave meaning to the words "love of God" for Lewis
•FL 37 ❖ FL 2:23

Longings, spiritual, include the desire to be accepted and welcomed by Nature ("into the heart of things")

•WG 14-17 (*see also* FL 78-79*; L 154-155*) ❖ WG 1:11-13 (*see also* FL 3:40*; L 14 Jun 32*)

Look for Christ and you will find Him, and with Him everything else thrown in
•MC 190 (*see also* GO 79*; MC 118-119) ❖ MC IV 11:15 (*see also* GO 4:21*; MC III 10:1)

Look for comfort and you will not get it; look for truth and you may find comfort in the end
•MC 39 ❖ MC I 5:4

"**Looking** along"—*consider also* Experience

"Looking along" as important as looking at, when attempting to understand reality
•GID 215 ❖ GID II 6:12

"Looking along" pleasures and blessings essential to our adoration of Him who gave them; without this experience, we will not have "tasted and seen"*
•LM 91 ❖ LM 17:13

"Looking along" vs. looking at (Experience of something, such as pain, vs. scientific-like knowledge about it)
•GID 212-215 (*see also* L 172*) ❖ GID II ch. 6 (*see also* L 3 Dec 39*)

Looking for God—*see* Search for God; Seeking God

Lord's Prayer: "Forgive us our trespasses": What to do about vague feelings of guilt which do not seem to be connected with particular wrong-doing
•LM 32-34 (*see also* LAL 77*) ❖ LM 6:11-17 (*see also* LAL Jul 21 58*)

Lord's Prayer: "Forgive us...as we forgive": "My resource is to look for some action of my own which is open to the same charge as the one I'm resenting"
•LM 27-28 ❖ LM 5:15

Lord's Prayer: "Kingdom" as sovereignty *de jure*; "power" as sovereignty *de facto*, and "glory" as—well, the glory; the "light from behind the sun"
•LM 28 ❖ LM 5:17

Lord's Prayer: "Lead us not into temptation" often means "Deny me those gratifying invitations [etc.] which I so often, at such risk, desire"*
•RP 74 ❖ RP 7:16

Lord's Prayer: "Lead us not into temptation": The Greek word means "trial"; thus this passage means "Spare us, where possible, from all crises..."
•LM 28 ❖ LM 5:16

Lord's Prayer: "Lead us not into temptation" adds a reservation to all preceding prayers, as if we said "Do not grant them if they would be snares or sorrows"
•LM 28 ❖ LM 5:16

Lord's Prayer probably longer than what was recorded; the disciples fell asleep
•L 211 ❖ L undated letter of 1947

Lord's Prayer: The prayer for our daily bread means all we need for the day—those things necessary for the body as well as for the soul
•LM 27 (*see also* SL 29; *consider also* Daily...*) ❖ LM 5:14 (*see also* SL 6:2; *consider also* Daily...)

Lord's Prayer: The prayer for our daily bread is a petitionary prayer; therefore man has definitely been told to ask for things
•SL 126 ❖ SL 27:2

Lord's Prayer: The words "Our Father" mean that you are putting yourself in the place of a son of God—you are pretending
•MC 161 ❖ MC IV 7:2

Lord's Prayer: "Thy kingdom come": "That is, may your reign be realised here, as it is realised there" ("here" includes in my heart)
•LM 24-25 ❖ LM 5:4

Lord's Prayer: "Thy will be done" gives us a pattern for prayer which seems inconsistent with another recommended pattern—that of asking with a sure belief
•CR 142-144 ❖ CR 12:1-9

Lord's Prayer: "Thy will be done": How can you have faith that you will get what you ask and then add this reservation?
•LM 58-59 (*see also* CR 142-151) ❖ LM 11:5 (*see also* CR ch. 12)

Lord's Prayer: "Thy will be done": I am asking that I may be enabled to *do* it, not merely that I will accept it; I must be an agent as well as a patient
•LM 25-26 ❖ LM 5:6-9

Lord's Prayer: "Thy will be done" should be the voice of joyful desire, free of hunger and thirst—not merely of submission or renunciation
•CR 143 ❖ CR 12:4

Lord's Prayer: We are told that if we don't forgive we will not be forgiven
•WG 121-122, 125 (*see also* Forgiveness) ❖ WG 8:2, 7 (*see also* Forgiveness)

Lord's Supper—*see* Communion, Holy

Loss—*see also* Bereavement; Grief

Loss: "When we lose one blessing, another is often most unexpectedly given in its place"
•LAL 86 ❖ LAL Aug 3/59

"Lost" may be those who dare not go to such a "public" place (as sins will be common knowledge to the universe)
•PP 61 (*see also* SL 148*)
❖ PP 4:9 (*see also* SL 31:5*)

Lost: Sooner or later they must know their own sinfulness; right must be asserted (re: the "intolerable" doctrine of Hell)*
•PP 120-122 ❖ PP 8:5

Lost (souls)—*see also* Destiny of lost Man; Wicked; *consider also* Hell

Lost souls, in Dante, are very concerned with their past; not so the saved
•LAL 99 ❖ LAL 5 Jun 61

Lost souls, the characteristic of, is "their rejection of everything that is not simply themselves"
•PP 123 ❖ PP 8:7

Love—*see also* Affection; Charity; Eros; Friendship; *consider also* Marriage

Love, activities of natural: Nothing is too trivial to be transformed into works of Charity...a game, a joke, a drink together...
•FL 184 ❖ FL 6:34

Love, actual experience of, precludes at that moment an intellectual understanding of love; humans cannot experience and intellectualize at the same time

•GID 65-66 (*see also* SJ 217-219)
❖ GID I 5:8 (*see also* SJ 14:9, 10)

Love, admiration as that element in, which wishes that its object should be what it is even if we were never to enjoy it
•FL 32-33 ❖ FL 2:12-14

Love, all kinds of, carry in them the seeds of hatred
•FL 82-83 (*see also* FL 64, 82, 160; SL 120) ❖ FL 3:45 (*see also* FL 3:17, 45; 5:46; SL 26:1)

Love: All lovers are eventually separated, even if both die at exactly the same moment
•GO 58-59, 63-64 ❖ GO 3:33, 40

Love and friendship: "No one can mark the exact moment at which friendship becomes love" (re: his relationship with Joy Davidman)
•LAL 65 ❖ LAL 17/2/57

Love, Appreciative, gazes and holds its breath and is silent; rejoices that such a wonder should exist even if not for him
•FL 33 ❖ FL 2:14

Love, Appreciative, not a basic element in Affection; but Affection can make appreciations possible which, but for it, might never have existed
•FL 56, 58-59 ❖ FL 3:7, 10

Love: "Baby talk" as it is used in both Affection and Eros not unique to humans; some birds use infantile sounds in the same way
•FL 58 ❖ FL 3:9

Love, being in, involves the feeling that *all* is at stake; "if we miss this chance we shall have lived in vain"; this is an illusion
•GID 320-321 ❖ GID III 9:23-25

Love, being in: Promise of permanent fidelity in marriage cannot depend on this
•MC 96-101 (*see also* L 184, 209; SL 81-84) ❖ MC III 6:3-13 (*see also* L 18 Apr 40; 2 Aug 46; SL ch. 18)

Love, bereavement is a universal and integral part of our experience of; it is not the interruption of the dance, but the next figure

•GO 58-59 (*see also* GO 14-15, 63-64)

❖ GO 3:33 (*see also* GO 1:28; 3:40)

Love between a man and a woman as an
analogy useful to our conception of
God's love for us
•PP 45-46, 47 (*see also* FL 112-113, 124)

❖ PP 3:13, 14 (*see also* FL 4:42, 58)

Love between God and Man rarely represented in Scripture as Friendship;
more often as Affection ("Father") and
Eros ("Bridegroom")
•FL 112-113, 124 (*see also* PP 44-46)

❖ FL 4:42, 58 (*see also* PP 3:12, 13)

Love: By a high paradox, God enables men
to have a Gift-love towards Himself
•FL 177 ❖ FL 6:24

Love, by definition, seeks to enjoy its object—that is why love for God makes
heaven its goal
•PP 145 ❖ PP 10:1

Love ceases to be a demon only when he
ceases to be a god (quote from M.
Denis de Rougemont)
•CR 35; FL 17-18, 39; L 182 (*see also* FL
83, 151*, 156-157*, 160, 166*) ❖ CR 2:55;
FL 1:13, 14, 29; L 16 Apr 40 (*see also* FL
3:45; 5:31*; 5:39-41*; 5:46; 6:5*)

Love, Christian, is an affair of the will
•MC 115, 117-118 (*see also* L 269; LM
115)

❖ MC III 9:2, 9, 10 (*see also* L undated
letter just after 13 Mar 56; LM 21:12)

Love, Christian virtue of, does not necessarily involve unselfishness in the
negative sense (going without things
ourselves)
•WG 3 (*see also* SL 121)

❖ WG 1:1 (*see also* SL 26:2)

Love compared to a garden: Both must be
tended, and our tending must be combined with God's grace
•FL 163-165 ❖ FL 6:2

Love, definition of: It is not an affectionate feeling, but a steady wish for
the loved person's ultimate good
•GID 49 (*see also* MC 108) ❖ GID I 4:3
(Ques. 1) (*see also* MC III 7:10)

Love, difficulty of receiving, which is not
based on our own attractiveness as
shown by a marriage in which one

person is ill
•FL 182 ❖ FL 6:30

Love: Distinction between Gift-love and
Need-love discussed
•FL 11-21, 33, 175-184

❖ FL ch. 1; 2:14; 6:21-34

Love: Eros tends to turn "being in love"
into a sort of religion; opposition
makes lovers feel like martyrs
•FL 154 ❖ FL 5:36

Love, erotic—*see* Eros

Love, even the imagining of supernatural,
towards God has at times made all
other objects of desire "look like broken toys and faded flowers"
•FL 192 (*see also* PP 106*)

❖ FL 6:47 (*see also* PP 6:17*)

Love, every, has its art of love
•FL 68 (*see also* FL 81)

❖ FL 3:25 (*see also* FL 3:44)

Love, exclusive focus on object of, is dangerous to that love; this illustrates a
universal law
•GID 280 ❖ GID III 2:6

Love: "Falling in love" not something that
just happens to one, like measles; it is
a choice
•MC 101 (*see also* SL 88, 93)

❖ MC III 6:13 (*see also* SL 19:3; 20:5)

Love, feelings of, are not enough; something else must come to the help of
mere feeling if it is to remain sweet
•FL 163 (*see also* FL 81-83, 124, 159-160;
GID 285; L 198-199; SL 124)

❖ FL 6:1 (*see also* FL 3:44, 45; 4:59; 5:45,
46; GID III 3:7; L undated letter just
before 20 Jan 42; SL 26:5)

Love, feelings of, not reliable in marriage;
hence the need for a promise
•MC 96-99 (*see also* L 184; SL 82- 84*)

❖ MC III 6:4-9 (*see also* L 18 Apr 40; SL
18:6)

Love for animals: "I think God wants us
to love Him *more*, not to love creatures
(even animals) *less*"
•LAL 61 (*see also* FL 165*, 170-171, 190-
191*)

❖ LAL 18/8/56 (*see also* FL 6:3, 4, 15, 44*)

Love for God—*consider also* Appetite for
God

Love for God, a man's spiritual health is exactly proportional to his
- FL 13 ❖ FL 1:7

Love for God and for your neighbor a state of the *will*; no man can love because he is told to
- L 269 (*see also* MC 115, 117-118; LM 115)
- ❖ L undated letter just before 2 Apr 56 (*see also* MC III 9:2, 9, 10; LM 21:12)

Love for God, do not sit trying to manufacture feelings of; act as if you love Him
- MC 117 (*see also* L 269; LM 115)
- ❖ MC III 9:9 (*see also* L undated letter just after 13 Mar 56; LM 21:12)

Love for God enables us to love the world better
- GID 150 ❖ GID I 17:7

Love for God, feeling: "...the only love that matters is His for you...He will see to the rest"
- L 192 ❖ L 4 Jan 41

Love for God finds its natural expression in praise; indeed the praise completes the enjoyment
- RP 94-97 (*see also* GO 72)
- ❖ RP 9:5, 6 (*see also* GO 4:5)

Love for God: "For most of us the true rivalry lies between the self and the human Other, not yet between the human Other and God"
- FL 165 (*see also* LAL 61)
- ❖ FL 6:3, 4 (*see also* LAL 18/8/56)

Love for God: God can, through Grace, awaken in man a supernatural Appreciative love towards Himself
- FL 191 ❖ FL 6:46

Love for God: God is our true Beloved, whom we have loved all our life
- FL 190-191; PP 147; SL 148
- ❖ FL 6:44, 45; PP 10:3; SL 31:5

Love for God, human, largely a form of Need-love; our need of Him can never end, but our awareness of it can
- FL 12-14, 31 ❖ FL 1:4-8; 2:9

Love for God: "I think God wants us to love Him *more*, not to love creatures (even animals) *less*"
- LAL 61 (*see also* FL 165, 170-171, 190-191)
- ❖ LAL 18/8/56 (*see also* FL 6:3, 4, 15, 44)

Love for God: In order to fully understand the doctrine of praise, we must suppose ourselves to be in perfect love with God...drunk with delight...
- RP 96 ❖ RP 9:6

Love for God: Loving God too little a greater danger than loving any human too much
- FL 170 ❖ FL 6:15

Love for God, natural loves as rivals to our
- FL 41-42, 61, 154-155, 165-174
- ❖ FL 2:33; 3:13; 5:36, 37; 6:3-19

Love for God: Need-love cries to God from our poverty; Gift-love longs to serve; Appreciative love says "We give thanks to Thee for Thy great glory"
- FL 33 ❖ FL 2:14

Love for God: Our Need-love for Him can never end—but our awareness of it can
- FL 31 ❖ FL 2:9

Love for God requires a knowledge of Him; if we do not love God it may be that what we are trying to love is not yet God
- PP 53 ❖ PP 3:18

Love for God, rivalry between natural loves and
- FL 41-42, 61, 154-155, 165-174 (*see also* SL 18*) ❖ FL 2:33; 3:13; 5:36, 37; 6:3-19 (*see also* SL 3:6*)

"Love for God" too easily suggests the word "spiritual" in all those negative senses which it has acquired (Lewis preferred "appetite for God")
- RP 51 (*see also* "Spiritual")
- ❖ RP 5:9 (*see also* "Spiritual")

Love for God: "...we shall not be well so long as we love and admire anything more than we love and admire God"
- MC 113 ❖ MC III 8:11

Love for God: "When I have learnt to love God better than my earthly dearest, I shall love my earthly dearest better than I do now"
- L 248 (*see also* GID 150)
- ❖ L 8 Nov 52 (*see also* GID I 17:7)

Love for God, whether we have enough:

God's love for us is a much safer subject to think about
- MC 117-118 ❖ MC III 9:10

Love: "For most of us the true rivalry lies between the self and the human Other, not yet between the human Other and God"
- FL 165 (see also LAL 61)
❖ FL 6:4 (see also LAL 18/8/56)

Love for my neighbor like love for myself: I might detest something I have done, yet I do not cease to love myself
- GID 49 ❖ GID I 4:3 (Ques. 1)

Love for one's country like love for one's family or school; the familiar is in itself ground for affection
- L 231
❖ L undated letter just after 19 Apr 51

Love for one's hometown: "No man loves his city because it is great, but because it is his" (quote from "one of the Greeks")
- FL 46 ❖ FL 2:40

Love for ourselves—see Self-love

Love, for those few years H. [Joy] and I feasted on; sometimes as dramatic as a thunderstorm, sometimes as comfortable and unemphatic as putting on soft slippers
- GO 6 ❖ GO 1:12

Love for what is not personal: Nature and natural beauty
- FL 34-39 (see also Beauty; Nature)
❖ FL 2:17-28 (see also Beauty; Nature)

Love for what is not personal: one's country
- FL 39-49 (see also Patriotism)
❖ FL 2:29-43 (see also Patriotism)

Love for your neighbor, do not waste time bothering whether you have; act as if you did
- MC 116 (see also L 269; LM 115; MC 161) ❖ MC III 9:5 (see also L undated letter just after 13 Mar 56; LM 21:12; MC IV 7:3)

Love: Gift-love (as in parenting) must work toward its own abdication; we must aim at making ourselves superfluous

- FL 76 ❖ FL 3:37

Love: Gift-love may become perverted, as in the need to be needed (story of Mrs. Fidget)
- FL 73-76, 82-83 (see also L 198-199*; MC 167; SL 121*, 123*)
❖ FL 3:33-37, 45 (see also L undated letter just before 20 Jan 42*; MC IV 7:3; SL 26:2*, 5*)

Love: Gift-love of Charity comes by Grace
- FL 178 ❖ FL 6:24, 25

Love: Gift-love the most God-like love
- FL 19 ❖ FL 1:16

Love: Gift-love to God includes our charity to those in need; "every stranger whom we feed or clothe is Christ"
- FL 178 ❖ FL 6:24

Love: Gift-loves are natural images of God Himself; Need-loves have no resemblance to the love which God is
- FL 175-176 (see also FL 11-12)
❖ FL 6:21, 22 (see also FL 1:1-3)

Love: God can give us a share of His Divine Gift-love, which is wholly disinterested and desires what is best for the beloved
- FL 177 ❖ FL 6:24

Love: God implants in each of us both Gift-loves and Need-loves; but this natural Gift-love is not yet Divine Gift-love
- FL 176-177 ❖ FL 6:22-24

Love: "God seems to build our higher loves round our merely natural impulses—sex, maternity, kinship, old acquaintances, etc."
- L 231-232
❖ L undated letter just after 19 Apr 51

Love, God will look to every soul like its first, because He is its first love
- PP 147 ❖ PP 10:3

Love, happiness achieved in, not by good lovers but by good people
- GID 321 (see also FL 159-160)
❖ GID III 9:24 (see also FL 5:45)

Love, human, has a tendency to claim for itself a divine authority
- FL 17-19 (see also FL 39, 83, 151, 156-157, 160, 166; CR 35*; L 182)
❖ FL 1:13-15 (see also FL 1:28, 29; 3:45; 5:31, 39-41, 46; 6:5; CR 2:56*; L 16 Apr 40)

Love, human, is caused by a real or supposed good in the beloved which the lover needs and desires; but God's love causes all the goodness we have
•PP 50 ❖ PP 3:17

Love, idolatry of: "Where a true Eros is present resistance to his commands feels like an apostasy," and temptations feel like duties
•FL 155-157 (see also FL 20-21, 151)
❖ FL 5:37-41 (see also FL 1:18; 5:31, 32)

Love: If a man really loved God and man, obedience could hardly be called obedience, for he would be unable to help it
•LM 115 (see also L 277; PP 100)
❖ LM 21:12 (see also L 18 Jul 57; PP 6:11)

Love: If we try to protect our hearts from breaking, they will become unbreakable, impenetrable, irredeemable
•FL 169 ❖ FL 6:13

Love: "If you would be loved, be lovable" (quote from Ovid)
•FL 65 ❖ FL 3:19

Love: In actual life the three elements of love (Gift-love, Appreciative love, and Need-love) are mixed; mostly they do not exist alone
•FL 33 (see also FL 57)
❖ FL 2:15 (see also FL 3:8)

Love, in all forms of, the great thing is to turn from the demand to be loved to the wish to love
•L 245 ❖ L 20 Oct 52

Love, in its own nature, demands the perfecting of the beloved (as God does with us)
•PP 46-48 (see also MC 172)
❖PP 3:13-15 (see also MC IV 9:4)

Love in the sense of natural affection not enough; not a cause of lasting happiness—requires charity
•FL 163; GID 285; SL 124 (see also FL 81-83, 124, 159-160; GID 285; L 198-199; SL 124)
❖ FL 6:1; GID III 3:7; SL 26:5 (see also FL 3:44, 45; 4:59; 5:45, 46; L undated letter just before 20 Jan 42)

Love involves trusting the beloved beyond the evidence, even against much

evidence (re: "obstinate" trust in God)
•WLN 26 (see also MC 123)
❖ WLN 2:13 (see also MC III 11:4, 5)

Love is parodied by indulgence as merriment is parodied by flippancy
•WG 19 ❖ WG 1:15

Love: "...it is better to love the self than to love nothing, and to pity the self than to pity no one"
•GID 195 ❖ GID II 2:4

Love: It would be undesirable, even if it were possible, for people to be "in love" all their lives
•L 184 (see also MC 98-99)
❖ L 18 Apr 40 (see also MC III 6:9)

Love makes the difference in all aspects of Vicariousness, and differentiates it from mere parasitism
•M 118-120 (see also GID 85-87*)
❖ M 14:19, 20 (see also GID I 9:8, 10*)

Love makes us generous and courageous; is the great conqueror of lust
•MC 98-99 ❖ MC III 6:9

Love may cause pain to its object, but only on the supposition that the object needs alteration to become fully lovable (re: God's love for us)
•PP 55 ❖ PP 4:1

Love may forgive all infirmities and love still in spite of them: but Love cannot cease to will their removal (re: God's love for us)
•PP 46 ❖ PP 3:13

Love: Need-love a real form of love, and the form our love for God must largely take
•FL 12-14, 31 ❖ FL 1:4-8; 2:9

Love: Need-love says of a woman "I cannot live without her"; Gift-love longs to give her happiness, comfort, etc.
•FL 33 ❖ FL 2:14

Love: Need-love will not last longer than the need, but another kind of love may be grafted onto it
•FL 30-31 ❖ FL 2:9

Love: "No one loves because he sees reason, but because he loves" (quote from George MacDonald)
•L 231
❖ L undated letter just after 19 Apr 51

Love, nothing so enriches erotic, as the discovery that the Beloved can deeply and truly enter into Friendship with the Friends you already had
- FL 99 (*consider also* Eros)
❖ FL 4:21 (*consider also* Eros)

Love of a father for his son as an analogy useful to our conception of God's love for us
- PP 44-45, 47 (*see also* FL 112-113, 124)
❖ PP 3:12, 14 (*see also* FL 4:42, 58)

Love, of all arguments against, none makes so strong an appeal to my nature as "Careful! This might lead you to suffering"
- FL 168 (*see also* Safety)
❖ FL 6:9 (*see also* Safety)

Love of God—*consider also* Love for God

Love of God, altruistic vs. egoistic love as regards the, (God has no needs, thus His love is bottomlessly selfless)
- PP 49-54, esp. 50
❖ PP 3:17-19, esp. 3:17

Love of God: "But who can duly adore that Love which will open the high gates to a prodigal who is brought in kicking, struggling, resentful..."
- SJ 229 (*see also* GID 261)
❖ SJ 14:23 (*see also* GID II 16:19-22)

Love of God: Christ did not die for men because of their merit, but because He is love and He loves infinitely
- M 52 (*see also* M 122; WLN 86)
❖ M 7:14 (*see also* M 14:24; WLN 6:10)

Love of God for Man, analogies from the various types of love between creatures can be useful to our conception of the, (examples listed)
- PP 41-46 ❖ PP 3:9-14

Love of God for Man defined and discussed
- PP 37-54 ❖ PP ch. 3

Love of God for Man: "It is certainly a burden of glory not only beyond our deserts but also, except in rare moments of grace, beyond our desiring"
- PP 47 ❖ PP 3:14

Love of God for Man: "The Impassible speaks as if it suffered passion..."
- PP 47 ❖ PP 3:14

Love of God for us is Gift-love rather than Need-love
- FL 11, 175-184 ❖ FL 1:1-3; 6:21-34

Love of God for us may involve allowing us to suffer*
- GO 49-50 ❖ GO 3:15-18

Love of God for us: We are a Divine work of art; an artist, over the most loved picture of his life, will spend much time and effort perfecting it
- PP 42-43, 47 (*see also* LM 34, 69; MC 44, 173) ❖ PP 3:10, 14 (*see also* LM 6:16; 13:4; MC II 1:4; IV 9:7)

Love of God for us, we like to believe, is because we are intrinsically lovable and attractive
- FL 180 ❖ FL 6:27

Love of God: God cannot be affected with love because He *is* love, in the same way that water is exempt from getting wet
- M 92-93 ❖ M 11:17

Love of God: God does not love us because we are good; He makes us good because He loves us
- MC 64 ❖ MC II 5:6

Love of God: God is "not a senile benevolence that drowsily wishes you to be happy in your own way," but a persistent, loving artist who desires our perfection
- PP 46-47 ❖ PP 3:14

Love of God: God is not proud, He stoops to conquer; He will have us even when we have shown that we prefer everything else to Him
- PP 97 (*see also* LAL 49; SJ 229) ❖ PP 6:8 (*see also* LAL 16/12/55; SJ 14:23)

Love of God: God loved into existence wholly superfluous creatures in order that He might love and perfect them
- FL 176 ❖ FL 6:21

Love of God: God loves each person individually, as if he were the only creature in existence
- L 243 ❖ L 20 Jun 52

Love of God: God loves us in spite of our faults, as we should our neighbors
- GID 154 (*see also* GID 123*)
❖ GID I 18:8, 9 (*see also* GID I 14:7, 8*)

Love of God: God loves us in spite of our faults, but He cannot cease to will their removal
- •PP 46 (*see also* MC 172)
- ❖ PP 3:13 (*see also* MC IV 9:4)

Love of God: God loves us, not because we are lovable but because He is love; not because He needs to receive but because He delights to give
- •L 231; WG 115 ❖ L undated letter just after 19 Apr 51; WG 7:14

Love of God: "He has paid us the intolerable compliment of loving us, in the deepest, most tragic, most inexorable sense"
- •PP 41, 42, 53 ❖ PP 3:8, 10, 18

Love of God: His love for us and His knowledge of us are not distinct from one another; He sees because He loves, and therefore loves although He sees
- •GO 84 ❖ GO 4:31

Love of God: How He loves us is how we should love each other (not for any nice, attractive qualities we have)
- •MC 108 ❖ MC III 7:11

Love of God: "...if nature had never awakened certain longings in me, huge areas of what I can now mean by the 'love' of God would never...have existed"
- •FL 37 ❖ FL 2:23

Love of God illustrated by parents who would rather see their children suffer much than be happy in contemptible and estranging modes
- •PP 41 ❖ PP 3:8

Love of God includes "wrath"; turn God's wrath into mere disapproval, and you also turn His love into mere humanitarianism
- •LM 96-97 (*see also* PP 58)
- ❖ LM 18:6-9 (*see also* PP 4:6)

Love of God is not wearied by our sins or our indifference; is quite relentless
- •MC 118 ❖ MC III 9:10

Love of God is something more than mere kindness (may cause pain to its object because it needs alteration)
- •PP 40-41, 46 ❖ PP 3:7, 8, 13

Love of God is surely as fertile in resource as it is measureless in condescension (re: possible redemption for other fallen races, if any)
- •WLN 87 ❖ WLN 6:5

Love of God: Nothing separates Pagan theology from Christianity so sharply as Aristotle's doctrine that God moves the universe to love Him, Himself unmoved
- •PP 51-52 (*see also* GID 174*)
- ❖ PP 3:17 (*see also* GID I 21:5*)

Love of God, Screwtape attempts to describe the "impossible," for humans
- •SL 65, 81-82, 85-87, 128
- ❖ SL 14:4; 18:4; 19:1-3; 27:4

Love of God toward Himself: "God loveth not Himself as Himself but as Goodness; and if there were aught better than God, He would love that and not Himself"
- •PP 152 (quote from *Theol. Germ.* XXXII) ❖ PP 10:10 (quote from *Theol. Germ.* XXXII)

Love of God: When pain is to be borne, courage helps more than knowledge, human sympathy more than courage, and the love of God more than all
- •PP 10 ❖ PP P:1

Love of self—*see* Self-love

Love, one of the miracles of, is that it gives—especially to the woman—a power of seeing through its own enchantments and yet not being disenchanted
- •GO 83-84 ❖ GO 4:30, 31

Love, only by being in some respect like God has any earthly beloved excited our
- •FL 190 ❖ FL 6:44

Love: Our experience is coloured through and through by books and plays and the cinema; it takes skill to disentangle the things we have learned for ourselves
- •MC 100, 101 (*see also* SL 88)
- ❖ MC III 6:10, 13 (*see also* SL 19:3)

Love, perhaps real, —like that in a society of pure intelligences—is not an emotion and does not need an attendant

emotion
- GO 85-88, esp. 87
- ❖ GO 4:33-35, esp. 4:35

Love, praise is the mode of, which always has some element of joy in it
- GO 72 ❖ GO 4:5

Love: Promise of permanence an illusion
- GID 320-321 (see also MC 98-101)
- ❖ GID III 9:23-25 (see also MC III 6:7-12)

Love, real, vs. "Christina dreams": The love dream makes a man incapable of real love
- L 76 (see also L 78)
- ❖ L 24 May 22 (see also L 30 Jun 22)

Love (regarding Charles Williams): "He was not only a lover himself but the cause that love was in other men"
- L 208
- ❖ L undated letter just after 10 Dec 45

Love, romantic—see Eros

Love, Screwtape advises causing humans to confuse sexual infatuation with, so they'll excuse themselves from guilt and consequences of improper marriages
- SL 84 ❖ SL 18:6

"Love," Screwtape advises causing humans in courtship to think they have solved their problems through, when in fact they have only waived or postponed them
- SL 120 ❖ SL 26:1

Love: Screwtape advises Wormwood on the kind of woman he ought to encourage his "patient" to fall in love with and marry
- SL 91-94 ❖ SL 20:2-5

Love, Screwtape attempts to define: "The good of one self is to be the good of another. This impossibility He [God] calls love..."
- SL 81-82 ❖ SL 18:4

Love, Screwtape describes being or falling in, as a neutral situation which can work either to God's or the devil's advantage
- SL 87-89 ❖ SL 19:3

Love, sexual—see Sexual love; Venus

Love that had never embodied Love Himself on earth would be irrelevant to you in Heaven
- FL 188 ❖ FL 6:39

Love: "The greed to be loved is a fearful thing..."
- GID 285 (see also FL 64-65)
- ❖ GID III 3:7 (see also FL 3:18)

Love, the pervert sees normal, as a mere milk and water substitute for the ghastly world of impossible fantasies which have become to him the "real thing"
- CR 40 ❖ CR 3:7

Love, the total commitment of Eros is an example of, we ought to exercise towards God and Man
- FL 153-154, 158 ❖ FL 5:35, 43

"Love," the word, is sometimes used when referring to a devilish desire to dominate—almost to digest—one's fellow; this is a principle of Hell
- SL xi (see also FL 160; SL 81; consider also Absorption)
- ❖ SL P:19, 20 (see also FL 5:46; SL 18:3, 4; consider also Absorption)

Love, there are four kinds of; Agape is the best kind, is good in all circumstances, and is the kind of love God has for us
- L 256 ❖ L 18 Feb 54

Love, those unlovable people who demand, produce in us a sense of guilt for a fault we could not have avoided and cannot cease to commit
- FL 65 (see also GID 285)
- ❖ FL 3:18 (see also GID III 3:7)

Love, though we can have erotic, and friendship for the same person, in some ways nothing is less like a Friendship than a love-affair
- FL 91 ❖ FL 4:8

Love: "To love at all is to be vulnerable. Love anything at all and your heart will certainly be wrung and possibly be broken"
- FL 169 ❖ FL 6:13

Love, two kinds of: for those we need, and for those who need us (which is how God loves us)
- L 231

❖ L undated letter just after 19 Apr 51

Love vs. "being in love": True love not merely a feeling, but a deep unity; it is on this that the engine of marriage is run
•MC 98-99 ❖ MC III 6:9

Love, we must join neither the idolators nor the debunkers of human
•FL 20 ❖ FL 1:18

Love: We must love others as God loves us (not for any nice, attractive qualities we have...)
•MC 108 ❖ MC III 7:11

Love: "When I have learnt to love God better than my earthly dearest, I shall love my earthly dearest better than I do now"
•L 248 (see also GID 150)
❖ L 8 Nov 52 (see also GID I 17:7)

"Love your neighbor as yourself" cannot be done until we learn to love God
•MC 82 (see also LM 114-115)
❖ MC III 3:8 (see also LM 21:11, 12)

Loves, Friendship the most spiritual of, so the danger which besets it is spiritual too (Pride); it must invoke the divine protection if it is to remain sweet
•FL 111-112, 123-124
❖ FL 4:38, 39, 57-59

Loves, human, can be glorious images of Divine love; can help or hinder our approach to God
•FL 20-21 ❖ FL 1:18

Loves, I believe that the most lawless and inordinate, are less contrary to God's will than self-protective lovelessness
•FL 169-170 ❖ FL 6:14

Loves, it is important so to order our, that the occasion for "hating" our loved one (to put God or honour first) need never arise
•FL 173-174 ❖ FL 6:19

Loves, natural, as rivals to the love of God
•FL 41-42, 61, 154-155, 165-174
❖ FL 2:33; 3:13; 5:36, 37; 6:3-19

Loves, natural, can become rivals to spiritual love—but can also be preparatory imitations of it
•FL 41-42 (see also FL 20-21, 158)
❖ FL 2:33 (see also FL 1:18; 5:43)

Loves, natural, can hope for eternity only in so far as they have allowed themselves to be taken into the eternity of Charity
•FL 187 ❖ FL 6:38

Loves, natural: "Left to themselves they either vanish or become demons"
•FL 166 (see also FL 47, 81-83, 124, 154, 160) ❖ FL 6:5 (see also FL 2:40; 3:44, 45; 4:59; 5:36, 46)

Loves, natural: "Much of the grubbiness is clean dirt if only you will leave it in the garden and not keep on sprinkling it over the library table"
•FL 20 ❖ FL 1:18

Loves, natural, need to be crucified and reborn; cannot of themselves lead to happiness
•L 198-199
❖ L undated letter just before 20 Jan 42

Loves, natural, prove that they are unworthy to take the place of God since they cannot even do what they promise to do without God's help
•FL 166 (see also FL 158-159)
❖ FL 6:5 (see also FL 5:42, 43)

Loves, natural: Some may have to be sacrificed; others will have to be transformed
•FL 183 (see also FL 154)
❖ FL 6:31 (see also FL 5:35)

Loves, natural, that are allowed to become gods do not remain loves but can become complicated forms of hatred
•FL 19-20 (see also FL 64, 82-83, 160; GID 285) ❖ FL 1:16 (see also FL 3:17, 45; 5:46; GID III 3:7)

Loves, natural: "When God arrives (and only then) the half-gods can remain"
•FL 166 ❖ FL 6:5

Loves, natural: When they become lawless they cease to be loves at all
•FL 47 (see also FL 154)
❖ FL 2:40 (see also FL 5:36)

Loves, need for transformation of our natural, by God may be overlooked
•FL 183 ❖ FL 6:31

Loves, setting priorities for our: Our deepest concern should be for first things, and our next deepest for second

things; this is called "ordinate loves"
- LM 22 (*see also* L 228, 248; FL 165, 170-171, 190-191; GID 150; Priorities)
- ❖ LM 4:14 (*see also* L 23 Apr 51; 8 Nov 52; FL 6:3, 4, 15, 44; GID I 17:7; Priorities)

Loves, the rivalry between all natural, and the love of God is something a Christian dare not forget
- FL 61 (*see also* FL 41-42, 70-73, 154-155, 170-174; SL 18*)
- ❖ FL 3:13 (*see also* FL 2:33; 3:27-32; 5:36, 37; 6:15-19; SL 3:6*)

Loves, transformation of our natural, by Divine Love not achieved by substitution but by being "taken up into... Love Himself"
- FL 183-184 ❖ FL 6:32, 33

Loved one that had never embodied Love Himself on earth would be irrelevant to you in Heaven (like meeting a childhood friend you had outgrown)
- FL 188 ❖ FL 6:39

Loved ones—*see also* Family members

Loved ones a reflection of God: "...of her, and of every created thing I praise, I should say, 'In some way, in its unique way, like Him who made it'"
- GO 73 (*see also* LM 90*)
- ❖ GO 4:7 (*see also* LM 17:8*)

Loved ones: After their death, a slow process begins in which they become more and more imaginary—the reality is no longer there to check us*
- GO 19-24 (*see also* GO 59, 64-65, 75-77) ❖ GO 2:3-7 (*see also* GO 3:33, 34, 41; 4:13-17)

Loved ones: By loving God more than them we shall love them more than we do now
- FL 191 ❖ FL 6:44

Loved one's conversion to Christianity (or any other profound change) may elicit a sense of outrage in family members
- L 274 (*see also* FL 70-73; SL 18*) ❖ L 10 Feb 57 (*see also* FL 3:27-32; SL 3:6*)

Loved ones, faces of our, are difficult to remember after they're gone; all the expressions crowd together in our memory and cancel out into a blur

- GO 16-17 ❖ GO 1:31

Loved ones, how to forgive
- LAL 92-93 ❖ LAL 28 Oct 60

Loved ones, I can't help suspecting that the dead also feel the pains of separation from their
- GO 58 (*see also* GO 31)
- ❖ GO 3:33 (*see also* GO 2:17)

Loved ones: "I think God wants us to love Him *more*, not to love creatures (even animals) *less*"
- LAL 61 (*see also* FL 165, 170-171, 190-191)
- ❖ LAL 18/8/56 (*see also* FL 6:3, 4, 15, 44)

Loved ones incessantly triumph over our mere idea of them; this reality is what we are to love still, after they are dead
- GO 77 (*see also* GO 19-22)
- ❖ GO 4:16 (*see also* GO 2:3-6)

Loved ones: "It is not that we have loved them too much, but that we did not quite understand what we were loving"
- FL 190-191 (*see also* LAL 61)
- ❖ FL 6:44 (*see also* LAL 18/8/56)

Loved ones must be turned down when they come between us and our obedience to God
- FL 171-172 ❖ FL 6:17

Loved ones: "Only by being in some respect like Him...has any earthly Beloved excited our love"
- FL 190 (*see also* L 274*)
- ❖ FL 6:44 (*see also* L 10 Feb 57*)

Loved ones, reunion with deceased, not to be the goal of our Christian life
- FL 189-191 (*see also* GO 28-30, 79; L 290; RP 41; SJ 231*)
- ❖ FL 6:41-43 (*see also* GO 2:13-16; 4:21; L 3 Dec 59; RP 4:16; SJ 15:3*)

Loved ones, reunion with deceased: The reality of it would probably blow all one's ideas about it into smithereens
- GO 82-83 ❖ GO 4:27-29

Loved ones: We (like God, with us) would rather see them suffer much than be happy in contemptible and estranging modes
- PP 41 ❖ PP 3:8

Loved ones: We shall find them all in God;

they are as portraits to the Original, and as rivulets to the Fountain
•FL 191 ❖ FL 6:44

Loved ones, whether we shall know our, in Heaven and whether those relationships will have any continued significance
•FL 187-188 ❖ FL 6:38, 39

Loved ones will be in Heaven only on a condition ("...nothing can enter there which cannot become heavenly")
•FL 187 ❖ FL 6:38

Loved ones, witnessing to: "We must be careful not to expect or demand that their salvation shd. conform to some ready-made pattern of our own"
•L 261 ❖ L 2 Feb 55

Loving and admiring anything outside ourselves is to take one step away from utter spiritual ruin—though we shall not be whole until we love God more
•MC 113 ❖ MC III 8:11

Loving God—*see* Love for God

"Loving" of Jacob seems to mean the acceptance of Jacob for a high (and painful) vocation; the "hating" of Esau, his rejection
•FL 172 ❖ FL 6:17

Loving your enemy (or "neighbor") does not necessarily mean feeling fond of him or thinking him nice; it means wishing his good
•MC 105, 108 (*see also* GID 49; MC 115-117) ❖ MC III 7:4, 5, 10 (*see also* GID I 4:3; MC III 9:2-6)

"**Low**" church: "I think the 'low' church milieu that I grew up in did tend to be too cosily at ease in Sion" (re: intimacy without awe in prayer)
•LM 13 ❖ LM 2:14

Low-brow(s)—*see also* Vulgar

Low-brow people who like hymns may be better Christians than ourselves
•L 224 ❖ L 7 Dec 50

Low-brow vs. High-brow music in church
•CR 94-99 ❖ CR ch. 8

Low-brows who genuinely enjoy art or literature vs. snobs who feign enjoyment of it ("I...prefer the live dog to

the dead lion")
•WLN 38-39 (*see also* CR 10)
❖ WLN 3:12 (*see also* CR 1:15)

Loyalty: A man "should never give all his heart to anything which will end when his life ends"*
•WLN 110 ❖ WLN 7:31

Lucretius' argument for atheism, I felt [in my youth] the force of: "'Had God designed the world, it would not be A world so frail and faulty as we see'"
•SJ 65 ❖ SJ 4:11

Lucretius mentioned: "That austere voluptuary gave it as his opinion that love actually impairs sexual pleasure"
•FL 135 ❖ FL 5:5

Lukewarm religion mentioned by Screwtape: "A moderated religion is as good for us as no religion at all—and more amusing"*
•SL 43 (*see also* SL 33, 75; Self-reservation) ❖ SL 9:3 (*see also* SL 7:2; 16:5; Self-reservation)

Lust—*see also* Sexual temptation; *consider also* Eros

Lust: "...a lascivious man thinks about women's bodies, [and] a lascivious woman thinks about her own. *What* a world we live in!"
•L 141 ❖ L 10 Jun 30

Lust, all the modern propaganda for, contributes to our feeling that the desires we are resisting are natural, healthy, and reasonable
•MC 92 ❖ MC III 5:8, 10

Lust causes a man to want, not a woman, but a pleasure for which a woman happens to be the necessary apparatus
•FL 134-135 ❖ FL 5:5

Lust, cruelty is surely more evil than, and the World at least as dangerous as the Flesh
•SJ 109 ❖ SJ 7:11

Lust described by Screwtape: "...the felt evil is what he wants; it is that 'tang' in the flavour which he is after"*
•SL 93 ❖ SL 20:4, 5

Lust: If our minds are full of novels and sentimental songs, and our bodies full

of alcohol, we can turn any kind of
love into that kind of love*
- •MC 100, 101 (*see also* SL 88)
- ❖ MC III 6:10, 13 (*see also* SL 19:3)

Lust: "If the imagination were obedient,
the appetites would give us very little
trouble"
- •GID 217; LAL 111; LM 17
- ❖ GID II 7:3; LAL 26 Nov 62; LM 3:9

Lust is conquered by real love
- •MC 98-99 ❖ MC III 6:9

Lust less likely to become a god than the
human loves at their best (but will still
corrupt its addict in a dozen other
ways)
- •FL 18 ❖ FL 1:14, 15

Lust: Lewis mentions the error of mistaking the dictates of passion for the decree of fate (as in a marriage between
unbelievers)
- •L 160-161 (*see also* MC 100, 101)
- ❖ L 10 Jun 38 (*see also* MC III 6:11, 13)

Lust, passion for the Occult is a spiritual;
and like the lust of the body it has the
fatal power of making everything else
in the world seem uninteresting
- •SJ 60 (*see also* SJ 177, 178)
- ❖ SJ 4:6 (*see also* SJ 11:14, 16)

Lust, resentment behaves just like a; draws
one back and back to nurse and fondle
and encourage it
- •LM 94 ❖ LM 18:1

Lust ("unchastity"): Sins of the flesh the
least bad of all sins*
- •MC 94-95 (*see also* L 175; LAL 111)
- ❖ MC III 5:14 (*see also* L 17 Jan 40; LAL
26 Nov 62)

Lust: The actual pleasure, when it arrives,
is not sinful (for pleasure is created by
God); the sin lies in the anticipation
- •SL 69 ❖ SL 15:3

Lust, the satisfaction of a tyrannous, described as something "past reason
hunted and, no sooner had, past reason hated"
- •FL 28 ❖ FL 2:6

Luther, Martin, compared humanity to a
drunkard who, after falling off his
horse on the right, falls off it next time
on the left (re: reactive errors)

- •WLN 94 ❖ WLN 7:4

Luther, quote from, regarding assurance
that we are chosen
- •L 252 ❖ L 3 Aug 53

Lying; Lie(s)—*see* Dishonesty

MacDonald, George
- •L 181, 205 ❖ L 26 Mar 40; 29 Oct 44

MacDonald, George, I had found when I was sixteen and never wavered in my allegiance—though I tried for a long time to ignore his Christianity
- •GID 203 ❖ GID II 4:5

MacDonald, George: Lewis mentions his own book, *George MacDonald: an Anthology*
- •L 299 ❖ L 9 May 61

MacDonald, George, mentioned with reference to the book *Phantastes*
- •L 27, 84, 167; SJ 179
- ❖ L undated letter of Oct 1915; 11 Jan 23; 9 Jul 39; SJ 11:18

MacDonald, George, my love for, has not extended to his poetry, though I have naturally made several attempts to like it
- •L 232 ❖ L 5 Jun 51

MacDonald, George: "...of course it was a pity he had that bee in his bonnet about Christianity"
- •SJ 213 ❖ SJ 14:3

MacDonald, George, parable from: Transformation of our nature is like the rebuilding of a house; God intends to come and live in it Himself
- •MC 174 ❖ MC IV 9:10

MacDonald, George (*Phantastes*): "... never had the wind of Joy blowing through any story been less separable from the story itself"
- •SJ 180 ❖ SJ 11:19

MacDonald, George (*Phantastes*): I did not yet know the name of the new quality that met me; it was Holiness
- •SJ 179 (*see also* L 167)
- ❖ SJ 11:18, 19 (*see also* L 9 Jul 39)

MacDonald, George, quote from: "... Obedience is the one key of life" (re: trying to guess when Christ will return)
- •WLN 108-109 ❖ WLN 7:28

MacDonald, George, quote from: "God is easy to please, but hard to satisfy" (like a father being pleased with baby's first steps)
- •MC 172 (*see also* PP 46*; SL 39)
- ❖ MC IV 9:5 (*see also* PP 3:13*; SL 8:4)

MacDonald, George, quote from: "The one principle of Hell is—'I am my own'"
- •SJ 212 ❖ SJ 14 prelim. quote

MacDonald, George, "represents God as saying to men 'You must be strong with my strength...*for I have no other to give you*'"
- •PP 53 ❖ PP 3:19

MacDonald, George: "That night [on reading *Phantastes*] my imagination was, in a certain sense, baptized; the rest of me, not unnaturally, took longer"
- •SJ 181 ❖ SJ 11:19

Machine, Christian morality claims to be a technique for putting the human, right (as does psychoanalysis)
- •MC 83 ❖ MC III 4:2

Machine, God Himself is the fuel for the human
- •MC 54 ❖ MC II 3:7

Machine, moral rules are like directions for running a
- •MC 69 (*see also* RP 60-61*)
- ❖ MC III 1:1 (*see also* RP 6:10, 11*)

Machine, we are the; God is the Inventor
- •MC 173 ❖ MC IV 9:7

Machines, our bodies are like; they wear out
- •LAL 110-111 (*see also* LAL 78)
- ❖ LAL 26 Nov 62 (*see also* LAL Sep 30 58)

Machines: "The more noise, heat, and smell a machine produces the more power is being wasted"
- •LAL 16 ❖ LAL May 30th 53

Maeterlinck, [Maurice], after Yeats I plunged into, and there came up against Spiritualism, Theosophy, and Pantheism
•SJ 175 ❖ SJ 11:12

Magazines, in a letter of advice to a child on writing, Lewis suggests avoiding the reading of
•L 291 ❖ L 14 Dec 59

Magazines, women's, described as having "a baneful influence on [one's] mind and imagination"
•L 279 ❖ L 2 Sep 57

Magdalen College, Oxford described
•L 104-105 ❖ L 21 Oct 25

Magdalen College, Oxford, Lewis relates his election to a Fellowship at
•L 100-103
❖ L undated letter of "April or May" 1925; 26 May 25; 14 Aug 25

Magdalene College, Cambridge, compared to Magdalen College, Oxford
•LAL 35 (*see also* LAL 32) ❖ LAL Nov 1st 54 (*see also* LAL Sep 19/54)

Magic and the Occult, Lewis's interest in, during his youth
•SJ 59-60, 174-178 ❖ SJ 4:6; 11:12-16

Magic, Yeats believed seriously in
•SJ 174 ❖ SJ 11:12

Magical element in Christianity, what is the value of, for me
•LM 104 ❖ LM 19:10

Magical element of Christianity can never be reduced to zero; if it is, what remains is only morality, or culture, or philosophy (re: Holy Communion)
•LM 104 ❖ LM 19:11

Magician, God as a kind of, to children: I imagine that disappointment of this kind of faith is of no religious importance
•SJ 20-21 ❖ SJ 1:22

Magnificat as a kind of Psalm
•CR 115, 120-121; RP 6
❖ CR 10:2, 13; RP 1:9

Magnificat as one of the things that link us to the Psalms
•CR 121 ❖ CR 10:15

Magnificat is terrifying; if there are two things in the Bible which should make

our blood run cold, it is one
•CR 120-121 ❖ CR 10:13

Magnificat, it is the humble and meek who have all the blessings in the
•LAL 29 ❖ LAL Mar 31st 54

Magnificat, the spark of desire for judgement seen first in the Psalms burns clear in the
•CR 122 ❖ CR 10:20

Mailing parcels as one of the things Lewis said he disliked most in the world
•LAL 46 ❖ LAL 9/10/55

Making and Begetting (chapter title)
•MC 135-140 ❖ MC IV ch. 1

Making vs. begetting (re: Jesus Christ as the "Son" of God)
•MC 135-140, 150-151 (*see also* Father and Son) ❖ MC IV ch. 1; 4:2, 3 (*see also* Father and Son)

Male aspects in women: "...there ought spiritually to be a man in every woman and a woman in every man"
•L 237 ❖ L 10 Jan 52

Malvern College, Lewis relates his election to the Board of Governors of
•L 134-135
❖ L undated letter postmarked 17 Jul 29

Mammon, quote regarding, from a pupil of Lewis's
•L 197 ❖ L 21 Dec 41

Mammon, Screwtape mentions
•SL 47 ❖ SL 10:3

Man—*see also* Humanity

"Man approaches God most nearly when he is in one sense least like God" (re: human Need-love)
•FL 14 ❖ FL 1:8

Man as a potential god: "If we let Him ...He will make the feeblest and filthiest of us into a god or goddess..."
•MC 174-175, 187 (*see also* Gods)
❖ MC IV 9:11; 11:9 (*see also* Gods)

Man, as a species, spoiled himself; therefore "good" to us must mean primarily remedial or corrective good
•PP 88 ❖ PP 5:14

Man as the "head" of woman given by St. Paul in a proportion sum ("God is to Christ as Christ is to man and man is to woman...")

•CR 4-5 ❖ CR 1:6

Man as the one lost sheep in the universe: In the parable, the lost sheep was not the only sheep in the flock, nor the most valuable
•GID 42-43, 100; M 122; WLN 86-87 (*see also* M 51-52*)
❖ GID I 3:9; I 10:42; M 14:24; WLN 6:11 (*see also* M 7:13, 14*)

Man, Christ as the archetypal, in whose suffering, resurrection, and victories all men (unless they refuse) can share
•RP 133-134 ❖ RP 12:12

Man, fall of—*see* Fall of Man; Fallen Man

Man has the completest resemblance to God which we know of
•MC 139 ❖ MC IV 1:15

Man, headship of, in Christian marriage is most fully embodied in him whose marriage is most like a crucifixion; his crown is made of thorns
•FL 148 ❖ FL 5:26

Man, history of, is largely a record of crime, war, disease, and terror; Reason has enabled men to inflict far greater pain than they otherwise could have done
•PP 14 ❖ PP 1:1

Man, how majestically indifferent most reality is to, (re: the vastness of the material universe)
•M 51 ❖ M 7:11

Man, insignificance of—*see* Insignificance of Man

Man is a composite being—a natural organism tenanted by a supernatural spirit
•M 126 ❖ M 14:30

Man is a finite creature who finds himself dwarfed by reality as a whole
•M 50-51 ❖ M 7:11

Man is an animal called or raised to be something more than an animal; there may be more than analogy between this and the taking up of man into God
•RP 115-116, 134 ❖ RP 11:11; 12:13

Man is on the borderline between the Natural and the Supernatural
•GID 276 ❖ GID III 1:18

Man is the highest of the things we meet in sensuous experience; therefore manlike images are the best we can use in describing God
•M 74-75 ❖ M 10:13

Man as the Prodigal Son of the universe
•M 122 ❖ M 14:24

Man meant to be the mediator through whom animals apprehend so much of the Divine splendour as their irrational nature allows
•PP 78 ❖ PP 5:6

Man, nature of, not totally depraved; if our depravity were total, we would not know ourselves to be depraved
•PP 66-67 (*see also* Depravity)
❖ PP 4:15 (*see also* Depravity)

Man not the centre of the universe; we were made not primarily that we may love God but that God may love us— and He will labour to make us lovable
•PP 47-48 ❖ PP 3:15

Man not the sole end of nature, nor the center of the universe—may be the one lost sheep whom the shepherd was sent to save
•GID 42-43, 100 (*see also* M 51-52, 122)
❖ GID I 3:9; 10:42 (*see also* M 7:12, 13; 14:24)

Man, one of the things that distinguishes, from the other animals is the desire for knowledge
•GID 108 ❖ GID I 12:1

Man or Rabbit? (chapter title)
•GID 108-113 ❖ GID I ch. 12

Man, possible redemptive function of, with regard to animals
•PP 136 (*see also* LAL 110)
❖ PP 9:8 (*see also* LAL 26 Nov 62)

Man, prehistoric, may have descended from the animals but was not necessarily inferior to modern man in character and other respects
•PP 72-74 ❖ PP 5:3

Man, prehistoric: We forget that they made all the most useful discoveries, except that of chloroform, that have ever been made (wheel, ship, fire, etc.)
•PP 74 ❖ PP 5:3

Man: Psalm 8 is an expression of wonder at man and man's place in Nature and

the universe—and therefore at God who appointed it
•RP 132-134 ❖ RP 12:11-13

Man, smallness of—*see* Insignificance of Man

Man, smallness of, when compared with the universe ("To puny man, the great nebula Andromeda owes in a sense its greatness")
•GID 39-42 ❖ GID I 3:4-8

Man, there ought spiritually to be a woman in every, and a man in every woman
•L 237 ❖ L 10 Jan 52

Man, unfallen—*see* Adam; Unfallen man

Man, when one considers the sky and all the stars it seems strange that God should be at all concerned with, —yet He has given us extraordinary honour (re: Psalm 8)
•RP 132 ❖ RP 12:11

Managerial Age, I live in the, where the greatest evil is not now done in "dens of crime" but rather in clean, carpeted offices by quiet men in white collars...
•SL x ❖ SL P:17

Managerial God, I will not believe in the, and his general laws; God's grand design has no unconsidered and undesired by-products or consequences
•LM 53-56 ❖ LM 10:4-11

Manichaean repudiation of nature (including human nature) differs from the Christian view of nature
•GID 148-149 ❖ GID I 17:5

Manichee, I am still smarting under the charge of being a
•LM 14, 18 ❖ LM 3:1, 10

Manicheeism, contempt for the world (*contemptus mundi*) is dangerous and may lead to
•L 183 ❖ L 16 Apr 40

Man-like images—*see* Anthropomorphic images; Imagery; Language, imaginative

Manners, discussion of domestic
•FL 66-70; GID 282-286
❖ FL 3:22-26; GID III ch. 3

Map, Theology is like a ; if you want to go anywhere it's absolutely necessary

•MC 135-136 ❖ MC IV 1:1-5

Mark 8, passage in, given as an example of a sequence which is logically, emotionally, and imaginatively perfect
•CR 155-156 ❖ CR 13:6

Marriage—*see also* Eros (romantic love); Love; *consider also* Family; Family relations; Home; Relations, interpersonal

Marriage: All the rubs and frustrations of a joint life—even at its worst—seem to me better than solitude
•LAL 109 (*see also* LAL 102, 117*, 120*)
❖ LAL 8 Nov 62 (*see also* LAL 17 Jan 62; 10 Jun 63*; 6 Jul 63*)

Marriage and home-making as a sea full of hidden rocks; we need a celestial chart
•GID 284 ❖ GID III 3:6

Marriage and sexual temptation, Screwtape speaks on
•SL 80-84 ❖ SL ch. 18

Marriage as "one flesh": Sexual union cannot be isolated from the total union, which is marriage
•MC 95-96; SL 82-83
❖ MC III 6:2, 3; SL 18:6

Marriage as "one ship" which must chug along on only a single engine after the death of one's spouse
•GO 39 ❖ GO 2:33

Marriage as "that fatal tomb of all lively and interesting men"
•L 55 ❖ L 13 Mar 21

Marriage, bereavement is a universal and integral part of our experience of; it is not the interruption of the dance, but the next figure
•GO 58-59 (*see also* GO 14-15, 63-64)
❖ GO 3:33 (*see also* GO 1:28; 3:40)

Marriage best between those who acknowledge the same law, where each are "related in the right way to Love Himself"
•FL 173-174 ❖ FL 6:19

Marriage, Christian (chapter title)
•MC 95-103 ❖ MC III ch. 6

Marriage, Christian, discussion of
•MC 95-103 ❖ MC III ch. 6

Marriage, Christian law has bestowed (in-

flicted?) upon the man a certain "headship" in the relationship of
•FL 148-149 (see also MC 102-103)
❖ FL 5:26-28 (see also MC III 6:15-17)

Marriage: Christianity insists on obedience and respect from wives to husbands
•MC 80 ❖ MC III 3:4

Marriage, Christianity more than any other religion has blessed
•GID 147; MC 91
❖ GID I 17:2; MC III 5:7

Marriage, entering into, which will certainly involve misery: "There is no wisdom or virtue in...deliberately courting persecution"
•FL 149 ❖ FL 5:27

Marriage, equality in, not the Divine plan but a necessity due to the Fall
•WG 114-115 (see also M 119-120*, 124*; MC 102-103) ❖ WG 7:12-15 (see also M 14:20*, 26*; MC III 6:17)

Marriage: Equality of the sexes as citizens or intellectual beings not absolutely repugnant to Pauline thought*
•CR 4 ❖ CR 1:6

Marriage, example of, in which one person is ill to show the difficulty of receiving love which is not based on our own attractiveness
•FL 182 ❖ FL 6:30

Marriage, fidelity/infidelity in
•GID 317-322; MC 95-101
❖ GID III ch. 9; MC III 6:1-13

Marriage for any reason causes two to become "one flesh"
•L 184; SL 82-83 ❖ L 18 Apr 40; SL 18:6

Marriage for the reason of "being in love" seems to me to be simply moonshine
•L 184 (see also L 209; MC 97-101; SL 82-84) ❖ L 18 Apr 40 (see also L 2 Aug 46; MC III 6:6-13; SL 18:6)

Marriage, happiness achieved in, not by good lovers but by good people
•GID 321 (see also FL 159-160; L 184) ❖ GID III 9:24 (see also FL 5:45; L 18 Apr 40)

Marriage: Headship (as Christ is to man and man is to woman) is divine virtue received by imitation*

•CR 4-5 ❖ CR 1:6

Marriage, headship in: The real danger is not that husbands may grasp it too eagerly, but that they will allow or compel their wives to usurp it
•FL 149 ❖ FL 5:28

Marriage, headship of the man in Christian, is most fully embodied in him whose marriage is most like a crucifixion; his crown is made of thorns
•FL 148-149 ❖ FL 5:26-28

Marriage heals the sword between the sexes; separately most men and women are poor, warped fragments of humanity—in marriage the two become fully human
•GO 57-58 ❖ GO 3:32

Marriage, image of, is not only profoundly natural but almost inevitable as a means of expressing the desired union between God and man
•RP 129 ❖ RP 12:9

Marriage: In this, as in every department of life, disappointment marks the transition between dreaming aspiration to laborious doing
•SL 13 (see also LM 26-27; MC 100)
❖ SL 2:3 (see also LM 5:11, 13; MC III 6:11, 12)

Marriage, infidelity in: A society which tolerates infidelity is a society adverse to women, who are more often the victims than the culprits
•GID 321 ❖ GID III 9:27

Marriage "is the mystical image of the union between God and Man," in which the sexual act is the body's share
•FL 139 ❖ FL 5:13

Marriage: It is we who must labor to bring it into closer accordance with what the glimpses [of Eros] have revealed
•FL 159 ❖ FL 5:45

Marriage, letters to a lady with the problem of infidelity in her
•L 218-221 (see also L 227-228, 236, 240) ❖ L 2 Sep 49 through 27 Sep 49 (see also L 5 Mar 51; 8 Jan 52; 13 May 52)

Marriage, Lewis describes the roles Joy played in their: "She was my daugh-

ter and my mother, my pupil and my teacher, my subject and my sovereign..."
•GO 55-56 ❖ GO 3:29

Marriage, Lewis mentions his, to Joy Davidman
•LAL 63, 64, 65 (*see also* Joy, Lewis's wife) ❖ LAL Nov 16/56; Dec 12th 56; 17/1/57 (*see also* Joy, Lewis's wife)

Marriage, Lewis's: I am tempted to say, "It was too perfect to last"—as if God said, "Good; you have mastered that exercise...and ready to go on to the next"
•GO 56-57 ❖ GO 3:31

Marriage, Lewis's: "[She was] my mistress; but at the same time all that any man friend (and I have good ones) has ever been to me. Perhaps more"
•GO 56 ❖ GO 3:29

Marriage: Living together perhaps better than making vows you do not intend to keep
•MC 97 ❖ MC III 6:5

Marriage: Man as the "head" of woman given by St. Paul in a proportion sum ("...God is to Christ as Christ is to man and man is to woman...")*
•CR 4 ❖ CR 1:6

Marriage ("monogamous family life") no guarantee of finding happiness and holiness; must be offered to God
•GID 284-285 ❖ GID III 3:6

Marriage, one of the functions of, is to express the nature of the union between Christ and the Church
•GID 238 ❖ GID II 11:10

Marriage: One of the miracles of love is that it gives—especially to the woman—a power of seeing through its own enchantments and yet not being disenchanted*
•GO 83-84 ❖ GO 4:30, 31

Marriage, promise of permanent fidelity in, cannot depend on "being in love"
•MC 96-101 (*see also* L 184; SL 81-84) ❖ MC III 6:3-13 (*see also* L 18 Apr 40; SL ch. 18)

Marriage proposals: A woman's decision to marry might be the *cause*, not the *result* of such a proposal (re: cause and effect in prayer)
•LM 48, 49; WLN 7 ❖ LM 9:7, 9; WLN 1:13

Marriage (quote from Johnson): "Marriage is not otherwise unhappy than as life is unhappy"
•L 128 ❖ L 2 Aug 28

Marriage, regarding the man who "just feels" that abstinence from, is obligatory
•WG 37-38 ❖ WG 3:8, 9

Marriage: Regarding wives who try to change their husbands by "cultivating" them*
•FL 107 ❖ FL 4:32

Marriage: Regarding wives who try to control their husbands (breaking up their Friendships)*
•FL 109-110 ❖ FL 4:35, 36

Marriage requires humility, charity and divine grace*
•FL 160 ❖ FL 5:45

Marriage ruefully defined by Screwtape as "a partnership for mutual help, for the preservation of chastity, and for the transmission of life"
•SL 83-84 ❖ SL 18:6

Marriage: Screwtape advises that if a human's sexuality fails to make him unchaste, it should be used for the promotion of a certain type of marriage
•SL 90-94 (*see also* SL 88) ❖ SL ch. 20 (*see also* SL 19:3)

Marriage service not a place for celebrating the flesh but for making a solemn agreement before God and society
•L 185 ❖ L 18 Apr 40

Marriage service, Screwtape advises causing humans to find the, "very offensive"
•SL 84 ❖ SL 18:6

Marriage, since my, I can never again believe that religion is...a substitute for sex
•GO 6 (*see also* SJ 170) ❖ GO 1:12 (*see also* SJ 11:6)

Marriage: Solomon calls his bride Sister;

could a woman be a complete wife unless she could also, at some moments, almost be called Brother?
•GO 56 ❖ GO 3:30

Marriage: Story of Mrs. Fidget illustrates how the attempt to be "the perfect wife and mother" may become perverted*
•FL 73-76, 82-83 (see also L 198-199*; MC 167*; SL 121*, 123*)
❖ FL 3:33-37, 45 (see also L undated letter just before 20 Jan 42*; MC IV 7:3*; SL 26:2*, 5*)

Marriage: Submission of wives to husbands discussed
•MC 102-103 ❖ MC III 6:15-17

Marriage, the couple whose, will be endangered by lapses of mere feeling are those who have idolised Eros (romantic love)
•FL 159 ❖ FL 5:45

Marriage, the great and permanent temptation of, is not to sensuality but to avarice
•FL 138 ❖ FL 5:10

Marriage: "The husband is the head of the wife just in so far as he is to her what Christ is to the Church"
•FL 148 ❖ FL 5:26

Marriage, the most precious gift that, gave me was this constant impact of something very close and intimate yet all the time unmistakably other—real
•GO 19-24 (see also GO 59, 64-65, 75-77) ❖ GO 2:3-7 (see also GO 3:33, 34, 41; 4:13-17)

Marriage: "There's a limit to the 'one flesh.' You can't really share someone else's weakness, or fear or pain"
•GO 13 ❖ GO 1:26

Marriage, thoughts regarding the headship of the man in
•L 184-185 ❖ L 18 Apr 40

Marriage, three reasons the Prayer Book gives for
•L 184 ❖ L 18 Apr 40

Marriage, to reach the state in which my years of, should appear in retrospect a charming episode in my interminable life would be the worst fate of all
•GO 70 ❖ GO 4:2

Marriage to unbelievers (quote from Johnson): "It was not difficult to discover the danger of committing myself forever..."
•L 160-161 ❖ L 10 Jun 38

Marriage, what St. Paul has to say on the hindrance of, has not to do with sex but with the multiple distractions of domesticity
•FL 137-138 ❖ FL 5:10

Marriage: Women are half-ashamed when they rule their husbands, and despise the husbands they rule
•MC 102-103 ❖ MC III 6:17

Marriages, Screwtape advises causing humans to confuse sexual infatuation with "love" so that they'll excuse themselves from guilt and consequences of improper
•SL 84 ❖ SL 18:6

Married life, the "deliciously plain prose and businesslike intimacy" of, renders absurd the idea that lovers might idolise each other
•FL 155 ❖ FL 5:37

Martlets mentioned
•L 48, 53, 63, 91 ❖ L 7 Feb 19; 21 Jan 21; 1 Jul 21; undated journal entry just after letter of 22 Nov 23

Martyr, Lazarus and not St. Stephen ought really to be celebrated as the first
•GO 48; LAL 119
❖ GO 3:12; LAL 25 Jun 63

Martyrs, opposition makes lovers feel like; Eros tends to turn "being in love" into a sort of religion
•FL 154 ❖ FL 5:36

Martyrs, the wounds of the, will turn into beauties in Heaven
•GID 216 ❖ GID II 7:1

Martyrs: Those who "live for others" but always in a discontented, grumbling way
•MC 167 (see also FL 73-76, 82; SL 121-124) ❖ MC IV 8:3 (see also FL 3:33-36, 45; SL 26:2-5)

Martyrdom: A man may be tempted to surrender benefits not that others may

be happy in having them but that he may be unselfish in forgoing them*
•SL 121 (see also WG 3)
❖ SL 26:2 (see also WG 1:1)

Martyrdom: All our offerings, whether of music or martyrdom, are like the intrinsically worthless present of a child, which the father values only for intent
•CR 99 ❖ CR 8:12

Martyrdom almost a specifically Christian action
•GID 148 ❖ GID I 17:3

Martyrdom, domestic: "What is commonly called 'sensitiveness' is the most powerful engine of domestic tyranny, sometimes a life-long tyranny"*
•RP 14 ❖ RP 2:9

Martyrdom: "...duty is always conditioned by evil"—in martyrdom, by evil in the persecutor
•LM 116 ❖ LM 21:14

Martyrdom: Goodness of Christ (and of Socrates) led to their death because of the nature of goodness and the nature of this world
•RP 105 ❖ RP 10:10

Martyrdom: I suppose the great saints really want to share the divine sufferings...but this is far beyond me*
•LAL 55-56 ❖ LAL 26/4/56

Martyrdom: "...it is...the persecuted or martyred Christian in whom the pattern of the Master is most unambiguously realized" (re: miserable marriages)
•FL 149 ❖ FL 5:27

Martyrdom, Lewis mentions the "gay, almost mocking courage" of Christian
•GID 206 ❖ GID II 4:9

Martyrdom ("sacrifice in its supreme realisation") not exacted of all; the causes of this distribution I do not know
•PP 104 ❖ PP 6:15

Martyrdom: Self-pity may cause the lives of some people (who are capable of real sacrifice) to be a misery to themselves and others*
•SJ 143-144 ❖ SJ 9:19

Martyrdom: Spare me the man "whose

very kindnesses are a continual reproach, a continual demand for pity, gratitude, and admiration"*
•SJ 144 ❖ SJ 9:19

Martyrdom: The ideal of courage (as found in literature) may provide temptation, but for some it may prove a schoolmaster to the ideal of martyrdom
•CR 22 ❖ CR 2:30

Martyrdom, the pleasures of domestic, (to feel ill-used and to harbor a continual resentment for it)*
•FL 82 (see also FL 73-77—story of Mrs. Fidget; SJ 143-144; SL 121-124)
❖ FL 3:45 (see also FL 3:33-36—story of Mrs. Fidget; SJ 9:19; SL 26:2-5)

Martyrdom the supreme enacting and perfection of Christianity; this great action has been done on our behalf by Christ on Calvary
•PP 102 ❖ PP 6:14

Martyrdom, there is no wisdom or virtue in seeking unnecessary, (re: deliberately making a marriage that involves misery)
•FL 149 ❖ FL 5:27

Martyrdoms and miracles tend to occur around the same areas of history
•M 167-168 ❖ M 17:5

Marxians have discovered that we exist as members of some economic class
•GID 271 ❖ GID III 1:2

Marxism, I very seldom meet consistent
•GID 241 ❖ GID II 12:2

Marxist finds himself in agreement with the Christians who say that poverty is blessed and yet ought to be removed
•PP 108-109 ❖ PP 6:18

Mary—consider also Immaculate Conception; Virgin Birth

Mary: Christians are unhappily divided about the kind of honour in which the Mother of the Lord should be held—but one truth is certain...
•CR 121 ❖ CR 10:14

Mary: Jesus' words to His Mother better understood if we realize that the iron element in His nature likely came

from her
•CR 121 (*see also* RP 6)
❖ CR 10:14 (*see also* RP 1:9)
Mary, Lewis explains why he doesn't say more about the Blessed Virgin
•MC 7-8 ❖ MC P:5
Mary Magdalene's action had an allegorical sense: The box which one must break over the Holy Feet is one's heart
•LAL 35-36 ❖ LAL Nov 1st 54
Mary, Mother of Jesus: "There is a fierceness...mixed with the sweetness in the *Magnificat* to which most painted Madonnas do little justice"
•RP 6 (*see also* CR 120-121)
❖ RP 1:9 (*see also* CR 10:13)
Mary, salutes to the Virgin, better avoided lest she begin to be treated as a divinity
•L 243 (*see also* GID 332-334; 337-338; Devotions to saints) ❖ L undated letter just after 20 Jun 52 (*see also* GID IV Letters 7, 10; Devotions to saints)
Mary: Use of reverential prefixes such as "Blessed" not necessary; more a matter of style
•GID 335 ❖ GID IV Letter 8
Mary, Virgin, became in the eyes of the Middle Ages almost "a fourth Person of the Trinity"
•GID 235 ❖ GID II 11:5
Masculine aspects in women: "...there ought spiritually to be a man in every woman and a woman in every man"
•L 237 ❖ L 10 Jan 52
Masculine uniform, only one wearing the, can represent the Lord to the Church; we men may make bad priests, but that is because we are insufficiently masculine
•GID 239 ❖ GID II 11:12
Masochism and Sadism mentioned with regard to Man's recognition of pain as evil
•PP 92-93, 94 ❖ PP 6:5, 6
Mass—*see also* Communion, Holy
Mass, God may be trusted to know when we need *bed* even more than
•LAL 24 (*see also* LAL 38) ❖ LAL Jan 1st 54 (*see also* LAL 20/2/55)

"Mass" vs. "Holy Communion": Screwtape relishes the quarrel over which of these labels to use
•SL 75 ❖ SL 16:5
Material prosperity as one of the values implicit in nineteenth-century fiction
•CR 16, 21-22 ❖ CR 2:13, 29
Material things—*see also* Matter
Material things, God uses, like bread and wine to put the new life into us
•MC 65 ❖ MC II 5:7
Materialism—*see also* Naturalism; Realism/ists; *consider also* Atheism; Commercialism; Possession(s); Worldliness
Materialism and disbelief in the supernatural
•GID 25-27 ❖ GID I 2:1, 2
Materialism: "...he who has God and everything else has no more than he who has God only"*
•WG 10 (*see also* PP 96*)
❖ WG 1:8 (*see also* PP 6:8*)
Materialism as a belief system which has an "obvious" attraction but meets insuperable obstacles later on
•M 131 ❖ M 14:36
Materialism: "At the moment it appears that the burden of proof rests, not on us, but on those who deny that nature has some cause beyond herself"
•GID 39 ❖ GID I 3:3
Materialism, books written in direct defence of, are not what make a man a materialist; it is the materialistic assumptions in all the other books
•GID 93 ❖ GID I 10:9
Materialism, danger of
•GID 110 ❖ GID I 12:4
Materialism, dogmatic, as a system of thought which moved out with its time (vs. Christianity, which has survived)
•GID 65 ❖ GID I 5:7
Materialism engraved in our thought from our earlier lives, like a rut
•L 227 (*see also* M 81-84*, 164-167*)
❖ L 5 Mar 51 (*see also* M 11:1-5*; 17:1-4*)
Materialism: If the solar system is an accident, thoughts are mere accidents too—including this one

•GID 52-53; M 12-24 (*see also* CR 60-61, 71, 72-81, 89; GID 21, 136-138; 272*; 274-276; M 34, 105; MC 45-46; SJ 208-209; WG 88-91

❖ GID I 4:20, 21 (Ques. 6); M ch. 3 (*see also* CR 5:9, 10, 27; ch. 6; 7:16; GID I 1:1; 16:13-17; III 1:4*, 9, 13-16; M 5:1; 13:16; MC II 1:6; SJ 13:17; WG 5:21-24)

Materialism, in approaching the Occult my fear gave me a fresh motive for wishing, to be true; that creed promises to exclude the bogies

•SJ 176, 177 ❖ SJ 11:14, 16

Materialism is a philosophy for boys
•CR 71 ❖ CR 5:26

Materialism, Lewis mentions that a "drop of disturbing doubt" fell into his, as he read Maeterlinck
•SJ 175 ❖ SJ 11:12

Materialism, my real fear is not of; if it were true, suicide could provide a way out
•GO 33 (*see also* SJ 171)
❖ GO 2:22 (*see also* SJ 11:8)

Materialism, my reason showed me the apparently insoluble difficulties of
•CR 41 ❖ CR 3:9

Materialism, no real victory possible over, as long as people deliberately refuse to understand the meaning of things
•WG 71-72 ❖ WG 4:29

Materialism not necessarily transmitted to the next generation; those who base all their hopes on the terrestrial future do not entrust much to it*
•GID 119 ❖ GID I 13:11

Materialism: "...one had to look out on a meaningless dance of atoms...to realize that all the apparent beauty was a subjective phosphorescence..."
•SJ 172-173 ❖ SJ 11:9

Materialism: Our fear of "having to depend solely on God" shows how very much we have been depending on things*
•LAL 49 ❖ LAL 16/12/55

Materialism refutes itself by discrediting the processes of reasoning
•M 15 (*see also* Reasoning)
❖ M 3:7 (*see also* Reasoning)

Materialism: Screwtape advises convincing humans, not that it is true, but that it is "the philosophy of the future"
•SL 7-8 ❖ SL 1:1

Materialism sees all experience as an illusion; thus it discredits miracles
•GID 25-26 (*see also* CR 59*)
❖ GID I 2:1 (*see also* CR 5:5*)

Materialism: "The great, permanent temptation of marriage is not to sensuality but (quite bluntly) to avarice"*
•FL 138 ❖ FL 5:10

Materialism: "...the word 'mine' in its fully possessive sense cannot be uttered by a human being about anything" (—Screwtape*)
•SL 98 ❖ SL 21:6

Materialism vs. Christianity: Ethical differences as they affect actions and social values
•GID 109-110 ❖ GID I 12:2-4

Materialism vs. Christianity: They can't both be true
•GID 110 ❖ GID I 12:4

Materialist Magician, Screwtape aims to produce: the man who worships what he vaguely calls "Forces" while denying the existence of "spirits"
•SL 33 ❖ SL 7:1

Materialist may understand the kind and degree of conviction expressed in a Christian's "I believe" if he thinks about his own "I don't believe it"
•WLN 15 ❖ WLN 2:4

Materialist, modern Western European, mentioned
•MC 43 ❖ MC II 1:2

Materialist sees all the facts but none of the meaning; his conclusions are the only ones possible on the evidence available to him
•WG 64; 71-72 (*see also* RP 116-117*)
❖ WG 4:15, 29 (*see also* RP 11:12*)

Materialist view, description of
•MC 31 ❖ MC I 4:2

Materialist vs. religious view of the universe: Neither can be proved by science*
•MC 32 ❖ MC I 4:2

Materialist's universe, to me, had the enor-

mous attraction that it offered you limited liabilities; death ended all
•SJ 171 (*see also* GO 33; *consider also* Limited liabilities)
❖ SJ 11:8 (*see also* GO 2:22; *consider also* Limited liabilities)

Materialistic account of thinking, the conclusion that logic is a real insight into reality and is not merely subjective rules out any
•CR 63 (*see also* Reason/ing)
❖ CR 5:14-16 (*see also* Reason/ing)

Materialistic ethic implied by Pacifism is that death and pain are the greatest evils; I do not think they are
•WG 43 (*see also* SL 131-132; Death)
❖ WG 3:18 (*see also* SL 28:1; Death)

Materialistic gain of being a Christian: a more complete enjoyment of literature
•L 173 ❖ L 18 Dec 39

Materialistic systems of the past all believed in eternity; but if anything emerges clearly from modern physics, it is that nature is not everlasting
•GID 39 ❖ GID I 3:3

Maternal instinct—*see* Motherhood

Mathematics analogy to show how the values of Universal Reason differ from ours (like a math calculation differs from a child's short sums)
•CR 68 (*see also* CR 70)
❖ CR 5:22 (*see also* CR 5:25)

Mathematics, I could never have gone far in any science because on the path of every science the lion of, lies in wait for you
•SJ 137 ❖ SJ 9:11

Mathematics: Lewis describes his failure to pass the Oxford Responsions exam which involved "elementary mathematics"
•SJ 186-187 ❖ SJ 12:6

Mathematics may be true about reality, but can hardly be reality itself, any more than contour lines are real mountains (re: attempting contact with ultimate Reality)
•CR 169-170 ❖ CR 14:24

Matter, Christianity is almost the only one of the great religions which believes

that, is good
•MC 91 (*see also* M 161-162)
❖ MC III 5:7 (*see also* M 16:30)

Matter enters our experience only by being perceived and understood
•LM 123 ❖ LM 22:19

Matter, fixed nature of, furnishes occasion for the abuse of free will
•PP 31-33 ❖ PP 2:12-14

Matter, God likes; He invented it
•MC 65 (*see also* M 162)
❖ MC II 5:7 (*see also* M 16:30)

Matter: God uses material things like bread and wine to put the new life into us
•MC 65 ❖ MC II 5:7

Matter, Hindus despise; but they don't know about the Sacraments nor the resurrection of the body
•LAL 60 ❖ LAL 3/8/56

Matter, like everything God made, has some likeness to God; matter is like Him in having energy
•MC 139 (*see also* L 175)
❖ MC IV 1:14 (*see also* L 17 Jan 40)

Matter listed as part of "the old field" of Nature which is not to be unmade, but remade
•M 149 (*see also* M 163)
❖ M 16:12 (*see also* M 16:32)

Matter must be subject to fixed laws if it is to serve as a neutral field for co-existent beings (re: Divine omnipotence)
•PP 31-32 ❖ PP 2:12

Matter (or "a neutral something" which can be manipulated) essential for communication between co-existent beings (re: Divine omnipotence)
•PP 31 ❖ PP 2:10

Matter (or "the creature"), contempt for, is dangerous while love of the creature is also dangerous ("Not bad you see, just very very small")*
•L 183 ❖ L 16 Apr 40

Matter, our resurrected body will not be made of the same; even in this life its actual ingredients change
•GID 33 (*see also* M 151—waterfall analogy) ❖ GID I 2:12 (*see also* M 16:15—waterfall analogy)

Matter, the things in Heaven originated with; let us therefore bless matter
•LM 123 ❖ LM 22:19

Matter would be nothing to us if it were not the source of sensations; we are more interested in a resurrection of the senses than a resurrection of the body
•LM 121 ❖ LM 22:13

Matthew 5:28: "He that but looketh on a plate of ham and eggs to lust after it, hath already committed breakfast with it in his heart" (re: having mumps)
•LAL 28 ❖ LAL Mar 10/54

McCarthy, [Joseph], mentioned: "A very intelligent American pupil said 'He is our potential Hitler'"
•LAL 36 ❖ LAL Nov 20 54

Meaning, if the universe has no, we should never have found out that it has no meaning—just as "dark" has no meaning to creatures without eyes
•MC 46 ❖ MC II 1:6

Meaning of existence, ultimate questions such as the, not part of most people's thinking
•GID 252-253 (see also SL 8-9*)
❖ GID II 14:10 (see also SL 1:2, 3*)

Meaning of life being questioned since the eschatological hopes of our ancestors have rather faded out
•CR 57 ❖ CR 5:1

Meaning of the Universe, Right and Wrong as a Clue to the (Book I of *Mere Christianity*)
•MC 17-39 ❖ MC Book I

Meanings: Almost anything can be read into any book if you are determined enough
•RP 99 ❖ RP 10:2

Meanings, hidden, in things written or said: "I am suggesting that different instances demand that we should regard them in different ways"
•RP 102 ❖ RP 10:7

Meanings, hidden or allegorical, in things written or said
•RP 99-108 ❖ RP ch. 10

Meanings, hidden or allegorical, in Scripture
•RP 109-117 ❖ RP 11:1-13

Meanings, if Old Testament is the Word of God we can set no limit to the multiplicity of, which may have been laid upon it
•RP 117 ❖ RP 11:13

Meanings: "Some of the allegories thus imposed on my own books have been so ingenious and interesting that I often wish I had thought of them myself"
•RP 99 ❖ RP 10:2

Meanings, the more "spiritual," in Scripture may not always have been intended by the author—but they also do not negate the first, plainer meaning
•RP 128-129 ❖ RP 12:9

Meanings, the "transposition" of higher, into lower objects or symbols
•WG 54-73 (see also RP 115-117)
❖ WG ch. 4 (see also RP 11:11-13)

Meanings, there are good reasons for not throwing away all second, as rubbish (e.g., connection between Pagan mythology and Christianity)
•RP 108 ❖ RP 10:13

Means and ends: Acts of worship may be distinguished from the vision of God; then they can become a substitute for, and a rival to, God Himself*
•RP 48-49 ❖ RP 5:7

Means and ends: Prayer is a means, but is also an end; the world was made partly that there might be prayer
•LM 56 ❖ LM 10:11

Means and ends: Screwtape discusses how Christianity, used merely as a means to social justice, can work to the devil's advantage
•SL 108-109 (see also MC 137)
❖ SL 23:4 (see also MC IV 1:6, 7)

Means and ends, Screwtape speaks on: "Once you have made the World an end, and faith a means, you have almost won your man..."
•SL 35 ❖ SL 7:4

Means and ends: Since God does not want us to make Change, any more than

eating, an end in itself He has balanced our love of change by desire for permanence*
•SL 116 ❖ SL 25:2

Means and ends: There is a tendency in all human activities for the means to hamper the very ends they were intended to serve
•WG 109 (*see also* GID 278-281)
❖ WG 7:5 (*see also* GID III ch. 2)

Means, to find which, are lawful God has given us natural light; to find which means are efficacious He has given us brains
•GID 199 ❖ GID II 3:6

Means, when the, are autonomous they are deadly (re: "sacred" activities as an end in themselves)
•LM 30-31 (*see also* SL 35)
❖ LM 6:4-6 (*see also* SL 7:4)

Means, when the, are autonomous they are deadly —quote from Charles Williams (Lewis uses it here regarding the Law and legalism)
•RP 58 ❖ RP 6:7

Mechanism, like all materialist systems, breaks down at the problem of knowledge: If thought is accidental, what reason have we to trust it?
•GID 21 (*consider also* Thought)
❖ GID I 1:1 (*consider also* Thought)

Meddling: "...no one can paddle his own canoe but everyone can paddle someone else's..."*
•L 235 ❖ L 26 Dec 51

Media—*consider* Art(s); Magazines; Newspaper(s); Radio; Television

Medicine—*consider also* Doctor(s)

Medicine, advance of: My guess is we shall remove old miseries and produce new ones; become more beneficent and more mischievous
•GID 312 ❖ GID III 8:6

Medicine and Christianity: No other religion leaves you free to fight death while knowing how all our real investments are beyond the grave
•GID 147-150 ❖ GID I ch. 17

Medicine: "I do wonder why the doctors inflict such torture to delay what can-

not in any case be very long delayed. Or why God does!"*
•LAL 118 ❖ LAL 25 Jun 63

Medicine: Let the doctor tell me I shall die unless I do so-and-so, but whether life is worth having on those terms is not a question for him or any other man
•GID 315 ❖ GID III 8:15

Medicine: My doctor says that most illnesses are either incurable or cure themselves in due course
•LAL 39 ❖ LAL 21/3/55

Medicine, role of, in healing (Doctors merely stimulate Nature's functions or remove what hinders them)
•GID 30; M 139-140
❖ GID I 2:8; M 15:14

Medieval allegory, Lewis mentions, as his own subject of study
•L 155-157 ❖ L 7 Jun 34

Meditation—*consider also* Mysticism

Meditation and solitude, we live in a world starved for
•WG 107 ❖ WG 7:2

Meditation in a Toolshed (chapter title)
•GID 212-215 ❖ GID II ch. 6

Meditation on the Third Commandment (chapter title)
•GID 196-199 ❖ GID II ch. 3

Meditation: "The stillness in which the mystics approach Him is intent and alert —at the opposite pole from sleep or reverie"*
•M 93 ❖ M 11:18

Meekness—*see* Humility

Megaphone, pain is God's, to rouse a deaf world
•PP 93 ❖ PP 6:5

Melchisedek mentioned as having been included in the Bible for people who were being led to the truth by the route Lewis was
•L 182 ❖ L 16 Apr 40

Melchizedek: The identification of this very mysterious person as a symbol or prophecy of Christ (as priest-king) is made in Hebrews 7
•RP 122-124 ❖ RP 12:4, 5

Mellontolatry (worship of the future) is a fuddled religion

•GID 21 ❖ GID I 1:1

Members, church: Screwtape advises tempting them to criticize their church, whereas the "Enemy" [God] wants pupils, not critics
•SL 72-73 ❖ SL 16:2

Members, we are, of one another whether we choose to recognise the fact or not (no one is truly "independent")
•LAL 112 (*see also* Interdependence) ❖ LAL 10 Dec 62 (*see also* Interdependence)

Membership—*see also* Body of Christ; Unity

Membership: As Christians we are not mere members of a group but organs in a body*
•MC 159 (*see also* GID 238; MC 65) ❖ MC IV 6:3 (*see also* GID II 11:10; MC II 5:8)

Membership (chapter title)
•WG 106-120 ❖ WG ch. 7

Membership, Christian definition of (Members are "things essentially different from, and complimentary to, one another")
•WG 110 ❖ WG 7:6

Membership, Christian, likened to the structure of a family (each person is almost a species in himself; they are not interchangeable)
•WG 110-112 ❖ WG 7:6-9

Membership, Christian, vs. secular collectivism
•WG 110-113 ❖ WG 7:5-13

Membership, importance of church (we become part of the Body of Christ)
•L 224; WG 106-120 (*see also* MC 65; *consider also* Church attendance) ❖ L 7 Dec 50; WG ch. 7 (*see also* MC II 5:8; *consider also* Church attendance)

Membership: The Church is not a society of people with common interests but the Body of Christ
•L 224 ❖ L 7 Dec 50

Membership: We are all "special" as members in the Body of Christ
•L 242-243 ❖ L 20 Jun 52

Memories and beauty are only good images of what we really desire

•WG 6-7 ❖ WG 1:5

Memories are nourishing if we are content to accept them for what they are; "Leave those bulbs alone and the new flowers will come up"
•LM 26-27 ❖ LM 5:10-13

Memories (e.g., of holidays) improve with time
•L 71-72 ❖ L 31 Aug 21

Memories: "It is not settled happiness but momentary joy that glorifies the past"
•SJ 8 ❖ SJ 1:5

Memories: Lewis mentions stowing them away "with the faintly melancholy feeling of things going past"
•L 117 ❖ L 26 Apr 27

Memory: After a loved one's death, a slow process begins in which they become more and more imaginary—the reality is no longer there to check us*
•GO 19-24 (*see also* GO 59, 64-65, 75-77) ❖ GO 2:3-7 (*see also* GO 3:33, 34, 41; 4:13-17)

Memory: After the death of a spouse, one may recall a passage of carnal love with no re-awakening of concupiscence; this is a kind of resurrection
•LM 123 ❖ LM 22:18

Memory: "...as we grow older we remember the distant past better than what is nearer"
•SJ 232 ❖ SJ 15:5

Memory as we now know it is a dim foretaste of a power which the soul will exercise hereafter
•LM 121-122 ❖ LM 22:15

Memory can transfigure; "how often some momentary glimpse of beauty in boyhood is 'a whisper Which memory will warehouse as a shout'"
•LM 122 ❖ LM 22:17

Memory, don't talk to me of the "illusions" of; why should what we see at the moment be more "real" than what we see from ten years' distance?
•LM 122 ❖ LM 22:17

Memory, general tendency of, is to minimize
•L 100 ❖ L undated letter of "April or May" 1925

Memory: I can now only tell you about the fields of my boyhood; perhaps the day is coming when I can take you for a walk through them
•LM 122 ❖ LM 22:15

Memory, Lewis describes a, of a certain instance of Joy: "...the remembering... was itself a new experience of just the same kind"
•SJ 73, 166 ❖ SJ 5:4; 11:3

Memory loss: "We have *always* been forgetting things: but now, when we do so, we attribute it to our age"
•LAL 93-94 ❖ LAL 24 Nov 60

Memory of a lost loved one: At the very moment when I mourned H. [Joy] least, I remembered her best...It was as if the lifting of the sorrow removed a barrier
•GO 52-53 (*see also* GO 64-65; LAL 92)
❖ GO 3:22-24 (*see also* GO 3:41; LAL 24 Sep 60)

Memory of a lost loved one: "The remembered voice—that can turn me at any moment to a whimpering child"
•GO 17 ❖ GO 1:31

"Memory of a memory" as the first instance of Lewis's experience of "Joy" (longing) —recalling his brother's toy garden
•SJ 16 (*see also* SJ 7)
❖ SJ 1:15 (*see also* SJ 1:4)

Memory: Our unconscious is largely responsible for our forgettings*
•RP 110 ❖ RP 11:3

Memory, then comes a sudden jab of red-hot, and all this "common sense" vanishes like an ant in the mouth of a furnace (re: bereavement)
•GO 2 ❖ GO 1:4

Men, according to Screwtape, are more often tempted to gluttony of Vanity, while women are more often tempted to gluttony of Delicacy ("All-I-Want...")
•SL 76-79 ❖ SL 17:1-3

Men, all, are haunted by desire for at least two imaginary women—a terrestrial and an infernal Venus (according to Screwtape)

•SL 93-94 ❖ SL 20:4

Men and women are quite diversely affected by illness; women worry that they can't do things, and men are grateful for the excuse *not* to do things
•LAL 105 ❖ LAL 31/7/62

Men and women, there will be a special exercise for, in Purgatory (a kitchen with things going wrong in it)
•LAL 105-106, 107
❖ LAL 31/7/62; 3 Sep 62

Men characterized as lazy; women as fidgets
•L 199 ❖ L 20 Jan 42

Men, domestic happiness more essential to women than to
•GID 321 ❖ GID III 9:27

Men, feminine as well as masculine traits in
•GO 58 ❖ GO 3:32

Men generally preferred by women to be the head of the household
•MC 102-103 ❖ MC III 6:17

Men hold women more by their personality, whereas women hold men by their beauty, which decreases as they get older
•GID 321-322 ❖ GID III 9:27

Men, lascivious, think about women's bodies while lascivious women think about their own
•L 141 ❖ L 10 Jun 30

Men loathe letter-writing and women love it
•LAL 104 ❖ LAL Ascension Day 1962

Men mean by "Unselfishness" not giving trouble to others; women mean chiefly taking trouble for others—therefore each sex regards the other as selfish
•SL 121 ❖ SL 26:2

Men, middle-aged, have "great powers of passive resistance" and may indulge wives who try to change them*
•FL 107 ❖ FL 4:32

Men more likely to hand their chores over to others; women more likely to do themselves what others wish they would leave alone (kitchen in Purgatory example)
•LAL 107 ❖ LAL 3 Sep 62

Men, my experience is that women rather

distrust and dislike beauty in
•LAL 112 ❖ LAL 2 Jan 63

Men: Screwtape relates the success which the devils have enjoyed at making certain secondary characteristics (such as the beard) disagreeable to women
•SL 91 ❖ SL 20:3

Men talk less and women talk more when fatigued; this can cause much secret resentment, even between lovers
•SL 142 ❖ SL 30:3

Men, the privilege or burden which Christianity lays upon, is one which most of us are inadequate to fill (re: women in the clergy)
•GID 238 ❖ GID II 11:12

Mephistopheles: This humorous and civilised image of the devil has helped to strengthen the illusion that evil is liberating
•SL ix (*see also* SL 33*)
❖ SL P:15 (*see also* SL 7:1*)

Mercy, all of God's, cannot remove the fact of Hell ("So much mercy, yet still there is Hell")
•PP 119-120 ❖ PP 8:3

Mercy, Christians must reject the covert attempt to drive, out of the world by calling it such names as "Sentimentality"
•PP 56 ❖ PP 4:2

Mercy detached from Justice grows unmerciful (re: "Humanitarian" concept of punishment)
•GID 294 ❖ GID III 4:13

Mercy, Divine: "The hardness of God is kinder than the softness of men, and His compulsion is our liberation"
•SJ 229 (*see also* GID 261*)
❖ SJ 14:23 (*see also* GID II 16:19-22*)

Mercy, essential act of, is to pardon; and pardon in its very essence involves the recognition of guilt and ill-desert in the recipient
•GID 294 ❖ GID III 4:13

Mercy, if one virtue must be cultivated at the expense of all the rest none has a higher claim than
•PP 56 ❖ PP 4:2

Mercy, in the Judgement we must pin all

our hopes on the, of God and the work of Christ
•RP 13 ❖ RP 2:8

Mercy which yields to danger will be merciful only on conditions; Pilate was merciful till it became risky
•SL 137-138 ❖ SL 29:6

"Mere" Christianity—*see* Christianity, "mere"

Mere Christianity, Lewis discusses some problems he had with writing the scripts for the BBC talks which later became
•L 197-198 ❖ L 21 Dec 41

Mere Christianity, mention of giving, as BBC talks
•L 193 ❖ L 15 May 41

Merton, Thomas: "I've been greatly impressed by the work of an American Trappist..." (re: the book *No Man Is An Island*)
•LAL 101 ❖ LAL 23 Dec 61

Merton, Thomas, mentioned (*No Man Is an Island*)
•L 302 ❖ L 20 Dec 61

Metaphorical language/Metaphor(s)— *see* Language, metaphorical; *consider also* Analogy(ies)

Methodists mentioned
•MC 63 ❖ MC II 5:3

Methods of evangelism—*see* Evangelism

Military: "I met there both the World and the great goddess Nonsense"
•SJ 194 ❖ SJ 12:16

Military, I try to keep in touch with life beyond the
•L 41 ❖ L 16 Feb 18

Military profession not said to be sinful by Christ (He praised the Centurion)
•L 248 ❖ L 8 Nov 52

Military service—*consider also* Pacifism; War

Military service as a possible obstacle to Christian faith*
•SL 28 ❖ SL 6:1

Military service in wartime includes the threat of every temporal evil—pain, death, isolation, injustice, etc.
•L 166 (*see also* WG 52)
❖ L 8 May 39 (*see also* WG 3:30)

Military service, Lewis describes his
- •SJ 186-198 (*see also* L 33-46)
- ❖ SJ 12:6-13:1 (*see also* L 28 Jan 17 to undated letter just before 27 Jan 19)

Miller, William, created a local "scare" (re: extreme views of the doctrine of the Second Coming)
- •WLN 94 ❖ WLN 7:3

Miller, William: "One's ears should be closed against any future William Miller in advance"
- •WLN 108 ❖ WLN 7:27

Miller, William, (whom I take to have been an honest fanatic), gave one of the most famous predictions for the Second Coming
- •WLN 107 ❖ WLN 7:25

Milton, John: His great success lies in practising the credal affirmation without losing the *quality* of myth
- •L 303 ❖ L 21 Mar 62

Milton, [John], I am very glad you have become a convert to
- •L 58 (*see also* L 64)
- ❖ L undated letter just before 23 Apr 21 (*see also* L 1 Jul 21)

Milton, [John], listed as one of the authors whom Lewis enjoyed as a scholar at Oxford, "in spite of" his being a Christian
- •SJ 213 (*see also* CR 39)
- ❖ SJ 14:3 (*see also* CR 3:7)

Milton, [John], Screwtape mentions the poet
- •SL 103 ❖ SL 22:6

Milton, [John]: The devils depicted in his literature, by their grandeur and high poetry, have done great harm
- •SL ix ❖ SL P:15

Milton, John, mentioned with regard to his view of "culture"
- •CR 17-18 ❖ CR 2:19

Milton's poem on the Nativity recaptures a little-emphasized aspect of Christmas: that Christ was expected to come as a hero or militant champion
- •RP 124-125 ❖ RP 12:5

Mind, human—*see* Human mind

"Minimal" religion—*see* Religion, "minimal"

Ministers—*see* Clergymen

Miracle, a definition of: "...an interference with Nature by supernatural power"
- •M 5 (*see also* M 43-44)
- ❖ M 2:1 (*see also* M 6:8)

Miracle at Cana sanctified an innocent, sensual pleasure and could be taken to sanctify at least a recreational use of "culture" as mere entertainment
- •CR 15 ❖ CR 2:7

Miracle, central, asserted by Christians is the Incarnation: They say that God became Man
- •M 108 (*see also* GID 80)
- ❖ M 14:1 (*see also* GID I 9:1)

Miracle, definition of: "It is inaccurate to define a miracle as something that breaks the laws of Nature. It doesn't"
- •M 59 (*see also* GID 72-74, 76-78*, 178)
- ❖ M 8:8 (*see also* GID I 7:1-28; 8:1-6*; 22:4)

Miracle, divine art of, not an art of suspending the pattern to which events conform but of feeding the new events into that pattern
- •M 59-60 ❖ M 8:8

Miracle: "Its cause is the activity of God: its results follow according to Natural law"
- •M 60 ❖ M 8:9

Miracle of calming the storm: Christ did what God has often done before, for in a sense all storms are stilled by God
- •M 141 ❖ M 15:16

Miracle of conception always an act of God: "The bed is barren where that great third party, Genius, is not present"
- •M 139 (*see also* GID 30-32)
- ❖ M 15:12 (*see also* GID I 2:9)

Miracle of conception: Human father is only a carrier of life that comes from the supreme Life
- •GID 31-32; M 137-139
- ❖ GID I 2:9; M 15:10-12

Miracle of Incarnation—*see also* Incarnation

Miracle of Incarnation discussed ("The Grand Miracle")

❖ M 7:4 (Compare with M 12:7)

Miracles are neither exceptions nor irrelevancies; they are the chapters in this great story on which the plot turns
•M 98-99 ❖ M 12:7

Miracles are not like fairy-tale magic, which would prove that (instead of the God of Nature) an alien power was invading Nature
•GID 32 (see also M 32*, 132)
❖ GID I 2:10 (see also M 4:14*; 15:1)

Miracles are part of the Christian faith, but the conception of a stable world demands that they be rare
•PP 33-34 ❖ PP 2:15

Miracles are "...the retelling in capital letters of the same message which Nature writes in her crabbed cursive hand"
•GID 206 (see also GID 29; M 134-135)
❖ GID II 4:9 (see also GID I 2:7; M 15:4)

Miracles as both reminders and prophecies
•GID 29 ❖ GID I 2:7

Miracles as small-scale models of large-scale activity—writing in small letters things God has written or will write in letters almost too large to be noticed
•GID 29-32; M 132-142
❖ GID I 2:7-9; M ch. 15

Miracles, case against, relies on two different grounds: thinking that the character of God or of Nature excludes them
•M 45 ❖ M 7:1

Miracles, Christian vs. mythological: Difference is that Christian miracles show invasion by a power which is not alien to Nature
•M 132 (see also M 32*; GID 32)
❖ M 15:1 (see also M 4:14*; GID I 2:10)

Miracles: Constant interference by God in the world to correct the results of our abuse of free will would result in the exclusion of free will
•PP 33-34, 71 (see also PP 84)
❖ PP 2:15; 5:1 (see also PP 5:11)

Miracles, current skepticism about, comes from two ideas: aesthetic dislike of miracles, and confusing "laws of nature" with "laws of thought"
•GID 28 ❖ GID I 2:5

Miracles do not break the laws of nature; Nature makes the event at home in her realm
•M 59 (see also GID 178)
❖ M 8:8 (see also GID I 22:4)

Miracles: Experience cannot prove or disprove the miraculous; what we learn from experience depends on the kind of philosophy we bring to it
•M 3 (see also GID 25-26)
❖ M 1:2 (see also GID I 2:1)

Miracles: History cannot prove the miraculous; if we believe miracles to be impossible, no amount of historical evidence will convince us
•M 3-4 (see also GID 27-28)
❖ M 1:3 (see also GID I 2:4)

Miracles, I do not in my book examine the historical evidence for Christian; I am not a trained historian
•M 4 ❖ M 1:5

Miracles: If they do occur, then not to have wrought them would be the real inconsistency
•M 97 ❖ M 12:5

Miracles, if they occur, must, like all events, be revelations of that total harmony of all that exists
•M 61 (see also M 96)
❖ M 8:10 (see also M 12:4)

Miracles in Buddhism vs. miracles in Christianity: Christ's miracles accord with Christian beliefs; Buddha's miracles do not accord with Buddhism
•M 133 ❖ M 15:2

Miracles, in studying the historical evidence for, begin with the New Testament and not with the books about it
•M 164 ❖ M 17:1

Miracles interrupt the usual course of Nature but, in doing so, they also assert the unity and self-consistency of total reality at some deeper level
•M 61, 95-99 ❖ M 8:10; ch. 12

Miracles, letter of response to a critic of Lewis's ideas about
•GID 327-328 ❖ GID IV Letter 3

Miracles, Lewis examines the view that, were accepted in earlier times because people didn't know the laws of Nature
•M 45-48 ❖ M 7:2-6

Miracles, Lewis examines the view that, were accepted in earlier times because people had a false conception of the universe and of Man's importance in it
•M 48-54 ❖ M 7:7-17

Miracles, Lewis explains why many desire a Christianity stripped of its
•M 154 ❖ M 16:20

Miracles, Lewis replies to a critique of his book, written by Dr. W. Norman Pittenger
•GID 177-183 ❖ GID I ch. 22

Miracles: Making stones into bread may have been impracticable, for the Son will do nothing but what He sees the Father do
•M 136 ❖ M 15:8

Miracles not contradictions of Nature, but Nature, left to her own resources, could never produce them
•M 61-62 ❖ M 8:10

Miracles not perceived until you believe that Nature works according to regular laws
•M 46-47 (*see also* GID 26-27, 45*, 72-73, 100; M 139) ❖ M 7:5 (*see also* GID I 2:2, 3; 3:15*; 7:1-10; 10:43; M 15:13)

Miracles of anticipation (e.g., walking on water, raising of Lazarus) give us hints of what the New Nature will be like
•M 150-153 ❖ M 16:13-19

Miracles of Christ, in all the, incarnate God does suddenly and locally something that God has done or will do in general
•M 134-135 (*see also* GID 29, 32, 206) ❖ M 15:4 (*see also* GID I 2:7, 10, 11; II 4:9)

Miracles of Christ, two ways of classifying, listed
•M 134 ❖ M 15:3

Miracles of Dominion over the Inorganic listed
•M 134, 141-142 ❖ M 15:3, 16

Miracles of Fertility listed

•M 136-139 ❖ M 15:7-12

Miracles of healing: "All who are ever cured are cured by Him, the healer within. But once He did it visibly, a Man meeting a man"
•GID 30; M 139-140
❖ GID I 2:8; M 15:14

Miracles of Jesus, essential likeness between, and the general order of Nature
•GID 36 ❖ GID I 2:15

Miracles of Jesus healing the sick: The Power that always was behind all healings puts on a face and hands
•M 139-140 (*see also* GID 30)
❖ M 15:13, 14 (*see also* GID I 2:8)

Miracles of Jesus healing the sick: Why it is idle to complain that He healed only those whom He happened to meet
•M 140 ❖ M 15:14

Miracles of Jesus, Lewis discusses the kinds of faith we see exercised in the
•CR 144-145 ❖ CR 12:10, 11

Miracles of Old Creation and Miracles of New Creation defined
•M 135, 141 ❖ M 15:4, 16

Miracles of raising the dead are miracles of reversal—early flowers which are prophetic of spring
•GID 32-33; M 142
❖ GID I 2:11; M 15:17

Miracles of the incarnate God do not need religious imagery; they are the sort of thing we can describe literally
•GID 71; M 79-80 ❖ GID I 6:10; M 10:19

Miracles of the New Creation (chapter title)
•M 143-163 ❖ M ch. 16

Miracles of the Old Creation (chapter title)
•M 132-142 ❖ M ch. 15

Miracles: Only faith vouches for the connection between prayer and event; "even a miracle, if one occurred, 'might have been going to happen anyway'"
•LM 48-49 ❖ LM 9:6-8

Miracles, "popular" religion excludes, because it excludes a God who does anything at all
•M 81 ❖ M 11:1, 2

•CR 5-7 ❖ CR 1:8-10

Mirror analogy: Enjoyment of God is no more separable from praise than the brightness a mirror receives is separable from the brightness it sheds
•RP 96 ❖ RP 9:6

Mirror analogy: Sunlight (like God) is reflected better in a clean mirror than a dusty one
•MC 144 ❖ MC IV 2:13, 14

Mirror, everyone in Heaven is filled with goodness as a, is filled with light
•MC 130-131 ❖ MC III 12:9

Mirror, we are to become a, reflecting God's own boundless power and delight and goodness
•MC 175 ❖ MC IV 9:11

Mirrors, our whole destiny lies in becoming—not "ourselves"—but clean, filled with the image of a face that is not ours
•CR 6-7 ❖ CR 1:10

Mirrors, we are, whose brightness is wholly derived from the sun that shines upon us
•FL 180 ❖ FL 6:27

Miserable Offenders: An Interpretation of Prayer Book Language" (chapter title)
•GID 120-125 ❖ GID I ch. 14

Miserific Vision mentioned by Screwtape
•SL 101 (*see also* CR x)
❖ SL 22:3 (*see also* CR P:9)

Misery: "I have learned that while those who speak about one's miseries usually hurt one, those who keep silence hurt more"
•L 289 ❖ L 3 Dec 59

Misery, part of every, is the fact that you don't merely suffer but have to keep on thinking about the fact that you suffer
•GO 9 (*see also* PP 14)
•GO 1:18 (*see also* PP 1:1)

Misery, the heartbreaking routine of monotonous: "If I knew any way of escape I would crawl through sewers to find it" (re: perfection through suffering)
•PP 105 ❖ PP 6:16

Misfortune(s)—*see also* Difficulties

Misfortune, men are not angered by mere, but by misfortune conceived as injury; the more claims on life we make, the more often we will feel injured
•SL 95-96 (*see also* LAL 96; SL 141)
❖ SL 21:2 (*see also* LAL 9 Jan 61; SL 30:2)

Misfortunes, if we could steadfastly remember God I suppose we should need no
•L 227 (*see also* L 161-162)
❖ L 5 Mar 51 (*see also* L 12 Sep 38)

Misogynist, Lewis mentions a musical, who shared his hospital room during the war
•SJ 190 ❖ SJ 12:11

Mission field, Great Britain is as much part of the, as China
•GID 94 ❖ GID I 10:12

Mission work: "If we are to convert our heathen neighbors, we must understand their culture. We must 'beat them at their own game'"*
•CR 17 (*see also* WG 28)
❖ CR 2:18 (*see also* WG 2:10)

Missionaries' holy desire to save souls not always distinct from an arrogant desire to "civilize" the "natives"
•WLN 90 ❖ WLN 6:21

Missionary to the priests of one's own church is an embarrassing role—though perhaps very urgently necessary (re: modern theology)
•CR 166 ❖ CR 13:36

Missions must involve meeting the people of each country on their own level
•L 254 ❖ L 16 Jan 54

Mockery, Eros involves good-natured; until they have a baby to laugh at, lovers are always laughing at each other
•FL 151 ❖ FL 5:30

Mocking—*see also* Opposition; Oppression

Mocking by unbelievers: "They know well enough what we are believing or trying to believe...and regard it as total illusion" (re: Psalmists' dark experience)
•CR 127-128 ❖ CR 10:38-40

Moderation—*see also* Balance; Temperance

Moderation: "A certain degree of a thing might be good and a further degree of the same thing bad"
•L 158 ❖ L 8 Mar 37

Moderation: All extremes except extreme devotion to God mentioned by Screwtape as serving his purposes (re: extreme Pacifism and extreme patriotism)*
•SL 33 (see also SL 25)
❖ SL 7:2 (see also SL 5:1)

"Moderation" in the area of religion mentioned by Screwtape: "A moderated religion is as good for us as no religion at all—and more amusing"
•SL 43 ❖ SL 9:3

Moderation regarding exclusive focus in love: "You can't get second things by putting them first..."*
•GID 280 ❖ GID III 2:6

Modern...—consider also Liberal...; Progress

Modern age, "dynamic" is one of the words invented by this, which sums up what it likes and I abominate
•L 179 (see also L 204*)
❖ L 22 Mar 40 (see also L undated letter of May 1944*)

Modern outlook sees human life merely as a development and complication of animal life*
•FL 90 ❖ FL 4:5

Modern outlook values the collective above the individual; this disparages Friendship*
•FL 90 ❖ FL 4:5

Modern theology—see Theology, liberal; Theology, modern

Modern Theology and Biblical Criticism (chapter title)
•CR 152-166 ❖ CR ch. 13

Modern Translations of the Bible (chapter title)
•GID 229-233 ❖ GID II ch. 10

Modern world as it is becoming is simply too much for people of the old squarerigged type like you and me (letter to his brother)
•L 177 (see also L 179)
❖ L 18 Feb 40 (see also L 22 Mar 40)

"Modernist" Christianity: I freely admit that it has played just the game of which the impatient sceptic accuses it (re: explaining away the use of imagery)
•M 70 ❖ M 10:4

Modernist "Christians" are the most arrogant and intolerant
•L 229 (see also GID 327)
❖ L 23 Apr 51 (see also GID IV Letter 2)

"Modernist dilutions of the faith" mentioned
•GID 335 (see also Christianity-and-water) ❖ GID IV Letter 7 (see also Christianity-and- water)

Modernist Movement and Alfred Loisy mentioned
•GID 67 (ftnt.) ❖ GID I 5:12 (ftnt.)

"Modernist," what unites the Evangelical and the Anglo-Catholic against the
•GID 336 ❖ GID IV Letter 9

Modernity: "...I am conscious of a partly pathological hostility to what is fashionable"*
•L 179 ❖ L 26 Mar 40

Modesty, false, never works with me; if a man tells me he can't do something I always believe him
•LAL 34 ❖ LAL Nov 1st 54

Modesty, perfect humility dispenses with
•WG 13 ❖ WG 1:10

Moffatt's translation of the Bible mentioned as being particularly good
•GID 231; L 181; RP 7
❖ GID II 10:5; L 26 Mar 40; RP 1:11

Mohammed never claimed to be God or the Son of God; there is no parallel to Jesus in other religions
•GID 157-158 ❖ GID I 19:3

Mohammedanism—see Islam

Monarchy of England mentioned as analogy to the retaining of Christianity because of its importance to us, in spite of its "inconvenience"
•GID 63-64 ❖ GID I 5:1-6

Monastic life, letter to a lady who was contemplating a
•L 249 ❖ L 6-7 Apr 53

Monastic life no guarantee of finding happiness and holiness; must be offered to God

•GID 284 ❖ GID III 3:6

Money—*see also* Riches; Wealth; *consider also* Ambition; Avarice

Money, concentrating on, listed as a means of avoiding God
•CR 168 ❖ CR 14:17, 18

Money, continual novelty costs, so that the desire for it spells avarice or unhappiness or both (—Screwtape)
•SL 117 ❖ SL 25:4

Money: Fear of financial insecurity must be recognised as a temptation; it hinders our charity
•MC 82 ❖ MC III 3:7

Money, giving, is only *one* way of showing charity; giving time and toil is better—and harder
•L 256 ❖ L 18 Feb 54

Money, greatest pleasure that, can give is to make it unnecessary to think about money
•L 227 ❖ L 5 Mar 51

Money, I'm a panic-y person about, myself; poverty frightens me more than anything else except large spiders and the tops of cliffs
•LAL 21 ❖ LAL Aug 10th 53

Money, lending, at interest is what our whole economic system is based on, yet Moses, Aristotle, and the Christians agreed in condemning it
•MC 81 ❖ MC III 3:6

Money, need for, of itself is apparently an innocent (though by no means a splendid) motive for any occupation (re: "cultural" occupations such as teaching)
•CR 20 ❖ CR 2:23

Money: "...of all claims to distinction money is, I suppose, the basest"
•LAL 111 ❖ LAL 10 Dec 62

Money, one of the dangers of having a lot of, is that you may be quite satisfied with the kinds of happiness it can give and so forget your need of God
•MC 180 ❖ MC IV 10:11

Money: The class system at Wyvern College was an answer to those who derive all the ills of society from economics

•SJ 110 ❖ SJ 7:13

Money, work which has no end in view except, vs. work which is worthwhile for its own sake
•WLN 74-81 ❖ WLN 5:9-22

Monism as a system of thought which moved out with its time (vs. Christianity, which has survived)
•GID 65 ❖ GID I 5:7

Monism as the theory that God Himself, being "above good and evil," impartially produces effects to which we give those two names
•PP 69 ❖ PP 5:1

Monism, definition of: the belief that everything is one (as "everything is God," or "everything is Nature")
•M 165 ❖ M 17:2

Monism, this sort of Stoical, was the philosophy of my New Look [at Oxford]; it gave me a great sense of peace
•SJ 205 ❖ SJ 13:11

Monist, if he starts from God, becomes a Pantheist; if he starts from Nature he becomes a Naturalist
•M 165 ❖ M 17:2

Monks, why are nuns nicer than, when women are not in general nicer than men?
•LAL 63 ❖ LAL Sep 14 [1956]

Monotheism, the Egyptian poem *Hymn to the Sun* was written by the Pharaoh Amenhetep IV; it shows an astonishing leap into
•RP 85-89 ❖ RP 8:16-19

Monotheism vs. Dualism
•GID 21-24 ❖ GID I ch. 1

Moods—*see* Feelings

Moon: "...he who reaches it first steals something from us all"
•CR 172-173 ❖ CR 14:38

Moon, I begin to be afraid that the villains will really contaminate the
•L 209-210 ❖ L 21 Oct 46

Moon, there (in the dormitory at "Belsen") I came to know the ghastly beauty of the full
•SJ 25 (*see also* SJ 34, 60, 171)
❖ SJ 2:4 (*see also* SJ 2:14; 4:6; 11:8)

Moore, Mrs., mentioned or referred to

•L 42, 56, 74, 79, 80, 86-87, 92, 112, 118, 150, 195, 204, 207, 212, 215; SJ 187*
❖ L 14 May 18; 14 Mar 21; 21 Apr 22; 2 Jul 22; 30 Sep 22; 22 Mar 23; 20 Jun 23; 22 Jun 23; 17-25 Mar 24; 15 Feb 27; 9 Jul 27; L 20 Mar 32; 9 Nov 41; 10 Aug 43; 28 May 45; 22 Dec 47; undated letter of Jan 1949; SJ 12:7*)

Moore, Mrs., probable reference to, in her later years
•L 212 ❖ L 22 Dec 47

Moral choice(s)—*see* Moral decisions

Moral code(s)—*see also* Ethics; Ethical code; Values

Moral code, all modern attempts at developing a new, consist of selecting and isolating one maxim of traditional morality as all-important*
•CR 75 ❖ CR 6:10

Moral code, idea that Christianity brought a new, into the world is a grave error; Jesus' commands are paralleled in classical, Egyptian, and Chinese texts
•CR 46-47, 51, 52-53, 44, 77 (*see also* Law of Nature; book *The Abolition of Man*) ❖ CR 4:5-7, 17, 20-22, 26; 6:16 (*see also* Law of Nature; book *The Abolition of Man*)

Moral code, Lewis refutes the argument that to tie ourselves to an immutable, is to cut off all progress and acquiesce in "stagnation"
•CR 76-77 ❖ CR 6:13-15

Moral codes, all the modern attempts at developing new, are contractions of something already given
•CR 53, 56 (*see also* Law of Nature)
❖ CR 4:22, 27 (*see also* Law of Nature)

Moral codes: "...may we not recognize in modern thought a very serious exaggeration of the ethical differences between different cultures?"
•CR 54-55 (*see also* CR 77-78; MC 19, 24) ❖ CR 4:24 (*see also* CR 6:16; MC I 1:6, 7; 2:7)

Moral collapse follows upon spiritual collapse
•GID 264-265 ❖ GID II 16:44

Moral decision(s)—*see also* Choices; Ethics; Moral judgement(s); Values

Moral decisions aided by having the imitation of Christ as our goal
•MC 162 ❖ MC IV 7:5

Moral decisions, arguable and inarguable processes of making
•WG 37-38 ❖ WG 3:7-9

Moral decisions (as in sexual morality) should not turn on "fine feelings" but on honesty, justice, charity, and obedience*
•FL 133 ❖ FL 5:2

Moral decisions do not admit of mathematical certainty
•WG 39, 53 ❖ WG 3:11, 31

Moral decisions: In this sphere we are bribed from the very beginning, since we have some wish either to do it or not to do it
•WG 36 ❖ WG 3:6

Moral decisions involve facts, intuition, reasoning, and regard for authority
•WG 33-39 ❖ WG 3:1-11

Moral decisions involve two things: 1) the act of choosing, and 2) the feelings and impulses which are the raw material of one's choice
•MC 84 ❖ MC III 4:4

Moral decisions: Many preferences which seem to the ignorant to be simply "matters of taste" are visible to a trained critic as choices between good and evil
•CR 29 ❖ CR 2:48

Moral decisions often influenced by peer pressure ("the lure of the caucus")
•WG 98 ❖ WG 6:7

Moral decline consists of small wrong choices*
•SL 156-157; WLN 54-55 (*see also* MC 86-87, 117; RP 136; SL 53-54; WG 101-103)
❖ SL 32:10; WLN 4:10 (*see also* MC III 4:8, 9; 9:8; RP 12:16; SL 12:1; WG 6:12)

Moral effort—*consider also* Righteousness by faith/grace; Will; Willpower; Works

Moral effort: A "deeper, less conscious Charity" can enable us to want to do the right thing*
•FL 185 ❖ FL 6:36

Moral effort, a serious, is the only thing that will bring you to the point where you throw up the sponge
•MC 129 ❖ MC III 12:6

Moral effort: After the Fall, man had no resource but to fight back the tidal wave of new thoughts and desires arising from mere nature by main strength
•PP 82 ❖ PP 5:10

Moral effort: "After the first few steps in the Christian life we realise that everything which really needs to be done in our souls can be done only by God"
•MC 165 ❖ MC IV 7:12

Moral effort: "All this trying leads up to the vital moment at which you turn to God and say, 'You must do this. I can't'"
•MC 128 ❖ MC III 12:5

Moral effort: As fully surrendered Christians, we will try to obey Him—but in a new, less worried way; not in order to be saved...
•MC 129 ❖ MC III 12:6

Moral effort cannot bring about the change we most need—a change in our motives and temperament; what we are matters even more than what we do
•MC 165 ❖ MC IV 7:12

Moral effort: Encouragement to those who have trouble being "good": You are one of the "poor" whom Christ blessed*
•MC 181-182 ❖ MC IV 10:12-14

Moral effort: "Even the best Christian that ever lived is not acting on his own steam..."
•MC 64 ❖ MC III 5:5, 6

Moral effort: "I know all about the despair of overcoming chronic temptations"*
•L 199 ❖ L 20 Jan 42

Moral effort: If we insist on retaining our natural self, either we will give up trying to be good or we will become very unhappy indeed
•MC 167 ❖ MC IV 8:3

Moral effort: In a sense, no temptation is ever overcome until we stop trying to overcome it
•MC 129 ❖ MC III 12:6

Moral effort, in one sense the road back to God is a road of, but in another sense it is not trying that is ever going to bring us home
•MC 128 ❖ MC III 12:5

Moral effort: In order to transcend the law we must first admit its claims upon us, try to meet those claims, and admit our failure
•PP 65 (see also LM 114-115)
❖ PP 4:13 (see also LM 21:11-13)

Moral effort to control one's appetites, inadequacy of, which Lewis thought was shown by his father's generation*
•L 126 ❖ L 1 Apr 28

Moral effort: It is God who does the work in us; we allow it to be done
•MC 165 ❖ MC IV 7:13

Moral effort: Lewis describes how he first came to realize that an attempt at complete virtue had to be made*
•SJ 225-226 ❖ SJ 14:18

Moral effort: "...'most' of the behaviour which is now duty would be spontaneous and delightful if we were, so to speak, good rose-trees"*
•LM 114-116 ❖ LM 21:11-14

Moral effort: My long-evaded encounter with God happened at a time when I was making a serious effort to obey my conscience
•CR 169 ❖ CR 14:20

Moral effort not effective in being "good"; if we could become moral by our own effort we should only perish in the ice and unbreathable air of the summit
•GID 112-113 ❖ GID I 12:10, 11

Moral effort: One of the first results of attempting obedience is to bring your picture of yourself down to something nearer life-size*
•CR 169 ❖ CR 14:21

Moral effort: Our efforts must be directed toward keeping the Christ-life which has been put into us*
•MC 64 ❖ MC II 5:5

Moral effort, our, is like a child's first at-

tempt to draw a wheel (when compared with God's goodness, which is as a perfect circle)*
•PP 39 ❖ PP 3:4

Moral effort: Our own unaided efforts can never carry us through twenty-four hours as "decent" people
•MC 173 ❖ MC IV 9:8

Moral effort: Screwtape advises getting humans to make their wandering mind in prayer a task for their will power rather than a subject of their prayer*
•SL 125-126 ❖ SL 27:1

Moral effort: "The main thing we learn from a serious attempt to practise the Christian virtues is that we fail"
•MC 125 ❖ MC III 11:7

Moral effort: The more one likes the right thing and the less one has to try to be good, the better
•L 277 (see also LM 114-116; PP 100) ❖ L 18 Jul 57 (see also LM 21:11-14; PP 100)

Moral effort to keep the Law of God springs, in the Psalmist, not from servile fear but from love of moral beauty
•RP 59-60 ❖ RP 6:9

Moral effort useful in that it cures our illusions about ourselves and teaches us to depend upon God
•MC 94, 124-125, 127-131 ❖ MC III 5:12; 11:7; 12:3-9

Moral effort: We can't change ourselves; we can only ask Our Lord to do so, keeping on meanwhile with one's sacraments, prayers, and ordinary rule of life*
•LAL 48* ❖ LAL 9/11/55

Moral effort, we have not got to try to climb up into spiritual life by our own
•MC 156-157 (see also L 284) ❖ MC IV 5:8 (see also L 20 Jan 59)

Moral effort: "Will" not to be mistaken for the conscious fume and fret of resolutions and clenched teeth; the will is our real centre, our heart*
•SL 31 (see also SL 15) ❖ SL 6:5 (see also SL 3:1)

Moral intuitions, basic, which cannot be

argued about: the ultimate preference of the will for love rather than hatred, and happiness rather than misery
•WG 37 ❖ WG 3:7

Moral issues, Screwtape observes that danger in the world (such as war) brings, to the point
•SL 137 ❖ SL 29:5, 6

Moral judgement(s)—see also Choices; Moral decisions

Moral judgement, how the modern error of "subjectivism" has affected our
•CR 72-81 (see also Subjectivism) ❖ CR ch. 6 (see also Subjectivism)

Moral judgement may be impaired due to the Fall, but our knowledge of the law was not depraved in the same degree as our power to fulfil it
•CR 79 (see also Depravity, doctrine of Total) ❖ CR 6:19 (see also Depravity, doctrine of Total)

Moral judgement referred to as "practical reason" by Lewis*
•CR 72-73, 75, 77, 79 ❖ CR 6:4, 12, 16, 19

Moral judgement that life is better than death is necessary before preservation of the human race can be deemed valuable
•M 37-38 (see also MC 29-30*; WG 43) ❖ M 5:9 (see also MC I 3:5*; WG 3:18)

Moral judgements and Naturalism: If Naturalism is true, "I ought" is the same sort of statement as "I'm going to be sick"
•M 36 (see also CR 67*; M 105*; MC 45-46*; PP 21*; Subjectivism) ❖ M 5:5 (see also CR 5:20*; M 13:16*; MC II 1:6*; PP 1:12*; Subjectivism)

Moral judgements: Regarding any proposed course of action, God wants men to ask simply, "Is it righteous? Is it prudent? Is it possible?"*
•SL 118 ❖ SL 25:6

Moral judgements vs. taste, in literary criticism: Danger of invoking "thus saith the Lord" at the end of every expression of our pet aversions*
•CR 30-31 (see also CR 34-35; RP 31) ❖ CR 2:51 (see also CR 2:55; RP 3:20)

Moral judgements, we must combine a firm belief in the objective validity of goodness with scepticism about all our particular, (as people make mistakes)
•CR 69 ❖ CR 5:23

Moral judgements, if we are to continue to make, then we must believe that conscience is not a product of Nature
•M 38 ❖ M 5:10

Moral law(s)—*see also* Ethics; Law(s); Law of Nature; Principles; Rules; Values; *consider also* Legalism

Moral law a better indication of God's character than the universe itself; universe is beautiful but also terrifying and dangerous
•MC 37 ❖ MC I 5:3

Moral law, Christianity is addressed only to those who admit their disobedience to the known; it introduces no new ethical code
•CR 46-47 (*see also* GID 243-244; MC 38-39)
❖ CR 4:7 (*see also* GID II 12:6; MC I 5:4)

Moral law, in order to transcend, we must first admit its claims upon us, try to meet those claims, and admit our failure
•PP 65 (*see also* LM 114-115; MC 94, 124-125, 127-131) ❖ PP 4:13 (*see also* LM 21:11-13; MC III 5:12; 11:7; 12:3-9)

Moral law known by all but broken by all
•MC 20-21 (*see also* MC 26-30)
❖ MC I 1:9-11 (*see also* MC I 3:1-6)

Moral law, Lewis attempts to describe the relationship between God and the, (Possibly God neither *obeys* nor *creates* the moral law; Good is uncreated)
•CR 79-80 ❖ CR 6:21

Moral law, objectivity of—*see also* Law of Nature; Subjectivism

Moral law, objectivity of, as a proof of the Supernatural discussed
•M 34-38; MC 17-39
❖ M ch. 5; MC Book I

Moral law, objectivity of, discussed
•CR 44-56, 72-81 (*see also* CR 67-71; M 105; MC 45-46; PP 21-22; book *The Abolition of Man*) ❖ CR ch. 4, 6 (*see also* CR 5:20-27; M 13:16; MC II 1:6; PP 1:12;

book *The Abolition of Man*)

Moral law: Question of whether these things are right because God commands them or He commands them because they are right ("Both views are intolerable")
•CR 79 (*see also* PP 100; RP 61)
❖ CR 6:20 (*see also* PP 6:12; RP 6:11)

Moral law seems to be agreed on by all people everywhere
•MC 17-26 (*see also* CR 44-45, 72-81; GID 318; M 34-38; RP 13; book *The Abolition of Man*)
❖ MC I 1:1 to 2:8 (*see also* CR 4:1-27, GID III 9:7, 8; 6:1-23; M 5:1-11; RP 2:8; book *The Abolition of Man*)

Moral laws are like directions for running a machine
•MC 69 (*see also* RP 60-61)
❖ MC III 1:1 (*see also* RP 6:10, 11)

Moral perfection—*see also* Perfection

Moral perfection, the Holiness of God is something more than, but it is not less; the road to the promised land runs past Sinai
•PP 65 (*see also* LM 114-115)
❖ PP 4:13 (*see also* LM 21:11-13)

Moral philosophy not taught by nature; if it were, it might be that of ruthless competition
•FL 35-36 ❖ FL 2:19-21

Moral principles, Lewis maintains that the primary, on which all others depend are rationally perceived and are intrinsically reasonable
•M 34-35 ❖ M 5:2

Moral progress, real, is made *from within* the existing moral tradition and in the spirit of that tradition
•CR 77 ❖ CR 6:15

Moral realm exists to be transcended; but until we are perfected we have the category of duty
•LM 115 (*see also* CR 45*; GID 144*; L 277; MC 130-131; PP 65, 100*)
❖ LM 21:11-14 (*see also* CR 4:2*; GID I 16:26*; L 18 Jul 57; MC III 12:9; PP 4:13; 6:11*)

Moral realm, situation which creates the whole, here on earth described (our

within different cultures
•CR 78 ❖ CR 6:17

Moral values: Within different cultures we find substantial agreement with considerable local differences of emphasis
•CR 77-78 (see also CR 54-55; MC 19, 24; PP 63; book The Abolition of Man)
❖ CR 6:16, 17 (see also CR 4:24; MC I 1:6, 7; 2:7; PP 4:10; book The Abolition of Man)

Moralists, all great, are sent not to inform men but to remind them—to restate the primeval moral platitudes which the devil attempts to conceal
•SL 107 ❖ SL 23:3

Moralities, activity of those who urge us to adopt new, is in the long run always directed against our freedom
•CR 56 (see also CR 81)
❖ CR 4:27 (see also CR 6:22)

Moralities of various civilizations have never been totally different
•CR 54-55; 77-78; MC 19, 24 (see also Law of Nature) ❖ CR 4:24; 6:16; MC I 1:6, 7; 2:7 (see also Law of Nature)

Moralities, the moment you say some, are better than others you are, in fact, comparing them both with some Real Morality, admitting there is a Real Right
•MC 24-25 ❖ MC I 2:7

Morality—consider also Goodness; Moral effort; Virtue; Works

Morality a mountain we cannot climb by our own efforts; even if we could, we should only perish in the ice and unbreathable air of the summit
•GID 112-113 ❖ GID I 12:10, 11

Morality, acknowledgement of some kind of, as the second stage or element of the development of religion
•PP 21-22 (consider also Moral law, objectivity of) ❖ PP 1:12 (consider also Moral law, objectivity of)

Morality, analogies of a musical band and of ships sailing in formation to illustrate the importance and operation of
•MC 70-73 ❖ MC III 1:3-8

Morality and human reason listed as "proofs of the Supernatural"
•M 43 (see also GID 275-276; MC 17-39; WG 88-89, 91)
❖ M 6:7 (see also GID III 1:13-16; MC Book I; WG 5:21, 24)

Morality and Psychoanalysis (chapter title)
•MC 83-87 ❖ MC III ch. 4

Morality, Christ did not preach any brand new
•MC 78 (see also CR 47, 51, 53, 77; MC 19; PP 63; RP 27; Law of Nature; book The Abolition of Man)
❖ MC III 3:1 (see also CR 4:7, 17, 22; 6:16; MC I 1:7; PP 4:10; RP 3:13; Law of Nature; book The Abolition of Man)

Morality, Christian, claims to be a technique for putting the human machine right, as does psychoanalysis
•MC 83 ❖ MC III 4:2

Morality, Christian, not a bargain in which God says, "If you keep a lot of rules, I'll reward you"
•MC 86-87 ❖ MC III 4:8

Morality, Christianity makes duty a self-transcending concept and endeavors to escape from the region of mere, in its ethics
•CR 45 (see also GID 112, 144; LM 114-115; MC 130-131; PP 65)
❖ CR 4:2 (see also GID I 12:10; 16:26; LM 21:11-14; MC III 12:9; PP 4:13)

Morality, Christianity seems at first to be all about, —duties and rules, guilt and virtue—yet it leads you out of all that, into something beyond
•MC 130-131 ❖ MC III 12:9

Morality concerned with three things: human relationships, individual character, and the purpose of human life as a whole
•MC 71, 73 ❖ MC III 1:5, 10

Morality connected with the Numinous (Law with Lawgiver) in the third stage or element of the development of religion
•PP 22-23 ❖ PP 1:13

Morality, duty, and the Law essential until a man really loves God and his fellow man
•LM 114-116 (see also L 277; PP 100*)

❖ LM 21:11-14 (see also L 18 Jul 57; PP 6:11*)

Morality, either the maxims of traditional, must be accepted as axioms of practical reason which cannot be argued, or else there are no values at all
•CR 75 ❖ CR 6:12

Morality: Faced with the great issues of Christianity, can you really remain wholly absorbed in you own blessed "moral development"?
•GID 112 ❖ GID I 12:9

Morality: "Good people know about both good and evil: bad people do not know about either"; a bad man understands his own badness less and less
•MC 87 (see also GID 56-57; LAL 95; PP 55, top; 67; Self-knowledge)
❖ MC III 4:10 (see also GID I 4:38; LAL 9 Jan 61; PP 4:prelim. quote; 4:15; Self-knowledge)

Morality: "Human beings judge one another by their external actions. God judges them by their moral choices"
•MC 85, 86 ❖ MC III 4:6, 7

Morality: "If wisdom turns out to be something objective and external, it is at least probable that goodness will turn out to be the same"
•CR 69 ❖ CR 5:23

Morality, legislation of: "You cannot make men good by law: and without good men you cannot have a good society"
•MC 72 ❖ MC III 1:7

Morality, Lewis maintains that all men accept the principles of primary, and agree on the reasonableness of them
•M 34-38 ❖ M ch. 5

Morality, Lewis refutes the argument that traditional, is different in different times and places ("The answer is that this is a lie...")
•CR 77-78 (see also CR 52, 54-55; MC 19, 24; PP 63; book The Abolition of Man) ❖ CR 6:16 (see also CR 4:21, 24; MC I 1:6, 7; 2:7; PP 4:10; book The Abolition of Man)

"Morality," meaning of the word, to modern minds ("chastity")
•GID 98 ❖ GID I 10:31

Morality, mere, is not the end of life— the purpose for which we were created
•GID 112-113 ❖ GID I 12:10, 11

Morality, objective, as a proof of the Supernatural discussed
•M 34-38; MC 17-39
❖ M ch. 5; MC I 1:1 to 5:4

Morality of Nietzsche is a mere innovation; can be accepted only if we are ready to scrap traditional morals as a mere error...
•CR 77 ❖ CR 6:15

Morality of the world increasingly gives Christians reason to value God's Law over current ways of thinking
•RP 64-65 (see also SL 110-113)
❖ RP 6:14 (see also SL 24:1-5)

Morality often seen as a word that means something that stops you having a good time
•MC 69 ❖ MC III 1:1

Morality: "People need to be reminded more often than they need to be instructed" (quote from Dr. Johnson)
•MC 78 (see also L 128; MC 124*)
❖ MC III 3:1 (see also L 2 Aug 28; MC III 11:6*)

Morality, piano analogy to illustrate: Moral law is the tune; instincts are the keys
•MC 22-23 ❖ MC I 2:2-4

Morality, primary principles of, unchanging in the face of increasing knowledge
•GID 44-45 ❖ GID I 3:13, 14

Morality, reason as the organ whereby objective, is apprehended*
•CR 78 ❖ CR 6:16

Morality, Sexual (chapter title)
•MC 88-95 ❖ MC III ch. 5

Morality, sexual, discussion of
•MC 88-95 ❖ MC III ch. 5

Morality, Social (chapter title)
•MC 78-83 ❖ MC III ch. 3

Morality, social, discussion of
•MC 78-83 ❖ MC III ch. 3

Morality, standard of, seems to be agreed on by all people everywhere
•MC 17-26 (see also CR 44-56, 72-81; M 34-38; MC 19; RP 13; Law of Na-

ture; book *The Abolition of Man*)

❖ MC I 1:1 to 2:8 (*see also* CR 44-56, 72-81; M 34-38; MC 9; RP 13; Law of Nature; book *The Abolition of Man*)

Morality, "subjectivism" regards, as a subjective sentiment to be altered at will
•CR 73 ❖ CR 6:5

Morality: The attempt to explain evil (having once accepted reality as moral) lies in the realm of theology
•CR 69-71, esp. 71
❖ CR 5:24-26; esp. 5:26

Morality: The man who says, "It can't be wrong because it doesn't hurt anyone" is only thinking of one aspect of morality
•MC 71-73 ❖ MC III 1:6-10

Morality, The Three Parts of (chapter title)
•MC 69-73 ❖ MC III ch. 1

Morality, there can be no moral motive for entering a new [system of], unless that motive is borrowed from traditional morality
•CR 52-53 ❖ CR 4:21

Morality, there is no, in Heaven; the angels never knew the meaning of the word "ought"
•LM 115 ❖ LM 21:13

Morality, traditional, does not necessarily provide an answer to every particular moral problem with which we may be confronted (chess game analogy)
•CR 56 ❖ CR 4:27

Morality, traditional, is neither Christian nor Pagan, neither Eastern nor Western, neither ancient nor modern, but general
•CR 51-53 (*see also* CR 47, 53, 77; MC 19, 78; PP 63; RP 27; Law of Nature)
❖ CR 4:17-21 (*see also* CR 4:7; 6:16; MC I 1:6, 7; III 3:1; PP 4:10; RP 3:13; Law of Nature)

Morality unconnected with a Law-giver yields "the cold, sad self-righteousness of sheer moralism"
•PP 23 ❖ PP 1:13

Morality: "Unless we allow ultimate reality to be moral, we cannot morally condemn it"

•CR 69-70 ❖ CR 5:24

Morality, use of the word "stagnant" rather than "permanent" to describe traditional, is to infer an unfair metaphor
•CR 76 (*see also* SL 119)
❖ CR 6:14 (*see also* SL 25:6)

Morality: What we are matters even more than what we do (and what we do matters chiefly as evidence of what we are)*
•MC 165 ❖ MC IV 7:12

Morally neutral ground: "There is no neutral ground in the universe: every square inch every split second, is claimed by God and counterclaimed by Satan"*
•CR 33 ❖ CR 2:54

Morally neutral things: "Sensitivity," like "experience," is a potentiality and therefore neutral; neither can be an end to Christians*
•CR 24 ❖ CR 2:38

Morning as "the cream of the day"
•LAL 48 ❖ LAL 26/10/55

Morning: "I get up early and try to dispose of my mail in the day's cool and silent hours..."
•LAL 87 ❖ LAL 21 Aug 59

Morning: "I love the empty, silent, dewy, cobwebby hours"
•LAL 78 ❖ LAL Sep 30 58

Morning, [someday] the bad dream will be over and it will be
•MC 170 (*see also* LAL 47, 57, 69; SL 147) ❖ MC IV 8:12 (*see also* LAL 26/10/55; 21/5/56; Oct 20 57; SL 31:3)

Morning, the dreadful thing is the waking each, —the moment at which it all flows back on one
•LAL 88 ❖ LAL 18 Oct 59

Morning, what our first job each, consists of
•MC 169 ❖ MC IV 8:8

Morris, William, my great author at this period was; I read all the Morris I could get
•SJ 163-164 (*see also* L 147, 205; SJ 102, 145, 173, 198)
❖ SJ 10:17 (*see also* L 17 Jan 32; 29 Oct 44; SJ 7:3; 9:21; 11:10; 13:1)

Mortal, you have never met a mere; we are all helping each other to one or the other of two eternal destinations
•WG 18-19 ❖ WG 1:15

Mortality, it is good to be always aware of our
•WG 31-32 ❖ WG 2:14

Mortification—*see also* Asceticism; Renunciation; Self-denial

Mortification, an imposed, can have all the merit of a voluntary one if it is taken in the right spirit
•LAL 20, 60, 105
❖ LAL Aug 10th 53; 3/8/56; 3/7/62

Mortification: It has been truly said that "only God can mortify"; ascetic practices and tribulation sent by God accomplish very different things
•PP 112 ❖ PP 7:3

Mortification: Where other systems (like Buddhism) expose our total nature to death, Christianity demands only that we set right a *misdirection* of our nature*
•PP 104 ❖ PP 6:15

Moses may have been influenced by Akhenaten's system of Monotheism as expressed in the Egyptian poem *Hymn to the Sun*
•RP 85-89 ❖ RP 8:16-19

Moslem, Christian, and Jewish view of the universe is that there is something beyond Nature which refutes the scientists' picture of futility
•CR 59 ❖ CR 5:5

Mother(s)—*see also* Parents; *consider also* Loved ones

Mother, a man may have to "hate" his, for the Lord's sake; this hard saying of our Lord is wholesome only to those who find it hard
•GID 191 (*see also* FL 165-166, 171-173; RP 131-132) ❖ GID II 1:4 (*see also* FL 6:4, 17, 18; RP 12:10)

Mother, example of a son rebuking his, to show how reluctantly "national repentance" should be preached by the Church
•GID 191 ❖ GID II 1:4

Mother, Lewis mentions going to his,

when he had a toothache
•MC 171; SJ 18 ❖ MC IV 9:2; SJ 1:19

Mother, Lewis mentions the death of his: "It was sea and islands now; the great continent had sunk like Atlantis"
•SJ 18-21 ❖ SJ 1:19-23

Mother, Lewis's
•SJ 3-5, 9, 11, 18-21
❖ SJ 1:1, 2, 7, 10, 19-23

Mother, Lewis's: Her death indirectly referred to as a source of Lewis's pessimism
•SJ 63 ❖ SJ 4:10

Mother, Lewis's: "Of my mother's religion I can say almost nothing from my own memory"
•SJ 8 ❖ SJ 1:5

Mother, narrow devotion of, who "lives for her son" mentioned as an example of a kind of love that can become a god
•FL 18 ❖ FL 1:15

Mother of Jesus—*see* Mary

Mothers: Her Affection is a Gift-love but it is also a Need-love because it needs to be needed
•FL 54 (*see also* FL 76)
❖ FL 3:3 (*see also* FL 3:37)

Mothers mentioned whose daughters spend all their years tending to "a maternal vampire who can never be caressed and obeyed enough"
•FL 66 ❖ FL 3:20

Mothers who "live for their family" may not be doing their family a favor (re: Gift-love based on a need to be needed; story of Mrs. Fidget)*
•FL 73-77, 82-83 (*see also* L 198-199*; MC 167*; SL 121*, 123*)
❖ FL 3:33-37, 45 (*see also* L undated letter just before 20 Jan 42*; MC IV 7:3*; SL 26:2, 5*)

Motherhood: In the loss of a child, a mother may find comfort in the idea of Heaven, but her specifically maternal happiness must be written off
•GO 29-30 ❖ GO 2:16

Motherhood: Maternal instinct liable to create a perversion of Gift-love (the need to be needed)

•FL 73-77 ❖ FL 3:33-37

Motherhood: Screwtape mentions the maternal jealousy which may be felt when a son develops a new interest (such as religion)
•SL 18 (see also FL 61, 70-73)
❖ SL 3:6 (see also FL 3:13, 27-32)

Motives for coming to God: "If God were a Kantian, who would not have us till we came to Him from the purest and best motives, who could be saved?"
•PP 98 ❖ PP 6:8

Motives for our good actions may not be so good; and we cannot change our motives by moral effort—must rely on God
•MC 165 (see also Moral effort)
❖ MC IV 7:12, 13 (see also Moral effort)

Motives of people usually mixed; people are seldom either totally sincere or totally hypocritical
•LAL 97 (see also LAL 95)
❖ LAL 28 Mar 61 (see also LAL 9 Jan 61)

Mountains of Mourne: "Here is the thing itself, utterly irresistible, the way to the world's end, the land of longing, the breaking and blessing of hearts"
•SJ 155-156 ❖ SJ 10:7, 8

Mountbracken and Campbell (chapter title)
•SJ 42-55 ❖ SJ ch. 3

Mourne Mountains: "Here is the thing itself, utterly irresistible, the way to the world's end, the land of longing, the breaking and blessing of hearts"
•SJ 155-156 ❖ SJ 10:7, 8

Mouse's search for the cat, Lewis says, was a better description for what he experienced near conversion than "man's search for God"
•SJ 227 (see also CR 169)
❖ SJ 14:21 (see also CR 14:19)

Movies/Movie stars—see Films/Film stars

Moving: "House-hunting is gruelling and heart-breaking work at the best of times"
•LAL 86, 87
❖ LAL 21 Aug 59; 21 Sep [1959]

Moving, Lewis's dislike for: "By nature I demand from the arrangements of this world just that permanence which God has...refused to give them"
•L 306 ❖ L 21 Nov 62

Moving: "Yes: moves are desolating things...and one's belongings have a sort of squalid pathos about them once they are packed"
•LAL 70 (see also LAL 86-87) ❖ LAL Nov 30th 57 (see also LAL 21 Aug 59)

Murder an offence not primarily against individuals but against society
•GID 339 ❖ GID IV Letter 12

Murder: In the commandment "Thou shalt not kill" the word "kill" means "murder" (re: pacifism and capital punishment)
•L 247; MC 106-107
❖ L 8 Nov 52; MC III 7:7

Murder is no better than cards if cards can do the trick (—Screwtape, on how to ruin a human soul)
•SL 56 ❖ SL 12:5

Muses mentioned: "The Muses will submit to no marriage of convenience" (re: genuine enjoyment of "culture" vs. an enjoyment that looks to remoter ends)
•WLN 35 ❖ WLN 3:7

Muses, Smewgy [Lewis's teacher] knew that courtesy was of the
•SJ 112 ❖ SJ 7:15

Music—consider also Culture

Music and silence listed by Screwtape as two of the things he detests; "We will make the whole universe a noise in the end"
•SL 102-103 (see also CR 168*)
❖ SL 22:5 (see also CR 14:17, 18*)

Music as a form of culture in which "culture" is irrelevant when the enjoyment is genuine
•WLN 33-34 ❖ WLN 3:5

Music as a medium of spiritual longing
•WG 6-7 ❖ WG 1:5

Music, choosing of church: Democracy is all very well as a political device, but it must not intrude into the spiritual, or even the aesthetic, world
•CR 98 ❖ CR 8:11

Music, choosing of church: Not the business of the Church to encourage the natural man's instinctive hatred of excellence
•CR 97-98 ❖ CR 8:11

Music, Christianity for me was associated with ugly
•SJ 172 ❖ SJ 11:8

Music, church—*see also* Hymns; *consider also* Praise; Worship

Music, church: A congregation whose intent is to glorify God will not complain if a good deal of the music they hear in church is above their heads
•CR 97 ❖ CR 8:11

Music, church: All our offerings are like the intrinsically worthless present of a child, which a father values indeed, but only for the intention
•CR 99 ❖ CR 8:12

Music, church: Case for abolishing all church music seems to me far stronger than the case for abolishing the choir and retaining the roar of the congregation
•CR 96 ❖ CR 8:7

Music, church: Excellence in a performance does not prove a good motive
•CR 98 ❖ CR 8:12

Music, church, "glorifies God by being excellent in its own kind; almost as the birds and flowers and the heavens themselves glorify Him"
•CR 95 (*see also* CR 98)
❖ CR 8:5 (*see also* CR 8:12)

Music, church: I have sometimes fancied God might ask, "If I wanted music...do you really think *you* are the source I would rely on?"
•RP 50 ❖ RP 5:7

Music, church: "In the composition and highly-trained execution of sacred music we offer our natural gifts at their highest to God..."
•CR 95 ❖ CR 8:5

Music, church: My conclusion is that both musical parties, the High Brows and the Low, assume far too easily the spiritual value of the music they want
•CR 96 ❖ CR

Music, church: Neither the best choir singing, nor the heartiest bellowing from the pews, must be taken to signify that any religious activity is going on
•CR 96 ❖ CR 8:8

Music, church: "...nothing should be done or sung or said in church which does not aim...either at glorifying God or edifying the people or both"
•CR 94 ❖ CR 8:2

Music, church: Regarding the organist of "trained and delicate taste" who decides to give the people what they want, feeling that he can thus bring them to God
•CR 96 ❖ CR 8:9

Music, church: Regarding the "stupid and unmusical layman" who sits patiently and humbly through a learned piece of music, feeling the defect to be in himself
•CR 96-97 ❖ CR 8:9

Music, church: Regarding unmusical laymen who look with the resentful hostility of an inferiority complex on all who would try to improve their taste
•CR 97 ❖ CR 8:9

Music, church: The problem is never a merely musical one; opportunities for charity and humility are provided by discrepancies of taste and capacity
•CR 96-97 ❖ CR 8:9, 10

Music, church: "We must beware of the naive idea that our music can 'please' God as it would please a cultivated human hearer"
•CR 98-99 ❖ CR 8:12

Music, church: "What I, like many other laymen, chiefly desire in church are fewer, better, and shorter hymns; especially fewer"
•CR 96 ❖ CR 8:6

Music, emotional vs. intellectual appreciation of: Both are ambivalent from the religious point of view
•L 268
❖ L undated letter just before 2 Apr 56

Music: "I have found my musical soul again...this time in the Preludes of Chopin"

•L 28 ❖ L undated letter just after letter of Oct 1915

Music: "If a musical phrase could be translated into words at all it would become an adjective"
•LM 86 ❖ LM 16:11

Music may be a preparation or medium for meeting God, *or* it may be a distraction or impediment
•L 268
❖ L undated letter just before 2 Apr 56

Music of Wagner as an avenue through which Lewis experienced "Joy"
•SJ 73-75 (*see also* SJ 102, 164, 165-166)
❖ SJ 5:5, 6 (*see also* SJ 7:3; 10:17; 11:1-3)

Music, On Church (chapter title)
•CR 94-99 ❖ CR ch. 8

Music or poetry, good taste in, not necessary to salvation (as evidenced by the humble charwoman in church who revels in hymns)
•L 224 ❖ L 7 Dec 50

Music: Records seemed more real than an orchestra to Lewis as a child; our taste and experience does not always confirm which is real and which is a substitute (re: religion as reality or substitute)*
•CR 39-41 ❖ CR 3:5-9

Music, Screwtape likens joyful human laughter to "that detestable art" which humans call
•SL 50 ❖ SL 11:2

Music: "The ears that are delighted with jazz cannot quite believe that 'classical music' is anything but a sort of 'vegetarian jazz'..."
•CR 40 ❖ CR 3:7

Music: The real musician is troublesome to the man who wishes to indulge in untaught "musical appreciation" (analogy to the "troublesome" complexity of God)
•M 85-86 ❖ M 11:7

Music: "We—even our poets and musicians and inventors—never, in the ultimate sense, *make*. We only build. We always have materials to build from"
•LM 73 (*see* Creativity)
❖ LM 14:3 (*see also* Creativity)

Musical instruments, of all, I liked (and like) the organ least
•SJ 234 ❖ SJ 15:6

Musicians, church: Regarding the musician filled with pride of skill, who looks with contempt on the unappreciative congregation
•CR 97 ❖ CR 8:9

Musicians, church: "There is...a sense in which all natural agents, even inanimate ones, glorify God continually by revealing the powers He has given them"
•CR 98 (*see also* CR 95)
❖ CR 8:11 (*see also* CR 8:5)

Musicians, church: When a performer's intention is to glorify God, and when it succeeds, he is the most enviable of men
•CR 98 ❖ CR 8:12

Must Our Image of God Go? (chapter title)
•GID 184-185 ❖ GID I ch. 23

"**Mutual** admiration society," Friendship must not become a, yet must be full of mutual admiration
•FL 124 (*see also* FL 112)
❖ FL 4:59 (*see also* FL 4:41)

"**Mystical**" element in the Church implies that we should expect to find something in it opaque to our reason though not contrary to it
•GID 238 ❖ GID II 11:11

Mysticism—*consider also* Asceticism; Meditation

Mysticism, activity a part of true; "...the ultimate Peace is silent through very density of life"*
•M 93 ❖ M 11:18

Mysticism discussed
•LM 63-65 ❖ LM 12:2-11

Mysticism, I do not attempt the precipices of; I don't think we are all "called" to that ascent
•LM 63 ❖ LM 12:2, 5

Mysticism likened to voyages whose "departures are all alike; it is the landfall that crowns the voyage"
•LM 64-65 ❖ LM 12:7-9

Mysticism, the destiny of redeemed Man

is not less but more unimaginable than, would lead us to suppose
•M 159 ❖ M 16:27

Mysticism, the true religion gives value to its own, but mysticism does not validate the religion in which it happens to occur
•LM 65 ❖ LM 12:8

Mysticism: To find God it is perhaps not always necessary to leave His creatures behind; the world is crowded with Him*
•LM 75 ❖ LM 14:11

Mystics mentioned (with regard to Pantheism) as "that ill-defined but popular class" who tend to generalize God
•M 86 ❖ M 11:8

Mystics, the stillness in which the, approach God is intent and alert—at the opposite pole from sleep or reverie
•M 93 ❖ M 11:18

Myth as "a real though unfocused gleam of divine truth falling on human imagination"
•M 133-134 (ftnt.) ❖ M 15:2 (ftnt.)

Myth as the partial solution to the problem that humans cannot experience a thing (such as Pain) and intellectualize about it at the same time
•GID 65-66 (see also SJ 217-219*)
❖ GID I 5:8 (see also SJ 14:9, 10*)

Myth Became Fact (chapter title)
•GID 63-67 (see also M 133-134, ftnt.; WG 84-85; SJ 236) ❖ GID I ch. 5 (see also M 15:2—ftnt; WG 5:15; SJ 15:7)

Myth, discussion of the nature of, (In myth "we come nearest to experiencing as a concrete what can otherwise be understood only as an abstraction")
•GID 65-66 (see also CR 130-131*)
❖ GID I 5:8-10 (see also CR 11:4*)

Myth, in becoming Fact, does not cease to be Myth; just as God, in becoming Man, does not cease to be God
•GID 66-67 (see also M 133-134, ftnt.)
❖ GID I 5:11, 13 (see also M 15:2—ftnt.)

Myth, into a, a writer puts what he does not yet know and could not come by in any other way
•L 271 ❖ L 22 Sep 56

Myth into Fact and God into Man both involve a certain humiliation, yet the humiliation in each case leads to a greater glory
•WG 84-85 (see also M 133-134, ftnt.)
❖ WG 5:15 (see also M 15:2—ftnt.)

Myth may be more spiritually sustaining than professed religion
•GID 67 ❖ GID I 5:11, 12

"Myth" may mean either an account of what may have been historical fact, or a symbolical representation of non-historic truth*
•PP 77 (ftnt.) ❖ PP 5:6 (ftnt.)

Myth of "dying god"—consider also Death and Rebirth pattern

Myth of "dying god" came true once
•GID 57-58, 66-67, 83-84; M 113-115; SJ 235-236 (see also GID 132*)
❖ GID I 4:42 (Ques. 10); 5:11-13; 9:5, 6; M 14:9-14; SJ 15:7 (see also GID I 16:4*)

Myth of "dying god": In 1926 the hardest boiled of all the atheists I knew remarked, "Rum thing. It almost looks as if it had really happened once"
•SJ 223-224, 235-236 ❖ SJ 14:15; 15:7

Myth, story of the Fall as an example of a, built into a systematic and fully believed theology (vis-a-vis myths told by primitive man)
•L 303 ❖ L 21 Mar 62

Myth, The Funeral of a Great (chapter title —re: popular Evolutionism)
•CR 82-93 ❖ CR ch. 7

Myth transcends thought and Incarnation transcends myth in conveying abstract reality to humans; Christ is more than Balder, not less
•GID 66-67 ❖ GID I 5:10-13

Myth, use of, in the Old Testament
•RP 111 (see also RP 116)
❖ RP 11:4 (see also RP 11:11)

Myth vs. Allegory: "A myth is a story out of which ever varying meanings will grow..."; an allegory has one meaning
•L 271 (see also L 283)
❖ L 22 Sep 56 (see also L 29 Dec 58)

Myth vs. history in the Incarnation of Jesus: "If ever a myth had become fact,

had been incarnated, it would be just like this"
•SJ 236 (*see also* GID 63-67; M 133-134, ftnt.; WG 84-85; Bible as literature)
❖ SJ 15:7 (*see also* GID I ch 5; M 15:2—ftnt.; WG 5:15; Bible as literature)

Myths, I was by now too experienced in literary criticism to regard the Gospels as; they had not the mythical taste
•SJ 236 (*see also* CR 154-155; GID 101, 158-159) ❖ SJ 15:7 (*see also* CR 13:4, 5; GID I 10:47; 19:4, 5)

Myths in Holy Scripture, I have the deepest respect even for Pagan myths—still more for, (re: story of the apple in Genesis)
•PP 71-72 (*see also* L 286; GID 42, 57-58; M 33, 133-134, ftnt.; RP 109-111)
❖ PP 5:2 (*see also* L 7 May 59; GID I 3:9; 4:42; M 4:15; 15:2—ftnt.; RP 11:1-4)

Myths, Lewis lists different views which have been held regarding, including his own
•GID 131-132 ❖ GID I 16:4

Mythologies, Creation as expressed in the various
•RP 78 ❖ RP 8:4

Mythologies, history as seen by the various Pagan, and the "Historicism" evident in them
•CR 102-104 ❖ CR 9:5-7

Mythology—*see also* Paganism

Mythology and Paganism, we should expect to find in, some glimpse of that theme which we believe to be the very plot of the whole cosmic story
•WG 83 ❖ WG 5:15

Mythology and poetry, so false as history, may be very near the truth as prophecy ("Some day, God willing, we shall get *in*")
•WG 16-17 ❖ WG 1:13

Mythology as bearing "a likeness permitted by God to that truth on which all depends" (Lewis's view)
•RP 106-107 (*see also* MC 54)
❖ RP 10:11 (*see also* MC II 3:9)

Mythology as the precursor to Biblical religion
•GID 57-58, 66-67, 83-84, 132; M 133-134, ftnt. (*see also* GID 175; L 258; M

113-114; PP 25; WG 82-85)
❖ GID I 4:42 (Ques. 10); 5:11-13; 9:5, 6; 16:4; M 15:2—ftnt. (*see also* GID I 21:7; L 1 Nov 54; M 14:9-14; PP 1:16; WG 5:14, 15)

Mythology, Celtic, soon became a rival (or at least a humble companion) to Norse
•SJ 114 (*see also* SJ 165)
❖ SJ 7:18 (*see also* SJ 11:1)

Mythology, Christianity referred to as the Christian, by Lewis while a scholar at Oxford (prior to his becoming a Christian)
•SJ 214, 215 ❖ SJ 14:4, 5

Mythology, death and rebirth pattern in, not accidental; it teaches the truth that man himself must undergo some sort of death if he would truly live
•RP 106-107 (*see also* Death and Rebirth pattern) ❖ RP 10:11 (*see also* Death and Rebirth pattern)

Mythology, desire for a "vague something" as seen in Pagan, shows a first and rudimentary form of "the idea of God"
•L 144 ❖ L 24 Oct 31

Mythology: I almost think I was sent back to the false gods to acquire some capacity for worship against the day when the true God should recall me*
•SJ 77 ❖ SJ 5:9

Mythology, I ought to have seen that the Desirable was further away and less subjective than a system of, —had, in fact, only shown through that system
•SJ 168-169 ❖ SJ 11:5

Mythology, if Christianity is only a, it is not the one I like best; I like Greek, Irish, and Norse mythology much better
•WG 76 ❖ WG 5:6

"Mythology" in Christianity: In trying to remove the imagery from Christianity, a poorer mythology is being substituted for a richer
•LM 52 (*see also* M 74-75)
❖ LM 10:2 (*see also* M 10:13)

Mythology, Norse—*see also* Norse literature

Mythology, Norse: "From these books again and again I received the stab of Joy"

●SJ 78 (*see also* SJ 211)
❖ SJ 5:11 (*see also* SJ 13:20)

Mythology, Norse, Lewis's taste for
●GID 278; L 110-111, 205; SJ 17, 72-78, 114-115, 130, 163-164, 165-169, 211; WG 76) ❖ GID III 2:1; L 8 Feb 27; 29 Oct 44; SJ 1:17; 5:3-11; 7:19, 20; 8:15-18; 10:17; 11:1-6; 13:20; WG 5:6)

Mythology of the Hebrews was the chosen mythology, just as the Hebrews were the chosen people
●M 133-134 (ftnt.) ❖ M 15:2 (ftnt.)

Mythology, our, [of Satan's existence, fall, and corruption of the Earth] may be much nearer to literal truth than we suppose
●PP 134-136 ❖ PP 9:7

Mythology, Pagan, seen by some as the direct work of the Devil; "he 'makes his lies as like the truth as he can'"
●RP 106 ❖ RP 10:11

Mythology, sources of, include true history, allegory, ritual, the human delight in story telling, *and* the supernatural—both diabolical and divine
●GID 132 ❖ GID I 16:4

Mythopoeic: "...as a mythopoeic poet he is incomparable" (re: Richard Wagner)
●CR 84 ❖ CR 7:7

Mythopoeic, if God chooses to be, shall we refuse to be *mythopathic*? (re: Christ as Myth become Fact)
●GID 67 (*see also* M 133-134, ftnt.*)
❖ GID I 5:13 (*see also* M 15:2—ftnt.*)

Mythopoeic: "...our mythopoeic...faculties"
●CR 105 ❖ CR 9:11

Mythopoeic: "...the final stroke of mythopoeic genius" (re: the "myth" of Evolutionism)
●CR 88 ❖ CR 7:14

"**Mythopoeics**," Lewis's invention of the word, to describe the "science of the nature of myths"
●L 163
❖ L undated letter just after 8 Feb 39

Name, God will give each man a new, which will always remain a secret between God and him
●PP 149-150 ❖ PP 10:7

Name of God, we cannot assume that all who use the, without reverential prefixes are making careless use of it
●GID 335-336 ❖ GID IV Letter 8

Name, our new, shall reflect that one aspect of the divine beauty which we will know and praise better than any other creature can
●PP 149-150 ❖ PP 10:7

Names, children calling parents by their first, a perverse practice
●WG 111 ❖ WG 7:7

Narnia—*see Chronicles of Narnia*

National Repentance, Dangers of (chapter title)
●GID 189-192 ❖ GID II ch. 1

Nationalism—*see* Patriotism

Nations, horrible, have horrible religions; have been looking at God through a dirty lens
●MC 144 ❖ MC IV 2:14

Natural...—*consider also* Temporal ...; Worldly ...

"**Natural**," a definition of what is: "The Natural is what springs up, or comes forth, or goes on, *of its own accord*..."
●M 6 ❖ M 2:4

Natural environment, Christianity does not teach us to desire a total release from our
●M 162 (*see also* Matter)

❖ M 16:30 (*see also* Matter)

Natural gifts—*see* Talents

Natural gifts can cause us to forget our need of God as surely as wealth
•MC 180-181 (*see also* L 221)
❖ MC IV 10:11-13 (*see also* L 22 Sep 49)

Natural Law(s)—*see* Law(s) of Nature

Natural self—*see* Self, natural

Natural thing, every, which is not in itself sinful can become the servant of the spiritual life, but none is automatically so
•L 268 ❖ L 2 Apr 56

"Natural" thoughts and desires, at the Fall the will had no resource but to force back the the new, arising from the tidal wave of mere nature, by main strength
•PP 82 ❖ PP 5:10

Naturalism—*see also* Materialism; Religion, "popular"; *consider also* Pantheism

Naturalism, a definition of: the belief that nothing exists except Nature*
•M 5 ❖ M 2:1

Naturalism, A Further Difficulty In (chapter title)
•M 34-38 ❖ M ch. 5

Naturalism and moral judgements: If Naturalism is true, "I ought" is the same sort of statement as "I'm going to be sick"
•M 36 (*see also* CR 67; PP 21*)
❖ M 5:5 (*see also* CR 5:20; PP 1:12*)

Naturalism believes in a one-floor reality; popular "religion" conceives two floors—a ground floor (Nature) and a mystical, indescribable Something
•M 154 ❖ M 16:20

Naturalism cannot accept the idea of a God who stands outside Nature and made it
•M 9 (*consider also* Creation)
❖ M 2:10 (*consider also* Creation)

Naturalism described (vs. Supernaturalism)
•M 5-11 ❖ M ch. 2

Naturalism discredits the processes of reasoning, thereby discrediting the reasoning of Naturalism itself
•M 12-24, 34, 105 (*see also* CR 60-61,

71, 72-81, 89; GID 21, 52-53, 136-138, 272*, 274-276; MC 45-46; SJ 208-209; WG 88-91) ❖ M ch. 3; 5:1; 13:16 (*see also* CR 5:9, 10, 27; ch. 6; 7:16; GID I 1:1; 4:21; 16:13-17; III 1:4*; 1:9, 13-16; MC II 1:6; SJ 13:17; WG 5:21- 24)

Naturalism: If true, our convictions are simply a fact *about* us, like the color of our hair—including our conviction that Nature is uniform
•M 105 (*see also* MC 45-46*)
❖ M 13:16 (*see also* MC II 1:6*)

Naturalism: If true, thoughts are mere accidents and we can know no truths
•GID 136-138; M 12-24
❖ GID I 16:12-17; M ch. 3

Naturalism, philosophical difficulties with the theory of
•M 12-44 (*see also* CR 60-71*)
❖ M ch. 3-6 (*see also* CR 5:9-27*)

Naturalism, pond without a bottom as analogy to
•M 29-30 ❖ M 4:9

Naturalism, The Cardinal Difficulty of (chapter title)
•M 12-24 ❖ M ch. 3

Naturalism, the conception that units of matter obey no laws seems a refutation of nineteenth-century, (re: science and miracles)
•GID 133 ❖ GID I 16:6

Naturalism: The point at which it can win its final victory or reveal its fatal philosophical defect is at the study of man himself
•GID 135 ❖ GID I 16:11

Naturalism: "Was it devised not to get in facts but to keep out God?"
•WG 89 ❖ WG 5:22

Naturalist and the Supernaturalist, The (chapter title)
•M 5-11 ❖ M ch. 2

"Naturalist" defined as someone who believes that nothing exists except Nature; "Supernaturalists" believe that there exists something else
•M 5-11, esp. 5 ❖ M ch. 2, esp. 2:1

Naturalist, if a Monist starts from Nature he becomes a, whereas if he starts from God he becomes a Pantheist

•M 165 ❖ M 17:2

Naturalistic assumptions, you will meet, even from the pens of clergymen
•M 164-165 (*see also* CR 152-166)
❖ M 17:1 (*see also* CR ch. 13)

Nature (chapter title)
•RP 76-89 ❖ RP ch. 8

Nature, a desire to be welcomed and accepted by, is part of our spiritual longing
•WG 14-16 (*see also* FL 78-79*; L 154-155*) ❖ WG 1:11, 12 (*see also* FL 3:40*; L 14 Jun 32*)

Nature, a great many things in, will begin to come right when we are drawn in to Christ
•MC 170 ❖ MC IV 8:12

Nature, a new, is being not merely made but made out of an old one
•M 155 ❖ M 16:21

Nature a partial system within reality; has been mistaken for the whole (fish tank analogy)
•M 60-61 ❖ M 8:9

Nature, aesthetic enjoyment of, was certainly hallowed by our Lord's praise of the lilies
•CR 15 ❖ CR 2:7

Nature ("all creation") will one day be rescued from decay and restored to shape, and will subserve the splendour of remade humanity
•GID 33 (*see also* M 149)
❖ GID I 2:11 (*see also* M 16:12)

Nature and God are in one sense separated by the fact that God created Nature—but in another sense she is a manifestation of the Divine
•RP 80-81 ❖ RP 8:8, 9

Nature and God have come into a certain relation; they have, at least, a common frontier—in every human mind
•M 31 ❖ M 4:12

Nature and Spirit will eventually be harmonised; hence Christians believe in the resurrection of the body*
•M 172 ❖ M App. A:11

Nature and Spirit will one day be fully harmonised
•M 159, 160-161 (*see also* WG 72-73)

❖ M 16:27, 29 (*see also* WG 4:30)

Nature and Supernature (chapter title)
•M 25-33 ❖ M ch. 4

Nature and the universe: "It is to be expected that [God's] creation should be, in the main, unintelligible to us"
•GID 43 ❖ GID I 3:9

Nature, appreciation of, can be both utilitarian and poetic, as seen in the Psalms
•RP 76-77, 83-84 ❖ RP 8:2, 13

Nature as a medium of spiritual longing*
•WG 16-17 ❖ WG 1:13

Nature as approached in the Psalms
•RP 76-89 ❖ RP ch. 8

Nature as incomplete revelation: "We must make a detour—leave the hills and woods and go back to our studies, to church, to our Bibles, to our knees"
•FL 38 ❖ FL 2:26

Nature as "the instrument for that music which will...arise between Christ and us"
•M 162 ❖ M 16:30

Nature, beauties of, may be a secret God has shared with humans alone; that may be one of the reasons why we were made
•LM 18 ❖ LM 3:9

Nature, beauty of: I was cured once and for all of the pernicious tendency to compare and prefer...
•SJ 145-146 (*see also* FL 34-35)
❖ SJ 9:22 (*see also* FL 2:17, 18)

Nature both fair and cruel; no more baffling than a man being both kind and dishonest, for both are creatures (created things)
•M 65 ❖ M 9:4

Nature, by emptying, of her divinity you may fill her with Deity, for she is now the bearer of messages; whereas Nature-worship silences her
•RP 82-83 ❖ RP 8:11

"Nature," Centaur as an illustration of how, might one day be fully harmonised with "Spirit"
•M 126, 161 ❖ M 14:30; 16:29

Nature, Christianity demands only that

•MC 17-21 ❖ MC I ch. 1

Nature: "I chewed endlessly on the problem: 'How can it be so beautiful and also so cruel, wasteful and futile?'"
•SJ 170 ❖ SJ 11:7

Nature: I learned that we should attempt a total surrender to whatever atmosphere is offering itself at the moment; to find the most dismal and dripping wood...*
•SJ 199 (see also SJ 146)
❖ SJ 13:3 (see also SJ 9:22)

Nature, if you take, as a teacher she will teach you exactly the lessons you had already decided to learn
•FL 35-37 ❖ FL 2:21-24

Nature illuminated by the Incarnation— her pattern of death and rebirth, her selectiveness, and her vicariousness
•GID 81-86; M 109-110
❖ GID I 9:3-8; M 14:3-20

Nature imperfect (in the sense of having room for improvement) as well as being positively depraved due to sin
•M 120-121 ❖ M 14:22

Nature is only a very small part of a very long and complicated story; miracles are those chapters on which the plot turns*
•M 98-99 ❖ M 12:7

Nature is the creature of God; He is her inventor and controller
•M 115 ❖ M 14:13

Nature, it is a remarkable fact that no canonical writer has ever used, to prove the existence of God (quote from Pascal)
•PP 13 ❖ PP 1 prelim. quote

Nature, knowing God through: We can get hints, but must not try to find a direct path through it and beyond it to an increasing knowledge of God
•FL 38 ❖ FL 2:26

Nature, law(s) of—see Law(s) of Nature

Nature, Lewis mentions developing a love for, which was not a studious love; "It was the mood of a scene that mattered to me..."
•SJ 78 ❖ SJ 5:10

Nature, Lewis worried that if, was created it was not fully wild: "I...asked, 'If Nature herself proves artificial, where will you go to seek wildness?'"
•M 63-64 ❖ M 9:2, 3

Nature, Lewis's appreciation of, in adolescence: "The mere smells were enough to make a man tipsy—cut grass, dew-dabbled mosses, sweet pea, autumn woods..."
•SJ 118 ❖ SJ 8:1

Nature, Lewis's love for, came partly from books read at an early age
•L 109-110 ❖ L 4 Jul 26

Nature, like ourselves, is to be redeemed and cured, but not tamed or sterilised; we shall still be able to recognise her
•M 66-67 ❖ M 9:7

Nature, love of
•FL 34-39 ❖ FL 2:17-28

Nature, love of, can turn into a nature religion which will lead us, if not to the Dark Gods, to a great deal of nonsense
•FL 38 ❖ FL 2:26

Nature, love of, need not be surrendered as long as it is chastened and limited
•FL 38-39 ❖ FL 2:27

Nature, man's attempt to win safety and ease from, seems to lead on to universal suburbia
•L 211 ❖ L 15 Oct 47

Nature, mentally limited beings studying a painting used to illustrate the impossibility of discovering by science how God works on (illustration borrowed from Bergson)
•M 97 ❖ M 12:5

Nature, miracles are the retelling in capital letters of the same message which, writes in her crabbed cursive hand
•GID 206 (see also GID 29; M 134-135)
❖ GID II 4:9 (see also GID I 2:7; M 15:4)

Nature, moral philosophy not taught by; if it were, it might be that of ruthless competition
•FL 35-36 ❖ FL 2:19-21

Nature, my brother's toy garden made me aware of, as something cool, dewy, fresh, exuberant
•SJ 7 ❖ SJ 1:4

Nature, my feelings for, had been too nar-

rowly romantic; I attended mostly to what I thought was awe-inspiring, or wild, or eerie, or distant
•SJ 152 ❖ SJ 10:4

Nature, my imaginative Renaissance almost at once produced a new appreciation of external
•SJ 77 ❖ SJ 5:10

Nature [Natural universe]: "When logic says a thing must be so, Nature always agrees"
•CR 64 ❖ CR 5:17

Nature never plays exactly the same tune twice (re: improbability of communication with loved ones who have died)
•GO 15-16 (see also GO 28-29)
❖ GO 1:29 (see also GO 2:14)

Nature "never taught me that there exists a God of glory and of infinite majesty...But nature gave the word 'glory' a meaning for me"
•FL 37 (see also FL 153-154)
❖ FL 2:23 (see also FL 5:35)

Nature, New: Jesus' miracles of anticipation (e.g., walking on water, raising of Lazarus) give us hints of what our New Nature will be like
•M 150-153 (see also Destiny of redeemed Man) ❖ M 16:13-19 (see also Destiny of redeemed Man)

Nature: No smallest part of her is there except because it expresses the character God chose to give her
•M 65 ❖ M 9:5

Nature "not an evil creature but a good creature corrupted, retaining many beauties but all tainted..."
•L 301 (see also M 66)
❖ L 20 Dec 61 (see also M 9:6)

Nature, not even Omnipotence could create a society of free souls without at the same time creating a relatively independent and "inexorable"
•PP 29 ❖ PP 2:6

Nature not irrelevant to spiritual beatitude; Heaven will involve a natural environment as well as a spiritual state
•M 161-162 (see also Matter)

❖ M 16:30 (see also Matter)

Nature not to be unmade but remade; the old field of space, time, matter, and the senses is to be weeded and sown for a new crop
•M 149 (see also GID 87)
❖ M 16:12 (see also GID I 9:11)

Nature of Christ—see Humanity of Christ; Incarnation

Nature: "...of every created thing I praise, I should say, 'In some way, in its unique way, like Him who made it'"*
•GO 73 (see also LM 90)
❖ GO 4:7 (see also LM 17:8)

Nature, one result of believing in Creation is to see, not as a mere datum but as an achievement
•RP 83 ❖ RP 8:12

Nature, only Supernaturalists really see; we must offer her neither worship nor contempt
•M 66-67 ❖ M 9:7

Nature only the commentary; in Christianity we find the real text or poem
•M 130 (see also GID 84*)
❖ M 14:35 (see also GID I 9:6*)

Nature only the image or symbol of what we really desire; fitfully reflects the splendour of God
•WG 17 ❖ WG 1:13

Nature, our conviction that, is uniform cannot be trusted if Naturalism is true
•M 105 ❖ M 13:16

Nature: "Our real journey to God involves constantly turning our backs on her; passing from the dawn-lit fields into some poky little church..."
•FL 39 ❖ FL 2:27

Nature, pantheistic or merely sensuous love of, as one of the values implicit in romantic poetry
•CR 16, 21-22 ❖ CR 2:13, 29, 32

Nature: Psalmist's appreciation for animals is almost certainly reached through the idea of God as Creator and sustainer of all; we are fellow-dependents on Him
•RP 84-85 (see also RP 88-89)
❖ RP 8:14 (see also RP 8:18)

Nature, regarding our longing to be united

with: We long to meet with some response, yet "we have been mere spectators"
•WG 14-17 ❖ WG 1:11-13

Nature religions, in the incarnated God we see Someone Who is behind all the
•GID 84; M 120 ❖ GID I 9:6; M 14:20

Nature religions simply affirm my natural desires; anti-natural religions (e.g., Buddhism or higher Hinduism) simply contradict them; Christianity does neither
•GID 86; M 119 ❖ GID I 9:9; M 14:20

Nature, religious language and imagery contains nothing that has not been borrowed from
•WG 57 ❖ WG 4:4

Nature shows a depraved vicariousness (e.g., cats living on mice), although the principle is of divine origin
•M 118 (see also GID 85-86)
❖ M 14:19 (see also GID I 9:8)

Nature: "Shut your mouth; open your eyes and ears. Take in what is there and give no thought to what might have been there..."
•SJ 146 ❖ SJ 9:22

Nature soon ceased to be (for me) a reminder of the books, and became herself a medium of the real joy
•SJ 77 ❖ SJ 5:10

Nature, subordination of, demanded only in the interests of Nature herself; the beauty withers when we try to make it an absolute
•L 228 ❖ L 23 Apr 51

Nature, talking and smoking interfere with one's appreciation of, (Lewis describes his afternoon walks, most of which were taken alone)
•SJ 142 (see also SJ 200*)
❖ SJ 9:18 (see also SJ 13:4*)

Nature, temptation to worship, as seen in a passage in Job ("Perhaps in certain times and places it was really innocent")
•RP 80-81 ❖ RP 8:8

Nature: "The created glory may be expected to give us hints of the uncreated; for the one is derived from the

other and in some fashion reflects it"
•FL 38 ❖ FL 2:25

Nature, the Jews (Psalmists) were agricultural and approached, with a gardener's and a farmer's interest— but we also find them led on beyond this
•RP 76-77, 83-84 ❖ RP 8:2, 13

Nature: "The night sky suggests that the inanimate also has for God some value we cannot imagine"*
•LM 55 ❖ LM 10:10

Nature, the same doctrine (Creation) which empties, of her divinity also makes her an index, a symbol, a manifestation of the Divine
•RP 81 ❖ RP 8:9, 10

Nature, this time [while walking] the face of, was not emptied of its beauty... (re: Lewis's recovery from the loss of his wife)
•GO 69 ❖ GO 4:2

Nature to be re-made, and this will not stop at Man, or even at this planet
•M 120 (see also GID 87; Destiny of Nature) ❖ M 14:21 (see also GID I 9:11; Destiny of Nature)

Nature, to shrink back from, into negative spirituality ("Heaven is a state of mind") is as if we ran away from horses instead of learning to ride
•M 163 ❖ M 16:32

Nature, "town" contrasted by "country" is part of our appreciation of; this was not the case with the Psalmists— towns were few and very small
•RP 76-77 ❖ RP 8:2

Nature, unity in: "...there are rules behind the rules, and a unity which is deeper than uniformity" (re: the "propriety" of miracles)
•M 96 ❖ M 12:4

Nature ("universe") does not appear to be in any sense good as a whole, though it throws up some good elements— strawberries and the sea and sunrise (re: question of futility)*
•CR 65 (see also PP 13-15)
❖ CR 5:19 (see also PP 1:1)

Nature, vague religion which attempts to

feel the presence of God in, is attractive because it is all thrills and no work
•MC 136 (see also MC 35; M 81; Pantheism; Religion, minimal)
❖ MC IV 1:4 (see also MC I 4:6; M 11:2; Pantheism; Religion, minimal)

Nature, vanity of, defined as "her futility, her ruinousness"
•M 151 ❖ M 16:16

Nature, vanity of, is her disease, not her essence
•M 66-67 ❖ M 9:7

Nature: Was it—space and time and matter—created in order to make manyness possible?
•MC 159 ❖ MC IV 6:2

Nature, whole world of, invented and formed by "that great Imagination...for Its own delight and for the delight of men and angels and...beasts"
•RP 5 ❖ RP 1:8

Nature: Wordsworthian contemplation can be the first and lowest form of recognition that there is something outside ourselves which demands reverence
•CR 22 ❖ CR 2:32

Nature works according to regular laws, and until you believe that you can perceive no miracles
•M 46-47 (see also GID 26-27; 45*, 72-73, 100; M 139) ❖ M 7:5 (see also GID I 2, 2, 3; 3:15*; 7:1-10; 10:43; M 15:13)

Nazis who made Norse mythology part of their ideology got that mythology all wrong
•GID 278-280 ❖ GID III 2:1-5

Nazism mentioned by Screwtape
•SL 161; WLN 59
❖ SL 32:17; WLN 4:17

Nearness by likeness vs. nearness of approach
•FL 14-19 ❖ FL 1:8-16

Necessary evils—see Evils, necessary

Need, a clamorous, seems to shut one off from the thing needed; the moments when you call most desperately to God for help are those when you seem to get none
•LAL 92 (see also GO 4-6; 53-54)

❖ LAL 24 Sep 60 (see also GO 1:7-11; 3:24-26)

Need, God has no; but God of mere miracle may have made Himself able to hunger and created in Himself that which we can satisfy
•PP 50-52 ❖ PP 3:17, 18

Need, God has no; His love is purely Gift-love
•FL 11-12, 175-176 ❖ FL 1:1-3; 6:21, 22

Need, God has no, of our praise; that miserable idea is answered by the words "If I be hungry I will not tell thee"
•CR 98-99; RP 93 (see also MC 113-114*)
❖ CR 8:12; RP 9:4 (see also MC III 8:12*)

Need to be needed, Friendship is utterly free from Affection's
•FL 102 ❖ FL 4:26

Need to be needed may lead to a perversion of Gift-love (story of Mrs. Fidget)
•FL 73-83 (see also SL 121*, 123*)
❖ FL 3:33-45 (see also SL 26:2, 5*)

Need to be needed often finds its outlet in pampering an animal
•FL 78-79 (see also FL 75-76)
❖ FL 3:40 (see also FL 3:35)

Need to be needed, we must get over our, (Women mentioned as especially susceptible to this temptation)
•MC 187-188 ❖ MC IV 11:10

Neediness, Grace imparts to us a childlike and delighted acceptance of our, and a joy in total dependence upon God
•FL 179-181 ❖ FL 6:26-28

Neediness, nothing about us except our, is in this life permanent
•FL 33 ❖ FL 2:15

Neediness of man: "...our whole being by its very nature is one vast need; incomplete, preparatory, empty yet cluttered ..."
•FL 13-14 ❖ FL 1:7

Neediness of those who demand to be loved seals up the very fountain for which they are thirsty
•FL 65 (see also GID 285)
❖ FL 3:18 (see also GID III 3:7)

Neediness: The desperateness of our need

may prevent our perception of God's presence*
•GO 53-54; LAL 92
❖ GO 3:24, 25; LAL 24 Sep 60

Need-love—*see also* Love

Need-love, Appreciative love, and Gift-love differentiated
•FL 11-21, 32-33 (*see also* FL 175-184)
❖ FL ch. 1; 2:13, 14 (*see also* FL 6:21-34)

Need-love, God has no; His love is purely Gift-love
•FL 11-12, 175-176 ❖ FL 1:1-3; 6:21, 22

Need-love: If God has created in Himself that which we can satisfy, this is because we need to be needed*
•PP 50-51 ❖ PP 3:17

Need-love is not mere selfishness
•FL 12-13 ❖ FL 1:6

Need-love says of a woman "I cannot live without her"; Gift-love longs to give her happiness, comfort, etc.
•FL 33 ❖ FL 2:14

Need-love, so far as I have been able to see, has no resemblance to the love which God is; God needs nothing
•FL 175-176 (*see also* FL 11-12; PP 50-52) ❖ FL 6:21, 22 (*see also* FL 1:1-3; PP 3:17, 18)

Need-love will not last longer than the need, but another kind of love may be grafted onto it
•FL 30-31 ❖ FL 2:9

Need-loves may be greedy and exacting, but they do not try to become gods as the more spiritual loves might
•FL 18-20, esp. 20
❖ FL 1:15-17, esp. 1:17

Need-pleasure, Eros transforms a, into an Appreciative pleasure
•FL 135-136 ❖ FL 5:6

Need-pleasure vs. Appreciative pleasure
•FL 25-30 ❖ FL 2:2-8

Neighbor, loving your, does not necessarily mean feeling fond of him
•MC 105 (*see also* MC 115-117)
❖ MC III 7:4, 5 (*see also* MC III 9:2-6)

Neighbor, when we have learned to love our, as ourself we may then be able to love ourself as our neighbor—with charity instead of partiality

•GID 194; SL 65 ❖ GID II 2:3; SL 14:4

Neighbor, your, is almost the holiest object presented to your senses
•WG 19 ❖ WG 1:15

Neighbors, you cannot put God off with speculations about your next-door; if there is a God you are, in a sense, alone with Him
•MC 183 ❖ MC IV 10:17

Nero, true tragedy of, was not that he fiddled while Rome burned; he fiddled on the brink of hell
•WG 20 ❖ WG 2:2

Neurosis—or the realistic fears of certain of the Psalmists—called "the Dark Night of the Flesh" by Lewis
•CR 125-128 ❖ CR 10:31-40

Neurosis as a condition which some may attribute to the Psalmists—but the belief that one is threatened by certain evils may be realistic
•CR 126 ❖ CR 10:32-35

Neutral ground, there is no, in the universe; every square inch, every split second, is claimed by God and counterclaimed by Satan
•CR 33 ❖ CR 2:54

Neutral things listed which can become the servant of the spiritual life or dangerous idols (music, poetry, etc.)
•L 268
❖ L undated letter just before 2 Apr 56

Neutral things, Screwtape mentions, which can work for either God's or the devil's purposes (love, health, sickness, war, peace, etc.)
•SL 87-89 ❖ SL 19:3

Neutral things: "Sensitivity," like "experience," is a potentiality, therefore neutral; neither can be an end to Christians
•CR 24 ❖ CR 2:38

Neutral things: Sex in itself cannot be immoral, but the sexual behaviour of human beings can*
•LM 14 ❖ LM 3:2

New Age—*consider also* Anthroposophy; Occult; Pantheism; Spiritualism; Theosophy

New Age: "A united Christendom should be the answer to the new Paganism"**
•L 165 ❖ L 8 May 39

New Age: Ironically, each new relapse into the immemorial "religion" of Pantheism is hailed as the last word in novelty and emancipation**
•M 82-83 ❖ M 11:4

New Birth—*see also* Conversion; *consider also* Growth, Christian

New Birth, according to some authors a symptom of, is a permanent and horrified perception of our sinfulness (but this can be taken too far)*
•LM 98-99 ❖ LM 18:13-16

New Birth: Individuals are immortal only as new creatures*
•WG 120 ❖ WG 7:19

New Birth is a redirection and revitalising of all the parts or elements in man—spirit, soul, and body
•M 172 ❖ M App. A:11

New Birth likened to an ordinary birth: Just as a baby might, if it had the choice, we may prefer to stay in the warmth and safety of the womb
•MC 187 (*see also* MC 154-155*, 173; SL 147*) ❖ MC IV 11:9 (*see also* MC IV 5:3*; 9:7; SL 31:3*)

New Birth, meaning of
•MC 164 ❖ MC IV 7:10

New Birth means surrendering ourselves back to God in Christ, after which we will have a life which is absolutely Supernatural, not created but begotten
•M 170 ❖ M App. A:2, 3

New Birth, practical aspects of
•MC 160-166 ❖ MC IV ch. 7

New Birth: "Regenerate" as the best adjective to describe the New Man
•M 172 ❖ M App. A:11

New Birth: The words "regeneration" and "the New Man" suggest that some tendencies in each natural man may have to be simply rejected*
•WG 118 ❖ WG 7:17

New Birth: "Ye must be born again" (Obedience as an imperative not really obedience at all)

•LM 115 ❖ LM 21:12

New Creation, Christ's resurrection as the "first fruits" of the
•M 145 ❖ M 16:5

New Look, The (chapter title)
•SJ 197-211 ❖ SJ ch. 13

New Man, "regenerate" as the best adjective to describe the, who has been "born again"
•M 170, 172 (*see also* WG 118)
❖ M App. A:3, 11 (*see also* WG 7:17)

Newman, according to, you cannot have a Christian literature; it is a contradiction in terms to attempt a sinless Literature of sinful man [John Henry Cardinal Newman]
•CR 16 ❖ CR 2:13

Newman felt culture might provide innocent distraction at those moments of spiritual relaxation which would otherwise lead to sin
•CR 18 (*see also* CR21)
❖ CR 2:20 (*see also* CR 2:27)

Newman's view of the cultivation of the intellect as a justifiable end in itself, while remaining wholly distinct from virtue, discussed by Lewis
•CR 18-19 ❖ CR 2:20, 21

New men, description of ("Every now and then one meets them...")
•MC 187-188 (*see also* Good people)
❖ MC IV 11:10 (*see also* Good people)

New Men, The (chapter title)
•MC 183-190 ❖ MC IV ch. 11

New Testament—*see* Bible—New Testament

News, war-time, is most likely distorted by the time it reaches the papers; reading it is surely a waste of time
•SJ 159 ❖ SJ 10:12

Newspaper extracts, one wouldn't condemn a dog on
•LM 29 ❖ LM 6:2

Newspaper, I never read the; why does anyone? They're nearly all lies...
•LAL 47 (*see also* SJ 136)
❖ LAL 26/10/55 (*see also* SJ 9:11)

Newspaper, Lewis mentions that he never developed a taste for reading the
•SJ 136 ❖ SJ 9:11

Newspapers, content of: "That is possibly the most phantasmal of all histories ..." (re: "Historicism")
•CR 113 ❖ CR 9:26

Newspapers, even in peacetime I think those are very wrong who say that schoolboys should be encouraged to read the
•SJ 159 ❖ SJ 10:12

Newspapers: If you wish to avoid God, select your books very carefully; safer to stick to the papers
•CR 168-169 ❖ CR 14:17, 18

Newspapers, people will go out of their way to buy a, whose editor is a rascal —thus paying the owner for his lies, blasphemies, etc. (re: "connivance")
•RP 67 ❖ RP 7:3

Newspapers: "...the great cataract of nonsense that pours from the press..."
•WG 29 ❖ WG 2:10

"Nice" people are just as much in need of salvation as miserable people—and possibly more difficult to save
•MC 182 ❖ MC IV 10:15

Nice People or New Men (chapter title)
•MC 175-183 ❖ MC IV ch. 10

"Nice" people, warning to: Much is expected from those to whom much is given
•MC 180-181 ❖ MC IV 10:11-13

Nietzsche mentioned as confirming our desire to be stronger or cleverer than other people (re: Christian vs. other views of equality)
•GID 87 (*consider also* Equality)
❖ GID I 9:10 (*consider also* Equality)

Nietzsche, the morality of, is a mere innovation; can be accepted only if we are ready to scrap traditional morals as a mere error...
•CR 77 ❖ CR 6:15

Night sky: Is anything more certain than that in all those vast times and spaces ...I should nowhere find her face? She died... (re: death of Lewis's wife, Joy)
•GO 16 ❖ GO 1:30

Night sky, Lewis describes watching the, from his dormitory at "Belsen"
•SJ 25, 34, 60, 171 ❖ SJ 2:4, 14; 4:6; 11:8

Night sky suggests that the inanimate also has for God some value we cannot imagine
•LM 55 ❖ LM 10:10

Night sky: When one considers the sky and stars, it seems strange that God should be at all concerned with man— yet He has given us extraordinary honour (re: Psalm 8)
•RP 132 ❖ RP 12:11

Nightmare, life as a
•LAL 57 (*see also* LAL 47, 119-120*; MC 170; SL 147; Pessimism, Lewis's)
❖ LAL 21/5/56 (*see also* LAL 26/10/ 55; 28 Jun 63*; MC IV 8:12; SL 31:3; Pessimism, Lewis's)

Nightmare, this life has something like, about it; it'll be nice when we all wake up
•LAL 69 ❖ LAL Oct 20th 57

Nobility lies not in the ancient descent but in having been for so many generations illustrious that more of the steps are *recorded*
•LAL 26 (*see also* LAL 27) ❖ LAL 26/ 1/54 (*see also* LAL Feb 22/54)

Nobility, one may enjoy the tinsel crown of, provided one takes it lightly enough*
•LAL 111 ❖ LAL 10 Dec 62

Noise, Hell referred to by Screwtape as the Kingdom of
•SL 146 ❖ SL 31:2

Noise, Screwtape advocates the use of, to "defend" the humans from "silly qualms, despairing scruples, and impossible desires"
•SL 102-103 (*see also* CR 168*, 170*)
❖ SL 22:5 (*see also* CR 14:18*, 27*)

Non-Christian countries, question of salvation for the people of
•L 152-153 (*see also* GID 265-266*; MC 65, 176-177; SL 26*)
❖ L 8 Apr 32 (*see also* GID II 16:50, 51*; MC II 5:8; IV 10:4; SL 5:2*)

Non-Christians—*see* Unbelievers

Nonsense draws evil after it; if we believe that wars must be fought purely on moral grounds, we will believe that just wars must be wars of annihilation

•FL 47-48 ❖ FL 2:41

Nonsense, Lewis mentions the "great cataract" of, that pours from the press
- •WG 29 (*see also* Newspaper/s)
- ❖ WG 2:10 (*see also* Newspaper/s)

Nonsense questions, all, are unanswerable—and probably half the questions we ask are like that
- •GO 81 (*see also* Questions)
- ❖ GO 4:25 (*see also* Questions)

Nonsense remains nonsense even when we talk it about God; God cannot carry out both of two mutually exclusive alternatives (re: Divine omnipotence)
- •PP 28 ❖ PP 2:4

Norse form of Dualism a manly creed, nobler by many degrees than most philosophies of the moment; yet still only a half-way house
- •GID 24 ❖ GID I 1:8

Norse gods, unlike the Homeric, are beings rooted in a historical process (re: "Historicism")
- •CR 103 ❖ CR 9:7

Norse literature, Lewis's taste for
- •GID 278; L 110-111, 205; SJ 17, 72-78, 114-115, 130, 163-164, 165-169, 211; WG 76 ❖ GID III 2:1; L 8 Feb 27; 29 Oct 44; SJ 1:17; 5:3-11; 7:19, 20; 8:15-18; 10:17; 11:1-6; 13:20; WG 5:6

Norse mythology: "From these books again and again I received the stab of Joy"
- •SJ 78 (*see also* SJ 165, 211)
- ❖ SJ 5:11 (*see also* SJ 11:2; 13:20)

Norse Mythology: When the Nazis made it part of their ideology, they got that mythology all wrong
- •GID 278-280 ❖ GID III 2:1-5

Norse Paganism possibly influenced by Christianity*
- •CR 103 ❖ CR 9:7

Norse theology, in, cosmic history is neither cycle nor flux; it is irreversible, tragic epic marching death-ward to the drumbeat of omens and prophecies (re: "Historicism")
- •CR 103 ❖ CR 9:7

North, Arthur and I both knew that the arrow [of Joy] was shot from the
- •SJ 130 ❖ SJ 8:18

Northernness—*see also* Norse...

Northernness and mythology, Lewis states that the Object of his desire had merely shown through, and that he ought to have seen that the Desirable was further away
- •SJ 168-169 ❖ SJ 11:5

"Northernness" engulfed me...remoteness ...severity... (on reading the words *Siegfried and the Twilight of the Gods*)
- •SJ 73, 75-76 (*see also* SJ 17, 114)
- ❖ SJ 5:4, 6, 7 (*see also* SJ 1:17; 7:19)

Northernness: "...my attitude toward it contained elements which my religion ought to have contained and did not"
- •SJ 76-77 ❖ SJ 5:9

"Northernness" was essentially a desire and implied the absence of its object
- •SJ 82 ❖ SJ 5:15

Nostalgia—*see* Past

Nothing: Screwtape points out that what really gladdens the Devil's heart is to get a man's soul and give him *nothing* in return
- •SL 42 (*see also* SL 144)
- ❖ SL 9:2 (*see also* SL 30:4)

Nothing: "The Christians describe the Enemy as one 'without whom Nothing is strong.' And Nothing is very strong..." (—Screwtape)
- •SL 56 ❖ SL 12:4

Nothingness—*see* Insignificance; Unworthiness

Novel, analogy of writing, to show that God is not in Time
- •MC 146-147 ❖ MC IV 3:6-8

Novel of history, Incarnation as "the missing chapter" in the
- •GID 80-88; M 109-110
- ❖ GID I ch. 9; M 14:3

Novel, the writing of a, as an analogy to our (partly) false picture of God contriving the physical "plot" of the universe
- •M 175-177 ❖ M App. B:8-10

Novels and sentimental songs, if our minds are full of, we can turn any kind of love into the wrong kind of love

•MC 100, 101 (*see also* SL 88)

❖ MC III 6:10, 13 (*see also* SL 19:3)

Novelty, continual, costs money so that the desire for it spells avarice or unhappiness or both (—Screwtape)

•SL 117 ❖ SL 25:4

Novelty, Screwtape describes how he has perverted the natural human enjoyment of change into a demand for continual

•SL 116-117 ❖ SL 25:2-4

Novelty: "...the more rapacious this desire, the sooner it must eat up all the innocent sources of pleasure..." (—Screwtape)

•SL 117 ❖ SL 25:4

Nuclear war—*see* War, nuclear

Nudity emphasizes common humanity and soft-pedals what is individual; in that way we are "more ourselves" when clothed

•FL 147 ❖ FL 5:25

Nudity, Screwtape speaks on

•SL 92 ❖ SL 20:3

Numinous—*see also* Awe; Supernatural

Numinous as "...the Something which is ...the awful haunter of nature"*

•PP 23 ❖ PP 1:14

Numinous awe, definition of: "...wonder and a certain shrinking...this feeling may be described as awe, and the object which excites it as the Numinous"

•PP 17 ❖ PP 1:5

Numinous Awe: Either it is a mere twist in the human mind (serving no biological function), or else it is a direct experience of the supernatural

•PP 20-21 ❖ PP 1:11

Numinous awe: The important thing is that it came into existence, is widespread, and does not disappear with the growth of knowledge and civilisation

•PP 19 ❖ PP 1:10

Numinous awe: We do not know how far back in human history this feeling goes, but it is probably as old as humanity itself

•PP 19 ❖ PP 1:10

Numinous defined as "the Awful"; later

became "the Holy" only in so far as it came to be connected with the morally good

•GID 174-175 ❖ GID I 21:7

Numinous, examples of the experience of, in literature

•PP 18-19 ❖ PP 1:7-9

Numinous, experience of, as the first element of all developed religion

•PP 16-20 ❖ PP 1:5-11

Numinous, man can close his spiritual eyes against the, if he is prepared to part company with poets, prophets, his own childhood, and experience

•PP 24-25 ❖ PP 1:16

"Numinous" used to describe the Person of the Gospels, "lit by a light from beyond the world"

•SJ 236 ❖ SJ 15:7

Nuns, why are, nicer than monks when women in general are not nicer than men?"

•LAL 63 ❖ LAL Sep 14 [1956]

Nurses and hospitals, Joy's description of, in a letter to an American lady

•LAL 75 ❖ LAL Jun 6th [1958]

Nurses: "Few of us have always, in full measure, given our pupils or patients or clients...what we were being paid for"*

•RP 13 ❖ RP 2:8

Nurses who lie to their patients about their terminal condition mentioned with satisfaction by Screwtape

•SL 26-27 (*see also* L 275)

❖ SL 5:2 (*see also* L 6 Mar 57)

Nursing homes: "In your position I myself would prefer a 'Home'—or almost anything—to solitude"

•LAL 102 ❖ LAL 17 Jan 62

Nursing homes ("Old People's Homes"): Sometimes the things we have most dreaded turn out to be quite nice

•LAL 94 ❖ LAL 24 Nov 60

Nursing homes ("Old People's Homes"): "If you ever do have to go to a Home, Christ will be there just as much as in any other place"

•LAL 94 ❖ LAL 24 Nov 60

Nursing homes, Screwtape mentions with

satisfaction humans who die in costly, amid doctors, nurses, and friends who all lie to them about their condition •SL 26-27 (*see also* L 275*; SL 146) ❖ SL 5:2 (*see also* L 6 Mar 57*; SL 31:3)

Obedience—*consider also* Moral effort; Will of God; Works

Obedience accepted with delight and authority exercised with humility are the very lines along which our spirits live •WG 115 ❖ WG 7:15

Obedience as an imperative not really obedience at all; "Ye must be born again" •LM 115 (*see also* L 277; PP 100*) ❖ LM 21:12 (*see also* L 18 Jul 57; PP 6:11*)

Obedience: At my conversion I did not yet believe in a future life; God was to be obeyed simply because He was God •SJ 231 (*see also* FL 189-190; LM 120; RP 39-42, esp. 42) ❖ SJ 15:3 (*see also* FL 6:42; LM 22:8; RP 4:12-17, esp. 4:17)

Obedience, attempting—*see also* Moral effort

Obedience, attempting, teaches us our dependence upon God •MC 94, 124-125, 127-131 (*see also* CR 169*: PP 65) ❖ MC III 5:12; 11:7; 12:3-9 (*see also* CR 14:20, 21*; PP 4:13)

Obedience brings true happiness* •PP 48, 52 (*see also* WG 118-119) ❖ PP 3:15, 18 (*see also* WG 7:18)

Obedience, by, man consciously acts his creaturely role and reverses the act by which he fell •PP 100-101 ❖ PP 6:12

Obedience, civil, not related to the kind and degree of obedience which a creature owes to its Creator; on the former I have nothing to say

•PP 115 ❖ PP 7:6

Obedience, external: "God is not deceived by externals"
•MC 76 ❖ MC III 2:6

Obedience, external, may be deceiving: "...a cold, self-righteous prig who goes regularly to church may be far nearer to hell than a prostitute"*
•MC 94-95 ❖ MC III 5:14

Obedience, external: Screwtape observes that this may be useful in a Christian's self-deception*
•SL 54 ❖ SL 12:2

Obedience, first reward of, is increasing power to desire the ultimate reward (schoolboy analogy)
•WG 5 ❖ WG 1:3

Obedience: "For he who does the will of the Father shall know the doctrine" (re: use of imagery to describe Heaven)*
•M 158 ❖ M 16:25

Obedience, God demands our; the call is not only to prostration and awe, it is to a creaturely participation in the Divine attributes
•PP 52-53 ❖ PP 3:18

Obedience: Golden Rule cannot really be carried out until we learn to love God, and we cannot learn to love God except by learning to obey Him
•MC 82 ❖ MC III 3:8

Obedience, human beings must be trained in, almost before they have moral intuitions
•WG 36-37 (see also L 179)
❖ WG 3:6 (see also L 26 Mar 40)

Obedience: "If the imagination were obedient, the appetites would give us very little trouble"
•LM 17 (see also GID 217; L 126; LAL 111) ❖ LM 3:9 (see also GID II 7:3; L 1 Apr 28; LAL 16 Nov 62)

Obedience: "If you ask why we should obey God, in the last resort the answer is, 'I am.' To know God is to know that our obedience is due to Him..."
•SJ 231-232 ❖ SJ 15:3

Obedience is the key to all doors; feelings come and go

•L 224-225 (see also L 216; Feelings)
❖ L 7 Dec 50 (see also L 3 Apr 49; Feelings)

Obedience is the one key of life (quote from G. MacDonald)
•WLN 109 ❖ WLN 7:28

Obedience is the road to freedom
•WG 113 (see also SL 37-38)
❖ WG 7:9 (see also SL 8:3)

Obedience leads to peace, and to knowledge about good and evil*
•MC 87, 94 (see also Self- knowledge)
❖ MC III 4:10; 5:13 (see also Self-knowledge)

Obedience mentioned by Screwtape as a "habit"
•SL 126 (see also CR 24-25*)
❖ SL 27:3 (see also CR 2:38*)

Obedience: My long-evaded encounter with God happened at a time when I was making a serious effort to obey my conscience
•CR 169 ❖ CR 14:20

Obedience not the main thing God wants; He wants people of a particular sort
•MC 77, 127 (see also MC 164-165)
❖ MC III 2:8; 12:3 (see also MC IV 7:12)

Obedience, omnipresence of, in a Christian's life is analogous to the omnipresence of God in space
•WG 26 ❖ WG 2:8

Obedience, one of the first results of attempting, is to bring your picture of yourself down to something nearer life-size
•CR 169 (see also MC 94, 124-125, 127-128) ❖ CR 14:21 (see also MC III 5:12, 13; 11:7; 12:3-5)

Obedience, Pauline epistles seem to indicate that perfect, to the moral law is not in fact possible to men
•PP 66 (see also Perfection)
❖ PP 4:14 (see also Perfection)

Obedience, Screwtape advises guarding against the human attitude in which temporal affairs are treated primarily as material for
•SL 35 ❖ SL 7:4

Obedience, Screwtape discusses the paradoxical freedom of, which humans

can experience
- •SL 37-38 ❖ SL 8:3

Obedience: Screwtape rues the man who feels that every trace of God has vanished, and asks why he has been forsaken, and still obeys
- •SL 39 ❖ SL 8:4

Obedience, simplest act of mere, is worship of a far more important sort than adoration of God for what He gives us
- •LM 91 ❖ LM 17:15

Obedience: "...the love that matters is His for you—yours for Him may at present exist only in the form of obedience"
- •L 192 ❖ L 4 Jan 41

Obedience: The Psalmist probably felt about the Law as he did about his poetry; both involved exact and loving conformity to an intricate pattern*
- •RP 59 ❖ RP 6:9

Obedience: The Psalmist's effort to keep the Law springs not from servile fear but from love of moral beauty*
- •RP 59-60 ❖ RP 6:9

Obedience: To act on the light one has is almost the only way to more light
- •L 191-192 ❖ L 4 Jan 41

Obedience to God's concrete law as a means to correct the growing emptiness of our idea of God
- •M 90 ❖ M 11:14

Obedience to God's will may become pleasurable to us, but then it can no longer be a means of learning self-surrender
- •PP 99, 101 ❖ PP 6:10, 13

Obedience: "To obey is the proper office of a rational soul" (quote from Montaigne)
- •PP 69, top ❖ PP 5 prelim. quote

Obedience vs. authority: A child can be trained in the art of obedience before it has reason and age enough to learn to command
- •L 179 (see also WG 36-37)
- ❖ L 26 Mar 40 (see also WG 3:6)

Obedience: We can perhaps train ourselves to ask how the thing which we are saying or doing will look when the irresistible light streams in upon it*

- •WLN 113 ❖ WLN 7:38

Obedience: We must sometimes act on our intellectual assent before we have real confidence (faith)
- •L 199 (see also Faith as confidence)
- ❖ L 20 Jan 42 (see also Faith as confidence)

Obedience, we owe God our; He is the ground of our existence and our benefactor, as well as being absolutely wise and good
- •CR 27 ❖ CR 2:42

Obedience, wherever the will is perfectly offered back to our Creator in delighted, there is Heaven
- •PP 91 ❖ PP 6:3

Object, emotion in religious experience is a by-product of our attention to a particular
- •CR 140 ❖ CR 11:22

Object of desire—see Desire, object of

Objects, holy: If they cease to remind us that all objects are holy, they will do us harm
- •LM 75 ❖ LM 14:10

Objections, Some (chapter title)
- •MC 21-26 ❖ MC I ch. 2

Objectivity of moral law—see Moral law, objectivity of; Subjectivism

Obscenity in literature a sign of a culture that has lost its faith
- •GID 264-265 ❖ GID II 16:43, 44

Obsession with people who have hurt us: "...that...is almost the greatest evil nasty people can do to us—to become an obsession, to haunt our minds"
- •LAL 28 ❖ LAL Mar 10/54

Obsolescence of products, built-in, becoming an economic necessity; this situation excludes the idea of Good Work from the outset
- •WLN 72 (see also CR 92)
- ❖ WLN 5:3 (see also CR 7:21)

Obstacle to conversion, I have often found an immoral, naive and sentimental pantheism to be in fact the chief
- •GID 181 ❖ GID I 22:10

Obstacles to Christian faith—see also Opposition to Christianity; consider also Evangelism, problems in

Obstacles to Christian faith: A high natural gift of reason has been identified with a greater tendency to refuse the life of Christ*
•CR 17 (quote from *Theologia Germanica*) ❖ CR 2:16 (quote from *Theologia Germanica*)

Obstacles to Christian faith: a "mere change of scene...God is less credible when I pray in a hotel bedroom than when I am in College"*
•CR 42 ❖ CR 3:10

Obstacles to Christian faith: adversity and prosperity (—Screwtape)*
•SL 132 ❖ SL 28:1

Obstacles to Christian faith: An atheist might feel that Jesus was really the same sort of charlatan as all the other writers of apocalyptic*
•WLN 95 ❖ WLN 7:5

Obstacles to Christian faith and practice: suspense and anxiety, such as are present in war-time (—Screwtape)*
•SL 28-29 ❖ SL 6:1, 2

Obstacles to Christian faith: anthropomorphism
•LM 21-22 ❖ LM 4:9

Obstacles to Christian faith: belief in vague, non-Christian creeds*
•GID 240-241 ❖ GID II 12:2

Obstacles to Christian faith: belief in a "historical Jesus"—Jesus as merely a teacher*
•SL 106-108 ❖ SL 23:3, 4

Obstacles to Christian faith: believing that one's wrong choices are trivial and revocable*
•SL 53 (*see also* WLN 54-55; Choices) ❖ SL 12:1 (*see also* WLN 4:10; Choices)

Obstacles to Christian faith: contented worldliness (Screwtape mentions that war prevents this, since it causes people to think about death)*
•SL 27 ❖ SL 5:2

Obstacles to Christian faith: Difficulties—"The conclusion I really dread is not, 'So there's no God after all,' but, 'So this is what God's really like...'"*
•GO 5 ❖ GO 1:9

Obstacles to Christian faith: "Do all theoretical problems conceal shirkings by the will?"*
•L 202 ❖ L 22 Dec 42

Obstacles to Christian faith: failure of the Apologist to translate it into the vernacular*
•GID 93, 94, 96-98, 254-257, 338 ❖ GID I 10:10, 12, 18-38; II ch. 15; IV Letter 11

Obstacles to Christian faith: fear of what God may require of you*
•GID 110-111 (*see also* Self-reservation) ❖ GID I 12:6-8 (*see also* Self-reservation)

Obstacles to Christian faith: feeling that we can lead a good life without believing in Christianity*
•GID 110-111 ❖ GID I 12:6

Obstacles to Christian faith: Flippancy mentioned by Screwtape as deadening the intellect and effectively armouring humans against God*
•SL 52 ❖ SL 11:6

Obstacles to Christian faith: "Floating is a very agreeable operation; a decision either way costs something"*
•GID 250 ❖ GID II 14:3

Obstacles to Christian faith: having never been told what the Christians say (re: British school system)*
•GID 115 ❖ GID I 13:3

Obstacles to Christian faith: I have often found that an immoral, naivë and sentimental Pantheism was the chief obstacle to conversion
•GID 181 ❖ GID I 22:10

Obstacles to Christian faith: ignorance of the Faith one is rejecting*
•GID 127 ❖ GID I 15:3

Obstacles to Christian faith: In the uneducated man, there is a scepticism about History, and therefore about the Gospels*
•GID 94-95, 241-242 ❖ GID I 10:13; II 12:3

Obstacles to Christian faith: It is not always an intellectual difficulty; may be small, irrational things*
•CR 42-43 (*see also* MC 124) ❖ CR 3:10-12 (*see also* MC III 11:6)

Obstacles to Christian faith: jealousy to-

ward God, who, we feel, may "steal" our loved one's heart; "the bitterness of some unbelief is really due to this"
•FL 61 (*see also* FL 70-73; L 274; SL 18)
❖ FL 3:13 (*see also* FL 3:27-32; L 10 Feb 57; SL 3:6)

Obstacles to Christian faith: Lewis lists many things which will help you to avoid God, if that is what you desire ("Avoid silence...Live in a crowd...")*
•CR 168-169 ❖ CR 14:17, 18

Obstacles to Christian faith: mere feeling, which continually assaults conviction (though this is also true for the atheist)*
•CR 41 (*see also* CR 42-43)
❖ CR 3:9 (*see also* CR 3:10, 11)

Obstacles to Christian faith: Noise ("Music and silence—how I detest them both!"—Screwtape)*
•SL 102-103 ❖ SL 22:5

Obstacles to Christian faith: Not necessarily "sweet sins"; may be just "a dreary flickering of the mind over it knows not what and knows not why..."*
•SL 56 ❖ SL 12:4

Obstacles to Christian faith: other people we see in church*
•SL 12-14 ❖ SL 2:2-4

Obstacles to Christian faith: reading the life of Christ as merely a human life*
•RP 116 ❖ RP 11:12

Obstacles to Christian faith: "Salvation is constantly associated with palms, crowns, white robes, thrones..."—makes no immediate appeal to me at all*
•WG 9, 11 ❖ WG 1:7, 9

Obstacles to Christian faith: Scripture can be read as merely human literature—no new discovery, no new method will ever prove either interpretation*
•RP 116-117 ❖ RP 11:12

Obstacles to Christian faith: "Spiritual things are spiritually discerned"*
•WG 64-65 ❖ WG 4:16

Obstacles to Christian faith: "Subjectivism"—the belief that morality is a subjective sentiment to be altered at will*
•CR 72-81 (*see also* CR 44-56; M 34-38; MC 17-35) ❖ CR ch. 6 (*see also* CR ch. 4; M ch. 5; MC I ch. 1-4)

Obstacles to Christian faith: "...the almost total absence from the minds of my audience of any sense of sin"
•GID 243-244 (*see also* GID 95-96, 181-182; MC 38-39; PP 55)
❖ GID II 12:6 (*see also* GID I 10:15-17; 22:13; MC I 5:4; PP 4:1)

Obstacles to Christian faith: The belief or disbelief of most people results from their upbringing and from the prevailing tone of the circles they live in*
•CR 170-171 ❖ CR 14:28

Obstacles to Christian faith: the case against prayer*
•GID 104-105, 217; LM 19-22, 35-39, 48; WLN 7 (*see also* CR 142-151)
❖ GID I 11:1-5; II 7:4; LM 4:1-9; ch. 7; 9:6, 7; WLN 1:14 (*see also* CR ch. 12)

Obstacles to Christian faith: the Church itself (incomprehensible liturgy, bad lyrics, errant church-goers, etc.)*
•SL 12-14 ❖ SL 2:2-4

Obstacles to Christian faith: the desire to call one's soul one's own"*
•SJ 237 (*see also* PP 80; SJ 172, 228; Self-reservation) ❖ SJ 15:8 (*see also* PP 5:8; SJ 11:8; 14:22; Self-reservation)

Obstacles to Christian faith: "The difficulty of converting an uneducated man nowadays lies in his complacency"
•CR 23 ❖ CR 2:35

Obstacles to Christian faith: the Myth of Evolutionism*
•CR 82-93 ❖ CR ch. 7

Obstacles to Christian faith: the pressure of the ordinary; "real life"*
•SL 8-10 ❖ SL 1:2-4

Obstacles to Christian faith: the problem of pain
•PP 26; GID 265 ❖ PP 2:1; GID II 16:47

Obstacles to Christian faith: "...the sceptic's conclusion that the so-called spiritual is really derived from the natural..."*
•WG 64 (*see also* RP 116-117)

❖ WG 4:15 (*see also* RP 11:12)

Obstacles to Christian faith: the secret wish that our faith should *not* be very strong*
•CR 43 (*see also* LM 114; SL 22-23)
❖ CR 3:12 (*see also* LM 21:7; SL 4:4)

Obstacles to Christian faith: the society of unbelievers*
•CR 42 (*see also* SL 45-49)
❖ CR 3:10 (*see also* SL ch. 10; 11:1)

Obstacles to Christian faith: the temptation to guard our worldly interests*
•WG 126-132 (*consider also* Self-reservation) ❖ WG ch. 9 (*consider also* Self-reservation)

Obstacles to Christian faith: The unbeliever's difficulties with the miraculous usually begin with his contempt or disgust for Christian imagery*
•M 68-70 ❖ M 10:2-4

Obstacles to Christian faith: "...this deliberate refusal to understand things from above"*
•WG 72 ❖ WG 4:29

Obstacles to Christian faith: Those who lose their Christian faith not usually reasoned out of it by honest argument; just drift away*
•MC 124 (*see also* CR 42)
❖ MC III 11:6 (*see also* CR 3:10)

Obstacles to Christian faith: Ultimate questions such as the meaning of existence not part of most people's thinking*
•GID 252-253 (*see also* SL 8-9*)
❖ GID II 14:10 (*see also* SL 1:2, 3*)

Obstacles to Christian faith: "...very little of the opposition we meet is inspired by malice or suspicion...It is based on genuine doubt..."*
•GID 242 ❖ GID II 12:3

Obstacles to Christian faith: "...we do not usually think about the next world till our hopes in this have been pretty well flattened out..."*
•CR 37 ❖ CR 3:2

Obstacles to Christian faith: We fear lest the demands of God may prove too inconvenient

•WG 127 (*see also* Self-reservation)
❖ WG 9:4 (*see also* Self-reservation)

Obstacles to Christian faith: "We feel, if we do not say, that the vision of God will come not to fulfill but to destroy our nature"*
•WG 67 (*see also* MC 141; SL 59; Personality) ❖ WG 4:21 (*see also* MC IV 2:3; SL 13:3, 4; Personality)

Obstacles to Christian faith: "We shrink from too naked a contact [in prayer], because we are afraid of the divine demands upon us which it might make too audible"*
•LM 114 (*see also* CR 43; LM 75; M 94; SL 22-23*, 54-55; WG 127-128)
❖ LM 21:8 (*see also* CR 3:12; LM 14:12; M 11:19; SL 4:4*; 12:3; WG 9:5)

Obstacles to Christian faith: "We *will* not turn to Him as long as He leaves us anything else to turn to"*
•LAL 49 (*see also* PP 97)
❖ LAL 16/12/55 (*see also* PP 6:8)

Obstacles to Christian perseverance: old habits*
•SL 11 ❖ SL 2:1

Obstacles to Christian perseverance: Suffering probably *not* among them, according to Screwtape, since humans have been told it is a part of Redemption*
•SL 27 ❖ SL 5:3

Obstacles to Christian perseverance listed by Screwtape ("The routine of adversity, the gradual decay of youthful loves and youthful hopes...")*
•SL 132 ❖ SL 28:1

Obstacles to Christian perseverance: vague guilt*
•SL 54-56 ❖ SL 12:3, 4

Obstacles to Lewis's acceptance of Christianity: "Christianity placed at the center what then seemed to me a transcendental Interferer"*
•SJ 171-172 ❖ SJ 11:8

Obstacles to Lewis's acceptance of Christianity: desire for "limited liabilities"*
•SJ 171 (*see also* WG 126-132; Limited Liabilities) ❖ SJ 11:8 (*see also* WG ch. 9; Limited Liabilities)

Obstacles to Lewis's acceptance of Christianity: his own intellect*
•SJ 173 (*see also* SJ 170)
❖ SJ 11:9, 10 (*see also* SJ 11:7)

Obstacles to Lewis's acceptance of Christianity: I tried to get the comforts both of a materialist and of a spiritual philosophy without the rigors*
•SJ 178 (*consider also* Religion, "popular") ❖ SJ 11:16 (*consider also* Religion, "popular")

Obstacles to Lewis's acceptance of Christianity: making a state of mind ("Joy") his aim and attempting to produce it*
•SJ 168 ❖ SJ 11:5

Obstacles to Lewis's acceptance of Christianity: "My lifelong fear of sentimentalism..."*
•SJ 173 (*see also* SJ 190)
❖ SJ 11:10 (*see also* SJ 12:12)

Obstacles to Lewis's acceptance of Christianity: "On the one side a many-islanded sea of poetry and myth; on the other a glib and shallow "rationalism"*
•SJ 170 ❖ SJ 11:7

Obstacles to Lewis's acceptance of Christianity: religious imagery
•WG 9, 11 ❖ WG 1:7, 9

Obstacles to Lewis's acceptance of Christianity: The Christian universe had no door marked "Exit" (whereas materialism offered limited liabilities)*
•SJ 171 (*see also* GO 33; SJ 228; *consider also* Limited liabilities)
❖ SJ 11:8 (*see also* GO 2:22; SJ 14:22; *consider also* Limited liabilities)

Obstacles to Lewis's acceptance of Christianity: "...the externals of Christianity made no appeal to my sense of beauty"*
•SJ 171-172 ❖ SJ 11:8

Obstacles to Lewis's acceptance of Christianity: the "sentimentality and cheapness" of much Christian hymnody
•CR 13 (*see also* SJ 172, 234; Hymns)
❖ CR 2:3 (*see also* SJ 11:8; 15:6; Hymns)

Obstacles to Lewis's acceptance of Christianity: the World, the Flesh, and the Devil*

•SJ 176, 178 ❖ SJ 11:13, 17

Obstacles to Lewis's acceptance of Christianity: What I wanted was some area of my soul of which I could say, "This is my business and mine only"*
•SJ 172 ❖ SJ 11:8

Obstacles to our perception of ordinary pleasures as blessings from God: inattention, greed, and conceit
•LM 90 ❖ LM 17:10

Obstacles to prayer: gravitation away from God to self, which is a product of the Fall*
•PP 76 (*see also* PP 83, 91)
❖ PP 5:5 (*see also* PP 5:10; 6:3)

Obstacles to prayer in an empty church: distractions of organ practice, etc.
•LM 17 ❖ LM 3:8

Obstacles to prayer: introspection (trying to make a feeling or a state of mind your aim)*
•L 256 (*see also* L 202; SJ 61-62; SL 20-21) ❖ L 31 Jul 54 (*see also* L 22 Dec 42; SJ 4:8; SL 4:3)

Obstacles to prayer: It is no use to ask God for "A" when our whole mind is in reality filled with desire for "B"*
•LM 22-23 ❖ LM 4:15-18

Obstacles to prayer: making our reluctance to pray and our wandering mind an object of our will-power rather than a subject of our prayers*
•SL 125-126 (*see also* LM 23)
❖ SL 27:1 (*see also* LM 4:18, 19)

Obstacles to prayer: money, sex, status, grievances, the radio, crowds, sedation, newspapers, etc.*
•CR 168-169 ❖ CR 14:17, 18

Obstacles to prayer: Perfect silence and solitude may leave one more open to the distractions which come from within*
•LM 18 ❖ LM 3:11

Obstacles to prayer: putting it last thing at night*
•L 256 (*see also* LM 16, 18)
❖ L 31 Jul 54 (*see also* LM 3:7, 10)

Obstacles to prayer: Screwtape himself (The Devil)*
•SL 19-23, 125-129 ❖ SL ch. 4; ch. 27

Obstacles to prayer, Screwtape lists: Noise ("Music and silence—how I detest them both!")*
•SL 102-103 ❖ SL 22:5

Obstacles to prayer: sins, avoidable immersion in worldly things, and neglect of mental discipline
•LM 114 ❖ LM 21:8

Obstacles to prayer: "...the man will not venture within reach of the eternal until he has made the things temporal safe in advance"
•WG 126-132, esp. 128 (consider also Safety; Self-reservation)
❖ WG ch. 9, esp. 9:5 (consider also Safety; Self-reservation)

Obstacles to prayer: the multiple distractions of domesticity; the practical and prudential cares of this world; petty anxieties and decisions
•FL 137-138 ❖ FL 5:10

Obstacles to prayer: We feel our time is "our own," and God's share in it is a tribute we must pay out of "our own" pocket*
•PP 75 ❖ PP 5:5

Obstacles to prayer: We may sometimes be deterred from small prayers by a sense of our own dignity rather than God's; we must not be too high-minded
•LM 23 ❖ LM 4:20

Obstacles to prayer: "We shrink from too naked a contact, because we are afraid of the divine demands upon us which it might make too audible"*
•LM 114 (see also CR 43; LM 75; M 94; SL 22-23*, 54-55; WG 127-128)
❖ LM 21:8 (see also CR 3:12; LM 14:12; M 11:19; SL 4:4*; 12:3; WG 9:4, 5)

Obstinacy in Belief, On (chapter title)
•WLN 13-30 (see also CR 42-43; MC 121-123) ❖ WLN ch. 2 (see also CR 3:10-12; MC III 11:1-5)

Obstinate Toy Soldiers, The (chapter title)
•MC 154-157 ❖ MC IV ch. 5

Occult—see also Spiritualism

Occult and Magic, Lewis's interest in, during his youth
•SJ 59-60, 174-178 ❖ SJ 4:6; 11:12-16

Occult as encountered by Lewis through the writings of Maeterlinck
•SJ 175-178 ❖ SJ 11:12-16

Occult, at "Chartres" I developed a passion for the
•SJ 59-60 (see also SJ 175)
❖ SJ 4:6 (see also SJ 11:12)

Occult, I had learned a wholesome antipathy to, which was to stand me in good stead when, at Oxford, I was to meet Magicians, Spiritualists, and the like
•SJ 178 ❖ SJ 11:16

Occult, I thought my friends [Harwood and Barfield] were falling under that ravenous salt lust for the
•SJ 207 ❖ SJ 13:15

Occult: Ignorance, incapacity, and cowardice as three things which Lewis said protected him as he became interested in the Occult
•SJ 176 ❖ SJ 11:14

Occult, in approaching the, my fear gave me a fresh motive for wishing Materialism to be true; that creed excludes the bogies
•SJ 176, 177 ❖ SJ 11:14, 16

Occult, "Joy" as it related (or did not relate) to Lewis's interest in the, during his youth
•SJ 175-177 (see also SJ 204)
❖ SJ 11:13-15 (see also SJ 13:10)

Occult: "My best protection was the known nature of Joy"
•SJ 177 ❖ SJ 11:14, 15

Occult: "Not that the ravenous lust was never to tempt me again but that I now knew it for a temptation"—and I now knew Joy did not point in that direction
•SJ 178 ❖ SJ 11:16

Occult, passion for, as "a spiritual lust; and like the lust of the body it has the fatal power of making everything else in the world seem uninteresting..."
•SJ 60 (see also SJ 177, 178)
❖ SJ 4:6 (see also SJ 11:14, 16)

Occult: Raising a spirit might have been extremely interesting, "but the real Desirable would have evaded one..."

•SJ 177 ❖ SJ 11:14

Occult vs. "Joy": "Slowly, and with many relapses, I came to see that the magical conclusion was just as irrelevant to Joy as the erotic conclusion had been"
•SJ 177 (see also SJ 203-204)
❖ SJ 11:14 (see also SJ 13:10)

Occupation(s)—see also Job; Work

Occupation, choice of: We must try to earn our living by doing well what would be worth doing even if we had not our living to earn
•WLN 78 (see also MC 80)
❖ WLN 5:16 (see also MC III 3:4)

Occupation, need for money of itself is apparently an innocent (though by no means a splendid) motive for any, (re: "cultural" occupations such as teaching)
•CR 20 ❖ CR 2:23

Occupations such as teaching, writing, reviewing, etc. may be justified provided there is a demand for "culture," and that culture is in fact harmless
•CR 20 ❖ CR 2:23

Occupations we naturally like may be as much a part of our "service" to God as our hardest duties
•WG 130 ❖ WG 9:9

Ocean—see Beach; Sea; consider Ship(s)

Odour "which is death to us until we allow it to become life" as that Christian element which Lewis met in various works of literature
•GID 203-204 ❖ GID II 4:5

Offerings to God, all our, are like the intrinsically worthless present of a child, which a father values indeed, but only for the intention (re: church music)
•CR 99 ❖ CR 8:12

Offerings: We cannot give God anything that is not His already*
•MC 125 (see also SL 96-99)
❖ MC III 11:9 (see also SL 21:2-6)

Old age—see Aging

Old People's Homes: "If you ever do have to go to a Home, Christ will be there just as much as in any other place"
•LAL 94 ❖ LAL 24 Nov 60

Old People's Homes: "In your position I myself would prefer a 'Home'—or almost anything—to solitude"
•LAL 102 ❖ LAL 17 Jan 62

Old People's Homes: Sometimes the things we have most dreaded turn out to be quite nice
•LAL 94 ❖ LAL 24 Nov 60

Old Testament—see Bible—Old Testament

Oldie's school (Lewis's first school, which he called "Belsen" for anonymity) described
•SJ 24-37, 49, 126 ❖ SJ 2:4-16; 3:8; 8:8

"Olympian" defined: tranquil and tolerant, vs. "Titanic" (restive, militant and embittered)—re: circles of Friends
•FL 120 ❖ FL 4:53

Omission, in parable of Sheep and Goats the "Goats" are condemned entirely for their sins of
•RP 9 ❖ RP 2:1

Omnipotence, Divine (chapter title)
•PP 26-36 ❖ PP ch. 2

Omnipotence of God means power to do all that is intrinsically possible, not to do the intrinsically impossible
•PP 26-28 ❖ PP 2:2-4

Omnipotence of God: Regarding the impossibility of "tinkering with the creation as though this or that element of it could have been removed"
•PP 35 ❖ PP 2:16

Omnipresence of God—consider also Pantheism

Omnipresence of God: Much wiser to think of the Divine presence being in particular objects than just of "omnipresence," which gives idea of something like a gas
•LM 74 (see also M 74-75, 87, 91-92)
❖ LM 14:9 (see also M 10:13; 11:10, 16)

Omnipresence of God: "The higher the creature, the more, and also the less, God is in it; the more present by grace, and the less present...as mere power"
•LM 74 ❖ LM 14:9

Omnipresence of God: "We may ignore, but we can nowhere evade, the presence of God. The world is crowded

with Him"
•LM 75 ❖ LM 14:11
Omniscience of Christ ("God Incarnate"):
"The answer of the theologians is that
the God-Man was omniscient as God,
and ignorant as Man"
•WLN 99 ❖ WLN 7:10
Omniscience of Christ: How the omni-
science of God was affected by His be-
coming a man
•MC 147-148 ❖ MC IV 3:10
Omniscience of Christ: I certainly think
that Christ was not omniscient, if only
because a human brain would not be
capable of omniscient consciousness
•PP 134 ❖ PP 9:6
Omniscience of God: God created the universe already foreseeing the Crucifixion
•FL 176 ❖ FL 6:21
Omniscience of God: How can God foresee our acts and yet leave us free not
to do them?
•MC 148-149 (*see also* SL 126-128; Free
will) ❖ MC IV 3:11 (*see also* SL 27:3, 4;
Free will)
Omniscience of God, Our Lord has reminded us not to pray as if we forgot
the
•LM 19 ❖ LM 4:2
Omniscience of God with regard to
prayer: If God is omniscient, why do
we need to confess our sins and "make
known" our requests?
•LM 19-22 (*see also* CR 142*; GID 104-
105; L 149, 217)
❖ LM 4:1-9 (*see also* CR 12:2*; GID I
11:1-5; L 21 Feb 32; 1 Aug 49)
Ontological Argument, I sometimes wonder whether the, did not arise as an
attempt at a translation of an experience without concepts or words
•CR 141 ❖ CR 11:25
Ontological Proof, Descartes', mentioned
with regard to the existence of God
•GID 173 (*see also* L 143)
❖ GID I 21:3 (*see also* L 24 Oct 31)
Opinion, I take a very low view of climates of; all discoveries are made and
all errors are corrected by those who
ignore the "climate of opinion"

•PP 134 ❖ PP 9:6
Opinion of others about ourselves: "Every now and then we discover what
our fellow creatures really think of
us"; God's opinion will be infallible
•WLN 112-113 ❖ WLN 7:36, 37
Opinion of others about ourselves: "... we
all wish to be judged by our peers...
theirs is the praise we really covet and
the blame we really dread"
•FL 114 ❖ FL 4:44
Opinion, the great thing is to make your
patient value an, for some quality
other than truth (—Screwtape)
•SL 64 ❖ SL 14:4
Opposites, devil always sends errors into
the world in pairs of; we must go
straight through between both errors
•MC 160 (*see also* WG 108; WLN 94-
95)
❖ MC IV 6:4 (*see also* WG 7:3; WLN 7:4)
Opposition, in my experience the bitterest, comes neither from thoroughgoing believers nor from atheists, but
from semi-believers of all complexions
•RP 7-8 ❖ RP 1:13
Opposition, Lewis describes some of the,
which he encountered after becoming
a Christian
•GID 252 ❖ GID II 14:9
Opposition to Christianity—*see also* Obstacles to Christian faith
Opposition to Christianity: Defenders are
opposed not by the irreligion of their
hearers but by their vague, Pantheistic religion*
•M 81 ❖ M 11:2
Opposition to Christianity may sometimes
call itself "Christianity"*
•GID 223 ❖ GID II 8:13
Opposition to Christianity: Much of the
bitterness against religion arises out
of the suffering of puzzled, jealous
loved ones of new converts
•L 274 (*see also* FL 61, 70-73; SL 18)
❖ L 10 Feb 57 (*see also* FL 3:13, 27-32;
SL 3:6)
Opposition to Christianity or Theism often inspired by genuine doubt

•GID 242 ❖ GID II 12:3

Opposition to Christianity: Our opponents had to correct their ignorance of
the faith they supposed themselves to
be rejecting (re: Socratic Club)
•GID 127 ❖ GID I 15:3

Opposition to Christianity, reasons for
development of, (its demand for total
surrender, etc.)
•GID 222-223 ❖ GID II 8:12

Oppression—*consider also* Persecution

Oppression, hardly any amount of, from
above takes the heart out of a boy like
oppression from his fellows
•SJ 31 ❖ SJ 2:11

Oppression ("humiliation"): We should
mind it less if we were humbler*
•LAL 29 ❖ LAL Mar 31st 54

Oppression tempts the oppressed to the
sin of hatred
•CR 118-120; RP 24-26
❖ CR 10:9-12; RP 3:9-11

Oppression: The modern man, having discovered that there is oppression, immediately asks how he can join the
ranks of the oppressors (re: current
lack of thirst for justice)
•CR 122 (*see also* RP 69-70)
❖ CR 10:19 (*see also* RP 7:7, 8)

Oppression: Where it does not completely
and permanently break the spirit, has
it not a natural tendency to produce
retaliatory pride and contempt?
•SJ 107 ❖ SJ 7:8

Optimism as a belief system which has an
"obvious" attraction but meets insuperable obstacles later on
•M 131 ❖ M 14:36

Optimism, cause for ultimate: "All will be
well and all manner of thing will be
well" (quote from Julian of Norwich)*
•CR 123; GID 169; GO 75; L 186
❖ CR 10:22; GID I 20:Reply-11; GO
4:12; L 2 Jun 40

Optimism, example of Lewis's: "Say what
you like, Barfield, the world is sillier
and better fun than they make out..."*
•L 217 ❖ L 4 Apr 49

"Optimism," Lewis's essay on, mentioned
•L 53, 61-63 ❖ L 21 Jan 21; 29 May 21;
27 Jun 21; 1 Jul 21

Optimism nor pessimism, Christianity
offers neither the attractions of
•WG 75 (*see also* GID 51-52; SJ 204)
❖ WG 5:5 (*see also* GID I 4:18, 19—
Ques. 5; SJ 13:11)

Optimist, it is hard being the only, (a
tongue-in-cheek reference to himself)
•L 163 ❖ L 8 Feb 39

Optimists and pessimists ("Imagine a set
of people all living in the same building. Half of them think it is a hotel...")*
•GID 52 ❖ GID I 4:18, 19 (Ques. 5)

Orchestra analogy: We are now merely
tuning our instruments, as Donne says
[learning to praise God, in anticipation of the "symphony" of Heaven]
•RP 97 (*see also* LM 116)
❖ RP 9:7 (*see also* LM 21:15)

Orchestra ("band") analogy to illustrate
importance and operation of morality
•MC 71 ❖ MC III 1:3-5

Orchestra, if all experienced God and
worshipped Him in the same way it
would be like an, in which all the instruments played the same note
•PP 150 ❖ PP 10:7

Orchestra ("symphony"): Our prayers are
known to us only as we pray them—
"But they are eternally in the score of
the great symphony"
•LM 110 (*see also* GID 79; L 217; LM
48, 50; M 176-180; SL 127-128) ❖ LM
20:16 (*see also* GID I 8:9; L 1 Aug 49;
LM 9:5, 12; M App. B:10-18; SL 27:4)

Organ, of all musical instruments I liked
(and like) the, least
•SJ 234 ❖ SJ 15:6

Organization(s)—*see also* Bureaucracy

Organization, church, vs. the congregational principle discussed by
Screwtape: The congregational principle makes each church into a kind
of club or faction
•SL 73 ❖ SL 16:2

Organization: Devil used to prevent
people from doing good works; now
he just *organizes* them

•LAL 58 ❖ LAL 5/7/56

Organization, since the Fall no, has a natural tendency to go right (re: the false sentiment that the home is a panacea bound to produce happiness)
•GID 284 ❖ GID III 3:6

Original sin, doctrine of*
•PP 69-88 ❖ PP ch. 5

Original sin, if I call our present condition one of, and not merely one of original misfortune, that is because our religious experience allows no other way
•PP 85 ❖ PP 5:12

Original sin: "...I'm not saying...that evil is inherent in finitude. That would identify the creation with the fall and make God the author of evil"*
•LM 44 ❖ LM 8:12

Original sin: "We inherit a whole system of desires which do not necessarily contradict God's will but which... steadfastly ignore it"*
•PP 98-99 ❖ PP 6:10

Originality can only come unsought; "No man who values originality will ever be original"
•WG 119 (*see also* MC 190)
❖ WG 7:19 (*see also* MC IV 11:15)

Originality: "Even in literature and art, no man who bothers about originality will ever be original"
•MC 190 ❖ MC IV 11:15

Originality: The basis of all literary criticism should be the maxim that an author never brings into existence beauty or wisdom which did not exist before
•CR 7 ❖ CR 1:11

Originality, the pother about, all comes from people who have nothing to say
•L 201
❖ L undated letter just before 13 Oct 42

Originality the prerogative of God alone; even seems to be confined to the Father (re: "originality" in literature)
•CR 6-7 ❖ CR 1:10

Originality: "...we can create nothing new, but can only rearrange our material provided through sense data"
•GID 276 ❖ GID III 1:19

Originality: We can never actually create anything new but can only recombine elements borrowed from the real universe
•M 32-33 ❖ M 4:14

Originality: "We—even our poets and musicians and inventors—never, in the ultimate sense, *make*. We only build. We always have materials to build from"
•LM 73 (*see also* L 203-204)
❖ LM 14:3 (*see also* L 20 Feb 43)

Orthodox listed among those who have retained more of the gusto of the Psalmists than the Anglicans
•RP 52 ❖ RP 5:10

Orual (*Till We Have Faces*) mentioned as an instance of human affection in its natural condition
•L 274 ❖ L 10 Feb 57

Orwell, George, mentioned as one who "preferred sexuality in its native condition, uncontaminated by Eros" (romantic love)
•FL 134 ❖ FL 5:4

Osteoporosis, Lewis refers to his
•LAL 67, 68, 70, 71, 83
❖ LAL Jun 18th; Aug 12th 57; Nov 3d 57; Nov 30th 57; 14/1/58; Jun 7th 59

Ostrich, you know you ought to be a Man and not an, hiding its head in the sand (re: evasion of Christ out of fear of duty)
•GID 111 ❖ GID I 12:8

Other, God as the naked
•SJ 221 ❖ SJ 14:12

Other people—*see* Human Beings; Neighbors; People; Relations, interpersonal; *consider* Judging

Otherness, sense of, was the most precious gift that marriage gave me—this constant impact of something very close and intimate yet unmistakably other; real
•GO 19-24, esp. 20 (*see also* GO 59, 64-65, 76-78) ❖ GO 2:3-7, esp. 2:4 (*see also* GO 3:33, 34, 41; 4:14-18)

Out of the Silent Planet: "...any amount of theology can now be smuggled into people's minds under cover of ro-

mance without their knowing it"
- •L 167 ❖ L 9 Jul 39

Out of the Silent Planet, Lewis mentions, as imagining "what God might be supposed to have done in other worlds"
- •L 261 ❖ L 2 Feb 55

Out of the Silent Planet: "…I tried to get the *good* element in the martial spirit, the discipline and freedom from anxiety"
- •L 209 ❖ L 31 Jan 46

Out of the Silent Planet: I was trying to redeem for genuinely imaginative purposes the form known as "science fiction"
- •L 295 ❖ L undated letter of Aug 1960

Out of the Silent Planet mentioned
- •LAL 27 ❖ LAL Feb 22/54

Out of the Silent Planet: Most reviewers thought my idea of the fall of the Bent One was an invention of my own
- •L 167 ❖ L 9 Jul 39

Out of the Silent Planet, reason for writing, explained
- •L 166-167 ❖ L 9 Jul 39

"**Outsiders**" and "Insiders" mentioned with reference to Inner Rings
- •WG 95-105 (*see also* Inner Rings)
- ❖ WG 6:4-18 (*see also* Inner Rings)

"Outsiders" mentioned with reference to circles of friends
- •FL 116-122 ❖ FL 4:47-55

Outsiders, there are two kinds of, whom the theologian needs to study: the uneducated, and those who are educated in some way but not in his way
- •CR 152-153 ❖ CR 13:1, 2

Overpopulation: "Unemployment" an alternative (and more charitable) term for "surplus population"*
- •WLN 79 ❖ WLN 5:20

Oversensitivity as "the most powerful engine of domestic tyranny…we should be merciless to its first appearance in ourselves"*
- •RP 14 ❖ RP 2:9

Overzealousness: We may embrace tasks never intended for us
- •WG 129-130 ❖ WG 9:8

Ownership forbidden in heaven; each soul will be eternally engaged in giving away to all the rest that which it receives
- •PP 149, 151 ❖ PP 10:7, 9

Ownership, men's belief in their, of their bodies causes much of the modern resistance to chastity
- •SL 97-98 ❖ SL 21:4

Ownership, Screwtape advises that the sense of, is always to be encouraged in humans
- •SL 97-99 ❖ SL 21:4-6

Ownership: We cannot give God anything that is not His already
- •MC 125 (*see also* SL 96-99)
- ❖MC III 11:9 (*see also* SL 21:2-6)

Oxford, after a really beautiful walk through an empty and twilit, I was in bed by five (re: Lewis's Home Guard duty during World War II)
- •L 189 ❖ L 11 Aug 40

Oxford, both a decline of "religion" and a revival of Christianity going on at
- •GID 218 ❖ GID II 8:1

Oxford, Lewis describes his first visit to, in which he sat for the entrance exam
- •L 32-33; SJ 184-185
- ❖ L Dec 1916; SJ 12:3, 4

Oxford, Lewis describes the growth of, in his day
- •WG 106-107 ❖ WG 7:2

Oxford, "dreaming spires" of
- •SJ 184 ❖ SJ 12:3

Oxford, Lewis describes an ordinary day for him while at
- •L 144 (*see also* L 214)
- ❖ L 22 Nov 31 (*see also* L 29 May 48)

Oxford, Lewis describes his work as a Don (professor) at
- •L 214 ❖ L 29 May 48

Oxford, Lewis relates his election to a Fellowship at Magdalen College of
- •L 100-103
- ❖ L undated letter of "April or May" 1925; 26 May 25; 14 Aug 25

Oxford, Lewis relates his return to, after serving in the war
- •L 46-47 ❖ L 27 Jan 19

Oxford: Magdalen College described
- •L 104-105 ❖ L 21 Oct 25

Oxford: Magdalene College, Cambridge, compared to Magdalen College, Oxford
- •LAL 35 (*see also* LAL 32)
- ❖ LAL Nov 1st 54 (*see also* LAL Sep 19/54)

Oxford professors described
- •L 59-60 ❖ L 10 May 21

Oxford Socratic Club, The Founding of the (chapter title)
- •GID 126-128 ❖ GID I ch. 15

Oxford in wartime described
- •L 34-38; SJ 187
- ❖ L undated letter postmarked 28 Apr 17 through undated letter postmarked 18 Jul 17; SJ 12:8

P

Pacifism—*consider also* War

Pacifism, ardent, and extreme patriotism both mentioned by Screwtape as serving his purposes
- •SL 25, 33-35 ❖ SL 5:1; 7:2, 3

Pacifism, as a Christian effort to deal with the evil of war, has always been a failure
- •GID 327 ❖ GID IV Letter 1

Pacifism either amounts to nothing or defeats itself
- •WG 44 ❖ WG 3:19

Pacifism: "I have no sympathy with the modern view that killing or being killed is a great evil"
- •L 176 ❖ L 17 Jan 40

Pacifism: If war is ever lawful, then peace is sometimes sinful
- •GID 326 ❖ GID IV Letter 1

Pacifism: "...if you cannot restrain a man by any method except by trying to kill him, then it seems to me a Christian must do that"
- •GID 49 ❖ GID I 4:3 (Ques. 1)

Pacifism implies a materialistic ethic—that death and pain are the greatest evils; I do not think they are
- •WG 43 (*see also* SL 131-132; Death)
- ❖ WG 3:18 (*see also* SL 28:1; Death)

Pacifism: In the commandment "Thou shalt not kill" the word "kill" means "murder"
- •L 247; MC 106-107
- ❖ L 8 Nov 52; MC III 7:7

Pacifism: "It is...in my opinion perfectly

right for a...Christian soldier to kill an enemy"
•MC 106 ❖ MC III 7:8

Pacifism, Lewis's case against
•WG 33-53 ❖ WG ch. 3

Pacifism, pure motives not likely in
•WG51-52❖WG3:30

Pacifism: Regarding the man who "just feels" that all killing of human beings is in all circumstances an absolute evil
•WG 39-41 ❖ WG 3:12-14

Pacifism, sayings of Our Lord as they relate to
•WG 48-51 ❖ WG 3:26-29

Pacifism, Screwtape mentions, which is adopted not on moral grounds but from a habit of belittling others and from "a dash of purely fashionable...communism"
•SL 45-46 ❖ SL 10:1

Pacifism: Screwtape speaks on conscientious objection to war
•SL 34-35 ❖ SL 7:3, 4

Pacifism: Three ways of taking the command to turn the other cheek
•WG 49-51 ❖ WG 3:28, 29

Pacifism: When Jesus praised the Centurion He never hinted that the military profession in itself was sinful
•L 248 ❖ L 8 Nov 52

Pacifist, Buddhism mentioned as the only civilised religion which is genuinely
•WG 47 ❖ WG 3:26

Pacifist, I can respect an honest, though I think he is entirely mistaken
•MC 106-107 ❖ MC III 7:8

Pacifist, I'm not a, but death would be better than to live through another war
•L 166 ❖ L 8 May 39

Pacifist, Why I Am Not A (chapter title)
•WG 33-53 ❖ WG ch. 3

Pacifists tolerated only in liberal societies
•WG 44 ❖ WG 3:19

Pacifists, we must respect and tolerate, but I think their view erroneous
•L 247-248 ❖ L 8 Nov 52

Pagan animism "an anthropomorphic failure of imagination"
•L 89 ❖ L 7 Jul 23

Pagan animism, the delicious variety of, is in a way more attractive than Christianity
•WG 76 ❖ WG 5:5

Pagan anticipation of the truth, Homer's idea that only a drink of sacrificial blood can restore a ghost to rationality may show
•RP 37-38 ❖ RP 4:8

Pagan deities, Law of God when compared with that of, must have shown with an extraordinary radiance
•RP 62, 64 ❖ RP 6:12, 14

Pagan hearers of the Gospel could be assumed to have a real consciousness of deserving the Divine anger
•PP 55 ❖ PP 4:1

"Pagan," Hindus as, —but not in the popular modern sense, which means pretty nearly "irreligious"
•LAL 60, 62 ❖ LAL 3/8/56; Sep 8/56

Pagan, I have been a converted, living among apostate Puritans
•SJ 69 ❖ SJ 4:18

"Pagan" in the proper sense means Polytheist
•LAL 62 ❖ Sep 8/56

Pagan literature vs. the Psalms: "One's first impression is that the Jews were much more vindictive and vitriolic than the Pagans"
•RP 27-31 ❖ RP 3:14-20

Pagan mythologies, history as seen by the various, and the "Historicism" evident in them
•CR 102-104 ❖ CR 9:5-7

Pagan mythology, death and rebirth pattern in, not accidental; it teaches the truth that man himself must undergo some sort of death if he would truly live
•RP 106-107 (*see also* Death and Rebirth pattern) ❖ RP 10:11 (*see also* Death and Rebirth pattern)

Pagan mythology, desire for a "vague something" as seen in, shows a first and rudimentary form of "the idea of God"
•L 144 ❖ L 24 Oct 31

Pagan mythology: Norse gods, unlike the

Homeric, are beings rooted in a historical process (re: Historicism)
•CR 103 ❖ CR 9:7

Pagan myths have similarities to the "myth" of Christ; this resemblance can be interpreted in different ways
•RP 106-108; WG 82-85 (see also MC 54) ❖ RP 10:11; WG 5:14, 15 (see also MC II 3:9)

Pagan sacramental element in sex as one of the serious elements of the sexual act ("...the marriage of Sky-Father and Earth-Mother")
•FL 139-140, 145-147 ❖ FL 5:13, 23-25

Pagan theology, nothing separates, from Christianity so sharply as Aristotle's doctrine that God moves the universe to love Him, Himself unmoved
•PP 51-52 (see also GID 174*)
❖ PP 3:17 (see also GID I 21:5*)

Pagans may belong to Christ without knowing it
•MC 176-177 (see also MC 65; L 152-153; SL 26*) ❖ MC IV 10:4 (see also MC II 5:8; L 8 Apr 32; SL 5:2*)

Pagans more responsive to Christianity than the modern, post-Christian man
•GID 172 ❖ GID I 21:1

Paganism—see also Polytheism; consider also Mythology

Paganism, agnostic argument from similarities between Christianity and, works only if you know the answer
•GID 132 ❖ GID I 16:4

Paganism, ancient Judaism more like, in its externals and attitudes than like all the stuffiness which the word "religion" now suggests
•RP 44 ❖ RP 5:2

Paganism and mythology, we should expect to find in, some glimpse of that theme which we believe to be the very plot of the whole cosmic story
•WG 83 ❖ WG 5:15

Paganism as bearing "a likeness permitted by God to that truth on which all depends"
•RP 106-107 (see also MC 54)
❖ RP 10:11 (see also MC II 3:9)

Paganism, attraction of: It is a distortion

of the truth, and therefore retains some of its flavour
•GID 143-144 ❖ GID I 16:26

Paganism: "...Christ, in transcending and thus abrogating, also fulfills, both Paganism and Judaism..."
•RP 129 ❖ RP 12:9

Paganism does not merely survive but first becomes really itself in the very heart of Christianity
•L 258 ❖ L 1 Nov 54 (second letter)

Paganism: Even in the creation-myths, gods have beginnings
•RP 82 ❖ RP 8:11

Paganism had been only the childhood of religion, or only a prophetic dream. Where was the thing full grown? or where was the awakening?
•SJ 235 ❖ SJ 15:7

Paganism: I almost think I was sent back to the false gods to acquire some capacity for worship against the day when the true God should recall me to Himself
•SJ 77 ❖ SJ 5:9

Paganism, in, the god is the bridegroom of the mother-goddess, the earth (another sense in which Christ fulfils Paganism)
•RP 129 ❖ RP 12:9

Paganism includes a hazy doctrine of the Fall, but no real doctrine of Creation
•GID 149 ❖ GID I 17:6

Paganism, morality is always breaking in—even on
•PP 23 ❖ PP 1:13

Paganism, no one [in my youth] ever attempted to show me in what sense Christianity fulfilled, or Paganism prefigured Christianity
•SJ 62 (see also Death and Rebirth pattern) ❖ SJ 4:9 (see also Death and Rebirth pattern)

Paganism, Norse, possibly influenced by Christianity*
•CR 103 ❖ CR 9:7

Paganism: Only a few world religions have a theology; Greeks were not agreed on a systematic series of beliefs about Zeus

•WG 74 ❖ WG 5:2

Paganism, real, is dead
•GID 102 ❖ GID I 10:49

Paganism seen by some as nothing but the direct work of the Devil; "he 'makes his lies as like the truth as he can'"
•RP 106 ❖ RP 10:11

Paganism, stories about Creation in, are often religiously unimportant
•RP 78 ❖ RP 8:4

Paganism: Those who believed in many gods very seldom regarded those gods as creators of the universe and self-existent
•M 8 (see also GID 149)
❖ M 2:9 (see also GID I 17:6)

Paganism, true, is hospitable to all gods; ready to take any shape but able to retain none
•L 285 (see also L 267*)
❖ L 30 Apr 59 (see also L 8 Feb 56*)

Paganism, unfortunately the folly and idiot-cunning of, seem to have far more power of surviving than its innocent or even beautiful elements (re: "bargaining" in the Psalms)
•RP 98 ❖ RP 9:8

Paganism: "We have to hurl down false gods and also elicit the peculiar truth preserved in the worship of each"
•L 300 ❖ L 3 Dec 61

Paganism, where had, reached its maturity? There were really only two answers possible—either in Hinduism or in Christianity
•SJ 235-236 (see also CR 71; GID 102, 132) ❖ SJ 15:7 (see also CR 5:26; GID I 10:49; 16:4)

Pain—see also Difficulties; Grief; Sorrow; Suffering

Pain, 1st operation of: It shatters the illusion that all is well
•PP 92-95, 106 ❖ PP 6:5-8

Pain, 2nd operation of: It shatters the illusion of self-sufficiency—that what we have, whether good or bad in itself, is our own and enough for us
•PP 95-98, 102 (see also LAL 49*)
❖ PP 6:8, 9, 14 (see also LAL 16/12/55*)

Pain, 3rd operation of: It enables the full acting out of the self's surrender to God
•PP 98-101 ❖ PP 6:10-13

Pain, a duly subordinated intention to avoid, using lawful means, is in accordance with "nature"
•PP 113 ❖ PP 7:3

Pain, actual experience of, has no effect on one's reading or writing about the problem of pain
•L 172 ❖ L 3 Dec 39

Pain and death not the greatest evils (re: Pacifism)
•WG 43 (see also GID 297, 311, L 166; M 125; SL 131-132)
❖ WG 3:18 (see also GID III 4:20; 8:1; L 8 May 39; M 14:28; SL 28:1)

Pain and pleasure, categories of, recede when we think of eternity—as vaster good and evil looms in sight
•PP 126 (see also PP 153; SL 148)
❖ PP 8:9 (see also PP 10:11; SL 31:5)

Pain and self-sacrifice in this life not limited to Christians
•GID 53 ❖ GID I 4:24, 25 (Ques. 8)

Pain and suffering of mankind largely brought on by ourselves
•PP 89 ❖ PP 6:1

Pain, animal—see Animal pain

Pain below a certain intensity is not feared or resented and may even be pleasurable
•PP 32, 90 ❖ PP 2:13; 6:2

Pain, Christianity (in a sense) creates rather than solves the problem of, for in the midst of a painful world it assures us that ultimate reality is loving
•PP 24 ❖ PP 1:15

Pain: Courage helps more than knowledge, human sympathy more than courage, and the least tincture of the love of God more than all
•PP 10 ❖ PP P:1

Pain, experience of, as example of "looking along"
•GID 214 (see also L 172*)
❖ GID II 6:8 (see also L 3 Dec 39*)

Pain, experience of, precludes at that moment an intellectual understanding of pain; humans cannot experience and

intellectualize at the same time
- •GID 65-66 (*see also* L 172, 221; SJ 217-219) ❖ GID I 5:8 (*see also* L 3 Dec 39; 27 Sep 49; SJ 14:9, 10)

Pain, fear and pity as forms of, which help us in our return to obedience and charity
- •PP 105-016 ❖ PP 6:17

Pain, fear of: "We are not necessarily doubting that God will do the best for us; we are wondering how painful the best will turn out to be"
- •L 285 ❖ L 29 Apr 59

"Pain" has two senses: 1) a kind of sensation which may or may not be objectionable, or 2) any experience one dislikes
- •PP 90 ❖ PP 6:2

Pain, Human (chapter title)
- •PP 89-109, 110-117 ❖ PP ch. 6, 7

Pain, I believe that all, is contrary to God's will, absolutely but not relatively (analogy of removing thorn from child's finger)
- •L 237-238 ❖ L 31 Jan 52

Pain: I suppose the great saints really *want* to share the divine sufferings and that is how they can actually desire pain—but this is far beyond me
- •LAL 55-56 ❖ LAL 26/4/56

Pain, I was [in my youth] far more eager to escape, than to achieve happiness
- •SJ 171, 228 (*see also* SJ 117*)
- ❖ SJ 11:8; 14:22 (*see also* SJ 7:21*)

Pain: "If any man is safe from under-estimating this adversary, I am that man"
- •PP 10 (*see also* PP 105)
- ❖ PP P:1 (*see also* PP 6:16)

Pain, infliction of, always requires justification (re: vivisection)
- •GID 224-225 ❖ GID II 9:3

Pain, intellectualizing God and the problem of, when one is grieving: "Do I hope that if feeling disguises itself as thought I shall feel less?"*
- •GO 38 (*see also* GO 41, 43)
- ❖ GO 2:31 (*see also* GO 3:3, 4)

Pain is God's megaphone to rouse a deaf world
- •PP 93 ❖ PP 6:5

Pain is sterilized or disinfected evil; does not breed more pain as sin breeds sin, and that is why it is chiefly used by God to produce "complex good"
- •PP 116-117 ❖ PP 7:9

Pain is terrible, but surely you need not have fear as well? Can you not see death as the friend and deliverer?
- •LAL 117 ❖ LAL 17 Jun 63

Pain is unmasked, unmistakable evil; not only immediately recognisable evil, but evil impossible to ignore
- •PP 92-93 ❖ PP 6:5, 6

Pain, Lewis describes various kinds of, such as anxiety, loneliness, etc., which make it difficult to discuss the justification of suffering
- •PP 104-105 ❖ PP 6:16

Pain, Lewis's view of, in his youth: "...I had very definitely formed the opinion that the universe was, in the main, a rather regrettable institution"*
- •SJ 63 ❖ SJ 4:10

Pain, like all that is given to a creature with free will, is two-edged (can lead to knowledge or to final and unrepented rebellion)
- •PP 107, 118 (*see also* L 257*; PP 95)
- ❖ PP 6:18; 8:1 (*see also* L 1 Nov 54—first letter*; PP 6:7)

Pain, love may cause, to its object but only on the supposition that the object needs alteration to become fully lovable (re: God's love for us)
- •PP 55 ❖ PP 4:1

Pain may rouse the bad man to a knowledge that all is not well, but it might also lead to a final and unrepented rebellion
- •PP 95, 118 (*see also* PP 120-123)
- ❖ PP 6:7; 8:1 (*see also* PP 8:5-7)

Pain, physical vs. mental: Physical pain can be continuous; the mind has some power of evasion
- •GO 46-47 ❖ GO 3:11

Pain, possibility of, is inherent in the very existence of a world where souls can meet
- •PP 31-33, 89 ❖ PP 2:11-14; 6:1

Pain, problem of—*see also* Evil

Pain, problem of, and the laws of Nature
•PP 29-34 ❖ PP 2:6-15

Pain, problem of: Constant interference by God in the world to correct the results of our abuse of free will would result in the exclusion of free will*
•PP 33-34, 71 (see also PP 84)
❖ PP 2:15; 5:1 (see also PP 5:11)

Pain, problem of, discussed in response to a question
•GID 51-52 ❖ GID I 4:17-19 (Ques. 5)

Pain, problem of: "...even a boy can recognize that there is desert all round him though he, for the nonce, sits in an oasis"*
•SJ 65 ❖ SJ 4:11

Pain, problem of: Evil comes from the abuse of free will*
•PP 135 (see also M 121-122; MC 52-53; PP 69) ❖ PP 9:7 (see also M 14:23; MC II 3:3, 4; PP 5:1)

Pain, problem of: God cannot give a creature free will, and at the same time withhold the results of its free will from it*
•PP 28 ❖ PP 2:4

Pain, problem of: "If God's goodness is inconsistent with hurting us, then either God is not good or there is no God..."
•GO 31 ❖ GO 2:18

Pain, problem of: "If there is a good God, then these tortures are necessary. For no even moderately good Being could possibly...permit them if they weren't"*
•GO 50 ❖ GO 3:17

Pain, problem of: If we come to believe that God is evil, we usually find ourselves asking the "Great God" to curse him and bring him to nought
•GID 171 ❖ GID I 20:Reply-17

Pain, problem of: Lewis reacts to a friend's book on the subject as being "Emotional reaction rather than rational conviction"
•L 302-303 ❖ L 29 Dec 61

Pain, problem of: Love of God illustrated by parents who would rather see their children suffer much than be happy

in contemptible and estranging modes
•PP 41 ❖ PP 3:8

Pain, problem of, makes strong case against Christianity
•GID 265 ❖ GID II 16:47

Pain, problem of, no more urgent for us than for the great majority of monotheists down through the ages*
•GID 22 ❖ GID I 1:2

Pain, problem of, not insoluble if we understand the nature of the love of God and the place of man
•PP 47-48 ❖ PP 3:15

Pain, problem of, stated "in its simplest form"
•PP 26 ❖ PP 2:1

Pain, problem of: Suffering makes relevant and personal the question of whether God exists and whether He is good*
•GO 43 ❖ GO 3:4

Pain, problem of: "The conclusion I dread is not, 'So there's no God after all,' but, 'So this is what God's really like'..."*
•GO 5 ❖ GO 1:9

Pain, problem of, unanswerable if the terms "good" and "happy" always mean the same thing; having happiness is not always the same as having what's good for you
•PP 26 (see also PP 37-54)
❖ PP 2:1 (see also PP ch. 3)

Pain, problem of: "What really matters is the argument that there must be an answer..."
•GID 170 (see also GID 167-168*)
❖ GID I 20:Reply-15 (see also GID I 20:Reply-6*)

Pain, problem of: What we regard as a hideous interruption and curtailment of life is really the concrete situation*
•L 221 (see also L 161-162; SL 21:2, 3*)
❖ L 22 Sep 49 (see also L 12 Sep 38; SL 21:2, 3*)

Pain, problem of: "When I lay these questions before God I get no answer... more like a silent, certainly not uncompassionate, gaze"*
•GO 80-81 (see also GO 83)
❖ GO 4:24 (see also GO 4:29)

Pain, "romance" of, is unmasked as non-sense by five minutes of genuine toothache; and with it goes self-pity for imaginary distresses
•SL 58 ❖ SL 13:3

Pain rouses an evil man to the presence of evil in his existence; he either rebels (with possibility of deeper repentance later) or decides to change
•PP 95 ❖ PP 6:7

Pain, self-surrender to God demands; is never pleasant to fallen creatures
•PP 99-101 ❖ PP 6:11-13

Pain, some, may be necessary to awaken us to the existence of evil and the necessity for self-surrender
•PP 92-98, 106-107 ❖ PP 6:5-9, 17

Pain, the actual moment of present, is only the centre of the whole tribulational system which includes fear and pity
•PP 105 (see also Present)
❖ PP 6:17 (see also Present)

Pain: "The great thing...is to live from day to day and hour to hour not adding the past or future to the present"
•LAL 69 (see also LAL 58, 60, 79, 103; SL 29, 67-71*) ❖ LAL Oct 20th 57 (see also LAL 14/6/56; 3/8/56; Oct 30 58; 4 May 62; SL 6:2; ch. 15*)

Pain: The real problem is not why some humble, pious, believing people suffer, but why some do not
•PP 104 ❖ PP 6:15

Pain: "To grin and bear it and (in some feeble, desperate way) to trust is the utmost most of us can manage"
•LAL 56 ❖ LAL 26/4/56

Pain, we must not make the problem of, worse than it is by talking of "the sum of human misery"; there is no such thing, for no one suffers it
•PP 115-116 (see also WG 30-31)
❖ PP 7:8 (see also WG 2:14)

Pain: "What do people mean when they say 'I am not afraid of God because I know He is good?' Have they never been to a dentist?"
•GO 50-51 (see also God as Dentist)
❖ GO 3:19 (see also God as Dentist)

Pain: Whatever misery God permits will be for our ultimate good unless by rebellion we convert it to evil
•L 166 (see also GID 52*) ❖ L 8 May 39 (see also GID I 4:18, 19 Ques. 5*)

Pain: Why the cure for our sinfulness and self-will must be a painful process
•PP 89-117 ❖ PP ch. 6, 7

Pain, you can't really share someone else's weakness or fear or; there's a limit to the "one flesh" [of marriage]
•GO 13 ❖ GO 1:26

Pain, you would like to know how I behave when I am experiencing, not writing books about it; I will tell you— I am a great coward
•PP 105 (see also SJ 117*, 171)
❖ PP 6:16 (see also SJ 7:21*; 11:8)

Pains, even if there were, in heaven all who understand would desire them
•PP 126 (see also PP 152; SL 148)
❖ PP 8:9 (see also PP 10:9; SL 31:5)

Pains of Animals, The (chapter title)
•GID 161-171 (see also Animal pain)
❖ GID I ch. 20 (see also Animal pain)

Painter, God is the; we are only the picture
•MC 173 (see also LM 34, 69; MC 44; PP 42-43) ❖ MC IV 9:7 (see also LM 6:16; 13:4; MC II 1:4; PP 3:10)

Painting, mentally limited beings studying a, used to illustrate the impossibility of discovering by science how God works on Nature (illustration borrowed from Bergson)
•M 97 ❖ M 12:5

Pantheism—see also Religion, "popular"; consider also Naturalism; Omnipresence of God

Pantheism as a belief system which has an "obvious" attraction but meets insuperable obstacles later on
•M 131 ❖ M 14:36

Pantheism attractive because its God does nothing, demands nothing; He will not pursue you
•M 81, 93-94 (see also GID 142-143; MC 35, 136; SJ 209-210*; consider also Cost)
❖ M 11:2, 19 (see also GID I 16:25; MC I 4:6; IV 1:4; SJ 13:18*; consider also Cost)

Pantheism concludes that God is equally

present in evil and good and therefore indifferent to both
•M 84-85 (see also LM 74*)
❖ M 11:6 (see also LM 14:9*)

Pantheism, discussion of
•M 81-94; MC 43-45
❖ M ch. 11; MC II 1:3, 4

Pantheism: I have often found an immoral, naive, and sentimental Pantheism to be the chief obstacle to conversion
•GID 181 ❖ GID I 22:10

Pantheism, implications of believing
•GID 139-141 ❖ GID I 16:21, 22

Pantheism: In modern English audiences, one often encounters a Christianity tainted with Pantheistic elements
•GID 240-241 (see also GID 252)
❖ GID II 12:2 (see also GID II 14:9)

Pantheism: "In Pantheism, God is all. But the whole point of creation surely is that He was not content to be all. He intends to be 'all in all'"
•LM 70 ❖ LM 13:9

Pantheism, in, the universe is never something God made; it is an emanation...
•GID 149 (consider also Creation)
❖ GID I 17:6 (consider also Creation)

Pantheism is a creed not so much false as hopelessly behind the times; before creation it would have been true to say that everything was God
•PP 150-151 ❖ PP 10:8

Pantheism is a "religion" if the word "religion" means simply what man says about God, and not what God does about man
•M 83 ❖ M 11:4

Pantheism is hostile to nature, and Polytheism is nature-worship; neither leaves you free to enjoy your breakfast and mortify inordinate appetites
•GID 149 ❖ GID I 17:6

Pantheism: Lewis explains why it is more popular than Christianity
•M 154 (see also M 81, 93-94; MC 35*, 136) ❖ M 16:20 (see also M 11:2, 19; MC I 4:6*; IV 1:4)

Pantheism may be a road out of Christianity, but it may also be a road into it   (re: possible value of "sub-Chris-

tian" literature)*
•CR 22 (see also L 297) ❖ CR 2:29, 32 (see also L undated letter of Feb 61)

Pantheism, modern philosophy and science have both proved powerless to curb the human impulse toward
•M 83 ❖ M 11:4

Pantheism, morality is always breaking in—even on
•PP 23 ❖ PP 1:13

Pantheism, popular "religion" which excludes a miracle-performing God may be called; is the permanent natural bent of the human mind
•M 81-84 (see also L 227*; M 164-167)
❖ M 11:2-5 (see also L 5 Mar 51*; M 17:1-4)

Pantheism: "The doctrine of Creation in one sense empties Nature of divinity"; the created and the Creator cannot be one*
•RP 80 (consider also Creation)
❖ RP 8:8 (consider also Creation)

Pantheism, the majestic simplifications of, make it in a way more attractive than Christianity
•WG 75-76 ❖ WG 5:5

Pantheism, Theosophy, and Spiritualism as encountered by Lewis in the writings of Maeterlinck
•SJ 175 ❖ SJ 11:12

Pantheism thinly veils a mass of spontaneous picture-thinking; not as profound and mysterious as it seems
•M 84 ❖ M 11:6

Pantheism, two forms of, are theosophy and the worship of the life-force
•M 83 ❖ M 11:4

Pantheism vs. Christian theology, old atomic theory vs. quantum physics as analogy to, (re: the attractive simplicity of man's first guess vs. the truth)
•M 83-84 (see also PP 25)
❖ M 11:5 (see also PP 1:16)

Pantheism: We believe that the Holy Spirit can be present in the human spirit, but not, like the Pantheists, that we are "parts" of God
•PP 87 (see also LM 68-70)
❖ PP 5:13 (see also LM 13:2-9)

Pantheist, if a Monist starts from God he becomes a, whereas if he starts from Nature he becomes a Naturalist
  •M 165 ❖ M 17:2

Pantheist's and Idealist's idea of the material universe is that it is not quite real; a kind of mirage
  •CR 59 ❖ CR 5:5

Pantheists and Christians agree that God is present everywhere, but the Christian says that while God is in every point of space and time, He is *locally* in none
  •M 84 (*see also* LM 74*)
  ❖ M 11:6 (*see also* LM 14:9*)

Pantheists and Deists: Among the former, we must emphasize the relative independence of creatures; among the latter, the divine presence in all things
  •LM 74 ❖ LM 14:8

Pantheistic love of nature as one of the values implicit in romantic poetry
  •CR 16, 21-22 ❖ CR 2:13, 29, 32

Papist, Tolkien was a, and I had been (implicitly) warned at my first coming into the world never to trust a Papist
  •SJ 216 ❖ SJ 14:6

Parable of Lost Sheep: Man may be the one lost sheep that the Shepherd went in search of; in the parable the lost sheep was not the only sheep in the flock
  •GID 42-43, 100; M 122; WLN 86-87 (*see also* M 51-52*)
  ❖ GID I 3:9; 10:42; M 14:24; WLN 6:11 (*see also* M 7:13, 14*)

Parable of Lost Sheep: Who the "lost sheep" are
  •MC 181 ❖ MC IV 10:12

Parable of Prodigal Son: Man is the Prodigal Son of the universe
  •M 122 ❖ M 14:24

Parable of Prodigal Son: Screwtape makes mention of the elder brother who felt his sibling was "getting in on very easy terms"
  •SL 18 ❖ SL 3:6

Parable of Rich Man and Lazarus
  •RP 34 ❖ RP 4:3

Parable of Sheep and Goats: "Charity...

seems to be the point on which everything turns"
  •MC 81 (*see also* PP 114*)
  ❖ MC III 3:7 (*see also* PP 7:4*)

Parable of Sheep and Goats: "I take the whole parable to be about the judgement of the heathen"
  •FL 178 ❖ FL 6:24

Parable of Sheep and Goats is Our Lord's comment on helping people in need
  •LM 73 ❖ LM 14:4

Parable of Sheep and Goats makes our duty perfectly plain (re: alms)
  •LAL 108 ❖ LAL 26 Oct 62

Parable of Sheep and Goats points to Judgement; in it, the "Goats" are condemned entirely for their sins of omission
  •RP 9 ❖ RP 2:1

Parable of Sheep and Goats suggests that virtuous unbelievers may have a very pleasant surprise coming to them
  •L 196 ❖ L 8 Dec 41

Parable of Sheep and Goats: The "sheep" in the parable had no idea of the God hidden in the prisoner whom they visited
  •FL 178 ❖ FL 6:24

Parable of Sheep and Goats: There we see nothing about Predestination or even faith—all depends on works
  •L 251 ❖ L 3 Aug 53

Parable of Sheep and Goats: Those saved do not seem to know that they have served Christ
  •L 247 ❖ L 8 Nov 52

Parable of Sheep and Goats vs. Parable of Unjust Judge: The one portrays a characteristically Christian picture of judgement, the other a Jewish picture
  •RP 10-11 ❖ RP 2:3

Parable of Unjust Judge not so much poetry as a philosophic illustration
  •CR 4 ❖ CR 1:5

Parable of Unjust Judge portrays a characteristically Jewish picture of judgement—it is clearly a civil action
  •RP 10; CR 123-124 ❖ RP 2:3; CR 10:25

Parable of Unjust Judge teaches us about "praying to the end"

•LAL 23 ❖ LAL 27/xi/53

Parable of Unjust Judge teaches us that no evil habit is so ingrained that it cannot, even in old age, be whisked away
•LM 107 ❖ LM 20:1

Parable of Unjust Judge: "...what has been vainly asked for years can suddenly be granted" (re: the ability to forgive someone)
•LAL 120 ❖ LAL 6 Jul 63

Parable of Unjust Steward, the Master in, is the *world*
•L 286, 301 ❖ L 30 Apr 59; 20 Dec 61

Parable of Unjust Steward: The point is that we are denied many graces that we ask for because they would be our ruin
•L 301 ❖ L 20 Dec 61

Parables of Christ as a means of learning about the love and goodness of God
•M 92 ❖ M 11:17

Parachute, we regard God as an airman regards his; it's there for emergencies but he hopes he'll never have to use it
•PP 96 ❖ PP 6:8

Paradisal man—*see* Adam; Unfallen man

Paradise—*see also* Heaven

Paradise, as long as I live my imagination of, will retain something of my brother's toy garden
•SJ 7 (*see also* SJ 8, 16)
❖ SJ 1:4 (*see also* SJ 1:5, 15)

Paradoxes, Dominical, such as the Sermon on the Mount and Luke 14:26 are wholesome only to those who find them hard
•GID 182, 191-192 ❖ GID I 22:13; II 1:4

Paradoxes: If the universe has no meaning, we should never have found out that it has no meaning—just as "dark" has no meaning to creatures without eyes*
•MC 46 ❖ MC II 1:6

Paradoxes in Christianity: A man may have to "hate" his mother for the Lord's sake*
•GID 191 (*see also* FL 165-166, 171-173; RP 131-132) ❖ GID II 1:4 (*see also* FL 6:4, 17, 18; RP 12:10)

Paradoxes in Christianity: "...a man's most genuinely Christian activities may fall entirely outside that part of his life which he calls 'religious'"*
•LM 30-31 ❖ LM 6:6

Paradoxes in Christianity: A moderately bad man knows he is not very good; a thoroughly bad man thinks he is all right*
•MC 87 (*see also* GID 56-57; LAL 95; PP 55, top; 67; Self-knowledge)
❖ MC III 4:10 (*see also* GID I 4:38; LAL 9 Jan 61; PP 4:prelim. quote; PP 4:15; Self-knowledge)

Paradoxes in Christianity: A rejection of the natural self is the passport to everlasting life; nothing that has not died will be resurrected*
•WG 117 (*see also* Personality)
❖ WG 7:16 (*see also* Personality)

Paradoxes in Christianity: Pharisees and spoiled saints make better sport in Hell than mere common tyrants or debauchees (—Screwtape)*
•SL 105-106 ❖ SL 23:1

Paradoxes in Christianity: "Aim at Heaven and you will get earth 'thrown in': aim at earth and you will get neither"*
•MC 118 ❖ MC III 10:1

Paradoxes in Christianity: All people experience peaks and troughs in life; Screwtape explains why Christians seem to experience longer and deeper troughs*
•SL 37-39 ❖ SL 8:3, 4

Paradoxes in Christianity: An author may be "original" and yet completely dependent on a supernatural teacher*
•CR 7-9 (*see also* Originality)
❖ CR 1:12-14 (*see also* Originality)

Paradoxes in Christianity: "'Any road out of Jerusalem must also be a road into Jerusalem'" (re: the possible value of "sub-Christian" literature)*
•CR 22, 23 (*see also* L 297)
❖ CR 2:29, 34 (*see also* L undated letter of Feb 61)

Paradoxes in Christianity: As mere biological entities, we are of no account; but as organs in the Body of Christ, we are assured of our eternal self-identity*

•WG 117 ❖ WG 7:16

Paradoxes in Christianity: Belief in Heaven and Hell, coming too soon, may render impossible the development of the appetite for God*

•RP 39-40 (see also FL 189-190; GID 130-131; LM 120; SJ 231)

❖ RP 4:13-15 (see also FL 6:41-44; GID I 16:2, 3; LM 22:8; SJ 15:3)

Paradoxes in Christianity: By a high paradox, God enables men to have a Gift-love towards Himself; "'Our wills are ours to make them Thine'"

•FL 177-178 ❖ FL 6:24

Paradoxes in Christianity: By loving God more than our earthly loved ones, we shall love our earthly loved ones more than we do now*

•FL 191 ❖ FL 6:44

Paradoxes in Christianity: "Can I meet H. [Joy] again only if I learn to love her so much that I don't care whether I meet her or not?"*

•GO 79-80 (see also GO 29)

❖ GO 4:22 (see also GO 2:16)

Paradoxes in Christianity: Christianity both world-affirming and world-denying

•GID 147-150 ❖ GID I ch. 17

Paradoxes in Christianity: Comfort is the only thing you cannot get by looking for it; but if you look for truth, you may find comfort in the end*

•MC 39 ❖ MC I 5:4

Paradoxes in Christianity: "Death and Rebirth—go down to go up—it is a key principle. Through this...the highroad nearly always lies"*

•M 112 (see also GID 82-84; M 98, 124-125, 130, 151, 161; PP 149)

❖ M 14:6 (see also GID I 9:4-6; M 12:7; 14:26-28, 35; 16:6; 16:29; PP 10:7)

Paradoxes in Christianity: Demands of God which we least like in fact marshall us where we would want to go if we knew what we wanted*

•PP 52 (see also PP 90; WG 118-119)

❖ PP 3:18 (see also PP 6:3; WG 7:18)

Paradoxes in Christianity: Eros "ceases to be a devil only when it ceases to be a god" (quote from M. de Rougemont)*

•CR 35; FL 17-18; L 182 (see also FL 83, 151*, 156-157*, 160, 166*) ❖ CR 2:55; FL 1:13, 14, 29; L 26 Apr 40 (see also FL 3:45; 5:31*; 5:39-41*; 5:46; 6:5*)

Paradoxes in Christianity: Even the desire itself [for Heaven] lives only if you abandon it*

•PP 148, 149 ❖ PP 10:5, 7

Paradoxes in Christianity: Evil usually contains or imitates some good, which accounts for its potency (re: Fascism and Communism)*

•L 176 ❖ L 17 Jan 40

Paradoxes in Christianity: First things, when put first, increase the value of second things; if we put second things first, we lose both*

•GID 280-281; L 248 (see also FL 166; GID 150*; L 228, 269; LM 22; MC 118-119; RP 49)

❖ GID III 2:5-10; L 8 Nov 52 (see also FL 6:5; GID I 17:7*; L 23 Apr 51; 2 Apr 56; LM 4:14; MC III 9:1; RP 5:7)

Paradoxes in Christianity: "Give up yourself, and you will find your real self"*

•MC 190 (consider also Personality)

❖ MC IV 11:14, 15 (consider also Personality)

Paradoxes in Christianity: God gives back with His right hand what He takes away with His left (re: restoration of our self-love in its proper form)*

•SL 65 (see also GID 194*; L 155)

❖ SL 14:4 (see also GID II 2:3; L undated letter of 1933)

Paradoxes in Christianity: God wants a world full of beings united to Him but still distinct*

•SL 38 (see also GID 131; MC 141; SL 59, 81; WG 67, 117-118; Personality)

❖ SL 8:3 (see also GID I 16:3; MC IV 2:3; SL 13:4; 18:3, 4; WG 4:21, 22; 7:16, 17; Personality)

Paradoxes in Christianity: Hard sayings of Our Lord are wholesome only to those who find them hard*

•GID 191-192 (see also GID 182*; RP

131-132) ❖ GID II 1:4 (*see also* GID I 22:13*; RP 12:10)

Paradoxes in Christianity: "He that loseth his life shall find it"; surely this is the main purpose of life—to "die," to lose one's freedom and independence*
•LAL 97-98 ❖ LAL 28 Mar 61

Paradoxes in Christianity: Holy Spirit may be most operative when you can feel it least*
•L 241 ❖ bL 15 May 52

Paradoxes in Christianity: "Human will becomes truly creative and truly our own when it is wholly God's..."; he that loses his soul shall find it*
•PP 102 (*consider also* Personality)
❖ PP 6:14 (*consider also* Personality)

Paradoxes in Christianity: Humility is the road to pleasure*
•WG 113 ❖ WG 7:9

Paradoxes in Christianity: Hypocrites more curable than "goody-goodies" who are content in their routine piety and are attempting no deception*
•WLN 47-48 ❖ WLN 3:25, 26

Paradoxes in Christianity: "I became my own only when I gave myself to Another"
•L 251 (*see also* MC 141, 188-190; PP 152; SL 59; WG 117-118)
❖ L 17 Jul 53 (*see also* MC IV 2:3; 11:11-15; PP 10:10; SL 13:4; WG 7:16, 17)

Paradoxes in Christianity: "If the Divine call does not make us better, it will make us very much worse; of all bad men religious bad men are the worst"*
•RP 31-32 (*see also* L 301; RP 28)
❖ RP 3:20 (*see also* L 20 Dec 61; RP 3:17)

Paradoxes in Christianity: "If you think you are not conceited, it means you are very conceited indeed"*
•MC 114 ❖ MC III 8:14

Paradoxes in Christianity: Image of a Child in a manger doesn't suggest a king or bridegroom—but it would not suggest the Word, either, if we didn't know*
•RP 130 ❖ RP 12:10

Paradoxes in Christianity: In Christianity, the learned and the adult have no ad-vantage over the simple and the child*
•PP 79 (*see also* LM 103; PP 75*)
❖ PP 5:7 (*see also* LM 19:7; PP 5:5*)

Paradoxes in Christianity: In prayer we ought to be simultaneously aware of closest proximity and infinite dis-tance*
•LM 13 ❖ LM 2:13

Paradoxes in Christianity: In the Church we recover our real inequalities, and are offered refreshing opportunities for reverence and worship
•WG 113-116 (*see also* GID 84-85*; Inequality) ❖ WG 7:10-15 (*see also* GID I 9:7*; Inequality)

Paradoxes in Christianity: It gives back to those who abandon individualism an eternal possession of their own per-sonal being, even of their bodies*
•WG 117 (*see also* MC 141, 188-190; SL 59; Body/ies; Personality)
❖ WG 7:16 (*see also* MC IV 2:3; 11:11-15; SL 13:4; Body/ies; Personality)

Paradoxes in Christianity: It is dangerous to draw nearer to God; possibility of blacker sins as well as brighter vir-tues*
•L 301 (*see also* L 164*; RP 28-32)
❖ L 20 Dec 61 (*see also* L 5 Apr 39*; RP 3:17-20)

Paradoxes in Christianity: "It is great men, potential saints, not little men, who become merciless fanatics"*
•RP 28 (*see also* L 301; RP 31-32)
❖ RP 3:17 (*see also* L 20 Dec 61; RP 3:20)

Paradoxes in Christianity: Jesus says, "Take up your Cross" and then, "My yoke is easy and my burden light"*
•MC 167-168 ❖ MC IV 8:5

Paradoxes in Christianity: Look for Christ and you will find Him, and with Him everything else thrown in*
•MC 190 (*see also* GO 79*; MC 118-119)
❖ MC IV 11:15 (*see also* GO 4:21*; MC III 10:1)

Paradoxes in Christianity: "Lose your life and you will save it"*
•MC 190 ❖ MC IV 11:15

Paradoxes in Christianity: Love ceases to be a demon only when it ceases to be a god (quote from M. Denis de Rougemont)

•FL 17-18, 39 (see also CR 35; FL 83, 151*, 156-157*, 160, 166*; L 182) ❖ FL 1:13, 14, 29 (see also CR 2:56; FL 3:45; 5:31*; 5:39-41*; 5:46; 6:5*; L 16 Apr 40)

Paradoxes in Christianity: "Man approaches God most nearly when he is in one sense least like God"—i.e., needy, powerless, and penitent

•FL 14-15 ❖ FL 1:8

Paradoxes in Christianity: Mercy, detached from Justice, grows unmerciful (as in the "Humanitarian theory" of punishment)*

•GID 294 ❖ GID III 4:13

Paradoxes in Christianity: Natural loves must submit to be second things if they are to remain the things they want to be; they are "taller when they bow"*

•FL 166 (see also L 198-199, 228)

❖ FL 6:5 (see also L undated letter just before 20 Jan 42; 23 Apr 51)

Paradoxes in Christianity: "Nature dies on those who try to live for a love of nature"*

•FL 39 (see also L 228)

❖ FL 2:28 (see also L 23 Apr 51)

Paradoxes in Christianity: "Nice" people are just as much in need of salvation as miserable people—and possibly more difficult to save*

•MC 182 ❖ MC IV 10:15

Paradoxes in Christianity: "Nothing that you have not given away will ever really be yours"*

•MC 190 (see also GID 216)

❖ MC IV 11:15 (see also GID II 7:1)

Paradoxes in Christianity: "Nothing in you that has not died will ever be raised from the dead"*

•MC 190 ❖ MC IV 11:15

Paradoxes in Christianity: Obedience is the road to freedom*

•WG 113 (see also SL 37-38)

❖ WG 7:9 (see also SL 8:3)

Paradoxes in Christianity: Our attitude toward death: "Of all men, we hope most of death; yet nothing will recon-

cile us to...its unnaturalness"*

•GID 150 ❖ GID I 17:7

Paradoxes in Christianity: Perfect humility dispenses with modesty; glory, in the sense of obtaining approval by God, is scriptural*

•WG 11-13 ❖ WG 1:9, 10

Paradoxes in Christianity: Poverty is blessed, yet ought to be removed; in this the Marxist agrees

•PP 108-109, 110 ❖ PP 6:18; 7:2

Paradoxes in Christianity: "Nowhere do we tempt so successfully as on the very steps of the altar" (—Screwtape)*

•SL 172; WLN 70 (see also L 227)

❖ SL 32:40; WLN 4:40 (see also L 5 Mar 51)

Paradoxes in Christianity (regarding spiritual enlightenment): "The entrance is low: we must stoop till we are no taller than children in order to get in"

•RP 88 ❖ RP 8:17

Paradoxes in Christianity: Screwtape discusses the paradoxical freedom of obedience which humans can experience*

•SL 37-38 ❖ SL 8:3

Paradoxes in Christianity: Screwtape observes that in order to be greatly and effectively wicked, a man needs some virtue*

•SL 135-136 (see also SL 105-106; WLN 56)

❖ SL 29:2 (see also SL 23:1; WLN 4:13)

Paradoxes in Christianity: Self-rejection will also be a self-finding, and to die is to live

•GID 131 (see also MC 141, 180, 188-190; SL 59; WG 67, 117-118)

❖ GID I 16:3 (see also MC IV 2:3; 10:10; 11:11-15; SL 13:4; WG 4:22; 7:16, 17)

Paradoxes in Christianity: Some of the last will be first, and some of the first will be last*

•MC 181-182 ❖ MC IV 10:14

Paradoxes in Christianity: "Submit to death...and you will find eternal life"*

•MC 190 ❖ MC IV 11:15

Paradoxes in Christianity: Sufferers are blessed, yet suffering ought to be re-

moved (not good in itself)
•PP 110 ❖ PP 7:2

Paradoxes in Christianity: "The best is perhaps what we understand least" (re: the resurrection of the body)*
•GO 89 ❖ GO 4:38

Paradoxes in Christianity: The better stuff a creature is made of, the better—and worse—it can become*
•MC 53 (see also MC 181)
❖ MC II 3:5 (see also MC IV 10:13)

Paradoxes in Christianity: "The fine flower of unholiness can grow only in the close neighborhood of the holy" (—Screwtape)*
•SL 172; WLN 70
❖ SL 32:40; WLN 4:40

Paradoxes in Christianity: The great sinners are conscious of real guilt, and are thus capable of real repentance (—Screwtape)
•SL 165-166; WLN 64
❖ SL 32:29; WLN 4:29

Paradoxes in Christianity: The great sinners are made out of the very same material as the great Saints (—Screwtape)*
•SL 158; WLN 56 (see also SL 105-106, 135-136*) ❖ SL 32:13; WLN 4:13 (see also SL 23:1; 29:2*)

Paradoxes in Christianity: "The hardness of God is kinder than the softness of men, and His compulsion is our liberation"*
•SJ 229 (see also GID 261*)
❖ SJ 14:23 (see also GID II 16:19-22*)

Paradoxes in Christianity: The higher you rise the lower you can descend; fully regenerate man will recover his body*
•M 172-173 ❖ M App. A:11

Paradoxes in Christianity: "The higher the more in danger" (e.g., the Jews, the chosen people, show more vindictiveness—in the Psalms—than the Pagans)
•RP 28 (see also L 164*, 301; RP 31-32)
❖ RP 3:17 (see also L 5 Apr 39*; 20 Dec 61; RP 3:20)

Paradoxes in Christianity: "The higher the creature, the more, and also the less,

God is in it" (the more present by grace, and the less as mere power)*
•LM 74 ❖ LM 14:9

Paradoxes in Christianity: "'The higher does not stand without the lower'" (re: petitionary prayer as a necessary ingredient in the practice of worship)*
•LM 87 ❖ LM 16:13

Paradoxes in Christianity: The higher can descend into the lower; because of this, Christ can descend into the death of the body for us*
•M 130 ❖ M 14:35

Paradoxes in Christianity: "The highest does not stand without the lowest" (quote from Imitation of Christ)*
•FL 14, 20, 25, 32, 124; RP 88
❖ FL 1:7, 18; 2:1, 13; 4:58; RP 8:17

Paradoxes in Christianity: "The highest does not stand without the lowest" (re: finding humor as well as high poetry in "the flesh")*
•FL 144 ❖ FL 5:20

Paradoxes in Christianity: The individualism in which we all begin is only a parody or shadow of our true personality, which lies ahead*
•WG 117-118 (see also MC 141, 188-190; SL 59; WG 67, 69, 72; Personality) ❖ WG 7:17 (see also MC IV 2:3; 11:11-15; SL 13:4; WG 4:21, 22, 24, 30; Personality)

Paradoxes in Christianity: The moral realm exists to be transcended; "Here is the paradox of Christianity"
•LM 115 (see also CR 45; GID 144; L 277; MC 130-131; PP 65, 100*) ❖ LM 21:11-14 (see also CR 4:2; GID I 16:26; L 18 Jul 57; MC III 12:9; PP 4:13; 6:11*)

Paradoxes in Christianity: The more pride one has, the more one dislikes pride in others
•MC 109 ❖ MC III 8:1, 3

Paradoxes in Christianity: The most deeply compelled action is also the freest
•GID 261 (see also LM 49-50*; SJ 224-225) ❖ GID II 16:19-22 (see also LM 9:11*; SJ 14:16)

Paradoxes in Christianity: The only things

we can keep are those we freely give to God
•MC 180, 190 ❖ MC IV 10:10; 11:14, 15

Paradoxes in Christianity: The seed dies to live, the bread must be cast upon the waters, he that loses his soul shall save it
•PP 149 ❖ PP 10:7

Paradoxes in Christianity: The two great commandments must be translated "Behave as *if you* loved God and man" —yet this is not really obedience
•LM 115 ❖ LM 21:12

Paradoxes in Christianity: The whole moral realm exists to be transcended; there is no morality in Heaven*
•LM 114-116 (*see also* L 277*; PP 100*) ❖ LM 21:11-14 (*see also* L 18 Jul 57*; PP 6:11*)

Paradoxes in Christianity: There are many things in our spiritual life where a thing has to be killed, and broken, in order to become bright and splendid*
•GID 82 (*see also* Death and Rebirth pattern) ❖ GID I 9:5 (*see also* Death and Rebirth pattern)

Paradoxes in Christianity: "There can be no surer proof of a confirmed pride than a belief that one is sufficiently humble" (quote from Law)*
•LAL 96; PP 55, top (*see also* CR 14; MC 114; SL 62-63) ❖ LAL 24 Feb 61; PP 4 prelim. quote (*see also* CR 2:4; MC III 8:14; SL 14:2)

Paradoxes in Christianity: There can be a merely impulsive, headstrong, greedy desire even for spiritual things—a desire which is "flesh" and not "spirit"*
•LM 65 ❖ LM 12:11

Paradoxes in Christianity: "Those who are readiest to die for a cause may easily become those who are readiest to kill for it"*
•RP 28 ❖ RP 3:17

Paradoxes in Christianity: Those who try to hold an optimistic view of this world become pessimists; those who hold a stern view of it become optimistic (Hotel/prison analogy)*
•GID 52 ❖ GID I 4:18, 19 (Ques. 5)

Paradoxes in Christianity: "To be high or central means to abdicate continually ...all good masters are servants..."*
•M 124 (*consider also* Equality; Hierarchy) ❖ M 14:26 (*consider also* Equality; Hierarchy)

Paradoxes in Christianity: Unity is the road to personality*
•WG 113 ❖ WG 7:9

Paradoxes in Christianity: Vicariousness, which is evil in the world of selfishness and necessity, is good in world of love and understanding*
•M 120 (*see also* GID 85-86*) ❖ M 14:20 (*see also* GID I 9:8*)

Paradoxes in Christianity: We become "taller than we bow," and lowlier when we instruct (re: refreshing return to inequality which the Church offers us)*
•WG 115-116 (*see also* FL 166*) ❖ WG 7:15 (*see also* FL 6:5*)

Paradoxes in Christianity: "...what seem our worst prayers may really be, in God's eyes, our best"*
•LM 116 (*see also* LAL 73) ❖ LM 21:16 (*see also* LAL 31/3/58)

Paradoxes in Christianity: What seem to us the easiest conditions (in life) may really be the hardest*
•L 221 ❖ L 22 Sep 49

Paradoxes in Christianity: "When God arrives (and only then) the half-gods can remain" (re: natural loves)*
•FL 166 (*see also* L 198-199) ❖ FL 6:5 (*see also* L undated letter just before 20 Jan 42)

Paradoxes in Christianity: "When I have learnt to love God better than my earthly dearest, I shall love my earthly dearest better than I do now"*
•L 248 (*see also* GID 150*) ❖ L 8 Nov 52 (*see also* GID I 17:7*)

Paradoxes in Christianity: "When natural things look most divine, the demoniac is just round the corner" (re: Venus, or sexual love)*
•FL 144-145 ❖ FL 5:21

Paradoxes in Christianity: "When we try to keep within us an area that is our

own, we try to keep an area of death"*
- WG 130-131 (*see also* MC 166-168*)
- ❖ WG 9:10 (*see also* MC IV 8:1-7*)

Paradoxes in Christianity: When you are most desperate for help may be just the time when God can't give it; you're like the drowning man who clutches and grabs*
- GO 53-54 (*see also* GO 4-6; LAL 92)
- ❖ GO 3:24, 25 (*see also* GO 1:7-11; LAL 24 Sep 60)

Paradoxes in Christianity: "'Work out your own salvation... for it is God that worketh in you'"
- GID 55; LM 49; MC 130 ❖ GID I 4:31 (Ques. 8); LM 9:11; MC III 12:8

Paradoxes in life, many, listed*
- MC 190 ❖ MC IV 11:15

Paradoxes: "The moment good taste knows itself, some of its goodness is lost"*
- SJ 104 ❖ SJ 7:4

Parallelism as the chief formal characteristic of the Psalms (and fortunately one that survives in translation)
- RP 3-5; L 188 ❖ RP 1:5-7; L 16 Jul 40

Parallelism as "the practice of saying the same thing twice in different words": Jesus used it as well as the Psalmists
- RP 3-6 ❖ RP 1:5-9

Paranoia ("neurosis") as a condition which some attribute to the Psalmists—but the belief that one is threatened by certain evils may be realistic
- CR 126 ❖ CR 10:32-35

Paranoia—or the realistic fears of certain of the Psalmists—called "the Dark Night of the Flesh" by Lewis*
- CR 125-128 ❖ CR 10:31-40

Parasitism in Nature does not forbid us to suppose that the principle of Vicariousness is itself of Divine origin
- M 118 (*see also* GID 85-87)
- ❖ M 14:19 (*see also* GID I 9:8-10)

Parcel, putting up a, as one of the things Lewis said he disliked most in the world
- LAL 46 ❖ LAL 9/10/55

Parent(s)—*see also* Father(s); Mother(s)

Parent, affection of a, may degenerate into a continued and ruthless demand for sympathy, affection, and appreciation
- GID 285 (*see also* FL 64-65, 073-76)
- ❖ GID III 3:7 (*see also* FL 3:18, 33-36)

Parent and ancestor, the "incalculable momentousness" of being a, (re: the serious side of Venus, or sexual love)
- FL 140 ❖ FL 5:13

Parents' anxiety about children "being a credit to them" is nothing compared to the anxiety of children that their parents should not be an absolute disgrace
- L 172 ❖ L 3 Dec 39

Parents, any doctor will tell you that even prosperous people refuse to look after their; we are growing less kind to the elderly
- GID 312 ❖ GID III 8:4

Parents, Christ's exhortation about hating your, profitable only to those who read it with horror
- RP 131-132 (*see also* FL 165-166, 171-173; GID 191-192) ❖ RP 12:10 (*see also* FL 6:4, 16-19; GID II 1:4)

Parents: "...every man has a grudge against his father and his first teacher. The process of being brought up, however well it is done, cannot fail to offend"*
- CR 92 ❖ CR 7:20

Parents, importance of courtesy of, toward children (especially young adults)
- FL 66 (*see also* GID 282-286)
- ❖ FL 3:22 (*see also* GID III ch. 3)

Parents, narrow devotion of, who "live for their children" mentioned as an example of a kind of love that can become a god*
- FL 18 ❖ FL 1:15

Parents, support of, is a most ancient and universally acknowledged duty
LAL 21 ❖ LAL Aug 10th 53

Parents, unlovable, who demand to be loved by their children illustrated by Mr. Pontifex in *The Way of All Flesh*
- FL 62-65 ❖ FL 3:16-18

Parents who keep at home for selfish reasons children who ought to be sent out

into the world as example of a needy kind of love which God does not have
- PP 49-50 (*see also* Need-love)
❖ PP 3:17 (*see also* Need-love)

Parents who "live for their family" may not be doing their family a favor (re: Gift-love based on a need to be needed; story of Mrs. Fidget)*
- FL 73-77, 82-83 (*see also* L 198-199*; MC 167*; SL 121*, 123*)
❖ FL 3:33-37, 45 (*see also* L undated letter just before 20 Jan 42*; MC IV 7:3*; SL 26:2, 5*)

Parenting—*see* Child-rearing

Parochial idea that man could be important to God as part of what some called the "absurdity" of Christianity if the universe is well inhabited
- WLN 83 ❖ WLN 6:2

Parochialism—*see* Provincialism

Parousia—*see* Second Coming

Parson(s)—*see* Clergy(men)

Parties, neighborhood, which young Lewis hated: Even adults, I fancy, would not find an evening party very endurable without the attraction of sex and of alcohol
- SJ 46-48 (*see also* SJ 160)
❖ SJ 3:5, 6 (*see also* SJ 10:13)

Pascal, quote from: "God instituted prayer in order to lend to His creatures the dignity of causality"
- GID 106; LM 52; WLN 9
❖ GID I 11:8; LM 10:3; WLN 1:17

Pascal referred to "'Error of Stoicism': thinking we can do always what we can do sometimes" (e.g., prayers without words)
- LM 11 ❖ LM 2:5

Passion—*see also* Lust

Passion, mistaking the dictates of, for the decree of fate (as in the problem of marrying unbelievers)
- L 160-161 (*see also* MC 100, 101)
❖ L 10 Jun 38 (*see also* MC III 6:11, 13)

Passion of Christ as "the human situation writ large" (anxiety, suspense, hope, loneliness—even feeling forsaken by God)
- LM 42-44 (*see also* GO 5; LAL 38, 77)

❖ LM 8:6-12 (*see also* GO 5:8; LAL 20/2/55; Jul 21st 58)

Passion of Christ: "The 'hiddenness' of God perhaps presses most painfully on those who are in another way nearest to Him..."
- LM 44 ❖ LM 8:12

Past, as we grow older we remember the distant, better than what is nearer
- SJ 232 ❖ SJ 15:5

Past, do not miserably try to conjure back the; "Leave those bulbs alone, and the new flowers will come up"
- LM 26-27 (*see also* L 161-162*, 306; WLN 110*; *Perelandra* 48*)
❖ LM 5:10-13 (*see also* L 12 Sep 38*; 21 Nov 62; WLN 7:31*; *Perelandra* 4:6*)

Past, I am a lover of the
- GID 264 ❖ GID II 16:42

Past, if you could go back to the, you would find the same desire or longing
- WG 6-7 (*see also The Pilgrim's Regress*, p. xi) ❖ WG 1:5 (*see also The Pilgrim's Regress*, P:16)

Past, in Dante the lost souls are entirely concerned with their; not so the saved
- LAL 99 ❖ LAL 5 Jun 61

Past, it is not settled happiness but momentary joy that glorifies the
- SJ 8 ❖ SJ 1:5

Past, "Joy" not a desire for our own, (though that may come into it)*
- SJ 16 ❖ SJ 1:15

Past, my primary field is the, ("I travel with my back to the engine")
- GID 266 (*see also* CR 106)
❖ GID II 16:55 (*see also* CR 9:14)

Past, nostalgia for: "There is a 'rumness,' a ghostliness, about even a Windsor chair when it says, 'You will not see me again'"*
- SJ 131 ❖ SJ 8:19

Past: Reality never repeats; the exact same thing is never taken away and given back (re: reunion with loved ones in Heaven)
- GO 28-29 (*see also* GO 15-16; "Encore")
❖ GO 2:14 (*see also* GO 1:29; "Encore")

Past, Screwtape advises tempting human thought away from the Present and having them dwell on the, and the Future*
•SL 67-71 ❖ SL 15:3-5

Past: The useless word is "encore"; we must sit light to life and all its phases
•L 306 (*see also* L 161-162*; LM 26-27; WLN 110) ❖ L 21 Nov 62 (*see also* L 12 Sep 38*; LM 5:10- 13; WLN 7:31)

Past, we must beware of the; any fixing of the mind on old evils (beyond what is necessary for repentance and forgiveness) is useless and usually bad for us
•LAL 98-99 (*see also* PP 67)
❖ LAL 5 Jun 61 (*see also* PP 4:15)

Patience in suffering: "It doesn't really matter whether you grip the arms of the dentist's chair or let your hands lie in your lap. The drill drills on"
•GO 38 ❖ GO 2:31

Patience, need for three kinds of: patience with God, with one's neighbor, with oneself
•LAL 29-30 ❖ LAL Mar 31st 54

Patience ("tolerance"), opportunities for practicing, are never lacking; in everyone, including ourselves, there is that which requires forbearance
•FL 186 ❖ FL 6:37

Patriotism, 1st ingredient in, is love of home and its particular way of life
•FL 41-42 ❖ FL 2:32-34

Patriotism, 2nd ingredient in, is a particular attitude to our country's past
•FL 42-44 ❖ FL 2:35-37

Patriotism, 3rd ingredient in, may be the belief that our nation is markedly superior to all others
•FL 44-45 ❖ FL 2:38

Patriotism, 4th ingredient in, may be the belief that as a superior nation our nation has rights and duties toward the others
•FL 45-46 ❖ FL 2:39

Patriotism, a pernicious type of, occurs when the young are indoctrinated in knowably false or biased history
•FL 44 ❖ FL 2:37

Patriotism and its claims must not supersede God's claims on us*
•WG 24-25 ❖ WG 2:6

Patriotism, Christ also exhibited
•FL 40 ❖ FL 2:29

Patriotism discussed (an attempt "to distinguish its innocent from its demoniac condition")
•FL 39-49 ❖ FL 2:29-43

Patriotism, extreme, and ardent pacifism both mentioned by Screwtape as serving his purposes
•SL 25, 33-35 ❖ SL 5:1; 7:2, 3

Patriotism, extreme, which believes that our nation is in fact markedly superior to all others may breed Racism, which Christianity and science forbid
•FL 44-45 ❖ FL 2:38

Patriotism, like the other loves, may claim for itself a divine authority and thus attempt to become a god
•FL 18 ❖ FL 1:14

Patriotism: Like the other natural loves, when it becomes lawless, it ceases to be a love at all
•FL 46-47 ❖ FL 2:40

Patriotism: Love for one's country means chiefly love for people who have a lot in common with oneself; the familiar is in itself ground for affection
•L 231
❖ L undated letter just after 19 Apr 51

Patriotism: Love of one's country becomes a demon when it becomes a god
•FL 39 ❖ FL 2:29

Patriotism: "'No man loves his city because it is great, but because it is his'" (quote from "one of the Greeks")
•FL 46 ❖ FL 2:40

Patriotism: "...no two writers have expressed it more vigorously than Kipling or Chesterton"
•FL 40, 46 ❖ FL 2:31, 40

Patriotism offers us the first step beyond family selfishness
•FL 41 ❖ FL 2:33

Patriotism, wars must be fought on the basis of, not purely on moral grounds as such
•FL 47-48 ❖ FL 2:41, 42

Paul, Saint: Even St. Peter admits being

stumped by the Pauline Epistles
•L 251 ❖ L 3 Aug 53

Paul, Saint, expresses the relationship of God to Christ and Christ to man and man to woman as a proportion
•CR 4-5 ❖ CR 1:6

Paul, Saint: "He is the Christian author whom no one can by-pass"
•GID 231-232 ❖ GID II 10:6

Paul, Saint: Humility in the saints not a false humility; when they say they are vile, they are recording truth with scientific accuracy*
•PP 67-68 ❖ PP 4:15

Paul, Saint: I cannot be the only reader to wonder why God withheld from Him the gift of lucidity and orderly exposition
•RP 113 ❖ RP 11:8

Paul, Saint, mentioned by a friend of Lewis's as an example of the Christian ideal at work, though "one would probably have disliked him in real life"
•L 82 ❖ L 18 Oct 22

Paul, Saint: Narrative of Tertullos' speech against him is an example of how only portions of certain events were recalled and recorded by Bible writers
•LM 47 ❖ LM 9:4

Paul, Saint: Perhaps his writings let through what matters more than ideas—a whole Christian life in operation
•RP 114 ❖ RP 11:9

Paul, Saint, recognized our inability to keep the Law but at the same time he asserted our power to perceive the Law's goodness and rejoice in it
•CR 79 ❖ CR 6:19

Paul, Saint: Screwtape mentions "that pestilent fellow Paul" (with reference to Paul's advice regarding scruples)
•SL 75 ❖ SL 16:5

Paul, Saint: The nineteenth-century attack on him was really only a stage in the revolt against Christ
•GID 232-233 ❖ GID II 10:7

Paul, Saint: What he had to say on the hindrance of marriage related not to sex but to the multiple distractions of domesticity
•FL 137-138 ❖ FL 5:10

Pauline epistles seem to indicate that perfect obedience to the moral law is not in fact possible to men
•PP 66 ❖ PP 4:14

Peace and war listed by Screwtape as neutral situations which can work either for God's or the devil's purposes
•SL 89 (see also SL 114)
❖ SL 19:3 (see also SL 24:6)

Peace: "Do you get sudden lucid intervals—islands of profound peace? I do..."
•L 186 ❖ L 2 Jun 40

Peace, it is one thing to see the land of, from a wooded ridge...and another to tread the road that leads to it (quote from St. Augustine)
•SJ 230 ❖ SJ 15 prelim. quote

Peace may not always be compatible with goodwill; may require justice
•GID 309-310 ❖ GID III 7:14

Peace: "Silences in the physical world occur in empty places: but the ultimate Peace is silent through very density of life"
•M 93 ❖ M 11:18

Peace: When I lay these questions before God I get no answer; it is as though He shook His head not in refusal but waiving the question: "Peace, child..."
•GO 80-81 ❖ GO 4:24

"Peaks" and "troughs" of human experience discussed by Screwtape
•SL 36-44 (see also SL 13-14*)
❖ SL ch. 8, 9 (see also SL 2:3*)

"Peaks" and "troughs" of human experience: Screwtape advises Wormwood how to exploit them for diabolical purposes
•SL 40-44 ❖ SL ch. 9

Pedantry, being accused of: "...there are circles in which only a man indifferent to all accuracy will escape being called a pedant"
•RP 74 ❖ RP 7:15

Pederasty among schoolboys at Wyvern College
•SJ 87-89, 92, 101, 108-110

❖ SJ 6:8, 9, 15; 7:1, 11, 12

Pederasty as one of the two sins Lewis mentioned that he was never tempted to commit (the other was gambling)
•SJ 101 ❖ SJ 7:1

Pederasty: "We attack this vice not because it is the worst but because it is, by adult standards, the most disreputable and unmentionable..."
•SJ 108-109 ❖ SJ 7:11, 12

Peer pressure—*see also* Conformity

Peer pressure: Tempters make use of the desire for conformity, especially in young people
•SL 163-164; WLN 62 (*see also* SL 45-48) ❖ SL 32:25, 26; WLN 4:25, 26 (*see also* SL ch. 10)

Peer pressure ("the lure of the caucus") a major factor in moral decisions
•WG 98 ❖ WG 6:7

Peers, we all wish to be judged by our: "Theirs is the praise we really covet and the blame we really dread"
•FL 114 (*see also* WLN 112)
❖ FL 4:44 (*see also* WLN 7:36)

Pelagianism mentioned (re: grace and free will)
•LM 49 ❖ LM 9:11

Penance: Suffering which falls upon us by necessity can be as meritorious as *voluntary* suffering, if embraced for Christ's sake*
•LAL 20, 60, 105
❖ LAL Aug 10th 53; 3/8/56; 3/7/62

Penance: You should at least make a list of your sins on a piece of paper, and make a serious act of penance about each one of them
•GID 123-124 ❖ GID I 14:9

Penitence—*see also* Repentance

Penitence, forgiveness ought not to rest on the quality of the other person's; it may no doubt be very imperfect (as is our own)
•LAL 95 ❖ LAL 9 Jan 61

Penitence in the Psalms shows a desire to placate God's wrath; this is not inconsistent with Christian liturgies of penitence
•LM 95 ❖ LM 18:4

Penitence ought to be an act; the high-minded views involve some danger of regarding it simply as a state of feeling
•LM 97 ❖ LM 18:12

Penitent, Christ as the perfect
•MC 56-61 ❖ MC II ch. 4

Penitent, The Perfect (chapter title)
•MC 56-61 ❖ MC II ch. 4

Penitential prayers, at their highest level, are an attempt to restore an infinitely valued and vulnerable personal relationship
•LM 95 (*see also* MC 59-60)
❖ LM 18:3 (*see also* MC II 4:7, 8)

Pentecost, application of Psalm 68 to
•RP 125-126 ❖ RP 12:6

Pentecost: Ascension (withdrawal of the incarnate God) may have been the necessary condition of God's presence in another mode
•RP 126 ❖ RP 12:6

Pentecost mentioned as an instance of "Transposition"
•WG 54-55, 64-65 ❖ WG 4:1-2, 15-17

People—*see also* Humans; Human beings; *consider also* Relations, interpersonal; Interdependence

People are immortal, not nations or civilizations (thus are incomparably more important)
•GID 109-110; MC 73; WG 19, 117; WLN 68 ❖ GID I 12:2, 3; MC III 1:9; WG 1:15; 7:16; WLN 4:39

People are immortal only as new creatures
•WG 120 ❖ WG 7:19

People, boring: "It's so much easier to pray for a bore than to go and see him"
•LM 66 ❖ LM 12:12

People, boring, mentioned "whose history you know well after a short acquaintance...because they had nothing to say and would not be silent"
•L 136 ❖ L 9 Sep 29

People, closeness of, (as in a family) makes hatred possible as well as affection
•FL 64 (*see also* FL 82-83, 160; GID 285*; SL 17-18, 120)
❖ FL 3:17 (*see also* FL 3:45; 5:46; GID III 3:7*; SL 3:4, 5; 26:1)

People, difficult: "We are *all* fallen creatures and *all* very hard to live with..."*
•LAL 110 ❖ LAL 8 Nov 62

People, difficulties of living with, reflect how it must be for God; He sees all His plans spoiled by the crookedness of people
•GID 151-155 (*see also* GID 121-123)
❖ GID I ch. 18 (*see also* GID I 14:4-8)

People: Each person is in reality far better *and* worse than is ever imagined*
•L 267 ❖ L 8 Feb 56

People, God designed, as a man invents an engine; God Himself is the fuel
•MC 54 (*see also* Human machine)
❖ MC II 3:7 (*see also* Human machine)

People, good—*see* Good people

People, I loathe "sensitive," who are easily hurt; they are a social pest...vanity is usually the real trouble
•LAL 59 ❖ LAL 3/8/56

People, I prefer tree-like, (staunch and knotty and storm-enduring) to flowerlike people (frilly and fragrant and easily withered)
•L 253 ❖ L 9 Jan 54

People: In order to find God, it is perhaps not always necessary to leave His creatures behind; the world is crowded with Him
•LM 75 ❖ LM 14:11

People: "It takes all sorts to make a world; or a church...Heaven will display far more variety than Hell"
•LM 10 ❖ LM 2:3

People met in books can become like members of one's own family
•L 173 ❖ L 18 Dec 39

People, ordinary: "[In the war] I came to know and pity and reverence the ordinary man..."
•SJ 196 ❖ SJ 12:17

People, real character of, seen best when they have been taken off their guard
•MC 164-165 ❖ MC IV 7:12

People, reality of, usually different from our idea of them: "We all think we've got one another taped"
•GO 75-78 (*see also* GID 249*; GO 19-22) ❖ GO 4:13-19 (*see also* GID II 13:18*; GO 2:3)

People: The better stuff they are made of the better—and worse—they can become
•MC 53 (*see also* MC 181)
❖ MC II 3:5 (*see also* MC IV 10:13)

People, there are no ordinary; you have never met a mere mortal
•WG 18-19 ❖ WG 1:15

People, we cannot rely on; they will let us down
•MC 163 ❖ MC IV 7:9

People we regard as historically important may turn out to be minor characters, having importance only by giving occasion to states of soul in others
•CR 110 ❖ CR 9:20

People who *appear* to lack all spirituality: "Somewhere under that glib surface there lurks, however atrophied, a human soul"
•WLN 85 ❖ WLN 6:9

People who are "a thorn in the flesh": Best to not press on the place where they are embedded; i.e., to stop one's thoughts from moving towards them
•LAL 44 (*see also* LAL 28, 47*)
❖ LAL 21/6/55 (*see also* LAL Mar 10/54; 26/10/55*)

People who are at the heart of each religion are all closer to one another than those who are at the fringes
•LAL 11-12 (*see also* GID 60; MC 9)
❖ LAL Nov 10th 52 (*see also* GID I 4:56—Ques. 14; MC P:9)

People who are capable of real sacrifice may lead lives which are a misery to themselves and to others, because of self-concern and self-pity
•SJ 143-144 ❖ SJ 9:19

People who are cruel, dishonest, etc.: We should avoid contact with them, not because we are too good for them, but because we are not good enough
•RP 71-74 (*see also* SL 45-48*)
❖ RP 7:9-16 (*see also* SL ch. 10*)

People who are jealous, how to deal with
•LAL 44 ❖ LAL 21/6/55

People who are merely disagreeable: Probable cause is inner insecurity

•LAL 27-28 (*see also* SL 162-163*; WLN 60-61*) ❖ LAL Mar 10/54 (*see also* SL 32:22, 23*; WLN 4:22, 23*)

People who are merely disagreeable are harder to understand than those who commit the great crimes, for the raw material of them exists in us all
•LAL 27-28 ❖ LAL Mar 10/54

People "who bore one another should meet seldom; people who interest one another, often"
•FL 116 ❖ FL 4:47

People who have hurt us, prayer for, and then forgetting it, better than allowing them to become an obsession, to haunt our minds
•LAL 28 (*see also* LAL 44) ❖ LAL Mar 10/54 (*see also* LAL 21/6/55)

People who have hurt us: "...that, after all, is almost the greatest evil nasty people can do to us—to become an obsession, to haunt our minds"
•LAL 28 ❖ LAL Mar 10/54

People who have never met Christ: We do not know what His arrangements about them are
•MC 65 (*see also* GID 265-266; L 152-153; MC 176-177; SL 26*) ❖ MC II 5:8 (*see also* GID II 16:50, 51; L 8 Apr 32; MC IV 10:4; SL 5:2*)

People who have trouble being "good," encouragement to: You are one of the "poor" whom Christ blessed
•MC 181-182 ❖ MC IV 10:12-14

People who lead "incomplete and crippled lives," having never been in love, etc. as illustration of the loss incurred by those who never learn to appreciate God
•RP 92 ❖ RP 9:3

People who think alike tend to gravitate together into coteries where they do not encounter much opposition; complacent dogmatism thrives
•GID 127 (*see also* L 106*; *consider also* Inner Rings)
❖ GID I 15:2 (*see also* L 5 Jan 26; *consider also* Inner Rings)

People will go out of their way to meet a celebrity, politician, etc. even when it is known that that person leads a vile and mischievous life
•RP 67, 71 (*see also* LAL 27*)
❖ RP 7:3, 9 (*see also* LAL Feb 22/54*)

People you dislike: If you do them a good turn, you will find yourself disliking them less
•MC 116-117 (*see also* MC 161)
❖ MC III 9:5, 6 (*see also* MC IV 7:3)

Pepys's Diary, Lewis makes comments on publishing, in its unexpurgated form
•L 293-294 ❖ L 17 Jun 60

Pepys's Diary, quote from, describing aesthetic delight
•WG 57 ❖ WG 4:5

Perelandra, mention of writing
•L 195, 200, 205
❖ L 9 Nov 41; 11 May 42; 29 Oct 44

Perelandra mentioned as doubtfully suitable for children
•LAL 25, 27
❖ LAL 24/1/54; Feb 22/54

Perelandra mentioned: "Suppose...in some other planet there were a first couple undergoing the same that Adam and Eve underwent...but successfully"
•L 283 ❖ L 29 Dec 58

Perfect Penitent, The (chapter title)
•MC 56-61 ❖ MC II ch. 4

Perfection—*see also* Moral effort; Morality; Works; *consider also* Growth, Christian; Righteousness by faith/grace; Transformation

Perfection: Faced with the great issues of Christianity, can you really remain wholly absorbed in your own blessed "moral development"?*
•GID 112 ❖ GID I 12:9

Perfection: If we could become moral by our own effort, we should only perish in the ice and unbreathable air of the summit*
•GID 112-113 ❖ GID I 12:10, 11

Perfection: Lewis suggests the meaning of Christ's words, "Be ye perfect"
•MC 171-175 ❖ MC IV ch. 9

Perfection: Looking for improvement in yourself puts you on the wrong track*
•MC 128 (*see also* LM 34; Introspection) ❖ MC III 12:5 (*see also* LM 6:16;

Introspection)

Perfection: "...Love, in its own nature, demands the perfecting of the beloved"; God is pleased with little, but demands all
•PP 46 (see also MC 172)
❖ PP 3:13 (see also MC IV 9:4, 5)

Perfection: Mere improvement is no redemption; the change must go deeper than that*
•MC 182, 183 ❖ MC IV 10:16; 11:1

Perfection: No human in history has ever quite succeeded in trying to obey their conscience*
•MC 54 ❖ MC II 3:9

Perfection of Christ must be interpreted in a sense which admits of His feeling the full range of temptations
•L 189
❖ L undated letter just after 11 Aug 40

Perfection: Pauline epistles seem to indicate that perfect obedience to the moral law is not in fact possible to men
•PP 66 ❖ PP 4:14

Perfection: The change will not be completed in this life
•MC 173-174, 175 ❖ MC IV 9:8; 10:1

Perfection: "The command 'Be ye perfect' is not idealist gas...[God] is going to make us into creatures that can obey that command"
•MC 174-175 ❖ MC IV 9:11

Perfection, the Holiness of God is something more and other than moral, but it is not less; the road to the promised land runs past Sinai
•PP 65 (see also LM 114-115)
❖ PP 4:13 (see also LM 21:11-13)

Perfection, the only fatal thing is to sit down content with anything less than
•MC 94 (see also L 199; WG 132)
❖ MC III 5:12 (see also L 20 Jan 40; WG 9:13)

Perfection: "To ask that God's love should be content with us as we are is to ask that God should cease to be God"*
•PP 48 ❖ PP 3:15

Perfection: Transformation of natural loves into Charity is a work so diffi-

cult that perhaps no fallen man has ever come close to doing it perfectly*
•FL 184-185 ❖ FL 6:35

Perfection: We are a Divine work of art; an artist, over the most loved picture of his life, will spend much time and effort perfecting it
•PP 42-43, 47 (see also LM 34, 69; MC 44, 173) ❖ PP 3:10, 14 (see also LM 6:16; 13:4; MC II 1:4; IV 9:7)

Perfection: "We are bidden to 'put on Christ,' to become like God"*
•PP 53-54 (see also SL 158*; WLN 56*)
❖ PP 3:18, 019 (see also SL 32:13*; WLN 4:13*)

Perfection: We can't change ourselves—we can only ask Our Lord to do so; one mustn't fuss too much about one's state*
•LAL 48 ❖ LAL 9/11/55

Perfection: "We know that none of us will ever come up to that standard...we must pin all our hopes on the mercy of God and the work of Christ"*
•RP 13 ❖ RP 2:8

Perfection, we may treat the regimental rules as a dead letter or counsel of, but neglect of them is going to cost every man his life
•PP 64 ❖ PP 4:10

Perfection: We must have at least allowed the process to begin here on earth (re: transformation of our natural loves into Charity)**
•FL 187 ❖ FL 6:38

Perfection: When Jesus said, "Be perfect," He meant it
•MC 169 ❖ MC IV 8:9

Period (of time)—see Age

Permanence, Lewis's preference for
•L 306 (consider also Change)
❖ L 21 Nov 62 (consider also Change)

Permanence not to be found in this life; we must "sit light" to life and all its phases
•L 306 (see also L 161-162; LM 26-27; WLN 110; Perelandra 48*)
❖ L 21 Nov 62 (see also L 12 Sep 38; LM 5:10- 13; WLN 7:31; Perelandra 4:6*)

Permanence: Screwtape mentions human

enjoyment of change, balanced by a desire for permanence—which enables people to appreciate Rhythm (such as seasons)
•SL 116 ❖ SL 25:2

Persecution—*consider also* Opposition; Oppression

Persecution: Christian movements always excite opposition eventually; claims of real Christianity are offensive to the World (re: Christian revival at Oxford)*
•GID 222-223 ❖ GID II 8:12, 13

Persecution: Christians themselves have been persecutors in the past; I detest every kind of religious compulsion
•GID 60-61 ❖ GID I 4:57, 58 (Ques. 15)

Persecution, ghastly record of Christian, shows that when Christianity does not make a man very much better, it makes him very much worse
•L 301 (*see also* RP 28-32)
❖ L 20 Dec 61 (*see also* RP 3:17-20)

Persecution: I suppose the great saints really *want* to share the divine sufferings...but this is far beyond me*
•LAL 55-56 ❖ LAL 26/4/56

Persecution: "...it is...the persecuted or martyred Christian in whom the pattern of the Master is most unambiguously realized" (re: miserable marriages)
•FL 149 ❖ FL 5:27

Persecution, likely process for the development of religious
•GID 198 ❖ GID II 3:5

Persecution: "Perhaps prayers as a secret indulgence which Father disapproves may have a charm they lacked in houses where they were commanded"*
•LAL 32 ❖ LAL Sep 19/54

Persecution, religious: Christendom must fully confess its specific contribution to the sum of human cruelty and treachery*
•FL 49 ❖ FL 2:43

Persecution, there is no wisdom or virtue in deliberately courting, (re: making a marriage that will certainly involve misery)

•FL 149 ❖ FL 5:27

Perseverance—*see* Steadfastness

Persians, the ancient, debated everything twice: once when they were sober, and once drunk (re: emotion vs. "coolness" in intellectual processes)
•LM 45 ❖ LM 8:14

Personal God—*see* God, personal

"**Personal**," meaning of the word, to modern minds ("Corporeal"—thus a "personal God" would only mean an anthropomorphic God)
•GID 98, 255 ❖ GID I 10:32; II 15:5

Personality, Beyond: or First Steps in the Doctrine of the Trinity (Book IV of *Mere Christianity*)
•MC 135-190 ❖ MC Book IV

Personality differences: It takes all sorts to make a world, or a church; Heaven will display far more variety than Hell
•LM 10 ❖ LM 2:3

Personality, even in heaven we shall have differences of, ("the blessed shall remain eternally different"); and each will communicate a unique vision of God
•PP 150-151 (*see also* FL 92-93)
❖ PP 10:7, 8 (*see also* FL 4:9)

Personality: Grace will expand all our natures into the full richness of the diversity which God intended when He made them
•LM 10 ❖ LM 2:3

Personality: "Human will becomes truly creative and truly our own when it is wholly God's...he that loses his soul shall find it"*
•PP 102 ❖ PP 6:14

Personality, in the Body of Christ we all have differences of, yet all are necessary to the whole and to one another
•L 242-243 ❖ L 20 Jun 52

Personality, individual: We may be at last reunited with God in a love offered from the height of the utter individualities which He has liberated us to be*
•SL xii ❖ SL P:20

Personality is God-given; the idea that each of us starts with a treasure called "personality" locked up inside him is

a pestilent notion
- WG 118-119 (*see also* PP 147-148)
- ❖ WG 7:19 (*see also* PP 10:3)

Personality, much of our, can be traced to such small things as books read at an early age*
- L 109-110 ❖ L 4 Jul 26

Personality of Jesus discussed (with regard to Biblical criticism)
- CR 156-157 ❖ CR 13:7, 8

Personality, our unique: No one is like anyone else; we are all "special" as members in the Body of Christ
- L 242-243 ❖ L 20 Jun 52

Personality, our unique: We can be taken into the life of God and yet remain ourselves
- MC 141 (*see also* GID 131; SL 38, 59, 81-82; WG 67, 117-118)
- ❖ MC IV 2:3 (*see also* GID I 16:3; SL 8:3; 13:4; 18:3, 4; WG 4:21, 22; 7:16, 17)

Personality, our unique, will live eternally
- WG 117-118 (*see also* MC 188-190)
- ❖ WG 7:16, 17 (*see also* MC IV 11:11-15)

Personality: "Our whole destiny [as Christians] seems to lie in...being as little as possible ourselves...in becoming clean mirrors filled..."
- CR 6-7 ❖ CR 1:10

Personality peculiarities, I wonder what prevents the growth of rich and strongly marked, now-a-days
- L 124 ❖ L 25 Feb 28

Personality, recovery of: "To enter heaven is to become more human than you ever succeeded in being on earth"*
- PP 125 (*see also* WG 117-119)
- ❖ PP 8:9 (*see also* WG 7:17, 18)

Personality: Self exists to be abdicated and, by that abdication, becomes the more truly self*
- PP 152 (*see also* L 251; MC 141, 188-190; SL 59; WG 117- 118)
- ❖ PP 10:10 (*see also* L 17 Jul 53; MC IV 2:3; 11:11-15; SL 13:4; WG 7:16, 17)

Personality, since I have begun to pray I find my extreme view of, changing...
- L 155
- ❖ L undated letter just before 7 Jun 34

Personality, the ins and outs of your, are

no mystery to God; and one day they will be no mystery to you
- PP 147 ❖ PP 10:3

Personality, true, lies ahead; present individualism is only a shadow of it
- WG 117-118 (*see also* MC 141, 188-190; SL 59; WG 67, 69, 72)
- ❖ WG 7:17 (*see also* MC IV 2:3; 11:11-15; SL 13:4; WG 4:21, 22, 24, 30)

Personality, unity is the road to
- WG 113 ❖ WG 7:9

Personality, when I give myself up to His, I first begin to have a real personality of my own
- MC 188-190 (*see also* GID 131; L 251; MC 141; WG 118)
- ❖ MC IV 11:11-15 (*see also* GID I 16:3; L 17 Jul 53; MC IV 2:3; WG 7:17)

Personality, Screwtape laments that when men abandon their self-will God gives them back their, and when they're wholly His, they'll be more themselves than ever
- SL 59 (*see also* SL 38)
- ❖ SL 13:4 (*see also* SL 8:3)

Personality, whether our, is nice or nasty is of secondary importance; question is whether we will offer it to God
- MC 179 ❖ MC IV 10:7, 8

Perspective—*consider also* Priorities

Perspective, eternal: "...how different the content of our faith will look when we see it in the total context"*
- L 267 ❖ L 8 Feb 56

Perspective: Every age has its own outlook; we therefore need older books that can correct the characteristic mistakes of our own period*
- GID 202 (*see also* Age/s)
- ❖ GID II 4:4 (*see also* Age/s)

Perspective, historical, gained through education protects one against the errors of the current age
- WG 28-29 ❖ WG 2:10

Perspective of eternity, in the, the categories of pain and pleasure recede as vaster good and evil looms in sight
- PP 126 (*see also* PP 153; SL 148)
- ❖ PP 8:9 (*see also* PP 10:11; SL 31:5)

Perspective of eternity: One sometimes

wonders why God thinks the game worth the candle; but we have not yet seen the game*
•LM 91-92 ❖ LM 17:15

Perspective of history lacking in the uneducated man; this is one problem in presenting the Christian faith to modern unbelievers
•GID 94-95, 241-242
❖ GID I 10:13; II 12:2

Perspective of time: "Why should what we see at the moment be more 'real' than what we see from ten years' distance?"
•LM 122 ❖ LM 22:17

Perversion, sexual: Pervert sees normal love as a milk and water substitute for the ghastly world of impossible fantasies which have become for him "real"*
•CR 40 ❖ CR 3:7

Pessimism—see also Futility

Pessimism and Atheism, my own, were fully formed before I went to Bookham [to study with Kirkpatrick]
•SJ 139-140 (see also SJ 190)
❖ SJ 9:16 (see also SJ 12:12)

Pessimism and timidity may prevent me from gambling, but they also tempt me to avoid those risks and adventures which every man ought to take
•RP 29 ❖ RP 3:18

Pessimism as a belief system which has an "obvious" attraction but meets insuperable obstacles later on
•M 131 ❖ M 14:36

Pessimism defined as the "judgement that life is not worth preserving"—or, the preference for non-existence*
•SJ 116, 117 ❖ SJ 7:21

Pessimism: Having once tasted life, even pessimists are subject to the impulse of self-preservation
•SJ 116 (see also LAL 114)
❖ SJ 7:21 (see also LAL 19 Mar 63)

Pessimism, Heroic, has a contradiction at its centre: If a Brute made the world, then he also made the standard by which we judge him to be a Brute
•CR 65-67 (see also CR 69-70; MC 45-

46*) ❖ CR 5:19 (see also CR 5:24; MC II 1:5, 6*)

Pessimism, Lewis describes his own, as "cowardice"
•SJ 117 (see also SJ 171*)
❖ SJ 7:21 (see also SJ 11:8*)

Pessimism, Lewis describes his, ("Perhaps because I had a not very happy boyhood...I am too familiar with the idea of futility to feel the shock of it...")*
•CR 57 ❖ CR 5:2

Pessimism, Lewis mentions his resolution (during his early years at Oxford) to disavow
•SJ 201 ❖ SJ 13:7

Pessimism, Lewis relates his feeling (while a student at Oxford) of materialistic
•L 77 ❖ L 24 May 22

Pessimism, Lewis writes of his, in his youth: "...even a boy can recognize that there is desert all round him though he, for the nonce, sits in an oasis"
•SJ 65 ❖ SJ 4:11

Pessimism, Lewis writes of his, in youth "...I had very definitely formed the opinion that the universe was, in the main, a rather regrettable institution"
•SJ 63 ❖ SJ 4:10

Pessimism, Lewis's: "...as the comic beatitude says, 'Blessed are they that expect little for they shall not be disappointed'"*
•LAL 96 (see also SL 95-96)
❖ LAL 24 Feb 61 (see also SL 21:2)

Pessimism, Lewis's, during World War II: "More and more sleep seems to be the best thing"*
•L 169 (see also SJ 100*)
❖ L 18 Sep 39 (see also SJ 6:27*)

Pessimism, Lewis's: "Has this world been so kind to you that you should leave it with regret? There are better things ahead..."*
•LAL 117 ❖ LAL 17 Jun 63

Pessimism, Lewis's: How any man can take it for granted that existence is not futile beats me...*
•CR 57 ❖ CR 5:2

Pessimism, Lewis's: "How wicked it would be, if we could, to call the dead back!"*

•GO 89 ❖ GO 4:40

Pessimism, Lewis's: "I am not sure that the great canyon of anguish which lies across our lives is *solely* due to some pre-historic catastrophe"*

•LM 91 ❖ LM 17:15

Pessimism, Lewis's: I felt it something of an outrage that I had been created without my own permission*

•SJ 171 (*see also* GO 32*; SJ 115)

❖ SJ 11:8 (*see also* GO 2:20*; SJ 7:19, 20)

Pessimism, Lewis's: "I had been warned ...not to reckon on worldly happiness. We were even promised sufferings. They were part of the program"*

•GO 41-42 ❖ GO 3:3

Pessimism, Lewis's: "I have even (I'm afraid) caught myself wishing that I had never been born, wh. is sinful. Also meaningless if you think it out"*

•L 166 (*see also* SJ 115-116)

❖ L 8 May 39 (*see also* SJ 7:19-21)

Pessimism, Lewis's: I maintained that God did not exist, I was very angry with God for not existing, and I was equally angry with Him for creating a world*

•SJ 115-117 (*see also* CR 65-67*, 70*; MC 45-46; SJ 171)

❖ SJ 7:20, 21 (*see also* CR 5:19-20*, 24-26*; MC II 1:5, 6; SJ 11:8)

Pessimism, Lewis's: I was [as a youth] far more eager to escape pain than to achieve happiness*

•SJ 171, 228 (*see also* SJ 117)

❖ SJ 11:8; 14:22 (*see also* SJ 7:21)

Pessimism, Lewis's: "I wish life and death were not the only alternatives, for I don't like either; one could imagine a via media"*

•L 73 ❖ L 7 Apr 22

Pessimism, Lewis's: If we really believe that our real home is elsewhere, why should we not look forward to the arrival?*

•LAL 83-84 (*see also* SL 132*)

❖ LAL Jun 7th 59 (*see also* SL 28:1*)

Pessimism, Lewis's: "It doesn't really mat-ter whether you grip the arms of the dentist's chair or let your hands lie in your lap. The drill drills on"*

•GO 38 ❖ GO 2:31

Pessimism, Lewis's: It (life) is not forever; wouldn't it be ghastly to be *immortal* on earth? It will all one day go away like a dream*

•LAL 47 (*see also* LAL 64-65, 66, 115-116, 120-121)

❖ LAL 26/10/55 (*see also* LAL 4/1/57; 17/2/57; 22 Apr 63; 6 Jul 63)

Pessimism, Lewis's: "It remains true that I have, almost all my life, been quite unable to feel that horror of nonentity, of annihilation..."*

•SJ 117 ❖ SJ 7:21

Pessimism, Lewis's: "It'll be nice when we all wake up from this life which has indeed something like nightmare about it"*

•LAL 69 (*see also* LAL 47, 57)

❖ LAL Oct 20th 57 (*see also* LAL 26/10/55; 21/5/56)

Pessimism, Lewis's: Lazarus and not St. Stephen ought to be celebrated as the first martyr (had it all over with, then had to come back and do it all again)*

•GO 48; LAL 119

❖ GO 3:12; LAL 25 Jun 63

Pessimism, Lewis's: Life as a bad dream which will not last forever*

•LAL 47, 57, 69 (*see also* MC 170; SL 147) ❖ LAL 26/10/55; 21/5/56; Oct 20th 57 (*see also* MC IV 8:12; SL 31:3)

Pessimism, Lewis's: Life as a "'valley of tears,' cursed with labour, hemmed round with necessities," etc.*

•LM 92 ❖ LM 17:17

Pessimism, Lewis's: "...my very early reading...had lodged very firmly in my imagination the vastness and cold of space, the littleness of Man"*

•SJ 65 ❖ SJ 4:11

Pessimism, Lewis's: One sometimes won-ders why God thinks the game worth the candle; but we have not yet seen the game*

•LM 91-92 ❖ LM 17:15

Pessimism, Lewis's: Ordinary men have

not been so much in love with life as is usually supposed; are more than half in love with easeful death*
- L 190-191
❖ L undated letter just after 11 Aug 40

Pessimism, Lewis's: "Pain is terrible, but surely you need not have fear as well? Can you not see death as the friend and deliverer?"*
- LAL 117 ❖ LAL 17 Jun 63

Pessimism, Lewis's (quote from Johnson): "Marriage is not otherwise unhappy than as life is unhappy"*
- L 128 ❖ L 2 Aug 28

Pessimism, Lewis's: "The bad dream will be over"*
- MC 170 ❖ MC IV 8:12

Pessimism, Lewis's: The killing of innocents in war seems, in a way, to make war not worse but better*
- WG 43 (see also SL 131-132)
❖ WG 3:18 (see also SL 28:1)

Pessimism, Lewis's: "...the less one can think about happiness on earth, the less, I believe, one suffers"*
- LAL 96 (see also SL 95-96)
❖ LAL 9 Jan 61 (see also SL 21:2)

Pessimism, Lewis's: "The sooner we are safely out of this world, the better"*
- L 166 (Compare with L 217*) ❖ L 8 May 39 (Compare with L 4 Apr 49*)

Pessimism, Lewis's: To me the materialist's universe had the enormous attraction that it offered limited liabilities; death ended all*
- SJ 171 (see also GO 33)
❖ SJ 11:8 (see also GO 2:22)

Pessimism, Lewis's: "We are under the harrow and can't escape. Reality, looked at steadily, is unbearable"*
- GO 32 ❖ GO 2:20

Pessimism, Lewis's: "...what a grim business even a happy human life is when you read it rapidly through to the inevitable end"*
- L 187 ❖ L 12 Jul 40

Pessimism, Lewis's: "What have you and I got to do but make our exit? When they told me I was in danger...I don't remember feeling distressed"*

- LAL 114 (see also LAL 115-116, 118)
❖ LAL 19 Mar 63 (see also LAL 22 Apr 63; 25 Jun 63)

Pessimism listed by Lewis as one of the causes for his rising doubt, as a youth, in the Christian faith
- SJ 63 (see also SJ 190)
❖ SJ 4:10 (see also SJ 12:12)

Pessimism nor optimism, Christianity offers neither the attractions of
- WG 75-76 (see also GID 51-52; SJ 204)
❖ WG 5:5 (see also GID I 4:18, 19-Ques. 5; SJ 13:11)

Pessimism, what Lewis believed were the sources of his, (the clumsiness of his hands; his mother's death; his fear of poverty; his very early reading)
- SJ 63-65 ❖ SJ 4:10

Pessimist, when once one has dropped the absurd notion that reality is an arbitrary alternative to "nothing," one gives up being a, (or even an optimist)
- SJ 204 ❖ SJ 13:11

Pessimist's case against the existence of God, and an answer to it
- PP 13-25 ❖ PP ch. 1

Pessimists, people who try to hold an optimistic view of this world become; the people who hold a pretty stern view of it become optimistic
- GID 52 ❖ GID I 4:19

Peter, Saint: What Christ meant when He said to him, "Get thee behind me"
- FL 171 ❖ FL 6:17

Peter walking on water, miracle of: I find no difficulty in accepting it as historical
- CR 145 ❖ CR 12:11

Peter walking on water: Surely the faith he lacked was faith in the particular event, not a general faith in God's goodness
- CR 145-146 ❖ CR 12:11

Peter's "momentary ruin" when Christ said to Him, "Get thee behind Me"
- CR 155 ❖ CR 13:6

Petitionary prayer—see Prayer, petitionary

Petitionary Prayer: A Problem Without an Answer (chapter title)

•CR 142-151 ❖ CR ch. 12

Pets—*see also* Animals; Cats; Dogs

Pets can be a "bridge" between us and the rest of nature
•FL 78-79 ❖ FL 3:40

Pets, euthanasia for: "...rejoice that God's law allows you to extend to Fanda that last mercy which...we are forbidden to extend to suffering humans"
•LAL 61 ❖ LAL 18/8/56

Pets: I never knew a guinea-pig that took any notice of humans
•L 265 ❖ L 16 Oct 55

Pets: "I will never laugh at anyone for grieving over a loved beast"
•LAL 61 ❖ LAL 18/8/56

Pets: If they seem "almost human" it is because we have made them so
•PP 139, 141 (*see also* MC 166, 170)
❖ PP 9:11, 13 (*see also* MC IV 7:13; 8:11)

Pets: If you want to make sure of keeping your heart intact, you must give it to no one, not even an animal*
•FL 169 ❖ FL 6:13

Pets: Of small animals I think Hamsters are the most amusing—and I am also fond of mice
•L 265 ❖ L 16 Oct 55

Pets, possible immortality of
•PP 136-142 (*see also* LAL 110)
❖ PP 9:9-13 (*see also* LAL 26 Nov 62)

Pets: Psychological diagnoses must be phoney when applied to animals
•LAL 97 ❖ LAL 24 Feb 61

Pets: The human need to be needed often finds its outlet in pampering an animal
•FL 78-79 (*see also* FL 75-76)
❖ FL 3:40 (*see also* FL 3:35)

Pets, the things we must sometimes do to our, suggest that the strange and terrifying things which happen to *us* are really for our benefit
•LAL 114 ❖ LAL 8 Feb 63

Pets: The woman who makes a dog the centre of her life loses not only her human usefulness but also the proper pleasure of dog-keeping
•GID 280 ❖ GID III 2:6

Phantastes, by George MacDonald: "...

never had the wind of Joy blowing through any story been less separable from the story itself"
•SJ 180 ❖ SJ 11:19

Phantastes, by George MacDonald, described by Lewis to his friend, Arthur Greeves
•L 27 ❖ L undated letter of Oct 1915

Phantastes, by George MacDonald, "fills for me the place of a devotional book"
•L 84 ❖ L 11 Jan 23

Phantastes, by George MacDonald: I did not yet know the name of the new quality that met me; it was Holiness
•SJ 179 (*see also* L 167)
❖ SJ 11:18, 19 (*see also* L 9 Jul 39)

Phantastes, on reading, by George MacDonald: "That night my imagination was, in a certain sense, baptized; the rest of me, not unnaturally, took longer"
•SJ 181 ❖ SJ 11:19

Pharisaism—*see also* Pride; Self-righteousness; *consider also* Hypocrisy; Snobbery

Pharisaism, I lacked the bloodhound sensitivity for, and have never felt the dislike of goodness quite common in better men than me
•SJ 191 ❖ SJ 12:12

Pharisaism: "I think that even in the Psalms this evil is already at work"
•RP 66-67 ❖ RP 7:1, 2

Pharisee, a cat is a; when he sits and stares you out of countenance he is thanking God that he is not as these dogs, or these humans, or as other cats
•LAL 40 ❖ LAL 21/3/55

Pharisee, two types of, described by Screwtape; "types that were most antagonistic to one another on earth"
•SL 171; WLN 69
❖ SL 32:40; WLN 4:40

Pharisees and spoiled saints make better sport in Hell than mere common tyrants or debauchees (—Screwtape)
•SL 105-106 ❖ SL 23:1

Pharisees, legalism was the sin and simultaneously the punishment of the Scribes and

•RP 57-58 ❖ RP 6:7

Pharisees, we must not be Pharisaical even to the, (re: self-righteousness in the Psalms)
•RP 66-67 ❖ RP 7:1, 2

"Phase," Screwtape advises Wormwood to get his patient to see his religious experience as a, which will pass
•SL 36, 43-44 ❖ SL 8:1; 9:4, 5

"Phases," humans tend to feel superior and patronizing to the, they have emerged from—not from healthy criticism but simply because they are in the past
•SL 43 ❖ SL 9:4

Philanthropy—see Charity; Humanitarianism

Philological Arm, Screwtape mentions the, —a department of Hell which attempts to change the meaning of words slightly to achieve diabolical ends
•SL 70 (see also SL 121, 161; WLN 59; Words and phrases...)
❖ SL 15:5 (see also SL 26:2; 32:19; WLN 4:19; Words and phrases...)

Philologist, even the shallowest, knows that the unconscious linguistic process is continually degrading good words and blunting useful distinctions
•GID 333 ❖ GID IV Letter 7

Philologist, Tolkien was a
•SJ 216 ❖ SJ 14:6

Philosophical argument no longer as effective as it used to be; people are more influenced by jargon than by argument for truth*
•SL 7-8 (see also SL 43)
❖ SL 1:1, 2 (see also SL 9:4)

Philosophical idealism turns out to be disguised Theism
•WG 91 ❖ WG 5:23

Philosophies, almost all our modern, have been devised to convince us that the good of man is to be found on this earth
•WG 7-8 ❖ WG 1:5

Philosophies, most modern, read human life merely as an animal life of unusual complexity; similarly, Scripture

can be read as merely human literature
•RP 116-117 (see also WG 64*)
❖ RP 11:12 (see also WG 4:15*)

Philosophies, of all the, I believe Hinduism and Christianity to be the two serious options for the adult mind
•CR 71 (see also GID 102; SJ 235-236)
❖ CR 5:26 (see also GID I 10:49; SJ 15:7)

Philosophy and art are but clumsy imitations of the soul's never-completed attempt to communicate its unique vision of God to all the others
•PP 150 (see also FL 92-93*)
❖ PP 10:7 (see also FL 4:9*)

Philosophy and science have both proved powerless to curb the human impulse toward Pantheism
•M 83 ❖ M 11:4

Philosophy and theology not learned from nature; in nature each man can clothe his own belief
•FL 35-37 ❖ FL 2:19-24

Philosophy as one of those things that are religiously ambivalent, i.e., it may be a preparation or medium for meeting God, or it may be an impediment
•L 268
❖ L undated letter just before 2 Apr 56

Philosophy, error of assuming the, of our own age to be correct as opposed to the thought of past ages
•WLN 96 (see also RP 121, 130; SJ 207-208; Age/s) ❖ WLN 7:6 (see also RP 12:3, 9; SJ 13:17; Age/s)

Philosophy, good, must exist to answer bad philosophy (re: value of education for the Christian)
•WG 28 ❖ WG 2:10

Philosophy, said Barfield, wasn't a subject to Plato; it was a way
•SJ 225 ❖ SJ 14:17

Philosophy, systems of—consider Buddhism; Christianity; Confucianism; Hinduism; Islam; Materialism; Stoicism

Philosophy, what we learn from experience depends on the kind of, we bring to it
•M 3 (see also GID 25-26)

❖ M 1:2 (*see also* GID I 2:1)

Phobias: I am inclined to think a real objective curiosity will usually have a cleansing effect (re: his own fear of spiders)*
•SJ 9 (*see also* Fear)
❖ SJ 1:6 (*see also* Fear)

Photograph, I have no, of her [Joy] that's any good; I cannot even see her face distinctly in my imagination (re: Lewis's grief for his wife)
•GO 16 ❖ GO 1:31

Photographs: "Of course no man ever approves the photos of the woman he loves!"
•LAL 68 ❖ LAL Aug 12th 57

Photographs [of deceased loved ones]: "Images, whether on paper or in the mind, are not important for themselves. Merely links"
•GO 75-76 ❖ GO 4:13, 14

Physical sensation(s)—*see* Sensation(s), physical

Physician(s)—*see also* Doctor(s)

Physician, they that are whole need not the; no creature that deserved Redemption would need to be redeemed
•WLN 86, 87 (*see also* M 52*, 122*)
❖ WLN 6:10, 12 (*see also* M 7:14*; 14:24*)

Physicist describes "reality" by mathematics, but mathematics can hardly be reality itself (re: attempting contact with ultimate Reality)
•CR 170 ❖ CR 14:24

Physics is replacing biology as the science *par excellence* in the mind of the plain man; this points to the decline of Evolutionism
•CR 89 ❖ CR 7:17

Physics, quantum, vs. the old atomic theory as analogy to Christian theology vs. Pantheism (re: the attractive simplicity of man's first guess vs. truth)
•M 83-84 (*see also* MC 137; PP 25, 86)
❖ M 11:5 (*see also* MC IV 1:9; PP 1:16; 5:13)

Piano analogy: Moral law is the tune; instincts are the keys

•MC 22-23 ❖ MC I 2:2-4

Picture, our natural experiences are like a; our risen life will be the reality
•WG 68-69 ❖ WG 4:22-24

Picture ["portrait"], living the Christian life is more like painting a, than like obeying a set of rules
•MC 162 (*consider also* Imitation of Christ) ❖ MC IV 7:5 (*consider also* Imitation of Christ)

Picture, the unfinished, would so like to jump off the easel and have a look at itself (re: extreme introspection)
•LM 34 (*see also* MC 128)
❖ LM 6:16 (*see also* MC III 12:5)

Picture, we are the; God is the painter
•MC 173 (*see also* LM 69; MC 44; PP 42-43) ❖ MC IV 9:7 (*see also* LM 13:4; MC II 1:4; PP 3:10)

Picture, world is like a, with a golden background; you must step off the background [into death] before you can see the gold
•PP 148 ❖ PP 10:5

Pictures as a form of Transposition (something which adapts a richer to a poorer medium); analogy to religious experience
•WG 60-62; 68-73 (*see also* M 85)
❖ WG 4:10-13, 23, 24 (*see also* M 11:6)

Pictures as an example of the difficulty inherent in representing a spiritual reality by earthly concepts and images
•WG 60-62; 68-69 (*see also* M 85; PP 86) ❖ WG 4:10-13, 23, 24 (*see also* M 11:6; PP 5:12)

Pictures of Jesus—*see also* Images

Pictures of Jesus: The artistic merits or demerits are a distraction (re: use of images in prayer and worship)*
•LM 84 ❖ LM 16:4

Pictures of Jesus: The use of images (in prayer), for me, is very limited; but focussing one's eyes on almost any object is a help towards concentration*
•LM 84 ❖ LM 16:3, 4

"Pie in the sky," we are shy of mentioning heaven nowadays—afraid of the jeer about
•PP 144 ❖ PP 10:1

Piety, one may bewail happier days when religion meant
- L 177 ❖ L 18 Feb 40

Piety ("sanctity") and culture: Both are hard to diagnose and easy to feign*
❖ WLN 47 ❖ WLN 3:24

Piety, undesirable states of, (such as the "goody-goody")
- WLN 47 ❖ WLN 3:25

Piety: Why it is a poor qualification for entry into a ruling class
- WLN 31-49 ❖ WLN ch. 3

Pilgrim's Progress, if you ignore some straw-splitting dialogues on Calvinist theology and concentrate on the story, is first-class
- L 299 ❖ L 9 May 61

Pilgrim's Progress, passage from, indicates how we can taste the illustrious experience of Friendship with safety
- FL 124-125 ❖ FL 4:59, 60

Pilgrim's Regress, I don't wonder that you got fogged in; it was my first religious book...
- L 248-249 ❖ L 19 Jan 53

Pilgrim's Regress: "The Tableland represents *all* high and dry states of mind, of which High Anglicanism then seemed to me to be one..."
- L 170 ❖ L 8 Nov 39

Pipe: People might find "that the heart sings unbidden while they are working their way through a tough bit of theology with a pipe in their teeth..."
- GID 205 ❖ GID II 4:7

Pittenger, Rejoinder to Dr. (chapter title)
❖ GID 177-183 ❖ GID I ch. 22

Pity as a form of pain which helps us in our return to obedience and charity (makes it easier for us to love the unlovely)
- PP 105-106 (*see also* PP 117)
❖ PP 6:17 (*see also* PP 7:9)

Pity (as for oppressed classes), if not controlled by charity and justice, leads through anger to cruelty
- PP 65 ❖ PP 4:12

Pity: My own idea is that all sadness not arising from either repentance (hastening to amendment) or pity (hastening to assistance) is simply bad
- PP 67 ❖ PP 4:15

Places, holy: If they cease to remind us that all places are holy, they will do us harm
- LM 75 ❖ LM 14:10

Plagiarism: How can any man prefer the galley-slave labour of transcription to the freeman's work of attempting an essay on his own?
- L 291 ❖ L 10 Dec 59

Plan of salvation—*see* Salvation, plan of

Planning—*consider also* Future

Planning for the future not inconsistent with a world where the future is unknown—we have been doing so in such a world for thousands of years
- LM 38 ❖ LM 7:9

Planning: Great thing is to be found at one's post, living each day as though it were our last, but planning as though our world might last a hundred years
- GID 266 (*see also* WLN 110-112)
❖ GID II 16:55 (*see also* WLN 7:31-34)

Planning, in the sense of thinking before one acts, is compatible with and demanded by Christian ethics
- L 226 ❖ L 7 Feb 51

Platitudes, truths may sound like barren, to those who have not had the relevant experience
- L 166 ❖ L 8 May 39

Plato described as "an overwhelming theological genius"
- RP 80 ❖ RP 8:6

Plato, I loved, before St. Augustine
- GID 132 ❖ GID I 16:4

Plato, in his *Republic*, talks of pure righteousness, the very same thing of which the Passion of Christ is the supreme illustration
- RP 104, 108 ❖ RP 10:9, 10, 12

Plato mentioned with regard to his view of the body
- PP 104 ❖ PP 6:15

Plato, philosophers like, have a vivid and positive doctrine of immortality
- RP 37 ❖ RP 4:8

Plato reached the concept of "the timeless

•GID 79; M 178-179

❖ GID I 8:10; M App. B:17

Play: "It is a serious matter to choose wholesome recreations: but they would no longer be recreations if we pursued them seriously"

•CR 33-34 ❖ CR 2:54

Play, making games organized and compulsory in school banished the element of

•SJ 98 (see also SJ 107)

❖ SJ 6:22, 23 (see also SJ 7:9)

Play: "We can play, as we can eat, to the glory of God" (re: the reading of comedies and tales)

•CR 10 ❖ CR 1:15

Playfulness and humour within Eros (Romantic love)

•FL 150-151 ❖ FL 5:30

Playfulness and humour within Venus (sexual love)

•FL 138-146 ❖ FL 5:11-21

Pleasure, critics must not judge a thing intended purely for, as something it was not meant to be (re: literature meant to be read lightly)

•CR 33-34 ❖ CR 2:54

Pleasure (e.g., sexual pleasure) is not what one is *really* looking for; you might as well offer a mutton chop to a man who is dying of thirst...

•SJ 170 (see also GO 6-7*; consider also Desire) ❖ SJ 11:6 (see also GO 1:12*; consider also Desire)

Pleasure, enjoyment of any, for its own sake is better than abandoning what you really like in favour of the "best" people, the "important" books, etc.*

•SL 58-60 (see also CR 10; L 216; LAL 54; WLN 31-35)

❖ SL 13:3, 4 (see also CR 1:15; L 3 Apr 49; LAL 20/3/56; WLN 3:2-7)

Pleasure, even if hell contained much, that black pleasure would be such as to send any soul, not already damned, flying to its prayers in nightmare terror

•PP 126 (see also PP 152)

❖ PP 8:9 (see also PP 10:9)

Pleasure, every, can be made a channel for

adoration; we can learn to recognise its divine source and give thanks for it in the same moment it is received

•LM 89-90 (see also GO 73*)

❖ LM 17:6-9 (see also GO 4:7, 8*)

Pleasure, experience of, precludes at that moment an intellectual understanding of pleasure; humans cannot experience and intellectualize at the same time

•GID 65-66 (see also SJ 217-219)

❖ GID I 5:8 (see also SJ 14:9, 10)

Pleasure: Flippancy parodies merriment as indulgence parodies love*

•WG 19 ❖ WG 1:15

Pleasure ("Fun") can sometimes be used to divert humans from duties

(—Screwtape)

•SL 50 ❖ SL 11:3

Pleasure ("Fun") defined by Screwtape as "a sort of emotional froth arising from the play instinct"

•SL 50 ❖ SL 11:3

Pleasure ("Fun") mentioned by Screwtape as having "wholly undesirable tendencies; it promotes charity, contentment, and many other evils"

•SL 50 ❖ SL 11:3

Pleasure ("Fun"): "Say what you like, Barfield, the world is sillier and better fun than they make out..."

•L 217 ❖ L 4 Apr 49

Pleasure, humility is the road to

•WG 113 ❖ WG 7:9

Pleasure in itself is good; a "sinful" pleasure means a good offered, and accepted, under conditions which involve a breach of the moral law

•CR 21 (see also MC 49; SL 41-42, 69)

❖ CR 2:27 (see also MC II 2:9; SL 9:2; 15:3)

Pleasure in the arts ("culture") possibly more varied, intense, and lasting than vulgar or "popular" pleasure (though this has not been proved)

•CR 21 ❖ CR 2:28

Pleasure is God's invention, not the devil's

(—Screwtape)

•SL 41 ❖ SL 9:2

Pleasure: "Joy" is distinct not only from

pleasure in general but even from aesthetic pleasure; it must have the stab, the pang, the longing
•SJ 72 (see also SJ 221)
❖ SJ 5:2 (see also SJ 14:12)

Pleasure, like all that is given to a creature with free will, is two-edged (as is pain)
•PP 107, 118 ❖ PP 6:18; 8:1

Pleasure: Need-pleasures, even when innocent, "die on us" with extraordinary abruptness
•FL 28 (see also MC 100-101)
❖ FL 2:6 (see also MC III 6:11, 12)

Pleasure not bad in itself; we will have bodies even in Heaven
•MC 91 (see also LM 89; M 159-163; SL 69; WG 18, 72-73*)
❖ MC III 5:7 (see also LM 17:5; M 16:27-32; SL 15:3; WG 1:14; 4:30*)

Pleasure of evil: "...how terrible that there should be even a kind of pleasure in thinking evil"
•L 222-223 ❖ L 12 Jan 50

Pleasure of exclusiveness: Friendship may be "about" almost nothing except the fact that it excludes others
•FL 121-122 ❖ FL 4:54, 55

Pleasure of hatred: "...creatures like us who actually find hatred such a pleasure that to give it up is like giving up beer or tobacco..."*
•MC 108 ❖ MC III 7:11

Pleasure of hatred: Hatred has its pleasures; may be a compensation for fear, or an anodyne for shame
•SL 136 ❖ SL 29:4

Pleasure of hatred: Lewis mentions that, on his conversion, he found within himself (among other things) "a harem of fondled hatreds"*
•SJ 226 (see also CR 169)
❖ SJ 14:19 (see also CR 14:21)

Pleasure of hatred: "...we all know the perilous charm of a shared hatred or grievance"*
•FL 113 ❖ FL 4:43

Pleasure of having a grievance
•LM 94 (see also FL 82, 113; LAL 92-93; SL ix) ❖ LM 18:1 (see also FL 3:45;

4:43; LAL 28 Oct 60; SL P:16)

Pleasure of poetic language is the pleasure at finding anything vividly conveyed to the imagination
•CR 130-131 (see also GID 66*)
❖ CR 11:4 (see also GID I 5:9*)

Pleasure of pride is like the pleasure of scratching; but much nicer to have neither the itch nor the scratch
•L 256 ❖ L 18 Feb 54

Pleasure of putting other people in the wrong, of bossing and patronising and spoiling sport, of backbiting, of power and of hatred mentioned
•MC 94-95 ❖ MC III 5:14

Pleasure of resentment: "How a resentment, while it lasts, draws one back and back to nurse and fondle and encourage it!"
•LM 94 ❖ LM 18:1

Pleasure of resentment: "...how madly one cherishes that base part as if it were one's dearest possession..."*
•LAL 93 ❖ LAL 28 Oct 60

Pleasure of resentment, if anyone says he does not know the, he is a liar or a saint
•FL 82 ❖ FL 3:45

Pleasure of resentment: "Resentment is pleasant only as a relief from, or alternative to, humiliation"
•LM 95 ❖ LM 18:1

Pleasure of resentment: We can recognise in ourselves the Psalmists' tendency to chew over and over the cud of some injury*
•RP 23-24 ❖ RP 3:8

Pleasure of resentment: "'Well,' we say, 'he'll live to be sorry for it'... not admitting that what we predict gives us a certain satisfaction"*
•RP 23 ❖ RP 3:8

Pleasure of sex, like the pleasure of eating, is not wrong but you must not try to isolate it from the total union which is marriage
•MC 96 ❖ MC III 6:2

Pleasure of thinking about other people's faults as "the most morbid pleasure in the world"

•GID 154 ❖ GID I 18:9

Pleasure: Screwtape mentions his Enemy [God] as being "a hedonist at heart" who offers "pleasures for evermore"
•SL 101-102, 116 ❖ SL 22:3; 25:2

Pleasure: Settled happiness and security God withholds from us, "but joy, pleasure, and merriment He has scattered broadcast"
•PP 115 ❖ PP 7:7

Pleasure, the miracle at Cana sanctified an innocent sensual, and could be taken to sanctify at least a recreational use of "culture" as mere entertainment
•CR 15 ❖ CR 2:7

Pleasure, the surest way to spoil a, is to start examining it (re: introspection as it relates to "Joy")
•SJ 218-219 (see also GID 65-66)
❖ SJ 14:10, 11 (see also GID I 5:8)

Pleasure vs. "Joy": I doubt whether anyone who has tasted Joy would exchange it for all the pleasures in the world
•SJ 18 (see also SL 148*; Joy)
❖ SJ 1:18 (see also SL 31:5*; Joy)

Pleasure vs. "Joy": "Joy" has only one characteristic in common with Pleasure: Anyone who has experienced it will want it again
•SJ 18 ❖ SJ 1:18

Pleasure vs. "Joy": "Joy is never in our power and pleasure often is"
•SJ 18 ❖ SJ 1:18

Pleasures, all the worst, are purely spiritual—pleasures of power, hatred, etc.
•MC 94-95 ❖ MC III 5:14

Pleasures are rendered at once less pleasant and harder to forgo by making a habit of them
•SL 55 (see also MC 100-101; SL 41-42, 116-117) ❖ SL 12:4 (see also MC III 6:12; SL 9:2; 25:3, 4)

Pleasures are shafts of the glory of God as it strikes our sensibility
•LM 89 ❖ LM 17:4

Pleasures are the results of God's creative rapture; even as now filtered, they are too much for our present management
❖ WG 7-18 ❖ WG 1:14

Pleasures, "bad," are really "pleasures snatched by unlawful acts"—stealing an apple is bad, not the sweetness
•LM 89 (see also SL 69*)
❖ LM 17:5 (see also SL 15:3*)

Pleasures, both sensuous and aesthetic, can be means for adoring God
•LM 90 ❖ LM 17:9-11

Pleasures, earthly, only suggest what we were really made for
•MC 120 ❖ MC III 10:5

Pleasures, experience of, essential to our adoration of Him who gave them (without it, we will not have "tasted and seen")
•LM 91 ❖ LM 17:13

Pleasures, I sometimes wonder whether all, are not substitutes for "Joy"
•SJ 170 ❖ SJ 11:6

Pleasures, no, ought to be too ordinary or usual to be perceived as blessings from God ("...down to one's soft slippers at bedtime")
•LM 89-90 ❖ LM 17:6-9

Pleasures, obstacles to our perception of ordinary, as blessings from God: inattention, greed, and conceit
•LM 90 ❖ LM 17:10

Pleasures of Appreciation make us feel that something has not merely gratified our senses but claimed our appreciation by right
•FL 29-30 ❖ FL 2:7, 8

Pleasures of Appreciation turn into Need-pleasures when they go bad (as in addiction)
•FL 26-27 ❖ FL 2:2, 3

Pleasures of childhood, you and I have kept, (such as fairy tales), and have added some grown-up ones as well
•LAL 17 ❖ LAL Jun 22d 53

Pleasures, real, create the feeling of coming home, of recovering oneself; this is mentioned by Screwtape as defeating his purpose
•SL 59 ❖ SL 13:3

Pleasures, two classes of: those not pleasurable unless preceded by desire, and those pleasurable in their own right (Need-pleasure vs. Appreciative plea-

sure)
•FL 25-26 ❖ FL 2:2

Pleasures: When we take them at times or in ways or in degrees which God has forbidden, we get an ever increasing craving for an ever diminishing pleasure*
•SL 41-42 (*see also* SL 55, 116-117)
❖ SL 9:2 (*see also* SL 12:4; 25:3, 4)

Pleasures which God allows humans listed by Screwtape
•SL 101-102 (*see also* SL 116)
❖ SL 22:2 (*see also* SL 25:2)

Pleasures, Wormwood's attempt to damn his patient by palming off "vanity, bustle, irony, and expensive tedium" as, failed by giving him a *real* pleasure
•SL 58-59 ❖ SL 13:3

Poached egg, a man who was merely a man and said the sort of things Jesus said would be on a level with the man who says he is a
•MC 56 ❖ MC II 3:13

Poem a symbol which can be seen only in its simplest interpretation, i.e., black marks on white paper (just as the Bible can be read merely as literature)
•RP 116-117 (*see also* RP 128-129)
❖ RP 11:12 (*see also* RP 12:9)

Poems, an anthology of love, for public and perpetual use would probably be as sore a trial to literary taste as *Hymns Ancient and Modern*
•RP 94 ❖ RP 9:5

Poems, Psalms must be read as, with all the licenses and hyperboles which are proper to lyric poetry
•RP 3 ❖ RP 1:4

Poet, Lewis mentions or refers to his aspiration to become a
•L 73, 86, 163, 260
❖ L 15 Apr 22; 9 Feb 23; 13 Feb 23; 8 Feb 39; undated letter just before 2 Feb 55

Poets, "Abracadabrist": "What gives the show away is that their professed admirers give quite contradictory interpretations of the same poem..."
•LAL 30 ❖ LAL Mar 31st 54

Poets and mythologies express our deep desire: to be united with the beauty we see
•WG 16 ❖ WG 1:13

Poetic language can convey to us the quality of experiences which we have not had, or perhaps can never have...
•CR 133 ❖ CR 11:8, 9

Poetic language is by no means merely an expression, nor a stimulant, of emotion, but a real medium of information
•CR 130-134, esp. 134
❖ CR 11:4-11, esp. 11:11

Poetic language, most human experiences cannot be communicated by Scientific language and require instead the use of
•CR 138, 140 ❖ CR 11:20, 23

Poetic language often expresses emotion not for its own sake but in order to inform us about the object which aroused the emotion
•CR 132, 134 ❖ CR 11:7, 11

Poetic language, pleasure of, is the pleasure at finding anything vividly conveyed to the imagination
•CR 130-131 (*see also* GID 66*)
❖ CR 11:4 (*see also* GID I 5:9*)

Poetic language, religious experiences cannot be conveyed to one another except by, —by hints, similes, metaphors, and emotions
•CR 137-138, 140 ❖ CR 11:19, 23

Poetic language, such information about religion as, has to give can be received only if you are prepared to meet it half-way—with good will
•CR 135, 137, 141
❖ CR 11:12, 16, 18, 25

Poetic language: There seems to be a difference between understanding a person's fear because he has expressed it well and being actually *infected* by it
•CR 132 ❖ CR 11:6

Poetic language uses factors within our experience so that they become pointers to something outside our experience
•CR 133 ❖ CR 11:9

Poetic language vs. Ordinary or Scientific language: Poetic language vividly

conveys factual information to the imagination
•CR 130-131 (*see also* GID 66*)
❖ CR 11:3, 4 (*see also* GID I 5:9*)

Poetical religious expressions like "God is love" not merely expressions of emotion; can convey real information if you will meet them half-way—with good will
•CR 136-137 (*see also* CR 135, 141)
❖ CR 11:16 (*see also* CR 11:12, 25)

Poetical religious language, emotion in: "Momentous matter, if believed, will arouse emotion whatever the language"
•CR 136 ❖ CR 11:16

Poetry—*consider also* Art; Culture; Literature

"Poetry" (aesthetic satisfaction) the result rather than the cause of religious belief
•WG 77-78 ❖ WG 5:9

Poetry: "...all the greatest poems have been made by men who valued something else much more than poetry"
•CR 10 ❖ CR 1:15

Poetry and ancient myths, so false as history, may be very near the truth as prophecy ("Some day, God willing, we shall get *in*")
•WG 16-17 ❖ WG 1:13

Poetry and the romances, Christianity prefigured in
•L 143 ❖ L 24 Oct 31

Poetry and theology: "In Akhenaten as in the Psalms, a certain kind of poetry seems to go with a certain kind of theology"
•RP 89 ❖ RP 8:18

Poetry as a form of culture in which "culture" is irrelevant when the enjoyment is genuine
•WLN 33-35 ❖ WLN 3:5-7

Poetry as "only a collection of mental pictures": These in reality are what the appreciation of poetry, when interrupted, leaves behind
•SJ 219 ❖ SJ 14:10

Poetry, Christianity for me was associated with bad

•SJ 172 ❖ SJ 11:8

"Poetry" defined for the question, "Is Theology Poetry?": "...writing which arouses and in part satisfies the imagination"
•WG 74-75 ❖ WG 5:3

Poetry, English, as something you can come to the end of, like a wood
•L 129 (*see also* GID 42*)
❖ L 2 Aug 28 (*see also* GID I 3:8*)

Poetry, except in bad, poets are not always telling us that things are shocking or delightful—though they do tell us that grass is green, etc.
•CR 131 ❖ CR 11:5

Poetry, for the modern student, is something assigned and tested on; he does not know that poetry ever had any other purpose
•WLN 47 ❖ WLN 3:25

Poetry, I am more and more convinced that there is no future [in writing]
•L 163 ❖ L 8 Feb 39

Poetry, I am told my mother cared for no, at all
•SJ 5 ❖ SJ 1:2

Poetry: "I began to see that the reader who misses syntactical points in a poem is missing aesthetic points as well"
•SJ 112 ❖ SJ 7:16

Poetry, I have leaned too much on the idea of being able to write
•L 73 (*see also* L 86, 260)
❖ L Apr 22 (*see also* L 9 Feb 23; 13 Feb 23; undated letter just before 2 Feb 55)

Poetry: "I think '*vers libre*' succeeds only in a few exceptional poems and its prevalence has really ruined the art"
•LAL 28 (*see also* L 48)
❖ LAL Mar 10/54 (*see also* L 25 May 19)

Poetry "is a little incarnation, giving body to what had been before invisible and inaudible" (e.g., Psalms and some of the sayings of Our Lord)
•RP 5 ❖ RP 1:8

Poetry is religiously ambivalent; i.e., may be a preparation or medium for meeting God, *or* it may be a distraction and impediment
•L 268

❖ L undated letter just before 2 Apr 56

Poetry, it does not matter at what point you first break into the system of European; only keep your ears open and your mouth shut
•SJ 53 ❖ SJ 3:12

Poetry, it seems to me appropriate that the speech of God should sometimes be, (e.g., Psalms)
•RP 5 ❖ RP 1:8

Poetry, mouthing of, an infallible mark of the man who really likes poetry
•L 152 ❖ L 8 Apr 32

Poetry, my father was fond of, provided it had elements of rhetoric or pathos or both
•SJ 4 ❖ SJ 1:2

Poetry, nearly all the greatest love, has been produced by Christians
•MC 91 ❖ MC III 5:7

Poetry of the Bible depends largely on parallelism, which translates into any language
•L 188; RP 3-5 ❖ L 16 Jul 40; RP 1:5-7

Poetry of the Psalms did not, like ours, seek to express those things in which individuals differ, and did not aim at novelty
•CR 115 ❖ CR 10:2

Poetry of the Psalms: "I take [Psalm 19] to be the greatest poem in the Psalter and one of the greatest lyrics in the world"
•RP 63 ❖ GID 6:13

Poetry, one obvious difference between, and straight prose is that poetry contains a great many more adjectives
•CR 131 ❖ CR 11:5

Poetry, only, can speak low enough to catch the faint murmur of the mind
•LM 112 ❖ LM 21:2

Poetry or music, good taste in, not necessary to salvation (as evidenced by the humble charwoman in church who revels in hymns)
•L 224 ❖ L 7 Dec 50

Poetry: Reading and eating are two pleasures that combine admirably, although it would be a kind of blasphemy to read poetry at table
•SJ 142 ❖ SJ 9:18

Poetry, rhyming, compared to architecture: "...a need, and the answer of it following so quickly that they make a single sensation"
•L 66 ❖ L 7 Aug 21

Poetry, Romantic, as a natural counterpart to the Myth of Evolutionism
•CR 90 ❖ CR 7:17

Poetry, sensuous imagery in, hints at the future complete healing of Spirit and Nature
•M 159 ❖ M 16:27

Poetry, Smewgy first taught me the right sensuality of; how it should be savored and mouthed in solitude
•SJ 111 ❖ SJ 7:15

Poetry, those who read, to improve their minds will never improve their minds by reading poetry—the true enjoyments must be spontaneous and look to no remoter end
•WLN 35 ❖ WLN 3:7

Poetry, values presupposed in romantic: enjoyment of nature; Sehnsucht awakened by the past, the remote, or the (imagined) supernatural
•CR 16, 21-23 ❖ CR 2:13, 29-34

Poetry, Vorticist
•L 51-52 ❖ L 6 Jun 20

Poetry vs. Science to convey information: Science gives us, out of the teeming complexity of every concrete reality only "the common measurable features"
•CR 135 ❖ CR 11:12

Poetry: "We—even our poets and musicians and inventors—never, in the ultimate sense, make. We only build. We always have materials to build from"
•LM 73 (see also Creativity)
❖ LM 14:3 (see also Creativity)

Poetry works with "subtle and sensitive exploitations of imagination and emotion" to convey information (re: language and religion)
•CR 137 ❖ CR 11:18

Poetry writing: "I began...to look for expressions which would not merely state but suggest...I had learned what writing means"

•SJ 74 ❖ SJ 5:5

Pointing as an example of an act which, without understanding the symbolism, cannot be understood (e.g., a dog will merely sniff at your finger)
•WG 71 ❖ WG 4:29

Poison of Subjectivism, The (chapter title)
•CR 72-81 ❖ CR ch. 6

Political argument, I see Bulverism at work in every
•GID 274 (*see also* Bulverism)
❖ GID III 1:8 (*see also* Bulverism)

Political corruption, Screwtape speaks on small-scale
•SL 154, 156; WLN 52, 54
❖ SL 32:5, 10; WLN 4:5, 10

Political ideologies cannot be compared if morality is a subjective sentiment to be altered at will*
•CR 73 (*see also* CR 75)
❖ CR 6:5 (*see also* CR 6:11)

Political ideology, penetration of, into theology: "Mark my words: you will presently see both a Leftist and a Rightist pseudo-theology developing..."
•L 176 ❖ L 17 Jan 40

Political opinions, such embryonic, as I had [in my youth] were vaguely socialistic
•SJ 173 ❖ SJ 11:10

Political parties, nearly all, agree on the desirable ends: security, a living wage, etc.; what they disagree on is the means of achieving them
•GID 196 ❖ GID II 3:2

Political parties: "The demon inherent in every party is at all times ready enough to disguise himself as the Holy Ghost"
•GID 198 ❖ GID II 3:5

Political party, problems inherent in the creation of a Christian
•GID 196-199 (*see also* WG 113-114*)
❖ GID II ch. 3 (*see also* WG 7:11, 12*)

Political power is at best a necessary evil, but it is least evil when its claims are modest and commonplace, setting itself strictly limited objectives
•WLN 40 (*see also* GID 315-316; L 281;

WLN 48) ❖ WLN 3:13 (*see also* GID III 8:16-21; L 1 Feb 58; WLN 3:27)

Political programme, Christianity does not profess to have a detailed, for applying the Golden Rule to a particular society at a particular moment
•MC 78-79 ❖ MC III 3: 2, 3

Political theory, classical, (we surrender our right of self-protection on the condition that the State will protect us) no longer a reality; has died
•GID 308, 314 ❖ GID III 7:8, 9; 8:11

Politician, people will go out of their way to meet a, or a celebrity, even when it is known that the person leads a vile and mischievous life
•RP 67, 71 ❖ RP 7:3, 9

Politicians: "Give me a man who will do a day's work for a day's pay, who will refuse bribes, who will not make up his facts, and who has learned his job"
•CR 81 ❖ CR 6:23

Politicians: If we believed in the objectivity of moral values we would value those who solicit our votes by other standards than are currently in fashion
•CR 81 ❖ CR 6:23

Politicians: Rhetorician, definition of: "...he...escapes from questions he doesn't want to answer into a cloud of eloquence"** (Lewis is here referring to a "rhetorician")
•L 113-114 ❖ L 30 Mar 27

Politicians: "The higher the pretensions of our rulers are, the more meddlesome and impertinent their rule is likely to be..."
•WLN 48 (*see also* WLN 40)
❖ WLN 3:27 (*see also* WLN 3:13)

Politicians: "...wisdom and virtue are not the only or the commonest qualifications for a place in the government..."
•GID 292 ❖ GID III 4:11

Politics—*see also* Government

Politics: A "Christian Party," being itself a minority and having factions within itself, could never be of much effect (and may be dangerous)
•GID 196-199 ❖ GID II ch. 3

Politics: "...a prudent society must spend at least as much energy on conserving what it has as on improvement"
•CR 92-93 ❖ CR 7:22

Politics and Christianity, Screwtape discusses a profitable relationship between, from his point of view
•SL 108-109 ❖ SL 23:4

Politics and economics discussed briefly with regard to Christianity
•MC 78-83 ❖ MC III 3:2-8

Politics: "...any change in society is at least as likely to destroy the liberties and amenities we already have as to add new ones..." (re: "progress")
•CR 92 ❖ CR 7:22

Politics: "I believe in God, but I detest theocracy. For every Government consists of mere men..."
•GID 315 ❖ GID III 8:16

Politics, modern, would be impossible without the Myth of Evolutionism, which obscures truisms which would be fatal to the political Left and Right
•CR 92-93 ❖ CR 7:22

Politics: Most of us are approaching the subject in the hope of finding support from Christianity for the views of our own party
•MC 82 ❖ MC III 3:8

Politics, practical problem of Christian, is that of living as innocently as we can with unbelieving fellow subjects under unbelieving rulers
•GID 292-293 ❖ GID III 4:12

Politics, the only ways in which Christianity can influence
•GID 199 ❖ GID II 3:7

Politics: There are fools who believe that my religious writings are all covert anti-Leftist propaganda
•L 235 ❖ L 3 Dec 51

Politics, we think about such things as, only in order to be able to think about something else
•WG 109 (see also GID 280-281*)
❖ WG 7:4 (see also GID III 2:6-10*)

Polytheism—consider also Paganism

Polytheism has no real doctrine of Creation; the gods are usually the product of a universe already in existence
•GID 149 (see also M 8; RP 78, 82)
❖ GID I 17:6 (see also M 2:9; RP 8:4, 11)

Polytheism is nature-worship, and Pantheism is hostile to nature; neither leaves you free to enjoy your breakfast and mortify inordinate appetites
•GID 149 ❖ GID I 17:6

Polytheism, richness of, lacking in the Christian story (re: Christian theology as "poetry")
•WG 75 ❖ WG 5:5

Polytheism: "The difference between believing in God and in many gods is not one of arithmetic"
•RP 82 ❖ RP 8:11

Polytheism: Those who believed in many gods very seldom regarded those gods as creators of the universe and self-existent
•M 8 (see also Gods)
❖ M 2:9 (see also Gods)

Polytheist, "Pagan" in the proper sense means
•LAL 62 ❖ LAL Sep 8/56

Pond without a bottom as analogy to Naturalism
•M 29-30 ❖ M 4:9

Poor, helping the—see Charity; Humanitarianism

Poor: More than one kind of poverty meant in the words, "Blessed are the poor"
•MC 180-181 ❖ MC IV 10:11, 12

Poor, the Christian knows that the, probably include most of his superiors
•CR 10 ❖ CR 1:15

Pope Gregory, on arriving in Heaven and discovering that a cherished theory of his was quite wrong: It was the funniest thing he'd ever heard (story from Paradiso)
•CR 11 ❖ CR 1:16

Pope John XXIII referred to
•LAL 117 ❖ LAL 10 Jun 63

Pope, nothing would give such strong support to the Papal claims as the, functioning as the head of Christendom
•L 165 (consider also Reunion)

❖ L 8 May 39 (*consider also* Reunion)

Pope's Managerial God, the God of the New Testament who takes into account the death of every sparrow is far less anthropomorphic than, (re: poet Alexander Pope)
•LM 53-56, esp. 55
❖ LM 10:4-11, esp. 10:9

Popularity as a gift which could cause us to forget our need of God
•MC 180-181 ❖ MC IV 10:11

Popularity, personal, can only come unsought; "Until you conquer the fear of being an outsider, an outsider you will remain"*
•WG 103 ❖ WG 6:14

Pornography: I treat the use of filth and obscenity in literature as a sign of a culture that has lost its faith*
•GID 264-265 ❖ GID II 16:43

Portrait(s)—*see* Picture(s)

Possession(s)—*see also* Ownership

Possession: Appreciation of beauty that we shall never ourselves see or enjoy (or possess) as a form of disinterested love*
•FL 32-33 ❖ FL 2:12-14

Possession: "...the word 'mine' in its fully possessive sense cannot be uttered by a human being about anything" (not even his own soul)—Screwtape
•SL 98 (*consider also* Soul)
❖ SL 21:6 (*consider also* Soul)

Possessions: "...he who has God and everything else has no more than he who has God only"*
•WG 10 (*see also* PP 96*)
❖ WG 1:8 (*see also* PP 6:8*)

Possessiveness a characteristic of affection without charity*
•GID 285 ❖ GID III 3:7

Possessiveness: Human affection cannot stand seeing the beloved passing into a sphere where it cannot follow
•L 274 (*see also* FL 70-73)
❖ L 10 Feb 57 (*see also* FL 3:27-32)

Post, great thing is to be found at one's, living each day as though it were our last but planning as though our world might last a hundred years

•GID 266 (*see also* WLN 111-112)
❖ GID II 16:55 (*see also* WLN 7:34)

Potter, Beatrix: The second instance of Lewis's experience of "Joy" or longing came through the book *Squirrel Nutkin* by Beatrix Potter
•SJ 16-17 ❖ SJ 1:16

Poverty and every other ill, lovingly accepted, has all the value of voluntary poverty or penance
•LAL 60 (*see also* LAL 20)
❖ LAL 3/8/56 (*see also* LAL Aug 10th 53)

Poverty and overwork brought on by human stupidity and avarice rather than by "the churlishness of nature"
•PP 89 ❖ PP 6:1

Poverty as "the affliction which actually or potentially includes all other afflictions"
•PP 108 ❖ PP 6:18

Poverty, fighting—*see* Charity; Humanitarianism

Poverty frightens me more than anything else...if God wanted us to live like the lilies of the field He might have given us an organism more like theirs
•LAL 21, 22, 79 (*see also* GO 84)
❖ LAL Aug 10th 53; Nov 6/53; Oct 30 58 (*see also* GO 4:32)

Poverty, Lewis describes the development of his fear of, as a child
•SJ 64-65 ❖ SJ 4:11

Poverty: Marxist finds himself in agreement with the Christians who say that poverty is blessed and yet ought to be removed
•PP 108-109 (*see also* PP 110)
❖ PP 6:18 (*see also* PP 7:2)

Poverty merely *reveals* the helpless dependence which has all the time been our real condition...we are members of one another
•LAL 111-112 ❖ LAL 10 Dec 62

Poverty, more than one kind of, meant in the words "Blessed are the poor"
•MC 180-181 ❖ MC IV 10:11, 12

Power, all, corrupts; Theocracy is the worst of all possible governments
•WLN 40 (*see also* GID 315-316; WLN

48) ❖ WLN 3:13 (*see also* GID III 8:16-21; WLN 3:27)

Power: "All power corrupts..." (quote from Lord Acton)
•WG 114 ❖ WG 7:12

Power corrupts; those who have little authority over others may be thankful
•CR 119-120 ❖ CR 10:10

Power, God gives the higher creatures, to will His will; the lower ones simply execute it automatically
•LM 74-75 ❖ LM 14:9

Power, let all of us who have never been in positions of, give hearty thanks for it (fewer opportunities of oppressing and embittering others)
•RP 25 ❖ RP 3:10

Power of choice—*see* Choice; Freedom of choice; Free will

Power of God to alter character limited by Himself
•GID 152-153 ❖ GID I 18:5

Power over others, some Christians believe that no one can be trusted with more than a minimum of
•GID 197 (*see also* GID 315-316; WG 113-114) ❖ GID II 3:3 (*see also* GID III 8:15-21; WG 7:11, 12)

Power: Pascal referred to "Error of Stoicism": thinking we can do always what we can do sometimes" (e.g., prayer without words)
•LM 11 ❖ LM 2:5

Practical aspects of "being born again"
•MC 160-166 (*see also* Christianity, practice of) ❖ MC IV ch. 7 (*see also* Christianity, practice of)

Practical Conclusion, The (chapter title)
❖ MC 62-66 ❖ MC II ch. 5

Practice may be imperfect yet the precept still profitable
•GID 283-284 ❖ GID III 3:4

Practice more important than preaching toward the conversion of others
•L 261 (*see also* L 247; LAL 96)
❖ L 2 Feb 55 (*see also* L 8 Nov 52; LAL 24 Feb 61)

Practice much harder than preaching (re: humility)
•LAL 29 ❖ LAL Mar 31st 54

Practice of Christianity—*see* Christianity, practice of

Praise—*see also* Adoration; Worship; *consider also* Church services; Glorifying; Music, church

Praise ("adoration"), more than any other kind of prayer, should be a communal act
•LM 100 ❖ LM 19:1

Praise and adoration in prayer: "Begin where you are"—with the pleasures and blessings you are apprehending right now
•LM 88-91 ❖ LM 17:1-13

Praise as "inner health made audible": The most balanced and capacious minds praise most, while the cranks and misfits praise least
•RP 94 ❖ RP 9:5

Praise, enjoyment of God no more separable from, than the brightness a mirror receives is separable from the brightness it sheds
•RP 96 ❖ RP 9:6

Praise, every pleasure can be made a channel for; we can learn to recognise its divine source and give thanks for it in the same moment it is received
•LM 89-90 (*see also* GO 73)
❖ LM 17:6-9 (*see also* GO 4:7, 8)

Praise for God, like admiration for a painting, is the correct and appropriate response; if we do not render it we shall have missed something
•RP 92 ❖ RP 9:3

Praise for small things: "We...shall not be able to adore God on the highest occasions if we have learned no habit of doing so on the lowest"
•LM 91 ❖ LM 17:13

Praise: "Fully to enjoy is to glorify. In commanding us to glorify Him, God is inviting us to enjoy Him"
•RP 96-97 ❖ RP 9:6

Praise God, in learning to, we are merely "tuning our instruments"—in anticipation of the "symphony" of Heaven
•RP 97 (*see also* LM 116)
❖ RP 9:7 (*see also* LM 21:15)

Praise: God is that Object to admire which

is simply to be awake, and not to appreciate which is to have lost the greatest experience
•RP 92 ❖ RP 9:3

Praise, how to approach the idea that God "demands"
•RP 90-98 ❖ RP ch. 9

Praise, I had thought of, in terms of compliment—but all enjoyment spontaneously overflows into praise unless something checks it
•RP 93-94 ❖ RP 9:5

Praise, I think we delight to, what we enjoy because the praise not merely expresses but completes the enjoyment (re: Psalms)
•RP 95 (see also GO 72)
❖ RP 9:6 (see also GO 4:5)

Praise: If we are in perfect love with God, our hardly tolerable bliss will flow from us in effortless expression
•RP 96 ❖ RP 9:6

Praise, importance of the body in: But for our body all that we receive through the senses would go unpraised
•LM 17-18 (see also LAL 110-111)
❖ LM 3:9 (see also LAL 26 Nov 62)

Praise, in order to fully understand the doctrine of, we must suppose ourselves to be in perfect love with God...drunk with, drowned in, dissolved by, delight
•RP 96 ❖ RP 9:6

Praise in the Psalms
•RP 90-98 ❖ RP ch. 9

Praise is the mode of love which always has some element of joy in it
•GO 72 ❖ GO 4:5

Praise: "...it is in the process of being worshipped that God communicates His presence to men"
•RP 93 ❖ RP 9:4

Praise: It is natural for men to spontaneously urge other men to join them in praising whatever they value; the Psalmists are no exception
•RP 94-95 ❖ RP 9:5

Praise, love for God finds its natural expression in; indeed praise completes the enjoyment

•RP 94-97 (see also GO 72)
❖ RP 9:5, 6 (see also GO 4:5)

Praise of a deceased loved one (and of God): "Don't we in praise somehow enjoy what we praise, however far we are from it?"
•GO 72 (see also RP 95)
❖ GO 4:5 (see also RP 9:6)

Praise: "...of every created thing I praise, I should say, 'In some way, in its unique way, like Him who made it'"
•GO 73 (see also LM 90)
❖ GO 4:7 (see also LM 17:8)

Praise: Pleasure in being praised is not Pride
•MC 112 ❖ MC III 8:10

Praise, proper delight in ("Nothing can eliminate from the parable the divine accolade, 'Well done, thou good and faithful servant'")
•WG 11-12 ❖ WG 1:10

Praise, the idea of God demanding, reminded me of the dictator or celebrity who demands continued assurance of his own virtue
•RP 90-91 ❖ RP 9:2

Praise, the miserable idea that God should need or want our, is answered by the words "If I be hungry I will not tell thee"
•RP 92-93 (see also CR 98-99; MC 113-114*)
❖ RP 9:4 (see also CR 8:12; MC III 8:12*)

Praise: The worthier the object, the more intense the delight in praising; in Heaven angels and men will be perpetually employed in praising God
•RP 96 ❖ RP 9:6

Praising, A Word about (chapter title)
•RP 90-98 ❖ RP ch. 9

Praising God, two levels of: One in which intention is irrelevant, and another in which all depends on intention (re: church music)*
•CR 98 ❖ CR 8:12

Praising the God you love as natural a thing to want to do as sharing your delight in a new author, a good joke, or a lovely landscape
•RP 95 ❖ RP 9:6

Prayer(s)—*see also* Lord's Prayer; Obstacles to prayer; *consider also* Devotional life; Devotions

Prayer: A clergyman once said to me that perfect silence and solitude left one more open to the distractions which come from within
•LM 18 ❖ LM 3:11

Prayer: A false spirituality can cause humans to believe piously that "praise and communion with God are the true prayer"
•SL 126 ❖ SL 27:2

Prayer: A mere change of scene can decrease my faith at first; God is less credible when I pray in a hotel bedroom than when I am in College
•CR 42 ❖ CR 3:10

Prayer: A possible reference to Lewis's wife, Joy, whose prayer for recovery was seemingly answered
•WLN 3-4 (*see also* GO 34-35; LAL 67, 81) ❖ WLN 1:3 (*see also* GO 2:25; LAL Jun 18th 57; Jan 26th 59)

Prayer, a silly sort of, is prayer for a sick person which amounts to a diagnosis followed by advice as to how God should treat the patient
•LM 20 ❖ LM 4:3

Prayer, absence of faith that your, will be answered not necessarily a sin; Our Lord had no such assurance when He prayed in Gethsemane
•LM 60 ❖ LM 11:12

Prayer: All events are equally Providential, but prayer always contributes to God's decision one way or the other*
•M 174, 181 ❖ M App. B:3, 21

Prayer and actions, through both, God gave us the dignity of causality
•GID 106 (*see also* LM 52; WLN 9) ❖ GID I 11:8 (*see also* LM 10:3; WLN 1:17)

Prayer and suffering for others: "... there's a lot scattered through 2d Corinthians which is well worth meditation"
•LAL 55 ❖ LAL 15/4/56

Prayer and work as the two methods by which we are allowed to produce events as yet unproduced by God
•GID 106 ❖ GID I 11:9

Prayer, answers to: Did God bring it about or would it have happened anyway? —An impossible question
•M 178-179 (*see also* SL 126-127) ❖ M App. B:17 (*see also* SL 27:3)

Prayer, answers to: "God gives where He finds empty hands" (quote from Saint Augustine)*
•LAL 73 (*see also* PP 96) ❖ LAL 31/3/58 (*see also* PP 6:8)

Prayer, anxieties and decisions of everyday domestic life more of a hindrance to, than any appetite or passion
•FL 137-138 ❖ FL 5:10

Prayer as a duty which often feels like a burden: "The fact that prayers are constantly set as penances tells its own tale"
•LM 113 ❖ LM 21:5

Prayer as cause: Affirmative answer not guaranteed; otherwise prayer would be dangerous
•GID 106 ❖ GID I 11:10, 11

Prayer as cause, even when events have already happened ("...we can at noon become part causes of an event occurring at ten a.m.")
•M 179-180 (*see also* LM 110) ❖ M App. B:18 (*see also* LM 20:16)

Prayer as cause: Hamlet illustration shows how all events are providential and also come about by natural causes
•GID 79; M 179 ❖ GID I 8:10; M App. B:17

Prayer as cause: Illustration of mother praying for her son in the war
•GID 76-77 ❖ GID I 8:1-3

Prayer as cause: In forgiveness of sins, a divine action is elicited by our petition
•LM 50 ❖ LM 9:12

Prayer as cause no more mysterious than our other actions as cause
•GID 106, 217; L 149; WLN 9 ❖ GID I 11:7; II 7:4; L 21 Feb 32; WLN 1:17, 18

Prayer as cause: "Only faith vouches for the connection. No empirical proof could establish it"

•LM 48-49 ❖ LM 9:6-8

Prayer as cause: play illustration— author fixes general outline only
•GID 105 ❖ GID I 11:7

Prayer as cause: unlimited by space and time
•GID 107 ❖ GID I 11:11

Prayer as request, not compulsion: The essence of request is that it may or may not be granted
•WLN 4-7 ❖ WLN 1:6-14

Prayer as request, not magic or a mechanical operation
•L 236 (*see also* L 226; WLN 8, 10)
❖ L 8 Jan 52 (*see also* L undated letter just before 7 Feb 51; WLN 1:16, 19)

Prayer as soliloquy: Prayer in its most perfect state is a soliloquy; if the Holy Spirit speaks in the man, then in prayer God speaks to God
•LM 67-68 (*see also* LAL 22, 23; LM 49-50*, 81; MC 142-143)
❖ LM 13:1, 2 (*see also* LAL Nov 6/53; 27/xi/53; LM 9:11*; 15:15; MC IV 2:9)

Prayer as worship or adoration: "Begin where you are"—with the pleasures and blessings you are apprehending right now
•LM 88-91 ❖ LM 17:1-13

Prayer, assurance about, (as in our requests of people), is not from knowing things about the Giver but from knowing *him*
•WLN 6-8 (*see also* LM 49; WLN 26-27*) ❖ WLN 1:12-15 (*see also* LM 9:8; WLN 2:14*)

Prayer: Audacity of asking God to take sides in a war, e.g., "Prosper Oh Lord, our righteous cause"
•L 168 (*see also* FL 47-48*; L 183*; WG 24*) ❖ L 10 Sep 39 (*see also* FL 2:41, 42*; L 16 Apr 40*; WG 2:6*)

Prayer: Avoid trying to decide whether your mind is in the right frame; turn your attention to God
•L 256 (*see also* LM 23; SJ 61-62*; SL 20-21, 125) ❖ L 31 Jul 54 (*see also* LM 4:19; SJ 4:8*; SL 4:3; 27:1)

Prayer, awe in: We ought to be simultaneously aware of closest proximity and infinite distance
•LM 13 ❖ LM 2:13

Prayer, bargaining with God in: I have often, on my knees, been shocked to find what absurd adjustments or compromises I was, half-consciously, proposing
•RP 97-98 ❖ RP 9:8

Prayer Book Language, An Interpretation of ("Miserable Offenders"—chapter title)
•GID 120-128 ❖ GID I ch. 14

Prayer Book language, difficulties with
•GID 254-255 ❖ GID II 15:3, 4, 6

Prayer Book, revision of: "The more 'up to date' the book is, the sooner it will be dated"
•LM 12 ❖ LM 2:11

Prayer Book: Revisions ought to be done very gradually and with great caution
•LM 6-8 ❖ LM 1:11-20

Prayer Book, we are taught in the, to "give thanks to God for His great glory" as if we owed Him thanks just for being what He is; and so indeed we do
•SJ 77 (*see also* GID 130*; SJ 211, 231)
❖ SJ 5:9 (*see also* GID I 16:2*; SJ 13:20; 15:3)

Prayer: Can it change God's will?
•L 236 ❖ L 8 Jan 52

Prayer, case against: Doesn't God know already what is best?
•GID 104-105 (*see also* CR 142*; L 149)
❖ GID I 11:1-5 (*see also* CR 12:2*; L 21 Feb 32)

Prayer, case against: If God is omniscient, why do we need to confess our sins and "make known" our requests?
•LM 19-22 (*see also* L 217)
❖ LM 4:1-9 (*see also* L 1 Aug 49)

Prayer, case against: If what you request is good, God will do it whether you pray or not
•GID 105, 217 ❖ GID I 11:5; II 7:4

Prayer, case against: "Whatever we get we might have been going to get anyway"—but it's the same with our requests of people
•WLN 6-7; LM 36-37; 48-49
❖ WLN 1:12-14; LM 7:4-6; 9:7-9

Prayer, causative power of: As creatures "we have nothing we have not received; but we have received the power of being something more than receptacles"
•LM 50 ❖ LM 9:12

Prayer, corporate—*see also* Church services; Worship, corporate

Prayer, corporate
•LM 3-8 ❖ LM ch. 1

Prayer, corporate ("liturgiology"): There is almost no subject in the world on which I have less to say
•LM 3-4 ❖ LM 1:2

Prayer, corporate: My whole position really boils down to an entreaty for permanence and uniformity
•LM 4-5 ❖ LM 1:3-8

Prayer does not change God's mind—that is, His overall purpose. But that purpose can be realized in different ways...
•WLN 9 ❖ WLN 1:17

Prayer, efficacy of, cannot be either asserted or denied without an exercise of the will—choosing or rejecting faith
•M 180-181 ❖ M App. B:20, 21

Prayer: Emotional intensity is in itself no proof of spiritual depth
•LM 82 ❖ LM 15:17

Prayer, empirical proof regarding the efficacy of, such as we have in the sciences can never be attained
•WLN 4-6 ❖ WLN 1:5-10

Prayer, every sincere, even to a false god is accepted by the true God
•L 247 ❖ L 8 Nov 52

Prayer: Example of the man who prayed "Oh Lord, make me chaste" while his heart added, "But please don't do it just yet"
•MC 92 ❖ MC III 5:9

Prayer, faith in, based upon having a certain idea of God's character
•LM 49 (*see also* WLN 7-8, 25-27*)
❖ LM 9:8 (*see also* WLN 1:14, 15; 2:13, 14*)

Prayer, faith in: "The faith that moves mountains is a gift from Him who created mountains"
•CR 150 ❖ CR 12:25

Prayer, faith in: "...we ought perhaps to regard the worker of miracles, however rare, as the true Christian norm and ourselves as spiritual cripples"
•CR 150 ❖ CR 12:25

Prayer, faith in: Whatever else faith may mean, I feel quite sure it does not mean psychological certitude manufactured from within
•CR 150 ❖ CR 12:25

Prayer, fixed form of, sets our devotions free; easier to keep one's thoughts from straying
•L 239 (*see also* L 245; SL 20)
❖ L 1 Apr 52 (*see also* L 20 Oct 52; SL 4:2)

Prayer for a reliving of our past likely to go unanswered; "Leave those bulbs alone, and the new flowers will come up"
•LM 26-27 ❖ LM 5:10-13

Prayer for God's return: "I wonder whether people who ask God to interfere openly and directly in our world quite realise what it will be like when He does"
•MC 66 (*consider also* Contact with God) ❖ MC II 5:9 (*consider also* Contact with God)

Prayer for others might be more effectual if one were a better Christian
•LAL 55 ❖ LAL 26/4/56

Prayer for our enemies: As Christians, we are under orders to pray for them
•MC 11-12 ❖ MC P:16

Prayer for our enemies: How to make it real
•L 183 ❖ L 16 Apr 40

Prayer for our enemies: "I'd sooner pray for God's mercy than for His justice on my friends, my enemies, and myself"
•LAL 14 ❖ LAL 17/4/53

Prayer: For our spiritual life, having our prayers considered means more than having them granted; we can bear to be refused but not to be ignored
•LM 52-53 ❖ LM 10:3

Prayer for people: "Don't you find that, if you keep your mind fixed upon God, you will automatically think of the

person you are praying for?"
•LM 66 ❖ LM 12:13

Prayer for people one dislikes: I find it helpful to remember that one is joining in *Christ's* prayer for them
•L 226
❖ L undated letter just before 7 Feb 51

Prayer for people: "The increasing list of people to be prayed for is...one of the burdens of old age"
•LM 66 ❖ LM 12:13

Prayer for people who have hurt us—and then forgetting it—better than allowing them to become an obsession, to haunt our minds
•LAL 28 (*see also* LAL 44) ❖ LAL Mar 10/54 (*see also* LAL 21/6/55)

Prayer for the sick is unquestionably right and can do real good
•L 226 (*see also* CR 148; L 224-225; SL 126)
❖ L undated letter just before 7 Feb 51 (*see also* CR 12:19; L 7 Dec 50; SL 27:2)

Prayer for unbelievers more important than speculation about their destiny
•L 247 ❖ L 8 Nov 52

Prayer: God and man cannot exclude one another as man excludes man; in prayer, "God said it" and "I said it" can both be true
•LM 08 (*see also* LAL 22, 23; LM 49-50, 81; MC 142-143)
❖ LM 13:2 (*see also* LAL Nov 6/53; 27/xi/53; LM 9:11; 15:15; MC IV 2:9)

Prayer: God (as Trinity) prompts us to pray, helps us to pray, and is who we are praying to
•MC 142-143 (*see also* Prayer as soliloquy)
❖ MC IV 2:9 (*see also* Prayer as soliloquy)

Prayer: God has infinite attention to spare for each one of us ("You are as much alone with Him as if you were the only being He had ever created")
•MC 147 ❖ MC IV 3:7

Prayer, God instituted, in order to lend to His creatures the dignity of causality (quote from Pascal)
•GID 106; LM 52; WLN 9
❖ GID I 11:8; LM 10:3; WLN 1:17

Prayer, God is met as a Person in, just as we, by confessing our sins and making known our requests, assume the high rank of persons before Him
•LM 20-21 ❖ LM 4:6-8

Prayer: God speaks to Himself through us; then when the need comes, *He* carries out in us His otherwise impossible instructions
•LAL 22, 23 (*see also* LM 49-50, 68-69; Prayer as soliloquy)
❖ LAL Nov 6/53; 27/xi/53 (*see also* LM 9:11; 13:3; Prayer as soliloquy)

Prayer, granting of, not dependent upon a state of mind we should describe as "faith"; real faith cannot be "worked up"
•LM 60 ❖ LM 11:11

Prayer, Huck Finn tried the experiment of, and then, not unnaturally, never gave Christianity a second thought
•LM 60 ❖ LM 11:10

Prayer, human distaste for, when one is feeling vague guilt mentioned by Screwtape
•SL 54-55 ❖ SL 12:3

Prayer: "I come to you, reverend Fathers, for guidance. How am I to pray this very night?"
•CR 151 ❖ CR 12:25

Prayer: "...I find it best to make 'my own words' the staple but introduce a modicum of the ready-made"
•LM 12 ❖ LM 2:7

Prayer, I have never met a book on, which was much use...
•LM 62 ❖ LM 12:1

Prayer, I think you are perfectly right to change your manner of, from time to time
•L 245 ❖ L 20 Oct 52

Prayer: "I'd sooner pray for God's mercy than for His justice on my friends, my enemies, and myself"
•LAL 14 ❖ LAL 17/4/53

Prayer: "If we were perfected, prayer would not be a duty, it would be delight. Some day, please God, it will be"
•LM 114 (*see also* L 277*)

❖ LM 21:11 (*see also* L 18 Jul 57*)

Prayer: Illustration of asking the Headmaster
•GID 107 ❖ GID I 11:11

Prayer: Importance of re-awakening an awareness of God and myself as real entities facing each other, in actual contact with each other
•LM 77-82 ❖ LM ch. 15

Prayer, importance of the body in: But for our body all that we receive through the senses would go unpraised
•LM 17-18 (*see also* LAL 110-111; SL 20)
❖ LM 3:9 (*see also* LAL 26 Nov 62; SL 4:2)

Prayer in bereavement: "There is no answer. Only the locked door, the iron curtain, the vacuum, absolute zero. Them as asks don't get"
•GO 7 (*see also* GO 4-6, 53-54, 71, 80; LAL 92) ❖ GO 1:13 (*see also* GO 1:7-11; 3:25, 26; 4:4, 24; LAL 24 Sep 60)

Prayer in Christ's name means prayers prayed in the spirit of Christ; but how are we to take the promise of invariable granting of these prayers?
•CR 149 ❖ CR 12:21

Prayer in Gethsemane: Disciples only heard the opening words—then fell asleep; they record those words as if they were the whole
•LM 47 ❖ LM 9:3

Prayer in Gethsemane: Fact that Jesus made His request with a reservation—"Not my will, but thine"—does not remove the prayer's petitionary character
•LM 36 ❖ LM 7:2

Prayer in Gethsemane, for most of us, is the only model; removing mountains can wait
•LM 60 ❖ LM 11:10

Prayer in Gethsemane, idea that the New Testament promises invariable granting of our prayers is dismissed by the instance of Christ's
•WLN 5 ❖ WLN 1:7

Prayer in Gethsemane: Our Lord descended into the humiliation of praying on His own behalf (but then certitude about His Father's will was withdrawn)
•LM 61 ❖ LM 11:14

Prayer in Gethsemane refutes the idea that people whose prayers are answered are "a sort of court favorites, people who have influence with the throne"
•WLN 10 ❖ WLN 1:20

Prayer in Gethsemane shows that anxiety is part of our human destiny; the perfect Man experienced it
•LM 42-43 ❖ LM 8:9

Prayer in Gethsemane: We may be sure Jesus prayed aloud; people did everything aloud in those days
•LM 47 ❖ LM 9:3

Prayer, in the stage-play of, God is the Author, the Producer, and the Audience
•LM 81 (*see also* Prayer as soliloquy) ❖ LM 15:15 (*see also* Prayer as soliloquy)

Prayer, invariable "success" in, would not prove the Christian doctrine at all — it would prove something more like magic
•WLN 4-5 ❖ WLN 1:6

Prayer, irksomeness of: An excuse to omit it is never unwelcome; let us come clean about this
•LM 112-113 (See entire chapter) ❖ LM 21:1-4 (See entire chapter)

Prayer, irksomeness of: I am not deeply worried by this; it is humiliating and frustrating—but we are still only at school
•LM 116 ❖ LM 21:15

Prayer is a means, but is also an end; the world was made partly that there might be prayer
•LM 56 ❖ LM 10:11

Prayer is an effort toward unity with God; here, at least, the distortion of God's voice through man is not total
•LM 69-70 ❖ LM 13:6

Prayer is either sheer illusion or personal contact between ourselves and God, as is confession, penitence, adoration, and the vision and enjoyment of God
•WLN 8 ❖ WLN 1:16

Prayer is most ours when most His ("The deeper the level within ourselves from which our prayer, or any other act, wells up, the more it is His...")
•LM 69 ❖ LM 13:3

Prayer is not magic, or a machine; it is not advice offered to God—the reality is doubtless not comprehensible to our faculties
•WLN 8, 10 (*see also* L 236)
❖ WLN 1:16, 19 (*see also* L 8 Jan 52)

Prayer is not the time for pressing our own favorite social or political panacea
•LM 25 ❖ LM 5:5

Prayer "is perhaps the only form of 'work for re-union' which never does anything but good" (re: ecumenicism)
•LAL 12 ❖ LAL Nov 10th 52

Prayer: It is no use to ask God for "A" when our whole mind is in reality filled with desire for "B"
•LM 22-23 ❖ LM 4:15, 16

Prayer, it is not possible to prove whether or not an event is an answer to; we are not even to ask
•M 180-181 (*see also* LM 48-49)
❖ M App. B:20, 21 (*see also* LM 9: 6-8)

Prayer: "It would be better not to be reverent at all than to have a reverence which denied the proximity [of God]"
•LM 13 ❖ LM 2:15

Prayer: "It's so much easier to pray for a bore than to go and see him"
•LM 66 ❖ LM 12:12

Prayer, Joy's remission of cancer after, mentioned
•LAL 81, 82, 88 (*see also* LAL 67; WLN 3-4*)
❖ LAL Jan 26th 59; 6/5/59; 18 Oct 59 (*see also* LAL Jun 18th 57; WLN 1:3*)

Prayer, kneeling in: "I won't say this doesn't matter. The body ought to pray as well as the soul"
•LM 17 (*see also* SL 20)
❖ LM 3:9 (*see also* SL 4:2)

Prayer, kneeling in: "The relevant point is that kneeling does matter, but other things matter even more"
•LM 18 ❖ LM 3:10

Prayer, Lewis describes his first experience with, during his mother's illness ("The thing hadn't worked, but I was used to things not working...")
•SJ 20-21 ❖ SJ 1:22

Prayer, Lewis describes his realization of the need for continual recourse to, for his virtue (though at the time he called the object "Spirit")
•SJ 226 (*see also* SL 62*; Daily...)
❖ SJ 14:20 (*see also* SL 14:1*; Daily...)

Prayer: Lewis mentions that he himself would be wholly content with the type of prayer that leaves everything to God's wisdom
•CR 143-144 ❖ CR 12:5-8

Prayer life—*see* Devotional life; Devotions

Prayer: Life as a school in which we must practice the "duty" of prayer, just as we must learn grammar if we are ever to read the poets
•LM 115-116 ❖ LM 21:12-15

Prayer, like all other actions, is an attempt to bring about a certain result
•GID 105 (*see also* LM 36-37)
❖ GID I 11:6 (*see also* LM 7:4-6)

Prayer, Lord's—*see* Lord's Prayer

Prayer may facilitate the continual correcting of our image of God which is so essential; "Every idea of Him we form, He must in mercy shatter"
•LM 82 (*see also* GO 76-78*, 82-83*; SL 22*) ❖ LM 15:17 (*see also* GO 4:15-18*, 27-28*; SL 4:4*)

Prayer, mental images in, give rise to problems yet play an important part
•LM 84-87 (*see also* SL 21-22)
❖ LM 16:5-13 (*see also* SL 4:4)

Prayer: Mental pictures seem to help me most when they are most fugitive and fragmentary
•LM 86-87 ❖ LM 16:11-13

Prayer: Never try to generate an emotion by will-power (re: a prayerful frame of mind)
•L 256 (*see also* L 202; LM 23*; SJ 61-62*; SL 20-21, 125)
❖ L 31 Jul 54 (*see also* L 22 Dec 42; LM 4:19*; SJ 4:8*; SL 4:3; 27:1)

Prayer: No use applying to Heaven for earthly comfort; there is no earthly

comfort in the long run—Heaven can give only heavenly comfort
•FL 190 (*see also* GO 28-30; L 290; LAL 49) ❖ FL 6:43 (*see also* GO 2:13-16; L 3 Dec 59; LAL 16/12/55)

Prayer not a magical cause; it doesn't act directly on nature, like a spell
•LM 48 ❖ LM 9:6

Prayer, obstacles to—*see* Obstacles to prayer

Prayer of adoration, more than any other kind of prayer, should be a communal act
•LM 100 (*see also* Praise)
❖ LM 19:1 (*see also* Praise)

Prayer, one cannot establish the efficacy of, by statistics; remains a matter of faith
•L 226
❖ L undated letter just before 7 Feb 51

Prayer, our backwardness in, is due to sins, avoidable immersion in worldly things, neglect of mental discipline, and fear of divine demands upon us
•LM 114 ❖ LM 21:8

Prayer, our imagining of God as a "bright blur" may be an obstacle to; this idol needs to be broken before we begin
•LM 78 (*see also* LM 82, 83, 91) ❖ LM 15:5 (*see also* LM 15:17; 16:1; 17:12)

Prayer: Our struggle is to believe that there *is* a Listener, and that He will listen to our prayers, and take them into account
•LM 61 (*see also* LM 67-68)
❖ LM 11:15 (*see also* LM 13:1)

Prayer, petitionary
•LM 22-23, 28, 35-39, 48-50, 52-56, 57-61; M 174-181 ❖ LM 4:10-20; 5:16; ch. 7; 9:5-12; 10:3-11; ch. 11; M App. B

Prayer, Petitionary: A Problem Without an Answer (chapter title)
•CR 142-151 ❖ CR ch. 12

Prayer, petitionary: An argument against it is that if answered, it would make the world unpredictable; and the world must be predictable if man is to be free
•LM 37-39 ❖ LM 7:7-11

Prayer, petitionary, as a necessary in-

gredient in any practice or discussion of worship: "The higher does not stand without the lower"
•LM 87 ❖ LM 16:13

Prayer, petitionary: Distance between philosophical questions about it and anxiety as to whether our own urgent prayer will be answered is infinite
•LM 40 (*see also* LM 48)
❖ LM 8:1 (*see also* LM 9:5)

Prayer, petitionary: I agree that there are many other and perhaps higher sorts of prayer
•CR 142 ❖ CR 12:1

Prayer, petitionary: I am not, in principle, puzzled by refusal: what I am puzzled by is the promise of granting
•CR 148 ❖ CR 12:18

Prayer, petitionary: "If God had granted all the silly prayers I've made in my life, where should I be now?"
•LM 28 (*see also* CR 144)
❖ LM 5:16 (*see also* CR 12:8)

Prayer, petitionary, is both allowed and commanded us—but can we believe that God ever really modifies His action in response to it?
•WLN 8-9 ❖ WLN 1:17, 18

Prayer, petitionary, is recommended in the New Testament both by precept and by example
•CR 142; LM 35-36 ❖ CR 12:1; LM 7:1-3

Prayer, petitionary: Omission or disdain of it may spring not from superior sanctity but from a lack of faith
•LM 87 ❖ LM 16:13

Prayer, petitionary: Our Lord in Gethsemane made a petitionary prayer (and did not get what He asked for)
•LM 35-36 ❖ LM 7:1, 2

Prayer, petitionary: Prayers that are invariably granted are likely the prayers of God's fellow-workers, demanding what is needed for the joint work
•LM 60-61 ❖ LM 11:13

Prayer, petitionary: Regarding the New Testament's embarrassing promises that what we pray for with faith we shall receive

•LM 57-61 ❖ LM ch. 11

Prayer, petitionary, Screwtape speaks on
•SL 126-128 ❖ SL 27:2-4

Prayer, petitionary: "That wisdom must sometimes refuse what ignorance may quite innocently ask seems to be self-evident"
•CR 142 ❖ CR 12:2

Prayer, petitionary: "The more we believe that God hurts only to heal, the less we can believe that there is any use in begging for tenderness"
•GO 49-50 ❖ GO 3:17

Prayer, petitionary: The real problem is not why refusal is so frequent, but why the opposite result is so lavishly promised
•LM 59 ❖ LM 11:7

Prayer, petitionary: Two seemingly inconsistent patterns recommended—praying "Thy will be done" and praying with sure belief that what we ask will be granted
•CR 142-151, esp. 142-144 (see also LM 58-59)
❖ CR ch. 12, esp. 12:1-9 (see also LM 11:5)

Prayer, petitionary: "Whatever the theoretical difficulties are, we must continue to make requests of God"
•LM 36 (see also SL 126)
❖ LM 7:3 (see also SL 27:2)

Prayer, petitionary: "When the event you prayed for occurs your prayer has always contributed to it"
•M 181 ❖ M App. B:21

Prayer, possible mechanism of
•GID 76-77, 79; M 174-181 (see also M 58-59*) ❖ GID I 8:12, 9-10; M App. B (see also M 8:6-8*)

Prayer, presence of God in: Screwtape points out that the humans do not desire it as much as they suppose
•SL 22-23 (see also LM 114; M 94)
❖ SL 4:4 (see also LM 21:8; M 11:19)

Prayer, promise of invariable granting: There is the faint suggestion of goods that look a little larger in the advertisement than they turn out to be
•CR 151 ❖ CR 12:25

Prayer puts us on a personal footing with God; instead of being merely known, we show, we tell, we offer ourselves to view
•LM 20-21 ❖ LM 4:6, 7

Prayer, "realness" of, vs. the facade of ourselves and the room we're in
•LM 77-82 ❖ LM ch. 15

Prayer, Screwtape advises getting humans to make their distractions and wandering mind a task for their will power rather than a subject of their
•SL 125-126 ❖ SL 27:1

Prayer, Screwtape describes how a granted, can become just as good a proof as a denied one that prayers are ineffective ("It would've happened anyway")
•SL 126-127 ❖ SL 27:3

Prayer, Screwtape discusses the effort to produce in, a vaguely devotional mood and other feelings
•SL 20-21 ❖ SL 4:2, 3

Prayer: "The best thing, where it is possible, is to keep the patient from the serious intention of praying altogether" (—Screwtape)
•SL 19-20 ❖ SL 4:2

Prayer: The devotional life is destroyed by belief in a "historical Jesus" because such a construct cannot in fact be worshipped
•SL 106-108 ❖ SL 23:3, 4

Prayer, The Efficacy of (chapter title)
•WLN 3-11 ❖ WLN ch. 1

Prayer, the lavish promises concerning, in the New Testament are the worst possible place to begin Christian instruction for a child or a Pagan
•LM 59-60 ❖ LM 11:10

Prayer: "The moments at which you call most desperately and clamorously to God for help are precisely those when you seem to get none"
•LAL 92 (see also GO 4-6; 53-54)
❖ LAL 24 Sep 60 (see also GO 1:7-11; 3:24-26)

Prayer: "The odd thing is that this reluctance [to pray] is not confined to periods of dryness"
•LM 113 ❖ LM 21:6

Prayer: "The ordinate frame of mind is one of the blessings we must pray for, not a fancy-dress we must put on when we pray"
•LM 23 (*see also* L 256; SJ 61-62*; SL 20-21*, 125-126) ❖ LM 4:19 (*see also* L 31 Jul 54; SJ 4:7, 8*; SL 4:2, 3*; 27:1)

Prayer: "The painful effort which prayer involves is no proof that we are doing something we were not created to do"
•LM 114 ❖ LM 21:10

Prayer: The point in Jesus' statement about moving mountains is that the condition of doing such a mighty work is unwavering, unhesitating faith
•CR 146-147 ❖ CR 12:13

Prayer: The point of the parable of the Unjust Steward is that we are denied many graces that we ask for because they would be our ruin
•L 301 ❖ L 20 Dec 61

Prayer: The pressure of things we are trying to keep out of our mind is a hopeless distraction; better to lay all the cards on the table
•LM 23 (*see also* SL 125-126)
❖ LM 4:18, 19 (*see also* SL 27:1)

Prayer: "The very question, 'Does prayer work?' puts us in the wrong frame of mind from the outset...as if it were magic, or a machine"
•WLN 8 ❖ WLN 1:16

Prayer: Thinking the outcome is already decided one way or the other is no good reason for ceasing our prayers
•M 179-180 ❖ M App. B:18

Prayer, through, God pours out a knowledge of Himself
•SL 21 ❖ SL 4:4

Prayer: "Thy will be done" should be the voice of joyful desire, free of hunger and thirst—not merely of submission or renunciation
•CR 143 ❖ CR 12:4

Prayer to saints, while Christendom is divided about, we are all agreed about praying *with* them
•LM 15 ❖ LM 3:4

Prayer, use of images in, for me is very limited; but focussing one's eyes on almost any object is a help towards concentration
•LM 84 ❖ LM 16:3, 4

Prayer: We can learn to make every pleasure a channel for adoration—to recognise its divine source and give thanks for it in the same moment it is received
•LM 89-90 (*see also* GO 73*)
❖ LM 17:6-9 (*see also* GO 4:7, 8*)

Prayer: We fear lest God's will should become too unmistakable if we prayed longer
•WG 127-128 (*see also* CR 43*; LM 114; SL 22-23*, 54-55) ❖ WG 9:5 (*see also* CR 3:12*; LM 21:8; SL 4:4*; 12:3)

Prayer, we must never in, strive to extort "by maistry" what God does not give (feelings of affection, etc.)
•SJ 61-62 (*see also* L 202, 256; LM 23; SL 20-21, 125; SJ 168)
❖ SJ 4:8 (*see also* L 22 Dec 42; 31 Jul 54; LM 4:19; SL 4:3; 27:1; SJ 11:5)

Prayer, what chokes every, is the memory of all the prayers H. [Joy] and I offered and all the false hopes we had
•GO 34 ❖ GO 2:25

Prayer: "When it is over, this casts a feeling of relief and holiday over the rest of the day. We are reluctant to begin. We are delighted to finish"
•LM 113 ❖ LM 21:4

Prayer: Whether we pray for the living or the dead, the causes which will prevent or exclude the events we pray for are already at work
•LM 110 ❖ LM 20:16

Prayer: Why we find it difficult to concentrate
•LM 114 (*see also* SL 19-23)
❖ LM 21:8, 9 (*see also* SL ch. 4)

Prayer, words in, are only an anchor—it does not matter very much who first put them together
•LM 11 ❖ LM 2:6

Prayer, Work and (chapter title)
•GID 104-107 (*see also* GID 217)
❖ GID I ch. 11 (*see also* GID II 7:4)

Prayer would be meaningless in the sort of universe Pope pictured (with a

Managerial God whose grand design drags undesirable consequences after it)
•LM 53-56 ❖ LM 10:4-11

Prayer: "Yes, I know how terrible that doubt is 'Perhaps He will not'"
•LAL 60 ❖ LAL 3/8/56

Prayer, you need not (unless you choose) believe in a causal connection between, and events that you pray for—such as the recovery of a sick person
•WLN 4 ❖ WLN 1:4

Prayers, addressing our, always to Jesus tends to what has been called "Jesus-worship"
•LM 84 ❖ LM 16:4

Prayers, all, are heard though not all are granted
•M 180-181 ❖ M App. B:21

Prayers, all our, are part of the Church's prayer, and are united with the perpetual prayer of Christ
•L 226 (see also CR 149; L 183)
❖ L undated letter just before 7 Feb 51 (see also CR 12:20; L 16 Apr 40)

Prayers and religious reading, importance of daily
•MC 124 (see also L 220; GID 266; SJ 226*; WG 132) ❖ MC III 11:6 (see also L undated letter just after 6 Sep 49; GID II 16:52, 53; SJ 14:20*; WG 9:13)

Prayers are always taken into account by God
•M 181 (see also GID 79)
❖ M App. B:21 (see also GID I 8:9)

Prayers are heard not only before we make them but before we are made ourselves
•LM 48 ❖ LM 9:5

Prayers as a secret indulgence which Father disapproves may have a charm they lacked in houses where they were commanded
•LAL 32 ❖ LAL Sep 19/54

Prayers at a time of acute distress are themselves a form of anguish
•LM 41 ❖ LM 8:4

Prayers, David's dancing a valuable contrast to the merely dutiful "church-going" and laborious saying of our, to which religion is often reduced

•RP 45-46 ❖ RP 5:4

Prayers, folly of estimating the value of our, by our success in producing the desired feeling (forgiveness, charity, courage)
•SL 21 ❖ SL 4:3

Prayers for family members, Screwtape discusses, ("Make sure they are always very 'spiritual'..."; keep attention on grievances, etc.)
•SL 16-17 ❖ SL 3:3

Prayers for the dead
•L 300, 302 (see also GID 335; LAL 119)
❖ L 28 Oct 61; 28 Dec 61 (see also GID IV Letter 7; LAL 25 Jun 63)

Prayers for the dead: "I have always been able to pray for the other dead...But when I try to pray for H. [Joy], I halt"
•GO 24-26 ❖ GO 2:8, 9

Prayers for the dead: "Of course I pray for the dead...What sort of intercourse with God could I have if what I love best were unmentionable to Him?"
•LM 107 ❖ LM 20:3

Prayers, God does not have to listen to all of our, at once; He is not in Time
•MC 145-147 (see also L 217; LM 109-110; M 176-177)
❖ MC IV 3:2-9 (see also L 1 Aug 49; LM 20:14-17; M App. B:10)

Prayers granted are not related to God's favor toward us: "If we were stronger, we might be less tenderly treated"
•WLN 10-11 ❖ WLN 1:21

Prayers, I don't think we ought to try to keep up our normal, when we are ill and over-tired (though I would not say this to a beginner)
•LAL 38 (see also LAL 24)
❖ LAL 20/2/55 (see also LAL Jan 1st 54)

Prayers, if our, are granted at all they are granted from the foundation of the world; God and His acts are not in Time
•LM 48, 50, 110 (see also GID 79; L 217; M 176-180; SL 127-128)
❖ LM 9:5, 12; 20:16 (see also GID I 8:9; L 1 Aug 49; M App. B:10-18; SL 27:4)

Prayers, if something is the subject of our thoughts it must be the subject of our

•LM 22-23 ❖ LM 4:15-18

Prayers, Lewis describes his efforts as a schoolboy to be utterly conscious of his, thus rendering his private practice of religion a "quite intolerable burden"
•SJ 61-62 (see also L 256*; SJ 168)
❖ SJ 4:7-9 (see also L 31 Jul 54*; SJ 11:5)

Prayers, main, should not be put 'last thing at night'
•L 256 ❖ L 31 Jul 54

Prayers, main, should not be reserved for bed-time—obviously the worst hour for any action which needs concentration
•LM 16-17 ❖ LM 3:7

Prayers: Many parishioners apparently just repeat whatever little formula they were taught in childhood
•LM 63 ❖ LM 12:3

Prayers may be offered sitting in a crowded train, on a bench in a park, or a back street where one can pace up and down
•LM 17 ❖ LM 3:7

Prayers may sometimes go wrong because we insist on trying to talk to God when He wants to talk to us
•LAL 73 ❖ LAL 31/3/58

Prayers offered in our "dry" periods are those which please God best
•SL 39 ❖ SL 8:4

Prayers, on the use of "ready-made"
•LM 10-13 (see also SL 20)
❖ LM 2:2-15 (see also SL 4:2)

Prayers, penitential, at their highest level are an attempt to restore an infinitely valued and vulnerable personal relationship
•LM 95 (see also MC 59-60)
❖ LM 18:3 (see also MC II 4:7, 8)

Prayers, "ready-made": "A ready-made form can't serve for my intercourse with God any more than it could serve for my intercourse with you"
•LM 12 ❖ LM 2:8

Prayers, "ready-made": "...I find it best to make 'my own words' the staple but introduce a modicum of the ready-made"

•LM 12 ❖ LM 2:7

Prayers, "ready-made," serve three purposes: keep me in touch with sound doctrine, remind me what I ought to ask, and provide an element of the ceremonial
•LM 12 ❖ LM 2:10-12

Prayers, "ready-made," serve to remind us of the necessity for reverence
•LM 13 ❖ LM 2:13-15

Prayers, saying private, in a church: Usually too many distractions
•LM 17 ❖ LM 3:8

Prayers, Screwtape rues the man who directs his, to God as "Not to what I think thou art but to what thou knowest thyself to be"
•SL 22 ❖ SL 4:4

Prayers, simply to say your, is not to pray; otherwise properly trained parrots would serve as well as men
•WLN 6 ❖ WLN 1:10

Prayers, we cannot rely on feeling to support our; what seem our worst prayers may really be, in God's eyes, our best
•LM 116 (see also LAL 73; SL 21)
❖ LM 21:16 (see also LAL 31/3/58; SL 4:3)

Prayers, we may sometimes be deterred from small, by a sense of our own dignity rather than of God's; we must not be too high-minded
•LM 23 ❖ LM 4:20

Prayers, what most often interrupts my, is not great distractions but tiny ones —things one will have to do or avoid in the course of the next hour
•LAL 73 ❖ LAL 31/3/58

Prayers without words, I find, are the best—when I can manage it
•L 245; LM 11 (see also L 256) ❖ L 20 Oct 52; LM 2:5, 6 (see also L 31 Jul 54)

Prayers without words: "I have often, on my knees, been shocked to find what sort of thoughts I have, for a moment, been addressing to God"
•RP 97-98 ❖ RP 9:8

Prayers without words: "I now see that in trying to make it my daily bread I was counting on a greater mental and

spiritual strength than I really have"
•LM 11 (see also SL 20*)
❖ LM 2:5 (see also SL 4:2*)
Prayers without words mentioned by
Screwtape as serving his purposes if
practiced by a novice
•SL 20 ❖ SL 4:2
Prayers without words, when I spoke of,
I didn't mean anything so exalted as
what the mystics call the "prayer of
silence"
•LM 16 ❖ LM 3:6
Praying for people by their names not nec-
essary
•LM 18 ❖ LM 3:12
Preacher(s)—see also Clergymen
"Preacher" in the full sense, the Evan-
gelist, the man on fire, represents the
Lord; the apologist represents John
Baptist
•GID 221-222 ❖ GID II 8:10
Preaching—see also Apologetic(s); consider
also Evangelism
Preaching by laymen: Most useful to start
from one's own position
•WG 126 ❖ WG 9:1
Preaching: I believe there are too many
accommodating preachers in the
church; The Gospel is directly op-
posed to the world
•GID 265 (see also GID 89-90, 260)
❖ GID II 16:46 (see also GID I 10:2; II
16:12)
Preaching: Lewis lists terms which are
used differently by the layman than
by the clergyman or theologian
•GID 96-98 ❖ GID I 10:20-37
Preaching much easier than practice (re:
humility)
•LAL 29 ❖ LAL Mar 31st 54
Preaching : "Our business is to present that
which is timeless...in the particular
language of our own age"
•GID 93, 94, 96-98 (see also GID 242-
243) ❖ GID I 10:10, 12, 18-38 (see also
GID II 12:4, 5)
Preaching: "People need to be reminded
more often than they need to be instructed" (quote from Dr. Johnson)*
•MC 78 (see also L 128; MC 124)

❖ MC III 3:1 (see also L 2 Aug 28; MC
III 11:6)
Preaching, practice of Christianity more
important than, toward the conversion of others
•L 261 (see also L 247*; LAL 96*)
❖ L 2 Feb 55 (see also L 8 Nov 52*; LAL
24 Feb 61*)
Preaching: Screwtape mentions the clergyman who waters down the faith so
much that he shocks his parishioners
with his unbelief*
•SL 73-74 (see also Christianity-and-
water) ❖ SL 16:3 (see also Christianity-
and-water)
Preaching: Screwtape mentions the clergyman who "revolves endlessly
round the little treadmill of his fifteen
favourite Psalms and twenty favourite
lessons"
•SL 74 ❖ SL 16:3
Preaching: The reading of a lecture sends
people to sleep**
•L 99
❖ L undated letter postmarked 28 Aug 24
Preaching, use of emotion in
•GID 99 ❖ GID I 10:39
Preaching: "What a wonderful power is
in the direct appeal which disregards
the temporary climate..."
•L 177 ❖ L 11 Feb 40
Predestination and Free-will, question of,
is to my mind indiscussible, insol-
uble; I suspect it is meaningless
•L 245-246 ❖ L 20 Oct 52
Predestination: God sees us doing things
in His unbounded Now; and obvi-
ously to watch a man doing some-
thing is not to make him do it
•SL 128 ❖ SL 27:4
Predestination, in the parable of the Sheep
and the Goats you see nothing about,
or even faith—all depends on works
•L 251 ❖ L 3 Aug 53
Predestination: Lewis's answer to the
puzzle of Divine foreknowledge and
free will explained through Screwtape*
•SL 127-128 (see also M 174-181)
❖ SL 27:4 (see also M App. B)
Predestination: "The real inter-relation

between God's omnipotence and Man's freedom is something we can't find out"
•L 252 ❖ L 3 Aug 53
"Pre-determined": The syllable "*pre*" lets in the notion of eternity as simply an older time—but for God, it is the endless present
•LM 110 (*see also* SL 127-128; Time)
❖ LM 20:16 (*see also* SL 27:4; Time)
Predictability belongs to the realm of science, not of human history (re: one objection to petitionary prayer)
•LM 37-39 (*see also* LM 42)
❖ LM 7:7-11 (*see also* LM 8:7)
Predictions about the future, doing our daily duty more important than, (play analogy)
•WLN 104-106 ❖ WLN 7:19-23
Predictions of future not useful: "The world might stop in ten minutes; meanwhile we are to go on doing our duty"
•GID 266 (*see also* WLN 111-112)
❖ GID II 16:54-56 (*see also* WLN 7:34)
Predictions of Jesus seen as being in a class with other apocalyptic writings, which to most modern tastes appear tedious and unedifying
•WLN 95 ❖ WLN 7:5
Predictions of the date a practical risk of belief in the Second Coming of Jesus; but it is impossible and we must be ready at all moments
•WLN 106-109 ❖ WLN 7:24-29
Predictions of the future: "To play well the scenes in which we are 'on' concerns us much more than to guess about the scenes that follow it"*
•WLN 104 ❖ WLN 7:19
Pre-existence—*see* Reincarnation
Preferences—*see also* Tastes
Preferences, matters of, not to be confused with matters of faith and morals (e.g., use of reverential prefixes before the Holy Name)
•GID 335-336 ❖ GID IV Letter 8
Prejudice, racial—*see* Racism
Presence of God—*consider also* Contact with God; Destiny of redeemed Man;

Heaven; Omnipresence of God; Seeking God
Presence of God, awareness of, has often been unwelcome—for He comes not only to raise up but to cast down; to deny, to rebuke, to interrupt
•LM 75 (*see also* Evasion)
❖ LM 14:12 (*see also* Evasion)
Presence of God, experienced by men in prayer and sacrament, is substituted by the devil with a vague, remote "historical Jesus" which cannot be worshipped*
•SL 107 ❖ SL 23:3
Presence of God: "I wonder whether people who ask God to interfere openly and directly in our world quite realise what it will be like when He does"*
•MC 66 ❖ MC II 5:9
Presence of God, if I never felt like fleeing from, I would suspect those moments when I seemed to delight in it of being wish-fulfilment dreams
•LM 75 ❖ LM 14:12, 13
Presence of God in prayer: Screwtape points out that the humans do not desire it as much as they suppose
•SL 22-23 (*see also* LM 114; M 94)
❖ SL 4:4 (*see also* LM 21:8; M 11:19)
Presence of God, in times of desperate need our very desperateness may prevent our perception of the
•GO 53-54; LAL 92 (*see also* Absence of God) ❖ GO 3:24, 25; LAL 24 Sep 60 (*see also* Absence of God)
Presence of God not the same as the *sense* of the presence of God; the latter may be due to imagination, and the former may not bring consolation
•LAL 38-39 ❖ LAL 20/2/55
Presence of God, real test of being in the, is that you either forget about yourself altogether or see yourself as a small, dirty object...
•MC 111 ❖ MC III 8:7
Presence of God revealed in any but the faintest and most mitigated degree would override our will and defeat His ultimate purpose

•SL 38-39 ❖ SL 8:4

Presence of God, Screwtape mentions, which comes to humans upon their repentance and protects them from the devil's assaults
•SL 57-58 ❖ SL 13:1, 2

Presence of God, sense of, and acts of worship were for the ancient Jew all one
•RP 46-48 ❖ RP 5:5, 6

Presence of God: The Psalmists asked of God no gift more urgently than His presence
•RP 52 ❖ RP 5:10

Presence of God, we may ignore but we can nowhere evade the; the world is crowded with Him...the real labour is to remember, to attend
•LM 75 ❖ LM 14:11

Present anxiety and suspense: It is about *this* that we are to say, "Thy will be done"—not all the things we are afraid of; this fear itself is our cross*
•SL 29 (*see also* LAL 60)
❖ SL 6:2 (*see also* LAL 3/8/56)

Present as the only part of history we have in which we may find divine comment or revelation (excepting the great events embodied in the creeds)
•CR 112-113 ❖ CR 9:26

Present as the only time in which any duty can be done or any grace received
•WG 30 ❖ WG 2:13

Present is the point at which time touches eternity; in it alone freedom and actuality are offered us
•SL 68 ❖ SL 15:2

Present, it is seldom the exact, that is unbearable; the great thing with unhappy times is to take them bit by bit, hour by hour
•LAL 58 (*see also* LAL 60, 69, 103)
❖ LAL 14/6/56 (*see also* LAL 3/8/56; Oct 20th 57; 4 May 62)

Present pain, actual moment of, is only the centre of the whole tribulational system which includes fear and pity
•PP 105 ❖ PP 6:17

Present, Screwtape advises tempting human thought away from the, and having them dwell on the Past and the Future
•SL 67-71 ❖ SL 15:3-5

Present: "...there, and there alone, all duty, all grace, all knowledge, and all pleasure dwell..."
•SL 70 ❖ SL 15:5

Present, we have nothing but the tiny little
•MC 148 ❖ MC IV 3:10

Present: "Where, except in the present, can the Eternal be met?"
•CR 113 ❖ CR 9:26

Preservation of the human race: An imperative imposed by instinct?
•CR 48-52 ❖ CR 4:12-19

Preservation of the human race as a basis for a code of ethics: Is it a duty, and if so, on what grounds do we assume it is a duty?
•CR 48 ❖ CR 4:10, 11

Preservation of the human race deemed valuable only if we accept the moral judgement that life is better than death
•M 37-38 (*see also* WG 43*)
❖ M 5:9 (*see also* WG 3:18*)

Preservation of the human race not desirable unless the people are people of a certain sort, behaving in a certain way
•GID 296-297 (*see also* GID 311)
❖ GID III 4:20 (*see also* GID III 8:1)

Preservation of the human race: Who or what is telling us that it ought to be preserved?
•CR 51; MC 29-30* (*see also* Ethics)
❖ CR 4:17; MC I 3:5* (*see also* Ethics)

Preservation of the human race: "Why should this instinct [if it is an instinct] be preferred to all my others? It is certainly not my strongest"
•CR 50, 55 ❖ CR 4:15, 25

Presumption: [Legalism] raises scruples when we don't keep the routine, and presumption when we do
•LAL 38 ❖ LAL 20/2/55

Presumption: "What the devil loves is that vague cloud of unspecified guilt feeling or unspecified virtue by which he lures us into despair or presumption"
•LAL 77 ❖ LAL Jul 21st 58

Pretend, Let's (chapter title)

•MC 160-166 ❖ MC IV ch. 7

Pretending—*see also* Imitation

Pretending: "A man is never so proud as when striking an attitude of humility"*
•CR 14 ❖ CR 2:4

Pretending: "All mortals tend to turn into the thing they are pretending to be" (—Screwtape, regarding association of believers with ungodly people)
•SL 46 ❖ SL 10:2

Pretending, it is really God who does the; He treats us as if we were His sons
•MC 165 ❖ MC IV 7:13

Pretending: Often the only way to get a quality is to start behaving as if you had it already
•MC 161-162 (*see also* SJ 192-193; Imitation of Christ) ❖ MC IV 7:2-4 (*see also* SJ 12:14; Imitation of Christ)

Pretending: "The distinction between pretending you are better than you are and beginning to be better in reality is finer than moral sleuthhounds conceive"
•SJ 192-193 ❖ SJ 12:14

Pretending to be better than one is: If this is hypocrisy, then I must conclude that hypocrisy can do a man good
•SJ 192-193 ❖ SJ 12:14

Pretending to be "cultured": Sanctity and culture are both hard to diagnose and easy to feign
•WLN 47 (*see also* Culture)
❖ WLN 3:24 (*see also* Culture)

Pretending, we all appear as dunces when, to have an interest in things we care nothing about (re: women trying to enter men's discussions)*
•FL 109 ❖ FL 4:33

Pretending: "When a boor first enters the society of courteous people what can he do, for a while, except imitate the motions?"
•SJ 193 ❖ SJ 12:14

Pretending: "Do not waste time bothering whether you 'love' your neighbor; act as if you did"*
•MC 116 (*see also* L 269; LM 115; MC 161) ❖ MC III 9:5 (*see also* L undated letter just after 13 Mar 56; LM 21:12; MC IV 7:3)

Pride—*see also* Arrogance; Self-righteousness; Self-satisfaction; Superiority; Vanity; *consider also* Humility; Snobbery; Priggery

Pride a danger in the love of knowledge and culture, or in the possession of talents
•WG 27-28 ❖ WG 2:9

Pride a danger in the pursuit of cultural activities*
•L 182-183 (*see also* CR 10, 14, 17*, 21*; LAL 54*; SL 60; WLN 31-39)
❖ L 16 Apr 40 (*see also* CR 1:15; 2:4-6, 16*, 28*; LAL 20/3/56*; SL 13:4; WLN 3:1-12)

Pride: A man can go on improving his talents to the best of his ability without forming an opinion of them or deciding his own niche in the temple of Fame
•SL 65 ❖ SL 14:5

Pride: "A man is never so proud as when striking an attitude of humility" (said in reference to himself)
•CR 14 ❖ CR 2:4

Pride, acceptable forms of
•MC 112-113 (*see also* SL 64-65)
❖ MC III 8:10-11 (*see also* SL 14:4, 5)

Pride and self-righteousness as the result of legalism
•RP 57-58 ❖ RP 6:6, 7

Pride and superiority, best book about, is Law's *Serious Call to a Devout and Holy Life*
•LAL 44-45 ❖ LAL 30/6/55

Pride ("arrogance") of the unmusical church-goers who look with resentful hostility on all who would try to improve their taste
•CR 97 ❖ CR 8:9, 11

Pride as a hindrance to charity (we are tempted to spend more on tipping, hospitality, etc. than on those who really need our help)
•MC 82 ❖ MC III 3:7

Pride, as long as one knows one is proud one is safe from the worst form of
•L 241 (*see also* Self-knowledge)

❖ L 15 May 52 (*see also* Self-knowledge)

Pride: "As long as you are proud you cannot know God"
- •MC 111 ❖ MC III 8:6

Pride as the cause of the first sin—the movement whereby a creature tries to set up on its own, to exist for itself
- •PP 75 ❖ PP 5:5

Pride as the danger to which Friendships are naturally liable: Friends may come to take pleasure in the exclusion of "Outsiders"
- •FL 114-127 (*see also* Inner Rings)
- ❖ FL 4:46-62 (*see also* Inner Rings)

Pride as the utmost evil; leads to every other vice
- •MC 109 ❖ MC III 8:2

Pride at our own humility, Screwtape advises tempting humans to
- •SL 62-63 ❖ SL 14:2

Pride best combatted not by the thought "I'm no more special than anyone else" but by the feeling "Everyone is as special as me"
- •L 242-243 (*see also* SL 64)
- ❖ L 20 Jun 52 (*see also* SL 14:4)

Pride can be the result of overcoming the temptation to conformity and determining to be different*
- •SL 164; WLN 62-63
- ❖ SL 32:27; WLN 4:27

Pride, Christian may come to feel himself part of an "inner ring" (vis-a-vis "the unbelievers") and thus develop a form of Spiritual
- •SL 110-113 (*see also* RP 64-65; SL 34)
- ❖ SL 24:1-5 (*see also* RP 6:14; SL 7:2)

Pride ("conceit") as an obstacle to a proper appreciation of all ordinary pleasures as means for adoring God
- •LM 90 ❖ LM 17:10

Pride, diabolical, comes when you look down on others so much that you do not care what they think of you
- •MC 112-113 ❖ MC III 8:10

Pride, discussion of
- •MC 108-114 ❖ MC III ch. 8

Pride does not only go before a fall but is a fall—a transfer of attention from God the Creator to ourselves, mere creatures (re: "originality")
- •CR 7 ❖ CR 1:10

Pride: God is not proud; "He is cynically indifferent to the dignity of His position..." (re: prayer)
- •SL 21 ❖ SL 4:4

Pride: God is not proud, He stoops to conquer; He will have us even when we have shown that we prefer everything else to Him
- •PP 97 (*see also* LAL 49; SJ 229) ❖ PP 6:8 (*see also* LAL 16/12/55; SJ 14:23)

Pride: God wants each man to be able to recognize all creatures (even himself) as glorious and excellent things; this is different from sinful pride*
- •SL 64 ❖ SL 14:4

Pride: I can hardly imagine a more deadly spiritual condition than that of the man who can read the Sermon on the Mount with tranquil pleasure*
- •GID 182 (*see also* GID 191-192*)
- ❖ GID I 22:13 (*see also* GID II 1:4*)

Pride, I exulted with youthful and vulgar, at what I thought was my enlightenment [after studying with Kirkpatrick]
- •SJ 173 ❖ SJ 11:9

Pride: "...if our heart flatter us, God is greater than our heart"*
- •LM 34 ❖ LM 6:14

Pride: If you want to know how much pride you have, ask yourself how much you dislike it in other people
- •MC 109 ❖ MC III 8:1, 3

Pride: If you think you're not conceited, it means that you are very conceited indeed; first step toward acquiring humility is to realize that one is proud
- •MC 114 ❖ MC III 8:14

Pride in one's talents: Talents are given to us; we might as well be proud of the color of our hair
- •SL 65 ❖ SL 14:5

Pride involved in enjoyment of helping others: "...for me it is much harder to receive than to give, but, I think, much more blessed" (—Joy Lewis)
- •LAL 76 ❖ LAL Jun 6th [1958]

Pride is competitive by its very nature; it

gets no pleasure out of having something, only out of having more of it than the next man
•MC 109-110 ❖ MC III 8:3

Pride is spiritual cancer
•MC 112 ❖ MC III 8:8

Pride may be a consequence of human courage, according to Screwtape
•SL 135 (see also SL 140)
❖ SL 29:1 (see also SL 30:1)

Pride means enmity to God; in God you come up against something immeasurably superior to yourself
•MC 111 ❖ MC III 8:6

Pride of activities such as reading a certain book in order to make clever comments about it to one's friends mentioned by Screwtape*
•SL 58, 60 (see also L 216)
❖ SL 13:3, 4 (see also L 3 Apr 49)

Pride of pursuing "culture": "...every real thing is good only if it will be humble and ordinate"
•L 182-183 ❖ L 16 Apr 40

Pride of pursuing "culture" for the sake of prestige or merit endangers the very enjoyment of the activities and impoverishes social life*
•WLN 34-36 (see also SL 58-60)
❖ WLN 3:6-8 (see also SL 13:3, 4)

Pride of pursuing "culture": "I have no 'cultural activities'. I like the Bacchae because it's exciting, not because it is––loathsome word—'cultured'!"*
•LAL 54 (see also SL 60)
❖ LAL 20/3/56 (see also SL 13:4)

Pride of pursuing "culture": Regarding the evil tendency to love knowledge and discernment more than the object known and discerned*
•CR 17; WG 28 ❖ CR 2:16; WG 2:9

Pride of pursuing "culture": The unbeliever mentioned who "commonly wishes to maintain his superiority to the great mass of mankind who turn to books for mere recreation"*
•CR 10 (see also WLN 38-39, 41; SL 58-60) ❖ CR 1:15 (see also WLN 3:11, 12, 14; SL 13:3-5)

Pride of pursuing "culture": We should

not regard pleasure in the arts as meritorious*
•CR 21 ❖ CR 2:28

Pride of the "goody-goody" more difficult to cure than that of the hypocrite*
•WLN 47-48 ❖ WLN 3:25, 26

Pride of the skilled church musician who looks with contempt on the unappreciative congregation
•CR 97 ❖ CR 8:9

Pride, pleasure in being praised is not
•MC 112 ❖ MC III 8:10

Pride, pleasure of, is like the pleasure of scratching; but much nicer to have neither the itch nor the scratch
•L 256 ❖ L 18 Feb 54

Pride, proper and improper kinds of
•WG 11-12 (see also SL 64-65*)
❖ WG 1:9, 10 (see also SL 14:4, 5*)

Pride, retaliatory, and contempt may be the products of cruelty and oppression ("We reimburse ourselves for cuffs and toil by a double dose of self-esteem")
•SJ 107 ❖ SJ 7:8

Pride: Screwtape observes that the devils have been successful in making men proud of most vices—but not yet of cowardice, at which they still feel shame
•SL 136-137 ❖ SL 29:5

Pride, snobbish, vs. the pride of Friendships (snobs wish to attach themselves to an "elite"; Friends may come to regard themselves as an "elite")
•FL 118 ❖ FL 4:51

Pride, spiritual, as one of the worst sins
•FL 111-112; LAL 111; MC 108-112
❖ FL 4:39; LAL 26 Nov 62; MC III 8:1-8

Pride, spiritual, Lewis describes an instance of his own, (in reacting against those who felt that good taste somehow defined the true Christian)
•CR 13-14 ❖ CR 2:4

Pride, spiritual, listed by Screwtape as "the strongest and most beautiful of the vices"
•SL 110-113 ❖ SL 24:1-5

Pride, spiritual: "One is sometimes (not often) glad not to be a great theo-

logian; one might so easily mistake it for being a good Christian"
•RP 57 ❖ RP 6:6

Pride, spiritual, ("priggery") as the danger to which Christians are exposed as they learn to value the Law of God over current ways of thinking
•RP 64-65 (see also SL 47-48, 110-113)
❖ RP 6:14 (see also SL 10:4; 24:1-5)

Pride, spiritual: The pride of being a Christian (vis-a-vis "the unbelievers") discussed by Screwtape and named "Spiritual Pride"
•SL 110-113 (see also RP 64-65; SL 34)
❖ SL 24:1-5 (see also RP 6:14; SL 7:2)

Pride: The devil laughs to see us overcoming cowardice, or lust, or ill-temper by learning to think that they are beneath our dignity
•MC 112 ❖ MC III 8:8

Pride is the eventual end of almost every activity we undertake; even "thoughts undertaken for God's sake" can become a source of pride
•PP 76 ❖ PP 5:5

Pride: "The moment good taste knows itself, some of its goodness is lost"*
•SJ 104 ❖ SJ 7:4

Pride: The prig who considers himself *above* enjoying his tinsel crown (beauty, talent, etc.) is perhaps as far astray as the paranoiac who mistakes it for gold
•LAL 111 ❖ LAL 10 Dec 62

Pride: "There can be intemperance in work just as in drink. What feels like zeal may be only fidgets or even the flattering of one's self-importance"*
•LAL 53 ❖ LAL 19/3/56

Pride: "There can be no surer proof of a confirmed pride than a belief that one is sufficiently humble" (quote from Law)
•LAL 96; PP 55, top (see also CR 14; MC 114; SL 62-63)
❖ LAL 24 Feb 61; PP 4 prelim. quote (see also CR 2:4; MC III 8:14; SL 14:2)

Pride: There is no fault which we are more unconscious of in ourselves and which we dislike more in others

•MC 109 ❖ MC III 8:1

Pride, transition from individual humility to corporate, is very easy (re: sets of Friends)
•FL 118 ❖ FL 4:50

Pride, vanity is the least bad and most pardonable sort of
•MC 112 ❖ MC III 8:10

Pride: We must be aware of our own sinfulness, but a continual poring over the "sink" might breed its own perverse pride
•LM 99 ❖ LM 18:15

Pride, wounded, often a part of what we call "feeling hurt"
•LAL 56-57 ❖ LAL 21/5/56

Priestesses in the Church? (chapter title)
•GID 234-239 ❖ GID II ch. 11

Priesthood of Christ prefigured by that of Melchizedek
•RP 122-124 ❖ RP 12:4, 5

Priests serve as representatives of God to us; therefore women are not suited for this role, since God is masculine
•GID 234-239 ❖ GID II ch. 11

Prig, I did not notice that Wyvern [College] was making me into an intellectual
•SJ 100, 104 (see also SJ 115, 185)
❖ SJ 6:27; 7:4 (see also SJ 7:19; 12:4)

Prig, I have now to tell you how Wyvern made me into a
•SJ 101 (101-117)
❖ SJ 7:3 (and entire chapter)

Prig, though it is bad to be a, there are times when we must risk seeming to be one (e.g., unprotesting participation in evil conversation)
•RP 73-74 ❖ RP 7:15

Prig who considers himself *above* enjoying his tinsel crown (beauty, talent, fame, etc.) is perhaps as far astray as the paranoiac who mistakes it for gold
•LAL 111 ❖ LAL 10 Dec 62

Prigs, sets of Friends thought to be stuck-up, by those who in their own lives have never known real Friendship
•FL 112 ❖ FL 4:41

Priggery—see also Pride; Snobbery
Priggery as the danger to which Chris-

tians are exposed as they learn to value the Law of God over the current ways of thinking
•RP 64-65 (see also SL 47-48, 110-113)
❖ RP 6:14 (see also SL 10:4; 24:1-5)

Priggery, fear of being accused of, increases the temptation to consort with people whose behaviour we disapprove
•RP 71-72 (see also SL 48)
❖ RP 7:10 (see also SL 10:4)

Prince Caspian mentioned
•LAL 14 ❖ LAL 17/4/53

Principles—see also Laws; Moral laws; Rules

Principles, Christian, stricter than others but we may get help towards obeying them
•MC 93 ❖ MC III 5:10

Principles, every sane man must have some set of, by which to make choices
•MC 93 ❖ MC III 5:10

Principles, evil, start out as small wrong choices
•SL 156-157; WLN 54-55 (see also MC 86-87, 117; RP 136; SL 53-54; WG 101-103)
❖ SL 32:10; WLN 4:10 (see also MC III 4:8, 9; 9:8; RP 12:16; SL 12:1; WG 6:12)

Principles of Christianity and morality unchanging in the face of increasing knowledge
•GID 45, 92 (see also GID 92)
❖ GID I 3:13, 14 (see also GID I 10:7)

Priorities—see also Values; consider also Perspective

Priorities: A man "should never give all his heart to anything which will end when his life ends"*
•WLN 110 ❖ WLN 7:31

Priorities and values change when doctrine of immortality is accepted*
•MC 73 ❖ MC III 1:9

Priorities: Choosing to put God first rather than an earthly beloved not a question of whom we feel greater love for*
•FL 170-171 ❖ FL 6:15

Priorities, importance of finding and setting
•GID 280-281 ❖ GID III 2:7-10

Priorities of Christians: Can education in secular subjects be justified?
•WG 21 ❖ WG 2:3

Priorities: Put first things first and you will get second things thrown in
•L 228 (see also FL 166*; GID 280-281; MC 118-119; RP 49*)
❖ L 23 Apr 51 (see also FL 6:5*; GID III 2:5-10; MC III 9:1; RP 5:7*)

Priorities: Putting first things first increases the value of second things
•L 248 (see also GID 150*)
❖ L 8 Nov 52 (see also GID I 17:7*)

Priorities: Putting second things first corrupts them (re: the over-valuing of "culture")
•L 269 ❖ L 2 Apr 56

Priorities: Salvation of a single soul more important than all the world's literature*
•CR 10 ❖ CR 1:15

Priorities: Ultimately what really matters is whether a thing or a circumstance moves us closer to God or to the devil*
•SL 87-89 (see also SL 56, 126)
❖ SL 19:3 (see also SL 12:5; 27:1)

Priority-setting for our loves: Our deepest concern should be for first things, and our next deepest for second things; this is called "ordinate loves"*
•LM 22 (see also L 228, 248; FL 165, 170-171, 190-191; GID 150)
❖ LM 4:14 (see also L 23 Apr 51; 8 Nov 52; FL 6:3, 4, 15, 44; GID I 17:7)

Prison/hotel analogy to illustrate how thinking of this world as a place intended for our happiness may bring disillusionment
•GID 52 ❖ GID I 4:18, 19 (Ques. 5)

Privacy—see also Solitude

Privacy, sacrifice of selfish, which is demanded in Christianity is repaid by growth in personality
•WG 113 ❖ WG 7:9

Privacy, the modern world attempts to banish all
•WG 107-108 ❖ WG 7:2, 3

Probability, On (chapter title) (re: Miracles)
•M 100-107 ❖ M ch. 13

Probability, on finding a criterion of, for judging any particular story of the miraculous
•M 100-107 (*see also* GID 81)
❖ M ch. 13 (*see also* GID I 9:2, 3)

Problem of pain—see Pain, problem of

Problem of Pain, Dr. Humphrey Havard noted as reading to the "Inklings" his paper on the clinical experience of pain which became the appendix to
•L 176 ❖ L 3 Feb 40

Problem of Pain: Lewis summarizes his book and answers an inquiry by C.E.M. Joad regarding the chapter on animal pain
•GID 166-171 ❖ GID I ch. 20

Problem of Pain, mention of writing
•L 172, 183, 234; LAL 110
❖ L 11 Nov 39; 3 Dec 39; 16 Apr 40; 12 Sep 51; LAL 26 Nov 62

Problems—*see* Difficulties

Problems, theological—*see* Doctrines, difficult; Difficulties in Scripture

Prodigal Son at least walked home on his own two feet; I was brought in kicking, struggling, resentful, eyes darting in every direction for a chance of escape
•SJ 229 (*see also* GID 261)
❖ SJ 14:23 (*see also* GID II 16:19-22)

Prodigal Son, Man is the, of the universe
•M 122 (*see also* GID 42-43*, 100*; WLN 86-87*) ❖ M 14:24 (*see also* GID I 3:9*; 10:42*; WLN 6:11*)

Prodigal Son, parable of: Screwtape makes mention of the elder brother who felt his sibling was "getting in on very easy terms"
•SL 18 ❖ SL 3:6

Profession(s)—*see* Job(s); Work

Professional circles, the only, that really matter are those which exist quite by accident and are composed merely of those who do good work
•WG 104-105 (*consider also* Inner Rings)
❖ WG 6:17 (*consider also* Inner Rings)

Progress—*consider also* Emergent Evolution; Evolutionism

"Progress": "...a prudent society must spend at least as much energy on conserving what it has as on improvement"
•CR 92-93 ❖ CR 7:22

Progress and Creative Evolution, philosophies of, bear reluctant witness to the truth that our real goal is elsewhere
•WG 8 ❖ WG 1:5

Progress and Development, Screwtape advises feeding humans hazy ideas of, to instill distrust of religion
•SL 43 ❖ SL 9:4

Progress: "...any given change in society is at least as likely to destroy the liberties and amenities we already have as to add new ones..."
•CR 92 ❖ CR 7:22

Progress assumed by television to be inevitable; the important thing seems to be to increase the comfort of man at all cost
•L 282 ❖ L 30 Oct 58

Progress, belief in, defined as the belief that human history is a simple, unilinear movement from worse to better
•WG 46-47 ❖ WG 3:24

Progress: Emergent evolution involves the belief that what is coming next will be an improvement; this belief is unwarranted
•GID 21 (*see also* WLN 101)
❖ GID I 1:1 (*see also* WLN 7:13)

Progress, for me, means increasing goodness and happiness of individual lives—not mere longevity
•GID 311 (*see also* GID 296-297; L 158*; SL 131*; WG 43*)
❖ GID III 8:1 (*see also* GID III 4:20; L 13 Jan 37*; SL 28:1*; WG 3:18*)

Progress, in my opinion the modern conception of, is simply a myth, supported by no evidence whatever
•WLN 100-104, esp. 101
❖ WLN 7:12-19, esp. 7:13

Progress, in true Evolution, is the exception rather than the rule (vs. the Myth of Evolutionism, in which the reverse is believed)

Proof rests upon the unprovable which has to be just "seen"
- WG 35 ❖ WG 3:4

Proof, scientific, not the same kind of proof required for belief in God, since belief is different from knowledge
- WLN 14-16, 20-21 (see also WLN 92)
- ❖ WLN 2:3, 4, 9 (see also WLN 6:28)

Prophecies, Jesus appropriated to Himself many Old Testament; this helps to show that Bible passages can and do have multiple meanings
- RP 117-119, 120 ❖ RP 11:14, 15; 12:1

Propriety, rule of, changes with time and place while the rule of chastity remains the same for all Christians at all times
- MC 88-89 ❖ MC III 5:1

Prosperity—see also Riches; Wealth

Prosperity and adversity both mentioned by Screwtape as possible means of separating men from God ("Prosperity knits a man to the World")
- SL 132 ❖ SL 28:1

Prosperity, dangers of
- GID 51-52 (see also L 221) ❖ GID I 4:18 (Ques. 5) (see also L 22 Sep 49)

Prosperity, earthly, not the reward of seeing God; the Jews were continually reminded of this
- RP 43 ❖ RP 4:19

Prosperity, material, as one of the values implicit in nineteenth-century fiction
- CR 16, 21-22 ❖ CR 2:13, 29

Prosperity, self-sufficiency the possible result of those views that lead to worldly
- PP 98 ❖ PP 6:9

Prostitute, a cold self-righteous prig may be nearer to hell than a
- MC 94-95 (see also L 175; LAL 111*
- ❖ MC III 5:14 (see also L 17 Jan 40; LAL 26 Nov 62*)

Prostitutes are in no danger of finding their present life so satisfactory that they cannot turn to God; the proud, the self-righteous are in that danger
- PP 98 ❖ PP 6:9

Prostitution, I feel it is a form of, for a clergyman to disbelieve what he preaches

- GID 260 (see also GID 89-90*, 265*)
- ❖ GID II 16:12 (see also GID I 10:2, 3*; II 16:46*)

Prostitution listed as an extreme example of unnecessary work: The reason it is worse than ordinary fornication is that it has no end in view except money
- WLN 75 ❖ WLN 5:11

Proverbs, what a dull and remote thing the Book of, seems at first glance
- CR 115 ❖ CR 10:3

Providences, On Special (title of Appendix B)
- M 174-181 ❖ M App. B

"Provincial" defined: to reject a thing "because it does not immediately appeal to our own age...to have the self-complacent blindness of the stay-at-home"
- RP 130 (see also Age)
- ❖ RP 12:9 (see also Age)

Provincialism: Theologians need to study outsiders; "The minds you daily meet have been conditioned by the same studies and prevalent opinions as your own"*
- CR 152 ❖ CR 13:1

Proving oneself: The claim to equality is made only by those who feel themselves to be in some way inferior
- SL 162-163; WLN 60-61 (see also LAL 27-28) ❖ SL 32:22; WLN 4:22 (see also LAL Mar 10/54)

Prudence, meaning and discussion of, as one of the "Cardinal virtues" ("Prudence means practical common sense...")
- MC 74-75 ❖ MC III 2:4

Psalm 8 is "an expression of wonder at man and man's place in Nature...and therefore at God who appointed it"
- RP 132-134 ❖ RP 12:11-13

Psalm 19: "I take this to be the greatest poem in the Psalter and one of the greatest lyrics in the world"
- RP 63 (Also quoted in GID 130)
- ❖ RP 6:13 (Also quoted in GID I 16:2)

Psalm 19, structure of: six verses about Nature, five about the Law, and four of personal prayer
- RP 63 ❖ RP 6:13

•RP 2 ❖ RP 1:2

Psalms, in Akhenaten as in the, a certain kind of poetry seems to go with a certain kind of theology
•RP 89 ❖ RP 8:18

Psalms: "...in reading them I suspect that we have our hands on the near end of a living cord that stretches far back into the past"
•CR 115 ❖ CR 10:2

Psalms, in the, I find an experience fully God-centred, asking of God no gift more urgently than His presence
•RP 52 ❖ RP 5:10

Psalms: It seems to me appropriate that the speech of God should sometimes be poetry
•RP 5 ❖ RP 1:8

Psalms, "Judgement" in the (chapter title)
•RP 9-19 (see also CR 122-128)
❖ RP ch. 2 (see also CR 10:22-40)

Psalms largely a closed book to many modern church-goers, due to the vindictiveness and self-righteousness in it
•RP 18-19 ❖ RP 2:14

Psalms, Law of God in the
•RP 54-65 (see also GID 130)
❖ RP ch. 6 (see also GID I 16:2)

Psalms, Lewis mentions Coverdale as the Bible translation he mainly worked from in studying the
•RP 7 ❖ RP 1:11

Psalms, most of the, are said to be "post-exilic," that is, from the sixth century B.C.
•CR 114-115 ❖ CR 10:2

Psalms, Nature as approached in the
•RP 76-89 ❖ RP ch. 8

Psalms of Judgement: For the Psalmists, judgement is apparently an occasion of universal rejoicing; they ask for it
•RP 9-10 ❖ RP 2:2

Psalms of Judgement: "It is for justice, for a hearing, far more often than for pardon, that the Psalmists pray"
•CR 125 (see also RP 9-19)
❖ CR 10:28 (see also RP ch. 2)

Psalms of Judgement: Judgement not something that the conscience-stricken believer fears but something

the downtrodden believer hopes for
•CR 123-124 ❖ CR 10:24-28

Psalms of Judgement: The Psalmists cried to God for justice instead of injustice; the Divine Judge is the defender, the rescuer
•RP 12 ❖ RP 2:6

Psalms of Judgement: "There are, indeed, some few passages in which a Psalmist thinks of 'judgement' with trembling..."
•CR 124-125 (see also RP 16-17)
❖ CR 10:28 (see also RP 2:11)

Psalms of the Nativity
•RP 124-125, 127-132 ❖ RP 12:5, 8-10

Psalms: Our Lord's mind and language were clearly steeped in the Psalter; we should be able to make some use even of the difficult passages
•RP 22 (see also CR 121)
❖ RP 3:4 (see also CR 10:15)

Psalms, penitence in, shows a desire to placate God's wrath; this is not inconsistent with Christian liturgies of penitence
•LM 95 ❖ LM 18:4

Psalms, poetry of, depends largely on parallelism, which translates into any language
•L 188; RP 3-5 ❖ L 16 Jul 40; RP 1:5-7

Psalms: "...poetry of that sort did not, like ours, seek to express those things in which individuals differ, and did not aim at novelty"
•CR 115 ❖ CR 10:2

Psalms, praise in the
•RP 90-98 (see also Praise)
❖ RP ch. 9 (see also Praise)

Psalms, protests against sins of the tongue are all over the
•RP 75 ❖ RP 7:16

Psalms, Resentment is expressed in the, without disguise, without self-consciousness, without shame—as few but children would express it today
•RP 23 (see also CR 118)
❖ RP 3:7 (see also CR 10:7)

Psalms, Second Meanings in the (chapter title)
•RP 120-138 ❖ RP ch. 12

Psalms, self-righteousness in the: It is important to make a distinction between being in the right and being "righteous"
•RP 17-18 (*see also* L 183)
❖ RP 2:13 (*see also* L 16 Apr 40)

Psalms, self-righteousness in the: "Our Lord...becomes the speaker in these passages"; He was in fact holy and innocent
•RP 135 ❖ RP 12:15

Psalms, spirit and technique of, may be very like those of much older sacred poetry which is now lost
•CR 114-115 ❖ CR 10:2

Psalms, The (chapter title)
•CR 114-128 ❖ CR ch. 10

Psalms, the cursing, can show us the proper object of utter hostility— wickedness, especially our own
•RP 136 ❖ RP 12:16

Psalms, the cursing: We ought to read them with fear, for who knows what imprecations of the same sort we have tempted someone to utter against us?
•CR 118-119 (*see also* RP 24)
❖ CR 10:9, 10 (*see also* RP 3:9)

Psalms, the cursing: What good can we find in reading them?
•CR 118-119; RP 18-33
❖ CR 10:9, 10; RP 2:14; ch. 3

Psalms: The cursings "may occur most disquietingly in the Psalms we love"
•RP 21 ❖ RP 3:3

Psalms, the delight expressed in the, is very much centred in the Temple and its services
•RP 45-48, 50 ❖ RP 5:3-6, 8

Psalms, the dominant impression I get from reading the, is one of antiquity
•CR 114 ❖ CR 10:1

Psalms: The ferocious parts serve as a reminder that there is in the world such a thing as wickedness and that it is hateful to God
•RP 32-33 ❖ RP 3:21

Psalms: The Hebrew poets are our predecessors in a way that the Pagan writers could not be; they have Something the Pagans have not

•CR 116 ❖ CR 10:4

Psalms: The most inevitable "second meaning" in them is that the expressions of suffering are all related to Christ's suffering
•RP 126-127 ❖ RP 12:7

Psalms: The most valuable thing they do for me is to express that same delight in God which made David dance
•RP 45 ❖ RP 5:4

Psalms, there is in many of the, a fatal confusion between the desire for justice and the desire for revenge
•RP 18 ❖ RP 2:14

Psalms: Through all the horrible distortions of the human medium, I have gained something I might not have gained from a flawless exposition
•RP 114 ❖ RP 11:10

Psalms, through the writings of Bergson I became capable of appreciating the more exultant
•SJ 198 ❖ SJ 13:1

Psalms, two figures meet us in the, that of the sufferer and the king; Our Lord identified Himself with both
•RP 120-121 ❖ RP 12:2

Psalms, two things link the, with us: One is the *Magnificat*, and the other is Our Lord's continued quotations from them
•CR 121 (*see also* RP 6, 22)
❖ CR 10:15 (*see also* RP 1:9; 3:4)

Psalms vs. Pagan literature: "One's first impression is that the Jews were much more vindictive and vitriolic than the Pagans"
•RP 27-31 ❖ RP 3:14-20

Psalms: We can recognize in ourselves the Psalmists' tendency to chew over and over the cud of some injury
•RP 23-24 ❖ RP 3:8

Psalms: We may learn·to see the good thing which the ferocity is mixed with: a passionate craving for justice
•CR 121-122 ❖ CR 10:17

Psalms were written by many poets and at many different times
•RP 2 ❖ RP 1:3

Psalms which address "connivance," or

unprotesting participation in evil
•RP 66-75 ❖ RP ch. 7

Psalms, while reading, two images come to mind: creatures of unrestrained emotion, and Anglican choir boys singing without personal emotion
•CR 114 (see also CR 121)
❖ CR 10:1 (see also CR 10:14)

Psalmist is nearly always the indignant plaintiff; as a Christian I can find the Jewish conception of a civil judgement useful by picturing myself as defendant
•RP 16-17 ❖ RP 2:11-13

Psalmist probably felt about the Law as he felt about his poetry; both involved exact and loving conformity to an intricate pattern
•RP 59 ❖ RP 6:9

Psalmists (and other Old Testament writers) probably had little or no belief in a future life
•RP 36, 38-39 ❖ RP 4:6, 9-12

Psalmist's appreciation for animals is almost certainly reached through the idea of God as Creator and sustainer of all; they are our fellow-dependents
•RP 84-85 (see also RP 88-89)
❖ RP 8:14 (see also RP 8:18)

Psalmists are eager for judgement because they believe themselves to be wholly in the right; Christian trembles because he knows he is a sinner
•CR 125 (see also RP 9-12)
❖ CR 10:29 (see also RP 11:1-6)

Psalmists' delight in the Law is a delight in having touched firmness—like a pedestrian weary of muddy short-cuts
•RP 62 ❖ RP 6:11

Psalmists did not know that God would die to offer them eternal joy—yet they express longing for Him, for His mere presence
•RP 50 ❖ RP 5:8

Psalmist's effort to keep the Law springs not from servile fear but from love of moral beauty
•RP 59-60 ❖ RP 6:9

Psalmists, like ourselves, include both good and bad members of the Church; the tares among them we have no authority to pull up
•CR 121 ❖ CR 10:16

Psalmists look forward to judgement because they think they have been wronged and hope to see their wrongs righted; this leads into self-righteousness
•RP 16-17 (see also RP 134-135)
❖ RP 2:11-13 (see also RP 12:15)

Psalmists, neurosis as a condition which some may attribute to the, —but the belief that one is threatened by certain evils may be realistic
•CR 126 ❖ CR 10:32-35

Psalmists, reaction of the, to injury— though profoundly natural—is profoundly wrong
•RP 26 (see also CR 118-120)
❖ RP 3:12 (see also CR 10:7-12)

Psalmists, self-righteous utterances of, grew out of their "Dark Night of the Flesh" which included ostracism, ineffectiveness, and humiliation
•CR 125-128 ❖ CR 10:30-40

Psalmists: "These poets lived in a world of savage punishments, of massacre and violence..."; they were "ferocious, self-pitying, barbaric men"
•RP 23-24 (see also CR 118)
❖ RP 3:8 (see also CR 10:8)

Psalmists: "What I see (so to speak) in the faces of these old poets tells me more about the God whom they and we adore"
•RP 52-53 ❖ RP 5:10

Psychiatrists, keep clear of, unless you know that they are also Christians
•L 211 ❖ L undated letter of 1947

"Psychical Research" mentioned by Screwtape as a useful addition to mere Christianity
•SL 115 ❖ SL 25:1

Psychoanalysis—consider also Advice

Psychoanalysis and Christian morality
•MC 83-87 ❖ MC III ch. 4

Psychoanalysis, attempting to practice obedience is a cheaper way to self-knowledge than, (though in some ways it may be more costly)

•CR 169 ❖ CR 14:21

Psychoanalysis claims to be a technique for putting the human machine right, as does Christian morality
•MC 83 ❖ MC III 4:2

Psychoanalysis: "I see no reason why a Christian should not be an analyst"
•L 180 ❖ L 26 Mar 40

Psychoanalysis: "Its technique overlaps with Christian morality at some points and it would not be a bad thing if every parson knew something about it"
•MC 84 ❖ MC III 4:3

Psychoanalysis, Morality and (chapter title)
•MC 83-87 ❖ MC III ch. 4

Psychoanalysis no doubt full of errors, but so long as it remains a science and doesn't set up to be a philosophy, I have no quarrel with it
•L 179-180 ❖ L 26 Mar 40

Psychoanalysis is partly to blame in the decline of our sense of guilt (by intimating that shame is a dangerous and mischievous thing)
•PP 56-57 ❖ PP 4:3

Psychoanalysis, some aspects of, mentioned by Screwtape as useful to his purposes
•SL 33 ❖ SL 7:1

Psychoanalysis: The patient is always influenced by the analyst's own values
•L 180 ❖ L 26 Mar 40

Psychoanalysis undertakes to give a man better raw material for his choices; morality is concerned with the choices themselves
•MC 84 ❖ MC III 4:4

Psychoanalysis: "We all know people who have undergone it and seem to have made themselves a life-long subject of research ever since"
•LM 34 ❖ LM 6:16

Psychological outfit, we may have made so little use of a good, that we are no better than those we regard as fiends
•MC 86 (see also L 183; MC 180-182) ❖ MC III 4:7 (see also L 16 Apr 40; MC IV 10:9-14)

Psychological situation, every, has its own peculiar temptations and advantages; the best could be abused, and the worst turned to good use
•L 180 ❖ L 26 Mar 40

Psychologists are talking nonsense when they tell us that all guilt-feelings are untrustworthy and pathological
•LM 32-33 ❖ LM 6:12

Psychologists have a good *prima facie* case against religion; the theory that our religion is a substitute has a great deal of plausibility
•CR 37-38 (see also GID 271-274*; WLN 19*) ❖ CR 3:2 (see also GID III 1:1-7*; WLN 2:8*)

Psychologists have made the error of underestimating the depth and variety of the contents of our subconscious (sex not the only element)
•LM 79 ❖ LM 15:8

Psychologists mentioned as seldom being religious; "It is as [scientists'] subject matter comes nearer to man himself that their anti-religious bias hardens"
•GID 135 ❖ GID I 16:9, 10

Psychology: Applying arguments to alter our own emotions as an example of how rational thoughts enable us to alter the course of Nature*
•M 25-26 ❖ M 4:2

Psychology: I do not think we see things more clearly by classifying all malefical states of Affection as pathological*
•FL 80-81 ❖ FL 3:43

Psychology: Jesus "was not at all like the psychologist's picture of the integrated, balanced, adjusted, happily married, employed popular citizen"*
•FL 81 ❖ FL 3:43

Psychology: Lewis speculates that at the Fall the mind fell under the psychological laws which God had made to rule the psychology of the higher anthropoids
•PP 82 ❖ PP 5:10

Psychology, the new, which was concerned about "Fantasy" or "wishful thinking" was sweeping through us all (re: Lewis's early years at Oxford)
•SJ 203 ❖ SJ 13:10

Psychotherapy mentioned with regard to the "Humanitarian" concept of punishment
- GID 288, 289, 290, 293, 313
- ❖ GID III 4:2, 5, 7, 12; 8:9

Publican who makes dishonest demands labelled "the ungodly" who "for his own lust doth persecute the poor" in the Psalms
- RP 15 ❖ RP 2:10

Publishing a dead person's correspondence indiscriminately, warning against
- L 108 ❖ L 5 Jun 26

Publishing *Pepys's Diary*, Lewis makes comments on, in its unexpurgated form
- L 293-294 ❖ L 17 Jun 60

Punishment—*consider also* Revenge

Punishment, capital: A man may sometimes be entitled to hurt or even kill his fellow, but only when the necessity is urgent (etc.)*
- PP 111-112 ❖ PP 7:2

Punishment, capital: I am not trying to show that it is certainly right; I am only maintaining that it is not certainly wrong
- WG 42-43 ❖ WG 3:17

Punishment, capital: I am on neither side in the controversy; but I think the abolitionists conduct their case very ill
- GID 340 ❖ GID IV Letter 12

Punishment, capital: I do not know whether the fear of death is an indispensable deterrent
- GID 287 ❖ GID III 4:1

Punishment, capital: I do not know when a murderer is more likely to repent—on the gallows or in the prison infirmary thirty years later
- GID 287 (*see also* GID 339; WG 42)
- ❖ GID III 4:1 (*see also* GID IV Letter 12; WG 3:17)

Punishment, capital: I do not think death and pain are the greatest evils (re: Pacifism)**
- WG 43 (*see also* GID 297, 311; L 176; M 125; SL 131-132)
- ❖ WG 3:8 (*see also* GID III 4:20; 8:1; L 17 Jan 40; M 14:28; SL 28:1)

Punishment, capital: "...if you cannot restrain a man except by trying to kill him, then it seems to me a Christian must do that"
- GID 49 ❖ GID I 4:3 (Ques. 1)

Punishment, capital: "In some instances ...death may be the only efficient method of restraint"
- WG 42 ❖ WG 3:17

Punishment, capital: In the commandment "Thou shalt not kill" the word "kill" means "murder"
- L 247; MC 106-107
- ❖ L 8 Nov 52; MC III 7:7

Punishment, capital: It is quite clear that St. Paul approved of this
- L 247-248 ❖ L 8 Nov 52

Punishment, capital, letter regarding
- GID 339-340 ❖ GID IV Letter 12

Punishment, capital, may be valuable as a deterrent through fear as well as an expression of the moral importance of certain crimes
- WG 42 ❖ WG 3:17

Punishment, capital, mentioned briefly ("Do you see we're abolishing capital punishment in this country? Do you think we're wise or foolish?")
- LAL 59 ❖ LAL 5/7/56

Punishment, capital: Neither natural light, nor scripture, nor ecclesiastical authority seems to tell me whether or not it should be abolished; I don't know
- GID 339 ❖ GID IV Letter 12

Punishment, capital: Whether it is a morally permissible deterrent is a question which I propose to leave untouched
- GID 287 ❖ GID III 4:1

Punishment, Christian forgiveness and love of one's enemy does not preclude the concept of
- MC 106-108 ❖ MC III 7:8-10

Punishment, classical theory of, (based on the concept of Desert) explained and defended
- GID 287-300, 313 (*see also* PP 93-94)
- ❖ GID III ch. 4 (*see also* PP 6:6)

Punishment: "Even while we kill and punish [a person] we must...wish that he

were not bad, to hope that he may, in this world or another, be cured..."
•MC 108 ❖ MC III 7:10

Punishment, "Humanitarian" theory of, (regards crime as a disease)
•GID 287-294 (*see also* GID 313; L 304) ❖ GID III 4:1-14 (*see also* GID III 8:7-9; L 25 May 62)

Punishment, "Humanitarian" theory of, carries on its front a semblance of mercy which is wholly false—thus it deceives men of good will
•GID 293 ❖ GID III 4:13

Punishment, I was brought up to believe that any fear of, or hope of reward contaminated the will; goodness must be disinterested
•SJ 231 (*see also* FL 189-190; LM 120; RP 39-42) ❖ SJ 15:3 (*see also* FL 6:42; LM 22:8; RP 4:12-17)

Punishment of an innocent man is wicked only if we grant the traditional view that righteous punishment means deserved punishment
•GID 291 ❖ GID III 4:9

Punishment of lost souls based on retribution (ill-desert), but is less a sentence imposed on one than the mere fact of being what one is
•PP 122-123 (*see also* GID 155; MC 77-78; PP 127*) ❖ PP 8:7 (*see also* GID I 18:11; MC III 2:12; PP 8:11*)

Punishment, only the concept of desert connects, with morality and justice; if crime is merely a disease, it cannot be pardoned—can only be cured
•GID 288, 294, 313, 339 (*see also* PP 93-94, 120-122; L 304) ❖ GID III 4:4, 13; 8:7; IV Letter 12 (*see also* PP 6:6; 8:5, 6; L 25 May 62)

Punishment, The Humanitarian Theory of (chapter title)
•GID 287-300 ❖ GID III ch. 4

Punishment: "The modern view, by excluding the retributive element and concentrating solely on deterrence and cure, is hideously immoral"
•L 304 ❖ L 25 May 62

Punishment, to be punishment, must be based on grounds of desert; otherwise

it is an instance of tyranny (or of war)
•GID 287-294, 298 (*see also* GID 313, 339; PP 120-122)
❖ GID III 4:1-14, 23 (*see also* GID III 8:7-9; IV Letter 12; PP 8:5, 6)

Punishment, under the humanitarian view of, (where crime is seen as a "disease" which must be "cured"), rulers become owners
•GID 313 ❖ GID III 8:8

Punishment: "We may punish if necessary, but we must not enjoy it"
•MC 107-108 ❖ MC III 7:10

Punishment, we must prefer the conversion rather than the, of very evil men, and prefer it infinitely—but to ask for justice may be a very ethical demand
•PP 121-122 ❖ PP 8:5

Punishments, Divine, are also mercies and particular good is worked out of particular evil
•SJ 77 ❖ SJ 5:9

Punishments, the moment you regard your troubles and sorrows as, they become easier to bear (as a dingy hotel may look good if thought to be a prison)
•GID 52 ❖ GID I 4:18 (Ques. 5)

Pure in heart, it is safe to tell the, that they shall see God, for only the pure in heart want to
•PP 145 ❖ PP 10:1

Purgatory as a process of purification which may involve suffering
•LM 108-109 ❖ LM 20:10-12

Purgatory described as a place "for souls already saved"
•PP 124 (ftnt.) ❖ PP 8:8 (ftnt.)

Purgatory, I believe in; our souls demand it, don't they?
•LM 108-109 ❖ LM 20:7-10

Purgatory: I can't help suspecting that the dead also feel the pains of separation from their loved ones (and this may be one of their purgatorial sufferings)
•GO 58 (*see also* GO 31) ❖ GO 3:33 (*see also* GO 2:17)

Purgatory: "I hope that when the tooth of life is drawn and I am 'coming round,' a voice will say, 'Rinse your mouth out

with this'"
•LAL 84; LM 109 (*see also* SL 146*, 147)
❖ LAL Jul 7th 59; LM 20:12 (*see also* SL 31:2*, 3)

Purgatory: "I know there are not only tears to be dried but stains to be scoured. The sword will be made even brighter"*
•GO 49 ❖ GO 3:15

Purgatory: "I never believed...that the faithfulest soul could leap straight into perfection and peace the moment death has rattled in the throat"*
•GO 48-49 ❖ GO 3:15

Purgatory mentioned as "a process by which the work of redemption continues..." vs."a second chance in the strict sense"
•L 246-247 ❖ L 8 Nov 52

Purgatory, one stage in, might be a big kitchen with things going wrong; women must learn to do nothing—men must learn to jump up and do something about it
•LAL 105-106, 107
❖ LAL 31/7/62; 3 Sep 62

Purgatory: "Shall we, perhaps, in Purgatory, see our own faces and hear our own voices as they really were?"
•RP 8 ❖ RP 1:13

Purgatory: "When you die, and if prison visiting is allowed, come down and look me up in Purgatory"
•L 307 ❖ L 17 Sep 63

"**Puritanism**" as a word which has decreased the value people place on temperance, chastity, and sobriety of life
•SL 47, 48 (*see also* SL 52, 118)
❖ SL 10:3 (*see also* SL 11:5; 25:5)

Purpose—*see also* Goal

Purpose of God—*see also* Will of God

Purpose of God becoming a man: to turn creatures into sons
•MC 182 (*see also* MC 185-186)
❖ MC IV 10:16 (*see also* MC IV 11:4-7)

Purpose of God in creating individuals includes the never-completed "attempt by each soul to communicate its unique vision [of God] to all the others"

•PP 150 (*see also* FL 92-93*)
❖ PP 10:7 (*see also* FL 4:9*)

Purpose of life—*see also* Goal of human life

Purpose of life, surely the main, is to reach the point at which "one's own life as a person" is at an end; "He that loseth his life shall find it"
•LAL 97-98 ❖ LAL 28 Mar 61

Purpose of our creation: We were made not primarily that we may love God but that God may love us
•PP 48 ❖ PP 3:15

Purpose of the Church is nothing else but to draw men into Christ
•MC 169-170 ❖ MC IV 8:10

Purposes of God, our conjectures about, are probably of no more value than my dog's ideas of what I am up to when I sit and read
•RP 115 ❖ RP 11:11

Quakers mentioned
 •L 229, 240, 289
 ❖ L 23 Apr 51; 1 Apr 52; 8 Sep 59
Quality of workmanship valued less and less as built-in obsolescence becomes an economic necessity
 •WLN 72, 78 ❖ WLN 5:3, 4, 15
Quarrelling can be unfair if we cause others to give in to us because we pretend to be "hurt"; in this way we win by cheating
 •RP 14 ❖ RP 2:9
Quarrelling: Domestic hatred may express itself more in the manner of speech than in the words themselves; thus a grievance may be had when offence is taken
 •SL 17-18 ❖ SL 3:5
Quarrelling: In a given quarrel (or war) the question "Who is righteous?" is quite distinct from the question "Who is in the right?"
 •L 183 (see also RP 17-18)
 ❖ L 16 Apr 40 (see also RP 2:13, 14)
Quarrelling—see also Family relations; Relations, interpersonal
Quarrelling: "Who would not rather live with those ordinary people who get over their tantrums (and ours) unemphatically letting a meal...or a joke mend all?"*
 •FL 185 ❖ FL 6:36
Queen of England, coronation of, seen as a symbol of the situation of humanity itself—called by God, yet inadequate

to the responsibility
 •LAL 18-19 ❖ LAL Jul 10 53
Questions—see also Difficulties in Scripture; Doctrinal differences; Doctrines, difficult
Questions, answers to our, about the problem of pain: "What really matters is the argument that there must be an answer..."
 •GID 170 (see also GID 167-168*)
 ❖ GID I 20:Reply-15 (see also GID I 20:Reply-6*)
Questions, answers to our (doctrinal): "...I might...be answered as a far greater questioner was answered: 'What is that to thee? Follow thou Me'"
 •MC 7 ❖ MC P:4
Questions, answers to our: "[I get] the sense that some shattering and disarming simplicity is the real answer"
 •GO 83 ❖ GO 4:29
Questions, answers to our: The Irresistible and the Indisputable are the two weapons which God's scheme forbids Him to use*
 •SL 38 ❖ SL 8:4
Questions can be very interesting without being answerable; one of my main efforts as a teacher has been to train people to say "We don't know"
 •L 295 ❖ L 26 Sep 60
Questions, do all our theoretical, conceal shirkings by the will?
 •L 202 ❖ L 22 Dec 42
Questions, Heaven will answer our, but not by showing us subtle reconciliations between our contradictory notions; the notions will be knocked from under us...
 •GO 83 ❖ GO 4:28
Questions: Jesus "hardly ever gave a straight answer to a straight question. He will not be, in the way we want, 'pinned down'"
 •RP 113 ❖ RP 11:7
Questions, our: If the Church is truly the bearer of revelation, we should expect to find in it things opaque to our reason though not contrary to it*
 •GID 238 ❖ GID II 11:11

Questions, probably half of the, we ask of God are unanswerable—nonsensical, like "Is yellow square or round?"
•GO 81 (*see also* GO 89)
❖ GO 4:25 (*see also* GO 4:39)
Questions, Scripture not intended to give true answers to all the, we might ask
•L 287 ❖ L 7 May 59
Questions: "The best is perhaps what we understand least"
•GO 89 ❖ GO 4:38
Questions we ask of God: "Our Lord's replies are never straight answers and never gratify curiosity"
•L 169-170 (*see also* PP 119)
❖ L 5 Nov 39 (*see also* PP 8:2)
Questions, when I lay these, before God, I get no answer; it is as though He shook His head not in refusal but waiving the question: "Peace, child..."
•GO 80-81 ❖ GO 4:24
Quotations may be misquoted, or misunderstood out of context; in reading (studying) one should find the source of quotes and look them up
•L 156 ❖ L 7 Jun 34

Rabbit, all the, in us is to disappear— the worried, conscientious, ethical rabbit as well as the cowardly and sensual rabbit
•GID 112 ❖ GID I 12:10
Rabbit, Man or (chapter title)
•GID 108-113 ❖ GID I ch. 12
Racine as "a mighty poet and steeped in the Bible"
•RP 54 (*see also* LAL 60)
❖ RP 6:1 (*see also* LAL 3/8/56)
Racism: "All over the earth the White Man's offence 'smells to heaven': massacres, broken treaties, theft, kidnappings, enslavement..."*
•CR 119 ❖ CR 10:10
Racism: I'm shocked to hear that a shop wouldn't serve a Chinese; but I have long known that the talk about Brotherhood, wherever it occurs, is hypocrisy*
•LAL 43 ❖ LAL 7/6/55
Racism ("oppression and injustice") provokes to the sin of hatred and prayers of vindictiveness*
•CR 119 (*see also* RP 24*)
❖ CR 10:9, 10 (*see also* RP 3:9*)
Racism ("Racialism"), extreme patriotism which believes that our nation is in fact markedly superior to all others may breed, which Christianity forbids
•FL 44-45 ❖ FL 2:38
Radio analogy to show relationship of man's rational thinking to the voice of eternal Reason

---

•M 39-40 (*see also* CR 68*)

❖ M 6:2 (*see also* CR 5:22*)

Radio has driven the Leprechauns away in Eire

•LAL 62 ❖ LAL Sep 8/56

Radio, if you wish to avoid God keep the, on; avoid silence and solitude...Live in a crowd

•CR 168 (*see also* SL 102-103*)

❖ CR 14:17, 18 (*see also* SL 22:5*)

Radio, in a letter of advice to a child (on writing) Lewis suggests turning off the

•L 291 ❖ L 14 Dec 59

Radio ("wireless") an instrument invented to destroy solitude

•WG 107 ❖ WG 7:2

Ransom plays the role of Christ as every Christian is called upon in some measure to *enact* Christ

•L 283 ❖ L 29 Dec 58

Rapture—*consider* Second Coming

Rationalism, my youthful, was based on what I believed to be the findings of the sciences—which I had to take on trusted authority

•SJ 174 (*see also* SJ 170)

❖ SJ 11:12 (*see also* SJ 11:7)

"Rationalist," Kirk was a, of the old, high and dry nineteenth-century type

•SJ 139 (*see also* SJ 171)

❖ SJ 9:15 (*see also* SJ 11:8)

Rationality—*see also* Reason(ing); Thinking; Thought

Rationality, argument for a supernatural source for human

•M 12-33; CR 57-71 (*see also* GID 275-276) ❖ M ch. 3, 4; CR ch. 5 (*see also* GID III 1:13-16)

Rationality: If dolphins are proved to be rational, we have no more right to enslave them than to enslave our fellowmen

•CR 174 ❖ CR 14:44

Rationality of a man is his share of eternal Reason only insofar as the state of his brain allows it to be (radio analogy)

•M 39-40 (*see also* CR 68)

❖ M 6:2 (*see also* CR 5:22)

Rationality of Man is the tell-tale rift in Nature which speaks of something beyond her

•M 29 (*see also* CR 60-71; GID 136-138; M 12-24, SJ 208-209)

❖ M 4:8 (*see also* CR ch. 5; GID 16:13-17; M ch. 3; SJ 13:17)

Rats in a trap, my real fear is that we are really, —or worse still, rats in a laboratory

•GO 33 ❖ GO 2:22

Raw material out of which a thing is made is not always that which would seem most promising to one who doesn't understand the process (re: "Chosen" people)

•CR 117 ❖ CR 10:6

Raw material: You can't judge Christianity simply by comparing the *product* in two people; you need to know what kind of raw material Christ is working on

•GID 59 (*see also* L 242*; MC 177-178)

❖ GID I 4:47-52 (*see also* L 28 May 52*; MC IV 10:5)

Reactions, I hate and distrust all types of, (e.g., extreme views of the doctrine of the Second Coming have caused it to be under-emphasized)

•WLN 94-95 (*see also* MC 160)

❖ WLN 7:4 (*see also* MC IV 6:4)

Reading—*consider also* Books; Literature; Poetry

Reading, a young man who wishes to be a sound atheist cannot be too careful of his; there are traps everywhere

•SJ 191 (*see also* CR 168-169)

❖ SJ 12:13 (*see also* CR 14:18)

Reading about recent improvements in theology important for the Apologist

•GID 91-92 ❖ GID I 10:7

Reading "all day for mere pleasure with a clear conscience" one of the rewards of a small illness

•L 106-107 (*see also* L 159-160, 202, 302; SJ 189)

❖ L undated letter postmarked 25 Jan 26 (*see also* L undated letter just after 2 Sep 37; 31 Jan 43; 20 Dec 61; SJ 12:11)

Reading and eating are two pleasures that combine admirably, although not all

books are suitable for mealtime reading
•SJ 142 ❖ SJ 9:18

Reading, devotional—*see* Devotional reading

Reading eight books and getting only what the one book behind those eight would have given you
•L 148 ❖ L 17 Jan 32

Reading: I could not doubt that the sub-Christian or anti-Christian values implicit in most literature did actually infect many readers
•CR 16 ❖ CR 2:13

Reading: "I should like to have...a new [Morris] romance always waiting for me the next time I am sick or sorry"*
•L 147-148 ❖ L 17 Jan 32

Reading: "I was by now a sufficiently experienced reader to distinguish liking from agreement" (re: reading G. K. Chesterton)
•SJ 190 ❖ SJ 12:12

Reading in "Schools" is difficult, even though theoretically three hours free from interruption and safe for reading ought to be a great blessing
•L 153 ❖ L 14 Jun 32

Reading isn't a strong enough drug now ... (re: grief Lewis felt after his wife's death)
•GO 10 ❖ GO 1:18

Reading: "It is a serious matter to choose wholesome recreations: but they would no longer be recreations if we pursued them seriously"
•CR 33-34 ❖ CR 2:54

Reading, it is important to acquire early in life the power of, wherever you happen to be
•SJ 56-57 ❖ SJ 4:1

Reading, Lewis makes suggestions for several types of Christian
•L 298-299 ❖ L 9 May 61

Reading, Lewis suggests sources for devotional
•L 192 ❖ L 4 Jan 41

Reading of Old Books, On the (chapter title)
•GID 200-207 ❖ GID II ch. 4

Reading of the classics listed by Lewis as one of the conscious causes for his rising doubt in the Christian faith (as a youth)
•SJ 62 ❖ SJ 4:9

Reading on trains: My brother and I soon learned that books can be taken on a journey and that hours of golden reading can so be added to its other delights
•SJ 56-57 (*see also* L 203, 265)
❖ SJ 4:1 (*see also* L 31 Jan 43; 5 Dec 55)

Reading, pride of activities such as, a certain book in order to make clever comments about it to one's friends mentioned by Screwtape
•SL 58, 60 (*see also* L 216; LAL 54; SJ 102-103; WLN 33-34)
❖ SL 13:3, 4 (*see also* L 3 Apr 49; LAL 20/3/56; SJ 7:3; WLN 3:5, 6)

Reading (studying): One should find the source of quotes and look them up, since they may be misquoted or misunderstood out of context
•L 156 ❖ L 7 Jun 34

Reading: The Christian has no objection to comedies that merely amuse and tales that merely refresh; we can play, as we can eat, to the glory of God
•CR 10 ❖ CR 1:15

Reading, those who like, for its own sake are those who truly enjoy the great literature
•L 152 ❖ L 8 Apr 32

Reading, what is the point in, contemporary authors because they happen to be alive?
•L 225-226
❖ L undated letter of Jan 1951

"**Real**" and "subjective" as words which Screwtape uses to his advantage, depending on the situation
•SL 142-144 ❖ SL 30:4

Real person seen best when he has been taken off his guard
•MC 164-165 ❖ MC IV 7:12

Realism—*see also* Materialism; Naturalism

Realism, I had abandoned
•SJ 216 ❖ SJ 14:7

"**Realists**," we had been; that is, we accepted as rock-bottom reality the universe revealed by the senses
•SJ 208 ❖ SJ 13:17

Reality—*see also* Truth

Reality, a cultured person is usually aware that, is very odd and that truth *must* have the characteristics of strangeness...
•CR 23 ❖ CR 2:35

Reality, all, is iconoclastic; our loved ones incessantly triumph over our mere idea of them
•GO 76-77 (*see also* GO 19-22, 83)
❖ GO 4:15, 16 (*see also* GO 2:3-6; 4:28)

Reality always complex, as is Christianity (re: the knotty and ambiguous doctrine of Hell)
•PP 119 (*see also* MC 46-48, 137, 145; PP 25) ❖ PP 8:3 (*see also* MC II 2:2, 4, 5; IV 1:9; 2:17; PP 1:16)

Reality, any conception of, which a sane mind can admit must favor some of its wishes and frustrate others
•SJ 172 ❖ SJ 11:9

Reality, as regards material, we are now being forced to the conclusion that we know nothing about it save its mathematics
•GID 46 ❖ GID I 3:16

Reality as seen from Heaven: "...how different the content of our faith will look when we see it in the total context"
•L 267 ❖ L 8 Feb 56

Reality, contact with ultimate: That voice which speaks in your conscience and in some of your intensest joys may be in fact the closest contact you have...
•CR 170 ❖ CR 14:27

Reality has sharp corners and rough edges; we dimly know at heart that nothing which is in every way agreeable to us can have objective reality
•LM 75-76 ❖ LM 14:13

Reality, Idealist's and Pantheist's view of, is that the material universe is, in the last resort, not quite real; a kind of mirage
•CR 59 ❖ CR 5:5

Reality, if our inferences do not give a

genuine insight into, then we can know nothing (re: reason)
•GID 274-275, 277
❖ GID III 1:11, 22-27

Reality is a very *long* story, with a complicated plot; what we know of reality through Nature is only a very small part*
•M 98-99 ❖ M 12:7

Reality is "incorrigibly plural"; all things come from one and all things are related, but all things are not one
•M 165 ❖ M 17:2

Reality lies "behind the scenes"; all our experience is only an "appearance," as illustrated by stage sets in a theatre
•GID 245-249 (*see also* CR 169-172; LM 78-81) ❖ GID II ch. 13 (*see also* CR 14:21-32; LM 15: 5-15)

Reality, looked at steadily, is unbearable
•GO 32 ❖ GO 2:20

Reality, in attempting to understand, "looking along" (i.e., experience of) a thing is as important as "looking at" it (i.e., scientific-like knowledge)
•GID 215 ❖ GID II 6:12

Reality may look simple, but is not; is complicated, and usually odd
•MC 46-48 (*see also* MC 137, 145; M 165; PP 25, 119) ❖ MC II 2:2-5 (*see also* MC IV 1:9; 2:16; M 17:2; PP 1:16; 8:3)

Reality must be self-consistent; but better to hold two inconsistent views than to ignore one side of the evidence
•L 252 ❖ L 3 Aug 53

Reality, myth transcends thought and Incarnation transcends myth in conveying abstract, to humans; Christ is more than Balder, not less
•GID 65-67 (*see also* M 133-134, ftnt.*)
❖ GID I 5:8-13 (*see also* M 15:2—ftnt.*)

Reality, Nature a partial system within, which has been mistaken for the whole (fish tank analogy)
•M 60-61 ❖ M 8:9

Reality never repeats; the exact same thing is never taken away and given back (re: reunion with loved ones in Heaven)
•GO 28-29 (*see also* GO 15-16; "En-

core")
❖ GO 2:14 (*see also* GO 1:29; "Encore")

Reality, there is no rational ground for the dogma that, must have no more than two levels—Nature, and a mystical, indescribable Something
•M 154-155 ❖ M 16:20, 21

Reality not fully knowable by us now
•GID 43-44 ❖ GID I 3:9, 10

Reality of God not the same as our image or idea of Him; He shatters this image time after time
•GO 76-78; LM 82 (*see also* GO 82-83; SL 22*) ❖ GO 4:15-18; LM 15:17 (*see also* GO 4:27, 28; SL 4:4*)

Reality of prayer vs. the facade of ourselves and the room we're in
•LM 77-82 ❖ LM ch. 15

Reality of the Law, The (chapter title)
•MC 26-30 ❖ MC I ch. 3

Reality of the mechanism of prayer is doubtless not comprehensible to our faculties
•WLN 10 ❖ WLN 1:19

Reality, science describes, by mathematics, but mathematics can hardly be reality itself (re: attempting contact with ultimate Reality)
•CR 170 ❖ CR 14:24

Reality, spiritual, difficult to picture by earthly concepts and images
•WG 60-62; 68-69 (*see also* M 85)
❖ WG 4:10-13, 23, 24 (*see also* M 11:6)

Reality, spiritual: We have no right to demand that it should be picturable, or even explicable in terms of our abstract thought
•PP 86-87 (*see also* M 83-86*)
❖ PP 5:13 (*see also* M 11:5-7*)

Reality, "tasting," through myth: In myth "we come nearest to experiencing as a concrete what can otherwise be understood only as an abstraction"
•GID 65-66 (*see also* CR 130-134, esp. 133) ❖ GID I 5:8-10 (*see also* CR 11:4-10, esp. 11:9)

Reality: The contemplation of what we take to be real is attended with a certain sort of aesthetic satisfaction
•WG 77-78 ❖ WG 5:9

Reality, the Jewish, Moslem, and Christian view of, is that there is something beyond Nature which refutes the scientists' picture of futility
•CR 59 ❖ CR 5:5

Reality vs. Truth: "...truth is always about something, but reality is that *about which* truth is"
•GID 66 ❖ GID I 5:10

Reality: "...we should never ask of anything 'Is it real?,' for everything is real. The proper question is 'A real what?'..." (re: the "realness" of prayer vs. the facade of a stage set)
•LM 80 ❖ LM 15:12

Reality, what appears to us as, is only a facade—both ourselves and the things around us (re: attempting contact with ultimate Reality)
•CR 169-170 (*see also* GID 245-249; LM 78-81) ❖ CR 14:21-24 (*see also* GID II ch. 13; LM 15: 5-15)

Reason(ing)—*see also* Rationality; Thinking; Thought

Reason, a belief in the objectivity and validity of, must be maintained *or* all thoughts are accidents and we can know no truths and have no knowledge*
•CR 60-63, 71, 72-81, 89; GID 21, 52-53, 136-138, 272, 274-276; M 12-24, 34, 105; MC 45-46; SJ 208; WG 88-91
❖ CR 5:9-13, 27; ch. 6; 7:16; GID I 1:1; 4:21; 16:13-17; GID III 1:4, 9, 13-16; M ch. 3; 5:1; 13:16; MC II 1:6; SJ 13:17; WG 5:21-24

Reason: A firm and settled belief is required because "though Reason is divine, human reasoners are not"
•CR 43 ❖ CR 3:12

Reason, a high natural gift of, identified with a greater tendency to refuse the life of Christ (quote from *Theologia Germanica*)
•CR 17 ❖ CR 2:16

Reason: A refutation of nineteenth-century philosophy which said that reason and moral values were subjective and had no basis in reality*
•CR 57-71 (*see also* CR 72-81—re:

moral subjectivism)

❖ CR ch. 5 (*see also* CR ch. 6—re: moral subjectivism)

Reason and authority: "One of the things my reason tells me is that I ought to check the results of my own thinking by the opinions of the wise"

•CR 26 ❖ CR 2:40

Reason and logic as objective rather than subjective rules out materialism but not idealism, theism, pantheism, or dualism*

•CR 63-65 ❖ CR 5:14-18

Reason and new beliefs must fight to maintain a foothold against our habitual ways of thinking (e.g., a rational belief in miracles)

•M 166-167 ❖ M 17:4

Reason and the Myth of Evolution: If my own mind is a product of the irrational, how shall I trust my own mind when it tells me about Evolution?

•CR 89 ❖ CR 7:16

Reason as an analogy to Conscience (both mean the whole man judging, either between truth and falsehood, or between good and evil)

•WG 34 ❖ WG 3:3

Reason as the organ whereby objective morality is apprehended*

•CR 78 ❖ CR 6:16

Reason, authority, and experience: "... on these three, mixed in varying proportions all our knowledge depends"

•CR 41 (*see also* CR 26*, 43)

❖ CR 3:9 (*see also* CR 2:40*; 3:12)

Reason enables Man to foresee his own pain and his own death, which causes acute mental suffering

•PP 14 (*see also* GO 9)

❖ PP 1:1 (*see also* GO 1:18)

Reason enables men to inflict a great deal more pain than they otherwise could have done on other men and on animals

•PP 14 ❖ PP 1:1

Reason, Evolution as a purely biological theorem does not discuss the origin and validity of

•CR 86 ❖ CR 7:12

Reason, human, and morality listed as "proofs of the Supernatural"

•M 43 (*see also* GID 275-276; MC 17-38; WG 88-89, 91)

❖ M 6:7 (*see also* GID III 1:13-16; MC Book I; WG 5:21, 24)

Reason, human, as an invasion of Nature by something outside her—or, in other words, a Miracle

•M 43 ❖ M 6:7

Reason, human, seen in modern religious thought as of no value at all

•L 177 ❖ L 18 Feb 40

Reason, I couldn't get at the universe if I couldn't trust my; if we couldn't trust inference we could know nothing...

•GID 274-275, 277

❖ GID III 1:11, 22-27

Reason, I thought that by definition God was, itself; but would He also be "reasonable" in that other, more comfortable sense?

•SJ 228 ❖ SJ 14:22

Reason: "...if our minds are totally alien to reality then all our thoughts, including this thought, are worthless"

•CR 71 ❖ CR 5:27

Reason: If the Church is truly the bearer of revelation, we should expect an element in it which is "opaque to our reason though not contrary to it"

•GID 238 ❖ GID II 11:11

Reason: In subjectivism, where reason is thought to be the by-product of a blind evolutionary process, there is no reason for supposing that logic yields truth

•CR 72 (*see also* Subjectivism)

❖ CR 6:2 (*see also* Subjectivism)

Reason may win truths; without Faith she will retain them just so long as Satan pleases

•CR 43 ❖ CR 3:12

Reason, natural gift of: Danger that it may come to think of itself as "the true Eternal Light" (quote from *Theologia Germanica*)

•CR 17 ❖ CR 2:16

Reason, practical, defined: "By practical reason I mean our judgement of good

and evil"
- CR 72-73 ❖ CR 6:4

Reason, relationship of theism to belief in
- GID 274-276 ❖ GID III 1:11-19

Reason, Screwtape warns against awakening, in humans: "...and once it is awake, who can foresee the result?"
- SL 8 ❖ SL 1:2

Reason, the materials for correcting our abstract conception of God cannot be supplied by, but by experience of Him
- M 90 (see also Experience)
❖ M 11:14 (see also Experience)

Reason: "To say that Reason is objective is to say that all our false reasonings could in principle be corrected by more Reason"
- CR 68 ❖ CR 5:22

Reason, Universal, apparently differs from ours in some ways, but cannot be radically different
- CR 67-69 (see also CR 79; GO 36-38; PP 37-39) ❖ CR 5:21-23 (see also CR 6:19; GO 2:28-30; PP 3:1-5)

Reason, Universal, differs from ours like a mathematical calculation differs from the short sums a child can do
- CR 68 (see also CR 70)
❖ CR 5:22 (see also CR 5:25)

Reason, use of, in evangelism: "Uneducated people are not irrational people..."
- GID 99 ❖ GID I 10:39, 40

Reason: We must combine a steadfast faith in inference as such with scepticism about each particular instance of inference (as people make mistakes)
- CR 67-68 ❖ CR 5:22

Reason: "When logic says a thing must be so, Nature always agrees"; this validity of knowledge cannot be explained by perpetual happy coincidence
- CR 64-65 ❖ CR 5:17

Reason: When reason itself becomes the object of study, it is as if we take out our own eyes to look at them; this yields "subjectivism"
- CR 72 (see also L 221*)
❖ CR 6:2 (see also L 27 Sep 49*)

Reasoning, all knowledge depends on the

validity of; Naturalism discredits our processes of reasoning, thereby discrediting Naturalism itself
- M 12-24, 34, 105 (see also CR 60-61, 71, 72-81, 89; GID 21, 52-53, 136-138, 272*, 274-276; MC 45-46, 52-53; SJ 108-209; WG 88-91)
❖ M ch. 3; 5:1; 13:16 (see also CR 5:9, 10, 27; ch. 6; 7:16; GID I 1:1; 4:21; 16:13-17; GID III 1:4*; 1:9, 13- 16; MC II 1:6; 3:4; SJ 13:17; WG 5:21-24)

Reasoning and rational argument no longer as effective as it used to be; people are more influenced by jargon than by argument for truth*
- SL 7-8 (see also SL 43)
❖ SL 1:1, 2 (see also SL 9:4)

Reasoning, God is the source for all your; when you argue against Him you are arguing against the very power that makes you able to argue at all
- MC 52-53 ❖ MC II 3:4

Reasoning, how the modern error of "subjectivism" has affected our moral
- CR 72-81 (see also Subjectivism)
❖ CR ch. 6 (see also Subjectivism)

Reasoning: I conclude that logic is a real insight into the way real things have to exist [and is not merely subjective]
- CR 63 ❖ CR 5:14

Reasoning involves three elements: reception of facts (from experience or authority), perception of self-evident truth, and arranging of facts...
- WG 34 ❖ WG 3:3

Reasoning necessary to give us all truth would be too complicated for any human mind; but that is due to a defect in the human instrument, not in Reason
- CR 68 (see also M 39-40)
❖ CR 5:22 (see also M 6:1, 2)

Reasoning, on the validity of human
- CR 57-71; M 3-44
❖ CR ch. 5; M ch. 1-6

Reasoning ("ratiocination"), I loved; though I could never have been a scientist, I had scientific as well as imaginative impulses
- SJ 137 ❖ SJ 9:11

Rebellion at one stage may yield the possibility of a clearer issue and deeper repentance at some later stage (re: pain as God's megaphone)*
•PP 95 ❖ PP 6:7

Rebellion, pain may rouse the bad man to a knowledge that all is not well or it might lead him to final and unrepented
•PP 95, 118 (*see also* PP 120-123)
❖ PP 6:7; 8:1 (*see also* PP 8:5-7)

Rebellion, the present situation is one of, not war (rebellion of "nature" against "spirit" in our bodies)
•M 126-127 ❖ M 14:30, 31

Rebels, we are, who must lay down our arms; we must render back the will which we have so long claimed for our own—this is a grievous pain
•PP 91 ❖ PP 6:3

Reconciliation between two people is fullest when the anger has been fully expressed; the "wrath" of God is likewise an essential part of His love
•LM 96-97 ❖ LM 18:8, 9

Recreation—*see also* Games; Play; *consider also* Pleasure(s)

Recreation: The miracle at Cana sanctified an innocent sensual pleasure and could be taken to sanctify at least a recreational use of "culture"
•CR 15 ❖ CR 2:7

Recreations, it is a serious matter to choose wholesome; but they would no longer be recreations if we pursued them seriously (re: reading and games)
•CR 33-34 ❖ CR 2:54

Red Herrings, A Chapter of (chapter title)
•M 45-54 ❖ M ch. 7

Redeemed—*consider* Destiny of redeemed Man

Redemption—*see also* Salvation

Redemption by sacrificial blood anticipated by Paganism; this may be seen in Homer*
•RP 37-38 ❖ RP 4:8

Redemption: Christ died, not for valuable men, but for sinners—human souls whose value, out of relation to God, is zero
•WG 115 (*see also* WLN 53)
❖ WG 7:14 (*see also* WLN 4:8)

Redemption, death as a means of: Christianity is unique in that it teaches that the terrible task has already in some sense been done for us
•PP 104 ❖ PP 6:15

Redemption, doctrine of death as means of, not peculiar to Christianity and cannot be escaped by ceasing to be a Christian
•PP 103 ❖ PP 6:15

Redemption: Free will has the result that Divine labour to redeem the world cannot be certain of succeeding; some souls will not be redeemed
•PP 118 (*see also* PP 127)
❖ PP 8:1 (*see also* PP 8:11)

Redemption: "It was not for societies or states that Christ died, but for men"
•WG 117 (*see also* GID 109-110; MC 73; WG 19; WLN 68)
❖ WG 7:16 (*see also* GID I 12:3; MC III 1:9; WG 1:15; WLN 4:39)

Redemption, mere improvement is no, though redemption always improves people; the change must go deeper than that
•MC 182, 183 ❖ MC IV 10:16; 11:1

Redemption, no creature that deserved, would need to be redeemed
•WLN 86 (*see also* M 52, 122*)
❖ WLN 6:10 (*see also* M 7:14; 14:24*)

Redemption of Man may be unique in the universe, yet spreads outward and exalts all creatures
•M 122-123 (*see also* WLN 87-88)
❖ M 14:24-26 (*see also* WLN 6:13, 14)

Redemption: Question of whether other rational species in the universe (if they exist) are fallen and, if so, whether they have been redeemed
•WLN 86-88 ❖ WLN 6:10-14

Redemption: "Redeemed humanity is to be something more glorious than unfallen humanity would have been..."
•M 122-123 ❖ M 14:24

Redemption, suffering an essential part of,

(therefore, says Screwtape, it is largely ineffective as an attack on faith)
  •SL 27 ❖ SL 5:3
Redemption through Christ's death, possible mechanism of
  •MC 56-61 (see also Atonement)
  ❖ MC II ch. 4 (see also Atonement)
Redemption through Christ's death: "... no explanation will ever be quite adequate to the reality"
  •MC 57 ❖ MC II 4:3
Redemption through Christ's death: Is this the only mode of Redemption that is possible? Here we ask what is wholly unknowable
  •WLN 87 ❖ WLN 6:12
Redemptive function of man, possible, with regard to animals
  •PP 136 (see also LAL 110)
  ❖ PP 9:8 (see also LAL 26 Nov 62)
Refinement—see also Culture
"Refinement," cultural: Where it is most named it is most absent
  •WLN 32 ❖ WLN 3:2
"Refinement," we all know those who shudder at the word, as a term of social approval (re: "culture" as a qualification for entry into the ruling class)
  •WLN 31-32 ❖ WLN 3:2
Reflection: "Part of every misery is...the fact that you don't merely suffer but have to keep on thinking about the fact that you suffer"
  •GO 9 (see also PP 14)
  ❖ GO 1:18 (see also PP 1:1)
"Regenerate" as the best adjective to describe the New Man
  •M 172 ❖ M App. A:11
Regenerate life, according to some authors a symptom of, is a permanent and horrified perception of our own sinfulness (but this can be taken too far)
  •LM 98-99 ❖ LM 18:13-16
Regeneration—see New Birth; Transformation
Regret for the consequences of our innocent blunders different from guilt for sins; we must try not to confuse the two

•LAL 106-107 ❖ LAL 3 Sep 62
Regret: "I now see that I spent most of my life doing *neither* what I ought *nor* what I liked" (said by a patient of Screwtape's, already in Hell)*
  •SL 56 (see also SL 42*, 144*)
  ❖ SL 12:4 (see also SL 9:2*; 30:4*)
"Rehearsal" (In a letter to a lady who thought she was dying): "Of course this may not be the end. Then make it a good rehearsal"
  •LAL 118 ❖ LAL 17 Jun 63
Reincarnation—see also Dead, state of the; Life after death
Reincarnation, belief about, in Buddhism: "Salvation from immortality, deliverance from reincarnation, is the very core of its message"
  •GID 130-131 ❖ GID I 16:2, 3
Reincarnation mentioned (as compared with Purgatory)
  •L 246-247 (consider also Purgatory)
  ❖ L 8 Nov 52 (consider also Purgatory)
Reincarnation: "...perhaps my pre-human past"*
  •LM 79 ❖ LM 15:8
Reincarnation ("spiritualism") offers only a vague comfort for our personal hankerings and adds a new horror to death—that of mere endless succession*
  •GID 142-143 ❖ GID I 16:25
Rejection by God, feeling of: We may imagine He has let us down at the very moment help was on its way
  •L 219 ❖ L 2 Sep 49
Rejection by God (quote from Law): "Many will be rejected because...they have not taken time and pains *enough*"
  •WG 131 ❖ WG 9:11
Rejection of God, what we miss by: "We shall have missed the end for which we are formed and rejected the only thing that satisfies"
  •WG 131 ❖ WG 9:11
Rejoinder to Dr. Pittenger (chapter title)
  •GID 177-183 ❖ GID I ch. 22
Relations, interpersonal—see also Domestic...; Family relations; Friendship; People; consider also Marriage; Men;

Women

Relations, interpersonal: A desire to believe all the good you can of others and to make others as comfortable as you can will solve most of the problems*
•MC 89 ❖ MC III 5:1

Relations, interpersonal: Affection creates a growing appreciation for the assorted people in our lives*
•FL 58-60 ❖ FL 3:10, 11

Relations, interpersonal: All the rubs and frustrations of a joint life—even at its worst—seem to me better than solitude*
•LAL 109 (see also LAL 102, 117, 120) ❖ LAL 8 Nov 62 (see also LAL 17 Jan 62; 10 Jun 63; 6 Jul 63)

Relations, interpersonal: All the same principles which are evil in the world of selfishness and necessity are good in the world of love and understanding* (re: dependence on others, self-sacrifice, etc.)
•M 119-120 ❖ M 14:20

Relations, interpersonal: Analogy of ships sailing in formation to illustrate importance and operation of morality*
•MC 70-73 ❖ MC III 1:3-8

Relations, interpersonal: Anger is love's renewal; reconciliation between two people is fullest when the anger has been fully expressed (re: wrath of God)*
•LM 96-97 ❖ LM 18:8, 9

Relations, interpersonal: Camaraderie among fellow sufferers (such as among soldiers) makes tribulation easier to bear*
•SJ 188 ❖ SJ 12:10

Relations, interpersonal, Christian attitude regarding: We must be continually concerned for the eternal destiny of each person*
•WG 18-19 ❖ WG 1:15

Relations, interpersonal: Closeness of people, as in a family, can make hatred possible as well as affection*
•FL 64 (see also FL 82-83, 160, GID 285*; SL 17-18, 120)

❖ FL 3:17 (see also FL 3:45; 5:46; GID III 3:7*; SL 3:4, 5; 26:1)

Relations, interpersonal: "...diabolical Pride comes when you look down on others so much that you do not care what they think of you"*
•MC 112-113 ❖ MC III 8:10

Relations, interpersonal, difficulties in ("The Trouble With 'X'"—chapter title)
•GID 151-155 ❖ GID I ch. 18

Relations, interpersonal: Do not waste time bothering whether you have love for your neighbor; act as if you did*
•MC 116 (see also L 269; LM 115; MC 161) ❖ MC III 9:5 (see also L undated letter just after 13 Mar 56; LM 21:12; MC IV 7:3)

Relations, interpersonal: Except for anxiety, nothing is more hostile to sleep than anger toward a loved one*
•LAL 92-93 ❖ LAL 28 Oct 60

Relations, interpersonal: Faults of our loved ones are opportunities for practicing tolerance and forgiveness*
•FL 186 ❖ FL 6:37

Relations, interpersonal: "Feeling hurt" so seldom means merely sorrow—usually mixed with wounded pride, self-justification, fright, desire for retaliation*
•LAL 56-57 ❖ LAL 21/5/56

Relations, interpersonal: Forgiveness ought not to rest on the quality of another person's penitence; it may no doubt be very imperfect, as is our own*
•LAL 95 ❖ LAL 9 Jan 61

Relations, interpersonal: Forgiveness must include that of the incessant provocations of daily life (bossy mother-in-law, bullying husband, nagging wife)*
•WG 125 ❖ WG 8:7

Relations, interpersonal: Gift-love may become perverted (story of Mrs. Fidget who gave unwanted service to her family in the name of "love")*
•FL 73-76, 82-83 (see also L 198-199; MC 167; SL 121, 123) ❖ FL 3:33-36, 45 (see also L undated letter just before 20

Jan 42; MC IV 7:3; SL 26:2, 5)

Relations, interpersonal: God loves us in spite of our faults, as we should love each other*
•GID 154 (see also GID 122-123*)
❖ GID I 18:8, 9 (see also GID I 14:7, 8*)

Relations, interpersonal: Hatred in humans is disappointing to Screwtape when it is directed against imaginary scapegoats rather than real persons*
•SL 30-31 ❖ SL 6:4, 5

Relations, interpersonal: How to forgive loved ones ("I find fear a great help—the fear that my own unforgivingness will exclude me from all the promises")*
•LAL 92-93 ❖ LAL 28 Oct 60

Relations, interpersonal: "I am often... praying for others when I should be doing things for them"*
•LM 66 ❖ LM 12:12

Relations, interpersonal: "I earnestly beseech all who conceive they have suffered an affront to believe that it is very much less than they suppose"
•LAL 96-97 ❖ LAL 24 Feb 61

Relations, interpersonal: I loathe "sensitive" people who are easily hurt; they are a social pest...vanity is usually the real trouble*
•LAL 59 ❖ LAL 3/8/56

Relations, interpersonal: If we are in the right relation to God, the right relation to one another will follow inevitably
•GID 51 ❖ GID I 4:18 (Ques. 5)

Relations, interpersonal: If you do someone you dislike a good turn, you will find yourself disliking them less*
•MC 116-117 (see also MC 161)
❖ MC III 9:5, 6 (see also MC IV 7:3)

Relations, interpersonal: "If you would be loved, be lovable" (quote from Ovid)*
•FL 65 ❖ FL 3:19

Relations, interpersonal: [In a heated conversation], slowing down the speed of the conversation is sometimes helpful; also sitting down*
•LAL 94 ❖ LAL 24 Nov 60

Relations, interpersonal: In praying for

people one dislikes, I find it helpful to remember that one is joining in Christ's prayer for them*
•L 226 (see also L 183)
❖ L undated letter just before 7 Feb 51 (see also L 16 Apr 40)

Relations, interpersonal: In this area, I could forgive much neglect more easily than the least degree of what I regarded as interference*
•SJ 116-117 (see also Interference)
❖ SJ 7:21 (see also Interference)

Relations, interpersonal: Inner insecurity as the probable cause of mere disagreeableness in people*
•LAL 27-28 (see also SL 162-163; WLN 60-61) ❖ LAL Mar 10/54 (see also SL 32:22, 23; WLN 4:22, 23)

Relations, interpersonal: Issues regarding quarrelling discussed in context of the differing Jewish and Christian conceptions of "judgement"*
•RP 14 ❖ RP 2:9

Relations, interpersonal: It is important to realize that there is some really fatal flaw in you which causes others the same despair*
•GID 123, 151-155 (see also FL 186)
❖ GID I 14:7, 8; ch. 18 (see also FL 6:37)

Relations, interpersonal: "It's the mixture, or alternation, of resentment and affection that is so very difficult, isn't it?"*
•LAL 92-93 ❖ LAL 28 Oct 60

Relations, interpersonal: Lewis speaks about people who "live for others," but always in a discontented, grumbling way*
•MC 167 (see also FL 73-77, 82; SL 121-124) ❖ MC IV 8:3 (see also FL 3:33-37, 45; SL 26:2-5)

Relations, interpersonal: Many instances of domestic nastiness come before me in my mail; the only "ordinary" homes seem to be the ones we don't know much about*
•LAL 45-46 ❖ LAL 5/10/55

Relations, interpersonal: Most times people who "hurt" us did not intend to, and are quite unconscious of the

whole thing*
•LAL 59 (*see also* LAL 96-97)
❖ LAL 3/8/56 (*see also* LAL 24 Feb 61)
Relations, interpersonal: Natural result of injuring another is to arouse resentment; thus in addition to the original injury I've also provoked him to sin*
•RP 24, 25-26 (*see also* CR 119-120)
❖ RP 3:9, 11 (*see also* CR 10:10)
Relations, interpersonal: Neediness of those who demand to be loved seals up the very fountain for which they are thirsty*
•FL 65 (*see also* GID 285)
❖ FL 3:18 (*see also* GID III 3:7)
Relations, interpersonal: "...no one can paddle his own canoe but everyone can paddle someone else's..."*
•L 236 ❖ L 26 Dec 51
Relations, interpersonal: "*one* trouble about habitual liars is that, since you can't believe anything they say, you can't feel the slightest interest in it"
•LAL 107 ❖ LAL 2 Oct 62
Relations, interpersonal: Others *may* be sinners; ask yourself, "Why should their vices prove hypocrisy if I can consider that I am in some sense a Christian?"*
•SL 14 (*consider also* Judging)
❖ SL 2:4 (*consider also* Judging)
Relations, interpersonal: People are very seldom either totally sincere or totally hypocritical; their motives are mixed*
•LAL 97 (*see also* LAL 95)
❖ LAL 28 Mar 61 (*see also* LAL 9 Jan 61)
Relations, interpersonal: Regarding those who make an elaborate show of always "unnecessarily asking, or insufferably offering, forgiveness"*
•FL 185 ❖ FL 6:36
Relations, interpersonal: Regarding exclusive Inner Rings or circles of people such as may form among those who work together*
•WG 93-105 (*see also* FL 115-127; Inner Rings) ❖ WG ch. 6 (*see also* FL 4:46-62; Inner Rings)
Relations, interpersonal: Regarding unlovable people who demand to be loved*
•FL 62-66 ❖ FL 3:15-20
Relations, interpersonal: Screwtape points out the difference between men and women in their understanding of the word "Unselfishness"*
•SL 121 ❖ SL 26:2
Relations, interpersonal: Screwtape advises causing humans in courtship to think they have solved problems through "love" when they've only postponed them*
•SL 120 ❖ SL 26:1
Relations, interpersonal: The reality of people is usually different from our idea of them; "We all think we've got one another taped"*
•GO 75-78 (*see also* GO 19-22)
❖ GO 4:13-19 (*see also* GO 2:3)
Relations, interpersonal: "Those who are, or can become, His sons, are our real brothers...It is spiritual, not biological, kinship that counts"*
•WLN 91 ❖ WLN 6:22
Relations, interpersonal: Those who have little authority over others may be thankful; it is hard to be just, and power corrupts*
•CR 119-110; RP 25 (*see also* WG 114)
❖ CR 10:10; RP 3:10 (*see also* WG 7:12)
Relations, interpersonal: "We are *all* fallen creatures and *all* very hard to live with..."*
•LAL 110 ❖ LAL 8 Nov 62
Relations, interpersonal: We can recognize in ourselves the Psalmists' tendency to chew over and over the cud of some injury...*
•RP 23-24 ❖ RP 3:8
Relations, interpersonal: We should read the cursing Psalms with fear, for who knows what similar imprecations we have tempted someone to utter against us?*
•CR 118-110 (*see also* RP 24)
❖ CR 10:9, 10 (*see also* RP 3:9)
Relations, interpersonal: What Christianity tells us about interdependence and vicariousness ("It will not, in any way, allow me to be an exploiter...")*

•GID 87 ❖ GID I 9:10

Relations, interpersonal: What Christianity tells us about equality*
•MC 102-103; WG 113-116 (see also GID 84-85, 87; SL 170*; WLN 68*)
❖ MC III 6:17; WG 7:10-15 (see also GID I 9:7, 10; SL 32:39*; WLN 4:39*)

Relations, interpersonal: When dealing with people who are "a thorn in the flesh," don't press on the place where they are embedded—don't dwell on it*
•LAL 44 (see also LAL 28, 47)
❖ LAL 21/6/55 (see also LAL Mar 10/54; 26/10/55)

Relations, interpersonal: When people have hurt us, prayer for them—and then forgetting it—is better than allowing them to become an obsession*
•LAL 28 (see also LAL 44) ❖ LAL Mar 10/54 (see also LAL 21/6/55)

Relations, interpersonal: When we talk to another about our difficulties, we should remember that that person may be full of troubles we know nothing about*
•LAL 40-41 ❖ LAL 24/3/55

Relations, interpersonal: [With habitual liars] "One has to keep on saying 'But for the grace of God, there go I'"*
•LAL 107 ❖ LAL 2 Oct 62

Relations, interpersonal: Women talk more and men talk less when fatigued; this can cause much secret resentment, even between lovers*
•SL 142 ❖ SL 30:3

Relations, interpersonal: You'll never make a good impression on people until you stop thinking about what kind of impression you are making*
•MC 190 ❖ MC IV 11:15.

Relationship between Creator and creature is unique but analogies from the various types of love between creatures can be useful (examples listed)
•PP 41-46 ❖ PP 3:9-14

Relationship between Man and God ideally something like the relation of a good dog to its master (except that Man has reason)

•GID 50 ❖ GID I 4:12 (Ques. 3)

Relationship of God to Christ and Christ to man and man to woman expressed by St. Paul as a proportion
•CR 4-5 ❖ CR 1:6, 7

Relationship: Scientific logic not the same logic required for trust in God, because once you accept that He is, you move from speculation to a relationship
•WLN 21-30, esp. 26-27, 30 (see also LM 49) ❖ WLN 2:10-18, esp. 2:14, 18 (see also LM 9:8)

Relationship with God—see also Knowing God; Knowledge of God; consider also Contact with God; Devotional life; Separation from God

Relationship with God became a painful effort after the Fall, since man's inclination had become self-ward*
•PP 83 (see also PP 91)
❖ PP 5:10 (see also PP 6:3)

Relationship with God by virtue of being created is different from the union of wills which, under grace, is reached by a life of sanctity
•LM 69 ❖ LM 13:5

Relationship with God, implicit trust the only mode in which our personal, can establish itself
•WLN 26-30, esp. 28
❖ WLN 2:13-18, esp. 2:16

Relationship with God, Lewis mentions that when he first came to belief in God as "the Absolute" he felt there was no possibility of being in a personal
•SJ 223 ❖ SJ 14:14

Relationship with God on a daily basis, necessity of
•GID 266 (see also L 220; MC 168-169; SL 62*; WG 132)
❖ GID II 16:52, 53 (see also L undated letter between 6 Sep 49 and 22 Sep 49; MC IV 8:8; SL 14:1*; WG 9:13)

Relationship with God on a daily basis, importance of, to train the habit of Faith
•MC 124 ❖ MC III 11:5, 6

Relationship with God: "Our relation to

those who trusted us only after proven innocent in court cannot be the same as...to those who trusted us all through" (re: steadfast belief)
•WLN 29 ❖ WLN 2:17

Relationship with God: Penitential prayers at their highest level are an attempt to restore an infinitely valued and vulnerable personal relationship
•LM 95 (see also MC 59-60)
❖ LM 18:3 (see also MC II 4:7, 8)

Relationship with God: Prosperity and adversity both mentioned by Screwtape as useful in separating men from God*
•SL 132 (consider also Obstacles to Christian perseverance)
❖ SL 28:1 (consider also Obstacles to Christian perseverance)

Relationship with God, right, cannot happen until we discover our bankruptcy
•MC 127 ❖ MC III 12:3, 4

Relationship with God, we receive the new life through; Lewis calls this "good infection"
•MC 153, 156-157, 162, 163, 186
❖ MC IV 4:8-10; 5:8; 7:5, 8; 11:7

Relativism [regarding moral values]—see Subjectivism

Release (chapter title)
•SJ 118-131 ❖ SJ ch. 8

Relief after a crisis: Emotions may be flat; that isn't ingratitude, only exhaustion
•LM 46 ❖ LM 9:2

Relief after a crisis: Like at sea, "once you have doubled the point and got into smooth water, the point doesn't take long to hide below the horizon"
•LM 46 ❖ LM 9:1

Religion, a "moderated," is as good as no religion at all (re: thinking that "religion is all very well up to a point")
•SL 43 (see also Self-reservation)
❖ SL 9:3 (see also Self-reservation)

Religion, aesthetic, ("of flowers and music") insufficient
•MC 136 (see also GID 328-329; consider also Cost) ❖ MC IV 1:4 (see also GID IV Letter 4; consider also Cost)

Religion and language: Poetry works with "subtle and sensitive exploitations of imagination and emotion" to convey information*
•CR 137 ❖ CR 11:18

Religion and Rocketry (chapter title)
•WLN 83-92 ❖ WLN ch. 6

Religion and Science (chapter title)
•GID 72-75 ❖ GID I ch. 7

Religion and war, analogy between the claims of, (neither will simply cancel the merely human life we were leading before)
•WG 24 ❖ WG 2:6

"Religion" as a topic for intellectual discussions: We must continually fall back from our arguments into Reality—from Christian apologetics into Christ*
•GID 103 ❖ GID I 10:50

"Religion" as an end instead of the means to an end is deadly
•LM 30-31 (see also RP 57-58; SL 35*)
❖ LM 6:4-6 (see also RP 6:6, 7; SL 7:4*)

Religion as reality or substitute: Experience and taste do not always confirm what is real and what is a substitute
•CR 38-41 ❖ CR 3:3-9

Religion, as such, is of interest as a topic for discussion only to the undecided; not of interest to the truly religious
•GID 250 ❖ GID II 14:2

Religion, by a sheer mistake in spiritual technique I had rendered my private practice of, a quite intolerable burden —and was anxious to get rid of it
•SJ 61-62 (see also SJ 168)
❖ SJ 4:7-9 (see also SJ 11:5)

Religion cannot operate as a bribe (in its promise of eternal life)
•GID 131 (see also FL 189-190*; LM 120; PP 145*; RP 39-42; SJ 231; WG 3-5*)
❖ GID I 16:3 (see also FL 6:42*; LM 22:8; PP 10:2*; RP 4:17; SJ 15:3; WG 1:1-3*)

"Religion," Christianity and (chapter title)
•M 81-94 ❖ M ch. 11

Religion, Christianity as the tradition in which we may most reasonably believe we have the consummation of all
•GID 144 ❖ GID I 16:26

Religion: Crusades, meetings, pamphlets,

movements, etc. as ends in themselves mentioned by Screwtape as serving his purposes
- •SL 35 (*see also* Means and ends)
- ❖ SL 7:4 (*see also* Means and ends)

Religion, David's dancing a valuable contrast to, which becomes merely dutiful "church-going" and laborious "saying our prayers"*
- •RP 45-46 ❖ RP 5:4

Religion, "decline" of, may be a misperception
- •GID 218-220, 253 ❖ GID II 8:1-7; 14:11

Religion dismissed on the ground that it is a substitute for sex: The experience of marriage disproved this for Lewis
- •GO 6 (*see also* SJ 170, 203-204*)
- ❖ GO 1:12 (*see also* SJ 11:6; 13:10*)

Religion dismissed on the grounds that for some it is tainted with desire for personal gain does not get us one inch nearer to deciding if it is true or not
- •GID 273-274 (*see also* WLN 18-20)
- ❖ GID III 1:7 (*see also* WLN 2:8)

Religion dismissed on the grounds that it is "wish-fulfilment" illogical: "...our wishes may favour either side or both"
- •WLN 18-20 (*see also* GID 272-274; GO 45; SJ 171, 172, 203*)
- ❖ WLN 2:8 (*see also* GID III 1:5-7; GO 3:9; SJ 11:7, 9; 13:10*)

Religion dismissed on the grounds that it is substitute for well-being we have failed to achieve on earth: Psychologists have a good *prima facie* case
- •CR 37-38 ❖ CR 3:2

Religion dismissed on the grounds that it is "imaginative enjoyment" not logical; God is not always delightful in men's imaginations
- •WG 76 ❖ WG 5:7

Religion, don't talk to me about the consolation of, or I shall suspect you don't understand
- •GO 28-30 (*see also* FL 190; L 290; LAL 49) ❖ GO 2:13-16 (*see also* FL 6:43; L 3 Dec 59; LAL 16/12/55)

"Religion" (e.g., having specifically holy places, things, and days) both neces-

sary and dangerous
- •LM 75 ❖ LM 14:10

Religion, elements of our, which seem puzzling or repellent must not be avoided (these conceal precisely what we do not yet know and need to know)
- •WG 9-10 ❖ WG 1:7

Religion, essence of, as defined by H. H. Price and cited (refuted) by Lewis: "...belief in God and immortality"
- •GID 129-131 ❖ GID I 16:1-3

Religion, essence of, defined by Lewis: "...the thirst for an end higher than natural ends..."
- •GID 131 ❖ GID I 16:3

Religion, essence of, is not belief in God *and* immortality; glory of God is to be worshipped for its own sake
- •GID 130 ❖ GID I 16:2

"Religion," futility and danger of empty, described by Screwtape
- •SL 171-172; WLN 69-70
- ❖ SL 32:40; WLN 4:40

Religion, happiness is found in which?— "While it lasts, the religion of worshipping oneself is best"
- •GID 58 ❖ GID I 4:43, 44 (Ques. 11)

Religion, I didn't go to, to make me happy; I always knew a bottle of port would do that
- •GID 58 ❖ GID I 4:45 (Ques. 11)

Religion: I *do* get that sudden feeling that the whole thing is hocus-pocus, but it hardly worries me now
- •L 227 ❖ L 5 Mar 51

Religion, I have the feeling (often on waking in the morning) that there is nothing I *dislike* so much as, —that it's all against the grain
- •L 195 ❖ L 19 Nov 41

"Religion," in a sense, must occupy the whole of life; there is no question of compromise between the claims of God and the claims of anything else
- •WG 25 ❖ WG 2:7

Religion, in all developed, we find three elements or stages: experience of the "Numinous"; sense of morality; Numinous Power seen as connected

be believed except what was comforting or exciting
•SJ 60 (*consider also* Cost)
❖ SJ 4:6 (*consider also* Cost)

Religion of "the Absolute": "This was a religion that cost nothing...There was nothing to fear; better still, nothing to obey"
•SJ 209-210 (*see also* GID 143; M 81, 93-94; MC 35, 136; Cost)
❖ SJ 13:18 (*see also* GID I 16:25; M 11:2, 19; MC I 4:6; IV 1:4; Cost)

Religion of "the Absolute" which Lewis adopted while a student at Oxford
•SJ 209-210, 215, 221, 222-223
❖ SJ 13:18; 14:5, 13, 14

Religion of "the Absolute" yielded a life of "'desire without hope'"
•SJ 210 ❖ SJ 13:19

Religion, one may bewail happier days when, meant piety
•L 177 ❖ L 18 Feb 40

Religion, opposition to—*see* Obstacles to Christian faith; Opposition to Christianity

Religion, "popular"—*see also* Naturalism; Pantheism

Religion, "popular," conceives a two-floor reality—a ground floor (Nature) and a mystical, spiritual, indescribable Something
•M 154 ❖ M 16:20

Religion, "popular," excludes miracles because it excludes a God who does anything at all
•M 81 ❖ M 11:1, 2

Religion, "popular," God of, not a concrete Being but "being in general" about which nothing can be truly asserted
•M 86-88 ❖ M 11:7-10

Religion, "popular," (Pantheism) attractive because its God does nothing, demands nothing; He will not pursue you
•M 81, 93-94 (*see also* GID 143; MC 35, 136; SJ 209-210; *consider also* Cost)
❖ M 11:2, 19 (*see also* GID I 16:25; MC I 4:6; IV 1:4; SJ 13:18; *consider also* Cost)

Religion (prayer, sacrament, repentance,

adoration) as our sole avenue to knowledge about the reality of God
•GID 46 ❖ GID I 3:16

Religion, quasi-, which enabled one to get all the conveniences of Theism without believing in God: it cost nothing; nothing to fear and nothing to obey
•SJ 209-210 (*see also* Cost; Religion, minimal) ❖ SJ 13:18 (*see also* Cost; Religion, minimal)

Religion: Question of whether our faith is a substitute for the real well-being we have failed to achieve on earth
•CR 37-43 ❖ CR ch. 3

Religion: Reality or Substitute? (chapter title)
•CR 37-43 ❖ CR ch. 3

Religion, Screwtape discusses how the Christian, used merely as a means to social justice, can work to the devil's advantage
•SL 108-109 (*see also* MC 137)
❖ SL 23:4 (*see also* MC IV 1:6, 7)

Religion, Screwtape mentions the law of Undulation which refers to the human tendency to experience peaks and troughs, especially in the area of
•SL 36-39 (*see also* SL 40-44)
❖ SL ch. 8 (*see also* SL ch. 9)

Religion, such information about, as Poetic language has to give can be received only if you are prepared to meet it half-way—with good will
•CR 135, 137, 141
❖ CR 11:12, 16, 18, 25

Religion, supposed "decline" of, not reflected in books; the outlook of nineteenth century authors was as secular as our own
•GID 219 ❖ GID II 8:3, 4

Religion: The belief or disbelief of most people results from their upbringing and from the prevailing tone of the circles they live in
•CR 170-171 ❖ CR 14:28

Religion, The Decline of (chapter title)
•GID 218-223 ❖ GID II ch. 8

Religion, the enemy attempts to make, a private affair
•WG 107-108 ❖ WG 7:3

Spiritualism, etc.)
- •GID 240-241, 252 ❖ GID II 12:2; 14:9

Religions and denominations: "It is at her centre, where her truest children dwell, that each communion is really closest to every other in spirit..."
- •MC 9 (see also LAL 11)
- ❖ MC P:9 (see also LAL Nov 10 52)

Religions cannot all be true
- •GID 101-102 ❖ GID I 10:48

Religions: Christianity and Hinduism the only two worth considering; most others are heresies of these
- •GID 102 (see also CR 71)
- ❖ GID I 10:49 (see also CR 5:26)

Religions, divisions between: How much more one has in common with a *real* Jew or Muslim than with a wretched liberalising specimen of the same categories
- •LAL 11-12 ❖ LAL Nov 10th 52

Religions, divisions between: "...those who are at the heart of each division are all closer to one another than those who are at the fringes"
- •LAL 11-12 (see also GID 60; MC 9)
- ❖ LAL Nov 10th 52 (see also GID I 4:56—Ques. 14; MC P:9)

Religions, horrible nations have horrible; have been looking at God through a dirty lens
- •MC 144 ❖ MC IV 2:14

Religions of countries outside the Western world: Buddha may be the form in which Christ appears to the Eastern mind
- •L 152-153 (see also GID 265-266*; MC 65, 176-177; SL 26*)
- ❖ L 8 Apr 32 (see also GID II 16:50, 51*; MC II 5:8; IV 10:4; SL 5:2*)

Religions, only if all other, are one hundred percent erroneous could Christianity avoid coincidental ideas
- •WG 82-83 (consider also Islam; Judaism; Mythology) ❖ WG 5:15 (consider also Islam; Judaism; Mythology)

Religions, other: Buddhist who concentrates on the Buddhist teaching about mercy as an example of those who belong to Christ without knowing it
- •MC 176-177 ❖ MC IV 10:4

Religions, other: "If you are a Christian you do not have to believe that all the other religions are simply wrong all through"
- •MC 43 (see also GID 54, 132; SJ 235)
- ❖ MC II 1:1 (see also GID I 4:27; 16:4; SJ 15:7)

Religions other than Christianity: Regarding the question of salvation for the people of non-Christian countries
- •L 152-153 (see also GID 265-266*; MC 65, 176-177; SL 26*)
- ❖ L 8 Apr 32 (see also GID II 16:50, 51*; MC II 5:8; IV 10:4; SL 5:2*)

Religions other than Christianity are all either nature religions (affirm my natural desires) or anti-nature religions (contradict them)
- •GID 86; M 119 ❖ GID I 9:9; M 14:20

Religions other than Christianity: Every sincere prayer, even to a false god, is accepted by the true God; Christ saves many who do not think they know Him
- •L 247 ❖ L 8 Nov 52

Religions other than Christianity not totally false
- •GID 101-102 (see also MC 43; GID 57-58*, 66-67*, 132*, 175*; WG 82-83)
- ❖ GID I 10:48, 49 (see also MC II 1:1; GID I 4:42*; 5:11-13*; 16:4*; 21:7, 8*; WG 5:15)

Religions, "Thick" (those which have orgies and ecstasies and mysteries) vs. "Clear" (those which are philosophical, ethical, and universalizing)
- •GID 102-103 ❖ GID I 10:49

Religions, we cannot compete in simplicity with people who are inventing; truth is never simple
- •MC 145 (see also MC 46-48, 137; PP 119) ❖ MC IV 2:17 (see also MC II 2:2, 4, 5; IV 1:9; PP 8:3)

Religions, we seethe with; they buzz about us like bees
- •GID 252, 253 ❖ GID II 14:9, 11

Religions: Where was Paganism full grown? There were really only two answers possible—either in Hinduism

or in Christianity
•SJ 235-236 (see also CR 71; GID 102, 132) ❖ SJ 15:7 (see also CR 5:26; GID I 10:49; 16:4)
Religions which have as their main doctrine the wickedness of other religions
•SL 171; WLN 69
❖ SL 32:40; WLN 4:40
Religiosity: "If the Divine call does not make us better, it will make us very much worse. Of all bad men religious bad men are the worst"*
•RP 31-32 (see also L 310; RP 28)
❖ RP 3:20 (see also L 20 Dec 61; RP 3:17)
"**Religious**," a man's most genuinely Christian activities may fall entirely outside that part of his life which he calls
•LM 30-31 ❖ LM 6:6
Religious activities, as an end in themselves, are infinitely dangerous—can become an idol that hides both God and my neighbors
•LM 30 (see also RP 57-58; SL 35)
❖ LM 6:4-6 (see also RP 6:6, 7; SL 7:4)
Religious and cultural activities should be undertaken for their own sakes, not for the sake of prestige or merit
•WLN 31-39 (see also CR 10*; SL 60; Pride of pursuing "culture")
❖ WLN 3:1-11 (see also CR 1:15*; SL 13:4; Pride of pursuing "culture")
Religious belief: theories about what it is (Freud: a complex; Frazer: a by-product of agriculture; Tylor: comes from dreams about the dead, etc.)
•WLN 18 ❖ WLN 2:7
Religious belief which is purely a result of conditioning mentioned by Screwtape
•SL 110-111 ❖ SL 24:1
Religious beliefs and experiences, language in which we express our, not a special language but something ranging between the Ordinary and the Poetical
•CR 135 ❖ CR 11:13
Religious concepts illustrated by mundane, earthly acts and language
•WG 56 (see also Imagery)

❖ WG 4:4 (see also Imagery)
"Religious," definition of: that which is ethical and numinous*
•GID 131 ❖ GID I 16:3
"Religious duties," when we carry out our, we are like people digging channels in a waterless land, so that when water [delight] comes we are ready for it
•RP 97 (see also LM 114-116)
❖ RP 9:7 (see also LM 21:10-15)
Religious education (for children) often has exactly the opposite effect to that which was intended; how many hard atheists come from pious homes
•LAL 32 ❖ LAL Sep 19/54
Religious experience, elements of, involve philosophical argument, our own moral and spiritual experience, and history
•GID 175 ❖ GID I 21:8, 9
Religious experience, emotion in, is a by-product of our attention to a particular Object
•CR 140 ❖ CR 11:22
Religious experience, feelings in, cannot be manufactured; and they are not, in themselves, of any importance*
•L 192, 202, 210, 216, 225, 256, 269 (see also LAL 38-39; LM 115; MC 105, 116-118; SJ 61-62, 168; SL 20-21; WLN 109; Feelings) ❖ L 4 Jan 41; 22 Dec 42; undated letter of 1947; 3 Apr 49; 7 Dec 50; 31 Jul 54; undated letter just before 2 Apr 56 (see also LAL 20/2/55; LM 21:12; MC III 7:5; 9:5-10; SJ 4:8; 11:5; SL 4:3; WLN 7:30; Feelings)
Religious experience, historical evidence, and authority as three of the things on which a Christian may base his belief
•WLN 17 ❖ WLN 2:6
Religious experience, Lewis describes his early, (while a student at "Belsen") as involving a great deal of fear
•SJ 33-34 ❖ SJ 2:14
Religious experience, Screwtape advises Wormwood to get his patient to see his, as a "phase" which will pass
•SL 36, 43-44 ❖ SL 8:1; 9:4, 5
Religious experience: Through it, Christians believe that they get a sort of

verification (or perhaps sometimes falsification) of their tenets
•CR 137-138 ❖ CR 11:19

Religious experiences cannot be conveyed to one another except by Poetic language—by hints, similes, metaphors, and emotions
•CR 137-138, 140 ❖ CR 11:19, 23

Religious experiences did not occur at all in my childhood, although I was taught the usual things and made to say my prayers and taken to church
•SJ 7 ❖ SJ 1:5

Religious expressions: Lewis attempts to show, not that they are true, but that they are significant—if you meet them "half-way," with a certain good will
•CR 129-141, esp. 135, 141
❖ CR ch. 11, esp. 11:12, 23

Religious expressions like "God is love" not merely expressions of emotion; they convey real information to you if you will meet them half-way—with good will
•CR 136-137 (see also CR 135, 141)
❖ CR 11:16 (see also CR 11:12, 25)

Religious festivals and acts of worship can be separated from the vision of God, thereby becoming a substitute for, and a rival to, God Himself (e.g., Christmas)
•RP 48-49 ❖ RP 5:7

Religious language and imagery contains nothing that has not been borrowed from Nature
•WG 57 (see also Imagery)
❖ WG 4:5 (see also Imagery)

Religious language, emotion in poetical: "Momentous matter, if believed, will arouse emotion whatever the language"
•CR 136 ❖ CR 11:16

Religious language, in my opinion there is no specifically
•CR 129 ❖ CR 11:1

"Religious people," truly regenerate people will not be very like the idea of, which you have formed from your general reading
•MC 187 ❖ MC IV 11:10

Religious persecution—see Persecution, religious

Religious piety: Why it is a poor qualification for entry into a ruling class
•WLN 31-49 ❖ WLN ch. 3

Religious sanctity and culture: Both are hard to diagnose and easy to feign
•WLN 47 ❖ WLN 3:24

Religious view of the universe vs. the materialist view
•MC 31-35 ❖ MC I ch. 4

Religious zeal may be confused with merely natural enthusiasms
•GID 198 ❖ GID II 3:5

Renaissance (chapter title)
•SJ 71-82 ❖ SJ ch. 5

Renaissance, I do not much believe in the, as generally described by historians
•SJ 71 ❖ SJ 5:1

Renewal, Christian—see New Birth

Renunciation—see also Asceticism; Mortification; Self-denial

Renunciation, Christian, does not mean stoic "Apathy" but a readiness to prefer God to inferior ends which are in themselves lawful
•PP 113 ❖ PP 7:3

Renunciation, the one hearty, is of everything which we realize does not lead us to God (quote from Brother Lawrence)
•PP 113 (ftnt.) ❖ PP 7:3 (ftnt.)

Renunciation, "total", as recommended by some saints can only mean a total readiness for every particular renunciation that may be demanded
•PP 113 ❖ PP 7:3

Repentance—consider also Surrender

Repentance: After we have repented, we should remember the price of our forgiveness and be humble
•PP 61 (see also L 236)
❖ PP 4:9 (see also L 8 Jan 52)

Repentance as "movement full speed astern"
•MC 59 (see also PP 101)
❖ MC II 4:7 (see also PP 6:13)

Repentance as one of the steps in conversion
•L 192 ❖ L 4 Jan 41

Repentance (as sorrow for being that kind of person) may continue after we have been forgiven
- L 236 (*see also* PP 61; SL 148*)
❖ L 8 Jan 52 (*see also* PP 4:9; SL 31:5*)

Repentance as what a Christian is enabled to do because the Christ-life is inside him
- MC 64 ❖ MC II 5:5

Repentance, at its highest level, is an attempt to restore an infinitely valued and vulnerable personal relationship
- LM 95 ❖ LM 18:3

Repentance can straighten out the twist in the soul which a sin leaves
- MC 87 ❖ MC III 4:9

Repentance, Dangers of National (chapter title)
- GID 189-192 ❖ GID II ch. 1

Repentance essential to understanding Christianity
- MC 38-39 (*see also* CR 46-47*; GID 95*, 181*, 243-244*, PP 55*)
❖ MC I 5:4 (*see also* CR 4:7*; GID I 10:15*; 22:13*; II 12:6*; PP 4:1*)

Repentance, explicit, of a definite and fully recognized sin vs. the vague, uneasy feeling that one hasn't been doing very well lately
- SL 54 ❖ SL 12:2

Repentance: I have found that my feelings of shame and disgust at my own sins do not correspond to what my reason tells me about their comparative gravity
- LM 99 ❖ LM 18:16

Repentance: "If there is a particular sin on your conscience, repent and confess it. If there isn't, tell the despondent devil not to be silly"
- LAL 77 (*see also* LM 32-34; SL 54-55*)
❖ LAL Jul 21st 58 (*see also* LM 6:11-17; SL 12:2-4*)

Repentance: My own idea is that all sadness not arising from either repentance (hastening to amendment) or pity (hastening to assistance) is simply bad
- PP 67 ❖ PP 4:15

Repentance not just fear—though fear is alright as a beginning
- L 196 (*see also* LM 76*)
❖ L 8 Dec 41 (*see also* LM 14:14*)

Repentance not something God demands of you before He will take you back, but a description of what going back is like
- MC 59-60 ❖ MC II 4:8

Repentance of past acts will have to be paid for; better to leave that issue undecided
- WG 127 ❖ WG 9:4

Repentance of sins in the long run a relief, like having a painful tooth out
- GID 124 (*see also* RP 32; Dentist analogy) ❖ GID I 14:10 (*see also* RP 3:21; Dentist analogy)

Repentance: Only God can do it perfectly
- MC 59-61 ❖ MC II 4:6-10

Repentance: Pain rouses men to the presence of evil in their existence; they may rebel (with the possibility of deeper repentance later) or make a change
- PP 95 ❖ PP 6:7

Repentance ("penitence"), forgiveness ought not to rest on the quality of the other person's; it may no doubt be very imperfect, as is our own
- LAL 95 ❖ LAL 9 Jan 61

Repentance ("penitence") in the Psalms shows a desire to placate God's wrath; this is not inconsistent with Christian liturgies of penitence
- LM 95 ❖ LM 18:4

Repentance ("penitence") ought to be an act; the more high-minded views involve the danger of regarding it simply as a state of feeling
- LM 97 ❖ LM 18:12

Repentance, Screwtape advises preventing any, from being converted into action: "The great thing is to prevent his doing anything"
- SL 60-61 ❖ SL 13:5

Repentance, Screwtape mentions the presence of God which comes to humans upon their, and protects them from the devil's assaults
- SL 57-58 ❖ SL 13:1, 2

Repentance, the biggest sinners are conscious of guilt and thereby capable of real
•SL 165-166; WLN 64
❖ SL 32:29; WLN 4:29

Repentance, the call to, would be meaningless if God's standard of goodness were sheerly different from our own
•PP 39 ❖ PP 3:5

"Repentance," the word, suggests that some tendencies in each natural man may have to be simply rejected
WG 118 ❖ WG 7:17

Repentance, true, often confused with mere disappointment in oneself
•L 195 ❖ L 19 Nov 41

Repentance, true, reflects acceptance of blame; making excuses reflects denial of blame*
•WG 122 ❖ WG 8:3

Repentance vs. asking God to accept our excuses
•GID 124; WG 122-124
❖ GID I 14:9; WG 8:3-5

Repentance: We must be aware of our own sinfulness, but a continual poring over the "sink" might breed its own perverse pride
•LM 98-99 ❖ LM 18:13-15

Repentance: You should at least make a list of your sins on a piece of paper, and make a serious act of penance about each one of them
•GID 123-124 ❖ GID I 14:9

Repented sin contributes to a complex good, though the sin itself remains evil
•PP 111 ❖ PP 7:2

Repenting our own sins may be evaded by bewailing and denouncing the conduct of others (re: "national repentance" of England's actions in the War)
•GID 190 ❖ GID II 1:2

Requirements of God/Christianity—see Demands of God/Christianity

Rescue analogy to show that trust may sometimes need to be maintained in the teeth of our senses (without the *feeling* of confidence)
•WLN 23-25 (*see also* CR 42-43; L 199;

MC 122-123) ❖ WLN 2:12, 13 (*see also* CR 3:11, 12; L 20 Jan 42; MC III 11:3)

Resentment and revenge, feelings of, must be killed
•MC 107-108 ❖ MC III 7:10

Resentment as one of the "deadly serious passions" lived out in Hell
•SL ix ❖ SL P:16

Resentment behaves just like a lust; draws one back and back to nurse and fondle and encourage it
•LM 94 ❖ LM 18:1

Resentment: "...how madly one cherishes that base part as if it were one's dearest possession..."
•LAL 93 ❖ LAL 28 Oct 60

Resentment, if anyone says he does not know the pleasures of, he is a liar or a saint
•FL 82 (*see also* FL 113; L 222-223; LAL 92-93; LM 94-95; MC 108; RP 22-24)
❖ FL 3:45 (*see also* FL 4:43; L 12 Jan 50; LAL 28 Oct 60; LM 18:1, 2; MC III 7:11; RP 3:6-8)

Resentment, if we cause, in another by injuring him we are guilty not only of the original injury but of provoking his hatred
•CR 119-120; RP 24-26
❖ CR 10:9-12; RP 3:9-11

Resentment is expressed in the Psalms without disguise, without self-consciousness, without shame—as few but children would express it today
•RP 23 ❖ RP 3:7

Resentment is like an itch: the temptation to scratch is very severe; but it is pleasant only as relief from, or alternative to, humiliation
•LM 94-95 ❖ LM 18:1

Resentment: "...that, after all, is almost the greatest evil nasty people can do to us—to become an obsession, to haunt our minds"*
•LAL 28 ❖ LAL Mar 10/54

Resentment: We can recognize in ourselves the Psalmists' tendency to chew over and over the cud of some injury...
•RP 23-24 ❖ RP 3:8

Reservation of ourselves—see Self-reservation

Resolutions, I don't want to be carried away into any, which I shall later regret
- •WG 127 ❖ WG 9:4

Resolutions, Lewis describes making a list of good, as a boy at school
- •SJ 119-120 ❖ SJ 8:2

Resolutions, on the making of
- •SL 62 ❖ SL 14:1

Response, our highest activity must be, not initiative
- •PP 51 ❖ PP 3:17

Response to Christ our choice
- •GID 87-88 (see also M 93-94*)
- ❖ GID I 9:11 (see also M 11:19, 20*)

Responsibility, each person has a, to come to terms with the claims of Jesus Christ—or be guilty of inattention or evasion
- •GID 265-266 ❖ GID II 16:50

Responsibility, personal: Doctrine that badness is an unavoidable legacy from our animal ancestors encourages us to shift responsibility for our behaviour
- •PP 65-66 ❖ PP 4:14

Responsibility, personal: I am sick of the modern assumption that, for all events, "we" are never responsible: it is always our rulers, or our parents, or...
- •LAL 15 ❖ LAL May 30th 53

Responsibility, personal: We must guard against the feeling that if all men are as bad as the Christians say, then badness must be very excusable
- •PP 62 ❖ PP 4:10

Responsibility to the One who made us, we have a
- •MC 73 ❖ MC III 1:8

Restitution as one of the steps in conversion
- •L 192 ❖ L 4 Jan 41

Restraint necessary for any happiness, even in this world
- •MC 93 ❖ MC III 5:10

Resurrected bodies, nature of, as seen in the body of Christ
- •M 145-163 ❖ M 16:5-32

Resurrected bodies will not be made of the same atoms; even in this life their actual ingredients change
- •GID 33; M 151 ❖ GID I 2:11; M 16:15

Resurrection as a prophetic miracle
- •GID 32-33 ❖ GID I 2:11

Resurrection as a reversal of natural processes
- •GID 33; M 146 ❖ GID I 2:11; M 16:6

Resurrection as one of the beliefs which unite all Christians everywhere
- •GID 336 ❖ GID IV Letter 9

Resurrection, I believe in the, but the state of the dead till the resurrection is unimaginable
- •L 294-295 (see also L 297)
- ❖ L 5 Aug 60 (see also L 16 Oct 60)

Resurrection, imagery associated with: Impossible to know how much of a representation is symbolical and how much is literal
- •CR 164-166 ❖ CR 13:30-35

Resurrection: Lewis explains what makes the descriptions of the resurrected Lord baffling to us
- •GID 34-35 ❖ GID I 2:13

Resurrection likened to a crocus: It is a harbinger of spring
- •GID 87-88 ❖ GID I 9:11

Resurrection, meaning of: Christ defeated death, and pulled the created universe up with Him
- •GID 159-160 ❖ GID I 19:6, 7

"Resurrection model," we can look forward to having the latest, (re: new bodies in Heaven)
- •LAL 78 (see also LAL 110) ❖ LAL Sep 30 58 (see also LAL 26 Nov 62)

Resurrection, no possibility of isolating the doctrine of, from that of the Ascension
- •M 145-149 ❖ M 16:4-11

Resurrection not simply an undoing of the Incarnation; Jesus still a man with a body
- •M 147 ❖ M 16:8

Resurrection of Christ (and of ourselves) likened to a tin soldier becoming alive
- •MC 155 ❖ MC IV 5:4, 5

"Resurrection of Christ" brings different imagery to different minds, but this

does not change the miraculous nature of the event
- •GID 45-46 ❖ GID I 3:15, 16

Resurrection of Christ likened to a diver bringing up a precious object from deep slime
- •M 111-112 (*see also* GID 82; M 135)
- ❖ M 14:5, 6 (*see also* GID I 9:4, 5; M 15:5)

Resurrection of Christ not evidence for the immortality of the soul
- •M 145-146 ❖ M 16:5

Resurrection of Christ the central theme in every Christian sermon reported in the book of Acts
- •M 143 ❖ M 16:2

Resurrection of Jesus clearly a *physical* resurrection, as shown in Luke 24
- •L 233 ❖ L 13 Jun 51

Resurrection of Lazarus anticipates the general resurrection of all men
- •M 150-151 ❖ M 16:15

Resurrection of men: We will not recover the same atoms we ruled before; even here our matter changes continually, like a waterfall
- •M 151 (*see also* GID 33)
- ❖ M 16:15 (*see also* GID I 2:11)

Resurrection of the body as a doctrine may have an importance connected with our unique appreciation as humans of the "beauties of nature"
- •LM 18 ❖ LM 3:9

Resurrection of the body, I feel that to make the life of the blessed dead strictly timeless is inconsistent with the
- •LM 110 ❖ LM 20:15

Resurrection of the body is a doctrine I take seriously, though it is very soft-pedalled now-a-days
- •LAL 110 ❖ LAL 26 Nov 62

Resurrection of the body, Lewis explains why many who believe in immortality cannot believe in the
- •M 154 ❖ M 16:20

Resurrection of the body: Naked spirituality is in accordance with the nature of angels; not, I think, with ours
- •LM 123-124 ❖ LM 22:20

Resurrection of the body, only Christians believe in the; ancient philosophers regard the body as a mere encumbrance
- •M 172 ❖ M App. A:11

Resurrection of the body: The reality will likely be very different from our idea of it; "The notions will all be knocked from under our feet"
- •GO 82-83 ❖ GO 4:28, 29

Resurrection of the body, Transposition throws a new light on the; all our earthly sensations are to be flooded with new meaning
- •WG 72 (*see also* WG 67-68)
- ❖ WG 4:30 (*see also* WG 4:22)

Resurrection of the body: "We are not, in this doctrine, concerned with matter as such at all...what the soul cries out for is the resurrection of the senses"
- •LM 121 ❖ LM 22:13

Resurrection of the body: "We cannot understand. The best is perhaps what we understand least"
- •GO 89 ❖ GO 4:38

Resurrection of the body, what Lewis thought was meant by
- •LM 121-124 ❖ LM 22:12-22

"Resurrection" refers not only to the act of rising from the dead but also to the state of having risen
- •M 144-145 ❖ M 16:3, 4

Resurrection: Some modern theologians, after swallowing the camel of the Resurrection, strain at such gnats as the feeding of the multitudes
- •CR 153 ❖ CR 13:2

Resurrection tends to confirm only one idea about death: that the righteous dead will return to earth one day as solid men (quote from Isaiah 26:19)
- •M 145-146 ❖ M 16:6

Resurrection: "The local appearances, the eating, the touching, the claim to be corporeal, must be either reality or sheer illusion"
- •M 153 ❖ M 16:19

Resurrection: "...the Risen Lord excites terror only when mistaken for a ghost, i.e., when not recognised as *risen*"
- •LAL 13 ❖ LAL 4/iii/53

Resurrection: We may hope it includes the general fabric of our earthly life with its affections and relationships
- FL 187-188 (*see also* PP 139)
- ❖ FL 6:38 (*see also* PP 9:11)

Retaliation—*see also* Revenge; Vindictiveness

Retaliation, Christianity commands absolute mortification of the desire for
- WG 49 ❖ WG 3:28

Retaliation, desire for, must be killed
- MC 107-108 ❖ MC III 7:10

Retaliation, desire for, often a part of what we call "feeling hurt"
- LAL 56-57 ❖ LAL 21/5/56

Retaliation: "If one I love is tortured or murdered my desire to avenge him must be given no quarter"
- L 247-248 (*see also* RP 18-19; ch. 3)
- ❖ L 8 Nov 52 (*see also* RP 2:14; ch. 3)

Retaliatory pride and contempt may be the products of cruelty and oppression
- SJ 107 ❖ SJ 7:8

Return of Christ—*see* Second Coming of Christ

Reunion [of churches]—*consider also* Division(s)

Reunion: "Discussions usually separate us; actions sometimes unite us"
- LM 16 ❖ LM 3:5

Reunion, I sometimes have a bright dream of, engulfing us unawares while our official representatives are still pronouncing it impossible
- LM 16 ❖ LM 3:5

Reunion, if I have not directly helped the cause of, I have perhaps made it clear why we ought to be reunited
- MC 9 ❖ MC P:9

Reunion of Christendom never more needed—but how it is to happen, I confess I cannot see
- L 165 ❖ L 8 May 39

Reunion: Pitfalls of ecumenical organizations listed*
- GID 197-198 ❖ GID II 3:5

Reunion, prayer is perhaps the only form of work toward, which never does anything but good
- LAL 12 ❖ LAL Nov 10th 52

Reunion: The divisions of Christendom are not so dispiriting when seen from without; Christianity still an immensely formidable unity*
- GID 204 ❖ GID II 4:6

Reunion, we must pray for; divisions between Christians are a sin and a scandal
- GID 60 ❖ GID I 4:55, 56 (Ques. 14)

Reunion with deceased loved ones not to be the goal of our Christian life
- FL 189-190 (*see also* GO 28-29, 79; L 290; L 3 Dec 59; RP 41; SJ 231*)
- ❖ FL 6:41-43 (*see also* GO 2:13-16; 4:21; L 3 Dec 59; RP 4:16; SJ 15:3*)

Reunion with deceased loved ones: The reality of it would probably blow all one's ideas about it into smithereens
- GO 82-83 ❖ GO 4:27-29

Revelation—*see also* Truth

Revelation as expressed through the Church: if true, "...there ought to be something opaque to our reason, though not contrary to it"
- GID 238 ❖ GID II 11:11

Revelation, Biblical, addressed not to our intellectual curiosity but to our conscience and our will (re: the Dominical utterances)*
- PP 119 (*see also* L 169-170)
- ❖ PP 8:2 (*see also* L 5 Nov 39)

Revelation, book of: Phrase "the wrath of the Lamb" as one of two phrases in the Bible which should make our blood run cold (the other is the *Magnificat*)
- CR 120 ❖ CR 10:13

Revelation may be derived from the experience of Awe if it is not a mere twist in the human mind (re: existence of the Supernatural)
- PP 20-21 ❖ PP 1:11

Revelation not meant for gratification of curiosity; is purely practical
- GID 43 ❖ GID I 3:10

Revelation of God—*consider also* Presence of God

Revelation of God in history may be seen in the great events of the creeds, and in "primary history"—our own expe-

rience (re: "Historicism")
- •CR 112-113 ❖ CR 9:26

Revelation of God: Screwtape offers an explanation of why God's presence is not more often revealed or revealed to a greater degree to humans
- •SL 38-39 ❖ SL 8:4

Revenge—*see also* Retaliation; Vindictiveness; *consider also* Punishment

Revenge, desire for, must be killed
- •MC 107-108 ❖ MC III 7:10

Revenge, desire for, ("vindictive passion") is evil and expressly forbidden to Christians
- •PP 94 ❖ PP 6:6

Revenge loses sight of the end in the means, but its end is not wholly bad
- •PP 94, 120 ❖ PP 6:6; 8:5

Revenge, the least indulgence of the passion for, is very deadly sin—but to ask for justice may be a truly ethical demand (re: doctrine of hell)
- •PP 121 ❖ PP 8:5

Revenge, there is in many of the Psalms a fatal confusion between the desire for justice and the desire for
- •RP 18 ❖ RP 2:14

Revenge: This natural impulse must be fought against by the Christian whenever it arises
- •L 247 ❖ L 8 Nov 52

Revengefulness, Hobbes's definition of: "Desire by doing hurt to another to make him condemn some fact of his own"
- •PP 94 ❖ PP 6:6

Reverence—*consider also* Awe

Reverence for a Divine being, which the church offers us opportunity for, is a refreshing change from the necessary democracy of the world
- •WG 116 (*see also* GID 84-85*; WG 113)
- ❖ WG 7:15 (*see also* GID I 9:7*; WG 7:10)

Reverence: I learned how a thing can be revered not for what it can do to us but for what it is in itself
- •SJ 231 (*see also* FL 189-190; LM 120; RP 39-42) ❖ SJ 15:3 (*see also* FL 6:42; LM 22:8; RP 4:12-17)

Reverence in prayer: "It would be better

not to be reverent at all than to have a reverence which denied the proximity [of God]"
- •LM 13 ❖ LM 2:15

Reverence in prayer, "ready-made" prayers remind us of the need for
- •LM 13 ❖ LM 2:13-15

"Revival," Christian: Ease of getting an audience for discussion of "religion" does not prove that more people are becoming religious
- •GID 250 ❖ GID II 14:2

Revival, Christian: If real, it works slowly and obscurely in small groups
- •GID 222 ❖ GID II 8:11

Revival or Decay? (chapter title)
- •GID 250-253 ❖ GID II ch. 14

Revolutions seldom cure the evil against which they are directed; they always beget a hundred others
- •GID 309 ❖ GID III 7:12

Reward, century after century it was hammered into the Jewish people that earthly prosperity is not the, of seeing God
- •RP 43 ❖ RP 4:19

Reward: I was brought up to believe that goodness must be disinterested, and that any hope of reward or fear of punishment contaminated the will
- •SJ 231 (*see also* FL 189-190; LM 120; RP 39-42; compare with WG 3-5*)
- ❖ SJ 15:3 (*see also* FL 6:42; LM 22:8; RP 4:12-17; compare with WG 1:1-3*)

Rewards promised in the Gospels seem to indicate that God finds our desires not too strong, but too weak
- •WG 3 (Compare with GID 131*)
- ❖ WG 1:1 (Compare with GID I 16:3*)

Rewards, proper, are the consummation of an activity, not simply "tacked on"
- •WG 4 ❖ WG 1:2

Rhetorician, definition of: "...he...escapes from questions he doesn't want to answer into a cloud of eloquence" (re: Mussolini)*
- •L 113-114 ❖ L 30 Mar 27

Rheumatism, Lewis mentions having
- •LAL 32 (*see also* LAL 35, 65, 66, 67*)
- ❖ LAL Sep 19/54 (*see also* LAL Nov

Righteousness by faith/grace: In the judgement we must pin all our hopes on the mercy of God and the work of Christ*
•RP 13 ❖ RP 2:8

Righteousness by faith/grace: Lewis describes his realization of the need for "continual, conscious recourse" to God (whom he then called "Spirit") for his virtue*
•SJ 226 (see also SL 62; Dependence upon God) ❖ SJ 14:20 (see also SL 14:1; Dependence upon God)

Righteousness by faith/grace: Moral effort cures our illusions about ourselves and teaches us to depend on God*
•MC 94, 124-125, 127-131 (see also CR 169; PP 65) ❖ MC III 5:12; 11:7; 12:3-9 (see also CR 14:20, 21; PP 4:13)

Righteousness by faith/grace: "Not only do we need to recognize that we are sinners; we need to believe in a Saviour who takes away sin"*
•GID 260 ❖ GID II 16:18

Righteousness by faith/grace: Out of faith in Christ, good actions will inevitably come*
•MC 129 ❖ MC III 12:7

Righteousness by faith/grace: Story of Irish woman in church to illustrate that as long as we are in connection with God, we cannot sin*
•WG 128 ❖ WG 9:5

Righteousness by faith/grace: "...the regenerate man will find his soul eventually harmonised with his spirit by the life of Christ that is in him"*
•M 172 ❖ M App. A:11

Righteousness by faith/grace: Virtues such as charity, submissiveness to God's will, etc. are graces—gifts from the Holy Spirit—not our own merits*
•L 219 ❖ L 2 Sep 49

Righteousness by faith/grace: "What God does for us, He does in us"—this process must begin again every day*
•WG 132 ❖ WG 9:13

Righteousness by faith/grace: What we are matters even more than what we do—and only God can change character*
•MC 165 ❖ MC IV 7:12, 13

Righteousness by grace: "...when the need comes he carries out in us His otherwise impossible instructions"*
•LAL 22 (see also LM 49-50, 68-69) ❖ LAL Nov 6/53 (see also LM 9:11; 13:3)

Righteousness by faith/grace: When we learn that we've pleased Him, there will be no room for vanity; we'll be free from the miserable illusion that it is our doing*
•WG 12-13 (see also FL 180) ❖ WG 1:10 (see also FL 6:27)

Righteousness, God commands, because He loves it; He enjoins what is good because it is good
•RP 60-61 (see also CR 79-80; PP 100) ❖ RP 6:10, 11 (see also CR 6:20, 21; PP 6:12)

Righteousness, Plato argues that, is often praised for the rewards it brings — honour, popularity, and the like...
•RP 104 ❖ RP 10:9

Righteousness vs. rightness: We may at times be "in the right," but this must be distinguished from being "righteous," which none of us ever are
•RP 17-18 (see also L 183) ❖ RP 2:13 (see also L 16 Apr 40)

Risk-taking—see also Safety

Risk-taking in love: "The only place outside Heaven where you can be perfectly safe from all the dangers and perturbations of love is Hell"*
•FL 169 ❖ FL 6:13

Risk-taking: The timidity and pessimism which prevent me from gambling also tempt me to avoid those risks and adventures which every man ought to take*
•RP 29 ❖ RP 3:18

Rival Conceptions of God, The (chapter title)
•MC 43-46 ❖ MC II ch. 1

River, even the weariest, winds somewhere safe to sea
•LAL 120-121 ❖ LAL 6 Jul 63

Road: "'Any road out of Jerusalem must

also be a road into Jerusalem'" (re: possible value of sub-Christian literature)
•CR 22, 23 ❖ CR 2:29, 34

Road: "For it is one thing to see the land of peace from a wooded ridge...and another to tread the road that leads to it" (quote from St. Augustine)
•SJ 230 ❖ SJ 15 prelim. quote

Road, God can't be used as a, to another end (such as reunion with our deceased loved ones)
•GO 79 (see also FL 189-190; GO 28-29; L 290; RP 41)
❖ GO 4:21 (see also FL 6:41-43; GO 2:14; L 3 Dec 59; RP 4:16)

Road into the city (Christianity) and the road out of it usually the same road; thus "semi-Christianity" may be useful at times
•L 297 ❖ L undated letter of Feb 61

Rocketry, Religion and (chapter title)
•WLN 83-92 ❖ WLN ch. 6

Roman Catholics—see Catholics

"**Romans**" listed among those who have retained more of the gusto of the Psalmists than the Anglicans
•RP 52 ❖ RP 5:10

Romantic, Lewis describes himself as a*
•SJ 5, 7, 173 (see also SJ 152, 201, 203)
❖ SJ 1:2, 5; 11:10 (see also SJ 10:4; 13:7, 9)

Romantics, the only non-Christian authors who seemed to me really to know anything were the, (and even they were tinged with something like religion)
•SJ 214 ❖ SJ 14:4

Romantic love—see also Eros

Romantic love, such as that valued in literature, may be a dangerous ideal but for some it has proved a schoolmaster to better things
•CR 22 (see also CR 16)
❖ CR 2:31 (see also CR 2:13)

Romanticism, I suppose my, was destined to divide me from the orthodox Intellectuals as soon as I met them
•SJ 173 ❖ SJ 11:10

Romanticism: Lewis mentions his retreat (at Oxford) from "all that sort of ro-

manticism which had hitherto been the chief concern of my life"
•SJ 201 (see also SJ 203)
❖ SJ 13:7 (see also SJ 13:9)

Romanticism: The country I grew up in had everything to encourage a romantic bent; my feelings for nature had been too narrowly romantic
•SJ 152 (see also SJ 155)
❖ SJ 10:4 (see also SJ 10:7)

Rope analogy to show that "You never know how much you really believe anything until its truth or falsehood becomes a matter of life and death to you"
•GO 25, 41-43 ❖ GO 2:9; 3:3

Rose-tree, what can be done for a, that dislikes producing roses? Surely it ought to want to? (re: our reluctance to pray)
•LM 113-114 ❖ LM 21:7

Rose-trees, most of the behaviour which is now duty would be spontaneous and delightful if we were, so to speak, good
•LM 116 (see also L 277*; LM 114-115; PP 100*) ❖ LM 21:14 (see also L 18 Jul 57*; LM 21:11; PP 6:11*)

Rousseau mentioned by Screwtape: "In his perfect democracy, you will remember, only the state religion is permitted..."
•SL 160-161; WLN 59
❖ SL 32:17; WLN 4:17

Rudeness in unbelievers may indicate fear that there "might be something in it after all"
•LAL 90 ❖ LAL 26 Mar 60

Rule of fair play seems to be known by all people everywhere
•MC 17-26 (see also CR 44-56, 72-81; M 34-38; RP 13; book The Abolition of Man) ❖ MC I 1:1 to 2:8 (see also CR 4:1-27, 6:1-23; M 5:1-11; RP 2:8; book The Abolition of Man)

Rules—see also Laws; Moral laws; Principles

Rules a necessity in common life (such as home life); alternative is not freedom but tyranny
•GID 286 ❖ GID III 3:10

Rules, Christianity leads you out of, into something beyond
•MC 130-131 (*see also* CR 45; GID 144; LM 114-115; PP 65)
❖ MC III 12:9 (*see also* CR 4:2; GID I 16:26; LM 21:11-14; PP 4:13)

Rules, difficult Christian, must be attempted, like compulsory exam questions*
•MC 93 ❖ MC III 5:11

Rules, God does not want simply obedience to a set of; He wants people of a particular sort
•MC 77, 127 (*see also* MC 164-165; Works) ❖ MC III 2:8; 12:3 (*see also* MC IV 7:12; Works)

Rules: God enjoins what is good because it is good; not an arbitrary toss-up*
•RP 60-61 (*see also* CR 79-80; PP 100)
❖ RP 6:10, 11 (*see also* CR 6:20, 21; PP 6:12)

Rules, nothing gives one a more spuriously good conscience than keeping, —even if there has been a total absence of all real charity and faith
•LAL 38 ❖ LAL 20/2/55

Rules ("principles"), Christian, are stricter than others but we may get help towards obeying them
•MC 93 ❖ MC III 5:10

Rules, spiritual life is more like painting a portrait than obeying a set of
•MC 162 ❖ MC IV 7:5

Rules, we may treat the regimental, as a dead letter or counsel of perfection, but neglect of them is going to cost every man his life
•PP 64 ❖ PP 4:10

Rushing about wherever I pleased, the deadly power of, had not been given me since I had no car
•SJ 156-157 ❖ SJ 10:9

Russia and America, space-race between: Great powers are seldom less dangerously employed than in fabricating costly objects and flinging them overboard
•CR 172; WLN 77
❖ CR 14:36; WLN 5:14

Russia, many people living in, today have never had to consider the claims of Christ because they have never heard of those claims
•GID 265 ❖ GID II 16:50

Rut, scepticism and materialism engraved in us from our earlier lives like a
•L 227 (*see also* M 81-84*, 164-167*)
❖ L 5 Mar 51 (*see also* M 11:1-5*; 17:1-4*)

Ruts: "Belief-feelings" do not follow reason except after long training; they follow the grooves and ruts which already exist in the mind
•M 167 ❖ M 17:4

Sabbath: If these holy days cease to remind us that all days are holy, they begin to do us harm (re: specifically holy places, things, and days)**
•LM 75 ❖ LM 14:10

Sabbath, Kirkpatrick came to disbelieve in God but still would not wear his weekday clothes on the
•SJ 139 ❖ SJ 9:14

"Sabbath-breach," letter-writing on Sunday as
•LAL 53 ❖ LAL 4/3/56

Sacrament of the Eucharist—see Communion, Holy

Sacraments show the value of matter and the senses in God's scheme
•M 163 ❖ M 16:32

Sacrifice—see also Renunciation; Self-denial

Sacrifice: A man may be tempted to surrender benefits, not that others may be happy in having them, but that he may be unselfish in forgoing them
•SL 121 (see also WG 3)
❖ SL 26:2 (see also WG 1:1)

Sacrifice, essence of, in Judaism was not that men gave animals to God but that by their doing so God gave Himself to men
•RP 93 ❖ RP 9:4

Sacrificial rites in Judaism became separated from unity with God; came to be seen as the only thing God wanted
•RP 49 ❖ RP 5:7

Sadducees were holding to the older Jew-

ish view of death which had apparently changed greatly by Our Lord's time
•RP 39 ❖ RP 4:12

Sadism and Masochism mentioned with regard to Man's recognition of pain as evil
•PP 92-93, 94 ❖ PP 6:5, 6

Sadist, God as Cosmic, vs. God as a kind surgeon whose intentions are wholly good
•GO 49-50 (see also GO 35, 43-44, 45-46, 49-50)
❖ GO 3:17 (see also GO 2:26; 3:4, 5, 9, 17)

Sadness, my own idea is that all, not arising from either repentance (hastening to amendment) or pity (hastening to assistance) is simply bad (re: emotion of shame)
•PP 67 ❖ PP 4:15

Safety—see also Security; consider also Independence; Self-reservation

Safety: "Christ did not teach and suffer that we might become...more careful of our own happiness"*
•FL 170 (see also CR 155)
❖ FL 6:14 (see also CR 13:6)

Safety: I am a safety-first creature...but Christ's teaching was never meant to confirm my preference for safe investments and limited liabilities
•FL 168 (see also SJ 203, 228; SL 133)
❖ FL 6:10 (see also SJ 13:9; 14:22; SL 28:2)

"Safety in numbers," we must guard against the feeling that there is, (re: all men being bad)
•PP 62 ❖ PP 4:10

Safety in regard to spiritual matters: "The man will not venture within reach of the eternal until he has made the things temporal safe in advance"
•WG 127-128 (see also Self-reservation)
❖ WG 9:5 (see also Self-reservation)

Safety: Only God can help us with our desire for "limited liabilities"
•WG 132 (see also CR 43*)
❖ WG 9:13 (see also CR 3:12*)

Safety: Our craving for "limited lia-

* These items reflect some interpretation on the part of the editor; the idea will not be found in these exact words. See Introduction, p. ix.
** These items are ideas of Lewis's which the editor has placed under a topic Lewis did not there intend to address. See Introduction, p. ix. Entries without asterisks are not necessarily exact quotes, but the idea should be easy to find as worded.

bilities"
- WG 126-132 (*see also* SJ 171)
- ❖ WG ch. 9 (*see also* SJ 11:8)

Safety: "There is no safe investment. To love at all is to be vulnerable…"
- FL 169 ❖ FL 6:13

Saint(s)—*consider also* Good people

Saint, a spoiled, makes better sport in Hell than a mere common tyrant or debauchee (—Screwtape)
- SL 105-106 ❖ SL 23:1

Saints, canonization of: I only hope there'll be no scheme for this in the Church of England
- LM 15 ❖ LM 3:3

Saints, comment on the Canonization of
- GID 337 ❖ GID IV Letter 10

Saints, devotions to—*see* Devotions to saints

Saints, humility in the, not a false humility; when they say they are vile, they are recording truth with scientific accuracy
- PP 67-68 ❖ PP 4:15

Saints, I get letters from, who have no notion they are any such thing, showing in every line radiant faith…in appalling suffering
- GID 252 ❖ GID II 14:9

Saints, I suppose the great, really *want* to share the divine sufferings and that is how they can actually desire pain (but this is far beyond me)
- LAL 56 ❖ LAL 26/4/56

Saints, invocation of: "I accept the authority of the Benedicite for the propriety of *invoking*…saints" [as opposed to *devotions to* saints]
- GID 334 ❖ GID IV Letter 7

Saints: "It is great men, potential saints, not little men, who become merciless fanatics"—may become ready to kill for their cause
- RP 28 (*see also* L 301; RP 31-32)
- ❖ RP 3:17 (*see also* L 20 Dec 61; RP 3:20)

Saints: Salvation apparently not dependent upon degree of tribulation in this life; some old saints seem to have got through their seventy years with surprising ease

- PP 104 ❖ PP 6:15

Saints, the great, (according to Screwtape) are made out of the very same material as the great sinners
- SL 158; WLN 56 (*see also* SL 105-106, 135-136*) ❖ SL 32:13; WLN 4:13 (*see also* SL 23:1; 29:2*)

Saints, while Christendom is divided about prayer *to*, we are all agreed about praying *with* them
- LM 15 ❖ LM 3:4

Salt analogy to show how, when Christ is added to our lives, we shall still remain ourselves and different from one another
- MC 188-189 ❖ MC IV 11:12

Salvation—*see also* Redemption; *consider also* Assurance; Destiny of redeemed Man; Eternal life; Immortality

Salvation: "…a life, by natural standards, crippled and thwarted [is] not only no bar to salvation, but might easily be one of its conditions"
- CR 14 ❖ CR 2:5

Salvation (according to Screwtape) may also go to people who gave their lives to wrong causes, thinking them to be right*
- SL 26 ❖ SL 5:2

Salvation: All are "saved" in principle; we have to appropriate that salvation
- MC 156 ❖ MC IV 5:8

Salvation: "…all the texts on which we can base such warrant as we have for hoping that all men will be saved come from St. Paul"
- GID 232 ❖ GID II 10:7

Salvation apparently not dependent upon degree of tribulation in this life; some old saints seem to have got through their seventy years with surprising ease
- PP 104 ❖ PP 6:15

Salvation Army listed among those who have retained more of the gusto of the Psalmists [than the Anglicans]
- RP 52 ❖ RP 5:10

Salvation as a free gift: "Christ offers us something for nothing; He even offers everything for nothing"

•MC 128-129 ❖ MC III 12:6

Salvation by faith/grace—*consider also* Righteousness by faith/grace; Works

Salvation by faith in Jesus (Article xviii in the Prayer Book) firmly disbelieved by many modern audiences
•GID 101-102 ❖ GID I 10:48

Salvation by faith: Lewis mentions a Methodist who complained that Lewis said nothing about "justification by faith" in his BBC talks
•L 198 ❖ L 21 Dec 41

Salvation by faith: "Not doing these things in order to be saved, but because He has begun to save you already"*
•MC 128-129 ❖ MC III 12:6

Salvation by faith vs. works: "I personally rely on the paradoxical text, 'Work out your own salvation...for it is God that worketh in you'"
•GID 55 (*see also* LM 49; MC 130)
❖ GID I 4:30, 31 (Ques. 8) (*see also* LM 9:11; MC III 12:8)

Salvation by grace another way of saying that we are creatures not creators, derived beings, living not of ourselves but from Christ*
•WG 119 ❖ WG 7:19

Salvation by grace: "...the approach, however initiated and supported by Grace, is something we must do"*
•FL 16-17 (*see also* FL 19)
❖ FL 1:12 (*see also* FL 1:16)

Salvation, essentials of, may not be the same for everyone; God has His own way with each soul
•L 261 ❖ L 2 Feb 55

Salvation for animals, possibility of*
•PP 136-143 (*see also* LAL 110)
❖ PP 9:9-14 (*see also* LAL 26 Nov 62)

Salvation for the people of non-Christian countries, question of
•L 152-153 (*see also* GID 265-266*; MC 65, 176-177, SL 26*)
❖ L 8 Apr 32 (*see also* GID II 16:50, 51*; MC II 5:8; IV 10:4; SL 5:2*)

Salvation for unbelievers: Every sincere prayer, even to a false god, is accepted by the true God; Christ saves many who do not think they know Him

•L 247 (*see also* Unbelievers)
❖ L 8 Nov 52 (*see also* Unbelievers)

Salvation: I would pay any price to be able to say "All will be saved" but my reason retorts, "Without their will, or with it?"
•PP 118-119 ❖ PP 8:1

Salvation: "If majority are damned, how can God be a good God?" as one of the questions discussed by Lewis and his friends
•L 169-170 (*see also* PP 118-119)
❖ L 5 Nov 39 (*see also* PP 8:1)

Salvation, is it possible for men to be too much concerned with their own?—in one sense, yes*
•RP 39-40 (*see also* WG 3, 18-19)
❖ RP 4:13-15 (*see also* WG 1:1, 15)

Salvation, it may be that, consists not in the cancelling of sins but in the perfected humility that bears the shame forever
•PP 61 (*see also* L 236; SL 148*)
❖ PP 4:9 (*see also* L 8 Jan 52; SL 31:5*)

Salvation, Lewis reacts against the notion that good taste is essential to
•CR 13-14 (*see also* L 224)
❖ CR 2:3, 4 (*see also* L 7 Dec 50)

Salvation may be harder to attain if we are faced with few difficult personality traits in our loved ones whereby we can practice forbearance and forgiveness*
•FL 186-187 ❖ FL 6:37

Salvation, nice world just as much in need of, as a miserable world—and possibly more difficult to save
•MC 182 ❖ MC IV 10:15

Salvation: Not everyone will be saved; "If the happiness of a creature lies in self-surrender, no one can make that surrender but himself...and he may refuse"
•PP 118-119 ❖ PP 8:1

Salvation not exclusively for those who have accepted Jesus explicitly in this life
•GID 101-102; MC 65 (*see also* GID 265-266*) ❖ GID I 10:48; MC II 5:8 (*see also* GID II 16:50, 51*)

Salvation of a single soul more important than all the world's literature
•CR 10 ❖ CR 1:15

Salvation of souls (as our only means to glorifying God) listed as "the business of life"
•CR 14 (see also CR 12, 26)
❖ CR 2:4 (see also CR 2:1, 42)

Salvation of those fortunate in this world, Christ explained, only by referring to the unsearchable omnipotence of God
•PP 104 (see also Riches)
❖ PP 6:15 (see also Riches)

Salvation, our own rejection of: "The point is not that God will refuse you admission..."*
•MC 77-78 ❖ MC III 2:12

Salvation, plan of, as the ultimate answer to all those who object to the doctrine of hell*
•PP 128 ❖ PP 8:12

Salvation, plan of, does not imply any superiority in man or favouritism in God—in fact it implies a particular demerit or depravity*
•WLN 86, 88 (see also M 52, 122)
❖ WLN 6:10, 15 (see also M 7:14; 14:24)

Salvation, plan of: "God saw the crucifixion in the act of creating the first nebula"*
•PP 84 ❖ PP 5:11

Salvation, plan of: We have been shown the plan only in so far as it concerns ourselves; we do not know about other life in the universe*
•MC 170 ❖ MC IV 8:10

Salvation, plan of: World is a dance in which good (from God) is disturbed by evil (from the creatures); resulting conflict resolved by God becoming Man
•PP 84 ❖ PP 5:11

Salvation: Psalmists (and other Old Testament writers) probably had little or no belief in a future life
•RP 36, 38-39 ❖ RP 4:6, 9-12

Salvation (quote from Law): "Many will be rejected because...they have not taken time and pains enough"
•WG 131 ❖ WG 9:11

Salvation, quote from Luther regarding our assurance of
•L 252 ❖ L 3 Aug 53

Salvation, regarding question of, for deceased unbelievers
•L 238 ❖ L 31 Jan 52

Salvation ("spiritual life"), we have not got to try to climb up into, by our own efforts; it has already come down into the human race
•MC 156-157 (see also Moral effort)
❖ MC IV 5:8 (see also Moral effort)

Salvation through Christ's death, possible mechanism of*
•MC 56-61 (see also Atonement)
❖ MC II ch. 4 (see also Atonement)

Salvationism and supernaturalism as essential parts of real religion (as opposed to all watered-down and modernist versions)
•L 170 (see also Christianity-and-water) ❖ L 8 Nov 39 (see also Christianity-and-water)

Same Old Thing, Screwtape mentions the humans' horror of, and demand for novelty which is a perversion of the natural enjoyment of change
•SL 116-119 ❖ SL 25:2-6

Sanctification—see also Growth, Christian; Transformation

Sanctification: Lewis describes the "union of wills" between a man and God which is reached, under grace, by a life of sanctity**
•LM 69 ❖ LM 13:5

Sanctification done in us and for us**
•MC 156-157, 165-166 (see also GID 112-113; M 172; Righteousness by faith/grace) ❖ MC IV 5:8; 7:12, 13 (see also GID I 12:10, 11; M App. A:11; Righteousness by faith/grace)

Sanctity—see also Piety

Sanctity and culture: Both are hard to diagnose and easy to feign
•WLN 47 ❖ WLN 3:24

Sanctity: Relationship of Creature and Creator different from the union of wills which is reached, under grace, by a life of sanctity
•LM 69 ❖ LM 13:5

Satan—*see also* Devil; *consider also* Angels, fallen

Satan and his associates have tampered with things inside our frontier, like Nature*
•M 121 ❖ M 14:22

Satan as the god of this world, the god we ask the "Great God" to curse for being evil*
•GID 171 ❖ GID I 20:Reply-17, 18

Satan associated with disease in Scripture; I by no means reject the view that disease may be caused by a created being other than man
•PP 89 (ftnt.), 136 ❖ PP 6:1 (ftnt.); 9:7

Satan can exploit even truths to our deception (re: corporate guilt or a social conscience as an excuse for evading our own personal faults)
•PP 60 ❖ PP 4:8

Satan did not frustrate the good that God intended when He created the world; rather evil provides the fuel for a second, more complex kind of good*
•PP 84 (*see also* PP 110-111)
❖ PP 5:11 (*see also* PP 7:2)

Satan has been tempting humans to try to run the human race on the wrong juice; God designed the human machine to run on Himself
•MC 54 ❖ MC II 3:8

Satan has no sense of humour, for humour involves a sense of proportion and a power of seeing yourself from the outside
•SL ix (*see also* SL xii-xiii)
❖ SL P:16 (*see also* SL P:22)

Satan: I don't think evil, in the strict sense, can *create*, but it can spoil something that Another has created
•L 257 (*see also* L 301) ❖ L 1 Nov 54 (first letter) (*see also* L 20 Dec 61)

Satan, Lewis describes his belief about, (As the leader or dictator of devils, he is the opposite, not of God, but of Michael)
•SL vii ❖ SL P:10

Satan, Lewis relates the story of the existence and fall of, (and his corruption of man and Earth) as it has been widely believed in the Church
•PP 133-136 ❖ PP 9:6, 7

Satan, modern clergymen are anxious to allow, every advantage he can with any show of fairness claim
•M 164-165 ❖ M 17:1

Satan: Most reviewers thought my idea of the fall of the Bent One [in *Out of the Silent Planet*] was an invention of my own
•L 167 ❖ L 9 Jul 39

Satan: "Reason may win truths; without Faith she will retain them just so long as Satan pleases"
•CR 43 ❖ CR 3:12

Satan, Screwtape describes his version of the initial quarrel between, and God*
•SL 86-87 ❖ SL 19:2

Satan, sin of: wanting to be the center
•MC 53 ❖ MC II 3:6

Satan: "There is no neutral ground in the universe: every square inch, every split second, is claimed by God and counterclaimed by Satan"
•CR 33 ❖ CR 2:54

Satan vs. Michael: If Michael is in the right and Satan in the wrong, this must mean they stand in relation to a more ultimate ground of reality (re: Dualism)
•GID 24 ❖ GID I 1:7

Satan, we have Scriptural authority for, originating diseases
•L 257 ❖ L 1 Nov 54 (first letter)

Satan's weapons, God uses certain of, such as Death, to defeat Satan himself (chess game analogy)
•M 128-129 ❖ M 14:34

Satisfaction—*see also* Desire; Happiness

Satisfaction, belief in any reality lends a certain sort of aesthetic; "poetry" is the result, not the cause, of religious belief
•WG 77-78 ❖ WG 5:9

Satisfaction, God is the true goal of men and the, of their needs
•RP 40-41 (*see also* GO 79*; WG 14-16)
❖ RP 4:15 (*see also* GO 4:21*; WG 1:11, 12)

Satisfaction of our desires: "All that you

are, sins apart, is destined, if you will let God have His good way, to utter satisfaction"
•PP 147 (*see also* Desire; Destiny of redeemed Man) ❖ PP 10:3 (*see also* Desire; Destiny of redeemed Man)

Satisfaction of poetic language is in the pleasure at finding anything vividly conveyed to the imagination*
•CR 130-131 (*see also* GID 66*) ❖ CR 11:4 (*see also* GID I 5:9*)

Satisfaction, what state of affairs in this life can we view with
•L 166 ❖ L 8 May 39

Satisfaction: "When we want to be something other than the thing God wants us to be, we must be wanting what, in fact, will not make us happy"*
•PP 52 (*see also* PP 90; WG 118-119) ❖ PP 3:18 (*see also* PP 6:3; WG 7:18)

Satisfactions, if you reject aesthetic, you will fall into sensual satisfactions (re: learning in war-time)
•WG 23-24 ❖ WG 2:5

Saved (souls)—*consider* Destiny of redeemed Man

Saviour, Christ as: His advantage is the only reason He can help us (drowning swimmer analogy)
•L 234-235; MC 61 ❖ L undated letter between 12 Sep 51 and 3 Dec 51; MC II 4:10

Saviour, we need to believe in a; it is not enough to want to get rid of our sins
•GID 260 ❖ GID II 16:18

Savoir (direct knowledge about) vs. *connaitre* (knowledge-by-acquaintance)—specifically regarding the love of God
•FL 174-175 (*see also* GID 170; WLN 25, 29, 30) ❖ FL 6:20 (*see also* GID I 20:Reply-15; WLN 2:13, 18)

Scenery around Belfast described
•SJ 7, 11, 152-156 ❖ SJ 1:4, 9; 10:4-8

Scenery: I attended mostly to what I thought was awe-inspiring, or wild, or eerie, or distant; hence mountains, clouds, and sky were my especial delight
•SJ 152 ❖ SJ 10:4

Scenery: I learned that we should attempt a total surrender to whatever atmosphere is offering itself at the moment...to find the most dismal wood...*
•SJ 199 (*see also* SJ 146) ❖ SJ 13:3 (*see also* SJ 9:22)

Scenery: It is frustrating to come upon a scene of unexpected grandeur, and then to realize those with you care nothing for it
•RP 95 ❖ RP 9:6

Scenery: "It was the mood of a scene that mattered to me; and in tasting that mood my skin and nose were as busy as my eyes"
•SJ 78 ❖ SJ 5:10

Scenery: Landscapes are religiously ambivalent; i.e., may be a preparation or medium for meeting God, *or* may be a distraction and impediment
•L 268 ❖ L undated letter just before 2 Apr 56

Scenery, natural: I was cured once and for all of the pernicious tendency to compare and prefer...
•SJ 145-146 (*see also* FL 34-35) ❖ SJ 9:22 (*see also* FL 2:17, 18)

Scenery of England described (Lewis's first impressions, at age nine)
•SJ 24-25 ❖ SJ 2:3, 4

Scenery of Ireland (Donegal): "All the mountains look like mountains in a story, and there are wooded valleys, and golden sands, and the smell of peat..."
•LAL 32 (*see also* LAL 45) ❖ LAL Sep 19/54 (*see also* LAL 5/10/55)

Scenery: "Of landscapes, as of people, one becomes more tolerant after one's twentieth year"
•L 63 ❖ L Jul 21

Scenery of Surrey described
•SJ 132, 134, 145-147 ❖ SJ 9:1, 6-8, 22

Scenery: "Shut your mouth; open your eyes and ears. Take in what is there and give no thought to what might have been there..."
•SJ 146 ❖ SJ 9:22

Scenery, why beautiful, is so unsatisfac-

tory when seen from a train or a car
- L 253 ❖ L 9 Jan 54

Scenery: You have stood before some landscape which seems to embody what you have been looking for all your life—but your friend sees something different*
- PP 145-146 ❖ PP 10:2

Sceptic(s)—*consider also* Agnostic(s); Atheist(s); Unbeliever(s)

Sceptic ("critic") who "sees all the facts but not the meaning," such as those who believe that religion is only psychological
- WG 71-72 ❖ WG 4:29

Sceptic who approaches a Transposition "from below": "On the evidence available to him his conclusion is the only one possible"
- WG 64; 71-72 ❖ WG 4:15, 29

Scepticism—*see also* Agnosticism; Doubt; *consider also* Atheism

Scepticism arising from the demand for "proof": God's presence in any but the faintest and most mitigated degree would override our will and defeat His purpose*
- SL 38-39 ❖ SL 8:4

Scepticism arising from the demand for "proof": The Irresistible and the Indisputable are the two weapons which God's scheme forbids Him to use*
- SL 38 ❖ SL 8:4

Scepticism engraved in our thought from our earlier lives, like a rut
- L 227 (*see also* M 81-84*, 164-167*)
❖ L 5 Mar 51 (*see also* M 11:1-5*; 17:1-4*)

Scepticism, everywhere except in theology there has been a vigorous growth of, about scepticism itself
- CR 162 ❖ CR 13:25

Scepticism, I do not wish to reduce; I am only suggesting that it need not be reserved for the New Testament—try doubting something else
- CR 164 (*see also* CR 162*)
❖ CR 13:29 (*see also* CR 13:25*)

Scepticism ("the psychological quality of being suspicious") as the result of not knowing God well enough*

- WLN 25-30, esp. 29
❖ WLN 2:13-18, esp. 2:17

Scepticism, we are prevented from accepting total, because it operates only by making a tacit exception in favour of the thought we're thinking at the moment
- CR 61; M 23 ❖ CR 5:10; 3:31

Scholarship—*see also* Intellectual life; Intellectualism; Knowledge

Scholarship, transitory nature of all, including that of theology
- CR 162 ❖ CR 13:25

Scholastic achievement: The only people who achieve much are those who want knowledge so badly that they seek it while conditions are still unfavourable
- WG 30 ❖ WG 2:12

School(s)—*see also* Education

School, a boy who is unhappy at, learns the habit of keeping the future in its place; thoughts of the coming term must not intrude on the present holiday
- SJ 158 ❖ SJ 10:11

School as a Preparation for Public Life (a tongue-in-cheek reference)
- SJ 88, 92, 93, 95 ❖ SJ 6:9, 14, 16, 19

School, it is difficult for most parents to realize the unimportance of most schoolmasters in the life of a
- SJ 99-100 ❖ SJ 6:26

School, Lewis's distaste for his early years at
- L 96, 138 (*see also* SJ 22-37, 41) ❖ L 4 Jul 24; 9 Sep 29 (*see also* SJ 2:1-16, 19)

School, life as a, in which we must practice the "duty" of prayer as we must learn grammar if we are ever to read the poets
- LM 115-116 ❖ LM 21:12-15

School, making games organized and compulsory in, banished the element of play
- SJ 98 (*see also* SJ 107)
❖ SJ 6:22, 23 (*see also* SJ 7:9)

School: Straight tribulation [such as being in the army] is easier to bear than tribulation which advertises itself as

pleasure [such as school]
•SJ 188 ❖ SJ 12:10
School system of Britain discussed with regard to the transmission of Christianity
•GID 114-119 ❖ GID I ch. 13
Schools, Christian, need for
•GID 118-119 ❖ GID I 13:9, 10
Schools, Public, of England criticized
•L 131-132 (see also L 134) ❖ L undated letter of Nov 1928 (see also L undated letter postmarked 17 Jul 29)
Schools, secular, not likely to tolerate radically Christian elements
•GID 118-119 ❖ GID I 13:9
Schoolboy analogy to show how strict, formal rules (as in rhyming) will eventually be seen as subject to a higher, subtler law—re: miracles/laws of Nature
•M 95-96 ❖ M 12:2, 3
Schoolboy analogy to show that the first reward of our obedience is our increasing power to desire the ultimate reward
•WG 4-6 ❖ WG 1:2-4
Schoolmaster, illustration of Socialist, who decided to give up Socialism for its tyranny but then wished to join the ranks of his oppressors in the Ministry of Education (re: current lack of thirst for justice)
•CR 122; RP 69-71
❖ CR 10:18, 19; RP 7:7, 8
Schoolteachers—see Teachers
School-term, all the sting had been drawn from the beginning of the, (re: Lewis's tutoring under William T. Kirkpatrick)
•SJ 159 ❖ SJ 10:13
Schweitzer, Dr. Albert, associated with a school of thought which sees the return of Christ and the end of the world as Christ's central message
•WLN 94 ❖ WLN 7:3
Science—consider also Laws of Nature
Science: A belief in the objectivity and validity of reason must be maintained or all thoughts are accidents and we can know no truths and have no knowledge*

•CR 60-63, 71, 72-81, 89; GID 21, 52-53, 136-138, 272, 274-276; M 12-24, 34, 105; MC 45-46; SJ 208; WG 88-92
❖ CR 5:9-13, 27; ch. 6; 7:16; GID I 1:1; 4:21; 16:13-17; III 1:4, 9, 13-16; M ch. 3; 5:1; 13:16; MC II 1:6; SJ 13:17; WG 5:21-24
Science, advance of: "We can become either more beneficent or more mischievous. My guess is we shall do both"
•GID 312 ❖ GID III 8:6
Science, advancement of, has not altered the question of miracles, or made them harder to accept
•M 46-48 (see also GID 72-75)
❖ M 7:5, 6 (see also GID I ch. 7)
Science alternately holds that life can only be supported on earth, and that the universe is well-inhabited; both used as arguments against Christianity
•CR 174; M 50; WLN 83-84
❖ CR 14:46; M 7:10; WLN 6:1-3
Science and eugenics as part of the false hope the devil wishes us to have for turning this Earth into Heaven
•SL 133 ❖ SL 28:2
Science and government, relationship between, in a "technocracy" ("I dread government in the name of science. That is how tyrannies come in")
•GID 314-315 ❖ GID III 8:15-18
Science and miracles: "[Miracle] introduces a new factor into the situation, namely supernatural force, which the scientist had not reckoned on"
•M 58 (see also GID 76-79*)
❖ M 8:6 (see also GID I ch. 8*)
Science and miracles: Nature a partial system within reality which has been mistaken for the whole (fish-tank analogy)
•M 60-61 ❖ M 8:9
Science and modern philosophy have both proved powerless to curb the human impulse toward Pantheism
•M 83 ❖ M 11:4
Science: "As regards material reality, we are now being forced to the conclusion that we know nothing about it save its mathematics"

•GID 46 ❖ GID I 3:16

Science, at least some value of the use of, was implied in St. Paul's demand that we should perceive the Invisible through the visible
•CR 15 ❖ CR 2:7

Science cannot prove or disprove miracles
•GID 134-135 ❖ GID I 16:7-9

Science: Christians and their opponents keep expecting that some new discovery will either turn matters of faith into knowledge or reduce them to absurdities
•WLN 92 ❖ WLN 6:27

"Science" considered reliable by the uneducated man, while history regarded with scepticism; this has implications for evangelism
•GID 241-242 (*see also* GID 94-95, 252) ❖ GID II 12:3 (*see also* GID I 10:13, 14; II 14:8, 9)

Science describes "reality" by mathematics, but mathematics can hardly be reality itself (re: attempting contact with ultimate Reality)
•CR 170 ❖ CR 14:24

Science, each new discovery in, seized by unbelievers for a new attack on Christianity—and by believers (more embarrassingly) for a new defence
•WLN 84 ❖ WLN 6:3

Science fiction, I was trying to redeem for imaginative purposes the form known as, (re: *Out of the Silent Planet*)
•L 295 ❖ L undated letter of Aug 1960

Science fiction, Lewis relates some of the reflections that first moved him to write
•CR 173-174 ❖ CR 14:40-43

Science fiction, Lewis's early interest in planetary, described as "something courser and stronger" than "Joy"; it was "ravenous, like a lust"
•SJ 35-36 ❖ SJ 2:15

Science fiction, modern, assumes moral thought to be merely a subjective thing like one's taste in food, which can vary from species to species
•CR 61 ❖ CR 5:11

Science fiction used to represent the inhabitants of other worlds as monsters and the terrestrial invaders as good; that is changing now
•CR 173-174 ❖ CR 14:43

Science: For modern physics, the universe is "running down"; science knows of no winding-up process
•GID 33-34; M 151-152 (*see also* Entropy) ❖ GID I 2:12; M 16:16, 17 (*see also* Entropy)

Science has nothing to say either for or against the doctrine of the Fall
•PP 72-74, esp. 74 ❖ PP 5:3

Science has parted company with classical forms of materialism; if anything emerges clearly from modern physics, it is that nature is not everlasting
•GID 38-39 ❖ GID I 3:3

Science, I could never have gone far in any, because on the path of every science the lion Mathematics lies in wait for you
•SJ 137 ❖ SJ 9:11

Science, in, we have been reading only the notes to a poem; in Christianity we find the poem itself
•M 130 ❖ M 14:35

Science is based on observation; cannot be expected to anticipate the reversal of entropy (i.e., the Resurrection)
•M 151-152; GID 33-34 ❖ M 16:16, 17; GID I 2:12

Science: Lewis examines the view that miracles were accepted in earlier times because people had a false conception of the universe and Man's importance in it
•M 48-54 ❖ M 7:7-17

Science: Lewis examines the view that miracles were accepted in earlier times because people didn't know the laws of Nature
•M 45-48 ❖ M 7:2-6

Science logically requires conviction that Nature will not be perpetually or meaninglessly altered; but in Naturalism convictions are untrustworthy
•M 105-106 ❖ M 13:16, 17

Science, mentally limited beings studying a painting used to illustrate the

impossibility of discovering by, how God works on Nature (illustration borrowed from Bergson)
•M 97 ❖ M 12:5

Science, methods of, do not discover facts like whether or not Christ was God [or how to find God]
•CR 172 ❖ CR 14:33, 34

Science not dependable for apologetic since it is always switching positions; "Science *twisted* in the interest of apologetics would be sin and folly"
•GID 92-98 (*see also* GID 39, 44; WLN 83-84) ❖ GID I 10:8,9 (*see also* GID I 3:3, 12; WLN 6:1-3)

Science: "Physics...is replacing biology as the science *par excellence* in the mind of the plain man"; this points to the decline of Evolutionism
•CR 89 ❖ CR 7:17

Science, predictability belongs to the realm of, not of human history (re: one objection to petitionary prayer)
•LM 38 ❖ LM 7:7-11

Science, probably every age gets (within certain limits) the, it desires (re: myth of popular Evolution)
•CR 84-85 ❖ CR 7:9

Science, Religion and (chapter title)
•GID 72-75 ❖ GID I ch. 7

Science: Strictly speaking, there is no such thing as "modern science"; there are only particular sciences, in rapid change, and sometimes inconsistent...
•CR 82-83 ❖ CR 7:4

Science unable to settle questions like "Why is there a universe?"
•MC 32 ❖ MC I 4:2

Science vs. (Christian) Theology: Long before I believed Theology to be true I had decided that the popular scientific picture was false
•WG 88 ❖ WG 5:21

Science vs. Christianity: Christian theology can fit in science, art, and morality; science cannot fit in any of these things, not even itself
•WG 91-92 ❖ WG 5:24

Science vs. history: "The scientist studies those elements in reality which repeat

themselves. The historian studies the unique" (re: "Historicism")
•CR 112 ❖ CR 9:25

Science vs. miracles: "I am afraid I have not understood why the miracles could never be accepted by one who accepted science"
•GID 133-135 ❖ GID I 16:5-9

Science vs. miracles: Laws of Nature tell what will happen provided there's no interference; a miracle is when something outside nature interferes
•GID 72-74 (*see also* M 5, 45-48) ❖ GID I 7:1-28 (*see also* M 2:1; 7:2-6)

Science vs. Poetry to convey information: Science gives us, out of the teeming complexity of every concrete reality, only the "common measurable features"
•CR 135 ❖ CR 11:12

Science vs. Religion: "To the man in the street the conflict is still perfectly real"
•GID 68 ❖ GID I 6:1

Science: We forget that prehistoric man made all the most useful discoveries, except that of chloroform, which have ever been made (wheel, fire, etc.)
•PP 74 ❖ PP 5:3

Science: "When logic says a thing must be so, Nature always agrees"*
•CR 64 ❖ CR 5:17

Science, you need much more faith in, than in theology (quote from unknown source)
•L 113 ❖ L 30 Mar 27

Sciences and arts, Christianity never intended to replace or supersede the ordinary; it is rather a director which will set them all to the right jobs
•MC 79 ❖ MC III 3:2

Sciences encourage people to think about realities they can't touch or see; Screwtape advises Wormwood not to use them as a defense against Christianity
•SL 10 ❖ SL 1:4

Sciences, my youthful rationalism was based on what I believed to be the findings of the, —which I had to take on trusted authority

•SJ 174 (*see also* SJ 170)

❖ SJ 11:12 (*see also* SJ 11:7)

Sciences, physical, depend on the validity of logic and inference just as much as metaphysics; if logic is discredited, science must go down with it (re: subjectivity vs. objectivity of human thought)

•CR 61-62, 72, 89 (*see also* Logic)

❖ CR 5:12; 6:3; 7:16 (*see also* Logic)

Sciences, physical, no less than theology, propose for our belief much that cannot be imagined (re: difficulty of imagining God as man)

•WLN 99 ❖ WLN 7:10

Scientific hope of defeating death a real rival to Christianity

•L 167 ❖ L 9 Jul 39

Scientific Humanism—*see* Humanism, scientific

Scientific knowledge, how Christian dogma can be unchanging in the face of growing

•GID 38-47 ❖ GID I ch. 3

Scientific language, most human experiences cannot be communicated by; require the use of Poetic language

•CR 138, 140 ❖ CR 11:20, 23

Scientific logic not the same logic required for trust in God because, once you accept that He is, you move from speculative thought to a *relationship*

•WLN 21-30, esp. 26-27, 30 (*see also* LM 49; MC 32) ❖ WLN 2:10-18, esp. 2:14, 18 (*see also* LM 9:8; MC I 4:2)

Scientific proof not the same kind of proof required for belief in God, since belief is different from knowledge

•WLN 14-16, 20-21 (*see also* WLN 92; MC 32-33) ❖ WLN 2:3, 4, 9 (*see also* WLN 6:28; MC I 4:2, 3)

Scientific view, Determinism seems to be implicit in a, of the world

•LM 36 ❖ LM 7:5

"**Scientism**" [the derivation of conclusions about God from science] vs. "Historicism" [the derivation of metahistorical meaning from history]

•CR 112 ❖ CR 9:25

Scientist, though I could never have been a, I had scientific as well as imaginative impulses; I loved ratiocination

•SJ 137 ❖ SJ 9:11

Scientists: As their subject matter comes nearer to man himself (e.g., psychologists), their anti-religious bias hardens

•GID 135 ❖ GID I 16:9, 10

Scientists have been increasingly engaged in specialised inquiries requiring a kind of thought which leads to Naturalism unless corrected

•M 41-42 ❖ M 6:5

Scientists' idea of long-term futility, three possible attitudes toward: to accept it; to deny that view of the universe; or to work against it

•CR 59 ❖ CR 5:5

Scientists, in most modern, the belief in a Legislator (of law in Nature) has died; will be interesting to see how long faith in uniformity survives

•M 106 ❖ M 13:17, 18

Scientists join hands with the theologians in predicting that the world will not always be habitable

•WLN 110 ❖ WLN 7:32

Scientists may flirt with the error of subjectivism, but in the main, subjectivism is an uncomfortable yokefellow for research

•CR 72 (*see also* Subjectivism)

❖ CR 6:3 (*see also* Subjectivism)

Scissors analogy: Asking whether good actions or Faith in Christ leads us home seems to me like asking which blade in a pair of scissors is most necessary

•MC 129 ❖ MC III 12:7

Scotch run awfully true to type and never change

•LAL 52 ❖ LAL 4/3/56

Scotch: "...the typically Scotch attitude consists not in being loud or quiet, or merry or sad, but just in being *Scotch*"

•L 133-134 ❖ L undated letter postmarked 13 Apr 29

Scotch were a people unusually tenacious of old memories; have retained a lot of traditional history

•L 133

❖ L undated letter postmarked 13 Apr 29

Scotland: "Edinburgh is a wonderful city, with a castle on a crag and mountains beyond it..."
- •LAL 52 ❖ LAL 4/3/56

Scoundrelism, the choice which could lead to, will come in no very dramatic colours
- •WG 101-102 ❖ WG 6:12

Scraps (chapter title)
- •GID 216-217 ❖ GID II ch. 7

Screwtape Letters, would you believe that an American schoolgirl has been expelled from her school for having a copy of
- •L 258 ❖ L 17 Dec 54

Screwtape Letters, conception of the idea for, mentioned
- •L 188 ❖ L 20 Jul 40

Screwtape Letters did not require many years' study in theology; "'My heart'—I need no other's—'showeth me the wickedness of the ungodly'"
- •SL xiii (*see also* RP 136*)
- ❖ SL P:24 (*see also* RP 12:16*)

Screwtape Letters: "...ethics served with an imaginative seasoning"
- •L 234
- ❖ L undated letter just before 3 Dec 51

Screwtape Letters: "...its purpose was not to speculate about diabolical life but to throw light from a new angle on the life of men"
- •SL xii ❖ SL P:21

Screwtape Letters: Lewis acknowledges a debt to the books *The Confessions of a Well-Meaning Woman* and *Voyage to Arcturus* for some ideas
- •SL xii-xiii ❖ SL P:22

Screwtape Letters: Lewis explains that in making up the names of the devils, he aimed merely at making them nasty by the sound
- •SL xiii ❖ SL P:23

Screwtape Letters mentioned as a book Lewis did not enjoy writing
- •GID 263 ❖ GID II 16:32-34

Screwtape Letters, probable indirect reference to the results of writing*
- •WG 94 ❖ WG 6:3

Screwtape Letters: "Though I had never written anything more easily, I never wrote with less enjoyment"
- •SL xiii-xiv ❖ SL P:25

Screwtape Proposes a Toast (chapter title)
- •SL 150-172; WLN 51-70
- ❖ SL ch. 32; WLN ch. 4

"Screwtape Proposes A Toast," Lewis mentions what finally caused him to write
- •SL xiv-xv ❖ SL P:27

Screwtape: The devil is a liar; not everything Screwtape says should be assumed to be true even from his own angle
- •SL 4 ❖ SL PP:3

Screwtape's official title given: "His Abysmal Sublimity Undersecretary Screwtape, T. E., B. S., etc."
- •SL 104 ❖ SL 22:6

Scripture(s)—*see also* Bible; *consider also* Gospel(s)

Scripture: Apocalyptic writings, to most modern tastes, appear tedious and unedifying; predictions of Jesus seen as "much the same sort of thing"
- •WLN 95 ❖ WLN 7:5

Scripture as a medium of the Holy Spirit to us
- •L 243 ❖ L 20 Jun 52

Scripture, baffling passages in, are to be expected; God speaks not only for us but for sages and mystics
- •L 253 ❖ L 8 Aug 53

Scripture can be read as merely human literature; nothing will ever prove either interpretation
- •RP 116-117 ❖ RP 11:12

Scripture (chapter title)
- •RP 109-119 ❖ RP ch. 11

Scripture, difficulties in—*see also* Questions

Scripture, difficulties in: "Behind the shocking passage be sure there lurks some great truth which you don't understand"
- •L 253 ❖ L 8 Aug 53

Scripture, difficulties in: If we are free to delete all inconvenient data, we shall have no theological difficulties; but

•SL 75 ❖ SL 16:5

Scrupulosity: "We can become scrupulous or fanatical; we can, in what seems zeal but is really presumption, embrace tasks never intended for us"
•WG 129 ❖ WG 9:8

Sculptor's shop, the world is a great; someday the statues are going to come to life
•MC 140 ❖ MC IV 1:16

Sea, even the weariest river winds somewhere safe to
•LAL 120-121 ❖ LAL 6 Jul 63

Sea, God described as a: We are tempted to be careful not to get out of our depth and lose our things temporal
•WG 128 (*see also* FL 181)
❖ WG 9:6 (*see also* FL 6:28)

Sea: I should think I *do* like salt water, and in all its forms
•L 218 (*see also* L 29)
❖ L 16 Aug 49 (*see also* L undated letter between Oct 1915 and 27 Sep 16)

Sea, Lewis's liking for, expressed
•L 41 (*see also* Beach; Ship/s)
❖ L 16 Feb 18 (*see also* Beach; Ship/s)

Sea ("where no Jew willingly went") appreciated in the Psalms
•RP 84 (*see also* RP 52)
❖ RP 8:13 (*see also* RP 5:9)

Search for God—*see also* Seeking God

Search for God, agnostics talk cheerfully about man's; to me, as I was then, they might as well have talked about the mouse's search for the cat
•SJ 227 (*see also* CR 169)
❖ SJ 14:21 (*see also* CR 14:19)

Search for God: Initiative lies wholly on God's side
•GID 143-144 (*see also* CR 169; MC 144; PP 51-52; SJ 216, 227)
❖ GID I 16:26 (*see also* CR 14:19; MC IV 2:13; PP 3:17; SJ 14:7, 20, 21)

Search for God, Man's, not what Christianity is about; it is about something done by God for, to, and about, Man
•M 116 (*see also* GID 144, top; M 83; PP 51; SJ 227) ❖ M 14:15 (*see also* GID I 16:26; M 11:4; PP 3:17; SJ 14:21)

Search for God: "Much depends on the seeing eye"; "What is required is a certain faculty of recognition"
•CR 171, 172 ❖ CR 14:29, 34

Search for God: Space travel has nothing to do with discovering God—to some, God is discoverable everywhere; to others, nowhere
•CR 171 ❖ CR 14:29

Search for God: That voice which speaks in your conscience and in some of your intensest joys may be in fact the closest contact you have with the mystery...*
•CR 170 ❖ CR 14:27

Search for God, the soul's, only a mode of His search for her, since all comes from Him
•PP 51 ❖ PP 3:17

Search for knowledge and beauty cannot be postponed until men are secure (re: education in time of war)
•WG 21-22 ❖ WG 2:4

Search for truth about God: "If He can be known it will be by self-revelation on His part, not by speculation on ours"
•GID 144 ❖ GID I 16:26

Search for Truth, importance of: If Christianity is untrue, no honest man will want to believe it; if it is true, every honest man will want to believe it
•GID 108-109, 111-112 (*see also* GID 265-266, 281; Truth) ❖ GID I 12:1, 9; (*see also* GID II 2:10; 16:50, 51; Truth)

Search for Truth, importance of, within various Christian denominations
•MC 11-12 ❖ MC P:15

Season, autumn mentioned as a, which Lewis enjoyed
•L 30, 31; LAL 45; SJ 16-17 ❖ L 27 Sep 16; 30 Oct 16; LAL 5/10/55; SJ 1:16

Seasons, change of, mentioned by Screwtape as an example of that union of change and permanence enjoyed by humans which is called Rhythm
•SL 116-117 ❖ SL 25:2, 3

Seasons: "It sounds fantastic to say that one can be enamored of a season, but that is something like what happened" (on reading *Squirrel Nutkin*)
•SJ 16-17 ❖ SJ 1:16

Seasons: Old age likened to autumn—the best of the seasons, but it doesn't last
•L 308 ❖ L 27 Oct 63

Seasons: "The first beginning of winter always excites me; it makes me want adventures. I expect our autumn has gentler colours than your fall..."
•L 264-265 ❖ L 16 Oct 55

Second chance, regarding the objection that there ought to be a: "Finality must come sometime..."

Second Coming—*see also* End of the World; *consider also* Destiny of lost Man; Destiny of redeemed Man

Second Coming: "Apparently many people find it difficult to believe in this great event without trying to guess its date"
•WLN 106-107 ❖ WLN 7:25

Second Coming as one of the beliefs which unite all Christians everywhere
•GID 336 ❖ GID IV Letter 9

Second Coming, Christ's teaching about: 1) that He will certainly return, 2) that we cannot know when, and 3) that therefore we must always be ready
•WLN 107 ❖ WLN 7:26

Second Coming, doctrine of: "If this is not an integral part of the faith once given to the saints, I do not know what is"
•WLN 93 ❖ WLN 7:1

Second Coming, doctrine of, is deeply uncongenial to the whole evolutionary or developmental character of modern thought
•WLN 100 ❖ WLN 7:12

Second Coming, doctrine of, ought to be more valued and made more frequently the subject of meditation
•WLN 106 ❖ WLN 7:23

Second Coming, doctrine of, teaches us that we do not and cannot know when the drama will end; curtain may be rung down at any moment
•WLN 105 (*see also* WLN 101)
❖ WLN 7:21 (*see also* WLN 7:12)

Second Coming, doctrine of, will have failed if it does not cause us to ask ourselves continuously, "What if the present were the world's last night?"

•WLN 109 (*see also* WLN 111-113)
❖ WLN 7:29 (*see also* WLN 7:34-38)

Second Coming: Escatological hope has rather faded out, leaving a certain vacuity—a widespread question as to what this hustling and crowded life is *about*
•CR 57 ❖ CR 5:1

Second Coming, exciting fear about, will not succeed in its purpose since it is impossible to maintain any emotion for very long
•WLN 109 (*see also* RP 41-42; LM 76)
❖ WLN 7:30 (*see also* RP 4:16; LM 14:15)

Second Coming: "I wonder whether people who ask God to interfere openly and directly in our world quite realise what it will be like when He does"
•MC 66 (*consider also* Contact with God) ❖ MC II 5:9 (*consider also* Contact with God)

Second Coming, imagery associated with: Impossible to know how much of a representation is symbolical and how much is literal
•CR 164-166 ❖ CR 13:30-35

Second Coming, it seems to me impossible to believe in the Divinity of Christ while abandoning or neglecting the doctrine of the
•WLN 93 ❖ WLN 7:1

Second Coming: It will strike either irresistible love or irresistible horror into every creature
•MC 66 (*see also* GID 47)
❖ MC II 5:9 (*see also* GID I 3:17)

Second Coming, Lewis addresses some thoughts that may deter modern men from a firm belief in
•WLN 93-113 ❖ WLN ch. 7

Second Coming: Many are shy of this doctrine because they are reacting against a school of thought which sees this as Christ's central message
•WLN 94 ❖ WLN 7:3

Second Coming of Christ and Restoration anticipated by the Resurrection
•M 145-146 ❖ M 16:6

Second Coming of Christ, current under-

emphasis of, a reaction to earlier over-emphasis
- •WLN 94-95 ❖ WLN 7:3, 4

Second Coming: "Precisely because we cannot predict the moment, we must be ready at all moments"
- •WLN 107 (see also GID 266)
- ❖ WLN 7:27 (see also GID II 16:54-56)

Second Coming: Regarding the embarrassing fact that Jesus told His disciples He would come back in their lifetime
- •WLN 97-100 ❖ WLN 7:8-11

Second Coming, the idea which shuts out the, from our minds—that the world is slowly ripening to perfection—is a myth
- •WLN 104 ❖ WLN 7:19

Second Coming, William Miller (whom I take to have been an honest fanatic) gave one of the most famous predictions for the
- •WLN 107 (see also WLN 94)
- ❖ WLN 7:25 (see also WLN 7:3)

Second Meanings (chapter title)
- •RP 99-108 ❖ RP ch. 10

Second meanings in Scripture (the "spiritual" ones) may not always have been intended by the author—but they also do not negate the first, plainer meaning
- •RP 128-129 ❖ RP 12:9

Second Meanings in the Psalms (chapter title)
- •RP 120-138 ❖ RP ch. 12

Secret we cannot hide and cannot tell... which pierces with such sweetness (re: "desire for our own far-off country")
- •WG 6-7 ❖ WG 1:5

Sectarianism—consider Christianity, "mere"; Denominations; Divisions within Christianity

Sects—see Denominations

Secular—see Temporal; Worldly

Security—see also Safety; consider also Self-reservation

Security, real, is in Heaven and thus earth affords only imitations
- •LAL 49 (see also FL 190)
- ❖ LAL 16/12/55 (see also FL 6:43)

Security, temptation to obtain temporal, ("Our real protection is to be sought elsewhere")
- •WG 129-130 ❖ WG 9:8

Security, the settled happiness and, which we all desire God withholds from us, for it would teach us to rest our hearts in this world
- •PP 115 ❖ PP 7:7

Seed, think of yourself as a, waiting to come up in the Gardener's good time, up into the real world
- •LAL 119 ❖ LAL 28 Jun 63

Seed, you don't teach a, how to die into treehood by throwing it into the fire: and it has to become a good seed before it's worth burying (re: the self)
- •L 155
- ❖ L undated letter just before 7 Jun 34

Seeing Eye, The (chapter title)
- •CR 167-176 ❖ CR ch. 14

Seeking God—see also Search for God; consider also Desire for God

Seeking God became a painful effort after the Fall, since man's inclination had become self-ward*
- •PP 83 (see also PP 91)
- ❖ PP 5:10 (see also PP 6:3)

Seeking God, continue, with seriousness; unless He wanted you, you would not be wanting Him
- •L 233 ❖ L 13 Jun 51

Seeking God daily vital to the Christian life*
- •GID 266 (see also L 220; MC 124, 168-169; SL 62; WG 132)
- ❖ GID II 16:52, 53 (see also L undated letter between 6 Sep 49 and 22 Sep 49; MC III 11:6; IV 8:8; SL 14:1; WG 9:13)

Seeking God: "...in order to find God it is perhaps not always necessary to leave the creatures behind...the world is crowded with Him"
- •LM 75 ❖ LM 14:11

Seeking God, obstacles to—see Obstacles to Christian faith

Seeking God: "People will find God if they consciously seek from Him the right attitude towards all unpleasant things"

15; SL 13:4; WG 4:21, 22, 24, 30)

Self, Screwtape advises keeping humans' attention on, and away from God
•SL 20-21 (see also SL 16, 29-30, 65-66)
❖ SL 4:3 (see also SL 3:2; 6:3; 14:5)

Self soon turns out to be not so dead as he pretended (in Eros, or after a religious conversion)
•FL 159 ❖ FL 5:44

Self, the instrument through which you see God is your whole
•MC 144 ❖ MC IV 2:14

Self, the journey homeward to habitual, (gravitation away from God) must be a product of the Fall
•PP 76 (see also PP 83, 91)
❖ PP 5:5 (see also PP 5:10; 6:3)

Self, the thing you long for summons you away from the, (re: desire for heaven)
•PP 149 (see also PP 151-153)
❖ PP 10:7 (see also PP 10:9-11)

Self, the wrong asceticism torments the; the right kind kills the selfness
•GID 195 ❖ GID II 2:4

Self, to hand over your whole, is almost impossible—yet easier than remaining "ourselves" and still being "good"
•MC 168 ❖ MC IV 8:7

Self, turning from God to, fulfills the necessary conditions for a sin possible to unfallen ("Paradisal") man
•PP 80-81 ❖ PP 5:9

Self, Two Ways With The (chapter title)
•GID 193-195 ❖ GID II ch. 2

Self, we fear the killing of our natural
•MC 154 (see also MC 164, 167, 174*; Self-reservation) ❖ MC IV 5:2 (see also MC IV 7:11; 8:4; 9:10*; Self-reservation)

Self, what we feel then has been well described by Keats as the journey homeward to habitual, (re: our spiritual longings)
•WG 14 ❖ WG 1:11

Self-admiration a poison although pleasure in being praised can be lawful
•WG 12 ❖ WG 1:10

Self-analysis—see Introspection; Self-examination; Self-knowledge

Self-centeredness–see also Selfishness

Self-centeredness as the characteristic of

the lost: They reject everything that is not simply themselves
•PP 123 ❖ PP 8:7

Self-centeredness as the state of Hell ("where everyone is perpetually concerned with his own dignity and advancement..."—etc.)
•SL ix ❖ SL P:16

Self-centeredness fundamental to our nature
•MC 154 ❖ MC IV 5:2

Self-centeredness instead of God-centeredness as the basic sin behind all particular sins
•PP 75 ❖ PP 5:5

Self-centeredness slowly permeates every one of our activities, even when they are begun with the best of intentions
•PP 75-76 ❖ PP 5:5

Self-centeredness : The moment you have a self, there is a possibility of putting yourself first—wanting to be the center; that was the sin of Satan
•MC 53 ❖ MC II 3:6

Self-complacency, the real danger to any order is not the man who speaks (within that order) of its faults but the man who flatters our corporate
•WLN 36 ❖ WLN 3:9

Self-concern—consider also Self-forgetfulness; Self-reservation

Self-concern and self-pity may cause the lives of some people (who are capable of real sacrifice) to be a misery to themselves and others
•SJ 143-144 ❖ SJ 9:19

Self-concern, as long as we have the itch of, we shall want the pleasure of self-approval; better to have neither and to forget our precious selves
•L 256 ❖ L 18 Feb 54

Self-concern as one of the "deadly serious passions" of Hell; Hell is a state where everyone is perpetually concerned about his own dignity and advancement
•SL ix ❖ SL P:16

Self-concern: "Christ did not teach and suffer that we might become, even in the natural loves, more careful of our

own happiness
•FL 170 ❖ FL 6:14

Self-concern: Christ's teaching was never meant to confirm my congenital preference for safe investments and limited liabilities
•FL 168 (see also CR 155; Limited liabilities) ❖ FL 6:10 (see also CR 13:6; Limited liabilities)

Self-concern: For the self-regarding caution and egoism of very bad people, death represents the final defeat
•L 190
❖ L undated letter just after 11 Aug 40

Self-condemnation: Screwtape mentions despair over one's own sinfulness as "a greater sin than any of the sins which provoke it"
•SL 138 ❖ SL 29:7

Self-condemnation: Screwtape points out that God does not want a person to think too much of his sins; the sooner the man turns his attention outward, the better*
•SL 66 (see also LM 33)
❖ SL 14:5 (see also LM 6:13)

Self-condemnation: We must be aware of our own sinfulness, but a continual poring over the "sink" can breed its own perverse pride*
•LM 98-99 ❖ LM 18:13-15

Self-conquest, we need not suppose that the necessity for, will ever be ended
•PP 151-152 ❖ PP 10:9, 10

Self-consciousness—see Introspection

Self-contempt as a source of cynicism or cruelty: "Even Christians...are not always free from the danger"
•GID 194-195 ❖ GID II 2:2, 3

Self-contempt can be the starting point for contempt for other selves, and thus for gloom, cynicism, and cruelty
•SL 63 ❖ SL 14:3

Self-contempt (or self-directed anger) "'worketh not the righteousness of God'. One must never be either content with, or impatient with, oneself"
•LAL 29 ❖ LAL Mar 31st 54

Self-contempt, right and wrong kinds of
•GID 193-195 (see also SL 62-66)

❖ GID II ch. 2 (see also SL ch.14)

Self-contentment—see Self-satisfaction

Self-deception—consider also Self-knowledge; Self-satisfaction

Self-deception: A man may console himself for his vices by a conviction that "his heart's in the right place" and "he wouldn't hurt a fly"*
•PP 56 ❖ PP 4:2

Self-deception: A moderately bad man knows he is not very good; a thoroughly bad man thinks he is all right*
•MC 87 (see also GID 56-57; LAL 95; PP 55, top; PP 67)
❖ MC III 4:10 (see also GID I 4:38; LAL 9 Jan 61; PP 4:prelim. quote; 4:15)

Self-deception: Corporate guilt (e.g., a "social conscience") can distract us from our own personal guilts
•PP 60-61 ❖ PP 4:8

Self-deception: We are far more subtle than the Psalmists in disguising our ill will from others and from ourselves
•RP 23 ❖ RP 3:8

Self-deception: We like to believe that our habitual vices are exceptional single acts, and make the opposite mistake about our virtues*
•PP 60 ❖ PP 4:7

Self-denial—see also Self-sacrifice; consider also Asceticism; Fasting; Renunciation

Self-denial: A man may be tempted to surrender benefits not that others may be happy in having them but that he may be unselfish in forgoing them
•SL 121 (see also WG 3)
❖ SL 26:2 (see also WG 1:1)

Self-denial: An imposed mortification can have all the merit of a voluntary one if it is taken in the right spirit
•LAL 20, 60, 105
❖ LAL Aug 10th 53; 3/8/56; 3/7/62

Self-denial ("asceticism"), right and wrong kinds of
•GID 193-195 (see also SL 63-66*)
❖ GID II ch. 2 (see also SL 14:3-5*)

Self-denial: It has been truly said that "only God can mortify"; ascetic practices and tribulation sent by God accomplish very different things*

•PP 112 ❖ PP 7:3

Self-denial, the New Testament has lots to say about, but not about self-denial as an end in itself
•WG 3 (*see also* SL 121*)
❖ WG 1:1 (*see also* SL 26:2*)

Self-denial: Where other systems (like Buddhism) expose our total nature to death, Christianity demands only that we set right a *misdirection* of our nature*
•PP 104 ❖ PP 6:15

Self-exaltation—*see* Pride

Self-examination—*see also* Introspection; Self-knowledge

Self-examination: A recollection of all one's own cruelty will help to make prayer for one's enemies real
•L 183 ❖ L 16 Apr 40

Self-examination, after his conversion to Theism Lewis's, became a discipline and a duty—"no longer a hobby or a habit"
•SJ 233 ❖ SJ 15:5

Self-examination as one of the steps in conversion
•L 192 ❖ L 4 Jan 41

Self-examination, chronic, a possible result of undergoing psychoanalysis
•LM 34 ❖ LM 6:16

Self-examination in such matters as faith or enjoyment not profitable; the moment I ask, "Do I believe?" all belief seems to go
•L 221 ❖ L 27 Sep 49

Self-examination, Lewis's, on conversion: "And there I found what appalled me; a zoo of lusts, a bedlam of ambitions, a nursery of fears..."
•SJ 226 (*see also* CR 169*)
❖ SJ 14:19 (*see also* CR 14:21*)

Self-examination seldom reveals our most obvious defects; humans tend toward a horror and neglect of the obvious*
•SL 16 (*see also* GID 121-124, 153)
❖ SL 3:2 (*see also* GID I 14:4-10; 18:6, 7)

Self-expression, Christian theory of literary criticism opposes the idea of literature as
•CR 7-8 ❖ CR 1:11-13

Self-finding—*see* Personality

Self-forgetfulness as a test of whether we are in the presence of God
•MC 111 ❖ MC III 8:7

Self-forgetfulness: God's whole effort is to get a man's mind off the subject of his own value altogether
•SL 64-66 ❖ SL 14:4, 5

Self-forgetfulness, humility means, rather than a low opinion of one's talents and character
•SL 63-65 (*see also* MC 114)
❖ SL 14:3-5 (*see also* MC III 8:12, 13)

Self-forgetfulness through the enjoyment of books*
•WLN 39 ❖ WLN 3:12

Self-forgiveness: "I think if God forgives us we must forgive ourselves. Otherwise it is almost like setting ourselves up as a higher tribunal than Him"
•L 230 ❖ L 19 Apr 51

Self-forgiveness: "Remember what St. John says 'If our *heart* condemn us, God is stronger than our heart'"
•LAL 77 ❖ LAL Jul 21st 58

Self-giving—*see* Self-sacrifice

Self-hatred—*see also* Self-contempt

Self-hatred, right and wrong kinds of
•GID 193-195 (*see also* SL 62-66)
❖ GID II ch. 2 (*see also* SL ch. 14)

Selfhood—*see also* Personality

Selfhood enhanced by being taken into the life of God
•MC 141 (*see also* GID 131; SL 38, 59, 81; WG 67, 117-118)
❖ MC IV 2:3 (*see also* GID I 16:3; SL 8:3; 13:4; 18:3, 4; WG 4:21, 22; 7:16, 17)

Self-identity—*see also* Personality

Self-identity given back to us for eternity when we abandon individualism
•WG 117-118 ❖ WG 7:17

Self-identity: "Human will becomes truly creative and truly our own when it is wholly God's..."
•PP 102 ❖ PP 6:14

Self-idolatry ("self-worship") as the best religion in which to find "happiness" —while it lasts
•GID 58 ❖ GID I 4:43, 44 (Ques. 11)

Self-idolatry, the mere existence of a self

includes the danger of; this is the "weak spot" in the very nature of creation
•PP 81 (see also PP 75)
❖ PP 5:9 (see also PP 5:5)

Self-importance as one of the "deadly serious passions" lived out in Hell
•SL ix ❖ SL P:16

Self-importance, what feels like zeal may be only fidgets or even; there can be intemperance in work as well as in drink
•LAL 53 ❖ LAL 19/3/56

Selfish, each sex regards the other as radically, since men's and women's interpretations of the word "unselfishness" are quite different
•SL 121 ❖ SL 26:2

Selfishness—see also Self-centeredness

Selfishness, a little frank, better than being a "martyr"
•MC 167 (see also FL 73-76, 82; SL 121-124) ❖ MC IV 8:3 (see also FL 3:33-37, 45; SL 26:2-5)

Selfishness, human Need-love is not mere
•FL 12-13 ❖ FL 1:6

Selfishness of those who are determined to get what they want, however troublesome it may be to others, described by Screwtape ("All-I-want" state of mind)
•SL 77-79 ❖ SL 17:1, 2

Selfishness vs. self-centeredness: "Either condition will destroy the soul in the end"
•SJ 143-144 ❖ SJ 9:19

Self-justification—see also Excuses; Excusing

Self-justification often a part of what we call "feeling hurt"
•LAL 56-57 ❖ LAL 21/5/56

Self-knowledge—see also Introspection; Self-examination

Self-knowledge: "A moderately bad man knows he is not very good; a thoroughly bad man thinks he is all right"*
•MC 87 (see also GID 56-57; LAL 95; PP 55, top; PP 67)
❖ MC III 4:10 (see also GID I 4:38; LAL 9 Jan 61; PP 4:prelim. quote; 4:15)

Self-knowledge: According to Alexander Whyte, the true Christian's nostril is to be continually attentive to the inner cesspool
•LM 97-98 ❖ LM 18:13

Self-knowledge: "As long as one knows one is proud one is safe from the worst form of pride"
•L 241 (see also LAL 96; PP 55)
❖ L 15 May 52 (see also LAL 24 Feb 61; PP quote at beginning of chapter 4)

Self-knowledge: As we begin to "put on Christ" we begin to notice our sinfulness*
•MC 164 ❖ MC IV 7:12

Self-knowledge: At the least we know enough of the spiritual to know that we have fallen short of it
•WG 65 ❖ WG 4:17

Self-knowledge: Attempting obedience brings to light not only snarling resentments and nagging lusts but also "radiant things, delights and inspirations"*
•CR 169 ❖ CR 14:21

Self-knowledge: "Each can reflect that his own heart is the specimen of that wickedness best known to him"*
•RP 136 (see also SL xiii)
❖ RP 12:16 (see also SL P:24)

Self-knowledge enables us to understand the "wrath" of God (as soon as we perceive our badness, it appears inevitable)*
•PP 58 ❖ PP 4:5, 6

Self-knowledge gained by Confession: "...most of us have never really faced the facts about ourselves until we uttered them aloud in plain words..."
•L 250 ❖ L 6-7 Apr 53

Self-knowledge: "...how many people in the whole world believe themselves to be snobs, prigs, bores, bullies or talebearers?"
•LAL 58-59 ❖ LAL 5/7/56

Self-knowledge: "I come back to St. John: 'If our heart condemn us, God is greater than our heart.' And equally, when our heart flatter us..."
•LM 34 ❖ LM 6:14

Self-knowledge: I have been trying to make the reader believe that we are, at present, creatures whose character is a horror to God
•PP 67 ❖ PP 4:15

Self-knowledge, I pray for just so much, as I can bear and use at the moment; the little daily dose
•LM 34 ❖ LM 6:14

Self-knowledge: "...if, on consideration, one can find no faults on one's own side, then cry for mercy: for this *must* be a most dangerous delusion..."*
•LAL 95 ❖ LAL 9 Jan 61

Self-knowledge important to the Christian life*
•GID 123-124 ❖ GID I 14:8-10

Self-knowledge: In attempting obedience "you find that what you called yourself is only a thin film on the surface of an unsounded and dangerous sea"*
•CR 169 ❖ CR 14:21

Self-knowledge: Introspection seldom reveals our most obvious defects; humans tend toward a horror and neglect of the obvious*
•SL 16 (*see also* GID 121-124, 153)
❖ SL 3:2 (*see also* GID I 14:4-10; 18:6, 7)

Self-knowledge is useful at least "to practice the absence of God, to become increasingly aware of our unawareness"*
•FL 192 ❖ FL 6:47

Self-knowledge: It is important to realize that there is some really fatal flaw in *you* which causes others to despair
•GID 123, 153 (*see also* FL 186)
❖ GID I 14:7, 8; 18:6, 7 (*see also* FL 6:37)

Self-knowledge: It is when we notice the dirt that God is most present in us; a realization of our badness is the very sign of God's presence
•L 199 ❖ L 20 Jan 42

Self-knowledge: Jesus Himself "plumbed the depths of that worst suffering which comes to evil men who at last know their own evil"*
•RP 127 ❖ RP 12:7

Self-knowledge: "No man knows how bad he is till he has tried very hard to be good"
•MC 124 ❖ MC III 11:7

Self-knowledge: One of the first results of attempting obedience is to bring your picture of yourself down to something nearer life-size*
•CR 169 ❖ CR 14:21

Self-knowledge: Purification of the will leads to enlightenment of the intelligence*
•L 255 ❖ L 30 Jan 54

Self-knowledge: Screwtape mentions "the peculiar kind of clarity which Hell affords"*
•SL 13 ❖ SL 2:2

Self-knowledge: Screwtape observes that humans shall gain an utter knowledge of their sinfulness and shall embrace the pain of it*
•SL 148 (*see also* PP 61; Pains)
❖ SL 31:5 (*see also* PP 4:9; Pains)

Self-knowledge: Screwtape relates his belief that what the new Christian says, even on his knees, about his own sinfulness is only parrot talk*
•SL 14 ❖ SL 2:4

Self-knowledge: "Shall we, perhaps, in Purgatory, see our own faces and hear our own voices as they really were?"*
•RP 8 ❖ RP 1:13

Self-knowledge: Sinfulness of ourselves is never fully known to us
•GID 121-123, 153; PP 59-60 (*see also* L 183; MC 87; SL 16)
❖ GID I 14:4-8; 18:6, 7; PP 4:7 (*see also* L 16 Apr 40; MC III 4:10; SL 3:2)

Self-knowledge: Someday we shall hear God's infallible judgment on us, and perhaps we will realise that in some dim fashion we could have known it all along
•WLN 112-113 ❖ WLN 7:36, 37

Self-knowledge: "The attempt to discover by introspective analysis our own spiritual condition...may be the quickest road to presumption or despair"
•WG 66 ❖ WG 4:18

Self-knowledge: "...the thing we know already...when said by *someone else* becomes suddenly operative"*

•L 236 (*see also* L 195)

❖ L 26 Dec 51 (*see also* L 19 Nov 41)

Self-knowledge: "To know that one is dreaming is to be no longer perfectly asleep" (re: a realization of our incomplete awareness of God)

•FL 192 ❖ FL 6:47

Self-knowledge, total: Have we any reason to suppose that it would, if it were given us, be for our good?

•LM 34 ❖ LM 6:15

Self-knowledge: "Unless Christianity is wholly false, the perception of ourselves which we have in moments of shame must be the only true one..."

•PP 57 ❖ PP 4:3

Self-knowledge: We are far more subtle than the Psalmists in disguising our ill will from others and from ourselves*

•RP 23 ❖ RP 3:8

Self-knowledge: We are slowest to recognise the faults of our own circle of friends*

•FL 122 ❖ FL 4:55

Self-knowledge: We must be aware of our own sinfulness—but a continual poring over the "sink" might breed its own perverse pride*

•LM 98-99 ❖ LM 18:13-15

Self-knowledge: When a man is getting better, he understands more clearly the evil left in him*

•MC 87 (*see also* GID 56-57; PP 55, top; PP 67) ❖ MC III 4:10 (*see also* GID I 4:38; PP 4: prelim. quote; 4:15)

Selflessness—*see also* Self-forgetfulness; Self-sacrifice; Unselfishness

Selflessness as the root principle behind public and domestic courtesy ("'that no one give any kind of preference to himself'")*

•FL 67 ❖ FL 3:24

Selflessness, Eros is driven to make promises which show a transitory

•FL 158-159 ❖ FL 5:43, 44

Selflessness: "For most of us the true rivalry lies between the self and the human Other, not yet between the human Other and God"*

•FL 165 (*see also* LAL 61)

❖ FL 6:4 (*see also* LAL 18/8/56)

Self-loathing—*see* Self-contempt; Self-hatred

Self-love, God wants to kill our animal, but then to restore to us a new kind of self-love—a charity and gratitude for all selves, including our own

•SL 64-65 (*see also* GID 193-195; L 242-243) ❖ SL 14:4 (*see also* GID II ch. 2; L 20 Jun 52)

Self-love: Love of the creature is dangerous ("Not bad you see, just very very small") while *contemptus mundi* is also dangerous*

•L 183 ❖ L 16 Apr 40

Self-love not right up to a certain point and wrong beyond that point; there are two kinds, one totally wrong and one totally right

•GID 193-195 (*see also* SL 63-66)

❖ GID II ch. 2 (*see also* SL 14:3-5)

Self-love of Eve in *Paradise Lost*: If she had been fallen she would have passed through the stage of finding the real, external lover a second best

•CR 39-40 ❖ CR 3:7

Self-love, the very, which a Christian has to reject is a specimen of how he ought to feel to all selves

•GID 194 ❖ GID II 2:3

Self-love: When we have learned to love our neighbor as ourself, we may then be able to love ourself as our neighbor—with charity instead of partiality

•GID 194; SL 65 ❖ GID II 2:3; SL 14:4

Self-pity for imaginary distresses, according to Screwtape, vanishes upon five minutes of genuine toothache; the "romance" of pain is unmasked as nonsense

•SL 58 ❖ SL 13:3

Self-pity, Lewis mentions his resolution (during his early years at Oxford) to forgo

•SJ 201 ❖ SJ 13:7

Self-pity may cause the lives of some people (who are capable of real sacrifice) to be a misery to themselves and others

•SJ 143-144 ❖ SJ 9:19

Self-pity: We can recognize in ourselves the Psalmists' tendency to chew over and over the cud of some injury...*
•RP 23-24 ❖ RP 3:8

Self-preference must not only be hated, but simply killed
•GID 193-194 (*see also* SL 64-65*)
❖ GID II 2:3 (*see also* SL 14:4*)

Self-preservation—*consider also* Self-reservation

Self-preservation, having once tasted life even pessimists are subject to the impulse of
•SJ 116 ❖ SJ 7:21

Self-preservation is awakened into fierce activity when our life is threatened (re: Lewis's attitude toward dying vs. being killed)
•LAL 114 ❖ LAL 19 Mar 63

Self-preservation not really what life is all about; all Jesus' followers must take up the cross
•CR 155 (*see also* FL 168, 170)
❖ CR 13:6 (*see also* FL 6:10, 14)

Self-protection—*see also* Safety; Self-concern; Self-reservation

Self-protection in love: "Christ did not teach and suffer that we might become...more careful of our own happiness"*
•FL 167-170, esp. 170 (*see also* CR 155)
❖ FL 6:8-14, esp. 6:14 (*see also* CR 13:6)

Self-protection in love: "I believe that the most lawless and inordinate loves are less contrary to God's will than...self-protective lovelessness"
•FL 169-170 ❖ FL 6:14

Self-regard—*see* Self-concern

Self-rejection will also be a self-finding, and to die is to live
•GID 131 (*see also* MC 141, 180, 188-190; SL 59; WG 67, 117-118)
❖ GID I 16:3 (*see also* MC IV 2:3; 10:10; 11:11-15; SL 13:4; WG 4:22; 7:16, 17)

Self-renunciation—*see* Asceticism; Self-denial

Self-reservation—*see also* Safety; *consider also* Cost; Independence

Self-reservation: A "moderated" religion is as good as no religion at all (re: thinking that "religion is all very well up to a point")*
•SL 43 ❖ SL 9:3

Self-reservation: Christian apologist is likely to encounter the belief that a certain amount of "religion" is desirable but one mustn't carry it too far*
•GID 101 ❖ GID I 10:48

Self-reservation: Christ's teaching "was never meant to confirm my congenital preference for safe investments and limited liabilities"
•FL 168 (*see also* CR 155; SJ 203; SL 133)
❖ FL 6:10 (*see also* CR 13:6; SJ 13:9; SL 28:2)

Self-reservation: Fear of duty as a reason for avoiding truth
•GID 110-111 (*see also* WG 3:4*)
❖ GID I 12:6-8 (*see also* WG 3:4*)

Self-reservation: If you want to make sure of keeping your heart intact, you must give it to no one, not even an animal*
•FL 167-170, esp. 169
❖ FL 6:8-14, esp. 6:13

Self-reservation, only God can help us with the temptation of
•WG 132 (*see also* CR 43*)
❖ WG 9:13 (*see also* CR 3:12*)

Self-reservation: Our craving for "limited liabilities"
•WG 126-132 (*see also* LM 114*)
❖ WG ch. 9 (*see also* LM 21:8*)

Self-reservation: "The one principle of Hell is—'I am my own'" (quote from G. MacDonald)*
•SJ 212 ❖ SJ 14 prelim. quote

Self-reservation: The secret wish that our faith should *not* be very strong may be one of the causes of our weak faith
•CR 43 ❖ CR 3:12

Self-reservation: There is no area in our lives on which God has no claim*
•WG 130 (*see also* MC 167*)
❖ WG 9:9 (*see also* MC IV 8:4*)

Self-reservation: "There is no safe investment. To love at all is to be vulnerable..."*
•FL 169 ❖ FL 6:13

Self-reservation: To me the materialist

universe had the enormous attraction that it offered you limited liabilities; death ended all*
- •SJ 171 (*see also* GO 33; SJ 228)
- ❖ SJ 11:8 (*see also* GO 2:22; SJ 14:22)

Self-reservation: We fear lest God's will should become too unmistakable if we prayed longer*
- •WG 127-128 (*see also* CR 43*; LM 114; SL 22-23*, 54-55) ❖ WG 9:5 (*see also* CR 3:12*; LM 21:8; SL 4:4*; 12:3)

Self-reservation: We fear the killing of our natural self by Christ; but He will replace it with the kind of self He has*
- •MC 154, 164, 167 (*see also* MC 174*)
- ❖ MC IV 5:2; 7:11; 8:4 (*see also* MC IV 9:10*)

Self-reservation: "We shrink from too naked a contact [in prayer], because we are afraid of the divine demands upon us which it might make too audible"*
- •LM 114 (*see also* CR 43; LM 75; M 94; SL 22-23*, 54-55; WG 127-128)
- ❖ LM 21:8 (*see also* CR 3:12; LM 14:12; M 11:19; SL 4:4*; 12:3; WG 9:5)

Self-reservation: What I wanted was some area in my soul of which I could say to all other beings, "This is my business and mine only"*
- •SJ 172 (*see also* SJ 228, 237)
- ❖ SJ 11:8 (*see also* SJ 14:22; 15:8)

Self-reservation: "When we try to keep within us an area that is our own, we try to keep an area of death"*
- •WG 130-131 ❖ WG 9:10

Self-righteous utterances of the Psalmists grew out of their "Dark Night of the Flesh" which included ostracism, ineffectiveness, and humiliation
- •CR 125-128 ❖ CR 10:30-40

Self-righteousness—*consider also* Hypocrisy; Piety; Pride; Snobbery

Self-righteousness: A cold, self-righteous prig may be nearer to hell than a prostitute
- •MC 94-95 (*see also* L 175; LAL 111)
- ❖ MC III 5:14 (*see also* L 17 Jan 40; LAL 26 Nov 62)

Self-righteousness: A Pharisee "makes better sport in Hell than a mere com-

mon tyrant or debauchee" (—Screwtape)*
- •SL 105-106 ❖ SL 23:1

Self-righteousness: "All virtues are less formidable to us once the man is aware that he has them, but this is specially true of humility" (—Screwtape)*
- •SL 62-63 ❖ SL 14:2

Self-righteousness and anxiety as the results of legalism
- •RP 57-58 ❖ RP 6:6, 7

Self-righteousness as the danger to which Christians are exposed as they learn to value the Law of God over the current ways of thinking*
- •RP 64-65 (*see also* SL 47-48*, 110-113*)
- ❖ RP 6:14 (*see also* SL 10:4*; 24:1-5*)

Self-righteousness: "How difficult it is to avoid having a special standard for oneself!"*
- •LAL 58 ❖ LAL 5/7/56

Self-righteousness: I can hardly imagine a more deadly spiritual condition than that of the man who can read the Sermon on the Mount with tranquil pleasure*
- •GID 182 (*see also* GID 191-192*)
- ❖ GID I 22:13 (*see also* GID II 1:4*)

Self-righteousness, in one sense we might say that Jewish confidence in the face of judgement is a by-product of Jewish, but this is far too summary (re: Judgement in the Psalms)
- •CR 125 ❖ CR 10:30

Self-righteousness in the Psalms: "...we must not be Pharisaical even to the Pharisees"
- •RP 67 ❖ RP 7:2

Self-righteousness in the Psalms more complete than anything in the classics
- •CR 116 ❖ CR 10:4

Self-righteousness in the Psalms: "Our Lord...becomes the speaker in these passages"; He was in fact holy and innocent
- •RP 135 ❖ RP 12:15

Self-righteousness, it is not, but mere prudence to avoid contact with wicked people when we can

•RP 74 (see also RP 71-72; SL 45-48*)
❖ RP 7:15, 16 (see also RP 7:10; SL ch. 10*)
Self-righteousness of asking God to take sides in a war, e.g., "Prosper Oh Lord, our righteous cause"
•L 168 (see also FL 47-48; L 183; WG 24) ❖ L 10 Sep 39 (see also FL 2:41, 42; L 16 Apr 40; WG 2:6)
Self-righteousness ("Pharisaism"): "I think that even in the Psalms this evil is already at work"
•RP 66-67 (see also RP 64-65)
❖ RP 7:1, 2 (see also RP 6:14)
Self-righteousness: We may at times be "in the right," but this must be distinguished from being "righteous," which none of us ever are (re: Psalmists)
•RP 17-18 (see also L 183)
❖ RP 2:13 (see also L 16 Apr 40)
Self-righteousness: Whenever we find our religious life is making us feel that we are good—or better than others—we may be sure we are being acted on by the devil
•MC 111 ❖ MC III 8:7
Self-sacrifice—see also Renunciation; Self-denial; Self-forgetfulness
Self-sacrifice and discomfort in this life not limited to Christians
•GID 53 ❖ GID I 4:24, 25 (Ques. 8)
Self-sacrifice, eternal dance of, "makes heaven drowsy with the harmony"; in self-giving we touch a rhythm not only of all creation but of all being
•PP 152-153 ❖ PP 10:10, 11
Self-sacrifice: People who "live for others" may end up making the "others" miserable*
•FL 73-76, 82-83; MC 167 (see also L 198-199; SL 121, 123) ❖ FL 3:33-37, 45; MC IV 7:3 (see also L undated letter just before 20 Jan 42; SL 26:2, 5)
Self-satisfaction: A man may console himself for his vices by a conviction that "his heart's in the right place" and "he wouldn't hurt a fly"*
•PP 56 ❖ PP 4:2
Self-satisfaction: "A moderately bad man knows he is not very good; a thor-

oughly bad man thinks he is all right"*
•MC 87 (see also GID 56-57; PP 55, top; PP 67) ❖ MC III 4:10 (see also GID I 4:38; PP 4: prelim. quote; PP 4:15)
Self-satisfaction: A person may believe that all his niceness is his own doing, and not feel the need for any better kind of goodness
•MC 180-181 ❖ MC IV 10:11-13
Self-satisfaction: "If, on consideration, one can find no faults on one's own side, then cry for mercy: for this must be a most dangerous delusion..."*
•LAL 95 (see also MC 87; PP 55, top; 67) ❖ LAL 9 Jan 61 (see also MC III 4:10; PP 4 prelim. quote; 4:15)
Self-satisfaction may be brought on by "riches" such as health, intelligence, popularity, etc. as well as monetary wealth
•MC 180-181 (see also Riches)
❖ MC IV 10:11, 12 (see also Riches)
Self-satisfaction: "One must never be either content with, or impatient with, oneself"
•LAL 29 ❖ LAL Mar 31st 54
Self-satisfaction: "There can be no surer proof of a confirmed pride than a belief that one is sufficiently humble" (quote from Law)*
•LAL 96; PP 55, top (see also CR 14; MC 114; SL 62-63)
❖ LAL 24 Feb 61; PP 4 prelim. quote (see also CR 2:4; MC III 8:14; SL 14:2)
Self-satisfaction: "...there remains some lingering idea of our own, our very own, attractiveness"—that God loves us because we are lovable*
•FL 180 ❖ FL 6:27
Self-satisfaction: "To ask that God's love should be content with us as we are is to ask that God should cease to be God"*
•PP 48 ❖ PP 3:15
Self-satisfaction vs. true repentance
•WG 122-123 ❖ WG 8:3
Self-satisfaction: When Christ has enabled us to overcome one or two obvious sins, we tend to feel that we are now good enough; this is a fatal mis-

take
•MC 172-173 ❖ MC IV 9:6

Self-sufficiency, if pain shatters a creature's false, it teaches him the kind he ought to have—the strength which God confers
•PP 102 ❖ PP 6:14

Self-sufficiency, pain shatters the illusion of
•PP 95-98 (*see also* LAL 49*)
❖ PP 6:8, 9 (*see also* LAL 16/12/55*)

Self-sufficiency the possible result of those vices that lead to worldly success (while the vices of the feckless and dissipated are not likely to so deceive)
•PP 98 ❖ PP 6:9

Self-surrender—*see also* Surrender

Self-surrender as "a grievous pain" and "a kind of death"
•PP 91 ❖ PP 6:3

Self-surrender as the proper good of a creature, and that which will make it happy
•PP 90 (*see also* PP 52; WG 118-119)
❖ PP 6:3 (*see also* PP 3:18; WG 7:18)

Self-surrender became a painful effort after the Fall, since man's inclination had become self-ward*
•PP 83 ❖ PP 5:10

Self-surrender described as "movement full speed astern"
•MC 59; PP 101 ❖ MC II 4:7; PP 6:13

Self-surrender: God demands not so much of our time and attention, but ourselves
•WG 130 (*see also* MC 167)
❖ WG 9:9 (*see also* MC IV 8:4)

Self-surrender of unfallen man meant no struggle but only a delicious overcoming of an infinitesimal self-adherence which delighted to be overcome
•PP 81 (*see also* PP 78)
❖ PP 5:9 (*see also* PP 5:6)

Self-surrender: One of the operations of pain is to enable the full acting out of the self's surrender to God
•PP 98-101 ❖ PP 6:10-13

Self-surrender, the happiness of a creature lies in; no one can make that surrender but himself, and he may refuse

(re: doctrine of hell)
•PP 118 ❖ PP 8:1

Self-surrender, the problem is how to recover; even in Paradise a minimal self-adherence had to be overcome
•PP 91 ❖ PP 6:3

Self-surrender to God demands pain; is never pleasant to fallen creatures
•PP 99-101 ❖ PP 6:11-13

Self-surrender: To hand over your whole self is almost impossible—yet easier than remaining "ourselves" and still being "good"
•MC 168 ❖ MC IV 8:7

Self-surrender will not even be attempted as long as all seems well; some pain may be necessary to awaken us to evil
•PP 92-98, 106-107 ❖ PP 6:5-9, 17

Self-uniqueness—*see* Personality

Self-will and sinfulness, why the cure for our, must be a painful process
•PP 89-117 ❖ PP ch. 6, 7

Self-will, death of, involves the necessity of dying daily; "...however often we think we have broken the rebellious self we shall still find it alive"
•PP 92 ❖ PP 6:3

Self-worship as the best religion in which to find "happiness"—while it lasts
•GID 58 ❖ GID I 4:43, 44 (Ques. 11)

Self-worship, the mere existence of a self includes the danger of; this is the "weak spot" in the very nature of creation
•PP 81 (*see also* PP 75)
❖ PP 5:9 (*see also* PP 5:5)

Selves, our real, are all waiting for us in Christ
•MC 188-190 (*see also* Personality)
❖ MC IV 11:11-15 (*see also* Personality)

Sensation, physical, of "Joy": "...a fluttering sensation in the diaphragm..."
•SJ 168, 219 (*see also* CR 139-140; WG 57-59) ❖ SJ 11:5; 14:10, 11 (*see also* CR 11:22; WG 4:5-8)

Sensations accompanying my emotions, by themselves, are of very mediocre interest to me—their value is in what they are about
•CR 139-140 (*see also* SJ 168, 218-220,

238; WG 57-59) ❖ CR 11:22 (*see also* SJ 11:5; 14:10-12; 15:10; WG 4:5-7)

Sensations, all our earthly, are to be flooded with new meaning (at the Resurrection)
- •WG 68-73, esp. 73 (*see also* WG 18)
- ❖ WG 4:23-30, esp. 4:30 (*see also* WG 1:14)

Sensations associated with "Joy": "I knew now that they were merely the mental track left by the passage of Joy...the wave's imprint on the sand"
- •SJ 219 ❖ SJ 14:11

Sensations of grief and fear are the same—the same fluttering in the stomach, the same restlessness
- •GO 1 (*see also* GO 38-39)
- ❖ GO 1:1 (*see also* GO 2:32)

Sensations, physical, of both joy and anguish are exactly the same; they are a "transposition" of our emotional life
- •WG 57-59, 63 ❖ WG 4:5-7, 13

Senses, but for our body all that we receive through the, would go unpraised; our senses are important to our realization of God's glory
- •LM 17-18 (*see also* LAL 110-111)
- ❖ LM 3:9 (*see also* LAL 26 Nov 62)

Senses, Lewis's awakening of, in adolescence: "The mere smells were enough to make a man tipsy—cut grass, dew-dabbled mosses, sweet pea, autumn woods..."
- •SJ 118 ❖ SJ 8:1

Senses listed as part of "the old field" of Nature which is not to be unmade, but remade
- •M 149 (*see also* M 163)
- ❖ M 16:12 (*see also* M 16:32)

Senses, we are more interested in the resurrection of the, than the resurrection of the body (as matter)
- •LM 121 ❖ LM 22:13

"Sensitive" people, I loathe, who are easily hurt; they are a social pest. Vanity is usually the real trouble
- •LAL 59 ❖ LAL 3/8/56

"Sensitiveness" as "the most powerful engine of domestic tyranny...we should be merciless to its first appearance in ourselves"
- •RP 14 ❖ RP 2:9

"Sensitivity" (as in cultural sensitivity) is a potentiality, therefore neutral; it can be no more an end to Christians than "experience"
- •CR 24 ❖ CR 2:38

Sensuality really arises more from the imagination than from the appetites
- •LAL 111 (*see also* GID 217; LM 17)
- ❖ LAL 26 Nov 62 (*see also* GID II 7:3; LM 3:9)

Sentimental feeling, Lewis describes a, even toward hated things when leaving them for the last time
- •SJ 131 ❖ SJ 8:19

Sentimentalism, Lewis's dislike of
- •SJ 66, 133, 173, 190 (*see also* SJ 4*, 33*, 158-159*) ❖ SJ 4:13; 9:2, 3; 11:10; 12:12 (*see also* SJ 1:1*; 2:13*; 10:11*)

Sentimentalism, my lifelong fear of, ought to have qualified me to become a vigorous "debunker"
- •SJ 173 ❖ SJ 11:10

"Sentimentality," Christians must reject the covert attempt to drive mercy out of the world by calling it such names as "Humanitarianism" and
- •PP 56 ❖ PP 4:2

Separation: All lovers are eventually separated, even if both die at exactly the same moment
- •GO 58-59, 63-64 ❖ GO 3:33, 40

Separation from God—*consider also* Abandonment

Separation from God causes death; unity with Him inevitably results in life
- •MC 153 (*see also* MC 157, 186)
- ❖ MC IV 4:8 (*see also* MC IV 5:8; 11:7)

Separation from God: Creatures, by being created, are in one sense separated from the Creator; Jesus experienced this aspect of humanity as well
- •LM 44 ❖ LM 8:12

Separation from God is horror and union with Him is bliss; thus Heaven and Hell come in
- •SJ 232 (*see also* GID 47)
- ❖ SJ 15:4 (*see also* GID I 3:17)

Separation from God: Prosperity and ad-

versity both mentioned by Screwtape as useful in separating men from God
•SL 132 (*consider also* Obstacles to Christian perseverance)
❖ SL 28:1 (*consider also* Obstacles to Christian perseverance)

Separation from God: The only importance of the size of a sin is the degree to which it separates a man from God (—Screwtape)
•SL 56 (*see also* SL 87-88)
❖ SL 12:5 (*see also* SL 19:3)

Separation of Church and State—*see also* Government; Politics

Separation of Church and State: Theocracy has been abolished because priests are wicked men like the rest of us*
•WG 114 ❖ WG 7:12

Separation of Church and State: Christianity an enemy of totalitarian government; gives the individual a standing ground against the State*
•GID 118 (*see also* MC 73)
❖ GID I 13:9 (*see also* MC III 1:9)

Separation of Church and State: "For every Government consists of mere men and...if it adds to its commands 'Thus saith the Lord,' it lies..."*
•GID 315 ❖ GID III 8:16

Separation of Church and State: "Government is at its best a necessary evil. Let's keep it in its place"*
•L 281 ❖ L 1 Feb 58

Separation of Church and State: "I detest every kind of religious compulsion"*
•GID 61 ❖ GID I 4:57, 58 (Ques. 15)

Separation of Church and State: "If Mr. Childe can find any passage in my works which favours religious or antireligious compulsion I will give..."*
•GID 329 ❖ GID IV Letter 4

Separation of Church and State: Some Christians believe that no one can be trusted with more than a minimum of power over others*
•GID 197-198 ❖ GID II 3:3-5

Separation of Church and State: "We are not such busybodies that we want to improve all our neighbors by force..."*

•GID 299 ❖ GID III 4:26

Separation of Church and State: When the "neurosis" of religion becomes inconvenient to government, what is to hinder government from proceeding to "cure" it?*
•GID 293, 313, 340
❖ GID III 4:12; 8:9; IV Letter 12

Separation of Church and State: "Who the deuce are our rulers to enforce their opinions about sin on us?" (re: homosexuality)*
•L 281 ❖ L 1 Feb 58

Seriousness ("solemnity"), I believe there is too much, in dealing with sacred matters (re: use of humour in Christian writing)
•GID 259 ❖ GID II 15:8

Sermon and the Lunch, The (chapter title)
•GID 282-286 ❖ GID III ch. 3

Sermon, last, which Lewis ever delivered: "A Slip of the Tongue"*
•WG 126-132 (see Introduction to book)
❖ WG ch. 9 (see Introduction to book)

Sermon on the Mount not something you can read with tranquil pleasure
•GID 182 (*see also* GID 191-192*)
❖ GID I 22:13 (*see also* GID II 1:4*)

Sermons—*see also* Preaching

Sermons: An uncritical attitude, a laying open of the mind in humble receptivity to any nourishment available, decried by Screwtape
•SL 73 ❖ SL 16:2

Servant is not greater, and must not be more high-minded, than the master (re: making requests of God, as Jesus did)
•LM 36 (*see also* LM 23, 35, 43)
❖ LM 7:3 (*see also* LM 4:20; 7:1; 8:9)

Service—*consider also* Duty(ies); Vocation

Service to God: "...a sacred calling is not limited to ecclesiastical functions. The man who is weeding a field of turnips is also serving God"
•GID 264 ❖ GID II 16:38

Service to God: "A vocation is a terrible thing. To be called out of nature into the supernatural life is at first...a costly

honour"*
•RP 131 ❖ RP 12:10

Service to God, activities we like may be as much a part of our, as our hardest duties
•WG 130 ❖ WG 9:9

Service to God was the keenest pleasure of Paradisal man; in following God's will, he also gratified his own desire
•PP 98 ❖ PP 6:10

Service to God: We cannot give God anything that is not His already
•MC 125 (see also SL 96-99)
❖ MC III 11:9 (see also SL 21:2-6)

Service to God: We must not fret about doing God those supposed services which He in fact does not allow us to do
•LAL 72 (see also LAL 53)
❖ LAL 22/2/58 (see also LAL 19/3/56)

Services, Church—see Church services

Seventh-day Adventists mentioned: "I fear it is very mixed up with attempts to interpret the Book of Daniel..."
•LAL 108 ❖ LAL 2 Oct 62

Seventh-day Adventists mentioned: "If they have so much charity there must be something very right about them..."
•LAL 109 ❖ LAL 26 Oct 62

Sex, analogy of boy wondering whether, involves eating chocolates to our wondering whether Heaven will be like things we know on earth
•M 160 (see also WG 67-69*)
❖ M 16:28 (see also WG 4:22-24*)

Sex and alcohol, without the attraction of, I fancy even adults would not find an evening party very endurable
•SJ 47 ❖ SJ 3:5

Sex: Finding the subject humorous a symptom of our estrangement, as spirits, from Nature and as animals, from Spirit; this estrangement is to be healed
•M 160 ❖ M 16:29

Sex: If Christianity is true, the mere fact of sexual intercourse sets up a human relationship which has transcendental repercussions

•L 184; SL 82-83 ❖ L 18 Apr 40; SL 18:6

Sex in its present state is a thing to be ashamed of, like gluttony
•MC 91-92 (see also MC 96-97)
❖ MC III 5:8 (see also MC III 6:4)

Sex in itself cannot be moral or immoral, but the sexual behaviour of human beings can
•LM 14 ❖ LM 3:2

Sex, jokes about, embody an attitude which endangers the Christian life far less than reverential gravity
•FL 140 ❖ FL 5:15

Sex, "Joy" is not a substitute for; sex may very often be a substitute for "Joy" ("Joy" meaning our longing—itself highly desirable—for the transtemporal)
•SJ 170 (see also GO 6; SJ 203-204; Joy)
❖ SJ 11:6 (see also GO 1:12; SJ 13:10; Joy)

Sex no longer hushed up, yet it is still in a mess
•MC 91 (see also GID 320)
❖ MC III 5:7 (see also GID III 9:17)

Sex not the only element of our subconscious; psychologists have made the error of underestimating the depth and variety of its contents*
•LM 79 ❖ LM 15:8

Sex: One of the ends for which it was created was to symbolize to us the hidden things of God
•GID 238 ❖ GID II 11:10

Sex or pleasure thought to be bad in themselves by some Christians; they are wrong
•MC 91, 92 (see also SL 69)
❖ MC III 5:7, 10 (see also SL 15:3)

Sex, Pagan sacramental element in, as one of the more serious elements of the sexual act ("...the marriage of Sky-Father and Earth-Mother")
•FL 139-140, 145-147 ❖ FL 5:13, 23-25

Sex: Rough play harmless and wholesome on one condition (that it is understood to be a charade)
•FL 145-147 ❖ FL 5:22-25

Sex, Screwtape decries: "The whole thing ...turns out to be simply one more device for dragging in Love"

•SL 82 ❖ SL 18:5

Sex, since my marriage I can never again
believe that religion is a substitute for
•GO 6 (*see also* SJ 170, 203-204*)
❖ GO 1:12 (*see also* SJ 11:6; 13:10*)

Sex ("the flesh"), finding humor as well
as high poetry in: "The highest does
not stand without the lowest"
•FL 144 ❖ FL 5:20

Sex, the "incalculable momentousness" of
being a parent and ancestor as one of
the serious elements in
•FL 140 ❖ FL 5:13

Sex: "...the moderns have achieved the
feat, which I should have thought impossible, of making the whole subject
a bore"
•LM 15 ❖ LM 3:2

Sex, we are half-hearted creatures fooling
about with, and drink and ambition
when infinite joy is offered us
•WG 3-4 ❖ WG 1:1

Sex: What St. Paul had to say on the hindrance of marriage related not to sex
but to the multiple distractions of domesticity
•FL 137-138 ❖ FL 5:10

Sex without Eros (romantic love) not nec-
essarily impure; and the presence of
Eros does not necessarily sanctify it
•FL 132-133 ❖ FL 5:2

Sex, worship of, as a serious "religion" of
modern times
•GID 253 ❖ GID II 14:11

Sex, worship of, mentioned by Screwtape
as useful to his purposes
•SL 33 ❖ SL 7:1

Sexism: "There is, hidden or flaunted, a
sword between the sexes till an entire
marriage reconciles them"*
•GO 57-58 ❖ GO 3:32

Sexual act in danger of being taken too
seriously; "We have reached the stage
at which nothing is more needed than
a roar of old-fashioned laughter"
•FL 138-144, esp. 138-139
❖ FL 5:11-21, esp. 5:11, 12

Sexual act is the body's share in marriage,
which is the mystical image of the
union between God and Man

•FL 139 ❖ FL 5:13

Sexual act may or may not be attended
with pleasure; in the same way we
may not always *sense* the Holy Spirit's
presence, which begets Christ in us
•LAL 38-39 ❖ LAL 20/2/55

Sexual act, when lawful, can, like all other
natural acts, be done to the glory of
God, and will then be holy
•LM 15 ❖ LM 3:2

Sexual appetite, like our other appetites,
grows by indulgence
•MC 90 ❖ MC III 5:5

Sexual corruption did not cause the fall of
man, but the book of Genesis suggests
that the fall of man caused sexual corruption
•MC 53 ❖ MC II 3:6

Sexual desire wants *it*, the thing in itself;
Eros wants the Beloved
•FL 134 ❖ FL 5:4

Sexual element within Eros (romantic
love) labelled "Venus"
•FL 131-132 ❖ FL 5:1

Sexual experience can occur without Eros,
or "being in love"
•FL 131-132 ❖ FL 5:1, 2

Sexual impulse ("Venus") may be less to
blame in the loss of many a virginity
than peer pressure ("the lure of the
caucus")
•WG 98 ❖ WG 6:7

Sexual impulses are being put in a position of preposterous privilege by society, possibly because this desire
seems to promise complete happiness
•GID 320-321 ❖ GID III 9:17-25

Sexual infatuation, Screwtape advises
causing humans to confuse, with
"love" so they'll excuse themselves
from guilt and consequences of improper marriages
•SL 84 ❖ SL 18:6

Sexual intercourse, Screwtape speaks on:
"...wherever a man lies with a
woman...a transcendental relation is
set up between them..."
•SL 83 (*see also* L 184)
❖ SL 18:6 (*see also* L 18 Apr 40)

Sexual life, the letter and spirit of Scrip-

ture forbid us to suppose that life in the New Creation will be a; something better will leave no room for it
•M 159-160 ❖ M 16:28

Sexual love—*see also* Eros

Sexual love as one of the glimpses we have of the future healing of Spirit and Nature
•M 159 ❖ M 16:27

Sexual love as one of the values implicit in both medieval romance and nineteenth-century fiction
•CR 16, 21-22 ❖ CR 2:13, 29, 31

Sexual love, humour a necessary ingredient in
•FL 138-144 ❖ FL 5:11-21

Sexual love, the body provides comic relief in; one if its functions in our lives is to play the part of buffoon
•FL 143-144 ❖ FL 5:19-21

Sexual love: "When natural things look most divine, the demoniac is just round the corner"
•FL 144-145 ❖ FL 5:21

Sexual morality—*see also* Chastity

Sexual Morality (chapter title)
•MC 88-95 ❖ MC III ch. 5

Sexual morality, adultery not an offense against, but against honesty, gratitude, and common humanity
•GID 320 (*see also* FL 132-133; Adultery) ❖ GID III 9:20 (*see also* FL 5:2; Adultery)

Sexual morality, discussion of
•MC 88-95 ❖ MC III ch. 5

Sexual morality: Distinction between sin and duty does not turn on "fine feelings" but on honesty, justice, charity, and obedience
•FL 133 ❖ FL 5:2

Sexual morality: "...we grow up surrounded by propaganda in favour of unchastity"
•MC 92 ❖ MC III 5:8, 10

Sexual motives replacing the early innocent desire for the beloved as an example of how "the bloom of innocence" is gradually rubbed off every activity
•PP 76 ❖ PP 5:5

Sexual perversion: Pervert sees normal love as a milk and water substitute for the ghastly world of impossible fantasies which have become for him "real"*
•CR 40 ❖ CR 3:7

Sexual perversion: "Plato was right after all. Eros, turned upside down, blackened, distorted, and filthy, still bore the traces of his divinity" (re: pederasty at Wyvern College
•SJ 109-110 ❖ SJ 7:12

Sexual perversion: Sadism and Masochism mentioned with regard to Man's recognition of pain as evil
•PP 92-93, 94 ❖ PP 6:5, 6

Sexual pleasure thought by some (including George Orwell and Lucretius) to actually be impaired by love
•FL 134-135 ❖ FL 5:4, 5

Sexual pleasure vs. "Joy": "You might as well offer a mutton chop to a man who is dying of thirst as offer sexual pleasure to the desire I am speaking of"
•SJ 170 (*see also* GO 6-7; SJ 203-204; Joy)
❖ SJ 11:6 (*see also* GO 1:12; SJ 13:10; Joy)

Sexual promiscuity, in the ruthless war of, women are at a double disadvantage
•GID 321-322 ❖ GID III 9:27

Sexual seduction: We should think it monstrous to dwell on the guilt of the party who yielded to temptation and ignore that of the party who tempted (re: the "seduction" to hatred to which every injury gives rise)
•CR 119 ❖ CR 10:9

Sexual temptation—*see also* Lust

Sexual temptation and marriage, Screwtape speaks on
•SL 80-84 ❖ SL ch. 18

Sexual temptation: "If the imagination were obedient, the appetites would give us very little trouble"
•GID 217; LAL 111; LM 17
❖ GID II 7:3; LAL 26 Nov 62; LM 3:9

Sexual temptation, Lewis mentions a "wholly successful" assault of, in his youth
•SJ 68-69 ❖ SJ 4:16-18

Sexual temptation: Screwtape advises Wormwood on the value of excess in food to attacks on human chastity
•SL 79 ❖ SL 17:4

Sexual temptation, Screwtape advises promoting the lie that an excess of physical exercise and consequent exhaustion is helpful in combatting
•SL 79 ❖ SL 17:4

Sexual temptation: Screwtape mentions "fornication and solitary vice"
•SL 94 ❖ SL 20:4

Sexual temptation: Screwtape mentions the devil's best weapon as being "the belief of ignorant humans that there is no hope of getting rid of us except by yielding"
•SL 90-91 ❖ SL 20:1

Sexual temptation: "The attack has a much better chance of success when the man's whole inner world is drab and cold and empty" (—Screwtape)
•SL 40-41 ❖ SL 9:2

Sexual temptation: Those who really wish for help will get it; but for many people even the wish is difficult
•MC 92 ❖ MC III 5:9

Sexual temptation: When the devil fails to tempt us in this area (his attacks don't last forever), he tries to persuade us that chastity is unhealthy*
•SL 90-91 ❖ SL 20:1

Sexual union cannot be isolated from the total union of marriage
•MC 95-96 ❖ MC III 6:2, 3

Sexuality is the transposition into a minor key of that creative joy which in God is unceasing and irresistible
•M 91 (see also M 112)
❖ M 11:15 (see also M 14:6, 7)

Sexuality: No need to suppose that the distinction between the sexes will disappear in Heaven
•M 160 ❖ M 16:28

Sexuality, Screwtape advises how to exploit a human's attitude toward, to advance the devil's cause
•SL 87-89 ❖ SL 19:3

Sexuality, Screwtape advises that if, fails to make a human unchaste it should be used for the promotion of a marriage useful to the devils' ends
•SL 90-94 (see also SL 88)
❖ SL ch. 20 (see also SL 19:3)

Sexuality: Screwtape mentions making the role of the eye more and more important, while making its demands more and more impossible
•SL 92 ❖ SL 20:3

Sexuality, what Eros does to our, ("Eros, without diminishing desire, makes abstinence easier")
•FL 138 ❖ FL 5:10

Shadows and light make up so much of the beauty of the world
•LAL 80 ❖ LAL Dec 25th 58

Shakespeare analogy: "God can no more be in competition with a creature than Shakespeare can be in competition with Viola"
•PP 49 ❖ PP 3:17

Shakespeare, creativity of, helps to illustrate God's creative freedom as "the freedom to create a consistent...thing with its own inimitable flavour" (re: the "realness" of Nature)
•M 65-66 ❖ M 9:4-6

Shakespeare: Every week a clever undergraduate or a dull American don discovers for the first time what some Shakesperean play really meant
•CR 157-158 ❖ CR 13:10

Shakespeare: In all his works the conception of good seems to be purely worldly; in Hamlet we see everything questioned *except* the duty of revenge
•CR 16 ❖ CR 2:13

Shakespeare: In King Lear there is a minor character who has no notion how the play is going to go, but he does his present duty well (as we should)
•WLN 104-105 ❖ WLN 7:20

Shakespeare: Lady Macbeth mentioned with regard to the will of God and the popular case against prayer
•GID 105 ❖ GID 11:6

Shakespeare play illustration (Hamlet) to show how all events are providential and also come about by natural causes
•GID 79; M 178-179

❖ GID I 8:10; M App. B:17

Shakespeare play illustration: "...if Shakespeare and Hamlet could ever meet, it must be Shakespeare's doing" (re: human contact with God)
•SJ 227 (*see also* SJ 223; *consider also* Initiative) ❖ SJ 14:20 (*see also* SJ 14:14; *consider also* Initiative)

Shakespeare, we value, for the glory of his language and his knowledge of the human heart; not for his belief in witches or the divine right of kings
•WLN 95-96 ❖ WLN 7:5

Shakespeare's plays, reading all, to find Shakespeare as analogy to exploring space to find God or Heaven
•CR 167-168 ❖ CR 14:10-14

Shame—*see also* Conscience; Guilt; Humiliation

Shame, cowardice is almost the only vice at which men still feel
•SL 137 ❖ SL 29:5

Shame (embarrassment), I sometimes think that, does as much towards preventing good acts and straightforward happiness as any of our vices can do
•GO 9 ❖ GO 1:17

Shame, emotion of, valuable not as an emotion but because of the insight to which it leads
•PP 67 ❖ PP 4:15

Shame, hatred is a great anodyne for
•SL 136 ❖ SL 29:4

Shame, I have found that the degree of, which I feel at my own sins does not at all correspond to what my reason tells me about their comparative gravity
•LM 99 ❖ LM 18:16

Shame: "It may be that salvation consists not in the cancelling of [sins] but in the perfected humility that bears the shame forever..."
•PP 61 (*see also* L 236; SL 148) ❖ PP 4:9 (*see also* L 8 Jan 52; SL 31:5)

Shame, mere emotion of: I believe that all sadness not arising from either repentance (hastening to amendment) or pity (hastening to assistance) is bad
•PP 67 ❖ PP 4:15

Shame, Psycho-analysis intimates that, is a dangerous and mischievous thing; this is partly to blame for the decline of our sense of guilt
•PP 56-57 ❖ PP 4:3

Shame: "Unless Christianity is wholly false, the perception of ourselves which we have in moments of shame must be the only true one..."
•PP 56-57 ❖ PP 4:3

Sharing one's delight in a new author, a good joke, or a lovely scene as an illustration of the naturalness of spontaneous praise
•RP 95 ❖ RP 9:6

Shaw, George Bernard: According to Shavian Romanticism the voice of Eros is the voice of the Life Force seeking parents or ancestors for superman
•FL 152-153 ❖ FL 5:34

Shaw, [George] Bernard: From him come the wittiest expositions of Creative Evolution (also called "Emergent Evolution" or "Life-Force philosophy")
•MC 35 ❖ MC I 4:6

Shaw, [George] Bernard, mentioned as having carried forward a popular form of nature religion started, in a sense, by [Henri] Bergson
•GID 86 ❖ GID I 9:9

Sheep and Goats, parable of—*see* Parable of Sheep and Goats

Sheep, I am a, telling shepherds what only a sheep can tell them (re: Lewis's thoughts on modern theology and Biblical criticism)
•CR 152 ❖ CR 13:1

Sheep, Man may be the only lost, in the universe—the one, therefore, whom the Shepherd came to seek
•GID 42-43; WLN 86-87 (*see also* GID 100; M 122) ❖ GID I 3:9; WLN 6:11 (*see also* GID I 10:42; M 14:24)

Sheol—*see also* Hell

Sheol defined as a shadowy world, a land of forgetfulness and imbecility
•M 145 ❖ M 16:6

Sheol, early Jewish doctrine of, described
•GID 130 ❖ GID I 16:2

Sheol in the Psalms simply means "the land of the dead"—the state of all

dead, good and bad alike
•RP 36, 38 ❖ RP 4:6, 9

Sheol, the ancient Jew was not encouraged to think about
•RP 36 ❖ RP 4:7

Ship, gospel replaces law and longing
transforms obedience as gradually as
the tide lifts a grounded
•WG 5 ❖ WG 1:3

Ship, I like to see salt water washing past
from the deck of a
•L 218 (*see also* SJ 23-24)
❖ L 16 Aug 49 (*see also* SJ 2:2)

Ship, it is a poor thing to strike our colours
to God when the, is going down un-
der us
•PP 97 ❖ PP 6:8

Ship, marriage as one, which must chug
along on a single engine after the
death of one's spouse
•GO 39 ❖ GO 2:33

Ship, the fact that the, is sinking is no reason for allowing her to be a floating
hell while she still floats
•CR 58-59 (*see also* World, improvement of) ❖ CR 5:4 (*see also* World,
improvement of)

Ship's cabin is snug in a way that is impossible for a mere room in a house
•L 95 ❖ L 3 Jul 24

Ships: "I have only to close my eyes to
see...the phosphorescence of a ship's
wash, the mast unmoving against the
stars..."
•SJ 149-150 ❖ SJ 10:1

Ships: Lewis describes his first trip by
ferry to England: "I was, and am, an
obstinately good sailor"
•SJ 24-25 ❖ SJ 2:2

Ships sailing in formation, analogy of, to
illustrate importance and operation of
morality
•MC 70-73 ❖ MC III 1:3-8

Ships: Since I crossed the Irish Sea six
times a year as a child, my memory is
stored with ship's-side images to a degree unusual for such an untraveled
man
•SJ 149 ❖ SJ 10:1

Ships: "The sound of a steamer's horn at

night still conjures up my whole boyhood"
•SJ 11 ❖ SJ 1:9

Shocking Alternative, The (chapter title)
•MC 51-56 ❖ MC II ch. 3

Sick, caring for—*see* Medicine; *consider*
Doctors

Sickness—*see* Disease; Illness

Siegfried and the Twilight of the Gods as an
avenue through which Lewis experienced "Joy"
•SJ 72-78 ❖ SJ 5:3-10

Signpost, "Joy" was a, to something other
and outer
•SJ 238 ❖ SJ 15:10

Silence a good refuge when, during evil
conversation, one does not wish to
offend or appear to agree (although
there is a limit)
•RP 72-73 (*see also* GID 262; SL 46)
❖ RP 7:11-13 (*see also* GID II 16:29; SL
10:2)

Silence and music listed by Screwtape as
two of the things he detests; "We will
make the whole universe a noise in the
end"
•SL 102-103 ❖ SL 22:5

Silence and solitude, avoid, if you wish to
avoid God...Live in a crowd...Keep the
radio on...
•CR 168 ❖ CR 14:17, 18

Silence during an argument or discussion
can be of an emphatic, audible and
even dialectical character*
•LM 77 (*see also* LAL 110)
❖ LM 15:1 (*see also* LAL 8 Nov 62)

Silence, people draw conclusions even
from, (re: Lewis's silence on Holy
Communion)
•LM 101 ❖ LM 19:3

Silence, we live in a world starved for
•WG 107 ❖ WG 7:2

Silences in the physical world occur in
empty places; but the ultimate Peace
is silent through very density of life
•M 93 ❖ M 11:18

Sin(s)—*see also* Fault(s); Vice(s); *consider
also* Free will

Sin: A man may console himself for his
vices by a conviction that "his heart's

in the right place" and "he wouldn't hurt a fly"*
•PP 56 ❖ PP 4:2

Sin, a recovery of the old sense of, is essential to Christianity
•PP 57 ❖ PP 4:4

Sin: A "sinful" pleasure means a good offered, and accepted, under conditions which involve a breach of the moral law
•CR 21 (see also MC 49; SL 41-42, 69)
❖ CR 2:27 (see also MC II 2:9; SL 9:2; 15:3)

Sin: "Bad" pleasures are really "pleasures snatched by unlawful acts"— stealing an apple is bad, not the sweetness*
•LM 89 (see also Pleasure/s)
❖ LM 17:5 (see also Pleasure/s)

Sin, body (i.e., physical desires) vs. soul (i.e., "imagination") in the fight of*
•GID 216-217 ❖ GID II 7:3

Sin, both of men and of angels, is made possible by the fact that God gave them free will
•M 121-122 (see also MC 52-53; PP 135)
❖ M 14:23 (see also MC II 3:3-5; PP 9:7)

Sin breeds more sin by strengthening sinful habit and weakening the conscience (vs. pain, which is "disinfected evil" having no tendency to proliferate)
•PP 116 ❖ PP 7:9

Sin can contribute to a complex good (by causing grace to abound) but the sin itself remains evil (example of Judas)
•PP 111 (see also PP 84)
❖ PP 7:2 (see also PP 5:11)

Sin, condemnation of, may result in danger to our charity and humility (but the alternative is to condone it, thus sharing guilt)
•PP 117 ❖ PP 7:9

Sin, dreariness of: A man's life may be stolen away not by sweet sins but in a dreary flickering of the mind over it knows not what and knows not why...
•SL 56 (see also SL 144*)
❖ SL 12:4 (see also SL 30:4*)

Sin, every, is the distortion of an energy breathed into us which would have otherwise blossomed into a holy act
•LM 69 ❖ LM 13:4

Sin, first, described by St. Augustine as the result of Pride, of the movement whereby a creature tries to set up on its own
•PP 75 ❖ PP 5:5

Sin, first: Question of whether the eating of the fruit [in Genesis] was literal or not is of no consequence
•PP 80 ❖ PP 5:8

Sin, God cannot remove by miracle the results of each, because then choice itself would soon cease
•PP 71 (see also PP 34)
❖ PP 5:1 (see also PP 2:15)

Sin, God's implacable hostility toward, (but not toward the sinner) is expressed in the ferocious parts of the Psalms
•RP 32-33 ❖ RP 3:21

Sin, greatest, is Pride; it leads to every other vice
•MC 109 ❖ MC III 8:2

Sin, guilt shared by those who observe, and do not condemn it
•PP 117 ❖ PP 7:9

Sin has its beginnings in small, wrong choices*
•MC 86-87, 117; RP 136; SL 53-54; WG 102-103; WLN 54-55
❖ MC III 4:8, 9; 9:8; RP 12:16; SL 12:1; WG 6:12; WLN 4:10

Sin, if there is a particular, on your conscience repent and confess it; if there isn't, tell the despondent devil not to be silly
•LAL 77 (see also LM 32-34; SL 54-55*)
❖ LAL Jul 21st 58 (see also LM 6:11-17; SL 12:2-4*)

Sin: Is it in accordance with the will of God?*
•MC 51-54 ❖ MC II 3:1-6

Sin, Lewis discusses the origin of, and the doctrine of original sin*
•PP 69-88 ❖ PP ch. 5

Sin, no, simply as such, should be made a crime ("Who the deuce are our rulers to enforce their opinions about sin on us?")—re: homosexuality

on the tiny central self
- MC 87 (*see also* MC 107; WLN 54-55)
- ❖ MC III 4:9 (*see also* MC III 7:10; WLN 4:10)

Sins ("crimes"), I find it easier to understand the great, for the raw material of them exists in us all; mere disagreeableness is mysterious*
- LAL 27-28 ❖ LAL Mar 10/54

Sins: Even the noblest of our natural activities will be sinful if not offered to God
- WG 25 ❖ WG 2:8

Sins, gambling and pederasty mentioned by Lewis as the two, which he was never tempted to commit
- SJ 101 (*see also* GID 59-60; SJ 89)
- ❖ SJ 7:1 (*see also* GID I 4:53, 54; SJ 6:9)

Sins, God loves us in spite of our, as we should love each other*
- GID 154 (*see also* GID 122-123*)
- ❖ GID I 18:8, 9 (*see also* GID I 14:7, 8*)

Sins, God may love us in spite of our, but He cannot cease to will their removal
- PP 46 (*see also* MC 172)
- ❖ PP 3:13 (*see also* MC IV 9:4)

Sins: God will be merciful to our failures, but cannot accept compromise or acquiescence
- WG 130, 132 ❖ WG 9:9, 13

Sins, I have found that my feelings of shame and disgust at my own, do not at all correspond to what my reason tells me about their comparative gravity
- LM 99 ❖ LM 18:16

Sins, in confessing our, we do give God information He already has—but in doing so, we put ourselves on a personal footing with Him
- LM 20-21 ❖ LM 4:6, 7

Sins, it is not enough to want to get rid of our; we need to believe in a Saviour
- GID 260 ❖ GID II 16:18

Sins, love of God is not wearied by our, or by our indifference; is quite relentless
- MC 118 ❖ MC III 9:10

Sins may never be cancelled but may always be common knowledge to the universe; "lost" may be those who

dare not go to such a "public" place
- PP 61 (*see also* SL 148)
- ❖ PP 4:9 (*see also* SL 31:5)

Sins, more important: "Cruelty is surely more evil than lust and the World at least as dangerous as the Flesh"
- SJ 109 ❖ SJ 7:11

Sins, more important: Hypocrites more curable than "goody-goodies" who are content in their routine piety and respectability, attempting no deception*
- WLN 47-48 ❖ WLN 3:25, 26

Sins, more important, may be seen as harmless next to sins of the flesh by people not very morally sensitive or instructed
- L 175 ❖ L 17 Jan 40

Sins, more important: Spiritual evils which we share with the devils (pride, spite) are far worse than the sensual evils which we share with the beasts
- LAL 111 (*see also* FL 111-112; GID 98; MC 94-95, 108-112)
- ❖ LAL 26 Nov 62 (*see also* FL 4:39; GID I 10:36; MC III 5:14; 8:1-8)

Sins, more important: The proud, the avaricious, the self-righteous are more in danger of finding life satisfactory than the feckless and dissipated*
- PP 98 ❖ PP 6:9

Sins, more important: We must try to get the mind of our audience off of public affairs and "crime" and on to their own spite, greed, envy, conceit, etc.
- GID 96 ❖ GID I 10:17

Sins of omission, in parable of Sheep and Goats the "Goats" are condemned entirely for their
- RP 9 ❖ RP 2:1

Sins of the flesh are bad, but they are the least bad of all sins
- MC 94-95 (*see also* FL 111-112*; L 175; LAL 111) ❖ MC III 5:14 (*see also* FL 4:39*; L 17 Jan 40; LAL 26 Nov 62)

Sins of the flesh: "Cruelty is surely more evil than lust and the World at least as dangerous as the Flesh"
- SJ 109 ❖ SJ 7:11

Sins of the flesh, temptations to, are more

successful during the "trough" periods of human experience—when men are dull and weary (—Screwtape)
•SL 41 ❖ SL 9:2

Sins of the tongue, protests against, are all over the Psalms
•RP 75 ❖ RP 7:16

Sins, repentance of—*see* Repentance

Sins, Screwtape points out that God does not want a person to think too much of his; the sooner the man turns his attention outward, the better
•SL 66 (*see also* LM 33)
❖ SL 14:5 (*see also* LM 6:13)

Sins: Screwtape reminds Wormwood that anything, even a sin, which has the total effect of moving a man closer to God works against the devils' purpose
•SL 125-126 (*see also* SL 56, 87-89)
❖ SL 27:1 (*see also* SL 12:5; 19:3)

Sins: The only thing that matters is the degree to which they separate us from God (Screwtape: "Murder is no better than cards if cards can do the trick")
•SL 56 (*see also* SL 87-88, 125-126)
❖ SL 12:5 (*see also* SL 19:3; 27:1)

Sins, those who do not think much about their own, make up for it by thinking incessantly about the sins of others
•GID 124 (*see also* GID 154)
❖ GID I 14:10 (*see also* GID I 18:10)

Sins, try not to think of others'; one's own are a much more profitable theme
•LAL 95 ❖ LAL 9 Jan 61

Sins, when one draws nearer to God there is the possibility of blacker, as well as brighter virtues
•L 301 (*see also* RP 28-32)
❖ L 20 Dec 61 (*see also* RP 3:17-20)

Sins, which, to emphasize to modern audiences in order to awaken conscience
•GID 244 ❖ GID II 12:8

Sins ("wrong choices"), Screwtape advocates leading humans to believe that their, are trivial and revocable
•SL 53-54 (*see also* WLN 54-55)
❖ SL 12:1 (*see also* WLN 4:10)

Sins, you should at least make a list of your, on a piece of paper and make a serious act of penance about each one

of them
•GID 123-124 ❖ GID I 14:9

Sinai, the road to the promised land runs past; the moral law may exist to be transcended, yet while God may be more than moral goodness, He is not less
•PP 65 (*see also* Law, moral)
❖ PP 4:13 (*see also* Law, moral)

Sinful habits: The parable of the Unjust Judge teaches us that no evil habit is so ingrained that it cannot, even in old age, be whisked away
•LM 107 ❖ LM 20:1

Sinful nature was transmitted by heredity from Adam to all later generations; "a new species, never created by God, had sinned itself into existence"
•PP 83 ❖ PP 5:10

Sinfulness—*see also* Badness; Evil; Wickedness; *consider also* Self-knowledge

Sinfulness and self-will, why the cure for our, must be a painful process
•PP 89-117 ❖ PP ch. 6, 7

Sinfulness, as soon as we perceive our, the "wrath" of God appears inevitable; otherwise it seems a barbarous doctrine
•PP 58 ❖ PP 4:6

Sinfulness, as we begin to "put on Christ" we begin to notice our
•MC 164 ❖ MC IV 7:12

Sinfulness, Christianity has nothing to say to people who do not feel a sense of their own
•MC 38-39 ❖ MC I 5:4

Sinfulness: "It may be that salvation consists not in the cancelling of [sins] but in the perfected humility that bears the shame forever..."
•PP 61 (*see also* L 236; SL 148)
❖ PP 4:9 (*see also* L 8 Jan 52; SL 31:5)

Sinfulness: Jesus Himself "plumbed the depths of that worst suffering which comes to evil men who at last know their own evil"*
•RP 127 ❖ RP 12:7

Sinfulness of every person: "...when the saints say that they—even they—are vile, they are recording truth with sci-

entific accuracy"
•PP 68 ❖ PP 4:15

Sinfulness of Man: Christ takes it for granted that men are bad; until we feel the truth of this, we are not part of the audience He addressed
•PP 57 ❖ PP 4:4

Sinfulness of ourselves never fully known to us
•GID 121-123, 153; PP 59-60 (see also L 183; MC 87; SL 16)
❖ GID I 14:4-8; 18:6, 7; PP 4:7 (see also L 16 Apr 40; MC III 4:10; SL 3:2)

Sinfulness, regarding the dead now having knowledge of all our: "Look your hardest, dear...I wouldn't hide if I could..."
•GO 83-84 ❖ GO 4:30

Sinfulness, Screwtape mentions despair over one's own, as "a greater sin than any of the sins which provoke it"
•SL 138 ❖ SL 29:7

Sinfulness, Screwtape observes that humans shall gain an utter knowledge of their, and shall embrace the pain of it
•SL 148 (see also PP 61, 126, 152; Self-knowledge) ❖ SL 31:5 (see also PP 10:3; 8:9; 10:9; Self-knowledge)

Sinfulness: Screwtape relates his belief that what the new Christian says, even on his knees, about his own sinfulness is only parrot talk
•SL 14 ❖ SL 2:4

Sinfulness, sense of—see also Conscience; Guilt; Self-knowledge

Sinfulness, sense of, lacking in modern audiences
•GID 95-96, 181-182, 243-244; PP 55-57 (see also MC 38-39)
❖ GID I 10:15-17; 22:13; II 12: 6-8; PP 4:1-4 (see also MC I 5:4)

Sinfulness, sense of: Method for awakening it in modern audiences
•GID 96 ❖ GID I 10:16, 17

Sinfulness, the holier a man is the more he is aware of his
•PP 67 (see also LAL 95; MC 87, 164; PP 55, top)
❖ PP 4:15 (see also LAL 9 Jan 61; MC III 4:10; IV 7:12; PP 4 prelim. quote)

Sinfulness, we must be aware of our own, but a continual poring over the "sink" might breed its own perverse pride
•LM 98-99 ❖ LM 18:13-15

Sinfulness: When a man is getting better he understands more clearly the evil left in him; when he is getting worse he understands his own badness less and less
•MC 87 (see also GID 56-57; LAL 95; PP 55, top; PP 67; Self-knowledge)
❖ MC III 4:10 (see also GID I 4:38; LAL 9 Jan 61; PP 4:prelim. quote; PP 4:15; Self-knowledge)

Singers, popular, and film stars mentioned by Screwtape as useful in drawing thousands of souls away from God
•SL 158-159; WLN 56-57
❖ SL 32:13; WLN 4:13

Sinner, God desireth not the death of a, but His implacable hostility toward sin is expressed in the ferocious parts of the Psalms
•RP 32-33 ❖ RP 3:21

Sinner, hating the sin but not the: We have no trouble doing this with ourselves
•MC 105-106 ❖ MC III 7:4-6

Sinner, it is better for a, even if he never becomes good, to know sooner or later that he is a failure—to realize his own sinfulness (re:doctrine of Hell)
•PP 120-122 ❖ PP 8:5

Sinners, Christ died not for valuable men but for, —human souls whose value, apart from God, is zero
•WG 115 (see also SL 155; WLN 53)
❖ WG 7:14 (see also SL 32:8; WLN 4:8)

Sinners, great, are conscious of guilt, thus capable of real repentance (Screwtape: "The great sinners seem easier to catch. But then they are incalculable")
•SL 165-166; WLN 64
❖ SL 32:29; WLN 4:29

Sinners: Jesus Himself "plumbed the depths of that worst suffering which comes to evil men who at last know their own evil"
•RP 127 (consider also Self-knowledge)
❖ RP 12:7 (consider also Self-knowl-

edge)

Sinners, the great, (according to Screwtape) are made out of the very same material as the great Saints
•SL 157-158; WLN 55-56 (*see also* SL 105-106, 135-136*) ❖ SL 32:12, 13; WLN 4:12, 13 (*see also* SL 23:1; 29:2*)

Sinning: Failures will be forgiven; it is acquiescence that is fatal
•L 199; MC 94; WG 132
❖ L 20 Jan 40; MC III 5:12; WG 9:13

Sinning: Humble souls will, after death, have the delightful surprise of finding that on certain occasions they sinned much less than they'd thought
•WG 123 ❖ WG 8:4

Sinning: Story of Irish woman in church to illustrate that as long as we are in connection with God we cannot sin*
•WG 128 ❖ WG 9:5

Size, argument from, illogical (in trying to show the unimportance of the earth in relation to the universe)
•GID 39-41 (*see also* GID 74-75; PP 13)
❖ GID I 3:4-7 (*see also* GID I 7:29-41; PP 1:1)

Size tells us nothing about importance or value (God's love for Man undiminished by our technical insignificance)
•M 48-54 (*see also* GID 100)
❖ M 7:7-17 (*see also* GID I 10:42)

Skepticism—*see* Scepticism

Sky is to me one of the principal elements in any landscape; clouds were my especial delight
•SJ 152 (*see also* L 110; LM 90)
❖ SJ 10:4 (*see also* L 10 Jan 27; LM 17:10)

Sky, Lewis describes watching the night, from his dormitory at "Belsen"
•SJ 25, 34, 60, 171 ❖ SJ 2:4, 14; 4:6; 11:8

Sky, the night, suggests that the inanimate also has for God some value we cannot imagine
•LM 55 ❖ LM 10:10

Sky: When God made space and worlds and air, He knew what the sky would mean to us; it is of all things sensuously perceived the most like infinity (re: our images of Heaven)
•M 157-158 ❖ M 16:25, 26

Sky, when one considers the, and all the stars it seems strange that God should be at all concerned with man—yet He has given us extraordinary honour (re: Psalm 8)
•RP 132 ❖ RP 12:11

Slang—*see also* Expressions

Slang of our own circle, we must be on guard against using; it may delude ourselves as well as mystify outsiders
•GID 256-257 ❖ GID II 15:11-13

Sleep: Conversion likened to the experience of a man who, after long sleep, still lying motionless in bed, becomes aware that he is awake
•SJ 237 ❖ SJ 15:8

Sleep: "Don't you simply love going to bed?"
•L 31 ❖ L 25 Oct 16

Sleep, except for anxiety there is nothing more hostile to, than anger toward a loved one ("...the alternation of resentment and affection...")
•LAL 92-93 ❖ LAL 28 Oct 60

Sleep: God "may be trusted to know when we need *bed* even more than Mass"
•LAL 24 (*see also* LAL 38)
❖ LAL Jan 1st 54 (*see also* LAL 20/2/55)

Sleep is a jade who scorns her suitors but woos her scorners; the great secret (if one can do it) is not to *care* whether you sleep
•LAL 23 ❖ LAL 27/xi/53

Sleep: "More and more sleep seems to be the best thing"
•L 169 (*see also* SJ 100)
❖ L 18 Sep 39 (*see also* SJ 6:27)

Sleep, to unfallen Man, was [possibly] not a stupor but willed and conscious repose—he remained awake to enjoy the pleasure and duty of sleep
•PP 78 ❖ PP 5:6

Sleeping, Lewis mentions having difficulty
•LAL 89, 98, 113, 120 ❖ LAL 13 Feb 60; 21 Apr 61; 26/1/63; 6 Jul 63

Slip of the Tongue, A (chapter title)
•WG 126-132 ❖ WG ch. 9

Slogans, plastering the landscape with re-

ligious: What we disagree with is their taste, not their doctrines
•L 268 ❖ L 13 Mar 56

Smell or odour ("...that almost unvarying *something*")—the Christian element—which Lewis met in various works of literature
•GID 203-204 ❖ GID II 4:5

Smell, pleasure of, as example of a Pleasure of Appreciation
•FL 26 ❖ FL 2:2

Smoke on the Mountain, reference to the book, by Joy Davidman (Lewis's wife)
•LAL 67 ❖ LAL Jul 3/57

Smoking and talking both interfere with one's appreciation of nature; walks should mostly be taken alone
•SJ 142 ❖ SJ 9:18

Smoking and temperance, mention of, with regard to the temptation to guard our worldly interests
•WG 127 ❖ WG 9:4

Smoking, Lewis makes a probable reference to his childhood, with his brother
•CR 38-39 ❖ CR 3:4

Smoking, mention of, with regard to our abuse of our bodies*
•GID 216 ❖ GID II 7:3

Smoking much harder to justify than drinking; but "not smoking is a whole-time job"
•L 267 ❖ L 13 Mar 56

Smoking: We should all like to believe that Heaven will mean the happy past restored, that there are cigars in Heaven
•GO 29 ❖ GO 2:14

Snob, there are circles where manners are so coarse that a man (whatever his social position) of any good taste will be called a
•RP 74 ❖ RP 7:15

Snobs who feign enjoyment of art or literature vs. low-brows who genuinely enjoy it ("I...prefer the live dog to the dead lion")
•WLN 38-39 (*see also* CR 10)
❖ WLN 3:12 (*see also* CR 1:15)

Snobbery—*consider also* Pride; Priggery

Snobbery as the desire to get inside that particular Inner Ring called "Society"

•WG 97 (*see also* Inner Rings)
❖ WG 6:6 (*see also* Inner Rings)

Snobbery, chronological: the uncritical acceptance of the intellectual climate common to our own age, and the arbitrary discrediting of past thought
•SJ 207-208 (*see also* RP 121, 130; SJ 206, 212-213, 216; SL 128-129; WLN 96)
❖ SJ 13:17 (*see also* RP 12:3, 9; SJ 13:14; 14:2, 7; SL 27:5; WLN 7:6)

"Snobbery" in the sense of a greedy desire to know people "of ancient and noble blood" distinguished from an interested appreciation of them
•LAL 27 ❖ LAL Feb 22/54

Snobbery: Most men do not like to be merely equal with other men; we find them building themselves into groups in which they can feel superior to others*
•WLN 41 ❖ WLN 3:14

Snobbery vs. true friendship: "...consort simply with the people you like"*
•WG 105-106 ❖ WG 6:17

Snobbery: "When [it] consists *only* of the admiring look upward and *not* of the contemptuous look downward, one need not be hard on it"
•L 113 ❖ L 30 Mar 27

Snobbish pride vs. the pride of friendships (snobs wish to attach themselves to an "elite"; Friends may come to regard themselves as an "elite")
•FL 118 ❖ FL 4:51

Snow: "One part of me almost envies you that deep snow: *real* snow"
•LAL 25 ❖ LAL 24/1/54

Snugness: I notice that a study in a hut or a cave or the cabin of a ship can be snug in a way that is impossible for a mere room in a house...
•L 95 ❖ L 3 Jul 24

Sobriety—*consider also* Alcohol

Sobriety mentioned by Lewis as one of the virtues attempted by his friends at Oxford, and a standard which he accepted in principle
•SJ 201 ❖ SJ 13:6

Social advancement—*consider also* Inner Ring(s)

Social advancement: Importance of getting onto the first rung—"And not then at peace either; for not to advance is to fall back"
•SJ 98 ❖ SJ 6:22

Social advancement, Lewis describes the system and importance of, at Wyvern College
•SJ 83-100, 108 ❖ SJ ch. 6; 7:10

Social and political programmes good only so far as they don't trample on people's rights for the sake of their good
•L 226-227 (see also WLN 111)
❖ L 7 Feb 51 (see also WLN 7:33)

Social causes—see also Causes

Social causes: Pity (as for oppressed classes), if not controlled by charity and justice, leads through anger to cruelty*
•PP 65 ❖ PP 4:12

Social changes and improvement of "the world": I remind the reader that a particular medicine is not to be mistaken for the elixir of life
•PP 114 ❖ PP 7:5

Social conscience as currently being reawakened can be used a mere excuse for evading our own personal faults
•PP 60-61 ❖ PP 4:8

Social engagements, your, seem to be almost as much of an affliction as anything else—but I can understand that
•LAL 59 (see also Collective)
❖ LAL 3/8/56 (see also Collective)

Social ethics of Christianity—see also World, improvement of

Social ethics of Christianity: We have a duty to leave the world (even in a temporal sense) "better" than we found it
•PP 113-114 (see also GID 49, 57, 147-150; MC 118; WLN 111)
❖ PP 7:4 (see also GID I 4:6, 7, 40; ch. 17; MC III 10:1; WLN 7:33, 34)

"Social functions," Lewis describes his distaste for, such as the neighborhood dances of his youth
•SJ 46-48, 160 ❖ SJ 3:5, 6; 10:13

Social gatherings, Christian principles regarding, (especially re: unprotesting participation in evil conversation)
•RP 71-74 (see also GID 262; SL 45-48*)
❖ RP 7:10-16 (see also GID II 16:29; SL ch. 10*)

Social gatherings: "People who bore one another should meet seldom; people who interest one another, often"*
•FL 116 ❖ FL 4:47

Social justice, Screwtape discusses how Christianity used merely as a means to, can work to the devil's advantage
•SL 108-109 (see also MC 137)
❖ SL 23:4 (see also MC IV 1:6, 7)

Social life, competitive egoisms can only impoverish, (re: the pursuit of "culture" for the sake of prestige or merit)
•WLN 35-36 (consider also Pride of pursuing "culture") ❖ WLN 3:8 (consider also Pride of pursuing "culture")

Social life: You'll never make a good impression on people until you stop thinking about what kind of impression you're making
•MC 190 ❖ MC IV 11:15

Social morality—see Morality, social

Social Morality (chapter title)
•MC 78-83 ❖ MC III ch. 3

Social problems, job of finding the Christian solution to our, is really on us laymen
•MC 79 ❖ MC III 3:3

Social struggle mentioned as the deadly thing about Lewis's college, Wyvern: "And from it, at school as in the world, all sorts of meanness flow..."
•SJ 108 ❖ SJ 7:10

Social values of the Christian vs. the Materialist (and the effect they have on the actions of each)
•GID 109-110 ❖ GID I 12:2-4

Social work: A strong sense of our common miseries as good a spur as any to the removal of all miseries we can (no need to believe in "heaven on earth")
•PP 114 ❖ PP 7:5

Socialism, Christian, mentioned by Screwtape
•SL 160; WLN 58
❖ SL 32:16; WLN 4:16

Socialism: "Is there any possibility of get-

ting the super Welfare State's honey and avoiding the sting? Let us make no mistake about the sting..."*
•GID 314-316, esp. 316
❖ GID III 8:11-22, esp. 20, 21
Socialism: Such embryonic political opinions as I had [in my youth] were vaguely socialistic
•SJ 173 (see also L 48)
❖ SJ 11:10 (see also L 25 May 19)
Socialist schoolmaster, illustration of, who decided to give up Socialism for its tyranny but then wished to join ranks of his oppressors in Ministry of Education (re: current lack of thirst for justice)
•CR 122; RP 69-71
❖ CR 10:18, 19; RP 7:7, 8
Societies, formation of, such as C. S. Lewis Societies: Lewis mentioned that he was "delighted" by the formation of a "Milton Society of America"**
•L 260
❖ L undated letter just before 2 Feb 55
Society—see also Collective
Society, a prudent, must spend at least as much energy on conserving what it has as on improvement
•CR 92-93 ❖ CR 7:22
Society, a sick, must think much about politics—as a sick man must think much about his digestion
•WG 109 ❖ WG 7:4
Society, any given change in, is at least as likely to destroy the liberties and amenities we already have as to add new ones (re: "progress")
•CR 92 ❖ CR 7:22
"Society" as one form of Inner Ring which people may desire to belong to; this desire takes the form of snobbery
•WG 97 (see also Inner Rings)
❖ WG 6:6 (see also Inner Rings)
Society, Christianity does not profess to have a detailed political programme for applying the Golden Rule to a particular, at a particular moment
•MC 78-79 ❖ MC III 3:2, 3
Society, heaven is a, because the blessed remain eternally different; and each

has something unique to tell all the others about God
•PP 150 (see also FL 92-93; L 242-243*)
❖ PP 10:7 (see also FL 4:9; L 20 Jun 52*)
Society, it may be asked whether a, which tolerates "rascals" (such as dishonest politicians or newspaper editors) is a healthy one
•RP 67 ❖ RP 7:3, 4
"Society," snobbery as the desire to get inside that particular Inner Ring called
•WG 97 ❖ WG 6:6
Society, the class system at Wyvern College was an answer to those who derive all the ills of, from economics
•SJ 110 ❖ SJ 7:13
Society, the New Testament (without going into details) gives us a pretty clear hint of what a fully Christian, would be like
•MC 80-82 ❖ MC III 3:4-6
Society, two determinants of the future of our: the advance of science, and the changed relationship between Government and subjects
•GID 312-313 ❖ GID III 8:5-7
Society, under views of "subjectivism" it is useless to compare the ideologies of one, with those of another; progress and decadence are meaningless words*
•CR 73 (see also CR 75)
❖ CR 6:5 (see also CR 6:11)
Society, without good men you cannot have a good
•MC 72 ❖ MC III 1:7
Socrates mentioned: All great moralists are sent not to inform men, but to remind them; to restate the primeval moral platitudes which the devil attempts to conceal (—Screwtape)
•SL 107 ❖ SL 23:3
Socrates never claimed to be God or the Son of God; there is no parallel to Jesus in other religions
•GID 157-158 ❖ GID I 19:3
Socrates, personality of: That union of "silly and scabrous titters about Greek pederasty with the highest mystical fervour and homeliest good sense"

•CR 156 ❖ CR 13:8

Socrates, the imperfect yet very venerable goodness of, led to his death
•RP 105 ❖ RP 10:10

Socratic Club mentioned in a letter to Dorothy Sayers
•L 208 ❖ L 10 Dec 45

Socratic Club not neutral; founded by Christians
•GID 128 ❖ GID I 15:4

Socratic Club, papers have been read to the, in which a contrast was drawn between a supposedly Christian and a supposedly scientific attitude to belief
•WLN 13 ❖ WLN 2:1

Socratic Club, probable mention of the formation of, described by Lewis to his father
•L 131 ❖ L undated letter of Nov 1928

Socratic Club: Purpose of existence was to discuss pros and cons of Christian religion
•GID 126 ❖ GID I 15:2

Socratic Club: Such an arena specially devoted to the conflict between Christian and unbeliever was a novelty at Oxford
•GID 127 ❖ GID I 15:2

Socratic Club, The Founding of the Oxford (chapter title)
•GID 126-128 ❖ GID I ch. 15

Sodomy—*consider also* Homosexual(ity)

Sodomy: "We attack this vice not because it is the worst but because it is, by adult standards, the most disreputable and unmentionable..."
•SJ 109 ❖ SJ 7:11

Soldier, tin, turning into a real man as analogy to Christian transformation
•MC 154-156, 162 ❖ MC IV 5:3-7; 7:7

Soldiers and Christians are still men; neither conversion nor enlistment in the army is really going to obliterate our human life (re: learning in war-time)
•WG 23-24 ❖ WG 2:5, 6

Soldiers on a train, illustration of, who seemed to have "no conception of good and evil whatsoever" because they showed an absence of indignation

•RP 29-30 ❖ RP 3:18

Soldiers, The Obstinate (chapter title)
•MC 154-157 ❖ MC IV ch. 5

Soldiers who kill each other in plain battle, each believing his own country to be right: This does not seem to me the most terrible thing
•WG 43 (*see also* MC 107; SL 131-132*; *consider also* Pacifism; War)
❖ WG 3:18 (*see also* MC III 7:9; SL 28:1*; *consider also* Pacifism; War)

Solemnity, I believe there is too much, in dealing with sacred matters (re: use of humor in Christian writing)
•GID 259 ❖ GID II 15:8

Soliloquy, prayer as: Prayer in its most perfect state is a soliloquy; if the Holy Spirit speaks in the man, then in prayer God speaks to God
•LM 67-68 (*see also* LAL 22, 23; LM 49-50*, 81; MC 142-143)
❖ LM 13:1, 2 (*see also* LAL Nov 6/53; 27/xi/53; LM 9:11*; 15:15; MC IV 2:9)

Solipsism mentioned
•WLN 16, 17 ❖ WLN 2:5

Solitary religion, Christianity not a
•WG 106 (*see also* L 224; Church attendance) ❖ WG 7:1 (*see also* L 7 Dec 50; Church attendance)

Solitude—*see also* Privacy; *consider also* Loneliness

Solitude, all the rubs and frustrations of a joint life—even at its worst—seem to me better than
•LAL 109 ❖ LAL 8 Nov 62

Solitude and silence, avoid, if you wish to avoid God...Live in a crowd...Keep the radio on...
•CR 168 (*see also* SL 102-103*)
❖ CR 14:17, 18 (*see also* SL 22:5*)

Solitude, education organizes a boy's whole life to the exclusion of all; if a Wordsworth were born today, he would be "cured" before he was twelve
•WLN 42 ❖ WLN 3:16

Solitude, friends find this, about them whether they like it or not; they would be glad to reduce it, and be joined by a third

•FL 97 (*see also* FL 91-92)

❖ FL 4:16, 17 (*see also* FL 4:8, 9)

Solitude, I [now] live in almost total

•LAL 120 ❖ LAL 6 Jul 63

Solitude, in your position I myself would prefer a "Home"—or almost anything—to

•LAL 102 ❖ LAL 17 Jan 62

Solitude, Lewis mentions his childhood enjoyment of

•SJ 54 ❖ SJ 3:13

Solitude, Lewis mentions his dislike of

•LAL 117 ❖ LAL 10 Jun 63

Solitude, some of us find it more natural to approach God in; but Christianity is not a solitary religion—we must go to church

•L 224 (*see also* GID 61-62)

❖ L 7 Dec 50 (*see also* GID I 4:59, 60)

Solitude: "There is a crowd of busy-bodies whose life is devoted to destroying solitude wherever solitude exists"

•WG 107 ❖ WG 7:2

Solitude, we live in a world starved for, and therefore starved for meditation and true friendship

•WG 107 ❖ WG 7:2, 3

Solomon calls his bride Sister; could a woman be a complete wife unless, for a moment, in a particular mood, a man may also be inclined to call her Brother?

•GO 56 ❖ GO 3:30

Some Objections (chapter title)

•MC 21-26 ❖ MC I ch. 2

Some Thoughts (chapter title)

•GID 147-150 ❖ GID I ch. 17

"Song of Solomon" mentioned with regard to its inspiration and spiritual truth

•GID 264 ❖ GID II 16:39, 40

Song of Songs, book of: Christ as Bridegroom to the Church

•RP 128-132 ❖ RP 12:9, 10

Song of Songs, poets of, probably never dreamed of any but a secular and natural purpose in what they composed

•RP 111 ❖ RP 11:4

Sons, could there have been many, begotten by God as Jesus was?

•MC 157-159 ❖ MC IV 6:2

Sons of God, becoming: "...the approach, however initiated and supported by Grace, is something we must do"

•FL 16-17 (*see also* FL 19)

❖ FL 1:12 (*see also* FL 1:16)

Sons of God, we can become, by attaching ourselves to Christ

•MC 137-138 ❖ MC IV 1:10

Sons (stepsons) of C. S. Lewis—*see* Gresham, David and Douglas

Sonship, Christ will share His, with us and will make us, like Himself, "Sons of God"

•MC 128 ❖ MC III 12:6

Sonship of Jesus the solid reality; biological sonship merely a diagrammatic representation of that

•M 91 (*consider also* Transposition)

❖ M 11:15 (*consider also* Transposition)

Sophists mentioned by Screwtape as being made by his fellow devils, whereas such men as Socrates are sent by God to answer them

•SL 107 ❖ SL 23:3

Sorrow—*see also* Difficulties; Grief; Pain; Suffering

Sorrow, after being forgiven we may continue to feel, for being that sort of person—and be humbled

•L 236 (*see also* PP 61; SL 148*)

❖ L 8 Jan 52 (*see also* PP 4:9; SL 31:5*)

Sorrow for Sin—*see* Repentance

Sorrow isn't a state but a process; it keeps on changing—like a winding road with quite a new landscape at each bend

•GO 68-69; LAL 92

❖ GO 4:1; LAL 24 Sep 60

Soul—*see also* Immortality of the Soul; Spirit

Soul, at present we tend to think of the, as "inside" the body; the resurrected body, as I conceive it, will be inside the soul

•LM 122 ❖ LM 22:16

Soul, he that loses his, shall find it; human will becomes truly creative and truly our own when it is wholly God's

•PP 102 (*consider also* Personality)

❖ PP 6:14 (*consider also* Personality)

Soul: I had wanted (mad wish) "to call my soul my own"; I wanted, above all things, not to be "interfered with"
- SJ 228 (*see also* SJ 172, 237)
- ❖ SJ 14:22 (*see also* SJ 11:8; 15:8)

Soul is but a hollow which God fills
- PP 151 (*see also* PP 147)
- ❖ PP 10:9 (*see also* PP 10:3)

Soul, no part of our, can be called "our own"; God claims all*
- WG 130 (*see also* SJ 172*; SL 98-99)
- ❖ WG 9:9 (*see also* SJ 11:8*; SL 21:5, 6)

Soul (or "ghost"), confusion between, and "Spirit" has done much harm
- M 92 ❖ M 11:16

"Soul," the word translated, in the Psalms simply means "life"
- RP 36 ❖ RP 4:6

Soul: To "call their souls their own" was what men desired from the beginning, but this was to live a lie for our souls are not our own
- PP 80 (*see also* L 251; SJ 172, 228, 237; SL 95-99; WG 130-131)
- ❖ PP 5:8 (*see also* L 17 Jul 53; SJ 11:8; 14:22; 15:8; SL ch. 21; WG 9:9, 10)

Soul vs. spirit as they relate to the values of "culture"
- CR 23 (*see also* CR xii for Walter Hooper's commentary on this)
- ❖ CR 2:34 (*see also* CR P:15 for Walter Hooper's commentary on this)

Soul, your, is a hollow made to fit a particular swelling in the infinite contours of the divine substance
- PP 147 (*see also* PP 151)
- ❖ PP 10:3(*see also* PP 10:9)

Sour grapes: Question of whether our rejection of the world is "only the disappointed fox's attempt to convince himself that unattainable grapes are sour"
- CR 37 ❖ CR 3:2

Sovereignty, the Creator has, *de facto* as well as *de jure*; He has the power as well as the kingdom and the glory
- SJ 232 (*see also* LM 28)
- ❖ SJ 15:3, 4 (*see also* LM 5:17)

Soviet Union—*see* Russia

Space—*see also* Extraterrestrial life

Space, God invented; to look for Him within it is nonsensical
- CR 168 ❖ CR 14:15

Space, God is not in, but space is in God
- LM 122 ❖ LM 22:16

Space, like everything God made, has some likeness to God; Space is like Him in its hugeness
- MC 139 ❖ MC IV 1:14

Space, looking for God or Heaven by exploring, is like seeing all Shakespeare's plays in the hope that you will find Shakespeare as one of the characters
- CR 167-168 ❖ CR 14:10-14

Space, mere movement in, will never bring you any nearer to God or any farther from Him than you are at this very moment
- CR 168 ❖ CR 14:16

Space, my very early reading had lodged very firmly in my imagination the vastness and coldness of, and the littleness of Man
- SJ 65 ❖ SJ 4:11

Space, presence or absence of extraterrestrial life in outer, both used as arguments against Christianity
- CR 174; M 50; WLN 83-84 (*see also* Extraterrestrial life)
- ❖ CR 14:46; M 7:10; WLN 6:1-3 (*see also* Extraterrestrial life)

"Space-race" between America and Russia: Great powers are seldom less dangerously employed than in fabricating costly objects and flinging them overboard
- CR 172; WLN 77
- ❖ CR 14:36; WLN 5:14

Space travel: At the very least we shall corrupt any alien rational species with our vices and infect it with our diseases
- CR 173 ❖ CR 14:40

Space travel has nothing to do with discovering God—to some, God is discoverable everywhere; to others, nowhere
- CR 171 ❖ CR 14:29

Space travel: He who first reaches the moon steals something from us all

•CR 172-173 ❖ CR 14:38

Space travel: "I begin to be afraid that the villains will really contaminate the moon"
•L 209-210 ❖ L 21 Oct 46

Space travel: "I have wondered...whether the vast astronomical distances may not be God's quarantine precautions"
•WLN 91 ❖ WLN 6:24

Space travel: If there is life on other planets, we shall hardly find it nearer than the stars
•CR 173 ❖ CR 14:39

Space travel: "...let us thank God that we are still very far from travel to other worlds"
•WLN 91 ❖ WLN 6:23

Space travel: "Once we find ourselves spiritually awakened, we can go to outer space and take the good things with us"
•GID 267 ❖ GID II 16:58

Space travel, there are three ways in which, will bother me if it reaches the stage for which most people are hoping
•CR 172-176 ❖ CR 14:37-52

Space travel to find God: "If you do not at all know God, of course you will not recognize Him, either in Jesus or in outer space"
•CR 172 ❖ CR 14:35

Space travel to other planets, dangers of (we would corrupt them)
•GID 267; WLN 88-91
❖ GID II 16:57, 58; WLN 6:16-24

Space travel: "...to travel in space and distribute upon new worlds the vomit of our own corruption..."— God forbid
•RP 103 ❖ RP 10:8

Space travel: "We are not fit yet to visit other worlds. We have filled our own with massacre, torture, syphilis, famine..."
•CR 173 ❖ CR 14:41

Space Trilogy: I was trying to redeem for genuinely imaginative purposes the form known as "science fiction" (re: *Out of the Silent Planet*)
•L 295 ❖ L undated letter of Aug 1960

Space Trilogy, Lewis acknowledges a "heavy debt" to Ezekiel for his characterization of angels in the
•LAL 13 (*see also* LAL 72)
❖ LAL 4/iii/53 (*see also* LAL 22/2/58)

Space Trilogy, Lewis describes, as "a kind of theologised science-fiction"
•L 260
❖ L undated letter just before 2 Feb 55

Space Trilogy, Lewis describes how he chose some of the words and names used in
•L 283-284 ❖ L 29 Dec 58

Space Trilogy, Lewis refers to, as imagining "what God might be supposed to have done in other worlds"
•L 261 ❖ L 2 Feb 55

Space Trilogy: Lewis relates some of the reflections that first moved him to write science fiction*
•CR 173-174 ❖ CR 14:40-43

Space Trilogy: Ransom plays the role of Christ as every Christian is called upon in some measure to *enact* Christ
•L 283 ❖ L 29 Dec 58

Space Trilogy: *Voyage to Arcturus*, by David Lindsay, mentioned by Lewis as the "real father" of his own planet books
•L 205 ❖ L 29 Oct 44

Speaking in tongues—*see* Tongues

"Special Providences," On (title of Appendix B)
•M 174-181 ❖ M App. B

Specialness—*see* Personality, our unique

Speculation about God vs. revelation about Him
•GID 143-144 ❖ GID I 16:26

Speculation about the date of the Second Coming not worthwhile; we must be ready at all moments
•WLN 106-109 (*see also* GID 266)
❖ WLN 7:24-29 (*see also* GID II 16:54-56)

Speculation about the nature and object of our Desire: "If this opinion is not true, something better is"
•PP 149 ❖ PP 10:6

Speculation about unbelievers less valuable than earnest prayer for them
•L 247 (*see also* L 196)
❖ L 8 Nov 52 (*see also* L 8 Dec 41)

Speculations about unknowns (in this case, the destiny of animals) intended by Lewis to liberate the imagination*
•GID 169, 170 ❖ GID I 20:Reply-11, 15

Speech—*see also* Conversation; Talk(ing)

Speech, delivering a: The reading of a lecture sends people to sleep
•L 99
❖ L undated letter postmarked 28 Aug 24

Speech, precision in: "One used to be told as a child: 'Think what you're saying.' Apparently we also need to be told, 'Think what you're thinking'"*
•LM 45 ❖ LM 8:14

Speech: "...real beliefs may differ from the professed and may lurk in the turn of a phrase or the choice of an epithet*
•CR 28-29 ❖ CR 2:48

Spell, you and I have need of the strongest, to wake us from the evil enchantment of worldliness
•WG 7 (*see also* CR 93—re: enchantment of Myth of Evolutionism)
❖ WG 1:5 (*see also* CR 7:23—re: enchantment of Myth of Evolutionism)

Spiders, poverty frightens me more than anything else except large, and the tops of cliffs
•LAL 21 (*see also* L 257; SJ 8-9)
❖ LAL Aug 10th 53 (*see also* L 1 Nov 54; SJ 1:6, 7)

Spirit—*see also* Soul

"Spirit" and "ghost" in conflict due to the Fall; "Nature" causes disintegration and death of the body, and for this Christ's death is the remedy
•M 125-126 ❖ M 14:28-30

Spirit and Nature will one day be fully harmonised
•M 159, 160-161 (*see also* WG 72-73)
❖ M 16:27, 29 (*see also* WG 4:30)

"Spirit" and "organism" not at home together, as can be seen by people finding sexual references to be comic or unfortunate; this estrangement will be healed
•M 160 ❖ M 16:29

"Spirit" and "organism" not at home together, as can be seen by men making jokes about death

•M 127 ❖ M 14:32

Spirit and soul will be eventually harmonised; hence Christians believe in the resurrection of the body
•M 172 ❖ M App. A:11

"Spirit" and "Spiritual" as words often used to mean merely the *relatively* supernatural element in man which is handed out to all (rational element)
•M 170-171 ❖ M App. A:4

"Spirit" and "Spiritual", On the Words (title of Appendix A)
•M 169-173 ❖ M App. A

"Spirit," Centaur as an illustration of how "Nature" might one day be fully harmonised with
•M 126, 161 ❖ M 14:30; 16:29

Spirit, confusion between, and "ghost" has done much harm
•M 92 ❖ M 11:16

Spirit, earth's beauty hints at the future healing of Nature and
•M 159 ❖ M 16:27

Spirit, Holy—*see* Holy Spirit

"Spirit," human, once had full control of the human organism; this was lost through the Fall
•PP 77-78*, 81-83 ❖ PP 5:6*, 10

Spirit, human, went [at the Fall] from being the master of human nature to a mere lodger in its own house, or even a prisoner
•PP 83 ❖ PP 5:10

Spirit of the Age: I take a low view of "climates of opinion"; all discoveries are made and all errors corrected by those who ignore the "climate of opinion"*
•PP 134 ❖ PP 9:6

"Spirit of the age" mentioned as one of the things which influence our habitual way of thinking
•M 166 ❖ M 17:4

"Spirit," "Spirits," and "Spiritual": Lewis lists the various meanings given to these words
•M 171 ❖ M App. A:5-10

Spirit vs. soul as they relate to the values of "culture"
•CR 23 (*see also* CR xii for Walter Hooper's commentary on this)

❖ CR 2:34 (*see also* CR P:15 for Walter Hooper's commentary on this)

Spirits in Bondage, Lewis refers to publishing his book of poems entitled
• L 45 (*see also* L 51)
❖ L 9 Sep 18 (*see also* L 6 Jun 20)

"**Spiritual**" as a word and a concept which Screwtape twists to his own ends*
• SL 16, 48, 105, 126
❖ SL 3:3; 10:4; 23:1; 27:2

"Spiritual" as a word which has unhappily acquired many negative or restrictive senses
• RP 51 (*see also* L 182; RP 46)
❖ RP 5:9 (*see also* L 16 Apr 40; RP 5:5)

Spiritual concepts illustrated by mundane, earthly acts and language
• WG 56 (*see also* Imagery)
❖ WG 4:4 (*see also* Imagery)

Spiritual condition, knowledge of our— *see also* Self-knowledge

Spiritual condition, knowledge of our: "The attempt to discover by introspective analysis our own spiritual condition is to me a horrible thing..."
• WG 66 ❖ WG 4:18

Spiritual creature, God never meant man to be a purely
• MC 65 (*see also* M 162; Matter; Nature) ❖ MC II 5:7 (*see also* M 16:30; Matter; Nature)

"Spiritual" defined in two different ways: 1) pertaining to the Holy Spirit (always good), and 2) opposite of corporeal (may be good or evil) (re: Friendship as a "spiritual" love)
• FL 111 ❖ FL 4:39

Spiritual evils (pride, spite) worse than sensual evils
• L 175; LAL 111 (*see also* FL 111-112; GID 98; MC 94-95, 108-112; SJ 109)
❖ L 17 Jan 40; LAL 26 Nov 62 (*see also* FL 4:39; GID I 10:36; MC III 5:14; 8:1-8; SJ 7:11)

Spiritual experience cannot abide introspection
• WG 65-66 (*see also* Introspection)
❖ WG 4:18 (*see also* Introspection)

Spiritual experiences, in our childhood we already had, as pure and momentous as any we have undergone since
• PP 79 (*see also* PP 24-25; SJ chapters 1-5)
❖ PP 5:7 (*see also* PP 1:16; SJ ch. 1-5)

Spiritual gifts—*consider* Glossolalia

Spiritual growth—*see* Growth, Christian

Spiritual health, a man's, is exactly proportional to his love for God
• FL 13 ❖ FL 1:7

Spiritual life and human activities, no essential quarrel between
• WG 25-26 (*see also* CR 24; L 228)
❖ WG 2:8 (*see also* CR 2:37; L 23 Apr 51)

Spiritual life, every advance in, opens to one the possibility of blacker sins as well as brighter virtues
• L 301 (*see also* RP 28-32)
❖ L 20 Dec 61 (*see also* RP 3:17-20)

Spiritual life, I haven't any language weak enough to describe the weakness of my
• LM 113 ❖ LM 21:2

Spiritual life, natural things which are not in themselves sinful can become the servant of the, but are not automatically so
• L 268
❖ L undated letter just before 2 Apr 56

Spiritual life, we have not got to try to climb up into, by our own efforts; it has already come down into the human race
• MC 156-157 ❖ MC IV 5:8

Spiritual life ("Zoe") defined and discussed
• M 169-173 ❖ M App. A

Spiritual life ("Zoe") mentioned
• MC 139-140, 143, 153, 154, 156-157, 162, 186
❖ MC IV 1:15; 2:9; 4:10; 5:1, 2, 8; 7:6; 11:7

Spiritual longing—*see* Desire; Longing(s)

"Spiritual," meaning of the word, to modern minds ("...they don't really believe that envy could be as bad as drunkenness")
• GID 98 ❖ GID I 10:36

Spiritual pride—*see* Pride, spiritual

Spiritual renewal—*see* New Birth

Spiritual things, experience of, is essential

to our understanding of them ("Spiritual things are spiritually discerned")
- •WG 54-73, esp. WG 65
- ❖ WG ch. 4, esp. WG 4:16

Spiritual things, there can be a merely impulsive, headstrong, greedy desire even for, —a desire which is "flesh" and not "spirit"
- •LM 65 ❖ LM 12:11

Spiritualism—*see also* Occult

Spiritualism as encountered by Lewis through the Matron at "Chartres"
- •SJ 59-60, 66 (*see also* SJ 175)
- ❖ SJ 4:6, 13 (*see also* SJ 11:12)

Spiritualism mentioned as one of many non-Christian creeds Lewis found among his audiences
- •GID 240-241, 252 ❖ GID II 14:9

Spiritualism offers only a vague comfort for our unredeemably personal hankerings and adds a new horror to death—that of mere endless succession
- •GID 142-143 ❖ GID I 16:25

Spiritualism: "Reality never repeats. The exact same thing is never taken away and given back"
- •GO 28-29 (*see also* GO 15-16)
- ❖ GO 2:14 (*see also* GO 1:29)

Spiritualism: The vast majority of spirit messages sink pitiably below the best that has been thought and said in this world
- •GID 142 ❖ GID I 16:24

Spiritualism, Theosophy, and Pantheism as encountered by Lewis in the writings of Maeterlinck
- •SJ 175-178 ❖ SJ 11:12-16

Spirituality, people who *appear* to lack all: "Somewhere under that glib surface there lurks, however atrophied, a human soul"*
- •WLN 85 ❖ WLN 6:9

Spirituality, Screwtape advises that if, cannot be removed from a human's life then it ought to be *corrupted*
- •SL 105 ❖ SL 23:1

"Spirituality": The Supernatural, on entering a human soul, opens to it new possibilities of both good and evil; of

all bad men religious bad men are the worst*
- •RP 31-32 (*see also* L 301; RP 28)
- ❖ RP 3:20 (*see also* L 20 Dec 61; RP 3:17)

Spirituality, to shrink back from all that can be called Nature into negative, is as if we ran away from horses instead of learning to ride (re: imagery)
- •M 162-163 ❖ M 16:31, 32

Sports: Games and dance are frivolous and unimportant down here, for "down here" is not their natural place; will be enjoyed without frivolity in Heaven*
- •LM 92-93 (*see also* LM 115-116*)
- ❖ LM 17:17 (*see also* LM 21:13*)

Sports: "Games...seem to me to lead to ambition, jealousy, and embittered partisan feeling, quite as often as to anything else"
- •SJ 129 ❖ SJ 8:13

Sports: I was useless at games
- •SJ 94 (*see also* L 75)
- ❖ SJ 6:18 (*see also* L 18 May 22)

Sports: "It is a serious matter to choose wholesome recreations: but they would no longer be recreations if we pursued them seriously"*
- •CR 33-34 ❖ CR 2:54

Sports, Lewis's dislike for
- •SJ 90, 96-98, 107, 113-114, 129-130 (*see also* L 61*, LAL 46, LM 3, 92)
- ❖ SJ 6:11, 20-23; 7:9, 18; 8:13 (*see also* L 29 May 21*; LAL 9/10/55; LM 1:2; 17:16)

Sports: Making them organized and compulsory in school banished the element of play
- •SJ 98 (*see also* SJ 107)
- ❖ SJ 6:22, 23 (*see also* SJ 7:9)

Sports: "Not to like them is a misfortune, because it cuts you off from companionship with many excellent people who can be approached in no other way"
- •SJ 129-130 ❖ SJ 8:13

Spring, Resurrection likened to a crocus— it is a harbinger of
- •GID 87-88 ❖ GID I 9:11

Squirrel Nutkin, the second instance of Lewis's experience of "Joy" or long-

ing came through the book, by Beatrix
Potter
•SJ 16-17 ❖ SJ 1:16

Standard(s)—*see also* Moral judgement(s);
Moral standards; Morality; Value(s);
consider also Virtue

Standard, how difficult it is to avoid having a special, for oneself (how many
people believe themselves to be snobs,
prigs, etc.?)
•LAL 58 ❖ LAL 5/7/56

Standard of behaviour strikingly similar
in the teachings of Zarathustra, Jeremiah, Socrates, Gautama, and
Christ—teachers widely separated in
time
•PP 63 (*see also* CR 44-56, 77; MC 19,
78; RP 27; Law of Nature; book *The
Abolition of Man*)
❖ PP 4:10 (*see also* CR ch. 4; 6:16; MC I
1:7; III 3:1; RP 3:13; Law of Nature;
book *The Abolition of Man*)

Standard of decency in the human race
may turn out to be vastly inferior to
that of the larger universe
•PP 62-63 ❖ PP 4:10

Standard of right and wrong, God's, may
differ from ours but not as white differs from black
•PP 37-39 (*see also* CR 67-69, 79; GO
36-38) ❖ PP 3:2-4 (*see also* CR 5:21-23;
6:19; GO 2:28-30)

Standard, ultimate, implied when accusing the universe of futility
•CR 65-66 ❖ CR 5:19

Standard, ultimate, implied when accusing the universe of being cruel and
unjust*
•MC 45-46 (*see also* Moral law, objectivity of) ❖ MC II 1:5, 6 (*see also* Moral
law, objectivity of)

Standard, ultimate, implied when advocating an ethic which furthers the
"preservation of the human race"
•CR 48-52, 74 (*see also* M 37-38; MC
29-30) ❖ CR 4:12-19; 6:7 (*see also* M 5:7-
10; MC I 3:5, 6)

Standard, ultimate, necessary in the creation of values*
•GID 23 ❖ GID I 1:5, 6

Standard, what alarms us in the Christian
picture of Judgement is the infinite
purity of the, against which our actions will be judged (re: Judgement in
the Psalms)
•RP 13 ❖ RP 2:8

Standards, Christian, permanent and unchanging in the face of increasing
knowledge
•GID 44-45, 92 ❖ GID I 3:13, 14; 10:7

Standards, I accepted the, of these friends
at Oxford; they believed that veracity,
public spirit, chastity, and sobriety
were all obligatory
•SJ 201 ❖ SJ 13:6

Standards, lowering your moral, in order
to prevent guilt (or "shame"): "It is
mad work to remove hypocrisy by
removing the temptation to hypocrisy"*
•PP 57 ❖ PP 4:3

Standards of propriety change with time
and place, but the rule of chastity remains the same for all Christians at all
times
•MC 88-89 ❖ MC III 5:1

Star(s)—*consider also* Film star(s); Universe
Stars: "The night sky suggests that the inanimate also has for God some value
we cannot imagine"*
•LM 55 ❖ LM 10:10

Stars, when one considers the sky and all
the, it seems strange that God should
be at all concerned with man—yet He
has given us extraordinary honour
(re: Psalm 8)
•RP 132 ❖ RP 12:11

State of the Dead—*see* Dead, state of

Steadfastness or perseverance in the
Christian life, Screwtape lists obstacles to, ("The routine of adversity,
the gradual decay of youthful
loves...")
•SL 132 (*see also* Obstacles to Christian perseverance) ❖ SL 28:1 (*see also*
Obstacles to Christian perseverance)

Steadfastness, Screwtape laments that suffering is probably not an obstacle to
Christian, since humans have been
told it is an essential part of Redemp-

tion*
- •SL 27 ❖ SL 5:3

Steadfastness: Screwtape rues the man who feels that every trace of God has vanished, and asks why he has been forsaken, and still obeys*
- •SL 39 ❖ SL 8:4

Stepsons, Lewis's—*see* Gresham, David and Douglas

Stewardship: We cannot give God anything that is not His already*
- •MC 125 (*see also* SL 96-99)
- ❖ MC III 11:9 (*see also* SL 21:2-6)

Stillness—*see* Peace; Silence

Stoic superiority toward nature (including human nature) differs from the Christian view of nature
- •GID 148-149 ❖ GID I 17:5

Stoics held that myths were allegorically true
- •GID 131 ❖ GID 16:4

Stoics, the notion that to desire our own good and the enjoyment of it is a bad thing has crept in from Kant and the
- •WG 3 ❖ WG 1:1

Stoics, works of, mentioned with regard to Need-pleasures vs. Appreciative pleasures
- •FL 27 ❖ FL 2:3

Stoical Ethics: two definitions
- •CR 44-45 ❖ CR 4:2

Stoical Monism, this sort of, was the philosophy of my New Look [at Oxford]; it gave me a great sense of peace
- •SJ 205 ❖ SJ 13:11

Stoicism and Confucianism, the purely moral systems like, are philosophies for aristocrats
- •CR 71 ❖ CR 5:26

Stoicism as an anti-nature religion which simply contradicts our natural desires (vs. Christianity, which neither contradicts nor affirms them)
- •GID 86 (*see also* M 119*)
- ❖ GID I 9:9 (*see also* M 14:20*)

Stoicism, even, finds itself willy-nilly bowing the knee to God (re: connection of morality with "the Numinous")
- •PP 23 ❖ PP 1:13

Stoicism mentioned with regard to the

doctrine of immortality
- •GID 130 ❖ GID I 16:2

Stoicism, Pascal referred to Error of: thinking we can do always what we can do sometimes (e.g., prayers without words)
- •LM 11 ❖ LM 2:5

Stone, the apparent, will be bread to us if we believe that a Father's hand put it into ours, in mercy or in justice or even in rebuke
- •LM 53 ❖ LM 10:3

Storge—*see* Affection

Story—*see* Myth; *consider* Allegory; Books; Literature; Writing

Studies in Words, probable reference to Lewis's book, ("a dull, academic, technical one, tho' exciting to me")
- •LAL 79 ❖ LAL Dec 25th 58

Studying—*see also* Learning

Studying and learning tough bits of theology can cause the heart to "sing unbidden"
- •GID 205 ❖ GID II 4:7

Subconscious, psychologists have made the error of underestimating the depth and variety of the contents of our, (sex not the only element)*
- •LM 79 ❖ LM 15:8

"Subjective" and "real" as words which Screwtape uses to his advantage, depending on the situation
- •SL 142-144 ❖ SL 30:4

Subjectivism—*consider also* Ethic(s); Law of Nature; Moral value(s); Value(s)

Subjectivism about values is eternally incompatible with democracy; the very idea of freedom presupposes an objective moral law over rulers and ruled alike
- •CR 81 (*see also* CR 56)
- ❖ CR 6:22 (*see also* CR 4:27)

Subjectivism defined: the view that reason is caused by chemical or electrical events in a cortex which is itself the result of a blind evolutionary process*
- •CR 72 (*see also* Reason)
- ❖ CR 6:2 (*see also* Reason)

Subjectivism, how the modern error of,

has affected our judgement of good and evil
•CR 72-81 ❖ CR ch. 6

Subjectivism: Out of this apparently innocent idea comes the fatal superstition that men can create values, and that a community can "choose" its ideology
•CR 73 ❖ CR 6:5

Subjectivism regards morality as a subjective sentiment to be altered at will
•CR 73 ❖ CR 6:5

Subjectivism, scientists may flirt with the error of, but in the main subjectivism is an uncomfortable yokefellow for research
•CR 72 ❖ CR 6:3

Subjectivism: The conclusion that logic is a real insight into reality and is not merely subjective rules out any materialistic account of thinking*
•CR 63 (see also Reason/ing)
❖ CR 5:14-16 (see also Reason/ing)

Subjectivism, The Poison of (chapter title)
•CR 72-81 ❖ CR ch. 6

Subjectivism: Under this view it is useless to compare moral ideas of one society or age with those of another; progress and decadence are meaningless words
•CR 73 (see also CR 75)
❖ CR 6:5 (see also CR 6:11)

Subjectivism: Where reason is thought to be the by-product of a blind evolutionary process, there is no reason for supposing that logic yields truth
•CR 72 (see also Reason)
❖ CR 6:2 (see also Reason)

Subjectivism yields the view that value judgements are not really judgements at all, but sentiments produced by social conditioning
•CR 73 ❖ CR 6:4

Subjectivity of moral value(s)—see Subjectivism

Subjectivity vs. objectivity of human thought: All knowledge depends on the validity of inference*
•CR 62-63 (see also Knowledge)
❖ CR 5:12, 13 (see also Knowledge)

Submission—consider also Will of God

Submission: In the Lord's Prayer, when I ask, "Thy will be done," I am asking that I may be enabled to do it (not merely that I may be able to accept it)
•LM 25-26 ❖ LM 5:6-9

Submission should be not only towards possible future afflictions but also towards possible future blessings
•LM 26 ❖ LM 5:10

Substitute, experience and taste do not always confirm what is real and what is a, (re: religion as reality or substitute)
•CR 38-41 ❖ CR 3:3-9

Substitute, "Joy" is not a, for sex; sex is very often a substitute for "Joy"—and I sometimes wonder whether all pleasures are not substitutes for "Joy"
•SJ 170 (see also SJ 203-204*; Joy)
❖ SJ 11:6 (see also SJ 13:10*; Joy)

Substitute, question of whether religion is only a, for the real well-being we have failed to achieve on earth
•CR 37-43 (see also GID 271-274*; WLN 19*) ❖ CR ch. 3 (see also GID III 1:1-7*; WLN 2:8*)

Substitute, since my marriage I can never again believe that religion is a, for sex
•GO 6 ❖ GO 1:12

Substitutes, acts of worship and religious festivals can become, for God Himself (e.g., Christmas)
•RP 48-49 ❖ RP 5:7

Substitution of Christ for us more like paying a debt than taking a punishment
•MC 59 (see also Atonement)
❖ MC II 4:7 (see also Atonement)

Success—see also Ambition

Success, self-sufficiency the possible result of those vices that lead to worldly
•PP 98 ❖ PP 6:9

Suffering—see also Difficulties; Pain

Suffering and prayer for others: "... there's a lot scattered through 2d Corinthians which is well worth meditation"
•LAL 55 ❖ LAL 15/4/56

Suffering, anticipation of pain and of death a cause of much acute mental,

in Man; is the result of Reason
•PP 14 (*see also* GO 9*)
❖ PP 1:1 (*see also* GO 1:18*)

Suffering: Aren't all these notes the sense-less writhings of a man who won't accept that there's nothing we can do with suffering except to suffer it?
•GO 38 ❖ GO 2:31

Suffering, as Christians we cannot cease to fight against all kinds of; Christian-ity is both world-affirming and world-denying*
•GID 147-150 (*see also* World, im-provement of) ❖ GID I ch. 17 (*see also* World, improvement of)

Suffering as used by God in soul-making: "I have seen men, for the most part, grow better not worse with advanc-ing years..."
•PP 108 ❖ PP 6:18

Suffering, avoidance of—*see also* Self-pro-tection

Suffering, avoidance of, not what life is really about; all Jesus' followers must take up the cross
•CR 155 (*see also* FL 168, 170)
❖ CR 13:6 (*see also* FL 6:10, 14)

Suffering: Bystanders must control their own indignation lest it steal patience and humility from those who suffer, and plant anger and cynicism in their stead
•PP 107-108 ❖ PP 6:18

Suffering: Camaraderie among fellow sufferers (such as among soldiers) makes tribulation easier to bear
•SJ 188 ❖ SJ 12:10

Suffering can contribute to a complex good when exploited by God—but is not simply good in itself
•PP 110-111 ❖ PP 7:2

Suffering: "Children suffer not (I think) less than their elders, but differently" (re: Lewis's grief on the loss of his mother)
•SJ 18-19 ❖ SJ 1:20

Suffering, even if all, were man-made, we should like to know the reason God seems to have given permission to men to torture their fellows
•PP 89 ❖ PP 6:1

Suffering furnishes an occasion for sub-mission to the Divine will, but also exposes us to the danger of rebellion
•PP 112 (*see also* L 257)
❖ PP 7:3 (*see also* L 1 Nov 54)

Suffering, good of, includes compassion aroused in the spectators and the acts of mercy to which it leads
•PP 110 ❖ PP 7:2

Suffering helps to cure us of the illusion of "independence"
•LAL 20-21 ❖ LAL Aug 10th 53

Suffering: Humans have been plainly told that it is an essential part of Redemp-tion; therefore, says Screwtape, it is largely ineffective as an attack on faith
•SL 27 ❖ SL 5:3

Suffering, humiliation as a form of: We should mind it less if we were hum-bler
•LAL 29 ❖ LAL Mar 31st 54

Suffering, I am not convinced that, has any natural tendency to produce anger and cynicism on its own; may have the opposite tendency
•PP 108 ❖ PP 6:18

Suffering, I assume that the process of purification [in Purgatory] will in-volve; most real good that has been done me in this life has involved it
•LM 109 ❖ LM 20:11

Suffering, I had been far more anxious to avoid, than to achieve delight
•SJ 228 (*see also* SJ 117*, 171)
❖ SJ 14:22 (*see also* SJ 7:21*; 11:8)

Suffering: "If there is a good God, then these tortures are necessary..." (re: loss and grief)
•GO 49-50 ❖ GO 3:15-18

Suffering: "It doesn't really matter whether you grip the arms of the dentist's chair or let your hands lie in your lap. The drill drills on"
•GO 38 (*see also* Dentist analogy)
❖ GO 2:31 (*see also* Dentist analogy)

Suffering, Jesus shared the, not only of the righteous but of the guilty—that which comes to evil men who at last know their own evil

•RP 127 (*consider also* Self-knowledge)
❖ RP 12:7 (*consider also* Self-knowledge)

Suffering makes relevant and personal the question of whether God exists and whether He is good; until then the question is of no serious importance
•GO 43 ❖ GO 3:4

Suffering may be necessary to turn finite creatures (with free wills) into Gods
•L 257 (*consider also* Gods) ❖ L 1 Nov 54—first letter (*consider also* Gods)

Suffering not always but sometimes may be sent as a punishment (as suggested by parts of the Old Testament and Revelation)
•L 237-238 ❖ L 31 Jan 52

Suffering not good in itself; what is good in any painful experience is, for the sufferer, his submission to the will of God
•PP 110 ❖ PP 7:2

Suffering, nothing we can do will eradicate; I think the best results are obtained by people who work quietly away at limited objectives
•WG 44-45 ❖ WG 3:20

Suffering of "decent, inoffensive, worthy people," possible reason for
•PP 96-97 ❖ PP 6:8

Suffering of the innocent less of a problem to me than that of the wicked, in whom it seems to produce only hate, resentment, blasphemy, and egoism
•L 257 ❖ L 1 Nov 54 (first letter)

Suffering, Our Lord suffers in all the, of His people
•L 234 ❖ L 12 Sep 51

Suffering: "Part of every misery is...the fact that you don't merely suffer but have to keep on thinking about the fact that you suffer"
•GO 9 (*see also* PP 14)
❖ GO 1:18 (*see also* PP 1:1)

Suffering, physical vs. mental: Physical pain can be continuous; the mind has some power of evasion*
•GO 46-47 ❖ GO 3:11

Suffering, reconciling human, with the existence of a God who loves is not insoluble if we understand the nature of that love and the place of Man
•PP 47-48 ❖ PP 3:15

Suffering: Salvation apparently not dependent upon degree of tribulation in this life; some old saints seem to have got through their seventy years with surprising ease
•PP 104 ❖ PP 6:15

Suffering: "Straight tribulation is easier to bear than tribulation which advertises itself as pleasure"*
•SJ 188 ❖ SJ 12:10

Suffering taught the Jewish people that earthly prosperity is not the probable reward of seeing God; the book of Job was grimly illustrated in practice
•RP 43 ❖ RP 4:19

Suffering teaches us not to rest our hearts in this world
•PP 106, 115 (*see also* CR 37; L 227; SL 132) ❖ PP 6:17; 7:7 (*see also* CR 3:2; L 5 Mar 51; SL 28:2)

Suffering: "...the less one can think about happiness on earth, the less, I believe, one suffers"
•LAL 96 (*see also* SL 95-96)
❖ LAL 9 Jan 61 (*see also* SL 21:2)

Suffering: "The more we believe that God hurts only to heal, the less we can believe that there is any use in begging for tenderness"
•GO 49-50 ❖ GO 3:17

Suffering, the most inevitable "second meaning" in the Psalms is that the expressions of, are all related to Christ's suffering
•RP 126-127 ❖ RP 12:7

Suffering, the old Christian doctrine of being made perfect through, is not incredible; but to prove it palatable is beyond my design
•PP 105 ❖ PP 6:16

Suffering: The real problem is not why some humble, pious, believing people suffer, but why some do not
•PP 104 ❖ PP 6:15

Suffering, the redemptive effect of, lies chiefly in its tendency to reduce the rebel will

•PP 112 ❖ PP 7:3

Suffering, the "romance" of, is unmasked by five minutes of genuine toothache; and with it goes self-pity for imaginary distresses
•SL 58 ❖ SL 13:3

Suffering: The sacrifice of Christ is repeated among His followers in varying degrees; the causes of this distribution I do not know
•PP 104 ❖ PP 6:15

Suffering, there is no such thing as a sum of human; two people suffering does not increase the amount of pain experienced
•PP 115-116 (see also L 186; WG 30-31)
❖ PP 7:8 (see also L 2 Jun 40; WG 2:14)

Suffering: "To grin and bear it and (in some feeble, desperate way) to trust is the utmost most of us can manage"
•LAL 56 ❖ LAL 26/4/56

Suffering, try to exclude the possibility of, (in a world with free will), and you find that you have excluded life itself
•PP 33-34 ❖ PP 2:15

Suffering ("unhappiness"), one of the fruits of, is that it forces us to think of life as something to go through—and out at the other end
•L 227 ❖ L 5 Mar 51

Suffering, vicariousness in: The Sinless Man suffers for the sinful, and, in their degree, all men for all bad men
•M 118 (see also GID 85-86)
❖ M 14:19 (see also GID I 9:8)

Suffering: We are taught to offer it to Christ as our share of His suffering—but it is so hard to do
•LAL 55-56 ❖ LAL 26/4/56

Suffering which falls upon us by necessity can be as meritorious as voluntary suffering, if embraced for Christ's sake
•LAL 20, 60, 105
❖ LAL Aug 10th 53; 3/8/56; 3/7/62

Suffering which we willingly accept for others and then offer to God may be united with the suffering of Our Lord and may help to their redemption
•L 234 ❖ L 12 Sep 51

Sufferings, each individual's personal, can never be more than those of one man
•L 186 (see also PP 115-116; WG 30-31)
❖ L 2 Jun 40 (see also PP 7:8; WG 2:14)

Sufferings, every movement in the Passion of Christ writes large some common element in the, of the human race
•LM 43 ❖ LM 8:10, 11

Sufferings of men, people's cruelty to one another perhaps account for four-fifths of the
•PP 89 ❖ PP 6:1

Sufferings, our human: "We are not on an untrodden path. Rather, on the main road"—shared also with our Master
•LM 44 ❖ LM 8:13

Sufferings, we were promised; they were part of the program—but it is different when the thing happens to oneself
•GO 41-42 ❖ GO 3:3

Suicide: If ever finite disasters proved greater than one wished to bear, suicide would always be possible—but Christianity had no door marked "Exit"
•SJ 171 (see also GO 33)
❖ SJ 11:8 (see also GO 2:22)

Suicide mentioned briefly
•LAL 50 ❖ LAL 19/12/55

Suicide: My real fear is not of materialism; if it were true, suicide could provide a way out
•GO 33 ❖ GO 2:22

Suicide, physician-assisted: ". . .rejoice that God's law allows you to extend to Fanda that last mercy which. . .we are forbidden to extend to suffering humans" (re: a friend's pet)**
•LAL 61 ❖ LAL 18/8/56

"Sum of human misery," there is no such thing as, for no one suffers it (each person can only suffer the pain of one person)
•PP 115-116 (see also L 186; WG 30-31)
❖ PP 7:8 (see also L 2 Jun 40; WG 2:14)

Summer, Lewis mentions his distaste for, (he preferred Autumn)*
•L 30, 31 (see also L 308*) ❖ L 27 Sep 16; 30 Oct 16 (see also L 27 Oct 63*)

Sun—see also Light

Sun, a blessed spirit is a body ever more completely uncovered to the meridian blaze of the spiritual
•PP 151 ❖ PP 10:9

Sun and the sun's reflection in a dew-drop as a comparison to the Christian experience and the merely imaginative experience
•SJ 167 ❖ SJ 11:4

Sun and the sun's reflection in a pond as analogy to the resemblance between Christian truth and Pagan myths
•RP 107 ❖ RP 10:11

Sun: God's glory cannot be diminished by our refusal to worship Him, just as the sun cannot be put out by writing the word "darkness" on a cell wall
•PP 53 ❖ PP 3:18

Sun, I believe in Christianity as I believe that the, has risen—not only because I see it, but because by it I see everything else
•WG 92 (see also M 110; SJ 180*; WG 69) ❖ WG 5:24 (see also M 14:3; SJ 11:19*; WG 4:24)

Sun, in a certain sense it is no more possible to invent a new ethics than to place a new, in the sky
•CR 53, 75 (consider also Ethics) ❖ CR 4:22; 6:9 (consider also Ethics)

Sun, in Adoration one's mind runs back up the sunbeam to the
•LM 90 (see also GO 73*) ❖ LM 17:8 (see also GO 4:7, 8*)

Sun, in the Monotheistic religion of Akhenaten of Egypt God was not identified with the; the visible disc was only His manifestation
•RP 86 ❖ RP 8:16

Sun, Law of God associated with the, in Psalm 19 ("...the all-piercing, all-detecting sunshine...luminous, severe, disinfectant, exultant")
•RP 63-64 (see also RP 81) ❖ RP 6:13 (see also RP 8:9)

Sun as parallel to "the real world": Our natural experiences are like pencil lines on flat paper which will someday be flooded by the sunshine of reality

•WG 69 (see also WG 72) ❖ WG 4:24 (see also WG 4:30)

Sun, we are mirrors whose brightness is wholly derived from the, which shines upon us
•FL 180 ❖ FL 6:27

Sun, we believe that the, is in the sky at midday not because we can clearly see the sun but because we can see everything else (re: Incarnation)
•M 110 ❖ M 14:3

Sunbeam, trying to grasp Our Lord's teaching by intellect alone like trying to bottle a; it demands a response from the whole man
•RP 113 ❖ RP 11:7, 9

Sunlight and shadows make up so much of the beauty of the world
•LAL 80 ❖ LAL Dec 25th 58

Sunlight, any patch of, will show you something about the sun which you could not get from books on astronomy (re: adoration of God via experience of pleasure)
•LM 91 ❖ LM 17:13

Sunlight, I hate indoor; it makes shadows across the page of your book
•LAL 46 ❖ LAL 9/10/55

Superiority—see also Pride

Superiority and pride, best book about, is Law's Serious Call to a Devout and Holy Life
•LAL 44-45 ❖ LAL 30/6/55

Superiority, feeling of, involved in helping others: "...for me it is much harder to receive than to give, but, I think, much more blessed" (—Joy Lewis)
•LAL 76 ❖ LAL Jun 6th [1958]

Superiority in others, Screwtape observes that humans tend to resent every kind of; to denigrate it, to wish its annihilation
•SL 163; WLN 61 (see also MC 109) ❖ SL 32:23; WLN 4:23 (see also MC III 8:1-3)

Superiority, in the New Testament I found a number of emphatic warnings against every kind of, (re: the pursuit of "culture")
•CR 14 ❖ CR 2:6

Superiority of Christian ethics over other ways of thinking: Our appreciation of this may lead to priggery
• RP 64-65 (see also SL 110-113)
❖ RP 6:14 (see also SL 24:1-5)

Superiority: Pride means enmity, not only toward our fellow man but toward God; in God we come up against something immeasurably superior to ourselves
• MC 111 ❖ MC III 8:6

Superiority, sense of corporate, which may develop in a circle of Friends
• FL 116-124 (see also Inner Rings)
❖ FL 4:48-57 (see also Inner Rings)

Superiority: Since men do not like to be merely equal with other men, we find them building themselves into groups in which they can feel superior to the mass
• WLN 41 ❖ WLN 3:14

Superiority: We want to keep well away from anything better or stronger or higher than ourselves
• MC 154 (see also MC 110-111)
❖ MC IV 5:2 (see also MC III 8:4, 5)

Superiority: Whenever we find that our religious life is making us feel that we are good, or better than others, we may be sure we are being acted on by the devil
• MC 111 ❖ MC III 8:7

Supernatural—see also Numinous

Supernatural, argument for, vs. Naturalism
• M 12-44 ❖ M ch. 3-6

Supernatural, belief in, as an essential part of real religion (as opposed to all watered down and modernist versions)
• L 170 (see also GID 099; Christianity-and-water) ❖ L 8 Nov 39 (see also GID I 10:41; Christianity-and-water)

Supernatural, evidence for, may become like windows are to gardens, or as grammar to language—the most obvious is the most easily forgotten
• M 40-42 ❖ M 6:3-5

Supernatural, existence of, may be deduced from the experience of Awe if it is not a mere twist in the human mind
• PP 20-21 ❖ PP 1:11

Supernatural: How can it loom less than large if it is believed in at all?
• LM 120 ❖ LM 22:7, 9

Supernatural, human reason along with morality listed as proofs of the
• M 43 (see also GID 275-276; MC 17-39; WG 88-89, 91; Reason)
❖ M 6:7 (see also GID III 1:13-16; MC Book I; WG 5:21, 24; Reason)

Supernatural, Lewis mentions his resolution (during his early years at Oxford) to disavow any idea of the
• SJ 201 ❖ SJ 13:7

Supernatural: Lewis's answer to the objection, "If so stupendous a thing exists, ought it not to be as obvious as the sun in the sky?"
• M 40-41 ❖ M 6:3-5

Supernatural, "liberal" Christians who disbelieve in the, genuinely believe that writers of my sort are doing a great deal of harm
• LM 118-119 ❖ LM 22:1-3

Supernatural life given to both good and bad angels vs. the kind of supernatural life given only to a creature who voluntarily surrenders himself to it
• M 170 (see also FL 15)
❖ M App. A:2, 3 (see also FL 1:9)

Supernatural ("magical") element of Christianity can never be reduced to zero; if it is, what remains is only morality, or culture, or philosophy (re: Holy Communion)
• LM 104 ❖ LM 19:11

Supernatural, Man is on the borderline between the Natural and the
• GID 276 ❖ GID III 1:18

"Supernatural" meaning something which invades, or is added to, the great interlocked event in space and time, instead of merely arising from it
• M 169 ❖ M App. A:1

Supernatural, on entering a human soul, opens to it new possibilities both of good and of evil; of all bad men religious bad men are the worst
• RP 31-32 (see also L 301; RP 28)
❖ RP 3:20 (see also L 20 Dec 61; RP 3:17)

Supernatural or "something beyond" hinted at by Man's rationality
•M 27-29 ❖ M 4:5-8

Supernaturalism, Lewis describes himself as committed to, "in its full rigour"
•CR 44 ❖ CR 4:1

Supernaturalism: Screwtape laments that disbelief in devils takes away their ability to terrorize, while belief in them precludes materialism and scepticism*
•SL 32-33 ❖ SL 7:1

Supernaturalism: The Jewish, Moslem, and Christian view of universe is that there is something beyond Nature which refutes the scientist's picture of futility*
•CR 59 ❖ CR 5:5

"Supernaturalist" defined as someone who believes that, besides Nature, there exists something else
•M 5-11, esp. 5 ❖ M ch. 2, esp. 2:1

Supernaturalist, Lewis mentions some of the factors which caused him to become a*
•CR 41 ❖ CR 3:9

Supernaturalist, Neville Coghill was a Christian and a thoroughgoing
•SJ 212 ❖ SJ 14:2

Supernaturalists, Evangelicals and Anglo-Catholics share the fact of being thoroughgoing
•GID 336 ❖ GID IV Letter 9

Superpersonal: God described as "living yet superpersonal" (re: relationship between God and the moral law)
•CR 80 ❖ CR 6:22

Superpersonal God: "...the Christians are the only people who offer any idea of what a being that is beyond personality could be like"
•MC 140-141 (see also God, personal)
❖ MC IV 2:2 (see also God, personal)

Surprised by Joy, commentary on Lewis's conversion experience as related in
•GID 261 (re: SJ 224, 229)
❖ GID II 16:19-22 (re: SJ 14:16, 23)

Surprised by Joy written "partly in answer to requests that I would tell how I passed from Atheism to Christianity"
•SJ vii ❖ SJ P:1

Surrender—*see also* Self-surrender; *consider also* Conversion; Repentance

Surrender as "movement full speed astern"—realizing you have been on the wrong track, and getting ready to start life over again
•MC 59 ❖ MC II 4:7 (see also PP 6:13)

Surrender: "Christ says 'Give me All. I don't want so much of your time and so much of your money and so much of your work: I want You'"
•MC 167 (see also WG 130)
❖ MC IV 8:4 (see also WG 9:9)

Surrender: "[God] may have to take all these 'riches' away from you; if He doesn't, you will go on relying on them"*
•GID 51-52 ❖ GID I 4:18 (Ques. 5)

Surrender: "...'having to depend solely on God' is what we all dread most"*
•LAL 49 ❖ LAL 16/12/55

Surrender in the perfect sense cannot (since the Fall) be learned by doing what is pleasurable; demands pain, or at least the absence of inclination
•PP 99, 101 ❖ PP 6:10, 13

Surrender: It is a poor thing to come to God as a last resort, to offer up "our own" when it is no longer worth keeping; but God is not proud, He will have us...
•PP 97 (see also LAL 49*; SJ 229) ❖ PP 6:8 (see also LAL 16/12/55*; SJ 14:23)

Surrender, Lewis talks about the reluctance we feel toward, and our desire to call our souls our own; our desire for "limited liabilities"*
•PP 80; SJ 171-172, 228, 237; SL 97-99; WG 126-132; *consider also* Self-reservation
❖ PP 5:8; SJ 11:8; 14:22; 15:8; SL 21:4-6; WG ch. 9; *consider also* Self-reservation

Surrender, Lewis mentions his realization of the need for total, on the eve of his conversion
•SJ 228 ❖ SJ 14:22

Surrender likened to having a tooth out: "Christ says...I don't want to drill the

tooth, or crown it, or stop it, but to have it out"
- •MC 167 (see also Dentist analogy)
- ❖ MC IV 8:4 (see also Dentist analogy)

Surrender: "Surely the main purpose of our life is to reach the point at which 'one's own life as a person' is at an end"*
- •LAL 97-98 ❖ LAL 28 Mar 61

Surrender, the perfect, was undergone in our behalf by Christ
- •MC 59-60, 62 ❖ MC II 4:6-9; 5:1

Surrender to God, importance and urgency of: "In each of us there is something growing up which will of itself be hell unless it is nipped in the bud"*
- •GID 155 ❖ GID I 18:11

Surrender: "We will not turn to Him as long as He leaves us anything else to turn to"*
- •LAL 49 ❖ LAL 16/12/55

Surrender: "While what we call 'our own life' remains agreeable we will not surrender it to Him"
- •PP 96 ❖ PP 6:8

Surrey, Lewis mentions a conversation in which he observed the "wildness" of
- •SJ 134 ❖ SJ 9:6-8

Surrey, scenery of, described
- •SJ 132, 134, 145-147 ❖ SJ 9:1, 6-8, 22

Survival can have no value apart from the prior value of what survives
- •L 158 (see also GID 297, 311; SL 131; WG 43*) ❖ L 13 Jan 37 (see also GID III 4:20; 8:1; SL 28:1; WG 3:18*)

Suspicion often creates what it suspects (e.g., people who are suspected of being prigs may decide to become prigs)
- •SL 164; WLN 62-63
- ❖ SL 32:27; WLN 4:27

"Sweeter than Honey" (chapter title)
- •RP 54-65 ❖ RP ch. 6

Swimmer, analogy of drowning, to show how Christ's advantage is the only reason He can help us
- •L 234-235; MC 61
- ❖ L undated letter between 12 Sep 51 and 3 Dec 51; MC II 4:10

Swimmer, analogy of drowning, to show that philosophical definiteness about

details is not the first necessity once a belief in God has been accepted (re: nature of God)
- •M 75-76 ❖ M 10:15

Swimming analogy: Faith as confidence vs. intellectual assent: This analogy shows how trust must sometimes operate without the feeling of confidence
- •L 199 (see also CR 42-43; GID 172-173*; MC 122-123; WLN 23-25)
- ❖ L 20 Jan 42 (see also CR 3:11; GID I 21:2*; MC III 11:3; WLN 2:12, 13)

Swimming analogy to show our fear of immersing ourselves in the Christian life (but "Swimming lessons are better than a lifeline to the shore")
- •WG 128, 130, 131 (see also FL 181; Self-reservation) ❖ WG 9:6, 8, 12 (see also FL 6:28; Self-reservation)

Swimming, Lewis's fondness for
- •SJ 178, 182 ❖ SJ 11:18; 12:1

Sword, Joy (Lewis's wife) described as being like a
- •GO 72-73 (see also GO 49)
- ❖ GO 4:6-9 (see also GO 3:15)

Sword, marriage heals the, between the sexes; separately most men and women are poor, warped fragments of humanity—in marriage the two become fully human
- •GO 57-58 ❖ GO 3:32

Sword of Damocles really hangs over all mortals
- •L 280 ❖ L 6 Nov 57

Sword of Damocles, we live always under the
- •LAL 65, 69
- ❖ LAL 17/1/57; Oct 20th 57

Symbolical vs. literal interpretation of Biblical conceptions such as Resurrection and Ascension: Impossible to know how much should be taken symbolically
- •CR 164-166 (see also Literalism)
- ❖ CR 13:30-35 (see also Literalism)

Symbolism—see also Imagery

Symbolism and Belief, book by Edwyn Bevan, mentioned as having been helpful to Lewis in his ideas about symbolism

•GID 181, 260; L 181, 298 (*see also* M 70; PP 127, ftnt.)

❖ GID I 22:10; II 16:16; L 26 Mar 40; 9 May 61 (*see also* M 10:5; PP 8:10— ftnt.)

Symbolism, Christian theology shares with poetry the use of
•WG 85 ❖ WG 5:16

Symbolism: Lewis describes the "transposition" of higher meanings into lower objects or symbols
•WG 54-73 (*see also* RP 115-117)

❖ WG ch. 4 (*see also* RP 11:11-13)

Symbolism: Pointing as an example of an act which, without understanding the symbolism, cannot be understood (as a dog will merely sniff at your finger)
•WG 71 ❖ WG 4:29

"Symbolism," the word, is not adequate in all cases to cover the relation between the higher medium and its transposition in the lower
•WG 62 ❖ WG 4:13

Symbolism used in the Bible to describe Heaven not to be misunderstood; it is merely an attempt to express the inexpressible
•MC 121 ❖ MC III 10:6

Sympathy for another's difficulty: Lewis demonstrates that it is more effective if we can admit our own particular handicap in being able to truly empathize*
•LM 40-41 ❖ LM 8:2

Sympathy: I think it is only in a shared darkness that you and I can meet at present—shared also with our Master*
•LM 44 ❖ LM 8:13

Sympathy: The temptation as we try to sympathize with another's difficulty is to attempt reassurances
•LM 41 ❖ LM 8:3

Sympathy: When pain is to be borne, courage helps more than knowledge, human sympathy more than courage, and the love of God more than all
•PP 10 ❖ PP P:1

Symphony analogy: Our prayers are known to us only as we pray them— "But they are eternally in the score of the great symphony"
•LM 110 (*see also* GID 79; L 217; LM 48, 50; M 176-180; SL 127-128) ❖ LM 20:16 (*see also* GID I 8:9; L 1 Aug 49; LM 9:5, 12; M App. B: 10-18; SL 27:4)

Symphony analogy: We are now merely tuning our instruments, as Donne says (learning to praise God, in anticipation of the "symphony" of Heaven)
•RP 97 (*see also* LM 116) ❖ RP 9:7 (*see also* LM 21:15)

Symphony ("band") analogy to illustrate importance and operation of morality
•MC 71 ❖ MC III 1:3-5

Symphony, if all experienced God and worshipped Him in the same way the song of the Church would have no
•PP 150 ❖ PP 10:7

Taking for granted, which is an outrage in erotic love, is in Affection right and proper up to a point
•FL 56 ❖ FL 3:7

Talent for happiness, my father's people were true Welshmen who had not much of the
•SJ 3 ❖ SJ 1:1

Talents in the parable might include "talents" in the modern sense; and secular learning might be embodied in the Magi (re: value of "culture")
•CR 14-15 ❖ CR 2:7

Talents, man can go on improving his, to the best of his ability without forming an opinion of them or deciding his own niche in the temple of Fame
•SL 65 ❖ SL 14:5

Talents, pride a danger in the possession of
•WG 27-28 ❖ WG 2:9

Talents, pride in one's: Talents are given to us; we might as well be proud of the colour of our hair
•SL 65 ❖ SL 14:5

Talents: We cannot give God anything that is not His already
•MC 125 (see also SL 96-99)
❖ MC III 11:9 (see also SL 21:2-6)

Talk(ing)—see also Conversation

Talk: "...ours was a very nice battalion... You could get as good talk there as anywhere"
•SJ 193 ❖ SJ 12:15

Talk, the only two kinds of, I wanted were the almost purely imaginative and the almost purely rational
•SJ 136-137 ❖ SJ 9:11

Talk: When things are of high value and easily destroyed, we must talk with great care, and perhaps the less we talk the better (re: "culture")
•WLN 34 (see also WLN 37)
❖ WLN 3:6 (see also WLN 3:11)

Talking (about oneself): The rule is, When in doubt, don't tell; I have nearly always regretted doing the opposite and never once regretted holding my tongue
•LAL 54-55 ❖ LAL 15/4/56

Talking and smoking both interfere with one's appreciation of nature (Lewis describes his afternoon walks, which he mostly took alone)
•SJ 142 ❖ SJ 9:18

Talking and walking are two very great pleasures, but it is a mistake to combine them; the noise blots out the sounds and silences of the outdoor world
•SJ 142 (see also SJ 200*)
❖ SJ 9:18 (see also SJ 13:4*)

Talking to others about our difficulties: "Often...the person we speak to is at the moment full of troubles we know nothing about"
•LAL 40-41 ❖ LAL 24/3/55

Talking too much is one of my vices
•LAL 55 ❖ LAL 15/4/56

Taste—see also Culture; Enjoyment

Taste, good, in poetry or music not necessary to salvation, as evidenced by the humble charwoman who revels in hymns
•L 224 (see also CR 13-14)
❖ L 7 Dec 50 (see also CR 2:3, 4)

Taste, I admit bad, to be in some sense "a bad thing" but I do not think it per se "evil" (re: literary criticism)
•CR 36 ❖ CR 2:57

Taste, Lewis reacts against the notion that good, somehow defines the true Church or that course, unimaginative people are less likely to be saved
•CR 13 (see also L 224)

---

* These items reflect some interpretation on the part of the editor; the idea will not be found in these exact words. See Introduction, p. ix.
** These items are ideas of Lewis's which the editor has placed under a topic Lewis did not there intend to address. See Introduction, p. ix.
Entries without asterisks are not necessarily exact quotes, but the idea should be easy to find as worded.

❖ CR 2:3 (*see also* L 7 Dec 50)

Taste, many preferences which seem to the ignorant to be simply matters of, are visible to the trained critic as choices between good and evil
•CR 29 ❖ CR 2:48

Taste, matters of, not to be confused with matters of faith and morals (e.g., use of reverential prefixes before the Holy Name)
•GID 335-336 ❖ GID IV Letter 8

Taste, matters of, not to be confused with matters of doctrine (e.g., styles of worship; the plastering of the landscape with religious slogans)
•L 268 (*see also* CR 96-97)
❖ L 13 Mar 56 (*see also* CR 8:9, 10)

Taste, the moment good, knows itself some of its goodness is lost
•SJ 104 ❖ SJ 7:4

Tastes, Brother Every maintained that our, are symptomatic of our real standards of value, which may differ from our professed standards
•CR 28 ❖ CR 2:47

Tastes, it would almost seem that Providence quite overrules our, when it decides to bring two minds together (re: improbability of one's taste in books)
•SJ 190 ❖ SJ 12:12

Tastes, the deepest, of any man are the raw material with which God ("the Enemy") has furnished him (— Screwtape)
•SL 59-60 ❖ SL 13:4

Tastes vs. moral judgement in Christian literary criticism: Danger of invoking "thus saith the Lord" at the end of every expression of our pet aversions
•CR 30-31 (*see also* CR 34-35; RP 31)
❖ CR 2:51 (*see also* CR 2:55; RP 3:20)

Tastes, we must lay our, along with other carnal baggage, at the church door or bring them in to be humbled
•GID 336 ❖ GID IV Letter 8

Tastes: Your friends do not see the common quality in all the books you really love, and often wonder why, liking this, you should also like that*
•PP 145 ❖ PP 10:2

"**Tasting**" reality through myth: "In...a great myth we come nearest to experiencing as a concrete what can otherwise only be experienced as an abstraction"
•GID 65-66 (*see also* CR 130-134, esp. 133) ❖ GID I 5:8-10 (*see also* CR 11:4-10, esp. 11:9)

Taunting by unbelievers: "They know well enough what we are believing or trying to believe...and regard it as total illusion" (re: Psalmists' dark experience)
•CR 127 ❖ CR 10:38

Tax collector who makes dishonest demands of tax-payers as "the ungodly" who "for his own lust doth persecute the poor" in the Psalms
•RP 15 ❖ RP 2:10

Taxpayer analogy: We dread a rise in the tax (God's claims on us)
•WG 129 (*consider also* Self-reservation)
❖ WG 9:7(*consider also* Self-reservation)

Taxpayer analogy: We hope there will be enough left over for us to live on (after we've become "good")
•MC 166-167 ❖ MC IV 8:2

Tea, Lewis describes, as part of his usual day at Oxford
•L 144-145 ❖ L 22 Nov 31

Tea mentioned by Screwtape as a "positive Pleasure" dangerous to his side
•SL 58 ❖ SL 13:3

Tea-time should be no later than quarter past four, and tea should be taken in solitude
•SJ 142 ❖ SJ 9:18

Teacher ("don"), I knew that there was hardly any position in the world save that of a, in which I was fitted to earn a living
•SJ 183 (*see also* CR 20)
❖ SJ 12:2 (*see also* CR 2:23)

Teacher, every man has a grudge against his father and his first
•CR 92 ❖ CR 7:20

Teachers are not now content to teach a subject but aim at creating Plasticine characters who can simulate orthodox

responses and have no tastes of their own
•WLN 42-44, 46 ❖ WLN 3:16-18, 20

Teachers: As they are, so they will teach (if Christian, they will transmit Christianity, even if forbidden to teach it explicitly)
•GID 117-118 ❖ GID I 13:7, 8

Teachers ("dons") mentioned as one group of "culture-sellers" whose ranks should probably include some Christians
•CR 20-21 ❖ CR 2:23-25

Teachers: "Few of us have always, in full measure, given our pupils or patients or clients...what we were being paid for"*
•RP 13 ❖ RP 2:8

Teachers: "...how much harm a loose-talking young man can do to innocent boys" (re: a teacher he had at "Chartres")
•SJ 68 ❖ SJ 4:16

Teachers: It is difficult for most parents to realize the unimportance of most schoolmasters in the life of a school*
•SJ 99-100 ❖ SJ 6:26

Teachers, my two greatest, were Smewgy and Kirk; Smewgy taught me Grammar and Rhetoric and Kirk taught me Dialectic
•SJ 148 ❖ SJ 9:24

Teachers often less helpful with problems in schoolwork than fellow-pupils are; I write as one amateur to another
•RP 1-2 ❖ RP 1:1, 2

Teachers: "...we must always be working towards the moment at which our pupils are fit to become our critics and rivals"
•FL 77-78 ❖ FL 3:38, 39

Teaching—see also Education

Teaching of Jesus—see Jesus, teaching of

Teaching: The reading of a lecture sends people to sleep
•L 99
❖ L undated letter postmarked 28 Aug 24

Teachings—see also Beliefs; Doctrines

Teachings regarding standard of behavior strikingly similar in Zarathustra, Jeremiah, Socrates, Gautama and

Christ— teachers widely separated in space and time
•PP 63 (see also CR 44-56, 77; MC 19, 78; RP 27; Law of Nature; book *The Abolition of Man*)
❖ PP 4:10 (see also CR ch. 4; 6:16; MC I 1:7; III 3:1; RP 3:13; Law of Nature; book *The Abolition of Man*)

Technology, Christianity does not replace; when it tells you to feed the hungry it doesn't give you lessons in cookery
•GID 48 ❖ GID I 4:1

Teetotalism—see also Alcohol

Teetotalism, I strongly object to the tyrannic and unscriptural insolence of anything that calls itself a church and makes, a condition of membership
•L 262 ❖ L 16 Mar 55

Teetotalism: "It is a mistake to think that Christians ought all to be teetotallers"
•MC 75 ❖ MC III 2:5

Teetotaller, Lewis mentions a woman who was a "rabid"
•GID 319 ❖ GID III 9:15

Tegner's Drapa as an avenue through which Lewis experienced "Joy"
•SJ 17 (see also SJ 73)
❖ SJ 1:17 (see also SJ 5:4)

Television as one of the instruments invented to destroy solitude "wherever solitude exists" (Lewis is here referring to the radio)**
•WG 107 ❖ WG 7:2

Television portrays progress as an inevitable process, and assumes that the important thing is to increase man's comfort at all costs
•L 282 ❖ L 30 Oct 58

Temperament—consider also Character

Temperament: "We may have made so little use of a good heredity and a good upbringing that we are no better than those whom we regard as fiends"
•MC 86 (see also L 183; MC 180-182)
❖ MC III 4:7 (see also L 16 Apr 40; MC IV 10:9-14)

Temperance—see also Balance; Moderation; consider also Alcohol

Temperance: "A thing may be morally

neutral and yet the desire for that thing may be dangerous" (re: Inner Rings)**
•WG 99 ❖ WG 6:8

Temperance and smoking, mention of, with regard to the temptation to guard our worldly interests
•WG 127 ❖ WG 9:4

Temperance as one of the things which has decreased in value by abuse of the word "Puritanism"
•SL 47 ❖ SL 10:3

Temperance fanatics who claim to have an unanswerable intuition that all strong drink is forbidden really can have nothing of the sort
•WG 37-38 (see also L 263)
❖ WG 3:8 (see also L 14 May 55)

Temperance not just a matter of drink; involves caution in the indulgence of bridge, clothes, golf, etc.
•MC 75-76 ❖ MC III 2:5, 6

Temperance: "There can be intemperance in work just as in drink. What feels like zeal may be only fidgets or even the flattering of one's self-importance"
•LAL 53 ❖ LAL 19/3/56

"Temperance," when made a Cardinal virtue, meant not abstaining but going the right length and no further
•MC 75 ❖ MC III 2:5

Temperance, people in the "All-I-want" state of mind are being gluttonous and self-concerned even as they believe they are practicing
•SL 76-78 ❖ SL 17:1-3

Temple, every, in the world (e.g., Parthenon and Temple at Jerusalem) was a sacred slaughterhouse; we would not have enjoyed the ancient rituals
•RP 44-45 ❖ RP 5:2

Temple, finally I awoke from building the, to find that the God had flown; I no longer got the old thrill [from literature]
•SJ 165-166 ❖ SJ 11:2

Temple, I insisted that [the Desirable] ought to appear in the, I had made for

him; but he cares only for temples building and not at all for temples built
•SJ 166-167 (see also SJ 165)
❖ SJ 11:3 (see also SJ 11:2)

Temple of Jerusalem did not serve the same function as the synagogues; our parish church is the descendent of both (place of sacrifice/learning)
•RP 45 ❖ RP 5:3

Temple, the delight expressed in the Psalms is very much centred on the, and its services
•RP 45-48, 50 ❖ RP 5:3-6, 8

Temporal—see also Worldly

Temporal affairs, Screwtape advises guarding against the human attitude in which, are treated primarily as material for obedience
•SL 35 ❖ SL 7:4

Temporal blessings (e.g., friends, books, or brains) not given us to keep; we must learn to care for something else more
•L 161-162 (see also L 306)
❖ L 12 Sep 38 (see also L 21 Nov 62)

Temporal blessings look like broken toys in times of fear and pain; we are reminded that they were never intended to possess our heart*
•PP 106 (see also FL 192)
❖ PP 6:17 (see also FL 6:47)

Temporal claims must not supersede God's claims on us (re: giving ourselves without reservation to the claims of a nation, a party, or a class)
•WG 24-25 ❖ WG 2:6

Temporal ("natural") thing, Lewis gives a way to test the spiritual value of any, (such as music, religion, etc.)
•L 268-269
❖ L undated letter just before 2 Apr 56

Temporal ("natural") things which are not in themselves sinful can become the servant of the spiritual life, but are not automatically so
•L 268
❖ L undated letter just before 2 Apr 56

Temporal pleasures only suggest what we were really made for

•MC 120 ❖ MC III 10:5

Temporal things, temptation to guard our
- WG 126-132 (*see also* Self-reservation)
- ❖ WG ch. 9 (*see also* Self-reservation)

Temporariness of life—*see* Life

Temptation, a "stock response" to, is precisely what we need to acquire (vs. a "sensitivity" which shows us how unique and unamenable to general rules each temptation is)
- CR 24-25 ❖ CR 2:38

Temptation: Appetites would give us very little trouble if the imagination were obedient*
- LM 17 (*see also* GID 217; LAL 111)
- ❖ LM 3:9 (*see also* GID II 7:3; LAL 26 Nov 62)

Temptation, avoiding: We should avoid contact with people who are cruel, etc., not because we are too good for them, but because we are not good enough
- RP 71-74 (*see also* SL 45-48*)
- ❖ RP 7:9-16 (*see also* SL ch. 10*)

Temptation, fighting: Grace may reveal itself in a person's ever renewed struggle, without presumption or despair, against an abnormal desire
- L 242 ❖ L 28 May 52

Temptation, in a sense no, is ever overcome until we stop trying to overcome it
- MC 129 ❖ MC III 12:6

Temptation: Lewis mentions that he learned how it works (in order to write *Screwtape Letters*) by his own experience with it
- SL xiii ❖ SL P:24

Temptation most successful, according to Screwtape, on the very steps of the altar (re: danger of empty "religion")
- SL 172; WLN 70 (*see also* L 227)
- ❖ SL 32:40; WLN 32:40 (*see also* L 5 Mar 51)

Temptation, our, is to look eagerly for the minimum that will be accepted— like honest but reluctant taxpayers
- WG 129 (*see also* Self-reservation)
- ❖ WG 9:7 (*see also* Self-reservation)

Temptation probably not the only mode in which the Devil can corrupt and impair
- GID 169 ❖ GID I 20:Reply-12

Temptation, Screwtape mentions "the quiet despair" humans feel of ever overcoming chronic
- SL 132 ❖ SL 28:1

Temptation, Screwtape observes that soon individual, will no longer be necessary; "Catch the bellwether, and his whole flock comes after him"
- SL 158-159; WLN 56-57
- ❖ SL 32:13; WLN 4:13

Temptation, Screwtape observes that the way to prepare for an assault of moral, upon a human is to darken his intellect
- SL 95 ❖ SL 21:2

Temptation: Screwtape points out that as humans become less dependent on emotion in their religious experience, they become much harder to tempt
- SL 13-14 ❖ SL 2:3

Temptation, sexual—*see* Lust; Sexual temptation

Temptation, strength of a, discovered not by giving in but by fighting it
- MC 124-125 ❖ MC III 1:7

Temptation: Tempters try to elicit small wrong choices which later harden into habit and then into evil principles
- SL 156-157; WLN 54-55 (*see also* MC 86-87, 117; RP 136; SL 53-54; WG 101-103)
- ❖ SL 32:10; WLN 4:10 (*see also* MC III 4:8, 9; 9:8; RP 12:16; SL 12:1; WG 6:12)

Temptation: The choice which could lead to becoming a scoundrel will come, when it does come, in no very dramatic colors (re: temptations of Inner Rings)
- WG 101-102 ❖ WG 6:12

Temptation: "The safest road to Hell is the gradual one—the gentle slope, soft underfoot, without sudden turnings, without milestones, without signposts"
- SL 56 (*see also* SL 53-54*)
- ❖ SL 12:5 (*see also* SL 12:1*)

Temptation, the sort of arguments against Christianity which our reason

can be persuaded to accept at the moment of yielding to, are often preposterous
•CR 43 ❖ CR 3:12

Temptation to fear of death attacks most fiercely the best and the worst of men; Lewis explains why (re: Christ's fear in Gethsemane)
•L 189-190
❖ L undated letter just after 11 Aug 40

Temptation to retain temporal security, to merely "dabble and splash" in spiritual things, contains the truth that we can be too fanatical
•WG 128-130 (see also FL 181; consider also Self-reservation)
❖ WG 9:6-8 (see also FL 6:28; consider also Self-reservation)

Temptation, unfallen man had no, to choose self over God because his will was wholly disposed (though not compelled) to turn to God
•PP 81 ❖ PP 5:9

Temptations, certain people are not above but below some; the higher, the more in danger
•RP 28-30 ❖ RP 3:17-19

Temptations felt by the Perfect Man, thoughts regarding
•L 189-191
❖ L undated letter just after 11 Aug 40

Temptations, I am suffering incessant, to uncharitable thoughts at present
•L 222-223 ❖ L 12 Jan 50

Temptations, I know all about the despair of overcoming chronic; the only fatal thing is to lose one's temper and give it up
•L 199 (see also MC 94; WG 132; Moral effort) ❖ L 20 Jan 42 (see also MC III 5:12; WG 9:13; Moral effort)

Temptations of Eros when we are "in love" speak with the voice of "quasi-religious duties, acts of pious zeal to love"
•FL 156-157 ❖ FL 5:40

Temptations of the flesh are more successful during the "trough" periods of human experience—when men are dull and weary (—Screwtape)
•SL 41 ❖ SL 9:2

Temptations to small indulgences or small resentments which "seem so tiny, so helpless that in resisting them we feel we are being cruel to animals"
•RP 136 (see also SL 53-54; WLN 54-55)
❖ RP 12:16 (see also SL 12:1; WLN 4:10)

Ten Commandments—see Commandment(s); Law(s); Moral law(s)

Tennis player analogy to show how right actions done for the wrong reason do not help to build the internal quality of character called a "virtue"
•MC 77 ❖ MC III 2:10

Terms—see also Words

Terms, list of, which are used differently by the layman than by the clergyman or theologian (includes the typical lay definition)
•GID 96-98 ❖ GID I 10:20-37

Terror—see also Fear

Terror, that day I noticed how a greater, overcomes a less; in the midst of the shelling, a poor shivering mouse made no attempt to run from me
•SJ 195 ❖ SJ 12:17

Test of "goodness" or "badness" of anything: Ultimately what really matters is whether a thing or a circumstance moves us closer to God or to the devil*
•SL 87-89 (see also SL 56, 126)
❖ SL 19:3 (see also SL 12:5; 27:1)

Test of the spiritual value of any natural thing (music, religion, etc.): Does it make one more obedient, more God- and neighbor-centred, less self-centred?
•L 268-269
❖ L undated letter just before 2 Apr 56

Tests of our faith not sent in order that God might find out its quality; God already knows that—they show us its quality
•GO 61 ❖ GO 3:36

Testing of Abraham did not show God what he could endure (God already knew that)—it showed Abraham
•PP 101-102 ❖ PP 6:13

Thackeray I positively dislike; He is the voice of "the world" and his supposedly "good" women are revolting
•L 255 ❖ L 23 Jan 54; 30 Jan 54

Thankfulness—*see* Gratitude

That Hideous Strength has been unanimously damned by all reviewers
•L 209 ❖ L 31 Jan 46

That Hideous Strength, Lewis makes reference to some of the characters in
•L 217 ❖ L 4 Apr 49

That Hideous Strength mentioned as unsuitable for children
•LAL 25, 27
❖ LAL 24/1/54; Feb 22/54

That Hideous Strength referred to
•L 244 ❖ L 2 Oct 52

That Hideous Strength: The N.I.C.E. was not quite the fantastic absurdity so many people think
•L 207 ❖ L 26 Sep 45

Theatre—*see also* Play

Theatre, analogy of stage sets in a, to illustrate how all our experience is only an "appearance"; the reality lies "behind the scenes"
•GID 245-249 (*see also* CR 169-172; LM 80-81) ❖ GID II ch. 13 (*see also* CR 14:21-32; LM 15: 12-15)

Theism: Both those who believe in God and those who disbelieve face many hours of doubt
•CR 41 (*consider also* Atheism)
❖ CR 3:9 (*consider also* Atheism)

Theism: Descartes' Ontological Proof mentioned
•GID 173 (*see also* L 143)
❖ GID I 21:3 (*see also* L 24 Oct 31)

Theism, Is, Important? (chapter title)
•GID 172-176 ❖ GID I ch. 21

Theism, Lewis writes of his free-choice conversion to, while riding on a bus
•SJ 224-225 (*see also* GID 261)
❖ SJ 14:16 (*see also* GID II 16:19-22)

Theism, Lewis's conversion to—*see also* Conversion, Lewis's

Theism, mere—*see* Religion, minimal

Theism, relationship of, to belief in Reason
•GID 274-276 (*see also* Reason)
❖ GID III 1:11-19 (*see also* Reason)

Theism, there were all sorts of blankets and insurances which enabled one to get all the conveniences of, without believing in God
•SJ 209 (*consider also* Cost)
❖ SJ 13:18 (*consider also* Cost)

Theism, vague, is the religion which has declined—not Christianity
•GID 219 ❖ GID II 8:5

Theism, various arguments for, mentioned
•GID 173 ❖ GID I 21:3

Theocracy has been abolished because priests are wicked men like ourselves
•WG 114 (*see also* GID 197)
❖ WG 7:12 (*see also* GID II 3:3)

Theocracy, I don't think we are in danger of a, but of something only one degree less intolerable: a "Charientocracy"
•WLN 40-41 ❖ WLN 3:13

Theocracy: "The higher the pretensions of our rulers are, the more meddlesome and impertinent their rule is likely to be..."
•WLN 48 (*see also* WLN 40)
❖ WLN 3:27 (*see also* WLN 3:13)

Theocracy the worst of all possible governments; the loftier the pretensions of power, the more meddlesome, inhuman and oppressive it will be
•WLN 40, 48 ❖ WLN 3:13, 27

Theodicy—*see* Evil; Pain, problem of

Theologian, I am not a real, but an amateur (or "layman")
•CR 94, 152; GID 60, 62, 89, 332-333; L 219, 223; LM 101; MC 6; PP 10; RP 1-2; WG 71; WLN 93-94
❖ CR 8:1; 13:1; GID I 4:56 (Ques. 14); 4:60 (Ques. 16); 10:1, 2; IV Letter 7; L 2 Sep 49; 28 Nov 50; LM 19:3; MC P:2; PP P:2; RP 1:1, 2; WG 4:28; WLN 7:1

Theologian, issue of intellectual honesty for the modern, who denies the miraculous in the Gospels*
•CR 153 (*see also* M 164)
❖ CR 13:2 (*see also* M 17:1)

Theologian, one can begin trying to be a disciple before one is a professed
•L 191 ❖ L 4 Jan 41

Theologian, one is sometimes (not often) glad not to be a great; one might so easily mistake it for being a good Christian
•RP 57 ❖ RP 6:6

Theologian, there are two kinds of outsiders whom the, needs to study: the uneducated, and those who are educated but not in his way
•CR 152-153 ❖ CR 13:1, 2

Theologians, I find in modern, a constant use of the principle that the miraculous does not occur
•CR 158 ❖ CR 13:11

Theologians ("scholars"), modern Christian, are anxious to allow to the enemy every advantage he can with any show of fairness claim*
•M 164-165 ❖ M 17:1

Theologians, modern, have been obviously influenced by (and perhaps insufficiently critical of) the spirit of the age they grew up in
•CR 158 ❖ CR 13:11

Theologians, modern: I distrust them as critics; their literary experience lacks a wide and deep experience of literature in general
•CR 154 (see also CR 161)
❖ CR 13:4 (see also CR 13:22)

Theologians, some modern, after swallowing the camel of the Resurrection strain at such gnats as the feeding of the multitudes
•CR 153 ❖ CR 13:2

Theological controversies—see also Doctrinal differences; Divisions within Christianity

Theological controversies can be put in perspective by reading old books
•GID 201-202 ❖ GID II 4:3, 4

Theological controversies must be put in their proper perspective by having a standard of plain, central ("mere") Christianity
•GID 201 (see also Christianity, "mere") ❖ GID II 4:3 (see also Christianity, "mere")

Theological controversies: "...there are two ways in which a controversy can cease: by being settled, or by gradual and imperceptible change of custom"
•GID 335 ❖ GID IV Letter 7

Theological controversy, letter regarding Anglican

•GID 327 ❖ GID IV Letter 2

Theological language, belief in God stated in: "I believe in incorporeal entity, personal in the sense that it can be the subject and object of love..."
•CR 135 ❖ CR 11:13

Theological language: "In it we are attempting...to state religious matter in a form more like that we use for scientific matter"
•CR 135 ❖ CR 11:13

Theological language is in a sense alien to religion, omitting nearly all that really matters by its very precision
•CR 135-136 ❖ CR 11:13-15

Theological language often necessary, but it is not the language religion naturally speaks
•CR 135 ❖ CR 11:13

Theological questions: "[I get] the sense that some shattering and disarming simplicity is the real answer"*
•GO 83 (see also Questions)
❖ GO 4:28, 29 (see also Questions)

Theology—consider also Biblical criticism; Difficulties in Scripture

Theology and philosophy not learned from nature; in nature each man can clothe his own belief
•FL 35-37 ❖ FL 2:19-24

Theology and poetry: "In Akhenaten as in the Psalms, a certain kind of poetry seems to go with a certain kind of theology"
•RP 89 ❖ RP 8:18

Theology, Christian, and that of other religions can hardly avoid coincidental ideas
•WG 82-83 (consider also Islam; Judaism; Mythology) ❖ WG 5:15 (consider also Islam; Judaism; Mythology)

Theology, Christian, not very good as poetry (not grand or rich enough)
•WG 75 ❖ WG 5:5

Theology, definition of: "...the systematic series of statements about God and about Man's relation to Him which the believers of a religion make"
•WG 74 ❖ WG 5:2

Theology: Do all theoretical problems con-

ceal shirkings by the will?*
•L 202 ❖ L 22 Dec 42

Theology: Drowning man analogy to show that philosophical definiteness about details can never be the *first* necessity once a belief in God has been accepted* (re: nature of God)
•M 75-76 ❖ M 10:15

Theology, errors in our: Example of Pope Gregory, on arriving in Heaven and finding he'd been wrong about something: It was the funniest thing he'd ever heard (story from *Paradiso*)
•CR 11 ❖ CR 1:16

Theology, everywhere except in, there has been a vigorous growth of scepticism about scepticism itself
•CR 162 ❖ CR 13:25

Theology is experimental knowledge (although the initiative lies on God's side)
•MC 143-144 ❖ MC IV 2:11-13

Theology, Is, Poetry? (chapter title)
•WG 74-92 ❖ WG ch. 5

Theology, it is unlikely that we can know much about the development of early Christian; one's own life is improbable by historical standards
•CR 164 ❖ CR 13:28

Theology, liberal—*see also* Liberal Christianity; Liberal Christians; Theology, modern

Theology, liberal: Regarding the claim that the real teaching of Christ was misunderstood by His followers and has been recovered only by modern scholars
•CR 157-158 ❖ CR 13:10

Theology, liberal, which denies the miraculous will make the unlearned man either a Roman Catholic (if he disagrees) or an atheist (if he agrees)
•CR 153 ❖ CR 13:2

Theology, many find that the heart sings unbidden while working their way through a tough bit of, with a pipe in their teeth and a pencil in their hand
•GID 205 ❖ GID II 4:7

Theology means "the science of God"; is like a map and is practical—if you want to go anywhere it's absolutely

necessary
•MC 135-136 ❖ MC IV 1:1-5

Theology, modern—*see also* Theology, liberal

Theology, Modern, and Biblical Criticism (chapter title)
•CR 152-166 ❖ CR ch. 13

Theology, modern: History of the Church of England is likely to be very short if the current trend of theological thought continues
•CR 166 ❖ CR 13:36

Theology, modern: I do not expect the present school of theological thought to be everlasting; perhaps wishfully, I think the whole thing may blow over
•CR 162 ❖ CR 13:24, 25

Theology, modern: I had [wrongly] believed that among Christians one could escape from the horrible ferocity and grimness of modern thought
•L 177 ❖ L 18 Feb 40

Theology, modern: I find in modern theologians a constant use of the principle that the miraculous does not occur
•CR 158 ❖ CR 13:11

Theology, modern: Lewis describes himself as "a dogmatic Christian untinged with Modernist reservations and committed to supernaturalism..."*
•CR 44 ❖ CR 4:1

Theology, modern: Some modern theologians, after swallowing the camel of the Resurrection, strain at such gnats as the feeding of the multitude
•CR 153 ❖ CR 13:2

Theology, modern: "The undermining of the old orthodoxy [belief in miraculous] has been mainly the work of divines engaged in New Testament criticism"
•CR 152 ❖ CR 13:1

Theology, only a minority of world religions have a
•WG 74 ❖ WG 5:2

Theology penetrated by political ideology: "Mark my words: you will presently see both a Leftist and a Rightist pseudo theology developing..."
•L 176 ❖ L 17 Jan 40

Theology regarding Our Lord: "No net

less wide than a man's whole heart, nor less fine of mesh than love, will hold the sacred fish"*
•RP 119 ❖ RP 11:15

Theology, the attempt to explain evil (having once accepted reality as moral) lies in the realm of
•CR 69-71, esp. 71
❖ CR 5:24-26, esp. 5:26

Theology, the revival of, has attained proportions that have to be reckoned with; this points to the decline of the "Myth of Evolutionism"
•CR 89-90 ❖ CR 7:17

Theology: Theories of the Atonement need not be used if not found to be helpful
•L 197 (see also MC 57-59; Atonement)
❖ L 21 Dec 41 (see also MC II 4:3-5; Atonement)

Theology: "...there is no question of learning a subject but of steeping ourselves in a Personality..."
•RP 113-114 ❖ RP 11:9

Theology, Thomas Aquinas said of all his own, "It reminds me of straw"
•LM 82 ❖ LM 15:17

Theology, transitory nature of all scholarship including that of
•CR 162 ❖ CR 13:25

Theology, translation into the vernacular a test of true understanding of one's own
•GID 98-99, 243, 256- 257, 338
❖ GID I 10:38; II 12:5; ch. 15; IV Letter 11

Theology, translation into the vernacular necessary in communicating one's, to the people
•GID 96-98, 183, 242-243, 254-257, 338
❖ GID I 10:18-38; 22:16, 17; II 12:4, 5; ch. 15; IV Letter 11

Theology: Truth is not "adjustable to contemporary thought," etc., as some theologians seem to believe—as if we were trying to make rather than to learn
•LM 104 ❖ LM 19:12

Theology vs. Politics: "Theology teaches us what ends are desirable and what means are lawful, while Politics teaches us what means are effective"

•GID 94 ❖ GID I 10:11

Theology, we often talk as if God were not very good at, (re: questioning things He has said)
•L 236 ❖ L 8 Dec 52

Theology which denies the miraculous will make the unlearned man either a Roman Catholic (if he disagrees) or an atheist (if he agrees)
•CR 153 ❖ CR 13:2

Theosophy as a form of Pantheism
•M 83 ❖ M 11:4

Theosophy as encountered by Lewis through the Matron at "Chartres"
•SJ 59-60 ❖ SJ 4:6

Theosophy mentioned as one of many non-Christian creeds Lewis found among his audiences
•GID 240-241, 252 ❖ GID II 12:2; 14:9

Theosophy, Pantheism, and Spiritualism as encountered by Lewis in the writings of Maeterlinck
•SJ 175 ❖ SJ 11:12

Things, our fear of "having to depend solely on God" shows how very much we have been depending on
•LAL 49 ❖ LAL 16/12/55

Thinking—see also Thought; Rationality; Reason(ing)

Thinking and thoughts are but "the thinnest possible film on the surface of a vast deep" (re: prayer)
•LM 79 ❖ LM 15:8

Thinking as other than the succession of linked concepts which we use when we successfully convey our "thought" to another
•CR 139-140 ❖ CR 11:22, 23

Thinking: "Do I hope that if feeling disguises itself as thought I shall feel less?" (re: intellectualizing God and the problem of pain when one is grieving)
•GO 38 (see also GO 41, 43*)
❖ GO 2:31 (see also GO 3:3, 4*)

Thinking, I fancy that most of those who think at all have done a great deal of their, in the first fourteen years
•SJ 63 ❖ SJ 4:10

Thinking, in, we are not reading ration-

ality into an irrational universe but responding to a rationality with which the universe has always been saturated
•CR 65 ❖ CR 5:18

Thinking, theoretical errors in, may remove ordinary checks to evil and deprive good intentions of their natural support (re: "subjectivism")
•CR 72 ❖ CR 6:1

Thirst—*see* Desire

"**Thou** has made us for Thyself, and our heart has no rest till it comes to Thee" (quote from St. Augustine)
•FL 189 (*see also* GID 252)
❖ FL 6:41 (*see also* GID II 14:7)

Thought—*see also* Rationality; Reason(ing)

Thought: A belief in the objectivity and validity of reason must be maintained *or* all thoughts are accidents and we can know no truths and have no knowledge*
•CR 60-63, 71, 72-81, 89; GID 21, 52-53, 136-138, 272, 274-276; M 12-24, 34, 105; MC 45-46; SJ 208; WG 88-92
❖ CR 5:9-13, 27; ch. 6; 7:16; GID I 1:1; 4:21; 16:13-17; III 1:4, 9, 13-16; M ch. 3; 5:1; 13:16; MC II 1:6; SJ 13:17; WG 5:21-24

Thought: "Chronological snobbery" as the uncritical acceptance of the intellectual climate of our own age and the arbitrary discrediting of past thought
•SJ 207-208 (*see also* RP 121, 130; SJ 206, 212-213, 216; SL 128-129; WLN 96)
❖ SJ 13:17 (*see also* RP 12:3, 9; SJ 13:14; 14:2, 7; SL 27:5; WLN 7:6)

Thought, Fashions in, according to Screwtape are useful to distract the attention of men from their real dangers
•SL 117-118 ❖ SL 25:5

Thought, human, is not God's but God-kindled
•M 29 ❖ M 4:7

Thought, human: Total scepticism about it operates only by making a tacit exception in favour of the thought we are thinking at the moment
•CR 61; M 23 ❖ CR 5:10; M 3:31

Thought, if human, is the undesigned and

irrelevant product of cerebral motions, what reason have we to trust it?
•GID 21 (*see also* CR 60-61, 71, 72-81, 89; GID 52-53, 136-138, 272*, 274-276; M 12-24, 34, 105; MC 45-46; SJ 208-209; WG 88-91) ❖ GID I 1:1 (*see also* CR 5:9, 10; 5:27; ch. 6; 7:16; GID 4:21; 16:13-17; III 1:4*; 1:9, 13-16; M ch. 3; 5:1; 13:16; MC II 1:6; SJ 13:17; WG 5:21-24)

Thought, if you wish to avoid God avoid any train of, that leads off the beaten track
•CR 168 ❖ CR 14:17, 18

Thought: "Instead of the twofold division into Conscious and Unconscious, we need a threefold division: the Unconscious, the Enjoyed, and the Contemplated"
•SJ 217-219 ❖ SJ 14:9, 10

Thought is distinct from imagination; thought may be sound while accompanying images are false
•GID 69-70; M 70-72, 73 (*see also* WG 85-87) ❖ GID I 6:5-7; M 10:6-9, 11 (*see also* WG 5:18)

Thought is never static; pain often is (re: grief vs. physical pain)
•GO 46-47 ❖ GO 3:11

Thought is the result of non-rational causes ("I am a Christian because my parents were") or reasons ("I am a Christian because I believe it is true")
•GID 271-281 (*see also* M 15-16, 26) ❖ GID III ch. 1 (*see also* M 3:9-14; 4:2)

Thought, modern science fiction assumes moral, to be merely a subjective thing like one's taste in food, which can vary from species to species
•CR 61 ❖ CR 5:11

Thought, moral, as one kind of human thought believed by some to be merely subjective, while scientific thought is believed to be objective
•CR 61 (*consider also* Subjectivism) ❖ CR 5:11 (*consider also* Subjectivism)

Thought of our own age, error of assuming, to be correct as opposed to the thought of past ages
•WLN 96 (*see also* RP 121, 130; SJ 207-208; Age) ❖ WLN 7:6 (*see also* RP 12:3,

9; SJ 13:17; Age)

Thought, only poetry can speak low enough to catch the subtle nuances of, ("...the faint murmur of the mind ...")*
•LM 112 ❖ LM 21:2

Thought processes and the use of language to convey thought may be changing (Wells' *Country of the Blind* used as illustration of this)
•CR 140-141 ❖ CR 11:23, 24

Thought, question of whether human, can be set aside as merely subjective and irrelevant to the real universe
•CR 60-71; M 12-24
❖ CR 5:8-27; M ch. 3

Thought, rational, is independent of Nature but not necessarily *absolutely* independent; may be dependent on something else (e.g., self-existent Reason)
•M 27 ❖ M 4:5

Thought, the Foundation of Twentieth Century, ("Bulverism")—chapter title
•GID 271-281 ❖ GID III ch. 1

Thought: Thinking as other than the succession of linked concepts which we use when we successfully convey our "thought" to another
•CR 139-140 ❖ CR 11:22, 23

Thought, "Western," not as homogeneous (nor as "Christian") as may be supposed
•GID 251-253 ❖ GID II 14:6-11

Thought: Where it is strictly rational it must be, in some sense, not ours but cosmic or super-cosmic
•CR 65 ❖ CR 5:18

Thoughts are mere accidents if Materialism is correct in saying that the solar system was an accident
•GID 52-53 (*see also* M 15)
❖ GID I 4:20, 21 (Ques. 6) (*see also* M 3:7)

Thoughts are mere accidents if Naturalism is true
•GID 136-138; M 12-24 (*see also* CR 60-61, 89; GID 21, 52-53, 275; M 34; SJ 208-209; WG 72*, 88-89, 91)
❖ GID I 16:12-17; M ch. 3 (*see also* CR 5:9, 10; 7:16; GID I 1:1; 4:21; III 1:13; M 5:1; SJ 13:17; WG 4:29*; 5:21, 24)

Thoughts, how terrible that there should be even a kind of *pleasure* in thinking uncharitable
•L 222-223 (*see also* FL 82, 113; LAL 92-93; LM 94-95; MC 108; RP 22-24)
❖ L 12 Jan 50 (*see also* FL 3:45; 4:43; LAL 28 Oct 60; LM 18:1, 2; MC III 7:11; RP 3:6-8)

Thoughts, new, until they become habitual, will affect your consciousness as a whole only while you are actually thinking them
•M 166 ❖ M 17:4

Three Parts of Morality, The (chapter title)
•MC 69-73 ❖ MC III ch. 1

Three-Personal God, The (chapter title)
•MC 140-145 ❖ MC IV ch. 2

"Thrill," to try and produce the, of Joy as a state of mind turns religion into a self-caressing luxury
•SJ 168 (*see also* "Joy")
❖ SJ 11:5 (*see also* "Joy")

Thrills, in marriage and other departments of life, come at the beginning and do not last
•MC 99-101 (*see also* FL 28*; GID 320-321; LM 26-27; SL 13)
❖ MC III 6:9-12 (*see also* FL 2:6*; GID III 9:23, 24; LM 5:11, 12; SL 2:3)

Till We Have Faces, explanation of some aspects of
•L 273-274 ❖ L 10 Feb 57

Till We Have Faces, mention of writing: "I've...talked thro' the mouth of, and lived in the mind of, an *ugly* woman for a whole book"
•LAL 52 ❖ LAL 4/3/56

Time, a single second of lived, contains more than can be recorded; therefore we know next to nothing about history (re: "Historicism")
•CR 107 ❖ CR 9:15

Time and Beyond Time (chapter title)
•MC 145-149 ❖ MC IV ch. 3

Time and toil, giving, is a better—and harder—way of showing charity than giving money
•L 256 ❖ L 18 Feb 54

Time as a straight line; God as the whole page on which the line is drawn

•MC 147 ❖ MC IV 3:9

Time: As nothing outlasts God, so nothing slips away from Him into a past (re: Psalm 84:10; 2 Peter 3:8)
•RP 137 ❖ RP 12:17

Time, brevity of, by cosmic scale (re: Resurrection as harbinger of coming spring)
•GID 87-88 ❖ GID I 9:11

Time: Concept of "the timeless as the eternal present" was reached by Plato before it was reached in Christian thought; is evident in 2 Peter 3:8
•RP 137 ❖ RP 12:17

Time, discussion of
•MC 145-149 ❖ MC IV ch. 3

Time, God and His acts are not in; if our prayers are granted at all they are granted from the foundation of the world
•LM 48, 50, 110 (see also GID 79; L 217; SL 127-128) ❖ LM 9:5, 12; 20:16 (see also GID I 8:9; L 1 Aug 49; SL 27:4)

Time: God enjoys an infinite present, where nothing has yet passed away and nothing is still to come
•LM 109 ❖ LM 20:14

Time, God has infinite, to spare for each one of us
•MC 147 ❖ MC IV 3:7

Time, God is not in; this removes some apparent difficulties in Christianity
•MC 145-149 (see also L 217)
❖ MC IV 3:2-12 (see also L 1 Aug 49)

Time, God is not in; To Him all the physical events and all the human acts are present in an eternal Now
•M 176-177 (see also SL 127-128)
❖ M App. B:10 (see also SL 27:4)

Time: God's creative act is timeless; in this sense God did not create the universe long ago but creates it at this minute—at every minute
•M 177, 178 ❖ M App. B:10, 15

Time: How much greater a mess we would make if more were entrusted to us (by having a longer life)
•PP 124 ❖ PP 8:8

Time, humans live in, and therefore experience reality successively; thus they must experience change (—Screwtape)
•SL 116 ❖ SL 25:2

Time, humans live in, but God destines them to eternity; He therefore wants them to attend to eternity and to the Present (—Screwtape)
•SL 67-68 ❖ SL 15:2

Time: "I found, as always, that...the most studious have most time to spare"
•SJ 216 ❖ SJ 14:6

Time, I see few of the old warnings about the Value of, (—Screwtape)
•SL 47 ❖ SL 10:3

Time, if the dead are not in, is there any clear difference—when we speak of them—between was and is and will be?
•GO 26 ❖ GO 2:10

Time, if we think of, as a line (no width, only length) we probably ought to think of eternity as a plane or solid, of which earthly life is the base-line
•PP 123-124 ❖ PP 8:8

Time is to the universe as the metre is to a poem or the key is to music; God cannot be in it if He created it
•CR 168 ❖ CR 14:15

Time itself is one more name for death; the past is the past and that is what time means
•GO 28 ❖ GO 2:12

Time listed as part of "the old field" of Nature which is not to be unmade, but remade
•M 149 (see also M 163)
❖ M 16:12 (see also M 16:32)

Time magazine, concerning his critics in: "To call them liars would be as undeserved a compliment as to say that a dog was bad at arithmetic"
•LAL 51 (see also LAL 43)
❖ LAL 8/2/56 (see also LAL 14/5/55)

Time may not always be for us, as it is now, unilinear and irreversible
•M 153 ❖ M 16:19

Time, nothing throws a man into a passion so easily than to have his free, unexpectedly taken from him
•SL 96 ❖ SL 21:2

Time, our tendency is to picture the time-

less life of God as simply another sort of
- •WLN 99-100 (*see also* SL 127)
- ❖ WLN 7:11 (*see also* SL 27:4)

Time, real worldliness is a work of; Screwtape observes that that is why God allows humans so little of it
- •SL 133 ❖ SL 28:2, 3

Time: "The man can neither make, nor retain, one moment of time; it all comes to him by pure gift"—Screwtape
- •SL 96-97 ❖ SL 21:3

Time: The Present is the moment at which time touches eternity; in it alone freedom and actuality are offered us
- •SL 68 ❖ SL 15:2

Time, to be in, means to change; therefore, according to Screwtape, humans experience "the law of Undulation"—series of troughs and peaks—throughout life
- •SL 36-37 ❖ SL 8:1, 2

Time, up till this I always had too little; now there is nothing but time (re: Lewis's wife's death)
- •GO 39 ❖ GO 2:32

Time, we are so little reconciled to, that we are astonished at how fast it flies—as though we were not made for it
- •RP 138 ❖ RP 12:17

Time, we cannot give God any part of our, that is not His already
- •MC 125 (*see also* SL 96-97*)
- ❖ MC III 11:9 (*see also* SL 21:2, 3*)

Time, we feel, is "our own," and God's share in it is a tribute we must pay out of "our own" pocket
- •PP 75 ❖ PP 5:5

Time, we have a strange illusion that mere, cancels sin
- •PP 61 ❖ PP 4:9

Time: We have nothing but the tiny little present
- •MC 148 (*see also* CR 112-113; SL 67-71; Present) ❖ MC IV 3:10 (*see also* CR 9:26; SL ch. 15; Present)

Time: We may hope "finally to emerge, if not from the tyranny, at any rate from the unilinear poverty, of time"
- •RP 137-138 ❖ RP 12:17

Time, when I say that we are in, I mean

that as creatures our fundamentally timeless reality can be experienced only in the mode of succession
- •LM 110 ❖ LM 20:16

Time, whether the dead are in
- •LM 109-111 ❖ LM 20:13-17

Times, all, are eternally present to God (therefore mere time cannot cancel sin)
- •PP 61 ❖ PP 4:9

Tin soldier turning into a real man as analogy to Christian transformation
- •MC 154-156, 162 ❖ MC IV 5:3-7; 7:7

Tipping as a showy form of generosity (vs. real charity)
- •MC 82 ❖ MC III 3:7

Tiredness after a crisis: Emotions may be flat rather than joyful after a crisis passes; that isn't ingratitude, only exhaustion
- •LM 46 ❖ LM 9:2

Tiredness: God "may be trusted to know when we need *bed* even more than Mass"
- •LAL 38 ❖ LAL 20/2/55

Tiredness makes women talk more and men talk less; this can cause much secret resentment, even between lovers
- •SL 142 ❖ SL 30:3

Tiredness, Screwtape advises promoting the lie that exercise and subsequent, are helpful in combatting sexual temptation
- •SL 79 ❖ SL 17:4

Tiredness, Screwtape mentions the evil uses that can be made of, (It is not fatigue as such that causes anger, but unexpected demands on men already tired)
- •SL 141-142 ❖ SL 30:2

Tiredness: "...though I get no more tired now than I did when I was younger, I take much longer to get un-tired afterwards"
- •LAL 86 ❖ LAL Aug 3/59

"Titanic" defined (restive, militant and embittered) vs. "Olympian" (tranquil and tolerant) re: circles of Friends
- •FL 120 ❖ FL 4:53

Tobacco—*see* Smoking

Together: "...it is then that Friendship is born. And instantly they stand together in an immense solitude"
•FL 97 ❖ FL 4:16

Together: "To this day the vision of the world which comes most naturally to me is one in which 'we two' or 'we few'...stand together against something..."
•SJ 32 (see also SJ 176: "...we few..."; 206) ❖ SJ 2:12 (see also SJ 11:13: "...we few..."; 13:14)

Tolerance: In our day it is the "undogmatic" and "liberal" so-called Christians that are the most arrogant and intolerant
•L 229 ❖ L 23 Apr 51

Tolerance: "Intolerance" as a word which Screwtape uses to his advantage
•SL 48 ❖ SL 10:4

Tolerance: "'Mind one's own business' is a good rule in religion as in other things..." (re: varying tastes in worship styles)
•L 268 (consider also Judging)
❖ L 13 Mar 56 (consider also Judging)

Tolerance, opportunities for practicing, are never lacking; in everyone, including ourselves, there is that which requires forbearance and forgiveness
•FL 186 ❖ FL 6:37

Tolkien, J.R.R.: "It has become a regular custom that Tolkien should drop in on me of a Monday morning..."
•L 145 ❖ L 22 Nov 31

Tolkien, [J.R.R.], mentioned as "that great, but dilatory and unmethodical man"
•L 222
❖ L undated letter just before 9 Jan 50

Tolkien, J.R.R., mentioned by Lewis as one who gave him "much help in getting over the last stile" on the road to Christianity
•SJ 216 (see also L 197; SJ 225)
❖ SJ 14:6 (see also L 21 Dec 41; SJ 14:17)

Tolkien, [J.R.R], no one ever influenced, — you might as well try to influence a bandersnatch
•L 287 ❖ L 15 May 59

Tolkien, [J.R.R.], was both a Papist and a philologist, both of whom I had been warned never to trust
•SJ 216 ❖ SJ 14:6

Tolstoi: "...his error lies in thinking [mere affection] will do instead of agape"
•L 254-255 ❖ L 23 Jan 54

Tolstoi mentioned as an author of books "where the doctrine is as good...as the art"
•L 222
❖ L undated letter just before 9 Jan 50

Tongues: It is very hard to believe that in all instances of glossolalia the Holy Ghost is operating
•WG 55 ❖ WG 4:2

Tongues, speaking in, as an example of how glorifying God may not always edify our neighbor
•CR 94 ❖ CR 8:3

Tongues, speaking in, "glorified God firstly by being miraculous and involuntary, and secondly by the ecstatic state of mind in which the speaker was"
•CR 95 ❖ CR 8:5

Tongues, speaking in, mentioned as an example of how "Transposition" works
•WG 54-55; 64-65 ❖ WG 4:1-2, 15-17

Tongues, whether all instances of speaking in, are manifestations of hysteria
•WG 54-66 ❖ WG 4:1-18

Toolshed, Meditation in a (chapter title)
•GID 212-215 ❖ GID II ch. 6

Tooth, I had a, out the other day...may we dare hope that the moment of death will be like that delicious moment when one realises the tooth is really out
•LAL 84 ❖ LAL Jul 7th 59

Tooth of life, I hope that when the, is drawn and I am "coming round," a voice will say, "Rinse your mouth out with this"
•LAL 84; LM 109 (see also SL 147)
❖ LAL Jul 7th 59; LM 20:12 (see also SL 31:3)

Tooth, repentance of sins like having a painful, out
•GID 124 (see also RP 32)

❖ GID I 14:10 (*see also* RP 3:21)

Tooth, self-surrender likened to having a, out: "Christ says...I don't want to drill the tooth, or crown it, or stop it, but to have it out"
•MC 167 (*see also* Dentist analogy)
❖ MC IV 8:4 (*see also* Dentist analogy)

Toothache—*consider also* God as Dentist

Toothache, the "romance" of pain is unmasked by five minutes of genuine, (—Screwtape)
•SL 58 ❖ SL 13:3

Toothache, when I was a child I often had
•MC 171 (*see also* SJ 18, 96)
❖ MC IV 171 (*see also* SJ 1:19; 6:20)

Toothpaste as analogy to judging a person's Christianity: How much better it makes a person's teeth depends upon what they were like when he started brushing
•GID 59; MC 177-178
❖ GID I 4:46-52 (Ques. 12); MC IV 10:5

Total Depravity, doctrine of—*see* Depravity, doctrine of Total

Totalitarian government, Christianity is the worst enemy of; gives the individual a standing ground against the State
•GID 118 ❖ GID I 13:9

Totalitarian or Individualist, a Christian must not be either
•MC 159-160 ❖ MC IV 6:3

Totalitarianism vs. Democracy: If Christianity is true, then the individual is incomparably more important than a civilisation; he is everlasting
•MC 73 (*see also* GID 109-110; SL 170; WG 19, 116-117; WLN 68)
❖ MC III 1:9 (*see also* GID I 12:2, 3; SL 32:39; WG 1:15; 7:16; WLN 4:39)

Toy garden, the first instance of Lewis's experience of "Joy" came through the memory of his brother's
•SJ 7, 16 (*see also* SJ 8)
❖ SJ 1:4, 15 (*see also* SJ 1:5)

Toy soldier turning into a real man as analogy to Christian transformation
•MC 154-156, 162 ❖ MC IV 5:3-7; 7:7

Trade Unions, Screwtape speaks about
•SL 155; WLN 53 ❖ SL 32:5; WLN 4:5

Train, Lewis describes an enjoyable journey by, which he took to Bookham
•L 30 ❖ L 27 Sep 16

Train station, beautiful description of, in a letter to his brother*
•L 174 ❖ L 9 Jan 40

Trains, Lewis's enjoyment of riding on: "I get through a lot of reading and sometimes say my prayers"
•L 265 (*see also* LM 17)
❖ L 5 Dec 55 (*see also* LM 3:7)

Trains: My brother and I soon learned that books can be taken on a journey and that hours of golden reading can so be added to its other delights
•SJ 56-57 (*see also* L 203, 265)
❖ SJ 4:1 (*see also* L 31 Jan 43; 5 Dec 55)

Training—*see also* Education

Training for anything whatever that is good will always help in the true training for the Christian life
•SJ 146 ❖ SJ 9:22

Transfiguration, in the story of, as in the Ascension, "cloud" means a vague luminosity
•M 156 ❖ M 16:23

Transfiguration is a glimpse of our future power
•GID 32-33 ❖ GID I 2:11

Transfiguration of Jesus is no doubt an anticipatory glimpse of something to come
•M 152-153 ❖ M 16:18

Transfiguration: What is meant by the statement that Christ went up and vanished
•M 156-159 ❖ M 16:22-26

Transformation—*see also* Change; Growth, Christian; Improvement; *consider also* Perfection

Transformation, according to Screwtape, proceeds from within and is a manifestation of a certain "Life Force"
•SL 103-104 ❖ SL 22:6

Transformation, Christian: "All the rabbit in us is to disappear—the worried, conscientious, ethical rabbit as well as the cowardly and sensual rabbit..."*
•GID 112 ❖ GID I 12:10

Transformation, Christian, likened to turn-

Transposition: "...the Scriptures proceed not by conversion of God's word into a literature but by taking up of a literature to be the vehicle of God's word"*
•RP 116 (see also RP 111)
❖ RP 11:11 (see also RP 11:4)
Transposition throws a new light on the doctrine of the resurrection of the body; all our earthly sensations are to be flooded with new meaning
•WG 72 (see also WG 67-68)
❖ WG 4:30 (see also WG 4:22)
Transubstantiation, discussion of the controversy over*
•LM 101-105 ❖ LM 19:4-13
Transubstantiation, doctrine of, mentioned with reference to the Grail legend
•L 264, 295-296 (see also L 266, 269-270) ❖ L 22 Sep 55; 26 Sep 60 (see also L 17 Dec 55; 9 May 56)
Transubstantiation: I need not be tormented by the question, "What is this?" The command, after all, was Take, eat: not Take, understand*
•LM 104-105 ❖ LM 19:13
Transubstantiation: Lewis mentions the Sacrament as a supernatural event*
•LM 9 ❖ LM 2:1
Travel to other planets—see Space travel
Travelling—see also Walk(ing)
Travelling: Delight of nearing the end of a day's journey
•L 117 ❖ L 26 Apr 27
Travelling in cars: "...a modern boy travels a hundred miles with less sense of liberation and...adventure than his grandfather got from traveling ten"
•SJ 157 ❖ SJ 10:9
Travelling: Lewis describes a trip to the Forest of Dean
•L 128-129 ❖ L 2 Aug 28
Travelling: Lewis describes an English holiday taken with relatives
•L 65-72 ❖ L 7 Aug 21; 31 Aug 21
Travelling: Lewis describes an enjoyable journey by train to Bookham
•L 30 ❖ L 27 Sep 16
Travelling: My brother and I soon learned that books can be taken on a journey

and that hours of golden reading can so be added to its other delights
•SJ 56-57 (see also L 203, 265)
❖ SJ 4:1 (see also L 31 Jan 43; 5 Dec 55)
Travelling with friends: "Those are the golden sessions, when four or five of us after a hard day's walking come to our inn..."
•FL 105 ❖ FL 4:30
Treatment, compromise is harder than going in for the full; we are like eggs—must be hatched or go bad
•MC 169 (see also Self-surrender; Surrender) ❖ MC IV 8:9 (see also Self-surrender; Surrender)
Treatment: Our Lord is like the dentist; once you call Him in, He will give you the full treatment
•MC 171 (see also God as Dentist)
❖ MC IV 9:2, 3 (see also God as Dentist)
Treatment: "What is going on in you at present is simply the beginning of the *treatment*"
•L 233 ❖ L 13 Jun 51
Trials—see also Difficulties
Trials not sent in order that God might find out the quality of our faith—God already knows that; they show *us* its quality
⠆ •GO 61; PP 101-102 ❖ GO 3:36; PP 6:13
Tribulation(s)—see also Difficulties
Tribulation: "God, who foresaw your tribulation, has specially armed you to go through it, not without pain but without stain..."
•L 219 ❖ L 2 Sep 49
Tribulation, straight, [such as being in the army] is easier to bear than tribulation which advertises itself as pleasure [such as school]
•SJ 188 ❖ SJ 12:10
Tribulation, the real difficulty is to adopt one's steady beliefs about, to this particular
•L 186 ❖ L 2 Jun 40
Tribulation, the terrible necessity of, [to show us our dependence upon God] is only too clear
•PP 106-107 ❖ PP 6:17
Tribulations cannot cease until God either

sees us remade or sees that our remaking is now hopeless
- •PP 107, 114 ❖ PP 6:17; 7:5

Tribulations which fall upon us by necessity, if embraced for Christ's sake, become as meritorious as *voluntary* sufferings
- •LAL 20, 60, 105
- ❖ LAL Aug 10th 53; 3/8/56; 3/7/62

Trinity: "Beyond Personality: or First Steps in the Doctrine of the Trinity" (Book IV of *Mere Christianity*)
- •MC 135-190 ❖ MC Book IV

Trinity as described in early Christian writings was never philosophically definite; those writers were not writing to satisfy curiosity about God's nature
- •M 75-76 ❖ M 10:15

Trinity, difficulty of imagining, without "falling into the heresy of Tritheism"
- •LAL 14 ❖ LAL 17/4/53

Trinity, doctrine of, discussed
- •MC 135-153 (*see also* L 305)
- ❖ MC IV ch. 1-5 (*see also* L undated letter just after 10 Aug 62)

Trinity, doctrine of, has neither the monolithic grandeur of Unitarian conceptions nor the richness of Polytheism (re: Christian theology as "poetry")
- •WG 75 ❖ WG 5:5

Trinity, doctrine of, helps to describe the positive structure of uncreated Reality
- •M 79 ❖ M 10:19

Trinity, doctrine of, shows God as "a person and more"
- •GID 185 (*see also* MC 140-141)
- ❖ GID I 23:2 (*see also* MC IV 2:2)

Trinity, function of, as shown by a man saying his prayers
- •MC 142-143 ❖ MC IV 2:9

Trinity: God is revealed to us as *super*-personal, which is very different from being *im*personal (re: God as three Persons instead of A Person)
- •L 305 ❖ L undated letter of Aug 1962

Trinity: God is three persons while remaining one Being, as a cube is six squares while remaining one cube
- •CR 79-80; M 85; MC 142 (*see also* GID 182) ❖ CR 6:21; M 11:6; MC IV 2:7 (*see also* GID I 22:14)

Trinity, helpful ways of thinking of the
- •MC 141-143, 149-152
- ❖ MC IV 2:5-10; 4:1-7

Trinity, in the, something analogous to "society" exists, making possible the reciprocity of love within the Divine Being
- •PP 29 (*see also* PP 151)
- ❖ PP 2:7 (*see also* PP 10:8)

Trinity: Lewis mentions his belief that the Son (as God) is subject to the Father
- •L 198 ❖ L 21 Dec 41

Trinity, regarding the relationship of God to Christ in the
- •CR 4-6 ❖ CR 1:6-10

Trinity, Screwtape speaks about: "[God] claims to be three as well as one, in order that this nonsense about Love may find a foothold in His own nature"
- •SL 81-82 ❖ SL 18:4

Trinity, second Person of, as God *and* man
- •L 210 (*see also* L 191, 200-201)
- ❖ L undated letter of 1947 (*see also* L undated letter just before 4 Jan 41; 29 Jul 42)

Trinity, self-surrender begins within the; this is the pattern man was made to imitate
- •PP 90-91 ❖ PP 6:3

Trinity, third Person of
- •MC 152 ❖ MC IV 4:6, 7

Trips—*see* Travelling; Walking tours; Walks

Tristram Shandy, illustration of really good domestic manners from
- •FL 69-70 ❖ FL 3:26

Tristram Shandy: "It gives you the impression of an escaped lunatic's conversation while chasing his hat on a windy day"
- •L 31 ❖ L 25 Oct 16

Tristram Shandy, relationship between "my father" and Uncle Toby in, as a good example of Affection
- •FL 55 (*see also* SJ 120)
- ❖ FL 3:5 (*see also* SJ 8:4)

Trouble(s)—*see also* Difficulties

Trouble and misery may eventually be seen as having brought us to dependence upon God
•L 220 (*see also* LAL 49)
❖ L undated letter just before 22 Sep 49 (*see also* LAL 16/12/55)

Trouble, why is God so present a commander in our time of prosperity and so very absent a help in time of ?
•GO 4-5 ❖ GO 1:7

Trouble with "X", The (chapter title)
•GID 151-155 ❖ GID I ch. 18

Troubles and sorrows, the moment you regard your, as punishments they become easier to bear (as a dingy hotel may look good if thought to be a prison)
•GID 52 ❖ GID I 4:18 (Ques. 5)

Troubles, part of oneself still regards, as interruptions
•L 161-162, 221
❖ L 12 Sep 38; 22 Sep 49

"**Troughs**" and "peaks" of human experience: Screwtape advises Wormwood on how to exploit them for diabolical purposes
•SL 40-44 ❖ SL ch. 9

"Troughs," Screwtape speaks about the, or periods of dryness which humans may experience in their Christian life
•SL 13-14, 36-44 ❖ SL 2:3; ch. 8, 9

Trust—*see also* Belief; Faith

Trust: "Are you struggling, resisting? Don't you think our Lord says to you 'Peace, child...let go, I will catch you. Do you trust me so little?'"
•LAL 117 ❖ LAL 17 Jun 63

Trust, complete, could have no room to grow except where there is also room for doubt (re: trust in God)
•WLN 25-26 ❖ WLN 2:13

Trust, implicit, is the only mode in which our personal response to God can establish itself
•WLN 26-30, esp. 28
❖ WLN 2:13-18, esp. 2:16

Trust in God, a Christian's, is often more than may be merited by philosophical premises, but less than He deserves
•GID 173, 176 ❖ GID I 21:4, 9

Trust in God based on knowledge-by-acquaintance; we (as Christians) trust not because "a God" exists, but because *this* God exists
•WLN 25, 29-30 ❖ WLN 2:13, 17, 18

Trust in God: "...it is senseless to say that you will trust if you are given demonstrative certainty"; no room for trust if demonstration given
•WLN 28 (*see also* WLN 92)
❖ WLN 2:16 (*see also* WLN 6:28)

Trust in God, lack of, the result of not knowing God well enough*
•WLN 25-30, esp. 29
❖ WLN 2:13-18, esp. 2:17

Trust in God: "No man is our friend who believes in our good intentions only when they are proved"
•WLN 26 ❖ WLN 2:13

Trust may sometimes need to be maintained in the teeth of our senses (rescue analogy)
•WLN 23-25 ❖ WLN 2:12, 13

Trust may sometimes need to operate without the *feeling* of confidence (swimming analogy)
•CR 42-43 (*see also* GID 172-173*; L 199; MC 122-123; WLN 23-25)
❖ CR 3:11 (*see also* GID I 21:2*; L 20 Jan 42; MC III 11:3; WLN 2:12, 13)

Trust or confidence in the God whose existence we assent to by faith involves an attitude of the will; it is like our confidence in a friend
•GID 172-173 ❖ GID I 21:2

Trust: To trust God means that you trust His advice and try to do what He says—not in order to be saved, but because He has begun to save you already
•MC 128-130 ❖ MC III 12:6, 7

Trust, we can learn the lesson of, from the animals; how well a sick dog trusts one if one has to do things to it that hurt it
•LAL 56 (*see also* WLN 23-24)
❖ LAL 26/4/56 (*see also* WLN 2:12)

Truth—*see also* Reality; *consider also* Understanding

Truth: A belief in the objectivity and validity of reason must be maintained *or* all thoughts are accidents and we can know no truths and have no knowledge*
•CR 60-63, 71, 72-81, 89; GID 21, 52-53, 136-138, 272, 274-276; M 12-24, 34, 105; MC 45-46; SJ 208; WG 88-92 ❖ CR 5:9-13, 27; ch. 6; 7:16; GID I 1:1; 4:21; 16:13-17; III 1:4, 9, 13-16; M ch. 3; 5:1; 13:16; MC II 1:6; SJ 13:17; WG 5:21-24

Truth: A cultured person is almost compelled to be aware that reality is very odd and that the ultimate truth *must* have the characteristics of strangeness
•CR 23 ❖ CR 2:35

Truth, a man can't always be defending; there must be a time to feed on it
•RP 7 ❖ RP 1:12

Truth about God, avenues for seeking, (miracles, inspired teachers, and enjoined ritual)
•GID 143-144 ❖ GID I 16:26

Truth about God: "If He can be known it will be by self-revelation on His part, not by speculation on ours"
•GID 144 ❖ GID I 16:26

Truth about God, religion (prayer, sacrament, repentance, adoration) as our sole avenue to*
•GID 46 ❖ GID I 3:16

Truth about ourselves—*see also* Self-knowledge

Truth about ourselves: "A moderately bad man knows he is not very good: a thoroughly bad man thinks he is all right"
•MC 87 (*see also* GID 56-57; LAL 95; PP 55, top; PP 67)
❖ MC III 4:10 (*see also* GID I 4:38; LAL 9 Jan 61; 61; PP 4:prelim. quote; 4:15)

Truth about ourselves: "Every now and then we discover what our fellow beings really think of us"; the absolute truth will someday be known to all
•WLN 112-113 ❖ WLN 7:36, 37

Truth about ourselves never fully known to us
•GID 121-123, 153; PP 59-60 (*see also*

L 183*; MC 87; SL 16)
❖ GID I 14:4-8; 18:6, 7; PP 4:7 (*see also* L 16 Apr 40*; MC III 4:10; SL 3:2)

Truth about ourselves: "We shall perhaps realise that in some dim fashion we could have known it all along"
•WLN 113 ❖ WLN 7:37

Truth always comes to men, regardless of the mode, from God (as Moses may have been influenced by Akhenaten's system of Monotheism)*
•RP 86 ❖ RP 8:17

Truth and error, many preferences which seem to the ignorant to be simply "matters of taste" are visible to a trained critic as choices between
•CR 29 ❖ CR 2:48

Truth and reality: "Who...want to see it and take pains to find it out...even though the sight of it makes an incurable ulcer in their hearts?" (re: those "who would have truth at any price")
•GO 32 ❖ GO 2:20

Truth arrived at through varying proportions of three things: Authority, reason, and experience
•CR 41, 43 ❖ CR 3:9, 12

Truth as expressed through revelation: "...there ought to be something opaque to our reason though not contrary to it"
•GID 238 ❖ GID II 11:11

Truth as objective and discoverable by logic and reasoning
•CR 60-71 ❖ CR 5:9-27

Truth as seen from Heaven: "...how different the content of our faith will look when we see it in the total context"
•L 267 ❖ L 8 Feb 56

Truth, avoidance of—*see* Evasion of truth

Truth, basic, which cannot be argued about: the ultimate preference of the will for love rather than hatred, and happiness rather than misery*
•WG 37 ❖ WG 3:7

Truth: Christians believe that through religious experience they get a sort of verification (or perhaps sometimes falsification) of their tenets*

•CR 137-138 ❖ CR 11:19

Truth, coming to a knowledge of: "For he who does the will of the Father shall know the doctrine" (re: use of imagery to describe Heaven)
•M 158 ❖ M 16:25

Truth, error usually contains or imitates some; that is what makes it potent (re: Fascism and Communism)*
•L 176 ❖ L 17 Jan 40

Truth, honesty in seeking, even when it may turn out to be inconvenient
•GID 110-112 (see also WG 35*)
❖ GID I 12:6-9 (see also WG 3:4*)

Truth, honesty in seeking: "If Christianity is untrue, then no honest man will want to believe it...if it is true, every honest man will want to believe it"
•GID 108-109 ❖ GID I 12:1

Truth, honesty in seeking, in a civilization like ours: "...I feel that everyone must come to terms with the claims of Jesus Christ upon his life..."
•GID 265-266 ❖ GID II 16:50, 51

Truth: I couldn't get at the universe if I couldn't trust my reason; if we couldn't trust inference we could know nothing...
•GID 274-275, 277
❖ GID III 1:11, 22-27

Truth, I think that all things reflect heavenly, the imagination not least
•SJ 167 ❖ SJ 11:4

Truth: If any message from the core of reality ever were to reach us, we should expect to find in it just that unexpectedness which we find in Christianity
•PP 25 (see also MC 46-47, 137, 145; PP 119) ❖ PP 1:16 (see also MC II 2:2-5; IV 1:9; 2:17; PP 8:3)

Truth, if you look for, you may find comfort in the end; if you look for comfort you will not get either comfort or truth
•MC 39 ❖ MC I 5:4

Truth, importance of searching for, within various Christian denominations
•MC 11-12 ❖ MC P:15

Truth: In deciding which denomination to join, our question should never be: "Do I like that kind of service?" but

"Are these doctrines true?"
•MC 12 ❖ MC P:15

Truth, instruments God uses to convey, may include Pagan authors (as Moses may have been influenced by Akhenaten's system of Monotheism)*
•RP 86 ❖ RP 8:17

Truth, intellectual dishonesty of the man who evades, out of fear of duty: "...He has lost his intellectual virginity"
•GID 110-111 (see also Self-reservation) ❖ GID I 12:6-8 (see also Self-reservation)

Truth is bound to be difficult, not simple
•MC 46-48, 137, 145 (see also M 165; PP 119) ❖ MC II 2:2, 4, 5; IV 1:9; 2:17 (see also M 17:2; PP 8:3)

Truth is more effective through any lips rather than our own
•L 195 (see also L 236)
❖ L 19 Nov 41 (see also L 26 Dec 51)

Truth is not "adjustable to contemporary thought," etc., as some theologians seem to believe—as if we were trying to make rather than to learn*
•LM 104 ❖ LM 19:12

Truth: "It is possible that a certain sort of enlightenment can come too soon and too easily" (re: Akhenaten's system of Monotheism)
•RP 87 ❖ RP 8:17

Truth, looking at light vs. looking "along" light as analogy to understanding
•GID 212-215 ❖ GID II ch. 6

Truth must involve exclusions; what do Hindus deny?
•L 267 (see also L 285)
❖ L 8 Feb 56 (see also L 30 Apr 59)

Truth must sometimes be accepted on the basis of trusted authority
•WG 35-36 (see also CR 26*, 41, 43; GID 276*; MC 63; SJ 174; WLN 17)
❖ WG 3:5, 6

Truth never superseded or outmoded by more knowledge*
•GID 44-45, 47 ❖ GID I 3:13, 14, 16

Truth of Christianity must be discovered by reasoning before it is asked whether people's motives for believing it are proper or improper

- •GID 273-274 (*see also* WLN 18-20)
- ❖ GID III 1:7 (*see also* WLN 2:8)

Truth of Our Lord's teaching: "...there is no question of learning a subject but of steeping ourselves in a Personality"
- •RP 113-114 ❖ RP 11:9

Truth, pain (as God's megaphone) plants the flag of, within the fortress of a rebel soul
- •PP 95, 120 ❖ PP 6:7; 8:5

Truth, people no longer as concerned with; more interested in what is "practical" and "contemporary"—thus argument is not as effective as it used to be*
- •SL 7-8 ❖ SL 1:1

Truth, pursuit of: Our feelings and moods tell us more about the state of our passions and even our digestion than about reality*
- •CR 43 (*see also* MC 123-124)
- ❖ CR 3:10-12 (*see also* MC III 11:5)

Truth, pursuit of: You may take any number of wrong turnings, but keep your eyes open and you will not be allowed to go very far without warnings*
- •SJ 177 ❖ SJ 11:14

Truth ("Revelation") may be derived from the experience of Awe if it is not a mere twist in the human mind (re: existence of the Supernatural)*
- •PP 20-21 ❖ PP 1:11

Truth ("Revelation") may be derived from the human consciousness of a moral law and of guilt (if they are not inexplicable illusions)*
- •PP 21-22 ❖ PP 1:12

Truth, Satan can exploit even, to our deception (re: corporate guilt or a social conscience as an excuse for evading our own personal faults)
- •PP 60 ❖ PP 4:8

Truth, searching for: "...to act on the light one has is almost the only way to more light"
- •L 191-192 ❖ L 4 Jan 41

Truth, self-evident, ("intuition") defined as that which "no good man has ever dreamed of doubting"
- •WG 38 (*see also* WG 37, 39, 41)
- ❖ WG 3:9 (*see also* WG 3:7, 11, 15)

Truth, self-evident, ("intuition"): "You cannot produce rational intuition by argument, because argument depends upon rational intuition"
- •WG 35 (*see also* CR 75*)
- ❖ WG 3:4 (*see also* CR 6:12*)

Truth, spiritual experience essential to understanding spiritual
- •WG 54-73 ❖ WG ch. 4

Truth, spiritual: "...what is meat for a grown person might be unsuited to the palate of a child" (re: Song of Solomon)
- •GID 264 ❖ GID II 16:40

Truth, the great thing is to make your patient value an opinion for some quality other than, (—Screwtape)
- •SL 64 ❖ SL 14:4

Truth: "The man who will neither obey wisdom in others nor adventure for her himself is fatal"*
- •M 43 (*see also* GID 276)
- ❖ M 6:6 (*see also* GID III 1:17)

Truth: "...the thing we know already... when said by *someone else* becomes suddenly operative"
- •L 236 (*see also* L 195)
- ❖ L 26 Dec 51 (*see also* L 19 Nov 41)

Truth: Those who have heard the claims of Christ must come to terms with them, or else be guilty of inattention or of evading the question*
- •GID 265-266 ❖ GID II 16:50

Truth, understanding of, requires "the help of Him who is the Father of lights" (re: various pieces of truth which have required this help)**
- •RP 80, 110 ❖ RP 8:7; 11:3

Truth vs. helpful beliefs, Christianity as
- •GID 108-109 (*see also* GID 101)
- ❖ GID I 12:1 (*see also* GID I 10:48)

Truth vs. Reality: "...truth is always about something, but reality is that *about which* truth is"
- •GID 66 ❖ GID I 5:10

Truth: We dimly know at heart that nothing which is in every way agreeable to us can have objective reality; reality has sharp corners and rough edges
- •LM 75-76 ❖ LM 14:13

Truth, we may pray that those who have discovered only bits of, in their lifetime now enjoy the truth which so far transcends their own glimpse of it*
•RP 89, 108 ❖ RP 8:19; 10:12

Truth, we no longer rely on tradition and authority for; we must get it ourselves or go without it
•M 42 (see also GID 276)
❖ M 6:6 (see also GID III 1:17)

Truth: "What are facts without interpretation?"
•SJ 121 ❖ SJ 8:4

Truths about life: No real teaching possible; every generation starts from scratch
•L 166 ❖ L 8 May 39

Truths all intertwined: "Divine reality is like a fugue. All His acts are different, but they all rhyme or echo to one another"
•GID 37 ❖ GID I 2:15

Truths: Few of us have followed the reasoning on which the truths we believe are based; most of us accept them on expert authority
•WG 35 ❖ WG 3:5

Truths may sound like barren platitudes to those who have not had the relevant experience
•L 166 ❖ L 8 May 39

Truths, we have no right to demand that the highest spiritual, should be picturable or even explicable in terms of our abstract thought
•PP 86-87 (see also M 83-86*)
❖ PP 5:13 (see also M 11:5-7*)

Truthfulness—see also Honesty

Truthfulness: "Strict veracity" mentioned as one of "the severer virtues" which Lewis came to realize might have relevance in his own life
•SJ 192 (see also SJ 201)
❖ SJ 12:14 (see also SJ 13:6)

Trying to be good—see Moral effort

Turning the other cheek, three ways to take the command of
•WG 49-51 ❖ WG 3:28, 29

Turning to God—see Surrender

TV—see Television

Twist in the central man caused by wrong actions
•MC 86-87, 107 (see also WLN 54-55; MC 117*) ❖ MC III 4:8, 9; 7:9 (see also WLN 4:10; MC III 9:8*)

Two Lectures (chapter title)
•GID 208-211 ❖ GID II ch. 5

Two Notes (chapter title)
•MC 157-160 ❖ MC IV ch. 6

Two Ways with the Self (chapter title)
•GID 193-195 ❖ GID II ch. 2

Tyranny—see Oppression

Ultimate issues, Lewis relates his early beliefs about, (no belief in immortality; feeling of materialistic pessimism)
•L 77 ❖ L 24 May 22

Ultimate issues, Screwtape emphasizes the importance of keeping human minds off of, and having them attend instead to immediate sense experiences*
•SL 8 ❖ SL 1:2

Ultimate issues such as the meaning of life not part of most people's thinking*
•GID 252-253 ❖ GID II 14:10

Unbelief—consider Obstacles to Christian faith

Unbeliever(s)—see also Agnostic(s); Atheist(s); Sceptic(s)

Unbeliever, debate between Christian and: There is evidence both for and against the Christian propositions which fully rational minds can assess differently
•WLN 20 ❖ WLN 2:8

Unbeliever, debate between Christian and: "There is no need to suppose stark unreason on either side. We need only suppose error"
•WLN 21 ❖ WLN 2:9

Unbeliever, it is the high-minded, with his "faith in human nature," who is really sad; humility, after the first shock, is a cheerful virtue
•PP 67 ❖ PP 4:15

Unbeliever, regarding the fate of the virtuous
•L 164, 196 ❖ L 5 Apr 39; 8 Dec 41

Unbelievers, association with: Association with wicked people to be avoided, not because we are "too good" but because in a sense we are not good enough
•RP 71-74 (see also SL 45-48*)
❖ RP 7:9-16 (see also SL ch. 10*)

Unbelievers, association with, makes faith harder even when their opinions on any other subject are known to be worthless
•CR 42 ❖ CR 3:10

Unbelievers, association with: "They know well enough what we are believing or trying to believe...and regard it as total illusion"* (re: Psalmists' dark experience)
•CR 127-128 ❖ CR 10:38-40

Unbelievers, disagreement with, may sometimes be necessary
•GID 262; RP 73-74 (see also SL 45-48*)
❖ GID II 16:29; RP 7:14, 15 (see also SL ch. 10*)

Unbelievers: Filth that our enemies fling at God either does not stick or, sticking, turns into glory (re: charge that God committed adultery with Mary)
•GID 32 ❖ GID I 2:9

Unbelievers, intellectual attacks of, must be met by intellectual answers (re: value of education for the Christian)
•WG 28 (see also CR 17)
❖ WG 2:10 (see also CR 2:18)

Unbelievers, our anxiety about, most usefully employed when it leads us not to speculation but to prayer for them
•L 247 ❖ L 8 Nov 52

Unbelievers, our worry about, is more reason to get inside oneself, where we can help; to add a new finger to the body of Christ
•L 196 ❖ L 8 Dec 41

Unbelievers ("outsiders"), there are two kinds of, whom the theologian needs to study: the uneducated, and those who are educated in some way but not in his way
•CR 152-153 ❖ CR 13:1, 2

Unbelievers, putting one's Christian point of view to unpromising: We sin if our

real reason for silence is fear of looking a fool
•L 249 (see also Witnessing)
❖ L 6-7 Apr 53 (see also Witnessing)
Unbelievers, regarding question of salvation for deceased
•L 238 ❖ L 31 Jan 52
Unbelievers, regarding the destiny of virtuous: Parable of Sheep and Goats suggests that they have a very pleasant surprise coming to them
•L 196 ❖ L 8 Dec 41
Unbelievers, salvation for: Every sincere prayer, even to a false God, is accepted by the true God; Christ saves many who do not think they know Him
•L 247 ❖ L 8 Nov 52
Unbelievers, salvation for: Salvation not exclusively for those who have accepted Jesus explicitly in this life
•GID 101-102; MC 65 (see also GID 265-266*) ❖ GID I 10:48; MC II 5:8 (see also GID II 16:50, 51*)
Unbelievers, while we know that all justice and mercy will be done for, it is nevertheless our duty to do all we can to convert them
•L 238 ❖ L 31 Jan 52
Unbelievers who always speak of Christianity with reverence vs. those who are rude: The rudeness shows fear that there "might be something in it after all"
•LAL 90 ❖ LAL 26 Mar 60
Uncertainty about the future as a barricade to the human mind against God (—Screwtape)
•SL 28-29 ❖ SL 6:1, 2
Uncertainty (or unprovableness) of certain doctrines, such as a future life: "There is our...chance for a little generosity, a little sportsmanship"*
•LM 120-121 ❖ LM 22:10
Understanding—consider also Truth
Understanding about Jesus: "No net less wide than a man's whole heart, nor less fine of mesh than love, will hold the sacred Fish"
•RP 119 ❖ RP 11:15
Understanding about such things as how

the Atonement works not essential to our acceptance of them; we might not know how they work until we've accepted them*
•MC 58-59 (see also L 197-198)
❖ MC II 4:4, 5 (see also L 21 Dec 41)
Understanding, experience is essential to full, of anything ("One must look both along and at everything")
•GID 212-215 ❖ GID II ch. 6
Understanding: "It is possible that a certain sort of enlightenment can come too soon and too easily" (re: Akhenaten's system of Monotheism)
•RP 87 ❖ RP 8:17
Understanding need not precede obedience; humans must be trained in obedience almost before they have moral intuitions
•WG 36-37 (see also L 179)
❖ WG 3:6 (see also L 26 Mar 40)
Understanding not always possible or essential, as in Holy Communion, where the command was, after all, Take, eat: not Take, understand*
•LM 104 ❖ LM 19:13
Understanding of individual doctrines best begun by reading the Bible on your own, with prayer for guidance*
•L 233 ❖ L 13 Jun 51
Understanding of truth requires "the help of Him who is the Father of lights" (re: an "amazing leap" in the theology of Plato)*
•RP 80, 110 ❖ RP 8:7; 11:3
Understanding: "The entrance is low: we must stoop till we are no taller than children in order to get in"
•RP 88 ❖ RP 8:17
Understanding: Whenever you find any statement in Christian writings which you can't understand, do not worry; leave it alone
•MC 126 ❖ MC III 12:1
Undulation, law of: Screwtape advises Wormwood on how to use this law for the devil's purposes
•SL 40-44 ❖ SL ch. 9
Undulation, Screwtape discusses the law of, which refers to the human ten-

dency to experience peaks and troughs in every department of life
•SL 36-39 ❖ SL ch. 8

Uneasy, We Have Cause to Be (chapter title)
•MC 36-39 ❖ MC I ch. 5

Uneducated people—*see also* Lowbrow(s)

Uneducated people, value of reasoning with, in evangelism
•GID 99 ❖ GID I 10:39, 40

"Unemployment" an alternative (and more charitable) term for "surplus population"*
•WLN 79 ❖ WLN 5:20

Unfallen humanity, redeemed humanity is to be something more glorious than, would have been
•M 122-123 (*see also* GID 87*)
❖ M 14:24 (*see also* GID I 9:11*)

Unfallen man—*see also* Adam

Unfallen man: God came first in his love and in his thought, without painful effort
•PP 78 ❖ PP 5:6

Unfallen man, self-surrender of, meant no struggle but only a delicious overcoming of an infinitesimal self-adherence which delighted to be overcome
•PP 81 ❖ PP 5:9

Unfallen man, service of God was the keenest pleasure of
•PP 98 ❖ PP 6:10

Unfallen man, speculation about the nature of
•PP 77-84 ❖ PP 5:6-10

Unfallen man, turning from God to self fulfills the necessary conditions for a sin possible to
•PP 80-81 ❖ PP 5:9

Unhappiness: An unhappy man wants distractions?—Only as a dog-tired man wants a blanket on a cold night; he'd rather lie there shivering...
•GO 4 ❖ GO 1:6

Unhappiness, I must try not to let my own present, harden my heart against the woes of others
•LAL 64 ❖ LAL 4/1/57

Unhappiness in marriage: "Marriage is

not otherwise unhappy than as life is unhappy" (quote from Johnson)
•L 128 ❖ L 2 Aug 28

Unhappiness, Lewis describes his early pessimism which would have preferred non-existence itself to even the mildest
•SJ 117 (*see also* SJ 171)
❖ SJ 7:21 (*see also* SJ 11:8)

Unhappiness, one of the fruits of, is that it forces us to think of life as something to go *through*—and out at the other end
•L 227 ❖ L 5 Mar 51

Unhappiness, Screwtape mentions one cause of human, as the perverted thirst for continual novelty
•SL 117 ❖ SL 25:4

Unhappy times, the great thing with, is to take them bit by bit and hour by hour; it is seldom the exact present that is unbearable
•LAL 58 (*see also* LAL 60, 69, 103; SL 29, 67-71*)
❖ LAL 14/6/56 (*see also* LAL 3/8/56; Oct 20th 57; 4 May 62; SL 6:2; ch. 15*)

Unimportance—*see* Insignificance

Unions, Screwtape speaks about Trade
•SL 155; WLN 53 ❖ SL 32:5; WLN 4:5

Uniqueness of our personality—*see* Personality

Unitarian conceptions, the Christian story lacks the monolithic grandeur of strictly, (re: Christian theology as "poetry")
•WG 75 ❖ WG 5:5

United States—*see* America

Unity—*consider also* Membership; Reunion

Unity between Creature and Creator which is "given" by the relation between them is different from the union of wills which is reached through grace
•LM 69 ❖ LM 13:5

Unity, differences in kind make for real, (re: Christian membership)
•WG 110-111 ❖ WG 7:6, 7

Unity in the ideal sense is a refuge both from solitude and from the collective

I 3:9; 10:42*; WLN 6:13, 14)

Universe, God is related to the, more as an author is related to a play than as one object in the universe is related to another
•CR 168 ❖ CR 14:14

Universe, I found in Bergson a refutation of the old idea that the, might not have existed (thus one gives up pessimism—or even optimism)
•SJ 204 ❖ SJ 13:11

Universe, I had very definitely formed the opinion [in my youth] that the, was, in the main, a rather regrettable institution
•SJ 63 ❖ SJ 4:10

Universe, Idealist's and Pantheist's view of the material, is that it is, in the last resort, not quite real; is a kind of mirage
•CR 59 ❖ CR 5:5

Universe, if the whole, has no meaning we should never have found out that it has no meaning—just as "dark" has no meaning to creatures without eyes
•MC 46 ❖ MC II 1:6

Universe, immensity of, not a recent discovery; yet used in modern times as a stock argument against Christianity
•GID 39, 74-75; M 48-49 (see also PP 15-16) ❖ GID I 3:4; 7:29-41; M 7:7-9 (see also PP 1:3)

Universe is beautiful but also terrifying and dangerous; is misleading if taken as our only source of information about God—moral law is better source
•MC 37 ❖ MC I 5:3

Universe, it says in the Bible that the, was made for Christ and that everything is to be gathered together in Him
•MC 170 ❖ MC IV 8:10

Universe, Man not the center of the; may be the one lost sheep who the Shepherd was sent to save
•GID 42-43, 100 (see also M 51-52, 122) ❖ GID I 3:9; 10:42 (see also M 7:12, 13; 14:24)

Universe, Man not the center of the; we were made not primarily that we may love God but that God may love us—

and He will labour to make us lovable
•PP 47-48 ❖ PP 3:15

Universe: "...my very early reading...had lodged very firmly in my imagination the vastness and coldness of space, the littleness of Man"
•SJ 65 ❖ SJ 4:11

Universe ("Nature") a partial system within reality; has been mistaken for the whole (fish tank analogy)*
•M 60-61 ❖ M 8:9

Universe, origin of—see also Creation; Evolution

Universe, origin of, has counted for less in popular thought than its character (vastness; indifference to man)
•GID 39 ❖ GID I 3:4

Universe, our sins will be common knowledge to the; "...when the term ends we might find ourselves facing the public opinion of that larger world"
•PP 61, 63 (see also SL 148*)
❖ PP 4:9, 10 (see also SL 31:5*)

Universe, Right and Wrong as a Clue to the Meaning of the, (Book I of Mere Christianity)
•MC 17-39 ❖ MC Book I

Universe, right size of: "I should be suffocated in a universe that I could see to the end of"
•GID 42 ❖ GID I 3:8

Universe rings true wherever you fairly test it; keep your eyes open and you will not be allowed to go very far in the wrong direction without warnings
•SJ 177 ❖ SJ 11:14

Universe, size and emptiness of the, symbolises great truth
•PP 153-154 ❖ PP 10:11

Universe, the horror of the Christian, was that it had no door marked "Exit"; materialist's universe was attractive because it offered limited liabilities
•SJ 171 (see also GO 33; consider also Limited liabilities)
❖ SJ 11:8 (see also GO 2:22; consider also Limited liabilities)

Universe, the Jewish, Moslem, and Christian view of the, is that there is something beyond nature which refutes the

scientists' picture of futility
•CR 59 ❖ CR 5:5

Universe, there is no neutral ground in the; every square inch, every split second, is claimed by God and counterclaimed by Satan
•CR 33 ❖ CR 2:54

Universe, time is to the, as the metre is to a poem or the key is to music; God cannot be in it if He created it (re: finding God in space)
•CR 168 ❖ CR 14:15

Universe, vast distances of, may be God's quarantine precautions
•WLN 91 ❖ WLN 6:24

Universe, vastness of: "...how majestically indifferent most reality is to man..."
•M 51 ❖ M 7:11

Universe, vastness of, shows greatness of God
•GID 42 (see also M 53*)
❖ GID I 3:8 (see also M 7:16*)

Universe, when one considers the, it seems strange that God should be at all concerned with man—yet He has given us extraordinary honour (re: Psalm 8)
•RP 132, 134 ❖ RP 12:11, 13

Unjust Judge, parable of—see Parable of Unjust Judge

Unselfishness—see also Selflessness; Self-sacrifice

Unselfishness in the negative sense (going without things ourselves) is not necessarily the Christian virtue of Love
•WG 3 ❖ WG 1:1

"Unselfishness" in the negative sense is substituted by the devil for the positive word "Charity" (—Screwtape)
•SL 121 ❖ SL 26:2

Unselfishness: Screwtape advises teaching a man to surrender benefits not that others may be happy in having them but that he'll be unselfish in forgoing them
•SL 121 ❖ SL 26:2

"Unselfishness" vs. real charity: The former may be a dishonest attempt to feel blameless and ill-used

•SL 121-124 (see also Martyr; Martyrdom) ❖ SL 26:2-5 (see also Martyr; Martyrdom)

"Unselfishness": Women generally mean by this taking trouble for others; men generally mean not giving trouble to others; each see the other as selfish
•SL 121 ❖ SL 26:2

Unworthiness of Man for the love of the Creator: Christ did not die for men because they were worth dying for, but because He is love and He loves infinitely
•M 52 (see also WLN 86)
❖ M 7:14 (see also WLN 6:10)

Unworthiness of Man for the sacrifice of the Son of God*
•M 122 ❖ M 14:24

Upbringing, we may have made so little use of a good, that we are no better than those we regard as fiends
•MC 86 (see also L 183; MC 180-182)
❖ MC III 4:7 (see also L 16 Apr 40; MC IV 10:11-14)

Usefulness of ourselves by God: "One must take comfort in remembering that God used an ass to convert the prophet..."
•L 193-194 ❖ L 15 May 41

Vacations, memories of, improve with time
•L 71-72 ❖ L 31 Aug 21

Vale of soul-making, if the world is a indeed a, [because of affliction] it seems on the whole to be doing its work
•PP 108 ❖ PP 6:18

"Valentines" have almost died out in this country; I have not seen one since I was a small boy
•LAL 72 ❖ LAL 22/2/58

"Valley of tears," life as a, cursed with labour, hemmed round with necessities, tripped up with frustrations, etc.
•LM 92 (*consider also* Pessimism, Lewis's) ❖ LM 17:17 (*consider also* Pessimism, Lewis's)

Value, a philosophy which does not accept, as eternal and objective can lead us only to ruin
•CR 80-81 ❖ CR 6:22

Value, a sound theory of, demands that good should be original and evil a mere perversion
•GID 23 ❖ GID I 1:5

Value based on size illogical, and a primitive error (in trying to show the unimportance of the earth and Man in relation to the universe)
•GID 39-41; M 48-54 (*see also* GID 74-75; PP 13) ❖ GID I 3:4-6; M 7:7-17 (*see also* GID I 7:29-41; PP 1:1)

Value, Brother Every maintained that our tastes are symptomatic of our real standards of, which may differ from our professed standards
•CR 28 ❖ CR 2:47

Value, circumstances may set a temporary excess of, on some one goal: when we are in love, the beloved; when we are poor, money; when we are sick, health
•CR 54 ❖ CR 4:23

Value judgements, how the modern error of "subjectivism" has affected our
•CR 72-81 (*see also* Subjectivism)
❖ CR ch. 6 (*see also* Subjectivism)

Value judgements, "subjectivism" yields the view that, are not really judgements at all, but sentiments produced by social conditioning
•CR 73 ❖ CR 6:4

Value judgements vs. taste, in literary criticism: Danger of invoking "thus saith the Lord" at the end of every expression of our pet aversions*
•CR 30-31 (*see also* CR 34-35; RP 31)
❖ CR 2:51 (*see also* CR 2:55; RP 3:20)

Value of an act measured by its unpleasantness as a frame of mind attributed to Kant
•PP 99-100 ❖ PP 6:11

Value of each human soul, apart from God, is zero
•WG 115 (*see also* WLN 53*)
❖ WG 7:14 (*see also* WLN 4:8*)

Value of Man: "It passes reason to explain why creatures, not to say creatures such as we, should have a value so prodigious in their Creator's eyes"
•PP 47 ❖ PP 3:14

Value of Man: When one considers the sky and stars, it seems strange that God should be at all concerned with man—yet He has given us extraordinary honour (re: Psalm 8)
•RP 132 ❖ RP 12:11

Value of the individual does not lie in himself; he is capable of receiving value, and he receives it by union with Christ
•WG 118-119 ❖ WG 7:18

Value: Whether it is objective or subjective is not a question of merely speculative importance; subjectivism is eternally incompatible with freedom

•CR 16 ❖ CR 2:13

Values presupposed in nineteenth-century fiction: sexual love and material prosperity
•CR 16, 21-23 ❖ CR 2:13, 29-34

Values presupposed in romantic poetry: enjoyment of nature; indulgence of a *Sehnsucht* [or longing] awakened by...
•CR 16, 21-23 ❖ CR 2:13, 29-34

Values: Put first things first and you will get second things thrown in
•L 228 (*see also* FL 166*; GID 280-281; MC 118-119; RP 49*)
❖ L 23 Apr 51 (*see also* FL 6:5*: GID III 2:5-10; MC III 9:1; RP 5:7*)

Values: Putting first things first increases the value of second things
•L 248 (*see also* GID 150*)
❖ L 8 Nov 52 (*see also* GID I 17:7*)

Values: Putting second things first corrupts them (re: the over-valuing of "culture")
•L 269 ❖ L 2 Apr 56

Values, real, may differ from professed values and may lurk in the turn of a phrase or the choice of an epithet (re: beliefs implicit in literature)*
•CR 28-29 ❖ CR 2:48

Values, social, of the Christian vs. the Materialist (and how they affect the actions of each)
•GID 109-110 ❖ GID I 12:2-4

Values, the attempt to jettison traditional, as subjective and to substitute a new scheme of values is like trying to lift yourself by your own coat collar
•CR 74 ❖ CR 6:8

Values: "...to be united with that Life in the eternal Sonship of Christ is...the only thing worth a moment's consideration"*
•M 155 ❖ M 16:22

Values: Ultimately what really matters is whether a thing or a circumstance moves us closer to God or to the devil*
•SL 87-89 (*see also* SL 56, 126)
❖ SL 19:3 (*see also* SL 12:5; 27:1)

Vanities, I see few of the old warnings about worldly, (—Screwtape)
•SL 46-47 ❖ SL 10:3

Vanity—*see also* Pride

Vanity as one cause of the shame we feel as the intense pain of grief begins to lessen ("We want to prove...that we are lovers on the grand scale...")
•GO 62-63 ❖ GO 3:38, 39

Vanity involved in wanting to meet a celebrated or "important" person, even one of whom you disapprove
•RP 67, 71 (*see also* LAL 27*; SL 46*)
❖ RP 7:3, 9 (*see also* LAL Feb 22/54*: SL 10:2*)

Vanity is the least bad and most pardonable sort of Pride
•MC 112 ❖ MC III 8:10

Vanity, there will be no room for, when we see that we have pleased Him
•WG 12-13 (*see also* FL 180)
❖ WG 1:10 (*see also* FL 6:27)

Vanity usually the problem in "sensitive" people who are easily hurt
•LAL 59 ❖ LAL 3/8/56

Variety—*see also* Differences; Novelty

Variety: "It takes all sorts to make a world; or a church...Heaven will display far more variety than Hell" (re: differences of worship style)
•LM 10 ❖ LM 2:3

Vegetarianism mentioned by Screwtape as a useful addition to "mere Christianity" ("If they must be Christians, let them...be Christians with a difference")
•SL 115-116 ❖ SL 25:1

Vegetarianism: Screwtape mentions "what that pestilent fellow Paul used to teach about food and other unessentials" (re: factional disagreement within churches on unimportant issues)**
•SL 75 ❖ SL 16:2

Venereal disease mentioned in response to a question about its prevention
•GID 51 ❖ GID I 4:13-16 (Ques. 4)

Vengefulness—*see* Revenge; Vindictiveness

"Venus"—*see also* Eros; Sex; Sexual love

"Venus" defined as "the carnally or animally sexual element within Eros"
•FL 131-132 ❖ FL 5:1

"Venus" may be less to blame in the loss of many a virginity than peer pressure ("the lure of the caucus")
•WG 98 ❖ WG 6:7

"Venus" (sexual love within Eros) mentioned or discussed
•FL 131-132, 137-150, 159
❖ FL 5:1, 10-30, 44

Venus the female deity mentioned
•L 141 ❖ L 10 Jun 30

Venus: "You will find...that [every man] is haunted by at least two imaginary women—a terrestrial and an infernal Venus..." (—Screwtape)
•SL 93 ❖ SL 20:4

Veracity—see Honesty

Verdict, someday an absolutely correct, will be passed on what each of us is; this is what is meant by "Judgment"
•WLN 112-113 ❖ WLN 7:35-37

Vernacular, translation into, a test of true understanding of one's own faith and doctrinal beliefs
•GID 98-99, 243, 256-257, 338
❖ GID I 10:38; II 12:5; ch. 15; IV Letter 11

Vernacular, use of, necessary in Christian apologetics and preaching
•GID 96-98, 183, 242-243, 254-257, 338
❖ GID I 10:18-38; 22:16, 17; II 12:4, 5; ch. 15; IV Letter 11

Versions of the Bible—see Bible translations

Vet, God as Eternal, whose operations may hurt but only for our own good
•GO 75 (see also GO 46-47)
❖ GO 4:12 (see also GO 3:10, 11)

Vicariousness a characteristic of all Nature; everything is indebted to everything else
•M 118 (see also GID 85)
❖ M 14:19 (see also GID I 9:8)

Vicariousness as part of the natural order—and the very centre of Christianity
•GID 85-86; M 118 ❖ GID I 9:8; M 14:19

Vicariousness, discussion of the principle of, (it is of divine origin although in Nature it is depraved— e.g., cat living on mouse)
•M 118 (see also GID 85-86, 87)

❖ M 14:19 (see also GID I 9:8, 10)

Vicariousness: "...I find I can now believe again, that [Christ] has done vicariously whatever can be done"
•GO 51 ❖ GO 3:21

Vicariousness is the very idiom of the reality God has created; therefore His death can become ours
•M 130 ❖ M 14:35

Vicariousness, only love makes the difference in all aspects of, and differentiates it from mere parasitism*
•M 118-120 (see also GID 85-87*)
❖ M 14:19, 20 (see also GID I 9:8, 10*)

Vicariousness, principle of, includes the Sinless Man suffering for the sinful and, in their degree, all men for all bad men
•M 118 (see also GID 85-86)
❖ M 14:19 (see also GID I 9:8)

Vicariousness, with true, the glory of redeemed humanity will exalt all creatures, including those who have never fallen
•M 122-123 ❖ M 14:24

Vice(s)—see also Fault(s); Sin(s)

Vice, cowardice is almost the only, at which men still feel shame (—Screwtape)
•SL 137 ❖ SL 29:5

Vice, every, leads to cruelty
•PP 65 ❖ PP 4:12

Vice, greatest, is Pride; it leads to every other vice
•MC 109 ❖ MC III 8:2

Vices, a man may console himself for his, by a conviction that "his heart's in the right place" and "he wouldn't hurt a fly"
•PP 56 ❖ PP 4:2

Vices, nearly all, are rooted in the Future; gratitude looks to the Past and love to the Present; fear, avarice, lust, and ambition look ahead
•SL 69 ❖ SL 15:3

Vices that lead to worldly success regarded less leniently by God than the vices of "the feckless and dissipated," who are less likely to be self-satisfied
•PP 98 ❖ PP 6:9

Vices, we like to believe that our habitual, are exceptional single acts, and make the opposite mistake about our virtues
•PP 60 ❖ PP 4:7

Vindictiveness—*see also* Retaliation; Revenge

Vindictiveness and hatred forbidden in Judaism just as in Christianity; the reaction of the Psalmists to injury, though natural, is profoundly wrong
•RP 26 ❖ RP 3:12, 13

Vindictiveness in the Psalms
•CR 116, 118-120; RP 18-33
❖ CR 10:4, 7-12; RP 2:14; ch. 3

Vindictiveness (in the Psalms) as "...that passion to which Our Lord's teaching allows no quarter"
•RP 18-19 (*see also* L 247-248)
❖ RP 2:14 (*see also* L 8 Nov 52)

Vindictiveness: We are far more subtle than the Psalmists in disguising our ill will from others and from ourselves
•RP 23 ❖ RP 3:8

Vindictiveness: We would be wicked if we in any way condoned or approved the vindictive hatred expressed in the Psalms
•RP 22 ❖ RP 3:6

Virgil mentioned by Lewis as one of the authors who contributed to his rising doubt, as a youth, in the Christian faith
•SJ 62 ❖ SJ 4:9

Virgil seen throughout the Middle Ages as a Pagan prophet; he had written a poem beginning with the mention of a child sent down from heaven
•RP 101 (*see also* RP 107-108)
❖ RP 10:6 (*see also* RP 10:12)

Virgin Birth, an anonymous postcard tells me I ought to be flogged for professing to believe in the
•GID 252 ❖ GID II 14:9

Virgin Birth: Conception of Jesus was a miracle not unlike that of human conception
•GID 31-32; M 137-139
❖ GID I 2:9; M 15:10-12

Virgin Birth defined as a doctrine in the Apostle's Creed that Jesus had no

physical father, and was not conceived as a result of sexual intercourse
•L 232-233 ❖ L 13 Jun 51

Virgin Birth, exact details of, are not part of the doctrine; everyone is free to speculate
•L 232-233 ❖ L 13 Jun 51

Virgin Birth, Joseph's reaction to, shows that early Christians perceived miracles as being contrary to Nature
•M 46-47 (*see also* GID 26, 72-73, 100)
❖ M 7:5 (*see also* GID I 2:2; 7:1-10; 10:43)

Virgin Birth: Laws of Nature not broken by God creating a miraculous spermatozoon in a virgin's body; Nature at once makes the event at home in her realm
•M 59 ❖ M 8:8

Virgin Birth: "...the supernatural begetting of Our Lord is the archetype and human marriage the ectype..."
•L 229 ❖ L 23 May 51

Virgin Mary—*see* Mary

Virginity, mention of Charles Williams' lecture on
•L 177 (*see also* L 178, 196) ❖ L 11 Feb 40 (*see also* L 3 Mar 40; 21 Dec 41)

Virtue—*see also* Goodness; Morality

Virtue as the quality of character that really counts (not just external behaviour)
•MC 77 (*see also* MC 127, 164-165)
❖ MC III 2:8 (*see also* MC III 12:3; IV 7:12)

Virtue, divine, received by imitation (for Christ as well as for man)
•CR 5-6 (*see also* Imitation of Christ)
❖ CR 1:6-10 (*see also* Imitation of Christ)

Virtue—even attempted virtue—brings light; indulgence brings fog
•MC 94 ❖ MC III 5:13

Virtue, every, is a *habitus*—i.e., a *good* stock response [to temptation]
•CR 24-25 ❖ CR 2:38

Virtue, if one, must be cultivated at the expense of all the rest, none has a higher claim than mercy or "kindness" (but this is deceptive)
•PP 56 ❖ PP 4:2

Virtue is one; you cannot be kind unless you have all the other virtues, as every vice leads to cruelty
•PP 65 ❖ PP 4:12

Virtue, Lewis describes his realization of the need for "continual, conscious recourse" to God (which he then called "Spirit") for his
•SJ 226 (see also SL 62; Daily...)
❖ SJ 14:20 (see also SL 14:1; Daily...)

Virtue, Lewis describes how he first came to realize that an attempt at complete, had to be made
•SJ 225-226 ❖ SJ 14:18

Virtue, Lewis describes how his "ideal" of, became a command when he became a Theist ("...and what might not be expected of one?")
•SJ 228 ❖ SJ 14:22

Virtue, only a clever human can make a real Joke about; more common to treat it with flippancy (—Screwtape)
•SL 52 ❖ SL 11:6

Virtue, Our Lord seems to reduce all, to active beneficence; this places beyond doubt the basic principles of the social ethics of Christianity
•PP 114 ❖ PP 7:4

Virtue, question of whether the cultivation of the intellect can be considered part of the content of, rather than absolutely distinct from virtue
•CR 12-25, esp. 18-19
❖ CR 2:1-38, esp. 2:20-22

Virtue: Regarding the fate of the virtuous unbeliever
•L 164, 196 ❖ L 5 Apr 39; 8 Dec 41

Virtue, Screwtape observes that in order to be greatly and effectively wicked a man needs some
•SL 135-136 (see also SL 105-106*; WLN 56*)
❖ SL 29:2 (see also SL 23:1*; WLN 4:13*)

Virtue, someday even the delights of, itself will seem half-nauseous in comparison to meeting our true Beloved*
•SL 148 ❖ SL 31:5

Virtue, the equable, of "some who are psychologically sound" vs. the "man of good will, saddled with an abnormal

desire which he never chose..."
•L 242 ❖ L 28 May 52

Virtue: "The more virtuous a man becomes the more he enjoys virtuous actions"
•PP 100 (see also L 277; LM 114-116)
❖ PP 6:11 (see also L 18 Jul 57; LM 21:11-14)

Virtues—consider also Standards

Virtues, all, are less formidable to us once the man is aware that he has them, but this is specially true of humility (—Screwtape)
•SL 62-63 ❖ SL 14:2

Virtues approved and loved and desired (but not acted) will not keep a man from Hell; indeed they may make him more amusing when he gets there (—Screwtape)
•SL 31 ❖ SL 6:5

Virtues, attempting—see also Moral Effort

Virtues, attempting, teaches us our dependence upon God
•MC 94; 124-125, 127-131 (see also CR 169*; PP 65) ❖ MC III 5:12; 11:7; 12:3-9 (see also CR 169*; PP 4:13)

Virtues, Cardinal, listed (Prudence, Temperance, Justice and Fortitude)
•MC 74 ❖ MC III 2:3

Virtues: "Courage is not simply one of the virtues, but the form of every virtue at the testing point..." (—Screwtape)
•SL 137 ❖ SL 29:6

Virtues, difficult, must be attempted, like compulsory exam questions
•MC 93 ❖ MC III 5:11

Virtues, it crossed my mind for the first time since my apostasy that the severer, might have some relevance to my life (e.g., strict veracity, chastity, duty)
•SJ 192 ❖ SJ 12:14

Virtues, it is God who produces, in us
•LAL 22 (see also LM 49-50, 68-69; consider also Works)
❖ LAL Nov 6/53 (see also LM 9:11; 13:3; consider also Works)

Virtues: "It is only in so far as they reach the will and are there embodied in habits that the virtues are really fatal

to us" (—Screwtape)
•SL 31 ❖ SL 6:5

Virtues, prevention of the formation of, and the undermining of faith listed by Screwtape as "the real business" of Hell
•SL 25 ❖ SL 5:1

Virtues, Screwtape advises working to keep a person's, all in the realm of fantasy and his vices all in the realm of his Will
•SL 31 ❖ SL 6:5

Virtues such as charity, submissiveness to God's will, etc. are *graces*—gifts from the Holy Spirit—not our own merits
•L 219 (*consider also* Righteousness by faith/grace) ❖ L 2 Sep 49 (*consider also* Righteousness by faith/grace)

Virtues, The Cardinal (chapter title)
•MC 74-78 ❖ MC III ch. 2

Virtues: These friends at Oxford all believed, and acted on the belief, that veracity, public spirit, chastity, and sobriety were all obligatory...
•SJ 201 ❖ SJ 13:6

Vision and enjoyment of God, a man is "nearest" to God when he is most surely and swiftly approaching his final union with God and the
•FL 15 ❖ FL 1:9

Vision and enjoyment of God will outweigh all the negations we now perceive of Heaven
•WG 66-67 ❖ WG 4:20

Vision of God, didn't people dispute once whether the final, was more an act of intelligence or of love?—Probably a nonsense question
•GO 89 ❖ GO 4:39

Vision of God, in Heaven every soul will communicate their unique, to all the others
•FL 92-93; PP 150 ❖ FL 4:9; PP 10:7

Vision, the old parson was not seeking the Beatific, and did not even believe in God
•SJ 202 (*see also* CR x)
❖ SJ 13:8 (*see also* CR P:9)

Visions, I have dreamed dreams but not seen; but don't think all that matters

a hoot
•L 251 (*see also* L 269*)
❖ L 17 Jul 53 (*see also* L undated letter just before 2 Apr 56*)

Vivisection (chapter title)
•GID 224-228 ❖ GID II ch. 9

Vivisection can only be defended if it is right that one species should suffer in order that another should be happier
•GID 225 ❖ GID II 9:4

Vivisection, discussion of
•GID 224-228 ❖ GID II ch. 9

Vivisection, even if right, must be carried out with the utmost care to avoid pain, and with trembling awe at the responsibility
•GID 226 ❖ GID II 9:6

Vivisection: If right at all, it is a duty
•GID 224 ❖ GID II 9:1

Vivisection, if right, must be carried out with a vivid sense of the high mode in which life is to be lived if it is to justify the sacrifices made
•GID 226 ❖ GID II 9:6

Vivisection: "In justifying cruelty to animals we put ourselves also on the animal level. We choose the jungle and must abide by our choice"
•GID 228 ❖ GID II 9:10

Vivisection, the victory of, marks a great advance in the triumph of ruthless, non-moral utilitarianism over the old world of ethical law
•GID 228 ❖ GID II 9:10

Vivisection, without Christian belief of differences between man and beast, cannot be justified without also justifying experiments on inferior men
•GID 227 ❖ GID II 9:8

Vivisector, is God a vet or a
•GO 46 (*see also* GO 33, 44, 75)
❖ GO 3:10, 11 (*see also* GO 2:22; 3:5; 4:12)

Vocation—*see also* Duty; Occupation; Service; Work

Vocation, a, is a terrible thing; to be called out of nature into the supernatural life is a costly honour—as a Bride must leave her home and family
•RP 130-132 ❖ RP 12:10

Vocation: "...a sacred calling is not limited

to ecclesiastical functions. The man who is weeding a field of turnips is also serving God"
- •GID 264 ❖ GID II 16:38

Vocation: "Don't be too easily convinced that God really wants you to do all sorts of work you needn't do"
- •LAL 53 (*see also* LAL 72)
- ❖ LAL 19/3/56 (*see also* LAL 22/2/58)

Vocation: "Each must do his duty 'in that state of life to which God has called him'"
- •LAL 53 ❖ LAL 19/3/56

Vocation: Most men must glorify God by doing to His glory something which is not *per se* an act of glorifying, but which becomes so by being offered*
- •CR 24 ❖ CR 2:37

Vocation, one must be careful lest the desire to be a busy-body should disguise itself as a, to help the "fallen"
- •RP 69 ❖ RP 7:5

Vocation: "One must take comfort in remembering that God used an *ass* to convert the prophet..."*
- •L 193-194 ❖ L 15 May 41

Vocation: "...one treats as an interruption of one's (self-chosen) vocation, the vocation actually imposed on one..."
- •L 212 ❖ L 22 Dec 47

Vocation: "The great thing is to be found at one's post as a child of God..."*
- •GID 266 (*see also* WLN 111-112)
- ❖ GID II 16:55 (*see also* WLN 7:34)

Vocation: "There can be intemperance in work just as in drink. What feels like zeal may be only fidgets or even the flattering of one's self-importance"*
- •LAL 53 (*see also* LAL 72)
- ❖ LAL 19/3/56 (*see also* LAL 22/2/58)

Vocation, we are differentiated members of one Body—each with his own
- •WG 26-27 (*consider also* Body)
- ❖ WG 2:9 (*consider also* Body)

Vocation: We picture God as a kind of employer who tries to find suitable careers for souls; but the place was there first—the man was created for it*
- •WG 118-119 (*see also* PP 52, 147- 148*)
- ❖ WG 7:18 (*see also* PP 3:18; 10:3*)

Vocation which God has in mind for us: We were made for it, rather than it being made for us; and we shall not be fully ourselves until we find it*
- •WG 118-119 (*see also* PP 52)
- ❖ WG 7:17, 18 (*see also* PP 3:18)

Voice which speaks in your conscience and in some of your intensest joys... sometimes so obstinately silent...at other times so loud and emphatic (re: attempting contact with ultimate Reality)
- •CR 170 ❖ CR 14:27

Void, God-shaped—*see* Hollow

Voyage of the Dawn Treader mentioned
- •LAL 14 ❖ LAL 17/4/53

Voyage to Arcturus, by David Lindsay, mentioned by Lewis as the "real father" of his own planet books
- •L 205 ❖ L 29 Oct 44

Voyage to Arcturus, by David Lindsay: Lewis acknowledges a debt to this book for the writing of *The Screwtape Letters*
- •SL xiii ❖ SL P:22

Vulgar—*see also* Low-brow(s)

"Vulgar" a social term which tends to be used by those who consider themselves "the cultured"
- •WLN 41 (*see also* L 64)
- ❖ WLN 3:14 (*see also* L 1 Jul 21)

Vulgar, the Christian knows that the, since they include most of the poor, probably include most of his superiors
- •CR 10 ❖ CR 1:15

Vulgar, Lewis describes as, a phase in which he aspired to be a flashy dresser
- •SJ 67 ❖ SJ 4:14

"**Vulgarity**," meaning of the word, to modern minds ("Usually means obscenity or 'smut'")
- •GID 98 ❖ GID I 10:37

Wagner, Richard—*consider also* Norse Literature

Wagner, Richard: "...as a mythopoeic poet he is incomparable"
- •CR 84 (*see also* L 205)
- ❖ CR 7:7 (*see also* 29 Oct 44)

Wagner's music caused in Lewis "a conflict of sensations without name'"
- •SJ 75 (*see also* L 110; SJ 165)
- ❖ SJ 5:6 (*see also* L 8 Feb 27; SJ 11:1)

Wagner's *Siegfried and the Twilight of the Gods* as an avenue through which Lewis experienced "Joy"
- •SJ 72-78 (*see also* SJ 102, 164, 165-166)
- ❖ SJ 5:3-10 (*see also* SJ 7:3; 10:17; 11:1-3)

Waking up: "The dreadful thing...is the waking each morning—the moment at which it all flows back on one"
- •LAL 88 ❖ LAL 18 Oct 59

Walk, Lewis describes an enjoyable
- •L 31-32, 174
- ❖ L 30 Oct 16; 9 Jan 40

Walk, Lewis's distaste for information- and fact-oriented conversation reflected in a description of a dull
- •L 150-151 (*see also* L 173)
- ❖ L 20 Mar 32 (*see also* L 1 Jan 40)

Walk with Arthur Greeves recalled: "...we...were for a short time perfectly happy..."
- •L 27 ❖ L undated letter of Oct 1915

Walks, Screwtape refers to the spiritual dangers to his side of, taken alone through enjoyable country
- •SL 58 ❖ SL 13:3

Walks, the modern undergraduate is seldom engaged in those solitary, or walks with one companion, which built the minds of previous generations
- •WG 106-107 ❖ WG 7:2

Walking and talking are two very great pleasures, but it is a mistake to combine them; the noise blots out the sounds and silences of the outdoor world
- •SJ 142 (*see also* SJ 200*)
- ❖ SJ 9:18 (*see also* SJ 13:4*)

Walking: Having no car, I measured distances by the standard of man walking on his two feet
- •SJ 156-157 ❖ SJ 10:9

Walking, I do all the, I can, for I'd be a fool not to go to bed tired (re: Lewis's grief at the loss of his wife)
- •GO 69 ❖ GO 4:2

Walking: "...I loved the hills, and even mountain walks, but I was no climber"
- •LM 63 ❖ LM 12:2

Walking: "I'll never be able to take real walks again...but it's wonderful how mercifully the desire goes when the power goes"
- •LAL 70 ❖ LAL Nov 30th 57

Walking in Surrey, with the whole weekend's reading ahead, I suppose I reached as much happiness as is ever to be reached on earth
- •SJ 146-147 ❖ SJ 9:22

Walking, Lewis expresses distaste for the word "hiking" to describe the ordinary activity of
- •L 259 ❖ L 2 Dec 54

Walking: The only friend to walk with is one who so exactly shares your taste for each mood of the countryside that you needn't talk
- •SJ 142 ❖ SJ 9:18

Walking tour, Lewis mentions a, taken with A. C. Harwood
- •SJ 200 ❖ SJ 13:5

Walking tour, Lewis mentions a, taken with friends
- •L 50-51, 114-117

❖ L 4 Apr 20; 11 Apr 20; 26 Apr 27

Walking tours: Delight of nearing the end of a day's journey
- •L 117 ❖ L 26 Apr 27

Walking tours: It is frustrating to come upon a scene of unexpected grandeur, and then to realize those with you care nothing for it*
- •RP 95 (see also PP 145-146)
- ❖ RP 9:6 (see also PP 10:2)

Walking tours with friends: "Those are the golden sessions; when four or five of us after a hard day's walking have come to our inn..."
- •FL 105 ❖ FL 4:30

War—see also Pacifism; consider also Military service; Patriotism

War and Peace is in my opinion the best novel
- •L 201 (see also WG 23)
- ❖ L 13 Oct 42 (see also WG 2:5)

War and peace listed by Screwtape as neutral situations which can work either for God's or the devil's purposes
- •SL 89 ❖ SL 19:3

War and Peace, quote from, to illustrate the concept of the "Inner Ring"
- •WG 93 ❖ WG 6:1

War and religion, analogy between the claims of, (neither will simply cancel the merely human life we were leading before)
- •WG 24 ❖ WG 2:6

War: Ardent pacifism and extreme patriotism both mentioned by Screwtape as serving his purposes
- •SL 25, 33-35 ❖ SL 5:1; 7:2, 3

War: Bacterial warfare mentioned
- •GID 312 ❖ GID III 8:6

War cannot be compared with "normal life"; life has never been normal (re: education in time of war)
- •WG 21-22 (see also WLN 108*)
- ❖ WG 2:4 (see also WLN 7:27*)

War, Christianity agrees that the universe is at, though it thinks it is not a war between independent powers but a civil war—a rebellion
- •MC 50-51 ❖ MC II 2:11, 12

War, comments regarding conscientious objection to
- •GID 325-327 ❖ GID IV Letter 1

War creates no absolutely new situation; it simply aggravates the permanent human situation so that we can no longer ignore it (re: education in time of war)
- •WG 21 ❖ WG 2:3

War, death would be better than to live through another
- •L 166 ❖ L 8 May 39

War does not make death more frequent or more painful
- •WG 30-31 (see also PP 115-116)
- ❖ WG 2:14 (see also PP 7:8)

War: Each individual's sufferings can never be more than those of one man, or more than an unlucky man might have suffered in peacetime
- •L 186 ❖ L 2 Jun 40

War, [First World], Lewis's attitude toward the
- •SJ 158-159 ❖ SJ 10:11, 12

War, First World, may have prevented a greater evil
- •WG 40-41 ❖ WG 3:13

War forces us to think about death; as Christians, that may be one of its blessings
- •WG 31-32 ❖ WG 2:14

War forces us to think about death; this Screwtape considers "disastrous" to his cause ("One of our best weapons, contented worldliness, is rendered useless")
- •SL 27 ❖ SL 5:2

War: Hatred and malice in humans are disappointing to Screwtape when they are directed against imaginary scapegoats ("the Germans") rather than real persons
- •SL 30-31 ❖ SL 6:4, 5

War: I have often wondered how it would have been if I and some young German had killed each other simultaneously and found ourselves together a moment after death
- •MC 107 (see also WG 43)
- ❖ MC III 7:9 (see also WG 3:18)

War: If it is ever lawful, then peace is

sometimes sinful
- •GID 326 ❖ GID IV Letter 1

War: "...if you cannot restrain a man by any method except by trying to kill him, then it seems to me a Christian must do that"
- •GID 49 ❖ GID I 4:3 (Ques. 1)

War, in time of, it was usually the reserve who had to *watch* the carnage, not the troops who were in it, whose nerve broke first (re: fear of future)
- •L 250 ❖ L 17 Jul 53

War includes the threat of every temporal evil—pain, death, isolation, injustice, etc.
- •L 166 ❖ L 8 May 39

War is a dreadful thing, and I can respect an honest pacifist, though I think he is mistaken
- •MC 106-107 ❖ MC III 7:8

War: "It is...in my opinion perfectly right for a...Christian soldier to kill an enemy"
- •MC 106 ❖ MC III 7:8

War, my memories of the last, haunted my dreams for years
- •L 166 ❖ L 8 May 39

War, nuclear: [Atomic] bomb mentioned
- •GID 312 ❖ GID III 8:2, 3, 6

War, nuclear: Small statement regarding the use of the atomic bomb in Japan
- •L 225
- ❖ L undated letter just after 7 Dec 50

War, personal threats of, include pain, death, and all kinds of adversity; Pacifism threatens you with almost nothing
- •WG 52 ❖ WG 3:30

War, possible Christian approach to
- •GID 325-327 ❖ GID IV Letter 1

War, Screwtape speaks on conscientious objection to
- •SL 34-35 ❖ SL 7:3, 4

War service, Lewis describes his
- •SJ 186-198 (*see also* L 33-46)
- ❖ SJ 12:6-13:1 (*see also* L 28 Jan 17 to undated letter just before 27 Jan 19)

War shows futility of trying to find happiness in this life
- •WG 31-32 ❖ WG 2:14

War, the audacity of asking God to take sides in, e.g., "Prosper Oh Lord, our righteous cause"
- •L 168 (*see also* FL 47-48; L 183; WG 24) ❖ L 10 Sep 39 (*see also* FL 2:41, 42; L 16 Apr 40; WG 2:6)

War, the good that may come out of, lamented by Screwtape (e.g., conversions, selflessness, etc.)
- •SL 26-27 ❖ SL 5:2

War, three enemies which, raises up against the scholar: excitement, frustration, and fear
- •WG 29-32 (*see also* SJ 183*; SL 67-71) ❖ WG 2:12-14 (*see also* SJ 12:2*; SL ch. 15)

War: We must be cautious of identifying the enemy with forces of evil; human conflicts are never unambiguously between good and evil
- •L 183 (*see also* RP 17-18) ❖ L 16 Apr 40 (*see also* RP 2:13, 14)

War: What becomes the indisguisable issue of cowardice vs. courage awakes many men from moral stupor
- •SL 137 ❖ SL 29:5

War, whether Divine Authority permits
- •WG 47-51 (*see also* GID 49) ❖ WG 3:26-29 (*see also* GID I 4:2, 3)

Wars: If we believe that they must be fought purely on moral grounds, we will believe that just wars must be wars of annihilation
- •FL 47-48 ❖ FL 2:41

Wars must be fought on the basis of patriotism, not purely on moral grounds as such
- •FL 47-48 ❖ FL 2:41, 42

Wars, regarding the Pacifists' contention that, always do more harm than good
- •WG 39-41 ❖ WG 3:12-14

Wartime army: "I met there both the World and the great goddess Nonsense"
- •SJ 194 ❖ SJ 12:16

War-Time, Learning In (chapter title)
- •WG 20-32 ❖ WG ch. 2

War-time news most likely very distorted by the time it reaches the papers; reading it is surely a waste of time
- •SJ 159 ❖ SJ 10:12

"**Warnie**" [Lewis's brother, Warren H. Lewis]—*see* Lewis, Warren Hamilton

Warren Hamilton Lewis—*see* Lewis, Warren Hamilton

Waterfall, analogy of, to the human body: My form remains one, though the matter in it changes continually (re: recovery of same atoms in Resurrection)
  •M 151 (*see also* GID 33)
  ❖ M 16:15 (*see also* GID I 2:11)

We Have Cause to Be Uneasy (chapter title)
  •MC 36-39 ❖ MC I ch. 5

We Have No "Right to Happiness" (chapter title)
  •GID 317-322 (*see also* L 221)
  ❖ GID III ch. 9 (*see also* L 22 Sep 49)

Weakness, God can use us in spite of our human, (God used an *ass* to convert the prophet)*
  •L 193-194 ❖ L 15 May 41

Wealth—*see also* Money; Riches

Wealth as a gift which could cause us to forget our need for God
  •MC 180 ❖ MC IV 10:11

Wealth, if we can't be trusted even with the perishable, of this world who will trust us with the real wealth?
  •L 301 ❖ L 20 Dec 61

Wealth, living on inherited, makes one not "independent" but more dependent than most
  •LAL 21, 57-58, 112
  ❖ LAL Aug 10th 53; 14/6/56; 10 Dec 62

Wealth: "...of all claims to distinction money is, I suppose, the basest"
  •LAL 111 ❖ LAL 10 Dec 62

Wealthy, hard to enter heaven if you are
  •GID 51-52 (*see also* L 221) ❖ GID I 4:18 (Ques. 5) (*see also* L 22 Sep 49)

Wealthy people described who are always thinking that their latest diversion is "the Real Thing"—the satisfaction of their desire—and are always disappointed
  •MC 119 ❖ MC III 10:3

Weariness—*see* Tiredness

Weather as an aspect of Nature specially addressed by the Psalmists
  •RP 77 ❖ RP 8:2

Weather, Lewis mentions that from a teacher he learned how bad, is to be treated—"as a rough joke, a romp"
  •SJ 67 ❖ SJ 4:13

Wedding ceremony, Screwtape advises causing humans to find the, "very offensive"
  •SL 84 ❖ SL 18:6

Weeping: "If you must weep, weep: a good honest howl! I suspect we—and especially my sex—don't cry enough now-a-days"
  •LAL 26 ❖ LAL Feb 22/54

Weight of Glory, Lewis describes the collection of addresses which are included in the book
  •WG xxv ❖ WG P:1

Weight of Glory, The (chapter title)
  •WG 3-19 ❖ WG ch. 1

Wells' *Country of the Blind* mentioned as illustration of how thought and the use of language to convey thought may be changing
  •CR 140-141 ❖ CR 11:23, 24

Wells, H. G., evolutionary world picture of such people as, described and refuted
  •CR 82-93; WG 79-81
  ❖ CR ch. 7; WG 5:11, 12

Wells, H. G., mentioned as being a Naturalist who contradicted himself by advocating certain moral behaviour
  •M 36-37 ❖ M 5:7

Wells, H. G.: I grew up on his science fiction
  •L 205; SJ 35 ❖ L 29 Oct 44; SJ 2:15

"**Wellsianity**" suggested as a name for the evolutionary world picture of such people as H. G. Wells
  •WG 79 (ftnt.) (*see also* CR 82)
  ❖ WG 5:11 (ftnt.) (*see also* CR 7:3)

"**Western**" thinking not as homogeneous (nor as "Christian") as may be supposed
  •GID 251-253 ❖ GID II 14:6-11

What Are We to Make of Jesus Christ? (chapter title)
  •GID 156-160 ❖ GID I ch. 19

What Christians Believe (Book II of *Mere*

Christianity)
•MC 43-66 ❖ MC Book II
What Christmas Means to Me (chapter title)
•GID 304-305 ❖ GID III ch. 6
What Lies Behind the Law (chapter title)
•MC 31-35 ❖ MC I ch. 4
"What? You too? I thought I was the only one" as the typical expression of opening Friendship
•FL 96, 113 (*see also* SJ vii)
❖ FL 4:16, 43 (*see also* SJ P:1)
Wheel analogy: If you are right with God (hub) you will inevitably be right with your fellow-men (spokes—all in right relation to one another)
•MC 127 ❖ MC III 12:3
Whipsnade Zoo, Lewis describes taking the final step in his conversion to Christianity while on a trip to
•SJ 237-238 ❖ SJ 15:8, 9
Whipsnade Zoo reminded Lewis of the world before the Fall (tame animals)
•L 154-155; SJ 237-238
❖ L 14 Jun 32; SJ 15:8, 9
Whisper, how often some momentary glimpse of beauty in boyhood is a, which memory will warehouse as a shout
•LM 122 ❖ LM 22:17
Whitsunday, the assignment of Psalm 68 to, has some obvious reasons (e.g., application to Pentecost)
•RP 125-126 ❖ RP 12:6
Wicked—*see also* Bad people; *consider also* Destiny of lost Man; Lost
Wicked, Lewis differentiates two kinds of, and our reaction to them: those who are powerful, prosperous and impenitent, and those whose wickedness has not paid
•RP 68 ❖ RP 7:5
Wicked lose all capacity for enjoying what is good*
•PP 123 ❖ PP 8:7
Wicked people, we should avoid contact with, when we can—not because we are "too good" for them, but because in a sense we are not good enough
•RP 71-74 (*see also* SL 45-48*)

❖ RP 7:9-16 (*see also* SL ch. 10*)
Wicked should eventually know their own sinfulness; right must be asserted (re: the "intolerable" doctrine of Hell)*
•PP 120-122 ❖ PP 8:5
Wickedness—*see also* Badness; Evil; Sinfulness
Wickedness (especially our own) is the proper object of our utter hostility; my own heart is the specimen of that wickedness best known to me
•RP 136 (*see also* SL xiii)
❖ RP 12:16 (*see also* SL P:24)
Wickedness, Human (chapter title)
•PP 55-68 ❖ PP ch. 4
Wickedness is the pursuit of some good in the wrong way
•MC 49-50 (*see also* CR 21; LM 89)
❖ MC II 2:9, 10 (*see also* CR 2:27; LM 17:5)
Wickedness: "'My heart'—I need no other's—'showeth me the wickedness of the ungodly'" (re: writing of *The Screwtape Letters*)
•SL xiii (*see also* RP 136)
❖ SL P:24 (*see also* RP 12:16)
Wickedness: Screwtape observes that in order to be greatly and effectively wicked, a man needs some virtue
•SL 135-136 (*see also* SL 105-106*; WLN 56*)
❖ SL 29:2 (*see also* SL 23:1*; WLN 4:13*)
Wickedness, the ferocious parts of the Psalms serve as a reminder that there is in the world such a thing as, and that it is hateful to God
•RP 32-33 ❖ RP 3:21
Wife, Lewis's—*see* Joy (Lewis's wife)
Wildness, Lewis mentions a conversation in which he observed the, of Surrey
•SJ 134 ❖ SJ 9:6-8
Wildness: Lewis relates his earlier fear that if Nature was created, it was not fully wild
•M 63-64 ❖ M 9:2
Will—*consider also* Free will; Moral effort
Will, ascetic practices (such as fasting) useful only to strengthen the, against the passions; the reward is self-mastery and the danger pride

•PP 112 ❖ PP 7:3

Will, at the Fall, had no resource but to force back by main strength the new thoughts and desires arising from the tidal wave of mere nature
•PP 82 ❖ PP 5:10

Will, Christ offers to give us His own
•MC 167 ❖ MC IV 8:4

Will, Christian love is an affair of the
•MC 115, 117-118 (see also L 269; LM 115)
❖ MC III 9:2, 9, 10 (see also L undated letter just after 13 Mar 56; LM 21:12)

Will, Christianity does not help us if it brings no healing to the impotent; a mere statement of even the highest ethical principles is not enough
•GID 328-329 ❖ GID IV Letter 4

Will, conversion requires an alteration of the, which does not occur without the intervention of the supernatural
•GID 221 ❖ GID II 8:10

Will, free—see Free will

Will, God has made our, in such a way that we can freely offer it back to Him; this is Gift-love of man toward God
•FL 178 ❖ FL 6:24

Will, he who does the, of the Father shall know the doctrine (re: use of imagery to describe Heaven)
•M 158 ❖ M 16:25

Will, human, becomes truly creative and truly our own when it is wholly God's; he that loses his soul shall find it
•PP 102 (consider also Personality)
❖ PP 6:14 (consider also Personality)

Will, I do not think any efforts of my own, can end once and for all this craving for limited liabilities, this fatal reservation; only God can help us
•WG 132 (consider also Limited liabilities) ❖ WG 9:13 (consider also Limited liabilities)

Will, it is by his, that man is good or bad; feelings not important in themselves
•L 210 ❖ L undated letter of 1947

"Will" not to be mistaken for the conscious fume and fret of resolutions and clenched teeth; the will is our real centre, our heart

•SL 31 (see also SL 15)
❖ SL 6:5 (see also SL 3:1)

Will, purification of the, leads to enlightenment of the intelligence (this concept the author Thackeray lacked)
•L 255 ❖ L 30 Jan 54

Will, Screwtape advises working to keep a person's virtues all in the realm of fantasy and his vices all in the realm of his
•SL 31 ❖ SL 6:5

Will: Screwtape observes that men must often "carry out from the will alone duties which have lost all relish"
•SL 39 (For a definition of the "will," see SL 31) ❖ SL 8:4 (For a definition of the "will," see SL 6:5)

Will, submission to God's, means accepting with patience the tribulation which has actually been dealt one—not all the things that might happen
•SL 29 (see also LAL 60)
❖ SL 6:2 (see also LAL 3/8/56)

Will of God—consider also Obedience

Will of God: "By grace He gives the higher creatures power to will His will ('and wield their little tridents')"
•LM 74-75 ❖ LM 14:9

Will of God, doing the, may become pleasurable to us but then it can no longer be a means of learning self-surrender
•PP 99, 101 ❖ PP 6:10, 13

Will of God for me (however changeless in some ultimate sense) must be related to what I am or do; e.g., surely He hasn't to forgive me for sins I didn't commit
•L 236 ❖ L 8 Jan 52

Will of God for us: Activities we naturally like may be as much a part of our "service" to God as our hardest duties*
•WG 130 ❖ WG 9:9

Will of God for us, how to know: Holy Spirit guides our decisions not only from within but also through Scripture, Church, Christian friends, books, etc.
•L 243 ❖ L 20 Jun 52

Will of God for us is always based upon what is intrinsically good

•PP 100-101 (*see also* CR 79-80; RP 61)
❖ PP 6:12 (*see also* CR 6:20, 21; RP 6:11)
Will of God for us is carried out by God Himself; our prayers are really His prayers*
•LAL 22, 23 (*see also* LM 49-50, 68-69; Prayer as soliloquy)
❖ LAL Nov 6/53; 27/xi/53 (*see also* LM 9:11; 13:3; Prayer as soliloquy)
Will of God for us sometimes seen as an interruption of our self-chosen vocation
•L 212 ❖ L 22 Dec 47
Will of God for us: "The deepest likings and impulses of any man are the raw material, the starting point, with which the Enemy [God] has furnished him" (—Screwtape)*
•SL 59-60 ❖ SL 13:4
Will of God for us, we are guided in discovering, by the ordinary rules of moral behaviour common to the human race; no supernatural vision needed
•GID 54-55 ❖ GID I 4:28, 29 (Ques. 8)
Will of God for us: We think of God as a kind of employer who tries to find careers for souls; but the place was there first—the man was created for it
•WG 118-119 ❖ WG 7:18
Will of God for us: We will not be fully ourselves until we find it*
•WG 118-119 ❖ WG 7:17, 18
Will of God for you may be difficult or painful, or something you will like; we can't know in advance
•GID 53-54 ❖ GID I 4:25 (Ques. 8)
Will of God: Imitation of Christ includes looking at everything as something that comes from Him*
•GID 50 ❖ GID I 4:11 (Ques. 3)
Will of God, in following, Paradisal man also gratified his own desires
•PP 98 ❖ PP 6:10
Will of God: In the Lord's Prayer, when I ask "Thy will be done," I am asking that I may be enabled to *do* it (not merely that I may be able to accept it)
•LM 25-26 ❖ LM 5:6-9
Will of God may become too unmistakable

if we prayed longer
•WG 127-128 (*see also* LM 114; SL 22-23*, 54-55)
❖ WG 9:5 (*see also* LM 21:8; SL 4:4*; 12:3)
Will of God: Mostly if the thing we like doing is the thing God wants us to do, that is not why we do it; it is a mere happy coincidence
•PP 99 ❖ PP 6:10
Will of God: Regarding any proposed course of action, God wants men to ask simply, "Is it righteous? Is it prudent? Is it possible?"*
•SL 118 ❖ SL 25:6
Will of God: The practice of Christianity includes referring every experience, pleasant or unpleasant, to God and asking His will
•GID 50 ❖ GID I 4:11 (Ques. 3)
Will of God, was the fall of Satan and the subsequent fall of Man in accordance with the ?
•MC 51-54 ❖ MC II 3:1-6
Will of God, we all carry out, but it makes a difference to us whether we serve like Judas or like John
•PP 111 ❖ PP 7:2
Will of God: "We inherit a whole system of desires which do not necessarily contradict God's will but which...steadfastly ignore it"*
•PP 98-99 ❖ PP 6:10
Will of God: We must expect that it will often appear to us far from beneficent and far from wise, since His knowledge of our needs exceeds our own
•WLN 24-25 ❖ WLN 2:13
Will of God: Whatever misery God permits will be for our ultimate good unless by rebellious will we convert it to evil
•L 166 (*see also* GID 52*; LAL 114)
❖ L 8 May 39 (*see also* GID I 4:18, 19 Ques. 5*; LAL 8 Feb 63)
Will of God: "When we want to be something other than the thing God wants us to be, we must be wanting what, in fact, will not make us happy"*
•PP 52 (*see also* PP 90; WG 118-119)
❖ PP 3:18 (*see also* PP 6:3; WG 7:18)

Will of God will be realized in different ways according to the actions, including the prayers, of His creatures (re: the efficacy of prayer)
•WLN 9 ❖ WLN 1:17

Will-power—*see also* Moral effort

Will-power, feelings cannot be manufactured by*
•MC 116-118 (*see also* L 225, 269; LM 115; MC 105; SL 42)
❖ MC III 9:5-10 (*see also* L 7 Dec 50; undated letter just after 13 Mar 56; LM 21:12; MC III 7:5; SL 9:3)

Will-power to control one's appetites, inadequacy of, which Lewis thought was shown by his father's generation*
•L 126 ❖ L 1 Apr 28

Will-power, Lewis describes his futile efforts as a schoolboy to produce by sheer, prayers which were vivid in the imagination and the affections
•SJ 61-62 (*see also* L 202, 256; LM 23; SL 20-21, 125; SJ 168)
❖ SJ 4:8 (*see also* L 22 Dec 42; 31 Jul 54; LM 4:19; SL 4:3; 27:1; SJ 11:5)

Will-power, never try to generate an emotion by, (re: introspection in prayer)
•L 202, 256 (*see also* LM 23*; SJ 61-62*)
❖ L 22 Dec 42; 31 Jul 54 (*see also* LM 4:19*; SJ 4:7, 8*)

Will-power, Screwtape advises getting humans to make their wandering mind in prayer a task for their, rather than a subject of their prayer
•SL 125-126 ❖ SL 27:1

Will-power, Screwtape discusses the effort to produce by sheer, a vaguely devotional mood and other feelings in prayer (feelings of being forgiven, etc.)
•SL 20-21 ❖ SL 4:2, 3

Williams, Charles
•L 163, 167, 168, 169-170, 177, 178, 195, 196-197, 212, 244, 247, 269, 287-288, 298, 299
❖ L 8 Feb 39; 9 Jul 39; 10 Sep 39; 5 Nov 39; 11 Feb 40; 3 Mar 40; 19 Nov 41; 21 Dec 41; 22 Dec 47; 2 Oct 52; 8 Nov 52; 9 May 56; 15 May 59; 9 May 61

Williams, Charles, death of, referred to
•L 206 ❖ L 18 May 45; 20 May 45

Williams, Charles: Mention of his move to Oxford
•L 168 ❖ L 10 Sep 39

Williams, Charles, mentioned as an author of books "where the doctrine is as good...as the art"
•L 222
❖ L undated letter just before 9 Jan 50

Williams, Charles, quote from: "The altar must often be built in one place in order that the fire from heaven may descend *somewhere else*"
•LM 117 ❖ LM 21:16

Williams, Charles, quoted with regard to the Appreciative nature of Eros
•FL 136 ❖ FL 5:7

Williams, Charles, referred to as "my friend of friends, the comforter of all our little set, the most angelic man"
•L 206 ❖ L 20 May 45

Williams, Charles: "He was not only a lover himself, but the cause that love was in other men"
•L 208 (*see also* L 196)
❖ L undated letter just after 10 Dec 45 (*see also* L 21 Dec 41)

Williams, Charles, the works of: "Rather wild, but full of love and excelling in the creation of convincing *good* characters"
•L 167 ❖ L 9 Jul 39

Williams, Charles, wrote "When the means are autonomous they are deadly" (re: the Law and legalism)
•RP 58 (*see also* LM 30-31; SL 35*)
❖ RP 6:7 (*see also* LM 6:6; SL 7:4*)

Wind in the Willows: Relationships between Mole, Rat, Badger, and Toad as examples of the amazing heterogeneity possible in Affection
•FL 55 ❖ FL 3:5

Window analogy to help explain why the Supernatural is not more obvious in our experience
•M 41-42 ❖ M 6:3-5

Windows: "I hate indoor sunlight. It makes shadows across the page of your book..."
•LAL 46 ❖ LAL 9/10/55

Windows: "The main charm of the view

from a room is the fact that it is framed in, and unified by, the window"
•LAL 46 ❖ LAL 9/10/55

Wine—*consider also* Alcohol; Miracle of water into wine; Moderation; Teetotalism; Temperance

Wine, I know that I should be very angry if the Mohammedans tried to prevent the rest of us from drinking
•MC 101 ❖ MC III 6:14

Wine of the Bible was real fermented wine and alcoholic
•L 262, 263 ❖ L 15 Mar 55; 14 May 55

Winter, first beginning of, always excites me; it makes me want *adventures*
•L 264 ❖ L 16 Oct 55

Wisdom, the man who will neither obey, in others nor adventure for her himself is fatal
•M 43 (*see also* GID 276)
❖ M 6:6 (*see also* GID III 1:17)

Wisdom, we are reminded in the New Testament that a man must become a fool by secular standards before he can attain real
•CR 14 ❖ CR 2:6

Wishes, any conception of reality which a sane mind can admit must favor some of its, and frustrate others
•SJ 172 ❖ SJ 11:9

"Wishful thinking" as a part of the new Psychology which Lewis describes as having influenced many including himself while he was at Oxford
•SJ 203-204 ❖ SJ 13:10

Wishful thinking, I was so far from, that I hardly thought anything true unless it contradicted my wishes
•SJ 171-172 (*see also* SJ 203)
❖ SJ 11:7, 8 (*see also* SJ 13:10)

Wish-fulfilment as a general explanation of religious assent seems to me quite useless; our wishes may favour either side or both
•WLN 18-20 (*see also* GID 272-274; GO 45; SJ 171, 172, 203; WG 76*)
❖ WLN 2:8 (*see also* GID III 1:5-7; GO 3:9; SJ 11:7, 9; 13:10; WG 5:6, 7*)

Wish-fulfilment, connection of morality with the Numinous in religious devel-

opment cannot be explained by, for it fulfils no wishes
•PP 22 ❖ PP 1:13

Wish-fulfilment dreams, if I never felt like fleeing from God's presence I would suspect those moments when I seemed to delight in it of being
•LM 75 ❖ LM 14:12, 13

Witnessing—*see also* Evangelism; *consider also* Apologetic(s)

Witnessing: "Don't think I don't know how much easier it is to preach than practice"*
•LAL 29 ❖ LAL Mar 31st 54

Witnessing: Lewis answers the question, "How can we foster the encounter of people with Jesus Christ?"
•GID 262 ❖ GID II 16:27-30

Witnessing: No need to make a nuisance of ourselves by witnessing at improper times, but there comes a time when we must show that we disagree
•GID 262 ❖ GID II 16:29

Witnessing on one's job: A Christian should not take money for supplying one thing and use the opportunity to supply a quite different thing*
•CR 21 ❖ CR 2:25

Witnessing on one's job: The mere presence of Christians in the ranks will inevitably provide an antidote*
•CR 21 ❖ CR 2:25

Witnessing: One has to be very careful lest the desire to patronise and the itch to be a busybody should disguise itself as a vocation to help the "fallen"*
•RP 69 ❖ RP 7:5

Witnessing: Our anxiety about unbelievers is most usefully employed if it leads us to the attempt, in our own lives, to be good advertisements for Christianity*
•L 247 ❖ L 8 Nov 52

Witnessing: Our worry about unbelievers ("people outside") is more reason to get *inside* oneself, where we can help; to add a new finger to Christ's body*
•L 196 ❖ L 8 Dec 41

Witnessing to "enemy champions," advice to a new Christian regarding: "You're

not David and no one has told you to fight Goliath. You've only just enlisted..."
•L 241 ❖ L 15 May 52

Witnessing to loved ones: "We must be careful not to expect or demand that their salvation shd. conform to some ready-made pattern of our own"
•L 261 ❖ L 2 Feb 55

Witnessing to "unpromising subjects": One sins if one's real reason for silence is fear of looking a fool (though silence *may* be appropriate)
•L 249 ❖ L 6-7 Apr 53

Witnessing: What we practise is more important than what we preach
•L 261 ❖ L 2 Feb 55

Witnessing: "...what will really influence them, for good or ill, is not anything I do or say but what I *am*"*
•LAL 96 ❖ LAL 24 Feb 61

Woman, a lascivious, thinks about her own body while a lascivious man thinks about women's bodies
•L 141 ❖ L 10 Jun 30

Woman, "cultivated," who is always trying to bring her husband "up to her level"
•FL 107 ❖ FL 4:32

Woman, Lewis mentions living in the mind of an ugly, as he wrote the book *Till We Have Faces*
•LAL 52 ❖ LAL 4/3/56

Woman, Man as the "head" of, given by St. Paul in a proportion sum ("...God is to Christ as Christ is to man and man is to woman...")
•CR 4-5 ❖ CR 1:6

Woman, Screwtape describes with loathing a true Christian young
•SL 101 ❖ SL 22:2

Woman, the first, who ever spoke to my blood was a dancing mistress at a school...
•SJ 45, 68-69 ❖ SJ 3:3; 4:16-18

Woman, there ought spiritually to be a man in every, and a woman in every man
•L 237 ❖ L 10 Jan 52

Woman, your "Second Friend" is as fascinating (and infuriating) as a, (re: "First" and "Second" Friends)
•SJ 200 ❖ SJ 13:4

Women—*consider also* Equality

Women, according to Screwtape, are more often tempted to gluttony of Delicacy (the "All-I-Want" state of mind); men tempted more often to gluttony of Vanity
•SL 76-79 ❖ SL 17:1-3

Women and marriage: "Do you really want a matriarchal world? Do you really like women in authority?"
•L 184 ❖ L 18 Apr 40

Women and men are quite diversely affected by illness; women worry that they can't do things, and men are grateful for the excuse *not* to do things
•LAL 105 ❖ LAL 31/7/62

Women and society: A society which tolerates infidelity is a society adverse to women
•GID 321-322 ❖ GID III 9:27

Women are at a double disadvantage in the ruthless war of sexual promiscuity
•GID 321-322 ❖ GID III 9:27

Women are half-ashamed when they rule their husbands, and despise the husbands they rule
•MC 102-103 ❖ MC III 6:17

Women as priests, argument against (Priests serve as representatives of God, who is masculine; therefore women not suited for this role)
•GID 234-239 ❖ GID II ch. 11

Women: "By the way, you are one of the *minority* of my numerous female correspondents who didn't gradually fade away as soon as they heard I was married!"*
•LAL 74 ❖ LAL 15/4/58

Women characterized as fidgets; men as lazy
•L 199 ❖ L 20 Jan 42

Women, domestic happiness more essential to, than to men
•GID 321 ❖ GID III 9:27

Women: Equality of the sexes as citizens or intellectual beings not absolutely repugnant to Pauline thought

•CR 4 (*see also* Equality)
❖ CR 1:6 (*see also* Equality)
Women hold men by their beauty, which decreases as they get older; men hold women more by their personality
•GID 321-322 ❖ GID III 9:27
Women: Lewis mentions a "musical misogynist" who shared his hospital room during the war
•SJ 190 ❖ SJ 12:11
Women, Lewis's fear of teaching: "A man who lectures to women takes his life in his hand..."
•L 110 (*see also* L 79) ❖ L 3 Feb 27 (*see also* L undated letter of Jul 1922)
Women, Lewis's fear of teaching: "...as a general rule, women marry their tutors"*
•L 108 ❖ L 5 Jun 26
Women love letter-writing and men loathe it
•LAL 104 ❖ LAL Ascension Day 1962
Women, masculine as well as feminine traits in
•GO 56-58 ❖ GO 3:29-32
Women mean by "Unselfishness" chiefly taking trouble for others; men mean not giving trouble to others—therefore each sex regards the other as radically selfish
•SL 121 ❖ SL 26:2
Women mentioned as especially vulnerable to the temptation of wanting to be needed
•MC 187-188 (*see also* FL 73-83*)
❖ MC IV 11:10 (*see also* FL 3:34-45*)
Women more likely to do themselves what others wish they would leave alone; men more likely to hand their chores over to others (kitchen in Purgatory example)
•LAL 107 ❖ LAL 3 Sep 62
Women more naturally monogamous than men; therefore they are more often the victims of infidelity than the culprits
•GID 321 ❖ GID III 9:27
Women, my correspondence is mostly with; the female is by nature a much more "epistolatory" animal than the male

•L 242 ❖ L 28 May 52
Women, my experience is that, rather distrust and dislike beauty in men
•LAL 112 ❖ LAL 2 Jan 63
Women of early societies: "Perhaps their world was never as emphatically feminine as that of their men-folk was masculine"
•FL 95 ❖ FL 4:13
Women of early societies: What were they doing while the men came together to talk shop? How should I know?
•FL 95 ❖ FL 4:13
Women pupils: "...the pretty ones are stupid and the interesting ones are ugly"
•L 108 ❖ L 5 Jun 26
Women, question of limiting number of, at Oxford mentioned
•L 117-118 ❖ L 9 Jul 27
Women: Screwtape advises how to aggravate the female's chronic horror of growing old
•SL 92 ❖ SL 20:3
Women: Screwtape advises Wormwood on the kind of woman he ought to encourage his patient to fall in love with and marry
•SL 91-94 ❖ SL 20:2-5
Women: Screwtape lauds the "exaggeratedly feminine type, faint and languishing..."
•SL 92 ❖ SL 20:3
Women: Screwtape lauds "the statuesque and aristocratic type of beauty...[of] the most arrogant and prodigal women"
•SL 91 ❖ SL 20:3
Women, Screwtape lauds, "whose bodies are scarcely distinguishable from those of boys"
•SL 92 ❖ SL 20:3
Women, Screwtape relates the success the devils have had at making certain secondary male characteristics (such as the beard) disagreeable to
•SL 91 ❖ SL 20:3
Women: Screwtape rues a female who "Looks as if butter wouldn't melt in her mouth, and yet has a satirical wit" (which "the Enemy" also grins at!)

•SL 101 (*see also* SL 124*)

❖ SL 22:2 (*see also* SL 26:5*)

Women, "sensible": "At a mixed party they gravitate to one end of the room and talk women's talk to one another"
•FL 110 ❖ FL 4:37

Women, "silly," who invade and spoil the social circles of men whose interests differ from theirs
•FL 107-110 ❖ FL 4:33-37

Women talk more and men talk less when fatigued; this can cause much secret resentment, even between lovers
•SL 142 ❖ SL 30:3

Women: The dominance of the female as seen in the insect world named as one of two things "that some of us most dread for our own species"
•SJ 8-9 ❖ SJ 1:6

Women trying to enter men's discussions: "We all appear as dunces when feigning an interest in things we know nothing about"
•FL 106-110 ❖ FL 4:32-37

Women who have lost "whatever tinge of culture" their schooling gave them, and whose conversation is almost wholly narrative, may invade male circles*
•FL 108 ❖ FL 4:33

Women who militantly attempt to banish male companionship
•FL 109-110 ❖ FL 4:35, 36

Women who never use the word "happiness" in any sense other than to mean "sexual happiness"
•GID 319 ❖ GID III 9:15

Women who try to change their husbands: "The middle-aged male has great powers of passive resistance and (if she but knew) of indulgence..."*
•FL 107 ❖ FL 4:32

Women: "Why are nuns nicer than monks and schoolgirls nicer than schoolboys, when women are not in general nicer than men?"
•LAL 63 ❖ LAL Sep 14 [1956]

Women's magazines described as having "a baneful influence on [one's] mind and imagination"

•L 279 ❖ L 2 Sep 57

"Women's rights" and feminism mentioned in the context of a vote to limit the number of "Wimmen" at Oxford (which Lewis applauded)
•L 117-118 ❖ L 9 Jul 27

Wood, English poetry mentioned as something you can come to the end of, like a
•L 129 ❖ L 2 Aug 28

Wood, have you never while walking in a, turned back deliberately for fear you should come out the other side, then to see it as a mere beggarly strip of trees?
•GID 42 (*see also* L 129*)

❖ GID I 3:8 (*see also* L 2 Aug 28*)

Wood: I learned that we should attempt a total surrender to whatever atmosphere is offering itself at the moment...to find the most dismal and dripping wood...
•SJ 199 (*see also* SJ 146)

❖ SJ 13:3 (*see also* SJ 9:22)

Word about Praising, A (chapter title)
•RP 90-98 ❖ RP ch. 9

Word of God, Christ Himself is the true; Bible will bring us to Him
•L 247 ❖ L 8 Nov 52

Words—*see also* Language

Words and phrases which Screwtape turns to his advantage: "academic," "practical," "outworn," "contemporary," "conventional," "ruthless"*
•SL 8 ❖ SL 1:1

Words and phrases which Screwtape turns to his advantage: "Cause(s)"*
•SL 34, 35 ❖ SL 7:2, 4

Words and phrases which Screwtape turns to his advantage: "Democracy"
•SL 161-170; WLN 59-68

❖ SL 32:19-39; WLN 4:19-39

Words and phrases which Screwtape turns to his advantage: "For the descriptive word 'unchanged' we have substituted the emotional adjective 'stagnant'"
•SL 119 (*see also* CR 76)

❖ SL 25:6 (*see also* CR 6:13, 14)

Words and phrases which Screwtape turns to his advantage: "Forces" and

"devils"*
- •SL 33 (see also SL ix)
- ❖ SL 7:1 (see also SL P:15)

Words and phrases which Screwtape turns to his advantage: "Good Sense, Maturity, Experience"*
- •SL 133 ❖ SL 28:2

Words and phrases which Screwtape turns to his advantage: "hypocrisy" and "convention"*
- •SL 14 ❖ SL 2:4

Words and phrases which Screwtape turns to his advantage: "lack of humour"*
- •SL 51-52 ❖ SL 11:5

Words and phrases which Screwtape turns to his advantage: "living in the Present"; "complacency"*
- •SL 70 ❖ SL 15:5

Words and phrases which Screwtape turns to his advantage: "Love"
- •SL 80-89, 93, 120
- ❖ SL ch. 18, 19; 20:5; 26:1

Words and phrases which Screwtape turns to his advantage: "moderation in all things"*
- •SL 43 ❖ SL 9:3

Words and phrases which Screwtape turns to his advantage: "priggish," "intolerant," and "Puritanical"*
- •SL 48, 52 ❖ SL 10:4; 11:5

Words and phrases which Screwtape turns to his advantage: "Progress," "Development," "the Historical Point of View"*
- •SL 43 (see also SL 106-108)
- ❖ SL 9:4 (see also SL 23:3, 4)

Words and phrases which Screwtape turns to his advantage: "Puritanism"*
- •SL 47, 48 (see also SL 118; WLN 55)
- ❖ SL 10:3, 4 (see also SL 25:5; WLN 4:10)

Words and phrases which Screwtape turns to his advantage: "real" and "subjective"
- •SL 142-144 ❖ SL 30:4

Words and phrases which Screwtape turns to his advantage: "real life"*
- •SL 8-10 (see also SL 149)
- ❖ SL 1:2-4 (see also SL 31:5)

Words and phrases which Screwtape turns

to his advantage: "religious phase"; "Adolescent"*
- •SL 43, 44 ❖ SL 9:4, 5

Words and phrases which Screwtape turns to his advantage: "spiritual"*
- •SL 16, 48 (see also RP 51; SL 105, 126)
- ❖ SL 3:3, 10:4 (see also RP 5:9; SL 23:1; 27:2)

Words and phrases which Screwtape turns to his advantage: "the results of modern investigation"*
- •SL 10 ❖ SL 1:4

Words and phrases which Screwtape turns to his advantage: Unselfishness (used as a substitute for the positive word "Charity")
- •SL 121 (see also WG 3)
- ❖ SL 26:2 (see also WG 1:1)

Words, changing: The words "humanism" and "liberalism" are coming to be used simply as terms of disapprobation
- •CR 78 (see also WLN 49)
- ❖ CR 6:18 (see also WLN 3:28)

Words, doesn't the mere act of putting something into, of itself involve an exaggeration?
- •LM 112-113, 116 (see also L 137)
- ❖ LM 21:2, 15 (see also L 9 Sep 29)

Words: Journalists mentioned who neither know nor care what words mean
- •GID 309 ❖ GID III 7:11

Words, Lewis's dislike for, which make "specialised and self-conscious stunts" out of activities which have before been ordinary (e.g., "hiking")
- •L 259 ❖ L 22 Dec 54

Words, list of, which are used differently by the layman than by the clergyman or theologian (includes the typical lay definition)
- •GID 96-98 ❖ GID I 10:20-37

Words, meaning of, always changing; sometimes become spoiled for practical use (such as "gentleman" and "Christian")
- •MC 10-11 (see also GID 333; L 288-289; RP 51, 54)
- ❖ MC P:12-14 (see also GID IV Letter 7; L 8 Sep 59; RP 5:9, 6:1)

Words "Spirit" and "Spiritual", On the (title of Appendix A)
•M 169-173 ❖ M App. A

Words such as "holy" and "pure" and "spiritual" tend to reinforce the idea that Heaven comes not to fulfill but to destroy our nature.
•WG 67 ❖ WG 4:21

Words, use of emotive vs. descriptive, in argument: Use of "stagnant" rather than "permanent" to describe traditional morality is to infer an unfair metaphor*
•CR 76 (see also SL 119)
❖ CR 6:14 (see also SL 25:6)

Words: "We had better not follow Humpty Dumpty in making words mean whatever we please" (re: "Need-love" as a genuine kind of love)
•FL 12 ❖ FL 1:5

Words: What is disastrous is when a word changes its sense during a discussion without our being aware of it
•M 171-172 ❖ M App. A:11

Words which lose their meaning by becoming spiritualized: "Christian"
•MC 11 ❖ MC P:13-14

Words which lose their meaning by becoming spiritualized: "love of God"
•RP 51 ❖ RP 5:9

Words which lose their meaning: "Charming" (now a tepid and even patronising word)
•RP 54 ❖ RP 6:1

Wordsworth, I believe, made the same mistake I did—I insisted that the Desirable ought to appear in the temple I had built him
•SJ 167 ❖ SJ 11:3

Wordsworth mentioned as "the romantic who made a good end" (also, a quote from The Recluse)
•CR 9 ❖ CR 1:13

Wordsworth mentioned with regard to the love of nature
•FL 34-35, 39 ❖ FL 2:17-20, 28

Wordsworthian contemplation can be the first and lowest form of recognition that there is something outside ourselves which demands reverence
•CR 22 ❖ CR 2:32

Work—see also Job; Occupation; Vocation

Work and Prayer (chapter title)
•GID 104-107 (see also GID 217)
❖ GID I ch. 11 (see also GID II 7:4)

Work as "'the only wisdom' for one 'haunted with the scent of unseen roses'"—quote from G. MacDonald (re: our secret desire for heaven)
•PP 148 ❖ PP 10:5

Work assigned by God: "...one treats as an interruption of one's (self-chosen) vocation, the vocation actually imposed on one..."
•L 212 ❖ L 22 Dec 47

Work: "By doing what one's 'station and its duties' does not demand, one can make oneself less fit for the duties it does demand..."
•LAL 53 ❖ LAL 19/3/56

Work, domestic, the most important in the world
•L 262 ❖ L 16 Mar 55

Work, don't be too easily convinced that God really wants you to do all sorts of, you needn't do
•LAL 53 (see also LAL 72)
❖ LAL 19/3/56 (see also LAL 22/2/58)

Work, fairness in our: We have not always done quite our fair share of tiresome work if we found a colleague who would do it
•RP 13-14 ❖ RP 2:8

Work, good, not extinct though not necessarily characteristic of religious people
•WLN 71 ❖ WLN 5:2

Work, good, vs. "good works"
•WLN 71-81 ❖ WLN ch. 5

Work, honesty and fairness in our: "Few of us have always, in full measure, given our pupils or patients or clients ...what we were being paid for"
•RP 13 ❖ RP 2:8

Work: I bet the things which "had to be done" in your room didn't really have to be done at all; very few things really do
•LAL 113 (see also LAL 105-106, 107)

❖ LAL 8 Jan 63 (*see also* LAL 31/7/62; 3 Sep 62)

Work, if a man does not, he ought not to eat (but Lewis makes it clear that charity is an essential part of Christian morality)
•MC 80, 81 (*see also* Charity)
❖ MC III 3:3:4, 7 (*see also* Charity)

Work in time of grief: "Except at my job—where the machine seems to run on much as usual—I loathe the slightest effort"
•GO 3 ❖ GO 1:6

Work, Lewis's feeling about, which is unnecessary and would not be done unless it were paid
•WLN 74-81 (*see also* MC 80)
❖ WLN 5:9-22 (*see also* MC III 3:4)

Work: Men more likely to hand their chores over to others; women more likely to do themselves what others wish they would leave alone*
•LAL 107 ❖ LAL 3 Sep 62

Work must be accomplished while conditions are still unfavourable (re: learning in war-time)
•WG 29-30 ❖ WG 2:12

Work never intended for us: One must be careful lest the desire to be a busybody should disguise itself as a vocation to help the "fallen"
•RP 69 ❖ RP 7:5

Work never intended for us, we may embrace
•WG 129-130 ❖ WG 9:8

Work nowadays must *not* be good; "Built-in obsolescence" an economic necessity
•WLN 72 (*see also* CR 92)
❖ WLN 5:3 (*see also* CR 7:21)

Work of all levels can become spiritual if offered to God
•WG 26 (*see also* CR 24)
❖ WG 2:9 (*see also* CR 2:37)

Work, originality in, can only come unsought
•WG 119 (*see also* MC 190)
❖ WG 7:19 (*see also* MC IV 11:15)

Work, our changed attitude to all, has resulted in the tendency to regard every trade as existing for the sake of those who practise it
•WLN 79 ❖ WLN 5:19

"'Work out your own salvation...for it is God that worketh in you'"
•GID 55; LM 49; MC 130 ❖ GID I 4:31 (Ques. 8); LM 9:11; MC III 12:8

Work, real interest in the subject of one's, seems to be greater for garage-hands than for those in the liberal professions
•L 174 ❖ L 1 Jan 40

Work: Story of Mrs. Fidget shows how unreasonable self-sacrifice and work for others may reveal a perverted kind of Gift-love*
•FL 73-76, 82-83 (*see also* L 198-199; MC 167; SL 121, 12) ❖ FL 3:33-37, 45 (*see also* L undated letter just before 20 Jan 42; MC IV 7:3; SL 26:2, 5)

Work, the genuine pleasure of doing good
•WG 104-105 ❖ WG 6:17

Work, the neglect of doing good, in our jobs not according to Biblical precept
•WLN 71 ❖ WLN 5:1

Work, there are always plenty of rivals to our, besides war: falling in love, becoming ill, etc.
•WG 29-30 ❖ WG 2:12

Work, there can be intemperance in, just as in drink; what feels like zeal may be only fidgets or even the flattering of one's self-importance
•LAL 53 ❖ LAL 19/3/56

Work to earn our living, Christianity can be delightfully humdrum about, in spite of its revolutionary and apocalyptic elements
•CR 20 ❖ CR 2:23

Work, we must distinguish two kinds of: one wholly good and necessary, the other a punitive result of the Fall
•L 187-188 ❖ L 16 Jul 40

Work we naturally like may be as much a part of our "service" to God as are our hardest duties
•WG 130 ❖ WG 9:9

Work: When we begin a new job, we have the discharge of the vocation as our end; by the third week, we have our

own personal goals in mind
- PP 75-76 ❖ PP 5:5

Work worth doing apart from its pay has become the privilege of a fortunate minority; in our economy, many jobs come from advertisement-created wants
- WLN 74-78 (see also MC 80)
- ❖ WLN 5:9-16 (see also MC III 3:4)

Work, worthwhile vs. useless: In a fully Christian society, there would be "no manufacture of silly luxuries and then of sillier advertisements..."
- MC 80 (see also WLN 74-76)
- ❖ MC III 3:4 (see also WLN 5:9-12)

Works—see also Moral effort; Perfection; consider also Growth, Christian; Righteousness by faith/grace

Works: "A perfect man would never act from a sense of duty; he'd always want the right thing more than the wrong one"
- L 277 (see also LM 114-116; PP 100)
- ❖ L 18 Jul 57 (see also LM 21:11-14; PP 6:11)

Works: A tree is known by its fruit; a genuine conversion will be known by an improvement in outward behaviour
- MC 175-176 ❖ MC IV 10:2

Works: A world of "nice" people would be just as much in need of salvation as a miserable world, and possibly more difficult to save*
- MC 182 ❖ MC IV 10:15

Works: Christianity does not help us if it brings no healing to the impotent will; a mere statement of even the highest ethical principles is not enough*
- GID 328-329 ❖ GID IV Letter 4

Works: Christianity makes duty a self-transcending concept and endeavors to escape from the region of mere morality in its ethics*
- CR 45 (see also LM 115; GID 144; MC 130-131; PP 65)
- ❖ CR 4:2 (see also LM 21:10-12; GID I 16:26; MC III 12:9; PP 4:13)

Works: Even the noblest of our natural activities will be sinful if not offered to God*

- WG 25 ❖ WG 2:8

Works: God will not love us because we are good, but He will make us good because He loves us*
- MC 64 ❖ MC II 5:6

Works, Good, and Good Work (chapter title)
- WLN 71-81 ❖ WLN ch. 5

Works, good, not necessarily the same as good work—as you can see by inspecting some of the objects made to be sold at charity bazaars
- WLN 71 ❖ WLN 5:1

Works: Hypocrites are more curable than "goody-goodies" who are content in their routine piety and respectability, attempting no deception*
- WLN 47-48 ❖ WLN 3:26

Works: If I want to produce wheat, the change must go deeper than the surface
- MC 168 ❖ MC IV 8:7

Works: If the Bride does not bear fruit, it may be supposed that the marriage was an illusion...*
- RP 132 ❖ RP 12:10

Works: If we are in the right relation to God, the right relation to one another will follow inevitably*
- GID 51 ❖ GID I 4:18 (Ques. 5)

Works: In a sense the world is right to judge Christianity by its results; when we behave badly, we make Christianity unbelievable to the outside world
- MC 175-176 ❖ MC IV 10:2

Works: It is God who does the work in us; we allow it to be done
- MC 165 ❖ MC IV 7:13

Works: Judging a person's Christianity by their behaviour is not possible; you need to know what kind of raw material Christ is working on (toothpaste analogy)
- GID 59; MC 177-178 (see also L 242*; Judging)
- ❖ GID I 4:46-52 (Ques. 12); MC IV 10:5 (see also L 28 May 52*; Judging)

Works: Lewis describes his realization of the need for "continual, conscious recourse" to God (whom he then called

"Spirit") for his virtue*
- SJ 226 (see also SL 62; Devotional life)
- ❖ SJ 14:20 (see also SL 14:1; Devotional life)

Works: Lewis discusses the "man of good will, saddled with an abnormal desire" vs. "the (to human eyes) equable virtue of some who are psychologically sound"*
- L 242 ❖ L 28 Man 52

Works: "Morality is a mountain which we cannot climb by our own efforts..."*
- GID 112-113 ❖ GID I 12:10, 11

Works: Most of the behaviour which is now duty would be spontaneous and delightful if we were, so to speak, good rose-trees*
- LM 114-116, esp. 116 (see also L 277; PP 100) ❖ LM 21:11-14, esp. 21:14 (see also L 18 Jul 57; PP 6:11)

Works: "No good work is done anywhere without aid from the Father of Lights"
- RP 110 (see also RP 80)
- ❖ RP 11:3 (see also RP 8:6)

Works: "Not doing these things in order to be saved, but because He has begun to save you already"*
- MC 128-129 ❖ MC III 12:6

Works: "Nothing gives one a more spuriously good conscience than keeping rules, even if there has been a total absence of all real charity and faith"*
- LAL 38 (see also Legalism)
- ❖ LAL 20/2/55 (see also Legalism)

Works: Obedience as an imperative not really obedience at all; "Ye must be born again"*
- LM 115 ❖ LM 21:12

Works: Religious festivals and acts of worship can be separated from the vision of God, thereby becoming a substitute for, and a rival to, God Himself*
- RP 48-49 ❖ RP 5:7

Works: "...right actions done for the wrong reason do not help to build the internal quality of character called a 'virtue'..."*
- MC 77 (see also MC 127)
- ❖ MC III 2:10 (see also MC III 12:3)

Works: "The Christian thinks any good he does comes from the Christ-life inside him"
- MC 64 ❖ MC II 5:5, 6

Works: "The more virtuous a man becomes the more he enjoys virtuous actions"
- PP 100 (see also L 277; LM 114-116)
- ❖ PP 6:11 (see also L 18 Jul 57; LM 21:11-14)

Works vs. faith: "I personally rely on the paradoxical text, 'Work out your own salvation...for it is God that worketh in you'"
- GID 55 (see also LM 49; MC 130)
- ❖ GID I 4:30, 31 (Ques. 8) (see also LM 9:11; MC III 12:8)

Works vs. faith: In the parable of the Sheep and the Goats, you see nothing about predestination or even faith—all depends on works
- L 251 ❖ L 3 Aug 53

Works vs. faith, question of, is like asking which blade in a pair of scissors is most necessary
- MC 129 ❖ MC III 12:7

Works: "We profanely assume that divine and human action exclude one another..."
- LM 49-50 (see also GID 55; LM 68-69; MC 130)
- ❖ LM 9:11, 12 (see also GID I 4:30, 31— Ques. 8; LM 13:2-5; MC III 12:8)

Works: "What God does for us, He does in us"*
- WG 132 ❖ WG 9:13

Works: What we are matters more than what we do (and what we do matters chiefly as evidence of what we are)
- MC 165 ❖ MC IV 7:12

Workmanship, quality of, valued less and less as built-in obsolescence becomes an economic necessity
- WLN 72, 78 ❖ WLN 5:3, 4, 15

World—see also Earth; consider also Life; Universe

World affords only imitations of real security, which is in Heaven
- LAL 49 (see also FL 190)
- ❖ LAL 16/12/55 (see also FL 6:43)

World as a great sculptor's shop: Some

day some of the statues are going to come to life
•MC 140 ❖ MC IV 1:16

World as a "valley of tears" cursed with labour, hemmed round with necessities, tripped up with frustrations, etc.
•LM 92 ❖ LM 17:17

World as the vestibule of eternity: a view not held by many 19th century authors
•GID 219 ❖ GID II 8:3

World, Christianity believes many things have gone wrong with the
•MC 45 ❖ MC II 1:4

World: Christianity does not teach us to desire a total release from environment (or "Nature")*
•M 162 ❖ M 16:30

World, Christianity's relation to the
•GID 49, 57, 147-150, 266; PP 113-114; WLN 111
❖ GID I 4:6-8 (Ques. 2), 39-40 (Ques. 9); ch. 17; II 16:55; PP 7:4; WLN 7:33, 34

World, Christians' ineffectiveness in this, a result of ceasing to think of the next
•MC 118 ❖ MC III 10:1

World, contempt for, is dangerous; love of the creature is also dangerous ("Not bad you see; just very, very small")
•L 183 ❖ L 16 Apr 40

World: Contemptus mundi has sometimes been reckoned a Christian virtue; but Christianity is both world-affirming and world-denying
•GID 147-150, esp. 148 (see also L 183)
❖ GID I ch. 17, esp. 17:3 (see also L 16 Apr 40)

World: Course of events not governed like a state but created like a work of art to which every being makes its contribution (including prayer)
•LM 54-56, esp. 56
❖ LM 10:7-11, esp. 10:11

World, creation of a, seems to require certain intrinsic necessities—matter, environment, fixed laws, etc. (re: Divine omnipotence)
•PP 29-35 (see also PP 71)
❖ PP 2:6-16 (see also PP 5:1)

World, creation of: "The great work of art

was made for the sake of all it does and is, down to the curve of every wave and the flight of every insect" (re: prayer as an end as well as a means)
•LM 56 ❖ LM 10:11

World, Determinism seems to be implicit in a scientific view of the*
•LM 36 ❖ LM 7:5

World, end of—see End of the world

World, for news of the fully waking, you must go to my betters
•FL 192 (see also LM 75; RP 92)
❖ FL 6:47 (see also LM 14:11; RP 9:3)

World, Gospel is directly opposed to
•GID 265 ❖ GID II 16:46

World, had God designed the, it would not be A world so frail and faulty as we see (Lucretius' argument for atheism)
•SJ 65 ❖ SJ 4:11

World, I wonder whether people who ask God to interfere openly and directly in our, quite realise what it will be like when He does
•MC 66 (consider also Contact with God) ❖ MC II 5:9 (consider also Contact with God)

World, if a Brute made the, then he also made the standard by which we judge him to be a Brute (thus Heroic Pessimism has a contradiction at its centre)
•CR 65-67 (see also CR 69-70; MC 45-46*) ❖ CR 5:19, 24 (see also CR 5:24; MC II 1:5, 6*)

World, if the, is indeed a "vale of soul-making" [through affliction], it seems on the whole to be doing its work
•PP 108 ❖ PP 6:18

World, if you think of this, as a place intended for our happiness, you will find it quite intolerable; think of it as a place of training and it's not so bad (hotel/prison analogy)
•GID 52 ❖ GID I 4:18, 19 (Ques. 5)

World, improvement of, a goal in Christianity
•GID 49, 57, 147-150; MC 118; WLN 111

❖ GID I 4:6-8 (Ques. 2), 39-40 (Ques. 9); ch. 17; MC III 10:1; WLN 7:33, 34

World, improvement of: A strong sense of our common miseries is an excellent spur to the removal of all the miseries we can; no need to believe in "heaven on earth"
•PP 114 ❖ PP 7:5

World, improvement of: As Christians we have a duty to leave the world (even in a temporal sense) "better" than we found it
•PP 113-114 ❖ PP 7:4

World, improvement of: I remind the reader that a particular medicine is not to be mistaken for the elixir of life
•PP 114 ❖ PP 7:5

World, improvement of: I think the best results are obtained by people who work quietly away at limited objectives
•WG 44-45 ❖ WG 3:20

World, improvement of: Long-term futility is no ground for diminishing our efforts to make human life, while it lasts, less painful and less unfair...*
•CR 58-59 ❖ CR 5:4

World, improvement of: Screwtape discusses how Christianity used merely as a means to social justice can work to the devil's advantage*
•SL 108-109 (see also MC 137)
❖ SL 23:4 (see also MC IV 1:6, 7)

World, improvement of: Screwtape mentions wanting men to be "hagridden by the Future"—absorbed by visions of an imminent heaven or hell upon earth
•SL 69 ❖ SL 15:4

World, improvement of: Social and political programmes good only so far as they don't trample on people's rights for the sake of the good
•L 226-227 (see also PP 65; WLN 111)
❖ L 7 Feb 51 (see also PP 4:12; WLN 7:33, 34)

World, improvement of: Social values of the Christian vs. the Materialist, and how they affect the actions of each*
•GID 109-110 ❖ GID I 12:2-4

World, improvement of: "The fact that the ship is sinking is no reason for allowing her to be a floating hell while she still floats"
•CR 49 ❖ CR 5:4

World, improvement of: The job of finding the Christian solution to our social problems is really on us laymen*
•MC 79 ❖ MC III 3:3

World, improvement of: The making of a Heaven on Earth is a temptation the devil uses, especially on youth
•SL 133 ❖ SL 28:2

World is a dance in which good, descending from God, is disturbed by evil arising from the creatures; resulting conflict resolved by God becoming Man
•PP 84 ❖ PP 5:11

World is at least as dangerous as the Flesh, and cruelty is surely more evil than lust
•SJ 109 ❖ SJ 7:11

World is enemy-occupied territory; Christianity tells how the rightful king has landed
•MC 51, 56 ❖ MC II 2:11, 12; 4:1

World is like a picture with a golden background; you must step off the picture [into death] before you can see the gold
•PP 148 ❖ PP 10:5

World is only a very small part of a very long and complicated story; miracles are those chapters on which the plot turns*
•M 98-99 ❖ M 12:7

World, it is not always necessary to leave the, and His creatures behind in order to find God; the world is crowded with Him*
•LM 75 ❖ LM 14:11

World: Loving God enables us to love the world better
•GID 147-150, esp. 150
❖ GID I ch. 17, esp. 17:7

World may be a "local pocket of evil" in which the standard of decency is vastly inferior to that of the larger universe
•PP 62-63 ❖ PP 4:10

World might stop in ten minutes; mean-
while we are to go on doing our duty
•GID 266 (see also WLN 111-112)
❖ GID II 16:55 (see also WLN 7:34)

World, modern, as it is becoming is simply *too much* for people of the old
square-rigged type like you and me
(letter to his brother)
•L 177 (see also L 179)
❖ L 18 Feb 40 (see also L 22 Mar 40)

World, our conformance to, must be limited*
•GID 262 (see also RP 71-74; SL 45-48*)
❖ GID II 16:29 (see also RP 7:9-16; SL
ch. 10*)

World, our whole education tends to fix
our minds on this
•MC 119 (see also WG 7)
❖ MC III 10:2 (see also WG 1:5)

World, present, will never be a permanent city satisfying the soul of man
•WG 32 ❖ WG 2:14

World, question of whether the Christian's rejection of, "is only the disappointed fox's attempt to convince
himself that unattainable grapes are
sour"
•CR 37-43, esp. 37 ❖ CR ch. 3, esp. 3:2

World: "Say what you like, Barfield, the
world is sillier and better fun than
they make out..."
•L 217 ❖ L 4 Apr 49

World, suffering teaches us not to rest our
hearts in this
•PP 106, 115 (see also CR 37; L 227; SL
132) ❖ PP 6:17; 7:7 (see also CR 3:2; L 5
Mar 51; SL 28:2)

World: The Flesh and the Devil could not
offer me the supreme bribe—and the
World never even pretended to have it
•SJ 178 (see also SJ 176)
❖ SJ 11:17 (see also SJ 11:13)

World, the sooner we are safely out of this,
the better
•L 166 ❖ L 8 May 39

World, up till now each visitation of Joy
had left the common, momentarily a
desert; now I saw the common things
drawn into the bright shadow (re:
Lewis's reading of *Phantastes*, by

George MacDonald)
•SJ 181 ❖ SJ 11:19

World, we are shy about mentioning
heaven nowadays—afraid of being
told that we are trying to escape the
duty of improving the
•PP 144 ❖ PP 10:1

World, whole life of humanity in this, is
precarious, temporary, provisional; all
worldly achievements and triumphs
will come to nothing in the end
•WLN 110 ❖ WLN 7:31, 32

World will never find peace and happiness apart from God, since God designed the human machine to run on
Himself
•MC 54 ❖ MC II 3:7, 8

World will not always be habitable; most
scientists here join hands with the
theologians
•WLN 110 ❖ WLN 7:32

Worldliness—*consider also* Materialism

Worldliness, contented, prevented by war
since war forces people to think about
death (—Screwtape)
•SL 27 ❖ SL 5:2

Worldliness, nothing but these forcible
shakings will cure us of our; we force
God to surgical treatment
•L 161-162 (see also L 227)
❖ L 12 Sep 38 (see also L 5 Mar 51)

Worldliness, real, is a work of time; the
young have an inveterate appetite for
Heaven (—Screwtape)
•SL 133 ❖ SL 28:2

Worldliness, we have need of the strongest spell to wake us from the evil enchantment of
•WG 7 ❖ WG 1:5

Worldly...—*see also* Temporal ...

Worldly achievements and triumphs will
all come to nothing in the end
•WLN 110 ❖ WLN 7:32

Worldly ambition: A man "should never
give all his heart to anything which
will end when his life ends"*
•WLN 110 ❖ WLN 7:31

Worldly attachments, the rightly precarious hold we have on all our
•L 161-162 (see also L 306; LM 27, 90*)

❖ L 12 Sep 38 (*see also* L 21 Nov 62; LM 5:12, 13; 17:10*)

Worldly blessings look like broken toys in times of fear and pain; we are reminded that they were never intended to possess our heart*
- •PP 106 (*see also* FL 192)
- ❖ PP 6:17 (*see also* FL 6:47)

Worldly happiness, I had been warned not to reckon on; we were even promised sufferings—they were part of the program
- •GO 41-42 ❖ GO 3:3

Worldly interests, regarding the temptation to guard our
- •WG 126-132 (*see also* Self-reservation)
- ❖ WG ch. 9 (*see also* Self-reservation)

Worldly prosperity, for long centuries it was hammered into the Jews that, is not the probable reward of seeing God
- •RP 43 ❖ RP 4:19

Worldly prosperity "knits a man to the World" (—Screwtape)
- •SL 132 (*see also* Prosperity)
- ❖ SL 28:1 (*see also* Prosperity)

Worldly success, self-sufficiency the possible result of those vices that lead to
- •PP 98 ❖ PP 6:9

Worldly things, our avoidable immersion in, contributes to our reluctance to pray
- •LM 114 ❖ LM 21:8

Worldly Vanities, I see few of the old warnings about, (—Screwtape)
- •SL 46-47 ❖ SL 10:3

Worldly ways of thinking, we as Christians shall perhaps find increasing reasons to value Christian ethics over
- •RP 64-65 (*see also* SL 110-113)
- ❖ RP 6:14 (*see also* SL 24:1-5)

World's Last Night, The (chapter title)
- •WLN 93-113 ❖ WLN ch. 7

World's last night, what if this present were the, (quote from Donne)
- •WLN 109 (*see also* WLN 111-113)
- ❖ WLN 7:29 (*see also* WLN 7:34-38)

World-view, Lewis's—*consider* Pessimism, Lewis's

World-views ("beliefs about the universe"), different, lead to different behaviour*
- •MC 72-73 ❖ MC III 1:8-10

World-views, errant: Progress may mean doing an about-turn and walking back to the right road*
- •MC 36 ❖ MC I 5:2

World-views: Religious view of the universe vs. the materialist's view*
- •MC 31-35 ❖ MC I ch. 4

Worry—*see also* Anxiety; *consider also* Difficulties; Faith

Worry: A Christian society is to be a cheerful society, full of singing and rejoicing, and regarding worry or anxiety as wrong
- •MC 80 ❖ MC III 3:4

Worry: "...a mind so little sanguine as mine about the future..."*
- •SJ 173 (*see also* SJ 183*)
- ❖ SJ 11:10 (*see also* SJ 12:2*)

Worry: A schoolboy learns to keep the future in its place; if he allowed infiltrations from the coming term into the present holidays he would despair*
- •SJ 158 ❖ SJ 10:11

Worry and care not limited to adult life; it seems to me there is more in an average schoolboy's week than in a grown man's average year
- •SJ 89 ❖ SJ 6:10

Worry and suspense in a crisis: "...if only one could go underground, hibernate, sleep it out"*
- •LM 41 ❖ LM 8:4

Worry, financial: "The great thing...is to live from day to day and hour to hour not adding the past or future to the present"
- •LAL 69 (*see also* LAL 58, 60, 79, 103; SL 29, 67-71) ❖ LAL Oct 20th 57 (*see also* LAL 14/6/56; 3/8/56; Oct 30 58; 4 May 62; SL 6:2; ch. 15)

Worry: Helpful to keep it particular, not general
- •L 186 ❖ L 2 Jun 40

Worry in a crisis: Like at sea, "once you have doubled the point and got into smooth water, the point doesn't take long to hide below the horizon"
- •LM 46 ❖ LM 9:1

Worry: [In a letter to his father] "...the worrying temperament of the family did not end with your generation"
•L 88 ❖ L 1 Jul 23

Worry: Not all the things you fear can happen to you; the one (if any) that does will perhaps turn out very different from what you think
•LAL 60 (see also SL 29)
❖ LAL 3/8/56 (see also SL 6:2)

Worry: "One of your fears...is of all the fears you will have to suffer before you are out of the wood"
•L 285 ❖ L 29 Apr 59

Worry: "We are not necessarily doubting that God will do the best for us; we are wondering how painful the best will turn out to be"*
•L 285 ❖ L 29 Apr 59

Worship—see also Adoration; Praise; Praising; consider also Devotional life; Devotions; Prayer(s)

Worship, acts of, and a sense of the presence of God were for the ancient Jew all one
•RP 46-48 ❖ RP 5:5, 6

Worship, acts of, may be distinguished from the vision of God; then they can become a substitute for, and a rival to, God Himself (e.g., Christmas)
•RP 48-49 ❖ RP 5:7

Worship and adoration in prayer: "Begin where you are"—with the pleasures and blessings you are apprehending right now
•LM 88-91 ❖ LM 17:1-13

Worship and praise, church services are merely an attempt at, never fully successful; only a dim reflection of how it will be in Heaven
•RP 96 ❖ RP 9:6

Worship as an element in love which is foreshadowed by our Appreciative pleasures
•FL 32-33 ❖ FL 2:13

Worship, as Christians there is a tragic depth in our, which Judaism lacked; our most joyous festivals centre upon the broken body and the shed blood
•RP 52 ❖ RP 5:10

Worship as one of the processes through which God communicates His presence and beauty to men
•RP 93 ❖ RP 9:4

Worship, corporate—see also Church services; consider also Music, church

Worship, corporate
•LM 3-8 ❖ LM ch. 1

Worship, corporate: "I think our business as laymen is to take what we are given and make the best of it"
•LM 4, 5 ❖ LM 1:3, 10

Worship, corporate: My whole position really boils down to an entreaty for permanence and uniformity
•LM 4-5 ❖ LM 1:3-8

Worship: David's dancing a valuable contrast to merely dutiful "churchgoing" and "saying our prayers"; we may regard it with envy and hope to be infected by it*
•RP 44, 45-46 ❖ RP 5:2, 4

Worship, for the ancient Jew, (as in Temple festivals), combined many elements into his "love of God"—social pleasure, anticipation of rest, etc.
•RP 46-48 ❖ RP 5:5-7

Worship: I learned how a thing can be revered not for what it can do to us but for what it is in itself*
•SJ 231 (see also FL 189-190; LM 120; RP 39-42) ❖ SJ 15:3 (see also FL 6:42; LM 22:8; RP 4:12-17)

Worship, incense as part of, merely a question of ritual, not of doctrine; some find it helpful and others don't
•L 243
❖ L undated letter just after 20 Jun 52

Worship of a Divine being, which the Church offers us, is a refreshing change from the necessary democracy of the world
•WG 116 (see also GID 84-85*; WG 113) ❖ WG 7:15 (see also GID I 9:7*; WG 7:10)

Worship styles: Judging of others who worship in a different fashion than we do ("It takes all sorts to make a world; or a church...")
•LM 10 ❖ LM 2:3

Worship styles: Matters of taste not to be confused with matters of doctrine*
- L 268 ❖ L 13 Mar 56

Worship: The simplest act of mere obedience is worship of a far more important sort than adoration of God for what He gives us
- LM 91 ❖ LM 17:15

Worship, the value of icons in, depends very little on their perfection as artefacts (unlike literature and hymns)*
- CR 2 ❖ CR 1:2

Worship, use of pictures and images of Jesus in: The artistic merits and demerits are a distraction
- LM 84 ❖ LM 16:4

Worship, value of images in
- LM 83-84 ❖ LM 16:2-4

Worship, value of mental images in
- LM 84-87 (see also SL 21-22*)
- ❖ LM 16:5-13 (see also SL 4:4*)

Wrath—see also Anger

"Wrath" can be attributed to God only by analogy; but turn His wrath into mere disapproval and you also turn His love into mere humanitarianism
- LM 96-97 ❖ LM 18:6-9

Wrath, fear tames, —the fear that my own unforgivingness will exclude me from all the promises
- LAL 93 ❖ LAL 28 Oct 60

Wrath of God—consider also Judgement

"Wrath" of God seems a barbarous doctrine until we truly perceive our sinfulness; then it appears inevitable
- PP 58 ❖ PP 4:6

Wrinkles, why shouldn't we have, —honorable insignia of long service in this warfare
- LAL 79 ❖ LAL Oct 30 58

Writer(s)—see also Author(s)

Writer ought not to use italics for emphasis; he has other means of bringing out key words and ought to use them
- MC 5 ❖ MC P:1

Writer, Christian: "...always, of every idea and of every method he will not ask, 'Is it mine?' but 'Is it good?'"
- CR 9 ❖ CR 1:14

Writer, to regard an ancient, as a possible source of knowledge would be rejected by learned men as unutterably simple-minded
- SL 128-129 ❖ SL 27:5

Writers, advice for: You must know what you want to say and say exactly that
- GID 263 ❖ GID II 16:35, 36

Writers, I prefer to make no judgement concerning the inspiration of, by the Holy Spirit
- GID 264 ❖ GID II 16:37, 38

Writers, liberal, who are continually whittling down the truth of the Gospel are turning people away from the church
- GID 260 (see also GID 99*; Liberal Christianity) ❖ GID II 16:12 (see also GID I 10:41*; Liberal Christianity)

Writing, advice to a child regarding
- L 270-271, 291-292
- ❖ L 26 Jun 56; 14 Dec 59

Writing, advice to a correspondent regarding
- L 278-280 ❖ L 2 Sep 57

Writing, advice to Arthur Greeves on: "...write something, anything, but at any rate *write*"
- L 28 ❖ L undated letter between Oct 1915 and 27 Sep 16

Writing: Always, of every idea and every method, the Christian author will ask not "Is it mine?", but "Is it good?"
- CR 9 ❖ CR 1:14

Writing: "...any amount of theology can now be smuggled into people's minds under cover of romance without their knowing it" (re: Out of the Silent Planet)
- L 167 ❖ L 9 Jul 39

Writing: "At bottom, every ideal of style dictates not only how we should say things but what sort of things we may say" (re: "functionalism")
- SL xiv ❖ SL P:26

Writing: Author should never conceive himself as bringing into existence beauty or wisdom which did not exist before; he reflects eternal Beauty and Wisdom
- CR 6-7 (see also Originality)
- ❖ CR 1:10, 11 (see also Originality)

Writing: Christian author sees his own temperament and experience as of no value except as a way by which something universally profitable appeared to him
•CR 8 ❖ CR 1:13

Writing Christian literature must be done using same rules as those used for writing secular literature
•CR 1 ❖ CR 1:1

Writing comes as a result of a very strong impulse, like a lust
•GID 258 (Compare with L 209)
❖ GID II 15:2 (Compare with L 2 Aug 46)

Writing: "Creation" as applied to human authorship a misleading term; we rearrange elements He has provided
•L 203-204 (see also CR 6-7; GID 276; LM 73; M 32-33; Originality)
❖ L 20 Feb 43 (see also CR 1:10, 11; GID III 1:19; LM 14:3; M 4:14; Originality)

Writing, exaggeration seems to be inherent in the mere act of
•L 137 ❖ L 9 Sep 29

Writing: Except in bad poetry, poets are not always telling us that things are shocking or delightful—though they do tell us that grass is green, etc.*
•CR 131 ❖ CR 11:5

Writing: "Fiction may be perfectly serious in that people often express their deepest thoughts, speculations, etc. in a story"
•L 261 ❖ L 2 Feb 55

Writing for children certainly modified my habits of composition; these restrictions did me great good—like writing in a strict metre
•L 307 ❖ L 2 Dec 62

Writing: Humour a dangerous thing to try when learning to write
•L 28 ❖ L undated letter between Oct 1915 and 27 Sep 16

Writing: "I began...to look for expressions which would not merely state but suggest...I had learned what writing means"
•SJ 74 ❖ SJ 5:5

Writing: I turned to fairy tales because that seemed the form best fitted for what I wanted to say
•L 260, 307 ❖ L undated letter just before 2 Feb 55; 2 Dec 62

Writing: In literature and art, no man who bothers about originality will ever be original
•MC 190 (see also WG 119)
❖ MC IV 11:15 (see also WG 7:19)

Writing: "In my experience the desire [to write] has no constant ratio to the value of the work done"
•L 209 (Compare with GID 258)
❖ L 2 Aug 46 (Compare with GID II 16:2)

Writing, Lewis's, as a child: He tried not to make his stories interesting from the start, or (he believed) they wouldn't be like grown-up stories
•CR 33 ❖ CR 2:53

Writing: More books needed by Christians on other subjects with Christianity latent
•GID 93; L 208
❖ GID I 10:9; L 10 Dec 45

Writing on Christian themes, comment on the use of humour in
•GID 259 ❖ GID II 15:7-10

Writing: "The pother about 'originality' all comes from people who have nothing to say; if they had, they'd be original without noticing it"
•L 201
❖ L undated letter just before 13 Oct 42

Writing this book (The Problem of Pain) now a pleasure ("temptation") rather than a duty; therefore can no longer be a means of my learning self-surrender
•PP 99 ❖ PP 6:10

Writing, usefulness of various kinds of Christian, ("God has shown us that He can use any instrument")
•GID 258-259 ❖ GID II 15:4

Writing: What you want is practice, practice, practice
•L 29 ❖ L undated letter between Oct 1915 and 27 Sep 16

Wyvern College described
•SJ 83-114, 126-128 ❖ SJ 6:1-18; 8:8-10

Wyvern Priory was the first building that I ever perceived to be beautiful
•SJ 58 ❖ SJ 4:4

Wyvern, the town of, healed my quarrel with England; the great blue plain below us and, behind, those green, peaked hills...
•SJ 58 ❖ SJ 4:4

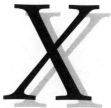

Xmas and Christmas (chapter title)
•GID 301-303 ❖ GID III ch. 5

* These items reflect some interpretation on the part of the editor; the idea will not be found in these exact words. *See Introduction, p. ix.*
** These items are ideas of Lewis's which the editor has placed under a topic Lewis did not there intend to address. *See Introduction, p. ix.*
Entries without asterisks are not necessarily exact quotes, but the idea should be easy to find as worded.

Yeats, [William Butler], I had been reading; to put it quite plainly, he believed seriously in Magic
•SJ 174-175 (*see also* SJ 114)
❖ SJ 11:12 (*see also* 7:18)

Yeats, William Butler, Lewis describes meeting
•L 56-58 ❖ L 14 Mar 21; 21 Mar 21

Youth—*see also* Childhood

Youth, agnosticism of, may be explained by ignorance; British school system no longer teaches Christianity
•GID 115 ❖ GID I 13:3,4

Youth and aging listed by Screwtape as neutral situations which can work either for God's or the devil's purposes
•SL 89 ❖ SL 19:3

Youth and generational differences in ideas of propriety: Lewis suggests believing all the good you can of others and making them as comfortable as you can
•MC 88-89 ❖ MC III 5:1

Youth are generally less unwilling to die than the middle-aged and the old; "prosperity knits a man to the World"
•SL 132 ❖ SL 28:1

Youth: "...Barfield was living through 'that whole year of youth   When life ached like an aching tooth'"
•SJ 205 ❖ SJ 13:13

Youth: Care and worry not limited to adult life; it seems to me there is more in an average schoolboy's week than in a grown man's average year

•SJ 89 ❖ SJ 6:10

Youth, desire for conformity in, made use of by the devil
•SL 163-164; WLN 62
❖ SL 32:25, 26; WLN 4:25, 26

Youth have an inveterate appetite for Heaven; "Real worldliness is a work of time..." (—Screwtape)
•SL 133 ❖ SL 28:2

Youth have the least sales-resistance; maybe that is why there is a tendency in the modern world to prolong that period
•LAL 19-20 ❖ LAL Aug 1st [1953]

Youth: "...how much harm a loose-talking young man can do to innocent boys" (re: a teacher he had at "Chartres")*
•SJ 68 ❖ SJ 4:16

Youth: "I fancy that most of those who think at all have done a great deal of their thinking in the first fourteen years"
•SJ 63 ❖ SJ 4:10

Youth, I feel the whole of one's, to be immensely important and of immense length
•L 266 (*see also* FL 56, top)
❖ L 8 Feb 56 (*see also* FL 3:6)

Youth, if we could go back to our, we would not find the thing we now long for; what we remember would turn out to be itself a remembering*
•WG 6-7 (*see also* preface to *The Pilgrim's Regress* p. xi) ❖ WG 1:5 (*see also The Pilgrim's Regress* P:16)

Youth, instruction of, about Christianity is remedy for agnosticism or indifference
•GID 115 ❖ GID I 13:3

Youth is neither the wisest, happiest, or most innocent period in life; the attempt to prolong it loses all the value of the *other* parts of life
•LAL 19 ❖ LAL Aug 1st [1953]

Youth of Lewis's time, communal sins of, listed
•GID 191 ❖ GID II 1:3

Youth: One answer to the question, "Why do they like every house better than their home?" (re: courtesy of parents

---

* These items reflect some interpretation on the part of the editor; the idea will not be found in these exact words. *See Introduction, p. ix.*
** These items are ideas of Lewis's which the editor has placed under a topic Lewis did not there intend to address. *See Introduction, p. ix. Entries without asterisks are not necessarily exact quotes, but the idea should be easy to find as worded.*

toward children)
- •FL 66 ❖ FL 3:22

Youth should not follow desire to enter "Inner Rings"
- •WG 104-105 (*see also* Inner Rings)
- ❖ WG 6:17, 18 (*see also* Inner Rings)

Youth, with the cruelty of, I allowed myself to be irritated by traits in my father which in other elderly men I have since regarded as lovable foibles
- •SJ 160 ❖ SJ 10:14

Youthful loves and youthful hopes, Screwtape mentions the gradual decay of, as providing "admirable opportunities of wearing out a soul by attrition"
- •SL 132 ❖ SL 28:1

Zeal, religious, may be confused with merely natural enthusiasms
- •GID 198 ❖ GID II 3:5

Zeal, what feels like, may be only fidgets or even the flattering of one's self-importance; there can be intemperance in work just as in drink
- •LAL 53 ❖ LAL 19/3/56

Zeal, what feels like, may be presumption; we may embrace tasks never intended for us
- •WG 129-130 ❖ WG 9:8

Zoë, or spiritual life, defined and discussed
- •M 169-173 ❖ M App. A

Zoë, or spiritual life, mentioned
- •MC 139-140, 143, 153, 154, 162, 186
- ❖ MC IV 1:15; 2:9; 4:10; 5:1, 2; 7:6; 11:7

Zoo, Lewis describes taking the final step in his conversion to Christianity while on a trip to the Whipsnade
- •SJ 237-238 ❖ SJ 15:8, 9

Zoo of lusts, a bedlam of ambitions, a nursery of fears, and a harem of fondled hatreds as what Lewis found within himself near his conversion
- •SJ 226 (*see also* CR 169*)
- ❖ SJ 14:19 (*see also* CR 14:21*)

Zoo, though I liked clergymen as I liked bears I had as little wish to be in the Church as in the, (re: Lewis's conversion to Theism)
- •SJ 234 ❖ SJ 15:6

Zoo, Whipsnade, reminded Lewis of the world before the Fall (tame animals)

* These items reflect some interpretation on the part of the editor; the idea will not be found in these exact words. *See Introduction, p. ix.*
** These items are ideas of Lewis's which the editor has placed under a topic Lewis did not there intend to address. *See Introduction, p. ix.*
Entries without asterisks are not necessarily exact quotes, but the idea should be easy to find as worded.